SINCE 1900

SINCE 1900

A HISTORY OF THE UNITED STATES IN OUR TIMES

FIFTH EDITION

OSCAR THEODORE BARCK, JR.

Professor of History, Emeritus, Syracuse University

NELSON MANFRED BLAKE

Professor of History, Syracuse University

MACMILLAN PUBLISHING CO., INC.

NEW YORK

COLLIER MACMILLAN PUBLISHERS

LONDON

Copyright © 1974, Macmillan Publishing Co., Inc.

Printed in the United States of America

Earlier editions copyright 1947 and 1952, © 1957, and copyright © 1965 by Macmillan Publishing Co., Inc.

Macmillan Publishing Co., Inc.
866 Third Avenue, New York, New York 10022

Collier-Macmillan Canada, Ltd.

Library of Congress Cataloging in Publication Data

Barck, Oscar Theodore (date)
  Since 1900; a history of the United States in our times.

  Includes bibliographical references.
  1. United States—History—20th century.
I. Blake, Nelson Manfred, (date) joint author.
II. Title.
E743.B343   1974   973.91   73-3894
ISBN 0-02-305930-3

Printing: 1 2 3 4 5 6 7 8   Year: 4 5 6 7 8 9 0

PREFACE TO FIFTH EDITION

This is a complete revision. We have tried to make the book more incisive and thoughtful by cutting out unnecessary detail and incorporating the results of recent scholarship. Five new chapters deal with such important topics as the Johnson and first Nixon administrations, the Vietnam war, the black revolution, space exploration, technological advance, student unrest, women's liberation, and the Nixon overtures to China and the Soviet Union. We end with an account of the election of 1972 and following developments from the Watergate affair.

We wish to express our gratitude to all those who have helped us in the preparation of the present edition. We are especially appreciative of the comments of those who have found earlier editions useful and have encouraged us to bring the book up to date once more.

OSCAR THEODORE BARCK, JR.
NELSON MANFRED BLAKE

PREFACE TO FIRST EDITION

The pitfalls in writing contemporary history are obvious, but the values of its study outweigh them. Never before has intelligent understanding of the role of the United States in world affairs been so much needed; never before has it been so imperative that the American government and the American economy be wisely guided. We are under no illusion that we know all the answers to urgent present day problems, but we are convinced that no one will ever find the answers without a study of the historical development of the issues—particularly since the turn of the century. This consideration has guided our choice of materials and greatest attention has been devoted to the problems that are of current importance. We are well aware of the significance of recent social and cultural trends and we have tried to give them ample treatment. But we have reserved a major portion of our space for the two lines of development which seem to us most impressive—the steady expansion of the functions of government to deal with the complex problems of a new age and the increasing involvement of the United States in global politics.

As far as is humanly possible, we have tried to keep this account free from partisan bias. Desirable in any case, this policy has been a practical necessity with us since we belong to different political parties and hold opposing convictions on many subjects; we have tried to state the facts and leave final judgments to the reader. This does not mean that we have shunned all responsibility for interpretation. On the contrary, we have tried to prepare the ground for fruitful discussion and thought by suggesting the most pertinent arguments for and against the more controversial propositions advanced during the period.

We are indebted to numerous colleagues and professional associates for encouragement and help in this enterprise. We wish to express particular gratitude to artists and newspapers all over the country for generous permission to reproduce cartoons. The opportunity to use these has greatly pleased us, since we are convinced that studying such material is one of the very best methods of projecting oneself back in time and seeing issues as they appeared to intelligent contemporary observers. To our loyal wives we want to pay sincere tribute both for their good sportsmanship in putting up with many inconveniences while we have been at work and for the long hours which they themselves contributed to helping us with proofreading and preparing the index. We of course must accept full responsibility for all errors of fact and judgment.

Oscar Theodore Barck, Jr.

Nelson Manfred Blake

Syracuse University, August 21, 1947

CONTENTS

Contents

1

THE GOOD OLD DAYS

The closing years of the nineteenth century and the opening ones of the twentieth were vastly significant in American history. In 1898 the United States abruptly advanced to the rank of first-class world power by waging war on Spain, liquidating that country's imperial possessions in the Caribbean Sea, and compelling her to cede the Philippine Islands, eight thousand miles across the Pacific from San Francisco. Three years later an assassin's bullet cut short the life of President William McKinley and ended an era in American domestic politics as well. The genial McKinley, like all his predecessors, Republican and Democratic, had been a conservative who believed that the nation's economic life should be subject to as little interference as possible at the hands of government. Theodore Roosevelt, his colorful successor, was sympathetic to new demands that were sweeping the country—demands that government should be more responsive to the popular will and should intervene where necessary to protect the public interest.

Thus were clearly foreshadowed the three themes that were to run through the history of the United States in the twentieth century. A people largely indifferent to international politics were to be pushed by men and events into increasing involvement in world affairs. They were to be compelled not only to defend democracy as a way of government and of life, but to re-examine their own institutions to determine whether they squared with the democratic ideal. And, finally, the American system of capitalism was to be subjected to acid testing. Succeeding generations were to raise the insistent cry that to produce wealth was not enough; a just economic system must provide security as well. Politics were to orient themselves around the rival claims of the parties to foster the well-being of the people.

The Momentum of American Growth

The emergence of the United States as a world power was an inevitable result of its astounding growth. In 1790 the new nation, extending westward to the Mississippi, had contained about 900,000 square miles of territory. By 1900 the Americans had extended their rule over a vast empire covering 3,738,000 square miles. The population growth had been even more remarkable. In 1790 the United States had fewer than 4 million inhabitants; the census of 1900 showed that there were some 76 million people in the continental United States and some 9 million living under the American flag in outlying territories.

Although by European or Asiatic standards much of the United States was thinly settled in 1900, the rate of American population growth had been extraordinary. For most of its history the country had been a rural society wherein early marriages and large families were customary. Yet the rapid increase in population was more directly traceable to large-scale immigration than to any other single factor. That the Americans of 1900 were an immigrant people, a glance at the census figures clearly proved. Over one third of the population was of immediate foreign stock—either foreign-born or of foreign parentage. The rest of the population was descended, almost without exception, from the immigration of earlier generations. Of the country's 76 million inhabitants, about 66.8 million were descended from white Europeans; some 8.8 million were of black African stock; and approximately 115,000 were of Oriental origin. The only truly 100 per cent Americans were some 237,000 Indians, mostly living on scattered reservations.

For three hundred years the stream of immigration had been flowing to America, but it was not until the middle of the nineteenth century that it reached huge proportions. For thirty years after 1850 foreigners entered the country at the rate of about 250,000 a year; after 1880 the annual average jumped to about 400,000; after 1900 there was a still more extraordinary increase. The peak year in the whole history of American immigration was 1907, when almost 1.3 million foreigners arrived, but this was only slightly more than the influx in five other years—1905, 1906, 1910, 1913, and 1914—in each of which there were more than a million immigrants.

What were the sources of this vast stream? As recently as 1880, about 80 per cent of the foreign-born Americans had come from Germany, Ireland, England, and Canada, but thereafter the proportion of immigrants from these traditional sources declined, while more and more newcomers from Italy, Russia, and Austria-Hungary arrived. The so-called new immigration outnumbered the old for the first time in 1896. During the decade 1901–1910 more than 92 per cent of the immigrants came from Europe. Of these, three quarters were from the countries of southern and eastern Europe. Among them, three groups bulked large. The first was that from southern Italy, an area impoverished by an archaic land system and burdensome taxes. A second group was Slavs, consisting of Poles, Czechs, Croats, and other subject peoples who had been living under either Austrian or Russian rule. The third was Jewish, principally refugees from the persecutions of Tsarist Russia.

Gloomy critics asserted that these people from eastern and southern Europe were of racial stock inferior to the northern Europeans who had been prominent in the earlier generation. Such assumptions were unscientific and dangerous, but a more valid indictment of the newcomers could be made: many of them manifested no intention of making America their permanent home. Indeed, nearly half of the 13 million immigrants admitted between 1901 and 1914 returned to the old country after a few years. American wage earners protested against having to compete with these temporary residents in the labor market.

American attitudes toward immigration were changing. Before the Civil War it had been generally believed that an open door to foreigners was essential to provide the population needed for national growth. After 1870, however, American wage earners became more and more concerned lest the uncontrolled flood of immigrant labor undermine wage scales and hamper unionization of the workers. All the large national labor unions included some restriction of immigration as one of their objectives. Most employers of this period still favored unrestricted immigration, but a few were changing their minds along with other worried members of the middle class. There was a growing fear of the serious social problems arising out of the poverty and ignorance of these unassimilated masses. Optimists placed their faith in the American "melting pot"; pessimists feared that the ingredients would never adequately blend. A more particular fear was that alien ideas as well as alien persons were entering the country; such anarchist-connected crimes as the assassination of President McKinley increased the fear of alien radicalism.

Congress responded to this growing pressure with a policy of qualitative restriction, barring from the country the groups to which there was the greatest objection. A series of laws passed between 1868 and 1903 denied admission to prostitutes, lunatics, idiots, convicts, paupers, contract laborers, and anarchists. Although Oriental immigration had never been large in comparison with European, it provoked a disproportionate clamor of opposition among native workers. Congress excluded Chinese laborers in 1882, but the Japanese did not arouse much alarm until they began coming over in larger numbers after 1900. Unable to ban the Japanese directly, legislatures and municipal bodies in the Pacific Coast states passed harassing legislation, limiting the right of Orientals to own land or segregating their children in the schools. By entering into the so-called Gentlemen's Agreement of 1907 with the Japanese government, President Theodore Roosevelt achieved a temporary solution, but it failed to satisfy the ultra-exclusionists.

In dealing with the larger immigration problem, advocates of drastic action pressed for a literacy test, which would exclude all foreigners who could not read or write some language. The restrictionists frankly admitted that such a test would sharply reduce the new immigration while affecting the old very little. Congress passed literacy test bills three times—in 1897, 1911, and 1915—only to have them vetoed by Presidents Cleveland, Taft, and Wilson, all of whom believed that the proposed test would unfairly penalize foreigners for not having had in the old country the very opportunities they were seeking in America. But in the end the restrictionists won their battle; in 1917 Congress enacted the literacy test over another Wilson veto.

As characteristic of American growth as the entrance of immigrants had been the movement of the population from section to section. After the Civil War came the final great frontier movement, which populated the vast area lying between eastern Kansas and such earlier-settled states as California and Oregon. The lure of gold and silver, abundant pasturage for cattle and sheep, and rich prairie soil attracted miners, cattlemen, sheepherders, and farmers in successive waves that finally erased the frontier line from the census map in 1890. By 1900 the roster of the fifty states was almost complete: three states (Idaho, Wyoming, and Utah) had been admitted to the Union during the nineties; only five more (Oklahoma, New Mexico, Arizona, Alaska, and Hawaii) remained to be added during the twentieth century. But the closing of the frontier in the 1890's was more theoretical than real. Much of the West was sparsely settled; there remained millions of acres of virgin soil to be broken to the plow or of fresh grazing lands to be opened up. With farmers continuing to seek new land, manufacturers moving to promising industrial sites, and the sick and the old seeking sunnier skies, the westward impulse still persisted.

Meanwhile, the nation was being transformed from a predominantly rural country to an urban one. In 1860, 83 per cent of the people had lived in communities of less than 2,500 inhabitants; by 1900 the percentage declined to 60. Urban population increased by over 16 million between 1880 and 1900; rural population by less than 10 million. This disparity of growth resulted from numerous factors, prominent among which were the thronging of immigrants to the cities and the tendency of farmers' sons and daughters to seek employment in the towns. The degree of urbanization was by no means uniform throughout the nation. Whereas Rhode Island, Massachusetts, and New York had, respectively, 95, 91, and 73 per cent of their population living under urban conditions in 1900, Idaho, North Dakota, Oklahoma, Mississippi, and Arkansas were still more than 90 per cent rural. American politics inevitably reflected the conflict between the points of view to which these far different environments gave rise.

The Afro-Americans

In 1900 there were more than 8.8 million black people in the United States, composing over 11 per cent of the entire population. For the most part, they were still living in the regions where their ancestors had once toiled as slaves. About 85 per cent of the blacks resided in the eleven states that had made up the Southern Confederacy;[1] another 8 per cent lived in the four border states of Delaware, Maryland, Kentucky, and Missouri.

During Reconstruction days, the Radical Republicans had attempted to guarantee to the freedmen full equality of citizenship and the right to vote, but this effort had failed. Federal troops had been withdrawn from Southern soil, the "carpetbag" state governments overthrown, and white supremacy restored. Weary of the issue, politicians of both parties had tacitly acquiesced in Southern policies that to all intents and purposes nullified the Fourteenth and Fifteenth amendments to the Federal Constitution.

For a time the Ku Klux Klan and similar groups had used force and intimidation to keep the blacks from the polls. These rough methods later gave way to other means of controlling the black vote. White landlords and employers were in a position to discourage their black tenants and workers from voting at all or to influence how they cast their ballots. Thus manipulated, the black vote became an instrument for maintaining

---

[1] Alabama, Arkansas, Florida, Georgia, Louisiana, Mississippi, North Carolina, South Carolina, Tennessee, Texas, and Virginia.

the rule of the so-called Bourbons, or conservatives. After 1890, when agrarian radicals challenged conservative control, the Populist leaders at first tried to build a united front of poor farmers, both black and white. But this competition for black support frightened the upholders of white supremacy of all classes and led to a strong countermovement to eliminate the black vote. When the newer politicians—men with their political base in the poorer sectors—gained control of the Democratic party, the state legislatures passed laws setting up literacy tests, poll tax requirements, and other devices for denying the ballot to the blacks. The legislatures also enacted so-called Jim Crow laws forbidding interracial marriages and requiring separation of the races in schools, trains, depots, hotels, barbershops, restaurants, and theaters. The Federal Supreme Court acquiesced in such legislation by a narrow interpretation of the Fourteenth Amendment. It ruled that the kind of private discrimination practiced by innkeepers or theater owners could not be forbidden by Federal law (Civil Rights Cases, 1883) and that state laws requiring the separation of the races in schools and on public conveyances were not unconstitutional so long as the accommodations provided were "separate but equal" (Plessey v. Ferguson, 1896). Behind this convenient separate-but-equal formula, state segregation laws were destined to enjoy more than fifty years of immunity despite the fact that the equality between black and white schools or between black and white railroad cars was usually fictional.

The two races did not enjoy the equal protection of the laws. By tacit consent of Southern authorities, blacks were kept off the jury lists. The courts dealt severely with blacks accused of killing or assaulting whites, whatever the provocation, but were singularly indulgent toward whites accused of similar crimes against blacks. Even with the scales of justice thus tilted by white prejudice, ugly mobs frequently took the law into their own hands, wreaking swift and terrible vengeance against blacks suspected of misdeeds. More than one hundred blacks were lynched in 1900 and a similar number in 1901; there were between fifty and one hundred such incidents annually thereafter until 1917.

Outside the South the black man's position was somewhat more secure. He exercised his right to vote and enjoyed general equality before the law. Yet private discrimination was almost universal. The blacks found many jobs closed to them; they were unable to buy and rent real estate except in certain districts; they were often excluded from hotels and restaurants. From the black man's point of view the situation in the early twentieth century was particularly discouraging. Most of the idealism that had sought to combat prejudice in the Civil War generation seemed to have spent itself; even in the North discrimination seemed to be increasing rather than declining.

By 1910 two basically different black strategies for dealing with the situation had evolved. One was that of Booker T. Washington, the best-known black leader of the time. He believed that the black man's best hope lay in demonstrating his worth through hard work and thrift. Consequently, Washington had developed at Tuskegee Institute in Alabama an excellent industrial school where black students were taught to be good farmers and mechanics. In a famous speech delivered at the Atlanta

Exposition in 1895, the educator offered his formula for amicable relations between blacks and whites: "In all things that are purely social we can be as separate as the five fingers, yet one as the hand in all things essential to mutual progress." Washington's apparent willingness to put up with unequal political and social status and to concentrate on economic improvement became increasingly distasteful to a militant black minority. W. E. Burghardt Du Bois of Atlanta University argued that vocational education was not enough. The "talented tenth" of the race ought to be able to obtain the classical and professional training essential to leadership, while the race as a whole should press for full equality of rights. In 1905 Du Bois and a small group of black intellectuals met at Niagara Falls, Canada, to formulate their demands. This Niagara Movement was at first small and little noticed. In 1910, however, a group of white liberals took the lead in organizing the National Association for the Advancement of Colored People (NAACP). Du Bois and many others of the Niagara group joined the movement, which pressed vigorously for court action and new laws to protect the black man in all his legal and constitutional rights. The National Urban League, also organized in 1910, was an interracial group committed to enlarging employment opportunities for blacks.

The Railroad Age

The most significant events of the period between the Civil War and World War I occurred not in diplomacy or in the halls of Congress, but in the economic sphere. Among the industrial nations of the world, the United States rose from fourth place in 1860 to first place in 1894. Between 1860 and 1899 the value of products manufactured in American factories rose from less than $2 billion annually to more than $11 billion. Industries that in 1860 scarcely existed at all grew to husky manhood by the end of the century. In earlier years steel had been made by hand processes, so costly that the product could be used only for fine weapons and tools. Mass production processes first adopted in the United States in 1864 and 1865 made possible the manufacture of steel at prices low enough to open up hundreds of new uses. American steel production expanded from less than 69,000 tons in 1870 to over 10 million tons in 1899. No less remarkable was the growth of the oil industry. In earlier years petroleum had been known only as a disagreeable substance sometimes befouling streams and wells. During the 1850's two revolutionary discoveries had been made. One was that by distilling petroleum, it was possible to manufacture kerosene, a cheap and satisfactory fuel for lamps and lanterns. The other was that by drilling wells, abundant supplies of underground oil could be brought to the surface. Kerosene lamps soon displaced tallow candles and whale-oil lamps in millions of American homes, and American kerosene found markets as remote as China. Meantime, the value of lubricating oils and other by-products was becoming evident, although the importance of gasoline was scarcely recognized until after 1900. The harnessing of electricity to such practical uses as the telegraph, the telephone, the incandescent lamp, and the streetcar provided great opportunities to manufacturers of generators, motors, and other types of electrical equipment and also to the power companies that supplied current to the public.

The rise of the United States to industrial supremacy resulted from the fortunate concurrence of many different factors: abundance of natural resources, political and economic freedom, widespread educational opportunities, common acceptance of the middle-class virtues of thrift and industry, and the accumulation of investment capital. Most important of all, perhaps, was the golden opportunity provided for the manufacturer to buy his raw material and sell his product in a great national market. In striking contrast to Europe, where national boundaries divided the continent into a score of independent sovereignties separated by tariff walls and other legal barriers, the United States offered a vast market, protected, of course, by its own tariff barriers, extending from the Atlantic Ocean to the Pacific in one direction and from the Canadian border to the Gulf of Mexico in in the other.

To move raw materials and finished goods over great distances, the nation depended largely upon the railroads. Although the first few miles of American railroad had been opened in 1830, the railroad age did not really commence until after 1850, when trunk lines linking one section of the country with another began to operate. After the Civil War the process of consolidating short lines into great systems went forward under the driving leadership of masterful men like Commodore Vanderbilt, Tom Scott, and Jay Gould. In the Far West, where railroad construction preceded rather than followed settlement, Federal land grants and loans encouraged the building of the Union Pacific and the other so-called transcontinentals—long systems from the start. Accompanying the process of consolidation was feverish new construction. In 1865 the United States had only 35,000 miles of track; by 1900 it had 193,000.

The railroads gave the nation tremendous advantages. Massachusetts shoes, New York clothing, and Illinois plows found their way to customers thousands of miles distant. Western cattle raisers and wheat farmers fed the nation and still had a surplus for export. Yet as producers became dependent upon the railroads, they began to fear the economic power of these great corporations. At first wholly arbitrary in their rate policies, the railroads might discriminate against entire communities, impoverish farmers or other economic groups by excessive charges, or bankrupt small businessmen by special concessions to their large competitors. Out of this fear arose the demand for governmental regulation of the railroads that swept the Middle West during the 1870's and 1880's, leading to the enactment of numerous state laws and the first great Federal regulatory measure, the Interstate Commerce Act of 1887. Unfortunately, Interstate Commerce Commission orders had to be implemented by court orders, which were seldom granted. Despite these various statutes, abuses in railroad management continued, and the problem of effective government regulation was still urgent in 1900.

Between 1900 and 1914 American railroads appeared to be enjoying a golden age. The laying of new track, largely halted during the depression of the nineties, was resumed; between 1900 and 1915 total American railroad trackage increased from 193,000 to 260,000 miles. The greatest figure in the railroad world was Edward H. Harriman. After achieving an outstanding success with the Illinois Central Railroad during the 1880's, Harriman had formed an alliance with the powerful banking house of Kuhn, Loeb, & Company to rehabilitate the historic but hitherto unprofitable Union Pacific Railroad. This success in turn helped Harriman gain control of the great Southern Pacific–Central Pacific system and extend his influence into the Pacific Northwest as well. The restless Harriman also invaded the eastern railroads, gaining substantial holdings in the New York Central, the Central of Georgia, and the Baltimore and Ohio. By this time his influence in transportation had become nationwide, and he was seeking new worlds to conquer in regions as remote as Manchuria.

Harriman's death in 1909 was followed by the sale of many of his holdings, so that the control exercised by his heirs was less Napoleonic in scope. The case of Harriman, although exceptional, typifies a general tendency toward railroad consolidation throughout the 1900–1917 period. In retrospect, the railroad prosperity of these years appears to have been built upon shaky foundations. Railroad mileage reached its maximum in 1916; thereafter, there was very little new construction and the general abandonment of many miles of unprofitable trackage.

Challenges to the Railroads

Rival means of transportation that would cause serious problems for the railroads were in the process of development early in the twentieth century. Most of the older waterways gave the railroads little to worry about, but the tremendous increase in Great Lakes shipping was a different matter. Between 1899 and 1916 the total annual shipments on the Lakes grew from 25 million to 125 million tons—most of it coal and iron. Interurban electric streetcar lines also enjoyed a mushroom growth for a few years.

The streetcar fad was short-lived, but a much more serious threat to the railroads was implicit in the birth and growth of the automobile industry. The key discovery of the internal-combustion engine powered with gasoline came through the experiments of French and German engineers between 1860 and 1890. Ingenious Americans soon entered the field. The nineties were a period of endless experimentation with all types of vehicles—steam, gasoline, and electric. It required many years for the superior advantages of the gasoline-driven cars to be generally recognized. Indeed as late as World War I, many people still considered the Stanley Steamer to be the last word in mechanical perfection. Pioneer builders of gasoline vehicles in America were Charles E. Duryea, who built the first such car in the United States, Henry Ford, Ransom Olds, Elwood Haynes, and the Apperson brothers. The new contraptions were extremely crude and undependable, but a moderate demand for them developed among people able to indulge themselves with rather expensive playthings. At first this trade was served by small shops where the horseless carriages were built to order. Production in quantity began near the turn of the century with the opening of such plants as those of the Locomobile Company of America, the Olds Motor Works, and the Cadillac Company.

The Ford Motor Company, destined to revolutionize the industry, began operations in 1903. Like other manufacturers, Ford at first experimented with a variety of motor types—two-, four-, and six-cylinder. In 1908, however, he began turning out the famous four-cylindered Model T. These "tin Lizzies," as they were affectionately called, were ugly to behold, clumsy to drive, and uncomfortable to ride in, yet they provided transportation at a price the average American could afford to pay. In 1908 the Model T was priced at $850; by 1917 it cost only $360. Ford was able to produce cars cheaply not only because he concentrated on a single model, but because he pioneered in many techniques of production. Standardized, interchangeable parts had been basic in American industrial success since Eli Whitney started manufacturing guns in 1798, but the assembly-line method of organizing production was largely a Ford innovation.

The General Motors Corporation, the other great giant of the industry, was organized in 1908 through the promotion of William C. Durant of the Buick Company. Durant was brilliant but reckless, expanding the company rapidly through the purchase of more and more separate concerns engaged in some phase of automotive manufacturing. He lost control of the company in 1910, regained command in 1915, and was finally ousted during the 1917 depression. Morgan and Du Pont interests thereafter dominated the corporation. As late as 1917, Ford was producing nearly four times as many cars annually as General Motors.

Despite the strength of Ford and General Motors, the automobile industry was still strongly competitive, with scores of independent companies producing for a rapidly expanding market. In 1895 there had been only four registered automobiles in the entire United States; in 1900 there were 8,000; in 1915 almost 2.5 million.

By 1917 the automobile's threat to the railroads was already alarming, but the challenge of the airplane still lay in the future. The famous experiments of Wilbur and Orville Wright at Kitty Hawk, North Carolina, demonstrated the feasibility of flying in heavier-than-air machines as early as 1903; but for the next decade only the most venturesome took to the skies. Not until 1911 did an airplane fly across the United States, and then the exploit required nearly seven weeks and was interrupted by numerous forced landings.

The Trust Problem

The growth of big business, first exemplified in the railroad field, was paralleled in many other areas of the American economy. The telegraph business, for example, had a natural tendency toward monopoly. The earlier situation, with competing lines between cities, resulted in a wasteful duplication of facilities, and the weaker telegraph companies had to go out of business or sell out to their stronger rivals. In this competition the Western Union Telegraph Company steadily forged ahead, thanks particularly to the mutually profitable contracts with the railroads, under which Western Union enjoyed the right to erect poles and wire along railroad rights of way and to have telegraph offices in the railroad stations in return for providing free wire services for train orders. The telephone business followed a somewhat similar evolution. Although there were many small, locally owned telephone companies in various parts of the country, the American Telephone and Telegraph Company, organized in 1900, held close control of long-distance lines.

In the manufacturing field, the same degree of monopoly was impossible, but the tendency toward consolidation was nevertheless strong. In 1860 industry was almost exclusively managed through partnerships and small corporations—organizations of modest capital, largely local in influence. By the opening years of the twentieth century, the situation was strikingly different. Through the great corporations, relatively small groups of powerful men controlled a major portion of the national economy. To be sure, there continued to be many small businesses; indeed as late as 1914, 88 per cent of the manufacturing establishments of the country were factories or shops with an annual output worth less than $100,000. The remaining 12 per cent, however, employed three quarters of the workers and turned out four fifths of the nation's manufactures.

The most famous example of these consolidation tendencies was provided by the oil industry. In 1863, when John D. Rockefeller entered the refining business in Cleveland, the industry was characterized by hundreds of fiercely competing small businessmen. It was an ideal situation for Rockefeller's particular type of organizing genius. Within five years he had built his refinery into the largest such establishment in the world. In 1870 he organized the Standard Oil Company of Ohio and began to buy out his competitors. By 1872 the Rockefeller combine controlled over 90 per cent of the refining capacity of the nation. Many factors contributed to this spectacular achievement. Rockefeller pleased customers by providing a product of dependable quality. He cut his costs through efficient management and utilization of by-products. Most important of all, through hard and often unscrupulous bargaining with the railroads, he obtained preferential rates his competitors could not match.

While Rockefeller's near monopoly of refining provided the most important example of horizontal combination, Andrew Carnegie was patiently piecing together a vertical integration of the steel industry. During the 1890's—twenty years after Carnegie entered the steel business, the Carnegie Steel Company was obtaining iron ore from its own mines in the rich Mesabi range in Minnesota, carrying it across the Great Lakes in its own steamships, and transporting it from Lake Erie to Pittsburgh on its own railroad. To provide fuel for its plants in the Pittsburgh suburbs, the Carnegie Company relied on rich coke fields under its control at Connelsville, Pennsylvania. Although Carnegie's share in the nation's steel production was only about two fifths, it was an extraordinarily profitable share —enough to make the one-time Scottish immigrant one of the wealthiest and most powerful men in the United States.

During the 1880's Americans began to worry about the "trust" problem. The original trust, in the strict sense of the word, was the Standard Oil

A dream of empire. The desire of the trusts to dominate the world. (By Opper in the *New York Journal.*)

Trust, organized in 1882 when the stockholders of some forty companies surrendered their stock to nine trustees and accepted in its place trust certificates entitling them to share in the profits of the combined operations, but not in their management. Through this device, Rockefeller and his fellow trustees were able to rule a huge economic empire. Similar trusts soon appeared in several other lines of business. This form of organization speedily fell under attack. In 1890 Congress passed the Sherman Antitrust Act, which declared illegal "every contract, combination in the form of trust or otherwise, or conspiracy in restraint of trade" in interstate or foreign commerce. For the next twelve years this Federal law was ineffective because of lax enforcement and narrow interpretations in the courts. But the trust form of organization received more damaging blows in the state courts, where abdication to trustees on the part of the stockholders was ruled to violate corporate charters.

Confronted with these legal setbacks, promoters devised new types of combination, made possible by changes in corporate laws of New Jersey and other states hospitable to big business. In outright consolidations, individual competing companies merged or amalgamated into a single corporation and lost their separate identities. In holding companies, the constituent concerns preserved their separate names and organizations but were integrated in management by a parent corporation that owned a controlling interest in the stock of each of them.

The word trust was now used in a loose sense to describe any industrial combination, whatever its form of organization, that sought to avoid competition by absorbing, controlling, or forcing out of business its competitors, or by acting together with them to fix prices and to regulate output. Absolute monopoly was difficult to achieve and seldom sought. The essential aim was to stabilize the industry and maintain prices. The trust movement entered its most aggressive phase between 1897 and 1903, when 234 combinations were formed, including such giants as the Standard Oil Company of New Jersey, the American Telephone and Telegraph Company, and the Amalgamated Copper Company. Particularly bold was the organization of the United States Steel Corporation by J. P. Morgan in 1901. The new holding company purchased the great Carnegie Steel Company for $400 million; to this it added some nine other large corporations owning mines and manufacturing steel, tubes, wire, tin plate, sheet steel, steel hoops, and bridges—about three fifths of the nation's steel business. The par value of United States Steel's stocks and bonds totaled some $1.4 billion, making it the country's first billion dollar corporation. Since the market value of such securities was less than $800 million, however, almost half the capitalization was "water." Such overcapitalization was characteristic of the big business methods of the period.

After a recession in 1903 and 1904, this passion for trust-building slackened off perceptibly. One reason was a change of political climate in Washington that threatened antitrust actions; another was the cooling off in investor enthusiasm for the new securities flooding the market. The most promising fields for consolidation had already been exploited; some of the new trust proposals were ill-disguised stock-jobbing schemes. Investor confidence was further shaken by several episodes indicating that some of the leading financial institutions were not above sharp dealing. In 1905 a committee of the New York legislature, with Charles Evans Hughes serving as counsel, demonstrated that executives of such leading life insurance companies as the Equitable, the Mutual, and the New York Life had jeopardized the interests of their policy holders by diverting funds into highly speculative investments—sometimes for the executives' personal benefit. During the panic of 1908, some large New York banks had to close their doors because stock market plungers had wormed their way into positions where they could use depositors' savings to finance their ventures. Even the great J. P. Morgan suffered a loss of confidence when the Morgan-controlled New York, New Haven, and Hartford Railroad went into liquidation in 1913 after a giddy decade that the Interstate Commerce Commission characterized as "one of the most glaring instances of maladministration provided in the history of American railroading."

Finance Capitalism

The big corporations dominated American economic life, but who dominated the big corporations? Not, as a usual thing, the experienced steelmaker or the expert in railroad transportation. The era was one of finance capitalism. Money was the lifeblood of the large combinations, and it was the private bankers who had access to the vast funds of accumulated wealth of the nation. The great corporations could not sell their securities without

J. P. Morgan, Sr. (with cane) in France. (Brown Bros.)

the services of the investment bankers, who took part of their compensation in stock and demanded a leading voice in management to protect their own interests and those of their clients.

To the ordinary American of 1900, the name J. P. Morgan suggested vast, but ill-understood, economic power. Morgan's leadership in the field began in 1860 when he became the New York agent for a London banking house of which his father was a partner. In 1871 the young banker made an advantageous alliance with the Drexel family of Philadelphia, another well-established banking dynasty. After the panic of 1873, the Morgan firm became the strongest banking house in the country. Wealthy Englishmen wishing to invest in American government bonds or other securities gave Morgan much of his early business. In 1879 the New York banker sold a large block of New York Central stock to English investors and accepted a position on the railroad's board of directors to represent the interests of the new holders.

Over the next twenty years Morgan's influence in the railroad field steadily mounted. The pattern of events was fairly predictable. A railroad company, guilty of reckless financing and overexpansion, would find itself in serious trouble, particularly during depression years. Unable to straighten out its own affairs, the railroad would have to accept a reorganization plan drafted by Morgan. Through painful surgery—a scaling down of bondholder claims, assessments against stockholders, and the sale of new securities—the railroad would be saved from liquidation, and the Morgan firm would collect liberal compensation for its services. Moreover, to protect the new investors, Morgan-designated directors would join the boards of the reorganized companies and Morgan-approved executives would be placed in charge of operations. By 1900 Morgan's influence, in one form or another, was strong in the New York Central, the Erie, the New Haven, the Reading, the Norfolk and Western, the Lehigh Valley, and the Southern Railway System. In alliance with James J. Hill, Morgan's power extended into the affairs of the Great Northern, the Northern Pacific, and the Baltimore and Ohio.

During the 1890's Morgan also became a key figure in the consolidation of industry. For several years before he achieved his masterpiece of corporate architecture in the United States Steel Corporation, he had been active in organizing holding companies like the Federal Steel Company, the National Tube Company, and the American Bridge Company. The House of Morgan undertook to sell the securities and mobilize the capital needed for these new ventures; inevitably, therefore, it became a powerful voice in the management of the companies.

Although Morgan was the most famous banker in the country, he was not the only man in his field any more than Rockefeller and Carnegie were in theirs. Such banking houses as Lee, Higginson & Company, of Boston, and Kuhn, Loeb & Company, of New York were private firms of great prestige, while commercial banks like the First National Bank and the National City Bank of New York, were also deeply involved in the growth of finance capitalism.

Whether big business and finance capitalism were regarded as good or bad depended on the point of view. The large corporations were usually able to produce more efficiently. The standardization of products and the frequent lowering of prices raised the standard of living for the whole population. Banker control was often a conservative, rationalizing influence. Despite all this, millions of Americans were uneasy in the realization that so much power rested in so few hands. Farmers, workers, consumers, and small businessmen shared this fear and looked increasingly to the government to bring these giants under some control.

The Lot of the Worker

By comparison with Europe, the United States was a land of good wages and humane working conditions. Opportunities for employment in American mines and factories appeared sufficiently attractive to draw millions of immigrants from Europe and even to tap the rural population of the United States itself. By present-day standards, however, the worker's share in American prosperity was a modest one. Hours were long: blast furnace laborers in the steel mills worked 84 hours a week; most factory employees were at their jobs 60 hours a week; and even the relatively fortunate construction workers put in a 48-hour week. Wages were low; one estimate is that the average annual earnings of all employed workers (excluding farm laborers) in 1900 was only $490—comparable to perhaps $2,200 in today's prices.

Throughout the nineteenth century the wage earners had made sporadic efforts to improve their position by forming unions and attempting strikes and boycotts. But labor's attempts to organize had been subject to many setbacks. Every period of economic boom brought a mushroom crop of local unions; every serious depression killed off all but the hardiest of these as the workers competed frantically for the few available jobs. The labor movement also suffered through confusion as to ends and means. Middle-class reformers sought working-class support for a variety of panaceas—utopian communities, producers' cooperatives, workingmen's parties, and the like. After the Civil War, labor demonstrated increasing restlessness but still had difficulty in establishing stable organizations. The National Labor Union enrolled an impressive membership around 1870 but then was shattered by a bungling attempt to establish a third party. The Knights of Labor claimed 700,000 members in 1886 and appeared to have achieved a stronger position than any preceding American labor organization. In a wave of strikes that resulted from this growth, however, the Knights revealed unsuspected weaknesses. Having enrolled a heterogeneous company of skilled and unskilled workers, farmers, physicians, small businessmen, feminists, and miscellaneous reformers, the Knights had neither the financial reserves nor the singleness of purpose necessary to impose the principle of collective bargaining upon unwilling employers.

Samuel Gompers was the organizing genius who led American labor out of this wilderness of frustration. Himself a skilled cigarmaker, Gompers believed that permanent organization could be built only upon the foundation of the many local craft unions that had grown up in the country despite the vicissitudes of national bodies. His first attempt to federate these bodies in 1881 was not very successful. He persisted, however, and in 1886 was able to establish the American Federation of Labor on a basis destined to be permanent. President of the AFL every year except one until his death in 1924, Gompers formulated the philosophy of "pure and simple unionism" that came to dominate all but a small segment of the American labor movement. He was uncompromising in his assertion of labor's right to organize—and when necessary to strike—in order to obtain higher wages, shorter hours, and better working conditions. By other standards, however, his leadership was conservative. Gompers advocated organization along lines of skilled crafts, a procedure that proved to be impossible for many of the mass-production industries. Unlike most European labor leaders, he was completely hostile to socialism. He opposed, moreover, the formation of an independent labor party, preferring that the Federation limit its political activities to endorsing or refusing to endorse candidates of the established parties. In seeking legislation, Gompers was also cautious because he feared making labor's position too dependent on government. The leadership of Gompers was not accepted in all quarters. The railroad employees, for example, maintained the independence of their own powerful Brotherhoods, while on the left of the labor movement were numerous small radical organizations. Of 800,000 union members in 1900, about 550,000 were part of the AFL.

Despite Gompers's achievement, the American labor movement was weak in comparison with its European counterparts. How did it happen that in a highly industrial nation, where perhaps 15 million persons were working for wages in nonagricultural jobs, only 800,000 were organized for collective bargaining? Or that the number of union members in 1900 was only slightly higher than it had been at the end of the Civil War despite a doubled national population? In part, the answer lies in Gompers's preference for organization along trade lines. Except for a few industrial unions like the coal miners' and brewers', the AFL had its strength in occupations where the old tradition of craftsmanship persisted, such as the building trades, the printing trades, and the metal industries. In the great mass-production industries like steel or textiles, where the bulk of the employees were unskilled or semiskilled workers, the unions were either nonexistent or impotent.

Other fundamental factors had handicapped the American labor movement. In many parts of Europe there was a more or less stable working class, composed of men who spent their whole lives in their jobs. Such men fitted well into the Marxian concept of an industrial proletariat and were easily organized for militant action. But the American labor force had different characteristics. Many native-born workers were fresh from American farms and villages; the more ambitious were likely to work themselves up to the rank of foreman or superintendent; the less successful would sometimes drift back to the rural environment whence they had come. Enjoying this mobility, the native workers rarely thought of themselves as permanent members of the toiling masses. Some of the foreign-born workers brought with them a sense of class-consciousness, but the majority accepted meekly whatever conditions of employment were offered them and turned an indifferent ear to the union organizer. The proportion of recent immigrants among the workers in Pennsylvania coal mines, Pittsburgh steel plants, and New England textile mills was very high in 1900; indeed, many employers deliberately preferred the newcomers as even less likely to make trouble than the old groups. Any American factory was likely to contain a miscellaneous collection of employees, each feeling more kinship with others of his own nationality group than with the working class as a whole.

The dominant American philosophy of individualism provided another formidable obstacle to the growth of labor unions. Employers argued that labor relations should be based on what they called "freedom of contract." They offered terms of employment to prospective employees, and the latter were free as individuals to accept or reject the proffered conditions. From the worker's point of view, this freedom of contract was a fiction. Employers and individual employees were hardly on an equal basis, since the industrialist who employed men by the hundreds could offer terms on a take-it-or-leave-it basis, while the employee—particularly in a company town where there was a single great industry—had to accept these terms or allow his family to go hungry. Nevertheless, most employers refused to concede the justice of the case for collective bargaining. They strongly opposed both labor unions and proposals for regulatory laws.

The prevailing faith in individualism assured the employer that most middle-class Americans would share his prejudice against unionism. The "walking delegate," or professional labor leader, was regarded as nothing but a troublemaker, and strikes, picket lines, and boycotts were condemned as threats to private property and public order. Government's intervention in labor disputes was almost invariably on the side of management. When President Cleveland helped to break the Pullman strike of 1894 with Federal court injunctions, the arrest and imprisonment of Eugene V. Debs and other strike leaders, and the use of Federal troops, his one-sided action won wide applause from the general public. Middle-class opinion was not yet ready to accept the labor unions as truly respectable institutions.

Despite this unfavorable climate of opinion, the labor unions continued to grow in the early twentieth century. Between 1900 and 1914 the AFL increased its membership from 550,000 to over 2 million, and the unaffiliated unions grew from 250,000 members to 625,000. The United Mine Workers, founded in 1890, increased steadily in power during these years. In 1897 the UMW won its first significant victory when it forced the operators of the so-called central bituminous field—western Pennsylvania, Ohio, Indiana, and Illinois—to recognize the union and enter into arrangements for periodic bargaining. The anthracite operators of eastern Pennsylvania were bitterly opposed to the union, but President Theodore Roosevelt's intervention during the strike of 1902 [2] helped the UMW, now under John Mitchell's able leadership, to win important concessions for the miners. Formal recognition of the union was not conceded at this time, but by 1916 the UMW was strong enough to obtain an important contract with the anthracite operators that granted recognition, the eight-hour day, and increased pay.

2 See Chap. 2.

Elsewhere the UMW was less successful. In the West Virginia bituminous mines, the operators, enjoying strong support from state and local government, were able to limit the union to small gains. The UMW's most costly defeat was in its attempt to organize the bituminous coal fields of southern Colorado. Here underpaid workers—80 per cent of them unable to speak English—lived under almost feudal conditions in primitive company towns without decent homes or sanitary provisions. The strike that began in September, 1913, and dragged on for some fifteen months, was one of the most bitter conflicts in labor history. In the Ludlow massacre of April 20, 1914, the National Guard attacked a strikers' tent colony and killed six men, two women, and eleven children. After appealing in vain to John D. Rockefeller, Jr., who controlled one of the principal coal companies, President Wilson had to send two thousand Federal troops into Colorado to restore order.

Unionism also made important gains in the clothing industry. Immigrant women, working under sweatshop conditions in New York City, manufactured most of the country's ready-made clothing. Hitherto these underpaid seamstresses had been largely unorganized, but under the leadership of the International Ladies Garment Workers Union, they waged successful strikes in 1909 and 1910. As a result, the workers achieved immediate gains, the industry set up machinery for arbitrating future disputes, and the ILGWU became a powerful arm of the labor movement.

Confronted by the increased strength of organized labor, businessmen showed a variety of responses. Mark Hanna, wealthy Ohio businessman and powerful Republican leader, was prominent among those who believed that the unions should be recognized as legitimate American institutions. Hanna, John D. Rockefeller, Jr., Samuel Gompers, and John Mitchell were all associated in the National Civic Federation, founded in 1901 to promote industrial peace by the acceptance of collective bargaining, as well as by the promotion of mediation and conciliation. This compromising spirit was, however, alien to most employers. The labor movement suffered a severe setback when the newly established United States Steel Corporation defeated the workers in two long strikes and freed itself from any need of dealing with the unions. This conspicuous victory encouraged the management of other heavy industries to pursue antiunion policies. Equally determined opponents of unionism were to be found among small employers. The National Association of Manufacturers, founded in 1895, turned its attention to the labor problem eight years later and was aggressive in its opposition to unions.

The unions had many unhappy experiences in the courts. Federal judges were particularly generous in granting injunctions, basing their action on the contention that picketing, boycotting, and other union activities were conspiracies in restraint of trade under the Sherman Act. Employers also enjoyed the usual support of the professional classes and other opinion-shapers. Small-town editors denounced labor organizers as troublemakers, and local vigilante groups sometimes ran the organizers out of town or broke up meetings that they tried to address.

An employer's antiunion policies did not always indicate a desire to subject his workers to ruthless exploitation. This was dramatically illustrated on January 5, 1914, when Henry Ford announced that he had established a minimum wage of $5.00 per eight-hour day. Ford's motives in proposing to pay twice the going rate for labor were partly altruistic and partly selfish, but some employers who followed his example worked out a plausible theory to justify the payment of reasonably good wages. Industries like the automobile business depended on a large market. How better could such a market be created than through lifting the income of American workers above the subsistence level? Better wages were supplemented with better working conditions. This became known as "welfare capitalism." It was still a trend in its infancy in 1914, but it served to strengthen the conviction of many middle-class Americans that workers would be better off if they ignored the siren song of the labor-union organizer and placed their faith in the good intentions of management. Wide acceptance of this belief hampered the work of union organizers and strengthened the position of antiunion employers, whether or not they were practitioners of welfare capitalism.

Meanwhile, the Gompers philosophy of conservative unionism had come under bitter attack from more radical leaders who wanted to mobilize all the workers, skilled and unskilled, into one big union, dedicated to the overthrow of capitalism. In 1897 the Western Federation of Miners seceded from the AFL and attempted to organize a rival movement. At first these efforts were not very effective, but in 1905 the leaders of the Western Federation joined with other radical unionists and such prominent socialists as Eugene V. Debs and Daniel DeLeon to found the Industrial Workers of the World (IWW). "The working class and the employing class have nothing in common," the preamble of the IWW constitution asserted. "Between these two classes a struggle must go on until all the toilers come together . . . and take hold of that which they produce by their labor through an economic organization of the working class, without affiliation with any political party."

The IWW was rent with factionalism from the beginning, and Debs, DeLeon, and several other leaders either dropped out or were expelled. At the height of its power, about 1912, the union probably had no more than sixty thousand members. Despite these handicaps, the "Wobblies" were much in the public eye in pre–World War I days when they were under the leadership of the militant "Big Bill" Haywood, a one-eyed former cowboy and miner. The IWW had its greatest success in the West, where poorly paid workers in the logging camps, mines, oil fields, canneries, and grain fields—many of them immigrants—were easy converts to a philosophy of sabotage and violence. In towns where the local police banned public meetings, IWW leaders would stage free speech demonstrations, sending in hundreds of Wobblies to make speeches and get themselves arrested, until the authorities had to reverse their policy in order to empty the overcrowded jails. In 1912, the IWW invaded the East and became involved in bitter strikes in Lawrence, Massachusetts, and Paterson, New Jersey.

Although here and there the IWW won some victories, the movement

was too radical in its objectives and methods to win over the rank and file of American workers. The AFL, committed to Gompers's philosophy of pure and simple unionism, continued to constitute the main stream of the American labor movement.

Problems of Agriculture

Changes in agriculture between 1861 and 1900 were scarcely less revolutionary than in transportation and industry. In an age of railroads, steamships, and cities, the farmer no longer thought primarily in terms of feeding and clothing his family from the produce of his own acres. Agriculture became increasingly commercial, with the farmer devoting most of his energy to the production of staples for distant markets while he purchased goods for his family at country stores or from mail-order houses. The new agriculture demanded new methods. To grow wheat or corn in profitable volume, the farmer needed many acres of land and horse-drawn harvesters and other machines. Most Middle Western farmers went heavily into debt during and after the Civil War to buy land and equipment. Although the growing of cotton in the South was not mechanized in anything like the same degree, the Southern farmer also struggled with the problem of debt. Thousands regularly mortgaged their crops to country merchants in exchange for seed and provisions.

The large volume of agricultural debt made American farmers particularly resentful of falling prices. Unfortunately for the rural population, the general trend of agricultural prices after the Civil War was downward, with especially serious declines during the periods 1872–1878 and 1887–1896. Many factors contributed to this situation. Because of increased acreage and mechanized methods, the supply of agricultural commodities expanded more rapidly than the market for them. In the world market, moreover, American farmers came into increasing competition with the producers of Russia, Argentina, Australia, and other countries.

In their own analysis of their difficulties, American farmers placed the principal blame on the businessmen with whom they dealt. They accused the railroads of fixing unfair rates, manufacturers of exacting monopolistic prices, middlemen of excessive handling charges, land speculators of withholding the best acreage, and bankers of usurious interest rates. Equally condemned were the state and Federal governments, whose monetary and fiscal policies were believed to favor bankers and industrialists while penalizing workers and farmers.

More than once during these years of agrarian discontent the farmers attempted concerted action to improve their lot. During the 1870's thousands joined the Patrons of Husbandry, popularly called the Grange. Through group purchasing and the establishment of cooperatives, the Grangers tried to free themselves from dependence on established merchants, middlemen, and manufacturers. Most of the ventures failed, but they partly served their purpose by scaring businessmen into treating their rural customers more fairly. Meantime, a number of Granger political parties sprang up in the Middle West, where they succeeded in obtaining state laws regulating the rates charged by railroads and grain elevators. The railroads soon secured the repeal of most of the regulatory laws, but the precedent of policing business in the public interest was of prime importance for the future, as evidenced by the passage of the Interstate Commerce Act of 1887.

Although better times in the early 1880's temporarily quieted agrarian agitation, the widespread agricultural depression of 1887–1896 resulted in new and stronger protest movements. The Farmers' Alliances established cooperatives and agitated for a broad program of government intervention to curb land speculation, nationalize the railroads, and provide more money and easier credit for farmers. Entering politics, these farmers' organizations won numerous local victories in the Middle West and the South, although their attempts on the national level, both under the Populist banner in 1892 and under the Democratic party label in 1896, failed. After the excitement of Bryan's Free Silver campaign died down, the agrarian ferment largely subsided.

From 1900 to 1920 American farmers were relatively free from those worries that had beset them throughout the preceding generation. The decline in farm prices ended, and a modest upward movement was in progress even before the dramatic rise during World War I. The farmer's relative prosperity was reflected in the estimated value of farm lands and buildings, which rose from a total of $16.6 billion in 1900 to $39.6 billion in 1910. The average price of farm land increased at an unprecedented rate: from $19.81 per acre in 1900 to $39.60 in 1910. For once, agricultural prices went up more than the prices of manufactured goods, thereby adding to the farmer's feeling of well-being.

Several factors combined to bring these benefits to agriculture. Many theorists emphasized the inflationary influence of discoveries of gold in the Klondike and South Africa and the new cyanide process of extracting the metal from low-grade ores. By 1914 the world's monetary stock of gold was about twice that of 1896. More fundamental, however, was the fact that the demand for agricultural products was expanding during these years more rapidly than the supply. Despite reclamation projects and new methods of dry farming, the opening of new lands in the West was proceeding at a rate much slower than it had in earlier decades. The production of staple crops continued to increase, but at a modest rate. Meantime, the number of consumers was rapidly increasing. The nonrural population of the country grew by 40 per cent from 1900 to 1910, thereby providing some twelve million more bodies to be fed and clothed with the products of agriculture. Indeed, the demands of the domestic market were such that the exports of American farm products were falling off sharply until World War I reversed this trend.

In other ways, also, life on the farm was becoming easier. The hard days of the first pioneers were over. Thousands of farmers now lived in comfortable homes near established villages with stores, churches, and schools. The railroad, rural free mail delivery, and the telephone had already taken much of the isolation and loneliness from rural life, and the cheap automobile offered even more promise for the future.

Yet despite these more hopeful days, the fundamental agricultural problem remained unsolved. The farmer was an individualist, who confidently believed that hard work and investment in more land and equipment would assure greater income. Yet the very energy with which millions of farmers sought to increase their output threatened to destroy their security. Again and again during the twentieth century American agriculture was destined to produce more than the world market could absorb at profitable prices. The precariousness of the farmer's position was increased by the rising cost of the things he had to purchase and heavier taxes and interest charges. The farm problem became a perennial political issue, as some legislators of both parties struggled to obtain measures that would help the farmer to borrow money on better terms, maintain prices on staple crops, and control production.

Religion in a Changing America

The religion of an earlier, largely rural America had manifested itself through rival denominations and forms of worship as diverse as the noisy frontier revival and the quiet Quaker meetinghouse. But certain generalizations could, nevertheless, be made. The predominant faith was Protestant, Bible-centered, and dedicated to the salvation of individual souls. Since the 1870's this old-time religion had been under assault by new intellectual forces. Darwin's theory of evolution and the "higher criticism"—a new type of critical study of the Scriptures—threatened the type of faith that was grounded upon a literal interpretation of the Bible. In the light of the new knowledge, Colonel "Bob" Ingersoll and other prominent agnostics doubted whether belief in God was any longer possible.

Yet those who thought the churches were dying underestimated religion's basic resilience and adaptability. Many churches responded to the challenge of the city by broadening their programs to include the sponsorship of scout troops and other youth groups, vocational classes, fresh-air camps for slum children, nurseries for the babies of working mothers, and temporary jobs for the unemployed. The bolder religious leaders went further than this. They asserted that it was not enough to preach salvation to the individual and to temper the lot of the poor with charitable works, but that Christians should try to reform society itself. In books like *Christianity and the Social Crisis* (1907) and *Prayers of the Social Awakening* (1910), Walter Rauschenbusch of the Rochester Theological Seminary condemned contemporary American economic life as un-Christian and advocated the establishment of a truly Christian society based upon socialistic principles. Only a minority of churchmen became Christian Socialists, but less sweeping expressions of the "social gospel" were frequent. The Federal Council of Churches, organized in 1908 through the cooperation of thirty-three Protestant bodies, adopted a "social creed" that urged the abolition of child labor, the reduction of the work day, the establishment of old-age insurance, and the "most equitable division of the products of industry that can ultimately be devised."

Meantime, many Protestant theologians had modified their teachings to accommodate the theory of evolution and other findings of modern science. In most of the leading Northern theological seminaries, the spirit of the higher criticism now pervaded Biblical study. Young ministers, thus trained, were likely to be "modernists." Although Protestant congregations were often more orthodox than their pastors, the sermons of the young liberals usually escaped criticism—provided they were not too long. Protestantism in the urban areas was quietly moving toward a milder and more tolerant creed.

In the rural districts, neither the social gospel nor modernism was popular. Asserting their faith in the "fundamentals" of old-time religion, rural preachers condemned the evils of the new day and warned of the wrath to come. When the local pastor's efforts seemed to falter, some traveling evangelist would visit the town to call sinners to repentance in highly emotional revival meetings. Most prominent among the revivalists after 1900 was the Reverend William A. ("Billy") Sunday, an ex-baseball player, who attracted tremendous crowds by his sensational and energetic preaching. He invaded the cities and inspired thousands of converts to throng to the front of the specially constructed tabernacles in which his meetings were held—to "hit the sawdust trail," in the slang phrase of the evangelist himself. Those who retained something of the old Puritan spirit were shocked at urban manners and morals. Dancing and card playing, long denounced as snares of the Devil, became increasingly popular, while newspapers, baseball games, moving pictures, and "joy riding" all intruded upon the quiet observance of the Sabbath.

The American religious situation was profoundly altered by immigration. In 1840 the Roman Catholic Church claimed about 600,000 members; by 1860 it had over 3 million; by 1910 about 16 million. Although still outnumbered by Protestants almost two to one, the Catholics had a unity that contrasted sharply with the multitude of Protestant denominations and sects. Crowded churches, large hospitals, imposing parochial schools, and numerous colleges and seminaries gave impressive evidence of Catholic strength. Fearful that the "Papists" were about to "take over" the government, excitable Protestants gave support from time to time to anti-Catholic movements like the American Protective Association of the late 1880's. Such manifestations of nativism were usually short-lived, however, and the prevalent spirit was one of tolerance.

Although the problem of modernism troubled the Catholics much less than the Protestants, the Roman Church could not avoid the challenge of the new economic conditions. The study of social problems had been encouraged by the encyclical *Rerum Novarum* (1891), in which Pope Leo XIII condemned the evils of the industrial system and advocated a Christian social order. The foremost American champion of Catholic social action was Father John A. Ryan of Catholic University. In *A Living Wage* (1906), Father Ryan deplored the fact that so many American workers were receiving wages inadequate to support their families in decent comfort and urged the enactment of minimum wage laws.

Immigration also greatly increased the number of Jews. During the middle of the nineteenth century, most Jewish immigrants came from Germany. Many of these organized "reformed" congregations, where numerous departures from strict Hebrew law and tradition were permitted. Of the 1.5 million Jews who entered the country in the new immigration of 1880–1910, over 70 per cent were from Russia and Russian Poland. Victims of persecution in the old country, most of the newcomers were strongly attached to orthodox Judaism. A substantial number of Jews took a middle stand between the reformed and orthodox congregations and attended "conservative" synagogues.

Among the reform causes taken up by religious people before World War I, none aroused more enthusiasm than the crusade against alcoholic beverages. So tragic were the broken homes and broken lives caused by intemperance, that millions of aroused people determined to drive the liquor business out of American life. While all the churches advocated temperance, the extreme goal of legislative prohibition gained most of its support from evangelical Protestants. Organized in 1874, the Woman's Christian Temperance Union had been conspicuously successful in obtaining state laws requiring that public schools give instruction in the evils of intemperance. Even more powerful was the American Anti-Saloon League, founded in 1893. By 1914 the League was employing hundreds of agents and speakers and spending hundreds of thousands of dollars annually in a many-pronged offensive. The League kept a careful record of the votes of all legislators and was singularly successful in rewarding its friends and punishing its enemies. The prohibition movement enjoyed particular success in the South, where many whites were eager to keep liquor from the blacks, and in the Middle West, where the Methodists and Baptists had their greatest strength.

By the end of 1914, nine states had banned the sale of intoxicants, while five others had voted to put prohibition into effect within the next two years. In many states where the dry forces had not yet gained statewide prohibition, local option laws permitted towns or counties to outlaw the trade. By one device or another, the saloon had been driven from most of rural America. In the cities, however, the enemy was still firmly entrenched. Since it was difficult to make local prohibition effective when liquor could be ordered by mail from neighboring communities, the Anti-Saloon League concentrated its activities on obtaining Federal legislation. In March, 1913, the Webb-Kenyon Act, passed over President Taft's veto, made it illegal to ship intoxicating liquors into any state, territory, or district where their consumption was in violation of local law. In December of the same year, the dry forces in Congress introduced a resolution providing for national prohibition by constitutional amendment. This proposal did not emerge from committee during that session, but it did fix an objective toward which all the militant foes of liquor could thenceforth drive.

Science and Education

Although the churches were still potent influences in shaping American society, they no longer dominated intellectual life. Much of the prestige which in an earlier generation had attached to the theologians now belonged to the scientists. Until the late nineteenth century, American science had been backward by European standards. Although ingenious in discovering practical applications like the telegraph or anesthesia, Americans had been lacking in the well-equipped laboratories and institutional support required for fundamental research. By 1900 the situation was changing, and a talented generation of American scientists—most of them European trained—were beginning to make contributions of great significance. Among these scholars, Albert A. Michelson, of the University of Chicago, enjoyed an international reputation for his ingenuity in measuring the speed of light and other experiments, some of which had a direct influence on Albert Einstein's famous theory of relativity. Of comparable stature were Willard Gibbs, of Yale University, founder of the science of physical chemistry, and Thomas Hunt Morgan, of Columbia University, a key figure in the field of genetics.

Much of this scientific research was along lines that seemed remote from the daily life of the average citizen. He could hardly fail to be impressed, however, by the miracles of synthetic chemistry, by which coal could now be transformed into coloring matter for cake frosting and wood pulp into sausage casings and rayon underwear.

It was when science joined hands with medicine that the most obvious contributions to human welfare became possible. Dr. Walter Reed's heroic experiment demonstrating that yellow fever was carried by mosquitoes saved thousands of lives and helped make possible the building of the Panama Canal. Medical science, working first in Puerto Rico and then in the South, discovered that hookworm was one of man's most insidious enemies, an enemy that did not kill its victim, but sapped his energies, leaving him tired, indolent, and despondent. A widespread campaign, aided by Rockefeller money, was waged to eradicate this disease and thus contribute to the rehabilitation of whole districts. Preventive medicine was meantime making smallpox, typhoid fever, and diphtheria very rare, instead of very common, diseases. No speedy magic dispelled the terrors of tuberculosis, but the work of Edward L. Trudeau at Saranac Lake, New York, demonstrated that nature would cure many cases if the patients were provided with proper rest and care in sanitariums. Through the activities of public health authorities and of the National Tuberculosis Association, founded in 1904, the annual death rate from tuberculosis of the lungs was reduced from 181.8 per hundred thousand population in 1900 to 128.2 in 1914.

The most influential American philosopher of the first half of the twentieth century was John Dewey, a gaunt Vermonter who taught first at the University of Chicago and then at Columbia. Dewey rejected belief in absolutes. Truth, he asserted, was the successfulness of ideas that men framed as instruments for the achievement of their purposes—or, in other words, as plans for solving problems. Dewey's greatest influence was in the field of education. Since truth was not fixed or complete, authoritarian methods of teaching fell into disrepute, and stress was placed on the importance of learning through experience. Social efficiency, and not mere knowledge, it was asserted, should be the aim of education. By 1914, Dewey's ideas of education had been put into practice in scores of private so-called progressive schools. Their penetration into teachers' training institutions and through these into the public schools had begun, although the period of their greatest influence still lay in the future.

Although Dewey's philosophy of education always encountered a substantial amount of conservative opposition, most Americans shared his faith that the solution of almost every national problem lay in improved schooling made available to more and more young people. The statistics of educational expansion were impressive. Between 1898 and 1914, enrollment in elementary schools grew from 16 million to more than 20 million, while that in high schools and colleges more than doubled. Much of the increase was in the South. As the number of students who went to high school and college increased, there were significant changes in the courses offered. Latin and Greek received less emphasis, and vocational training along different lines became available.

Colleges and universities became less dependent on the churches for support than they had been a generation before. New patrons were found among men who had gained wealth in banking and industry. The Rockefellers generously endowed the University of Chicago; Edward S. Harkness bestowed princely gifts on Yale; George F. Baker gave $6 million to found the Harvard Graduate School of Business Administration. Although such gifts were of inestimable value to the cause of higher education, they were not without their dangers. Some university presidents and deans, it was suspected, placed more importance on keeping the money rolling in from wealthy benefactors than in defending academic freedom. In several publicized incidents, college instructors lost their positions not because they were poor teachers, but because they were suspected of being unorthodox in their economic or political views. Concern over tenure was one of the things that led to the organization of the American Association of University Professors in 1914.

The desire to learn continued past the years of formal schooling. Many American women found an opportunity to widen their intellectual horizons through lectures and study classes sponsored by women's clubs. Large and small communities both received annual concentrated doses of education and entertainment when traveling Chautauqua companies set up their big tents in town. There such notables as Theodore Roosevelt and William Jennings Bryan might be seen and heard.

The periodical press constituted the most powerful influence working upon the adult mind. In the fourteen largest cities alone, daily newspapers had reached a circulation of over 40 million by 1914, while the circulation per issue of all periodicals—daily, weekly, monthly, and quarterly—went over the 200 million mark. American newspapers were larger, contained more news, and were more readable than most English or European papers. They made frequent crusades for good causes. The New York *World,* for example, forced the legislature to investigate the mismanagement of the life insurance companies, exposed police corruption in New York City, and aroused the public conscience on the issue of campaign contributions by the large corporations. The weekly and monthly magazines pointed out many evils in the political and business world.

There was, however, another side to the picture. The newspapers were heavily dependent upon advertising, and this situation often influenced editorial policy and decisions upon whether to play up or suppress specific news stories. The desire to expand circulation led many publishers to give an unwarranted amount of space and emphasis to stories of scandal and crime. Paradoxically, the same Joseph Pulitzer who had made the New York *World* an outstanding champion of reform contributed much to the development of "yellow journalism." He was speedily outdone, however, by William Randolph Hearst. By 1914, Hearst owned papers in New York, Chicago, Boston, Atlanta, San Francisco, and Los Angeles. Wherever they appeared, they were easily identified by their cheap sensationalism, their pseudoradicalism, and their irresponsible jingoism.

The newspapers expanded their circulation not only by featuring murders and divorces, but by introducing so-called features—comic strips, recipes, puzzles, bedtime stories, and advice to the lovelorn. This development, combined with the growth of newspaper chains and the increasing dependence of all papers on the great news services like the Associated Press and the United Press, imposed a monotonous sameness upon most American papers. The day of colorful editors and famous reporters was passing; the newspapers were gradually becoming impersonal products of machinelike journalism.

Literature and Art

The same demand for easy, rather than challenging, reading material carried over from the world of newspapers into the realm of books. Historical novels had a tremendous vogue around the turn of the century; by 1914 the trend was toward sentimental stories like those by Kate Douglas Wiggin and Gene Stratton Porter, entertaining studies of American character like those by Booth Tarkington, red-blooded tales of the North like those by Rex Beach, and earnest narratives conveying a rather obvious moral like those by Harold Bell Wright. Probably the best of the popular writers was Winston Churchill.[3] His historical novels, *Richard Carvel* and *The Crisis,* had enjoyed great success in 1899 and 1901, and his popularity was still great in 1913 and 1914 when his fictional appeal for Social Christianity, *The Inside of the Cup,* led the list of best sellers.

The minority of readers who were repelled by the shallow romanticism of the popular novelists applauded the growth of realism. The pioneers of the new school, William Dean Howells and Henry James, were firmly established by 1900. The former's most important work was already done; the latter wrote three of his greatest novels—*The Wings of the Dove, The Ambassadors,* and *The Golden Bowl*—early in the twentieth century. Among the younger writers, Edith Wharton and Willa Cather were outstanding. Most of Mrs. Wharton's novels were penetrating studies of New York society, but *Ethan Frome* (1911) was a powerful tragedy laid in a rural New England setting. Miss Cather won respect with *O Pioneers!* (1913), a finely written story of Bohemian and Scandinavian immigrants in Nebraska. Another group of novelists wrote realistic works much more sober in character. As "naturalists," they regarded human life as a Darwinian struggle for survival where the weak suffered inevitable defeat and moral choice was an illusion. Having written a few naturalist works of real power,

---

[3] Not to be confused with the famous English statesman with the same name.

two promising careers were suddenly cut short in 1900 and 1902 when Stephen Crane and Frank Norris died. Jack London lived longer, but his early promise was not fulfilled; he could not resist the temptation to gain wealth by giving the public the romantic stuff it craved. The greatest of the early naturalists was Theodore Dreiser. His first novel, *Sister Carrie* (1900), dealt with illicit love in so frank a fashion that the first editions were suppressed. Later novels, *The Financier* (1912) and *The Titan* (1914), told the story of a ruthless American businessman.

American poetry suffered from the same shallowness as American fiction. The popular poets were such genial versifiers as James Whitcomb Riley. Largely unrecognized by the general public, however, a young and singularly gifted generation of poets was learning its craft just before World War I. The oldest of the new school was Edwin Arlington Robinson, who was helped by the patronage of President Theodore Roosevelt. Less fortunate was Robert Frost, whose early work was rejected by American editors and publishers. Not until *A Boy's Will* (1913) and *North of Boston* (1914) were published and acclaimed in England did Frost find honor in his own country. Both Robinson and Frost wrote poems remarkable for their beauty of diction and their insight into life, but their work showed no radical departure from earlier verse forms. Three Chicago poets—Vachel Lindsay, Carl Sandburg, and Edgar Lee Masters—attracted attention with their bold and free techniques, as well as their unusual themes.

To serious readers this was an exciting period in which American literature seemed to be gaining a vitality and freedom that had been all too scarce since the 1840's and 1850's. Yet the "little renaissance," as the literary movement was sometimes called, never achieved broad recognition from the American public.

American achievement in the fine arts was still small. Painters were hardly recognized as useful members of society, and indeed they often preferred to live abroad. This was the case with James McNeill Whistler and John Singer Sargent, who gained fame in England. Some of the most notable of Sargent's work was nevertheless done in the United States, where he accepted lucrative commissions to paint the lords of Wall Street and their wives and daughters. Boston was vastly proud of the murals with which Sargent decorated her Public Library and her Museum of Fine Arts. More authentically American painters were Winslow Homer, who conveyed to canvas the rugged beauty of the Maine coast, Albert Ryder, who created dark, mysterious fantasies with his brush, and Thomas Eakins, who discovered significant new themes in hospital operating rooms and sports scenes. Even more realistic was the work of John Sloan and George Bellows, who recorded everyday life in New York City—its bars, prize fights, and slums.

Although the lot of the serious artists was not easy, some individuals won both fame and fortune through their dexterity with pencil and brush. The magazine illustrations of Charles Dana Gibson, James Montgomery Flagg, and Howard Chandler Christy enjoyed a tremendous vogue. The "Gibson girl" was indeed an influence to be reckoned with. She was the lovely, smartly dressed young lady that every American girl imagined herself to be.

Sculpture interested the general public more than did painting. After all, a people proud of its history could not fail to think it appropriate that the figures of its famous statesmen and generals should be carved in stone for the adornment of its parks and public buildings. Fortunately, a generation of talented American sculptors was available for the task. The most prominent was Augustus Saint-Gaudens, but George Gray Barnard, Daniel Chester French, and Lorado Taft also did memorable work.

American cities were losing some of their earlier ugliness with the development of fine parks and broad avenues and by the erection of impressive buildings. The prevalent taste in architecture was for the traditional styles, either neoclassical or Gothic. Monumental structures like the Pennsylvania Station in New York City found their inspiration in ancient Roman buildings. Many of the new "skyscrapers," like the fifty-seven-story Woolworth Building, completed in 1912, were given a Gothic cloak. Largely unrecognized by the general public were the two Chicago architects destined to exert a great future influence. Louis Sullivan and Frank Lloyd Wright rejected the prevalent traditionalism and advocated a more "functional," or "organic," style.

The state of American music was peculiar. Millions of little Americans were industriously practicing on the parlor piano; thousands of Caruso records were being purchased for the new phonographs; the Metropolitan Opera Company of New York was the finest in the world; the symphony orchestras of Boston, Philadelphia, Chicago, and New York were among the world's greatest. These facts suggested that the United States was a nation of music lovers. But piano playing was mostly a polite accomplishment with which young ladies were expected to impress their young gentlemen callers; the phonograph was a novelty; the opera and symphonies brought real pleasure to only a select few. Before World War I, Americans seldom became great musicians, more seldom still great composers.

But Americans did thoroughly enjoy music in its lighter forms. Operettas and musical comedies had long runs, and millions of Americans hummed their hit tunes. The public taste for this type of music was well served. In all the world there was no more skilled creator of captivating melodies than Victor Herbert. A new type of dance music destined to conquer the world was just evolving in 1914. Jazz was born in New Orleans; thence it spread to the big excursion boats that plied the Mississippi River ports. Jazz captured Chicago, and then moved east to New York. The first great combination, the Dixieland Band, was organized in New Orleans about 1905, moved from city to city, and finally took both New York and London by storm in the years following 1916. About 1912 W. C. Handy published the "Memphis Blues" and the "St. Louis Blues"—both destined for jazz immortality.

These then were the "good old days." Viewed in close perspective, they do not seem a golden age. The United States was prosperous, but its prosperity did not extend to all groups. The nation was religious, but its church members did not invariably practice righteousness. The country was full of schoolhouses, newspapers, and books, but popular taste in literature, art, and music was shallow. The days between 1900 and 1917 linger in affectionate memory not because they were perfect, but because they were untroubled by the most acute of present anxieties.

2

ROOSEVELT AND REFORM

An exciting period in American politics began on September 14, 1901, the day when the young and colorful Theodore Roosevelt became President of the United States. During the course of the next seven and a half years, Roosevelt was the dominant figure on the national and international scene. At home he won fame as the first chief executive to achieve many of the goals of progressivism. Yet historians have hotly disputed whether Roosevelt deserved such fame as a reformer. Certainly the demand for reform was much older and bigger than the popular President. When he took office a ferment was already at work that found its outlet in a demand for purging whatever seemed corrupt and unjust in American government and life. Many progressives denied that Roosevelt was a progressive at all. From their point of view, he was a highly intelligent conservative who used his popularity to capture the progressive movement and appease the voters with halfway measures, while safeguarding the interests of his business friends against any serious threats to their interests.

Business and Politics

During the presidency of William McKinley, the millionaire Ohio industrialist Mark Hanna played the role of national Republican boss and kept the Federal government safely quarantined from the contagion of reform. Hanna's prominence in national politics dramatized a situation that was far from new. Since the Civil War, businessmen had exerted a dominant influence over both state and national government. This was in contrast to the pre–Civil War situation in which the agrarian interests had usually been paramount. The shift in power, which paralleled new economic developments, was hastened by the Civil War. Taking advantage of the absence of legislators from the South, Republicans from the Northeast and the Middle West had enacted a series of tariff, banking, and railroad subsidy laws that benefited business.

With the end of the Civil War, the business interests felt some uneasiness lest a premature revival of the Democratic party should endanger their gains. Radical Reconstruction policies, however, kept at least a part of the South under Republican domination until the last Federal troops were withdrawn in 1877. Thereafter, resentful Dixie voted solidly Democratic for many years. This development weakened Republican control of the national government but did not destroy it. During the 36 years between

1865 and 1901, the Republicans controlled the House of Representatives 20 years and the Democrats 16. Republicans sat in the White House 28 of these 36 years; they controlled the Senate 32 of them. There was, moreover, very little distinction between the parties on most economic issues. Conservative Southern Democrats often collaborated with the Republicans in Congress. Furthermore, conservative leaders like Samuel J. Tilden and Grover Cleveland dominated the Northern wing of the Democratic party during most of these years.

Republican dominance was, in fact, based on something more solid than alliance with the business interests and the tenuous cooperation of conservative Democrats. The farmers of the East and Middle West usually voted Republican in gratitude for Republican-sponsored homestead legislation, land grants for agricultural colleges, and creation of the Department of Agriculture. The labor vote was divided, but the Republican convinced a substantial proportion of the industrial workers that a high protective tariff was their guarantee of high wages and "a full dinner pail." Probably a majority of the voters of every class were politically regular, casting their ballots for the party that had always held the loyalty of their family. The Democrats could thus depend upon many groups in the large cities of the North, particularly those of recent immigrant origin. Similarly, millions of Northern and Midwestern families were traditionally Republicans—still loyal to the "Grand Old Party" that had saved the Union.

Prominent in both Republican and Democratic party circles were the political bosses. These experienced politicians obtained campaign gifts from corporations and wealthy individuals and levied assessments upon public employees. By manipulating the machinery of nomination, they saw to it that none but "safe" men became candidates for public office. Party regularity demanded that legislators vote for or against bills as the bosses directed. Governors were expected to give jobs to faithful party workers. The state bosses exercised great influence over the Federal government as well. Their particular citadel was the Senate—until 1913 elected by the state legislatures rather than directly by the people. Such bosses as Thomas C. Platt of New York and Matthew Quay and Boies Penrose of Pennsylvania sat in the Senate themselves, while many of their fellow Senators were wealthy men enjoying this reward for generous campaign contributions. As members of the upper house, the bosses and their lieutenants not only exercised a veto on unwanted legislation, but used their power to control the Federal patronage. In the House of Representatives, the dictatorial rule of speakers like "Czar" Reed and "Uncle Joe" Cannon speedily schooled Congressmen in the virtues of party regularity and the perils of insurgency.

So long as political machines did not overreach themselves and engage in crude graft that raised taxes and antagonized the voters, many businessmen welcomed their existence. To the boss the businessman made his political contribution; to the boss he went when he wanted some law enacted, or—as more frequently happened—he wanted some legislative proposal defeated. Although businessmen usually professed their devotion to the philosophy of laissez faire, this did not inhibit them from seeking governmental aid in the form of tariffs, land grants, and franchises.

Practical politicians had to temper their ardor for the business interests with occasional concessions to other groups. Yet these proved to be only small breaches in the conservative dike. The silver purchase laws fell far short of the wholesale issuance of greenbacks and the free coinage of silver demanded by Western inflationists. The Federal civil service system was dependent upon presidential action for its implementation and still left much patronage under the control of the political leaders. The powers granted to the Interstate Commerce Commission were so narrow that shippers still found themselves without adequate remedy against unfair treatment by the railroads. At the same time, the Sherman Act became almost a dead letter through the unwillingness of the Attorneys General to initiate suits and the narrow interpretation given the law by the courts.

Indeed, the conservatism of state and Federal courts proved to be one of the most important lines of defense against legislation unwanted by the businessmen. The Fourteenth Amendment provided only shaky protection to black people but was so interpreted that it gave corporations immunity from many types of "unreasonable" regulation. Similarly, the Sherman Act, although ineffective in breaking up trusts, proved a useful weapon for prosecuting leaders of strikes and boycotts for "conspiracy in restraint of trade." In one of the most controversial decisions in its history, the Supreme Court in 1895 held a Federal income tax to be unconstitutional.

When it sometimes seemed to read the philosophy of laissez faire into the Federal Constitution itself, the Supreme Court revealed the influence of a tradition of American thought as old as Thomas Jefferson. In his inaugural address in 1801, the third President had argued that American happiness and prosperity depended upon "a wise and frugal Government, which shall restrain men from injuring one another, which shall leave them otherwise free to regulate their own pursuits of industry and improvement, and shall not take from the mouth of labor the bread it has earned." From the beginning, this philosophy had been challenged by another point of view, first articulated by the brilliant Alexander Hamilton and maintained with more or less consistency by the Federalists, the Whigs, and the Republicans. Less fearful of government and more nationalistic, the Hamiltonian tradition had favored positive Federal action to promote economic prosperity.

After the Civil War, the dominant business classes skillfully extracted what was most useful to their interests from both the Jeffersonian and Hamiltonian traditions. In their opposition to government regulation of economic affairs, business leaders could cite the warnings of Jefferson, while in their requests for protective tariffs, land grants to railroads, and government loans they could quote Hamilton. The orthodox philosophy was one of laissez faire—that is, a hands-off policy by government that would allow businessmen a maximum amount of liberty to run their own affairs— but it was a distinctly American version of laissez faire, with ample leeway for business to get what positive government assistance it could. To put this American version in another way, the business leaders scrupulously preserved laissez faire for the farmers and workers, while for themselves they tried to avoid its perils by private consolidations and government assistance.

The traditional Jeffersonian argument for laissez faire was powerfully buttressed during the 1880's and 1890's by a system of thought known as Social Darwinism. This depicted social evolution as the result of a struggle for existence among fiercely competing individuals. In this contest, the strong and efficient won out; the weak and inefficient fell by the wayside; only thus could progress be achieved. Legislation to hamper the strong or to help the weak was, therefore, both futile and harmful. Wise statesmanship should permit a maximum of individual liberty, restricting the function of government to the protection of lives and property and the enforcement of contracts. Conservative—or so-called hard—Social Darwinism received its first persuasive statement in the works of Herbert Spencer, an English philosopher with an amazingly large American following. The American writer who stated the case most forcefully was William Graham Sumner, famous Yale professor who rebuked all projects for social reform that involved limiting the liberty of the rich in order to equalize the opportunities of the poor.

The traditional social values preached from Protestant pulpits provided still a third support for laissez faire. Since the days of John Calvin, most Protestants had emphasized a doctrine of extreme individualism. Each man had a moral obligation to work hard in his chosen occupation or "calling," to save his money, and to abstain from waste and luxury. The rich man was assumed to have been blessed by God with rewards appropriate to his superior industry and thrift; the poor man suffered the consequences of his own laziness and lack of foresight. To Americans schooled in these simple precepts, the idea that government had a responsibility to protect the poor from exploitation and to restrain the rich from using their power unjustly seemed almost impious.

The Rising Tide of Protest

Although the conservatives appeared to be firmly in the saddle of government, they were really insecurely mounted. For three decades before 1900 there had been a growing discontent with many aspects of American political and economic life. Both workers and farmers had participated in sporadic attempts to organize third parties in order to demonstrate their resentment against conservative control of the two major parties. These efforts culminated in the Populist movement of the 1890's. In its platform of 1892, the "People's Party" demanded the issuance of more money (both paper and silver), a graduated income tax, government ownership of railroads and telegraphs, conservation of the national domain, government loans to farmers, restriction of immigration, election of Senators by direct vote of the people, adoption of the initiative and referendum, and use of the secret ballot. James B. Weaver, the Populist candidate for President, received more than a million votes and twenty-two electoral ballots. This impressive gesture of protest would have been greater still if the industrial workers had given wholehearted support to the movement.

In 1896 agrarian radicals captured the Democratic party. William Jennings Bryan made a spirited campaign for the presidency on a platform that incorporated many of the Populist demands of 1892, although it subordinated all other planks to the demand for the unlimited coinage of silver. Despite sweeping victories in the West and South, Bryan went down to defeat, and the revolt of the farmers subsided during the ensuing period of prosperity. Although free silver was dead as a political issue, a vestige of populism survived. The farmers had been imbued with fear of corporate wealth and monopoly, and this fear of big business was destined to be one of the principal ingredients of the progressive movement after 1900.

William Jennings Bryan. (Brown Bros.)

The citadels of American capitalism were under assault from another direction as well. For decades a few Americans had been familiar with the teachings of Karl Marx. In 1877 various local Marxist groups merged to form the Socialist Labor party—at first more a propagandists' group than a political party. From 1900 to 1914 the brilliant Daniel DeLeon dominated this Marxist faction. Opposing all halfway measures, DeLeon demanded a proletarian revolution aimed at the "unconditional surrender of capitalism." His militancy and hostility to the established labor union movements repelled all but a small group of faithful followers. The rival Socialist party, organized by Eugene V. Debs and others in 1901, was more moderate in its program and tactics. A sincere and eloquent Midwesterner, Debs was well equipped to present socialism in a way that largely cleared it of the taint of foreign ideology. As presidential candidate of his party, Debs's popular vote steadily increased from 95,000 in 1900 and 900,000 in 1912.

By other standards also, the Socialists seemed to be making themselves a force in American life. Victor Berger, who had helped found the party, went to Washington as Congressman from Wisconsin; the voters of Milwaukee elected a Socialist mayor, Emil Seidel. Many Socialist periodicals were published, and there was a large Socialist faction within the AFL.

Although the ultimate Socialist goal was the establishment of a cooperative commonwealth, they presented a series of immediate demands that were in reality only an advanced brand of populism. In addition to public ownership of railroads, utilities, and mines, they sought government relief for the unemployed, a shorter work week, abolition of child labor, social security legislation, income and inheritance taxes, equal suffrage, initiative and referendum, proportional representation, and abolition of the Supreme Court's power to pass upon the constitutionality of laws. While never more than a minority of Americans called themselves Socialists, the followers of Debs, like the Populists, helped to educate the American public to the idea that government should intervene in American economic life to promote social justice.

Although most middle-class people scorned populism and socialism as manifest absurdities, certain powerful intellectual forces were shaking the very foundations on which the philosophy of laissez faire rested. In contrast to Sumner's hard Social Darwinism, thinkers such as Lester Frank Ward had developed a soft, or liberal, Social Darwinism. Ward emphasized the idea that men could use their intelligence to direct social evolution toward definite goals. He repudiated laissez faire and argued for a program of bold government action to promote the general welfare. The philosophy of pragmatism, given its first persuasive statement by William James, threatened not only the sanctity of laissez faire, but all the other orthodoxies of the day. Pragmatism rejected the idea of a single, absolute truth. All ideas, according to James, must be tested by their practical results. In its origins, pragmatism supported extreme individualism, but in the hands of John Dewey, the new philosophy became an instrument of social criticism and an encouragement to social experimentation.

In provoking Americans to consider whether there might not be serious flaws in the existing social system and whether government might not be utilized to remedy these flaws, the writers of the late nineteenth century were particularly important. In *Progress and Poverty* (1879), Henry George found the cause for increasing want in the private ownership of land. As the remedy, he advocated the so-called single tax, a levy to take away from the landlord for the benefit of society the increase in the value of land that was created by no labor of its owner, but arose through the growth of cities, proximity to markets, or the discovery of mineral resources. Even those who regarded George's prescription as oversimple found his graphic description of the inequalities of American life profoundly moving. Similarly provocative was Edward Bellamy's *Looking Backward: 2000–1887* (1888). This fascinating novel contrasted the injustices of contemporary society with a Utopian America of the year 2000, when all industry would be merged into one great trust, or national syndicate. Repudiating the ideas of class struggle and proletarian dictatorship, Bellamy made socialism appear respectable to many middle-class idealists who shied away from the more ruthless aspects of Marxism.

Conservatives could not even rely on religion as an unyielding bulwark for the old order. As described in the previous chapter, many churchmen, both Protestant and Catholic, were becoming outspoken critics of un-Christlike features in the nation's political and economic structure.

The Muckrakers

After 1900, the reform movement gained much of its impetus from the activities of a talented group of writers known as the "muckrakers." This label was intended to convey a rebuke when it was applied to these authors by President Theodore Roosevelt in 1906, and the more irresponsible of them may have deserved such condemnation. The more important muckrakers, however, were scrupulously honest. They painted a dark picture of contemporary political and economic life only because they had discovered unpleasant truths.

The earliest of the great exposures appeared in *McClure's Magazine.* Eager to increase his circulation, S. S. McClure employed the most capable journalists he could and advanced thousands of dollars for their investigations. In October, 1902, appeared the first of Lincoln Steffens's revealing articles on municipal corruption. St. Louis, Minneapolis, Philadelphia— one city after another provided shocking case studies for what the author called *The Shame of the Cities.* Only a month after the first Steffens article, *McClure's* began the publication of Ida M. Tarbell's *History of the Standard Oil Company*—a muckraking classic based upon five years of patient research into the devious transactions that had built up that huge business. In Ray Stannard Baker, McClure discovered still another talented factfinder, who wrote effective articles on labor relations, railroad rate practices, and the status of black people.

Other magazines soon followed *McClure's* lead. In *Everybody's Magazine, Collier's,* and Hearst's *Cosmopolitan,* there were articles by Thomas V. Lawson on stock market speculation, by Charles Edward Russell on the meat industry, and by Samuel Hopkins Adams on patent medicines. Most sensational of all was David Graham Phillips's *The Treason of the Senate,* an exposé of the close ties between well-known legislators and the vested interests. This was the series that prompted Roosevelt's stinging denunciation at a Gridiron Club banquet in April, 1906.

Roosevelt's disapproval was not enough to kill the literature of exposure. Muckraking articles were still an important political influence during Taft's administration. Several factors, however, finally brought muckraking to an end. The earliest writers had exhausted the richest veins of material; later investigators found less rewarding subjects and often did their work less carefully. Exposure of corruption lost some of its novelty and was less effective in selling magazines. Financiers and advertisers exerted an increasingly costly pressure against the muckraking periodicals. The final blow was World War I, which diverted attention from domestic issues and divided the reformers into prowar and antiwar factions.

Although muckraking found its most characteristic medium in magazine articles, it flowed through other channels as well. Gustavus Myers's three-volume *History of the Great American Fortunes* (1910) was based on years of thorough research by a scholarly Socialist. One of the most effective documents of the period was Upton Sinclair's novel *The Jungle* (1906)— a shocking revelation of labor relations and sanitary conditions in the meat industry. The muckraking spirit also pervaded much of the fiction written by Jack London, Brand Whitlock, David Graham Phillips, and Winston Churchill.

The Rise of Progressivism

Grangers, Greenbackers, Single-Taxers, Bellamyites, Populists, and Socialists had all challenged the conservative control of government. Despite their vigor, however, these groups were indisputably minority elements, regarded by general middle-class opinion as visionary and dangerous. What was chiefly to distinguish progressivism from these earlier manifestations of protest was its broad appeal—its respectability in the eyes of a majority of the people.

Both in its leadership and its rank and file, the progressive movement was primarily middle class. The men who became reform mayors, governors, and legislators were often relatively young. Although a few were "self-made" men who had risen out of poverty, the larger number came from moderately well-to-do families. Most of them were Anglo-Saxon and Protestant; most had gone to college. Many of them came from small towns and even those who were urban-born usually felt a nostalgic loyalty to the supposed virtues of small-town life. They romanticized the integrity and high-mindedness of small-town people and looked down upon the foreign-born urban masses as ignorant, corrupt, and criminal. Although the progressives boldly proclaimed that the cure for democracy was more democracy, there was a paradoxical core of elitism in the movement. The progressives believed it necessary to wrest power from the bosses and place it in the hands of men of high principle like themselves. They placed great faith in the nonpolitical expert. Many progressives were clergymen, lawyers, and editors—members of professions that had once provided most of the political and social leadership of the country, who had now lost it to men of different background—political bosses, manipulators of trusts, and stock market operators. The progressives tended to think in highly moralistic terms: they saw themselves as the champions of virtue doing battle with the enemies of the people.

Although the progressives are often portrayed as defenders of the public interest forcing regulation upon an unwilling business community, the true situation was much more complicated. Many of those calling for reform were themselves wealthy businessmen: merchants and industrialists involved in the export trade were often tariff reformers; middlemen shipping goods by rail called for lower rates; railroad executives disgusted with the shippers' demands for special rates often welcomed regulation as a means of stabilizing the rate structure and abolishing the nuisance of rebates. Executives of well-established companies often wanted to suppress the cutthroat competitive methods of the newer and smaller firms. Businessmen harassed by conflicting state laws often agitated for national regulation instead.

It is similarly misleading to depict the progressives as always antiurban and anti-immigrant. Even within boss-ridden Tammany Hall, younger leaders like Alfred E. Smith and Robert F. Wagner were demanding progressive legislation that would improve working conditions for their immigrant constituents. Settlement house workers like Chicago's Jane Addams and New York's Lillian Wald often supported these demands. So amorphous was the progressive movement that it can only be defined in very broad terms. The progressives included liberals of all political parties who were seeking to purify politics and to eliminate the worst abuses in American business life.

The growing demand for reform became effective at the local and state level before it did in national politics. Samuel M. Jones, a successful factory owner, was elected mayor of Toledo, Ohio, in 1897. He rebelled against becoming a party to graft, thereby provoking a bitter fight with the Republican machine. He had gained the nickname of "Golden-Rule" because he endeavored to apply that Christian principle in his business dealings; he carried the same spirit into his administration of the city government. He took night sticks away from the policemen, introduced free kindergartens into the public schools, and established public playgrounds. He continued to win re-election until his death in 1904; the next year his disciple and former secretary, Brand Whitlock, was elected mayor. Whitlock's most notable achievement was a new city charter providing for initiative, referendum, recall, and direct nominations.

Events followed a similar pattern in Cleveland. Tom L. Johnson had had a highly successful business career during the eighties and nineties. A monopolist himself, he entered the crusade against monopoly after reading the works of Henry George. In 1901 he was elected mayor of Cleveland, where he gave the people an administration so energetic and efficient that Lincoln Steffens described him as "the best mayor of the best governed city in America." After eight years in office Johnson was defeated, but in 1911 a new reform mayor, Newton D. Baker, was elected to continue Johnson's policies.

Jones and Johnson were the most picturesque of the municipal reformers, but there were many others. Attempts were made to clean out such Augean stables as Chicago, St. Louis, Minneapolis, Jersey City, San Francisco, and even New York. Many brave victories were won, but few of them proved to be permanent. All too often the grafters took cover while public indignation waxed strong, only to emerge again almost as arrogant when the voters returned to complacency.

One of the weaknesses in the municipal reform movement was that the crusaders for decency often limited their indignation to the crooked politicians, shutting their eyes to the fact that the bribe-givers were as responsible as the bribe-takers for the low state of city government. Realistic reformers like Tom Johnson recognized that their most powerful enemies were respected businessmen who manipulated city councilmen, tax assessors, and judges to get profitable streetcar franchises, low tax assessments, and similar special privileges. Johnson therefore believed that the jailing of a few political grafters was much less important than fundamental changes like government ownership of railroads and city transit lines and the elimination of land monopoly through the single tax. Yet the average American, traditionally respectful to the rights of private property, was reluctant to consider these more radical remedies.

A second shortcoming of moralists who focused all their wrath on individual malefactors was that they failed to give serious consideration to the structure of municipal government. Most cities had antiquated charters providing for large, unwieldy city councils, weak mayors, and a dispersion of executive responsibility among separately elected department heads and independent boards. Many reformers believed that the solution lay in new forms of city government. Galveston, Texas, devised one such innovation following a disastrous flood and hurricane in 1900. To meet the emergency, extraordinary powers were placed in the hands of a commission of five. The experiment was so successful that a new city charter made the commission form of government permanent. Another widely copied plan was that devised for Dayton, Ohio, under which a commission acted like a board of directors for the city, while the actual municipal administration was entrusted to a city manager, a nonpolitical executive hired to run the government along lines of business efficiency. In one form or another, commission government had been introduced in 210 American cities by 1912, with varying degrees of success.

The progressives found a particularly fruitful field for activity within the state governments. The major political bosses maintained themselves through their control of the state capitals; they could best be forced to abdicate by popular revolts within their own feudal preserves. In these years, moreover, it seemed that reformers could obtain the bulk of the necessary regulation of business through state legislation enacted under the so-called police power—that is, the power that enabled a legislature to pass laws for the protection of the public health, morals, safety, or general welfare.

The career of Robert M. LaFollette of Wisconsin best exemplified the campaign against the bosses. Elected to Congress as a young man, he discovered that he was supposed to take orders from Senator Philetus Sawyer, wealthy lumber man and political boss. As punishment for his independence, LaFollette was kept out of office for nine years, but during that period he worked doggedly to build an anti-Sawyer bloc within the Republican party of the state. To defeat the old machine, it was necessary to create a new one, committed to the interests of the people as against those of the great corporations. LaFollette's triumph came in 1900 when he was elected governor by the largest majority in Wisconsin's history. He was re-elected in 1902 and 1904; from 1906 until his death in 1925 he represented his state in the United States Senate.

The program that LaFollette carried into effect in his home state was given wide publicity as the "Wisconsin idea." To curb the power of the bosses, he obtained a law that took the naming of candidates out of the control of party caucuses and conventions and gave it to the voters in direct primary elections. He attacked the privileged position of the railroads by getting legislation requiring the corporations to pay a larger

The Robert M. LaFollettes, Junior and Senior. (World Wide Photos.)

share of taxes, enlarging the power of the state railroad commission, and prohibiting the acceptance of railroad passes. Other laws subjected inheritances to a progressive tax, provided for workmen's compensation in case of industrial accidents, and aimed at the conservation of the forests and water power.

No less important than Wisconsin as a laboratory for trying out new ideas was the state of Oregon. In 1891 the legislature introduced the Australian, or secret, ballot; in 1899 it passed a new registration law; in 1902 it introduced the initiative and referendum; in 1904, 1908, and 1910, respectively, it enacted a direct primary law, a corrupt practices act, and a measure providing for the recall. William U'Ren, a quiet man who avoided public positions and campaigned for reform through the agency of voters' organizations, led the fight for all these Oregon innovations.

Everywhere the progressives placed great importance on the adoption of new devices of democratic government. All the states eventually resorted to some form of the direct primary; twenty-one states adopted initiative and referendum procedures; eleven states provided for recall of state officials. Women's suffrage also became a part of the progressive program; by 1914 eleven states—all west of the Mississippi—had granted women the right to vote. The direct election of United States Senators was an almost universal progressive demand. Since, as a constitutional amendment, it required a two-thirds vote of the very chamber it sought to reform, direct election was not finally achieved until 1913. Prior to that time, however, twenty-nine states adopted senatorial preference primaries, which in effect took the power of election out of the hands of state legislatures and put it in the hands of the voters.

Humanitarians were particularly disturbed by the prevalence of child labor—an evil that seemed to be on the increase. In 1900 more than 1.7 million children—almost one out of five in the ten-to-fifteen age bracket—were gainfully employed. New Jersey berry fields, Kentucky coal mines, Vermont granite quarries, and Carolina textile mills were all employing children, usually for long hours at pitifully small wages. In 1904 a National Child Labor Committee was organized to press for reform. During the next ten years most of the states set minimum ages for employment, ranging from twelve to fifteen years; they specified maximum hours for youthful employees and forbade night work and work in certain dangerous jobs; and they established educational requirements. Yet much remained to be done: some states had set higher standards than others, thereby risking an exodus of industries to their more lenient neighbors. Many reformers believed that a Federal law was necessary, and Senator Albert Beveridge of Indiana introduced such a bill in 1906. Not until the Wilson administration, however, did Congress take the desired action.

Another area of significant progress was in protecting industrial workers against the hazard of injury on the job. Until the 1890's victims of industrial accidents found it impossible to recover damages from their employers. A new crop of employers' liability acts passed during the 1890's and early 1900's corrected some of the old injustices but still required the injured worker to collect his claims through expensive litigation in the courts. Workmen's compensation acts, requiring employers to carry insurance against industrial accidents, provided a much more satisfactory remedy. Some thirty-five such measures were passed in various states between 1910 and 1917.

Similar advances were made in other areas. During the first thirty years of the century all except five states enacted laws limiting the number of hours that women could work. Statutes limiting the workday for men were less frequent, but several states restricted the hours in certain occupations, such as mining. About one third of the states enacted measures embodying maximum-wage standards for women and children. Conditions that had long been taken for granted suddenly aroused the public conscience and brought remedial legislation. Thus in the three years between 1911 and 1913, twenty states passed mothers' assistance acts providing pensions for widows with dependent children. The first state to set up an old-age pension system was Arizona, in 1914, but the state supreme court found the act unconstitutional.

The Road to the White House

Theodore Roosevelt, member of a prominent old New York City family, had been in a hurry from the start. In 1880 he was graduated from Harvard; in 1881 he was elected to the New York Assembly; the following year he published *The Naval War of 1812,* the first of his several books. After three years in the legislature he purchased two cattle ranches in the Bad Lands of North Dakota. Although this venture was not an economic success, his residence in the West helped to develop his philosophy of "the strenuous life." After his return to the East Roosevelt was nominated as Republican candidate for mayor of New York City in 1886. He ran a poor third to Abram Hewitt, the successful Democratic candidate, and Henry George, who had the support of the labor unions. Not disheartened by this setback, Roosevelt found a new outlet for his energy in a period of service on the Federal Civil Service Commission, to which he was appointed by President Benjamin Harrison and reappointed by President Cleveland. His next important post was the presidency of the New York City board of police commissioners, where he displayed independence, vigor, and a flair for provoking controversy.

In the election of 1896, Roosevelt campaigned for William McKinley, for which he was rewarded with appointment as Assistant Secretary of the Navy. There he played a conspicuous part in building up the strength of the service and preparing it for effective participation in the war with Spain—a conflict he welcomed with enthusiasm. Not content with a desk job during hostilities, the young politician resigned to obtain a commission as lieutenant colonel of the First Volunteer Cavalry—the famous Rough Riders, composed in large part of recruits from Roosevelt's beloved West. The new colonel eventually saw action in Cuba, particularly in the battle of San Juan Hill, where a disproportionate share of the glory fell upon his willing shoulders.

Roosevelt returned to the United States a hero, and Boss Thomas C. Platt succeeded in having him elected governor of New York. Platt soon repented of his action, however; although he and the new governor did not quarrel openly—Roosevelt was too well aware of the requirements for practical political achievement to do this—they did not get along well. Roosevelt refused to give the boss anything approaching a free hand; he insisted on reasonably honest appointments and he advocated certain reforms that Platt disliked. From the boss's point of view, the governor was irresponsible and impulsive. The presidential election of 1900 offered Platt an opportunity to get Roosevelt out of Albany.

The Republicans certainly did not intend to make progressivism an issue in the 1900 campaign. Astutely manipulated by Mark Hanna, the Republican convention renominated the safe and respectable William McKinley and adopted an equally safe and respectable platform, which praised the administration's foreign and domestic policies and pledged the party to the gold standard, the protective tariff, the maintenance of American rule over Hawaii and the Philippines, and the construction and control of an interoceanic canal by the United States.

At only one point were Hanna's wishes ignored. Vice President Garret Hobart had died in 1899, thereby leaving the race for the second post wide open. Hanna wanted to dictate this nomination also, but a number of factors took the decision out of his hands. Matthew Quay, Republican boss of Pennsylvania, disliked Hanna and welcomed an opportunity to oppose him. Platt had no quarrel with Hanna, but longed to remove Roosevelt from the governorship. Thus several state bosses decided to support Roosevelt, whom the disapproving Hanna referred to as that "damned cowboy." When news of this plan to "kick him upstairs" reached the governor's ears, he objected strenuously. He felt he was too young to take an office traditionally regarded as a dead-end street in politics. But the rank and file of convention delegates—particularly those from the West—took up the idea of Roosevelt for Vice President with marked enthusiasm and refused to allow his name to be withdrawn. Flattered by this acclaim, the reluctant candidate accepted the nomination, much to the displeasure of Hanna, who regretted—according to reports—that there would be only one life "between this madman and the Presidency."

To oppose this Republican ticket of McKinley and Roosevelt, the Democrats nominated William Jennings Bryan and Adlai E. Stevenson (grandfather of the Democratic presidential candidate in 1952 and 1956). Their platform once again demanded the free coinage of silver and reduction of the tariff but placed major emphasis on the issue of imperialism. Warning the country that "imperialism abroad will lead quickly and inevitably to despotism at home," the party pledged itself to grant independence to the Philippines as soon as a stable government could be established on the islands.

The election resulted in a more decisive victory for McKinley than he had achieved over the same opponent in 1896. In the electoral college the vote was 292 to 155; in the popular total it was 7,200,000 for McKinley and 6,360,000 for Bryan.[1] Thus Hanna and his conservative friends had reason to hope that the threat of popular revolt against their dominance had been thoroughly smashed. There were two weaknesses, however, in this assumption. One was the country's desire for reform that was much stronger than the electoral vote—reflecting national pride in the military victories and joy over the return of prosperity—seemed to indicate. For example, to Bryan's popular vote must be added the nearly 100,000 ballots cast for Debs, the Socialist candidate. The second was the fact that the new Vice President was an able and ambitious man, who clearly perceived, the changing direction from which the political winds of the twentieth century were likely to blow. McKinley served only six months of his second term. On September 6, 1901, Leon Czolgosz, a demented Polish fanatic, shot the President while the latter was attending a Pan-American Exposition at Buffalo, New York. Eight days later McKinley succumbed to the wound.

Roosevelt the Man

Theodore Roosevelt achieved the presidency at the age of forty-two, the youngest man to assume that post. He brought to it courage, independence, and a unique confidence in his own righteousness. Not a profound nor particularly original thinker, he had the happy faculty of anticipating the

---

[1] In 1896 it had been 271 to 176 in the electoral college and 7,036,000 to 6,470,000 in the popular vote.

Theodore Roosevelt. (Brown Bros.)

trend of public opinion, thereby appearing to be leading it. Not basically a progressive, he nevertheless succeeded in capturing the progressive movement. He combined caution and rashness. He could cleverly avoid taking up matters on which he had little—or even superficial—knowledge, notably in the field of economics, and yet on other issues he sometimes rushed in fearlessly. Although a firm believer in the party system, he bitterly fought party bosses whom he accused of placing selfish interests above national welfare. Yet he knew when to break off such battles and to compromise with the party leaders when this was necessary to achieve his goals, at least in part. He liked to regard himself as a practical idealist. Despite the fact that he frequently preferred words to deed, that he glittered in undeserved spotlights, and that he often claimed the credit that was due other men, Roosevelt was one of the most popular and versatile men ever to occupy the White House. As historian, rancher, editor, explorer, hunter, naturalist, and soldier, he captured the imagination of an entire generation as embodying all that was vigorously efficient in the American character.

After taking the oath of office, President Roosevelt immediately announced: "I wish to say that it shall be my aim to continue, absolutely unbroken, the policy of President McKinley for the peace, the prosperity, and the honor of our beloved country." In line with this assertion, he asked his predecessor's cabinet to continue in office. This initial decision to tread cautiously in another man's footprints was not typical of Roosevelt. It was, however, the traditional piety expected of Vice Presidents when they came to office under tragic circumstances. Moreover, Roosevelt was shrewd enough to realize that he needed time to win the support of party leaders and the public before he ventured out in new directions.

Roosevelt and the Trusts

The new President's first annual message to Congress in December, 1901, reassured the business community. It praised the captains of industry as men who "have on the whole done great good to our people." It attacked "the reckless agitator" who might tamper with the delicate mechanisms of business "in a spirit of rashness or ignorance." Yet in a linking of yes-and-no statements that was characteristic of the Roosevelt style, the President combined these conservative statements with a criticism of certain corporate sins like overcapitalization and unfair railroad rates. Even in these cases, however, he declared that "publicity" offered "the only sure remedy." Therefore, his principal recommendation was for a new Department of Commerce and Labor with investigatory powers.

Wall Street's complacency received a rude shock on February 18, 1902, when the administration announced its decision to proceed against the recently organized Northern Securities Company as a combination in restraint of trade. Prices on the stock market fell sharply, and J. P. Morgan hurried to Washington in an unsuccessful attempt to induce the President to halt the action. In attacking the Northern Securities Company, Roosevelt was challenging the interests of the great Morgan himself, as well as those of two of the country's most powerful railroad magnates, James J. Hill and Edward H. Harriman. This $400 million holding company was the device through which these three titans had made peace after a famous financial battle in 1901. At that time Hill and Morgan, who dominated the Great Northern and Northern Pacific railroads, had aroused the anger of Harriman, who controlled the third of the large transcontinental lines, the Union Pacific, by buying the Chicago, Burlington, and Quincy, on which all three of the systems were dependent for connections with Chicago. Harriman fought back by purchasing enormous blocks of Northern Pacific stock. Since Morgan's domination over this company rested upon an insecure minority interest, he became involved in a wide buying campaign to prevent control from passing into his rival's hands. The struggle became so desperate that the price of Northern Pacific shares rose from 110 to 1,000, and a panic gripped the stock market, where shorts were striving to

The fatted steer: "I just wonder what he is going to do." (By Rehse in the *St. Paul Pioneer Press.)*

fulfill their contracts. So confused did the situation become that only through court litigation would it have been possible to determine which party had won. Characteristically, the contestants abruptly decided to join hands rather than to continue their costly contest. In November, 1901, the three principals organized the Northern Securities Company as a holding corporation to unify the managements of the Great Northern, the Northern Pacific, and the Chicago, Burlington, and Quincy.

The government charged that the new combination would obtain an illegal monopoly over transportation in the whole Northwest. Proceeding cautiously because of the hitherto conservative attitude of the courts, Attorney General Philander Knox spent two years collecting evidence against the company. Roosevelt appealed for popular support for his challenge to the trusts in a speaking tour that took him to New England and the Middle West in the late summer and fall of 1902. He distinguished between good and bad trusts; the bad ones must be disciplined, but "wisdom and restraint" must be shown in dealing with the whole problem. The President took advantage of a vacancy on the Supreme Court to appoint one of the outstanding jurists of the twentieth century, Oliver Wendell Holmes, of Massachusetts, whom Roosevelt believed to be "absolutely sane and sound on the general national policies for which we stand in public life." In other words, the President fully expected that Holmes would share his views on all the great issues of the day, including the trust problem.

When the Supreme Court finally handed down its decision in 1904, it sustained the government's case—but by the narrowest of margins. Justice John Harlan, speaking for five judges, ordered the dissolution of the Northern Securities Company. "If the Anti-Trust Act is held not to embrace a case such as is now before us, the plain intention of the legislative branch of the Government will be defeated." A minority of four judges, headed by Holmes, dissented. "Great cases like hard cases make bad law," the new appointee wrote. The mere organization of a holding company, he believed, could not be illegal even though the intent of the incorporation was to end competition between competing railroads. Roosevelt was annoyed by Holmes's stand. "I could carve out of a banana," the President snapped, "a judge with more backbone than that."

But Roosevelt's unhappiness with the dissenters did not mar his feeling of triumph at the outcome of the case. To be sure, the triumvirate of Morgan, Hill, and Harriman speedily found ways to evade the administration's policy. By "community of interest," or unwritten agreement, they achieved most of the purposes they would have gained through the forbidden holding company. Yet for the politically astute President this was not the important thing. By his vigorous effort he had demonstrated to a doubting citizenry that even the rich and powerful were answerable to the laws. The Sherman Act, which appeared to be moribund, was brought back to life. Now hailed as "the trust-buster," Roosevelt lashed out in his speeches at the "malefactors of great wealth."

In February, 1903, Congress enacted three statutes intended to strengthen the government's hand in dealing with business. One measure authorized the establishment of the Department of Commerce and Labor, giving its head cabinet status. Within the new department, a Bureau of Corporations was to gather facts and figures concerning the great industries of the nation—information that might provide evidence needed by the Justice Department in antitrust suits. While the bureau had no regulatory authority, its first head, James R. Garfield, publicized some of the facts he collected and, in some instances, induced the "evil" corporations to reform themselves. The second law was the Expediting Act, passed at the request of Attorney General Knox, to prevent delays in prosecution under the antitrust and interstate commerce laws by giving government cases a preferred place on the circuit court calendars. The last of the three was the Elkins Anti-Rebate Act that closed certain loopholes in the old Interstate Commerce Act.

None of these laws of 1903, it should be understood, really challenged the dominant elements in the business community. On the contrary, the National Association of Manufacturers and other industry spokesmen strongly favored the establishment of the Department of Commerce with its toothless Bureau of Corporations. And it was the railroads themselves that wanted strong legislation against rebating to protect themselves against the importunities of their shippers.

The Roosevelt administration brought a number of powerful lawbreakers to book—though it waited until after the election of 1904 had given the President impressive evidence of popular support. In Swift & Company v. United States (1905), the Supreme Court ordered the dissolution of the so-called Beef Trust—a combination of leading packers who had agreed not to bid against each other in the livestock market, to restrict the output of meat in order to raise prices, and to obtain illegal rates from the railroads to the exclusion of competitors. In speaking for the unanimous court, Justice Holmes asserted the important "stream of commerce" doctrine.

Even when the stockyards were entirely within a single state, the buying and selling of cattle were to be considered as transactions in interstate commerce since the cattle had been shipped in from different states and were destined for eventual use in still other states. This "stream of commerce" doctrine provided a concept under which a much wider Federal regulation of business would eventually be possible. The government also instituted proceedings to obtain a dissolution of the American Tobacco and Standard Oil trusts—cases that were not eventually decided until the Taft administration.

In the most spectacular of several prosecutions under the Elkins Act, the Standard Oil Company was found guilty of accepting rebates on 1,462 separate counts and was fined $29,240,000 by Judge Kenesaw Mountain Landis. This verdict, however, was set aside by a higher court. In another notorious instance, officials and employees of the American Sugar Refining Company were convicted of tampering with their scales in order to avoid import duties. The Federal government recovered more than $4 million, plus a fine of $300,000 from the guilty corporation.

The significance of these activities has often been overrated. The Justice Department instituted fewer suits under the long Roosevelt administration than during the four-year Taft term. Moreover, Roosevelt constantly emphasized that not all trusts were bad; the good ones that were the result of natural developments in the business world should be left alone so long as they operated within the law. He came increasingly to believe that regulation rather than destruction was the answer to the trust problem. "We do not wish to destroy corporations," he asserted, "but we do wish to make them subserve the public good." He advocated measures that would require all businesses engaged in interstate commerce to be incorporated under Federal law. This idea also was more probusiness than antibusiness. Badgered by conflicting state laws and fly-by-night competitors, many powerful companies favored national incorporation and regulation at the national, rather than the state, level.

Roosevelt and Labor

In the period following the Civil War, the several administrations, both Republican and Democratic, had shown a certain degree of hostility toward organized labor. This attitude had its most dramatic illustration when President Cleveland took action to break the Pullman strike in 1894. In his first annual message, President Roosevelt had struck a somewhat more sympathetic note toward the rights of labor. He was soon given an opportunity to demonstrate his sincerity as a result of a serious strike in the Pennsylvania anthracite coal fields.

This upheaval was not entirely unexpected, for the miners had been unhappy with their lot for several years. The big coal-carrying railroads owned most of the mines of Ohio, Illinois, West Virginia, and Pennsylvania. The miners worked long hours for pay that lagged behind the rising cost of living; they had to patronize company stores where they paid tribute in the form of higher prices to their employers; they lived in squalid shacks. Resentful of these conditions, the miners flocked into the United Mine Workers, then under the leadership of the energetic young John Mitchell.

In the summer of 1900, Mitchell threatened to call a strike unless wages, stationary since 1880, were increased 10 per cent. Mark Hanna, who disliked labor troubles in an election year when his party was stressing the "full dinner pail," pressured the operators to yield to the miners' demands. Considering the raise inadequate, the miners broadened their demands in the spring of 1902, this time seeking a 20 per cent wage increase, an eight-hour day, improved working conditions, and union recognition. The operators, headed by George Baer, president of the Reading Railroad, were determined not only to resist these demands, but to break the obnoxious union. Baer's opinion of collective bargaining was immortalized in a widely quoted letter in which he asserted that the interests of the workers would be taken care of not by "labor agitators," but by "the Christian men to whom God in his infinite wisdom has given the control of the property interests of the country."

The strike involving 140,000 men began on May 12, 1902. By mid-September no progress had been made toward a settlement, the price of anthracite had risen from $5.00 a ton to over $30.00, and worried householders began to fear a coalless winter. The public placed most of the blame on the operators, for Mitchell had warned his followers to refrain from acts of violence. Even to most businessmen and politicians, it seemed imperative that the President do something about the situation. Neither law nor precedent, however, offered any satisfactory basis for executive action. At Roosevelt's request, Mark Hanna conducted secret negotiations with Mitchell and J. P. Morgan, who had extensive railroad interests at stake, but "Divine Right" Baer refused all proposals for compromise.

Finally the President summoned representatives of both sides to meet with him at the White House on October 3. Mitchell there offered to submit the miners' demands to an impartial commission to be appointed by Roosevelt. Baer and his colleagues not only refused this suggestion, but rebuked the President for his unwillingness to use Federal force to break the strike. In the following days, Roosevelt made no secret of his disapproval of the operators' conduct. He let it be known that he was contemplating calling out the army to take over the mines and operate them. If this were a bluff, the mine owners did not care to call it. After negotiations conducted by Secretary of War Elihu Root with J. P. Morgan, the operators finally consented to arbitration. Root and Morgan insisted, however, that the President's commission should include no representatives of organized labor. The miners protested this reservation and a new deadlock was threatened. But Roosevelt adroitly overcame the difficulty by appointing E. E. Clark, head of the railway conductors' union, describing him as an "eminent sociologist" rather than as a representative of labor.

The commission, headed by Judge George Gray, eventually granted some, but by no means all, of the miners' demands. The workers received a 10 per cent raise, a nine-hour day, and the right to submit future grievances to a board of conciliation representing both owners and miners, but they failed to get union recognition and other concessions. The miners' victory was a modest one, yet Roosevelt's departure from earlier precedents was important. For the first time the Federal government intervened in a labor controversy not to uphold the employers against their rebellious workmen, but in a way careful to protect the interests of the general public and bring about a peaceful solution without prejudice to either party.

Roosevelt's sympathy with the miners by no means indicated an unqualified approval of labor unionism. On the contrary, he publicly opposed the closed shop and denounced the radicalism of the more aggressive labor leaders. He frequently expressed the opinion that it was his duty to steer a middle course, thus saving the country from socialism by punishing the excesses of predatory wealth on the one hand and of lawless agitators on the other.

The Election of 1904

As President, Roosevelt continued the policy he had followed as governor of New York in alternately defying and appeasing the Republican bosses and the wealthy business interests. He did many things of which the Old Guard disapproved, and yet he avoided any break serious enough to endanger his chances for re-election or the success of his legislative program. Despite his caution, there was some talk that the Republicans should nominate some less impulsive candidate in 1904. The man most often mentioned was Hanna himself, although the Ohioan refused to avow his candidacy. The conservatives would not take Hanna's refusal seriously, but on February 15, 1904, the powerful boss died, and the President's control over the party machinery became complete. The Old Guard no longer had anyone who could seriously challenge the popular Teddy.

Consequently, when the convention met in Chicago, Roosevelt was renominated without opposition. The naming of Charles Fairbanks, Senator from Indiana, as his running mate was a sop to the conservative wing. The platform was largely confined to recounting the achievements of the administration, with emphasis upon trust-busting and the acquisition of Panama Canal rights rather than on specific pledges for the future.

Bryan's two defeats made his renomination in 1904 unlikely. Democratic conservatives talked about drafting Grover Cleveland again, but the ex-President ruled himself out and threw his support behind Judge Gray, who had headed the coal arbitration commission. The Bryan element supported the millionaire publisher William Randolph Hearst. In the end, the St. Louis convention nominated Judge Alton B. Parker of New York, a representative of the conservative Cleveland wing. Although Parker was rather colorless, the party leaders hoped he might be able to carry New York state, a requisite for victory. Like the candidate, the platform was a cautious compromise that omitted the usual silver plank because Parker refused to run unless the gold standard were "firmly and irrevocably established."

The only exciting incident in a dull campaign occurred when Parker charged that George Cortelyou, who was both Secretary of Commerce and Labor and Republican National Chairman, had used information gained from the Bureau of Corporations to extort money for the Republican campaign chest and had promised immunity from antitrust prosecutions to the corporate donors. Roosevelt admitted that his party had accepted the usual donations from big business but indignantly denied that this had involved a kind of blackmail. He was, he said, "unhampered by any pledge, promise or understanding of any kind, save my promise, made openly to the American people, that so far as in my power lies I shall see to it that every man has a square deal, no less and no more."

Roosevelt won a sweeping victory in November. Parker did not carry a single state outside of the Solid South, and even lost Missouri, which had been in the Democratic column consistently since the Civil War. The Roosevelt popular vote was 7,628,834 to Parker's 5,084,491, whereas the electoral count was 336 to 140.

Rooseveltian Reforms

Conscious now of the full extent of his popularity, Roosevelt moved further toward progressivism. In this he was clearly responding to the mood of the nation, now insistently demanding reform of the abuses exposed by the muckrakers. Moreover, although Bryan had never won the presidency, he had greatly influenced the Democratic party, a majority of whose legislators were now committed to government regulation of business.

As in earlier upsurges of popular protest, the railroads were the most conspicuous targets for criticism. The Interstate Commerce Act, the Elkins Act, and various state regulatory laws had been ineffective in curing the long-existent abuses of exorbitant rates, discriminations, disregard of safety, and excessive political influence. Roosevelt called for greater regulation but was opposed by the conservative Senate leadership of his own party. The Townshend-Esch Bill, incorporating presidential recommendations, passed the House early in 1905, but died in the upper house. A year later the President gave his support to a stronger measure introduced into the new Congress by Peter Hepburn of Iowa. Although the bill speedily passed the House by a vote of 346 to 7, it faced bitter opposition in the Senate. Since Republican leaders such as Aldrich of Rhode Island, Elkins of West Virginia, and Foraker of Ohio were against effective regulation, Roosevelt had to ally himself with men like "Pitchfork Ben" Tillman of South Carolina, the famous Populist-Democrat, and Jonathan Dolliver of Iowa, a progressive Republican. In the end, the President felt compelled to compromise with the conservatives, and the bill passed, 71 to 3, in a form somewhat disappointing to the progressives. The Hepburn Act expanded the Interstate Commerce Commission from five to seven members and extended its authority to cover express companies, sleeping-car companies, pipe lines, and railroad terminals. The most important new power bestowed upon the commission was that of nullifying rates found, upon complaint of shippers, to be unreasonable and, in such cases, stating the maximum rate that would be reasonable. The commission's orders were to be binding upon the carriers unless set aside by the courts, with the burden of initiating such litigation being transferred from the commission to the carriers. The act forbade free passes, except to railroad personnel, and attempted to compel the lines to give up other forms of business.

Progressive Westerners criticized the Hepburn Act because it permitted courts to delay and reverse the orders of the commission and because it did not authorize the commission to appraise the value of railroad properties—a step that Senator LaFollette argued was an essential preliminary to determining whether rates were bringing more than a fair return to the carrier. Whatever may have been its shortcomings, the Hepburn Act saved the Interstate Commerce Commission from oblivion and gave it its first really important powers. It was the most important piece of economic legislation of the Roosevelt administration, since it established Federal regulation as a major influence on the operation of the American transportation system. Another act of 1906 made the railroads liable for injuries sustained by their employees. Although this measure was declared unconstitutional by the Supreme Court, a law somewhat more strictly drawn was passed in 1908 and upheld.

Popular demand for reform, at a peak in 1906, found a new focus in concern about adulterated and injurious foods and drugs. Dr. Harvey W. Wiley, chief chemist of the Department of Agriculture, had been warning the public about such abuses for many years and urging remedial legislation. He found some of his most energetic coworkers among women like Alice Lakey of the Consumers' League. The usually conservative Edward Bok crusaded against patent medicines in the *Ladies Home Journal,* while Samuel Hopkins Adams applied the muckrake in articles in *Collier's.* Rather than opposing regulation, most businessmen involved in the food industry favored it to protect themselves against the unfair competition of the manufacturers of adulterated products. Indeed, business opposition to Federal action was limited to a few special groups, especially those connected with trade in patent medicines and whiskey.

The problems of the meat industry were particularly urgent. In the 1880's American meat had been so suspect abroad that the leading European nations had banned its importation. To reopen these markets, Congress had in 1891 passed a law requiring Federal inspection of meat in all slaughtering plants exporting any part of their products. The large packers welcomed this regulation, but were dissatisfied because it did not include the small establishments not involved in the export business. The effort of the big firms to get a more comprehensive law received an unanticipated assist from the publication of Upton Sinclair's *The Jungle* in 1906. Although the author had hoped to advance the cause of socialism by exposing the exploitation of immigrant workers, readers were usually more shocked by his vivid descriptions of disgustingly unsanitary conditions in the packing houses. At first skeptical of the book's accuracy, President Roosevelt was moved to action when Sinclair's charges were largely confirmed by investigators from the Department of Agriculture. Responding to pressure from both the White House and the nation, Congress passed the Pure Food and Drugs Act on June 23, 1906, and the Meat Inspection Act a week later. The former prohibited the manufacture, sale, or transportation of adulterated, misbranded, or harmful foods, drugs, or liquors and required that medicines containing dangerous drugs should carry a label listing them. The latter authorized Federal inspectors to examine meat shipped in interstate commerce and to enforce adequate sanitary standards in the slaughtering houses. Although the laws fell short of the demands of the progressives for penalties against false and misleading advertising, they represented a significant advance for the principle of regulation of industry in the public interest.

President Roosevelt also tried during his second administration to help the cause of the worker, although he had considerably less success here than in other areas. For example, he urged a thorough investigation of the child labor situation; he warned that the use of injunctions in labor disputes might result in "grave abuses" to the strikers; and he proposed a workmen's compensation measure for Federal employees. Congress took no action on any of these matters. The President's only victory came with the passage of a measure in 1908 for the regulation of hours for telegraph operators and trainmen employed by railroads crossing state lines.

Conservation

Theodore Roosevelt's most enduring contributions to national development may well have been in the field of conservation. For decades the national domain had been passing out of the hands of the Federal government into those of private owners. With careless generosity administrators had been giving up not only agricultural lands, but forest regions, mineral deposits, oil fields, and water-power sites without thought for the future needs of the country. Roosevelt's great love for the outdoors and for the West ideally equipped him for the task of laying down a new policy.

Early in his presidency, Roosevelt threw his support to a bill sponsored by Senator Francis Newlands, a Nevada Democrat, for a Federal reclamation program. The resulting Newlands Act of 1902 provided that the proceeds of Western land sales be applied to the construction of dams and other works necessary to irrigate arid tracts. Settlers on the reclaimed land were to repay the government, and these revenues would constitute a revolving fund for further irrigation projects. Under this important law great dams like the Shoshone in Wyoming and the Roosevelt in Arizona were built and nearly 1.2 million acres of land were opened to cultivation by 1920.

Taking advantage of legislation that had been on the books since 1891 but applied only on a small scale by his cautious predecessors, Roosevelt withdrew from public sale 150 million acres of forest land—an area considerably larger than France. Roosevelt's adviser and most enthusiastic lieutenant in this policy was Gifford Pinchot, chief of the Forestry Service in the Department of Agriculture. The President was equally interested in protecting mineral and water-power sites. In 1903 he vetoed a bill awarding to private interests the right to build a dam and generating system at Muscle Shoals on the Tennessee River—a location destined to be famous in future debates on the public versus private power issue.

Despite questionable legal authority, he ordered the withdrawal from public entry of millions of acres of coal and phosphate lands and water-power sites.

Roosevelt had a great flair for publicity; by numerous expedients he succeeded in making the American public conservation-conscious. In December, 1907, his annual message to Congress contained a striking survey of the whole problem of conservation and the development of the nation's resources. The next year he convened an important conservation conference at Washington, with governors, legislators, scientific experts, and prominent citizens from all parts of the country in attendance. The resulting declaration of principles urged the extension of the forest fire fighting service, protection for sources of navigable waterways, control of timber cutting on both public and private lands, and government retention of subsoil rights, especially in coal, oil, and natural gas. Inspired by this conference and other factors, forty-one of the states established conservation commissions before 1909. To coordinate these activities and compile an inventory of national resources, Roosevelt appointed a National Conservation Commission with Pinchot as chairman. Just before Roosevelt left office, an international conference, representing several of the countries of North America, agreed to cooperate in preserving the natural resources of the continent.

As was the case with other progressive causes, businessmen were divided on the conservation issue. Some of the lumbering firms feared depletion of the forests and favored a policy of Federal regulation that would provide an adequate annual yield of timber, while at the same time requiring new plantings and scientific care of the forests. They respected and supported the expert knowledge of Gifford Pinchot. Indeed, business groups interested in the efficient use of the forests were much more pleased with the Roosevelt conservation policies than were the conservationists of a different school, the "preservationists" who wanted to halt all lumbering in the national forests to preserve their natural beauty. Despite the conservative character of the Roosevelt policies, they nevertheless encountered bitter opposition from lumbermen and other businessmen who were more interested in short-run profits than long-time gains. Many Western politicians opposed the conservation program as retarding the growth of their states. Congressmen resented the President's failure to gain legislative authorization for many of his actions. Congress passed laws to prohibit further reservations of forest lands in certain states and to deny funds for the continuance of commissions established without congressional approval. Despite such harassments, Roosevelt succeeded in advancing the ideal of conservation to the point where public opinion would permit no major reversal of policy after he left the White House.

The Panic of 1907

In 1907 the country suffered a brief interruption of the unrivaled prosperity it had been enjoying for ten years. The stock market began to decline in March as a warning of troubles ahead. Later in the year several railroads went into receivership, thirteen New York City banks failed, and elsewhere serious unemployment and wage cuts were suffered. It was largely a bankers' panic brought about through speculation and rash management, but conservatives did not miss the opportunity to lay their troubles on the shoulders of the President; they blamed the depression on lack of confidence in administration policies. Roosevelt denied this responsibility, but he did make certain concessions to Wall Street.

One morning during the worst phase of the panic, Roosevelt was called from his breakfast table to meet two envoys from J. P. Morgan. They warned the President that a large New York financial institution would fail unless it could dispose of a large quantity of shares in the Tennessee Coal and Iron Company. The United States Steel Corporation stood ready to make the purchase, but its management desired to know whether the government would regard this action as a violation of the Sherman Antitrust Act. The President replied that he did not feel it his duty "to interpose any objections." Thus did the "trust-buster" give his tacit blessing to a transaction whereby the country's largest corporation acquired control of one of its most important competitors.

The panic focused attention on two major deficiencies of the national banking system: the inelasticity of the national bank notes, whose volume depended not on the needs of business but upon holdings of government bonds, and the lack of an adequate system of reserves upon which banks could draw in time of stringency. As a first step toward reform, the Aldrich-Vreeland Act of 1908 permitted national banks to form associations for the issuance of temporary currency in times of financial emergency. The act also authorized the establishment of a National Monetary Commission to investigate the currency systems of the United States and foreign countries. This prepared the ground for the establishment of the Federal Reserve System in 1913.

The economic setback of 1907 was brief and the country soon resumed its normal pursuits—one of which was to debate the virtues and vices of its colorful chief executive. One episode after another—many of them now almost forgotten—became matters of heated controversy. When he invited Booker T. Washington, prominent black educator, to have a meal at the White House, Roosevelt provoked bitter denunciations from Southern whites, as he did also by appointing blacks to Federal offices in the South. But black people themselves heatedly condemned the President for his hasty and indiscriminate punishment of black soldiers unjustly accused of provoking a racial affray in Brownsville, Texas. When news was scarce, reporters could always play up the President's latest pronouncement, whether it be condemnation of "nature-fakers" or "race-suicide" or a boost for "simplified spelling."

On issues more clearly within his field of responsibility, Roosevelt drew both praise and blame. Admirers praised his support of civil service reform: he was given credit for increasing the number of positions filled through competitive examinations and for promptly removing corrupt or dishonest officials. On the other hand, critics accused the President of using his power of appointment to build up the strength of his party and his own personal machine.

The more advanced liberals were often disappointed with Roosevelt.

He refused to be drawn into any really serious quarrel with the "stand-patters" of his party, men like Speaker "Uncle Joe" Cannon of the House and Senator Aldrich. He shunned the cause of tariff revision, which was, in the opinion of many progressives, the most promising way of attacking monopoly, although there was, in truth, no widespread popular demand for such reform. Obviously Roosevelt was no radical. He was by his own description an intelligent conservative, seeking to preserve free enterprise by curbing the most flagrant abuses in the system, abuses that were likely to lead to revolutionary discontent. He had numerous defects of character—vanity, bellicosity, impulsiveness. But his faults were easily forgotten by the great American public, which loved him for his youthful energy, his zest for adventure, his gift for vivid phrase-making, and his staunch patriotism.

Judicial Conservatism

The progressives were much more successful in infusing their spirit into the executive and legislative branches of government than into the judiciary. The tremendous power wielded by the courts in holding laws invalid on the grounds of unconstitutionality was a peculiarity of the American system, both state and Federal. Since judges were appointed or elected from the ranks of successful lawyers, they were likely to be social conservatives, both by training and by professional ties.

In giving judicial blessing to the doctrine of laissez faire, the judges found a handy formula in the familiar words: no persons shall be deprived of life, liberty, or property without due process of law. These or similar words were to be found in three significant places: in the Fifth Amendment to the Federal Constitution, where they constituted a limitation on Congress; in the Fourteenth Amendment, where they limited the states; and in most state constitutions as restraints upon the legislatures. Originally intended as a guarantee that men should not be punished nor have their property confiscated without fair trial in the courts, judicial interpretation had extended "due process" clauses to mean that certain types of legislation were invalid. In 1885, for example, the New York Court of Appeals had declared unconstitutional a state statute prohibiting cigar-manufacturing in tenement houses on the ground "that it arbitrarily interferes with personal liberty and private property without due process of law." A similar fate befell an Illinois eight-hour law for women in 1895, a Colorado eight-hour law for smelting workers in 1899, and a New York workmen's compensation act in 1911.

Even when state laws cleared the hurdles erected by the state courts, they often suffered invalidation by the United States Supreme Court. Although the highest tribunal had in the Granger cases of the 1870's laid down the general principle that private property devoted to public use was subject to public regulation, it had subsequently qualified this in ways that made effective action difficult. Corporations were held to be "persons" entitled to the protection of the due process clause; they had the right to appeal to the courts as to the "reasonableness" of rates fixed by state legislatures or commissions; rates that did not provide a fair return on the investment were set aside as deprivations of property in violation of the Fourteenth Amendment.

The extreme to which the Supreme Court was ready to go in reading the philosophy of laissez faire into the Constitution is best illustrated by the case of Lochner *v.* New York, decided by a five-to-four vote in 1905. Here the issue was the validity of a New York law limiting the hours of labor for bakery employees to ten a day or sixty a week. Speaking for the majority, Justice Rufus Peckham emphasized that the right to make labor contracts was "part of the liberty of the individual protected by the Fourteenth Amendment of the Federal Constitution." The act in question was "an illegal interference with the rights of individuals, both employers and employees, to make contracts regarding labor upon such terms as they may think best. . . ." In his famous dissent, Justice Holmes pointed out that laws restricting liberty of contract were not uncommon:

> Some of these laws embody convictions or prejudices which judges are likely to share. Some may not. But a constitution is not intended to embody a particular theory, whether of paternalism and the organic relation of the citizen to the state or of laissez faire. It is made for people of fundamentally differing views, and the accident of our finding certain opinions natural and familiar, or novel, and even shocking, ought not to conclude our judgment upon the question whether statutes embodying them conflict with the Constitution of the United States.

The changing temper of the times did eventually modify the court's position. On the question of maximum-hour laws it gradually gave way. In Muller *v.* Oregon (1908), it upheld a ten-hour law applying to female factory workers on the ground that women might need this special protection. The Muller case was memorable because of the forceful presentation of Louis D. Brandeis, a Boston lawyer who was gaining fame in these years as "the people's attorney." Brandeis's brief dealt with the legal precedents in two pages but devoted more than a hundred pages to mustering economic and sociological data drawn from both American and European sources to demonstrate that protective legislation for women was reasonable to protect the health and welfare of the people. The Brandeis-type, or sociological, brief became the most useful weapon in the arsenal of the progressive lawyers. When the Supreme Court upheld a general ten-hour law applying to men as well as women in Bunting *v.* Oregon (1917), another significant victory for the advocates of state regulation was achieved.

Yet the state and Federal courts continued to antagonize the progressives on many issues. Organized labor complained that the courts were lax in enforcing the antitrust laws against business but vigorous in using the same laws to prohibit boycotts and picketing and to jail union leaders who violated injunctions. This situation was hard to tolerate for progressives determined to make government more responsive to the popular will. Moderate reformers placed their hope on the appointment and election of more liberal judges, who would understand the needs of the new age. But to many other progressives this process was too slow. They advocated machinery either for the recall of judges whose behavior displeased the voters or for the recall of the decisions. By permitting the voters to re-enact laws that had been held unconstitutional by the courts, the recall of judicial decisions promised a new and speedier method of constitutional amendment by popular referendum.

Conservatives opposed such proposals for tampering with the court system more resolutely than they did any other part of the progressive program. They defended the power of judicial review and the independence of the judiciary as the greatest safeguards of constitutional rights of liberty and property. The struggle between the progressives and conservatives on this issue was deeply significant because it involved the whole conflict between the older and the newer views of the proper function of government.

THE BATTLE OF THE PROGRESSIVES

The progressive movement, heralded before 1900 by prophets in advance of their time and by rumblings of protest among the farmers and laborers, became a popular religion during the presidency of Theodore Roosevelt. During his seven and a half years in the White House, the Rough Rider contrived to make himself the embodiment of reform. Since the crusade had not gained all its objectives, William Howard Taft, Roosevelt's hand-picked successor, undertook to carry it on. Unfortunately, Taft did not have his predecessor's happy faculty for conciliating both supporters and opponents of progressivism. As a result, the progressives within his own party, growing steadily in strength, set up such a clamor as to disrupt the regular Republican organization. These insurgents forced the movement to a climax in the campaign of 1912, when three parties competed for the approval of the voters, each claiming to be more devoted to the cause of true reform than were its rivals.

The Crown Prince

Such was Roosevelt's popularity and power that he could easily have won a third term, but immediately after the election of 1904 he had publicly renounced any intention of seeking such an honor. Like other strong Presidents, however, Roosevelt was able virtually to name his successor. There were several men who might have been chosen to take over his mantle. Many people believed that Secretary of State Elihu Root was the greatest intellectual force in the Roosevelt cabinet, but the President realized that Root's career as a corporation lawyer made him suspect to the progressives. Governor Charles Evans Hughes was another very able man, admired by the progressives for his earlier investigation of insurance rackets, but Roosevelt disliked his stubborn independence. The outgoing President eventually threw his support to Secretary of War William Howard Taft, member of a prominent Ohio family. Taft had gained respect as a Federal judge and as governor-general of the Philippines before his appointment to the cabinet. Fat and genial, he seemed to have good potentialities as a vote getter—even though he had never run for elective office. Yielding to both presidential and family pressures, Taft agreed to seek the presidency instead of the Supreme Court post that would have been his own preference.

The Republican national convention, meeting in Chicago, nominated Taft on the first ballot, with James S. Sherman of New York as his running mate. The platform was a moderately progressive document that praised the Roosevelt record, emphasizing the war against the trusts and the quest for social justice. It called for a strengthening of the Interstate Commerce and Sherman Antitrust acts, for conservation and good roads, for a postal savings system, and even for tariff reform. Not accepted, however, were more radical planks advocated by LaFollette and his friends, which would have pledged the party to legislation requiring public reports of campaign expenditures, the valuation of railroad properties, and the direct election of United States Senators.

Having suffered an overwhelming defeat with a conservative candidate in 1904, the Democrats returned to the leadership of William Jennings Bryan, nominating him on the first ballot at their Denver convention—a remarkable tribute to a two-time loser. The platform condemned the Republican party as the organization of "privileges and private monopoly." It demanded laws prohibiting corporations from contributing to campaign funds, new antitrust legislation, and measures limiting the issuance of injunctions in labor disputes. Especially firm was the plank advocating a reduction of the Dingley Tariff.

The Labor Issue

The election of 1908 was notable for the more prominent part taken by organized labor. Samuel Gompers had always placed the achievement of collective bargaining above the enactment of legislation, but a situation had now arisen that could only be met by political action. The resort to Federal court injunctions to break strikes had become increasingly common since Attorney General Richard Olney's well-publicized success in dealing with the Pullman strike of 1894. Indeed, the interference of the courts with labor union activities took extreme forms after 1900.

A notable example of this was the so-called Danbury Hatters' case (Loewe v. Lawlor, 1908). In 1902 the United Hatters of America, attempting to support a strike by the employees of D. E. Loewe and Company of Danbury, Connecticut, declared a nation-wide boycott against the company's products. Subsequently the company filed suit in the Federal district court for triple damages of $240,000 against the officers and members of the union. Although the case dragged on until 1917, the union lost the principal bastions of its defense in February, 1908, when the Supreme Court ruled that such a boycott constituted a conspiracy in restraint of trade under the Sherman Act. The implications of this decision were most alarming to organized labor. Not only might a union be rendered liable for civil damages for its strike and boycott activities, but individual union members might be held responsible for the actions of union officers and might suffer the attachment of their homes and savings.[1]

---

[1] The case was finally settled for $234,000 in 1917; the greater part of this amount was raised by organized labor.

William Howard Taft (third from left). (Brown Bros.)

The Buck's Stove case gave additional evidence of the vulnerability of labor union activity to attack through the courts. A controversy between the foundrymen's union and the Buck's Stove and Range Company resulted in the inclusion of the company's name among the eighty or more firms on the *American Federationist*'s list of concerns deemed unfair to labor and from whom AFL members should not buy. In December, 1907, the Supreme Court of the District of Columbia issued an injunction ordering the AFL and its affiliated bodies to desist from their boycott. In 1909, the court imposed jail sentences upon Gompers and two other AFL officers for contempt of court in disobeying the injunction. A technicality saved Gompers from serving this sentence, but the long litigation riveted attention on the legal status of the unions.

Gompers and his followers tried to get both party conventions to commit themselves to legislation that would limit the issuance of injunctions in labor cases and require jury trial in contempt cases except when the alleged contempt occurred in the courtroom. Instead of complying, the Republicans pledged themselves to uphold "the authority and integrity of the courts" and insisted that the courts' "powers to enforce their process and to protect life, liberty, and property . . . be preserved inviolate." On the other hand, the Democrats received the Gompers delegation cordially and incorporated most of its requests in the party platform. The AFL followed its traditional nonpartisan policy to the extent of refraining from a formal endorsement of the Democratic party, but it pointed out the inadequacy of the Republican platform and Taft's alleged antiunion bias as a judge.

Gompers's support of Bryan, however, was a poor counterweight to Roosevelt's support of Taft. When the votes were counted in November, the crown prince's victory appeared to be scarcely less sweeping than that of his sponsor four years before. The electoral count was 321 to 162; the popular vote, 7,700,000 to 6,410,000; and the Republicans continued in secure control of both houses of Congress. Yet there were storm clouds on the Republican horizon. Even though Taft's popular vote was about 75,000 larger than Roosevelt's in 1904, the Democratic vote was 1,375,000 higher than it had been four years earlier. Moreover, Taft had found it difficult during the campaign to hold together the conservative and progressive wings of his own party. The progressives, who were sometimes highly critical of Taft's stand on important issues, gained additional seats in Congress. And the Democrats had won several Midwestern and Western states that Roosevelt had easily carried in 1904.

An Unfortunate Beginning

The enthusiasm of victory, however, made the Republican leaders overlook the danger signals, and Taft took office with every prospect of a peaceful, successful term. Roosevelt and the rest of the country assumed that the personnel and policies of the new administration would be almost identical with those of the old. In his inaugural, Taft, as expected, promised to carry on his predecessor's program. Shortly after the ceremony was over, Roosevelt departed for a big game hunt in Africa, confident that the nation was in good hands.

To follow Roosevelt in the White House, however, was far from easy. The new President shunned the publicity that his predecessor had sought. Whereas Roosevelt could enlist the support of the party liberals without antagonizing the conservatives, Taft found himself compelled to choose sides. Although sympathetic to many of the progressive objectives, he cast his lot chiefly with the Old Guard. Roosevelt had refused to consider the Constitution as a "straightjacket" and often stretched the powers of the executive, but Taft, strongly influenced by his judicial experience, placed strong value on the separation of powers and considered the executive branch to be one of three coequals. Taft's approach to progressivism was therefore cautious and legalistic in contrast to Roosevelt's dashing performance.

The progressives voiced their first serious doubts about the new administration when Taft made his cabinet selections. Roosevelt had been under the impression that Taft intended to retain five of the Roosevelt cabinet, but the new President kept only two of them. Roosevelt particularly resented the rejection of Secretary of the Interior James R. Garfield, a champion of conservation, and of Attorney General Luke Wright, to whom Roosevelt had offered the post in 1908 with the assurance that he would be retained by the incoming President. In substituting his own men, Taft drew largely on the legal profession. Philander Knox, the new Secretary of State, had once been Roosevelt's Attorney General, but the progressives emphasized his earlier career as a corporation lawyer. George

B. Wickersham, the new Attorney General, had a similar background and was regarded as a partisan of big business.

The Republican party had promised to revise the tariff, and Taft called the new Congress into special session to redeem this pledge. The House Ways and Means Committee, under the chairmanship of Sereno Payne of New York, prepared a bill that, though far from radical, provided for considerable reductions, particularly on steel and iron, and also placed more raw materials on the free list. Other progressive provisions included a tariff commission with power to suggest changes in the rates, partial free trade with the Philippines, and an income tax on corporations engaged in interstate commerce. The Payne Bill passed the House in practically its original form, but in the Senate it had to run the gauntlet of the Finance Committee headed by Senator Aldrich, a rigid protectionist. The committee made 847 amendments, generally in the direction of higher rates. Debate on the floor of the Senate was unusually acrimonious. Western Republicans led by LaFollette denounced what they regarded as a betrayal of the campaign pledge, while the Aldrich faction argued that only "a revision" of the tariff had been promised and that the legislators were free to revise it either upward or downward. Ten insurgents carried their revolt to the point of voting with the Democrats against the amended measure, but they could not prevent its passage.

Since the House and Senate had passed the bill in different forms, a conference committee was necessary. Warned by President Taft that he

The temptation of William. Speaker Cannon and Senator Aldrich attempting to persuade President Taft to support high protection. (By Rehse in the *St. Paul Pioneer Press.*)

would veto the measure unless reasonable concessions were made, the conferees reduced a few of the Senate schedules. Nevertheless, the Payne-Aldrich Tariff, as finally passed and signed by the President on August 5, 1909, was a bitter disappointment to the progressives. Taft did not like the measure, but he believed that his signature might avoid further strife and restore Republican harmony. The reverse was the case, for the insurgents, most of them ardent admirers of Roosevelt, asserted that Taft had sold out to the Old Guard. Their indignation was only intensified when the President attempted to defend the act in a speech at Winona, Minnesota. "I would say without hesitation," Taft told his audience, "that this is the best tariff bill that the Republican party has ever passed, and therefore the best tariff bill that has been passed at all. . . ."

The Struggle Over Reciprocity

Taft did attempt to lower the tariff wall and at the same time restore the harmony disrupted by the Payne-Aldrich Act by signing a reciprocity agreement with Canada on January 21, 1911. More than one hundred items were placed on the free list, and duties were reduced on more than four hundred other articles. Taft hoped that this arrangement would please all factions: Democrats and insurgent Republicans would like the lowering of the tariff wall; regular Republicans would welcome closer ties with Canada and a wider market for American manufacturers. To his surprise, Taft found himself involved in one of the most heated battles of his administration. Instead of supporting reciprocity, LaFollette and his followers charged that the arrangements would benefit only Eastern industrialists, while Western interests would suffer from the importation of Canadian cattle, hides, and grain. A strange alliance of insurgents and ultraconservatives opposed the treaty, while Republicans loyal to the President and many Democrats supported it.

Because of the well-known difficulties in obtaining a two-thirds majority in the Senate for the approval of formal treaties, the agreement stipulated that the tariff changes should be made by independent legislation in the two countries. In the United States, the House of Representatives passed the necessary bill in February, 1911, but the Senate failed to take action before it adjourned on March 4. Refusing to be thwarted, the President called the newly elected Congress into special session in April. Once again the House, now controlled by the Democrats, approved the measure, but in the Senate a bitter fight developed. Various farm organizations lobbied against reciprocity, while Taft sought to enlist public support by vigorous speeches. On June 21, 1911, the Senate finally passed the bill by a vote of 53 to 27. For the moment it was a great triumph for Taft, although one that would have been impossible without Democratic support; of the President's own party members, 12 insurgents and 12 regulars voted against the measure.

But the ill fate that pursued so many of Taft's ventures overtook this one as well. For almost half a century Canadian statesmen had sought a reciprocity treaty with the United States in order to enjoy again the benefits that had followed an earlier agreement between the two countries in effect from 1854 to 1866. Now that the American Congress had actually accepted such an agreement, the whole project failed because of its involvement in Canadian domestic politics. The treaty had been the work of the veteran Liberal Prime Minister, Sir Wilfrid Laurier; it was opposed by Sir Robert Borden and the Conservatives. The latter asserted that reciprocity would injure the British mother country, that it would result in American exploitation of Canadian resources, and, above all, that it would pave the way for the eventual annexation of the Dominion by the United States. The issue forced a dissolution of the Canadian Parliament and, in the resulting general election, the Liberals and the cause of reciprocity went down together in humiliating defeat.

Rise of Insurgency

While the controversy over the Payne-Aldrich Tariff was still raging, the administration fell under violent attack for its alleged sabotage of the Roosevelt conservation policies. The new Secretary of the Interior, Richard A. Ballinger, was, like the President, a cautious lawyer. He believed that the Roosevelt administration in its enthusiasm for conservation had sometimes exceeded its legal authority. With Taft's support, Ballinger proposed to proceed in the future with much more scrupulous regard for legal niceties. The ardent Gifford Pinchot was still head of the Forestry Service, and such circumspection immediately aroused his suspicions that the new Secretary was in league with large corporate interests greedy to gain control of the nation's mineral reserves and water-power sites.

Ballinger's integrity was also doubted by one of his own subordinates, Louis R. Glavis. Ballinger insisted upon approving the claims of one Clarence Cunningham and others to extensive coal and timber lands in Alaska. Glavis had been investigating these claims and had become convinced that they were fraudulent and that the whole affair was a conspiracy designed to enable a Morgan-Guggenheim syndicate—the embodiment of sinister big business—to gain control of a valuable portion of the public domain. Rebuffed in his protests to Ballinger, Glavis confided his suspicions to Pinchot, who took the unusual step of sending the young man directly to the President. Unmindful of the explosive possibilities of the affair, Taft dealt with it in a hasty and superficial manner. Accepting Ballinger's assurances that the charges were unfounded, the President wrote a public letter to the Secretary, exonerating him and directing the dismissal of Glavis.

Conservation—already a holy cause to millions of Americans—now had a martyr. The insurgent bloc in Congress took up Glavis's case with enthusiasm, while the muckraking magazines published sensational attacks upon the Interior Department. Taking up the cause with characteristic zeal, Pinchot took the serious step of writing an indignant letter, which Senator Jonathan Dolliver of Iowa read on the floor of the Senate. Suffering the same fate as Glavis, the Chief Forester was dismissed for insubordination. This was a much more serious matter. Glavis's name had been known to only a few; Pinchot's name was a household word synonymous with the whole cause of conservation. Furthermore, Pinchot, as everyone knew, was the intimate friend of Theodore Roosevelt.

This was not the end of the embarrassing ramifications of the Ballinger affair. During 1910 a congressional committee held extended hearings, in which the brilliant liberal lawyer Louis D. Brandeis pressed the Glavis-Pinchot charges. Although the committee's standpat majority supported the conduct of Taft and Ballinger, a minority report sharply criticized the President and advised the censure and removal of the Secretary. Moreover, new facts about the case brought to light under the sharp questioning of Brandeis provided ammunition for further newspaper attacks upon the administration. In March, 1911, Ballinger decided that his health would not let him continue in office, and Taft appointed as his successor Walter Fisher, a conservationist of the more zealous school.

Each succeeding month widened the gulf between the Republican conservatives and progressives. In the Senate, serious insurgency dated from the fight over the Payne-Aldrich Tariff, while in the House the incident most clearly foreshadowing a party split was the fight in 1910 over the powers of Speaker "Uncle Joe" Cannon. Following precedents laid down by Speaker "Czar" Reed in the early nineties, Cannon had ruled the House with an iron hand since he first gained the Speaker's post in 1901. He appointed the Republican majority on all committees and named their chairmen. Moreover, he himself served as chairman of the powerful Rules Committee, which determined procedure and made whatever special orders might be necessary. To call up a bill, a Representative had to negotiate with the Speaker in his private chambers. Otherwise measures never emerged from committee, nor did their sponsors obtain permission to address the House.

Not discouraged by earlier failure, Representative George W. Norris, a Republican from Nebraska, launched a new attack upon the Speaker's autocratic powers in March, 1910. He moved that the Committee on Rules be henceforth elected by the House and that the Speaker be excluded from membership upon it. Although caught momentarily off guard, Cannon fought desperately to retain his full powers, and he had the support of all the standpatters. But after an excited debate that continued for almost thirty hours, the Speaker was beaten. About forty insurgent Republicans voted with the Democrats for Norris's motion. Cannon thereupon dramatically offered to vacate the Speakership, but the insurgents, including Norris himself, voted to retain the old veteran, personally a likeable character. The following year, the Democrats, placed in a majority by the election of 1910, voted still further restrictions upon the Speaker's powers. All committees were henceforth to be chosen by the Ways and Means Committee, which, in its turn, was made up of members designated by the caucuses of the majority and minority parties.

Throughout 1910 insurgent indignation against the conservatives continued to mount. In the intraparty strife the disaster-prone President chose the losing side. In his private correspondence he alluded to men like LaFollette and Norris as "yellow dogs," and he discriminated against the insurgents in distributing patronage. A battle for control of Congress began with the Republican primaries, in which progressive candidates dislodged conservative incumbents in many states. In the November elections Taft's unpopularity aided the Democrats, who won control of the House of Representatives for the first time in sixteen years. The Republicans still had a nominal majority in the Senate, but the insurgent Republicans actually held the balance of power between the two parties.

Taft and Reform

Despite dissension within Republican ranks and reviving Democratic strength, the Taft administration achieved a number of reforms. Even the unfortunate Ballinger had to his credit several conservation laws enacted by Congress upon his advice. The President was given authority to withdraw from entry other lands in addition to forest reserves; the public lands were reclassified according to a scientific survey of their resources, and the title to surface holdings was separated from the coal, oil, natural gas, asphalt, or phosphates below the surface, rights to which were to be leased rather than sold. In 1911 the Appalachian Forest Reserve Act was passed, appropriating $8 million over a period of four years for the purchase of land controlling the sources of important streams in the White Mountains and the southern part of the Appalachian chain.

To deal with the trusts, President Taft advocated Federal incorporation of firms engaged in interstate commerce, but Congress took no action on these suggestions. Consequently, the administration had to proceed through antitrust actions. Attorney General Wickersham, though accounted a conservative, initiated some eighty suits under the Sherman Act. His most notable victories came in 1911 when the Supreme Court ordered the dissolution of the American Tobacco Company and the Standard Oil Company of New Jersey in the forms that these combinations had then attained. Gratifying though these decisions were to those who feared the trusts, jubilation could not be complete. These corporate monsters, chopped into pieces, showed a discouraging vitality in their dismembered parts; indeed they often continued to act like single organisms. Moreover, the Standard' Oil decision revealed an inclination upon the part of Chief Justice Edward White and a majority of his colleagues to narrow the scope of the Sherman Act by judicial interpretation. Because of the act's broad and general terms, said the Chief Justice, it seemed clear that the courts should apply "the standard of reason" to determine whether or not the statute had been violated in any particular case. In a dissenting opinion, Justice John Harlan condemned the so-called rule of reason as a usurpation of power upon the part of the Court; in effect, argued Harlan, the Court was amending the statute. Many legislators were convinced that this made new antitrust legislation imperative, but Taft defended the principle laid down by the Court.

Congress passed new railroad legislation in 1910. Under the Hepburn Act, railroads fixed and collected rates until some shipper complained that they were unreasonable and the commission, on investigation, ordered them changed. The new Mann-Elkins Act empowered the commission to suspend announced rates for periods not exceeding ten months, during which it would decide whether the rates were reasonable. Furthermore, the commission might act upon its own initiative without waiting for some shipper to complain. The act established a Commerce Court to expedite appeals from commission orders, but the court proved unpopular and was abolished by Congress before Taft left office. LaFollette failed in 1910, as he had in 1906, to have the commission authorized to appraise the property of railroads as a basis for determining rates, but Congress finally incorporated this principle in the Physical Valuations Act of 1913.

Congress also passed the Sixteenth (1909) and Seventeenth (1912) Amendments to the Federal Constitution. The former granted to Congress the power to levy taxes on income from whatever source derived; the latter provided for the direct election of United States Senators. Both proposals had long been on the program of American progressives. In 1913 both amendments, having been ratified by the required number of states, were proclaimed in effect.

In 1910 Congress established postal savings banks, which proved of great benefit to small investors who were suspicious of large private banks. Two years later the parcel post system was begun, a blow to the monopolistic express companies. Taft approved both these measures, despite charges by the banks and express companies that they were socialistic. The Department of Commerce and Labor was now divided, with two new cabinet posts resulting. In an effort to publicize the child labor problem and related issues, Congress established the Federal Children's Bureau. The merit system was extended to include the lesser postmastership, and Alaska received territorial status and greater powers of self-government.

But these good deeds were not enough to make Taft a hero to the progressives. Two things in particular brought political disaster to the President. In the first place, Taft was not Roosevelt; he lacked the explosive energy and color of his famous predecessor and he failed to publicize his own accomplishments. More important still, the reform movement had turned toward new objectives. The Taft administration was progressive according to the standards of 1900 or 1905; it was not when judged by those of 1910—the standards of Senator LaFollette or of Governor Hiram Johnson of California.

Illustrative of the limits beyond which Taft's progressivism would not go was the Arizona constitution issue. In 1911 both Arizona and New Mexico, having drawn up constitutions imbued with the liberal spirit then pervading the West, applied for statehood. Congress approved a joint measure, the New Mexico–Arizona Enabling Act, but Taft vetoed it, because the Arizona document provided for the recall of judges. He regarded that clause as "so pernicious in its effect, so destructive of independence in the judiciary, so likely to subject the rights of the individual to the possible tyranny of a popular majority" that he could not give his assent. Not until Arizona removed the objectionable provision was it granted admission—along with New Mexico—in 1912. Once in the Union, the Arizona citizens proceeded to re-enact the questioned clause and there was nothing Taft could do about it.

The Progressives Organize

On January 21, 1911, a group opposed to the renomination of Taft organized the National Progressive League. Senator Jonathan Bourne of Oregon was elected president of the League, but it derived most of its energy from the tireless LaFollette. Throughout 1911 a LaFollette-for-President boom appeared to be making great progress. In April a conference of congressional insurgents invited the Wisconsin Senator to become a candidate for the Republican nomination. At a progressive convention held in October in Chicago, informally chosen representatives from many states endorsed LaFollette's candidacy. Lincoln Steffens, of muckraking fame, was active in this movement, as were Gifford Pinchot, his brother Amos, and James R. Garfield, Roosevelt's Secretary of the Interior. A group of millionaire liberals, including Medill McCormick of Chicago, Joseph Fels of Philadelphia, and Rudolph Spreckels of San Francisco, gave financial support, while LaFollette poured out his energy in touring the country and making speeches.

How would Theodore Roosevelt stand in the coming contest? No question in American politics aroused as much interest as this. Following his hunting trip to Africa, Roosevelt toured Europe, where emperors, kings, politicians, and educators heaped honors·upon him. But the most gratifying tribute of all was the enthusiastic welcome he received from his own

Splitting. The break between Republican regulars and insurgents. (From the *Brooklyn Eagle.*)

people when he returned to America in June, 1910. While he was still abroad, standpatters and insurgents had bombarded him with indignant accounts of their opponents' conduct and, with the popular hero home again, these efforts were redoubled.

Although no longer feeling the cordial friendship that had once marked his relations with Taft, Roosevelt for many months refrained from any public criticism of his successor. Without taking sides between the two factions, he participated in the campaign of 1910—with unhappy results. Induced by his friends to accept nomination as chairman of the New York Republican state convention, he found his election opposed by conservatives and only secured the post after a close vote. His friend, the progressive Henry L. Stimson, won the nomination for governor, but was defeated in the November election by the Democrat, John A. Dix.

The former President's Western speaking tour in behalf of his party was equally ill-starred. His references to Taft were so noncommittal as to offend both standpatters and insurgents, while conservative opinion was shocked by his speech on the "New Nationalism," delivered at Osawatomie, Kansas, on August 31, 1910. Here Roosevelt said that property, which man's labor had created, must be "the servant and not the master of the commonwealth." The people "must effectively control the mighty forces which they have themselves called into being." The New Nationalism put national need before sectional or personal advantage, regarded the executive power as the steward of the public welfare, and demanded of the judiciary that it "be interested primarily in human welfare rather than in property." Despite these ultraprogressive expressions, Roosevelt declined to join the National Progressive Republican League after its organization in 1911. Throughout most of the year he remained silent in the face of pleas from his liberal friends that he become a candidate for the Republican presidential nomination. LaFollette still stood unchallenged as the hope of those who wanted to deny renomination to President Taft.

Although Roosevelt revealed growing irritation with Taft in his private conversations, he did not make a public attack upon him until November 16, 1911. On that date the *Outlook* carried Roosevelt's caustic comments on the recently announced antitrust suit against the United States Steel Corporation. He took violent exception to the Taft administration's contention that he had been misled during his presidency when he gave approval to the Steel Corporation's purchase of control of the Tennessee Coal and Iron Company.[2] He criticized the whole direction that the Taft antitrust campaign was taking. Nothing was gained, he said, "by breaking up a huge industrial organization *which has not offended otherwise than by its size.*" Unless they were guilty of wrongdoing, the large corporations should be handled by regulation, not by "destructive litigation" in the courts.

This public blast at the administration stirred the hopes of Roosevelt's admirers that he would try for the nomination. By January, 1912, it was becoming clear that the progressive rank and file, as well as most of its leadership, would swing over from LaFollette to Roosevelt if the latter

[2] See above, p. 55.

said the word. The Wisconsin Senator's fortunes were already sinking fast when they were finally destroyed by an unfortunate episode. On February 2, 1912, LaFollette spoke at a banquet given by the Publishers Association in Philadelphia. Overtired from his numerous activities and worried over the illness of one of his daughters, the insurgent leader shoved aside his prepared manuscript and indulged in a two-hour tirade against the big newspaper interests represented by his listeners. LaFollette's loss of self-control was only temporary, but the incident provided an opportunity for progressives who wanted to shift their support to Roosevelt to assert that they had no choice in the matter because of LaFollette's condition.

The truth was that Roosevelt had already decided to seek the nomination for himself. During January he dispatched a devoted follower, Frank Knox of Michigan (later to be Secretary of the Navy under another Roosevelt), to obtain the signatures of seven progressive governors to a letter—composed by the Rough Rider himself—begging him to make the race against Taft. On February 24, 1912, Roosevelt's reply to the appeal of the seven governors was made public: "I will accept the nomination for President if it is tendered to me, and I will adhere to this decision until the convention has expressed its preference." This was the formal announcement of his candidacy, but his campaign had actually begun three days before. In his so-called Charter of Democracy speech at Columbus, Ohio, he had come out for the initiative, the referendum, and the recall of judicial decisions. The same day he had replied to a reporter's question with the vivid phrase: "My hat is in the ring, the fight is on and I am stripped to the buff."

Taft Versus Roosevelt

The quarrel between the former President and the man he had put in the White House now became a bitter one. Speaking of extreme progressives, Taft condemned them as "neurotics"—a word that Roosevelt indignantly assumed was aimed at him. In April the President denounced his predecessor in an angry two-hour speech at Boston, while Roosevelt replied twenty-four hours later in a meeting at Worcester, Massachusetts. He said that Taft would never have become President had not Roosevelt kept his promise in spite of infinite pressure to break it. "It is a bad trait," the colonel said, "to bite the hand that feeds you."

Throughout the spring there was a feverish campaign for delegates. Within the Republican rank and file Roosevelt's popularity was still great. In thirteen states where presidential primaries were held, Roosevelt obtained 281 delegates as against 71 for Taft and 36 for LaFollette. In the remaining states, where the delegates were chosen by older, less democratic means, the Old Guard was able to muster most of the delegations for Taft. Preconvention polls indicated that Taft had about 550 delegates, enough to nominate him, while Roosevelt had about 100 less. Twelve days before the convention, the Republican National Committee convened to decide 238 disputed cases. The progressives hoped to win enough of these—many of them trumped up for this purpose—to overturn the Taft majority. But the National Committee, dominated by conservatives, decided against the Rooseveltians in almost every contest.

The progressives refused to surrender. Two days before the convention opened, Roosevelt went to Chicago, the convention city, where he received a fervent welcome from his followers. That night in addressing a crowded meeting, he closed with words that were quoted throughout the country:

> We fight in honorable fashion for the good of mankind; fearless of the future, unheeding of our individual fates, with unflinching hearts and undimmed eyes; we stand at Armageddon, and we battle for the Lord.

On June 18 the convention began and was immediately thrown into an uproar over two issues. The progressives challenged the right of seventy-two Taft delegates to their seats and moved to substitute Roosevelt adherents. The motion was declared out of order, and the Taft delegates were allowed to occupy their seats while the convention voted for a permanent chairman; their ballots helped to elect the conservative Elihu Root by a vote of 552 to 502 over the progressive Francis E. McGovern, governor of Wisconsin. The Old Guard's all-important victory kept them in control of the convention machinery. When the Rooseveltians renewed their attempt to unseat the Taft delegates, Root, following good legal precedents, allowed the latter to vote on their own cases despite angry cries of "theft," "fraud," and "steam roller" from the floor and galleries. Most of the Roosevelt backers, on orders from the candidate himself, refused to recognize the legitimacy of the convention and declined to vote on either the platform or the candidates. Thus Taft was nominated on the first ballot, and James Sherman was again selected as his running mate.[3] The platform recognized the popular demand for reform by advocating maximum-hour laws for women and children, workmen's compensation acts, reforms in legal procedure, a simpler process than impeachment for the removal of judges, additions to the antitrust laws, revision of the currency system, publicity of campaign contributions, and parcel post.

On June 22, the night following the renomination of Taft, the defeated faction held an informal meeting, at which Roosevelt announced plans for the organization of a new Progressive party. He asked the delegates to return to their homes, ascertain the sentiments of their communities, and reconvene on August 5.

The Rise of Wilson

With a Republican split assured, the nation watched with eager interest for the results of the Democratic National Convention, which opened in Baltimore on June 25. The leading contenders for the nomination were Champ Clark of Missouri, the popular Speaker of the House, Governor Judson Harmon of Ohio, Representative Oscar W. Underwood of Alabama,

---

[3] Sherman died before election day and the Republicans substituted Nicholas Murray Butler, president of Columbia University.

and Governor Woodrow Wilson of New Jersey. The first three were veteran politicians; Wilson, on the contrary, had been elected to his first public office only two years before.

The New Jersey governor had been born in Staunton, Virginia, in 1856. His father was a Presbyterian clergyman of Scotch-Irish stock—a fact that goes far toward explaining the austere sense of duty, the frequent stubbornness, and the deep religious conviction that were to be so characteristic of Wilson as President. After graduating from Princeton, Wilson studied law and practiced briefly, but soon substituted a career in college teaching. After earning a doctorate at Johns Hopkins and teaching at several institutions, he returned to Princeton as professor of government and history. A competent scholar and prolific writer, he displayed his real genius in the spoken word. He was a lecturer and public speaker of captivating grace and power.

In 1902 Wilson became president of Princeton, but his career as a university administrator was anything but placid. For seven years he struggled with Dean Andrew F. West over the administration and expansion of the graduate school. When Wilson tried to democratize undergraduate life by eliminating exclusive eating clubs, he became involved in another bitter controversy. The president's activities alienated many rich patrons of the university and created a powerful opposition among the trustees. By 1910 Wilson's position had become so difficult that he required little urging to accept the Democratic nomination for governor of New Jersey, thus launching out on a new career.

Colonel George Harvey, the publisher of the *North American Review* and *Harper's Weekly,* sold the idea of nominating Wilson to the Democratic state bosses. As early as 1906 Harvey had publicly expressed his conviction that the Princeton educator would make an excellent President of the United States. What attracted the publisher, a man with powerful friends in Wall Street, was not Wilson's liberalism but his apparent conservatism. Up to this point in his career Wilson had given little indication of sympathy with the progressives; he had condemned Roosevelt's regulatory proposals and opposed Bryan's leadership of the Democratic party as dangerously radical. Through Wilson, Harvey hoped that conservative Easterners would regain control of the Democratic organization. The election of Wilson to the New Jersey governorship was the necessary preliminary to Harvey's further plans, and to this end he obtained the cooperation of ex-Senator Jim Smith and Jim Nugent, the state's Democratic bosses. In November, 1910, Wilson was one of twenty-six Democratic governors elected in the great uprising against the Republicans.

Although New Jersey progressives at first regarded Wilson with suspicion, his sturdy independence soon won them to his side. First of all, the governor successfully prevented Jim Smith from stealing the senatorship from James Martine, whom the voters had supported in a preferential primary. Next, Wilson prevailed upon the state legislature to enact a program of progressive legislation. During an effective speaking tour of the West during the summer of 1911, Wilson advocated the initiative, referendum, and recall—all favorite progressive demands.

In this swing toward liberalism, Wilson found Harvey's support embarrassing and took steps to shake him off. He turned instead to Colonel Edward M. House, a prominent Texas politician. House was a quiet man of refinement and wealth, who loved to play the political game from behind the scene; unlike Harvey his sympathies were with the progressives. Relying heavily on House's advice, Wilson made a complete break with Harvey and began to court the Western faction of the party in general and Bryan in particular. Fortunately for the governor, Bryan forgave him for having one time expressed the wish that the Great Commoner might be knocked "once for all, into a cocked hat."

Although having no chance to be nominated himself, Bryan proved to be a powerful figure at the Baltimore convention. His influence was evident in the bold platform that called for immediate downward revision of the tariff, strengthening of the antitrust laws, presidential preference primaries, prohibition of corporation contributions to campaign chests, a single term for the President, and revision of banking and currency laws. Bryan's most dramatic maneuver came when he unexpectedly offered a resolution that opposed the nomination of any candidate "who is the representative of or under obligation to J. Pierpont Morgan, Thomas F. Ryan, August Belmont, or any other member of the privilege-hunting and favor-seeking class." This direct challenge to Tammany and Wall Street threw the convention into an uproar. While Bryan consented to delete its most offensive parts, the amended resolution was overwhelmingly adopted.

Champ Clark led in the early balloting and had an actual majority on the second day of voting when Charles Murphy, boss of Tammany, shifted the New York delegation to the Missourian at the expense of Harmon. But a variety of circumstances kept Clark from receiving the two-thirds vote necessary for nomination. Bryan, unwilling to be on the same side with Tammany, countered Murphy's move to Clark by shifting his own support from Clark to Wilson. More important than Bryan's action, however, were certain backstage maneuvers of the Wilson managers. Gradually they won away some of the Speaker's less resolute followers; finally by gaining the votes of the Illinois delegation, controlled by Chicago boss Roger Sullivan, a Wilson bandwagon was put in motion that gave the New Jersey governor the nomination on the forty-sixth ballot. Governor Thomas R. Marshall of Indiana was selected as the candidate for Vice President.

Three-Way Contest

The National Progressive party's first convention opened in Chicago in a unique atmosphere of religious enthusiasm. The inspired delegates sang "John Brown's Body" and "Onward, Christian Soldiers," and former Senator Albert Beveridge delivered a passionately eloquent keynote address. Roosevelt's speech accepting the nomination the next day was in the same spirit. Second place on the ticket went to Hiram Johnson of California. The platform called for the whole calendar of reform: direct primaries, direct election of Senators, initiative, referendum, and recall, a speedier method of amending the Constitution, woman suffrage, limitation of campaign expenditures, prohibition of child labor, a "living wage," the eight-hour day, a Department of Labor, conservation, strong regulation of interstate corporations, and the establishment of a Federal industrial commission comparable to the Interstate Commerce Commission.

Republicans throughout the country now had to choose between loyalty to the historic party or alignment with the secessionists. Naturally the bulk of the machine politicians as well as the businessmen supported Taft, while idealists and reformers rallied happily to the so-called Bull Moose standard. Many individuals, however, took an unpredictable course. Such outstanding insurgents as LaFollette and Borah refused to support the third-party movement, while among Roosevelt's most active supporters were Boss Bill Flinn of Pittsburgh, millionaire publisher Frank A. Munsey, and George W. Perkins, former partner of J. P. Morgan, who became chairman of the Progressive National Committee.

The campaign was a curious one. All three major candidates claimed to be friendly to the cause of reform; all three party platforms were liberal documents. Taft's liberalism was obviously more cautious than that of his rivals, but what was the difference between the New Nationalism proclaimed by Colonel Roosevelt and the New Freedom promised by Governor Wilson? Actually the similar-sounding slogans reflected some rather fundamental differences in point of view. Roosevelt's program was frankly Hamiltonian, based on the assumption that a bold enlargement of Federal functions was necessary to meet new economic and social conditions. On the trust issue, for example, Roosevelt enlarged upon his old distinction between good and bad trusts. What was needed, he now insisted, was not new legislation and prosecutions designed to break large corporations into small, but Federal regulation of the trusts to preserve their good points and eradicate their evil.

Wilson, on the other hand, considered himself a faithful disciple of Jefferson. He feared the growth of the Federal government and wanted to see the progressive objectives achieved as largely as possible through state action. Moreover, he still hoped for a minimum of government intervention in economic life and pinned his hopes on the restoration of competition. Wilson rejected Roosevelt's contention that bigness in business might sometimes be a good thing. He believed, on the contrary, that excessive size was in itself bad because it often produced inefficiency and gave the corporation too much power, both economic and political. The antitrust laws should therefore be strengthened and clarified, the tariff should be drastically reduced, and the national banking system should be reformed to free farmers and small businessmen from the clutches of the money trust. Both Roosevelt's New Nationalism and Wilson's New Freedom showed the influence of other men's thinking upon the issues of the day. Roosevelt's convictions had been fortified by the arguments of Herbert Croly, whose influential book, *The Promise of American Life,* had appeared in 1909; Wilson accepted many of the ideas developed by Louis D. Brandeis in his studies of the interrelations of finance and business.

Perplexed by these conflicting brands of progressivism, the voters considered the contest one of personalities. They were impressed by Wilson's lofty idealism; they were entertained by the vigor with which the former friends, Taft and Roosevelt, ripped into each other. They were shocked by the near tragedy of October 14, when an unbalanced assailant shot and wounded Roosevelt in Milwaukee.

Yet all the oratory and unexpected drama of the campaign could not exert much influence on the election results. The Democrats had only to hold their ranks to vanquish their divided enemy. By an overwhelming electoral majority Woodrow Wilson won the presidency; he had 435 ballots, Roosevelt 88, and Taft 8. Of the popular votes, Wilson received 6.3 million, or 42 per cent; Roosevelt, 4 million, or 27 per cent; and Taft, 3.5 million, or 23 per cent. The schism had enabled a candidate with a minority of the popular vote to win. Almost a million Americans showed their distrust of all three major candidates by backing Eugene V. Debs, the Socialist. The new Congress also showed the effects of the Republican split: the House would consist of 290 Democrats to 145 Republicans and Progressives; the Senate, 51 Democrats to 45 of the opposition.

4

THE AMERICAN EMPIRE

The closing years of the nineteenth century marked the end of comparative isolation and the beginning of an epoch during which the United States emerged as a world power. Although the successful war with Spain is generally considered the dividing line between the two periods, actually the shift was gradual; the war merely hastened and accentuated it.

As a result of that war, the United States acquired several insular possessions and, appetite whetted, obtained others in which it had been previously interested. The administration of some of the new overseas territories—particularly in the Far East—raised unusual problems and turned American diplomatic interest again toward that part of the world. To solve these problems, the United States became increasingly involved with other nations, thereby emerging from its shell of isolation.

The Rise of Imperialistic Thought

Since 1900 a series of events combined to make the United States a world-minded nation. By this time the American frontier was disappearing. While there were still millions of acres available for homesteading, Americans were beginning to seek new opportunities. Industry, growing mightily since the Civil War, was now producing more goods than the home market could sustain. Consequently, new markets were sought to buy the surplus. At the same time, these mercantile interests were looking for new sources of raw materials to keep their ever-expanding factories operating at full capacity. This combination of desire for new markets and for new investment areas could not long be held in check.

"Manifest Destiny," dormant since the early 1870's as Americans moved into the West, rehabilitated the South, and promoted industry, once more emerged—but in new form, one motivated both by economics and by needs of national defense. The foremost proponent was Captain Alfred Thayer Mahan, a prominent naval officer and writer, who firmly believed that the bulwark of American defense was a strong navy—and to be strong it required additional bases from which to operate. Therefore he revived the theories once advocated by William Seward, Secretary of State during the Lincoln-Johnson era. He did not believe in territorial expansion as such, for the United States had enough land as it was; but the acquisition of bases in both the Caribbean and the Pacific was essential to maintain the United States as a world power. To Mahan, the original Monroe Doctrine was not so important now, because the United States could not adequately defend southern South America. It should concentrate primarily upon the West Indies and the Gulf of Mexico. He also firmly believed that an interoceanic canal, under complete American control and strongly defended by Caribbean bases, would furnish the avenue to the Pacific, where the United States must also have naval outposts.

The captain was likewise convinced that America must develop markets in the Far East, and that China, the center of that trade, must be kept politically independent. By the middle of the 1890's, Mahan strongly supported close cooperation with Great Britain, whose outlook he deemed similar to that of his own country.

A more vociferous and vocal apostle of these views was the young Henry Cabot Lodge of Massachusetts, an out-and-out jingoist at this time, with considerable influence among the young generation. He lacked Mahan's breadth of vision and was much less cautious, being in many ways like the War Hawks of 1812. Lodge advocated annexing Canada, taking Cuba by force from Spain, and snatching certain Pacific islands from the grasping hands of European nations. Yet Lodge did not contemplate how these objectives could be obtained—nor the effects.

Combining the strategic intuitions of Mahan with the rashness of Lodge was Theodore Roosevelt, who first made his presence felt on the national scene as McKinley's Assistant Secretary of the Navy. Like Mahan, he was a crusader for a bigger and better navy, and the efficiency of the naval forces during the war with Spain was partly the result of his efforts. The larger navy demanded by the expansionists was already materializing, helped by increased appropriations, the troubles with Chile that had shown naval deficiencies, and difficulties with Britain and Germany over Samoa.

In the 1890's political scientists, sociologists, and religious leaders were teaching doctrines that tended to support imperialism. From Darwin's theory of evolution, students of society drew the analogy that there was a world struggle for existence and that the fittest races were destined to survive and dominate. Thus it was an easy step to conclude, as did Professor John Burgess of Columbia, that nations like England, Germany, and the United States, especially endowed with "the capacity for establishing nation states," had a historic mission "to carry the political civilization of the modern world into those parts of the world inhabited by unpolitical and barbaric races." In similar fashion, clergymen like the Reverend Josiah Strong thought it was God's will to expand Anglo-Saxon rule and Protestant Christianity throughout the world.

Many newspapers also pounded the Manifest Destiny drum. Some liked the increased circulation that followed war-scare stories; others joined the jingo parade to satisfy their readers. Thus the demand for colonial expansion intensified throughout the 1890's, as naval leaders, politicians, educational and religious leaders, investors, and industrialists all added their voices to the chorus.

True, there was vigorous opposition to this form of imperialism. In his second term (1893–1897), President Grover Cleveland withdrew the Hawaiian annexation treaty from senatorial consideration. Critics of big business saw in imperialism another medium for promoting greater capitalistic profits. Even some businessmen opposed colonial growth as likely to involve the nation in war, with resulting heavier taxes. And isolationists warned that distant annexations might entangle the United States in the web of world politics.

Thus, if the advocates of expansion were to succeed, they needed an issue to unite their varied, scattered forces. The event that coalesced those elements, that won new converts, and that launched the nation definitely on an imperialist course and made it a world power was the Spanish-American War.

The War with Spain

The "splendid little war," as John Hay called it, had both deep and surface roots. For about a century the Spaniards had feared that the United States might seize rich and strategic Cuba, a situation causing numerous diplomatic crises, particularly in the 1850's and 1870's. But the immediate cause of the war grew out of the Cuban revolt starting in 1895. Spanish repressive measures were harsh, and the atrocity stories that horrified America had an unfortunate basis in fact, although they were often exaggerated by Cuban juntas and the "yellow" press. American investments of $50 million and trade worth $100 million were imperiled by the insurrection, and American health was endangered by plague conditions in Cuban "reconcentration camps." American public opinion increasingly demanded that Spain cease hostilities and grant the Cubans independence. President McKinley tried to achieve these ends without hostilities, but the DeLôme letter episode, in which the Spanish ambassador's unflattering description of McKinley made its way into American newspapers, and the tragic destruction of the *Maine* in Havana harbor, aroused an American war spirit that neither the President nor Congress could withstand.

On April 11, 1898, McKinley asked for authority to intervene; on April 19, Congress responded by passing four resolutions that amounted to a declaration of war. The fourth, the so-called Teller Amendment, however, was a concession to the anti-imperialists; it disclaimed any intention by the United States to annex Cuba; the ultimate objective of the war was "to leave the government and control of the Island to its people."

Judged by twentieth-century standards, the Spanish War was not a great military contest. The American army was woefully deficient in leadership, manpower, and modern equipment. The navy, greatly increased in size and efficiency since 1890, was in much better condition and, thanks to the foresight of Secretary of the Navy John Long and his assistant, Theodore Roosevelt, the various fleets were at strategic points when hostilities began. Fortunately, Spain was worse off, despite an apparent supremacy on paper.

Although the United States entered this war for Cuba's sake, the first fighting took place in Manila Bay on May 1, when Admiral George Dewey, ordered to the Far East shortly after the *Maine* was blown up, successfully attacked the Spanish fleet there. What was considered the major campaign, however, did not open until about June 1, when the Atlantic fleet under Admirals Winfield Schley and William Sampson bottled up the Spanish navy at Santiago, Cuba. Not until three weeks later did the American army invade that island and, after some setbacks, was in practical control of all of Cuba by the middle of July. General Nelson Miles had an even easier time subduing nearby Puerto Rico. Although fighting still continued in the Philippines, the disastrous blows of the Americans elsewhere, added to political and economic troubles at home, compelled Spain to seek armistice terms on July 26. This speedy victory gave Americans a new sense of power. Had not a European power been brought to its knees in less than three months? Now it was the destiny—perhaps even the duty—of the United States to assume its rightful place in world affairs and make its wishes and interests felt everywhere.

The Treaty of Paris

This feeling of destiny was expressed at the Paris peace conference from October to December, 1898. The United States emerged not only with its prime objectives—a guardianship over Cuba until its inhabitants could govern themselves—but also with complete ownership of Puerto Rico, Guam, and the Philippines.

The decision to annex the Philippines was a momentous one. Although most Americans scarcely knew where these islands were when Dewey won his dramatic victory, a demand to bring them under the American flag soon developed. Businessmen were interested in the trade both of the Philippines and of nearby China; naval experts stressed the islands' strategic importance; missionaries were inspired by the rich harvest of souls to be converted. McKinley, cautious by nature, was won over to annexation largely because there was no attractive alternative. To turn the islanders back to Spain seemed unjust in view of her recent inability to govern her colonies, but, on the other hand, the Filipinos were not believed ready for independence. Unless the United States accepted the responsibility of ruling the islands, it appeared likely that they would fall under the imperial domination of Germany, England, France, or Japan. McKinley himself related how late one night, after agonizing prayer, it was revealed to him "that there was nothing left for us to do but to take them all, and to educate the Filipinos and uplift and civilize and Christianize them, and by God's grace do the very best we could by them, as our fellow-men for whom Christ also died."

The treaty encountered a rough time in the Senate, where the anti-imperialists rallied under George Hoar of Massachusetts to delay ratification. They argued that acquisition of colonies was inconsistent with the Declaration of Independence, which asserted that all governments derived their just powers from the consent of the governed. The administration forces, however, basing their treaty support on a variety of arguments, finally won the day, aided in part by William Jennings Bryan. Although a professed anti-imperialist, he wanted to end the state of war and deliver the Filipinos from Spanish rule as a first step toward granting them independence. Therefore he influenced some treaty opponents to change their minds, saying that the American voters could settle the issue of imperialism in the election of 1900. Even so, the treaty just squeezed through by a vote of 57 to 27 on February 6, 1899.

Before the century was over, imperialism had achieved additional triumphs. In 1898 the United States annexed Hawaii by joint resolution of Congress and similar action by Hawaii; the following year Britain, Germany, and the United States agreed to partition the Samoan Islands, with the United States gaining Tutuila, with its excellent coaling station and naval base of Pago Pago; and in 1900, the United States formally occupied Wake Island, valuable as a cable station. Dealing with the new responsibilities that these acquisitions entailed became the major task of American diplomacy in the opening years of the new century.

Keeping the Pledge with Cuba

The Teller Amendment of April, 1898, had stated: "That the United States hereby disclaims any disposition or intention to exercise sovereignty, jurisdiction, or control" over Cuba "except for the pacification thereof, and asserts its determination, when that is accomplished, to leave the government and control of the island to its people." When the war ended, however, the United States was not immediately ready to withdraw from Cuba. Possibility of a counterrevolution by the Spanish residents, the appalling illiteracy of the Cubans and their lack of training in self-government, and fear that American withdrawal might allow some other power, perhaps Germany, to step in combined to delay fulfillment of the promise.

Instead, an American military regime was established, with General Leonard Wood eventually serving as governor general. His administration brought many benefits to the Cubans. Construction of a road from one end of the island to the other and other public works improved transportion facilities; the Army Medical Corps, and particularly Major Walter Reed's efforts to destroy yellow-fever-carrying mosquitoes, cut down the death rate; and the new educational system reduced illiteracy and prepared the Cubans for their new responsibilities.

By mid-1900, Governor Wood believed the islanders were ready for self-government. A constituent assembly, selected by limited franchise, convened in November, and by February, 1901, had drawn up, under Wood's guidance, a constitution that provided for three branches of government and separation of powers, but failed to mention Cuba's future relationship with the United States. When the War Department refused to approve this document, Secretary of War Root and Governor Wood collaborated in drawing up the so-called Platt Amendment that was made a rider to the Army Appropriation Act of March, 1901. Of the seven articles in this amendment, the most important were: (1) "Cuba shall never enter into any treaty or other compact with any foreign power . . . which will impair . . . the independence of Cuba, nor . . . authorize . . . any foreign power . . . to obtain . . . control over any portion of the said island"; (2) Cuba shall not "contract any public debt to pay the interest on which . . . the ordinary revenues . . . shall be inadequate"; (3) "the United States may exercise the right to intervene for the preservation of Cuban independence, the maintenance of a government adequate for the protection of life, property, and individual liberty"; and (5) Cuba will lease or sell coaling stations and naval bases to the United States to aid in Cuban defense.

Acceptance of the Platt Amendment meant that Cuba would be a protectorate of the United States, enjoying something less than full independence. Although the Cubans resented this, they realized that if they did not comply with American wishes, they would not achieve cherished self-government. Therefore, with many misgivings, they made the necessary additions to their constitution. Then, to strengthen the right of American intervention, the Platt Amendment was made the basis of a treaty between the two countries in 1903.

As soon as Congress approved the Cuban constitution, preparations were made for the first election. The presidency was won by Tomás Estrada Palma, whose long exile in the United States had acquainted him with democratic procedures. Following his inauguration in May, 1902, American troops were withdrawn and the island left to its destiny. The ending of the military occupation occasioned some grumbling among the more zealous American imperialists and those who had investments in Cuba. Most Americans, however, realized that the honor of the United States was at stake in living up to its promise. The withdrawal was a

Cuba the beginner. Uncle Sam getting Cuba ready for self-government. (By Bart in the *Minneapolis Journal*.)

great surprise to many Europeans, who did not believe the United States would relinquish such a valuable prize.

During Palma's first administration Cuban progress continued with friendly American assistance. President Roosevelt, realizing that the high Dingley Tariff rates tended to exclude sugar, Cuba's principal crop, from its natural American market, asked Congress to grant preferential rates to the new republic. Despite opposition from Louisiana sugar interests and other protectionists, Congress, in December, 1903, reduced rates on imports from Cuba from 20 to 40 per cent and terminated sugar reciprocity agreements with other nations. Cuba was not only greatly aided by this, but American exporters benefited as well because the nearby republic became a leading purchaser of American goods.

When Palma was re-elected in 1905, his opponents, charging him with potential dictatorship, threatened to start a civil war. To meet this danger, American troops were sent to the island in 1906 and a military government was re-established. American annexationists eagerly believed that independence had failed, and even Roosevelt wrote to a friend: "I am so angry with that infernal little Cuban republic that I would like to wipe its people off the face of the earth."

During this intervention the governorship was chiefly in the hands of Charles Magoon, who had had experience as an executive in the Canal Zone. He undertook to stimulate Cuban economic life, to build more roads, to better the educational system, and to improve the election laws. This paternalism was opposed by some Cubans, who accused him of extravagant abuse of the pardoning power and even of corruption—charges subsequently dismissed as groundless by American investigators.

When the Cubans were again thought ready to govern themselves, an election brought victory to José Gomez, a Liberal. In January, 1909, the American intervention ended. Once again the United States had lived up to its promise, yet its policy clearly demonstrated that the Platt Amendment was no empty formula. Cuban independence was contingent upon the Cubans behaving themselves—from the American point of view.

The Puerto Rican Experiment

Puerto Rico, with its 3,435 square miles of territory and population of a million, was another postwar responsibility of the United States. The islanders were largely illiterate, with no training whatever in self-government. The Paris treaty provided that "the civil rights and political status of the native inhabitants . . . shall be determined by Congress," with no promise about future status. Therefore, Puerto Rico's case was radically different from Cuba's.

When annexed, the island was in a bad way economically, and the situation was soon made worse by a severe hurricane in the summer of 1899. The several American military governors of this period did commendable work in laying the foundations for improved economics, education, and sanitation.

Then in April, 1900, the Foraker Act established permanent civil government, providing for a governor and an executive council of eleven (of whom five were to be Puerto Ricans), named by the President with Senate approval. Six executive departments were created, each headed by a council member, usually an American. The insular legislature consisted of the council, serving as the upper house, and the House of Delegates, elected by the qualified voters. The court system followed the American model. The inhabitants were designated as "citizens of Puerto Rico," entitled to United States protection but not to all the privileges of American citizenship. This form of government was strikingly similar to that which the Americans themselves had once "enjoyed" under British rule and remained in force without essential change until 1917, even though it did not work altogether smoothly.

The Puerto Ricans were dissatisfied because they were placed in an inferior position through the denial of American citizenship and because control of the executive departments was kept from the assembly. Consequently, there were constant petty quarrels between the governor and his council on the one hand and the House of Delegates on the other, reminiscent of the eighteenth-century conflicts between British colonial executives and the American colonists. Just as in those cases the popular branch of the legislature tried to tighten the purse strings. In 1909 the American Congress foiled such tactics, however, by providing that the amount approved the preceding year would be collected if the House of Delegates failed at any time to vote necessary appropriations. Although better administrators were sent out and the government now worked more smoothly, it cannot be said that the Puerto Ricans were any more enthusiastic over American control.

In spite of bickering, there is no doubt that Puerto Rican economic conditions, though still far from prosperous, developed beyond anything the island had previously known. True, the important coffee industry declined somewhat, but the total exports and imports were considerably larger than in the past. In addition, the island obtained improved transportation, modern sanitation that thwarted the dreaded hookworm, and better schools that decreased the widespread illiteracy. While the United States assuredly showed its good intentions, the primary problem of government is to obtain the consent of the governed, and in that regard she was deficient.

Difficulties in the Philippines

The most novel and immediate problem raised by the war was that of the Philippines, consisting of seven thousand islands of varying size and inhabited by seven million people, many of them uncivilized, speaking many dialects, and practicing a variety of religions. The great American majority regarded the rule of these islands as a trust and wished to educate the Filipinos to self-government in the American sense as quickly as possible, although leading Republicans believed that would take a long time. On the other hand, it was inevitable that the Filipinos, after their experience with Spain, would not appreciate an American effort to dictate their future.

When Spain surrendered, American control did not extend beyond the environs of Manila and, when it became evident that the United States would not recognize the Philippine Republic under Emilio Aguinaldo, he and his supporters resorted to arms. Two days before the peace treaty was ratified, the Filipino insurgents, numerous and fairly well equipped, attacked the American troops at Manila, thereby promoting a serious situation.

In regular warfare, however, the Filipinos could not offer effective resistance to the soon heavily reinforced Americans. In a few months all the chief officers of the insurgent government were captured except Aguinaldo, who eluded his pursuers. In this struggle, the efficiency and zeal of the American forces were sometimes offset by the rainy season, the topography of the country, and the difficulty in controlling large districts with small garrisons.

The spirit of the insurgents was not broken, and they decided in November, 1899, to resort to guerrilla warfare exclusively. This action increased the American problems, and the fighting was now carried on with mounting ferocity. Public opinion at home became so disturbed by persistent reports of outrages committed by American troops against Filipino captives that a senatorial investigation was begun. The testimony clearly showed that American soldiers had in many cases been ruthless, yet in extenuation the situation was difficult and officers as a rule had tried to prevent atrocities. Such incidents are unfortunately the almost inevitable result of guerrilla warfare.

Meantime, military operations were actively pushed and, in March, 1901, Aguinaldo himself was captured. The remaining insurgents still fought desperately, but their defeat was now a matter of time, and the last resistance ended in April, 1902.

The first American rule in the archipelago was necessarily military, with first General Elwell Otis and then General Arthur MacArthur—father of the famous World War II General Douglas MacArthur—serving as military governor. Even before ratification of the peace treaty, however, President McKinley named the First Philippine Commission of five members, headed by President Jacob Schurman of Cornell University, to investigate the situation. After careful study, the members concluded the natives were not yet capable of self-government, although they ultimately should have their independence. The commissioners' report also included a very useful account of the conditions and resources of the Philippines, about which Americans knew little.

Also on this commission's recommendation, McKinley, as commander-in-chief, named a second commission of Chairman William Howard Taft and four others in April, 1901. Unlike the first board, this was a permanent administrative body especially charged with the delicate task of organizing a governmental system beginning with the conquered municipalities and then extending to the provinces. When the commissioners believed a civil, as distinct from a military, central government could be established, they were to submit the necessary recommendations. This Second Philippine

Commission became the supreme legislative authority in the islands, subject to the President through the Secretary of War, but the military governor remained as chief executive.

Because a firmer legal basis was desirable for such an important action, Congress added the Spooner Amendment to the Military Appropriation Act of March, 1901, which granted the President complete military, civil, and judicial power over the Philippines until Congress provided otherwise. This measure, although filling an immediate need, was a rather remarkable step for Congress to take—that of making McKinley a virtual dictator in the archipelago.

Taking advantage of this authority, McKinley wisely made certain governmental alterations. Taft was appointed civil governor and MacArthur's authority was limited to the districts still in revolt. A little later three Filipino members were added to the commission, and the administration was divided into four executive departments, each in charge of an American commissioner. In carrying out his difficult assignment, Governor Taft gained a reputation for executive ability that later helped make him President. To train the natives in civil responsibilities, he organized the local governments in such a way that elected officials served under careful American supervision.

As these arrangements generally worked well, Congress passed the Philippine Government, or Organic, Act in July, 1902, which confirmed what had been done, although specifying that the civil officers named thereafter by the President must have Senate approval. This measure also paved the way for future progress: two years after a census was taken, a general assembly was to be elected. This act further declared the natives to be citizens of the Philippines and extended to them most of the provisions of the American Constitution, including the guarantee of life, liberty, and property, but not trial by jury.

Although somewhat delayed, the election plans were finally completed. More than 100,000 Filipinos voted in the fall of 1907, and soon after the Philippine Assembly met. The Nationalist party, seeking speedy independence, gained a majority of seats over the Progressives, who favored evolution under American control. The upper house of this bicameral legislature consisted of the commissioners. The Nationalists, while still expressing their desire for freedom, wisely refrained from aggressive or violent tactics, and so the establishment of the assembly did not complicate the situation.

Creation of this best possible government was, however, only one of the numerous tasks that had to be faced. Particularly important were the settlement of the Friars' land problem and the introduction of a new educational system. Under the Spanish regime, three prominent religious orders—the Dominicans, the Augustinians, and the Recollectos—held about 400,000 acres of the best land in the islands, which the Filipinos could cultivate only by renting it on shares for long periods. The revolt against Spain in 1896 had been largely the outgrowth of Filipino hostility to this situation, as well as to the alleged immorality among the members of these religious orders. During the revolt the Friars had been largely dispossessed, but they still claimed the land, while the natives naturally regarded the captured soil as their own. According to the Philippine Commission, the best solution was to purchase the disputed acreage—which it was authorized to do under the Act of 1902, but the orders demanded too high a price. Lengthy negotiations, including a trip by Taft to the Vatican, lowered the price to $7,239,000, a sum admittedly more than the actual value of the land, but the commissioners agreed to pay it to end the controversy. Eventually the land was sold to the natives on very liberal terms.

Perhaps no aspect of American control deserves more praise than the development of an educational system vastly superior to that of the Spaniards. Because of the differences in tribal speech and the absence of a written literature, English was made the basis of instruction. Normal schools were quickly established to train native teachers, and a university modeled after American state universities was founded at Manila. Under the Spanish regime all manual toil had been considered something to be avoided, but, despite deep-seated prejudice, the new system made commendable progress in popularizing technical and agricultural education. The results should not be exaggerated, however, for the difficulties to be faced were still great. Oriental peoples change slowly, and some measures devised to force upon the Filipinos a premature enthusiasm for "American liberty" had the reverse effect. Moreover, Congress's failure to provide adequate financial aid for the schools retarded the work and limited to a disappointing degree the number of natives reached.

The Insular Cases

Meantime, the United States came face to face with some of the most complicated questions of political theory and constitutional law that the Americans ever had to meet. While the United States had acquired territory before, with the exception of Alaska it had been contiguous to the United States and was clearly destined to be eventually admitted to the Union. The case of Alaska caused little trouble as most of it remained so long unoccupied, but it seemed absurd to many Americans that distant islands, inhabited by races so dissimilar as those of the Philippines, should ever become states. On the other hand, the idea of the Stars and Stripes waving over permanently subject peoples was abhorrent to many anti-imperialists such as Senator Hoar and Carl Schurz.

Nor, after the deed was done, did the complications cease. Many well-informed persons held that new lands became at once part of the United States, and their inhabitants were just as much citizens as were those of the older American territories. While to some it seemed absurd that Moros and headhunters should have all the privileges of the Bill of Rights and the Fourteenth Amendment, to others nothing else was possible under the American form of government. The Constitution spoke nowhere of subjects, but only of citizens.

In the opposing view, the Constitution did not extend automatically to the new acquisitions, which were "dependencies" subject to the rule of Congress. Therefore, the Constitution would not apply to them until extended by act of the "sovereign legislature." While this view appeared to be good common sense, it was not easy to find a constitutional basis for it. Especially was it hard to think of Congress bound by constitutional limitations within the continental United States but doing anything it pleased outside of those geographical limits.

These vital questions came before the Supreme Court in the so-called Insular Cases of 1901. The first, DeLima v. Bidwell, turned on whether duties on goods from Puerto Rico could be collected under the Dingley Tariff Act. In a five-to-four decision, the court held that Puerto Rico was not a foreign country and therefore those duties could not be collected. This, however, did not reach the real heart of the matter: whether Congress had the right to place special duties on goods imported from the islands.

This further question arose at once. When the Foraker Act was passed, many Americans wanted Puerto Rican products to come in free. The sugar interests, however, were able to insert a 15 per cent duty on Puerto Rican imports until 1902. The validity of this requirement was now tested in Downes v. Bidwell, decided in May, 1901. The crux of the matter lay in this question: Did the constitutional provision that all duties must be uniform throughout the United States apply to Puerto Rico? By upholding the validity of the Foraker Act, the Supreme Court ruled that the Constitution did not automatically follow the flag; it was extended to outlying territories only when Congress so ordered. In many ways this was an unsatisfactory decision, and even the five judges forming the majority could not agree in their reasoning. Nevertheless, the imperialists welcomed the outcome of the litigation, and the way seemed open to extend American rule over peoples regarded as inferior without any requirement that they must be granted full rights of citizenship. But even Supreme Court decisions could not control irrevocably the thinking of the American people. In the minds of many, permanent American domination over colonial populations was inconsistent with American principles, nor could the implied pledge of independence for the Filipinos be forgotten.

American Interests in the Far East

The occupation of the Philippines and, to a lesser extent, of Hawaii, Guam, Wake, and Samoa revived an American interest in the Far East that had been largely dormant since before the Civil War, when Secretary of State Daniel Webster and his immediate successors had worked for equality of privileges and commercial facilities for all nations doing business with China.

Even as late as March, 1898, a British proposal for joint action in the Far East to protect the open door was sidetracked by the United States. But then came the war with Spain and the resultant annexation of Far Eastern territory. Quickly did the American attitude change, partly because American exporters sought new markets and importers needed raw materials, and partly because the region must be kept at peace so that the new possessions could be defended more easily and at less cost.

The major trouble spot was China, whose weakness had been clearly revealed by her overwhelming defeat in the Sino-Japanese War of 1894–

1895. Japan and the major European powers quickly seized advantage by acquiring spheres of influence in Chinese territory. France obtained a ninety-nine-year lease to Kwangchow-wan; Britain gained Wei-hai-wei and Kowloon; Russia took over Port Arthur; Germany secured Kiaochow; Japan sought Fukhien and Korea; and Italy was striving to keep pace. It was no coincidence that these spheres centered around important ports. While not sharing in these spoils, the United States was greatly concerned over what might follow. Suppose each trespassing power closed its ports to the commerce of all but its own ships? Certainly American trade would suffer increasingly, the closed-port theory might lead to war among the contestants, and the American hold on the Philippines might be lost or, at the least, the United States would have to increase her military and naval establishments in the Far East.

Although Britain had scrambled for concessions in China, she greatly preferred her traditional Open Door policy under which English merchants had gained a lion's share of Far Eastern trade. On several occasions, therefore, her government proposed to the reluctant McKinley administration some kind of joint action on the Chinese situation. An active propagandist was Lord Charles Beresford, a British naval hero who visited the United States in February, 1898, after a Far Eastern tour. Meanwhile, American businessmen were also clamoring for a change in American policy.

Finally, Secretary of State John Hay adopted ideas formulated by W. W. Rockhill, one of his American advisers on the Far East, and by Rockhill's friend, Alfred Hippisley, an Englishman employed in the Chinese customs service. In the fall of 1899, Hay sent to all six nations concerned similar notes, the gist of which was that no country should interfere "with any treaty port or vested interest within any so-called 'spheres of interest' or leased territory it may have in China"; within each sphere the Chinese government should collect all duties provided for in its tariff treaties; and each power was asked not only to approve these statements but try to persuade the others to agree also.

It will be observed that Hay's notes gave only a strictly limited definition to the Open Door and made no attempt to halt the partition of China. All Hay asked was that in any such partition American treaty rights in Chinese ports should be respected. Even for this modest proposal he received only faltering support. The replies were generally equivocal, with assent contingent upon approval by all the other powers, and the Russian answer, indeed, was practically a rejection. Displeased with this result, Hay determined on a bold stroke. On March 20, 1899, he publicly announced that all the nations concerned had supported his proposal in "final and definitive" terms. No power cared to challenge his statement lest the others consider it grasping. Thus Hay enjoyed a diplomatic victory of some real significance, although much less than that credited to him by the enthusiastic American press.

The Secretary of State carried his policy a step further within a few months. In June, 1900, a Chinese nationalistic faction, popularly known as the "Boxers," began a fanatical attempt to drive the invaders from their precious land. Several hundred "foreign devils" were killed, and the British legation at Peking, where many found refuge, was for weeks besieged by the Boxers. An international army of 20,000, of whom 2,500 were American troops from the Philippines, was finally needed to raise the siege by mid-August and to disperse the Boxer rebels.

Again the United States had to go to China's aid. On July 3, 1900, Hay added to the Open Door the additional policy of preserving Chinese territorial integrity and independence. The other powers did not formally accept Hay's principles, but the dismemberment of the empire was prevented by working one country's territorial greed against that of another. Furthermore, the possible bankruptcy of China through payment of a billion-dollar indemnity was prevented when the United States persuaded the other nations to cut their demands by two thirds. China showed her gratitude by signing a commercial treaty particularly favorable to her benefactor, and the good relations were further accentuated when the United States later returned most of her $24 million share of the Boxer indemnity. In turn, China used this money for scholarships in the United States granted to worthy Chinese students.

Hay was not always consistent in his policies. At the close of 1900—the very year in which he publicly talked about preserving Chinese territorial integrity—he secretly tried to obtain an American naval base in southern China. The deal was frustrated by the Japanese government, which chided Hay for his forgetfulness.

Since Hay's little flirtation with imperialism was not revealed until many years after his death, he continued to enjoy a great reputation as the statesman who had saved a helpless China from the ravenous clutches of other powers. This reputation was partly deserved and partly not. Hay had in truth shown considerable diplomatic skill in notifying the world that his country stood committed both to equality of trading opportunity in China and the preservation of that country's independence. Yet the policy was not primarily altruistic; it was designed more to promote American trade and investment and to preserve the general peace in the Far East. Moreover, two other factors were probably more important than Hay's diplomacy in saving China from further encroachment: the warning of outraged nationalism sounded by the Boxer uprising itself and the balance of power taking shape in the Far East between Russia and France on one side and England and Japan on the other.

Relations with Japan

After 1900 English and American proponents of the Open Door watched with growing concern as Russia extended more and more domination over Manchuria and even made gestures toward Korea. Britain, with the approval of most Americans, countered Russian imperialism by an alliance with Japan in 1902, which encouraged the Nipponese suddenly to attack Port Arthur in 1904, thus precipitating the Russo-Japanese War. Outwardly the United States maintained an official neutrality but made little attempt to disguise its pro-Japanese sympathies. Indeed, according to Roosevelt's own story—which has been questioned—he warned France and Germany that the United States might go to Japan's assistance if either entered on the side of Russia. Whatever the truth of this tale, Roosevelt did respond eagerly when Japan intimated to him in ultrasecrecy that it would welcome his good offices in bringing the war to an early conclusion whereby the fruits of initial Japanese victories would be assured. Fortunately for the President, Russia—convulsed by internal revolution—was also eager for peace. Roosevelt was thus on sure ground when he publicly invited the belligerents to a peace conference in the United States. The resultant Treaty of Portsmouth of 1905 pleased him, since it was moderate enough to maintain a balance of power and because he received the Nobel Peace Prize for bringing it about.

The surprising military strength of Japan impressed on the Roosevelt administration the desirability of an understanding to safeguard the Philippines. Accordingly, Secretary of War Taft and Prime Minister Katsura concluded the so-called Agreed Memorandum in July, 1905, under which the United States would allow Japan a free hand in Korea in return for a promise that Japan had no designs on the Philippines. Before the year was over, Secretary Root fully supported this memorandum when he told the Japanese ambassador to the United States that the United States would deal with Korean problems only through Japan.

This Agreed Memorandum, kept secret from the American people for many years, was not in accord with the Open Door. Later, Root tried to defend this secret diplomacy by saying that war was the only way to have stopped the Japanese trespass in Korea. He inferred that Congress would not have declared war and, even if it had, the people would not have stood for it. Therefore, "all we might have done was to make threats which we could not carry out."

Although the memorandum normally would be considered an indication of full accord between the two nations, actually beneath the surface there were signs of ill-feeling. Japanese jingoists, not knowing about the initiative taken by their own government, believed that American diplomatic intervention in their war with Russia had deprived them of both territory and large financial indemnity. On the other hand, Americans on the Pacific coast were worried over increased Japanese immigration, particularly of unskilled labor with a low standard of living. While a congressional bill for complete Japanese exclusion failed when Roosevelt opposed it, the San Francisco authorities in October, 1906, passed an ordinance preventing Orientals from attending the regular city schools. Immediately Japan declared that an earlier treaty gave her nationals the same rights as those enjoyed by the most favored nation.

Roosevelt supported this contention, but the Constitution gave him no authority to intervene in a local matter. He used, however, other means to end this "wicked absurdity." In a White House conference, he successfully persuaded the Republican leaders of California to use their influence to have the obnoxious statute repealed. And in this stand the President was backed by most of the nation's press, which feared war, so great was the Japanese resentment. The San Francisco authorities amended the school law so that Japanese children "of proper age and preparation" could attend the regular schools.

In an effort to stop further local or state actions of a similar nature,

Roosevelt arranged with the Japanese government the so-called Gentlemen's Agreement of 1907, under which Japan promised to refuse passports to the United States to Japanese laborers. By this face-saving device the Japanese government assumed responsibility for halting the type of emigration that had aroused antagonism.

The President, not wishing the Japanese to mistake his intervention in the school law case as a sign of weakness, wrote to a friend in July, 1907: "I am none the less anxious that they would realize that I am not afraid of them, and that the United States will no more submit to bullying than it will to bully." Consequently, he decided to send the American battle fleet of sixteen warships around the world. This would warn Japanese jingoists that the United States, with the world's second largest navy, was prepared for any trouble. When his announcement was made in the summer of 1907, the Eastern press immediately asserted that such a foolhardy move would leave the Atlantic shores unprotected and expose the fleet to Japanese attack. When Congress refused to furnish the money necessary for the venture, Roosevelt bluntly declared that enough funds were available to get the fleet to the Pacific, where it would stay until Congress changed its mind—and it quickly did.

This spectacular voyage had more behind it than simply brandishing a sword under the nose of Japan. Roosevelt, still an avid advocate of naval expansion, hoped to give the fleet practice in large-scale operations and at the same time publicize the need for larger appropriations for both the navy and the Panama Canal. As far as Japan was concerned, the expedition seemed to work out well, for the fleet accepted an invitation to visit Tokyo, where it received an enthusiastic welcome. The President could therefore claim that his action had promoted the cause of peace, but it is questionable whether it had actually done so. Secretly resentful of the American demonstration, Japan redoubled her efforts to build up her own naval strength to the point where she could dominate the Far East.

Even while the fleet was still on the high seas, Secretary Root completed a promising agreement with Japanese Ambassador Takahira in November, 1908. Its terms provided for mutual support for the Pacific status quo, noninterference with each other's possessions, mutual backing for the independence and territorial integrity of China, and general reiteration of the Open Door. While this was simply an executive agreement, Japan at least gave her most adequate endorsement of the Hay theory up to that time.

Despite the measures taken to ease Japanese-American tension, there was still a growing antagonism between the more nationalistic elements in both nations. Among certain Americans it was popular to depict Japan as the inevitable future enemy and to ask whether the United States should not embark upon a preventive war before her rival became too strong. This attitude was accentuated during the Taft administration when a Japanese syndicate sought to gain control of Magdalena Bay in Lower California in 1911. Immediately the cry was raised that the syndicate was really a Japanese governmental agency wanting the Bay as a future naval base from which to attack the United States. So great was the furor that the syndicate dropped its plans, but to prevent a similar threat in the future,

Senator Henry Cabot Lodge introduced the so-called Lodge Corollary to the Monroe Doctrine, which the upper house approved by a vote of 51 to 4 in August, 1912. It declared that "when any harbor or other place in the American continents is so situated that the occupation thereof for naval or military purposes that might threaten . . . the safety of the United States, the Government of the United States could not see without grave concern the actual or potential possession of such harbor or other place by any Government, not American." While this corollary was not endorsed by Taft, the American people welcomed it as a new version of the Monroe Doctrine—an attitude that did not improve Japanese-American relations.

Dollar Diplomacy in China

The Open Door was in jeopardy again during Taft's administration. In 1910 the Chinese revolution overthrew the Manchu dynasty and made China nominally a republic. Immediately the Chinese were submerged in problems of reorganization, particularly economic. Taft, along with Secretary of State Philander Knox, became worried that the proposal by French, German, and British bankers to construct the Hukuang Railroad through southern and central China might destroy the Open Door. Consequently, the State Department persuaded J. P. Morgan to establish an American syndicate to participate in the railway development. About the only effect of this action was to make Europe suspicious of American designs, and even the Morgan interests were not enthusiastic about entering the project.

Taft also worried about the Russo-Japanese railroad interests in Manchuria, which might endanger China's territorial integrity. Therefore he proposed that the European and Japanese bankers combine with those from America to lend China sufficient money to buy the railroads in question. The other powers were unsympathetic, however, and the American bankers were practically forced to participate. Finally, a six-power loan of $125 million was arranged, but before it could go through, Woodrow Wilson became President. In March, 1913, he announced that such a loan would weaken China's sovereignty and might lead to future intervention. If the American bankers wanted to go ahead, they would do so at their own risk; they could expect no support from his administration. Thus did Taft's attempt at so-called dollar diplomacy in China fail. His honest intentions could not be doubted, but his methods only served to promote closer Russo-Japanese accord and to weaken the earlier status quo arrangements.

By thus plunging into Far Eastern troubles, the United States was inviting serious trouble. Since in a showdown the American government would have neither the popular support nor the military strength needed to back up its policies by force, it had to rely on diplomatic maneuvering and the game of playing one nation against another. This worked so long as a balance of power could be maintained. When Europe became locked in the titanic struggles of World Wars I and II, however, the American position became untenable. Finally, during the crisis of 1941, the United States was compelled either to retire in humiliation or to fight.

5

SEARCH FOR SECURITY AND PEACE

American diplomacy in the first decade of the twentieth century found matters other than those of colonial administration, the Open Door, and peace in the Far East that demanded equal attention. In order to maintain its new position as a world power, the United States felt the need to construct and protect an interoceanic canal and to develop closer accord in the Western Hemisphere. Likewise, she assumed the responsibility of promoting world peace by continuing to be a prime supporter of the settlement of international disputes by arbitration.

Clearing the Way for the Panama Canal

The dream of a canal across Central America to link the Atlantic and Pacific oceans had appealed to Spanish imagination during the Age of Discovery. In later days Thomas Jefferson had proposed such a waterway, and mid-nineteenth-century advocates of Manifest Destiny had taken up the idea to speed transportation to California and Oregon. Indeed, in 1846 Minister Benjamin Bidlack concluded a treaty with New Granada, the predecessor of Colombia, that granted the United States a right of way across the Isthmus of Panama. Although no canal was built at this time, an American-controlled Panama railroad did result from the Bidlack diplomacy. At about the same time the rivalry of England and the United States in Central America threatened serious trouble, but the two nations, in the Clayton-Bulwer Treaty of 1850, agreed that neither would fortify nor exercise exclusive control over any isthmian canal.

Next, in 1879, when French promoters sought to follow up their triumph in building the Suez Canal by organizing a Panama Canal Company, it appeared that the long-dreamed-of waterway might soon became a reality under a control neither British nor American. Acquiring a concession from Colombia, the French promoters began construction in a great burst of energy. Long before the project could be completed, however, the company, plagued by graft and mismanagement, went bankrupt—to the immense relief of jealously watching Americans.

Meantime, the United States had become thoroughly dissatisfied with the limitations of the Clayton-Bulwer Treaty. In 1880, President Rutherford Hayes declared that any canal connecting the Atlantic and the Pacific must be under exclusive American control because it would form "a part of the coastline of the United States." During the administrations of James Garfield and Chester Arthur efforts were made to modify that treaty, but Britain refused to waive her rights—greatly to the displeasure of American expansionists who threatened to have the United States tear up the document and proceed on its own willful way. The anti-imperialist Grover Cleveland, although sternly opposed to such unilateral action, nevertheless impressed upon the English the desirability of modifying their position. By 1897, the latter were beginning to face up to the realities of the new situation. Eager to improve Anglo-American relations and wishing to encourage the building of a canal that would benefit English commerce as much as American, the British government was now ready to negotiate the issue.

This was the situation when the Spanish-American War provided dramatic evidence for building the waterway without further delay. The sixty-eight-day voyage of the *Oregon* around the Horn and the acquisition of Pacific islands demonstrated the need to link the two oceans if the new possessions were to be adequately protected.

Under these circumstances Secretary Hay had relatively little difficulty in reaching an agreement with Lord Pauncefote, the British ambassador. The so-called First Hay-Pauncefote Treaty (February, 1900) provided that the United States might build and manage a canal through Central America, but it must be neutralized and unfortified under approximately the same rules that governed the Suez Canal. The Senate, refusing to ratify this document as it stood, made a number of changes, the most important of which denied the international character of the canal and provided for American defense of it. Britain would not accept these amendments, however, and Hay had to start all over again.

On November 18, 1901, a compromise was reached in the Second Hay-Pauncefote Treaty: the Clayton-Bulwer arrangement was definitely superseded; the United States could build and manage a canal that, though theoretically neutralized, would be under her protection; and the clause barring fortifications was erased. The only important restriction provided that the canal be open to the nations of the world on an equality. This time the Senate offered no opposition to ratification. Britain somewhat later conceded America's right to fortify the canal since nothing in the treaty forbade it. These British concessions indicated the growing accord between the two nations. Another friendly sign was the gradual reduction of the British fleet and garrisons in Caribbean waters, tacit admission of American supremacy there.

Meanwhile, a spirited controversy had developed over the route of the proposed canal. The two most promising alternatives were to connect the various natural waterways of Nicaragua or to cut directly across the narrow waist of Panama. For various reasons the American preference had always been the Nicaragua project, but the partisans of Panama were now engaged in a widespread campaign to advertise what they claimed were the superior advantages of their shorter route. Deeply interested in the outcome was the New Panama Canal Company, which had taken over the assets of the old French corporation. The stockholders' only hope of salvaging something from the financial wreck was to sell their rights to the

The man behind the egg. The intrigue promoting the Panama revolution. (By Drake in the *New York Times*.)

United States for as much as they could get. In Philippe Bunau-Varilla, a French engineer who had worked for the old company, and William Cromwell, an astute New York lawyer, the new company had two highly ingenious lobbyists.

President McKinley appointed a commission headed by Admiral John Walker to study the competing routes. In a report submitted two days before the Second Hay-Pauncefote Treaty was concluded, the Walker Commission recommended the Nicaragua route, mainly because the New Panama Canal Company demanded $109 million for its rights across the isthmus.

The new chief executive, Theodore Roosevelt, was most anxious to begin canal construction. While he probably preferred the Panama route, he refused to pay the outrageous sum the Canal Company was asking. Consequently, in December, 1901, he gave his outward blessing to the Hepburn Bill for a Nicaragua canal, which passed the lower house early in January, 1902, by the one-sided vote of 308 to 2. Meantime, the company stockholders, realizing their own rights would be worthless were a canal built through Nicaragua, offered to sell their privileges for $40 million, which, according to the Walker Commission, was a reasonable figure. Thereupon the Senate added the Spooner Amendment to the Hepburn Bill, substituting the Panama route if the United States could get the company's rights for that amount and obtain satisfactory permission from Colombia. Thanks to administration pressure and volcanic eruptions near the proposed Nicaragua route, the amended Hepburn Bill passed both houses by overwhelming majorities and was signed by the President in June, 1902.

The remaining obstacle, Colombian permission, was the most difficult of all. After long negotiations, Hay concluded the Hay-Herrán Treaty in January, 1903, under which the United States would lease a six-mile-wide strip across the isthmus with full construction rights in return for a cash payment of $10 million and an annual rental of $250,000. The Senate ratified this agreement in March, despite some protests that it failed to give the United States sovereignty over the canal zone.

In Colombia, on the other hand, the treaty proved highly unpopular. Suspicious Latin Americans regarded the lease arrangements as an ingenious lever by which *Yanqui* imperialists would eventually pry Panama from Colombia; moreover, they considered the financial aspect as niggardly. Colombian finances were in a wretched condition, and it was hoped the United States would raise its price or the canal company would give some of its $40 million to Colombia. Because of explosive public opinion, President José Marroquín prudently left the decision to the Colombian Congress, even though he had acted without that body for several years. Special elections were held and for several weeks the new legislature debated the problem before the Colombian Senate rejected the treaty almost unanimously.

Although as a sovereign nation Colombia was within its rights, Roosevelt was so incensed that he described the leaders as "the foolish and homicidal corruptionists at Bogotá." Even though he still had the Nicaragua alternative, he was so strongly committed to the Panama route that he was reluctant to give it up.

The Colombian rejection was also greatly resented by the Panamanians, who had long dreamed of secession. Fear of losing the economic benefits a canal would bring now stirred them to active plotting for revolt. Such was the disparity of strength between Colombia and Panama, however, that any uprising would fail if it did not have the immediate protection of the United States. Thus it became the delicate mission of Bunau-Varilla to sound out American attitude in case of a Panama revolt. Although Roosevelt and Hay carefully avoided a definite commitment, Bunau-Varilla left Washington fully convinced of American support.

With the ground thus prepared, events moved rapidly. On November 2, 1903, the U.S.S. *Nashville* arrived at Colon, the Atlantic terminal of the Panama Railroad, the first of several naval vessels ordered into the expected trouble spot. The next day the rebels struck against the weak Colombian garrison at Panama City on the Pacific Coast. There were enough Colombian troops at Colon to have suppressed the movement, but they were not permitted to use the railroad. Cowed by the *Nashville*'s guns, the Colombian commander accepted a Panamanian bribe of $8,000 and two cases of champagne and evacuated the city. By November 5, the rebels were in complete control of the isthmus and any possibility Colombia might reconquer the territory was ruled out by the warning that American warships now guarding both coasts would not allow any Colombian troops to land. The United States justified its intervention by the old Bidlack Treaty, under which it had guaranteed free transit across the isthmus. Naturally Colombia refused to concede that the United States could deny the right of a sovereign state to put down an insurrection on its own soil.

Roosevelt brushed aside these protests and recognized the Republic of Panama on November 6, 1903. Thirteen days later, Bunau-Varilla, now a special envoy of the new republic, signed the Hay–Bunau-Varilla Treaty,[1] under which the United States guaranteed the independence of Panama, obtained a perpetual lease to a ten-mile-wide canal zone, and agreed to pay Panama the same amounts offered Colombia in the rejected Hay-Herrán Treaty.

Although the Senate approved the treaty without serious opposition, Roosevelt's conduct in the Panama affair was seriously criticized not only by Colombians, but by many Americans as well. The President, however, denied he had any direct complicity in the revolt and justified what had been done on the grounds of the Bidlack Treaty, American national interests, and the need of the world for a canal. In later years, on the other hand, Roosevelt declared: "I took the Canal Zone and let Congress debate." Quite apart from the moral issue of whether the end justified the means, what happened cannot escape condemnation for other reasons. It damaged United States reputation in the eyes of Latin America as a whole, causing injury that took many years to repair.

With the diplomatic problems solved, those of construction now had to be faced. Differences of opinion about the type of canal, congressional red tape, disputes over control and methods, and the search for an efficient labor force delayed the work in the early years. Finally, in 1907, Roosevelt placed construction in the hands of army engineers under Colonel George Goethals, while Colonial William Gorgas of the Army Medical Corps supervised the improvement of sanitary and health conditions in the Canal Zone. Then, as Roosevelt put it, "the dirt began to fly" and, despite many landslides and other obstructions, the Panama Canal was finally opened to traffic on August 15, 1914. The cost, $375 million, although higher than anticipated, was well worth the price, considering the advantages of the waterway to the United States and the rest of the world.

In anticipation of the opening, Congress passed the Panama Canal Act in August, 1912, to establish the toll rates. When it exempted American ships engaged in the coastwise trade from any payment, Britain protested that this was contrary to the Hay-Pauncefote Treaty clause providing that the canal be open to all nations on an equality. Not until March, 1914, was President Wilson able to persuade Congress to remove this exemption, thereby properly placing a treaty obligation ahead of national self-interest.

Caribbean Diplomacy

A favorite maxim of Theodore Roosevelt was "Speak softly but carry a big stick." To him, one was as important as the other, but to critics it usually seemed that the big stick was more characteristically Rooseveltian than soft speaking. At any event, the President believed that, while bluff and bluster should be avoided, a readiness to use necessary force was a vital element in foreign policy. In no field was this more evident than

[1] The fact that the New Panama Canal Company's rights would expire in 1904 helps to account for Colombia's desire to delay negotiations and for Bunau-Varilla's wish for haste in obtaining United States recognition of Panama's independence. Those rights, of course, were worth $40 million..

in his dealing with the Caribbean region, whose importance to American security was magnified by the construction of the canal. No potentially dangerous foreign power could be allowed to gain a foothold near the approaches to that waterway; no little hemisphere republic could be permitted to fall into such a condition of disorder or bankruptcy as to provoke foreign intervention; and the Monroe Doctrine must be modernized to meet such threats.

True, Roosevelt was not the first to employ big-stick diplomacy. During the 1890's, American nationalists, worried lest, under the guise of a boundary dispute between British Guiana and Venezuela, Britain might extend its control over strategically important Caribbean territory. Cleveland's Secretary of State, Richard Olney, in demanding arbitration of this controversy, flatly stated: "Today the United States is practically sovereign on this continent, and its fiat is law upon the subjects to which it confines its interposition." The British at first denied the right of the United States to intervene, but, when Cleveland sent a special message to Congress stating that all the nation's power would be used to prevent British encroachment on Venezuelan territory, Britain began to retreat. Not that she feared the United States—her navy, for instance, was five times larger—but as Minister Thomas Bayard wrote: "The United States is the last nation on earth with whom the British people or their rulers desire to quarrel." The English were worried about the European situation, and their traditional isolation no longer appeared so splendid.

Britain therefore submitted to the American demand, with a few face-saving safeguards, and the arbitral tribunal of 1899 awarded her most of the disputed territory. She was paying the price of American friendship by accepting the supremacy of the United States in the Western Hemisphere. One such evidence was her ratification of the Second Hay-Pauncefote Treaty.

Even while the canal negotiations were proceeding, Venezuela again became a trouble spot, this time over debts owed to the citizens of at least ten countries. British and German creditors, tired of being refused payment of either interest or principal, appealed to their respective governments in 1901 to intervene in their behalf. Germany took the lead by offering to submit the debt question to the Hague Court for arbitration, but Cipriano Castro, the Venezuelan dictator, who was largely responsible for the extravagance causing the debt, refused to accept. Consequently, Britain, with more at stake financially, suggested forcible collection, a move Roosevelt did not oppose, for he accepted British and German assurances that such action would not result in annexation of territory. Thus the Monroe Doctrine would not be at stake; furthermore, he believed Venezuela was wrong in refusing arbitration. Indeed, he had already written that if a Latin-American country misbehaved, "let the European country spank it."

Encouraged by Roosevelt's hands-off policy, Britain and Germany, soon followed by Italy, began a blockade of Venezuela in December, 1902. Although there was no declaration of war, ships of the little Venezuelan navy were captured, two were sunk, and coastal towns were bombarded. Castro then abruptly changed his tune and requested arbitration. The creditor nations agreed in principle but insisted on continuing the blockade until all details were arranged. Finally, in February, 1903, an arbitration agreement was signed. American public opinion was extremely irritated during the two-month blockade and, significantly, the Germans were the principal targets. Even Roosevelt became restive and suspicious, urging the German ambassador to end the blockade as soon as possible. Although openly professing faith that the Kaiser would live up to his pledge not to acquire any territory, the President kept the navy mobilized at Puerto Rico as additional insurance that the Monroe Doctrine would be respected. In later years Roosevelt claimed he forced the Kaiser to arbitrate by threatening to send the fleet to Venezuela, but contemporary evidence does not support this account. Be that as it may, the importance of this incident was that the European powers did not start the blockade until they learned the American position, and their decision to arbitrate was hastened by adverse American public opinion. Thus this co-called second Venezuelan affair, like the first, resulted in an impressive recognition of United States strength in the Western Hemisphere.

Roosevelt, however was made wary by this affair. With canal diplomacy concluded, he did not want similar incidents to develop in other Latin-American countries that might enable creditor nations to intervene and gain a foothold dangerous to the security of the proposed canal. He believed the United States must use its police power to prevent chronic wrongdoing within the republics along the approaches to that waterway. This need became evident in 1903 when the Dominican Republic, after years of dictatorship and civil war, could not meet its financial obligations to several European countries, notably France and Italy, or to the American-controlled San Domingo Improvement Company. After numerous attempts to arbitrate, the United States declared that if the republic did not pay its debts, the American government would take over the administration of Dominican customs receipts. The Dominican authorities did not heed this warning, and both France and Italy considered possible intervention. Consequently, in October, 1904, an American financial agent was placed in charge of the customs houses.

Roosevelt justified his action in his annual message to Congress in December, 1904, and again a year later. Telling passages in these two messages were:

If a nation shows that it knows how to act with reasonable efficiency and decency in social and political matters, if it keeps order and pays its obligations, it need fear no interference from the United States. Chronic wrongdoing . . . in the Western Hemisphere . . . may force the United States, however reluctantly, in flagrant cases of wrongdoing or impotence, to the exercise of an international police power. . . . We must make it evident that we do not intend to permit the Monroe Doctrine to be used by any nation on this Continent as a shield to protect it from the consequences of its own misdeeds against foreign nations. . . .

This Roosevelt, or Big-Stick, Corollary of the Monroe Doctrine was the logical extension of the Olney interpretation. Its promulgation was further proof that the United States realized its position as a world power; in view of the European deferment to the Doctrine in the second Venezuela incident, it was only natural that the United States should also expect the big-stick theory to be recognized.

Under this doctrine of hemisphere police power and to make the temporary arrangement with the Dominican Republic more satisfactory, Secretary Hay and President Carlos Morales agreed in February, 1905, that 45 per cent of the customs should be used for Dominican government expense and the rest to help amortize the debt; in addition, the United States was empowered "to restore the credit, preserve the order, increase the efficiency of the civil administration, and advance the material progress and welfare of the Dominican Republic." When the Senate, believing the executive branch was overstepping its authority, refused to ratify this arrangement in treaty form, Roosevelt made it effective by executive order.

Acting under this arrangement, the United States did efficient work. The Dominican government received more income from its 45 per cent share of the customs than it had earlier from the full receipts, and at the same time its debt was scaled down materially. Consequently, in 1907 the Senate temporarily put aside partisan bickering and ratified a treaty providing that the Dominican debt, now fixed at $17 million, should be paid with the help of a $20 million loan from American bankers. This financial protocol continued until 1924.

During the remainder of Roosevelt's administration and throughout the greater part of Taft's, the Dominican Republic was politically peaceful. Her trade developed rapidly and her program of public works benefited the inhabitants. Although the United States disclaimed any intention of exploiting the country, by 1911 her political leaders began to chafe under restraint. An era of rebellions started, which subsequently led to the establishment of American military and political control.

This intervention in the Dominican Republic under Roosevelt was the forerunner of the so-called dollar diplomacy that reached its zenith under Taft. As in later instances of such diplomacy, a chaotic and nearly bankrupt country, facing possible intervention by a European nation, had to be saved from such fate by the United States, using the Roosevelt Corollary as justification and following a fairly standard procedure. The United States would set up a financial protectorate and persuade private bankers to lend money to the backward state, and these bankers in turn would demand safeguards for their loans. The United States would therefore establish a political protectorate as well, usually with the aid of American marines. Supervised elections would result in victory for a presidential candidate favorably disposed toward the United States and the American banker creditors. He would then grant concessions to American investors who would subsequently reap the profits. This dollar diplomacy insofar as it affected Latin America was promoted under the guise of safeguarding the Panama Canal. As Taft's Secretary of State, Philander Knox said: "Thus the malady of revolutions and financial collapse is most acute precisely in the region where it is most dangerous to us. It is here we seek to apply a remedy." At another time, however, he tried to place such diplomacy on a higher plane: "If the American dollar can aid suffering humanity and lift the burden of financial difficulty from states with which we live on terms of intimate intercourse and earnest friendship, and replace insecurity and devastation by stability and peaceful self-development, all I can say is that it would be hard to find better employment."

The remedy that Taft and Knox advocated was administered to Honduras in 1909 when it could not pay the interest on its bonds, held mostly by British investors. Fearing possible British intervention, Knox persuaded American bankers to take over the Honduran debt in 1911. Similar trouble coupled with political chaos in Nicaragua led to the placing of that nation's customs houses under an American collector, a move aided in no small measure by the presence of an American warship and marines. The Taft administration then refused to recognize the new Nicaraguan president until he obtained enough American loans to pay off his country's foreign debt. Haiti was also beginning to show signs of economic troubles. Consequently, the State Department in 1910 persuaded four American banks to buy up many bonds of Haiti's National Bank, thereby opening the way for further intervention under Wilson.

There is no doubt that dollar diplomacy was a form of economic imperialism. While Taft used the excuse that only through American interventions and investments could the backward republics be made stable, peaceful, and civilized, one of the primary motives was to give American bankers and other investors a profit. And it cannot be said that dollar diplomacy did anything to improve Pan-American relations.

Pan-Americanism

The attempt to bring the hemisphere republics more closely together diplomatically, economically, and culturally—the objectives of Pan-Americanism—had originated under James G. Blaine, Secretary of State under Garfield and Benjamin Harrison. The first modern Pan-American meeting, held in Washington in 1889–1890, discussed arbitration agreements, a customs union, uniform weights and measures, copyright and patent laws, and a trade dollar, but did not accomplish much. The novelty of the plan, suspicion of American motives, and mutual jealousies all combined to prevent this conference from attaining its objectives. The meeting, however, did smooth the way for future sessions and established the forerunner of the Pan American Union, a clearinghouse for varied information of value to the republics.

The first conference of the new century, held at Mexico City in 1901–1902, did not open auspiciously. The United States had just finished its war with Spain, a war that, to the Latin-American mind, had turned from an altruistic effort to free Cuba into an imperialistic contest. It was feared that American imperialism had not been satisfied and that the next objective might be the smaller states of the Western Hemisphere. The United States delegates tried to quiet these apprehensions by proposing that all international disputes be submitted to arbitration. Unfortunately this suggestion did not receive unanimous backing, although a goodly minority supported it. A majority, however, agreed that financial problems not settled by normal diplomatic procedure should be submitted to arbitration through the channels suggested at The Hague in 1899.

Nor did the next session (Rio de Janeiro in 1906) open on a friendly note. The forcing of the Platt Amendment upon Cuba, the Panama revolution, intervention in the Dominican Republic, and the promulgation of the Roosevelt Corollary created widespread suspicion of American intentions. Furthermore, Argentina, rival of the United States for hemisphere leadership, had her own solution for the controversial debt problem. This Drago Doctrine stated that armed force must not be used to collect financial obligations, a theory in a sense opposed to the Roosevelt Corollary. Disagreement might have broken up the meeting had not the conciliatory Elihu Root, chairman of the United States delegation, promised to submit the matter of debt collection to the Second Hague Conference to meet the next year. He was also able to keep diplomatic discussions at Rio to a minimum and to concentrate on promoting economic and cultural accord.

Following this meeting, Root visited seven other Latin-American countries, where he was well received in his effort to promote better hemisphere relations through greater sympathy and understanding. President Roosevelt, commenting on this trip, wrote: "We in this country do not realize how wonderful it was and how much good he has done." It was also Root who persuaded Andrew Carnegie to contribute a large sum for the construction of a building to house the Pan American Union.

On the other hand, the Buenos Aires Conference of 1910 gave evidence of greater harmony than heretofore among the twenty-one republics. All the members signed a pact to arbitrate any financial differences among them. The Pan American Union was reorganized to satisfy most of the previous objections. Uniform patents, copyrights, and trademarks, the improvement of communications, health, and sanitation, and the interchange of students and professors occupied the major attention of the delegates.

The United States also tried to effect better accord among the constantly battling Central American republics. After a war between Guatemala on one side and El Salvador and Honduras on the other in 1906, President Roosevelt, aided by President Porfirio Díaz of Mexico, sought a solution. When opposition from dictator José Zelaya of Nicaragua, who feared United States domination of Central America, prevented a satisfactory settlement, the strife broadened. Consequently, in 1907, Roosevelt and Díaz again called a Washington conference of the republics, which established the Central American International Bureau to promote unity and organized the Central American Court of Justice to arbitrate quarrels among the members. The Bureau did excellent work along the lines of the Pan American Union, but unfortunately the Court was not a success.

Arbitration Efforts

The growing interest in world affairs and, more particularly, in the pacific settlement of controversies was well demonstrated under both Roosevelt and Taft. The first sign of this attitude had been shown at the First Hague Conference, called by the Russian Tsar in November, 1899. The United States, with Ambassador to Germany Andrew White heading its delegation, was one of twenty-six nations represented. A "Convention for the Peaceful Adjustment of International Differences" provided for the settlement of disputes between nations either by mediation, by international tribunals of inquiry, or by a Permanent Court of Arbitration (which was not a court in the real sense, but a panel of jurists from which arbiters could be chosen for a specific controversy) established by the Hague conferees. In ratifying the work of this meeting, however, the United States Senate insisted that incidents arising under the Monroe Doctrine were outside the jurisdiction of the new court.

The first case to come before the Hague Court involved the so-called Pious Fund. In the seventeenth century the Catholic Church had established a trust fund to help convert the Indians of California to Christianity. After its original administrators, the Jesuits, were expelled from the Spanish Indies, the King of Spain dispensed this fund until the Wars of Independence, when the new Mexican government took charge. In 1848, after the United States gained California, the Catholic bishops there sought control of the money. Mexico, however, refused to relinquish it, and the bishops brought the case before a mixed commission, which decided in their favor. Mexico then paid some of the interest, but stopped after a few years. At the end of the century, the United States interceded at the behest of the California Catholic leaders, and Mexico promised to abide by the decision of the anticipated Permanent Court. In 1902 its judgment favored the clerics, a decision to which Mexico conformed. Thus the combined efforts of the two neighbors showed that the Hague plan of arbitration could work.

The Alaska Boundary Settlement

Another long-standing difference settled by peaceful means was the controversial boundary between southern Alaska and Canada. The Klondike gold rush at the end of the century had made Canadians eager to control the Lynn Canal and the port of Skagway. The United States insisted, however, on an interpretation of earlier treaties that would maintain exclusive American domination over this stretch of coast.

Since 1899, Secretary Hay had tried unsuccessfully to reach a settlement. The British government, at Canadian insistence, demanded that the issue be submitted to arbitration in which a foreign umpire would have the deciding voice, but Hay wanted the question decided by a commission of three Americans and three British members. No decision could then be reached unless a commissioner voted against the contentions of his own government. When in 1903 Britain finally consented to this Hay proposition, President Roosevelt appointed to the commission not impartial jurists, but politicians: Secretary of War Root, Senator Lodge, and ex-Senator George Turner of Washington, on whom he could depend to hold out for the American claims. The British government named Lord Alverstone, the Lord Chief Justice of England, and two prominent Canadians. With such a tribunal the United States could scarcely lose its case, but Roosevelt left nothing to chance. He impressed upon the British government how unfortunate the consequences might be if Lord Alverstone did not vote against the Canadian contentions. In the end the British jurist did vote with the Americans and despite Canadian protests, the issue was ultimately settled on that basis.

The Hay Arbitration Treaties

After taking such a prominent part in setting up the Hague Permanent Court, the Roosevelt administration not only showed the way in referring special cases to it, but tried hard to establish agreements with other nations to submit to this tribunal all cases coming within what international jurists then regarded as the scope of arbitration. The First Hague Conference had already prepared a model treaty under which the contracting parties would promise to refer all such problems to the Permanent Court.

By December, 1904, Secretary Hay had negotiated fourteen treaties on this model, chiefly with Britain, France, and Germany, in which they excepted from arbitration questions affecting the vital interests, independence, or honor of the contracting parties. As these exceptions were precisely those that might cause war, the negotiation of such instruments did not go very far. And as for Great Britain, the United States had already arbitrated to great mutual advantage matters that might fairly be called vital. Nevertheless, Hay's efforts at least helped to advertise the idea of arbitration.

When these treaties were submitted to the Senate, there was trouble. Some Senators feared that its constitutional power over all treaties was being threatened. Others professed doubt lest questions arising out of the repudiation of debts by some states would be subjected to arbitration. The upper house therefore amended the treaties to alter the "special agreements" under which the various questions were in each case to be arbitrated into special treaties subject individually to the advice and consent of the Senate. Angered by this action, Roosevelt withdrew the treaties from further consideration, saying:

> I think that this amendment makes the treaties shams, and my present impression is that we had better abandon the whole business rather than give the impression of trickiness and insincerity which would be produced by solemnly promulgating a sham.

The Second Hague Conference

The Second Hague Conference of 1907, also called by the Tsar, was signalized by the fact that the Latin-American nations were invited at the insistence of Elihu Root. As far as limitation of armaments and formation of a real world court were concerned, this meeting accomplished little more than had the first. The American representatives, headed by Joseph Choate and General Horace Porter, concentrated their efforts on obtaining guarantees of the rights of neutrals and neutral commerce during war, but there were such differences of opinion that the best they could do was to refer the matter to a supplementary naval conference, scheduled to meet in London in 1908.

That naval gathering produced in 1909 the famous Declaration of London, which was practically a maritime code defining absolute and

The angel of peace: "Help, help!" Can the big stick work at the Second Hague Conference? (From the *New York World*.)

conditional contraband, blockades, and the right of search. It also laid down clear rules for the conduct of belligerents and neutrals in wartime. Great Britain, however, refused to ratify this declaration. Thus, at the outbreak of World War I, it could be regarded as international law only by a tremendous stretch of the imagination.

The Second Hague Conference likewise took up a problem of special interest to the United States and its Latin-American neighbors—the Drago Doctrine. The delegates refused to accept it as it stood, but instead amended it to read that armed force could not be used to collect debts unless the debtor country refused to arbitrate.

Shortly after the 1907 meeting adjourned, Secretary Root began to negotiate treaties similar to those engineered by Hay. During the remainder of Roosevelt's second administration he completed twenty-five of them with all the leading powers except Germany. Since they each guaranteed the rights of the Senate, they were duly ratified by the upper house.

The Taft-Knox Treaties

Taft and Philander Knox, his Secretary of State, were ready to go further than to adopt documents rendering lip service to arbitration but actually excepting everything that might cause war. As Taft said in October, 1911:

We now have treaties of arbitration . . . in which we agree to submit all questions that do not affect our national honor and do not affect our vital interest. Well, that seems to me to be an agreement to arbitrate everything that is highly unimportant. . . . If arbitration is worth anything it is an instrumentality for avoiding war. But, it is asked, would you arbitrate a question of national honor? I am not afraid of that question. Of course I would.

Following this theory, Knox negotiated two remarkable treaties with France and Britain, popularly known as the Taft-Knox Treaties, which went the whole way in providing for submission to arbitration all justiciable disputes whatsoever. Again there was much criticism from the more nationalistic elements. Former President Roosevelt became an outspoken opponent of agreements that might involve "national honor," and the Senate emasculated the documents by exempting from arbitration questions involving immigration, state debts, and the Monroe Doctrine. Thoroughly disgusted, Taft withdrew the treaties from further consideration.

However disappointing was the progress toward general arbitration, the peaceful settlement of specific controversies continued. In 1909 the United States and Britain agreed to submit to the Hague Court the troublesome question of American fishing in Newfoundland waters—a question vexing the diplomats since 1782. The court's decision in 1910 provided a workable compromise that safeguarded the rights of both Americans and Newfoundlanders.

The Algeciras Conference

In 1905 President Roosevelt became deeply involved in a tangled web of European diplomacy. By a dramatic visit to Tangier, Morocco, in that year, the German Kaiser made clear his objections to the steps France was taking to extend a protectorate over that North African country. He brusquely demanded that the Morocco question be submitted to an international conference. When France, strongly supported by Great Britain, refused, there was grave danger of a European war. The Kaiser, who had been courting Roosevelt ever since he became President, urged the American chief executive to back Germany. Roosevelt at first refused to take the problem seriously and ridiculed the "pipe dreams" of the German emperor. When he became convinced that the danger of war was actually great, however, he sought to mediate between the angry governments. Fortunately Roosevelt was on intimate terms with Jules Jusserand, the French ambassador in Washington, and Baron Speck von Sternburg, the German envoy, and through them he finally suggested an acceptable formula under which the conference could be held.

Early in 1906 diplomatic representatives of the powers interested in the Morocco question met at Algeciras, Spain. Roosevelt justified the sending of an American delegation, headed by Ambassador to Italy Henry White, on the grounds that the United States had treaty rights in Morocco and some slight trade to protect, as well as on the more defensible principle that America had an important interest in preserving world peace.

Both White in Algeciras and Roosevelt in Washington worked hard to bring about a settlement. While striving to maintain his role as a friendly mediator, the President had from the beginning believed that France was in the right. Consequently, on critical issues the American weight was thrown to the side of France and England. The resulting General Act of Algeciras saved German face by paying lip service to the independence of Morocco and to the principle of the Open Door for trade, but actually left France free to increase her influence over the disputed country. The reluctant Kaiser was informed that were he to accept the settlement, Roosevelt would pay public tribute to the German monarch's contribution to peace. The Kaiser agreed, and within a few days Roosevelt announced to a delegation of German war veterans at the White House that he gave Wilhelm credit for the Moroccan settlement.

Roosevelt's actions during this crisis were criticized in some quarters as a departure from the traditional American policy of noninvolvement in European affairs. The President, however, was wise enough to see how dangerous a general European war would be to all Western civilization.[2] Both he and his successor, working earnestly during these years to dispel mutual fears and suspicions, believed that peace was more important than tradition.

[2] While conceding Roosevelt's good intentions in the Algeciras affair, some historians consider the effects of his action to have been unfortunate. They contend he failed to understand the justice of Germany's complaints against French and English policy. Furthermore, Germany, having been compelled to back down on this occasion, might be more stubborn in the future—thereby increasing rather than decreasing the likelihood of war.

6
THE NEW FREEDOM

So many Americans had been absorbed by the Taft-Roosevelt feud in 1912 that they paid scant attention to the Democratic candidate. With his spare, angular body, thin face, and pince-nez glasses, Woodrow Wilson seemed to fit perfectly the popular stereotype of a college professor. Thus it was easy to assume that he would be a spineless intellectual, certain to be dominated by his party's practical politicians. Such a judgment, however, showed little knowledge of Wilson's actual record as college professor, university president, and New Jersey governor. The new President possessed an inflexible will and a fighting heart, along with fervent democratic convictions he wished to see carried into effective action.

As a close student of American government, Wilson was convinced that strong leadership was necessary to make the system work. In earlier years he had favored adoption of the British cabinet plan, but by the time he reached the White House, he believed that the President already had ample power if he would use it boldly. From the beginning of his term Wilson acted as the leader of the Democratic party. He formulated an ambitious legislative program, consulted regularly with congressional leaders, exerted personal pressure to bring wavering party members into line, and frequently appealed directly to the country on important issues.

In the early years of his administration, Wilson was strikingly successful. With wide support both in Congress and from the general public, he was able to reach his objectives in both the domestic and foreign fields. In later years, however, he encountered increasing opposition. Much of this was inevitable in the American system, yet some of it resulted from the hostility aroused by certain traits in Wilson's character. While he had great virtues—high-mindedness, faith in the democratic process, respect for human rights, and lofty eloquence—he also possessed some closely related defects. Certain that he was always right, he was apt to attribute unworthy motives to honest opposition. Even his close associates complained that he seemed cold and aloof, that he resented criticism and bore grudges, and that he was stubborn and reluctant to compromise.

The New Administration

Influenced by Colonel House, who was somewhat fearful that in an excess of idealism the new President might ignore orthodox Democrats

Woodrow Wilson. (Brown Bros.)

and fill his cabinet with independents. Wilson selected an official family representing the various sections of the country and the different factions within the party in a traditional way. Steeling himself to what the situation seemed to demand, he appointed as Secretary of State William Jennings Bryan, the man whom in earlier years he had sharply criticized. Sophisticated Easterners were inclined to ridicule the new Secretary, to laugh at his dinners where parched diplomats were served nothing stronger than grape juice, and to be vastly amused when Bryan took time off from his official duties to lecture in Chautauqua tents. But Wilson himself quickly learned to respect Bryan's sincerity, to value his sturdy common sense, and to accept gratefully his advice on political matters—a subject on which the Secretary certainly spoke from experience, whatever the deficiencies in his diplomatic education. The ablest man in the new cabinet was probably William Gibbs McAdoo, originally a Georgian, who had moved to New York where he achieved outstanding business success by promoting construction of railroad tunnels under the Hudson River. As Secretary of the Treasury, McAdoo demonstrated both administrative skill and an ability to formulate policy.

Besides his cabinet, Wilson consulted regularly with certain unofficial advisers, who often exerted more influence on administration policies than did the department heads. Colonel House was then the President's closest friend, often acting as Wilson's spokesman in conferring with both politicians and businessmen. And on the outbreak of World War I in 1914, House acted as unofficial roving diplomat at the various belligerent capitals.

Another powerful adviser was Louis Brandeis. Wilson wanted this Boston lawyer in his cabinet either as Attorney General or as Secretary of Commerce, but practical politicians were strongly opposed because Brandeis was a recent convert to the Democratic party and his supposed radicalism would antagonize businessmen. Nevertheless, Brandeis's keen legal mind was extremely useful to the administration in framing its legislative program. In 1916 Wilson risked conservative ire by nominating Brandeis to the Supreme Court, despite the bitter opposition of no fewer than six former presidents of the American Bar Association, including Taft and Root, who contended Brandeis was "not a fit person to be a member of the Supreme Court of the United States." Wilson stuck by his nominee, however, and obtained Senate confirmation after a hard battle.

Although the new President was firmly committed to progressive reform, he avoided any declaration of war against old-line Democrats whose votes he would need. By courting Speaker Champ Clark and Representative Oscar Underwood, he sought to heal the wounds left by the Baltimore convention. Moreover, he learned to acquiesce when Postmaster General Albert Burleson dispensed patronage with a practiced hand and Secretary Bryan found posts for "deserving Democrats."

If much of the old in political practice survived under Wilson, much that was strikingly new was also introduced. His inaugural address was both eloquent and bold. After itemizing the need for tariff and currency reform, for further regulation of business, and for measures beneficial to agriculture and labor, he concluded with these stirring words:

This is not a day of triumph; it is a day of dedication. Here muster, not the forces of party, but the forces of humanity. Men's hearts wait upon us; men's lives hang in the balance; men's hopes call upon us to say what we will do. Who shall live up to the great trust? Who dares fail to try? I summon all honest men, all patriotic, all forward-looking men, to my side. God helping me, I will not fail them, if they will but counsel and sustain me!

Scarcely a month after taking office, Wilson strikingly demonstrated the role he believed the chief executive should play. When the new Congress met in special session, he appeared in person before the legislature and packed galleries to appeal for tariff reform. By personally delivering his message instead of sending the written copy to be droned out by a reading clerk to an indifferent and largely empty chamber, the President boldly broke a precedent established by Thomas Jefferson and followed religiously by succeeding executives for more than a century. This was only the first of such appearances, for time and time again during the next eight years Wilson went before Congress to ask for legislation or to outline his policies.

Tariff Reform

At this special session, Congress provided the first dividend from the Democratic victory—the Underwood Tariff of 1913. In its initial form, the Underwood Bill tried to reduce the cost of living by placing wheat, corn, sugar, meat, eggs, and milk on the free list, along with raw wool, flax, and shoes. Duty-free also were iron ore, pig iron, steel rails, rough lumber, paper, and wood pulp. On hundreds of other items the protective principle was maintained, but rates were reduced in accordance with Wilson's theory that "the object of tariff duties henceforth laid must be effective competition, the whetting of American wits by contest with the wits of the rest of the world." On luxuries, such as precious stones, furs, and perfumes, the old rates were left unchanged. Taken as a whole, the Underwood Bill was not a radical abandonment of protection, but it did propose the first genuine downward revision since the Civil War.

Thanks to Underwood's skillful leadership, the bill passed the House in May without significant change, but in the Senate a hard fight developed. There the Democratic majority was small and many Senators sought amendments that would continue the protection enjoyed by their constituents. So active were the lobbyists that the President had to enter the picture by appealing to the people in the following press statement:

> It is of serious interest to the country that the people at large have no lobby and be voiceless in these matters, while great lobbies of astute men seek to create an artificial opinion and to overcome the interests of the public for their private profit. . . . Only public opinion can check and destroy it. . . .

In the end, wavering Democrats were kept in line, and the measure was passed in substantially its original form; indeed, in some schedules the final rates were even lower than those first proposed. As signed by the President on October 3, 1913, the Underwood Tariff lowered the average ad valorem rates from the Payne-Aldrich level of over 40 per cent to about 25 per cent, besides providing an extensive free list. One important feature was the provision engineered by Representative Cordell Hull of Tennessee for a graduated income tax, made possible by the Sixteenth Amendment, ratified in February, 1913. The rates were moderate—disappointingly so according to Senator LaFollette and other progressives. Incomes of less than $3,000 for single persons and of less than $4,000 for married ones were exempted; incomes in excess of those figures paid a normal tax of 1 per cent and graduated surtaxes reaching a level of 6 per cent on incomes exceeding $500,000. Altogether, the Underwood Tariff was a tremendous victory for Wilson—one gained on an issue Roosevelt had avoided and Taft had taken up to his own hurt.

Economists watched with interest to see how the new tariff would affect American economic life, but they were prevented from obtaining adequate data because within ten months after the Underwood schedules went into effect, international trade was largely disrupted by World War I. Conditions continued to be highly abnormal as late as 1921, when the Republicans, back in power, rewrote the tariff laws to fit their own doctrines.

The income tax at first disappointed as a revenue producer, but it did disclose interesting information on the concentration of wealth in the nation. Of 120 individuals paying taxes on $1 million or more, 74 lived in New York, 16 in Illinois, and 10 in Pennsylvania.

The Federal Reserve System

Even while the tariff debates were continuing, Congress was given a new assignment—the complicated and difficult task of banking and currency reform. Serious defects in the nation's banking structure had been obvious for years. National banks still functioned under antiquated Civil War legislation; state banks went their own way under a hodgepodge of conflicting statutes; there was no control agency over the system as a whole. Bank reserves were not mobilized in a way to meet depositors' runs on fundamentally sound institutions. Small-town banks deposited their reserve funds principally in large-city banks; these in turn deposited in the great New York City banks. Since these funds were available for speculative loans, the entire country's banking structure was apt to be jeopardized by troubles in the securities market. Furthermore, the system tended to drain funds from rural districts where credit was badly needed and concentrate them in the cities where they encouraged speculation. Credit was inelastic; banks unable to borrow themselves often had to refuse new loans to their clients or to renew old ones, even when perfectly good security was offered. Currency was also inelastic; instead of expanding and contracting as business increased or diminished, national bank notes were fixed in amount by the number of government bonds available for purchase by the banks.

Following the bankers' panic of 1907, a National Monetary Commission, headed by Senator Aldrich, had studied the situation for four years. Its analysis of the situation was valuable, but its suggested remedy, a strong central banking association controlled by private bankers, was politically impossible. Progressives regarded Aldrich as ultraconservative and a spokesman for special interests; the great bankers, moreover, were in particular disrepute because of revelations concerning the "money trust" made in 1912 by a special congressional committee headed by Representative Arsène Pujo of Louisiana.[1]

Some Democratic leaders opened an intensive study of this banking problem soon after the 1912 election, including discussions with leading financiers. The bill initially drafted by Representative Carter Glass of Virginia, chairman of the House Banking and Currency Committee, assisted by Paul Warburg, a big banker, was so conservative that Secretary Bryan insisted it was a surrender to the "money trust." A countermeasure was then drawn up by Senator Robert Owen of Oklahoma, head of the Senate Banking and Currency Committee, with the aid of Samuel Untermeyer, a progressive New York lawyer. Wilson's first impulse was to side with the Glass version, but Brandeis persuaded him that two principles in the Owen

[1] The Pujo Committee had revealed that three New York banking institutions—J. P. Morgan and Company, the First National Bank, and the National City Bank—had combined resources of over $600 million and control of seven other New York banks as well as of the Equitable Life Assurance Company. Direction over the investment of funds totaling some $2 billion thus lay within the power of a few individuals. The banking triumvirate was represented by 341 directors in 112 corporations having aggregate resources exceeding $22 billion. This so-called money trust included banks, insurance companies, transportation systems, public utility corporations, and manufacturing establishments.

draft were a must: the central governing board of the new system should be government appointees exclusively and the new currency should be an obligation of the United States government rather than of the banks. Out of all these differences the compromise Glass-Owen, or Federal Reserve, bill emerged to provide most of the facilities of a central banking system and to bring banking under a form of government control. Despite misgivings on the part of both Western radicals and Wall Streeters, the measure became law in December, 1913.

Instead of a single central bank, the Federal Reserve Act established twelve regional banks to serve the so-called Federal reserve districts. The stock of these Federal reserve banks was to be entirely owned by the member banks, consisting of all the country's national banks and such state banks and trust companies as cared to join. The Federal reserve banks were primarily bankers' banks. They received deposits from the member banks that had to be large enough to cover the reserves the law required to be maintained against the deposits in the member banks. The banking reserves of the nation were thus concentrated in a few large reservoirs and could not be used for speculation.

Member banks might borrow from the Federal reserve banks through rediscounting commercial paper. This meant that member banks could use high-grade notes, drafts, and bills of exchange on which they had advanced money to their own customers as the basis for obtaining loans for themselves. Unexpectedly important were the open market operations, under which reserve banks could deal in government bonds and domestic bills of exchange. A special Open Market Committee, chosen by the reserve banks, could sell such bonds and bills to member banks, thereby increasing their reserves and enabling them to extend more credit; when the committee was purchasing such bills, the member banks sold, thus reducing their reserves and decreasing their ability to give credit. Thus credit could be eased or tightened, depending on the economic situation. Likewise, through these processes the banking funds of the country became mobile, moving quickly to the areas of greatest business activity.

A most important function of the Federal reserve notes was to put into circulation a new kind of currency, the Federal reserve note. As Bryan had insisted, the new notes were made a direct United States government obligation, redeemable in gold and acceptable for all public dues. In issuing them, the government received and held in security commercial paper that the Federal reserve banks had taken in through their rediscounting activities. Although the law required a 40 per cent gold reserve to be maintained, the new currency possessed an elasticity so lacking in the old national bank notes. When business flourished, commercial paper increased in volume. This paper, through discounting, flowed into the Federal reserve banks and served as collateral for the issuance of Federal reserve notes. When business lagged, this process was reversed and the volume of notes in circulation was reduced.

The Federal reserve banks also received deposits of the Federal government and acted as its financial agents. This permitted eventual abandonment of the unsatisfactory system of keeping Federal funds in independent treasuries (which were terminated by Congress in 1920).

Despite strong banker opposition, an independent agency was created to supervise the new system. This Federal Reserve Board consisted of the Secretary of the Treasury, the Comptroller of the Currency, and five others appointed by the President for ten years with Senate consent. Each Federal reserve bank had nine directors, six of whom were elected by the member banks and three appointed by the Federal Reserve Board. This directorial board had extensive powers to examine the books of the Federal reserve banks, to remove their officers, and even to order them to suspend operations. Probably the most important board function, however, was to approve the rediscount rates fixed by the Federal reserve banks and provide a governor on the economic machinery of the country: a low discount rate encouraged borrowing and business expansion; a high rate discouraged them.

On the whole the Federal Reserve Act proved very satisfactory. The shock of World War I to American economic life was cushioned by the new system, and the Federal government could scarcely have financed United States participation in the hostilities had not this new organization been substantially completed by 1917.

Nevertheless, numerous weaknesses still remained in the American banking system. The country had many more state banks than national; for the former, membership in the Federal Reserve System was not compulsory and a majority stayed outside. Thus nonmember banks outnumbered member banks two to one, even though 80 per cent of the combined banking resources of the nation was held by the latter. Proposals for compulsory membership were opposed because such action would violate states' rights. Even over the practices of member banks themselves the Federal Reserve Board had little control, as the banking abuses of the 1920's were to show.

The Trust Problem

On January 20, 1914, President Wilson appeared again before Congress, this time seeking new antitrust legislation. The issue thus posed was a perplexing one. During the 1912 campaign, Roosevelt and Wilson had taken positions that seemed sharply opposed. The former's New Nationalism assumed big business was here to stay, to be strongly policed by the Federal government; the latter's New Freedom believed competition could be restored by a vigorous antitrust policy without expanding Federal power at the expense of the states. Now faced with the responsibility of office, however, the Democrats found this antithesis entirely too simple. The legislative program they eventually evolved was neither as broadly Hamiltonian as Roosevelt's proposals nor as purely Jeffersonian as Wilson's, but a middle ground between the two.

The original antitrust bills, drafted by Henry Clayton of Alabama, chairman of the House Judiciary Committee, were Jeffersonian in philosophy. The vague and general language of the Sherman Act was now to be strengthened by explicit prohibitions against interlocking directorates and other monopolistic practices, while a new interstate trade commission was to have investigatory rather than regulatory powers. Businessmen criticized the new prohibitions because they would hamper legitimate corporation growth; union leaders protested that labor would not have its promised exemption from antitrust prosecution; and many progressives repeated their conviction that what was needed was Federal regulation, not more antitrust suits.

In his perplexity, Wilson turned for guidance to Brandeis, whose thought upon the trust problem had been changing to favor a strong Federal commission. With the help of a New York lawyer friend, Brandeis drafted a new bill that Wilson strongly supported.

The resulting Federal Trade Commission Act of September, 1914, provided for a bipartisan commission of five members appointed by the President with Senate approval for a seven-year term, with extensive powers to compile information concerning the organization and conduct of corporations engaged in interstate commerce. Furthermore, it was to investigate the manner in which corporations adjudged guilty of violating antitrust laws carried out the court decrees. Unfair methods of competition were declared to be unlawful, and the commission could order any person or

Oliver Wendell Holmes and Louis D. Brandeis. (Brown Bros.)

corporation using unfair methods to "cease and desist." Such orders, how-ever, were subject to review in Federal courts.

As the trade commission approach gained ascendancy, enthusiasm for giving the Sherman Act new and sharper teeth declined. The Clayton Act of October, 1914, was considerably weaker than the original draft. Al-though there was an imposing list of prohibitions against price discrimi-nations, exclusive selling or leasing contracts, and the purchasing by one corporation of the stock of a competitor, the bans were not absolute, but limited to cases where the effect of such action might be "to substantially lessen competition or tend to create a monopoly in any line of commerce." Similarly limited were the prohibitions on interlocking directorates: no person might be a director or officer of more than one bank if one of the banks had assets of more than $5 million; nor could a person be a director of more than one corporation if the corporations were competitors and if one of them had assets of more than $1 million. In contrast with the Sher-man Act, the new law was primarily preventive, not punitive. Forbidden corporate practices were declared illegal per se without proof of actual monopoly or conspiracy.

Particularly important were the Clayton Act provisions dealing with the rights of workers. "The labor of a human being," the measure declared, "is not a commodity or article of commerce." Neither labor unions nor farmers' organizations engaged in lawful pursuit of their objectives were to be considered illegal combinations in restraint of trade. The rights of laborers to strike, to picket peaceably, to pay out strike benefits, and to boycott an employer were recognized. No Federal judge could grant an injunction in any case growing out of a labor controversy unless necessary to prevent irreparable injury to property; and trial by jury was granted in contempt cases unless the contempt was committed in the presence of the court. Samuel Gompers hailed these provisions as the "Magna Carta" for labor, but time proved that these rights had definite limitations. Judicial interpretations of the Clayton Act so narrowed its scope that many anti-labor injunctions continued to be granted by Federal courts.

The underlying philosophy of both the Federal Trade Commission Act and the Clayton Act was obvious. The liberals of 1914 refused to accept the socialist assumption that the trend toward monopoly was inevitable and that the public could safeguard its interests only by nationalizing the trusts. They believed, on the contrary, that competition was the answer to the nation's economic ills. If the corporations were compelled to compete and the competition kept open and fair, monopolies would be impossible, small business would survive, and consumers would be protected. This legislation of 1914, while no more successful than the Sherman Act in halt-ing the trend toward business consolidation, did protect the public against the sequeeze of economic power in many of its cruder forms.

In administering the new laws Wilson showed a desire not to alarm unduly the business world. From the beginning the Federal Trade Com-mission was criticized by LaFollette and other progressives as lacking in reforming zeal and all too eager to cooperate with the corporations it was supposed to be policing. Nevertheless, the Justice Department brought a number of important antitrust suits, while the Federal Trade Commission between 1914 and 1921 issued 379 "cease and desist" orders against false advertising, false statements against competitors, bribery, adulteration of goods, and misbranding of fabrics. The commission, together with the Justice Department, also obtained dissolution of the International Harvester Company in 1918 and the Corn Products Refining Company the following year.

American involvement in World War I had an inevitable influence. With popular attention focused on new issues, the antitrust crusade lost much of its fervor. Moreover, national economic mobilization tremendously accelerated the rate of corporate growth. Evidence of this change was the failure of the government's case against the Steel Trust in 1920. The Supreme Court refused to break up the United States Steel Corporation because, despite its size, it was not monopolistic.

Benefits for Agriculture and Labor

By creating the Federal Reserve Board and the Federal Trade Commission, the New Freedom had taken two cautious steps in the direction of the New Nationalism. In extending Federal authority to benefit agriculture and labor, the Democrats departed still further from their traditional states' rights philosophy.

Congress granted increased appropriations for the Department of Agriculture, which now took on broader activities, including a market news service. New Federal legislation provided for uniform grading of staple crops, for regulating trade in agricultural staples, and for better warehousing. The Agricultural Extension Act of 1914 made it possible through Federal and state cooperation to place in each of the 2,850 rural counties of the nation two agents to do farm demonstration work. Roadbuilding was stimulated by the Federal Highway Act of 1916, under which the Federal government expended money for rural roads if its appropriations were matched by the states.

One of the most urgent of the farmer's demands was for facilities for obtaining more favorable loans. The Federal Reserve Act provided for some improvement, but the need for long-term credit required new machinery. During his early presidency, Wilson's laissez-faire scruples prevented his accepting the idea that the Federal government should take on this additional function, but by 1916 he had changed his mind. The Federal Farm Loan Act, passed in that year with the President's strong support, established twelve Federal Land Banks in various sections of the country, which could loan money to cooperative farm-loan associates made up of farmers wanting to borrow. The farmer gave a mortgage on his real estate to the association, which in turn deposited the mortgage with the Land Bank. The initial capital of the Land Banks was to be subscribed by private investors, with the government making up any deficiency. Additional funds would come from the sale of tax-exempt bonds secured by the mortgages held by the Land Banks. Supervising this system was the Federal Farm Board, composed of the Secretary of Agriculture and four other members appointed by the President.

Although private capital was at first suspicious of the project and supplied only $200,000 of the $9 million required to set it up, a steadily larger proportion of private investment developed until by 1930 the government had disposed of most of its stock. Local farm-loan associations numbered 4,659 in 1930, while the Federal Farm Land Banks held about $1 billion worth of farm mortgages.

The Wilson administration was also responsive to the demands of labor, as the AFL leadership had supported Wilson in 1912. Its most appreciated reward came in the amendment of the antitrust laws to protect labor union activity from judicial interference, but other legislation in which labor was interested was also passed. Despite objections of some State Department officials who feared complications with other maritime nations, the La-Follette Seamen's Act of 1915 protected merchant sailors from many injustices. In 1913 a Board of Mediation and Conciliation was established to deal with railroad labor controversies, while in 1916, under circumstances to be discussed later, the Adamson Act, instituting an eight-hour day for railroad employees, was pushed through Congress under Wilson's urgings.

The movement for a Federal child labor law, a project Senator Beveridge had vainly urged during the Roosevelt administration, became more and more insistent after the Democratic victory of 1912. As on other issues, Wilson changed his mind. At first he believed that such a law would be an unconstitutional invasion of states' rights, but he later used the full weight of his influence to obtain Congressional approval of the Keating-Owen Child Labor Act of 1916. This measure excluded from interstate commerce goods produced in factories where child labor was employed. When it was held unconstitutional by the Supreme Court in 1918 (Hammer v. Dagenhart et al.), a second child labor act was passed in 1919. But this statute, which levied a 10 per cent tax on the income of factories and mines employing children, was likewise held invalid (Bailey v. Drexel Furniture Company, 1922). As a result a child labor amendment to the Constitution was approved by both houses in 1924, but it was never ratified by the states.

By the time of the 1916 presidential election, the Democrats had enacted a large part of the Progressive party platform of 1912. To some extent this heavy borrowing from the New Nationalism program was political, a conscious bid to win the progressive vote in this important election. But undoubtedly Wilson's drift away from states' rights and laissez faire toward federalism and regulation was the result of a greater understanding of how government must respond to changing conditions of modern life.

Wilson and the Dependencies

The spirit of the New Freedom was carried into the administration of outlying possessions. In an early message to Congress, Wilson insisted that the United States must move toward independence for the Philippines "as steadily as the way can be cleared." In naming the Philippine Commission, the President gave a majority of places to Filipinos and appointed as governor general Francis Harrison of New York, who administered the islands in a liberal spirit that promoted the nationalist ambitions of the natives. Wilson and Harrison were severely criticized by Taft and other prominent citizens because they encouraged an early independence for which the Filipinos were not ready.

The administration, however, refused to deviate from its course. In 1916, after hot debate, Congress passed the Jones, or Philippine Organic, Act, whose preamble stated that "it is, as it has always been, the purpose of the people of the United States to withdraw their sovereignty over the Philippine Islands and to recognize their independence as soon as stable government can be established therein. . . ." To speed that day, the government was reorganized to increase native participation and responsibility. The old Philippine Commission and Assembly were abolished in favor of a senate and house of representatives, both elected by Filipino citizens meeting certain property or literacy qualifications. Executive power was exercised by a governor general appointed by the President with consent of the Senate. Most of the other executive officers were named by the governor general with the consent of the Filipino senate.

The Jones Act took a long step toward delivering the islands to native rule, despite extensive veto powers retained by the governor general and the President. In execution the new organic law proved even more liberal than it appeared on paper because of the policies Harrison followed. By executive order, he created a council of state consisting of the governor general, the presidents of both legislative houses, and the six Filipinos who headed the executive departments.

Wilson also believed something should be done to answer the complaints of the Puerto Ricans. Consequently, in March, 1917, the Jones, or Puerto Rican Organic, Act was passed to make the island a United States territory and the inhabitants American citizens, with all the privileges of the Bill of Rights except trial by jury. Governmentally, the major change enabled the qualified male voters to elect the upper house of the insular legislature. The executive and judicial branches were still appointed by the President, who also had veto power over acts of the legislature. The Jones Act did quiet many unhappy Puerto Ricans, but others continued to seek a greater degree of self-government.

The New Diplomacy

President Wilson aspired to bring the same spirit of reform into the conduct of foreign affairs that he applied to domestic problems. Ever the idealist, he hoped to base his foreign policy on enduring principles of justice and morality. He was deeply suspicious of professional diplomats, who all too often advocated what was expedient rather than what was right. Wilson was particularly disturbed by the close alliance of the State Department and Wall Street that had developed during Taft's administration—the era of frankly avowed dollar diplomacy.

Scarcely two weeks after his inauguration, Wilson made plain his intention to repudiate this alliance. At Taft's invitation, some American bankers had arranged to cooperate with bankers of five other powers in a consortium or international loan to China. When representatives of J. P. Morgan and Company sought a statement of the new administration's attitude toward this project, Wilson expressed his emphatic disapproval on March 13, 1913. The conditions of the loan, he said, threatened the administrative independence of China; the United States government, through connection with the project, might become involved in a forcible intervention. Altogether, the plan "was obnoxious to the principles upon which the government of our people rests." Unenthusiastic about the proposition anyway, the American bankers thereupon withdrew from the consortium.

Economic imperialism in Latin America was even more bluntly condemned. First in a press statement on March 11, 1913, and later in a speech at Mobile, Alabama, the following October, Wilson lashed out at "special groups and interests." At Mobile, the President said of the relations of Latin-American governments with foreign capitalists:

They have had harder bargains driven with them in the matter of loans than any other people in the world. Interest has been exacted of them that was not exacted of anybody else, because the risk was said to be greater; and then securities were taken that destroyed the risk—an admirable arrangement for those who were forcing the terms! I rejoice in nothing so much as in the prospect that they will now be emancipated from these conditions, and we ought to be the first to take part in assisting that emancipation.

Wilson then went on to make an important policy statement: "I want to take this occasion to say that the United States will never again seek one additional foot of territory by conquest."

Such were the standards on which Wilsonian foreign policy was based. Like most idealists, however, the President often found the practical application of his principles most perplexingly difficult. More than once, indeed, the Wilson administration became involved in a line of conduct quite incompatible with Wilsonian ideals.

In Behalf of Peace

Despite the striking differences between Wilson and Bryan, they saw eye to eye on many issues. The Secretary was delighted by his chief's repudiation of imperialism, and the President in turn heartily supported a project Bryan had been sponsoring for many years. Under the latter's plan, the United States would make treaties with as many other nations as possible, pledging that all questions in dispute between the signatories not settled by diplomacy would be submitted to an international commission. The nations would agree not to resort to force until the commission had investigated and reported—a proceeding that must be completed within one year. These became known as "cooling-off treaties," since one advantage of the plan was believed to be the unlikelihood of two nations going to war over an issue if they had waited a year for the commission's report. England, France, and most of the other great powers were among the thirty nations making such treaties with the United States. Germany rejected the proposition because she would be deprived of the advantages of her superior military preparedness. The Senate ratified all but one or two of the "cooling-off treaties," but only twenty-two went into effect because of ratification difficulties with the signatory states.

Like most of Bryan's activities, these treaties were subjected to considerable ridicule, and they were, to be sure, frail bulwarks against the whirlwinds of war unloosed in 1914. As late as 1939, however, nineteen of them were still in force and had some influence on the diplomats striving to build more effective peace machinery.

A more ambitious proposal pushed by the administration in 1915 and 1916 was for a Pan-American pact in which the twenty-one republics would mutually guarantee each other's independence and territorial integrity. The project, the brainchild of Colonel House, failed largely because of Chile's opposition, but even more than the Bryan treaties it influenced Wilson in his later work on the League of Nations Covenant.

Wilson and the Canal

The Panama Canal, opened to traffic in 1914 although not fully completed until 1920, continued to involve the United States in tangled diplomatic problems. Colombia had never ceased to protest the steps by which Roosevelt "took" the Canal Zone. Taft tried unsuccessfully to placate this neighbor, and the problem was still acute when Wilson took over. In 1914 a treaty was arranged whereby the United States expressed "sincere regret" for the 1903 incident and promised to pay Colombia $25 million. This typically Wilsonian effort to right an old wrong was blocked in the Senate, where Roosevelt's friends indignantly opposed any American acknowledgment of guilt. Not until 1921, when Roosevelt was dead and Wilson had left the White House, did a similar treaty, but without the expression of regret, obtain ratification—this time sponsored by a Republican administration probably not unmindful of the recent discovery of oil in Colombia.

Another problem inherited from the Taft regime was the tolls issue. In 1912, it will be recalled, Congress fixed the tolls to be charged, and exempted American ships using the canal in sailing from one American port to another from any charges. The British government protested that this exemption violated the Hay-Pauncefote Treaty clause that stated the canal should be "free and open to the vessels . . . of all nations . . . on terms of entire equality." President Taft and Secretary Knox, both excellent lawyers, had held that the words "all nations" meant all nations other than the United States and that the American government was within its rights in giving preference to its own citizens. Foreign experts in international law almost unanimously disputed this, however, as did many Americans, among them Elihu Root, who had assisted Hay in the 1901 negotiations. The British were particularly resentful of Taft's refusal to submit the case to arbitration.

Wilson did not give the subject much attention before he became President, but then he gradually became convinced that the exemption clause was a breach of good faith with Britain. Despite the embarrassing fact that the 1912 Democratic platform had upheld the exemption principle, Wilson requested Congress in March, 1914, for "a voluntary withdrawal from a position everywhere questioned and misunderstood. I ask this of you in support of the foreign policy of the administration. I shall not know how to deal with other matters of even greater delicacy and nearer consequence if you do not grant it to me in ungrudging measure." This somewhat cryptic language probably referred both to Wilson's general aspiration to make the United States the moral leader in world affairs and to his more specific need of Britain's support for his Mexican policy, soon to be discussed. Although the bill to repeal the exemption clause precipitated stormy debate, it was finally passed, thereby increasing the American reputation for fair dealing in foreign, and particularly British, eyes.

Protecting the Caribbean Life Line

Despite Wilson's repudiation of imperialism in theory, the exigencies of canal diplomacy drew him into more than a little imperialism in fact. Indeed, his administration became involved in more interventions in Latin America than had any of its predecessors—interventions in Mexico, Cuba, Haiti, and the Dominican Republic—and tended, like those of the Roosevelt and Taft administrations, to reduce the Caribbean states to protectorates of the United States. The American empire was enlarged, moreover, by the purchase of the Danish West Indies—promptly renamed the Virgin Islands—from Denmark in 1917 for $25 million. The administration's Caribbean policy, seemingly so inconsistent with Wilsonian principles, is to be explained in part by the outbreak of World War I. Both the State and Navy departments were seriously alarmed lest Germany or some other belligerent seize territory for use as a base of operations against the Panama Canal. American intervention was also motivated by the desire to help Latin Americans achieve genuinely democratic government—an idealistic goal that Wilson and Bryan shared.

The most serious intervention was in Haiti, where conditions approaching anarchy had developed by 1914. Politics were characterized by civil war, assassinations, and mass executions. This situation endangered the lives and property of foreigners and threatened to bring European intervention. In particular jeopardy were certain American financial interests, specifically those the National City Bank of New York held in the National Bank of Haiti. To protect the gold reserve of the latter institution, American naval officers landed in December, 1914, removed $500,000 from its vaults, and deposited the money in the National City Bank of New York pending a reform of Haitian finances. Meantime, pressure was exerted on the insular government to accept a financial arrangement with the United States like that of the neighboring Dominican Republic. This pressure brought no result, and affairs reached a climax on July 27, 1915, when President Vilbrun Guillaume Sam summarily executed some 160 political prisoners. This bloody massacre was followed the next day by a mob uprising, in which the Haitian executive was literally torn limb from limb. That afternoon American marines landed and began an occupation lasting nineteen years.

Under the supervision of Admiral W. B. Caperton of the American Navy, the Haitian legislature elected a president acceptable to the United States. The new government than signed a treaty providing not only for American receivership of Haitian finances, but for the organization of a constabulary trained and officered by Americans and for restrictions upon Haitian sovereignty more extensive than those embodied in the Platt Amendment. In 1918 the islanders, cowed by the new constabulary, obediently voted 69,377 to 355 to adopted a new constitution primarily drafted by Americans.[2]

This intervention brought many material reforms to Haiti. A sanitary program improved health conditions, roads were built, and currency was stabilized, and the government's financial house put in order. On the dark side, Haitian resistance to foreign control brought drastic action; more than two thousand natives were shot by American marines in pacifying the country. American public opinion was shocked by stories of atrocities and forced labor.

Events in the Dominican Republic followed a similar, but less spectacular, course. Financial receivership proved insufficient by itself to assure stable political conditions. Civil war brought intervention by American marines in 1916, which lasted until 1924. Once again an American protectorate meant material benefits for the population but brought uneasy consciences to Americans who believed in "government by consent of the governed." In 1917 the United States once again sent troops to Cuba, where they remained until 1922. They did not, however, establish military rule as in 1906, but merely served as a warning to Cubans to maintain order.

Nicaragua had been one of the most active fields of Taft's dollar diplomacy, and at the end of his term a treaty was drafted granting the United States a renewable ninety-nine-year lease of the Great and Little Corn islands, the right to establish a naval base on the Gulf of Fonseca, and a grant in perpetuity of the exclusive right to build an interoceanic canal across Nicaraguan territory. In return, the United States would pay Nicaragua $3 million, but American consent would be necessary to the disbursement of this payment, a stipulation obviously to the interest of American bankers who had loaned money to Nicaragua. The advantage of the guarantee that no foreign country would control a water route rivaling the Panama Canal was so obvious that Wilson and Bryan supported the treaty and even agreed to a Nicaraguan suggestion that clauses similar to the Platt Amendment be incorporated. When the Senate rejected this proposal to establish so undisguised a protectorate, a new agreement, the Bryan-Chamorro Treaty of 1916 incorporating the original claims without the protectorate clause was substituted.

---

[2] Assistant Secretary of the Navy Franklin D. Roosevelt claimed in a campaign speech in 1920 that he had written this constitution. Actually, however, he had nothing to do with drawing it up, and the Republicans used his statement against him throughout the remainder of the campaign.

The Acid Test: Mexico

Although these events seemed to belie the sincerity of Wilson's repudiation of imperialism, the President's forbearance in dealing with a difficult situation in neighboring Mexico marked a sharp departure from the methods of dollar diplomacy. From 1876 to 1911 Mexico was ruled by Porfirio Díaz, a military dictator who maintained strict order and encouraged foreign investment. To Americans resident in that country or doing business there, Mexico under Díaz seemed in happy contrast to strife-ridden nations elsewhere in Latin America. But the beneficence of the dictator's rule was more apparent to foreigners exploiting Mexico's resources and to the privileged few among the Mexicans themselves who had amassed fabulous wealth than it was to the masses. The peasants, sunk in ignorance, remained in a condition of peonage that was almost slavery, and much of the land was converted into enormous estates by wealthy aristocrats.

Revolution broke out in 1910, and the following year Díaz fled to Europe, where he soon died. His successor was Francisco Madero, an idealistic reformer, but a gentle soul hardly equipped to control the explosive forces now unleashed. Civil war swept the country, and foreigners, fearing for their lives and property, longingly remembered happy days under Díaz.

In February, 1913, Madero was the victim of shocking treachery. One of his generals, Victoriano Huerta, rebelled against him, put him in jail, and proclaimed himself president. A few days later Madero was killed, almost in cold blood. Foreign diplomats in Mexico, shrugging off the murder as an unfortunate, but understandable act of Latin violence, recommended that their governments recognize the new regime—an action likely to restore the conditions of the Díaz dictatorship. Most European powers, including Britain, acted upon this advice. Had it not been the last month of Taft's term, the United States probably would have followed suit, but instead the decision was left to the incoming administration.

Wilson believed that Huerta's seizure of power created grave doubts as to whether his government should be recognized. He regarded Huerta as a murderer and suspected he was more popular with the foreign oil interests than he was with the Mexican people. Evidence of this was the continuing civil war in which Venustiano Carranza, governor of Coahuila, was becoming a formidable rival. Despite widespread American criticism that denial of recognition to a *de facto* government was contrary to American diplomatic precedent dating back to Jefferson's day, Wilson delayed recognizing the Huerta regime. Instead, he sought to have Mexican factions agree to an armistice in the civil war, to an early free election in which Huerta would not be a candidate, and to abide by the election results.

When Huerta refused to remove himself from Mexican politics, Wilson resorted to "watchful waiting"—that is, refusing to recognize Huerta but resisting the demand of American jingoes for United States military intervention to set the Mexican house in order. By refusing recognition, Wilson expected Huerta could not long remain in power. Defending this policy before Congress on August 27, 1913, Wilson declared:

We can afford to exercise the self-restraint of a really great nation which realizes its own strength and scorns to misuse it. It was our duty to offer our active assistance. It is now our duty to show what true neutrality will do to enable the people of Mexico to set their affairs in order again, and wait for a further opportunity to offer our friendly counsels.

Waiting proved unpopular in many quarters, especially since Mexican civil strife brought damage to American property and death to more than seventy American citizens between 1913 and 1915. Roosevelt demanded intervention, and Wilson's stand was vigorously denounced in Congress. At the end of 1913, the President modified his policy by adopting active measures to force Huerta out. Britain, thankful for Wilson's fight against the Panama tolls exemption clause, agreed to withdraw its support for Huerta. Moreover, in February, 1914, the President lifted the arms embargo of the previous years, thus greatly assisting the rebel leaders, Carranza and Francisco ("Pancho") Villa. But Huerta still defied the "Colossus of the North," an important factor in winning for him considerable backing from his own people.

In April, 1914, a crisis developed that seemed almost certain to bring full-scale American intervention. On the ninth, some American sailors were arrested at Tampico by a Mexican force and jailed for having allegedly violated martial law. The men were soon released by the Mexican commanding officer, who apologized for the arrests. But Admiral Henry Mayo, in command of the American fleet at the scene, demanded that within twenty-four hours the Mexican authorities must submit a formal apology and disavowal of the act, together with assurance that the officer responsible be severely punished. Also the admiral demanded that the Mexicans "publicly hoist the American flag in a prominent position on shore and salute it with twenty-one guns." The expression of regret was forthcoming, but Huerta refused to give the salute.

Wilson could scarcely refuse to back up his admiral, despite the dubious wisdom of the unauthorized ultimatum. On April 20, the President asked Congress to approve the use of armed force "in such ways and to such an extent as may be necessary to obtain from General Huerta and his adherents the fullest recognition of the rights and dignity of the United States." After a two-day debate, Wilson was granted this authority by an overwhelming vote.

Full-scale war now appeared likely. "I'd make them salute the flag if we had to blow up the whole place," asserted Senator William Chilton of West Virginia, while Senator William Borah of Idaho said: "This is the beginning of the march of the United States to the Panama Canal." Indeed, events beyond Wilson's power to control seemed to be forcing his hand. Even before Congress authorized force, the President learned that a German ship was about to deliver a cargo of arms to the Huerta faction at Vera Cruz. Fearful lest Huerta use those munitions against the United States, Wilson ordered armed action. On April 21, Vera Cruz was bombarded and occupied by American marines after considerable bloodshed.

Because the seizure of Vera Cruz served only to strengthen Huerta's defiance, further military operations appeared inevitable until a way out of the situation was offered from an unexpected quarter. On April 25, the diplomatic representatives of Argentina, Brazil, and Chile (the so-called ABC powers) offered to mediate the imbroglio. Wilson's immediate acceptance brought him enthusiastic praise throughout Latin America. Not only did it show friendly United States deference to the wishes of the republics to the South, but it indicated that Wilson's repudiation of aggressive designs toward Latin America was sincere. In the opinion of the Springfield (Massachusetts) *Republican* it was "worth dozens of Pan-American conferences. . . . It establishes a precedent; possibly it opens a new era."

The chief contribution of the mediation proposal was to ease the crisis caused by the Tampico and Vera Cruz incidents. The plan for a general Mexican settlement, worked out at a conference of the ABC powers, the United States, and Mexico at Niagara Falls, Canada, failed because Carranza refused to accept it. The United States, however, evacuated Vera Cruz without receiving the demanded salute, and in July, 1914, Huerta fled the country. To Wilson's admirers, the dictator's downfall seemed complete vindication of the President's actions.

Unfortunately, however, the embarrassing Mexican complications had not yet been exhausted. A new civil war broke out between Carranza and Villa over which should wear the mantle of the martyred Madero. Although Carranza held the stronger position, Wilson at first encouraged Villa in the mistaken belief that he would be more cooperative than his stiff-necked opponent. By October, 1915, however, Carranza's power became so great the President granted him *de facto* recognition. The now resentful Villa, gambling desperately to discredit his rival by provoking American intervention, began a policy of deliberate provocation. In January, 1916, his followers murdered sixteen American engineers at Santa Ysabel, Mexico, and the following March Villa led a raid across the border to sack Columbus, New Mexico, killing seventeen Americans. Wilson now had to act. He ordered General John J. Pershing to lead a cavalry force into Mexico to capture Villa dead or alive.

For the next eleven months the situation was explosive. Villa proved to be extraordinarily elusive, and Pershing was several times reinforced, to the great consternation of Carranza, who had given grudging consent to the original expedition, but now wished to rid Mexico soil of the Americans as quickly as possible. With American opinion turning strongly against Carranza for his unwillingness to cooperate and with Mexican opinion becoming bitterly anti-American, the danger of full-scale war between the two countries was great.

Wilson was especially worried because of World War I. If the United States became involved in the European struggle, it could not have a major portion of its small army tied up in Mexico. The sudden worsening of German-American relations in February, 1917, finally convinced the administration that Pershing's troops must be withdrawn. Once again Wilson's critics denounced his failure to adopt a policy of wholesale intervention and thorough housecleaning in Mexico, asserting that the Villa episode had been humiliating to American prestige. Ironically, at the same time many Americans criticized the President for not being sufficiently vigorous, Mexicans of all parties were denouncing him for having interfered too much.

Although the continuance of the Mexican revolution after 1917 involved still more diplomatic problems, American entry into World War I shifted attention away from the maelstrom of Mexican politics. Whether the whole course of American policy was to be praised or condemned depended largely on the partisan sympathies of the critic. Wilson's own evaluation was embodied in his message to Congress in December, 1916:

> We have been put to the acid test in Mexico, and we have stood the test. Whether we have benefited Mexico . . . remains to be seen. But we have at least proved that we will not take advantage of her in her distress and undertake to impose on her an order and government of our choosing . . . that we seek no political suzerainty or selfish control.

Reform Interrupted

For leadership in domestic reform, Wilson had unusual training. He was a student of government and of the new economic and social problems with which government had to deal. For leadership in foreign affairs, however, his education was much less adequate. His interests had been largely focused on purely American issues. Yet through one of history's ironies, Wilson was destined to deal not only with vexatious Latin-American issues, but with problems of world politics more momentous than those any previous President had faced. In August, 1914, Germany invaded Belgium to involve Europe in the first general war since the defeat of Napoleon a century before. From that time on, America's relationship to the great conflict increasingly absorbed the attention of the President and the nation.

The progressive movement did not end abruptly with the advent of war. Liberal legislation continued to be enacted and, as late as 1920, the Nineteenth Amendment, granting women's suffrage, was added to the Constitution, but the crusading spirit of earlier years was gone. After the United States belatedly entered the war, the country passed into a period of indifference and then of hostility to progressivism that lasted until the Great Depression brought a new demand for reform and change.

7
THE ROAD TO WAR

World War I came as an unexpected shock to the American people, who had paid little attention to the European scene during the years preceding 1914. Their first reaction was that the United States would not be affected by these hostilities, and President Wilson immediately issued the traditional proclamation of neutrality. As the contest in Europe progressed, however, its reverberations were felt in all parts of the world. America's industrial output was in growing demand, its struggles to obtain recognition of its concept of neutral rights were not successful, and its efforts to mediate the war were thwarted. While the Allies were the greater culprits in infringing international law, it was Germany that caused the loss of American lives. This fact, plus the belief that the Allies were the European guardians of democracy, promoted a growing feeling in the United States that the Central Powers must be defeated. Only by American entrance into the war could this be accomplished—but the road to war was slow and tortuous.

European Rivalry

The war in Europe found the American people ill-prepared to understand its causes and implications. For many years they had been concerned primarily with domestic matters: the tariff, banking reform, antitrust legislation, and social justice generally. Their chief diplomatic interests centered on hemisphere affairs: the construction of the Panama Canal, intervention in the smaller republics, and, more immediately, the Mexican problem

Consequently, the public did not realize that since about 1870 dangerous antagonisms among the European powers had led to alliances that needed but one little incident to arouse long-engendered animosities to a state of war. One alliance included Germany, Austria, and Italy; the other, France, Russia, and Britain. Balance of power, spheres of influence, nationalism, and commercial rivalry were prominent in the growing unrest between the two rival groups.

The assassination of Austrian Archduke Francis Ferdinand at Sarajevo, capital of Bosnia, on June 28, 1914, was the incident that touched off the spark. The average American thought it was another local flare-up following the Balkan Wars and would soon blow over. Nor did the State Department seem especially worried about the whole affair. Secretary Bryan was busy with his "cooling-off" treaties, while the President was trying to mediate the

Mexican trouble. True, he was "deeply shocked at the atrocious murder," but there is no indication he realized its potentialities.

Wilson and His Diplomatic Advisers

As a practical idealist, Wilson was firmly convinced that the United States had a mission to perform in the world. It must serve as a model of righteousness. If the nation boldly promoted international law and followed all its precepts, then other nations would have to follow suit. Force should be used to protect American citizens in their international rights only as a last resort. Diplomacy, plus the firm assertion of right, would accomplish more than arms. Unfortunately, a stubborn streak, added to a reluctance to accept advice, prevented the President from accomplishing as much as he might have.

The State Department was largely staffed by men of little diplomatic experience. Secretary Bryan was appointed more because of his prominence in the Democratic party and his support of Wilson in the 1912 convention than because of his diplomatic training. Although not an unconditional pacifist, he thoroughly disliked war. His eventual successor, Robert Lansing, a specialist in international law, posed as a vigorous champion of American rights, but he became more sympathetic toward the British as the war progressed; consequently, when controversies arose with England, he plunged them into an endless tangle of legalisms so that the Allied cause would be little embarrassed.

Walter Hines Page, ambassador to Britain, was so convinced England was entirely in the right that he did his best to bring the United States into the war on her side. James Gerard, ambassador to Germany, was a wealthy socialite who did little to improve German-American relations. Despite greater diplomatic experience, Myron Herrick, the envoy to France, displayed no real understanding of the European situation.

Neither the State Department nor the ambassadors abroad, however, played as important roles as might have been expected. More than most Presidents, Wilson himself decided questions of foreign policy and even drafted many important diplomatic documents. Distrusting conventional diplomacy, he relied upon unofficial agents, such as Colonel Edward House of Texas, who was entrusted with important confidential missions to foreign capitals.

As animosities grew in Europe in the spring of 1914, House persuaded Wilson to send him across the Atlantic to establish a concert of powers, with the United States as a member, to ensure a long-range peace. Despite his visits with major power leaders in the hectic days of June and July, his messages to Wilson did not even mention the archduke's assassination. After the peace dam broke, House soon believed the Allied cause was just, thus seeing eye to eye with Page and Lansing.

The Decision for Neutrality

On July 26, 1914, came the first intimation that war in Europe might develop when Austria severed relations with Serbia because the latter failed to accede to a twenty-four-hour ultimatum. Not until July 28, when Ambassador Herrick described the situation as "the gravest in history," did Wilson, who had been primarily concerned with his wife's health, realize the urgency of the problem, and even then he took no positive step. Meantime, Austria declared war on Serbia, Germany on Russia, France, and Belgium, and Britain on Germany. The unforeseen hostilities had burst in full fury.

No American doubted the wisdom of neutrality at this point. European troubles should be of no more concern now than they had been when Washington issued his famous proclamation in 1793. Wilson believed he must preserve this American tradition, in part so that he might achieve all the New Freedom reforms. Consequently, on August 4 he announced that no one in the United States "shall take part, directly or indirectly, in the said wars, but shall maintain a strict and impartial neutrality." There would be no interference, however, "with the free expression of opinion and sympathy, or with the commercial manufacture or sale of arms or munitions of war." At the same time, belligerents were warned against using American waters or territory for hostile purpose.

The President refused to believe the conflict would seriously implicate the United States, and at the outset he constantly spoke of World War I as one "which cannot touch us" or "with which we have nothing to do." Nonetheless, as the head of the most important neutral nation, Wilson offered his services as a mediator, only to be promptly rejected.

At this time American opinion was strongly behind the President, and even Theodore Roosevelt praised his stand, saying Americans should be thankful to be safe from the horrors of war. Despite this support, Wilson realized that about one third of the nation's 92 million inhabitants were of foreign birth or had one or both parents foreign born. Consequently, he appealed directly to the people on August 19 to "act and speak in the true spirit of neutrality, which is the spirit of impartiality and fairness and friendliness to all concerned. . . . The United States must be neutral in fact as well as in name. . . . We must be neutral in thought as well as in act. . . ." Again Roosevelt gave his support: "Nothing but urgent need would warrant breaking our neutrality and taking sides one way or another."

Pro-Ally Trend

While most Americans probably did honestly strive to be "neutral in fact as well as in name," there was a definite swing to the Allied cause as the war progressed. Although the Germans as a people were not disliked, their leaders' demands for their rightful place in the sun, their boasts of the supremacy of their *Kultur,* the strutting of Prussian officers, and the Kaiser's references to "Me und Gott" did not appeal to the average American, who was also revolted by the Germanic acts of violence. The disregard of Belgium's neutrality was the most heinous of all, accentuated by the German chancellor's reference to the nearly century-old neutrality treaty as a mere "scrap of paper." Furthermore, the atrocity stories about the mistreatment of Belgian civilians, although subsequently proved to be propagandist fabrications, were then wholly believed.

On the other side of the picture, the kinship of Americans to Britons, based on common language and institutions, had been strengthened by the growing diplomatic accord of recent years. The accounts of the progress of World War I came chiefly from Allied sources and stressed Allied victories and heroism. The taxi-transported French army, the first "hundred thousand" Britons who went to Belgium's defense, the slogan "They Shall Not Pass" all stirred Americans emotionally to favor the Allied cause.

Monetary considerations also closely linked Britain and America. American bankers loaned money to Britain and naturally felt that an Allied victory would mean speedier repayment. Thanks to British control of the seas, the American munitions trade was entirely with the Allies and brought a pro-Ally feeling—and the same can be said for trade in general.

The British also maintained a well-organized propaganda distribution center, known as Wellington House, that played up the righteousness of the Allied cause, the duty of the United States to join the Allies to ensure the triumph of democracy, and the danger of a German victory to the whole world. On the other hand, German propagandist efforts were amateurish, feeble, and ineffective. France was probably better liked by most Americans than was Britain because they remembered enough of their history to know that France had aided the United States during the Revolution. Perhaps the time had come to repay that debt. Also there was great sympathy because France was the victim of vicious invasion. Russia, on the other hand, was little known or liked by the general public.

In the long run, however, the invasion of Belgium, the German submarine warfare that destroyed American lives, and the belief that the Allied cause represented democracy and right were the prime factors in the gradual swing from neutrality in thought and action to a definite feeling that the Allies must win.

Economic Effects of the War

As the foremost maritime and industrial neutral, the United States was bound to be affected by the war. Even the President realized that American trade would boom, for the belligerents must necessarily seek supplies of all kinds from the United States, and European neutrals, formerly buying from the nations at war, would have to turn to America to stock their larders.

To meet the expected shipping shortage, Congress passed in August, 1914, the Ship Registry Act that enabled American-owned foreign-built ships to be more quickly admitted to United States registry. Two weeks later, the Bureau of War Risk Insurance was established with a fund of $5 million to provide insurance for American merchant vessels and their cargoes unable to obtain reasonable terms from private firms. Congress was not then ready, however, to authorize the government to buy, build, or lease ships.

The expected increase in American exports did not materialize at once. Instead there was a decided drop, particularly in wheat, cotton, copper, and steel, while the textile industry was hurt when German dyes became unavailable. As the president of the New York Chamber of Commerce said in mid-August, 1914: "Europe has placed an embargo on the commerce of the world."

When the first shock of war wore off, however, and the nation realized that events in Europe would help, not hurt, American industry, confidence was gradually restored by the spring of 1915. The Allies, now turning their industrial machinery to the war effort and expending their backlog of prewar commodities, sought more and more American supplies; an increasing number of ships became available to take care of the demand: and in turn American production in many fields was speeded up. Germany could have used the American output as well, but British control of the seas precluded delivery. Indeed, only one German ship, the large submarine *Deutschland,* was able to make the round trip across the Atlantic after Britain established its blockade. Thus during the period between 1914 and 1916, exports to the Allies nearly quadrupled (from $824 million to more than $3 billion), whereas in 1916 the Central Powers obtained only $1.1 million—less than 1 per cent of their 1914 imports ($169 million) from the United States.

The biggest export increases were in so-called war necessities. In 1914, about $6 million worth of explosives were sold; in 1917, more than $800 million. Iron and steel exports rose from $25 million in 1914 to more than $1 billion in 1917. Wheat sales jumped from $88 million to nearly $300 million in the same period. Prices rose almost in the same proportion as export values. For example, a bushel of wheat sold for less than $1.00 at the opening of the war; early in 1917 the price had risen to about $3.00. To meet the demands, American production of iron ore grew from 40 million tons in 1914 to 75 million in 1917; copper production increased from 1.1 billion pounds to 1.8 billion in the same period; and wheat from 760 million bushels to about 900 million.

The embittered Germans asserted that since only the Allies were being helped, the United States should lay an embargo, at least on munitions. But the Wilson administration pointed out that to impose an embargo during wartime would obviously be an unneutral act. Under international law, the fact that the Allies could obtain American goods and Germany could not was simply the fortunes of war. Even Ambassador Bernstorff had to admit that "no exceptions can be taken to neutral states letting war materials go to Germany's enemies."

Stocks and Loans

Fear that the $2.7 billion European-owned American securities might be dumped in the United States caused the New York Stock Exchange to close down on July 31, 1914. Not until December 12 was the danger sufficiently eased to allow limited trading, although it was not until the following April that full regular stock dealings were resumed. Thereafter, stock prices, especially of the so-called war babies, mounted rapidly, but whatever European-owned securities were sold did not materially affect the American exchange.

Nevertheless, the enormously expanded purchases of American commodities threatened serious trouble. The Allies could not afford to ship all their gold to America to pay for what they bought, nor did the United States want to dislocate its own and the European economy by such a transfer. Thus only about $1 billion in gold reached America, and approximately $1.5 billion worth of European-owned American securities were sold to offset the unfavorable balance. Not for long, however, could the Allies count on these limited resources to pay for their purchases.

If the trade were to continue, the Allies must obtain loans in America. When the issue was first raised, however, Secretary Bryan informed J. P. Morgan in August, 1914, that "loans by American bankers to any foreign nation which is at war is inconsistent with the true spirit of neutrality." At first the bankers considered this statement official, but in October, 1914, the President informed them indirectly that he would not oppose commercial short-term loans to belligerent nations. Then, in September, 1915, Secretary Lansing and Secretary McAdoo announced that "the flotation of large bond issues by the belligerent countries" was the only solution to the unfavorable balance of trade.

Before the month was over, Morgan, representing a syndicate of more than sixty New York banks, subscribed to a $500 million loan for the French and British governments. The only collateral was those governments' promise to repay—a sure indication that American bankers were convinced of eventual Allied victory. In 1916 four more Allied loans were floated, totaling another $500 million and backed by American securities still owned by the Allies. In addition, $75 million in Russian bonds were sold in the American market. A warning from the Federal Reserve Board about the effect of these sales suspended loans for the rest of the year, but in January, 1917, England sold $250 million worth of gold notes, and two months later France disposed of $100 million in similar securities.

On the other hand, Germany sold less than $20 million in short-term bonds in the early days of the war. Since she was unable to obtain war supplies in return, she used most of the proceeds for propaganda and sabotage.

Anglo-American Controversies

The longtime friendship between the United States and Britain was sorely tried early in the war. Insular Britain, insisting from the outset that she must dominate the seas to maintain her lifeline and to prevent supplies from reaching the enemy, refused to accept the Declaration of London of 1909, the maritime code drawn up under the auspices of the Second Hague Conference that had defined what belligerent nations could and could not do on the high seas. On the other hand, the United States, the outstanding champion of neutral rights, had agreed to the Declaration and, at the opening of the war, insisted that belligerents observe its terms. These opposite positions were bound to result in frequent controveries between the two nations.

One of the first involved the various types of cargoes, defined at London as: (1) absolute contraband, consisting of actual war materials destined for the enemy and seizable, even from a neutral vessel, without compensation; (2) conditional contraband, made up of goods that might be used for purposes of both war and peace, but which were contraband only if proven they were destined for enemy governments and their military forces; and (3) noncontraband or free goods, including commodities like food, wood and certain ores, which were essential to the life and industry of civilians.

When in August, 1914, Britain first announced the list of commodities she considered absolute and conditional contraband, the United States had no cause for complaint because the items were practically the same as those in the Declaration. As the war progressed, however, and England's position became precarious, she gradually added to the absolute list a number of materials previously conditional—notably gasoline, cotton, and rubber—because new methods of warfare required their use directly by the fighting forces. The most unusual addition was food, because of the German order commandeering all wheat, flour, and corn within Germany. Britain concluded this was done to ensure edibles for the German army; *ipso facto,* food must be contraband and could be seized by British blockaders. The ultimate was reached in April, 1916, when England removed all distinctions between types of contraband; thereafter more than 225 commodities might be seized from neutral ships.

Had Wilson taken a firm stand from the beginning, Britain might not have so acted. The administration's only response, however, was to warn England that her actions were contrary to neutral rights and might arouse "bitter feeling among the American people." Ambassador Page told Foreign Minister Sir Edward Grey that England could get around this warning, and American exporters did not complain because England gave them adequate compensation for any goods seized.

Blockade and Search Problems

Another controversy concerned the definition of a blockade. According to the London Declaration, it must be effective and impartial; it must be formally proclaimed; it must be established in the vicinity of the area under blockade; and it must not prevent access to neutral ports nor allow capture of ships going to nonblockaded ones. Nor did the Declaration recognize the doctrine of continuous voyage or ultimate destination—that is, that goods could be seized on the way to neutral ports if it could be proved they were ultimately destined for enemy territory.

Britain soon disregarded all these provisions. Her blockade, never formally announced, was not established near the German coast because of the submarine menace, but at the mouth of the North Sea. Her blockading ships could thereby control all traffic to the neutral countries of northern Europe and apply the doctrine of continuous voyage. Wilson's protests were answered with the claim that British measures did "conform to the spirit and principles of the essence of the rules of war." Grey also pointed out that the United States had used the doctrine of continuous voyage during the Civil War and had been upheld by the Supreme Court. Was the present British position any different? In fact that position, simply stated, was: "We have necessity on our side; you have the law—what is left of it—on your side; we'll not seriously quarrel"—and Wilson didn't.

Closely related to the blockade issue was that of visit and search. Under the declaration, a belligerent ship that stopped a neutral merchantman suspected of carrying contraband must make the search on the scene. After any contraband was removed, the merchantman must be allowed to continue its voyage. Again Britain defied this procedure, claiming German submarines made it dangerous for destroyers to conduct searches at sea. Therefore merchantmen were usually taken to British ports for examination that might entail a week or more because contraband goods, sometimes cleverly concealed, could not be discovered without such equipment as X-ray machines. Usually Britain compensated the ship owners for the time lost. American protests were as unavailing as in other controversies.

Another source of complaint was the British practice of raising the American flag over their ships to escape from German submarines. The first American protest was in February, 1915, against the "general use" of the flag, but Bryan admitted that "occasional use" of the flag as a *ruse de guerre* might be condoned. Lord Grey replied that Britain was merely following common usage; indeed, he said, Union ships had flown neutral flags during the Civil War. Consequently, Britain would not abandon the practice, and nothing further was said about it.

British and French censoring of American mail also gave rise to protests. In the war's early stages, the Allies examined only letters going through their territory, but by the end of 1915 the inspection included mail on ships merely stopping at their ports. In this controversy, most complaints came from businessmen who asserted that Britain obtained valuable trade information and delayed completion of American contract bids. Wilson, on the other hand, virtually admitted the belligerent right to seize merchandise in packages. Thus in the absence of forceful official demand on America's part, the Allies continued their widespread censorship.

The British practice of arming merchantmen for defense against submarine attacks led to three delicate questions: Did Germany have to give warning before trying to sink such vessels? What was the status of American passengers on those ships? And could such vessel rightly enter American ports? Even Lansing admitted that "merchant vessels . . . carrying an armament . . . should not possess the immunities attaching to private vessels of belligerent nationality." But again the Wilson administration failed to change Britain's position.

A particularly irritating issue arose in July, 1916, when the British published a "blacklist" of more than four hundred firms in neutral countries, including more than eighty in the United States, suspected of doing business with the Central Powers. No loyal Briton could have dealings with those companies. Wilson believed this was "the last straw" and privately alluded to those responsible for the blacklist as "poor boobs." When Congress authorized retaliatory measures, Wilson, primarily occupied with the campaign of 1916 and mediation plans, refused to use them.

For several weeks in 1916 England lost much ground in American public opinion by mishandling events in Ireland. Radical nationalists there sought to take advantage of Britain's involvement in the war to gain full independence; some even urged a military alliance with Germany to attain this goal. Because the radicals' aspirations obviously depended on a German victory, Irish-American supporters tried to prevent the United States from going to England's assistance. They joined the German-American groups in mass protests against the Wilson pro-British policies. Moreover, a small group of Irish-American leaders tried to gain Bernstorff's backing for the proposed Irish revolt. But a succession of disasters befell the Irish volunteers in their bid for independence during Easter week, 1916. The British quelled the uprising, 15 Irish leaders were executed, 145 were sentenced to long prison terms, and 1,841 were interned in England.

This severe British retribution shocked many Americans. Irish-Americans regarded the executed Irish leaders as martyrs in a holy cause. Even the staunchly pro-Ally *New York Times* called the executions "incredibly stupid." The Senate hoped that Britain would extend clemency to Irish political prisoners. The journalist David Lawrence wrote: "The truth is, Great Britain in a few days has alienated many of her sympathizers—almost as many as Germany alienated when the *Lusitania* sank."

Although several of these controversies threatened to get out of hand, this did not happen for several reasons. In the first place, pro-Ally feeling grew as the war progressed; American conceptions of international law would tie British hands, thereby weakening the Allies. Secondly, British infringements may have resulted in loss of time and inconvenience for American shippers, but not in loss of lives and seldom of money; when Wilson sent vigorous protest notes, Page usually softened them by saying they were written primarily for the American public. Finally, when England committed some flagrant deed, Germany would perform an inhumane act that overshadowed the British violation.

German Sabotage

Among the German acts that stirred up American resentment were those of sabotage and espionage. Early in the war, agents of the Central Powers tried to disrupt American industrial life, especially in the fields of munitions and transportation, in retaliation for American shipments to the Allies. Directed chiefly from the German Embassy with money supplied by the German government, the sabotage leaders were German Ambassador Johann von Bernstorff, Austrian Ambassador Constantin Dumba, Captain Franz von Papen, military attaché to the German Embassy, Captain Karl Boy-Ed, the naval attaché, and Dr. Heinrich Albert, commercial attaché.

Espionage and sabotage took many forms. German agents tried to send their government information about the quantity of munitions produced in the United States. They sought to prevent exportation of military supplies or to destroy the ships that carried them. Strikes were fomented in munitions plants. Passports were falsified so that German reservists might reach the Fatherland in the guise of American citizens. Manifests were forged to get supplies, like fuel, to German warships and submarines attacking Allied merchantmen. German agents also cooperated with Irish revolutionists in America and, through such organizations as the American Embargo Conference and the German-American National Alliance, tried to persuade Congress to pass measures inimical to the Allies.

American newspapers had a field day playing up sabotage cases, real or fanciful. Many incidents blamed on German agents were normal accidents, but, as in the case of Belgian atrocities, the public was more than ready to believe that every large fire or explosion was another instance of sabotage. Yet there is no doubt that saboteurs were responsible for some of these incidents, for the millions of dollars dispensed from the Central Power embassies could not all have been wasted. When the British seized the luggage of the lecturer-journalist James Archibald as he landed at Falmouth, they found numerous letters indicating the scope of the plans. One written by Ambassador Dumba read in part: "It is my impression that we can disorganize and hold up for months, if not entirely prevent, the manufacture of munitions in Bethlehem and the Middle West. . . ." This message, plus Dumba's unfortunate reference to Wilson's "self-willed temperament," forced the administration to demand the Austrian's recall in the fall of 1915. Another document revealed that von Papen had referred to "these idiotic Yankees"; he escaped dismissal then, but by the end of the year both he and Boy-Ed proved so obnoxious that Wilson insisted they leave the country. And the briefcase of Dr. Albert, absent-mindedly left on a New York City elevated train, contained documents showing that Germany was trying to stir up strikes and prevent munitions shipments.

The watchful American secret service thwarted most of the German plots. At least two attempts to blow up the Welland Canal were frustrated, as were bomb plots against numerous munitions plants. On the other hand, the July 30, 1916, explosion at the Black Tom (New Jersey) docks of the Lehigh Valley Railroad brought death to two persons and property damage of $22 million. Subsequently Germany admitted her responsibility and paid for the destruction.

On the whole, however, whatever the extent of these and other disruptive actions, Germany did not cripple American industry. Indeed, she lost ground because American opinion turned more against her.

The Early Submarine Threat

Much more important in causing the ultimate break with Germany was her submarine warfare, which threatened the safety of American lives on the high seas. The German proposal to isolate the British Isles by means of the submarine was first made in late 1914, but it was not until January, 1915, when the British navy had established a tighter ring around Germany, that several British merchantmen were torpedoed without warning. Encouraged by this success, Germany officially announced on February 4 that after the 18th "the waters surrounding Great Britain and Ireland including the whole English Channel are hereby declared to be comprised within the seat of war. . . . All enemy merchant ships found in these waters . . . will be destroyed although it may not always be possible to save crews and passengers. . . ." Because British ships were wont to fly neutral flags, non-belligerent vessels would expose themselves to danger if they entered this zone.

To President Wilson, this new German policy presented a delicate problem. As an ardent advocate of neutral rights, he felt he must nip the plan in the bud. In his note to Germany on February 10, he declared that the sinking of any merchant ship, even one owned by a belligerent, without preliminary visit and search, was "unprecedented in naval warfare." Were Germany to sink an American one, even by mistake, the United States would regard the act as an "indefensible violation of neutral rights" for which the perpetrator would be held to "strict accountability."

This message was received in Germany with mixed feelings. Some wanted to placate the United States; others thought that a month and a half would end the British blockade. The Kaiser made the ultimate decision: the submarine war on enemy merchantmen must continue, but U-boat captains must abstain "from violence to American merchant ships when they were recognizable as such." Thus he tried to show it was not Germany's intention "to destroy neutral lives and neutral property . . . as the American Government appear to have erroneously understood."

Wilson then tried to end the submarine menace by compromise. He suggested that if all American food shipments to Germany were distributed only to civilians by American agents, England should promise not to interfere with the shipments. Germany, in turn, would stop her submarine warfare, and both sides would cease indiscriminate mine laying and the use of neutral flags. The replies to these proposals were anything but satisfactory, and the situation became more discouraging as Britain tightened her own blockade.

American Lives Are Lost

Although many Allied ships were torpedoed after this compromise failed, the first incident to arouse the American public was the sinking of the British *Falaba,* carrying both passengers and munitions, on March 28, 1915, with the loss of one American life. Warning had been given by the submarine captain, who also allowed twenty-three minutes for the passengers to get off. The fatal torpedo, however, was fired before they were all safe because other British vessels were nearby.

There was disagreement over the protest to be sent. While Lansing favored severing relations and Wilson believed the German act was "an unquestionable violation of the just rules of international law," Bryan believed Americans traveling on belligerent ships did so at their own risk. He wanted the President to forbid such travel, but Wilson declared that citizens of a neutral country had a right to travel on the high seas, even aboard a belligerent-owned merchant vessel.

During these discussions, the *Cushing,* a clearly marked American steamer, was attacked by a German plane, but without loss of life, and three days later, the *Gulflight* was torpedoed. Although the tanker reached port, two crewmen drowned and the captain died of shock. Germany promptly "regretted" the "unfortunate, unintentional" incidents, for which she promised "full recompense." In addition, the German admiralty grudgingly agreed that future attacks on neutral ships would be avoided "under all circumstances"; thus no more American ships were sunk until February, 1917.

The "Lusitania" Tragedy

Meantime, the British liner *Lusitania* was sunk off the coast of Ireland on May 7, 1915, with the loss of 1,198 lives, of which 124 were American. An immediate demand for war developed in the United States. The press made much of the deaths of helpless women and children, and Theodore Roosevelt called the sinking an act of piracy. While it has since been shown that the sinking was not planned, the fact that the German Embassy through the newspapers had warned neutral citizens not to sail on belligerent ships and had sent telegrams similar in nature to those who had booked passage on the *Lusitania* convinced many Americans it was a deliberate crime.

Refusing to be influenced by the war element or by British pressure, Wilson made known his position in a Philadelphia speech on May 14:

The example of America must be the example not merely of peace because it will not fight, but of peace because peace is the healing and elevating influence of the world and strife is not. There is such a thing as a man being too proud to fight . . . a nation being so right that it does not need to convince others by force that it is right.

Many Americans condemned his stand, especially Theodore Roosevelt, who referred to him as a "Byzantine logothete," surrounded by "flubdubs, molly-coddles, and flapdoodle pacifists." Yet these and others failed to swerve the President.

On May 13, Bryan sent the first *Lusitania* note with the greatest reluctance. It stated that Germany had been previously warned against such incidents, and then emphasized that a submarine could not adhere to the following points of international law: the right of visit and search, the right to take prizes, the ability to take care of passengers and crews, and the need to give adequate warning. Therefore Germany must prevent "the recurrence of anything so obviously subversive to the principles of warfare. . . ." Bryan somewhat offset the note's severity by informing Dumba that it was sent merely to satisfy American public opinion.

The German reply was noncommital, although it did say that the sinking was perfectly justified because the *Lusitania* was armed and carried munitions.[1] To this, a second American note was drafted, denying that the ship was armed and carried explosives and refusing to concede that Germany might violate "the rights of humanity" in retaliation for England's non-observance of property rights; the two violations had nothing in common. Nor was it a valid excuse that the submarine was a new weapon, not covered by the Declaration of London.

Bryan refused to approve this draft and, when the rest of the Cabinet did not support him, he resigned on June 8, to be succeeded by Robert Lansing,

[1] There has been great controversy about whether the *Lusitania* was armed; the most thorough investigator asserts definitely that it was not. The fact is, however, that the submarine captain did not know whether it was armed, nor did he make any effort to find out. And he did break the rules of war by not giving warning. There is no doubt it carried several thousand cases of rifle cartridges, but they were not "explosives" in the terminology of international law.

definitely pro-Ally and certainly less of a pacifist. Then the second note, practically in its original form, was sent to Germany. Again the reply failed to meet the American points, much to the disgust of many citizens such as Roosevelt, who believed there should be less writing and more fighting.[2]

The "Arabic" Promise

Fruitless notes were still being exchanged over the *Lusitania* incident when the British *Arabic* was sunk on August 19, 1915, with the death of two Americans. So belligerent was American opinion that Bernstorff, on his own responsibility, promptly gave the State Department what has been called the *Arabic* pledge: "Liners will not be sunk by our submarines without warning and without safety of the lives of non-combatants, provided that the liners do not try to escape or offer resistance." Even though subsequently reprimanded for his promise, he succeeded in temporarily quieting American opposition. When the State Department renewed its protests of the violations of the "rights of humanity," Bethmann-Hollweg expressed regret for the *Arabic* sinking, promised an indemnity, and assured the United States that such stringent orders had been given to submarine captains "that a recurrence of incidents similar to the *Arabic* case is considered out of the question."

Wilson regarded the *Arabic* pledge as a victory for his note-writing diplomacy. The war spirit quickly died down; even the belligerent Roosevelt called the result "most gratifying." And Wilson could write toward the close of September: "The country is undoubtedly back of me in the whole matter." Yet Germany still had not admitted that search must precede an attack upon a merchant vessel not trying to resist, nor that such an attack must not cause death or injury to neutral citizens. Moreover, the American contention had been pressed to the point where the United States could hardly avoid drastic steps were German sinkings resumed.

The House-Grey Memorandum

Wilson still hoped to be a peacemaker. Encouraged by certain statements by Sir Edward Grey in the early fall of 1915, he sent Colonel House to find out whether the Allies were ready for a peace based upon justice. If they were, Wilson would send invitations to a peace meeting. If Germany accepted the olive branch and, at a subsequent conference, an accord were reached, hostilities would end, prewar boundaries would be re-established, and future peace assured through disarmament and a league of nations.

House set out on this "great adventure" in December, 1915, and for the next two and a half months he conferred with British, French, and German officials. His Berlin reception, none too cordial, convinced him that Germany

2 In February, 1916, Germany did agree to pay indemnity for the American losses in the *Lusitania* sinking, thereby admitting her liability. But since this offer was not accompanied by a statement that the act was illegal, Wilson refused to accept its adequacy. Therefore the affair was still unsettled when the United States entered the war.

did not favor a peace satisfactory either to the Allies or to Wilson. In Paris, he found the government noncommittal, largely because of the belief Germany would never submit to Allied wishes. In London, however, after lengthy sessions, Grey and House agreed on February 22, 1916, to the famous House-Grey Memorandum, the heart of which was:

> President Wilson was ready to propose that a Conference should be summoned to put an end to the war. Should the Allies accept this proposal and should Germany refuse it, the United States would probably enter the war against Germany.
> If such a Conference met, it would secure peace on terms not unfavorable to the Allies; and, if it failed to secure peace, the United States would leave the Conference as a belligerent on the side of the Allies, if Germany were unreasonable. . . .

Wilson approved the memorandum with one significant amendment: he inserted the word *probably* before the statement that in case Germany were unreasonable, the United States would leave the meeting as a belligerent. Wilson hoped the Allies would now support his peace move, but even the assurance that the United States might enter the war was not tangible enough to induce the British to act upon the proposal.

The Gore-McLemore Resolutions

Although Congress was unaware of the House-Grey negotiations, some members believed Wilson was planning to bring the nation into war. Moreover, some Democratic leaders were disposed to challenge Wilson's leadership in anticipation of the 1916 election; if they forced the President to reveal his policy toward the war, they might make a strong case against him with the voters.

While numerous resolutions concerning control of munitions makers, embargoes on armaments exports, and the like were introduced, the real fight was staged over the so-called Gore-McLemore Resolutions. On the premise that the loss of American lives on belligerent ships might bring the nation into war, the anti-Wilson faction insisted American citizens be barred from such travel. On January 5, 1916, Democratic Senator Thomas Gore of Oklahoma proposed to deny passports to citizens contemplating sailing on belligerent-owned ships; several days later he added the principle that American noncontraband must be fully protected on the high seas. While the Upper House discussed these propositions, Representative Jeff McLemore of Texas was working on a similar proposal to forbid Americans from traveling on armed belligerent ships.

The President vigorously opposed these resolutions because they would restrict the neutral rights for which he had been struggling and because a defeat on this issue would undermine his leadership. On the other hand, many Congressmen, especially Democrats, were just as insistent that the resolutions be passed. By mid-February it appeared Wilson might be defeated, but he still had a strong string to his bow. In conference with the party leaders and in letters to key men in Congress, he made the defeat of the resolutions a matter of party loyalty. One letter specifically explained the President's position:

I shall do everything in my power to keep the United States out of war. I think the country will feel no uneasiness about my course in that respect. . . . But in any event our duty is clear. No nation, no group of nations, has the right . . . to alter or disregard the principles which all nations have agreed upon in mitigation of the horrors and sufferings of war; and if the clear rights of American citizens should ever unhappily be abridged . . . we should . . . have in honor no choice as to what our own course should be. . . . We covet peace, and we shall preserve it at any cost but the loss of honor. . . .

As a result of these efforts, the Senate rejected the Gore-McLemore proposals by 68 to 14, and the House by 276 to 142. The disappointed Gore then tried to force the administration's hand by resolving that when American lives were lost as a result of submarine action without warning, war should be declared. The President, still in the driver's seat, had this proposal tabled.

The "Sussex" Pledge

Scarcely had this home opposition been stilled when the unarmed French *Sussex* was torpedoed without warning in the English Channel on March 24, 1916. Although the ship limped into port, a number of lives were lost and many passengers, including several Americans, were injured. Secretary Lansing promptly advocated an immediate rupture of diplomatic relations with Germany.

Wilson refused to take this action, but he did warn Bernstorff that a break would come unless Germany mended her ways. When Germany explained that the submarine captain claimed he had attacked a war vessel, Wilson declared this was a "direct untruth" and sent the first *Sussex* note on April 18. After calling the submarine attacks the "most terrible examples of . . . inhumanity," it warned that unless Germany abandoned "its present methods of submarine warfare against passenger and freight-carrying vessels, the Government of the United States can have no other choice but to sever relations with the German Government altogether." Although this would be done "with the greatest reluctance," it would be a necessary step "in behalf of humanity and the rights of neutral nations."

Germany, anxious to keep the United States at peace, replied on May 4 that she would do her "utmost to confine the operation of the war for the rest of its duration to the fighting forces of the belligerents." No more merchantmen would be sunk without warning or without an effort to save lives unless such ships resisted or tried to escape. Before this pledge became operative, however, Britain must end her restrictions upon neutrals; otherwise Germany "would then be facing a new situation in which it must reserve [to] itself complete liberty of decision."

Wilson was not satisfied with Germany's apparent change of heart. He insisted that American rights be respected by Germany regardless of what other countries did. "Responsibility in such matters," he concluded, "is single, not joint; absolute, not relative." Since Germany made no reply, Wilson assumed she would keep the *Sussex* pledge, temporarily at least, without the proviso. The war spirit again faded as no more American lives or property were lost until the following year, and relations with Germany perceptibly improved during the remainder of 1916.

The Preparedness Struggle

From the beginning of hostilities, Americans had been sharply divided on how the United States could best avoid involvement. Some thought it best not to supply the belligerents with war materials; others considered that the preventive was to work for mediation between the antagonists to bring an early peace. Still another group felt America should turn the other cheek to belligerent infractions of neutral rights and to various insults. And another element believed preparedness was the best method of avoiding war because other powers would think twice before antagonizing a strong United States. These conflicting points of view were vigorously debated during the early days of the war.

Numerous organizations were devoting their energies against war when World War I broke out, notably the Carnegie Endowment for International Peace and the World Peace Foundation. The number of such peace societies grew after hostilities started. In addition to the American Society for the Judicial Settlement of Disputes, the American School Peace League, and the Church Peace Union, there were the Women's Peace Party, with Jane Addams and Carrie Chapman Catt as sponsors, the Anti-Militarist League, backed chiefly by the colleges, and the National Peace Council. The majority of these societies were fully loyal and patriotic. Not all were against preparedness, but preparedness must be aimed at keeping the country out of war. That might be difficult, however, because an increased army and navy could promote a martial spirit among Americans; or belligerents, seeing America arming, might attack before preparedness was complete. Therefore, the best course was to keep preparedness at a minimum and concentrate upon mediation between warring groups.

In another category was the American Embargo Congress, supported by pro-German sympathizers, which tried to influence Congress to ban shipments of munitions and supplies to the belligerents. Germany would be helped were the United States to remain neutral, and the more Americans were influenced to join any peace organization, the less would be the chance that the United States might join the Allies.

Considerable publicity attended the mediation efforts of Henry Ford, who was convinced that "the fighting nations are sick of war." He chartered the Scandinavian liner *Oscar II* and set out for Europe in December, 1915, to "get the boys out of the trenches before Christmas." The sixty delegates who went along were a heterogeneous group, and the accompanying newspapermen had a field day poking fun at the "Peace Ship." Although Ford's motives could not be questioned, the movement, needless to say, did not accomplish its objectives and served only to hurt later peace projects.

The outstanding pacifist was William Jennings Bryan, particularly after he left the State Department. In speeches and in the columns of his paper, the *Commoner,* he preached the folly of both war and preparedness. He hurt his case, however, by becoming more bitter with the passage of time—and thus less convincing. Moreover, by unwittingly playing into the hands of the pro-German elements, he exposed himself to charges of disloyalty.

On the other hand, the first prominent advocate of preparedness as an anti-war measure was Henry Cabot Lodge's son-in-law, Congressman Augustus Gardner of Massachusetts. On October 15, 1914, he asked Congress to form a National Security Commission to determine how close the army and navy were to war strength. He warned that the United States was totally unprepared to defend itself and that the belligerents might some day attack America. The legislature refused to approve this project, but Gardner kept the plan alive with his frequent public appeals and by helping to establish preparedness organizations.

Two of the earliest such agencies were the National Security League and the American Legion, Incorporated, both promoted by General Leonard Wood and Theodore Roosevelt. The League's chief objective was to "insure for the nation an adequate system of national defense." The American Legion organized a military training program and advocated the enrollment of a variety of specialists like engineers, automobile drivers, and telegraph operators. Thus several hundred thousand trained volunteers would be ready in case of attack; if war did not materialize, they could be used to prevent sabotage.

Backed by many prominent Americans, Wood started his plan for voluntary military training for businessmen in Plattsburg, New York, in the summer of 1915. At the outset this was a small-scale project attracting only about 1,200 men, but the following summer some 12,000 men were trained in four camps. Even so, the Plattsburg plan touched only a small number of Americans and never gained Wilson's support.

Meantime, Roosevelt, tired of what he called Wilson's milk-and-water policy, became the President's outstanding critic and the most vigorous preparedness advocate. In January, 1915, he explained the need for adequate defense in *America and the World War,* and followed the next year with *Fear God and Take Your Own Part,* in which he decried the folly of turning the other cheek. This thesis was also upheld by Frederick Huldekoper in *The Military Unpreparedness of the United States,* who pointed out that in past wars many American soldiers had needlessly been slaughtered because they lacked military training.

Because Wilson at first believed the preparedness movement might weaken America's role as potential peacemaker, he opposed the efforts of the National Security League. In a speech to Congress in December, 1914, Wilson said: "We shall not alter our attitude . . . because some amongst us are nervous and excited. Such a change would merely mean that we had lost our self-possession." He continued to place national reliance upon a "citizenry trained and accustomed to arms," rather than on a large standing army. The navy should be a medium of defense, not of attack. Thus without executive approval, military appropriations were kept at the low prewar level.

As the war progressed, however, the President gradually changed his position. With American rights increasingly denied on the high seas, perhaps the preparedness advocates were correct in believing that armed force would do the most good in upholding international law. By May, 1915, Wilson was talking about improving national defense, but it was not until the end of that year that he asked Congress for larger appropriations for the army and navy, as well as increased control over the merchant marine. The President insisted he was not seeking war, for "we regard war merely as a means of asserting the rights of a people against aggression. . . . But we do believe in a body of free citizens ready and sufficient to take care of themselves. . . . At least so much by way of preparation for defense seems to me to be absolutely imperative now."

The First Preparedness Measures

To test the popularity of his new thesis and in anticipation of the 1916 election, Wilson made a series of speeches in key cities, especially in the Middle West, during January and February, 1916. Important sentences from some of his addresses were: "We must be ready . . . upon the shortest possible notice . . ."; "This country should prepare herself, not for war . . . but for adequate national defense"; we must build "a great navy second to none in the world." The enthusiastic reception, even in the supposedly antiwar Middle West, convinced Wilson he must press for preparedness legislation without delay.

Consequently, early in March, 1916, there were introduced in both houses similar bills to increase the armed forces. Delayed by disagreement over details but aided by Villa's raids on American territory, the Hay or National Defense Act of June, 1916, provided for a gradual increase in the regular army from the existing 90,000 to a minimum of 175,000 and a maximum of 220,000 men; federalization of the National Guard, to be built up to a complement of 400,000; establishment of officers' reserve corps; and compulsory training for high school and college youths over the age of sixteen. General support of the Hay Act was demonstrated by the numerous preparedness-day parades throughout the land.

With this successful opening wedge, several other preparedness measures were soon passed. On August 29, 1916, the Naval Construction Act appropriated more than $500 million during the next three years to build at least five battle cruisers, together with numerous lesser craft. About a week later, Congress, after nearly two years of debate, established the United States Shipping Board, with power to lease, buy, build, and operate merchant ships through an Emergency Fleet Corporation.

The Adamson Act

The preparedness campaign carried the national government much further than ever into the field of labor relations. In March, 1916, the four railway brotherhoods sought an eight-hour day and additional overtime pay. When the operators refused to agree and likewise failed to arbitrate the differences, the unions scheduled a strike to begin on Labor Day. The government, fearful lest the proposed walkout tie up national transportation facilities and thereby delay the preparedness program, tried to settle the controversy through the Board of Mediation and Conciliation established under the

Newlands Act of 1913, but without success. Wilson also failed to persuade the operators to grant the eight-hour day, which, he said, had "the sanction of the judgment of society in its favor."

Consequently, he went before Congress on August 29, explained the gravity of the situation, and quickly obtained passage of the Adamson Act four days later. This statute guaranteed union members the working day they sought, although overtime pay was to be prorated. Furthermore, a fact-finding commission was to consider overhauling the ICC and the Newlands Act. This measure satisfied the brotherhoods, who called off the strike. The President was widely criticized by business for surrendering to the threats of labor, but Wilson felt justified in order to keep preparedness rolling and to prevent an embarrassing strike during his presidential campaign.

The Campaign of 1916

Even while Congress was passing these measures, the presidential campaign of 1916 was getting well under way. Wilson's election in 1912 had been possible only because of the split in Republican ranks. Now, however, the Progressives had little vitality except as they drew upon that of the dynamic Theodore Roosevelt—and his interest in quixotic politics rapidly subsided. Much though the former President hated the Republican Old Guard, he detested Wilson more. The congressional elections of 1914 had clearly shown that the Progressive party was dying; some supporters went over to the Democrats and others returned to the Republican fold.

During the next two years the Progressive disintegration continued. Roosevelt was still the party's idol, but he wanted no three-way contest such as had led to Wilson's victory in 1912. He hoped rather that the split might be healed and that he would be triumphantly returned to the White House as the candidate of both the Republicans and Progressives. But the still bitter Old Guard wanted the Progressive vote without the Progressive hero. Another obstacle confronting Roosevelt was that no man in America was hated more by the German-Americans, whose votes were needed to beat Wilson.

What the Republicans required was a candidate who had not bolted, but whose record, nevertheless, was sufficiently liberal to attract the Progressives. He must not have alienated the German vote, yet he could not be open to the charge of being pro-German. Automatically ruled out were such men as ex-President Taft, Elihu Root, and Henry Cabot Lodge. The field, in fact, soon reduced itself to one—Justice Charles Evans Hughes of the Supreme Court. Hughes had first gained prominence in 1905 by his fearless investigation of insurance company scandals in New York; from 1907 to 1910 he had been a successful governor of that state. This part of his record would appeal to liberals. On the other hand, conservative Republicans noted with approval that Hughes had been appointed to the Supreme Court by Taft in 1910, that he had been a sound judge, and that his judical position had prevented his taking any stand in the party quarrel of 1912. Both conservative Republicans and German-Americans noted with distinct satisfaction one final fact about Hughes—it was common knowledge that Roosevelt did not like him.

Early in June, 1916, the Republicans and Progressives held their separate conventions in Chicago. The younger party marked time to see whether the Republicans would accept Roosevelt after all, but the voting soon demonstrated Hughes's strength and he was nominated on the third ballot. The brief platform denounced the Democratic administration for failing to protect the rights of American citizens, especially in Mexico, stressed the need for preparedness, and attacked both the Underwood Tariff and the merchant marine program.

The Progressives then nominated Roosevelt on a platform that repeated the slogans of 1912 and attacked Wilson's foreign policy, while demanding military and naval preparedness. But the party the Rough Rider had created was killed by its own parent. Roosevelt declined the nomination and announced his support of Hughes too late for the convention to name another candidate. The Progressive National Committee, by a divided vote, then endorsed Hughes and adjourned, never to meet again. Most Progressives returned to the Republican fold.

The Democratic convention, assembling later in June in St. Louis, proved a triumph for the President. Not only was he renominated by a vote of 1092 to 1, but the platform was largely his handiwork. It pointed with pride to the legislation passed by two Democratic Congresses and acclaimed the adminstration's patient Mexican policy. It praised American neutrality, and proclaimed the duty of the United States to join an association of nations.

Because Wilson believed there was "disloyalty active in the United States" that "must be absolutely crushed," he wanted to campaign on a ringing assertion of Americanism linked with a denunciation of "hyphenism"—the divided loyalty of some German-Americans and others of recent foreign stock. Events in St. Louis, however, proved the greater popularity of a different slogan. In his keynote speech, Martin Glynn of New York remarked: "In particular we commend to the American people the splendid diplomatic victories of our great President, who has preserved the vital interests of our Government and its citizens, and kept us out of war." The delegates gave their enthusiastic approval and it was obvious that Wilson's strongest political asset was his success in keeping the country insulated from the world conflagration. As a summary of the President's past policy, the slogan "He kept us out of war" was true; yet it was a dangerous guarantee for the future. Wilson had already said: "I can't keep the country out of war. . . . Any little German lieutenant can put us into war at any time by some calculated outrage."

The campaign itself was more notable for colorful incidents than for the quality of debate on the issues. Several incidents involved the hyphenate problem. Radical Irish- and German-Americans claimed credit for persuading the New Jersey Democratic voters to renominate Senator Martine in September despite Wilson's opposition. Jeremiah O'Leary, head of the rabid Anglophobe organization known as the American Truth Society, sent an exuberant telegram to the President:

Senator Martine won because the voters of New Jersey do not want any truckling to the British Empire nor do they approve of dictatorship over Congress. Your foreign policies, your failure to secure compliance with all American rights, your leniency with the British Empire, your approval of war loans, the ammunition traffic, are issues in this campaign.

Wilson's reply was immediate and crushing:

> I would feel deeply mortified to have you or anybody like you vote for me. Since you have access to many disloyal Americans and I have not, I will ask you to convey this message to them.

This O'Leary incident captured headlines throughout the country, and the Democratic National Committee sought to capitalize further on it by charging that Hughes had made a deal with the wicked O'Leary and a group of his followers. Hughes admitted he had met O'Leary, but denied he had promised him anything. The *New York Times,* supporting Wilson, chortled: "A few days ago who would have suspected in the bustling Jeremiah O'Leary the successor, as a candidate slayer, of the grave and reverend Burchard?"

Hughes's campaign was full of other embarrassments. His speeches, vigorously critical of the President, were vague as to any alternative policy. His cautious dealing with the submarine issue was in sharp contrast with the fiery speeches of Roosevelt, who likened Wilson to Pontius Pilate, and then apologized to Pilate. Roosevelt's language dismayed the Irish and German groups working for Hughes, and Bernstorff said that Germany had more to lose than to gain in a Republican victory.

The costliest blunder was committed in California, where Hughes shunned Governor Hiram Johnson, the Progressive vice-presidential candidate in 1912, who was now running for the United States Senate. Therefore Johnson made no effort to have his own followers support Hughes. When the ballots were counted in November, Johnson carried the state by almost 300,000 while Hughes was losing it by 4,000.

The first editions of the newspapers on the morning after election announced that Hughes had won, for he had carried all the large Eastern states, as well as the strategic Midwestern states of Illinois, Indiana, and Michigan. To win all these and yet lose the election seemed impossible, but Hughes did it. To Wilson went the Solid South, plus Maryland, New Hampshire, and Ohio; the balance of power proved to be the states west of the Mississippi, all of which the President carried except Oregon, Iowa, South Dakota, and Minnesota. After several days of uncertainty, the final electoral vote gave Wilson 277 to 254 for Hughes; the popular vote showed Wilson with 9.1 million and Hughes with 8.5 million.

The defeat of Hughes obviously depended on other factors than the snub of Johnson. Had he carried Ohio or Kansas, he could have afforded to lose California. The general weakness of his campaign was that it depended on appealing both to those who desired a more genuine neutrality than Wilson offered and to those who were pro-Ally. On domestic issues also Hughes was unconvincing. Wilson, on the other hand, had the support of labor, which liked the Adamson Act, and of the farmers, grateful for the Farm Loan Bank Act. Furthermore, women, now voting in most Western states, were particularly responsive to "He kept us out of war." The effect of the O'Leary incident is not clear; Wilson's condemnation of hyphenism probably won him many votes, but he lost the six states (New York, Pennsylvania, New Jersey, Massachusetts, Connecticut, and Illinois) that had the largest number of Irish votes.

The Democrats, with 53 seats, maintained control of the Senate, but the House went Republican, 216 to 210. Enough of the nine independents, holding the balance of power, allied with the Democrats to re-elect Champ Clark as House Speaker.

The Appeal for Peace

It was after his re-election that Wilson made his most vigorous effort to act as peacemaker or mediator. One reason was that Germany, in an apparent change of heart, had announced during the summer of 1916 that she was ready to ask the President to call a peace conference. More important was Wilson's realization that the longer the war lasted, the more difficult American neutrality would become; indeed, during the campaign he had said that "this is the last war . . . that involves the world that the United States can keep out of. . . . I mean this, that war now has such a scale that the position of neutrals sooner or later becomes intolerable." He had also privately informed Colonel House that unless peace were soon restored, America would "inevitably drift into war with Germany upon the submarine issue."

On December 18, 1916, Wilson asked each belligerent government to state the specific terms upon which it would agree to end hostilities and what it would require for future security. The responses were anything but satisfactory. The Allied reply of January 10, 1917, placed all the blame for the war on the Central Powers and insisted that the peace settlement must protect Europe from another outbreak of such "brutal covetousness." To do this the Central Powers must be deprived of all lands they had conquered and the peoples they had enslaved must be liberated.

Despite Germany's earlier interest in peace negotiations, she now refused to state any specific terms. Perhaps she was concerned about Lansing's tactless statement that the dispatch of Wilson's invitations "will indicate the possibility of our being forced into the war." Perhaps it was because Wilson's mediation would prevent the annexations she desired. At any event, Germany announced she would deal only with Allied delegates in some neutral European city free from "American indiscreetness and intermeddling."

Faced with this situation, Wilson reacted in a way completely characteristic of his own conception of democratic leadership. His carefully prepared address to the Senate on January 22, 1917, was really a direct appeal to the peoples of the warring nations over the heads of their governments. He took it for granted, he said, that mere terms of peace between the belligerents would not satisfy them for long. Any lasting peace must be " a peace without victory. . . . Victory would mean peace forced upon a loser, a victor's peace imposed upon the vanquished. . . . Only a peace between equals can last." Also a durable peace must be based upon the principles of government by the consent of the governed, freedom of the sea, and disarmament. Most important of all, "peace must be followed by some concert of powers which will make it virtually impossible that any such catastrophe should ever overwhelm us again." And such a league must include the United States, for otherwise it would not be sufficiently strong.

By many critics this is considered the greatest of Wilson's public papers— a message of prophetic power that, had it been heeded, might have saved the people of the world from untold suffering. But, despite the heartfelt American approval and that of liberals even in the belligerent nations, the speech was widely denounced. Several leading Republicans attacked bitterly American participation in a league of nations. The phrase "peace without victory" greatly offended the Allies. Government by consent of the governed seemed dangerous to the Central Powers. But the President did not give up his efforts; he renewed pressure on Germany to state the terms on which it would be willing to end the war.

End of the "Sussex" Pledge

Germany, however, wanted peace only on her own terms. As January, 1917, progressed, her military leaders were won over by the admirals to favor ruthless submarine warfare. Consequently, the Kaiser ordered "that the unrestricted submarine warfare be launched with the greatest vigor on the 1st of February." The German authorities realized this step would most probably bring the United States into the war on the Allied side, but the risk had to be chanced. Some Germans even believed America would remain neutral, for had not the voters given a mandate in the recent election to stay out of war? But were that mandate broken, the assistance the United States could give the Allies over and above what she had already furnished in the way of supplies and loans would, according to German military leaders, "amount to nothing." On the other hand, ruthless submarine warfare would soon bring England to her knees and the Allied cause would be lost.

Not until January 31 did Bernstorff hand Lansing a brusque note: after February 1, Germany would forcibly prevent all navigation, that of neutrals included, in a zone around Britain, France, and Italy. All ships in that zone would be sunk on sight. As a concession to the United States, however, one American steamer, not carrying contraband, might sail to and from Falmouth, England, each week, provided three "vertical stripes, one meter wide," alternately red and white, were painted on the hull; furthermore, that ship must fly a red-and white checkered flag fore and aft, it must be lighted at night and follow a course mapped out by Germany. To indignant Americans, this patronizing concession seemed the ultimate in insult.

Wilson's answer was to appear before Congress on February 3 to announce the severance of all diplomatic relations with Germany. Yet, he added, "I refuse to believe it is the intention of the German authorities to do in fact what they have warned us they will feel at liberty to do. . . . Only actual overt acts on their part can make me believe it even now." Should such acts occur, however, Wilson would ask authority necessary "for the protection of our seamen and our people." The Senate quickly endorsed his action by a vote of 78 to 5.

Armed Neutrality

Although the only two American ships sunk in February were given warning so that no lives were lost, American shipping was badly demoralized. Many vessels remained in port, and the demand was made that navy guns and gunners be provided for their protection. At first Wilson opposed, for such a step would obviously bring war closer.

Just at this critical moment, the President learned of an act of intrigue that more than any other single thing destroyed his faith in German good intentions. In mid-January, 1917, German Foreign Minister Alfred Zimmermann had sent a coded message to the German minister in Mexico telling of the decision to resume unrestricted submarine warfare. If war with the United States resulted, the minister was to propose an alliance with Mexico on the following terms: the two countries should make war and peace together; Germany would give Mexico financial support; and Mexico would use the war against the United States "to reconquer the lost territory in New Mexico, Texas, and Arizona." The Zimmermann note further proposed "that the President of Mexico . . . should communicate with Japan suggesting adherence at once to this plan; at the same time offer to mediate between Germany and Japan."

British intelligence had intercepted the message when it left Germany, but had shrewdly refrained from giving it to American officials until German-American relations neared a breaking point. On February 25, Wilson received the note; the next day he sought congressional approval to arm American merchantmen. To bolster his request, he made public the note, which immediately contributed to the war spirit. Although some Americans insisted the note was a British forgery, the possibility was ruled out when Zimmermann admitted his authorship.

Despite Wilson's personal appeal and the militant mood of the country, the armed ship bill did not become law. True, the House passed it by a vote of 403 to 14, but in the Senate eleven legislators, headed by LaFollette and Norris, successfully filibustered to prevent the measure from coming to a vote before Congress adjourned on March 4. The President bitterly condemned these obstructionists as "a little group of willful men, representing no opinion but their own" who "have rendered the great Government of the United States helpless and contemptible." Consequently, much against his original wish but because of the need for speedy action, Wilson on March 12 ordered the arming of merchant ships on his own responsibility, using as his authority a statute originally passed in 1797.

By this time most American opinion was demanding more drastic action, for news of the sinking of several American ships, mostly without warning, and the resultant loss of American lives, brought the nation to a fighting pitch. Just at that moment the dramatic information came that the Russian people had forced the abdication of the Tsar and established a constitutional government. America emphatically approved; indeed, the United States was the first to recognize the new regime. The event also clarified the issues of the war; now the Allied cause appeared to be truly that of democracy struggling against absolutism. No one felt this more keenly than did Wilson, who said: "If our entering the war would hasten and fix the movements in Russia and Germany, it would be a marked gain to the world and would tend to give additional justification to the whole struggle."

With these two developments—the sinking of more American ships and the Russian Revolution—Wilson at last concluded that America must enter the war. To make doubly sure he was right, he called a special Cabinet meeting on March 20, and, without telling the members his own position, he asked them what should be done. With but little discussion, they quickly recommended a declaration of war against Germany. Immediately the President called the new Congress into special session because of "grave questions of national policy."

Since this could mean but one thing—war—it was an impressive assembly that Wilson faced in the House on the evening of April 2. There were the Justices of the Supreme Court, the Cabinet officials, and the diplomatic corps, while other distinguished visitors crowded the galleries. After the Representatives had taken their seats, the Senators filed in, most of them wearing or carrying little American flags.

Wilson's address was worthy of the occasion. First, he reviewed the history of the submarine controversy, stressing "the wanton and wholesale destruction of the lives of non-combatants, men, women, and children, engaged in pursuits which have always, even in the darkest periods of modern history, been deemed innocent and legitimate." Next, he asked Congress to declare the recent course of the Imperial German Government to be in fact nothing less than war against the government and people of the United States and that it formally accept the status of belligerent. Then followed an eloquent statement of America's war objectives. With the German people, Wilson asserted, the United States had no quarrel; it was not upon their impulse that their government had acted in entering the war. The United States would fight for the ultimate peace of the world and for the liberation of its peoples, the Germans included, "The world must," he said, "be made safe for democracy." After admitting that it was a fearful thing to lead a peaceful people into war, he concluded with these stirring words:

> But the right is more precious than peace, and we shall fight for the things which we have always carried nearest to our hearts—for democracy, for the right of those who submit to authority to have a voice in their own Governments, for the rights and liberties of small nations, for a universal dominion of right by such a concert of free peoples as shall bring peace and safety to all nations and make the world itself at last free. To such a task we can dedicate our lives and our fortunes, everything that we are and everything that we have, with the pride of those who know that the day has come when America is privileged to spend her blood and her might for the principles that gave her birth and happiness and the peace which she has treasured. God helping her, she can do no other.

The President's address was frequently interrupted by wild applause; there was no question that Congress and the country would follow his leadership. By the morning of April 6, Congress had approved the declaration of war, the Senate by a vote of 82 to 6, the House by 373 to 50.

Why America Fought

In later years much was said and written about why the United States went to war in 1917. One school of thought held that Americans had been tricked by British propaganda; another, that bankers and munitions-makers were responsible in order to save the money they had loaned the Allies and to make bigger profits; and a third, that Wilson, wanting war from the beginning, had deliberately adopted policies to bring about this result. There has been, however, no real substantiation for any of these theories. Instead, the conclusion is inescapable that it was the submarine issue that was decisive. Had not the German government resumed unrestricted submarine warfare, the United States might easily have remained neutral; but with that German decision, there was nothing honorable left for Wilson to do except ask for war, particularly after the stand he had taken in the *Sussex* affair. Only through war, Wilson believed, could the United States maintain the long-cherished doctrine of freedom of the seas.

A more effective criticism of Wilson is that, although he really desired to keep his country out of the war, he followed policies that defeated his purpose. According to Senator LaFollette in the debate on the declaration of war, the Democratic administration made a fatal mistake. It had "assumed and acted upon the policy that it could enforce to the very letter of the law the principles of international law against one belligerent and relax them to the other." No nation could do this without losing the rights that went with "strict and absolute neutrality."

In the final analysis the question to be answered is this: Was World War I a struggle of such character that the United States could afford the kind of "strict and absolute neutrality" that LaFollette was thinking about? Such neutrality might have resulted in a crushing defeat of Britain and France and so resounding a victory for the Central Powers that the German military caste would have been encouraged to seek further triumphs. Would such an outcome to the war have been desirable from the standpoint of American interests? Looking back from our present vantage point, the answer seems obvious. Complete German dominance of Europe, followed as it must inevitably have been by mastery of the Atlantic Ocean, would have created such a new situation in world politics as to affect most seriously the security of the United States. Since this was so, "strict and absolute neutrality" was as unrealistic in the years following 1914 as it was in the years following 1939.[3] Wilson may be criticized for not having stressed the issue more clearly in his war messages. Probably he himself did not see it clearly. It was characteristic of him that he thought and talked more in terms of legal rights and moral principles than in those of national interests.

Once having accepted the idea of war, Wilson stressed the objectives he hoped to gain: the furtherance of democracy, insurance of the rights and liberties of small nations, and the establishment of a league of nations.

---

[3] Many scholars, however, still regard American involvement in World War I as a tragic mistake, since by contributing to total Allied victory Wilson lost the chance of achieving "the peace without victory" of which he had been dreaming. Such critics deny that Germany would necessarily have won if America had remained neutral. The more likely outcome of the war, they believe, would have been a stalemate. This school of thought believes that Wilson could have avoided the pitfalls implicit in his position on submarine warfare if he had simply warned Americans not to travel on belligerent ships.

He assumed that he spoke for the entire nation in stating these war aims, and in the exaltation of the moment it seemed he did. As time went on, however, many Americans, while accepting the necessity of war against Germany, rejected the Wilsonian conception of the ultimate war objectives.

8

THE WAR FOR DEMOCRACY

The United States was now at war, but what did war under such circumstances mean? How did one nation fight another three thousand miles away? Americans both in official positions and in civilian life were not sure, for this was the first major struggle involving the United States that entailed sending military forces outside the Western Hemisphere. Moreover, the navy was still being enlarged, while the National Defense Act of 1916 provided for an army of only 220,000, together with a possible 400,000 national guardsmen. Neither armed branch had had any experience in the modern type of warfare being waged in Europe. Transportation for troops and supplies was inadequate, and the German submarine menace was potent. Perhaps, as Germany believed, the United States would be limited to providing loans and supplies to the Allies. Despite all these difficulties, however, the desperate needs of the hour spurred the nation to greater and greater efforts.

First Aid to the Allies

The navy was thrown into the struggle at once. Indeed, even before the declaration of war, Admiral William Sims had been quietly sent to England; by April, 1917, he was already planning joint operations with the British navy. In May, the first American destroyers reached British waters, gradually to be followed by most of the growing navy. These ships were desperately needed by the English to help destroy enemy submarines, which were sinking several hundred thousand tons of Allied shipping each month.

The Allies were not slow in making other requirements known through the British and French missions sent to the United States within three weeks of the declaration of war. Their first need was money. The British had served as Allied bankers for almost three years, but now they were hard pressed for further assets to purchase food and munitions. Anticipating the requests of these missions, Congress had already passed the Emergency Loan Act, authorizing the issuance of $5 billion worth of bonds bearing 3.5 per cent interest. Three billion of this amount might be loaned to nations "engaged in war with the enemies of the United States." Many more loans—to a total of $7 billion—were to follow during the next year and a half, not only to England and France, but to Italy, Russia, Yugoslavia, and Cuba as well. The borrowers spent most of the money in the United States for products of American factories and farms.

Naval support, money, and goods—these the United States could obviously contribute to the campaign against the Central Powers, but most observers in April, 1917, felt this was about all the nation could do. It seemed fantastic to believe that America could create a large army, train it, equip it, and transport it across three thousand miles of submarine-infested waters to the western front. Yet such an army was needed, for the French were dangerously weary of war and their burdens appeared too heavy to be borne much longer. During the visit of the French war mission, Marshal Joseph Joffre appealed for at least an American token force to stiffen sagging morale.

As early as May 8, 1917, President Wilson and Secretary of War Newton Baker responded to this appeal by naming General John Pershing to command the proposed American Expeditionary Force. On June 26, the first American regiments, numbering 14,500 men, landed at St. Nazaire, France. While this handful received a joyous welcome, it was not sufficient to enable the Allies, weakened by three years of war, to launch a winning offensive. Concluding that only a large-scale American intervention could break the stalemate and crush the enemy, Pershing informed the War Department on July 6 that plans "should contemplate sending over one million men" by the spring of 1918, with additional millions to follow. In short, the impossible would have to be accomplished.

Raising an Army

Although sending a million soldiers to France was a new and breath-taking project, the idea that war would require a greatly enlarged army for national defense was not. When war was declared, the General Staff advocated immediate conscription, and both Wilson and Baker concurred at once, for they believed that in a democracy the obligation for military service should be universal. Furthermore, they knew the difficulties involved in recruiting as a result of the recent experiences of the British, who had depended on volunteers during the first years of the war. The greatest weakness of the system had been not that it failed to bring in enough recruits into the armed forces, but that all too often it brought the wrong men, or the right men at the wrong time. Manpower was wasted as volunteers gave up vital production jobs, or as fine potential officer material left school to serve as privates and to become an appallingly large proportion of the early war casualties. As a result of this British experience, Wilson said: "The idea of a selective draft is that those should be chosen . . . who can be most readily spared from the prosecution of the other activities which the country must engage in and to which it must devote a great deal of its best energy and capacity."

The Selective Service Bill, introduced in April, 1917, was based on the principle that the draft should be administered by public-spirited civilians serving in their own communities. Despite this suggested democratic machinery, the bill was not passed without a struggle. Speaker Champ Clark bluntly stated that "in the estimation of Missourians there is precious little difference between a conscript and a convict," while the Democratic chairman of the House Military Affairs Committee vigorously opposed the measure. One controversial point concerned the age limits for registrants; the War Department preferred men from nineteen to twenty-five; Congress, rebelling at drafting youths too young to vote, placed the limits at twenty-one to thirty.

The most bitter issue involved an amendment proposed by admirers of Theodore Roosevelt, which would have made it mandatory to accept volunteer units under their own officers. This project reflected the patriotic ambitions of the ex-President to raise a division of volunteers similar to the Rough Riders of 1898. The idea was enthusiastically supported by many Americans, but the army was thoroughly opposed. Modern warfare was for professionals; to commission a civilian to command an expeditionary force would be a dangerous precedent. Therefore Congress left the President at liberty to accept or reject volunteer units.

The Selective Service Bill finally became law on May 12, 1917. Without further delay the President settled the Roosevelt issue by declaring that this was "not the time for compliment or for any action not calculated to contribute to the immediate success of the war." Many critics attributed his action to petty jealousy and partisanship. Similar accusations were made when General Leonard Wood was not given active command in France; but here again civilian army heads were basing their policy upon professional advice. Pershing was chosen for the European command because he had had more experience, was younger, and in better health. Given a free hand in selecting his subordinates, Pershing opposed using Wood in any capacity.

June 5, registration day, was awaited with considerable anxiety. Memories of Civil War draft riots haunted some gloomy souls; Senator Reed of Missouri predicted that enforced conscription would cause American cities to run with blood. Nothing of the kind occurred, however, and on the appointed day more than 9.5 million young men received their serial numbers at 4,557 local selective service boards. On July 20, Secretary Baker drew from a large bowl the first serial number—258; the registrants having that number in each local district were to be the first called for classifica-

Selective conscription will pan out well. (From the *Chicago Tribune*.)

tion. The drawing continued until each registrant had been assigned a call number. Eventually all were grouped into five classes, based upon their availability for armed service, their obligation toward dependents, and the degree of importance attached to their civilian occupations. A total of 3,706,544 men were placed in Class I—subject to military duty. Later, when the needs of the services increased, all men between eighteen and forty-five not previously registered were enrolled in September, 1918. All told, 24,234,021 were registered under Selective Service during the war.

Thousands did not wait for the draft, but enlisted in the Regular Army, the National Guard, the Navy, or the Marine Corps. This continued until August 9, 1918, when volunteering was discontinued for all services. On April 2, 1917, just before Wilson's war message, the total number in the armed services was 378,619; on Armistice Day, 1918, the number had grown to 4,791,172.

Training the Armed Forces

Finding the men was comparatively easy, but transforming them into soldiers was immeasurably more difficult. First of all, they had to be housed. In June, 1917, construction was started on sixteen camps—each to be a complete city, equipped to quarter and feed 48,000 recruits. Impatient critics sniffed at the wooden barracks, recreation centers, and modern plumbing. Soldiers pampered with these luxuries, they asserted, would be too soft for battlefield conditions. The experience of other wars, however, had taught that unhealthy training centers might kill more soldiers than enemy bullets. The building of these camps was a miracle of speedy construction. Even so, they were far from completed by September, 1917, when the first men of the new National Army were mobilized. Not all of the first 687,000 draftees were in cantonments by Christmas.

The problem of finding enough instructors to teach the new methods of warfare was difficult. In part it was solved by employing British and French officers, loaned for this purpose. One of the most serious needs was for officers. The process of giving officer training to intelligent civilians had been started under the Plattsburg plan, well before war came. The War Department set up special officer training camps where university students and other carefully selected young men were given intensive three-month courses, after which those found competent were commissioned as second lieutenants.

Economic Mobilization

The Army Appropriation Act of August 29, 1916, had created a Council of National Defense, comprising the Secretaries of War, Navy, Interior, Agriculture, Commerce, and Labor. With advisory powers only, this council was charged with the "coordination of industries and resources for the national security and welfare" and with the "creation of relations which will render possible in time of need the immediate concentration and utilization of the resources of the Nation." To provide this council with essential information, Wilson appointed an Advisory Commission of seven specially qualified experts to serve without compensation: Daniel Willard of the Baltimore and Ohio Railroad, who advised on transportation problems; President Hollis Godfrey of Drexel Institute, engineering and education; Howard Coffin, a leading automotive engineer, manufacturing and munitions; Dr. Franklin Martin, medicine and surgery; Bernard Baruch, a successful Wall Street operator, raw materials; Julius Rosenwald of Sears, Roebuck, supplies; and Samuel Gompers, AFL president, labor relations.

By March, 1917, the commission had developed a considerable organization of experts drawn from varied lines of industry. But in transforming the national economy from a peacetime to a wartime basis, the National Defense Council and its dollar-a-year advisers lacked authority, their advice was often ignored, and the various agencies worked at cross-purposes. Moreover, there was criticism that in counseling the government while still on the payrolls of private corporations, Advisory Commission members were serving two masters, whose interests did not coincide. Gradually more and more work was assumed by new independent administrative bodies, staffed by men who had cut their ties with private business, which in turn were eventually dominated by individual administrators with vast power.

One such independent agency was already in existence when war was declared—the United States Shipping Board, organized in January, 1917, under the chairmanship of William Denman of California, to buy, lease, or build ships and operate them through the Emergency Fleet Corporation. The increasing emphasis placed on expansion of the merchant marine may be measured by the growth of government-supplied capital poured into the enterprise; originally fixed at $50 million, it was increased to nearly $2 billion by October, 1917.

As soon as war was declared, 105 enemy-owned vessels interned in American ports were turned over to the Shipping Board. Although sabotaged by their crews, they were quickly repaired and put in service within a few months. The Emergency Fleet Corporation also commandeered some four hundred ships being constructed in American shipyards, mostly for British and Norwegian buyers.

The necessity of building new ships in large volume led to a bitter controversy between Chairman Denman, who believed wooden ships could be built quickly and cheaply, and General George Goethals of Panama Canal construction fame and now manager of the Emergency Fleet Corporation, who insisted priority be given to steel vessels. Eventually the President replaced both men with Edward Hurley, a Chicago businessman, under whose leadership not only were steel and wooden ships built, but even concrete vessels. Many new shipyards were opened, the largest being at Hog Island, near Philadelphia, and many new ingenious methods to speed construction were devised. Ship design was standardized, many parts were prefabricated in various factories, and the work of the shipyards simplified to the point where it was primarily one of assembly. As a result, by the fall of 1918, 44 steel and 96 wooden ships were coming off the ways each month. Despite these striking achievements, not many new ships actually went into service before the armistice. The most effective work of the Shipping Board was coordinating the use of existing vessels.

A second powerful agency of economic mobilization was the Food Administration. As early as April, 1917, the Council of National Defense created a committee on food supply and prices with Herbert Hoover as chairman. Successful as a mining engineer in the United States, China, and Australia, he was representing extensive business interests in London at the outbreak of the war. Heading a committee organized to aid Americans caught in Europe, Hoover handled the job so effectively that he was placed in charge of the newly created Belgian Relief Commission. Within a few weeks he became a world figure through his success in helping the Belgians without arousing the opposition of either the Allies or the Germans. When the United States abandoned neutrality, however, Hoover had to return to America. His recent experiences made him the ideal man to head the food administration.

Hoover immediately objected to the purely advisory character of his committee. In May, 1917, he was named Food Commissioner and made independent of the Council of National Defense, but he still did not have sufficient legal authority to take the drastic steps he believed necessary. Therefore, in August, 1917, Congress passed the Lever Act, granting unprecedented powers over a broad area of American life. The President could establish controls over food, fuel, and fertilizers, as well as over the machinery and equipment to produce them. A minimum of $2.00 a bushel was fixed for the 1918 wheat crop, with the President to set in advance the minimum price for succeeding years. A striking victory for the anti-liquor forces was included in the section that prohibited the use of food to manufacture "distilled spirits for beverage purposes" or for "malt or vinous liquors." Chief criticism of the Lever Act came from the farmers who claimed it established a "dictatorship"—a result of the administration's subservience to organized labor.

Hoover now became Food Administrator, and his volunteer organization was given legal basis. Much of the agency's activity was educational. Housewives were not subjected to formal rationing, but they were enjoined to use leftovers, to substitute dark bread for white, and to observe wheatless Mondays and Wednesdays, meatless Tuesdays, and porkless Thursdays and Saturdays. The menfolk were exhorted to plant victory gardens even at the sacrifice of the front lawn. The activities of millers were conducted under a strict licensing system, and hoarding and profiteering were severely dealt with. Farmers were encouraged to produce more wheat by fixing its price at $2.20—twenty cents above the minimum guaranteed by the Lever Act. To stabilize the market, a government-owned Grain Corporation was established, soon followed by the Sugar Equalization Board. Increased production and conservation made possible the exportation to the Allied nations of three times the amount of foodstuffs shipped to them prior to 1914.

Another war agency set up under the Lever Act was the Fuel Administration, headed by Harry Garfield, son of a former United States President and himself president of Williams College. The price of coal was fixed sufficiently high to stimulate production and the public was implored to use fuel sparingly. The importance of gasoline was reflected in the ban, enforced by public opinion alone, upon all but essential driving on Sundays.

The fuel problem was closely linked with that of transportation. One of the voluntary organizations under the Council of National Defense had been a Railroads War Board, made up of prominent railroad executives. This agency did much to coordinate the operations of independent lines, and a system of freight priorities expedited the movement of vital supplies. Yet serious problems arose when tremendous quantities of freight, moved to the Atlantic coast for shipment to Europe, could not be unloaded fast enough. As a result, Eastern terminal yards were jammed with full cars while the rest of the country was starved for "empties." Therefore, on December 28, 1917, the President, under the authority of the Army Appropriation Act of 1916, placed the management of all the country's rail lines in the hands of William McAdoo, who was named Director General of the Railroads. McAdoo then operated them as a single consolidated system.

Meantime, these transportation tie-ups had caused thirty-seven ships loaded with munitions to be held up in New York harbor for lack of coal. Before the public became aware of this serious situation, Garfield announced that for five days starting January 18, 1918, all factories east of the Mississippi, except plants making munitions or other essential supplies, were to be closed and that thereafter "heatless Mondays" were to be observed for the next nine weeks. At first denounced as both arbitrary and unnecessary, Garfield's order was soon conceded to be essential for the

And, by ginger, he can play 'em all! But it keeps Uncle Sam busy these days. (By Donahey in the *Cleveland Plain Dealer*.)

success of the war effort. "Daylight saving" was one of the lasting features of Garfield's program to conserve coal and electricity.

Less known to the general public was the work of the War Trade Board, headed by Vance McCormick. A number of laws, culminating in the Trading-with-the-Enemy Act of October, 1917, gave it control over all American exports and imports. Through a system of licenses and blacklisting of firms in neutral countries, the British blockade of Germany was powerfully implemented and each month the economic strangulation of the enemy came closer to fulfillment.

Bernard Baruch: Economic Dictator

Meantime, the need to arm and equip a vast military machine had made the government the most important customer of American industry. The difficulty was that the government contracted for the products of the nation's factories not as a single unit, but through numerous separate and competing agencies. The confusion was increased by the separate purchasing activities of the Allies and by shortages that inevitably developed as one industry bid against another for essential raw materials. After struggling with various expedients, the Council of National Defense finally created the War Industries Board in July, 1917, under the chairmanship of Frank Scott, a Cleveland manufacturer, to set up a system of priorities and fix prices for necessary raw materials.

The War Industries Board had at first merely advisory powers, and neither government purchasing agencies nor businessmen were legally obliged to follow its orders. The need for independent status having become increasingly apparent, in 1918 Bernard Baruch was named chairman and given vast powers, while the board was made directly responsible to the President.

In the end, Baruch's organization served as a clearinghouse to which all government and Allied purchasing bureaus submitted their requirements. The board then planned how these were to be met and which were to be given priority. The search for new sources of critical raw materials led Baruch's lieutenants to survey not only the resources of the United States, but those of the rest of the world. New industrial plants were constructed and existing ones were guided in their conversion from civilian to war production. The country had come under a planned economy, with Baruch wielding the broad powers of an economic dictator.

Continued criticism of governmental inefficiency by Democrats and Republicans alike brought the passage of the Overman Act in May, 1918, which empowered Wilson to reorganize the wartime agencies and consolidate more effectively their functions. Making prompt use of this authority, Wilson met regularly with the Secretaries of War and the Navy and the heads of the six most prominent boards; in effect this group could be considered a war cabinet, which operated more efficiently than had the previous more or less separate agencies.

There were still many disappointments in war production. To create a vast aircraft industry proved much more difficult than was anticipated.

By Armistice Day about 1,100 planes and 32,000 "Liberty" motors had been manufactured, but only 200 of them reached American combat aviators. Not until three months before the armistice were Browning machine guns available in quantities sufficient to equip American troops at the front, while the war was over before American-made artillery appeared in France. In many lines, as in shipping, American production was just beginning to achieve large volume when hostilities ceased. This led to pointed criticism of the administration in both Congress and the press, but to the Germans the wonder was not that the Yankees had produced so little, but that they produced so much. When the Kaiser's generals undertook in later years to explain why the Fatherland lost the war, they gave full credit to American industry, and they uttered the name "Baruch" with regretful awe. Strangely enough, it had remained for the United States—antimilitary in tradition though it was—to develop the organization of "total war."

Labor and the War

One of the country's greatest assets during 1917 and 1918 was the patriotism and loyalty of Samuel Gompers. Not only did the AFL president efficiently combat radical socialists who sought to convince the workers that the war was merely for capitalistic aggrandizement, but he prevented many strikes and allayed the natural uneasiness with which union members saw women and nonunion labor streaming into war plant jobs. The general public, observing Gompers fraternizing with important industrialists of the Council of National Defense, was as much amazed as if the vision of the wolf dwelling with the lamb had suddenly became reality.

On the wage issue, however, labor's patience had definite limits. With the cost of living rising rapidly and the country's wage scale none too generous to begin with, there were demands for pay increases on every side. In taking over the railroads, the government found itself faced with a particularly serious situation. Despite increases during 1916 and 1917, 80 per cent of the railroad employees received $100 a month or less. The government granted substantial raises, not only to meet the rising cost of living, but "to find a just and equitable basis which would outlive the war and which would give a living wage and decent working conditions to every railroad employee." The war had made the government the country's greatest employer, with thousands of workers receiving pay in government-owned shipyards and war plants. Moreover, many private construction companies and factories were working on war contracts on a cost-plus basis. On every hand, payment of higher wages seemed infinitely preferable to serious labor controversy.

Since disputes and strikes still threatened production in many areas, a National War Labor Board was appointed in April, 1918, with ex-President Taft and Frank Walsh, a prominent labor lawyer, as joint chairmen. During the first year this board held more than a thousand hearings and made recommendations when all other methods of settlement had failed. In a few instances where the rulings were ignored, the President used or threatened coercion. Thus the War Department commandeered the Smith and Wesson plant at Springfield, Massachusetts, after noncompliance by its management, and workers at Bridgeport, Connecticut, were threatened with cancellation of their draft deferments for resisting orders of the board.

Other important new agencies were the Labor Policies Board, chaired by Felix Frankfurter, which worked out uniform labor standards for government employees, and the United States Employment Service, which found jobs for 3.7 million men and women.

Where the Money Came From

Waging modern war involved expenditures of money in amounts that seemed fabulous to Americans accustomed to annual peacetime national budgets of less than $750 million. Between July 1, 1917, and June 30, 1920, the outlays of the United States government averaged $12.5 billion each year.

Some prominent citizens believed the war could be financed on a "pay-as-you-go" basis. The American Committee on War Finance advocated such a policy, as did Robert LaFollette in the Senate—largely because it would penalize war manufacturers he suspected of having forced the country into hostilities. Most Americans, however, believed that taxes sufficiently heavy to pay current war bills would paralyze the national economy. Secretary McAdoo eventually recommended that one third of the costs be met by taxation and the remainder by loans. Most businessmen preferred the ratio of taxes to loans to be about one to five—the ratio of Federal financing during the Civil War.

The Revenue Act of 1917 levied excise taxes on nearly everything in sight; in addition to such familiar tax victims as tobacco and alcoholic beverages, the list now included transportation, communication, insurance, automobiles, pianos, phonographs, amusements, jewelry, patent medicines, and even chewing gum. The principal controversy was over rates for income and war profits taxes; no one knew just how much the recipients of large incomes could or should pay. After allowing $1,000 exemption for unmarried persons and $2,000 for heads of families, the final schedule provided for graduated taxes rising from 2 per cent on the lowest taxable income to 67 per cent on those in excess of $2 million. Corporations were taxed 6 per cent of their net incomes, while profits in excess of what was considered normal both on the basis of invested capital and prewar earnings were taxed at rates graduated from 20 to 60 per cent.

Never before had the government laid such heavy taxes directly on individuals and corporations, yet the war machine demanded still more. The Revenue Act of 1918 raised income taxes to 6 per cent on the lowest brackets and to 77 per cent on incomes over $1 million. The corporation tax was doubled, while excess profits were subjected to an 80 per cent level in the highest bracket.

Meantime, the government was borrowing from its own citizens in amounts hitherto deemed impossible by practical financiers. When the first Liberty Loan drive was being planned, J. P. Morgan advised $1 billion as the goal, but the optimistic McAdoo sought twice that amount. When the books were closed on this loan, the McAdoo quota was oversubscribed by more than $1 billion. Succeeding loans were equally successful and the four Liberty Loans and the Victory Loan—sold just after the armistice— brought in almost $21.5 billion. School children and others of small means contributed another $800 million by buying thrift stamps and war-savings certificates.

The Liberty Bond campaigns were skillfully organized by committees in every city, town, and village. Moving-picture programs were interrupted to enable "four-minute" speakers to make patriotic appeals from the stage, while in the larger cities, stage and screen celebrities contributed their services to sell bonds. So successfully was the message hammered home that more than 21 million individuals purchased bonds during the fourth drive.

The United States spent almost $21 billion in direct war expenditures and loaned another $10 billion to its cobelligerents. Just about one third of the total outlay was raised by taxes and the remainder by loans, thereby following closely McAdoo's recommendation.

Witch-Hunting

As soon as war was declared, many Americans became acutely spy-conscious. They imagined they saw mysterious lights at night, or asserted that German agents were plotting to poison Red Cross bandages or to wipe out entire communities by planting germs in public drinking water. Such hysterical ideas were not entirely unnatural, because there had been some evidence of German sabotage during the days of neutrality. German-Americans were suspected of disloyalty and were victims of numerous local persecutions.

Congress enacted new laws to deal drastically with treasonable activities. The Espionage Act of June, 1917, provided penalties running to $10,000 in fines and twenty years' imprisonment for those willfully causing or attempting to cause insubordination in the armed services or obstructing recruiting. Also subject to punishment were persons who willfully made false reports and statements with intent to interfere with the operations or success of the armed forces. The Postmaster General could bar from the mails any letter, pamphlet, book, or newspaper that violated any provision of the act or that advocated treason, insurrection, or forcible resistance to any United States law.

Drastic though the Espionage Act was, especially as vigorously administered by Attorney General Thomas Gregory and Postmaster General Burleson, still more powers were granted in the Trading-with-the-Enemy Act of October, 1917. In addition to dealing with the control of foreign trade, the law authorized the appointment of an Alien Property Custodian to take over and administer the property of enemy aliens resident in the United States and that of corporations controlled by enemy nationals. Furthermore, the President could set up a censorship over all channels of communication between the United States and other countries, and the

Post Office Department could exclude materials from the mails in a manner that amounted to an effective censorship of the foreign-language press. In April, 1918, the Sabotage Act made it a Federal offense to damage or destroy war material, utilities, or transportation, whether public or private.

Still the advocates of ruthless suppression of all subversive activities were not satisfied. In May, 1918, the so-called Sedition Act amended the Espionage Act to provide penalties for saying or doing anything to obstruct the sale of Liberty Bonds; for uttering, writing, or printing "any disloyal, scurrilous, or abusive language" about the form of government of the United States, the Constitution, the armed forces, or the flag, or any language intended to bring these institutions into contempt or disrepute; or for advocating curtailment of war production. The Postmaster General might also exclude any written matter of this description from the mails. The Sedition Act was far more drastic than the Espionage Act because the government now only need prove that an accused person had used disloyal language; it was no longer necessary to establish that some harmful consequence to the war effort had resulted.

The Department of Justice, acting vigorously under these laws, arrested 1,532 persons for disloyal utterances, 65 for threats against the President, and 10 for sabotage. Actual plots, however, were few. Now that the unwanted war had come, all but a few German-Americans proved thoroughly loyal. Such pro-Germanism as survived was not often expressed where unsympathetic neighbors might hear.

The principal victims of these laws were Socialists and other radicals who opposed war on ideological grounds, rather than because of sympathy for the enemy. Mrs. Rose Pastor Stokes received a ten-year sentence for asserting, "I am for the people and the government is for profiteers." A higher court set aside her conviction, but Eugene V. Debs was not so fortunate. Before he was finally pardoned by President Harding on Christmas Day, 1921, the veteran head of American Socialism served thirty-two months of his ten-year sentence for saying that the war was the supreme curse of capitalism. Leaders of the IWW, accused of using the war situation to destroy the existing economic system, were dealt with even more severely. One hundred of them were brought before Judge Kenesaw Mountain Landis in Chicago. After a trial lasting 138 days, the jury took but four hours to find them all guilty. Landis sentenced the fifteen most prominent leaders to twenty-year terms, thirty-five others to ten years, and the rest to less drastic penalties. Their fines aggregated $2.3 million—a blow from which the IWW never recovered.

Freedom of the press suffered even more than freedom of speech. The watchful eyes of Burleson's assistants were everywhere. Papers accused of violating the espionage acts were penalized, not only by having the single offending issue barred from the mails, but by being declared unmailable for the future no matter how circumspect their conduct. Such was the fate of German-American newspapers like the Philadelphia *Tagenblatt*, Irish-American papers like the *Gaelic American,* and radical periodicals like the *Masses* and the Milwaukee *Leader*. Although the witch-hunting record of the Wilson administration was inconsistent with its notable progressive achievements of earlier years, it must be remembered that the government was acting in response to insistent public opinion and was widely criticized as being too lenient. "Disloyalty"—a word of dangerously vague meaning—was for the time being considered the most heinous of crimes.

The unpopularity of all things German reached ludicrous extremes. Public demand compelled the statute of Frederick the Great in Washington to be taken down and ignominiously stored away in a basement. Local officials ordered instruction in German to be halted in many public schools; German operas and opera singers were boycotted; the great violinist Fritz Kreisler was not allowed to perform at East Orange, New Jersey. To the ultrapatriots, German measles became "liberty measles," dachshunds "liberty pups," and sauerkraut "liberty cabbage."

Advertising America

Soon after the United States entered the war, the Army and Navy departments urged a strict news censorship to prevent vital information from reaching the enemy. The newspapers, however, vigorously protested such controls. In his perplexity, Wilson turned with relief to the suggestion of George Creel, a dynamic free-lance journalist and editor, who asserted that what was needed was not censorship in the conventional sense of the word, but an agency to provide the press with the fullest possible information, relying upon voluntary cooperation of the newspapers not to publish material that might help the enemy.

The President promptly appointed a Committee on Public Information, with the Secretaries of State, War, and the Navy as members and Creel as executive head. Like so many other war agencies, the Committee on Public Information quickly became a one-man enterprise. Unencumbered by his fellow committeemen and loyally supported by Wilson, Creel built up a vast organization engaged in a great variety of activities.

The first modest function was to serve as a liaison agency between the various government departments and Washington reporters. The CPI's offices were open twenty-four hours a day, grinding out mimeographed releases for the newspapers, releases soon given a more pretentious form by being published daily in a new periodical, the *Official Journal*.

But Creel soon organized more ambitious projects. His job, as he conceived it, was to sell the war to the American people and Wilson's ideals of a democratic peace to the world. On the domestic front, leading American illustrators such as Charles Dana Gibson, James Montgomery Flagg, and Howard Chandler Christy prepared a remarkable series of war posters. College professors, led by Guy Stanton Ford, professor of history at the University of Minnesota, wrote popular pamphlets explaining the nation's war aims. The varied talents of novelists, dramatists, musicians, actors, and motion-picture directors were all employed in arousing the patriotic enthusiasm of the country. Perhaps the most remarkable of Creel's feats at home was the enlistment of 75,000 speakers, or "Four-Minute Men." These privates in the CPI army fired 7,555,190 speeches at their fellow countrymen assembled in moving-picture theaters, lodge meetings, schools, and churches; they even invaded lumber camps and Indian reservations, where they found some of their most enthusiastic audiences. The Four-Minute Men sold Liberty Bonds, explained the draft, urged food and fuel conservation, and attacked rumor-mongers.

Creel, a devoted disciple of Wilson, believed that the great war speeches in which the President expressed his abiding faith in democracy, his hatred of militarism, and his hope for future peace should be given the widest possible circulation. Through CPI agencies abroad, the speeches were translated and published in almost every country. A volume of Wilson's messages became a best seller in China, and the text of one address was used as a schoolbook in Madrid.

But the audiences Creel wanted to reach most were the German army and the German home front. Therefore CPI pamphlets printed in German were showered down from airplanes and shot over no man's land from guns. Some propaganda bombs consisted of facts, figures, and pictures designed to impress the enemy with the magnitude of the American war effort and the hopelessness of further resistance; others were translations of Wilson's speeches offering a just peace if the Germans rebelled against their war lords. Their effectiveness was evidenced by the frantic efforts of the German government to prevent its subjects from reading such literature.

Creel did make mistakes. He believed truth was his best weapon; yet under pressure of war psychology, he sometimes distorted facts. He sold Wilsonian idealism so completely to the common people of the world that they were bitterly disillusioned when the peace settlement fell short of perfection. He was worse than tactless in dealing with Congress, where he made dangerous enemies for both himself and Wilson. Despite these shortcomings, Creel's accomplishments were remarkable. He was a pioneer in the field of political warfare and, as truly as Pershing and Baruch, he was one of the architects of German defeat.

The War Fronts

The German High Command had resorted to unlimited submarine warfare in the twin beliefs that it would bring speedy victory and that the United States, even though it might enter the war, could not exert any effective military pressure. During the spring and summer of 1917 both premises seemed all too sound. The submarine campaign was dangerously effective, while America's unreadiness for real combat was evident to friend and foe alike.

Unless the seas were made safe for Allied shipping, Germany's defeat appeared impossible. When Admiral Sims took over his European command, there was no convoy system because the British did not have enough destroyers for the task, and they doubted, moreover, whether merchant ships could be kept moving in formation at the same speed. Even the antisubmarine patrols then in use needed many more ships. In answer to frantic appeals from Sims, the Navy Department hurried into service every vessel that could be used against U-boats, and destroyers and sub-chasers were given priority in naval construction.

The ensuing battle against underwater raiders became a grim contest in which new methods and tactics were constantly tried. Improved means of detection and more powerful depth charges helped in this struggle. Despite the difficulties, more and more shipping moved in convoys protected by destroyers and other small craft. The most ingenious stratagem was that of bottling up the submarines in the North Sea with a string of mines from Scotland to Norway. The gigantic task had not been completed when the war ended, but already it had proved effective. One out of every ten German submarines trying to cross the barrier was destroyed, and many more were so badly damaged that they had to return to port. The morale of the crews was thereby seriously shaken.

The success of the antisubmarine campaign was to be measured not alone by the steadily declining toll of Allied shipping losses after April, 1917, but also by the safety in which American soldiers were ferried across the Atlantic. It was the proud navy boast that not a single troopship was lost on its way to Europe. Three troopships, however, were torpedoed on the return voyage, and a Cunard liner was sunk off Ireland in February, 1918, with the loss of about 175 American lives.

Although Pershing had asked for a million men by the end of May, 1918, up to March 1, 1918, only 291,000 had been sent across. The delay was caused partly by the need to build camps and train men in America, and partly by the scarcity of shipping to carry the troops. American facilities were entirely inadequate, and the British found it difficult to help because of their own losses. They could spare vessels to transport American soldiers only by diverting them from carrying vital supplies to England itself. This they were at first reluctant to do.

This British hesitancy was closely linked with a delicate issue being violently contested behind the scenes: the disposition of the troops when they reached France. From the beginning, Pershing had insisted on a separate American army, fighting on its own sector of the front under its own commanders. British and French authorities opposed this, however, because they feared Pershing would hoard his men until he had enough for an effective army; thus Germany might achieve victory before the Americans were ready. Moreover, with untested troops and inexperienced officers, it might be actually dangerous to entrust any sizable section of the front to Pershing. Instead, the Allies wanted American units to support the British and French armies already in the field. Despite appeals by Lloyd George and Clemenceau, Wilson stood by his commander. So long as this controversy continued, the British disliked to gamble their precious shipping on the American Expeditionary Force.

Pershing was not unwilling to loan units to the Allies for limited periods or to meet special emergencies, because this would provide valuable training for his troops. Consequently, battalions of the American First Division participated in combat with the French forces in Lorraine as early as October 21, 1917. This experience enabled the Americans under General Robert Bullock to take over a quiet sector near Toul in mid-January, 1918.

In early 1918 the Germans staged a drive they hoped would win the war, hopes re-enforced by several factors. The Bolsheviks, who had overthrown the Kerensky government in November, 1917, were forced to agree to the harsh Treaty of Brest-Litovsk in May, 1918, which took Russia out of the war and gave Germany access to the agricultural wealth of the Ukraine. Moreover, the bulk of the Kaiser's armies was shifted to the western front to add weight to the offensive. For four months the Allied lines were subjected to terrific hammer blows that threatened complete disaster. The peril was increased by the lack of British and French reserves, by the fact they were still under separate commands, and by the hesitancy of one army to divert units to rescue some sector held by another.

The German offensive, beginning along the Somme on March 21, drove more than thirty miles in six days—greater gains than either side had achieved since 1914, and a wide gap was torn in the Allied lines. Desperate British countermeasures were required to stabilize the front. Ludendorff threw a second juggernaut into motion on April 9, this time in Flanders. Although deep penetrations were made, the Germans failed to keep their offensive rolling.

These near-disasters drove home to the Allies both the necessity of unified command and the desperate need for American reinforcements. After numerous conferences, General Ferdinand Foch was named Commander-in-Chief of the Allied Armies in April. Pershing at once offered him all American resources overseas and agreed to delay establishing a separate American army until the military situation improved.

Herculean efforts were now made to move American troops across the Atlantic, with the British diverting as much of their shipping to this service as possible. Thus 85,000 soldiers were transported to France in March, 120,000 in April, and a monthly average of 263,000 for the next six months. The first million men arrived by July 1, and a million more had come by Armistice Day. The new arrivals required more training behind the lines before they were ready for active combat, but by summer more and more Americans were moving to the fighting zones.

Up to this time, neither friend nor foe had had the opportunity to measure the quality of the American forces. The first real test came when the First Division attacked Cantigny, strategically located near the tip of the Somme salient. Not only did the division take the village on May 28, but held it against seven German counterattacks during the next two days.

Meantime, the third and most dangerous German drive had struck against the French left flank west of Reims. In the first three days the offensive reached Château-Thierry on the Marne, only fifty miles from Paris. Once again American troops were thrown into battle, and with the French they halted the advance. After a week of desperate fighting, the Americans regained Belleau Wood and thereby stabilized the line again.

Still maintaining the initiative, the Germans launched two more offensives. The first, directed west of the Marne salient in June, was stopped after a gain of six miles. The second, begun on July 14 in the sector around Reims, hoped to roll down the Marne Valley to Paris. "If my offensive at Reims succeeds, we have won the war," declared Ludendorff; but once again a combined Franco-American defense prevented a breakthrough.

American participation in the Allied offensive of 1918. (Adapted from
The War with Germany, A Statistical Summary, Washington, Office of the
Chief of Staff, 1919.)

Foch Strikes Back

This was the final turning point of the war. The Germans had thrown
all their resources into these five mighty blows; thereafter the preponderance
of strength lay with the Allies as more and more American divisions became ready for action. As soon as the enemy had been stopped at Reims,
Foch directed his first great counterblow at the Marne salient. American
troops, now well regarded, spearheaded the drive on July 18, and after
three weeks they controlled the entire salient.

At long last on August 10, Pershing gained command of an army of his
own, the First American Army, made up of divisions that had been
strengthening the British and French lines for the past crucial months.
This new army was assigned to eliminate the St. Mihiel salient west of
Verdun, which the Germans had held since 1914. Thirty-six hours after
the initial attack on September 12, the salient was wiped out.

Pershing hoped to keep his offensive rolling toward the great fortress
of Metz, a vital nerve center in the German communications system, but

Foch had other plans. His earlier limited offensive had aimed at eventually launching a grand assault on the Hindenburg Line, the deep defense zone the Germans had been preparing for four years. The new task of the American First Army was to attack west of Verdun in the Meuse-Argonne sector through a heavily fortified terrain filled with hills, ravines, rivers, and forests. It was a vital zone because not far beyond lay the Mézières-Metz railroad, on which the whole German front was dependent.

On September 26, Foch's grand assault began, with the Americans holding twenty-four miles of the flaming two-hundred mile front. The First Army found the initial going desperately difficult, its attack soon bogged down, and a reorganization of forces became necessary. The offensive was renewed on October 4, and continued for the next four weeks. This was the greatest battle in which Americans had ever been engaged. The weight of ammunition fired was more than that used by the Union forces in the entire Civil War, and each day's gains were measured in yards, not miles. But by October 20, the Argonne Forest lay behind and Pershing's men were ready for their next objective—cutting the Mézières-Metz railroad. This new attack, opening on November 1, brought decisive results. Within a week the German line was broken, the outskirts of Sedan were reached, bridgeheads were established across the Meuse, and the vital railroad had been cut.

Elsewhere along the broad front the French, British, and Belgians were equally successful. The Hindenburg Line was everywhere broken, and the Germans had been pushed back toward their own borders. Disasters even more catastrophic had befallen the Central Powers in the Balkan and Italian theaters. On September 29 Bulgaria accepted Allied armistice terms, Turkey followed suit on October 30, and Austria-Hungary surrendered on November 3.

Acknowledging that the war was lost, the German High Command sought an armistice as early as October 1. Preliminary negotiations began two days later and were hastened by the crumbling of the western front and the spread of revolution throughout Germany. On November 7, German delegates passed through the lines to receive Foch's terms. In a dramatic meeting in the forest of Compiègne on November 11, the armistice was signed and, at 11 A.M. of that day, the military phase of World War I ended.

This victory was not achieved without cost. Total American casualties were 321,000, of whom 39,000 were killed in action, 62,700 died of disease, 201,000 were wounded, and 4,400 were taken prisoner. Seven per cent of all those mobilized were on the casualty list. Compared to the 73 per cent casualties suffered by the French and the 36 per cent by the British Empire, American losses were extremely light. It should be remembered that American troops were in the front lines only a few months, but the actual battles in which they were engaged were among the most bitterly fought and most bloody in American history.

9

PEACE AND DISILLUSIONMENT

With the military battle won, the next great challenge to the world's statesmen was to negotiate a satisfactory peace. Woodrow Wilson's dearest dream was to be the architect of a new world order, founded upon justice and buttressed by a universal league of nations. Of all the President's goals, this proved the hardest to achieve. First, he had to struggle with the heads of the Allied governments, each eager to advance his own nation's special interests. More formidable still was the opposition in his own country, especially among certain Republican Senators. The American enemies ultimately gained the upper hand and destroyed most of Wilson's handiwork.

The country also deserted Wilson's leadership in domestic affairs. For months the President's attention had been absorbed by the struggle over the peace. Then his physical collapse and long illness prevented his giving effective attention to domestic reconstruction. The loneliness of his position was accentuated by estrangement from his long-time advisers. In February, 1920, Secretary Lansing was asked to resign because the two men had not agreed on fundamental policies for many months. Wilson's break with Colonel House is less easy to understand. Perhaps it arose from House's fondness for compromise at a time the President hated to make concessions to his opponents.

Quite apart from Wilson's physical inability to provide his old-time leadership, the nation was in no mood to accept his advice. Already disillusionment was widespread. The returning soldier found little glamor in his recent experiences. Those who had stayed at home were disgusted by the greedy scramble for the spoils of war at the Peace Conference. They were more immediately irritated by continued wartime controls and unchecked rising prices. Veterans and civilians alike wanted nothing so much as the return of prewar standards of living, but the road back was a rocky one.

The Evolution of War Aims

When the European war began, shocked Americans started to consider how future conflicts might be prevented. In June, 1915, the League to Enforce Peace was organized in Independence Hall, Philadelphia, under the leadership of former President Taft and President A. Lawrence Lowell of Harvard. It advocated the establishment of an international court of justice to which all "justiciable" questions arising between nations should be submitted and a league of nations that would employ its joint forces against any state rejecting these procedures. Local chapters of this league were founded throughout the country, and hundreds of speakers supported its program.

Even before this new organization was founded, Wilson had been thinking along the same general lines and, as time went on, he made it abundantly clear that he considered some kind of league of nations the essential foundation to any permanent peace after the war. The British government also favored such a league and British opinion appeared to demand it.

By January, 1917, Wilson had formulated other principles for a durable postwar settlement. In his "Peace Without Victory" speech, he asserted it must be a peace between equals and one that recognized the ideal of government by consent of the governed, freedom of the seas, and disarmament. His war message three months later declared that America was entering the contest to make the world safe for democracy.

By the end of 1917, an insistent public demand arose for a much more specific statement of war aims, partly because of the publication by the Bolshevik government in Russia of secret treaties found in the Tsarist archives, which pointed to an old-fashioned division of spoils if the Allies won. Repudiating these pacts, the Bolsheviks widely publicized their own ideals for a just peace: no annexations nor indemnities, and self-determination for subject nationalities. These developments gave rise to searching questions. To what end were the peoples of all the belligerent nations being called upon to make such terrible sacrifices? Was it simply to serve the territorial ambitions of the rival powers? Or was there a happier alternative —some hope that, when the guns were stilled, a better world would emerge?

Wilson's answer was embodied in his speech to Congress on January 9, 1918, in which the "Fourteen Points" were set forth as the basis for an enduring peace: (1) "Open covenants of peace, openly arrived at . . ."; (2) "Absolute freedom of navigation upon the sea . . . alike in peace and in war," except as the seas may be closed by international action for the enforcement of international covenants; (3) "The removal, as far as possible, of all economic barriers and the establishment of an equality of trade conditions . . ."; (4) Reduction of armaments "to the lowest point consistent with domestic safety"; (5) Impartial adjustment of all colonial claims in which "the interests of the populations concerned must have equal weight with the equitable claims of the government whose title is to be determined"; (6–13) Provided for the evacuation of Russian territory; the evacuation and restoration of Belgium; the evacuation of France (which should regain Alsace-Lorraine); the readjustment of Italy's frontiers "along clearly recognizable lines of nationality"; the autonomous development of the peoples of Austria-Hungary; Rumania, Serbia, and Montenegro to be evacuated and Serbia granted free access to the sea; the restoration of Poland with access to the sea; and the development of Turkey along autonomous lines, with the Dardenelles "opened as a free passage to the ships and commerce of all nations under international guarantees"; and (14) "A general association of nations must be formed under specific covenants" to afford "mutual guarantees of political independence and territorial integrity to great and small nations alike."

This speech made a tremendous impression because it stated in memorable phrases the thoughts running in the minds of people of many countries. Indeed, only three days earlier, Prime Minister Lloyd George had stated British objectives in very similar terms.

Wilson also discussed the bases of a just peace in several other speeches during 1918. On February 11 he clarified the Fourteen Points with his "Four Principles"; on the fourth of July, he spoke of the "Four Ends," which could be summed up in a single sentence: "What we seek is the reign of law, based upon the consent of the governed and sustained by the organized opinion of mankind." The last great war speech, delivered on September 27, stressed the "Five Particulars," one of which was that "there can be no leagues or special covenants and understandings within the general and common family of the League of Nations."

Armistice Negotiations

In the fall of 1918 when the German officials realized they had lost the war, they turned to the Fourteen Points in the desperate hope they might obtain lenient treatment. Accordingly, it was to Wilson that Prince Max addressed his request of October 3 for an armistice. Wilson, however, demanded categorical acceptance of the principles he had laid down in his war speeches, a promise to evacuate all Allied territory, a cessation of submarine attacks on passenger liners, and an assurance that the arbitrary power of the Kaiser and his generals had been placed under constitutional checks. Only after his adroit diplomacy had obtained these promises did the President transmit the armistice request to the Allies.

Now the problem was transferred to the European capitals. The military commanders had to decide whether it was expedient to halt hostilities and, if so, on what terms. British General Douglas Haig thought mild terms should be offered to ensure their acceptance; Pershing preferred no armistice at all; and Foch, whose decision was final, favored terms so drastic that Germany could not possibly renew the war. Meantime, the heads of the Allied governments were at first reluctant to accept the Fourteen Points as the basis for peace, and Colonel House had to warn them that refusal might cause the United States to drop out of the war. Only then did the Allied statesmen accept the Wilsonian principles with one reservation and one elucidation. Because the second of the Fourteen Points, relating to freedom of the seas, was "open to various interpretations, some of which they could not accept, they must, therefore, reserve to themselves complete freedom in this subject when they enter the peace conference"; this reservation obviously reflected the ideas of the British. The French stipulated that Germany must not only evacuate invaded territory, but compensate "for all damage done to the civilian population of the Allies and their property by the aggression of Germany by land, by sea, and from the air."

On November 5, Wilson informed the Germans of the Allied reply;

they would learn the actual armistice provisions by meeting with General Foch. Their envoys received Foch's terms on November 8, appealed to Berlin for further instructions, and finally signed the armistice agreement on November 11. It provided for a cessation of hostilities, German evacuation of all non-German territory, Allied occupation of both banks of the Rhine, and German delivery to the Allies of vast amounts of military equipment. Compliance would make it virtually impossible for Germany to renew hostilities.

The first Armistice Day was one of delirious rejoicing. Wilson's own happiness was reflected in his exultant statement:

Everything for which America fought has been accomplished. It will now be our fortunate duty to assist by example, by sober friendly counsel and by material aid in the establishment of a just democracy throughout the world.

It is no wonder the President used such phrases. The triumph of his principles appeared to be as complete as the victory of Allied arms. Not only had the Fourteen Points been accepted as the basis of peace by friend and foe alike, but German military autocracy seemed utterly vanquished. The peace-hungry German people, convinced that the Kaiser's continued presence on the throne was a barrier to an armistice, had risen in revolt. On November 9 the government was turned over to the Socialists, who proclaimed a German republic, and the emperor fled to Holland. It was another great victory for the American statesman who had called for "the destruction of every arbitrary power."

The Rise of Republican Opposition

Actually, however, Wilson's position was less impregnable than these diplomatic victories would indicate. Not only in Europe but in America powerful elements resented his leadership and were awaiting the first opportunity to make their opposition felt.

The most influential Republican was still Theodore Roosevelt, and his hatred for Wilson had grown with the passing years. Thoroughly loyal and patriotic, Roosevelt supported the war in vigorous speeches, but at the same time he maintained a constant barrage of criticism of the President, especially of his peace proposals. By 1918, his dislike for Wilson was so great that he tried to sabotage the President's October negotiations with the Germans by calling upon the Senate to repudiate the Fourteen Points. "Let us dictate the peace by the hammering of guns," he declared, "and not chat about peace to the accompaniment of clicking typewriters."

Equally hostile was Senator Lodge, who, like his close friend Roosevelt, had earlier believed that an association of nations to enforce peace was an excellent idea. In 1915, for example, he had asserted: "The great nations must be so united as to be able to say to any single country, you must not go to war, and they can only say that effectively when the country desiring war knows that the force . . . is irresistible." But following Wilson's fervent plea for a league in his "Peace Without Victory" speech of January, 1917, the Massachusetts Senator reversed himself completely, warning the upper house that such an international organization "might plunge us into war at any moment at the bidding of other nations."

The Republican leaders naturally wished to return to power in the national government. They believed the country was normally Republican and that the Democrats had enjoyed their brief hour of glory only because of animosities within the ranks of the dominant party. Therefore every effort was made to patch up the old quarrel as the congressional election of 1918 approached. A new and energetic national chairman, Will Hays of Indiana, was named, and Roosevelt and Taft appeared together on public platforms to show that the 1912 schism had ended. Wilson was accused of desiring a negotiated peace with the Kaiser rather than unconditional surrender, and the third of the Fourteen Points was depicted as a threat to the protective-tariff system. Worried Democratic Congressmen thereupon begged the President for help. Somewhat reluctantly, Wilson appealed to the voters on October 24:

If you have approved of my leadership and wish me to continue to be your unembarrassed spokesman at home and abroad, I earnestly beg that you will express yourself unmistakably to that effect by returning a Democratic majority to both the Senate and the House of Representatives. . . . The return of a Republican majority to either house of the Congress would . . . be interpreted on the other side of the water as a repudiation of my leadership.

This appeal proved to be a blunder, for it gave the Republicans an excuse to cast off the restraint they might have felt over attacking the President during wartime. Chairman Hays denounced Wilson's words as "ungracious . . . wanton . . . mendacious." To many, the President had slurred Republican patriotism.

After the ballots were counted on November 5, it was found that the new House would have 237 Republicans, 191 Democrats, and 7 independents, while in the Senate there would be 49 Republicans and 47 Democrats. It was a defeat not only for the President's party, but for the President himself because Wilson had defined confidence in his leadership as a campaign issue. Although the exultant victors asserted the President had been decisively repudiated, in reality it was by no means certain this was so. The war was almost over, and many voters were expressing their impatience with wartime restrictions or their sentiments on local issues. Republican victory under the circumstances was probably inevitable, but it was made more damaging to the President than it needed to be by the role he had assumed during the campaign.

Wilson Goes to Europe

Before November was over, the names of the American peace commissioners were announced. Wilson had long before decided to attend the peace conference in person; to accompany him he now named Secretary Lansing, Colonel House, General Tasker Bliss, and Henry White, a competent group.

Next to the President himself, Lansing and House were obviously the two best-informed men on recent diplomatic developments. Bliss was not only a military expert, but a scholar with an excellent grasp of European economic and political problems, and White had held important posts in London, Paris, and Rome.

The President's opponents, however, criticized these appointments severely. Natural though it might seem that Wilson should go to Paris himself, he was breaking a precedent. Earlier Presidents had left to others the actual negotiation of peace treaties. Wilson's decision to lead his own delegation was attributed to his vanity or to his "Messiah complex." The commission was further criticized as giving inadequate recognition to the Republicans. True, White was a Republican, but not an active partisan. Why had the President ignored such distinguished leaders as Hughes, Taft, and Root? Finally, the absence of Senators was resented as a slight to the body that must ratify any peace treaty. Although much of this criticism was partisan, Wilson's failure to take with him at least one prominent Senator from each party was a serious mistake that played directly into the hands of his enemies.

On December 4, 1918, the *George Washington* left New York, bearing the peace commission and scores of advisers and experts on various problems. Key men from the war administration were aboard, as well as numerous college professors and other specialists in history, geography, and economics who had been gathering facts and figures for many months under the leadership of Colonel House. Even this evidence of earnest preparation was ridiculed by unfriendly newspapers, which sneered at the Colonel's "troupe of performing professors."

The *George Washington* docked at Brest on December 13, but not for another month did the peace conference begin its work. During this interval, Wilson visited Paris, London, and Rome, where he received a most extraordinary welcome. The enthusiastic crowds lining the streets surpassed anything that men could remember. With pathetic trust, common people everywhere were counting on the American President to achieve an impossible goal—a perfect peace settlement.

Lions in the Path

But even while Wilson was enjoying his greatest triumphs, the dangers confronting him were clearly evident. Behind him in America opponents were ceaseless in their activity. Even before the President sailed, Roosevelt had warned "that Mr. Wilson has no authority whatever to speak for the American people at this time. His leadership has just been emphatically repudiated by them." This bitter statement was one of Roosevelt's last contributions to American political discussion, for the former President, a desperately sick man, fighting a losing struggle with a tropical ailment contracted during his trip to the Amazon in 1913, died on January 6, 1919.

Henry Cabot Lodge, however, remained very much alive. In an address to the Senate on December 21, 1918, he stated that the Allies should be permitted to make any territorial settlement they desired without Wilson's interference, and that the League of Nations should not be included in any peace treaty. The Senate, he continued, often had refused to ratify treaties; many other agreements—and these were significant words—had been "virtually amended." Without waiting to see what kind of a league would be proposed, Lodge was already planning to oppose it. He even suggested to Henry White that the latter encourage Allied statesmen to oppose the President, but White honorably refrained from so doing.

On the European front, several major obstacles lay in the President's path. Four years of bitter struggle had created a large public demand for stern punishment of the country held guilty for the war. There had been a 1918 election in England as well as in the United States; Lloyd George was victorious, using such popular slogans as "Hang the Kaiser," "Squeeze the Germans until the pips squeak," and "Make Germany pay for the War." In France, Clemenceau had received an impressive vote of confidence from the Chamber of Deputies under the popular expectation he would demand vigorous treatment of the hated *Boche*.

Equally dangerous to Wilsonian idealism was the network of secret treaties made by the Allied governments before the United States declared war. Italy, as her reward for entering the struggle against her former allies in 1915, had been promised a strategic frontier in the Alps and along the Adriatic, which would extend her rule not only over "unredeemed" Italians, but over thousands of Germans and Slavs as well. Rumania was to gain a large section of Hungary, while Russia, France, and Britain were to partition the Turkish Empire. Japan was to keep Germany's Pacific islands north of the equator, as well as German political and economic rights in the Shantung Peninsula.

Wilson, long aware of the existence of these documents, expressed his disapproval of such bargains in his appeal for "open covenants of peace, openly arrived at," but he refrained from any study of their details. He considered that American entry into the war, as well as the armistice negotiations, created a new situation in which the secret treaties should be ignored. Each part of the settlement should be made on its merits, without regard to previous agreements. Wilson soon discovered, however, that the Allied statesmen would insist stubbornly on fulfilling these earlier pledges.

The work of peacemaking had to be carried on in an atmosphere of haste and confusion hardly conducive to long and patient consideration of any single problem. Treaties had to be made not only with Germany, but also with Austria, Hungary, Turkey, and Bulgaria. The new states appearing on the map had to be committed by a separate series of treaties to the decent treatment of their minorities. Furthermore, all Europe appeared to be tottering on the edge of chaos. Not only had a score of petty wars broken out—both civil wars between rival factions and wars between neighboring countries over disputed boundaries, but there were unemployment, hunger, and discontent everywhere.

Such unrest seemed doubly dangerous because of the situation in Russia. Might not the wildfire of Communism spread across the whole continent? This was the greatest fear haunting the peacemakers, impelling them to make important decisions in frantic haste. That great country was also convulsed by civil war, and the Allies were uncomfortably involved. After the Soviet government had made its separate peace with Germany, Allied expeditionary forces were sent into various parts of Russia to prevent military supplies from falling into German hands. American troops participated in these operations, both around Archangel and in eastern Siberia. The armistice ended the need to protect military supplies, but by then the Allies were entangled in virtual alliances with anti-Bolshevik armies resisting the Soviet government in several parts of Russia.

No question confronting the statesmen at Paris was more perplexing than that of trying to shape a Russian policy. The French favored all-out military action against the Communist regime, but Lloyd George and Wilson urged instead that the rival leaders compromise their differences. When this effort failed, Wilson, with British approval, sent William C. Bullitt to Moscow on an unofficial, highly confidential mission. He brought back a Bolshevik offer to make an armistice, come to a conference, and acknowledge Russia's debts to the Allies if the latter would restore diplomatic relations and terminate their intervention in Russian internal affairs. When news of these negotiations leaked out, however, there was such loud condemnation that the whole matter was dropped.

The consequence of these failures was most unfortunate. The Allied policy of supplying and encouraging the anti-Bolsheviks continued—not sufficiently to be effective, but just enough to make the Soviet leaders bitterly suspicious of the Western democracies—suspicions that would plague international relations for the next generation. The Wilson administration, reluctant from the beginning to send American troops into Russia, began evacuating them in May, 1919, but not until 1933 did the United States recognize the Soviet regime diplomatically. Since the hated government was not represented at the Peace Conference, Allied statesmen found it impossible to draw boundary lines in eastern Europe and, what was still more important, vast Russia had no place in the League of Nations or in the concert of powers that would have an interest in preserving the peace settlement.

Planning the League

On January 18, 1919, the Peace Conference held its first plenary session. Such open meetings, where the delegates of all the nations that had broken relations with Germany were represented, were held on only a few occasions thereafter, and then merely to ratify decisions reached elsewhere. All the important work was done by smaller groups. From January to March the most important was the Council of Ten, which Wilson and Lansing attended along with the two highest ranking delegates from Britain, France, Italy, and Japan. Even this proved too cumbersome a body, so from March to June, when the most important issues were threshed out, the Council of Four— Lloyd George, Clemenceau, Wilson, and Vittorio Orlando (Premier of Italy)—dominated the scene. Most conference work was done behind carefully guarded doors, with only brief communiqués issued to the press. Critics protested that this was hardly the open diplomacy Wilson had advocated, but although the President tried to obtain more privileges for the journalists, the other leaders contended that full publicity would advertise each difference among the victors and stiffen the resistance of the vanquished.

Wilson, however, won two important points early in the negotiations.

The Big Four at Paris. Lloyd George, Orlando, Clemenceau, and Wilson.
(Brown Bros.)

Against the wishes of France, Australia, and South Africa, he prevented outright annexation of the German colonies and the Arab territories of the
Turkish Empire. Instead, the mandate principle was accepted. This meant
that those areas should be held under a form of trusteeship; the mandatory
power should administer them under conditions that would protect the
rights of the natives and provide for general supervision by the League of
Nations.

The President's second early achievement was obtaining immediate consideration for the League of Nations and acceptance of the principle that
the League be made an integral part of the peace treaty. A League of Nations
Commission, with Wilson as chairman, began drafting a constitution for this
body. Much preliminary work had already been done by British, French, and
American experts and, after long, exhausting night sessions, the document
was finally presented to a plenary session on February 14.

The proposed Covenant provided for an assembly in which every member
state, large and small, would have one vote, and for a council on which the
Big Five—Britain, France, Italy, Japan, and the United States—would have
permanent representation, with nonpermanent seats allotted to four of the
smaller powers. In addition to the assembly and council, which were to meet
at stated intervals and might be specially convened to deal with emergencies,
there was to be a permanent secretariat to assemble information for the

League's use and to publish the texts of any treaties signed by member states. Many functions were to be undertaken by the League, including the establishment of a Permanent Court of International Justice (the World Court), the formulation of plans for international disarmament, the supervision of mandates, the safeguarding of world health, and the promotion of fair conditions for labor. The League's most important responsibility, however, was to preserve peace. Any future war or threat of war was to be a matter of concern to the whole League; League members agreed to submit any controversy among them likely to lead to war either to arbitration or to council inquiry, and not to resort to war until three months after an award or report had been made. Moreover, if all council members other than those representing parties to the dispute agreed to certain recommendations, League members were bound not to go to war against any nation that complied with these recommendations. Should any League member go to war in disregard of these pledges, it was to be punished by economic sanctions; and the council, as a last resort, might recommend military action against the offending country. What Wilson regarded as "the heart of the Covenant" was Article 10:

The Members of the League undertake to respect and preserve as against external aggression the territorial integrity and existing political independence of all Members of the League. In case of any threat of danger of such aggression the Council shall advise upon the means by which this obligation shall be fulfilled.

The day after this draft of the Convenant was presented, Wilson embarked for America. Congress was ready to adjourn and the President had to be available to sign bills and attend to various matters accumulating during his absence. At House's suggestion, Wilson entertained the members of the Senate Foreign Relations Committee at a White House dinner on February 26. Until nearly midnight the President explained the Covenant and answered the Senators' questions. The Democratic members were much impressed; the Republicans were not. It was hard to say whose attitude was most ominous: that of Frank Brandegee of Connecticut, who cross-examined Wilson like a district attorney; that of Lodge, who kept silent most of the evening; or that of Borah of Idaho and Albert Fall of New Mexico, who refused to attend the meeting.

Wilson's failure to win over the skeptics was made all too clear less than a week later. On March 4, the last day of the session, Lodge requested unanimous consent to consider a resolution asserting that "the constitution of the League of Nations in the form now proposed to the peace conference should not be accepted by the United States" and that the whole proposal be postponed until after peace was made. Immediate objection was registered by a Democratic member—just as Lodge had hoped. This gave him his chance to read into the *Congressional Record* the names of thirty-nine Republican Senators or Senators-elect who would have voted for his resolution had they been given the opportunity. This challenge to the President, henceforth known as the "Round Robin," was of serious import, since but thirty-three votes were needed to block ratification of a treaty.

The President was entirely unwilling to separate the Covenant from the peace treaty. Were this done, he feared that the world's best opportunity to obtain a League would be lost. On the evening of the same March 4, Wilson addressed a huge, enthusiastic audience in New York City in which he accepted the gauge of battle flung down by his opponents. When the treaty was completed, he said, not only would the Covenant be in it, but so many threads of the treaty would be tied to the Covenant that it could not be separated from the treaty without destroying the whole vital structure. That the treaty itself might be rejected, the President apparently had no fear.

On the other hand, Wilson was not hostile to really constructive criticism. Following his return to Paris, a careful study was made of all the suggestions offered by prominent Republicans like Taft, Hughes, and Root, and by Democrats like Bryan and Senator Gilbert Hitchcock of Nebraska. Although the President believed the plan already drafted adequately safeguarded American rights, he did seek a number of amendments to satisfy hesitant Senators. The League of Nations Commission thereupon wrote into the Covenant numerous concessions to the United States. The right of a member to withdraw from the League was recognized, as was the right to refuse a mandate. Domestic questions such as immigration control and tariffs were specifically exempted from League jurisdiction, and, for all important questions, the council and the assembly would have to agree unanimously upon any course of action. Finally, and most important, nothing in the Covenant should be deemed "to affect the validity . . . of regional understandings like the Monroe Doctrine." This formal recognition of this historic American policy was a striking diplomatic victory. Thus Wilson won safeguards demanded by American opinion, but in so doing he had to moderate his opposition to certain demands by the other powers.

Completing the Treaty

The period from March 14, when Wilson returned to Paris, to June 28, when the Treaty of Versailles was finally signed, was one of great and exasperating difficulties. Always in frail health, Wilson aged perceptibly during these weeks of anxiety and overwork. For several days in April he was confined to his bed with an attack of the deadly influenza sweeping both Europe and America.

Clemenceau fought savagely for drastic treaty provisions he believed vital to French security, provisions that would have weakened Germany completely. Wilson opposed these demands as not only inconsistent with the Fourteen Points, but as providing for future war. Compromises were finally arranged. In the Saar Basin, only the coal mines went to France; the League would administer the area for fifteen years, after which a plebiscite would determine its final disposition. The Rhineland remained part of Germany but was to be permanently demilitarized. Allied troops were to occupy territory along the Rhine for fifteen years. To obtain Clemenceau's consent, security treaties were signed under which Britain and the United States promised to go to France's support were she the victim of unprovoked aggression; neither Britain nor the United States ever ratified these treaties.

On the reparations issue, both Lloyd George and Clemenceau opposed Wilson, who contended that a definite sum should be fixed in the treaty, based upon a reasonable estimate of Germany's ability to pay, that the payment should not be longer than thirty years, and that Germany's responsibility should be limited to paying for the restoration of devastated areas. Although the President successfully withstood pressure to have Germany's obligations cover the whole cost of the war, he had to give in to the British contention that Allied pension bills be added to civilian damages. In the end, the treaty compelled Germany to sign a blank check—a promise to accept a bill presented to her by a Reparations Commission in 1921. The sum eventually demanded, $33 billion, proved far more than Germany could or would pay.

Two issues provoking particular anxiety were the Italian demand for Fiume and the Japanese determination to take over Germany's political and economic rights in the Shantung peninsula. When the Allied statesmen could not agree on the first controversy, the Fiume question had to be left unsettled in the Paris treaties. It was not until 1924 that Yugoslavia acquiesced in Italian annexation of Fiume, in return for which she obtained port concessions and an outlet to the sea. On the Shantung question, Japan, after a bitter fight with Wilson, obtained Germany's economic rights, but promised that her troops would eventually be withdrawn and that China's sovereign rights in Shantung would be restored. The protesting Chinese thereupon refused to sign the treaty.

After many stormy sessions, the victorious powers finally agreed on the treaty terms, which were presented to the German representatives on May 7, 1919. No oral discussion was permitted, but the Germans were allowed to present written protests and counterproposals. A few concessions were made, but the final crisis came in June, when the German cabinet resigned rather than approve the document. Foch was then ordered to march into the heart of Germany unless the Allied terms were accepted within three days. Only then did Germany bow to the ultimatum and on June 28 the treaty was signed at a dramatic ceremony in the Hall of Mirrors at Versailles.

The Treaty of Versailles has been severely criticized by those who think it was too soft and by those who believe it was too harsh. The former regret that Wilson opposed Clemenceau's plan for the complete crippling of the enemy; the latter denounce the President for not having persuaded the other leaders to accept his ideas in every detail. To the first line of criticism it may be answered that the almost complete disarmament of Germany as well as the absolute demilitarization of its western frontier should have given ample security to France and the rest of Europe. That it did not was not because of deficiencies in the treaty itself, but because of divisions of opinion and weakness of will that permitted Hitlerite Germany to flout its provisions with impunity.

A more valid indictment of the treaty is that it broke faith with Germany, which had accepted the 1918 armistice after receiving an explicit stipulation that the Fourteen Points would be the basis of the peace settlement. As finally drafted, the treaty sinned against the spirit if not the letter of those Points. The terms imposed on Germany were severe: loss of her colonial empire, loss of considerable territory in Europe, loss of important economic resources, limitations on her sovereignty, acknowledgment of war guilt, and a crushing reparations obligation. Two unfortunate results followed: German opinion was easily aroused by demagogues to regard the settlement as so intolerable as to require repudiation at any cost; on the other hand, a guilt complex obsessed English and American liberals who became so acutely conscious of the treaty's shortcomings that they failed to see how dangerous it was not to insist upon the fulfillment of its terms. But if the treaty were too harsh, this at least can be said: it would have been harsher still had not Wilson fought for his principles. That the great idealist had to compromise was unfortunate, but not to be avoided under the conditions of 1919.

The Versailles Treaty has, unhappily, been more closely examined for its sins than for its virtues, yet it did not lack for the latter. More nearly than any preceding map of Europe, boundary lines now followed the principle of nationality. Moreover, the League Covenant offered a more promising opportunity for international cooperation than the world had ever known. Indeed, the President, who was not blind to the treaty's faults, consoled himself with the thought that whatever was unjust in the settlement might eventually be adjusted through procedures provided in the Covenant. That the League did not in practice function this way was not his fault.

Shortly after signing the treaty, the weary Wilson sailed for home, leaving Colonel House to deal with the great volume of unsettled business. Months of bitter controversy with the Senate lay ahead.

Delay on the Treaty

The President's confidence that the concessions he had obtained during his second stay at Paris would disarm his opponents proved entirely unwarranted. Lodge announced that the League in its revised form was worse than before and continued his attack on the whole Wilsonian settlement. His first achievement was to have the newly elected Senate organized in a way certain to create difficulties for Wilson. Through a well-planned filibuster the Republicans had held up passage of necessary appropriation bills before the old legislature adjourned on March 4, 1919. This made it necessary for Wilson to call the new Congress into special session in May, thereby giving the opposition ample time to form its battle lines before the President returned with the completed treaty. Not only was Lodge chairman of the powerful Senate Foreign Relations Committee, but the latter was packed with anti-League Republicans.

On July 10, the President went before the upper house to make a personal appeal for the treaty's approval. His position still seemed strong, for even his most bitter opponents believed that were the treaty to come to an immediate vote it would probably be ratified without change. Therefore their strategy had to be one of delay. The Foreign Relations Committee began a leisurely consideration of the document that consumed two months. Lodge himself killed two weeks by reading the entire treaty line by line, sometimes to an empty committee room. Six weeks more were devoted to public hearings during which self-appointed spokesmen of Ireland, China, India, Egypt, Persia, and the Ukraine, together with "experts" on specific problems, were allowed to protest various details of the settlement.

The committee then requested the President to place all his records of the

Getting a taste of it. Wilson giving Congress the first sample of the League of Nations. (By Donahey in the *Cleveland Plain Dealer.*)

Paris negotiations at its disposal. This Wilson refused to do—a refusal giving credence to the charge he was concealing something. Instead, he invited the members to the White House on August 19, where he was questioned for more than three hours. He tried to defend Article 10 of the Covenant, already under bitter attack, by saying that the League council could only "advise upon" the means of supplementing it, and no advice could be given without American consent. To him, Article 10 constituted "the very backbone of the whole Covenant. Without it the League would be scarcely more than an influential debating society."

He could see no objection to the Senate's passing resolutions interpreting the sense in which the United States accepted the obligations of the Covenant, provided they were not made part of the formal ratification itself. But if any reservations were made that had to be accepted by other signatories, they would not only delay ratification, but would cause other governments to follow the American example so that "the meaning and operative force of the treaty would presently be clouded from one end of its clauses to the other."

During this session, however, the President made no converts. As in the February conference, the Democrats went away convinced that Wilson had met every reasonable objection, while Lodge and his followers contended that the treaty should be ratified only with important reservations, if at all.

Public Opinion and the League

Both supporters and opponents of the League counted on a vast tide of popular sentiment to overwhelm the opposing faction. At first the pro-League forces seemed to have the better of it. Out of 1,377 newspaper editors polled by the *Literary Digest* in April, 1919, 718 unconditionally favored the League, 478 favored it conditionally, and only 181 opposed it. Thirty-two states legislatures passed resolutions favoring entrance into some form of international organization, thirty-three governors were similarly on record, while pro-League sentiment was also strong among Protestant clergymen. The League to Enforce Peace, at the height of its power and influence, staged nationwide meetings to urge ratification without reservations. Prominent in this movement was Taft, who sharply denounced the partisan maneuvers of his fellow Republicans.

But the anti-Leaguers were also active. A self-constituted general staff held frequent meetings—usually in the Washington home of Senator Brandegee. Important in the so-called cabal were Senators Borah, Johnson of California, Knox of Pennsylvania, and McCormick of Illinois, and Colonel George Harvey, publisher of the influential *Harper's Weekly* and bitter enemy of Wilson since their break in 1911. Two Pennsylvania millionaires, Henry Clay Frick and Andrew Mellon, provided the group with ample funds. The Hearst press was already violently denouncing the League; its efforts were supplemented by a large mass of literature warning against the perils of foreign entanglements. A League for the Preservation of American Independence held protest meetings against "the evil thing with a holy name."

Opponents of the League found willing allies among the American Irish, who would probably have regarded the League as a sinister Anglo-American alliance under any circumstances. A series of events in 1919, however, intensified their hostility. In February, a nationwide convention of Irish-Americans adopted a resolution asking the Peace Conference "to recognize the right of the people of Ireland to select for themselves . . . the form of government under which in the future they shall live." Wilson, not unsympathetic to the idea of Irish nationalism, tried to persuade Lloyd George to confer with a distinguished delegation of Irish-Americans, headed by Frank Walsh of the War Labor Board, which wanted to have Eamon de Valera, president of the so-called Irish Republic, present the cause of his government to the Conference. Lloyd George refused to do so, and Wilson did not press the issue to avoid offending the British. Disillusioned, the Irish-Americans returned home, convinced that the peace negotiators were spurning the rights of small nations for whom the war had supposedly been fought. Naturally the anti-Leaguers increased this Irish-American hostility by portraying the League as a menace both to Irish and American independence.

Alarmed by the success of his opponents in delaying action and beclouding the issue, Wilson set out in September on a speaking trip to carry his cause directly to the people. He visited the states of the Midwest, of the Pacific Coast, and of the Rocky Mountains. During the space of 22 days he traveled more than 8,000 miles and delivered 37 speeches averaging an hour in length.

For a frail man of 63, already overtaxed by his labors, this was too much. After his speech at Pueblo, Colorado, on September 25, Wilson suffered a serious breakdown. All thought of further activity had to be abandoned, and his special train speeded back to Washington. Stricken with partial paralysis the day after his return, Wilson was never again a well man. During the crucial rounds of the battle over the treaty, he was confined to his bedroom where he received little news from the outside world except through his wife and his doctor. Observers disagreed as to whether or not the heroic effort that had cost the President his health strengthened his cause. He had been greeted by large and enthusiastic crowds, many of his speeches were remarkably eloquent, and thousands of listeners were impressed by his impassioned earnestness; but he gained no additional support in the one place he most needed it—in the Senate—and big crowds also applauded the anti-League speeches of Borah, Johnson, and McCormick who pressed hard on the President's heels during the tour.

The Defeat of the Treaty

The Senate Foreign Relations Committee finally made its recommendations on September 10, 1919. The majority report, concurred in by nine of the ten Republican members, advocated no less than forty-five amendments and four reservations to the treaty. On the other hand, six of the seven Democrats signed a minority report calling for ratification without change.

The stage was now set for a long debate on the Senate floor. For purposes of clarity and convenience, the upper house members may be divided into four major groups. All but about seven Democrats were willing to vote for the treaty without change—either out of devotion to the League idea itself or out of loyalty to Wilson. The Republicans, on the other hand, were divided into three roughly equal factions. Some fourteen were staunch isolationists—the so called irreconcilables, determined to vote against the treaty so long as it incorporated the League in any form. A second faction, headed by Lodge, consisted of strong reservationists; some of them believed in an association of nations, but felt that the Wilson version must be drastically amended to safeguard American interests; others were probably against any League, but believed it was better strategy to emasculate the treaty with amendments than to reject it outright. The remainder were mild reservationists, at heart pro-League, yet believing that Wilson's work needed some clarification.

The initial advantage seemed to lie with the friends of the treaty. All the amendments originally recommended in the majority report were voted down by an alliance of Democrats with mild reservationists, but Lodge made a remarkable recovery from this setback. He now presented a battery of fourteen reservations and won a majority of the Senate to their support. The strong reservationists favored them as minimum safeguards were the United States to accept the suspect treaty; the irreconcilables voted for them to weaken the treaty if they could not kill it outright; the mild reservationists approved them to get the treaty ratified and believed the reservations would serve that end. The Democrats made their worst tactical error in not developing an alternate program to hold the support of these pro-League Republicans.

Senators supported the reservations for a variety of motives. Staunch Republicans were reluctant to let Wilson's treaty go through without change lest the Democratic party get too much political credit. Sticklers for congressional prerogatives feared that League membership might weaken the legislature's sole authority to declare war. The bogy that Article 10 constituted an entangling alliance impressed isolationists generally and particularly the Irish, who argued that the United States might help suppress the Irish Republic. Much was made of the British Empire's six votes in the League assembly to one for the United States (although English influence over the votes of South Africa or Canada was not likely to be as great as that of the United States over the votes of a dozen small neighboring republics). Wilson was accused of insulting the Senate in his choice of peace commissioners, of thwarting the aspirations of Italy and China, and of lying in his denial that he had known about the secret treaties before he went to Paris.

In the end, the Lodge reservations were approved by the Senate. All but one Republican voted for them; most Democrats voted against them. The most important reservation practically nullified Article 10 of the Covenant: the United States would assume no obligation under it unless Congress acted in a particular case. Other reservations claimed for the United States complete freedom to exclude any domestic issue from League jurisdiction, the sole right to interpret the Monroe Doctrine, refusal to agree to the Shantung settlement, and refusal to be bound by any League decision in which member states of the British Commonwealth cast in the aggregate more than one vote.

Lodge's motives in pushing through these reservations are still a matter of controversy. Those who believe in the Senator's sincerity insist he really wanted an association of nations such as he had championed in earlier years and was seeking only to protect American interests. Those who doubt Lodge's sincerity regard him as a bitter partisan determined to kill Wilson's project by maneuvering its Senate approval in such mutilated form that Wilson would not attempt to obtain its ratification by other powers. They point out that Lodge helped kill arbitration treaties in 1905 and 1911 by similar methods.

The question now was: Would the treaty with the Lodge reservations obtain the two-thirds vote needed for final Senate approval? Wilson's position was made clear in a letter expressing hope that friends and supporters of the treaty would vote against the proposal because it provided "for nullification of the treaty."

On November 19, when the important roll call was finally taken, only 39 Senators approved the treaty with the Lodge reservations, with 55 opposed. The nays were cast by 42 Democrats, most of them guided by the advice from the White House, and 13 Republican irreconcilables, who opposed any league. On ratification without reservations, only 38 Senators, all but one of them Democrats, supported the treaty in unadulterated form, while 55 opposed it, both groups of reservationists joining forces with the irreconcilables.

It seemed fantastic that, although there were only 17 Senators completely opposed to the treaty, ratification could not be obtained. Moderates from both parties sought escape from the impasse through a bipartisan conference in January, 1920, in which the Democrats offered to accept several reservations, including one to Article 10 drafted by Taft. This meeting made such apparent progress that the irreconcilables threatened to bolt the party if Lodge gave ground. In the end, the Massachusetts Senator refused all terms except complete Democratic acquiesence in his reservations, and the compromise attempt failed.

On March 19, 1920, the Senate took the final vote on the treaty. The 14 Lodge reservations had been strengthened and a fifteenth reservation of Democratic parentage had been adopted, stating that the Irish were entitled to a government of their own choice. The treaty with these 15 reservations came within 7 of the two-thirds vote necessary for ratification; now 49 Senators voted for it and 35 against it. Half of the Democrats who had voted earlier against the treaty with reservations now voted for it, convinced that approval in this form was better than no ratification at all. But the other half voted against it, following Wilson's advice. Once again it was their votes, added to those of the irreconcilables, that defeated the treaty.

An interesting speculation is whether the result would have been different had Wilson retained his health. Perhaps pro-League public opinion would have been more effectively rallied. Perhaps the President, more conscious of the realities of the situation, might, through compromise, have won the support of the more reasonable reservationists. But to compromise was impossible for the Wilson of 1920; many critics consider this to be his fatal mistake, although his admirers have insisted that compromise would have been equivalent to surrender.

Failure to ratify left the United States legally at war with Germany. The Republicans, anxious to end Wilson's wartime powers, passed the so-called Knox Resolution that simply repealed the declaration of war, but the President vetoed it with the stinging statement that this expedient was an "ineffaceable stain upon the gallantry and honor of the United States." Consequently, the official state of war continued until Harding was in office.

President Wilson never lost faith that American opinion would eventually override the obstructionists, and he looked forward to the 1920 election as "a solemn referendum" on the issue. But as will be shown later, that election proved meaningless as such a referendum. What the American people really thought of the League is difficult to determine. Undoubtedly time worked to the advantage of the anti-Leaguers. Over the course of the months, the combined efforts of the irreconcilable Senators, the nationalist press, the Irish, and other groups convinced millions of Americans that the League was a sinister plot against American independence. Millions of others did not lose their faith in the ideal, but they became hopelessly divided as to how to realize it. Taft and other leaders of the League to Enforce Peace shifted their ground, giving up their fight to obtain the treaty without change and urging ratification with the Lodge reservations, even though they considered some of them "harmful." On the other hand, many believed Wilson was right and that the Lodge reservations really nullified the treaty. Whether other signatories of the treaty would have accepted the reservations is uncertain, although there is some evidence that they were willing to do so. Baffled and confused, more and more Americans tired of the whole debate and were more than willing to forget the war and the League. Sadly commenting on this, Wilson declared: "They will have to learn now by bitter experience just what they have lost. . . . We had a chance to gain the leadership of the world. We have lost it, and soon we shall be witnessing the tragedy of it all."

Postwar Reform

The reaction against Wilsonian diplomatic idealism did not prevent certain prewar reform movements from achieving their goals in the months after the armistice. Indeed, the demand for both prohibition and women's suffrage had been accentuated by the war itself. The Anti-Saloon League and its allies, already strong, took immediate advantage of the opportunity offered by the war. The brewery business was denounced as unpatriotic because of its domination by German-Americans, while great stress was laid on the danger of the liquor trade to soldiers' morale and on the iniquity of diverting scarce grain into the manufacture of intoxicants. The Lever Act of 1917 prohibited using grain to make distilled liquors and permitted the President to extend the ban to beer, ale, and wine. Wilson ordered the breweries to close in October, 1918. Ten days after the armistice a law—curiously known as the "War Prohibition Act"—made it unlawful to sell intoxicants after June 30, 1919, until the war was proclaimed at an end.

This date, in fact, was the last day on which intoxicating beverages were legally sold in the United States for more than fourteen years. On December 18, 1917, Congress had passed and sent to the states the Eighteenth Amendment, by which "the manufacture, sale, or transportation of intoxicating liquors within, the transportation thereof into, or the exportation thereof from the United States and all territory subject to the jurisdiction thereof for beverage purposes" was prohibited. Congress and the several states were to have concurrent power to enforce the amendment by appropriate legislation. By January 16, 1919, the necessary thirty-six states had approved the amendment, which was proclaimed in force a year later. Eventually all the states except Connecticut and Rhode Island joined in ratification.

The actual definition of intoxicating beverages, as well as drastic penalties for their manufacture or sale, was provided by the Volstead Act, passed over Wilson's veto in October, 1919. The banning of all liquors containing more than 0.5 per cent alcohol was criticized by many who denied that light wines and beer were in fact intoxicating, but the Supreme Court upheld the law (Hawke v. Smith, 1920, and Rhode Island v. Palmer, 1920). Enforcement of legislation that a large section of the public considered a violation of personal liberty proved one of the most troublesome problems of the 1920's.

Meantime, the nation's participation in a crusade to make the world safe for democracy and the magnificent support women gave to the war effort had undermined male resistance to the demand for women's suffrage.

Can she live up to expectations? (By McCutcheon in the *Chicago Tribune*.)

In June, 1919, Congress accepted the Nineteenth Amendment, which specified that the right to vote should not be denied by the United States or any state "on account of sex." Woman suffrage was strongly opposed in many sections of the South, where nine states rejected the amendment. The fact, however, that 1920 was an election year worked to the advantage of the suffrage advocates. Republicans vied with Democrats for the political credit of having given women the vote, and in August, 1920, the consent of the thirty-sixth state was gained. The amendment was declared in effect in time for the ladies to cast their ballots for Harding or Cox. The feminine vote did not bring the immediate purification of politics that the more ardent suffragettes had promised, but neither did it produce the dreadful consequences predicted by misogynists.

Demobilization

The demobilization of more than four million men in the armed services was accomplished quickly. By mid-April, 1919, four thousand men a day were being discharged, and nearly half of those in training camps in the United States had been dismissed. Even before Wilson returned from Paris, a million and a half members of the AEF were back on American shores. This was almost as spectacular an achievement as getting them overseas, because only American ships were used on the return voyage. With the exception of fewer than twenty thousand men serving under General Henry Allen as an Army of Occupation in the Rhineland, all the expeditionary forces were home again by January, 1920.

It is questionable whether so rapid a demobilization was wise. Because soldiers were discharged by military units, without any consideration of employment opportunities in their home communities, many veterans faced weeks without work. The problem was accentuated by the abrupt and planless termination of war contracts, which threatened many industrial units with bankruptcy. Along with the returned veterans, moreover, thousands of war workers were seeking new jobs. According to Labor Department estimates, there were a million unemployed on January 31,

1919, a number that increased at the rate of a hundred thousand a week for more than two months thereafter.

The Federal government did little to help during the crisis. Wilson said that the American people knew their own business, were quick and resourceful in making adjustments, and were self-reliant in action. He advocated, therefore, a minimum of governmental direction over the processes of reconstruction. Baruch concurred in this judgment, and by January 1, 1919, the powerful War Industries Board had closed shop. Even the limited program the President did recommend was jettisoned by the Republican-dominated Congress. The United States Employment Service, which had placed more than 4.5 million workers in jobs over the course of sixteen months, had to scrap 60 per cent of its machinery in March, 1919, when Congress refused to make sufficient appropriations to support it, because of both the general impulse to cut down the huge governmental expenditures and the unpopularity of this particular agency with employers who accused it of being staffed with doctrinaire social workers, oversympathetic with the cause of labor unionism. The congressional economy drive also caused rejection of proposals to expand public works and to rehabilitate the railroads, in bad condition because of overuse during the war.

Similar motives combined with the opposition of the National Grange to defeat the so-called Lane Plan for Federal and state cooperation in a bold reclamation project to provide both employment and farms for returned veterans. One of the few measures actually passed by Congress was the Vocational Rehabilitation Act of June, 1918, which set up the Federal Board of Vocational Education to train disabled veterans for jobs. Although several thousand men were placed in colleges and schools throughout the country, the program proved a great disappointment because it benefited only a small percentage of the 230,000 Americans disabled during the war.

Many states and municipalities took a broader view of their responsibilities during the reconstruction period. New York, Oregon, and Indiana made generous appropriations for state employment services to serve both veterans and displaced civilian workers. Employment bureaus were also maintained by welfare agencies all over the nation. The task of coordinating these activities was entrusted to Colonel Arthur Woods, formerly New York City police commissioner and at this time assistant to Secretary of War Baker. In the end more than a million men obtained jobs through these channels. Seventeen states passed bonus acts for the benefit of veterans. New York and Oregon aided veterans in obtaining an education; several Western states promised cooperation with the Lane Plan for settling veterans on reclaimed lands and, when Congress failed to act, California went ahead with its own land settlement program.

The greatest help, however, in carrying the country safely through the demobilization period came from an unexpected quarter. By the summer of 1919 the postarmistice depression was giving way to an extraordinary postwar prosperity. Because the war had ruined for the time being the German export trade and seriously injured the British, American exports soared to dizzy heights for several months. They totaled slightly less than $8 billion in 1919 and considerably more than that in 1920—over three times their 1913 level. The domestic market was similarly active, as an orgy of spending of wartime savings were poured out for commodities difficult to buy during the war. Particularly prosperous was the automobile business. The boom, however, was not healthy. With all Europe impoverished by the war, the export business was cut in half as sharply as it had risen. As wartime controls relaxed, domestic prices jumped to such unreasonable levels as to dry up demand, while warehouses bulged with the huge inventories carried by overoptimistic businessmen. Although the country suffered a serious economic depression in 1921, the short-lived prosperity of the fall of 1919 and the following winter had at least eased the problems created by rapid demobilization.

Getting the Government Out of Business

During the war advanced liberals had watched with approval while the Federal government not only built and operated millions of tons of shipping, but took over management of the railroad, telegraph, telephone, cable, and radio systems of the country. Some at least of these economic activities, they hoped, would remain permanently nationalized or at least subjected to more rigorous public control than before the war. Conservatives, on the other hand, had acquiesced in government operation of these enterprises with great misgivings and, as soon as the armistice was signed, they demanded that business be turned back to private control as speedily as possible. In the case of electrical communications they had a complete victory. At midnight, July 31, 1919, Congress returned these properties to their owners without any condition other than that the rates established by the Postmaster General be continued for four months.

The railroads, however, constituted a somewhat different problem. Although high wartime costs caused the Railroad Administration to suffer a loss of $1 billion during the twenty-six months of its existence, government operation by certain other standards proved an interesting and not unsuccessful experiment. Particularly impressive was the greatly improved efficiency made possible by operating the railroads as a single system without wasteful duplication of facilities. Progressives demanded either the continuance of government operation or the return of the roads under conditions that would consolidate the wartime gains. McAdoo, who headed the Railroad Administration until January, 1919, and Walter Hines, his successor, both recommended that Federal control be continued for five years while the whole railroad problem was intensively investigated. The Railroad Brotherhoods vigorously supported a plan drafted by Glenn Plumb, their legal representative, under which the government would purchase the roads and operate them through a tripartite board representative of the government, management, and the employees.

Congress, however, opposed all such proposals. On March 1, 1920, the lines were returned to private management under the terms of the Esch-Cummins, or Transportation, Act of 1920. This important law not only provided for government support to the railroads during the difficult transition period, but laid down significant principles for the future regulation of transportation. For six months after the return of the lines, the government guaranteed the carriers a net return equal to the rentals they had been receiving from the Railroad Administration; rates, fares, wages, and salaries were all to be frozen at existing levels during the guarantee period unless the government authorized changes. As a further help, a revolving fund of $300 million was set up from which the railroads might obtain loans upon approval of the ICC for two years after resumption of private control. The ICC was enlarged from nine to eleven members and given important additional powers.

The most striking policy change in the 1920 railroad legislation was that under which cooperation and consolidation of the carriers were favored. Not only could the ICC relax the long-short haul clause and permit forms of pooling formerly prohibited, but it was directed to prepare a plan under which the railroad properties of the nation would be consolidated into a limited number of systems. Thus it was frankly recognized that enforced competition as the panacea for all railroad abuses had failed and that the public interest would best be served by encouraging strong carriers to take over the weak under strict government regulation.

Finally, the Esch-Cummins Transportation Act provided new machinery to handle labor disputes. There had been considerable congressional support for compulsory arbitration and the outlawing of railroad strikes; indeed, the Senate had passed the Esch Bill in a form incorporating these principles. The House rejected this extreme procedure, however, and the act provided instead for the establishment of both railroad boards of arbitration and a national Railroad Labor Board. The former was to hear grievances over rules and working conditions. Wage disputes and any grievances not settled by the adjustment boards were to be referred to the Railroad Labor Board, composed of nine members appointed by the President; three of them represented the employers, three the employees, and three the public. The board was given wide powers to compel testimony, but its findings were not binding on either party. A discussion of the problems confronting the board during its short life is included in a later chapter.

In many ways the shipping problem was even more complex than the railroad situation. Here was not a question of the government's returning to private management enterprises that had all along been privately owned; rather it was a problem of deciding what should be done with some two thousand ships built or purchased with government money. During the export boom of 1919 the problem was not acute; some three hundred operating companies willingly kept existing routes in operation and developed new ones on a cost-plus basis under supervision of the Merchant Fleet Corporation and the Shipping Board. But the collapse of international trade in 1920 brought unpleasant results. There was no longer enough business to provide attractive commissions to the operating companies, and their number fell to forty. Often government-owned ships were simply abandoned in foreign ports and government losses from its shipping operations reached $16 million a month by 1921.

Once again congressional conservatives favored a speedy return to private enterprise. The Merchant Marine Act of 1920 directed the Shipping Board to transfer government-owned ships quickly and on easy terms to private ownership. Except under special circumstances, the ships could be sold only to corporations in which a majority of the stock was held by American citizens; indeed, if the ships were to be used in the coasting trade, the companies had to be at least 75 per cent American controlled. The Merchant Fleet Corporation was to operate the ships that could not be sold; it was to establish new shipping routes and maintain them until private capital could be induced to take them over and could use a revolving fund of $25 million to make loans to companies willing to operate the new routes.

The shipping problem was too complex to be solved by a single wave of the wand. The nub of the problem was this: high costs made it unprofitable for American shipping to compete with foreign lines; yet an American merchant marine was vital to national defense. The only possible answers were government operation at a loss or private ownership and operation with subsidies. It required many years for American opinion to accept the inevitability of choosing between these alternatives.

Labor Unrest

During the war labor relations had been abnormal. AFL leaders were fairly successful in preventing strikes. At the same time, however, workers demanded substantial wage increases and the Federal war administrations approved their requests to keep industrial peace and maintain production. From the standpoint of most employers, labor became entirely too assertive, and it seemed imperative to resist firmly the trend toward increased power for labor union leaders once the war was over. The unions, on the other hand, were determined not only to preserve their wartime gains, but to obtain new concessions. They pointed out that the cost of living after the armistice was constantly rising and that many workers, even after pay raises, were worse off than they had been before the war. With both management and labor in an uncompromising mood, all the elements for serious industrial warfare were present. During 1919 more than four million workers were at one time or another out on strike, and the number of such disputes reached 3,630.

In many of these contests labor was victorious. Such was the result of walkouts of New York clothing workers, New York harbor workers, New England textile employees, New England telegraph operators, and New York actors. But these victories—mostly won early in 1919—hardened public opinion against labor, and the strikes later in the year were much less successful.

Particularly damaging to the cause of unionism was the nationwide alarm when Seattle, Washington, became the scene of a general strike in February. The trouble, starting in the shipyards, reached serious proportions when sixty thousand workers in all trades struck on February 6 to support the shipworkers' demands. Strict order was maintained by the strikers and an attempt was made to carry on essential services. But even though the strike was called off after five days, the spectacle of the economic life of a large city being thus tied up was widely cited as evidence of the danger of Bolshevism in the country—an interpretation given wide publicity by the speeches of Seattle's Mayor Ole Hansen. This feeling that labor was getting out of hand and threatening revolution received additional impetus by a serious general strike across the border in Winnipeg, Canada, in May.

The Steel Strike

Against this background, the story of the three most important labor controversies of 1919 must be considered. In the steel industry the workers were most discontented over their conditions. Their working day was frequently 12 hours, and the average in some plants was about 69 hours for a 7-day week. Nor was it unusual for the operators to call upon the men to labor on 24-hour shifts.

To remedy the situation, 24 AFL unions established a steelworkers' organizing committee that tried to unionize the men during the summer of 1919. Prominent in the movement was William Z. Foster, reputed to be anything from a Communist to a syndicalist. When the committee demanded an 8-hour day, a 6-day week, the ending of 24-hour shifts, and collective bargaining, Judge Elbert Gary, chairman of the board of United States Steel and general spokesman for the whole industry, refused to recognize the right of the group to speak for the men.

Consequently, a strike was scheduled for September 22. President Wilson's effort to avert the walkout failed when union officials rejected his plea to postpone the strike. On the appointed day, some 280,000 men left their jobs, chiefly in Chicago, Youngstown, Buffalo, and several plants in Pennsylvania. Gradually more workers joined the walkout until there were at least 300,000 in the strikers' ranks. There was disorder around some of the steel mills, at least four persons were killed and more than fifty wounded. At one time Federal troops were moved into Gary, Indiana, where martial law was declared and picketing limited.

Public opinion, influenced in no so small part by an antilabor press, turned increasingly against the strikers. There was widespread feeling that Foster was promoting un-American agitation and also that the workers had gained enough during the war. A back-to-work movement gained momentum by January, 1920, the organizing committee acknowledged failure, and the strike was declared at an end.

The strike, however, had a curious aftermath. Public opinion showed signs of reversal after it was over. In large part this was because of the harrowing picture of actual labor conditions in the steel industry in the report of a special investigating committee of the Interchurch World Movement. This report, signed by an impressive list of prominent Protestant churchmen, denied the strike had been Red-inspired: instead, it was the natural result of the labor policies of United States Steel—policies based not alone on low wages and long hours, but on arbitrary management, bribery, spying on the workers, and stirring up racial animosities to prevent employees from forming a common front. The corporation indignantly denied this indictment, but under pressure of public opinion and proddings by President Harding, the twelve-hour day was eliminated from the steel industry in 1923.

The Boston Police Strike

After the armistice, Boston policemen were in a rebellious mood. Their station houses were crowded, they had to buy their own uniforms, and, worst of all, they were still paid according to prewar scales based on a minimum of $1,100. In the summer of 1919, the Boston Social Club, to which the police had belonged for thirteen years, applied for an AFL charter. Since Police Commissioner Edwin Curtis had forbidden any such affiliation, he now took stern disciplinary action against the club's officers. Nineteen were threatened with suspension, bringing on a crisis. Mayor Andrew Peters and a Citizens' Committee sought to mediate under the following formula: the leaders were to be reinstated, the police were to be permitted to maintain a union but without outside affiliations, and the men were to be allowed to present their grievances. When Curtis refused to compromise and carried through the threatened suspensions, the police, by a vote of 1,134 to 2, decided to strike.

On September 9 the police left their posts and shortly after, ruffians, hoodlums, and lawbreakers of every description began looting stores and homes. The next day Mayor Peters called out the local state guard and was thus able to restore order. On the third day of the strike, Governor Calvin Coolidge took the situation into his own hands by calling out the rest of the state guard and appealing to the Secretary of War for Federal troops in case a general strike was attempted.

The policemen, realizing their defeat, were ready to return to work, but Curtis refused to take back any strikers and proposed enlisting an entirely new force. Samuel Gompers tried to intercede, but Coolidge, standing firmly behind the commissioner, rebuked the AFL head with a stinging telegram: "There is no right to strike against the public safety by anybody, anywhere, any time."

It reveals much about the prevailing mood of the country that Coolidge's actions made him a national hero and a possibility for the Republican presidential nomination in 1920. Even President Wilson added his congratulations to those showered upon this Yankee champion of law and order.

Enter John L. Lewis

John L. Lewis, destined to be a prominent figure in labor circles for the next four decades, became president of the United Mine Workers in 1919. His first task was to lead the workers in the bituminous coal fields in their struggle for a national contract, a 60 per cent wage increase, and a thirty-hour minimum work week. The pay demand was large because the bituminous miners, unlike the anthracite workers, had had no increase since September, 1917, even though the cost of living had risen sharply.

When the operators rejected these terms, a strike was called for November 1, 1919. Lewis was solidly supported by the miners, but on November 9, Attorney General A. Mitchell Palmer obtained a sweeping injunction based on the Lever Act, which gave the government extraordinary powers over food and fuel. The UMW officers were ordered to cease all efforts to encourage and maintain the strike. To the reporters Lewis commented: "We cannot fight the government," and he issued orders to end the walkout.

The miners, however, did not actually go back to work until a month later when the union accepted President Wilson's proposal that the controversial issues be submitted to arbitration. After extended hearings, the arbitral body awarded the miners a 27 per cent increase, but no shortening of working hours.

The Red Scare

The strike epidemic alone would have been enough to convince many conservative Americans that dangerous radicalism was rampant in the land—a feeling many times intensified by events in Europe. The Bolsheviks had not only clung to power in Russia, but had boldly raised the banner of world revolution; German Communists held control of Berlin for a few days; Hungarian Communists ruled their country for five months; unrest boiled high in Italy and elsewhere in Europe; and there were ominous rumblings in India and the British Empire. For a time during 1919 universal proletarian revolt seemed a definite possibility.

There was an intoxicating quality in the news that led a few extremists in the United States to the point of dangerous action. Late in April, 1919, a bomb was found in the mail of Mayor Hansen of Seattle, a conspicuous Red-baiter. The next day the black maid of Senator Thomas Hardwick of Georgia, an advocate of immigration restriction, had her hands blown off on opening a mysterious package addressed to her employer. Timely investigation in the New York City post office disclosed sixteen bomb packages addressed to prominent persons in public life. Some twenty other deadly bundles were discovered in the mails being sent to Attorney General Palmer, Supreme Court Justice Holmes, Federal Judge Landis, J. P. Morgan, John D. Rockefeller, and other well-known citizens. A month later several explosions occurred in widely scattered parts of the country, one of them wrecking the Washington home of Attorney General Palmer. The worst of these outrages took place on September 16, 1920, when a terrific blast in noonday-crowded Wall Street caused the death of thirty-eight persons, injury to hundreds of others, property damage of $2 million, and untold harm to the nerves of the masters of capital.

These and other similar incidents were more an index of the unusual strain of the times than of the real strength of the revolutionary movement in the United States. Actually radical ranks were divided and confused by the turn of events. A right-wing minority of the Socialists led by John Spargo had withdrawn in 1917 when the party condemned American participation in the war. This loss had not been serious, but in 1919 a more important crisis developed, Left-wing Socialists tried to capture the party

The Wall Street explosion, September 16, 1920. (Brown Bros.)

and affiliate with the Communist Third International; when this failed, the extremists split off into two new groups: the Communist party and the slightly less radical Communist Labor party. On orders from Moscow, the two were united in the spring of 1920 as the United Communist party. Meantime, the Socialist Labor group still regarded itself as the true Marxian party, the IWW continued on its separate way, and the Anarchists would have nothing to do with any of the others. The total of all these radical groups has been estimated at less than 0.2 per cent of the American population. There could be little menace from that small a minority.

To middle-class Americans, however, a Red was a Red. They were ignorant of or indifferent to the fact that the Socialists had purged Communists from their own ranks or that Anarchists were anti-Bolshevik. All radicals were branded as un-American because of their hostility to the war and the preponderance of recent immigrant stock in their ranks. In Weirton, West Virginia, 118 foreigners, members of the IWW and involved in the steel strike, were compelled by the police to kiss the flag. In New York City, a mob of ex-soldiers and civilians wrecked the office of the *New York Call,* a leading Socialist newspaper. Most serious of all was the clash at Centralia, Washington, on Armistice Day, 1919. Three parading members of the American Legion were killed by gunfire from IWW headquarters and another lost his life in the ensuing turmoil. This incident was surrounded by great controversy. The Legionnaires insisted the attack was unprovoked; the IWW members claimed they were defending their hall against an attempt to wreck it as it had been wrecked the year before. Guilty or innocent, the IWW was severely punished. Of twelve members accused of complicity in the shooting, one was taken from his cell by a mob, mutilated, and brutally lynched, while the others were sentenced from twenty-five to forty years in prison. But this was not all. Throughout the Northwest IWW halls were demolished by irate citizens; over a thousand of the detested group were arrested, and it was difficult to find lawyers to defend them.

Prosecution of individuals for merely belonging to the IWW or any other radical organization was made possible by the enactment of criminal syndicalist laws in thirty-two states declaring it illegal to belong to organizations advocating the forceful overthrow of the government. Twenty-eight states made it a punishable offense to display the Red flag as a political emblem.

Although ultrapatriots failed in their attempts to have passed a new Federal sedition law even more severe than the wartime legislation, the Federal government did enforce existing laws drastically against the radicals. Wilson could not forgive the Socialists for opposing the war and refused to pardon Debs and others sent to prison for their activities. Not until Christmas, 1933, were the Federal prisons cleared of the last of the fifteen hundred originally convicted.

A particularly effective weapon was a law of October, 1918, authorizing the Secretary of Labor to deport any alien who advocated revolution or belonged to any organization that advocated the forcible overthrow of the government, assassination of public officials, or the unlawful destruction of property. In 1920, the Secretary's authority was extended to permit the deportation of aliens convicted under the espionage laws. The first wholesale deportation took place in December, 1919, when the *Buford,* popularly known as the Red, or Soviet, Ark, left for Russia with 249 radicals aboard.

Meantime, Attorney General Palmer was preparing a drastic blow. For many weeks in 1919 Department of Justice operatives gathered data on Communists and Anarchists. Spies attended secret meetings of these radicals and obtained the names of the leaders. Palmer was supplied with three thousand deportation warrants that were served on January 2, 1920, in carefully planned simultaneous raids on radical meetings in all parts of the country. Everyone found on the premises was arrested whether or not the agents had a warrant for the particular individual, whether or not he was a Communist party member, and whether he was an alien or citizen. Other radicals were apprehended in their homes. Even persons trying to visit the jailed suspects were themselves arrested on suspicion of affiliation with the proscribed groups. Some four thousand in all were rounded up. Their treatment after arrest was often harsh, and the deportation hearings were conducted without counsel or other judicial safeguards. Only 556 of those arrested were in the end deported; some of the others were turned over to state authorities for punishment under the criminal syndicalist laws, but the majority were eventually released for want of evidence. Palmer's high-handed procedure was enthusiastically applauded by most of the public, who hated and feared the alien radicals; a few thoughtful citizens, like Charles Evans Hughes, spoke gravely, however, of "violations of personal rights which savor of the worst practices of tyranny."

While these events were transpiring, the New York Assembly tried to outdo the Attorney General in asserting its 100 per cent Americanism.

Five regularly elected assemblymen from New York City were expelled simply because they were Socialists. Hughes led the New York Bar Association in a vigorous, but ineffective protest; he declared:

> This is not, in my judgment, American government. . . . I count it a most serious mistake to proceed . . . against masses of our citizens combined for political action, by denying them the only source of peaceful government; that is, action by the ballot box and through duly elected representatives in legislative bodies.

The Assembly attempted to follow up its action by passing several drastic antiradical laws proposed by the Lusk Committee, but they were vetoed by Governor Alfred E. Smith.

The Congress also refused to be contaminated by the presence of Socialists. Victor Berger, second only to Debs in party prominence, had been an outspoken opponent of the war. He was convicted and sentenced by Judge Landis to twenty years in prison in December, 1918, under the Espionage Act, but this conviction was later set aside by the Supreme Court. In November, 1918, he had been duly elected to the House of Representatives, but the following spring his right to sit in the House was promptly challenged. The case was referred to a special committee that reported against him, and in November, 1919, the seat was declared vacant. The next month the voters of Berger's district again elected him in a special election, even though Democrats and Republicans united on a single candidate to oppose him. Once more the House voted to exclude him, despite the plea of James Mann of Illinois, the Republican floor manager, who said:

> I do not share the views of Mr. Berger, but I am willing to meet his views in an argument before the people rather than to say we shall deny him the opportunity to be heard when selected by the people in the legal form and invite them, in effect, to resort to violence.

Not until Berger was elected for a third time in 1922 did the House finally allow him to take his rightful seat.

Thus in an atmosphere of narrow nationalism and intolerance, the Wilson administration, which in better days had been dedicated to much different ideals, drew to a close.

10

THE REPUBLICAN RESTORATION

Humiliated in the election of 1912, the conservative wing of the Republican party came back to Washington in triumph after the election of 1920. American participation in World War I, the frustrating struggle over the League of Nations, and the anxieties of the postwar period had reversed the current of public opinion. Fed up with appeals to idealism and sacrifice, a majority of the voters wanted nothing so much as to forget politics and return to their private concerns. After 1922, when the country emerged from its postwar economic confusions into a period of general prosperity, the conservative mood deepened. The voters shrugged off revelations of corruption under Harding and discovered an unlikely hero in the tight-lipped Calvin Coolidge, who sagely proclaimed that the business of the country was business. Progressive Republicans and Democrats shrilly condemned popular complacency, but not until the Great Depression intervened did reform again become popular.

Republican Strategy

Realizing that the political tide which had turned with the congressional elections of 1918 was now running in their favor, the Republican delegates gathered in a mood of optimism at their national convention in Chicago on June 8, 1920. Henry Cabot Lodge provided the theme with his keynote speech. "Mr. Wilson and his dynasty," Lodge said, "his heirs and assigns, or anybody that is his, anybody who with bent knee has served his purpose, must be driven from all control of the government and all influence in it."

There had been a spirited contest for delegates to the convention. Indeed, so numerous were the Republican aspirants for the presidency that as early as February, 1920, Harry M. Daugherty, a small-town Ohio lawyer who yearned for the role of President-maker, had predicted a deadlocked convention. Then, he said, "at the proper time . . . some fifteen men, bleary with loss of sleep and perspiring profusely with the excessive heat, will sit down at a big table. I will be with them and will present the name of Senator Harding to them, and before we get through they will put him over." As it turned out, Daugherty was substantially correct in his prediction, but in putting over Senator Warren G. Harding of Ohio, he was aided by a variety of circumstances.

If Theodore Roosevelt had lived, he probably would have won the nomination, but his death in January, 1919, threw the race wide open. The front-runner was General Leonard Wood, because many Republicans regarded him as Roosevelt's political heir. Wood had gained widespread sympathy when Wilson refused to give him an overseas command during World War I. On the other hand, his military background and advocacy of preparedness aroused opposition among a war-weary electorate. Governor Frank Lowden of Illinois and Hiram Johnson, a leader among the irreconcilables in the fight over the treaty, also had strong support for the nomination. Besides these three, there were minor booms for several other candidates, Senator Harding among them.

One of the main factors leading to the deadlock was the adverse publicity created by the lavish campaign spending of the rival Wood and Lowden forces. Colonel William C. Procter, the soap manufacturer, undertook to raise a million dollars for Wood from his wealthy friends, and the Lowden supporters solicited money with the same abandon. As an ally of Johnson, Senator Borah prompted an investigation of campaign expenditures. A congressional committee report, made public just before the convention, revealed that the Wood forces had spent $1,773,300, while the Lowden group had expended $414,000. Despite this damaging disclosure, Wood led on the first ballot, with Lowden a close second. When three subsequent ballots followed a similar pattern, the party's elder statesmen arranged an overnight adjournment to seek a way out of the demoralizing impasse.

Thus it was that a group of party leaders huddled for hours in a room of the Blackstone Hotel, assessing the "availability" of various alternatives. Eventually they chose Harding. He was a stalwart party regular, yet he had not antagonized the progressives. He had followed a safe middle course by voting for the Treaty of Versailles with the Lodge reservations. While more convention balloting was required the next day, the result was not long in doubt. On the tenth ballot Harding received the nomination. The delegates then chose Governor Calvin Coolidge as their vice-presidential candidate.

The platform took few risks. The party, so it declared, stood "for agreement among the nations to preserve the peace of the world," which could "be done without the compromise of national independence." It denounced Wilson's Covenant as "certain to produce the injustice, hostility, and controversy among nations which it proposed to prevent." By such ambivalent wording the platform writers hoped to retain the allegiance of the irreconcilables by denouncing the Covenant, while appeasing the Taft-Root group by promising to work for the preservation of peace. The platform endorsed the return of the railroads and merchant marine to private ownership and advocated immigration restriction and greater tariff protection.

No Solemn Referendum

For a time Wilson evidently hoped to run for a third term in order to continue his battle for the League, but his illness and the turn of public opinion made this impossible. Thus the quest for the nomination developed into a struggle largely among Attorney General A. Mitchell Palmer of Red-baiting fame, William Gibbs McAdoo, well known both as a cabinet officer and as Wilson's son-in-law, and Governor James Cox of Ohio. For thirty-nine ballots at the San Francisco convention the issue was in doubt. Then the shift toward Cox began, and he finally won on the forty-fourth ballot. The convention nominated Assistant Secretary of the Navy Franklin D. Roosevelt for Vice President, partly to capitalize on the magic Roosevelt name.

The platform took an unequivocal stand on the League: "We advocate the immediate ratification of the treaty without reservations which would impair its essential integrity." The convention endorsed the domestic features of the New Freedom as well as woman suffrage, statehood for Puerto Rico, and independence for the Philippines.

At Wilson's request the Democrats tried to make the election a "solemn referendum" on the League. Cox's tour of the country, however, aroused little enthusiasm. Fearful of what Harding might say, the party leaders encouraged him to restrict himself to a front-porch campaign. He condemned the Wilsonian League with sufficient vigor to retain the support of the Johnson-Borah faction, while he made ambiguous references to the desirability of a real "association of nations" in order to encourage the hopes of the internationally minded Republicans. To reassure the pro-League group, Root, Hughes, Hoover, and Stimson among others issued a statement denying that the issue was "between a league and no league," thus implying that a vote for Harding was a vote for the League with reservations. The issue was thus hopelessly confused, with voters who wanted the League supporting Harding as well as those who did not. But it made little difference. With most voters the League had become a dead issue.

The electorate wanted a change and believed that it would come sooner and more completely under Republican rule. Harding received 16 million popular votes to Cox's 9 million; the 61 per cent of the total that went to the Republicans constituted one of the most impressive majorities in American history. The electoral totals gave Harding 404 to 127 for Cox. In the Senate the Republicans gained a majority of 22 seats; in the House, of 167. But the victory was not one of party; it was brought about by war-born resentments and the desire to repudiate Wilson.

Harding and His Helpers

The new President readily admitted that he was poorly fitted for his position. Born and brought up in rural Ohio, he had finally settled down in Marion, married an ambitious, fairly wealthy widow who urged him on to greater things, and become owner-editor of the local *Star*. Eventually he entered politics, where he was at first affiliated with the Foraker, or Standard Oil, faction. He served in the state legislature and as lieutenant governor, but was defeated for the governorship in 1910. During the 1912 split, he took the conservative side; indeed, he made the nominating speech for Taft. In 1914 he was elected to the United States Senate, where he

Governor Fuller of Massachusetts, President Harding, and Senator Lodge. (Acme.)

voted as a party regular, thus opposing the League as drafted but favoring it with the Lodge reservations.

Harding presented a noble appearance and was an effective orator of the old school, although his speeches were more remarkable for their verbosity than for their content. An unreflective man, he knew little about domestic problems and less about international ones. He was genial and easygoing to the point of weakness. The new President delighted to reward his many friends, but some of them were unworthy of his trust. This was the fatal flaw of the new regime.

Harding wanted to make Senator Albert Fall of New Mexico his Secretary of State, but this suggestion aroused so much protest that he appointed the high-minded Charles Evans Hughes instead. The President made Herbert Hoover of Food Administration fame his Secretary of Commerce and Andrew D. Mellon, wealthy Pittsburgh banker and industrialist, his Secretary of the Treasury. All three of these men were persons of great ability, but Harding also put into the Cabinet representatives of the worst elements within the party. He made the slippery Harry Daugherty his Attorney General and the unscrupulous Albert Fall his Secretary of the Interior.

Conservative Legislation

In the return to normalcy one of the first steps was to raise the tariff. In addition to the wish to overthrow everything connected with Wilson and to return to Republican protectionist principles, more tangible factors were at work. The postwar reaction had fostered a stronger feeling of nationalism and a desire for greater self-sufficiency. Particularly eager for protection was a new American chemical industry, fostered by war production and the seizure of German patents, as well as some infant metallurgical enterprises. The farmers joined in the demand for higher import duties. Having increased their acreage and production to meet wartime needs, they were now suffering from overproduction and falling prices. Sympathetic Senators and Congressmen had organized the so-called Farm Bloc by the spring of 1921 to demand tariff protection and other remedies.

Even before President Wilson returned from Versailles the movement to raise the Underwood rates had begun. The President sought to combat protectionism by pointing out to Congress that the United States was now a creditor nation. As such, it could only maintain its exports to Europe by one of three policies. It could demand payment in gold, which would adversely affect economic life on both sides of the Atlantic; it could extend further credit, which was unwise in view of Europe's huge war debts; or it could exchange goods. The last was the most beneficial policy for all parties concerned. "If we want to sell," Wilson concluded, "we must be prepared to buy."

American groups hard hit by the depression of 1920, especially the farmers, were not in a mood to listen to presidential moralizing. Anxious to quiet the farmers, Congress rushed through a bill to increase the rates on agricultural imports, but Wilson vetoed the measure on March 3—his last day in office. The advent of Harding brought a speedy change in policy. In a special message to Congress on April 12, 1921, the new executive said: "I believe in protection of American industry, and it is our purpose to prosper America first." Congress readily repassed the Wilson-vetoed measure, and Harding signed it on May 17. This so-called Emergency Tariff raised the duties on corn, wheat, meat, wool, and sugar to about the Payne-Aldrich levels.

The tariff law of 1921 was only a temporary measure, to last until a broader act could be worked out. The House Ways and Means Committee, under the chairmanship of Joseph W. Fordney of Michigan, now went to work in earnest. In July, 1921, the House passed the Fordney bill, establishing rates considerably higher than the Underwood Tariff. The Senate Finance Committee, headed by Porter McCumber of North Dakota, was even more protectionist and revised the schedules upward. Urged on by lobbyists for the chemical industry and advocates of military preparedness, Senators amended the measure greatly during four months of debate. As finally approved on September 22, 1922, the Fordney-McCumber Tariff gave the nation its highest import rates in peacetime history. In addition to agricultural products, such industrial commodities as dyes, chemicals, chinaware, and cotton textiles received high protection.

Academic economists deplored the return to high tariffs. Farmers gained very little, because their troubles arose not out of foreign imports, but out of overproduction that was flooding the home market. American exports suffered because European countries raised their tariff barriers in retaliation. As the decade progressed, more and more American manufacturers established branches in foreign countries to evade these customs walls. In the United States the lessening of foreign competition encouraged the concentration of industrial control in fewer hands. European debtor nations, unable to sell in the American market, found it increasingly difficult to pay their wartime obligations. The Tariff Commission, empowered to recommend changes in the rates, became a target of criticism for its alleged political partisanship. Acting upon the Commission's advice, Harding and Coolidge raised the duties on thirty-two commodities and lowered them on only five.

Yet there was no concerted demand for revision of the Fordney-McCumber Tariff during the rest of the twenties; indeed, in the campaign of 1928, both major parties urged continued protection. Until 1929 the country continued to enjoy prosperity and feared any change in tariff policy. Moreover, the South, once the champion of free trade, was now becoming industrialized and protariff. Even the farmers, who were not sharing in the good times, were not disposed to blame the tariff for their troubles.

For many years advocates of more efficient and economical government had been urging a better budget system for the Federal government. The existing practice under which the various executive departments made their independent requests for congressional appropriations was wasteful, extravagant, and haphazard. The need to deal with postwar problems of debt and tax reduction led President Wilson to ask Congress for the more efficient planning of Federal expenditures. He recommended that the responsibility for drawing up the budget be placed in the hands of the executive branch, which would obtain estimates from the different departments for the ensuing fiscal year. The only changes that Congress would make would be through a special appropriations committee in each house. In the fall of 1920 Congress passed a measure that conformed in general with Wilson's wishes, but the President vetoed it because of a clause that he believed placed an unconstitutional check upon the executive.

Harding promptly renewed the Wilsonian request, and in June, 1921, Congress passed the Budget and Accounting Act. This provided that each department, bureau, and agency of the government should submit to the President an estimate of its fiscal needs. He would then consider the feasibility of each and submit the finished budget to Congress on the opening day of each regular session, along with a financial report on the nation. That report should include an estimate of income and expenditures for the coming year and the financial summary for the preceding year. Only through a special committee of each house could departments appeal for a change. To assist the President, Congress provided for a new Budget Bureau and a Director of the Budget. Charles G. Dawes, who had gained fame as purchasing agent for the Expenditionary Force during the war, was the first Director of the Budget, a position that he filled both colorfully and efficiently.

The Harding administration had also to struggle with such difficult issues as immigration restriction, veterans' benefits, farm relief, tax reduction, and reduction of the national debt. All of these provoked sharp controversy, and all were still outstanding when the congressional elections of November, 1922, were held. In this first test the voters demonstrated no great enthusiasm for the dominant party. The Republican majority in the Senate was cut from 22 to 6, and in the House from 167 to 15.

From Harding to Coolidge

Accustomed to a life of comparative freedom and ease, Warren Harding did not take readily to his burdensome life in the White House. In his own way he tried to fulfill the obligations of the office, but he matched the time devoted to public affairs with hours spent on golf, poker, and other diversions. The combination of harder work and more strenuous play was bad enough for a constitution that had been allowed to run down; the situation became worse when Harding began to realize that the friends he had appointed to office were betraying his trust. By early 1923 Harding was becoming increasingly worried about rumors that things were amiss in various departments.

As a release from his mental and physical troubles and as an effort to strengthen his political position, Harding set out upon a speechmaking tour in June, 1923. At first, things seemed to go well. Enthusiastic crowds cheered his speeches in the cities of the Middle West and the Rocky Mountain states; the newspapers published appealing photographs of the President in informal roles—driving a binder in Kansas, visiting miners in Montana, attending rodeos and pageants. But such activities did not give his tired body the rest and relaxation it needed, nor did a sea voyage to Alaska do anything to restore him. Returning to Seattle on July 27, he was stricken with an illness first diagnosed as ptomaine poisoning. His aides hurried him to San Francisco for treatment, but he failed rapidly. Pneumonia set in, followed by a stroke of apoplexy that brought death on August 2. The nation's grief was sincere. Mourning millions watched the long trip of the funeral cortège from San Francisco to Washington, and then to Marion for burial. Not for some time after his death did the storm finally break, and only then did the public realize that the scandals of the affable President's administration had been the worst in American history. These sensations encouraged the circulation of all kinds of rumors about his "mysterious" death, among them the story that his jealous wife had poisoned him. The truth was much less melodramatic: the strain of office, a weakened constitution, and worry about the future had combined to bring about Harding's death.

On the morning of August 3, 1923, Calvin Coolidge's own father administered the oath of office to the new chief executive in the family home at Plymouth, Vermont, where the Vice President had been vacationing. A graduate of Amherst College and trained for the law, Coolidge had made politics practically his vocation. He filled a number of local posts, served in the Massachusetts legislature, and finally as governor. His stand in the Boston police strike made him a national figure and brought him the vice-presidential nomination in 1920.

There was nothing spectacular about Coolidge. He lacked the energy of Roosevelt, the idealism of Wilson, and the glad-handedness of Harding.

He made up for these deficiencies, however, by having the confidence of the people, to whom he appeared as an average American who would bring caution and common sense to the White House. Coolidge was primarily a party man of the conservative school. A faithful believer in laissez faire, he relied for advice, not upon the Republican liberals, but upon businessmen and lawyers. Economy in government was the overriding goal, and he vetoed many bills because of the proposed expenditures. Congress enacted little social legislation during his administration, and the government made little effort to enforce the existing regulatory measures against big business. This seemed to fit the mood of the country. The vast majority of Americans appeared to be concerned with matters materialistic rather than idealistic, and Coolidge suited them well. While he was on the bridge, the skipper was never to venture into uncharted seas, but the ship of state was never to be in danger.

The Harding Scandals

The first problem that President Coolidge faced was how to handle revelations of corruption about his predecessor's administration. It is impossible to judge whether Coolidge, who had attended frequent Cabinet meetings during his vice-presidency and was in close contact with some of the malefactors, knew anything about what was going on. At all events, he took no energetic action after he became President. He kept Harding's appointees in office until congressional pressure and the force of public opinion compelled the resignation or removal of those involved in scandal, and he hesitated to press charges against them until the approach of the 1924 election spurred him into action. The most charitable thing to be said about Coolidge's laxity is that he may have believed the charges against Fall, Daugherty, and others were primarily political, brought by the opposition to weaken his party.

The most spectacular of the Harding scandals involved the naval oil reserves. In 1912 President Taft had ordered set aside for the use of the navy some 70,000 acres of oil lands in the Elk Hills region of California, and three years later Wilson had added nearly 10,000 acres at Teapot Dome, Wyoming. As part of the general conservation policy, the oil in these reserves was to be maintained until some future time when the navy might find difficulty in obtaining it from other sources. When operations in privately owned neighboring fields endangered the naval reserves during the latter part of the Wilson administration, Congress passed the General Leasing Act of 1920, empowering the Secretary of the Navy, at his discretion, to "use, store, exchange or sell" the oil for the benefit of the United States. Secretary Daniels did lease a small percentage, but he kept the vast majority under naval control.

Shortly after Harding's inauguration, Secretary of the Interior Fall persuaded him to issue a secret executive order transferring the reserves to the Interior Department. Secretary of the Navy Edwin Denby concurred in the transfer. Fall explained that the reserves were losing oil through drainage so the government might better lease them to private companies and profit

Will it prove more than a tempest in a teapot? (From the *San Francisco Chronicle*.)

from the rentals. In 1922 Fall leased the reserves to powerful oil operators: Teapot Dome to Harry F. Sinclair and Elk Hills to Edward L. Doheny. Again these were secret transactions, but rumors of Fall's actions eventually came to the ears of the vigilant Senator LaFollette. The veteran progressive forced through the Senate a resolution setting up an investigating committee.

After a year and a half of investigation, Senator Thomas J. Walsh of Montana, the committee chairman, began open hearings on October 9, 1923. Secretary Denby was not shown guilty of any corrupt act, but the furor aroused over his complacency and lack of responsibility caused him to resign in March, 1924. The evidence concerning Fall was much more damaging. He had recently spent some $170,000 on his New Mexico ranch. How had he acquired this sudden wealth? After weeks of questioning, Walsh ferreted out the information that Fall had received "loans" of $100,000 from Doheny and of nearly $250,000 from Sinclair—who had also contributed lavishly to the Republican campaign fund. Fall resigned, but this did not save him from criminal prosecution. Since the Department of Justice was itself under suspicion, Coolidge named special government prosecutors, Owen J. Roberts of Pennsylvania and Atlee Pomerene of Ohio.

Although indictments for conspiracy and bribery were brought against Fall, Doheny, and Sinclair in June, 1924, delays of various kinds held up the trials for years. All were found not guilty of conspiracy to defraud, but Fall was convicted of accepting a bribe and sentenced to one year in prison and a fine of $100,000. Paradoxically, Doheny and Sinclair were both acquitted of having paid the bribes that Fall was convicted of having accepted. Sinclair did not, however, go off scot-free: he was found guilty of contempt of the Senate for refusing to answer questions and also of contempt of court for having his jurors shadowed; he was fined $1,000 and sentenced to nine months in jail. In December, 1927, the United States Supreme Court finally invalidated the leases on the ground that they had been obtained through fraud and corruption.

Other betrayals of the public faith were revealed. Custodian of Alien Property Thomas W. Miller, a member of the so-called Ohio gang that trailed Harding to Washington, was found guilty of having obtained $50,000 through disposal of patents and other property in his care; he was fined $5,000 and sentenced to eighteen months in prison. Jess Smith, Harry Daugherty's right-hand man, committed suicide when he became involved in the scandal. The Department of Justice was under suspicion of selling judgeships and pardons and of collaborating with corrupt business interests. For some months Coolidge resisted pressure to remove Daugherty from office, but when the Attorney General refused to answer the questions of a congressional committee on the grounds that he might incriminate himself, the President demanded his resignation in March, 1924. Charged with conspiracy to defraud the government, Daugherty escaped prison only because the jury disagreed. Colonel Charles R. Forbes, Director of the Veterans' Bureau, was found guilty of diverting at least $250 million from his agency into the pockets of himself and his friends through corrupt contract and building practices.

If Harding had still been President while these investigations and trials were taking place, the Republican party might have been critically affected. While it is true that Coolidge did not do much to bring perpetrators to account, he did enough apparently to satisfy the voters. The ease with which the general public shook off not only evidence of governmental corruption but of the sabotage of the conservation, veterans' aid, and preparedness programs is impressive evidence of the postwar retreat from idealism. The country seemed to have lost its capacity for indignation on such issues. And to make matters worse, individuals connected with the investigations were hounded unmercifully and subjected to trials on fraudulent charges; fortunately, they all survived these attempts to besmirch them.

America for Americans

Among the problems of the twenties, none was more significant than the shaping of a new immigration policy. Although the arrival of foreigners had

The new gate. The Senate and the House viewing with delight the effect of the literacy test upon immigration. (From the *Minneapolis Journal*.)

been reduced by the literacy test of 1917 and the disturbed conditions of World War I, immigration seemed likely to assume huge volume again after the end of hostilities. The AFL and other worker groups demanded more effective dikes against the anticipated flood and they now found strong allies. Before the war most employers' associations had opposed legislation that would bar sturdy foreign workers; now employer opinion tended to swing over to restriction—largely because of the fear of Communism and labor violence that swept the country during the Red scare of 1919 and 1920. Also alarmed were the Daughters of the American Revolution and other patriotic societies.

Responding to these pressures, Congress passed a bill that would have fixed immigrant quotas for each European country, but Wilson vetoed the measure. Harding strongly favored this proposal, however, and in May, 1921, the Emergency Quota Act received the new President's approval. This first effort to apply a radically different principle in immigration policy provided that the number of aliens of any nationality who might be admitted to the United States in any year should be limited to 3 per cent of the foreign-born population of that nationality in the United States according to the census of 1910. The effects of the act were felt almost immediately. For the year ending June 30, 1921, 805,228 immigrants were admitted; for the following year the number dropped to 309,556. The restrictionists, however, were far from satisfied. They considered the total volume of immigration still excessive; they believed that the quotas assigned to southern and eastern European countries, although smaller than those alloted to western and northern countries, were yet too large.

Accordingly Congress passed and President Coolidge signed on May 26, 1924, the Johnson Immigration Act, fixing the quotas at 2 per cent of the foreign-born of each nationality according to the census of 1890. This reduced the total number of immigrants from about 350,000 to 164,000, while discriminating much more drastically against southern and eastern Europe. The new immigration, which had contributed 75 per cent of the total between 1901 and 1910, was now restricted to less than 15 per cent. Immigration from nations in the Western Hemisphere was not brought under the quota system. The new law corrected many abuses in administration by placing responsibility for the primary selection of immigrants on United States consuls in the ports of embarkation rather than on American immigration officials in stations like Ellis Island.

Certain provisions of the Act of 1924 caused serious controversy. Anti-Japanese agitation in California and elsewhere led to a clause excluding all aliens ineligible for citizenship. Since the Supreme Court had ruled as recently as 1923 that Japanese, being neither "free white persons" nor persons of African descent, might not be naturalized under existing statutes, the purpose of the exclusion clause was obvious. President Coolidge and Secretary of State Hughes opposed this affront to Japanese national pride, and Japanese Ambassador Hanihara warned that "grave consequences" might follow the termination of the Gentlemen's Agreement, to which Japan had faithfully adhered. But the Hanihara note only stiffened the determination of the exclusionists, despite the fact that the Japanese quota would have been a mere 250 immigrants a year. In Japan the day that the act went into effect was observed as one of mourning, punctuated by ominous anti-American demonstrations.

A second highly debatable provision of the Johnson Act stipulated that the quotas based on 2 per cent of the foreign-born population in 1890 should be temporary. After July 1, 1927, the annual quota should be "a number which bears the same ratio to 150,000 as the number of inhabitants in continental United States in 1920 having that national origin . . . bears to the number of inhabitants in continental United States in 1920." Congress delegated to the Secretaries of States, Commerce, and Labor the virtually impossible task of determining the national origins of the entire American population of 1920. Although these unhappy officials more than once asked to be relieved of responsibility for trying to make a quantitative analysis of the American melting pot after three hundred years of immigration and intermarriage, Congress refused to repeal the national origins clause.

When the experts announced their preliminary findings, the general public gained its first real understanding of what was involved in the national origins quotas. This formula would almost double the quota allotted to Great Britain, while reducing the German and Irish quotas by almost one half and the Scandinavian by two thirds. A cry of protest arose from the affected groups, and Herbert Hoover and Alfred E. Smith both advocated repeal of the national origins provision during the presidential campaign of 1928. But narrow nationalists in Congress with the support of patriotic societies and organized labor refused to reconsider the issue. After several postponements, the new quotas finally became effective on July 1, 1929.

Total quota immigration, fixed at about 350,000 in 1921 and reduced to 164,000 in 1924, was established at about 150,000 in 1929. Yet this was not the end. The Great Depression strongly discouraged immigration, while in 1931 President Hoover, fearing any enlargement of unemployment, reduced the total quota to 48,500 by executive action. At the same time, Mexican immigration, normally exempt from the quota system, was drastically reduced by bans against "floaters" who crossed the border in search of jobs. Through rigid screening of newcomers and a severe deportation policy, the Hoover administration actually permitted less than 36,000 aliens to enter the country in 1932, while more than 103,000 were leaving, either voluntarily or involuntarily. Depression and war continued to hold immigration to small proportions for more than a decade. Not until 1946 did annual arrivals again exceed 100,000.

The radical curtailment of immigration was one of the most decisive events in twentieth-century American history. It brought certain apparent advantages: American workers no longer had to fear competition from cheap immigrant labor, and the cities were spared some of the social problems involved in large-scale assimilation of people brought up in a foreign culture. On the other hand, a quota system that admitted over 65,000 immigrants from Great Britain in a year but less than 6,000 from Italy and none at all from Japan was based upon racial assumptions that had their foundations not in science and reason, but in nativist prejudice. A more rational policy would have been to hold total immigration within manageable limits, but to permit the selection of actual immigrants on the basis of individual merit.

The Veterans and the Bonus

Even before the Armistice was signed, Colonel Theodore Roosevelt, Jr. son of the ex-President, had dreamed of a vast veterans' organization to be formed from all men who had been in uniform during the great conflict. On February 16, 1919, Roosevelt entertained twenty officers at a Paris dinner party where he enlisted their support for his plan. One month later an organization meeting in Paris attended by a thousand soldiers adopted the name "American Legion." On September 16, 1919, Congress granted a charter to the new organization. The American Legion became a powerful proponent of patriotism and preparedness, a promoter of many worthy charities, and a sponsor of an active social and recreational program for its members. But to the general public the Legion became best known as a tremendously effective pressure group seeking legislation to benefit the veterans.

Through the efforts of the Legion's lobbyists, the House passed in 1920 a bill providing "adjusted compensation" for the veterans in one of four ways land settlement, aid in purchasing a home, vocational training, or bonds on the basis of $1.50 for each day of military service. The Senate Finance Committee buried the bill, but the bonus, as the proposal was soon popularly tagged, became one of the most controversial political issues of the twenties. Congressmen found it a delicate matter. Most of them wanted to cut expenses and taxes, but feared to antagonize their many constituents who had served in the armed forces. Furthermore, the argument of the veterans was persua sive: they had served for approximately $1.00 a day. Those who had remained in civilian life had received high wages and dividends. Were not the veterans therefore entitled to "adjusted compensation" for the time they had spent in their country's service? The payment need not be in cash; it could be in long-term bonds or certificates.

President Harding was able to delay the movement for a time, but in 1922 the veterans' demands could no longer be ignored. Representative Fordney reintroduced the 1920 bill, together with a plan to pay the adjusted compensation by issuing paid-up twenty-year endowment policies, or certificates. The value would be determined at the rate of $1.00 a day for military service in the United States and $1.25 for service overseas. A veteran might borrow up to one half the face value of his policy and use this amount to purchase land or a home. On March 22 the House approved the Fordney bill by the one-sided vote of 333 to 70, while the galleries, packed with Legionnaires and other veterans, cheered as each affirmative vote was cast. The Senate was slower to act, but on August 30 it gave its approval by a vote of 47 to 22. Harding refused to sign the measure, pointing out in his veto message that Congress had made no provisions for paying the bonus. He sympathized with the bill's purpose, yet argued that the cost, estimated at $3 billion— one sixth of the public debt—should not be added to the already heavy financial burdens of the total population to help less than five million people. The House quickly overrode Harding's veto, 258 to 54; the Senate sustained it although by only four votes—44 to 28.

This defeat only strengthened the determination of the veterans. In April, 1924, Congress passed the World War Adjusted Compensation Act, providing twenty-year paid-up endowment policies on the basis of $1.00 a day for home and $1.25 a day for overseas service. Veterans entitled to $50 or less were to be paid in cash. Others were to receive certificates, on which they could borrow up to 22.5 per cent of face value. These certificates averaged about $1,500 and bore interest of 4 per cent; they were expected to total $3.5 billion. Following the precedent of Harding, Coolidge vetoed the bill, but Congress repassed it by overwhelming votes. In an election year few members cared to endanger their chances of re-election by voting against the measure.

The bonus was not the only form of assistance given the veterans of World War I. In August, 1921, Congress established the Veterans' Bureau, which consolidated programs dealing with vocational training, war risk insurance, and medical care. Through its various branches the Veterans' Bureau eventually administered more than forty hospitals and a dozen soldiers' homes. Unfortunately, the activities of Colonel Forbes, the first administrator, gave the agency a bad name in its early years; but a change of personnel enabled the bureau to perform excellent services. By 1931 the number of veterans receiving compensation was nearly 300,000; approximately 100,000 widows were being helped; and more than 500,000 had received hospital treatment. The cost of this care, the borrowings on the certificates, and the administration of the vocational program raised the price of World War I considerably. By 1931 the Veterans' Bureau had paid out $14 billion. Worthy though the expenditure was, it added to the problems of the economy-minded President and Secretary of the Treasury.

The Triumph of Calvin Coolidge

The Republican party entered the campaign of 1924 with some misgivings. There had been signs of discontent in the congressional elections of 1922 when the party's majorities had been materially cut. Coolidge's support in Congress was shaky, as the overriding of his bonus veto and the rejection of some of his legislative proposals demonstrated. The continuing revelations about Teapot Dome and other scandals seemed particularly threatening to the party prospects. The nation, however, did not appear to blame Coolidge for the weakness of his predecessor. He seemed to have given the nation a Midas touch—and growing prosperity covered a multitude of party sins.

When the Republican convention met in Cleveland early in June, the renomination of Coolidge was not in doubt. An experienced politician, Coolidge had started the machinery moving as soon as he moved into the White House. By Thanksgiving, 1923, he had obtained the support of most of the Republican wheelhorses. Not content, he then turned to the business interests and, with the assistance of William M. Butler, a textile industrialist in Massachusetts, he received most of their backing. The convention obediently gave an overwhelming, although not unanimous, nomination to Coolidge on the first ballot. After Frank Lowden refused the proffered vice-presidential nomination, it went to Charles G. Dawes, former Director of the Budget.

The Republican platform emphasized the party's "record unsurpassed" in economy and debt reduction and praised the Fordney-McCumber Tariff as a contribution to prosperity. The party favored regulation of public utilities but opposed government ownership; it opposed compulsory arbitration of labor disputes and favored the eight-hour day and the prohibition of child labor by constitutional amendment. It praised the work of the Washington disarmament conference and favored joining the World Court. The platform, like the candidate, was unexciting, but comfortably safe.

The Democratic party was by no means united when its convention opened in Madison Square Garden, New York City, on June 24, and the cleavages that developed during its marathon deliberations accentuated the hostilities. The Southern delegates, fearing racial and labor problems, opposed the revival of anything that savored of the New Freedom; the eastern elements of the party tended to be heavily Catholic and bitterly attacked the Ku Klux Klan. The South, with its growing industrialization, was losing interest in the principle of tariff for revenue only, and with that defection one of the few unifying issues died. The delegates from the urban districts were against prohibition, but those from the rural sections were drys. The two leading candidates were William Gibbs McAdoo, backed by the West and the South, and Governor Alfred E. Smith, the hero of the urban voters of the East.

The convention went through ballot after ballot without reaching a decision. The delegates' nerves were on edge; the galleries, vociferously for Al Smith, got out of hand; and the heat was terrific. On the one-hundred-third ballot the tired and unhappy delegates finally chose a compromise candidate, John W. Davis, a wealthy New York corporation lawyer and diplomat. Although able and distinguished, Davis could scarcely be advertised as a

How could McAdoo hope to win? (By Darling in the *New York Tribune*.)

great liberal to rally the anti-Coolidge vote. In naming as their vice-presidential candidate Charles W. Bryan, little-known brother of William Jennings, the delegates did nothing to strengthen the ticket.

The deep party divisions also caused dissension over the platform. By more than two to one the convention voted down a plank calling for American entry into the League of Nations; by the close vote of 546 to 541 it refused to denounce the Klan as un-American; it breached the gap between wets and drys by merely criticizing the Republicans for failure to enforce prohibition. The platform denounced the tariff of 1922 as an aid to monopolies and a detriment to trade; it said little about labor and the farm problem that was different from the Republican platform, but it condemned Republican corruption with proper indignation. All in all, this document was no more constructive than that of the opposition.

Senator LaFollette had long been disappointed in the trend away from liberalism. To stem this reaction, he formed the Conference for Progressive Political Action in 1922, reminiscent of his National Progressive League of a decade before. He hoped thereby to capture the 1924 nomination for himself. When Coolidge instead became the nominee, LaFollette called a second Cleveland convention on July 4, for the purpose of consolidating the various progressive forces and reviving the movement for social justice. This convention quickly named LaFollette for the presidency, with Democratic Senator Burton K. Wheeler of Montana, who had played a prominent part in exposing some of the Harding scandals, as running mate. The Socialist party, the Farmer-Labor party, and the AFL endorsed this Progressive ticket. The Communists tried to lend their support, but LaFollette refused it.

The brief fourteen-point program was the handiwork of LaFollette. The power of the Federal government, it asserted, must be used to crush, not to foster, monopolies. There must be public ownership of water power and public control over all natural resources, rapidly progressive taxes upon large incomes and inheritances, reform of the Federal Reserve System, and farm relief. Particularly significant planks called for the direct election of Federal judges and congressional power to override judicial decisions. The child labor amendment should be quickly ratified and injunctions in labor disputes prohibited. Denouncing Republican foreign policy as primarily in the "interests of financial imperialists, oil monopolists, and international bankers," the Progressives called for revision of the Treaty of Versailles, the outlawry of war, and a popular referendum before the United States could become involved in hostilities.

The Republican slogan, "Keep Cool with Coolidge," satisfied most of the listless electorate. The general question seemed to be, "Why swap horses in the middle of prosperity?" and no adequate reason could be found. The November returns gave Coolidge 15.7 million votes, Davis nearly 8.4 million, and LaFollette 4.8 million. The electoral college showed Coolidge with 382 votes, Davis with 136—all from the South—and LaFollette with 13 from Wisconsin. The good showing of LaFollette in twelve states of the West, in which he ran ahead of Davis, indicated that old-fashioned progressivism was not dead, but it was not strong enough to support a third party. Coolidge's triumph, though impressive, was largely a negative one; only about half of the qualified electorate bothered to cast their votes. The Republicans also maintained their control of Congress. The division in the new Senate was 50 Republicans, 40 Democrats, 6 LaFollette men; in the House, 232 Republicans, 183 Democrats, 20 in the LaFollette bloc.

Factional Differences

On March 4, 1925, more people than had ever before heard an inaugural address listened to that of Calvin Coolidge, broadcast by radio. In it he set the keynote for the next four years. "I favor the policy of economy," he said, "not because I wish to save money, but because I wish to save people." Then he continued:

> Economy is idealism in its most practical form. . . . The wise and correct course to follow in taxation and all other economic legislation is not to destroy those who have already secured success but to create conditions under which everyone will have a better chance to be successful. . . . We are not without our problems, but our most important problem is not to secure new advantages but to maintain those which we already possess.

His was to be an administration in which the government did its best to encourage private enterprise and to keep government control at a minimum. In carrying out this program he continued to have the services of two able holdovers from the Harding period—Secretary of the Treasury Mellon and Secretary of Commerce Hoover. But he lost Secretary of State Hughes, who

President Coolidge and his cabinet. *Seated, left to right:* Secretary of War Weeks, Secretary of State Hughes, President Coolidge, Secretary of the Treasury Mellon, Attorney General Stone, Secretary of the Navy Wilbur; *standing:* Secretary of Agriculture Wallace, Secretary of Commerce Hoover, Secretary of the Interior Work. *Not shown:* Postmaster General New and Secretary of Labor Davis. (Acme.)

was succeeded in March, 1925, by Frank B. Kellogg of Minnesota. Although Kellogg was a hard-working lawyer who had had diplomatic experience as ambassador to Great Britain, he lacked the ability and farsightedness of Hughes.

Coolidge had many difficulties with Congress despite its Republican majority. The Progressive legislators combined with the Democrats to attack administration measures, sometimes with success. One of the President's first setbacks came when he nominated Charles B. Warren of Michigan as Attorney General to succeed Harlan Stone, recently appointed to the Supreme Court. Democrats and Progressives, led by George Norris of Nebraska, asserted that Warren's Michigan State Sugar Trust had broken the antitrust laws and that the nominee had defended his company's actions. When the vote was taken on March 10, 1925, Vice President Dawes was absent, and without his influence the Senate turned the appointment down, 41 to 39. Contrary to the advice of his party leaders, Coolidge resubmitted the nomination a week later, only to be turned down once again by the more decisive vote of 46 to 39. The President then offered Warren a recess appointment that would not need Senate appointment, but Warren refused to accept it. Consequently, Coolidge nominated John Garibaldi Sargent of Vermont, a little-known lawyer with whom the Senate found no fault. Thereafter, Coolidge tried to ascertain beforehand whether his appointees were acceptable. Although some lesser appointments were rejected, the Senate generally approved the President's nominees from this time on.

The Republican regulars took steps to punish those who had bolted the party to support LaFollette. The Progressives lost their key positions on committees, had no chance for chairmanships, or were demoted to the bottom of committee lists. This purge of the Republican insurgents accounts in part for the opposition Coolidge encountered during the first half of his second administration. The election of 1926 showed a swing to the left, especially in the Middle West. Robert LaFollette, Jr., took the seat of his famous father, who had died in June, 1925, and several other Progressives won seats. In the East, the swing enabled a Democrat, David Walsh of Massachusetts, to defeat William Butler for the United States Senate, despite Coolidge's active support for his friend. While the Republicans retained a majority of 40 members in the House of Representatives, their hold over the Senate was extremely precarious. There were 48 Republican Senators, 47 Democrats, and 1 Farm-Laborite. In order to maintain their small majority, the Republican regulars had to restore the purged insurgents to their committee posts and to promise them legislative concessions.

Government and Business

The Coolidge administration showed an increasing tendency to give business a free hand. One of the early indications was in the appointments to governmental departments and agencies entrusted with the regulation of business activities. The most significant addition to the Interstate Commerce Commission was Thomas F. Woodlock of New York, who had made his money from railroad stocks. The liberals, led by Senator Norris, failed to defeat his confirmation; they believed that the railroads would now dominate the commission. In similar fashion the appointment of William E. Humphrey of Washington to the Federal Trade Commission gave the friends of big business a majority and diverted the commission's function from that of regulating business to one of giving advice. The Tariff Commission also underwent an overhauling, with the new appointees proving to be sympathetic to the wishes of manufacturing groups. Although Coolidge's packing of the commissions was deliberate, it merely strengthened a tendency already evident in the history of progressive reform. Regulatory bodies, originally intended as watchdogs, usually became domesticated; that is, they more and more adopted the points of view prevalent in the industries they were supposed to be regulating.

Not only did businessmen encounter a minimum of government interference, but they found much positive encouragement, especially from the Department of Commerce. Secretary Hoover gave the trade association movement his enthusiastic support; in the stabilization of production through voluntary cooperation he saw hope for the survival of small business. The Department published a handbook designed to promote the movement and sponsored many industrial conferences. It collected statistical information, which the government itself published, even though the exchange of such data was one of the chief devices through which trade associations hoped to induce members to restrict production and maintain prices.

What one branch of government was actively promoting, other branches for a time regarded with suspicion. Attorney General Daugherty prosecuted the Hardwood Manufacturers' Association for price-fixing activities. In this case the Supreme Court ruled that the gathering of information and statistics among members of such an association violated the Sherman Antitrust Act. This and other decisions discouraged the trade association movement, but presently the situation changed. The Supreme Court greatly weakened the antitrust laws in a series of five-to-four decisions. In 1925, for example, it decided that exchange of statistical information not involving any agreement as to production was legal.

The Justice Department became more lenient, although the several Attorneys General in the 1921–1929 era did bring a total of 138 antitrust suits to the courts. Public indifference, plus the attitude of the judiciary, resulted in fewer convictions after 1925, and many persons expressed the opinion that the Sherman and Clayton Acts were outmoded and should be repealed. Indeed, the Justice Department adopted the practice of advising organizers of trade associations in advance on the legality of their activities.

There was also a definite change in the policy of the Federal Trade Commission after Humphrey's appointment in 1925. "So far as I can prevent it," announced the new chairman, "the Federal Trade Commission is not going to be used as a publicity bureau to spread socialistic propaganda." Humphrey's changes in the rules were vigorously fought by the commission's minority members and by liberals generally. Senators Borah and Norris asserted that the FTC might as well be dissolved, so completely was it under big business domination. The commission actively participated in drafting codes of ethics and trade-association practice agreements under which members of an industry promised not to use unfair methods of competition such as bribery, misbranding, misrepresentation of products, refunds, discounts, freight allowances, and the like. Sometimes the producers secretly added clauses forbidding price cutting; in any case, the general tendency of these associations was toward restrictions on production and price fixing. So far indeed was this true that even while the Republicans were still in power, the government somewhat modified its policy. In 1930 the Department of Justice brought suit against eight of the associations; the next year the Department reported that an investigation of fifty trade associations revealed that the majority of them were violating the Sherman Act.

By that time, however, the trade association movement had grown too strong to be wiped out easily. The encouragement of the several agencies of government—the Supreme Court, the Department of Commerce, the Department of Justice, and the FTC—and their preference for modifying questionable business practices through quiet admonitions and conferences rather than through the use of more aggressive methods had built up a huge network of business associations. Industrialists, both large and small, praised the government practice of cooperating with business rather than regulating it.

Debt and Tax Reduction

The struggles between conservatives and liberals during the twenties are best exemplified in connection with three issues: fiscal policy, the disposition of Muscle Shoals, and the farm problem.

On August 31, 1919, the gross United States debt reached a peak of $26.6 billion—then considered a staggering amount. President Wilson and his successors regarded the reduction of this debt to be one of the principal duties of the Federal government. At the same time, however, the several administrations deemed it essential to decrease taxes, which had mounted sharply during the war years. Conservatives desired to have the burden lifted most quickly from the wealthy so that they could develop the national economy through investment. The liberals, on the other hand, wanted to continue high rates on excess profits, incomes, and inheritances and to give major relief to persons in the lower brackets in order to stimulate purchasing power. In his postwar messages President Wilson favored some tax concessions to business but emphasized his belief that the first step should be to help the average taxpayer by eliminating the nuisance taxes, while retaining the income tax, the excess-profits tax, and the estate tax as the mainstays of government revenue. The Revenue Act of 1919 followed in general the Wilsonian principles.

Under President Harding, administration policy changed. In a series of recommendations to Congress, Secretary Mellon urged repeal of excess-profits taxes, a compensatory increase in corporation levies, ending most of the nuisance taxes, and gradual reduction of both normal and surtaxes on individual incomes. Harding supported Mellon in strongly urging repeal of the excess-profits tax. Instead of following the Harding-Mellon recommendations, Congress, under the influence of the Farm Bloc and the Democrats, refused any substantial lowering of taxes upon the rich. In 1923 Mellon urged a revision of the whole tax program. He argued that the wealthy would not invest their money in new industries when the government was taking so large a percentage of their profits. Instead they were investing more and more in tax-exempt securities or in foreign fields to avoid the American levies. President Coolidge, of course, gave Mellon strong support, but progressive opposition in Congress was still strong. The Revenue Act of 1924 lowered taxes in the lower brackets and allowed a 25 per cent rebate on earned income, but it left corporation taxes unchanged and raised estate taxes. Particularly obnoxious to conservatives was a clause providing for the publication of the names of income tax payers, together with the amount of tax paid—a provision intended to make tax evasion more difficult.

Although Coolidge signed this 1924 act, he was highly critical of it. To him the law was "tax reduction, not tax reform," and both reduction and reform should be promoted "upon an economic and not a political basis." He attacked the publicity feature as an "unwarranted interference with the right of a citizen to privacy," which would not attain its objective because evaders would conceal their assets more cleverly. Republican victory in the election of 1924 and the prosperity of the immediately ensuing years finally won congressional approval for the Coolidge-Mellon tax theories in several revenue measures from 1926 to 1928. These acts lowered normal and surtaxes as well as the corporation tax; they cut the estate tax approximately in half and wiped out the excess-profits levy and most of the remaining nuisance taxes. Another administration victory came with the repeal of the clause requiring publicity of tax returns. Despite Democratic charges that the Republicans wanted only to relieve the wealthy, the administration succeeded in keeping the existing income-tax exemptions, thereby following the Mellon theory that as many citizens as possible should contribute to the running of the government.

Although the administration anticipated a drop in revenue as a result of the tax cuts, such a drop did not materialize. Surpluses piled up as the government became the beneficiary of payments on the war debts, back taxes, and the like. The opposition took advantage of the surplus to denounce the administration for not cutting taxes even more. As proof of the soundness of their policies, the Republicans pointed with pride at the record. Not only had they reduced taxes, but by June 30, 1930, they had cut the national debt to $16.2 billion. This decrease of approximately one third of the debt in a decade led conservative admirers to describe Andrew Mellon as the greatest Secretary of the Treasury since Alexander Hamilton.

From the standpoint of later theory, both the Republicans and the Democrats were wrong in this controversy. A new school of economists argued that tax policies should follow the ups and downs of the economic cycle. During depressions the government should reduce taxes to encourage investment; it should spend more than it receives in revenues in order to create purchasing power. During boom times, according to this line of reasoning, the government should raise taxes and reduce expenditures as a curb upon inflation. It may, therefore, be argued that the whole effort to reduce taxes during the twenties was misdirected. Much of the money saved by wealthy taxpayers went not into healthy investment but into speculation in land and securities, thereby contributing to the cycle of inflation and the crash of 1929. Sounder policy would have been to retain high rates and to retire even more of the public debt. Conservatives, however, have never accepted this contention. They have continued to regard the Coolidge-Mellon policy as a model of sound government finance.

The Battle Over Muscle Shoals

As part of the preparedness program, the National Defense Act of 1916 had empowered the President to construct and operate power facilities for the manufacture of explosives and fertilizers. Nothing was done until February, 1918, when Wilson ordered the use of the thirty-five-mile Muscle Shoals section of the Tennessee River for these purposes. By the end of Wilson's term the government had almost completed Wilson Dam and had constructed plants for the production of atmospheric nitrogen.

As another step toward normalcy, President Harding was determined to get the government out of the hydroelectric power business. He ordered a stop to work on Wilson Dam, and Secretary of War John W. Weeks asked for bids from private industry on the nitrate plants and uncompleted dams on which the government had already spent more than $100 million. In July, 1921, Henry Ford offered to take a hundred-year lease of Muscle Shoals at a rental of 4 per cent of the construction costs to buy the nitrate plants, which he promised to have constantly available for the manufacture of explosives, and to provide 40,000 tons of nitrogen annually for fertilizer if the government would complete the dams already started.

Ford's proposal was well received by the administration, especially by Secretary Hoover, by the Republican and Democratic leaders in Congress, and by farm groups who looked forward to getting cheap fertilizer. But Senator Norris began a long fight, against tremendous odds, to defeat the proposed lease. Norris believed that Ford was using the cloak of fertilizer manufacturing to obtain hydroelectric power for his own use at a ridiculously low rental. This would circumvent the aims of the Federal Power Act of 1920. Norris believed that the government should complete the Muscle Shoals project and then operate it for the manufacture of power, explosives, and fertilizers for the primary use of the army and navy. A special government corporation should operate Muscle Shoals and sell any surplus power to either public or private corporations. Norris had been studying the power problem for years and had reached the conclusion that public-run plants could supply electricity more cheaply than could private concerns. He pointed out that the government-operated hydroelectric company of the Province of Ontario furnished electricity to local consumers at about one seventh the rates charged in Washington, D.C., by privately owned utility companies.

In December, 1923, President Coolidge urged that Muscle Shoals should be sold to the highest bidder, who could then operate the power and fertilizer business under private control. In March, 1924, the House approved the Ford lease by a vote of 227 to 143. But by this time the issue was further complicated because several private utilities companies had organized as the Associated Power Companies of the South and made their own offer for a lease of the Muscle Shoals property.

Norris persuaded his fellow Senators not to act upon either the Ford or Associated Power proposals and succeeded in shelving Coolidge's plan. Indeed, before 1924 was over Ford withdrew his offer in the face of certain defeat, saying, "We have lost our interest in Muscle Shoals. Productive business cannot wait on politics." Nevertheless, President Coolidge and the conservatives in Congress were able to frustrate Norris's plan for government operation. In 1928 the two houses of Congress approved a resolution embodying the Norris project, but Coolidge killed it with a pocket veto.

This Muscle Shoals controversy was the most notable battle between conservatives and liberals during the twenties. By 1928 the contest had developed into a stalemate, with neither Coolidge nor Norris able to have his way. But the issue did not die; it was to be very much alive during the Hoover administration and to result in eventual victory for Norris under the New Deal.

The failure of the various Muscle Shoals proposals did not prevent progress in related fields. Frequent floods in the Mississippi Valley, culminating in the disastrous one of 1927, made the Coolidge administration realize the need for action. The President appointed a special commission to help alleviate suffering and propose new methods of flood control. Its chairman, Herbert

Hoover, visited the devastated areas and, with Red Cross aid, provided relief and prevented epidemics. Sensitive to the widespread demand that something be done to prevent future floods, Congress finally passed the Jones-Reid Act of May, 1928, under which more than $300 million was appropriated to construct levees, drainage basins, and spillways along the dangerous parts of the river.

The movement to regulate the Colorado River combined flood control, power development, and irrigation. In 1921 Congress authorized seven states [1] to try to reach an agreement apportioning the Colorado waters. Although the states reached a tentative agreement in 1922, Congress did not sanction it until six years later. The delay was caused by disputes between Arizona and California over their water allotments and disagreements over engineering problems, operating principles, and the division of authority between the states and the Federal government.

Finally, however, these problems were solved, and in December, 1928, Congress passed the Boulder Dam Project Act. This provided for construction of a 750-foot dam near Las Vegas, Nevada, capable of storing at least 20 million acre-feet of water, for building a canal to carry water to the arid Imperial Valley of California, and for erecting hydroelectric power plants. The cost of the undertaking, estimated at $165 million, would be met by the sale of electric power and water privileges to the neighboring states during the next half century. In such sales, local government agencies were to be granted preference over private concerns. The passage of this act marked the beginning of the Federal government's active participation in the production of hydroelectric power, a participation that was to grow during the next decade. It also indicated a partial breakdown of the laissez faire attitude that had been so characteristic of the Coolidge regime.

The Farm Problem

In many ways American farming showed remarkable progress in the twenties. New methods permitted the cultivation of the semiarid belt of the Great Plains. Gasoline-powered equipment was taking the place of the horse-drawn machinery of prewar days; the number of tractors increased from 230,000 in 1920 to 920,000 in 1930. With new combines that cut, bound, threshed, and sacked wheat as they were pulled through the fields, one man could harvest forty acres in a day and do work that would formerly have required the labor of fifty men. In planting, similar if less dramatic economies were introduced through the use of disk plows and power drills. Nor was wheat the only crop thus mechanized. The corn belt witnessed an increasing use of machinery, while in the cotton states one man using a sled could harvest as much as fifteen hand workers. The seed that the farmer sowed was much improved. Hybrid corn, for example, grew more quickly than older varieties, yielded heavier crops, and was resistant to disease. The farmer also profited by better fertilizers and insecticides. Livestock raisers made parallel progress. Partly as a result of scientific breeding, but more because of better

---

[1] Colorado, Arizona, New Mexico, Utah, Nevada, California, and Wyoming.

care and feeding, hogs produced more pork and lard, steers more beef, and cows more milk.

But as agriculture became more scientific, it likewise became more expensive. Only farmers cultivating many acres could afford the large investments necessary to take full advantage of the new methods. By 1928 there were 9,000 corporation-owned farms in the United States. The corporate form of organization, however, was unusual. Most farms continued to be owned by individuals, but they were becoming larger. By 1930 the average size of farms in the corn belt was already 239 acres, and experts were advocating 640 acres as the minimum desirable size for a family enterprise, while for maximum efficiency they were saying that a farmer would need 1,000 or even 2,500 acres. The small farmer, usually tilling the less fertile soil, found it increasingly difficult to, make a living. Many of these small farmers lost their holdings through mortgage foreclosures, or sold or abandoned them and became tenant farmers, agricultural laborers, or factory workers in the cities. Farm tenancy increased 4 per cent during the twenties, so that by 1929 more than 42 per cent of the farmers were tenants. Moreover, migration to the cities reduced the nation's agricultural population by 3 million during the seven years after 1921.

The mechanization of agriculture, however, more than made up for the decline in the number of farmers. Acreage under cultivation had greatly expanded during the war under the stimulation of large export markets and government-guaranteed prices. During the twenties acreage expanded still further. Production of all the great staples remained at high levels.

Yet, while the supply of American farm products remained high, effective market demand for them declined soon after the war was over. Between December, 1919, and December, 1920, wheat dropped from $2.15 a bushel to $1.44, corn from $1.25 to $0.68, and cotton from $0.36 a pound to $0.14. Nor did the foreign market revive. In this age of economic nationalism, the various countries were resorting to tariffs and bounties—often in retaliation against the American tariff—in an effort to promote their own agriculture and cut down on imports. In this shrinking market, moreover, American foodstuffs were competing with those grown in Canada, Australia, and Argentina.

The domestic demand for agricultural products failed to expand as in earlier generations. Immigration restriction and a declining birth rate meant fewer new Americans to be fed and clothed. Changes in diet and style likewise affected the market. As a larger proportion of the population followed sedentary callings, they ate less bread and meat. To be sure, a vitamin-conscious generation consumed more fruits and vegetables, but the contraction of one type of agriculture and the expansion of another was not an easy transition. The cotton grower was injured as women began to wear less clothing and rejected cotton in favor of silk and rayon. Finally, the displacement of perhaps 8 million horses by automobiles, trucks, and tractors profoundly affected the agricultural situation. Some 35 million acres had been required to grow feed for these animals, and most of this acreage was now planted with crops suitable for human consumption.

Denying the urgency of the problem, some critics pointed out that farm prices during the twenties were 25 to 50 per cent higher than they had been in prewar days and that agricultural exports maintained a substantially higher level than before 1915. Spokesmen for the farmers, however, emphasized a number of important points. In the first place, the prices of manufactured goods had risen much more than had the prices of agricultural products. The farmers' real income, therefore, was less than it had been before the war. Moreover, a substantial proportion of the nation's farmers had bought land—usually with borrowed money—at the inflated values of the war years. The collapse of prices in 1921 not only gave these farmers a very small return upon the invested capital, but made it extremely difficult for them to make their interest and principal payments. Indeed, the growth of mortagage indebtedness on American farms from $3.8 billion in 1912 to $9.2 billion in 1930 was one of the most serious aspects of the situation. Higher taxes, higher wages for farm labor, higher freight rates, and higher distribution costs also added substantially to the farmers' burdens.

The spokesmen for the farmers insisted that prices must be raised to save American agriculture from disaster, but the problem was a difficult one. Tariff protection was ineffective because of the annual surplus that had to be sold in the world markets. To raise prices, either the surplus would have to be reduced or exports would have to be subsidized in some manner. The various legislative projects whereby the farmers sought these ends occupied much of Congress's attention during the Harding and Coolidge administrations.

In August, 1921, Congress passed the Packers and Stockyards Act. This declared it unlawful for packers to monopolize the market, to control prices, to establish territorial pools, or to engage in other unfair practices. The Secretary of Agriculture was empowered to issue "cease and desist" orders to packers and stockyard operators in somewhat the same fashion as the Federal Trade Commission. Less than two weeks later Congress enacted the Grain Futures Act, which gave the Secretary of Agriculture similar control over dealers in wheat and other grains. At the same time, the Agriculture Credits Act broadened the powers of the War Finance Corporation to allow larger loans to agriculture, so that farm surpluses could be more effectively handled. During the life of this measure (until 1924), nearly $300 million was loaned to farm associations. Completing this early legislative program in February, 1922, the Farm Bloc forced through Congress after ten months of debate the Capper-Volstead Cooperative Act. This reinforced the Clayton Act in exempting agricultural organizations from the provisions of the Sherman Antitrust Act and permitted farm associations to process and market their staples in interstate commerce under the supervision of the Secretary of Agriculture.

None of this legislation provided effective relief, nor did the Fordney-McCumber Tariff, so Congress added another measure, the Federal Intermediate Credit Act, in March, 1923. Under this legislation, the Federal Farm Loan Board established twelve new banks, known as the Federal Intermediate Credit Banks. The government contributed the $5 million capital for each institution, and each bank had the right to rediscount agricultural paper and to loan money to farm cooperatives for as little as six months and as long as three years. The collateral for these loans comprised the agricultural products the cooperatives had in their warehouses. In addition, the farmers' associations were allowed to establish their own credit corporations, while the maximum loans permitted to be made by the Farm Loan and Federal Reserve Banks were increased. By the end of the decade farmers had borrowed more than $3 billion from these various sources. But the increase in agricultural debt was a two-edged sword, both dangerous and helpful to the farmer.

In further efforts to help the farmer, the Coolidge administration used its authority under the Fordney-McCumber Act to raise the tariff on wheat in 1924 and on butter in 1926. But farmers were coming to the conclusion that a tariff increase would not help a commodity that had an exportable surplus. Demand in the world market determined the price in most such cases. George Peek and Hugh S. Johnson, president and attorney, respectively, of the Moline Plow Company of Illinois, proposed a radically different kind of farm relief. As first advocated in 1922, the Peek-Johnson plan proposed that some government agency should purchase the exportable surplus at a fair domestic price and then sell it abroad at the world market price. The losses incurred in pegging domestic prices above their world level could be covered by a special tax or equalization fee levied upon the producers of the benefited staples.

This proposal was the basis for several measures sponsored in Congress by Senator Charles McNary of Oregon and Representative Gilbert Haugen of Iowa. The McNary-Haugen bills provoked stormy controversy, and the original plan was several times amended between 1924 and 1928. Each new amendment brought additional support. Originally the plan had the backing primarily of the Middle West. Gradually the Southern representatives joined the other members of the Farm Bloc as cotton and tobacco were added to the staples whose price was to be protected, and more votes were gained among legislators from the Far West. An increasing number of liberals and men prominent in government circles like Vice President Dawes, Secretary of Agriculture Henry C. Wallace, and Frank Lowden added their names to the growing list of McNary-Haugen adherents.

Despite the increased backing for the plan, President Coolidge refused to give his approval and he was supported by Wallace's successor, Secretary of Agriculture William Jardine, as well as by Eastern conservatives. In February, 1927, Congress passed the McNary-Haugen bill, but Coolidge vetoed it with a caustic message. He asserted that the scheme benefited the growers of a few staples such as wheat, cotton, tobacco, and corn, but did not help agriculture in general. It provided for government price fixing, which never worked. It was unconstitutional because it enabled the Farm Board to levy a tax—the equalization fee—a power reserved to Congress. The President also argued that the plan would result in further overproduction of the staples involved and would lead to dumping of foreign crops in the American market to take advantage of the artificial prices. Finally, he declared that the Farm Board personnel throughout the country might develop into "an enormous bureaucracy . . . offering infinite opportunities to fraud and incapacity."

Paying little attention to the President's preachments, the McNary-Haugen advocates rounded up support for still another version of the project. This measure, passed by both houses in May, 1928, contained the major parts of each of its defeated predecessors. It provided for the establishment of a Federal Farm Board, which would have a $400 million revolving fund available for loans to agricultural cooperatives in the marketing of staples. If losses were suffered when the surplus was sold in the world market, then an equalization fee would be collected. Using the same arguments as in his 1927 message, Coolidge vetoed this new version, and the legislature could not muster the necessary votes to override him.

Coolidge justified his stubborn adherence to laissez faire on the contention that the best solution for the agricultural problem would be for the farmers to reduce their production voluntarily, a course that he repeatedly advised them to take. Yet to expect any concerted movement to cut acreage on the part of millions of individual farm operators was obviously unrealistic. Nor could the farm cooperatives, so much favored by Republican policy, achieve the desired goal so long as the government abstained from measures of either coercion or inducement. Thus the farm problem remained critical at the end of the Coolidge regime. Farm income had dropped from 15 per cent of the national total in 1920 to but 9 per cent in 1929. The farmers' purchasing power was steadily diminishing. Both major parties were consequently forced to bid for the farm vote by incorporating promises of agricultural aid in their platforms of 1928.

The Coolidge period was one of conservative supremacy, but the liberals had developed a counterprogram on taxation, power, and agriculture. So long as prosperity continued, the country generally was not greatly interested in these issues, but the economic collapse of the next few years was to transform completely the balance of political power.

11

FOREIGN AFFAIRS, 1921-1929

While economic materialism held sway at home, the United States played a varied role in the world of diplomacy. Numerous inconsistencies developed, which were to be expected in a nation that never had any well-defined, long-range international policy. The League was rejected and membership in the World Court postponed, yet the United States tried to find some other road to world peace. Extreme nationalism was shown in the erection of high protective walls against imports and immigrants on the one hand, while on the other the United States showed a willingness to make concessions in the matter of debts, reparations, and disarmament. In Latin-American affairs, Uncle Sam also played a dual role as dollar diplomat and as good neighbor.

The Knox Resolution

President Harding's Secretary of State Hughes was immediately faced with the problem of ending the state of war with the Central Powers, not only as a diplomatic necessity, but to answer the public demand that domestic wartime controls be concluded. There was no interest in reviving the Treaty of Versailles issue. Indeed, Harding undoubtedly voiced the opinion of the American majority when he said on April 12, 1921: "We can have no part in a committal to an agency of force in unknown contingencies; we can recognize no super-authority."

Consequently, the Knox Resolution, vetoed successfully by Wilson the year before, was passed again and signed by Harding in July, 1921. It asserted the state of war "to be at an end" and reserved for the United States "all rights, privileges, indemnities, reparations, or advantages" accruing from its part in the war and the armistice arrangements, as well as those it would have obtained had it ratified the Treaty of Versailles.

To Hughes this one-sided arrangement might not stand up in a court of international law. Therefore, in August, 1921, treaties were drawn up with Germany, Austria, and Hungary, which reiterated the rights claimed by the United States without any commitment to the Versailles Treaty. They were all duty ratified before the year was over.

The World Court

So terrorized was the administration by the Republican irreconcilables that at first the State Department declined even to acknowledge receipt of

232

League of Nations communications. Gradually, however, this extreme policy gave way to quiet cooperation with many activities of the new body. Unofficial observers, sent to League sessions from the beginning, were frequently called on for advisory consultation on nonpolitical matters. Then in 1924 the country was officially represented at the Second Opium Conference. Thereafter, the United States participated actively in nearly fifty meetings of a similar nonpolitical nature and five envoys were permanently stationed at Geneva to take care of American interests.

The Harding and Coolidge administrations hoped to associate the United States with the Permanent Court of International Justice provided for in Article 14 of the League Covenant. A stimulus for American admission to this so-called World Court was the League Council's decision that membership would be open to all nations, regardless of their membership in the League.

The Court represented an idea in which Americans had been interested since at least 1832, when Massachusetts suggested establishing a tribunal to settle peacefully international disputes. Then in 1899 the American delegates to the Hague Conference proposed a permanent tribunal. The American government, however, was disappointed in the makeshift substitute that was then adopted and attempted—again unsuccessfully—to establish a real World Court during the Hague Conference of 1907. Secretary of State Root had been particularly interested in the project, and in 1920, when the protocol establishing the postwar tribunal was drafted, he took a leading part. Far from being a sinister foreign conspiracy, the Court was peculiarly American in philosophy and origin. John Basset Moore, an American expert on international law, was one of the eleven judges chosen in the first election to the Court bench, and later, Charles Evans Hughes and Frank Kellogg, both former Secretaries of States, as well as Manley Hudson, a prominent professor of international law, also served as World Court judges.

As Secretary of State, Hughes ardently supported American entrance into the Court and gained Harding's backing. Hughes believed, however, that the United States should append certain reservations to the World Court protocol to further guarantee the American position. On February 17, 1923, four such reservations were announced: (1) American membership must not commit the United States to any Treaty of Versailles or League obligations; (2) the United States must have equality with League members in selecting the Court judges; (3) the United States would pay its fair share of Court expenses; and (4) the Court protocol could not be amended without the approval of the United States, which could withdraw from the Court at any time.

A week after receiving these Hughes reservations, Harding submitted the Court plan to the Senate, saying: "Our deliberate public opinion of today is overwhelmingly in favor of participation"; but Henry Cabot Lodge, caring little for public opinion, kept the project shelved in the Foreign Relations Committee, of which he was still chairman. The disappointed Harding renewed his pleas in numerous speeches, but the committee still took no action. Harding's death did not end the matter, for Coolidge renewed the issue in his first message to Congress in December, 1923, with an even more urgent request for senatorial support. By that time other factors underlined the need for joining. Several bilateral arbitration treaties were up for renewal, and the other signatories, notably Britain, France, and Japan, were requesting that disputes be submitted to the World Court for adjudication.

As a result of strong public opinion, both major parties advocated joining the Court in their 1924 platforms. Lodge died during the year, but the chairmanship of the Senate Foreign Relations Committee fell to William Borah, an even more determined obstructionist. So the issue was still postponed, despite a resolution advocating membership overwhelmingly adopted by the lower house in March, 1925, and despite the emphasis Coolidge gave to the cause in his inaugural address: "The weight of our enormous influence must be cast upon the side of a reign, not of force but of law; and trial, not by battle but by reason."

Not until December, 1925, did the Court issue reach the Senate floor. There the so-called battalion of death put up a bitter fight, but the measure was finally adopted by a vote of 76 to 17. Suspicious Senators, however, added a fifth reservation, which constituted a veritable omnibus of safeguards for American sovereignty and dealt particularly with the Court's power to give advisory opinions.

Immediately Secretary Kellogg forwarded the reservations to both the Court membership and the League Council. The Council, concluding that some reservations might "hamper the work of the Council and prejudice the rights of the members of the League," asked the United States to meet with the League members to arrange a compromise. This opinion made the battalion of death jubilant since it supported their charge that the Court was merely a League tool. Kellogg refused the proposed meeting because "the reservations are plain and unequivocal." Nevertheless, at a Geneva conference in December, 1926, it was finally agreed to accept the reservations with the exception of that part of the fifth that read: ". . . nor shall it, without the consent of the United States, entertain any request for an advisory opinion touching any dispute or question in which the United States has or claims an interest."

The Senate refused to approve this compromise, and Coolidge stood by the upper house, saying he considered the whole matter closed. Perhaps he was influenced by the election results of the previous month; ten out of fifteen Senators seeking re-election who had voted for the Court were defeated in campaigns that were interpreted in some quarters as referendums on the issue.

The Washington Conference

Even though refusing to associate itself with the League and the Court, the United States tried other means to promote world peace during the twenties. The first effort was through the Washington Conference of 1921–1922, the brainchild of Senator Borah, who as early as December, 1920, became worried about existing conditions. Japan was already beginning a naval construction program to place her at least on a par with Britain and the United States. Borah feared lest this lead to a world-wide naval armaments race that might bring on another war—and war would end the American isolation for which he had struggled.

In December, 1920, he therefore added a rider to a pending naval construction bill authorizing the President to call a conference among the United States, Britain, and Japan to obtain a mutual agreement for annual naval reductions over a five-year period. Not until July, 1921, however, was this bill enacted into law. By that time the new Secretary of State Hughes realized that naval armament was only one phase of potential trouble. As he subsequently said: "Without better understanding of the Far East, it would have been idle to deal with proposals of limitation of armament." He was disturbed by Japan's aggressive policy since the war when she had entrenched herself in the Shantung peninsula, gained additional rights in Manchuria, and generally threatened the Open Door and the territorial integrity and independence of China. Nor was the United States satisfied—despite the safeguards of the League Covenant—that Japan would actually refrain from fortifying the former German islands in the Pacific she had received as mandates. Hughes hoped to have Yap internationalized because of its importance as a cable station.

Britain desired a conference on Pacific affairs even more than did the United States. Its particular problem was whether to renew the Anglo-Japanese alliance of 1902. The British were well aware that it was unpopular in America despite British declarations that their country would never join Japan in a war against the United States. Canada and Australia, suspicious of Japan and hoping for closer relations with the United States, were outspoken in their demand that the alliance be ended. Indeed their insistence led Britain to suggest a conference on the Pacific situation even before Hughes's project could be presented in London.

Thus Harding's formal invitations to the naval limitations conference included the proposal to discuss as well Far Eastern and Pacific problems. That being the case, the list of the invited was expanded to include France, Italy, the Netherlands, Portugal, Belgium, and China. All accepted, although Japan much less enthusiastically than the others.

On November 12, 1921, an impressive group of delegates gathered in Washington. Each country sent its most prominent envoys, indicating the importance it attached to this meeting. Secretary Hughes, Henry Cabot Lodge, Oscar Underwood, and Elihu Root represented the United States. After Harding's welcoming address, Chairman Hughes took over the leadership of the conference and his initial speech proved a bombshell. "The time has come," he said, "and this Conference has been called, not for a general resolution or mutual advice, but for action." And the action he proposed was drastic reduction of naval armaments. Construction of all capital ships should cease for ten years; this holiday must affect not only the building programs, but the ships still on the ways. Moreover, old ships in service above a certain total tonnage must be scrapped.[1] The comparative naval strength of the nations concerned must be maintained, and the capital ship tonnage should be approximately 500,000 for Britain and the United States, 300,000 for Japan, and 175,000 for France and Italy. Hughes also hoped that this 5:5:3:1.75:1.75 ratio would be observed for lesser naval craft.

[1] The United States should scrap 15 old ships and stop work on 15 new ones having a total tonnage of 845,740; Britain, 19 old and 4 new totaling 583,375 tons; and Japan, 10 old and 7 new of 448,958 tons.

This proposition to scrap almost two million tons of combat ships came as a decided surprise. British delegates, with their country's long tradition of naval supremacy, and the Japanese envoys, who had hoped for naval equality with the other two powers, did not at first appear to favor the plan. But the galleries, filled with prominent persons from many countries, were much more enthusiastic. Taking advantage of the shock his speech had occasioned, Hughes quickly obtained an adjournment over the weekend before the delegates could praise or criticize, and before the conferees met again, the press in all parts of the world came out in favor of what he had proposed.

On November 15 the discussion began in earnest among the delegates, who generally were very cooperative. The main exception were the French, who opposed a quota system for lesser naval craft and refused to consider the reduction of armies and land fortifications. Otherwise there was considerable unanimity on general terms, despite some differences over detail.

During the twelve weeks of discussion, several important agreements were reached. The foremost was the Five-Power Naval Treaty, signed February 6, 1922. This listed the capital ships that were to be scrapped by the United States, Britain, Japan, France, and Italy. For ten years no new capital ships were to be built except as replacements for vessels at least twenty years old. The total replacements were not to exceed 525,000 tons for the United States and England, 315,000 tons for Japan, and 175,000 tons for France and Italy. Nor was any replacement vessel to exceed 35,000 tons or carry guns of more than 16 inches. Aircraft-carrier tonnage was also limited, and no carrier was to be bigger than 27,000 tons. No lesser naval ships, except transports, should exceed 10,000 tons, and merchant vessels should not be prepared for possible armaments.

Britain, Japan, and the United States also agreed to maintain the status quo on fortifications and naval bases in the Pacific, except for the islands lying off their respective mainlands and certain of the larger island groups. The primary American exception was the Hawaiian Islands. This Naval Treaty was to remain in force until 1936 unless a signatory gave a two-year notice of intention to terminate it.

Another important agreement was the Four-Power Pact, signed by Britain, France, Japan, and the United States, which provided for mutual recognition of insular rights in the Pacific. Were any controversy to arise during the ten-year life of the pact that might result in war, the signatories promised to confer jointly to adjust the differences. Were the rights of the signatories threatened by some other power; they would confer on the proper measures to be taken. When the Four-Power Pact was ratified, the Anglo-Japanese alliance came to an end.

The Nine-Power Treaty, signed by all the delegations at Washington, was "to stabilize conditions in the Far East, to safeguard the rights and interests of China, and to promote intercourse between China and the other Powers upon the basis of equality of opportunity." Therefore the signatories promised to respect the political independence and territorial integrity of China and to preserve the Open Door, while China agreed not to discriminate against the nationals of any other power using her railroads or otherwise passing through her territory.

Lesser arrangements at Washington provided that (1) the United States

More up to date. The Four-Power Treaty replaces the cloak of isolation.
(By Harding in the *Brooklyn Eagle*.)

would have free access to the island of Yap, as well as equality with Japan in the cable communications there; (2) Japan would give up her political rights in Shantung and withdraw from Siberia; (3) the Lansing-Ishii agreement would be abrogated;[2] and (4) a commission would be appointed to consider extraterritorial rights in China.

The achievements of the Washington Conference seemed great at the time and won the immediate acclaim of most Americans. Actual limitations of armaments by international agreement was a goal often sought but never before achieved. Subsequent events, however, have made a later generation dubious of the wisdom of many of those decisions. Japan's navy, though smaller than those of Britain and the United States, was large enough to dominate the western Pacific. After Japanese militarists gained control of Japan's destinies in the thirties, it became obvious that the Naval Treaty had rendered Britain and the United States impotent to challenge her. Disarmament proved a feeble foundation for peace without some effective collective security system to prevent an aggressor state from taking advantage of the military and naval weaknesses of other powers.

[2] The Lansing-Ishii agreement of November, 1917, was a wartime effort to find a formula reconciling the conflicting China policies of the United States and Japan, then cobelligerents against Germany. It pledged mutual adherence to the principles of the Open Door and the territorial integrity and political independence of China but recognized that "Japan has special interests in China, particularly in that part to which her possessions are contiguous."

The Geneva Conference

The failure of the Washington Conference to extend the quota system to destroyers, cruisers, and submarines led to a race among some nations in those construction fields. The United States, primarily interested in domestic matters, did not participate and even failed to keep its capital-ship tonnage up to its allotted ratio. Yet by early 1927, President Coolidge became concerned about the increase in lesser armament, as well as about the strained relations developing between his country and Japan since the passage of the 1924 immigration law. Since these were potential causes for war, would it not be wise to hold another disarmament conference? Accordingly, on February 10, 1927, he invited the other four signatories of the Washington Treaty to another discussion to be held at Geneva.

This Geneva Conference, opening in June, 1927, proved a disappointing failure. France and Italy refused to attend, and Britain, Japan, and the United States could not agree on a formula to extend the quota system to smaller naval craft. England, with world-wide commitments and a network of island bases, wanted a large number of small cruisers, while the United States, poor in overseas possessions, held out for a small number of large cruisers. The difficulties were multiplied by the presence of professional naval officers who opposed the whole principle of limitation, and by the activities of lobbyists working to sabotage the project in the interests of munitions and armament firms. The conference's failure had serious results. Anglo-American relations were more strained than they had been for many years, and American isolationism and nationalism were given strong nourishment.

War Debts

Another matter of controversy was the payment of war debts. During the war, the United States had loaned over $7 billion to seven countries that were fighting Germany. After the armistice, about $3.3 billion more was granted to these nations and thirteen others hard hit by the ravages of war and in need of cash and supplies to speed rehabilitation.

The twenty debtor states started a movement as early as 1919 to have this $10.3 billion obligation canceled or at least reduced, asserting that these loans were, in effect, America's contribution to the war effort before she participated actively in the military conflict. Furthermore, since the borrowers had used the loans primarily to buy supplies in the United States, the profits accruing to American industry should be considered sufficient repayment. Then, too, it would be impossible to pay back in gold, for most of the bullion had been drained to the United States in the early days of the war. What little was left in Europe was needed for currency stabilization. The only way to repay, therefore, was in goods, but American tariff barriers precluded that possibility. France had her own reason for requesting cancellation. During the American Revolution she had loaned the young republic what were then large sums, which had not been fully repaid. Was it not the time now for America to reciprocate?

The United States refused to heed these arguments. Wilson and his successors would not concede there was any relationship between German reparations to the Allies and their obligations to the United States. Since the money had been loaned by the United States government to European governments without any strings attached, the debtors had both a legal and moral obligation to repay in full. Nor did assertions that the loans constituted America's contribution to the war effort hold good for the postwar aid. Moreover, at the Peace Conference the other victors had obtained land and promises of reparations, while the United States had received nothing tangible.

The debtors considered America greedy, and there were numerous references to Uncle Shylock and the pound of flesh he was collecting from unfortunate Europe. Yet it was not until December 6, 1921, that Harding sought congressional authority to settle the debt principal and interest of 5 per cent that was in default. The legislature responded on February 9, 1922, with provision for the appointment of the World War Debt Commission, empowered

to refund or convert, and to extend time of payment of the principal or the interest, or both, of any obligation of any foreign government now held by the United States, or any obligation of any foreign government hereafter received by the United States arising out of the World War.

This commission, headed by Secretary Mellon, immediately started holding conferences with envoys of the debtor nations, trying to reach a compromise based on the debtor's ability to pay. Britain, the first to reach an agreement, promised to pay the $4 billion she owed in semiannual installments over a sixty-two-year period at interest of 3.3 per cent. During the next three years, twelve other borrowers made varied arrangements at different interest rates.[3] A most stubborn negotiator was France, who did not come to terms until 1926, when she agreed to pay interest of only 1.6 per cent. Italy made an even better bargain with a 0.4 per cent charge. From the point of view of Americans who regarded the war debts as purely commercial transactions, the United States was more than generous in these settlements. Some of the unpaid interest was forgiven, thereby reducing a paper indebtedness of $12 billion to $11.6 billion. More important, the original interest rate of 5 per cent was reduced to an average of 2.1 per cent, even though the United States was paying 4.25 per cent interest on Liberty Bonds held by its own citizens. Figured over sixty-two years, the debt had been reduced to about half the original obligation.

The fact remains, however, that these were not ordinary commercial debts, but were American expenditures to support American foreign policy comparable to foreign aid grants during and after World War II. From Europe's point of view, the United States was exacting sixty-two years of tribute from

---

[3] Of the remaining seven debtors, Russia, Greece, and Armenia sent no envoys as their new governments had not been recognized by the United States; Cuba and Nicaragua had already paid most of their obligations; Liberia was about to receive an American loan to take care of her debts; and it was agreed that consideration of the Austrian debt would be postponed twenty years.

her former allies, thereby adding to their already desperate postwar problems. Furthermore, Europeans justly complained that America's high tariff policy was completely inconsistent with insistence upon war debt payments.

Many American liberals could understand and sympathize with this attitude, but politically any talk of debt cancellation was anathema. The American majority regarded the Europeans as virtual defaulters. Thus the isolationist trend was strengthened; if war brought repudiation, then it was best to stay out of European troubles. Whether wise or not, the temporary settlement of the debt question did at least clear the air and contribute to better international understanding.

The Dawes and Young Plans

Despite its continued insistence that the European obligations were not contingent upon Germany's payment of reparations, the United States did help speed up the reparations payments. In turn, America would benefit because the sooner the reparations problem was taken care of, the sooner European debtors would reach an agreement with the United States on war debts. Thus in August, 1924, Germany and the Allies ratified the Dawes Plan, for which three Americans—Charles Dawes, Henry Robinson, a prominent banker, and Owen D. Young, an outstanding industrialist—were largely responsible. It provided that the following year Germany pay the Allies $250 million out of income from railroads, industry, and loans, with larger amounts in ensuing years. American and Allied bankers would loan Germany $200 million in gold to facilitate the first payments, to speed up her industrial recovery, and to back a new currency issue.

The Dawes Plan worked well at first, but as the payments became larger and Germany realized that no ultimate date had been set to complete her reparations, she urged a new program. Again the United States came forward with the Young Plan of December 22, 1928. Germany was to pay $153 million a year for fifty-nine years, plus a varied scale of "conditional payments" determined by her prosperity. In turn, the Allies agreed to evacuate all German territory by 1930 and to end the supervision of her actions. If the United States lowered the obligations of her own debtors, Germany would be relieved of some of her reparations.

The claims of the American government and American citizens against Germany, Austria, and Hungary were taken care of in a complicated series of agreements, culminating in the War Claims Act of March, 1923. Various commissions and umpires awarded, with interest, some $233 million in settlement.

Nonrecognition of Russia

The one nation with which the United States did not negotiate for a debt settlement was the Soviet Union. Ever since the Bolsheviks had gained control in November, 1917, and repudiated all debts contracted by previous regimes, relations with the United States had been strained.

The immediate cause for America's failure to recognize the Soviet government was the latter's refusal to admit responsibility for an American loan of $178 million to the Kerensky administration, the confiscation of American property in Russia worth $443 million, and the failure to pay either principal or interest on the $75 million worth of bonds of the old regime sold in the United States. But there were other factors as well. Americans generally were shocked by the way the Communists had gained power and did not believe that they represented the will of the Russian people. Furthermore, the United States charged the Soviet with spreading propaganda in America calculated to overthrow the government.

This Wilson nonrecognition policy continued throughout the twenties, even though European neighbors did accept Russia into the family of nations. True, there was considerable pressure from American liberals to change this attitude, but to no avail.

The Paris Pact

Even before the Geneva Conference had demonstrated that naval limitation was not a sure path to peace, some Americans urged that the nations of the world band together to legislate against war. This view was also upheld by Aristide Briand, the French Foreign Minister. To publicize his belief, he devoted part of his address to the American people on April 6, 1927—the anniversary of America's entrance into the World War—to a proposal that the two countries agree to outlaw war between themselves.

Kellogg was slow to accept the Briand proposal. Perhaps he was not interested; perhaps he felt it was too limited in scope to do much for world peace. Yet a number of prominent Americans led by President Nicholas Butler of Columbia University gave their support, the press played it up, the Grange endorsed it, and the public became enthusiastic. Petition after petition was sent to the administration with signatures reaching into the millions.

This enormous tide of opinion forced Kellogg to change his hesitant policy, but it was not until December, 1927, that he agreed to consider Briand's suggestion were it broadened to include other nations. France consented to extend the invitation, and thus at Paris on August 27, 1928, Britain, her Dominions, Germany, Japan, Poland, Belgium, and Czechoslovakia joined with France and the United States in signing the Paris, or Kellogg-Briand, Pact. Under its terms, the signatories declared "that they condemn recourse to war as an instrument of national policy in their relations with one another." Furthermore, "the settlement or solution of all disputes or conflicts of whatever nature or of whatever origin they may be, which shall arise among them, shall never be sought except by pacific means." No termination date was set—the obligation was expected to be perpetual. The ratifying agencies of the fifteen signatories subsequently gave their approval, but usually with reservations. The chief American ones were that the pact did not cover defensive wars and that the United States considered the safeguarding of the Monroe Doctrine as necessary for its "national security and self-defense." Backed by overwhelming public opinion, the Senate approved in January, 1929, with only one dissenting vote.

In many ways the Paris Pact now seems a pious fraud. In the first place, since most nations reserved the right to defend not only themselves but certain cherished spheres of interest, the agreement "outlawed" not all wars, but only aggressive ones. Any history student knows that aggressor states never admit their aggression; they invariably justify their military measures as defensive. Therefore, it is not surprising that the aggressors of the 1930's—Japan, Germany, Italy, and Russia—were all solemn signatories of the Pact. An even more fatal weakness was that it provided no means of enforcement. It represented in purest form the isolationist dream that war could be abolished merely by general acceptance of a pledge not to go to war.

Absurd though all this seems today, the American public applauded the Paris Pact as a major achievement in the search for peace. Secretary Kellogg sought to capitalize on this spirit by reviving the Root arbitration-treaty plan. Eighteen such bilateral treaties were negotiated before 1931, each committing the contracting parties to submit all justiciable differences to some international tribunal, preferably the Hague Court. The Senate, still jealous of its prerogatives, continued to insist on the right to determine what matters should be submitted to arbitration.

The United States and Latin America

At the immediate close of World War I, relations between Latin America and the United States were more friendly than ever before. For the time being the United States had assumed first place among the nations exporting to and importing from the Latin-American states. The total value of exports and imports had grown from about $200 million in 1913 to nearly $3 billion in early 1919. United States loans and investments more than kept pace with this commercial interchange. Influenced largely by the actions of the United States, eight other hemisphere republics had declared war on Germany, with five others severing relations. Wilson's efforts to make the world safe for democracy and his subsequent Fourteen Points were well received in the rest of the hemisphere and helped the other republics lose for the time being their fear of the "Colossus of the North."

The League of Nations was considered an additional safeguard for Latin America, and seventeen of the states joined at once. They saw in it an opportunity to participate in world affairs, to settle international differences by peaceful means, and to have their independence and territorial integrity better protected. The dark spot was Article 21 of the Covenant, which asserted that nothing in the document should "affect the validity of international engagements . . . such as the Monroe Doctrine." All Latin-American efforts to amend that article were unavailing.

By 1920, however, the old fear of *Yanqui* imperialism was returning. The failure of the United States to join the League seemed to indicate she was not sincere in her wish for international cooperation. Then, to make that fear doubly great, came the repudiation of Wilson by Congress and by the voters in the election of 1920. The wartime trade boom gradually diminished with the return of peace. This decline of business with the United States was in part due to the failure of American exporters to live up to promises of speedy delivery and of high-quality goods. Latin America consequently turned again to European markets or, as a result of wartime specialization in that part of the hemisphere, to the neighboring republics. The Americans felt they should sell to, not buy from, Latin America.

Mexican Oil

Throughout most of the twenties, there was tension between the United States and Mexico, brought on by unstable Mexican politics and complications arising out of the extremely liberal 1917 Mexican constitution.

In 1920, Alvaro Obregón became president of Mexico by revolt and subsequent election. Immediately American investors in Mexican oil and land worried lest he make retroactive Article 27 of the constitution, which stated that subsoil rights belonged to the Mexican nation. They demanded that he approve a treaty guaranteeing their property rights. This Obregón would not do because he said foreigners would then have more security than Mexican citizens. Furthermore, Mexico seemed unable to pay her debts, mostly owed abroad, which had been greatly increased by the recent political chaos. Consequently, the United States would not recognize the new president.

American nonrecognition not only weakened Obregón's position, but made it difficult for Mexico to obtain new loans. Therefore in 1922 the Mexican Supreme Court decided that Article 27 would not affect oil leases acquired prior to 1917, which was followed by a similar executive decree the next year. Then in the summer of 1923, a meeting of an American-Mexican joint committee decided that subsoil rights gained by Americans prior to 1917 would not be interfered with, that Americans owning land in Mexico who lost their property through expropriation should be paid a fair price, and that American monetary claims would be settled by future joint commissions. These promises satisfied the United States, which recognized Obregón in August, 1923. Other major powers quickly followed America's lead.

The next year Plutarco Calles was elected to the presidency. At first it appeared that the improved relations would continue, but Secretary Kellogg presently charged that Mexico was not taking sufficient steps to indemnify American citizens for seized property. In addition, he implied that the Calles administration was threatened by revolt and warned: "The government of Mexico is now on trial before the world."

Angered by Kellogg's criticism, Calles instituted more drastic policies. Thus, in December, 1925, the so-called Petroleum Law and the Land Law were passed, placing so many conditions on oil leases and property rights that they made Article 27 in effect retroactive. Although the smaller American oil companies and landowners complied with this legislation, the more important ones refused to do so and appealed for United States protection. Kellogg, with Coolidge's backing, was inclined to support them. There followed a year of vigorous note writing between the two governments that did not ease the situation. Indeed, war seemed a possibility, especially in January, 1927, when Kellogg claimed he had proof Mexico was the center of Bolshevik activities in the hemisphere.

The Senate refused to believe these charges and on January 27, 1927, unanimously approved a resolution to arbitrate the whole oil problem. The administration, realizing it had gone too far, named as ambassador Dwight Morrow, who, though a business associate of J. P. Morgan, was an able conciliator. His friendly spirit, plus the need of the Calles administration for money, brought a change in Mexican policy. In December, 1927, the Mexican legislature rescinded most of the objectionable 1925 and 1926 measures, so that in effect Article 27 was no longer retroactive. Moreover, a Mexican statute prohibiting the purchase of American goods was repealed. With tensions eased, Morrow obtained some justice for Americans whose Mexican lands had been seized and helped temporarily in the troublesome religious situation in Mexico. Another step in the improvement of relations was the goodwill flight to Mexico City by Charles Lindbergh, soon to become Morrow's son-in-law.

Thus the air was cleared and friendship restored between the two neighbors. But the problem of debts, oil, and land were not settled; they were to cause more controversy during the next decade.

Meddling in Nicaragua

American dollar diplomacy in Nicaragua was a constant source of trouble throughout the twenties. Only the presence of American marines kept political peace there, and at times even they could not preserve order. In an effort to end the chaos, Nicaragua agreed in 1923 to use a new election law, drawn up by an American, in the next year's balloting. This reform, plus an improvement in Nicaraguan finances, thanks in part to the efficient American collector of customs, brought Hughes's promise that the marines would be withdrawn after the inauguration of the new president. The 1924 election, said to be the most fair and honest in Nicaragua's history, brought victory to a "Conservative-Liberal" coalition, and in August, 1925, the American troops left. Scarcely had they been withdrawn, however, when a revolt forced President Solórzano to resign and Vice President Juan Sacasa to flee. The rebel leader, Emiliano Chammoro, set himself up as chief, but the United States would not recognize him.

Heartened by the American position, Sacasa returned and civil war broke out anew. Therefore, in June, 1926, American troops, in greater numbers than before, were sent in. After considerable political maneuvering, hostilities ceased in the early fall, and a new election brought victory to "Conservative" Adopho Díaz, who was recognized by the United States. But Sacasa, still claiming the presidency and recognized by Mexico, established his own regime, and fighting broke out again. More American troops were then landed to protect Díaz, despite protests from other Latin-American republics.

In early 1927, Coolidge sent Henry Stimson to solve the imbroglio. Stimson decided that Díaz should finish his term, with the American marines, now nearly 6,000 strong, keeping the opposition in check. Sacasa bowed to the inevitable, but his fellow "Liberal," Augusto Sandino, continued the revolt. Then Stimson arranged a new election law under which the 1928 campaign was held under the supervision of the American military. The winner, "Liberal" José Moncada, promised to establish a national guard, trained by an American officer. When this force was competent to police the country, Coolidge agreed to withdraw the marines. Sandino, however, continued to be a source of trouble, even though Moncada disavowed his actions.

Military intervention in Nicaragua did not help the position of the United States in the hemisphere. The Coolidge excuse for it, however, was given on January 20, 1927:

> The United States cannot fail to view with deep concern any serious threat to stability and constitutional government in Nicaragua tending toward anarchy and jeopardizing American interests, especially if such state of affairs is contributed to or brought about by outside influence or by any foreign power.

He was referring to charges that Communists from Mexico were contributing to the Nicaraguan unrest.

Growing Neighborliness

Fortunately for the United States–Latin-American relations, several incidents during the twenties offset the ill-feeling promoted by affairs in Mexico and Nicaragua. Mention has already been made of the satisfactory settlement of the long-standing differences with Colombia through an American payment of $25 million and the grant to Colombia of equal rights to the use of the Panama Canal. This was followed by a rapid increase of American investments—between 1922 and 1929 more than $260 million in American capital was so invested—in that Latin-American republic, and by the signing of a commercial treaty advantageous to both parties.

In 1924 the last American marines were withdrawn from the Dominican Republic. The Dominican government promised to continue the political and economic improvements achieved during the American protectorate and to allow the American customs collector to supervise local finances until the American loans were repaid.[4] And in Cuba, the American General Enoch Crowder drew up new election laws that temporarily ended chaotic conditions without the use of military force.

The long-standing problem of the Tacna-Arica territory, which had alienated Chile and Peru for decades, was presented to the United States for mediation in 1922. For the next seven years the State Department struggled with the problem, suggesting procedures for settlement that ranged

---

[4] In September, 1940, the United States ended its control over Dominican finances when that government agreed that the payments to American bondholders would form the first lien on general government revenues.

all the way from a plebiscite of the inhabitants to direct negotiations between the two claimants. Finally, in May, 1929, the disputants asked President Hoover to submit his own solution. It was accepted and the United States had finally succeeded as an impartial mediator in a prominent South American dispute.

Two regular Pan-American conferences were held during the twenties. The first, delayed since 1914 by the war, convened at Santiago, Chile, in 1923. Although the United States refused to make the Monroe Doctrine multilateral, she did give full support to the so-called Gondra Treaty, which provided for the peaceful settlement of all disputes among the hemisphere republics. Should a conflict develop, a commission of inquiry was to be established as quickly as possible. While its findings were not binding, they might lead to a settlement.

The second meeting was at Havana, Cuba, in 1928. A feature was the opening speech by President Coolidge, in which he stressed the importance of hemisphere cooperation to develop human rights and pledged that the United States would do her part. He declared that "All nations here represented stand on an exact footing of equality," but this principle was not carried to its logical conclusion. When the right of one republic to intervene in the affairs of another was questioned, Hughes vigorously opposed discussion of the issue since it involved not only the recent United States activities in Mexico and Nicaragua, but the whole trend of its Caribbean policy since 1905. The United States was supported by Brazil, Bolivia, Chile, and Peru, so the explosive proposal was dropped. Another suggestion that the governing board of the Pan American Union serve as a hemisphere court of justice was likewise rejected, largely through American opposition. Despite United States contrariness in these matters, Hughes proved an able conciliator in other respects. Primarily through his efforts, the delegates agreed to hold a special conference in Washington the following December to consider possible extension of arbitration in the hemisphere.

This Washington meeting, called the Pan-American Conference on Conciliation and Arbitration, resulted in long steps toward peaceful settlement of disputes among the republics. First of all, the Gondra Treaty was reaffirmed with an amendment providing that disputing nations would not resort to war while the commissioners of inquiry were making their investigation. To this was added a General Treaty of Inter-American Arbitration, under which the states agreed to arbitrate all disputes of a juridical nature, but not domestic differences or those arising under the Monroe Doctrine. The decisions of the arbitral tribunal were to be final. And the Protocol for Progressive Arbitration attempted to set the stage for the abandonment of exceptions to arbitration. Shortly after the session, Argentina offered her South American Anti-War Pact, similar in content to the Paris Pact, which all the republics signed.

While these events were taking place, Coolidge asked J. Reuben Clark of the State Department to define the proper scope of the Monroe Doctrine. Although not published until 1930, the resulting Clark Memorandum did much to improve Latin American relations. It asserted that (1) the Monroe Doctrine was still unilateral—the United States alone would determine when it was being violated; (2) "the Doctrine does not concern itself with purely inter-American relations"; (3) "the Doctrine states a case of the United States versus Europe, not of the United States versus Latin America"; (4) "so far as Latin America is concerned, the Doctrine is now, and always has been, not an instrument of violence and oppression, but an unbought, freely bestowed and wholly effective guaranty of their freedom, independence, and territorial integrity against the imperialist designs of Europe"; and (5) "it is not believed that this [Roosevelt] corollary is justified by the terms of the Monroe Doctrine, however much it may be justified by the application of the doctrine of self-preservation." These statements, especially the repudiation of the Roosevelt Corollary, were welcome news to the other republics and could be called the basis for better relations—relations subsequently known as the Good Neighbor Policy.

Colonial Unrest

The Puerto Ricans had served their guardian well during World War I by participation in military service, buying war bonds, and aiding the Red Cross. Therefore it was a distinct shock when they were rewarded with the appointment of E. Mont Reily as governor by President Harding in 1921. Reily's failure to consider the wishes and needs of the Puerto Ricans, his replacement of competent judges and other local officials by his own untrained friends, and his budget increases to raise these newcomers' salaries brought protest after protest from the inhabitants. Threat of a congressional investigation brought Reily's resignation in early 1923, and he was succeeded by Horace Towner, described as "one of the best governors the island has ever had."

The Puerto Ricans realized Towner could not remain in office indefinitely and that he might be replaced by a man like Reily. Therefore, in 1924, a delegation went to Washington to seek a greater degree of autonomy, including the right to elect their own governor, with power to appoint local officials. Although Coolidge was in partial sympathy with this request, he would not approve all of it, saying, "Puerto Rico has a greater degree of sovereignty over its internal affairs than does the government of any State or Territory of the United States," but he did not try to explain how citizens of one of the states would react to having their governor appointed by the President. And Congress, through failure to agree, would not support the insular requests.

Then in 1928, the Puerto Ricans employed Charles Lindbergh to request Washington that they become a "free state," but again nothing came of this petition. Coolidge again said they had a more liberal government than was to be found in the United States proper.

Although the Coolidge administration showed little sympathy for changes in the administrative system, it was not lacking in humanity. When a disastrous hurricane swept over Puerto Rico in the fall of 1928, killing hundreds of people, rendering several hundred thousands homeless, and destroying millions of dollars worth of property, the United States quickly appropriated $8 million for repairs and for loans to hard-hit farmers. At the same time the Red Cross sent over workers and spent more than $3 million to alleviate the suffering.

The Harding-Coolidge regime also turned deaf ears toward Filipino demands for independence. Harding appointed Leonard Wood as governor of the Philippines, and he proceeded to undo most of the liberal work of his predecessor, Francis Harrison. With the Philippine Organic Act of 1916 as his authority, Wood used his veto power extensively to thwart the plans of his department heads. Therefore, the Filipino legislature approved a resolution in October, 1923, calling for Wood's dismissal. Coolidge, however, gave the governor his unlimited backing, saying, "You are entitled to the support of the Administration and shall have it."

Undismayed by this rebuff, the Filipinos then asked that one of their number be appointed governor and at the same time asserted that Wood's arbitrary actions made it impossible for them to work with him in any capacity. These resolutions concluded with the statement "that the immediate and absolute independence of the Philippines, which the whole country demands, is the only complete and satisfactory settlement of the Philippine problem."

Coolidge's answer was similar to his reply to the Puerto Ricans. Under American rule, the Filipinos were much better off than they would be if they wholly governed themselves. They did not have sufficient experience for independence and they failed to consider that they would not have the advantage of free trade with the United States.

On Wood's death early in 1928, Coolidge named Henry Stimson to replace him. Before the year was over, Stimson established another Council of State, consisting of himself, the heads of the Philippine Senate and House and their majority leaders, and the chairmen of the executive departments, to serve as an advisory board for the governor when he felt disposed to call the council into session. While this council was not so free and powerful as the one under Harrison, it was the first step in almost a decade toward autonomy.

On the whole, the diplomacy of the twenties was not vigorous. Harding left most of the duties in that field to the State Department—fortunately under the capable Charles Evans Hughes. The Washington Conference was more of a paper than an actual victory for peace, and the settlement of the debts and reparations problem was only temporary. Coolidge, in his early years in office, based his diplomacy on the same laissez faire principles as his domestic policies. When he did act, he favored American business interests. Toward the close of his administration, however, he took a more liberal view of colonial and world affairs, thereby setting the stage for the more internationally minded Hoover and Roosevelt regimes.

12

REACTIONARIES AND REBELS

American social and cultural life during the twenties displayed contrasting tendencies. It was a period of intolerance and narrow nationalism, when the Ku Klux Klan and all that it represented flourished. At the other extreme, it was an age of revolt, when women bobbed their hair and took up smoking, when flaming youth drank excessively and went mad over jazz, and when intellectuals ridiculed the conventions of earlier days. But probably to most Americans it was simply a happy, carefree period—a period of apparent prosperity—when the exploits of Babe Ruth, Jack Dempsey, and Red Grange seemed infinitely more interesting than the activities of the politicians.

The Unions Lose Ground

Labor shortages and government favor had helped labor unions to almost double their membership between 1914 and 1920. In 1920 more than 5 million workers were affiliated with unions; four fifths of these belonged to groups within the American Federation of Labor, the remainder to the Railroad Brotherhoods and various other independents. These gains, however, proved impossible to hold. By 1923 total trade-union membership had dropped to about 3.6 million.

To a certain degree, the losses of the early twenties were natural. Many workers had joined unions during the period of rapid growth simply because of temporary factors and neglected to pay their dues thereafter. The depression of 1921, moreover, hurt the unions. With labor in abundance, employers could give preference to nonunion men, while the unions lost their popularity when they could not prevent wage cuts and layoffs. Of equal importance was the aggressive campaign waged by many businessmen to curb what they regarded as labor's excessive power. Trade associations, chambers of commerce, and farmers' groups gave support to a well-organized open-shop movement. In January, 1921, representatives from twenty-two manufacturers' associations met in Chicago and adopted the name "American Plan" for their campaign to combat the unions. During the next several months organized labor suffered a number of bad defeats.

The unions also had serious setbacks in the courts. Judges interpreted very narrowly the provisions of the Clayton Act that Samuel Gompers had greeted as "Labor's Magna Carta." In the Duplex case of 1921, the Supreme Court ruled that the immunities granted by the act applied only to employees directly involved in a dispute and that it was illegal for fellow unionists to attempt to support those employees by refusing to service the employer's products. In another case of the same year (American Steel Foundries *v.* Tri-City Trades Council), labor's right to picket was rigorously limited, while in Truax *v.* Corrigan, also in 1921, the Supreme Court upheld the right of state courts to issue injunctions in labor disputes, even when the state legislatures had forbidden such injunctions. Particularly hated by the unions were the "yellow dog" contracts—agreements under which employees were obliged to promise that they would not become members of any union. The courts used the existence of such contracts as grounds for issuing injunctions forbidding union organizers to make any attempts, however peaceful, to enlist new members.

For the unions to lose membership during periods of depression was natural; the remarkable thing during the twenties was that they failed to make up their lost ground during the ensuing years of prosperity. Instead, their total membership in 1929 was only 3.45 million, about 150,000 less than in 1923. Organized labor's most conspicuous failure was its inability to penetrate such major industries as iron and steel, food packing, automobiles, rubber products, chemicals, and electrical equipment. This failure resulted on one side from the determined opposition of the employers; on the other, from the union leaders' uncertainty as to what tactics should be pursued. Since these were mass-production industries, employing for the most part workers without individual skills, the old-line unions that constituted the major strength of the AFL were ill-suited to the task of organizing them. Although the Federation did have a few industrial unions such as the United Mine Workers, the attempt to establish new ones aroused the jealousy of existing craft unions fearing an infringement on their jurisdictions. The AFL witnessed many sharp fights between the progressives who advocated more aggressive tactics and the conservatives who counseled caution. Throughout the decade the latter faction, led by Gompers until his death in 1924 and then by William Green, who succeeded him in the AFL presidency, kept control of the national organization.

Communist attempts to capture existing labor unions by "boring from within" injured the progressive cause. William Z. Foster of steel-strike fame organized the Trade Union Educational League to serve this purpose. Determined to keep Communists out of the AFL, Gompers took stern measures, ousting from conventions individuals who had sided with Foster and revoking the charters of unions that had fallen under Communist control. So far did the Federation go in its anti-Red campaign that it repeatedly opposed recognition of the Soviet government by the United States; in 1930 it even asked for an embargo on imports from Russia because they were "convict made." Although most of the progressives within the AFL were scarcely less opposed to Communism than were Gompers and Green, their efforts to advance industrial unionism fell into disrepute when the Communists began to demand the same things.

The United Mine Workers, under John L. Lewis, encountered many difficulties. In 1922 when the operators sought to cut wages, there were prolonged and bitter strikes in both the hard- and soft-coal fields. So high did feeling run at Herrin, Illinois, that twenty-five men, most of them strikebreakers, were killed. Although the miners won satisfactory settlements in 1922, they were unable to hold their gains during later years. The bituminous miners were compelled to take severe cuts and to suffer much unemployment because of competition with the nonunion fields in West Virginia, Kentucky, and Alabama. Attempts to organize these areas were sternly opposed by hired mine guards and company-controlled local officials. When the miners also resorted to violence, gun battles and bloodshed resulted. Such was the case in Harlan County, Kentucky, where three deputies and a miner were killed in a pitched battle on May 5, 1931; seven of the miners were sentenced to life imprisonment as an aftermath of the affray. The defeats suffered under Lewis led to rebellions against his leadership. Rival unions were formed, and the IWW and the Communists took their turns in organizing campaigns, but they had no greater success.

Serious strife also erupted in the textile field. The workers in the woolen mills of Passaic, New Jersey, rebelled against low wages and bad working conditions in a strike that began in January, 1927, and did not end until March, 1928. The vigorous role played by radicals tended to divert attention from the legitimate grievances of the workers, and eventually the Communists consented to retire from the struggle. But even after an old-line union, the United Textile Workers, took over the leadership, they found it impossible to obtain any important concessions.

During 1929 there were bitterly contested strikes in the Tennessee textile town of Elizabethton and in the North Carolina towns of Gastonia and Marion. At Elizabethton mobs attacked the labor organizers; at Gastonia local authorities used drastic tactics against the strikers and the chief of police was killed in the resulting clash; at Marion the sheriff and his deputies fired upon unarmed pickets, killing five and wounding nineteen. Against the alliance of company, local government authorities, and antiunion mobs, all campaigns to organize the Southern textile workers broke down, whether led by Communists as at Gastonia, or by the United Textile Workers as at Elizabethton and Marion.

Welfare Capitalism

Neither the shortcomings of union leadership nor the determination of the antiunion forces completely explain the weakness of the labor union movement during the twenties. Much of labor's docility resulted from the fact that many workers seemed to be bettering their lot without organization. Although there were wage cuts during the depression of 1921, pay usually remained substantially higher than before the war. The farmers' bad fortune, moreover, was to a certain extent the workers' good. Food prices, though higher than they had been in 1914, rose proportionately less than wages; the result was an increase in purchasing power. According to the calculation of a leading economist, the workers' real earnings averaged 32 per cent higher in 1929 than they had in 1914.

Sometimes the better wages were no more than a price grudgingly paid to keep workers reasonably satisfied and indifferent to the union organizers. For many businessmen, however, they reflected a new philosophy that defended high wages not merely as a necessary evil, but as a positive good since they attracted the more enterprising workers to a particular plant and developed the purchasing power that gave industry a mass market for automobiles, radios, and the like. Similarly, employers accepted the shorter work week as a contribution to higher efficiency and more leisure time for the workers to consume the products of industry.

Welfare capitalism sought also to improve the conditions under which the laborers worked. Employers were more careful in fixing piece rates and working rules and sometimes made provision for vacations with pay. Recreation halls and cafeterias also helped to keep the employees contented. A favorite device of the twenties was the company union, which provided for the election of labor representatives with power to consult with management and present worker grievances. Such unions, however, were kept strictly under the control of the employer and the extent of their activities was rigidly restricted.

In order to prevent the extension of the company-union movement, many old-line unions felt the necessity of cooperating closely with management. But union conservatism provided no more than a defensive tactic. Employers in industries not already organized continued to recognize only company unions and to base their labor policies on the tenets of welfare capitalism. Often they sought to ensure the loyalty of their men through stock-purchase plans—a policy that had some unfortunate repercussions when stock prices collapsed in 1929.

Suppressing Radicalism

The anti-Red hysteria of 1919 gradually subsided as the extremely small number of real radicals in the country became more apparent. But the IWW and the Communists continued to be highly unpopular. Criminal syndicalism laws remained on the books and, at least in California, they were actively enforced. In that state there were 504 arrests under these laws between 1919 and 1924.

Radicals arrested on any charge were likely to find judge and jury prejudiced against them. Such at least was the conclusion of thousands of Americans who interested themselves in the Sacco-Vanzetti case. Nicola Sacco and Bartolomeo Vanzetti, two anarchists who had been active in strikes during earlier years, were arrested in 1920 on the charge of having held up and murdered the paymaster of a shoe factory in South Braintree, Massachusetts. During their trial, the presiding judge, Webster Thayer, made clear his strong distaste for anarchists in general and these two in particular. He permitted the district attorney to drive home to the jury the radical beliefs and activities of the defendants. After the two were found guilty and sentenced to death, defense lawyers started a long campaign to obtain a new trial on the ground that the first had been unfair. Despite the weakness of the case against the two radicals and the

Sacco and Vanzetti (second and third figures walking in front row). (Brown Bros.)

discovery of new evidence, Judge Thayer refused all motions for retrial. Controversy over the case reached a climax in 1927. After a committee of prominent citizens headed by President A. Lawrence Lowell of Harvard had recommended against executive clemency, Governor Alvan T. Fuller allowed the executions to be carried out on August 23, 1927. Prominent in efforts to save the two had been newspapermen such as Heywood Broun, literary figures such as Edna St. Vincent Millay and John Dos Passos, and outstanding lawyers such as Felix Frankfurter and Arthur Garfield Hayes. News of the executions brought demonstrations thousands of miles away—in England, France, Italy, Russia, and Latin America. Rightly or wrongly, countless people throughout the world were convinced that Sacco and Vanzetti had gone to the electric chair not because they were guilty of murder, but because of their unpopular opinions.

In California two radical unionists, Thomas J. Mooney and Warren K. Billings, escaped death but nevertheless suffered long imprisonment for a crime of which many Americans believed them innocent. Accused of participating in a bomb outrage that took the lives of eight persons in a San Francisco Preparedness Day parade in 1916, Mooney was convicted and sentenced to be hanged, while Billings was given a life term. As a result of President Wilson's intercession, the governor of California commuted Mooney's sentence to life imprisonment. The men remained in prison despite the fact that the convictions had been obtained on flimsy evidence and perhaps on perjured testimony. As in the Sacco-Vanzetti case, the circumstance that thousands of liberals were demanding their release only seemed to stiffen the determination of the state authorities to allow the law to take its course. Not until 1939 were the California prisoners granted a pardon.

The Ku Klux Klan

On Thanksgiving night, 1915, Colonel William J. Simmons and some thirty friends gathered under a fiery cross on Stone Mountain near Atlanta, Georgia, and swore allegiance to the Invisible Empire, Knights of the Ku Klux Klan. During the next ten years such weird scenes were repeated thousands of times in every part of the country. Simmons's attempt to found a new organization employing the name and paraphernalia of the old Klan of Reconstruction days had no great success at first, but it received a new lease on life in 1920 when Edward Clarke and Mrs. Elizabeth Tyler were put in charge of its promotional activities. The country was divided into domains headed by Grand Goblins and realms or states each supervised by a King Kleagle. At the bottom of the organizational pyramid were thousands of local Kleagles who rounded up new members and collected their $10.00 initiation fees. With this streamlined machinery the Klan had a spectacular growth. Its days of greatest prosperity came between 1923 and 1925, during the regime of Simmons's successor, Hiram Wesley Evans, a Texas dentist.

Defenders of the Klan asserted that it was simply a fraternal order devoted to the praiseworthy ideals of patriotism and Christian morality. Many of its members were attracted either by these professed objectives or by the opportunity that the Klan offered for dressing up in mysterious robes and hoods, for participating in melodramatic rituals, or for talking a strange jargon that featured words starting with the letter K. Yet the movement, which had perhaps four or five million adherents by 1925, had many sinister aspects. It was fed by group hatred—white hatred of the black, Christian hatred of the Jew, and, above all, Protestant hatred of the Catholic. The ends to which the Klan was devoted and the methods it used depended upon the local situation. In some areas its activities were confined to burning crosses at night, holding mysterious konklaves, and parading through the streets; in others it acted as a vigilance committee, sending warning messages to bootleggers, persons accused of immorality, blacks lacking in humility, or labor union organizers. Spokesmen for the Klan always denied that it was guilty of violence, but there appears little doubt that local groups using the costume of the Klan were involved in floggings, tar-and-feather parties, mutilations, and even killings.

Physical violence, however, was less characteristic of the Klan than were other methods. Catholic and Jewish merchants suffered from boycotts; schoolteachers who failed to present their subjects in the Klan-prescribed way were dismissed by local school boards; ministers brave enough to condemn the Klan were forced to resign. The Klan became more and more involved in politics until it exerted power in states as widely scattered as Oregon, Texas, Oklahoma, Louisiana, Maine, and Kansas. Particularly notorious was the situation in Indiana, where David C. Stephenson used the Klan to establish a virtual dictatorship. But Stephenson's fall was as dramatic as his rise. The suicide of a girl whom he had abducted led to his arrest and conviction for murder. With its state leader condemned to prison for life, the Klan's reputation as the guardian of morality was shattered. This scandal was followed by revelations of corruption involving the Klan-elected governor of Indiana and several prominent members of Stephenson's machine. Decent people who had been taken in by the Klan organizers resigned in haste, while others sought to cut their connection with a group so thoroughly in disgrace.

Elsewhere the decline of the organization was not so rapid, but by 1926 the movement had passed its peak. Two years later Imperial Wizard Evans tried to rescue the Klan by banning the use of masks and visors. Yet the removal of much of the secrecy simply marked a further step in the Klan's disintegration. The Invisible Empire's greatest success had come through convincing misguided individuals that its activities were somehow patriotic; its collapse followed the belated discovery of what should have been evident from the first—that whatever the Klan's professed ideals, its actual objectives and methods were the antithesis of "good Americanism."

Fundamentalists Versus Modernists

Among the dangerous ideas that certain Americans hoped to repress were those that challenged old standards of religious orthodoxy. The tendency of a younger generation of Protestant clergymen to doubt the Virgin birth of Jesus, the reality of the Devil and Hell, and the literal truth of every word of the Bible, alarmed conservatives who believed that the essential foundations of Christianity were being undermined. As early as 1910 an influential pamphlet, entitled *The Fundamentals, a Testimony of Truth,* had been published and, with the backing of two wealthy laymen, millions of copies were distributed. This encouraged the growth of a faction calling themselves fundamentalists, who sought to purge the churches of hated modernism. Fundamentalists clashed with modernists in church conventions, in theological schools, and in individual churches.

William Jennings Bryan, a leading Presbyterian layman, devoted his last years to crusading against modernism with the same zeal that he had shown in his earlier onslaughts against the gold standard, imperialism, war, and liquor. Bryan's campaigning was influential in the introduction of bills to forbid the teaching of evolution in the public schools. Such measures were presented to the legislatures in almost half the states, and in Tennessee, Mississippi, and Arkansas the proposal actually became law.

The Tennessee antievolution act of March, 1925, led at once to interesting consequences. The American Civil Liberties Union announced that it would back any schoolteacher who would test the law. Enterprising citizens of Dayton acted quickly to obtain a promising show for their home town. A young high school teacher, John T. Scopes, readily agreed to cooperate. For teaching a departure from the story "of the divine creation of man as taught in the Bible," Scopes was brought to trial in Dayton during July, 1925. The young defendant was largely forgotten in the battle of giants drawn into the case. Bryan threw all his energies into the prosecution, while the defense was in the hands of Clarence Darrow, the most famous criminal lawyer in America.

The trial's most dramatic moment came when the defense summoned Bryan to the stand to testify as an expert on the Bible. Under Darrow's sharp questioning, Bryan proclaimed his belief that the whale swallowed Jonah, that Joshua made the sun stand still, and that the world was created in the year 4004 B.C. The courtroom audience supported the Commoner's defense of the literal truth of the Bible with loud hurrahs and amens, although Darrow contended that the examination had exposed "fool ideas that no intelligent Christian on earth believes." The defense attempted to bring to the stand religious-minded scientists who would have testified that the doctrine of evolution was not inconsistent with Christianity, but the judge ruled that the only question at issue was whether Scopes had taught evolution. Since this was admitted, his conviction was a foregone conclusion.

The Supreme Court of Tennessee upheld the constitutionality of the antievolution law, but set aside Scopes's hundred dollar fine on a technicality. This closed the door to carrying the case to the United States Supreme Court as the defense had hoped. Bryan was not on hand to witness the final disposition of the case. About a week after the end of the Dayton trial he suddenly died—his demise no doubt hastened by overexcitement and overwork.

Fortunately for the churches, a large middle party existed between the fundamentalist and modernist factions. This group was more interested in the church's work than in its doctrines and helped to prevent the quarrel from reaching the point of schism. The controversy gradually quieted down without a clear-cut victory for either side.

Just how strong the churches really were is difficult to say. A poll of newspaper readers taken in 1927 indicated that nearly 91 per cent professed a belief in God and that this belief was more nearly unanimous among college students than among their elders. Open skepticism was rare—rarer than during some earlier periods of national history. Despite this fact, the number of Americans who were casual and indifferent in their religious attitudes seemed to be growing. No longer was it taken for granted that a solid citizen would be found sedately occupying the family pew each Sunday morning. He was as likely to be found on the golf course, in his car speeding through the countryside, or in bed reading the Sunday paper. Nor would college students any longer tamely accept the institution of compulsory chapel; on campuses everywhere student newspapers were campaigning—usually with success—for making chapel attendance voluntary. Statistically the churches made a good record: the number of church members continued to grow; the churches gained in wealth and enlarged their social programs at home and their missionary efforts. To many spiritually minded individuals, nevertheless, it appeared that the majority of Americans were more interested in making money and having a good time than they were in seeking the Kingdom of God.

Problems of Prohibition

Millions of good people believed that the ratification of the Eighteenth Amendment had miraculously ended the liquor problem; the sale of intoxicants would at once cease and, with that cessation, poverty and crime would largely disappear. But millions of other Americans had an entirely different attitude toward alcoholic beverages. They had been brought up in households where beer or wine was served with the family meal, where birthday and wedding celebrations were incomplete without plenty of drinks, and where the problem of how much a person should imbibe was a question of personal morals. To such people national prohibition was an interference with personal liberty. They felt that the law was unreasonable and that they were justified in continuing to buy liquor whenever it was available.

This hostility to the law—particularly to be found in the large cities— was the nub of the enforcement problem. With millions of thirsty citizens ready to pay high prices for any kind of alcoholic beverage, it was not long before other citizens decided to profit by the situation. To provide an abundant supply of illegal liquor, there were, in the first place, 18,700 miles of border—land, sea, lake, and river—across which smugglers could operate. Some of the nation's largest cities were nearby. For example, ships could stand off Long Island, outside United States territorial limits, while motorboats ran their illegal cargoes onto deserted beaches within an hour's drive of New York City. In the second place, wholesale manufacture within the country soon developed. Illicit stills, built to evade the revenue laws, long antedated prohibition. Now they multiplied to meet the new demand. Stills were inexpensive and easily constructed—in fact, thousand of householders experimented with their own equipment in the kitchen or the cellar. Finally, large amounts of industrial alcohol and medicinal liquor were diverted from legitimate channels. Physicians were issuing eleven million prescriptions for alcoholic beverages annually, while druggists often diluted their medicinal stock and sold the balance illegally. The distribution of this vast supply of illicit liquor was largely in the hands of bootleggers, who retailed their wares to the doorsteps of customers or who disposed of it wholesale to speakeasies.

Assigned to combat all this was the Prohibition Bureau of the Treasury Department, employing about three thousand agents. The bureau was too small and too poorly supplied with money to plug up the sources of the illegal supply. General Lincoln C. Andrews, one of many administrators who attempted to direct the bureau during its troubled history, testified in 1925 that only about 5 per cent of the liquor smuggled into the country was being stopped and that only about one out of every ten stills was being seized. To add to the difficulties of enforcement, the extraordinary opportunities for graft made it necessary to dismiss in disgrace about one out of every twelve agents hired. Prosecutions under the law created forty or fifty thousand cases annually. Because of the congestion in their dockets, the Federal courts had to accept pleas of guilty in return for light penalties; prosecutors disposed of over 90 per cent of the cases with these "bargain-day" procedures.

Despite the difficulties of enforcement, the drys claimed that prohibition had brought important benefits. The open saloon had disappeared in most places, and drinking, particularly by the poor, had been materially reduced. The respected economist Professor Irving Fisher of Yale believed that prohibition had contributed largely to the prosperity of the twenties, and many employers noted a decline in the absenteeism and inefficiency that had been a problem—particularly on "blue Mondays"—in pre-Volstead days. Other businessmen praised prohibition because of the added purchasing power that was created when money formerly spent for liquor was available for Fords and radios. But the wets asserted that the evils of prohibition far outweighed its advantages. They emphasized the widespread violation of the law as evidence that the experiment had been a complete failure.

Organized Crime

The consolidation of business so characteristic in legitimate lines was duplicated in business carried on in defiance of the law. Gambling and prostitution were already highly organized; bootlegging became increasingly so. The profits to be made by monopolizing the illicit liquor trade were fabulous, and hardened criminals were prepared either to beat up speakeasy proprietors who refused to buy from them or to wreck their property, while they were ready to employ even more drastic measures against their competitors. Such men naturally intervened in politics, bribing their friends and intimidating their enemies until they gained almost complete immunity from the law.

The most spectacular criminal career of the twenties was that of Al Capone, who moved from New York to Chicago in 1920. By 1929 Capone had replaced Johnny Torrio as the "big shot" in Chicago; he had at his command several hundred ruthless gunmen armed with submachine guns and sawed-off shotguns; he largely controlled the sale of liquor in the city's ten thousand speakeasies; he was in complete political control of the suburb of Cicero; and he had useful ties with many Chicago politicians and judges. How much money he had made and concealed no one knew, but Federal agents estimated the sum at $20 million. Capone's wealth and power had not been achieved without the plentiful spilling of blood. Particularly bitter was the gang war fought between Capone's henchmen and those of his ambitious rival, Dion O'Banion. Gunmen masquerading as customers shot O'Banion to death in his own florist shop, but his gangsters continued to oppose Capone and made a lurid attempt to assassinate him in 1926, when in broad daylight eight touring cars paraded slowly past his Cicero headquarters, raking the building with machine-gun fire. In the most gruesome of all the killings, the St. Valentine's Day Massacre of 1929, strangers disguised as policemen lined up seven of the O'Banions against a garage wall and then mowed them down with machine guns. Between 1920 and 1929 there were more than five hundred gang murders in Chicago, and few of those responsible were ever brought to justice. Not until 1931 did Federal officers finally arrest Capone—and then the charge was not murder, extortion, bribery, or violation of the Volstead Act, but merely tax evasion.

Capone and his numerous imitators in New York, Detroit, and other cities gained much of their wealth through the opportunities created by prohibition. They soon expanded into other lines. They operated or demanded tribute from gambling houses, dog tracks, houses of prostitution, and road houses. The ancient crime of kidnapping had an unpleasant revival, with wealthy adults often the victims. Innumerable were the so-called rackets of the decade. Small businessmen were compelled to pay for "protection," and those who refused had their trucks wrecked, their shops bombed, or were themselves beaten up or killed. Unfortunately for the reputation of the legitimate labor union movement, these rackets were often operated through the connivance of corrupt union leaders. Sometimes they organized new unions for no other purpose than to levy tribute upon unfortunate workers and employers. Only less common than the racketeering labor union was the racketeering trade association that terrorized small businessmen until they signed up and meekly paid their assessments.

The crime that caused so much alarm during the twenties was more a change in the character of criminal activities than an absolute increase in their amount. America had always had murder, robbery, assault, and extortion, and statistics showed no greater increase in the aggregate number of such offenses than might have been expected with the growing population and urbanization of the nation. What was new and frightening was the large amount of organization among criminals and their wholesale use of high-powered automobiles, machine guns, and explosives. Crime had become big business—and to many thoughtful citizens the most serious aspect of prohibition was that by turning the liquor business over to criminals, vast new opportunities to make crime pay had been opened up.

Flaming Youth

Worry over children must be as old as human parenthood, but the older generation of the twenties perhaps worried over the young rather more than usual. They were shocked in the first place at the revolution in women's dress. Corsets and other undergarments were no longer considered essential. The amount of cloth necessary to garb a woman declined from $19\frac{1}{4}$ yards in 1913 to 7 yards in 1928. During 1919 and 1920 much shorter than ankle-length skirts had appeared, to the alarm of moralists. Fashion ordered them down again, but women were reluctant to obey, and by 1925 the designers had surrendered; skirts became shorter and shorter until they reached the knee in 1927. To aggravate the scandal, many bold young ladies began to roll their stockings. The flappers—as these pert females were now called—also bobbed their hair. Short-haired women in 1918 were assumed to be Bolsheviks, but by 1924 the new vogue was sweeping the nation. Before the war convention had decreed that no nice woman used rouge or lipstick, or, if she did, she tried to conceal the fact. During the postwar decade, however, the use of these and other cosmetics increased until their manufacture and sale became a million dollar business.

The young woman of the twenties not only looked different; she acted differently. In Theodore Roosevelt's time, when his daughter Alice wanted to experiment with tobacco she sought to escape parental wrath by blowing her smoke rings up the chimneys of White House fireplaces. Only the most sophisticated women used cigarettes. But during the postwar decade the taboo against women smoking broke down. Shocking as this was to the older generation, women's increasing use of alcoholic beverages was even more so. Among the smart set it became the accepted thing for men and women to drink together at cocktail parties, country club dances, and speakeasies.

All this was a further stage in the feminine revolt that had been in progress for many decades. Women had successfully rebelled against their inadequate educational opportunities, against their unfavorable legal status, against their disenfranchisement. Now they were asserting their right to smoke and drink because men did, and to cut their hair, rouge their cheeks, and wear scanty clothing because it symbolized their independence. Not for long, moreover, were these new manners to be found solely among the young. To an increasing degree older women moved into the territory that the younger shock troops had captured.

Though many parents were troubled over such issues as these, what kept them awake nights was their children's rebelliousness in other matters. Sons boldly demanded the use of the family car; daughters hotly asserted their intention of driving off with their boy friends without chaperonage. Often the youngsters did not get home until almost morning and indignantly refused to divulge where they had been or what they had been doing. Significantly enough, Samuel Hopkins Adams, one of the muckrakers of prewar days, found a theme in this rebellion. Under the pseudonym Warner Fabian, he wrote the lurid novel *Flaming Youth,* which had a huge popular sale and was syndicated in many newspapers. Shocked parents read about wild parties, midnight swimming excursions, and "petting" on lonely lanes. Similarly upsetting were *The Plastic Age,* by Percy Marks, and—on a distinctly higher literary level—the novels of F. Scott Fitzgerald. A sensation of another sort was provided by Judge Ben B. Lindsey, who believed that the breakdown in the old moral conventions was so serious that the situation should be frankly faced and a system of "companionate marriage" legalized—a sort of trial marriage that could be terminated at any time by mutual consent, provided there were no children.

Undoubtedly such writers as these exaggerated the situation. For the most part, the great revolution in morals probably amounted to simply this: girls were much easier to kiss than they once had been, and the automobile offered a much better opportunity. But many of the petting parties went further; just how large a proportion no one could say. Whatever the actual state of sexual morals might be, one thing was crystal clear. The new generation talked about sex with a frankness that would have been unthinkable to the old. The subject was endlessly discussed, not only because of its interest, but because of its fashionableness. American psychologists had been familiar with the teachings of Sigmund Freud for some time, but the general public was dabbling in the Freudian ideas for the first time during the postwar decade. Exactly what they meant would have been a little hard for most people to explain, but this did not prevent glib usage of such fascinating new expressions as "Oedipus complex," "inhibition," and "libido." In general, laymen gathered the impression that scientists had decided that sex was not only exciting but important, and that it was dangerous to repress the sexual impulses. This offered a comforting rationalization to those who wanted to defy the old conventions.

The Changing Family

For better or worse, American family life was being transformed into newer patterns. The home was less important as an economic, educational, and recreational center. Outside agencies were taking over more and more of the functions that the family had once performed.

Married women, particularly those of the middle-income group, were now relieved of much of the drudgery that had always been their lot. Bread was a highly commercialized product purchased in stores instead of a masterpiece laboriously fashioned in the kitchen, while many other foods hitherto prepared in the home were now obtained at bakeries or delicatessens. Commercial laundries did an increasing share of the nation's washing. The housewife, to be sure, still had many tasks, but she performed them more quickly and easily with the new electrical equipment. Husbands and children had their own crowded schedules of activities, and home often became scarcely more than a place where the members of the family checked in for a few hours of sleep each night.

An increasing number of American marriages were ending in divorce. In 1900 there were 20 divorces for each 10,000 married persons; in 1930 there were 36; by the latter year the chances that any particular marriage would eventually break up were about one in six. Divorce was more common in the United States than in any other country for which statistics were available, with the possible exception of the Soviet Union. But the conclusions to be drawn from this fact were disputed. Many regarded it as evidence that unhappiness in marriage was greater than ever before. Others asserted that there had always been many unhappy marriages and that the high divorce rate meant only that more people were taking this way out of their unhappy situation. Few denied that there was some connection between the increasing number of broken homes and the youth problem.

Another undeniable fact about family life was the declining birth rate. The rate had been 26.6 per thousand population in 1910 and had fluctuated within narrow limits until 1921, when it was 27.1; thereafter it fell until it was 19.7 in 1931—a decline of one quarter during the decade. Many Americans considered this a healthy situation, asserting that if the poor as well as the rich would practice birth control, this would remove a prime cause of poverty. The American Birth Control League, organized in 1917, carried on an active propaganda under the leadership of Margaret Sanger.

Her attempt to open a birth-control clinic in Brooklyn led to her arrest in 1921, but the New York courts ruled that physicians could legally give such information for health purposes. A permanent clinic was opened in New York City in 1923, and others followed in many cities, although in some states they were not permitted. Protestant churchmen disagreed on the moral issues involved. The Committee on Marriage and Home of the Federal Council of Churches recommended in 1930 that "the church should not seek to impose its point of view as to the use of contraceptives upon the public by legislation or any other form of coercion; and especially should not seek to prohibit physicians from imparting such information to those who in the judgment of the medical profession are entitled to receive it." The General Assembly of the Presbyterian Church, however, criticized this statement of policy as dangerous to morals.

The Roman Catholic Church was uncompromising in its condemnation of both divorce and birth control. In the encyclical *Casti Conubii,* issued in 1930, Pope Pius XI asserted that marriage was a "perpetual and indissoluble bond which cannot be dissolved by any civil law"; that companionate and experimental marriages were "hateful abdominations . . . which reduce our truly cultured natures to the barbarous standards of savage people"; and that contraceptive devices were "an offense against the law of God and nature."

Literature During the Twenties

The postwar reaction from idealism, notable in so many different areas of American life, markedly affected literature. The nation had an unusually talented group of novelists and poets during the twenties, but they used their gifts largely to attack contemporary American culture.

The reading public had its first rude jolt in 1920 with the publication of Sinclair Lewis's *Main Street.* The small Midwestern town, usually sentimentalized in literature, was here depicted as dreary, narrow, and hypocritical. Inasmuch as the character of American life was still so largely reflective of such small towns, Lewis's attack appeared to be a general disparagement of American civilization. A succession of other brilliant, but caustic, novels from the same author broadened the indictment. *Babbitt* (1922) satirized the self-satisfaction and crude self-advertisement of the American businessman. In the young doctor of *Arrowsmith* (1925), Lewis created a hero whom he could admire, yet he found much to criticize in the medical profession. *Elmer Gantry* (1927), the novelist's caricature of a go-getter religionist, gave ample proof—if any were needed—that the church could expect no immunity from his idol-smashing.

The great city, no less than the small, was the subject of literary attack. John Dos Passos, in *Manhattan Transfer* (1925), depicted life in New York City as hard and meaningless for the individuals thrown together in the vast network of urban society. An earlier Dos Passos novel, *Three Soldiers* (1921), struck the note of revulsion against war that was to recur through the decade.

The novels and short stories of Ernest Hemingway revealed disillusionment not only with the war, but with the general complexity of modern life. *The Sun Also Rises* (1926), *Men Without Women* (1927), and *A Farewell to Arms* (1929) reflected apparent indifference to idealistic aspirations or to the problems of society. The Hemingway characters found life's fleeting pleasures in only the most elemental experiences, particularly in physical combat and sex. Hemingway was one of the not inconsiderable group of American intellectuals who spent most of the decade in Europe.

William Faulkner, a writer of exceptional literary power, began to depict the tragic decline of Southern aristocracy in *The Sound and the Fury* (1929) and *Sartoris* (1929). Faulkner's South was the Deep South of Mississippi's decaying mansions and poverty-stricken sharecroppers. The South of Thomas Wolfe's *Look Homeward, Angel* (1929) was the middle-class, money-loving Newer South of Asheville, North Carolina.

Both the outer shell of sophistication and the inner kernel of unhappiness characteristic of the young people of "the lost generation" were exposed in the novels and short stories of F. Scott Fitzgerald. The critics regarded his early works, such as *This Side of Paradise* (1920) and *The Beautiful and Damned* (1922), as little more than popular fiction, but they hailed *The Great Gatsby* (1926) as one of the finest novels of the century.

Readers who were looking for ruthless realism admired one of the older novelists, Theodore Dreiser. *An American Tragedy* (1925), based upon a true murder case, depicted the influence of the American environment on a handsome weakling. Those who disliked the crudities of Dreiser's style took delight in three gifted women writers still in their prime: Willa Cather, Edith Wharton, and Ellen Glasgow.

The revival of poetry, which had just been beginning in 1914, more than fulfilled its early promise. Edwin Arlington Robinson and Robert Frost reflected their New England background in the austere beauty of their writing; they often found their themes in the frustrations and tragedies of life, but they differed from most of the novelists of the period in upholding the dignity of man in the face of suffering. Similar qualities were to be found in Stephen Vincent Benét, whose attempt at an American epic, *John Brown's Body,* aroused great interest in 1929. Poetry was not immune, however, to the spirit of the times. Indeed, no work of literature more completely reflected the generation's disillusionment and loss of faith than T. S. Eliot's *The Waste Land* (1922). Ezra Pound's contempt for American democracy was so complete that he not only lived the life of an expatriate, but became a glorifier of fascism. Thus there disappeared from the American scene one of the boldest experimenters with new verse forms. More frequent than such complete repudiation was poetry written in a spirit of detached cynicism and sophistication. In such a vein was Edna St. Vincent Millay's *A Few Figs from Thistles* (1920). Other works by this poet displayed higher sensitivity to beauty and a larger sense of social responsibility but failed to enjoy the popularity of this lighter work.

Writing for the American stage has rarely won lasting acclaim as literature, yet Eugene O'Neill gained that distinction. His plays *Emperor Jones* (1921), *Desire Under the Elms* (1924), and *Strange Interlude* (1929) showed great psychological insight and much ingenuity in the use of dramatic innovations to convey his meaning. Like so many of his contemporaries, however, O'Neill emphasized the least healthy aspects of American life.

H. L. Mencken, the editor of the *American Mercury*, exercised a powerful influence on the literary life of the twenties. This outspoken critic of the American scene regarded most of his fellow countrymen as "boobs," "morons," and "yokels" and said so month after month to the delight of his sophisticated readers. One of the leading features of Mencken's magazine was "Americana," a department made up of excerpts from the press chronicling the more idiotic deeds and pronouncements of Americans. A moderate sampling of Mencken's criticism often provided a healthy antidote for the reader's complacency, but an excessive dose was likely to leave him with a cynical contempt for democracy.

High- and Low-Brow Reading

The number of Americans who prided themselves on reading good books increased during the decade, but they showed a certain timidity in choosing their own reading matter. The Book-of-the-Month Club broadened its list of subscribers until by the end of the twenties some hundred thousand Americans were accepting the judgment of its board of experts in making their periodic purchases. The Literary Guild and other organizations distributed books on the same basis. To be selected through this system was to guarantee the success of any book. One of the unfortunate results, however, was that many scarcely less worthy books that had failed to appeal to the experts were doomed to small sales.

On the other hand, many readers chose books for their entertainment value and were indifferent to their rating as literature. The detective stories of Mary Roberts Rinehart, S. S. Van Dine, and others enjoyed a tremendous popularity, as did sexy romances such as *The Sheik,* by Mrs. E. M. Hull. There was also a good market for biographies, which varied in treatment from Albert J. Beveridge's scholarly *Life of John Marshall* (1916–1919) and Carl Sandburg's beautifully written *Abraham Lincoln: The Prairie Years* (1926) to popular works that attempted to "debunk" national heroes and to glamorize national villains. Significantly successful was *The Man Nobody Knows* (1925), in which Bruce Barton, an expert in advertising, portrayed Jesus as a model businessman. Self-improvement continued to be the aim of many earnest readers. For them a diversified fare was offered during the twenties, ranging from excellent popularizations like Will Durant's *Story of Philosophy* (1926) to the fabulously successful Emily Post's *Etiquette* (1922).

No other reading matter, however, was so widely distributed as daily newspapers, whose aggregate circulation in the United States and Canada reached forty million in 1929. The trend away from personal journalism and toward standardized, large-scale production methods, already pronounced in 1914, was much accelerated during the next fifteen years—in part caused by the rising cost of paper. Newspapers became increasingly dependent upon syndicated material, advertising revenue, and mass distribution. The number of newspaper chains doubled between 1923 and 1927. Within each city, moreover, there was a tendency to merge competing journals; five out of seven Chicago morning papers disappeared in fifteen years, while in Detroit the number of morning papers dropped from three to one. There were two thousand fewer publications in 1929 than in 1914. Sensational stories of crime and scandal still provided a dependable formula for making a paper popular, as demonstrated by the striking growth of the New York *Daily News.* This first New York tabloid, which began publication in 1919, achieved a circulation of 1.3 million ten years later. The success of this brash pioneer invited competition. Hearst's *Mirror* and Bernarr MacFadden's *Evening Graphic* entered the New York field, while similar papers multiplied in other cities.

Magazines also increased their sales. Muckraking articles, so popular a generation earlier, rarely appeared in the magazines of large circulation like the *Saturday Evening Post, Collier's,* or the *Ladies Home Journal.* Instead, their pages were devoted to fiction, light but frequently excellent within its limitations, and to articles praising the achievements of American businessmen. Three new magazines, founded within the decade, were different enough to grow rapidly. *Reader's Digest* offered capsules of information and inspiration condensed from other magazines; *Time* summarized the news of the week in a breezy, confident manner; the *New Yorker* delighted sophisticated readers with its cartoons, critical reviews, short stories, and light verse. Less educated readers found an escape from their own drab lives through reading *True Stories* and other "confession" magazines that had an enormous sale.

Education and Learning

Most American parents yearned to provide their children with greater educational opportunities than they themselves had received. The result was a remarkable increase in the number of pupils attending public high schools: in 1900 public secondary school enrollment stood at 519,000; in 1910, 915,000; in 1920, 2,199,000; and in 1930, 4,399,000. With rapidly expanding attendance went important modifications of curriculum to meet the needs of the new pupils. Whereas in 1900 over 50 per cent of high school students studied Latin and over 56 per cent algebra, the percentages were only 22 and 35, respectively, in 1928. Many subjects that had not been a part of the old high school course were now offered. Most of these were vocational in character, such as home economics, manual training, bookkeeping, shorthand, typewriting, and agriculture, but others, notably art and music, were cultural by any definition.

The advent of the automobile made it possible to close many of the one-room schoolhouses. Buses now transported the children from rural families to well-equipped central schools where each grade could be taught in a separate room. In order to enrich elementary education in the higher grades, many communities organized junior high schools to include the seventh, eighth, and ninth grades, the senior high school course being then reduced to three years.

Colleges and universities also grew rapidly. In 1900 college enrollment was 168,000; in 1910, 266,000; in 1920, 517,000; and in 1930, 1,085,800. Some critics believed that this expansion made advisable a division of higher education between the first two and the last two years. Junior colleges, of which there had been only 132 in 1917, numbered 450 in 1930. An increasing number of students now devoted more than four years to their higher education. Training in theology, medicine, dentistry, law, engineering, and business administration was based to an increasing degree on a foundation of three or four years of general education in a liberal arts college. A growing number of graduate degrees were granted; the annual crop of Ph.D.'s quadrupled during the decade. Most of this increase resulted from the demand for more and better trained college instructors, but a growing number of positions in industry became available to men who had graduate training—notably in chemistry.

University faculty members placed increasing emphasis on their responsibility to develop the body of knowledge rather than merely to transmit the cultural heritage. To catalogue the significant achievements of research in all the specialized branches of learning would be impossible, but a few landmarks should be noted because of their importance to general American thought during the decade. Charles and Mary Beard surveyed the whole field of American history from a new and stimulating viewpoint in *The Rise of American Civilization* (1927). Of equal significance as an interpretation of the roots of American culture was Vernon L. Parrington's *Main Currents in American Thought* (1927). The reader who wished to learn how people of every income level and background lived in a typical American community was fascinated by *Middletown* (1929), by Robert S. and Helen Lynd. Profoundly influential in its effect upon thinking in such diverse fields as education, morals, criminology, and philosophy was the purely mechanistic explanation of human behavior presented by John B. Watson in *Behaviorism* (1925).

In the field of physical sciences, Americans such as Robert A. Millikan and Arthur H. Compton helped fill in the details of the newer conceptions of the universe that were finding shape following the pioneer work of the great German, Albert Einstein. Two important astronomical observatories in California, Mt. Hamilton and Mt. Wilson, provided international science with data of great value in testing the new theories. Medical research was generously endowed and achieved many goals. Important advances in surgical technique grew out of the work of the doctors during the war. New uses for the X-ray were developed in both diagnosis and therapy. The importance of vitamins in nutrition was demonstrated, and the consumption of these health-givers later became a national fad. Public health measures virtually eliminated typhoid fever, while diphtheria, scarlet fever, and tuberculosis came under steadily increasing control. Life expectancy was raised from 49.24 years in 1901 to 59.1 years in 1927—largely through reduction of the death rate among infants and children.

The Arts

The prosperity of the twenties encouraged construction, and many of the new edifices displayed striking beauty. Some American architects continued to find their inspiration in classical and medieval models. Henry Bacon's Lincoln Memorial in Washington demonstrated once more the appeal of the Greek qualities of simplicity, balance, and proportion. Ralph Adams

Cram was deeply interested in promoting use of the Gothic style in ecclesiastical and university architecture. The Cathedral of St. John the Divine in New York City, as well as buildings on the Princeton, Yale, and West Point campuses, demonstrated Cram's strong influence.

America's most distinctive contribution to architecture, however, lay along more original lines. The ten years that followed the armistice were the great age of the skyscraper. In 1922 architects from all countries were invited to submit their designs for the *Chicago Tribune* tower. The competition, which attracted 260 plans from 23 nations, was won by the Gothic design of John Mead Howells and Raymond Hood. But later architects abandoned the pseudo-Gothic shell and designed their skyscrapers as lofty towers with clean-cut, unadorned forms. New York City, where the technical requirements of the building ordinances had much to do with the development of setback architecture, prided itself on the grandeur of the great buildings constructed during the twenties. This movement culminated in the Empire State Building, designed by Shreve, Lamb, and Harmon.

Outside the United States the best-known American architect was Frank Lloyd Wright, who boldly discarded older conventions and carried functional design to its logical limits. His "prairie houses" with their emphasis on horizontal lines hugging the earth pointed toward a revolution in residential design. Wright's influence was international in scope, but until late in his career he was too innovative for most of his timid countrymen.

American painters lacked the originality of American artists. Many took their cues from European art during this era and found an outlet for their talents in cubism, expressionism, and surrealism. Yet despite the weakness of the Americans for imported fads, a number of gifted artists were at work. Among these were John Marin, Max Weber, and Georgia O'Keeffe.

Musical appreciation seemed to deepen after the war. The radio brought concerts by the country's great orchestras and soloists into millions of homes, and individuals like Walter Damrosch worked tirelessly to educate the people to understand and enjoy good music. American-born singers such as Marion Talley and Lawrence Tibbett now sang with the Metropolitan Opera Company, and symphony orchestras in New York, Philadelphia, and Boston attained extraordinary virtuosity. In the light music field, Sigmund Romberg, Rudolf Friml, and Jerome Kern proved worthy successors to Victor Herbert. Jazz began to demand attention as an authentic form of musical expression. Orchestras playing in the new rhythms became increasingly pretentious, with Paul Whiteman's taking the lead in presenting jazz in "symphonic" arrangements. The most influential figure was George Gershwin, who wrote the music for a number of successful musical comedies during the twenties but then moved on to more ambitious things. From his talented pen came the ingenious symphonic works *Rhapsody in Blue, Concerto in F,* and *An American in Paris.*

There Were Giants in Those Days

Despite the cynicism of the intellectuals, the age was one of hero worship. Rudolph Valentino, the great screen lover, died in 1926, and the crowd attracted to the New York funeral parlor where he lay in state extended for eleven blocks. The whole country wept when efforts were unavailing to extricate Floyd Collins alive from a Kentucky cave where he had been trapped. And when the Lone Eagle, Charles Lindbergh, flew nonstop from New York to Paris the nation went wild.

Perhaps the most typical heroes of the twenties were to be found in the world of sport. Shrewd promotion, willingly abetted by newspaper and radio reporters, aroused the American people to a unique enthusiasm for athletics. Their work was made easier by the circumstance that the sports world had an unusually large number of competitors who were not only capable performers, but colorful personalities as well.

In 1919 "Babe" Ruth, playing for the Boston Red Sox, set a new record by hitting twenty-nine home runs in a season. Sensing the opportunity for profitable investment, the New York Yankees purchased the young pitcher-outfielder for $125,000. The Babe's employers never regretted their decision, nor did they refuse the slugger's eventual demand for a salary almost as large as that of the President of the United States. The exploits of Ruth, who hit fifty-nine homers in 1921 and sixty in 1927, brought customers to the Yankee Stadium by the thousands and enabled baseball to retain its popularity despite the growing interest in other sports.

The public avidly followed college football. So great was the demand to see games that new stadiums were built, many of them large enough to hold seventy or eighty thousand spectators. Despite complaints that the game had become professionalized, alumni insisted on highly paid coaches who could produce winning teams, and the coaches in turn demanded athletic scholarships and other inducements to attract promising material. The best players, men such as "Red" Grange of Illinois, and the most successful coaches such as Knute Rockne of Notre Dame received unlimited publicity.

Sports taste was catholic, however, and thousands of Americans who did not know the difference between a mashie and a putter followed breathlessly the progress of the great amateur, Bobby Jones, through various tournaments. Tennis, once thought like golf to be a high-brow game, became popularized through the dynamic play of Big Bill Tilden, while women's athletic prowess was demonstrated by Helen Wills. In most sports, women's performances could not be compared with those of the stronger sex, but when the American Gertrude Ederle swam the English Channel in 1926, her time was better than that of any of the five men who had completed the difficult feat before her.

No sport of the twenties could secure more publicity for a single contest than heavyweight boxing. The golden days of the prize ring were attained when the master promoter Tex Rickard had as his drawing card the superb performer Jack Dempsey. On July 4, 1919, Dempsey gained the heavyweight title by knocking out the giant Jess Willard in Toledo, Ohio. The new champion, colorful and aggressive, seemed to carry dynamite in his gloves. Attending prize fights became suddenly respectable, and the crowds that saw subsequent Dempsey fights were notable not only for their size but for the extraordinary number of politicians and socialites who were present. After Dempsey lost his title unexpectedly to Gene Tunney in 1926, the stage was set the next year for what was perhaps the most highly publicized sports

Babe Ruth. (Brown Bros.)

spectacle of the decade, the second Tunney-Dempsey fight in Chicago, when the gate receipts totaled $2,650,000. After the fight the newspapers devoted endless columns to the important question of whether Tunney had been the beneficiary of a "long count" in retaining his title.

Such were the twenties. American prosperity was built on a shaky foundation that threatened to collapse. The rest of the world struggled with

The "long count." Tunney-Dempsey fight in Chicago, 1927. (Acme.)

problems too difficult to be solved that were destined to involve the United States. But oblivious to the storm clouds on the horizon, the average American had a wonderful time during the age of the supercolossal.

13

PROSPERITY

When, in a speech during the 1928 campaign, Herbert Hoover said, "We in America today are nearer to the final triumph over poverty than ever before in the history of any land," he was expressing the belief of almost all Americans. The United States had enjoyed seven years of extraordinary prosperity, and few indeed were the prophets gloomy enough to predict danger ahead.

Economic Trends, 1914–1929

In 1914 when the European war broke out, the United States was in what seemed to be the incipient stage of a serious depression. At first hostilities abroad increased the nation's economic troubles, but French and English war orders reversed the trend in 1915 and produced a great wartime prosperity, intensified by actual American participation in 1917. The armistice had a temporarily upsetting effect, and serious unemployment prevailed for several months. This gave way, however, to a postwar boom lasting from the late spring of 1919 to the middle of 1920. This bubble burst suddenly, to be succeeded during the last half of 1920 and most of 1921 by a severe depression. In the latter year some seven million unemployed were walking the streets. National income fell from $75 billion in 1920 to $59 billion in 1921.

Although grave, this depression was short-lived. Recovery set in during 1922; by 1925 national income had passed the 1920 level, and it continued to rise until it reached more than $84 billion in 1929. In a proud catalogue of progress that candidate Hoover recited in 1928 he listed these items: over 25 per cent increase in the production of goods since 1921; the construction of more than 3.5 million new dwellings; the electrification of nearly 9 million homes; the installation of 6 million telephones; the manufacture of 7 million radio sets; the production of 14 million automobiles; and the building of parks, playgrounds, and highways. And in human terms Hoover reported:

We have doubled the use of electrical power and with it we have taken sweat from the backs of man. The purchasing power of wages has steadily increased. The hours of labor have decreased. The twelve-hour day has been abolished. Great progress has been made in the stabilization of commerce and industry. The job of every man has thus been made more secure. Unemployment in the sense of distress is widely disappearing.

Such was the impressive evidence of prosperity. It was small wonder that few Americans were seriously troubled by darker aspects of the picture that Hoover failed to mention.

America Takes to the Road

Much of the prosperity of the period reflected the rapid growth of new industries, and, of these, the automobile business was the most astonishing in the degree of its expansion.

Henry Ford continued to be the dominant personality in the industry. Still producing the famous Model T that had brought the price of an automobile down to a figure the ordinary farmer or workingman could afford, Ford built upon the success that he had achieved in prewar years. In 1924 a Ford could be bought for $290—if its owner was not too proud to crank it by hand. The Ford joke had become a staple commodity in American humor, and the canny Detroit industrialist accepted without complaint this free advertising. Yet Ford's position was not impregnable. The General Motors Corporation, now allied with the powerful Du Pont and Morgan empires and producing a well-balanced line of cars, grew rapidly during the twenties. The Chevrolet, priced to compete with the Ford, was equipped with conventional gear shift, good body lines, and other features that made it more attrac-

Henry Ford with his first and ten-millionth Fords, 1924. (Acme.)

tive than the ugly Model T. For a time Ford's famous business acumen seemed to have deserted him, as he stuck with his old model despite sharply declining sales. In 1928, however, he finally acknowledged changing times and brought out the new and more conventional Model A.

Between 1903 and 1928, 191 companies at one time or another manufactured passenger cars, but the mortality was exceptionally heavy. By 1926 the number of automobile manufacturers had been reduced to 44; during the new few years many more had to quit. By 1930, six companies were doing 90 per cent of the business. The "big two" had become a "big three" after the organization of the Chrysler Corporation in 1923 and its purchase of Dodge Brothers five years later. In 1929 Chrysler brought out the Plymouth to compete with the Ford and Chevrolet. That year Chrysler produced about 450,000 cars as compared with Ford's 1,950,000 and General Motors's 1,900,000, but its share in the business was destined to become larger during the thirties.

Annual production of motor cars in the United States rose from 1.9 million in 1920 to a peak of almost 4.8 million in 1929. By the latter year there was one car for every six inhabitants. The automobile industry had become the nation's leading business as measured by the value of its annual product; in 1929 that value was nearly $3.5 billion. The production of motor cars required vast quantities of steel, plate glass, rubber, leather, aluminum, and copper, while their operation consumed the lion's share of the nation's petroleum products. In terms of labor, the automobile industry not only provided direct employment to some 350,000 factory executives and employees, but gave indirect employment to workers in accessory and tire factories, salesmen, repair men, filling station attendants, truck drivers, and others. In the calculation of one authority, some five million persons had jobs in some way dependent upon the automobile business. This was one out every nine persons gainfully employed in the United States.

Because the nation's roads were pitifully inadequate for an automobile age, Federal, state, and local governments found it necessary to spend close to $10 billion on highway construction during the twenties. So heavy was the traffic that only well-built macadam or cement roads would hold up. Motorists paid a major part of the bill. Not only did they have to pay heavy registration and license fees, but between 1919 and 1930 every state followed the example of Oregon, which pioneered in the levying of a gasoline tax. In 1930 direct and indirect taxes upon those who used the roads accounted for approximately four fifths of the funds expended on state highways.

It would be difficult to catalogue completely the economic, political, and social implications of the expansion of the automobile industry. Although Americans traveled more, they depended less on older modes of transportation. The horse and buggy became symbols of the quaint past; even the electric streetcar and the railroad felt the competition of the motor vehicles speeding across the countryside, particularly when bus companies and commercial trucking concerns began to expand their operations. Many new problems confronted government. The automobile made the prohibition and immigration laws more difficult to enforce and helped murderers and bank robbers to make their getaways. For the farmer the new means of transportation brought many benefits; it lessened his isolation and provided an admirable means for him to carry his product to market. As Americans took to the road, enterprising businessmen made an earnest bid to take their money. Billboards, filling stations, tourist camps, and hot-dog stands lined the new state highways. Most citizens accepted this as merely further evidence of the healthy competition of rugged individualism, but the more sensitive complained bitterly that commercialism was destroying the beauty of the American countryside.

The Age of Electricity

In 1902 less than 5 billion kilowatt-hours of electricity were produced in the United States. This rate of production had more than tripled by 1912 when 17 billion kilowatt-hours were generated. This, however, was only a beginning. In 1920, 43 billion, and in 1929, 97 billion kilowatt-hours of electricity flowed into American homes and factories. Capital investment in the industry was less than $6 billion in 1910, over $12 billion in 1920, and more than $23 billion in 1930.

Who was using this current? Much of it went into domestic lighting. In 1912, only 16 per cent of the population lived in electrically lighted dwellings, but by 1927 63 per cent enjoyed this convenience. And once the home was wired, the housewife was almost certain to demand electrical appliances to lighten her domestic chores. According to a calculation of 1926, of 16 million households served by electricity, 80 per cent had electric irons, 37 per cent vacuum cleaners, and more than 25 per cent washing machines, fans, or toasters. Electric refrigerators, clocks, and stoves likewise became more and more common. Obviously, the rapidly increasing use of electricity offered a huge volume of business for manufacturers of household appliances.

But the factory no less than the home was being transformed. In 1914 only about 30 per cent of factory machines had been electrified; in 1929 approximately 70 per cent were run by electrical power. This permitted a much more efficient organization of production without cumbersome and dangerous systems of belts and pulleys. One of the industrial marvels of the day was the photoelectric eye, which counted products, detected flaws, and performed many other functions with uncanny accuracy. Electricity also had important special uses in the metallurgical and chemical industries.

The rapid growth of the power business presented new problems for government. Advanced liberals insisted that the public stake in the production and distribution of electricity was so great as to require public ownership. For a time there seemed to be a considerable trend in that direction. In 1902, 815 American municipalities operated their own utility systems; by 1922 the number had increased to 2,581. During the balance of the twenties, however, the number declined, largely because power could be more economically generated by large plants serving many cities and industries than by small local plants. What was required, in the opinion of public power advocates, was the generation of hydroelectric power in large volume by state or Federal authorities and its transmission and sale at reasonable rates to municipal distributing systems. Senator George Norris believed that public power production would provide a "yardstick" for measuring the rates of the private companies, and he hoped to have Muscle Shoals developed in this way. Other widely discussed plans called for the production of public power in connection with the building of a proposed St. Lawrence seaway, as well as for combined irrigation-power projects along the Colorado, Columbia, and Missouri rivers. Private power corporations opposed such government competition with private enterprise, and they had the support of the Coolidge and Hoover administrations. Not until the thirties were the advocates of public power development given much opportunity to try out their theories.

Meantime, the private power industry was being consolidated into larger and larger units. Not only did local distributing companies find that they could purchase power from the larger producing companies more economically than they could generate it themselves, but the operating companies were to an increasing degree brought under the control of holding corporations. The holding companies were themselves often controlled by other holding companies, and this process of pyramiding was carried so far that oftentimes six or more companies were piled on top of one another. By 1929 twelve large systems controlled approximately 76 per cent of the electricity generated in the United States. Finance capitalism was strongly in evidence, since corporations under the influence of Morgan and National City Bank of New York controlled some 37 per cent of the business, while companies within the sphere of influence of the Chase National Bank of New York accounted for about 11 per cent more. Samuel Insull of Chicago controlled a third major group. The Insull empire, comprising 10 per cent of the industry, was a fantastic affair. A labyrinth of holding and investment companies had been built up to include concerns serving 4,741 communities in 30 different states. Insull himself was chairman of the board of directors in 65 concerns and president of 11 others.

Although consolidation through holding companies served some economic purpose when judiciously carried out, much of the pyramiding characteristic of the twenties was against the public interest. Promoters flooded the market with grossly watered securities on which small investors lost millions of dollars during the Wall Street crash of 1929. Control of local operating companies, furthermore, rested in the hands of bankers remote from the scene and often insensitive to the interests of the consumers. Finally, the overcapitalization of the industry and its control by holding companies incorporated in many different states made the problem of rate regulation by state public-utilities commissions extremely difficult.

In 1920 Congress had made a cautious beginning in Federal regulation by establishing a Federal Power Commission to include three cabinet members—the Secretaries of War, Interior, and Agriculture. Congress empowered the commission to issue fifty-year licenses for electric projects on the public lands, reservations, and navigable streams. It could regulate rates on power moved across state lines by the licensed companies and their subsidiaries. The results were not very satisfactory. The cabinet members were too busy with other duties to give the commission's activities much attention, and only a very small proportion of the country's power was being produced under Federal license. Legislation in 1930 reorganized the commission by giving it five full-time members and increased funds but did not increase its regulatory powers. Although the liberals failed to get the FPC's control extended to all electricity crossing state lines, they did succeed in bringing about an important investigation of the whole utilities problem by the Federal Trade Commission. This revealed that utilities companies were spending millions of dollars every year to obtain newspaper comment favorable to the private control of the electricity business and opposing government ownership. The industry was artfully feeding similar propaganda into the educational system at every level from the kindergarten to the university.

Movies and Radio

Electricity made possible the development of two new forms of entertainment that themselves became big business. The first of these to evolve, largely through the experiments of Thomas A. Edison, was the moving picture. Crude machines capable of throwing animated pictures upon a screen were developed by 1896. In that year an audience in a New York music hall saw the first short movie show—some breaking waves, a bit of boxing, and a dancer. Thereafter vaudeville houses occasionally interspersed short interludes of movies into their regular programs, but the pictures were too hard on the eyes to have much popularity except as a curiosity. They improved, however, and in 1903 the first screen story was made under the intriguing title of *The Great Train Robbery*. Two years later a Pittsburgh real-estate operator, one Harry Davis, had the inspiration of putting a movie projector, a piano, and ninety-nine seats into a vacant store and charging five cents to see a one-reel show. The idea caught on and by 1907 there were five thousand similar "nickelodeons" in various parts of the country. After 1910 movie theaters became more pretentious; the Strand Theater, which opened on Broadway, New York City, in 1914, was the first of the really large ones.

As the motion picture began to capture the popular fancy, the business of producing films grew. The first large studios, those of the Biograph and the Edison companies, were opened in 1906. Within the next decade such favorite stars as Mary Pickford, Charlie Chaplin, Norma Talmadge, and Lillian and Dorothy Gish had emerged. David Wark Griffith was the most celebrated of the early directors. In 1915 he produced *The Birth of a Nation*, an exciting story of the Civil War and Reconstruction. Although the picture exalted the old Ku Klux Klan and stirred up racial prejudice, it enjoyed huge popularity. Cutting loose from stage conventions, Griffith demonstrated the dramatic possibilities of such screen techniques as distant views and close-ups, fade-outs and switchbacks, mob and battle scenes, and exciting flights and pursuits.

The industry had at first been located largely on Long Island, but the superior photographic advantages of California sunlight, as well as certain legal complications, resulted in a wholesale removal to Hollywood. There in 1922 the producers sought to avoid threatened public censorship by organizing the Motion Picture Producers and Distributors of America. Postmaster General Will H. Hays was induced to resign from Harding's cabinet

Mary Pickford in an early movie studio. (Acme.)

to head the new project. Under the guidance of the so-called Hays office, the industry sought zealously to avoid offending public taste. It sternly forbade overpassionate love scenes, the ridicule of any religious group, and the portrayal of crime or sin in which the culprit escaped just retribution.

The problem of making the movies talk was a difficult one, but eventually successful systems for synchronizing picture and sound were developed. *The Jazz Singer*, starring Al Jolson in 1927, was the first great hit in the "talkies." Some two years more elapsed before the wiring of theaters for sound became general.

By the end of the twenties all but the smallest American communities had motion-picture theaters, and between eighty and one hundred million customers each week were paying their money to ride the Western ranges with William S. Hart and Tom Mix, to sigh through the romances of Rudolph Valentino, Greta Garbo, Gloria Swanson, and other screen lovers, or to be instructed concerning "It"—a mysterious power supposedly possessed by Clara Bow. The popularity of these actors and actresses was in fact international. A large export business in films developed, and a majority of the pictures shown in almost every country were American-made.

As early as 1903 Reginald Fessenden was demonstrating the possibility of radio telephony in experiments in Washington, D.C. Other pioneers were also at work in the field, and in 1910 Dr. Lee De Forest successfully broadcast Enrico Caruso's voice from the Metropolitan Opera House. Six years later De Forest began experimental broadcasts from High Bridge, New York.

Then in August, 1920, the Detroit *Daily News* started the practice of broadcasting news bulletins regularly for the benefit of amateurs in the Detroit area.

Meantime, the Pittsburgh, Pennsylvania, amateurs had become interested in tuning in the experimental broadcasts made by the transmitters of the Westinghouse Electric Company. A department store in the city started selling receiving sets, and the Westinghouse Company presently decided to provide daily programs for the general public. Radio station KDKA began regular broadcasting on November 2, 1920. The Harding-Cox election returns provided the first program material. The success of this venture induced Westinghouse to erect stations the next year in Springfield, Massachusetts, Newark, New Jersey, and Chicago. Interest in the new form of entertainment swept the country and, by 1929, ten million sets were in use in the United States.

In 1922 the American Telephone and Telegraph Company's New York station, WEAF, began using advertising sponsors for its programs, thus solving the problem of who was to pay the expenses of broadcasting. The radio business promptly became highly remunerative; by 1927 there were some seven hundred stations in operation. Chaos on the air waves threatened, and Congress had to establish the Federal Radio Commission with authority to grant licenses to broadcasting stations and fix their wave lengths and hours of operation.

The almost inevitable trend of all business toward consolidation was evident in the organization of the Radio Corporation of America in 1919. This company, largely controlled by General Electric and Westinghouse, achieved a commanding position in the sale of radio sets and equipment. In 1926 the National Broadcasting Company, dominated by RCA, was established and soon controlled a chain of broadcasting stations from coast to coast. The rival Columbia Broadcasting System was organized the following year.

More Boom Industries

The manufacture of chemicals was scarcely a new industry in the sense that the automobile, movie, and radio businesses were. During the seventeenth century the colonists had begun the production of such commodities as potash and saltpeter. By 1900, moreover, there was extensive manufacture of the so-called heavy chemicals, products like sulfuric acid, soda ash, and caustic soda that were put to important industrial use. Up to 1914, however, the United States was almost completely dependent on imports from Germany for aniline dyes and other synthetic supplies.

The outbreak of war in Europe brought great opportunities. Cut off from imports, American textile manufacturers had to turn to American-made dyes, poor though they were at first. A vast amount of important technical information became available when the Alien Property Custodian seized and assigned to the newly organized Chemical Foundation some four thousand enemy-owned patents for dyes, drugs, and other products. Chemical companies were prospering meanwhile through the huge wartime expenditures for explosives and fertilizers; E. I. Du Pont de Nemours manufactured some 40 per cent of all the explosives used by the Allies. Wartime contracts permitted vast plant expansion and provided ample funds for research.

Already in a powerful position as it entered the postwar period, the industry received additional stimulus by the high rates of the Emergency Tariff Act of 1921 and the Fordney-McCumber Act. By 1929 four of the great American chemical concerns were larger than any of their European rivals. Greatest of all was Du Pont, which in 1930 was making 1,100 different products in 80 different factories located in 30 states.

The chemical industry seemed to have almost unlimited possibilities. Plastics had increased in number and utility since the pioneer discovery of celluloid by an American in 1869, until an appropriate product was now available for radio panels, fountain pens, buttons, combs, and hundreds of other uses. Although rayon was not at first satisfactory, it improved in quality and grew rapidly in popularity. New lacquers made of synthetic resins permitted the application of a fine finish to automobiles in two days instead of the twenty-six days formerly required. Other applications of chemistry made possible cheaper fertilizers for the farmer and more durable aluminum pots and pans for the housewife.

Wholesale industrial expansion afforded large profits to the construction business during the twenties. The erection of ever higher skyscrapers testified to the prevailing optimism. New York led the country, but throughout the nation the construction of lofty office building bolstered local pride. The construction of homes also boomed, particularly since very little house building had been done during the war. As automobiles became more common, suburban developments were particularly popular, and city workers accepted this opportunity to acquire homes in quieter, more country-like surroundings. On the other hand, the building of luxurious apartment houses was evidence that many families preferred to live in the cities and escape the inconvenience of commuting. Like the automobile business, the construction industry was notable for the stimulus that it gave to other lines—to steel, cement, lumber, electrical appliances, plumbing, and heating concerns, for example.

Sick and Subsidized Industries

Some industries did not share in the prevailing prosperity. This was notably true of agriculture, which has been described in an earlier chapter,[1] but it was also true of bituminous coal mining and cotton textile manufacture.

A combination of factors kept the bituminous coal industry in the doldrums. Fundamentally, the situation was one of overexpansion and overproduction. Coal was feeling the competition of newer sources of energy. Whereas coal had provided 87 per cent of all energy utilized in the United States at the end of the nineteenth century, the use of petroleum, natural gas, and hydroelectric power had reduced the proportion of coal-produced

[1] See Chap. 10.

energy to 45 per cent by the thirties. The declining price of bituminous coal resulted in bankruptcy, unemployment, and other difficulties. To make matters worse, many of the older mines that had accepted union contracts calling for reasonably good wages found themselves unable to compete effectively with newer mines opened in West Virginia, Kentucky, and elsewhere, where an aggressive antiunion policy made it possible to pay low wages.

The cotton textile industry suffered in part from loss of export markets. The growth of textile manufacturing in Japan, India, South America, and China had serious repercussions both in England and in the United States. To this blow was added certain changes in feminine apparel. Women wore shorter skirts, less clothing, and preferred silk or rayon to cotton for most of their lingerie and dresses. The total number of spindles actively employed in cotton textile manufacturing in the United States declined by about 12 per cent between 1920 and 1930. Prices fell, mills went bankrupt, and unemployment grew. As in the bituminous coal industry, Northern industrialists found themselves at a very serious disadvantage in competing with newer Southern concerns. The latter had the advantages of proximity to the market, an abundent labor supply willing to work long hours for a low wage, and the use of new machinery, much more efficient than the old equipment of Northern factories. Thus the Southern mills were able to expand despite the unfavorable circumstances in which the industry as a whole was placed; the number of spindles in the South was 4.3 million in 1900, 15.2 million in 1920, and 18.5 million in 1930. This development, of course, multiplied the troubles besetting the industry in New England, where spindles in operation declined by almost one third during the decade.

Businessmen fervently pledged their allegiance to laissez faire, but few interpreted the term to mean that government should abstain from measures directly helping them. The high tariffs of the twenties provided in reality a subsidy paid by the consumer to thousands of industries. Where it seemed necessary, moreover, the Republican administrations of the day did not hesitate to have the government make direct payments to private business enterprises. This proved to be the case with both the merchant marine and the aviation industries.

The value of a large merchant marine in case the United States became involved in war was obvious, yet the difficulties in maintaining one proved great. In conformity with the Merchant Marine Act of 1920, the Shipping Board sold 1,141 government-owned ships to private corporations between 1920 and 1928. The Board sold ships that had cost during the war as much as $200 a ton to build for $30, $20, and occasionally as low as $8 a ton. Even at these bargain prices, several hundred ships found no purchasers. Almost five hundred were allowed to lie idle; the remainder were operated by private companies under contracts so generous that the companies could not lose but the government could—and did in sums fluctuating between $12 and $50 million annually. The concerns that had purchased government ships had scarcely better success. They were competing with foreign shipping companies that enjoyed government subsidies, had lower operating costs, and used newer, faster, and more efficient vessels. In 1921 American ships carried almost 43 per cent of American exports; by 1928 the proportion had dropped to 32 per cent.

Congress tried to rescue the industry with the Jones-White Act of 1928. To modernize American shipping, the Shipping Board's loan fund was increased to $250 million, from which advances could be made at very low interest rates to private concerns for the construction of new ships or the rehabilitation of old ones. The government was also authorized to enter into long-term contracts with the shipping companies for carrying the mail. These contracts provided a generous if indirect subsidy. By 1933 these payments for carrying the mail reached about $23 million annually, many times what it cost to perform the service. Meanwhile, the government continued to sell its own ships to private companies at a great loss and to loan large sums of money for new construction. Such measures managed to keep the American merchant marine alive and even to provide it with a few new ships, but the situation was obviously far from healthy. Many stockholders and executives connected with the shipping business grew wealthy on government money, yet the nation did not acquire an effective merchant marine.

Aviation was a new industry, but it was far from being a boom enterprise. World War I had speeded its development immeasurably; planes had to be produced in quantity, and thousands of young Americans were trained as pilots. In 1918 the first regular air-mail service in the world was instituted between New York and Washington, and the following year a United States Navy seaplane, the NC-4, made the first crossing of the Atlantic by air.

But the early postwar years were discouraging ones for the industry. The government was no longer a customer for any substantial number of planes; indeed it was dumping its own surplus aircraft on the market. General William ("Billy") Mitchell preached the importance of aviation for national defense and even demonstrated that aerial bombing could sink a battleship. His superiors were unimpressed, however, and demoted Mitchell in rank, then court-martialed him and required him to retire from the service on charges that he had been insubordinate during his heated campaign to unify the army and navy air forces. Nor was there any extensive private market for aircraft. Aviation was still largely a curiosity; its principal vocational opportunity was to reckless young "barnstormers" who looped the loop and did barrel rolls at county fairs and then sold rides to anyone courageous enough to go up.

The Post Office gradually expanded its air-mail service, but up to 1925 the flying was done by its own pilots. In that year Congress passed the Kelly Act authorizing the government to make contracts for carrying the mail with private lines. In further recognition of the importance of the new industry, the Air Commerce Act of 1926 vested extensive powers over commercial aviation in the Department of Commerce.

The year 1927 was a turning point for the industry. On May 20 Charles A. Lindbergh took off in his plane, "The Spirit of St. Louis," from the New York airport; thirty-three and a half hours later he landed safely at Le Bourget Field near Paris. The flight, so quietly and competently performed, captured the imagination of the American public and demonstrated the possibilities of aviation as no previous event had done. The "Flying Colonel" became a national hero overnight, and aviation securities took off on a seemingly nonstop flight of their own; in nineteen months the Wright Aeronautical Company's stock soared from 25 to 245. Air-mindedness was stimulated still further by several other notable flights: in 1926 Commander Richard E. Byrd and Floyd Bennett flew over the North Pole; the next year Byrd organized a trans-Atlantic flight; in 1928 he flew over the South Pole. Meantime, the Atlantic had been crossed also by Clarence Chamberlain and Charles A. Levine and by the famous woman pilot, Amelia Earhart.

By the end of 1928, there were 48 airlines in the United States with a combined length of 20,000 miles that served 355 cities. Licensed aviators numbered 11,000. To an extraordinary degree, however, the industry was dependent upon the patronage of government. Between 1927 and 1933 the army and navy purchased over 50 per cent of the output of the aircraft factories, and as late as 1931, 85 per cent of the income of the transport companies came not from carrying passengers or freight, but from mail contracts. The rates of payment authorized by the Kelly Act were considered inadequate, and Congress raised them several times. Finally in 1930 the McNary-Watres Act empowered the Postmaster General to make contracts under which the companies would be paid for providing space for mail irrespective of the weight or volume of the mail actually carried. By 1932 payments on these contracts had risen to nearly $20 million annually, some three times what the Post Office was taking in through the sale of air-mail stamps.

The development of aviation was probably important enough to the national welfare to justify a policy of subsidies, but the actual administration of the system brought much criticism. Not only were the payments often excessive, but there seemed to be favoritism in their distribution. Hoover's Postmaster General, Walter F. Brown, was accused of having evaded the clauses in the McNary-Watres Act that required competitive bidding, of having allotted the contracts in such a manner that 90 per cent of the government payments were made to three major groups in the industry, and of having brought pressure to bear upon the smaller independents to compel them to merge with the larger ones.

The Railroads

Air transportation was a potential, rather than an actual, threat to the railroads during the twenties. Their more immediate difficulties lay in the growth of other forms of competition. Automobiles were scurrying over the roads on innumerable errands that a decade before would have provided business for the trains. The problem became still more serious as bus lines and trucking companies expanded their activities. Railroad executives complained that, whereas their companies had to expend huge sums in maintaining their tracks and roadbeds, these new competitors enjoyed the use of highways built at the taxpayers' expense. To make matters worse from the railroads' point of view, interstate motor transportation was not yet subject to Federal regulation. The railroads also felt increased competition from waterways. The building of the Panama Canal stimulated interest in similar projects within the national borders. In 1918 the new New York State Barge

Canal, superseding the historic Erie Canal, was opened to traffic. The Federal government expended large sums in projects designed to improve nagivation along the Ohio, Missouri, and Mississippi rivers. Most of these projects, the railroad executives charged, did not pay for themselves; a form of government-subsidized competition was further injuring the railroads.

The long-range prospects of the railroads looked anything but promising, and the railroads were hard hit by the depression of 1921. Yet prosperity postponed for a little while the day of reckoning. Despite the continued falling off of passenger receipts, freight revenues reflected the satisfactory state of general business activity. The railroads, moreover, achieved substantial economies in operation through the introduction of large freight cars, more powerful locomotives, diesel engines, electrification, and automatic systems of sorting cars in freight yards. One and a half million railroad employees were operating the country's lines in 1930, whereas two million had been required a decade before. Increased efficiency, however, was not enough to save the carriers from the devastating effects of the Great Depression when most of the railroads failed to earn their fixed charges, while over forty thousand miles went into the hands of receivers. Had it not been for life-saving loans by Hoover's Reconstruction Finance Corporation, bankrupt mileage would have been much greater—greater, in fact, than in any previous period of railroad history.

The Transportation Act of 1920 proved in certain of its provisions hard to administer. The organization of labor adjustment boards proceeded very slowly because of differences between the carriers and their employees. This added to the crushing weight of the problems confronting the National Railroad Labor Board. The board gained the hostility of the unions by recommending wage cuts in 1921 and 1922. When the shopmen walked out in protest against the second cut, their strike was broken with the assistance of an injunction obtained by Attorney General Daugherty. Labor's opposition to the Labor Board, combined with an attack upon it by many railroad executives, resulted in the passage of the Railroad Labor Act of 1926. This abolished the old board and substituted a permanent Board of Mediation composed of five members chosen by the President. The board's primary duty was to attempt to mediate in railroad labor disputes not settled by direct negotiations or by adjustment boards; if the board's effort at settlement also failed, it was then to urge the parties to submit the dispute to arbitration. Should either of the parties refuse to arbitrate and an interuption in interstate commerce be threatened, the President was empowered to appoint an emergency board to investigate. The parties were required not to make any change in conditions until thirty days after the emergency board's report. Despite pessimistic predictions by those who remembered the failure of similar legislation passed in 1913, this machinery worked surprisingly well.

As directed by the Transporation Act of 1920, the ICC twice proposed plans for consolidating the railroads of the country into some twenty great systems, but the companies objected to some provisions and made their own counterproposals. In the resulting deadlock none of the consolidation contemplated in the legislation of 1920 was actually achieved. For a time the railroads appeared to have found in holding-company organization a device for securing their own kind of consolidation—one that would escape the regulatory powers of the ICC. Particularly notorious were the activities of the Van Sweringen brothers of Cleveland, who used pyramided holding companies to gain control over railroads having aggregate assets of $2.5 billion with an investment of less than $20 million. The ICC was threatened with the undermining of much of its power until the situation was remedied by legislation in 1933.

The railroad question continued, obviously, to be one of the major national issues. As time went on, however, the problem changed from protecting the public against railroad abuses to keeping the roads operating in reasonably solvent fashion.

Business Becomes Bigger

The decade of the twenties was an age of consolidation. Not since the years 1897 to 1903 had the political, economic, and social elements blended in an atmosphere so exhilarating to the promoters of vast enterprises. The movement profited particularly from the increasing number of Americans eager to invest in stocks and willing to buy up almost any new issue thrown upon the market.

The extent to which business concentration had grown is shown by the fact that in 1930 the 200 largest nonfinancial corporations of the country—45 railroads, 58 public utilities, and 97 industrials—had gross assets of $67 billion. This was almost one half of all the assets owned by corporations of this character in the country. By 1930 there were 15 companies, each of which had assets of over $1 billion. Mergers resulted in the disappearance of 6,000 manufacturing and mining enterprises between 1919 and 1928, while 4,000 public utilities and more than 1,800 banks were absorbed by other concerns. Giant chain stores like the A & P, Woolworth's, the United Cigar Stores, and Walgreen's Drug Stores spread across the country. In 1929 these chains made 27 per cent of American food sales, 19 per cent of drugstore sales, and 93 per cent of variety-store sales.

Although outright mergers were frequent, the most popular device for consolidating business during the decade was the holding company. This form of combination had lost its popularity following the adverse decisions of the Supreme Court in the Northern Securities case in 1904 and the Standard Oil case in 1911, but after 1920, when the Court refused to order the dissolution of the United States Steel Corporation, promoters returned to it with great enthusiasm. Not only were about one quarter of all the nation's industrial concerns brought under holding-company organization during the next twelve years, but the method was used with increasing frequency in the railroad and banking fields.

As corporations became larger, they fell more and more under management control. Stockholders were so numerous and the proportion of stock that most of them held was so small that they seldom tried to influence the policies of the company; instead they willingly mailed in their proxies to be voted by a committee of the management. Unwilling to run even a remote risk of stockholders' revolt, corporation lawyers specialized in so organizing the com panies that the investing public put up the capital through the purchase of bonds, preferred stock, and nonvoting common stock, while a little group of insiders held tight control of the enterprise through a small issue of voting stock never put on public sale. The growing divorce between corporate ownership and control sometimes made for irresponsibility and bad management.

Despite this trend toward consolidation, the single corporation threatening to monopolize a whole field of economic endeavor was less characteristic of the twenties than it had been of the early years of the century. The various Standard Oil companies, for example, controlled only about 43 per cent of the oil business in 1926 as compared with the 80 per cent that had been theirs in 1911, while the United States Steel Corporation's output declined from 65 per cent of the nation's total in 1902 to approximately 40 per cent. But this did not mean a revival of small business. Instead, a situation was developing wherein there were three or four great companies in a field, competing with each other but far outdistancing smaller rivals. This condition, called oligopoly, was illustrated by the dominance of the automobile field by Ford, General Motors, and Chrysler; in the chemical field by Du Pont, Allied Chemical and Dye, and Union Carbide and Carbon; and by similar situations in the movie, oil, steel, cigarette, aviation, and electrical industries.

The competition of the giants was a great boon to the advertising business. Manufacturers spent enormous sums in an attempt to impress upon the buying public the sterling merits of Lucky Strike, Camel, and Chesterfield cigarettes, or the prodigious power of Esso, Gulf, or Texaco gasoline. Advertising, however, emphasized the quality of the competing products rather than their price. Indeed, it was taken for granted that the popular brands of gasoline, bread, and cigarettes would all sell at the same price. Businessmen came to look upon price cutting as unethical. It was assumed, for example, that the figure set by Standard Oil would fix the price charged for gasoline by all the other companies.

The organization of trade associations also reflected the desire to stabilize business. Such groupings had been in existence since the Civil War, but they increased greatly in number and importance during and after World War I. In 1925 there were approximately a thousand of them. Trade association activities took many different forms. Sometimes they did advertising in the interest of the whole industry. For example, when the American Tobacco Company featured the slogan, "Reach for a Lucky instead of a sweet," the candymakers' association responded with a series of advertisements emphasizing the healthful food values in their products. Many trade associations undertook to simplify the prevalent business practices in their fields or to standardize products. In such activities they had the cooperation of Secretary of Commerce Herbert Hoover. The varieties of paving brick were thus reduced from 66 to 4, of sheet steel from 1,819 to 261, and of range boilers from 130 to 13.

The temptation was great, however, to direct trade association activities into less legitimate channels—channels tending toward price fixing, restriction of production, and restraint of competition. Particularly controversial was the so-called open-price movement, which had its original impetus in 1912 from a book entitled *The New Competition,* written by a Chicago lawyer, A. J. Eddy. Upon its title page were these words: "Competition is War and 'War is Hell.' " Eddy's thesis was that cutthroat competition could be avoided and business stabilized if producers would provide each other with complete information about all their transactions—about sales, customers, shipments, production, and prices. By 1921 there were more than one hundred open-price associations engaged in collecting and distributing such information.

Foreign Trade and Investments

About one tenth of the annual production of goods in the United States was sold abroad. As compared with the proportion destined for the domestic market, these exports were not large, but to many industries they represented the difference between prosperity and depression. Hoover, as Secretary of Commerce, was particularly zealous in promoting American sales abroad. Requests to his department for information about foreign markets rose from 700 to 10,000 a day, and he sent a large corps of commercial attachés and trade experts abroad to advance the interests of the exporters. Other agencies for promoting foreign trade were some fifty export associations, which had been granted exemption from the antitrust laws by the Webb-Pomerene Act of 1918, and numerous American banks, which were permitted under the Federal Reserve Act to maintain foreign branches.

Thus encouraged, American exports rose from their depression low of $3.8 billion in 1922 to $5.2 billion in 1929. Certain interesting trends may be noted. Up to 1900 the leading exports had been cotton, wheat, and meat; by 1929 only cotton maintained its leading place—wheat and meat exports being far surpassed by petroleum products, machinery, and automobiles. In 1900 about two thirds of sales abroad had been agricultural products; by 1929 the proportion of these was not more than one third. In 1900, moreover, over three quarters of American exports went to Europe; by 1929 less than one half did so because of increased sales to Canada, Latin America, and Asia.

Imports, no less than exports, were important to the nation's economy. Increasing industrialization led to large purchases of newsprint, vegetable oils, rubber, and certain metals like copper, nickel, and tin. As in the case of sales abroad, American purchases from Europe were becoming proportionately less, while those from Canada and Asia were showing notable increases. Republican tariff policies, however, were reflected in the continued excess of exports over imports. In 1929, goods entering the United States were valued at only $4.4 billion, which fell short by $800 million of balancing the country's sales abroad.

Such an annual excess of exports over imports had been usual before World War I. Then it had served a useful function, since the United States was a debtor nation and required funds to pay dividends and interest to foreign investors who had loaned their money for building American railroads and factories. But the war radically altered the situation. Many foreigners had to liquidate their holdings of American securities, while American bankers and the United States government itself loaned large sums to the belligerents. Even excluding the large intergovernmental debts, the change in the situation was striking; foreign investments in the United States between 1914 and 1919 fell from $6.75 billion to $2.2 billion, while American investments abroad increased from $3.5 billion to $6.5 billion. The United States, in short, had become a creditor nation.

Ten years after the war, conditions were still more radically altered. Foreign investment in the United States had risen again to $6.7 billion—attracted by the dazzling prospects of American industry. But it by no means kept pace with American investment abroad, which, with the blessing of the American State Department, had risen by 1929 to $15.4 billion. The excess of American exports over imports provided funds for American loans to many foreign governments, as well as for the financing of tin-mine operations in Bolivia, oil development in Mexico, Venezuela, and Iraq, rubber plantations in the Netherlands East Indies, banana plantations in Central America, and sugar plantations in Cuba. Particularly notable was the large amount of American capital—$1.5 billion—invested in manufacturing enterprises in foreign countries, often in foreign branches of American companies. The export of American capital to build foreign factories was so extensive as to threaten the export market for goods manufactured in the United States.

So long as American capital continued to flow into foreign investments, world economic conditions appeared to be in a state of healthy convalescence. Germany successfully met the reparations payments fixed under the Dawes Plan of 1924, and her creditors in turn made their war-debt payments to the United States. American exports continued in large volume since they were in truth being financed by expanding American investments. But the foundation of this convalescence remained precarious. Should American loans abroad cease, disastrous consequences would be inevitable.

The Balance Sheet of the Twenties

Seen in perspective, the prosperity of the twenties was by no means fictitious. On the contrary, there was much solid economic achievement. Not only was there a substantial increase in the gross national income, but there were measurable gains both in per capita real income and in the real wages of American laborers. Particularly impressive was the increased efficiency to be found in manufacturing, mining, transportation, and agriculture. Scientific management and improved machinery had made human labor more productive than ever before.

Unfortunately, however, certain other developments of the period proved in the long run so unhealthy as to threaten the whole economic structure. The failure of agricultural prices to maintain an equitable relationship with other prices undermined the security of millions of American farmers, while sick industries like bituminous coal mining and cotton textile manufacturing involved hardship for many others. Particularly disquieting was the growth of technological unemployment; new machinery seemed to be taking away jobs faster than it created them. It was cold comfort to the man thrown out of work to assure him that his plight was temporary and that ultimately he might expect a new and better job from expanding industry. The transition period was often long and painful, and the rugged individualism of the twenties was entirely opposed to the principle of unemployment insurance to provide for such cases.

During the Coolidge period men liked to dream that the business cycle had been broken and that the country had entered a period of perpetual prosperity. But the continuance of good times required that distribution keep pace with production, demand with increased supply. Since this was fundamental, the seriousness of a situation in which millions of farmers, miners, and workers failed to obtain an ample and stable income is obvious. The price policies of many manufacturers added to the difficulty. The comparative stability of the general price level during the twenties is misleading, suggesting as it does that there was no general inflation. Yet in many lines reductions in cost were effected that failed to be reflected in reductions in price; the result was a concealed inflation. Instead of savings being handed on to the consumers, they were largely diverted to increased profits. Many businessmen preferred to take a large profit on a small volume of business rather than a small profit on a large volume. But prices higher than they needed to be seriously reduced the purchasing power of the consumers upon which continued prosperity depended. The inflexibility of prices, of course, reflected the restraints upon competition that were so common during the twenties—monopoly, oligopoly, price leadership, and trade association agreements.

In certain other lines the inflation was not concealed at all. By 1927 the price of most common stock was purely speculative and had lost all contact with the actual earning power of the corporation involved. Yet the great bull market was merely gathering momentum; up and up it went until it reached the fantastic peaks of September, 1929. The housing and real estate boom of the earlier twenties likewise drove prices up to unnatural levels; the most notorious situation was that in the Florida land market, where thousands of Northerners were feverishly engaged in buying and selling land, much of which they had never seen. Before the hurricane of 1926 and other factors combined to cool the excessive ardor of the speculators, prices had been pushed to grotesque levels.

Speculation in stocks and real estate was particularly dangerous to the continuance of prosperity because it was carried on largely upon credit. The investor preferred to borrow from his broker and buy a large amount of stock on margin rather than purchase a smaller amount outright; the real estate buyer gave a mortgage for most of the sales price and obligated himself for an indefinite period in the future to make heavy interest payments based upon an inflated valuation of his property. The overextension of credit was, in fact, to be seen on every hand. The ubiquitous salesman persuaded his prospects to "buy now and pay in easy installments." Many a young couple was making payments simultaneously on a bungalow, household furniture, radio, washing machine, vacuum cleaner, and automobile. It was an expensive process because it involved large interest payments; it was precarious since illness, unexpected expenses, or loss of one's job might make it impossible to continue the payments, in which case the unhappy householder might lose both his purchases and the payments he had already made. But the great banker was often as imprudent as the small householder; many of the securi-

The progress of civilization. Pioneers of the nineteenth and twentieth centuries.
(From the *Rochester Democrat and Chronicle*.)

ties—particularly the foreign ones—that he bought for himself and sold to
his customers proved to be worthless.

The final weakness in the prosperity of the twenties was its narrow base.
In 1929 there were 16,350,000 families in the United States receiving less than
$2,000 in annual income. This was nearly 60 per cent of all the families in
the country, yet they received less than 24 per cent of the national total. A
still greater drag on the country's economy was the lowest income group—
the 21 per cent of American families who received less than $1,000 a year
and less than 4 per cent of the national income. Here were the customers
who would have to obtain greater purchasing power before the nation would
really achieve Hoover's noble goal, "the final triumph over poverty."

14

HOOVER AND THE GREAT DEPRESSION

In October, 1929, a calamitous break in the New York stock market marked the dramatic beginning of the greatest depression in world history. Its repercussions were momentous in both domestic and international politics. In England, a Labor government was swept from power; in Germany, the political parties upholding the republic were overwhelmed by their anti-republican enemies; in France, no ministry could remain long in authority; in ten Latin-American states there were revolutions. And in the United States the Great Depression blasted the political fortunes of Herbert Hoover, despite the fact that few American presidents have entered the White House with greater prestige than was his in March, 1929.

The Election of 1928

On August 2, 1927, reporters covering Coolidge's vacation in the Black Hills of South Dakota were given an unexpected scoop when the President handed out the terse statement: "I do not choose to run for President in 1928." It was headline news because the country was prosperous and contented, Coolidge was at the height of his popularity, and political experts freely predicted he would easily be elected to a third term. Some of the President's most enthusiastic admirers refused to take this announcement as final and hoped that the movement to renominate him would assume such proportions that he would accept after all. Without any encouragement from the White House, however, the "draft-Coolidge" plan lasted only long enough to induce Coolidge's Senate opponents—Democrats and Republican progressives— to pass a resolution on February 10, 1928, that any departure from the time-honored custom established by Washington of retiring after two terms "would be unwise, unpatriotic and fraught with peril to our free institutions." Coolidge did not give his reasons for not seeking re-election. His decision may have been based upon respect for the anti-third-term tradition, upon the knowledge that his health was failing, or upon a canny recognition that prosperity might not last forever.

Coolidge's announcement was the signal for various Republican factions to start promoting their candidates. Former Governor Lowden of Illinois had a faithful following, but his chances were injured by his age (68) and by the scars left from the 1920 convention. Vice President Dawes had demonstrated executive ability during his career and possessed an unusually colorful personality, but the Senators had never forgiven him for lecturing them on the obsolescence of their rules when he took up the gavel in 1925. Senator Borah, a hero to many Republican liberals, was anathema to most conservative Eastern leaders. The aspirations of all these rivals were doomed to defeat by the irresistible tide that set in for the nomination of Herbert Hoover. Although the Secretary of Commerce was unpopular with many Republican leaders, he had tremendous strength among the party rank and file. His administration of Belgian war relief had established his reputation as a great humanitarian, his work as wartime Food Administrator had made his name a household word, and his long term in the Commerce Department had given him thousands of contacts with the business community. Hoover was assured of administration support when he praised Coolidge's veto of the McNary-Haugen bill.

At the Kansas City convention, Hoover won the nomination on the first ballot. The vice-presidential candidate was Charles Curtis of Kansas, the Senate majority leader. The cautious platform promised to continue the sound Republican policies that were responsible for the nation's prosperity. The troublesome farm problem was recognized in a plank assuring governmental assistance in establishing a farm marketing system, while prohibition was dealt with in a pledge to observe and vigorously enforce the Eighteenth Amendment. In international affairs, the platform advocated the outlawing of war and further limitation of armaments, but opposed entry into the League of Nations.

Several candidates, among them Governor Albert Ritchie of Maryland and Senator Thomas Walsh of Montana, were backed for the Democratic nomination. Their support was weak, however, compared with that of Governor Alfred E. Smith of New York. Since his unsuccessful bid for the nomination four years earlier, Smith had continued to grow in political stature. In 1924 he had been re-elected governor despite the fact that Coolidge had carried the state by a large majority; in 1926 he was elected for an unprecedented fourth term. Not only had he proved to be an effective campaigner, but his reform of his state government and his advocacy of progressive measures gained him nation-wide publicity. True he was disliked in the South as a Catholic and a wet, but no bitter-end opposition to him—such as had wrecked the party's chances in 1924— was allowed to develop. Instead, the "Happy Warrior," as Franklin D. Roosevelt had described him, received a first-ballot nomination at the Houston convention. An attempt to sugar-coat the pill for the South was made by naming Senator Joseph Robinson of Arkansas as his running mate.

The Democratic platform was no more inspiring than the Republican. The League of Nations was not mentioned, and prohibition was dealt with only in a pledge to make "an honest effort to enforce the Eighteenth Amendment and all other provisions of the Federal Constitution and all laws enacted pursuant thereto." Even on the tariff the Democrats sought no radical change, promising, on the contrary, duties to maintain legitimate business and a high standard of wages while permitting effective competition and preventing monopoly. Although Coolidge's farm policy was severely criticized, the Democratic alternative was left vague.

Fortunately the candidates proved somewhat less evasive than the party

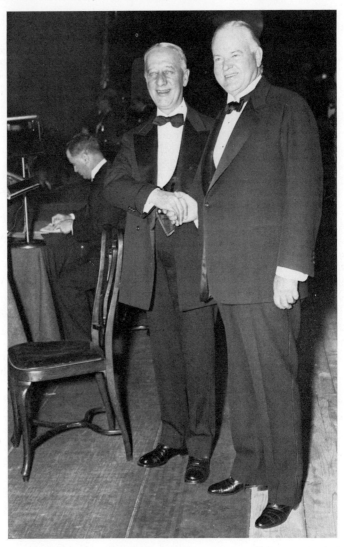

Alfred E. Smith and Herbert Hoover. (Acme.)

platforms. Smith promised to enforce the prohibition laws so long as they were on the books, but he advocated speedy modification of the Volstead Act and eventual repeal of the Eighteenth Amendment. His alternative was a system under which each state would handle its own liquor problem, yet he opposed the return of the saloon and urged the sale of liquor through state stores. Hoover, on the other hand, defended prohibition as "a great social and economic experiment, noble in motive and far-reaching in purpose." Smith bid for the farmers' vote by accepting the principle of the McNary-Haugen bill; he advocated also public operation of Muscle Shoals and gained thereby the support of Senator Norris. Hoover outdid

Coolidge in condemning such proposals, warning solemnly: "You cannot extend the mastery of government over the daily working life of a people without at the same time making it the master of the people's souls and thoughts." In spite of his stand on prohibition, farm relief, and public power, Smith was no radical. He sought to reassure the country that he would do nothing to interfere with prosperity, and in particular that he would not seek drastic tariff revision. The Smith campaign was essentially conservative, deriving its tone perhaps from the unusual circumstance that a wealthy General Motors executive, John J. Raskob, was serving as Democratic campaign manager.

The contest was a heated one, but not because of any widespread interest in the issues. What created excitement was the unorthodox background of the Democratic candidate. A product of Tammany Hall, boasting of his affection for "the sidewalks of New York," he was viewed with inevitable suspicion by millions of small-town Americans. That suspicion was doubled by the knowledge that he was a wet and multipled many times over because he was a Roman Catholic. Never before had a member of that faith been nominated for the presidency by a major party, and many narrow-minded Protestants—their prejudices heightened by recent Klan propaganda—predicted terrible consequences were Smith successful. A vicious whispering campaign was directed against the New York governor.

The Republicans' best argument was prosperity, for which the party orators naturally took complete credit, and the election returns showed the strength of that argument. Hoover received 444 electoral votes to Smith's 87. The unusual degree of hostility to the Democratic candidate in the South was demonstrated by Hoover's victory in Florida, North Carolina, Texas, and Virginia—states never carried by a Republican since Reconstruction days, and Smith suffered further disappointment when he lost his home state. Despite the fact that the Democrats won only eight states, Smith's popular vote of 15 million compared very favorably with the 9 million votes given Cox in 1920 and the 8 million to Davis in 1924. Hoover's popular vote was over 21 million. The Progressives made no effort to revive their party during this campaign. As in 1900, the election results were somewhat deceptive. The conservatives seemed completely triumphant, yet the onset of the depression was soon to restore progressivism to its old vigor.

Hoover: Assets and Liabilities

The President who took office on March 4, 1929, had many assets. Before he became a well-known public figure, Hoover had had years of experience in the business world. Trained as an engineer at Stanford University, he had begun in his profession at the bottom, but speedily acquired a fortune as a mining and railroad expert and promoter. He spent many years abroad in China, South Africa, and England. Both as businessman and government executive, he developed a passion for facts. He campaigned by quoting statistics; as President, he was continually organizing commissions of experts to study and report on problems—reports of great interest and importance as, for example, the Committees on Recent Economic Change, on Child Health and Protection, and on Recent Social Trends. Most famous of all was the Commission on Law Enforcement, better known as the Wickersham Commission, which prepared an exhaustive report on prohibition and related problems. Hoover had an outstanding talent for organizing cooperative enterprises. As a cabinet officer under Harding and Coolidge, he had been conspicuously successful in helping businessmen to help themselves. In the White House he sought to solve important national problems through the same method. Hoover had, moreover, a well-formulated philosophy of government, which he upheld with sincerity, if not always with consistency. He objected to government intervention in the business world as not alone injurious to economic life, but to liberty. "Economic freedom," he asserted during the campaign, "cannot be sacrificed if political freedom is to be preserved."

But Hoover had serious liabilities as well. His convictions regarding the proper functions of government were destined to be much more popular during days of prosperity than during the depression. Moreover, the new President's training, rich in so many respects, was dangerously weak in the field of practical politics. Never before had he held an elective office; never before had he had to deal directly with a legislative body, jealous of its prerogatives. He was sensitive to criticism, stiff in his personal contacts, cold to newspapermen, and colorless in his public appearances. Most serious of all, perhaps, he—like so many products during the golden age of salesmanship—had been overadvertised to the electorate. Depicted as a sort of superman, Hoover's popularity evaporated when the depression did not disappear at the magician's wand; by 1932 the words "Great Engineer" were usually uttered in a tone of bitterness.

The New Administration

Hoover's inaugural address listed the ideals to which he had devoted his leadership. They included:

The preservation of self-government . . .; the maintenance of ordered liberty; . . . the building up and preservation of equality of opportunity; the stimulation of initiative and individuality; . . . the direction of economic progress toward prosperity and the further lessening of poverty; . . . the sustaining of education and of the advancement of knowledge; . . . the strengthening of the home; the advancement of peace.

In selecting his cabinet, Hoover retained two of his associates in the Coolidge administration: Secretary of the Treasury Mellon and Secretary of Labor James Davis. Most important among the new faces were Secretary of State Henry Stimson, who had been Secretary of War under Taft and Governor General of the Philippines under Coolidge, and Secretary of the Interior Ray Lyman Wilbur, a close friend of the President and previously president of Stanford University. The retiring Vice President, Charles Dawes, was named Ambassador to Great Britain, an important post at any time and in 1929 particularly so because of Anglo-American disagreements on naval limitation.

The Great Bull Market

During Coolidge's presidency stock-market prices had risen almost without interruption. Up to 1927 the advance had been normal because business was expanding and profits were increasing, but thereafter an unnatural and unhealthy trend developed. While business activity leveled off and commodity prices tended to decline, the price of common stock soared ever higher. On several occasions the market threatened to break, but in a few days it would steady itself and then leap upward again. Hoover's victory in November, 1928, led to one of the most enthusiastic of these spurts, and by September 3, 1929, the bull market reached its final, fantastic peak. Over the course of eighteen months—taking account of split-ups and the issuance of special rights—the stock of United States Steel and Union Carbide had more than doubled in price, that of GE, Westinghouse, and Montgomery Ward had tripled, and that of RCA had quintupled. Such prices obviously represented speculative, rather than investment, values, for American corporations, though enjoying good profits, were not earning the gigantic sums that alone would have justified these transactions. Stock purchasers were gambling recklessly, buying in hope of making huge profits as the market continued to rise.

The situation was as remarkable for the number of people involved as for the strange behavior of prices. Back in 1919 when an earlier bull market had been in progress, there had been only six days in which as many as two million shares had been traded on the Exchange. During 1928 and 1929, however, five-million-share days were frequent, and on September 3, 1929, when prices were at their highest, more than eight million shares were traded. Before World War 1 the realm of stocks and bonds was a mysterious arena into which the average citizen did not care to venture. The great Liberty Loan drives of war days, however, gave thousands of Americans their first interest in other forms of investment outside of savings-bank accounts. Further education was provided when large corporations like United States Steel encouraged their own employees to purchase company stock as a form of welfare capitalism. As interest in the stock market grew, Wall Street brokerages opened branches in all the large cities, while important banks had closely affiliated investment agencies scouring the country for new customers. Investment trusts were organized on the plausible principle that purchase of their securities would permit small investors to share in the ownership of diversified holdings chosen by experts. Never before has so many people owned corporation securities. Between 1912 and 1931 the number of stockholders in the Pennsylvania Railroad multiplied three times, in United States Steel five, and in ATT over thirteen. Some of the political conservatism of the twenties is probably to be explained by this development.

The most disquieting aspect was the increasing proportion of stocks held on margin—that is, not owned outright, but purchased through a loan from one's broker who held the stock as security. The technique fascinated the uninitiated since one could apparently buy a great deal of stock with a small investment and then pay for it from the profit realized by its rise. Too late did many small investors discover the catch: if the price went down they had to put up more and more margin to keep their equity; when they could no longer do so, they lost both investment and stock. The banks were involved in these transactions through extensive loans to brokers who financed marginal buying. Such brokers' loans rose from $3.5 billion in mid-1927 to over $8 billion in September, 1929.

The Coolidge administration had watched the bull market with equanimity. Speculators from time to time drew fresh courage from Secretary Mellon's optimistic comments on business conditions, while the usually close-mouthed Coolidge gave the inflationary forces new strength in January, 1928, when he stated publicly that he did not consider brokers' loans too high. The Federal Reserve Board, moreover, loosened credit during the summer of 1927. The motive was worthy since the central banks of England, France, and Germany requested such action to assist European business through a threatened crisis. The lowered interest rates, however, greatly increased speculation in Wall Street. So powerful, indeed, was the magnet of the stock boom that Americans reduced their investments and loans in Europe to buy stocks; worse still, Europeans sent their own funds to America for this purpose. This trend, long continued, presaged disaster for the shaky European economy.

A worried Federal Reserve Board tried to stem the trend in 1928 by raising the rediscount rate several times—yet the bull market continued, fed by more and more brokers' loans. Two days after he took office, Hoover conferred with Federal Reserve officials and the result was an unprecedented action—the Board refused credit to banks directly or indirectly financing speculation. Shortly thereafter Mellon issued a curiously veiled warning: "The present situation in the financial markets offers an opportunity for the prudent investors to buy bonds. Bonds are low in price compared to stocks." These actions and warnings halted the bull market only temporarily. Many banks defied the Board's program by offering large credits to the stock market. The government's action caused a boost in stock-exchange loan rates up to 15 or 20 per cent, but these high rates only diverted money to the call market in preference to less remunerative investments. Even corporations made such loans from their surplus funds. Throughout the first half of 1929 the Federal Reserve Board continued to raise rediscount rates, but bankers and other moneylenders would not heed the warning.

The American people likewise still refused to believe that disaster lay ahead, and for the most part this was as true of experts as of laymen. Businessmen and college professors talked convincingly of "a new economic era"; the old truism of "what goes up must come down" was amended to read that what goes up will remain on "a permanently high plateau."

The Crash

The stock market began to flutter in September. On the 3rd, prices were at a peak, then they went down but recovered so quickly that on the 19th some established new highs. This respite was short-lived, and for a month prices fluctuated, but the trend was strongly downward. This decline was not considered alarming and the newspapers were full of reassuring statements. For example, an official of the National City Bank, on his arrival from Europe on October 22, assured reporters: "I know of nothing fundamentally wrong with the stock market or with the underlying business and credit structure."

The next day, however, the situation became suddenly serious when stocks dropped an average of 18 points. On October 24 panic developed. There were more than 12 million transactions on the Stock Exchange and a $240 million bankers' pool, hastily organized by the city's largest financial institutions, had to come to the rescue. Prices were temporarily stabilized, but a few days later they plunged down again. The blackest day in stock market history was October 29, 1929, when an unprecedented 16,410,030 transactions took place, and the average prices of fifty leading stocks fell nearly 40 points. Brokers were deluged with orders to sell from customers wanting to unload before the market went any lower. Many sales were involuntary; traders operating on margin were unable to raise enough money to save their accounts and were sold out. Thousands of Americans saw their life savings thus disappear.

After this terrible day there was no further panic. A stabilizing influence was the welter of comforting statements coming out of Washington and Wall Street. John D. Rockefeller announced: "Believing that financial conditions of the country are sound and there is nothing in the business situation to warrant the destruction of values that has taken place on the exchanges during the past week, my son and I have for some days been purchasing sound common stocks." But even with confidence somewhat restored, the liquidation of unfortunate marginal traders continued to depress the market and on November 13, prices reached their 1929 lows. In the seventy-one days since September 3, ATT had fallen from 304 to $197\frac{1}{4}$, GE from $396\frac{1}{4}$ to $168\frac{1}{8}$, Montgomery Ward from $137\frac{7}{8}$ to $49\frac{1}{4}$, and RCA from 101 to 28.

Depression

So persistent was the belief that America was in a new economic era of perpetual prosperity that even the stock market catastrophe failed at first to shake it. On New Year's Day, 1930, Secretary Mellon declared: "I see nothing in the situation that warrants pessimism," and Secretary of Commerce Robert Lamont predicted "for the long run" a continuance of prosperity and progress.

It soon became apparent, however, that the market collapse was merely the opening thunder crash for an economic storm of hurricane proportions. Manufacturers saw their orders falling off alarmingly, and price cuts failed to revive them. The net income of the nation's 550 largest industrial corporations declined 68 per cent during the next two years. Weak companies were forced out of business, strong ones operated only part time with sharply reduced personnel. By 1932 industrial production was approximately half what it had been in 1929. The construction business was even harder hit as residential and commercial building fell to one fifth of its 1929 volume. The railroads, dependent upon a high level of business activity for adequate revenues, were in a desperate situation; one third of the nation's mileage passed into receivership. National income dropped from $82 billion in 1928 to $40 billion in 1932.

Wage workers suffered greatly. Until September, 1931, employers generally avoided wage cuts in the belief that their effect would prolong the depression. But even while hourly rates were maintained, labor's take-home pay was sharply curtailed either because factories operated only part time or because what work was available was spread to provide for as many employees as possible—a practice encouraged by the AFL. Despite this staggering of employment, more and more workers found themselves laid off. At least 10 million Americans were jobless in 1932, while in the following spring the number increased to about 14 million. Moreover, between 1931 and 1933 substantial wage cuts were suffered by those fortunate enough to have jobs. The reduction in hourly rates was in most cases less than the reduction in the cost of living, but only a small proportion of the workers enjoyed steady enough employment to benefit by this.

People in all walks of life found themselves either without any income at all or with income sharply reduced. Ministers, teachers, salesmen, salaried executives, and farmers suffered along with industrial workers. Savings painfully accumulated were soon exhausted. People in debt—and there were millions of them—were confronted with especially serious problems. Thousands of farmers and homeowners lost their property, and there would have been many more foreclosures had not the real estate market been so depressed that the creditors postponed taking action. Stock given as collateral for loans was sold when the debts could not be paid, while furniture and automobiles were repossessed by finance companies.

If it was a hard time to owe money, it was no great privilege to be a creditor either. Banks were placed in great jeopardy when their debtors defaulted wholesale at a time when stock and real estate values were so low that the collateral the banks held was often insufficient to cover their outstanding loans. Even during the years of prosperity banks had failed with alarming frequency, averaging about 700 a year. In 1930, the number almost doubled when 1,326 institutions had to close their doors, while in 1931 the figure rose to 2,294 and in 1932 to 1,456. It was the smaller state banks, unaffiliated with the Federal Reserve, that failed most frequently, but large city institutions often found themselves in serious difficulty. Their troubles were multiplied when frightened depositors began to withdraw and hoard their money.

Unfair though it was, the farmers, who had shared very little in the prosperity of the twenties, were particularly hard hit by the depression. Agricultural prices had been considered low in comparison to other prices in 1929, yet by the spring of 1933 the former had fallen 64 per cent from their 1929 level, while the prices of manufactured goods had gone down only 34 per cent. Farmers' cash income declined from $11 billion in 1929 to $5 billion in 1932. Industrialists were able to maintain prices to some extent by reducing production, but the farmers, doing business under ruthlessly competitive conditions, could not follow suit. Instead, warehouses groaned with agricultural surpluses.

Causes of the Disaster

It should be stressed that the economic collapse was world-wide. Some roots were to be found in the maladjustment brought about by the war. Millions of lives had been lost and untold property damage inflicted. A tremendous volume of debt, both internal and intergovernmental, had been created in all the belligerent countries. Europe was crisscrossed by new political frontiers along which economic barriers were speedily erected. Fear for each nation's security led to expensive military establishments. For a few years the seriousness of the fundamental situation was shrouded from view by the fictitious prosperity created by American loans. When this stream of American investment dried up, in part because of the superior attractions of the stock market, the European economy deteriorated rapidly. Stocks fell in price, unemployment grew ominously, and debts were defaulted. America felt the repercussions in many ways, but most directly by a 69 per cent decline in the dollar value of her exports between 1920 and 1932.

Another important factor in the world situation was the enormous expansion of production in the primary industries during the twenties. For a time international cartels and marketing agreements succeeded in maintaining prices, but in 1929 and thereafter the market broke disastrously. Coffee fell off one third in three months and nearly 40 per cent in a year. Other prices declined less rapidly, but eventually all foodstuffs and raw materials showed the same downward trend. Such great primary producing countries as Canada, Australia, and Brazil were grievously hurt, and their difficulties reacted on the entire world.

America's economic troubles, however, could not all be blamed on outside forces. Factors already discussed—speculation, credit overextension, inflexible prices, the faulty balance between agriculture and the rest of the economy, inadequate income of millions of American families—all contributed to the debacle. The nation's economic woes were increased by abuses in the banking system that permitted dangerous credit inflation during prosperity and endangered the savings of depositors during depression.

During the late thirties much discussion was provoked by the explanation of the depression advanced by Professor Alvin Hansen of Harvard University. Adapting an analysis derived from John Maynard Keynes, famous English economist, Hansen stressed the fundamental changes brought about in the American situation by the closing of the frontier, immigration restriction, and the declining birth rate—all of which tended to reduce opportunities for private investment. The housing shortage caused by World War I and the new industries of the twenties offered temporary outlets, but their possibilities were largely exhausted by 1929. Nearly all the homes that people could afford had been built, skyscraper office buildings could not find tenants, factories had been so greatly expanded that their output could not be sold in a market where income did not keep pace with production. Automobiles, radios, refrigerators, and the like had been purchased by most Americans who could afford them—and by some who could not. Since these were relatively durable goods for which the market in the future would have to be largely a replacement one, there was little inducement to invest in plants for expanding their production. Savings lay idle in banks or were gambled in Wall Street because investment outlets were so largely saturated. And as capital expenditures declined, the market for basic goods like steel contracted and the country fell into a declining economic spiral. This Keynesian theory drew the conclusion that capitalism could be preserved only by government planning and government investment. This Hansen thesis was one of the most powerful influences at work during the later period of the New Deal.

The Federal Farm Board

In April, 1929, six months before the stock-market crash, Congress met in special session to redeem Republican pledges for farm relief. The administration program called for increased tariff protection and the establishment of a farm board to promote orderly agricultural marketing. The Hawley-Smoot Tariff was not passed until June, 1930, but the Agricultural Marketing Act was rapidly whipped into shape and Hoover signed it on June 15, 1929.

The new law created a Federal Farm Board of nine members appointed by the President. A $500 million revolving fund was made available for loans to cooperative marketing associations, owned and controlled by the farmers themselves. If more drastic measures were needed, the Farm Board could establish stabilization corporations to buy and take off the market a sufficient portion of the crop to maintain prices. The Farm Bloc, dubious of the effectiveness of the measure, tried to amend it by providing for export debentures—a plan whereby the government would pay a subsidy on farm exports equivalent to one half of the American tariff rate, but Hoover successfully prevented this. On signing the bill, the President pronounced it "the most important measure ever passed by Congress in aid of a single industry." He then appointed Alexander Legge, president of the International Harvester Company, as chairman of the new Farm Board.

The basic idea incorporated in this act was typical of Hoover. He hoped to help the farmers to help themselves or, in his own words, "with government assistance and an initial advance of capital to enable the agricultural industry to reach a stature of modern business operations by which the farmer will attain his independence and maintain his individuality." Under the act, existing cooperative associations were strengthened and expanded; local and state bodies were merged into nation-wide organizations like the Farmers National Grain Corporation, the American Cotton Cooperative Association, and the National Livestock Marketing Association. From the revolving fund the cooperatives could borrow to build storage facilities, creameries, canning, packing, and processing plants, as well as to finance the marketing of members' crops.

Such activities, however, would benefit farmers more in the future than immediately, and by the end of 1929 the stock-market crash had so upset agricultural prices that immediate relief was paramount. To an increasing degree, therefore, the Farm Board was diverted from a program of long-range assistance to desperate piecemeal efforts to halt the ruinous price fall. Willy-nilly, it had become the first of the great emergency agencies.

In October, 1929, the Farm Board authorized the marketing associations to make loans on wheat and cotton at fixed prices and later to purchase some of these commodities. It felt sufficiently encouraged by this first venture to enlarge its price-pegging policy in 1930. A Grain Stabilization Corporation and a Cotton Stabilization Corporation were established and both began large-scale operations in the market. During the next three years, 370 million bushels of wheat and 1.3 million bales of cotton were purchased with money advanced by the Farm Board.

During the first two years the Hoover administration was able to defend these activities on the ground that they held American prices at a level somewhat higher than those in the world market, but as time passed, the Farm Board's efforts became progressively less effective. The huge surpluses purchased by the stabilization corporations hung over the market with depressing effect. Moreover, the farmers, trying desperately to maintain their income despite falling prices, continued to produce a large surplus. The Board sought to correct this by asking the farmers for a voluntary 30 per cent reduction of their acreage. Because each farmer hesitated to do so unless assured that all other farmers also would, the plan inevitably failed. More instead of less acreage was planted in 1932.

By the spring of 1932, the need to dispose of the Farm Board's surplus was obvious. Special sales to China, Germany, and Brazil were made, and about half the Board's stock was given to the Red Cross for distribution to depression victims.

The Farm Board was eventually abolished by executive order of Hoover's Democratic successor. Losses sustained through unrecovered loans and through disposal of wheat and cotton holdings brought the total cost of the experiment to about $345 million. This was not large compared with other relief expenditures the government was destined to make, but the Farm Board policy was, nevertheless, a failure because it did not solve the fundamental agricultural problem: that of either reducing production or opening up new markets where American staples could be sold to provide farmers with an adequate income.

The Hawley-Smoot Tariff

The other measure of farm relief promised by the Hoover administration was an increase in the tariff schedules covering agricultural products. The President hoped that the revision would be a limited one and that rates on industrial goods would be changed only in those exceptional cases where existing duties did not conform with his favorite tariff formula, "the difference in the cost of production at home and abroad." In the House, however, the familiar process of logrolling was soon in evidence. Out of a thousand tariff raises proposed in the Hawley bill, 75 were on farm products and 925 on manufactured goods. A farm paper thereupon warned that if the farmer was not careful, he would find himself "paying out $2.00 in increased tariffs on manufactured products, which he must buy, for every $1.00 gain received on farm products." Such warnings were ineffective as agricultural pressure groups vied with manufacturers' lobbyists in seeking benefits.

Hoover's principal anxiety was to keep the bill free from farm-relief riders and to expand its "flexibility" by enlarging the powers of the Tariff Commission. On both issues he had difficulty with the Senate. The Farm Bloc succeeded in amending the House bill to include the export debenture plan, while Senator Borah, ever fearful of executive encroachments on the legislative branch, headed a Progressive-Democratic-Old Guard Republican campaign to compel all Tariff Commission recommendations to be passed upon by Congress. When a deadlock between the House and Senate versions of the bill necessitated a conference committee, however, Hoover succeeded in getting the flexible provisions in and the debenture plan out.

Progressive strength in the Senate had been sufficient to obstruct some of the more excessive demands of the manufacturers' lobbies. Senator Joseph Grundy of Pennsylvania, spokesman of the ultraprotectionists, was disappointed because the measure did not go far enough, but the country's leading economists believed the new rates were far too high; more than a thousand of them signed an appeal to the President to veto the bill. They asserted the measure would raise prices for the American consumer, would hamper the export of both farm and manufactured goods, would not help producers of staples that had to be sold in the world market, would make it difficult for the principal and interest on American loans abroad to be paid, and would lead to reprisals by foreign governments. Prominent bankers and spokesmen for the export industries also opposed the bill, but it was defended by the American Farm Bureau, the National Grange, the AFL, and the National Association of Manufacturers. On June 15, 1930, the President signed the Hawley-Smoot Tariff into law.

This measure raised the general average of duties from the 33 per cent of the Fordney-McCumber Act to 40 per cent. Rates on farm products were increased from less than 20 per cent to more than 33 per cent. The advantage to agriculture, however, was dubious. On the most important staples where an exportable surplus was produced, the tariff was ineffective in raising prices, while the farmers' cost of living was affected by higher duties on shoes, harnesses, saddles, shovels, spades, lumber, shingles, bricks, and cement. Moreover, the retaliatory measures in foreign countries against which the economists had warned followed quickly. The road of extreme economic nationalism on which the United States had elected to journey was crowded with fellow travelers.

Fighting the Depression

More than once in American history the Republicans have had the good fortune to witness the beginning of a great upsweep of prosperity coinciding with the passage of one of their tariff laws. Such, however, was not the experience of the architects of the Hawley-Smoot Tariff, for the business indexes continued their relentless downward spiral.

Careful you don't upset things! A warning against the Hawley-Smoot tariff. (From the *New York World-Telegram*.)

The President had already responded to the crisis with a program typically Hooverian. On November 21, 1929, Henry Ford, Alfred Sloane of General Motors, Owen D. Young of General Electric, Walter Gifford of ATT, Pierre Du Pont of the great chemical company, and other important leaders met with him in a confidential White House conference. He asked their cooperation in maintaining existing wage scales, in continuing construction, and in spreading available work as widely as possible among employees. The industrialists agreed, providing organized labor pledged not to seek pay increases and to avoid strikes during the crisis. A group of prominent trade-union officials, including William Green and John L. Lewis, met with Hoover later the same day and gave the required assurances, even going so far as to agree to withdraw certain demands already made. Announcement of this promise of cooperation between industry and labor was given to the press, and two weeks later the President's program was ratified at a White House meeting attended by several hundred representatives of the employers and the labor unions.

These pledges were substantially kept for almost two years. During 1930 an average of only 7 out of each 100 firms reporting to the Bureau of Labor Statistics recorded pay cuts as against 92 cuts per 100 during the depression of 1921. The workers' record was equally good. Early in October, 1930, Hoover, speaking to the AFL, congratulated the unions on having held strikes to less than 300 since their agreement.

Hoover had long been an advocate of expanding public works during periods of depression. In November, 1929, he requested governors and mayors all over the country to increase governmental construction, while in his message to Congress the next month he asked larger Federal appropriations for this purpose. Public-works expenditures by the Federal government rose from their predepression level of around $250 million annually to $412 million in the fiscal year ending June 30, 1930. Thereafter they increased until they reached more than $725 million for the year ending June 30, 1933.

To coordinate the relief activities of private charities and local and state agencies, Hoover established in October, 1930, the President's Committee for Unemployment Relief under the chairmanship of Colonel Arthur Woods of New York City. Similar committees of prominent citizens to mobilize relief efforts were set up in various states and local communities.

In September, 1930, the President determined to stop all immigration into the United States because, under existing conditions, the newcomers were likely to become public charges. Over the course of the next eight months the influx of foreigners, already sharply cut by the 1924 legislation, was reduced from a monthly rate of about 22,000 to one of 3,000. Meantime, departures from America, both voluntary and involuntary, reached 7,000 monthly. This later figure reflected the vigorous deportation policy of the administration. In 1929, 279,678 immigrants had arrived and 69,203 had left the United States; in 1932, there were 35,576 arrivals and 103,295 departures. This revolution in immigration resulted not solely from administration policies, but from the disillusionment of foreigners with the United States as a land of unlimited opportunity.

The Depression Grows Worse

The President and his advisers hoped that these initial steps would tide over the crisis until recovery could set in. At times victory seemed within grasp, confidence revived, and production climbed. Inevitably, however, a relapse would occur. Stocks would plunge down again, factories would lay off more men, and farm prices would decline once more. By the fall of 1931 wage cuts were the rule everywhere. The world-wide character of the depression became steadily more apparent, and Hoover struggled during 1931 with crises caused by the threatened economic collapse of Central Europe and England's departure from the gold standard.

As conditions grew worse, new problems arose. Bank failures and general business uncertainty led to large-scale hoarding of both currency and gold, while foreigners withdrew funds from America in alarming volume. This embarrassed the operations of the Federal reserve banks. Although the law required them to maintain only a 40 per cent gold reserve against the Federal reserve notes, the scarcity of eligible commercial paper made it necessary in practice to increase the gold reserve to 75 per cent. This combination of circumstances threatened to force the nation off the gold standard—a possibility as terrifying to Hoover as it had been to Cleveland in the 1890's.

Elsewhere the contraction of credit brought serious consequences. Home owners and farmers faced foreclosures. Manufacturers and railroads could not borrow. Banks found it difficult to obtain additional funds because they could not present eligible collateral to Federal reserve banks.

Confronted with this situation, the Hoover administration was obliged to expand its range of activities. At the President's urging, the banks of the country organized in October, 1931, the National Credit Association with a capital of $500 million. Its functions were to rediscount bank assets not eligible in the Federal Reserve System in order to assure the stability of banks against runs and to make loans against the assets of closed banks so that dividends to depositors might be made. Since the situation was too serious to be met by this form of self-help, in January, 1932, Congress created the Reconstruction Finance Corporation (RFC), headed by Charles Dawes. Capital of $500 million was advanced by the government, while additional sums up to $1.5 billion might be borrowed by the new agency, whose function was to loan money to railroads, banks, insurance companies, and industrial corporations. In July, the Emergency Relief and Construction Act gave the RFC greatly broadened powers. The amount it could borrow on the credit of the United States was doubled and it could now lend money to agricultural-credit banks, to states, counties, or cities unable to handle their own relief problems, and to public or private construction projects that would be self-liquidating.

The Hoover policy for easing the credit situation was further developed by extending the activities of the Federal Land Banks and creating a new system of Federal Home Loan Banks. Since the latter could only loan up to 50 per cent of the appraised value of the mortgagor's property, however, they did little business. To assist the Federal reserve banks and their member banks, the Glass-Steagall Act of February, 1932, permitted the Federal reserve banks to accept a much larger variety of collateral from their borrowers; this served the double purpose of freeing vast amounts of gold being held in excess of the legal reserve behind Federal reserve notes and at the same time making available to the member banks large amounts of credit. The Federal reserve banks also engaged in vast open-market operations, buying more than $1 billion worth of government bonds during the next few months; this operation expanded credit for the benefit of the whole country. Simultaneously, a vast antihoarding campaign was organized at Hoover's request by Colonel Frank Knox, a prominent Chicago publisher.

Progressive and Democratic Opposition

The continuance of the depression despite all Hoover had done naturally turned public attention more and more to the President's critics. During the first two years, the conservative Republicans were in control of the House, but in the Senate about a dozen of the 56 Republicans were progressives who held the balance of power. By allying with the 39 Democrats and the sole Farmer-Laborite, they could outvote the administration supporters. The coalition's strength was demonstrated when Senators Norris and Borah opposed the appointment of Charles Evans Hughes as Chief Justice of the United States in February, 1930, because his recent legal work had been largely in the employ of the great corporations. True, Hughes was confirmed, 52 to 26, but the size of the opposition was a warning of rising discontent with the conservative trend of recent Supreme Court decisions. Hoover's second appointment to the Court created a still greater controversy. The nominee, John Parker of North Carolina, was opposed by organized labor because of his decisions as a circuit court judge upholding "yellow-dog" contracts. Negro groups also protested the appointment, and in the end it was rejected, 39 to 41. Hoover then substituted Owen Roberts of Pennsylvania, who was confirmed by unanimous vote. When still another vacancy occurred in 1932, the President prevented another bitter fight by naming the liberal and universally respected Benjamin Cardozo of New York.

Hoover's difficulties with Congress were greatly increased by the elections of 1930. The new Senate contained 48 Republicans, of whom 12 were progressives, 47 Democrats, and 1 Farmer-Laborite. At first the Republicans appeared to have maintained their control of the House by a very narrow margin, but a number of deaths occurred before the Seventy-second Congress finally met in December, 1931. The Democrats then had a majority of four and elected John Nance Garner of Texas to the speakership.

The progressives found the political currents running their way for the first time since the Wilson administration. Even during the "lame-duck" session of the old Congress, they showed their strength by pushing through Norris's bill for government operation of Muscle Shoals. The President, however, subjected the measure to a stinging veto:

This bill would launch the Federal Government upon a policy of ownership and operation of power utilities upon a basis of competition instead of by the proper government function of regulation for the protection of all the people. I hesitate to contemplate the future of our institutions, of our government, and of our country if the preoccupation of its officials is to be no longer the promotion of justice and equal opportunity but is to be devoted to barter in the markets. This is not liberalism, it is degeneration.

Although the Senate upheld the veto, the insurgents were not disheartened by this setback. A week after Congress adjourned in March, 1931, a conference of progressives met in Washington to formulate a program. Prominent in the movement were Senators LaFollette, Norris, and Borah, historian Charles A. Beard, future New Dealers Harold Ickes of Chicago and Mayor Frank Murphy of Detroit, and labor leader Sidney Hillman. Among the proposals discussed were such anti-Hoover ideas as a large public works program, compulsory unemployment insurance, minimum wages, a five-day week, a six-hour day, wider distribution of wealth, social security, child labor laws, and a national economic council.

Neither Democrats nor progressives had any opportunity to attempt to attain their objectives until December, 1931, because Hoover refused to call the new Congress into special session to deal with the emergency. When the Seventy-second Congress finally met, conflicts between the legislators and the President were frequent. Hoover regarded a balanced budget as an essential step toward recovery. To this principle few Congressmen openly objected, because deficit spending to combat depressions had as yet few proponents. Nevertheless, it required months of discussion to frame a new revenue bill. The Southern Democrats advocated a manufacturers' sales tax, but the progressive Republican Representative Fiorello La Guardia of New York obtained enough votes to defeat it. In the end, income-tax rates were raised and nuisance taxes imposed; the new bill was calculated to increase revenues by $1 billion, but it fell short of what the President requested by some $400 million. Hoover and Congress similarly agreed in principle on the necessity of economy, but differed on where the axe should be applied. Finally, Congress reduced appropriations by only $300 million instead of by the $700 million the President had asked.

During this stormy session the President's congressional opponents raised many issues. One group attempted to challenge the Hawley-Smoot Tariff with bills that would have made the Tariff Commission answerable to Congress instead of to the executive, would have directed the President to invite other powers to an international tariff conference, and would have authorized him to negotiate reciprocal trade agreements. Another faction advocated the issuance of more money. The Goldsborough bill, for example, which passed the House but failed in the Senate, would have directed expanded currency and credit until prices rose to the average prevailing between 1921 and 1929. A third group insisted that the Federal government make large appropriations to provide either work or relief for the unemployed. Speaker Garner and Representative Rainey of Illinois sponsored a bill to provide a vastly expanded program of public works, while Senators Robert Wagner of New York, Costigan of Colorado, and LaFollette, along with Representative La Guardia, demanded a more adequate program of unemployment relief. All these measures, however, were successfully blocked by Hoover.

Not all the work of the progressives was frustrated. They enjoyed an important triumph in passing the Norris-La Guardia Anti-Injunction Act in March, 1932, under which yellow-dog contracts, whereby employees agreed not to join a labor union as a condition of employment, were declared to be against the public policy and not enforceable in any Federal court. Then followed a listing of specific union activities that might not be prohibited by any Federal court injunction. Such orders in labor disputes were not entirely banned, but the circumstances under which they could be issued were strictly defined and provision was made for jury trial in any contempt-of-court case arising out of such instances, unless the alleged contempt occurred in the presence of the court. By this important law, organized labor obtained the substance of rights of which the Clayton Act of 1914 had provided only the shadow. With some reluctance Hoover signed this measure.

The Bonus Issue Revived

From World War I veterans came an appeal for immediate payment of the bonus. A year before, Congress had enacted a measure over Hoover's veto permitting veterans to borrow up to 50 per cent on their certificates. In 1932, when the depression was even more severe, a demand went up for payment of the whole amount. A bill to this end, introduced by Representative Wright Patman of Texas, passed the House, but, under pressure from the President, was rejected by the Senate in June, 1932. The incident had an unhappy sequel. Starting in May, an increasingly large "Bonus Army" of unemployed veterans congregated in Washington to lobby for the Patman bill. On July 16 Congress adjourned without conceding the veterans' demands, but the Bonus Army lingered on disconsolately in their shanty villages on the outskirts of the capital. Hoover tried to get rid of the unwelcome horde by using government funds to pay their fares home. Some six thousand accepted this help, but five thousand others remained in the city, many of them with their wives and children.

On July 28 they became involved in a fracas with the police in which two veterans were killed and several policemen were injured. Acting immediately upon a request from the District Commissioners, the President called out the army to restore order. Under command of General Douglas MacArthur, four troops of cavalry, four of infantry, a machine-gun squadron, and six tanks completely dispersed the Bonus Army and evicted the men from their camps. Whether by accident or design, the shacks in which they lived were burned to the ground. Hoover's defenders stressed the patience he had hitherto shown in handling the situation and the fact that no lives were lost in the final eviction; they asserted that a large proportion of the demonstrators were Communists or hoodlums—not veterans at all. Moreover, they said, the shanty village was becoming a health menace to Washington. Whatever justification there might have been for the action, however, the incident did untold damage to the President's reputation as a great humanitarian and gave shocking evidence of the seriousness of the nation's economic situation.

Between Hoover and his liberal critics there was a clear-cut difference of principle. Hoover believed in using Federal funds and credit to combat the depression, but he thought that the proper place for the money to be expended was in strengthening banks, railroads, and other corporations. By so doing, small depositors and investors would be protected, employment would be maintained and expanded, and a process of economic recovery set in motion that would in the end benefit everyone. His philosophy also accepted public works so long as they fulfilled a real need, the distribution of food and clothing to prevent actual physical suffering, and the advance of Federal funds to the states under careful restrictions. But he opposed direct expenditure of Federal funds to relieve either the unemployed or the farmers because such direct relief would create a burdensome bureaucracy and destroy the initiative and self-reliance of the recipients.

But Hoover's critics contended that by 1931 and 1932 a condition and not a theory confronted the nation. Panhandlers lined the streets, and discouraged men sold apples on the corners. Long breadlines were everywhere to be seen outside private and local relief headquarters. Private charity was near the end of its resources; local governments were threatened with insolvency; the states were without adequate funds. The problem was too big for any lesser agency than the Federal government itself. Moreover, these opponents of the President asserted that money poured into the financial pyramid at the top through the RFC never seeped down to the bottom. A demand arose for measures to put purchasing power into the hands of the individual victims of the depression.

As the 1932 election approached, it was clear that not only the harassed President but bankers and businessmen generally had suffered an enormous loss of prestige. A revolution in public opinion had occurred, and those who had been the lords of creation in 1929 were now in disrepute.

15

HOOVER'S QUEST FOR WORLD STABILITY

In dealing with matters international, Hoover showed bolder leadership than he did in his domestic policies. His earlier experience as engineer and relief administrator had given him an unusually broad knowledge of world affairs, and, as Secretary of Commerce, he had become a leading authority in the field of international economics.

During the 1928 campaign, Hoover set the stage for the promotion of world peace when he said: "Our foreign policy has one primary object, and that is peace. We have no hates; we wish no further possessions; we harbor no military threats." And in his inaugural he promised that the United States would take "a practical part in supporting all useful international undertakings. We not only desire peace with the world, but to see peace maintained throughout the world."

In working toward these goals, Quaker-raised Hoover made real progress. The extension of naval disarmament, the moratorium on war debt payments, and the more liberal Latin-American policy were all first-class achievements. Yet ironically the structure of world peace was torn down in other parts of the world much more rapidly than Hoover could build it up. Even while he was still in the White House, Japan began its course of aggression and Germany fell under the rule of Hitler. To deal with such challenges, neither the prevalent American isolationism nor Hoover's cautious internationalism was adequate.

Further Rejection of the League and the Court

President Hoover did not believe the League of Nations would promote the peace he desired. In his inaugural address he asserted:

Our people have determined that we should make no political engagements such as membership in the League of Nations, which may commit us in advance as a nation to become involved in the settlement of controversies between other countries. They adhere to the belief that the independence of America from such obligations increases its ability and availability for service in all fields of human progress.

On the other hand, he wished the United States to participate in certain League activities not of a political nature. For example, in that same address he strongly urged adherence to the World Court, which was "peculiarly identified with American ideals and American statesmanship." Then he concluded with the hope that "we may take our proper place in a movement so fundamental to the progress of peace."

This action was to be based upon the so-called Root formula, worked out by a League-sponsored committee of which Elihu Root was a leading member. Completed by the fall of 1929, it tried to solve the differences between the Senate and the League Council that had developed back in 1926. First of all, it provided that all requests for advisory opinions be submitted to the United States. Next, any American objections to such opinions might be discussed with the parties concerned. Finally, the United States might withdraw from the Court were other members to deny that it had a "vital" interest without endangering such interest.

Both the League members and the American State Department found this formula satisfactory, so in December, 1929, Secretary of State Stimson signed the protocols for American admission to the World Court with the Root reservations. In appealing to the Senate for speedy approval, Hoover had the apparent support of a majority of public opinion and 75 per cent of the press, but a determined group of Senators prevented the issue from coming to a vote. The obstructionists had fervent backing from the isolationist press, headed by the Hearst papers, which charged that the Court was nothing more than a League agency with a membership of "international robbers."

The Renewal of Naval Disarmament

Following the failure of the Geneva Conference of 1927, the so-called Butler Cruiser bill, introduced into Congress in November, 1927, provided for construction of 25 cruisers, 5 aircraft carriers, and other vessels at the cost of $725 million. It stipulated, however, that the building of these ships was subject to the provisions of the Washington Treaty and, if another conference were called, the President might suspend all or part of this program.

While Congress debated this measure, the British announced abandonment of two thirds of their proposed naval-building projects. To many Americans, especially the big-navy advocates, this step came too late. The United States should complete the Cruiser bill provisions within five years and follow a replacement program during the next twenty years. Senator Borah, however, led the attack on the bill, declaring it would lead to "immediate and inevitable war." He was supported by Quakers, the Federal Council of Churches, and many other groups. This opposition forced the Butler bill to be withdrawn in favor of a substitute that cut the program to 15 cruisers and 1 carrier at a cost of $274 million. The new Navy Cruiser bill passed the House in March, 1928, but the Senate, thanks to Borah's continued opposition, held it up until February, 1929. While this measure avoided a direct challenge to Britain, it did threaten a new naval race.

Such was the situation when Hoover became President. The problem was then further complicated by the fact that England and France were having their troubles over parity definitions, while the League was facing the difficult task of trying to arrange a general disarmament conference. True to his inaugural promise, Hoover opened negotiations for another meeting of the Washington Treaty signatories. First, Ambassador Dawes and Labor Prime Minister Ramsay MacDonald ironed out most of the differences that had developed between their two countries at Geneva. Then MacDonald visited President Hoover in early October to reach substantial agreement on many issues. And, finally, Britain's formal invitation to another disarmament meeting in London was quickly accepted by the other four signatories of the Washington Treaty.

The London Naval Conference opened on January 21, 1930, with high hopes of success because the Anglo-American preliminary discussions had developed an understanding that had been lacking at Geneva. Moreover, the admirals and other big-navy advocates were conspicuous by their absence. Despite the favorable auguries, the meeting did not start off smoothly. There was wrangling over unessential details, and France almost broke up the conference by seeking defensive military agreements with the others before she would consider continuing naval limitations.

Navalism. Japan tilts the scales in her own favor despite the 5-5-3 ratio. (By Bishop in the *St. Louis Star-Times*.)

Gradually, however, the three largest naval powers agreed to the London Naval Treaty of April 22, 1930, which provided first of all for foregoing the construction of capital ships allowed under the Washington Treaty and for having Britain scrap five capital ships, the United States three, and Japan one before the end of 1931. Thus the total capital-ship tonnage would be for Britain, 474,750 (15 ships); for the United States, 464,300 (15 ships); and for Japan, 272,070 (9 ships). Aircraft-carrier tonnage would be at approximately the same ratio. Next, Class A cruisers with 8-inch guns were limited to 10,000 tons each, with the United States allotted 18, Britain 15, and Japan 12. The number of Class B cruisers with 6-inch guns was not allotted, but the United States could have 143,500 tons, Britain, 192,200, and Japan, 100,450. The ratio for destroyers was 10:10:7, and each country was allowed 52,700 tons of submarines, whose maximum size was limited.

An unusual feature of the treaty was the "escape" or "escalator" clause that allowed any signatory to build above treaty limits if some other power, not bound by this London agreement, started a construction program that might threaten the safety of the signatory. The London Treaty was to be in force until the end of 1936, with another conference called for 1935 to discuss extending the arrangements beyond that date.

The London Treay had serious weaknesses. France and Italy refused to enter the pact, a threat to the whole agreement since either French or Italian construction might provoke countermeasures under the escape clause. American admirals and naval experts, moreover, warned that the limitations would prevent the American navy from satisfactorily defending the United States and its possessions.

On the other hand, the long-desired parity with Britain in all naval categories was at last achieved. Furthermore, if the signatories lived up to the agreement, the menace of a naval construction race was ended at least until 1936. Savings of at least $300 million were thereby assured to American taxpayers. Actually the United States did not build up to treaty strength and thus lost much of its naval superiority over Japan, which took full advantage of its quota.

The reception of the London Treaty in the United States was, on the whole, good. True, there was some complaint about the cost of bringing the navy up to parity, but that quickly disappeared. Navy men opposing the agreement were backed by the jingo press, which asserted that American envoys, headed by Secretary Stimson, had become dupes of Britain and Japan. Some newspapers even insisted that the United States had a secret entangling agreement with the other signatories.

When the treaty was submitted to the Senate in July, 1930, some members demanded that Hoover turn over to them all the London meeting documents, but he refused to do so because it was contrary to precedent and might impede future treaty making. Enough members were satisfied to approve the treaty on July 21 by a vote of 58 to 9. To make doubly sure there were no strings attached, the Senate then resolved that the nation was not bound by any secret commitment.

Hoover was not content to stop with the London Treaty. When the World Disarmament Conference, sponsored by the League of Nations, met in Geneva in 1932, the American delegation sought international approval for scrapping all offensive weapons. France, however, led the way in tabling it; she refused to reduce her military arm without adequate guarantees that she would not be attacked. Next, the nations present were asked to reduce their armaments 50 per cent. Despite widespread support, nothing came of this proposal. Even while this meeting was in session, world peace was threatened by hostilities between Japan and China on the other side of the world.

The Moratorium

The quest for improved international relations was complicated by events in the economic field that disrupted war debts and reparations settlements. By the summer of 1931, France feared that a proposed customs union between Germany and Austria might develop into a political and military alliance. To prevent it, France withdrew her credit from a large Austrian bank, already hard hit by the depression. When that bank failed, several financially associated German banks and insurance companies tottered on the brink of bankruptcy. In turn, foreign credit, particularly American, was quickly withdrawn from Germany to escape the threatened economic collapse, and American banks holding large amounts of German short-term notes were greatly alarmed.

Fearing an economic catastrophe greater than the 1929 stock-market crash, Hoover acted quickly to avert it. Congress was not in session, but the President gained the assent of twenty-one prominent Senators and eighteen Representatives on June 20, 1931, for "the postponement during one year of all payments on intergovernmental debts, reparations, and relief payments, both principal and interest." By July 6, the European nations concerned agreed, and about two weeks later, at the London Conference on Recovery from the Depression, the international bankers approved a similar moratorium on private international obligations. Then in December, 1931, Congress supported Hoover's moratorium with the stipulation that the suspended payment be paid over a ten-year period at 4 per cent interest.

There is little doubt that the moratorium eased the international situation. Moreover, for the first time the United States recognized a relationship between war debts and reparations, but there were still dangers ahead. Since German banks were still in dire straits, several foreign banks, including the Federal Reserve of New York, loaned approximately $100 million in short-term notes to the ailing institutions. While this action saved the German banks, it did not prevent the withdrawal of gold from one country to another. Nation after nation was forced off the gold standard, culminating in the September, 1931, British decision to cease redeeming her currency with that bullion. Thereafter it seemed that nothing could be done to avert international disaster. Each nation thought primarily of itself, tariff walls were raised higher to protect domestic conditions, and local currency was inflated to spur a return to prosperity.

While the moratorium was still in effect, Pierre Laval, the French premier, held a series of conferences with Hoover in October, 1931, at which they agreed that the question of intergovernmental debts must be reconsidered before the moratorium was over to alleviate the depression and save the gold standard. While there were no actual commitments, the two men pledged to do all they could to assist in a solution, but the initiative must be taken by Europe in connection with German reparations.

Now if he just doesn't try to bring his trunk along. (Copyright, 1931, by the *Chicago Tribune.*)

Acting on this proposal, Germany's creditors met with German envoys at Lausanne, Switzerland, in June, 1932. By early July they had agreed to wipe out more than 90 per cent of the original reparations demands, cutting down their claims to about $700 million, payable in 5 per cent German bonds. This Lausanne Agreement, however, had a string attached: the creditors would not ratify until their own obligations to the United States were scaled down.

Their appeal for war debt reduction reached the United States during the presidential contest of 1932, and the Democrats had already gone on record against cancellation of those debts. Moreover, neither party dared favor the European proposal because they feared that the voters, hard hit by the depression, considered the payments a means of alleviating their own economic distress. Likewise linked with the issue was the matter of reducing armaments. Since Europe showed no inclination to limit theirs, Americans were all the more unwilling to follow up the Lausanne proposition with parallel reductions.

When Britain asked for an opportunity to discuss a reduction of the December, 1932, payment, President Hoover and President-elect Roosevelt could not agree and nothing was done. Consequently, France and four other nations defaulted on their payments; Britain and the remaining debtors sent the full amounts of their semiannual obligations with the warning that this might be the last time they could do so unless new arrangements were made. None was, and thereafter the whole problem was left to the new administration.

As things worked out, Hoover's moratorium, originally intended merely to postpone war debt and reparations payments for one year, resulted in a permanent halt to all but a small trickle of installments. From the economic point of view, this was an excellent thing because reparations and war debts had hung like millstones around the neck of the postwar world. From the political point of view, however, the outcome was bad. The United States had not made the generous gesture in canceling the debts that might have earned her some gratitude in Europe. Instead, Europe had simply ceased to pay, thereby playing into the hands of American isolationists.

The New Pan-Americanism

The same spirit Hoover showed in trying to ease world tensions was evinced in his Latin-American policy. Shortly after his election, he visited many Latin-American countries, where he made contacts that proved important later. Indeed, while on this trip he was approached by leaders of Peru, Bolivia, and Chile about the Tacna-Arica controversy. Partly through the knowledge he acquired during his visit, he found the solution to that long-standing problem. Moreover, the journey aided in bettering relations with Latin America; its citizens appreciated the visit of such a prominent American.

During his presidency, Hoover did his best to remove the fears and suspicions Latin America held toward his country and thereby fostered an improved feeling of cooperation and friendship in the Western Hemisphere. True, he was aided by some incidents near the close of Coolidge's administration—the naming of Dwight Morrow as Ambassador to Mexico, the Clark Memorandum, and the Washington Conference on Conciliation and Arbitration, for example, but they would not have helped for long had Hoover not carried on and extended the policy of neighborliness.

The first official pronouncement of this desire came in Hoover's inaugural address:

I have lately returned from a journey among our sister Republics of the Western Hemisphere. I have received unbounded hospitality and courtesy as their expression of friendliness to our country. We are held by particular bonds of sympathy and common interest with them. . . . We wish only for maintenance of their independence, the growth of their stability, and their prosperity. . . . Fortunately the New World is largely free from the inheritance of fear and distrust which have so troubled the Old World. We should keep it so.

Yet it was difficult for Hoover to allay distrust completely because the depression hit some Latin republics hard and, to make matters worse, the Hawley-Smoot Tariff hurt Latin-American commerce. Largely as a result of economic troubles, half the republics witnessed the overturn of their governments. Several Latin-American states had to suspend interest payments on their foreign obligations in October, 1931. Hoover did not press for payment, however, nor threaten military intervention for forcible collection as had some of his predecessors under similar circumstances. Moreover, the new revolu tionary governments were almost immediately recognized by the United States.

Withdrawal from Haiti

It was Hoover's attitude toward countries in which the United States had previously intervened, and in some of which marines were still stationed, that proved the sincerity of his professions of good will. In Haiti, for example, President Louis Borno became increasingly unpopular as 1929 progressed because of popular belief he was subservient to American wishes. In December, a strike of students, supported by Haitian politicians, attacked the American marines near Port-au-Prince; in the ensuing struggle six Haitians were killed and some thirty wounded.

On hearing of this outbreak, Congress, on Hoover's appeal, established the so-called Forbes Commission in February, 1930, to conduct a thorough investigation of Haiti's problems, to learn how United States obligations could be fulfilled, and to suggest when American troops might be withdrawn. After a two-month study, this commission praised the work of American officials in the field of transportation, health, and sanitation, but concluded that little progress had been made in training the Haitians to govern themselves because the American policy had been based "upon the assumption that the occupation would continue indefinitely." The commissioners recommended that the 1915 treaty rights remain in force until 1936 except where mutual agreement might modify them, that the military high commissioner be replaced by a civilian, that the Haitians be trained to take over control of their civil administration and national guard, that the Haitian legislature elect a new president, and that the American marines be gradually withdrawn.

With congressional backing, Hoover quickly carried these recommendations into effect. The little-liked Borno was replaced by Provisional President Eugene Roy at the end of April, 1930, and in October the legislature elected Stenio Vincent as the regular executive. Meantime, High Commissioner General Russell was replaced by Dana Munro, a civilian authority on Latin-American affairs. Then, under an agreement of August, 1931, Americans were withdrawn from the various government departments. Differences over financial control, the national guard, and the marine withdrawal delayed final settlement until September, 1932, when a treaty provided for complete civil and military retirement from Haiti before the end of 1934, although the United States might keep a watchful eye on Haitian finances after that date. Some Haitian opposition delayed treaty acceptance until after Hoover left office, but President Roosevelt found a satisfactory solution and the last marines left Haiti on August 15, 1934.

Ending Military Intervention in Nicaragua

Shortly before Hoover entered office, Nicaraguan President Moncada agreed to substitute a national guard for the army, and the United States promised to withdraw its marines when that guard was ready to police the country. In April, 1931, however, the difficulty of the American position was increased when Augusto Sandino, the rebel leader, openly attacked the Moncada administration. All efforts of the national guard and the American marines failed to curb his raids on local communities and at least nine American civilians lost their lives. So serious was the problem that Secretary Stimson advised Americans living in the interior to retire to the coast because marines could not protect them. In answer to a critical Congress, Stimson explained that the marines were not equipped for jungle fighting, but promised that the American navy, standing off the coast, was ready to protect "the lives of our nationals wherever they may be found."

When Sandino's men killed five marines during a raid in April, 1932, there were new senatorial protests against risking American troops merely to defend a handful of American businessmen, and a resolution called for the immediate withdrawal of the marines. Since the American forces had already been reduced from almost 6,000 to less than 1,000, complete evacuation might have been ordered had not the United States previously promised to supervise the following fall election. Living up to this pledge, 500 marines guarded the polls on November 6, 1932, and prevented disorders that had been so characteristic in the past. Admiral Clark Woodward of the United States Navy headed the election board.

The victor was Liberal Juan Sacasa, who took office on January 2, 1933, despite Sandino's assertion he would not recognize the new president. Shortly after, the last American marines left Nicaragua, ending another venture in dollar diplomacy.

Mexican Problems

Emilio Portes Gil became provisional executive of Mexico in November, 1928, as a man not particularly well liked because he was considered a puppet of the powerful Plutarco Calles. Shortly after, a regular election was scheduled for November, 1929. Administration political opponents, feeling they had little chance in the ensuing campaign, appealed to the element dissatisfied with the government's antichurch attitude to participate in a revolution. The Catholic group agreed, and on March 3, 1929, the day before Hoover took office, the uprising began.

President Hoover promptly acted to support the Gil government by not only proclaiming an embargo on all exports of arms and ammunition to the rebels in line with the Arms Embargo Resolution of 1922, but also allowing the Mexican government to buy military supplies in the United States. Furthermore, the State Department refused to consider the rebels as belligerents or to receive any of their representatives. Thanks in part to this position, Gil was able to crush the uprising by early May, 1929.

Hoover likewise helped to improve relations by naming the able J. Reuben Clark to succeed Dwight Morrow as American ambassador. Clark continued the friendship policy Morrow had instituted. Moreover, the United States immediately recognized Ortiz Rubio, victor in the presidential election of November, 1929. The new executive showed his gratitude by visiting the United States, where he was well received.

Just before Hoover left office, another action was taken to strengthen the accord between the two neighbors. On February 1, 1933, a treaty settled some of the differences over control of the Rio Grande in the El Paso region, which, it was hoped, would end the danger of floods.

Nonintervention in Cuba

The situation in Cuba was difficult during the Hoover administration. Because President Gerardo Machado had become a virtual dictator, popular unrest grew, much aggravated by falling sugar prices during the depression. Unfortunately, Hoover appointed as envoy Harry Guggenheim, an inexperienced diplomat, who did his best to keep Machado in office by aiding him financially and otherwise.

As the unrest mounted, it became evident that civil war might break out at any time. Consequently, some Senators urged American intervention near the close of 1930, but Stimson refused, asserting that only actual chaos warranted such a step. Until that chaos developed, the United States would merely maintain "close watch" of the situation. In the summer of 1931 an abortive revolt did take place, but Hoover would not use the Platt Amendment as an excuse for re-establishing military control. Instead, a "hands-off" policy was followed, with no attempt made to establish an arms embargo.

Many Cubans criticized Hoover's stand. Although pleased there was no intervention, they felt the United States was trying to maintain the dictatorial Machado in office. At the same time a demand arose in both countries to abrogate the Platt Amendment.

For Latin America generally, Hoover recognized *de facto* presidents without ascertaining how they obtained office. While no regular Pan-American conferences were held, he helped the cause by proclaiming in 1930 that thereafter April 14 would be celebrated as Pan-American Day.

Hoover tried to alleviate conditions in Puerto Rico as a result of his visit there where he saw at first hand its great poverty. On his return home, he obtained increased congressional appropriations for the improvement of conditions on that island. Theodore Roosevelt, Jr., new governor general of Puerto Rico, showed great energy and vigor in trying to end the sickness, hunger, and economic hardships prevalent throughout the island. The Puerto Ricans appreciated this assistance, so there were few political controversies during the Hoover regime.

The Movement Toward Philippine Independence

The question of Philippine independence arose once again during Hoover's term. This time, however, the impetus came largely from the United States, with the depression, rather than altruism, playing a large part in the revival of the issue. American farmers, their income falling rapidly, did not like the competition from Filipino cottonseed oil, sugar, dairy products, and cordage, which were allowed to enter duty free, and American workers did not care to see their jobs taken by cheap Filipino labor. Moreover, the threat of Japanese aggression in the Far East caused many Americans to believe the Philippines could not be protected without vast expenditures the American taxpayers were not eager to pay.

This combination of farmers, workers, and anti-imperialists exerted sufficient pressure on Congress to pass the Hawes-Cutting bill on January 12, 1933, despite the objections of another bloc, consisting of American investors in Filipino resources, big-navy advocates who saw in the retention of the islands an opportunity to press their cause, and supporters of imperialism.

The Hawes-Cutting bill provided that a specially convened Philippine convention frame a constitution, which was to be submitted to the Filipino voters for approval, along with the question of whether independence was desired. Were approval obtained, the Philippines would then begin a ten-year intermediate, or probationary, period, during which the governor generalship was to be abolished and American civil control ended except for the supervisory powers exercised by a new American official, the high commissioner. Throughout the probationary period, however, the United States President was to be allowed some regulation of Philippine legislation, the Supreme Court could review legal cases, and the islands' foreign problems would be supervised by the United States. The right to send commodities to the United States duty free was to be gradually reduced and competitive commodities placed under a quota system. Immigration to America would practically end.

At the conclusion of the ten-year probation, complete independence would automatically begin. Then all free trade with the United States would stop, unless some commercial arrangement effected reciprocity. The United States could maintain military establishments and naval bases in the islands and would try to neutralize the Philippines by international agreement.

President Hoover, in a long veto message on January 13, 1933, criticized the bill because of its economic provisions, which he believed would lead to "a degenerating economic and social life, with all its governmental difficulties." He also asserted that during probation American civil control would be weakened "to a point of practical impotence." Nor did he think the Philippines were prepared to preserve internal order or external defense.

The opposition was strong enough to pass the Hawes-Cutting bill over the executive veto. When the plan was presented to the Philippine legislature, however, it was rejected, primarily because of the restrictions on immigration and the failure to continue free trade. Therefore, although Hoover favored Philippine independence, Congress's failure to follow his suggestions delayed that independence until the next administration.

Far Eastern Troubles

Hoover's quest for international cooperation and peace received a rude jolt in the Orient. Throughout the 1920's revolutionary ferment and civil war in China resulted in incidents that threatened to bring outside intervention reminiscent of Boxer Rebellion days. For example, there were riots in Shanghai and Canton in 1925 that endangered foreign property. Two years later Chinese mobs attacked the British concession in Hankow, and later that year Chinese Nationalist, or Kuomintang, troops looted the foreign holdings in Nanking, with resulting loss of life to foreigners, including Americans. The United States joined other powers in demanding punishment for the guilty, but unsatisfactory replies were received. Then some nations, notably France, Britain, and Italy, urged economic sanctions against China until they received complete restitution. When the United States refused to cooperate, however, the proposal was dropped.

Coolidge and Secretary Kellogg undoubtedly realized that Chinese domestic unrest would continue until a single leader had won out in the civil war and that no settlement could be effected until that time. The administration's general policy was to cooperate with Chiang Kai-shek, head of the Nationalist element, to hasten the return to peace. For instance, in July, 1927, in a treaty with Chiang, the United States recognized China's complete control of her tariff. Yet Coolidge was ready to protect American lives and property in China, as shown by the constant presence of American gunboats in Chinese waters.

By the time Hoover was elected, Chiang had defeated most of his domestic foes except the Communists, and his government had been recognized by most of the great powers, including the United States. To show his good faith and desire for peace, Chiang signed the Paris Pact in August, 1928. Yet these incidents did not settle all the problems, particularly the Russo-Chinese controversy over North Manchuria, from which Russia refused to withdraw its dominant influence.

The Sino-Russian Controversy

In the spring and summer of 1929 a series of incidents widened the breach between the two countries. The Chinese, aided by the Manchurians, raided Russian consulates in several Manchurian cities, arresting the consuls and Communists for breaking a 1924 treaty by spreading anti-Chinese propaganda. Then followed the seizure of the communications systems of the Chinese Eastern Railways, hitherto under joint management, the substitution of Chinese for Russian officials, and the deportation of Russian employees.

In an ultimatum to Chiang, Russia demanded a prompt conference to settle the problem, insisting that a solution could not be reached until China revoked her action and restored Russian control over the railway. When Chiang's answer was unsatisfactory, Russia severed relations in July, 1929. There was an immediate troop mobilization along the border and it appeared war would soon break out.

The Paris Pact, which both nations had signed, left the responsibility of maintaining peace to each signatory; there was no machinery for conciliation and mediation. Stimson, however, insisted the Pact "necessarily carries with it the implication of consultation" and urged both parties to settle their troubles by peaceful means, and he was backed by the major European powers. When both potential contestants then claimed they would not fight except in self-defense, it appeared Stimson had won a victory for peace under the Pact.

The ensuing Sino-Soviet conference broke down, however, over the future of Manchuria, and neither party would accept outside mediation. Consequently, fighting broke out, the Manchurian provincial forces were defeated, and Chiang had to recognize Russian rights in North Manchuria.

Meantime, Stimson was hard at work trying to effect mediation. Though Germany and Japan refused to apply pressure, Britain, France, and Italy agreed to cooperate with the United States. The four nations sent identical notes to the two disputants on December 2, stressing the importance of abiding by the terms of the Paris Pact. In reply, China refused to admit it had broken the Pact and insisted it was ready to mediate. Russia placed the blame for the failure of negotiations squarely at the doors of China and the United States; China was blamed for not being conciliatory, the United States for meddling after the joint conference was under way. Moreover, Russia contended, the issue could not be settled by a third party, particularly if it was the United States, "which by its own will has no official relations with the Soviet."

Thus the energetic efforts of Stimson to resolve this Manchurian problem ended in failure. The first test of the Paris Pact had shown its weaknesses— the absence of any machinery to force a settlement of international disputes. Moreover, external interference, especially by the United States, helped to cause Russia to insist, even by force, upon regaining her former rights in North Manchuria and obtaining additional privileges.

The Menace of Japan

Soon after the American failure, another problem arose that indicated still more clearly the weakness of both the Paris Pact and the League of Nations. Beneath the surface, Japanese-American relations had not been satisfactory for many years. Japan blamed the United States for its failure to obtain all the Twenty-One Demands from China in 1915, for the retreat from Shantung after the war, and for its inferior naval position in the Washington Treaty, while the breaking of the Gentlemen's Agreement in the Johnson-Lodge Immigration Act of 1924 did not help the situation. On the other hand, the Japanese desire to dominate the Far East was clearly shown in 1923, when Baron Ishii asserted: "Japan's special interests in China continue to live in all their vigor." He insisted that they did not result from "benefits conferred upon Japan by the United States," but from "realities deriving from nature and geography."

Although maintaining a facade of parliamentary institutions, Japan was by no means a democracy. The government was dominated by old aristocratic families, army and navy officers, and industrial and commercial groups, particularly the Mitsui and Mitsubishi families. These dominant elements wished to extend Japanese power and influence, although differing considerably on methods. The moderates, found especially among big businessmen, thought in terms of economic penetration. By a "friendship policy" toward China, a subtle mixture of diplomatic pressure oiled by judicious bribery, they hoped to win an increasing share in the trade and investing opportunities of the undeveloped country, while avoiding serious trouble with the Western powers through a reasonable degree of collaboration with the League of Nations and the various international conferences. These moderates maintained an uneasy ascendancy through most of the twenties but were increasingly threatened by the militaristic factions who were impatient with these tactics. The extremists wanted to extend Japanese political control to dominate the more valuable parts of China and to expel the hated Occidentals from the western Pacific. China's progress toward unification and modernization late in the twenties was not at all to their liking.

The moderates' position was greatly weakened after 1929. The Great Depression accentuated Japan's economic problems, already serious because seventy million people were trying to make a living in a small and essentially poor country. The extremists considered this final proof of the need for Japanese expansion, and their discontent was increased when Britain and the United States refused Japan naval parity at the London Conference of 1930. The temptation to embark on an aggressive program was great because of the obvious demoralization of the Occident, where monetary chaos, governmental deficits, debt and armament controversies, and general loss of nerve made it unlikely that the Western powers could take any preventive step. As for the United States and its Open Door policy, Japanese realists thought it had been based on bluff from the beginning.

The showdown came in Manchuria—long a trouble spot. Since the war with Russia, Japan had had extensive treaty rights in the southern part of that province, particularly in the South Manchuria Railroad zone. For some time there had been a quiet struggle for power there between the Japanese and Chinese. The incident that gave the Japanese army its excuse for drastic action was the alleged blowing up of a section of track along the main line of the South Manchuria Railroad near the important center of Mukden on September 18, 1931. Despite China's denial of the deed, Japanese troops guarding the line quickly attacked the small Chinese force in the vicinity, and just as promptly the Japanese army in Manchuria seized Mukden and several other strategic places. Although Japan insisted her troops were acting in self-defense, many observers considered this was the beginning of a well-laid plan to conquer all of Manchuria.

Three days later China appealed both to the League and to the United States to effect a settlement. Secretary Stimson immediately announced he was trying to learn whether the Mukden incident contravened the Paris Pact and the Nine-Power Treaty, and he notified the League's Secretary General that America would cooperate with the League in trying to end the strife. He refused to believe that the attacks had been made without Tokyo's knowledge.

For the next few days Stimson took no further action, hoping the contestants might reach a satisfactory settlement, but on September 25 he urged them not to extend the conflict. Neither the League nor the American request for a peaceful solution succeeded and fighting broke out anew in early October. Consequently, on October 5, Stimson began an independent investigation to uphold the Pact and the Treaty, as well as cooperating with the League "to reinforce what the League does." For the latter purpose, the American consul at Geneva, Prentiss Gilbert, sat in on the League meetings—an arrangement supported by most of the American press, a far cry from its position of the previous decade.

Despite Sino-Japanese charges and countercharges, the United States concluded on October 8 that Japan was the aggressor. On that date Japanese planes bombed the unfortified city of Chinchow, bringing death to many civilians. Stimson promptly sent the following note to the Japanese Foreign Office:

> The Secretary of State cannot understand how the bombing of Chinchow can be minimized. . . . Chinchow is more than 50 miles from the Japanese railway zone and is situated in territory where the Chinese have an entire right to maintain troops. . . . Bombing of an unfortified and unwarned town is one of the most extreme military actions, deprecated even in time of war. . . .

Japan paid no attention to this note nor did she heed the League warning that she was breaking the Paris Pact. Moreover, it was her negative vote that prevented the League Council from calling for the withdrawal of Japanese troops from the Manchurian region outside of the railway zone before November 15 and for the immediate beginning of direct negotiations between China and Japan.

Since Gilbert's attendance at League sessions was not accomplishing much, the United States returned to its policy of independent cooperation. Ambassador Dawes was ordered to be in Paris during the Council meetings for purposes of consultation, and on December 10, 1931, the League set up a commission, headed by Lord Lytton of Britain, to make an on-the-scene study of the Sino-Japanese conflict and report its findings to the Council. General Frank McCoy was the American member.

At the same time, Hoover, in his annual message to Congress, declared the United States was committed to maintaining China's territorial integrity. This objective could best be accomplished by cooperating fully with the League, for "unity of effort to maintain peace" would thus be achieved. Such cooperation, he insisted, would not lead to American membership in the League because "in all the negotiations the Department of State has maintained complete freedom of judgment and action as to participation in any measure which might finally be determined upon."

The threat of League action, even with American cooperation, did not deter Japan from her objective. By early 1932, all South Manchuria was in her hands. The United States refused to recognize this conquest, and on January 7 Stimson notified the signatories of the Nine-Power Treaty that his country

> can not admit the legality of any situation *de facto* nor does it intend to recognize any treaty or agreement entered into . . . which may impair the treaty rights of the United States or its citizens in China, including those which relate to the sovereignty, the independence, or the territorial and administrative integrity of the Republic of China, commonly known as the open-door treaty; and that it does not intend to recognize . . . any situation . . . brought about by means contrary . . . to . . . the pact of Paris. . . .

This became known as the Stimson Doctrine, even though the policy of nonrecognition did not originate with him. Yet Stimson tried to make it international in scope by basing it in part on the Paris Pact, which so many nations had signed.

At home the doctrine was received with mixed feelings. Some believed it worthless because no real force backed it up. Another faction feared it would lead to trouble for the United States. To others, however, it was the natural sequel to the Paris Pact, through which an aggressor might be deterred from waging war.

Stimson believed his announcement would be well received in Europe, but he was in for a rude shock when British spokesmen expressed confidence in Japan's promise to respect the Open Door. As a result of British complacency, the Stimson Doctrine was weakened when Japan realized her opposition, was divided. Moreover, she concluded that the United States, torn by partisan strife and hard hit by the depression, was not in a position to force her to back down. While it is true most Americans thought China mistreated, this opinion did not extend beyond expressions of sympathy. Nor was the State Department ready to make an issue of the Doctrine.

Encouraged by the lack of Western cooperation, Japan broadened her aggression. In late January, 1932, she bombed Shanghai, killing thousands of civilians. Only then did American opinion really express itself against Japanese actions. Stimson likened the feeling to that in 1914 when Germany invaded Belgium. Even Britain was alarmed because Japan was striking closer to British spheres of influence.

When Stimson requested British collaboration in a stern and forceful note to Japan, stressing simply the breaking of the Nine-Power Treaty, the reply was noncommittal. This may have been because Britain still had faith in the Lytton Commission or because of a desire to appease Japan and thereby save Hong Kong and British interests generally in central China.

Realizing that American unilateral action would not bring results, Stimson decided to express the American position in an open letter to Senator Borah, chairman of the Foreign Relations Committee. This letter would be widely published, would probably be read by the governments concerned, and, Stimson hoped, might stir up public opinion in many parts of the world in support of the American stand. Since it was a letter to an American rather than an official note to Japan, failure would not be so injurious to American prestige.

On February 23, 1932, this long message to Borah was released. After tracing the history of Far Eastern relations from the Open Door through the recent attack on Shanghai, Stimson stressed the importance of upholding the Nine-Power Treaty and the Paris Pact. Then he continued:

We see no reason for abandoning the enlightened principles which are embodied in these treaties. We believe that this situation would have been avoided had these covenants been faithfully observed, and no evidence has come to us to indicate that a due compliance with them would have interfered with the adequate protection of the legitimate rights in China of the signatories of those treaties. . . . If a similar decision should be reached and a similar position taken by the other governments of the world, a caveat will be placed upon such action which . . .

will effectively bar the legality hereafter of any title or right sought to be obtained by pressure or treaty violation.

The American press generally praised the policy expressed in this letter, and on March 11, 1932, the League Assembly unanimously approved a resolution similar to the Stimson Doctrine. Many believe the letter partly influenced Japan to effect a compromise with China, under which Japanese troops withdrew from Shanghai by the end of May, 1932.

Japan still controlled Manchuria, although she attempted to forestall criticism by establishing a government that declared itself independent. Early in March, 1932, this "independent" state adopted the name of "Manchukuo" and selected Henry Pu-yi, deposed emperor of China, as regent. All the other powers, including the United States, refused to recognize the new state, knowing that Japan was responsible for the "independence" movement and that Pu-yi was only a Japanese puppet.

The next six months saw Japan trying to defend her actions and the other powers refusing to change their positions. On September 15, 1932, Japan made a more definite break by recognizing Manchukuo and making an alliance with it. Then on October 1 the long-awaited Lytton Report was published. After condemning Japan's defiance of existing commitments, the Report refused to accept Manchukuo as a sovereign state. Manchuria should be returned to China, but certain Russian and Japanese rights should be recognized. The League Assembly approved these findings, and the United States was in substantial agreement. Japan, however, defied the League by maintaining her dominant control over Manchuria.

During the whole controversy, the United States consistently upheld the Paris Pact and the Nine-Power Treaty and was ready to cooperate with the League or with other powers generally. When collaboration failed, she was ready to play a lone hand in supporting the Stimson Doctrine of nonrecognition. Whether the American public would have supported the administration had force been attempted is problematical; in all probability it would have not. The whole affair proved that the Kellogg-Briand Pact was powerless as a medium of peace, and the League was not much better.

Throughout the Hoover regime, the United States showed a greater degree of international cooperation than previously, as indicated by the support of the London Naval Conference, the moratorium on debts, improved relations with Latin America, and efforts to settle Far Eastern problems. Nevertheless, the United States refused membership in the League and even failed to join the World Court. The machinery of international cooperation was far too frail to deal with the rude forces rising in Japan, Germany, Italy, and Russia.

16

NEW DEAL TRIUMPHANT

Politics during the thirties revolved in a strikingly different orbit from those of the twenties. Old issues, seemingly dead during the complacent years of prosperity, suddenly came to life again, while a multitude of new demands came to the fore. Out of this conflict of forces came the New Deal—a simple name to describe a complex thing, composed of emergency measures, fundamental reforms, practical politics, and idealistic experiments. So heated was the partisanship evoked by the New Deal that balanced judgments were rare; it was either praised as wholly good or damned as entirely bad. Fully as controversial as the measures themselves was their sponsor, Franklin D. Roosevelt, the only man to be elected four times to the presidency of the United States.

The Emergence of Franklin Roosevelt

Franklin Delano Roosevelt, born in 1882 at Hyde Park, New York, was descended from the same seventeenth-century Dutch ancestor, Nicholas Roosevelt, from whom Theodore Roosevelt also traced descent. James Roosevelt, his father, was a wealthy landowner and businessman; Sara Delano, his mother, belonged to a still wealthier family. Instructed by private tutors until the age of fourteen, young Franklin then attended the exclusive Groton School and received his collegiate training at Harvard. He subsequently studied law at Columbia University Law School and, after being admitted to the bar, was employed by a Wall Street legal firm.

Yet the legal profession had small appeal for him. He spent much time at the Hyde Park family home and, when an opportunity arose to enter local politics, he eagerly took it. The assignment was not a promising one—to run as a Democrat for the state senate in a district in which no Democrat was supposed to have a chance for election—but Roosevelt threw himself wholeheartedly into the contest. His vigorous campaigning and the strongly anti-Republican trend of 1910 combined to win for him his first public office. Soon after going to Albany, he earned a reputation for progressivism by leading an insurgent revolt against Charles Murphy, the Tammany boss.

Because he had energetically campaigned for Wilson in 1912 and because of the magic of the Roosevelt name, the young politician moved to Washington in 1913 as Assistant Secretary of the Navy, a position once held by his cousin Theodore. He performed his duties in competent fashion, made important friends, and, what was most valuable, received an invaluable education in national politics. In 1920, he was nominated for the vice-presidency, an honor that many shrewd politicians would have declined because of almost certain Democratic defeat, but Roosevelt accepted it as an opportunity to make himself better known throughout the country. He made a long campaign tour during which thousands of people saw for the first time a handsome young man with a fascinating smile and an attractive voice. Despite the party's humiliating defeat, many predicted a brilliant future for this candidate.

The next year, however, Roosevelt was stricken with infantile paralysis. For months he was a helpless invalid, and it was generally assumed his political career was ended. Yet the disaster was not without its compensation. Although he was never again strong enough to walk without support, his struggle with invalidism demonstrated the courage that was to be his most valuable asset in days of crisis. Rest and exercise at Warm Springs, Georgia, restored Roosevelt's health and in 1928, at the urging of Al Smith, he ran for governor of New York. Gaining election in the year of a Republican landslide, Roosevelt quickly returned to the center of the political stage. When he was re-elected in 1930 by a margin greater than any previously won by the popular Smith, Governor Roosevelt became a leading contender for the presidency.

Long before the Democratic convention of 1932, an astute campaign to nominate the New York governor was in progress. James Farley traveled throughout the country, making friends and lining up delegates; Louis Howe, Roosevelt's secretary and shrewd political adviser, was coaching his protégé in practical politics; and a group of college professors—presently to be known as the Brain Trust—was assembling data on government and economics Roosevelt was eager to have. The governor himself was the movement's best asset. In an April, 1932, speech, he put his finger on what many felt was the fundamental fallacy of Hoover's policies when he called for plans "that build from the bottom up and not from the top down, that put their faith once more in the forgotten man at the bottom of the economic pyramid." Even more did he identify himself with the mood of the hour in a speech a month later when he said: "The country needs and, unless I mistake its temper, the country demands bold, persistent experimentation. It is common sense to take a method and try it. If it fails, admit it frankly and try another. But above all, try something."

The Election of 1932

On June 14, 1932, when the Republican National Convention opened at Chicago, there was no question of Hoover's renomination—he was still titular head and, in face of probable defeat, no one seriously challenged him. So, on the first ballot, he was renamed with only light and scattered opposition. The platform was largely devoted to praise of the Hoover record. Not only was the Hawley-Smoot Tariff upheld, but a pledge was made to extend the protectionist principle. The Federal Farm Board was defended and, in a sharp fight over the prohibition issue, the majority report favored a vague formula under which the voters were to pass upon a proposed amendment "which, while retaining in the Federal Government power to preserve the gains already made in dealing with the evils inherent in the liquor traffic, shall allow States to deal with the problem as their citizens may determine"; this so-called wet-dry plank was carried by a vote of 690 to 460 against the minority report favoring repeal of the Eighteenth Amendment.

The Democratic Convention, also meeting in Chicago, approved a platform in refreshing contrast to most such documents. It was both brief and clear—embarrassingly clear in the case of some commitments that later failed to be carried out. It called for repeal of the Eighteenth Amendment, a 25 per cent reduction in government expenses, a balanced budget, an enlarged program of public works and unemployment relief, state unemployment and old-age pension laws, banking reform, control of farm crop surpluses, reciprocal trade agreements, and Philippine independence.

Roosevelt had the support of more than half the delegates, but the two-thirds rule was still in effect. His most formidable opponent was Alfred E. Smith, eager for vindication after his 1928 defeat and strongly backed by a faction of wealthy conservatives, headed by John Raskob, the party chairman. A third figure with strong support was Speaker of the House John Nance Garner of Texas. The anti-Roosevelt forces hoped to block the New York governor's nomination and obtain the prize for some compromise candidate. But after Roosevelt's vote climbed from 666 to 682 on the first three ballots, Garner withdrew to prevent any such disastrous deadlock as that of 1924. The Texas and California delegations then swung to Roosevelt and the resulting band wagon brought the New York governor the coveted nomination on the fourth ballot. Garner's reward was unanimous nomination for the vice-presidency.

Roosevelt demonstrated his impatience with meaningless tradition by flying at once to Chicago to accept his nomination instead of waiting for the customary notification ceremony. He brought the tired delegates to a high state of enthusiasm with an aggressive speech concluding with these words: "I pledge you, I pledge myself, to a new deal for the American people. . . . Give me your help, not to win votes alone, but to win in this crusade to restore America to its own people."

By this bold gesture Roosevelt captured the attention of the electorate, and he never lost it during the long campaign. His speeches made the most of the weaknesses in the Republican record, while offering only the outlines of an alternative policy. They were progressive enough on the issues of farm relief and public utilities to win the support of Republicans like Senators Norris, Hiram Johnson, and Bronson Cutting of New Mexico, as well as Progressive LaFollette, son of "Fighting Bob" of earlier days. At the same time, however, Roosevelt's promise to balance the budget and his cautiousness on the tariff held in line the conservatives of his own party. Throughout the contest he demonstrated a mastery of the difficult art of maintaining the backing of widely divergent elements.

Late in the campaign Hoover became aware of the precarious position of the Republicans. He abandoned his own front-porch tactics and made an extensive tour, climaxing his efforts with a fighting speech in New York

Harry Hopkins and daughter Diane, President Roosevelt, Secretary of State Hull, and Secretary of the Treasury Morgenthau. (Acme.)

City. Were the Democratic tariff proposals to be adopted, he asserted, grass would grow in the streets of a hundred cities. The Democratic promise to put the unemployed to work he characterized as "cruel" because it was "absolutely impossible of realization." He defined the issue of the campaign as to whether or not the "American system" was to be maintained.

The election gave convincing evidence of the revolution in American opinion. Hoover, who had carried forty states in 1928, now took but six: Connecticut, Delaware, Maine, New Hampshire, Pennsylvania, and Vermont. The electoral vote was Roosevelt, 472; Hoover, 59; the popular vote was Roosevelt, 22,829,501; Hoover, 15,760,684. The congressional elections were equally decisive: the Democrats won 59 Senate seats to 36 for the Republicans and 1 for the Farmer-Laborites; in the House the division was 313 Democrats, 117 Republicans, and 5 independents. Political observers commented that these results were not so much a Democratic victory as they were a Republican defeat. So dissatisfied were the voters that they cast their ballots for Roosevelt to turn the Republicans out, believing a change could not be for the worse and might conceivably be for the better.

The Lame Ducks

During the twenties Senator Norris had campaigned for a constitutional amendment to inaugurate the President in January rather than in March and to eliminate lame-duck sessions of the old Congress. Despite the fact that the Senate passed the proposal five times between 1923 and 1931, it failed to obtain House approval largely because of the opposition of Speaker Nicholas Longworth and the Republican Old Guard. After Garner became Speaker, however, the amendment passed both chambers and was submitted to the states in March, 1932, and the Twentieth, or "Lame-Duck," Amendment was declared in effect on February 6, 1933.

Unfortunately the reform came too late to prevent the most glaring illustration of the evils of the old system. For four months after a decisive vote of no confidence had been registered, the Hoover administration continued in office, and for three of those months a lame-duck Congress was in session. It is little wonder that the resulting confusion and uncertainty plunged the nation into the most critical phase of the whole depression.

Congress and the President could not agree on measures for balancing the budget nor on banking reform. Among the few legislative acts of a positive character was the approval of the Twenty-first Amendment, providing for repeal of the Eighteenth Amendment, but prohibiting the transportation or importation of intoxicating liquors into any state in violation of the laws thereof. The amendment was unique in stipulating that it must be ratified by special state conventions.

Within a week after the election, Hoover felt the embarrassment of his position. A world disarmament conference was intermittently in progress, a world economic meeting was in prospect, and the war debts question was pressing for settlement. On November 22, 1932, Hoover and Secretary of the Treasury Ogden Mills conferred on these problems with Roosevelt and his adviser, Professor Raymond Moley of Columbia University. Neither at this meeting nor in subsequent correspondence did Hoover and Roosevelt achieve a good understanding. Hoover felt he could not initiate new policies without a pledge from the President-elect not to repudiate them after March 4; but Roosevelt replied: "I think you will realize that it would be unwise for me to accept an apparent joint responsibility with you when, as a matter of constitutional fact, I would be wholly lacking in any attendant authority." Both men were right; the difficulty lay not with them, but with the constitutional provision that required so long an interregnum. This did not mean, however, that there was no cooperation at all between the outgoing and incoming administrations. On the contrary, there was agreement on many points, and Hoover was assured there would be no major reorientation of American foreign policy.

Banking Chaos

Problems of foreign relations were as nothing compared with the crucial domestic issues that arose during the last month of Hoover's term. Depositors who had lost confidence in banks withdrew their savings; many who trusted banks did not trust the incoming administration and the result was the same—they hoarded their money. This situation threatened disaster for the whole country. The Federal reserve banks were under great strain as they had to put constantly larger amounts of currency into circulation while their gold stocks were seriously depleted. Gold was not only being hoarded at home, but was being exported in large volume.

Fear grew that sound institutions would be pulled under along with unsound ones. Some state governments resorted to temporary bank holidays —periods during which all transactions between banks and the public were halted to ease the situation. During 1932 there were several such local holidays in the Middle West, but they did not alarm the general public until early 1933. On February 4, the governor of Louisiana had to declare a weekend bank holiday for New Orleans; ten days later the Michigan governor announced an eight-day state-wide holiday to save the Detroit banks—a crisis that had a serious effect in other states.

To Hoover the crisis reflected only the nation's alarm over what the new administration would do. On February 17, he asked Roosevelt to assure the country "that there will be no tampering or inflation of the currency; that the budget will be unquestionably balanced, even if further taxation is necessary; that the Government credit will be maintained by refusal to exhaust it in the issue of securities." This request was an astonishing one, whose implication Hoover fully realized, for he wrote to Senator David Reed of Pennsylvania: "I realize that if these declarations be made by the President-elect, he will have ratified the whole major program of the Republicans; that is, it means the abandonment of 90 per cent of the so-called new deal." Although Roosevelt refused to allow his hands to be thus tied, he did use the occasion to announce the appointment of Senator Cordell Hull of Tennessee as Secretary of State and of William Woodin, president of the American Car and Foundry Company, as Secretary of the Treasury, neither of whom could be portrayed as radicals. Several weeks before the inaugural, Woodin and a number of Democratic experts were in earnest conference with Secretary Mills and other Treasury officials over the banking crisis.

Meantime the situation went from bad to worse. By March 3 more than twenty states had placed restrictions on bank withdrawals. That evening officials of the old and new administrations agreed that the banking holiday must be made general and together they pressured Governor Herbert Lehman of New York and other state executives to proclaim temporary holidays. By noon of inauguration day scarcely a bank in the country was engaged in normal operations.

The New President

Throughout the morning of March 4, 1933, news of the crisis spread across the nation, and those who crowded around radios at noon to listen to Roosevelt's inaugural were bewildered and somber. What they heard was tonic not only in phraseology, but in the calm, courageous manner of its delivery:

This great Nation will endure as it has endured, will revive and will prosper. So, first of all, let me assert my belief that the only thing we have to fear is fear itself—nameless, unreasoning, unjustified terror which paralyzes needed efforts to convert retreat into advance.

Roosevelt announced that Congress would meet at once in special session. If it failed to act on necessary measures, he would ask "for the one remaining instrument to meet the crisis—broad Executive power to wage a war against the emergency, as great as the power that would be given me if we were in fact invaded by a foreign foe."

Roosevelt appointed his cabinet with the usual geographical and political considerations in mind. Besides Hull and Woodin, prominent members were Henry A. Wallace of Iowa and Harold Ickes of Illinois, two converted Republicans who became, respectively, Secretary of Agriculture and Secretary of the Interior. Frances Perkins of New York, the first woman cabinet member, headed the Labor Department. The new President showed a lively interest in the ideas presented by college professors and young lawyers—many of the latter being recommended by Professor Felix Frankfurter of Harvard Law School. The resulting Brain Trust gained a horrendous reputation among businessmen and old line politicians for radicalism, but in reality Moley, the most powerful of FDR's advisers in 1933, was conservative on most issues and the others were less radical than they were generally painted.

On March 5 the President called Congress into special session. Meantime, in a sweeping executive proclamation, he ordered a national bank holiday, with all banking transactions suspended except those permitted by the Secretary of the Treasury. By the time Congress convened on March 9, an Emergency Banking bill had been drafted by a team of the old and new administrations; it was passed almost unanimously by both houses and signed by the President the same day. It not only confirmed all the steps already taken, but gave the President further emergency powers to control foreign exchange, gold and currency movements, and banking in general.

Throughout the week the Treasury Department worked day and night on the banking problem. With cooperation from Federal reserve banks, the financial condition of all the nation's institutions was reviewed to determine as quickly as possible which ones might be allowed to reopen and which must remain closed while their affairs were set in order. Finally, on March 13, the sound banks located in the twelve Federal reserve bank cities were permitted to open, and the next day those situated in some 250 cities where there were recognized clearinghouse associations were also given the green light. Those elsewhere were to be licensed as rapidly as their financial condition could be determined.

After all possible safeguards had been provided, there still remained a grave psychological obstacle to be surmounted. Would the public have confidence in the reopened banks? Or would bank runs and hoarding bring on a new crisis? It was at this point that Roosevelt made his own most important contribution. On Sunday evening, March 12, he delivered the first of his so-called fireside chats—an informal radio talk addressed to the common man. Simply and clearly he explained the measures that had been taken and promised his listeners that they could trust the institutions to be opened during the week. "I can assure you," he said, "that it is safer to keep your money in a reopened bank than under the mattress."

The reopening proved successful. Within three days about 76 per cent of the Federal Reserve member banks were doing business again. Since nonmembers had to be licensed by state banking authorities, this process took longer, but 72 per cent of them had reopened by April 12. More than 4,000 banks failed to obtain licenses during these early weeks; many of these reorganized and opened later, sometimes with no loss to their depositors. Hundreds were so hopelessly insolvent that they had to be liquidated, but even here the depositors' losses were rarely 100 per cent. Yet more than 1,700 banks failed, with losses to their customers of over $1 billion. As gratifying as the successful reopening of so many banks was the renewed public confidence. Hoarding ceased, paper currency and gold flowed back to the banks, and deposits by mid-April increased over $1 billion.

First aid had been successfully administered to the banking system, but as yet the abuses leading to the crisis remained uncorrected. It was a problem to which the administration returned at a later date.

The executive orders under which the banks had been closed and reopened contained several important restrictions. No gold, gold bullion, or gold certificates might be paid out by banks without the Secretary of the Treasury's authorization, nor could gold in any form be exported without Treasury license. The purpose was not only to conserve the nation's gold stock, but to allow the dollar to depreciate in its relationship to foreign currencies so as to raise the domestic price level and stimulate exports. For the first time since 1879 United States currency could not be redeemed in gold.

The Hundred Days

The special session of Congress that opened on March 9, 1933, adjourned on June 16, only 104 days after Roosevelt's inauguration. During these "Hundred Days," Congress passed more important pieces of legislation than any previous legislature in American history. This unusual record was possible because of the new President's great prestige and the willingness of a Congress sobered by the emergency to accept a great degree of executive leadership. Public opinion throughout the nation favored a maximum of action and a minimum of debate.

On March 20, the Economy Act gave the President wide powers to cut the salaries of Federal employees by as much as 15 per cent and to reduce as well pensions and allowances of war veterans. Roosevelt made prompt use of his authority, and his courage in braving the wrath of politically powerful groups did much to restore business confidence.

Inconsistent though it seemed to many, Federal emergency appropriations were increased at the same time that other expenditures were being reduced. The President gained early congressional approval for a project that would also have appealed to the first Roosevelt. The Civilian Conservation Corps (CCC) gave temporary employment to 250,000 unmarried men between the ages of 18 and 25, 25,000 World War I veterans, and 25,000 experienced woodsmen. Most of the young men received but $30 a month, $25 of which was sent to their families. They were taken off the streets, given board and lodgings in camp, and put to work on useful projects in the national forests

Since the RFC funds made available in 1932 for loans to the states for relief activities were now almost exhausted, Congress made a new appropriation of $500 million, with a few significant changes. Money was advanced to the states as grants rather than loans, and a new agency, the Federal Emergency Relief Administration (FERA), carried out the provisions of the law. Harry Hopkins of Iowa, long engaged in social work and who had directed the New York State Unemployment Relief Administration when Roosevelt was at Albany, headed the FERA.

Meantime, advocates of a large public-works program impressed upon the President the benefits that would flow from their proposals. Not only would employment be given to many workers, but a demand for steel, cement, and other materials would be stimulated. The final appropriation, embodied in Title II of the National Industrial Recovery Act (NIRA), was $3.3 billion—the largest peacetime appropriation by any government. The Public Works Administration (PWA) was under the chairmanship of Secretary of the Interior Ickes, an outspoken and honest official, whose deliberation and care in perusing each project were the despair of many other New Dealers.

The unemployed were not the only group needing immediate help. Unmanageable private debts threatened to crush debtors and creditors alike. The Emergency Farm Mortgage Act authorized the Federal Land Banks to undertake wholesale refinancing of farm mortgages. The law not only enabled thousands of farmers to escape foreclosure proceedings, but served equally the banks and insurance companies holding defaulted obligations. Similar in purpose was the Home Owners Loan Corporation (HOLC), which relieved both mortgagors and mortgagees of residential real estate. During its three-year life, the HOLC advanced more than $3 billion to over a million homeowners.

The RFC was not only continued under Roosevelt but was given much broader powers. Besides loaning money to banks in distress, it could now strengthen them by purchasing capital stock. Money was made available for payments to depositors who had funds tied up in closed banks. Direct loans to small businessmen were also permitted and large advances made to farmers on the security of their crops. Indeed, RFC loans proved to be the lifeblood for almost every phase of the recovery program.

It will be noted that the measures so far discussed differed from the Hoover depression policies more in the scale upon which they were carried out than in the underlying philosophy. Like Hoover, Roosevelt was trying to bolster the credit structure of the country and prevent wholesale liquidation. Capitalism had been granted a reprieve.

The First AAA

The New Dealers believed, however, that all such measures to save the banks, the corporations, the railroads, the homeowners, and the farmers would be futile unless economic activity could be stimulated and maintained. The income of millions of farmers and workers must be substantially raised if real recovery were to be attained. This was the primary purpose of the two most controversial measures passed during the Hundred Days—the Agricultural Adjustment Act and the National Industrial Recovery Act.

Roosevelt took quick steps to carry out the party's pledge to aid the farmers. A speedily gathered conference of some fifty representative farm leaders presented a set of recommendations to the President on March 11, which, together with those of various braintrusters and legislators, were finally combined in the Agricultural Adjustment Act of May 12, 1933. One section of this measure gave the President broad inflationary powers to be discussed later in the chapter. Principal interest, however, lay in Title I, under which the Secretary of Agriculture was granted extraordinary powers to raise the farmers' income by giving agricultural commodities a purchasing power with respect to articles farmers bought equivalent to the purchasing power of agricultural commodities in the base period, 1909–1914. To gain this end, two principal methods were provided. In the case of seven basic commodities,[1] the Secretary could make agreements with individual farmers who would receive benefit payments for reducing their crop acreage or their livestock production. The revenue for these payments would come from a "processing tax"—an excise paid by the manufacturers on the first processing of the basic commodities for the domestic market. The other method allowed the Secretary to make voluntary marketing quotas—exempt from the antitrust laws—with processors, farmers' associations, and others engaged in handling farm products that would maintain prices by curbing the sale of surpluses. The Secretary also had broad powers to loan money on the security of crops, to purchase surplus commodities, and to subsidize exports.

George Peek, one of the authors of the bill and an advocate of farm-relief measures since McNary-Haugen days, was appointed to head the Agricultural Adjustment Agency (AAA). Peek disagreed with Wallace, however, on fundamental policy. The former was an economic nationalist who believed in selling the agricultural surplus abroad and favored benefit payments, not curbs on production. Secretary Wallace wanted farm production immediately curtailed, although he hoped that reciprocal trade agreements and tariff concessions might eventually restore foreign markets for American farm products. Increasing friction between the two men led to the appointment of Chester Davis as Peek's successor in December, 1933.

The first steps taken under AAA were particularly controversial because they involved destruction of commodities already growing. This was believed necessary since the program began too late in the year to prevent the planting of crops and the breeding of livestock that threatened to glut the market. Cotton growers were asked to rent to the Secretary of Agriculture at least one quarter of their acreage. More than a million such contracts were made and about 10.4 million acres of cotton were plowed under. For not producing 4.4 million bales, cotton growers were paid $113 million in benefits. Even more shocking to Eastern conservatives was the slaughter of thousands of little pigs and pregnant sows to prevent a surplus.

[1] These basic commodities were wheat, cotton, corn, hogs, rice, tobacco, and milk. The act was amended in 1934 to add sugar, beef and dairy cattle, peanuts, rye, flax, barley, and grass sorghums.

How would they like to trade doctors? (By Darling in the *New York Herald Tribune*.)

The plowing under of crops and the slaughtering of animals were only emergency procedures. The AAA long-range plans called for limitations on production in advance. During the next three years the system had an extensive trial. Reduced production and better prices plus benefit payments increased farm income from $4.5 billion in 1932 to $6.9 billion in 1935. Even allowing for a substantial rise in the prices the farmer had to pay for his purchases, this was equivalent to a 35 per cent increase in his real income. The reduced output and increased prices could not be attributed solely to AAA. Since government spending for relief, dollar devaluation, increased purchasing power through NRA, and natural forces of recovery were all at work, it is impossible to isolate the effect of any one factor. Of great importance also was the serious drought of 1934, which reduced production more drastically than AAA had planned.

Farmers grumbled about many aspects of the program. Despite efforts to administer it democratically, producers of the basic commodities usually gained more than other growers, while large farmers gained more than the small. Also it interfered with the farmer's cherished individualism and established precedents that might lead to more distasteful forms of future regimentation. Some farmers worried about the ultimate effect on exports of a policy reducing production and raising prices. But whatever the farmers' misgivings, referendums revealed that the overwhelming majority wanted the AAA experiment continued at least until something better was devised.

Consumers were less enthusiastic, for they had to contribute to agricultural rehabilitation both in increased prices and in the processing taxes the manufacturers passed on to them. But agricultural spokesmen pointed out that for many decades consumers had been paying a similar, if less obvious, subsidy to manufacturers through the protective tariff, and they also asserted that "the economics of scarcity" had not originated with them, but with industrialists who by fair means or foul controlled production to maintain prices.

The New Deal was also interested in another type of agricultural legislation. Congress passed the Farm Mortgage Foreclosure Act in June, 1934, enabling farmers to borrow from the government to forestall the loss of their holdings in foreclosure proceedings. About the same time the Frazier-Lemke Bankruptcy Act became law, a controversial measure permitting a farmer to demand a reappraisal of his property lost through foreclosure and to buy it back at the new figure, paying for it over a six-year period with interest of only 1 per cent. Were the creditor to object, the farmer might halt the proceedings and keep his property for five years at a reasonable rental. This act led to bitter contests in the Middle West between bankrupt farmers and the mortgage holders until the Supreme Court in 1935 found the measure in conflict with the Fifth Amendment (Louisville Joint Stock Co. *v.* Radford). The following year the Frazier-Lemke Act was passed in amended form that changed the retention period to only three years. Because of changes in Supreme Court personnel, its validity was now upheld.

NRA: Experiment in Industrial Self-government

During the campaign, Roosevelt expressed interest in a movement for industrial self-government that had the support of many business leaders. Competition, at least in its most aggressive forms, had grown unpopular—particularly during the depression. This led to a demand that trade associations be expanded and allowed to stabilize production, prices, and marketing practices. Since such activities were illegal under the antitrust laws, the latter should be amended, suspended, or repealed. A concrete proposal was put forward by Gerard Swope, president of General Electric, in the autumn of 1931, and a somewhat similar plan was developed by the United States Chamber of Commerce. Although Hoover had been cold to the movement, Roosevelt gave the idea his sympathetic consideration.

Meantime, labor leaders were asserting that the principal cause of the depression was unemployment brought on by the increased productivity of the individual worker. To create purchasing power, hours should be radically shortened and employment spread as widely as possible. To achieve this end Senator Hugo Black of Alabama had introduced in

December, 1932, a bill to limit work in factories to thirty hours a week. Although strongly opposed by the Chamber of Commerce, the Black Thirty-Hour bill passed the Senate in April, 1933. In the House it had the support of William Connery of Massachusetts, chairman of the Committee on Labor, who suggested strengthening amendments. Secretary of Labor Perkins, however, declared that any bill fixing maximum hours would be dangerous to labor unless it also dealt with minimum wages.

As this Black-Connery-Perkins project took form, businessmen became greatly alarmed. Bowing to this opposition, the President asked his advisers to draft a measure reconciling the demands of the industrialists with those of labor. Despite opposition from old-line progressives who disliked the relaxation of the antitrust laws, Congress passed the resulting National Industrial Recovery Act and the President signed the measure on June 13, 1933. In an enthusiastic statement, Roosevelt said:

History probably will record the National Industrial Recovery Act as the most important and far-reaching legislation ever enacted by the American Congress. It represents a supreme effort to stabilize for all time the many factors which make for the prosperity of the Nation, and the preservation of American standards.

The act provided for the drafting of "codes of fair competition" by industrial groups or associations. These codes were to be submitted to the President or one of his representatives to make sure that the associations were "truly representative" and that the codes were "not designed to promote monopolies, or to eliminate or oppress enterprises." Once satisfied with a particular code, the President would give his formal approval; then all units in the industry were bound to the code and might be punished for violations, whether or not they had helped formulate it. Protection to labor was provided by Section 7-A, which guaranteed to employees the right of collective bargaining by representatives of their own choosing, free from restraint or coercion by employers. The measure was to be in force for two years, during which approved code activities were exempt from antitrust laws.

With the launching of this experiment, the New Deal veered sharply from the traditions of Wilson's New Freedom toward those of Theodore Roosevelt's New Nationalism. The inevitability of big business was accepted and the protection of the public was entrusted, not primarily to trust-busting and strict regulation, but to enlightened cooperation between business and government.

The National Recovery Administration (NRA), headed by General Hugh Johnson, was established to carry out the provisions of the act. Johnson had a colorful personality, great zeal for work, and a flair for pungent expression. The high point of his earlier career was in World War I when he organized the draft and also served on the War Industries Board. As NRA administrator, he used the same methods that had made his earlier ventures successful.

With more than two hundred codes submitted to NRA during July, 1933, alone, it was obvious that it would be many months before the whole industrial field could be covered. A short cut was provided by the President's

Re-employment Agreement (PRA) of July, 1933, under which employers pledged not to employ children, to limit hours of labor in stores and banks to forty and in factories to thirty-five, and to pay minimum wages of at least 30 cents an hour. This so-called Blanket Code was aimed at creating purchasing power to sustain the industrial recovery that had been developing.

Employers abiding by either the PRA or the code of their particular industry were entitled to display an official symbol featuring a blue eagle and the words "NRA—We do our part." Within four months, Johnson claimed that 96 per cent of commerce and industry were displaying the Blue Eagle, 2.8 million workers had been put back on payrolls, and annual purchasing power had been increased by $3 billion.

By February, 1934, when the code-making process was virtually completed, 557 basic codes had received NRA approval. They differed greatly, yet some of their more characteristic features may be listed. They always forbade child labor; maximum hours of work were variously fixed at between 35 and 48 weekly, with the average about 40; minimum wages were established usually at about 40 cents an hour; and the right of collective bargaining was recognized as required by Section 7-A. Most codes banned false advertising, commercial bribery, harassing litigation, and the like— practices already unlawful but that still prevailed in certain areas. More controversial were the provisions permitting control of production or limitations on pricing. The cotton textile code limited the number of hours plants could operate. Several codes forbade the acquisition of new machinery or the entry of new units into the industry without special authorization. In a few natural-resource industries like lumber, copper, and petroleum, definite production quotas were set. In the lumber, bituminous coal, and petroleum codes, moreover, prices were fixed. Most codes merely provided that goods must not be sold "below cost"—a formula difficult of application. Contrary to NRA advice, the tendency was to make codes increasingly elaborate, dealing with trade practices in bewildering detail.

The Tennessee Valley Authority

In April, 1933, the President appealed to Congress to carry out Senator Norris's Muscle Shoals project in a form that surpassed the dreams of that veteran progressive. Instead of a single power plant, Roosevelt asked Congress to create a Tennessee Valley Authority, "a corporation clothed with the power of Government but possessed of the flexibility and initiative of private enterprise," to be "charged with the broadest duty of planning for the proper use, conservation and development of the natural resources of the Tennessee River drainage basin and its adjoining territory for the general social and economic welfare of the Nation."

Congress passed the Tennessee Valley Authority Act in May, 1933, and Arthur Morgan, president of Antioch College, served as chairman of TVA until 1938, when a quarrel led to his removal and the elevation of David Lilienthal of Wisconsin, who had been an influential figure in the TVA since its organization, to the chairmanship. The agency's first great activity was dam building. Thirty dams eventually came under TVA's control, twenty of them new ones constructed by TVA itself.

Highly controversial was the authority Congress gave TVA to generate and sell electricity. The private power companies would not have objected so much if the power had been sold wholesale to them for transmission and distribution, but Congress directed TVA to "give preference to states, municipalities, and cooperative organizations of citizens or members." Thereupon, the utility companies put up a stubborn fight in the courts. Although the constitutionality of the provision permitting TVA to sell surplus electric power was upheld by the Supreme Court in 1936 (Ashwander *v.* TVA), this did not end the legal battle. A score of issues was raised, lower courts issued sweeping injunctions, and several cases were taken to the Supreme Court. On every major issue TVA was sustained, but the litigation, costing millions of dollars, hampered the agency's activities for years. Eventually, in 1939, Commonwealth and Southern, the holding company whose subsidiaries were most affected, sold its Tennessee electrical properties to TVA and local public agencies for $78.6 million, a substantially larger sum than TVA wanted to pay. Wendell Willkie, the company's president, gained nationwide publicity for his winning fight in behalf of the investors. Parallel negotiations led to the purchase of private utility properties in Mississippi and Alabama.

TVA did not deal directly with domestic consumers, but sold its power to municipalities and cooperative associations. In 1950 it was doing business with 95 of the former, including Knoxville, Nashville, Memphis, and Chattanooga, and 50 of the latter. Since it also sold directly to big industrial plants, many new enterprises were attracted to the area, particularly during World War II.

A most interesting aspect of the TVA experiment was its pioneering with a radically low rate structure, which encouraged the much wider use of electricity. In twelve communities served by TVA from 1934 to 1942, home electricity consumption increased by 196 per cent as compared with 53 per cent for the nation. Public power advocates contended that the TVA experiment provided a "yardstick" whereby the reasonableness of private utility rates all over the country could be measured. Private industry spokesmen replied that the comparison was unfair because TVA did not have to pay taxes or make a profit. This was not entirely true; TVA made annual payments of some $2 million to state and county governments in lieu of taxes. Yet it did remain true that the comparison between TVA rates and private ones was sometimes misleading, and that the fairness of the rates in any particular part of the country had to be judged on the basis of the local situation.

Whether TVA had provided a fair yardstick or not, private utilities responded to its challenge. An emphasis on rate reduction and increased consumption characterized the entire industry during the thirties. According to Lilienthal, electric rates dropped only 2 per cent in the seven years before TVA as compared with a decrease of about 33 per cent during the seven years after 1933.

Public attention was largely concentrated on TVA's power program because of its challenging and controversial character. Less known were its other activities. The great TVA dams were multipurpose structures. A principal objective was to promote navigation; huge artificial lakes connected by locks provided 650 miles of navigable waterways. These dams also prevented floods. No major river in the world was so fully controlled as the Tennessee; by holding back or releasing the waters impounded behind dams on the main stream and its tributaries, a vast region could be protected against inundation. Moreover, TVA manufactured fertilizer, rehabilitated impoverished farmers, and promoted reforestation.

Monetary Policy

Nothing better illustrates the difference in viewpoint between Hoover and Roosevelt than their attitudes toward the country's monetary system. Hoover considered the maintenance of the gold standard as perhaps his most important trust; he viewed with horror the slightest deviation from it. Roosevelt refused to adopt this fetish. While in his campaign speeches he pledged himself to "sound money," it was obvious he was leaving himself free to accept a moderate and controlled inflation if it seemed advisable. To him money was a means to an end rather than an end in itself. If one kind of money contributed more to recovery than another, then by pragmatic test the "soundness" of that money was demonstrated.

If Roosevelt's ideas on money were unorthodox, they were moderate when contrasted with the extreme inflationary demands of many members of his party. Senator Burton Wheeler of Montana had revived Bryan's old demand for free and unlimited coinage of silver at the ratio of sixteen to one. Other inflationists wanted the Treasury to issue several billion dollars in greenbacks. Because some form of currency or monetary experimentation was inevitable, Roosevelt induced Congress to grant him wide discretionary powers to choose whatever procedure seemed best.

Having obtained this unprecedented authority, Roosevelt acted cautiously. Shunning both the greenback and free-silver panaceas, he continued with the passive devaluation of the dollar. Since the Emergency Banking Act had given him power to control transactions in gold, on April 5, 1933, he ordered all persons owning gold coin, gold certificates, or gold bullion to deliver the same to the Federal reserve banks in exchange for an equivalent amount of any other form of coin or currency. Two weeks later the Treasury announced that no further licenses for exporting gold would be granted.

These steps had a dual purpose: to reduce the value of the dollar in foreign exchange and to raise the domestic price level. The first of these goals appeared necessary because of the abnormal conditions of 1933. England and most of the other countries had abandoned the gold standard. So long as the United States clung to it, the American dollar was expensive in terms of these foreign currencies. To reduce the foreign exchange value of the dollar, therefore, would encourage American exports. Raising the domestic price level seemed equally necessary. The downward spiral of prices made it increasingly difficult for debtors to meet their obligations, besides discouraging industrialists from manufacturing for future sale and merchants from buying more than they could quickly sell. The 1933 price level could be fairly described as deflated; the policies undertaken to raise that level were more accurately labeled reflationary than inflationary.

Obviously the cheapening of the dollar would result in a windfall to creditors if they could force their debtors to pay in gold rather than in currency. To prevent this, a joint resolution of Congress on June 5, 1933, voided any clause requiring payment in gold in any past or future obligation, whether government or private. This action was upheld by the Supreme Court in the Gold Clause cases of 1935.

The London Economic Conference—discussed more fully in a later chapter—forced Roosevelt to decide early in July, 1933, whether recovery could best be served by entering a stabilization agreement with other nations or by continuing his policy of lowering the value of the dollar and raising the domestic price level. He chose the latter path despite its lethal effect on the Conference.

Until October, 1933, the administration simply divorced the dollar from gold to allow its value to sink in terms of other currencies. But during the autumn the President, presumably influenced by Professor George Warren of Cornell University, initiated a more aggressive campaign to achieve his aims. The RFC began to buy gold at a price substantially above the world market. The first purchases were at $31.36 per ounce; by January, 1934 the price reached $34.45. Since an ounce of gold before March 4, 1933, had been worth $20.67, this was equivalent to a devaluation of the dollar by approximately 40 per cent.

This experiment was terminated by the Gold Reserve Act of January 30, 1934.[2] By presidential proclamation the next day, the weight of the gold dollar was finally fixed at 15 $\frac{5}{21}$ grains. Measured by the old gold dollar (25.8 grains), the new dollar was worth 59.06 cents; gold was priced at $35 an ounce as against the old price of $20.67.

Although the President still had power to change the weight of the dollar, he abstained from any further action. Instead, his policy was now to hold the dollar steady through the operations of the stabilization fund. When in 1936 a new wave of competitive currency depreciation threatened to develop, the United States joined Britain and France in an agreement to maintain an equilibrium among their respective currencies.

It is impossible to say how successful the gold policy was. Domestic prices rose and exports increased, but many other factors contributed. Furthermore, prices did not follow a uniform course. While manufactured goods held their price gains of the spring and early summer of 1933, agricultural prices, after a rapid upward spurt, drifted downward again for the rest of the year. Experience with the gold purchase plan indicated that the general price

[2] Title to all gold owned by the Federal reserve banks was transferred to the United States Treasury in return for dollar certificates; gold coin was abolished as a component of the monetary system, but gold in bullion form was to be held in the Treasury as a reserve against the currency; the President was authorized to fix the gold content of the dollar between 50 and 60 per cent of its weight; $2 billion of the profit accruing to the Treasury through the revaluation of its gold holdings was to be used as a stabilization fund to enable the Treasury to maintain the dollar at a reasonable ratio with foreign currencies through operations in the foreign exchange market.

level did not respond as directly to a change in the gold value of the dollar as the Warren school of theorists had believed. Too many factors—among them the volume of credit, the rate of government spending, the supply of and demand for goods, and the activities of speculators—were at work.

Perhaps the most serious criticism of the gold policy is that it represented a type of economic nationalism all too common in the world of 1933. To be sure, the steps the United States took in the foreign exchange market were essentially defensive since most of the other nations had already resorted to currency depreciation, but the American policy was, nevertheless, a source of anxiety to other countries. Despite world-wide restrictions on transactions in gold, the purchasing program drew an abnormally large proportion of the world's gold supply to the United States. In terms of domestic policies, Roosevelt's unorthodoxy on the monetary question cost him much of the business support he had enjoyed earlier. Conservatives never forgave him for abandoning the gold standard in favor of what Al Smith called the "baloney dollar."

On the other hand, monetary experimentation had at least one healthy result. Most of the dire predictions about what would follow any deviation from the old gold standard proved to be groundless. When Americans learned that life went on as usual when they could not redeem their currency in gold coin, another inhibiting fear that had shackled the country in 1932 was conquered.

The administration's silver policy, although somewhat resembling the gold plan, had this fundamental difference: it was forced upon the President somewhat against his will. Congressmen from silver-producing states wanted to remonetize silver in order to rescue the white metal from its disastrously low price at the beginning of 1933. Their position in Congress was strong because they held the balance of power between the inflationists and the anti-inflationists. They soon compelled Roosevelt to make important concessions lest some much more drastic step be forced upon him.

The silverites won their most important victory in the passage of the Silver Purchase Act of June 19, 1934. Congress fixed the objective of increasing the proportion of silver to gold in the national monetary stocks until one quarter of such stocks was in silver. The Treasury was directed to purchase domestic and foreign silver until either the prescribed proportion of the two metals was reached or the price of silver rose above its monetary value of $1.293 per ounce. Thus the Treasury had to buy the entire output of the domestic silver mines at an artificially high price and to make extensive purchases of foreign silver as well. The policy caused grave difficulties for China, Mexico, and other countries on a silver standard. Among its few satisfactory results was the creation of foreign purchasing power for the benefit of American exporters.

The Second New Deal

The nation's psychological response to the Hundred Days was striking. Most of the dark pessimism of the preceding winter was replaced with the optimistic belief that recovery would now be both speedy and complete.

Stock-market prices rose rapidly, and industrial activity expanded greatly. Much of this activity, however, was speculative in character. Manufacturers and merchants, anticipating higher costs, were filling their warehouses with products they hoped to sell at higher prices. Since purchasing power had not yet been created to sustain this increased production, business activity began to decline again during the summer and fall of 1933.

The failure of the New Deal to bring immediate prosperity had inevitable consequences. Roosevelt felt compelled to move on to further experiments to prime the economic pump. Meanwhile, business was in a state of cranky convalescence—no longer fearing the worst, but irritable with Doctor New Deal because recovery was not more rapid. It was soon evident that the era of good feeling under which the Democratic administration had begun could not last much longer.

In November, 1934, the voters had their first chance to register their opinion of the New Deal. The results were a Roosevelt triumph. The Democratic majority in the Senate increased from 22 to 42 and in the House from 191 to 209.

Strengthened by this victory, Roosevelt obtained from Congress in 1935 and 1936 legislation comparable in importance to the measures of 1933. But not for this reason alone were the policies now instituted often described as the Second New Deal. They represented an important shift of emphasis. Whereas the First New Deal had been dedicated primarily to recovery, and only incidentally to reform, the emphasis was now reversed. "When a man is convalescing from illness," Roosevelt declared in his first message to the new Congress, "wisdom dictates not only cure of the symptoms, but removal of their cause." The administration had shifted to the left by this time; under increasing attack from business, it derived its most dependable support from labor. The shift had its visible embodiment in the resignation of such conservative advisers as Raymond Moley, Hugh Johnson, and George Peek. Most prominent among the new faces were Harry Hopkins and two able protégés of Professor Frankfurter, Thomas Corcoran and Benjamin Cohen.

Many factors now contributed to shaping a more far-reaching program of reform. The hope that the administration's social objectives could be achieved through NRA was destroyed by increasing discontent with that agency and its overthrow by the Supreme Court. Still dissatisfied with the degree of economic recovery, the administration had to take more aggressive steps to create purchasing power. There was, moreover, growing danger that discontented groups would abandon the New Deal and support such extremist programs as those being agitated by Huey Long, Dr. Townsend, Upton Sinclair, and Father Coughlin. Among the fruits of the Second New Deal were the establishment of a large work-relief program, the passage of the National Labor Relations and Social Security Acts, and stricter regulation of the electrical utilities business.

Work for the Unemployed

A most troublesome problem of the Roosevelt administration was continued large-scale unemployment. Although the number of workers in private industry rose slowly from depression lows, the population was meanwhile increasing and jobs were not being created as rapidly as new workers were available to fill them. Throughout the eight years, 1933–1940, unemployment figures did not drop below eight million and averaged about ten million.

As unemployment remedies, both PWA and FERA had serious limitations. Large public-works projects were expensive, they were not always available in areas of greatest economic need, and they gave employment primarily to construction workers, whereas many of the unemployed were in the white-collar group—clerks, teachers, actors, musicians, artists, and even doctors and nurses. On the other hand, most of the locally administered FERA money went for direct relief—doles that provided only a bare subsistence. Such relief was cheaper in money than any other form of assistance but was expensive in other terms. The reliefers were given no real purchasing power to stimulate the country's economy, while protracted idleness deprived them both of the will to work and whatever skills they might once have possessed.

A short experiment in still a third method of dealing with unemployment had been tried during the winter of 1933–1934 through the Civil Works Administration (CWA), under Harry Hopkins. Under it, temporary employment was given four million men in painting and repairing schools, resurfacing highways, building flood control works, and similar projects of civic value.

CWA was sufficiently successful to serve as the inspiration for a much more ambitious program during the Second New Deal. On May 6, 1935, the Works Progress Administration (WPA) was established, with Hopkins as administrator. With characteristic speed, he had 2.7 million on the WPA payroll by December, 1935. Up to October 1, 1937, the WPA built 11,000 public buildings and repaired 30,000 others, laid over 43,000 miles of roads and repaired 146,000 miles, and constructed thousands of bridges, culverts, sidewalks, athletic fields, playgrounds, swimming pools, dams, levees, and sewers. Women were given work on sewing and canning projects; doctors and nurses operated clinics; musicians organized WPA orchestras; actors, writers, and teachers were given opportunities to practice their professions. Those employed in these multifarious activities received wages substantially higher than FERA payments, but not so high as those of PWA and CWA. The lower wages of WPA were set both as a measure of economy and as an inducement to the workers to obtain private employment wherever possible.

A particularly disquieting problem was that of 2.9 million young people in families on relief in 1935. The natural course for such youngsters was to quit school and look for jobs. This was deplored because it aggravated the unemployment problem and interrupted the education of the young people with potentially serious results for themselves and the community. Therefore the National Youth Administration (NYA) was set up within WPA under which high school and college students were given part-time employment on projects helpful to the institutions they were attending. The amount they earned was small, but was enough in many cases to enable them to stay in school.

New Deal spending was hotly attacked and as resolutely defended. Critics asserted that much of the work relief was what some cynic called "boondoggling"—made work of no value. Popular jokes depicted the WPA worker as leaning on his shovel much more than he dug with it. It was alleged that relief spending jeopardized the solvency of the Federal government and was manipulated to serve political purposes. But New Deal supporters, while not claiming all WPA projects were worth while or all WPA workers were conscientious, declared that no government responsibility was more important than that of preventing suffering. The great justification of the Hopkins program was that it served this end and at the same time produced an immense amount of useful work. The cost was well within the capacity of the government and small when compared with what would be spent in a wartime emergency. Politics and graft undoubtedly existed in some local WPA situations, but defenders argued that such abuses were really not very great in view of the program's magnitude.

The End of NRA

Only for a brief period did NRA enjoy almost universal support. As time passed it became the target for increasingly serious criticism. Employers protested that the agency was prolabor; union leaders that it was promanagement. Small businessmen were divided in their attitude. Many operators of small coal mines and sawmills were saved from disaster; many small merchants were grateful for NRA protection against cutthroat competitive practices. Nevertheless, the codes were often bitterly resented. The wage and hour requirements were more burdensome to small employers than to large, while big business was much better represented than small in the formulation and administration of the codes.

Because of this widespread criticism, Roosevelt appointed a National Review Board under the chairmanship of Clarence Darrow, famous criminal lawyer, in early 1934. Much to the disappointment of NRA officials, the Darrow Board, ignoring the considerable evidence showing that the codes had protected small business, concentrated on assembling proof that pointed to the contrary. The result was not a judicious appraisal of the actual situation, but a blistering indictment of the whole experiment. NRA enemies greatly publicized the adverse findings of this report, yet overlooked its most remarkable conclusion—that oppression of small businessmen was inevitable under capitalism and that the only answer was socialism.

Meantime, consumers had their own grievances against NRA. Just how much of the sharp price advances in many areas was fairly attributable to the codes and how much to other factors it is impossible to say; consumer resentment, however, was focused almost exclusively on NRA. The administration realized the seriousness of this resentment, but efforts to protect the consumer only alienated the industrialists.

The decline in NRA's popularity was a serious matter. The agency's success in obtaining the initial cooperation of the business world resulted from its overwhelming public support during the first months. Fear of public opinion was likewise a powerful force in gaining general compliance with code provisions; a threat to deprive a violator of his Blue Eagle usually brought him into line. As criticism of NRA mounted, however, more and more businessmen felt they could abrogate code provisions with impunity.

Business, an almost unwilling groom. But, you see, he met her only a few days ago. (By Darling in the *New York Herald Tribune.*)

Since open defiance of the codes threatened the whole experiment, the agency ordered "crackdowns" and prosecuted more and more offenders. Such coercion, however, angered still further the agency's critics.

Whether to continue the experiment after the expiration of the original law in June, 1935, was a principal problem confronting Congress. The President asked that NRA be extended for another two years because the fundamental purposes and principles were sound and abandoning them would "spell the return of industrial and labor chaos." He acknowledged, however, the need for amendments "to clarify the legislative purpose and to guide the execution of the law."

Even to this reformed NRA there was strong congressional opposition. Some kind of extension, however, would probably have been provided had not the Supreme Court on May 27, 1935, applied the *coup de grâce* to the whole undertaking. In the case of A. L. A. Schechter Poultry Corporation *v.* United States, the Court declared that the National Industrial Recovery Act was unconstitutional insofar as it delegated legislative power to the President without adequate standards to guide him and insofar as it provided for Federal regulation of hours and wages in enterprises like the Schechter concern whose business was entirely intrastate in character.

From the outset NRA was handicapped by the incompatibility of its main objectives—stimulating recovery and drafting rules of permanent benefit. The first called for the utmost haste; the second for caution and deliberation. Given the conditions of 1933, it is not surprising that the demands of recovery received priority. The result was that NRA had considerable success in its short-term objectives—speeding production, increasing purchasing power, and establishing a truce on cutthroat competition. But the excitement and haste that contributed to immediate success were prejudicial to the achievement of the long-range objectives. The codes attempted too much and contained too many ill-advised provisions. The resulting deterioration of public support even more than the Supreme Court's decision foretold NRA's eventual collapse. Nevertheless, the agency's failure was far from complete. Public opinion and subsequent legislation consolidated many of its gains: abolition of child labor, recognition of labor's right to organize, establishment of certain standards of maximum hours and minimum wages, and restraint upon ruthless exploitation of the nation's natural resources.

Labor's Right to Organize

The overthrow of NRA forced the Roosevelt administration to clarify its labor policy for, after a long period of retreat, the unions were now attempting a militant advance. Total union membership, below 3 million in 1933, jumped to 4.2 million in 1935. Much of this growth could be attributed to Section 7-A of the National Industrial Recovery Act, which declared "employees shall have the right to organize and bargain collectively through representatives of their own choosing" and no employee "shall be required as a condition of employment to join any company union or to refrain from joining . . . a labor organization of his own choosing."

Union organizers made skillful use of this clause. In the coal mines, for example, the news was carried from pit to pit with large banners bearing the legend: "President Roosevelt wants you to join a union." The response astonished even the labor leaders themselves. Not only did total membership increase rapidly, but hundreds of local unions were organized in the mass production industries where there had been practically no earlier unionization.

But labor's rejoicing proved somewhat premature. Many employers sought to fulfill the collective bargaining stipulation of Section 7-A by encouraging company unions. These more than doubled between 1933 and 1935, with their membership increasing from 1.3 million to about 2.5 million. Moreover, despite NRA, many antiunion employers prevented organization altogether. Labor protested many code provisions, asserting that in both the drafting and administering of these management had too much power. In the wage and hour provisions, labor usually fared poorly in unorganized industries. Innumerable disputes arose among AFL unions, unaffiliated independent unions, and company unions over the right to bargain in particular plants.

These grievances, plus wage and hour demands to be expected during a period of increasing production and rising prices, led to an epidemic of strikes in 1933 and 1934. Because these threatened to retard recovery and injure the NRA experiment, Roosevelt appointed in August, 1933, a National Labor Board, composed of three representatives of industry and three of labor with Senator Robert Wagner of New York as impartial chairman. This body heard complaints, settled strikes, and conducted elections to determine collective-bargaining representatives. As long as the prestige of NRA was high, the panel had reasonable success. During 1934, however, when NRA was under severe attack, management and labor were unwilling to accept its jurisdiction and to abide by its decisions.

Disillusioned unionists dubbed NRA the "National Run Around" and demanded additional protection for their right to organize. A bill for this purpose, introduced by Senator Wagner, failed to pass Congress, and shortly afterward the Supreme Court destroyed NRA. Left now without even the safeguards of Section 7-A, labor redoubled its efforts and on July 5, 1935, the Wagner-Connery, or National Labor Relations, Act was passed.

This measure provided for a National Labor Relations Board (NLRB) of three members appointed by the President with Senate consent. Section 7-A was re-enacted in almost identical language and was implemented with specified rules. Five unfair labor practices were listed; employers were forbidden (1) to interfere with employees' right to bargain collectively; (2) to dominate any labor organization or to support it financially; (3) to encourage or discourage membership in any labor organization; (4) to discriminate against any employee who filed charges or testified before the NLRB; and (5) to refuse to bargain collectively with employees' representatives. The act also provided that in any bargaining unit the representatives chosen by the majority should be the exclusive representatives of all the employees. In case of dispute, the NLRB would certify the proper representatives. To assist in this decision, the board might take a secret ballot or use any other suitable method. The NLRB could issue "cease and desist" orders against employers violating the act, but these were enforceable only through the Federal courts.

The National Association of Manufacturers and other business spokesmen vigorously protested this legislation, contending it was one-sided since it defined unfair conduct only on the part of employers. Asserting that the act was unconstitutional, most large employers ignored it pending a test of the legal issues. In 1937, however, the Supreme Court upheld its validity in Associated Press v. NLRB, NLRB v. Jones and Laughlin Steel Corporation, and several other cases.

Thereupon, the NLRB became a powerful agency. By the end of 1939 it had banned 340 company unions, and old company unions were reorganized to give them more independence. Meantime, trade-union membership continued to grow so that by 1941 about eleven million workers were affiliated with some organization. This increase could not be attributed solely to the Wagner-Connery Act and the NLRB, but these served at least as a strong deterrent to such methods as employers had previously used to counteract the efforts of the organizers.

Social Security

Another foundation stone of the Second New Deal was the Social Security Act of August, 1935. Old-age pensions, unemployment insurance, and provisions for sickness and accident benefits under government administration had been commonplace in Europe before World War I, but most Americans believed that saving against old age and misfortune was an individual problem. The depression, however, provided a cruel disillusionment. Thrifty citizens saw their life savings swept away by bank failures, while the average individual's inability to guarantee his own security was demonstrated in many other ways as well. By 1932 there was a widespread demand for government action. The AFL passed resolutions asking unemployment insurance with compulsory payments by employers and the state, and the Democratic national platform included a plank advocating both unemployment and old-age insurance under state laws.

But building a social security system exclusively on state legislation offered many difficulties. Each state hesitated to burden employers with payroll taxes lest factories be moved to other states having no such levies. Since some Federal program seemed to be required, in June, 1934, Roosevelt appointed a Committee on Economic Security with Secretary of Labor Perkins as chairman and numerous advisory groups of technical experts. The following January, the President sent to Congress this committee's recommendations for joint Federal-state action.

This action came none too soon. Local clubs throughout the country were already agitating for the Townsend Old Age Revolving Pension Plan, concocted by Dr. Francis Townsend, under which those over sixty years of age were to be paid $200 each month to be entirely spent within the next thirty days. Thus at one step, argued its sponsors, security for the aged would be provided along with perpetual prosperity for the nation. Upton Sinclair's EPIC (End Poverty in California) plan would levy special taxes to pay $50 a month to the needy aged. Even more extreme programs were advanced by Senator Huey Long of Louisiana with his Share-the-Wealth plan for guaranteeing each citizen an annual income of $5,000 and by the radio priest, Father Charles Coughlin of Royal Oak, Michigan, with his demands for radical inflation. In comparison with these reckless proposals the administration's recommendations seemed mild. The Social Security Act, passed by substantial majorities, became law on August 14, 1935.

This measure dealt with old-age pensions, unemployment insurance, public assistance to the needy aged, the needy blind, and dependent children, and additional aid for maternal and child welfare services and public health facilities. The only program exclusively administered by the Federal government was for old-age insurance. All employers and employees except those in certain exempted categories must pay a payroll tax equivalent to 1 per cent of each employee's salary, a tax to be gradually increased until it reached 3 per cent in 1949. The revenues would build up reserves in the Federal Treasury out of which after January 1, 1942, retired workers would receive monthly pensions of $10 to $85, depending upon their average wages and the length of time they had been contributing.

Bringing the prodigal home. (By Bishop in the *St. Louis Star-Times.*)

Unemployment insurance was left to the states, but to encourage the establishment of such plans, a Federal unemployment tax was levied upon all employers except those in exempted categories. The employers were to be allowed a credit up to 90 per cent for any contributions made to state unemployment funds. From the 10 per cent retained in such cases, the Federal government made grants to the states to assist them with administrative expenses. This inducement proved adequate for all the states to enact unemployment insurance laws by July 31, 1937.

The Social Security Act also provided for Federal grants-in-aid up to $15 a month for states matching this contribution and administering public assistance to old people in need of relief who were not covered by the insurance plan. Similar Federal grants were available to the states for aiding the blind and dependent children. On a somewhat different basis Federal aid was extended for certain health and welfare activities and for vocational rehabilitation.

The law was criticized in various quarters. Employers complained of their new tax burdens and bookkeeping problems. Liberals were unhappy because so many had not been included and because the benefits were small. Economists regarded the payroll tax as deflationary and unnecessarily heavy, since the Federal government with its power to tax was not under the same necessity as private insurance companies to accumulate huge reserves.

But whatever the misgivings about details, the idea of social security in principle soon won general acceptance. Republican efforts during the 1930 campaign to turn the workers against the law found little response, and it became apparent that the popular demand was not for repeal but for liberalization. In 1939, therefore, Congress enlarged the benefits and provided for protecting the widow and children of the worker in case of his death.

Regulation and Reform

Some of the most important New Deal measures dealt with the protection of depositors, investors, and consumers from abuses to which the depression had called attention. The Glass-Steagall Banking Act of June, 1933, strengthened the banking structure with three principal provisions: Federal reserve banks were given greater authority to curb speculative credit expansion by member banks; commercial banks were prohibited from engaging in investment banking or maintaining security affiliates; and a Federal Deposit Insurance Corporation (FDIC) guaranteed depositors against losses to the extent of $2,500. Although somewhat skeptically regarded at first, the insurance of bank deposits proved entirely feasible, and the coverage was increased to $5,000 in 1934, to $10,000 in 1950, to $15,000 in 1966, and to $20,000 in 1969.

No area of economic life was more in need of regulation and reform than the business of trading in securities. Elementary safeguards to assure the investor of adequate information had never been set up in the United States, even though England had had such laws since 1844. Shocking abuses were revealed in the Senate Committee on Banking and Currency, for which Ferdinand Pecora of New York served as counsel. The committee's hearings, held from 1932 until 1934, prepared the way for the banking legislation just described and also for the Securities Act of 1933 and the Securities Exchange Act of 1934.

These laws added another regulatory body, the Securities Exchange Commission (SEC), to the galaxy of Federal agencies. Corporations whose securities were traded on the exchanges had to register with the SEC and provide accurate and up-to-date information, especially in the case of new issues. Although not guaranteeing the investor against loss, these requirements did ensure that he had access to certain reliable information. The SEC also had broad powers to curb manipulations and other abuses in the stock market, and both the Federal Reserve Board and the SEC could fix margin requirements and otherwise control brokers' loans.

The New York Stock Exchange, jealous of its powers of self-government, regarded the SEC with great suspicion, but the situation did not come to a showdown until 1937, when William Douglas took over as SEC chairman. He insisted that the Exchange be completely reorganized to take control out of the hands of men who were dealing in stocks primarily on their own account and to place it with those doing business with the general public. This proposal was bitterly opposed by the Old Guard. At this junction, however, came a shocking revelation of the abuses possible under the old system. Richard Whitney, a former president of the Exchange, was indicted for grand larceny for having misappropriated his customers' securities over a period of many months. Fearing new regulatory laws in the face of these disclosures, the Stock Exchange was completely reorganized, with William Martin, a leader of the reform movement, as its new president.

The SEC was given additional responsibilities under the Public Utility Holding Company Act of 1935, which required all public-utility holding companies to register and file specified information on their corporate organization. After January 1, 1938, the SEC required each holding company to limit its operation to a single integrated public-utility system, although permission might be granted to control more than one system if it was necessary to economical management, was exercised over a contiguous geographical area, and did not constitute so large a combination as to impair localized management, efficient operation, or effective regulation. Even in the case of integrated systems, however, the new law did not allow holding companies beyond the second degree—meaning that an operating company might be controlled by a holding company and this first holding company by a second, but further pyramiding was prohibited.

One of the most bitter battles of the thirties was fought over this legislation. To liberals, utility abuses had long been a familiar story, and the 1935 law contained only the minimum safeguards that the situation demanded. But the corporations under attack protested that the outlawing of nonintegrated companies and companies pyramided beyond the second degree was a "death sentence." Congress was deluged with telegrams of protest from investors, but a Senate investigation revealed that many of the messages had originated with holding-company lobbyists rather than their supposed senders.

The corporations' resistance to the measure did not end with its passage. Most of them refused to register with the SEC until the validity of this requirement was upheld by the Supreme Court in the Electric Bond and Share case in 1938. In actually enforcing the "death sentence," however, the commission sought to promote voluntary reorganization to as large a degree as possible. Less publicized but more immediately effective provisions of the law authorized the SEC to discourage the issuance of unnecessarily risky securities and the assumption of fixed charges beyond the normal earning capacity of the companies.

The principle of government regulation already established in other areas was strengthened by the establishment of the Federal Communications Commission (FCC) in 1934 to supervise the telephone, telegraph, and radio industries, and by the much expanded powers given to the Federal Power Commission by the Federal Power Act of 1935. Consumers were also given greater protection under the Food, Drug, and Cosmetic Act of 1938, a considerably stronger law than the pioneer act of 1906.

Problems of the Budget

The New Deal was expensive; from March, 1933, to December, 1936, $13.9 billion was added to the national debt, whose total rose to $33.9 billion. This sum was by no means unmanageable. As a matter of fact, through lower interest rates, the Treasury reduced the annual carrying charges so that it cost the Federal government less for interest payments in 1936 than it had in 1934. The continuing deficit was, nevertheless, embarrassing to an administration that had originally pledged economy. So to emphasize the emergency character of the excess spending, Treasury reports differentiated between ordinary expenditures and recovery and relief costs. This point was stressed that the ordinary budget was in balance and that borrowing was necessitated entirely by the relief items. The administration argued that as national income increased, emergency expenditures would taper off and revenue would automatically increase until the budget was balanced again.

To try to keep the ordinary budget in balance, Roosevelt obtained new tax levies and resisted pressure to restore the cuts made in 1933 in Federal salaries and in benefit payments to veterans. But on the economy issue Congress rebelled. On March 28, 1934, the Independent Offices Appropriations Act—passed over the President's veto—reduced the maximum pay cut for government employees from 15 per cent to 10 per cent from February 1, 1934, to June 30, 1934, and to 5 per cent thereafter. This final 5 per cent cut was ended on July 1, 1935. Meantime, pressure from the veterans' lobby had resulted in restoring their benefit payments.

The most serious issue involving the veterans was the increasing demand for immediate payment of the bonus. In 1935, when Congress authorized the issuance of Treasury notes, or greenbacks, to pay the full maturity value of the certificates, not only did Roosevelt veto the measure, but he went before Congress on May 22, 1935, to state his objections. His principal argument was that the government's obligation during the depression was to all the unemployed and that able-bodied veterans should not be entitled to special treatment. The House overrode the veto, but in the Senate the President's action was sustained, although by a close vote.

Roosevelt's opposition only delayed the measure's passage. In January, 1936, a new bill, the Adjusted Payment Compensation bill, passed Congress. In its latest form it was less objectionable than the 1932 or 1935 versions since it eliminated the inflationary provision for paying the bonuses in greenbacks and stipulated that the veterans receive redeemable nine-year, interest-bearing bonds. Although Roosevelt still refused to approve the measure, it was enacted into law over his veto by overwhelming votes. Congressional generosity had made the government liable to immediate demands of about $2.4 billion, and of this total the veterans collected about $1.7 billion during the next few months.

The 1936 Boom

Whether as a result of the New Deal, as the administration supporters insisted, or in spite of the New Deal, as Republican critics charged, the fact was undeniable that by election day, 1936, the country was enjoying a substantial degree of prosperity. National income had been $41 billion in 1932; it was $64 billion in 1936. Industrial production by the end of 1936 was not only double the 1932 level, but somewhat higher than it had been in the fabulous year of 1929. In October, 1936, Roosevelt announced that for the first time in fifty-five years an entire year had passed without a single national bank failure. Conditions were sufficiently good to assure the triumphant re-election of the President, but New Deal policies had, nevertheless, aroused opposition in many influential quarters and bitter battles lay ahead.

17

NEW DEAL ON THE DEFENSIVE

Between 1936 to 1939 the Roosevelt liberals engaged in a bitter struggle with their conservative critics. The fight crossed party lines, with many one-time Republicans supporting the President while right-wing Democrats rebelled against him. In the first round, Roosevelt won the election of 1936 in decisive fashion, but succeeding rounds were less astutely fought. In the contest over judicial reform, in the attempted purge of right-wing Democrats, and in the 1938 congressional election Roosevelt suffered setbacks. Despite minor victories, however, the conservatives were unable to regain control of the government or to force the reversal of any basic New Deal policy. On the contrary, new legislation during Roosevelt's second term extended government regulation still further in several directions.

The Election of 1936

The first determined effort to unseat the Roosevelt faction was through the Liberty League, organized in August, 1934. The Du Ponts and other wealthy industrial and financial leaders furnished the movement with ample funds, while conservative Democrats like Al Smith, ex-Governor Joseph Ely of Massachusetts, and Jouett Shouse, former Democratic Executive Committee chairman, cooperated in trying to break the President's hold over his own party. Although the League's attempts were unsuccessful in the congressional election of 1934, it redoubled its efforts the next year. The climax of the campaign occurred in January, 1936, when Al Smith belabored the administration for an hour to the delight of a Washington banquet hall full of rich Liberty Leaguers. Nevertheless, the affair had unexpected repercussions. No less than twelve members of the Du Pont family were among Smith's audience, and the spectacle of the rich and privileged now making a hero of the Happy Warrior whom most of them had opposed in 1928 appeared ridiculous to the rest of the country.

As the Liberty League lost ground, wealthy anti–New Dealers turned to other expedients. Thousands of dollars were advanced to Governor Eugene Talmadge of Georgia, spokesman for the most narrow and demagogic Southern conservatives, to organize a revolt against Roosevelt in his section. It was hoped that by feeding this and other local quarrels within the Democratic ranks a substantial anti-Roosevelt bloc could be sent to the national convention. Postmaster General Farley, however, directed such an astute campaign that all the presidential preference primaries demonstrated Roosevelt's un-diminished popularity with the Democratic rank and file.

The Democratic convention at Philadelphia was also a triumph for Roose-velt. Not only were he and Garner renominated without opposition, but the platform was a thoroughly New Deal document. "We hold this truth to be self-evident," it proclaimed, "that government in a modern civilization has certain inescapable obligations to its citizens, among which are (1) protection of the family and the home; (2) establishment of a democracy of opportunity for all the people; (3) aid to those overtaken by disaster." And the platform pointed with pride to the administration's achievements under each of these headings, while promising more progress in the future. As another New Deal triumph, the selection of party nominees by a simple majority vote was substituted for the two-thirds rule.

Once again Roosevelt appeared before the convention to accept the nomination. The delegates were roused to great enthusiasm by his condemna-tion of "economic royalists" and by the stirring conclusion in which he declared: "This generation of Americans has a rendezvous with destiny."

The leading contenders for the Republican nomination were Herbert Hoover, Senator Borah, Senator Arthur Vandenberg of Michigan, Colonel Frank Knox, wealthy Chicago newspaper publisher and former Bull Mooser, and Governor Alfred Landon of Kansas. Despite the greater prominence of the other candidates, Landon won a first ballot nomination at the Cleveland convention because he seemed to have many assets for leading the anti–New Deal fight. Conservatives were impressed by his success in balancing the Kansas state budget, while liberals accepted him because he came from the farm belt and had supported Theodore Roosevelt in 1912. His background as a small Midwestern businessman would dramatize the contention that the New Deal was the enemy of small business. The candidate's lack of color was obvious, but this might be an asset were the voters tired of Roosevelt exuberance. Besides, the ticket was balanced by nominating the aggressive Colonel Knox for the vice-presidency.

Although hopefully undertaken, the Republican compaign was ill-starred from the start. The platform and the candidates' speeches illustrated the party dilemma. The New Deal had to be denounced as a whole while being accepted in most of its significant parts. Democratic violation of the Consti-tution, extravagance, bureaucracy, and appeal to class prejudice were cited as evidence that America was "in peril." Nevertheless, the Republicans pledged themselves to the effective regulation of business, to emergency benefit pay-ments to farmers, to guaranteeing labor's right to organize, and to relief for the unemployed. Clear-cut issues were largely confined to promises to balance the budget immediately, to repeal the Reciprocal Trade Agreements Act, and to sell the agricultural surplus abroad with governmental assistance.

For a time, great importance was laid on the emergence of a new third party. Old-line politicians had long feared that the admirers of Huey Long, Dr. Townsend, and Father Coughlin might unite in a single mass movement, and the formation of the Union party in June, 1936, was intended to bring about exactly this result. Several factors, however, made this party much less formidable than expected. Huey Long was dead, after one of the most curious careers in American politics. An enormously clever and effective demagogue, he had been elected governor of Louisiana in 1928. Although his political machine was corrupt and dictatorial, he gave better roads and schools to his poor constituents. Elected United States Senator in 1930, his Senate and radio speeches, though rambling and violent, were highly entertaining and never lacked for auditors. His "Share the Wealth" movement with its slogan "Every Man a King" won thousands of adherents in 1935, and his ambition to gain the White House seriously worried the Democratic high command. While not believing Huey could achieve this goal, they did fear he might win enough votes to throw the election to the Republicans. In September, 1935, he was assassinated in his home state. The Union party thereupon chose as its standard-bearer Representative William Lemke, a rather drab North Dakota legislator, hitherto little known except as an advocate of farm relief and inflation. Father Coughlin was so confident of his own influence that he promised to retire from broadcasting if Lemke did not poll at least 12 million votes, but the priest's attempts to create enthusiasm for "Liberty Bill" were unavailing. In the end the Union party received only 900,000 votes. Small though this was when compared with Coughlin's prediction, it was larger than the 190,000 that went to Norman Thomas, the Socialist candidate, and the 80,000 to Earl Browder, the Communist.

The only real contest was between Roosevelt and Landon, and even that proved a very unequal one. Despite the number of prominent Democrats who followed Al Smith in "taking a walk"—deserting their party nominee and supporting Landon, the mass of voters moved in the opposite direction. Landon's campaigning proved ineffective, while Roosevelt's was adroit and bold. Thus Landon was defeated more decisively than any previous Republican presidential candidate. He carried only two states and won only eight electorial votes as against Roosevelt's 523; the popular vote was Roosevelt, 27,751,597; Landon, 16,679,583.

The Second Inaugural

Roosevelt took his second presidential oath on January 20, 1937—the first inauguration on the new date provided by the Lame Duck Amendment. The ceremony took place in a heavy rainstorm—an appropriate setting for the first act of a tempestuous period in national politics. There was little of complacency in the inaugural address. In response to his own question— have we reached "the goal of our vision"?—the President stated:

I see a great nation, upon a great continent, blessed with a great wealth of natural resources. . . .
But here is the challenge to our democracy: In this nation I see tens of millions of its citizens—a substantial part of its whole population—who at this very moment are denied the greater part of what the very lowest standards of today call the necessities of life. . . .
I see one-third of a nation ill-housed, ill-clad, ill-nourished.

Obviously the second Roosevelt administration was being dedicated to new offensives under the standard of social justice. The President's conservative opponents, speculating uneasily on where the first blow would be struck, did not have long to wait.

The Supreme Court and the Progressive Movement

On February 5, 1937, the chief executive sent a message to Congress calling for reorganization of the entire Federal judiciary. Even a country conditioned to expect the unexpected was stunned by the audacity of the maneuver.

No discussion of the President's proposals and the great debate they precipated would be meaningful unless the issue were placed in its historical perspective. The Supreme Court's power to declare Federal and state laws unconstitutional was not explicitly granted in the Constitution, and it is debatable whether the framers intended the Court to perform such a function. When under the strong leadership of John Marshall the Supreme Court actually began to invalidate Federal and state laws, there were protests, but the precedents for its doing so were successfully established. Nevertheless, during the first seventy years of national history the Supreme Court declared acts of Congress unconstitutional on only two occasions.

Following the Civil War, however, the Court became much bolder, invalidating 23 Federal laws between 1860 and 1900, and 35 from 1900 to 1930. One disallowed law, the income-tax provision of 1894, was the embodiment of a great popular demand, and the Court was accused of shielding the wealthy against paying their proper share of Federal taxes. Such censure was all the more bitter because of the increasing frequency with which the Federal judiciary set aside state legislation regulating business. Between 1890 and 1937, 228 state laws were invalidated because they deprived "persons"—frequently corporations—of property "without due process of law."

By 1900 it was already apparent that the Supreme Court provided a conservative stronghold for property interests threatened by either Federal or state legislation. The progressives became increasingly dismayed over these judicial obstacles, and the recall of judges and of judicial decisions became progressive demands before World War I.

Theodore Roosevelt sought to liberalize the judiciary in 1902 by appointing Oliver Wendell Holmes, Jr., of Massachusetts to the Supreme Court because of Holmes's prolabor decisions as a state judge. Although the Rough Rider was much disappointed when the new judge dissented from the majority decision in the Northern Securities case, Holmes soon proved an important liberal influence. Again and again during his thirty years on the Supreme Court, he cheered progressives with his bold and brilliantly phrased opinions, the most memorable being dissents from the decisions of his more conservative colleagues. Roosevelt's other two appointments were much less effective for his purpose.

That Roosevelt named only three men to the highest court in almost eight years in the White House illustrates the conservatives' good fortune in maintaining their influence. The conservative Taft appointed six justices during his four-year term, while the liberal Wilson named only three during the next eight years. On the other hand, Old Guard Harding made four appointments and his successors, Coolidge and Hoover, made one and three appointments, respectively. The assumption that progressive Presidents always name progressive judges and conservative Presidents conservative judges is not always valid—as the choice of the reactionary James McReynolds by Wilson and the appointments of the liberal Stone and Cardozo by Coolidge and Hoover illustrate. Yet in general chief executives have selected judges who incline toward their own philosophy of government. The jealousy with which the conservatives regarded their control of the Court was best shown by the bitter fight against the confirmation of Brandeis in 1916.

Conservative success in controlling the Court showed its results in that body's decisions. In an earlier chapter, the judicial obstacles in the way of state regulation of hours of labor have been discussed. While eventually the Court gave way on this issue, it still remained hostile to minimum-wage laws, even those to protect women. In Adkins *v.* Children's Hospital (1923), the Supreme Court declared unconstitutional an act of Congress establishing minimum wages for women and children in the District of Columbia. Since the majority's line of reasoning made it certain that similar state laws would be invalidated, the decision stood as an effective barrier to the protection of workers from sweatshop conditions. State laws regulating child labor were not interfered with, but two Federal measures of the Wilson administration on the subject were negated by the Court (Hammer *v.* Dagenhart, 1918, and Bailey *v.* Drexel Furniture Company, 1921).

Organized labor's grievances against the judiciary have been frequently alluded to, but it should be added that the Supreme Court invalidated Federal and state laws specifically protecting the right of collective bargaining. In 1908 a Federal prohibition of "yellow-dog" contracts between the railroads and their employees was declared unconstitutional (Adair *v.* United States), while in 1915 a similar state law was invalidated (Coppage *v.* Kansas). The Court even denied the right of a state legislature to limit the power of its own state judges to issue injunctions in labor disputes (Truax *v.* Corrigan, 1921). This decision provoked Justice Holmes to say in his dissenting opinion:

There is nothing that I more deprecate than the use of the Fourteenth Amendment beyond the absolute compulsion of its words to prevent the making of social experiments that an important part of the community desires, in the insulated chambers afforded by the several States, even though the experiments may seem futile or even noxious to me and to those whose judgment I most respect.

Even during the twenties, when the progressive movement was in eclipse, the Federal judiciary was under chronic attack because of its conservatism. LaFollette's platform in 1924 urged a constitutional amendment under which a law declared unconstitutional by the Supreme Court might be re-enacted by Congress. Senator Borah authored a bill requiring the concurrence of seven Court members to declare an act of Congress unconstitutional. Such proposals were doomed to failure, but in 1930 the progressive bloc prevented the confirmation of the supposedly antilabor John Parker as a Supreme Court justice and strongly, though unsuccessfully, fought against the confirmation of Chief Justice Hughes.

The Supreme Court and the New Deal

Not until 1934 did cases involving the New Deal begin to reach the Supreme Court. Both friends and foes of the Roosevelt measures watched eagerly for an indication of the attitude the justices would take. Nervous New Dealers found some reassurance in the decisions upholding a Minnesota mortgage-moratorium act (Home Building and Loan Association v. Blaisdell) and a New York milk-control law (Nebbia v. New York). While neither case involved a Federal measure, both involved the powers of government to deal with an economic emergency. Realistic observers noted, however, that these were both five-to-four decisions. Those familiar with the record of the judges were not surprised at this; the Court was readily analyzed as containing four ultraconservatives (McReynolds, George Sutherland, Willis Van Devanter, and Pierce Butler), three liberals (Brandeis, Benjamin Cardozo, and Harlan Stone), and two middle-of-the-roaders (Chief Justice Hughes and Owen Roberts). The fate of the New Deal depended largely on how the last two exercised their balance of power.

The administration received its first serious setback in January, 1935, in the "Hot Oil" case (Panama Refining Company v. Ryan), in which all the judges except Cardozo concurred in negating Section 9-A of the National Industrial Recovery Act because it delegated legislative power to the executive—the first time an act of Congress was set aside for this reason. Because delegation of emergency powers to the President had been a prominent feature of the legislation of the Hundred Days, the decision had serious implications.

The next important New Deal measure to pass under review was the congressional resolution of June 5, 1933, under which any clause in a public or private contract specifying payment in gold was voided and the obligation must be paid dollar for dollar in any legal tender currency. The windfall to creditors and the utter financial confusion that would have followed the invalidation of this law were obvious, yet such a disaster was only narrowly averted. By five-to-four decisions in February, 1935, the Court upheld the resolution as regards private contracts, but denied Congress the power to modify the obligations of the United States bonds. The plaintiff, however, was not allowed to recover against the government because he had not proved any actual damage (the Gold Clause cases—Norman v. Ohio Railroad Company, Perry v. United States, and so on).

The New Deal's "Black Monday" in court came on May 27, 1935. In three unanimous decisions the Frazier-Lemke Farm Mortgage Act of 1934 was found invalid (Louisville Bank v. Radford), the President's removal of William Humphrey from the FTC was declared illegal (Humphrey's Executor v. United States), and the general code-making procedure under NRA was ruled unconstitutional (A. L. A. Schechter Corporation v. United States). Roosevelt found the last of these decisions most upsetting. Not only did it destroy an agency from which he hoped much good could still eventuate, but, what was more serious, the Court's opinion construed the commerce clause more narrowly than any decision had for decades. "We have been relegated," Roosevelt said, "to the horse-and-buggy definition of interstate commerce."

1936 was equally difficult for those arguing New Deal cases before the courts. In January the first Agricultural Adjustment Act was declared unconstitutional by a six-to-three decision (United States *v.* Butler)—perhaps the most criticized of all anti-Roosevelt decisions. In February the government won one of its few victories when the right of the TVA to sell surplus electricity generated at Wilson Dam was recognized (Ashwander *v.* TVA). But in June the power of the SEC was narrowly circumscribed (Jones *v.* SEC), while a month later the New Deal suffered another major defeat when the first Bituminous Coal Conservation Act was invalidated (Carter *v.* Carter Coal Company). Hughes joined the liberal minority in dissenting from this and from a subsequent decision declaring the New York Minimum Wage Act unconstitutional (Morehead *v.* Tipaldo). The latter case emphasized the predicament in which liberals now found themselves. Whereas on the one hand the Court was setting aside Federal laws establishing minimum labor standards because they invaded the powers of the states, on the other hand it was denying the state legislatures the right to pass similar laws because these violated the Fourteenth Amendment. Thus a legal "no man's land" had been created where neither Federal nor state governments could act.

The extent of the administration's difficulties is not adequately indicated by this account of Supreme Court cases. The lower Federal courts were largely staffed with conservatives no less eager to hamstring the Roosevelt reforms. Sixteen hundred injunctions restraining Federal officers from carrying out acts of Congress were granted. Anti–New Deal lawyers resorted to a variety of legal devices to invite judicial intervention. Such agencies at TVA, SEC, and NLRB found themselves almost powerless to carry out the functions for which they had been created.

The Judicial Reorganization Bill

Behind the scenes the administration was quietly considering how to remove these judicial obstacles. The judicial issue was avoided during the campaign not only for political expediency, but because of the difficulty of framing a concrete plan. The most logical remedy would be a constitutional amendment whereby the power of Congress and the state legislatures to deal effectively with twentieth-century economic problems would be affirmed in unequivocal language, but this did not seem practical. Drafting an amendment acceptable to two thirds of Congress would have been difficult in the first place; its acceptance by three quarters of the states would have been next to impossible. Another proposal would require seven, eight, or all of the judges to concur in a decision before the Supreme Court could invalidate a law. Roosevelt and his advisers decided, however, that any such measure would probably be declared unconstitutional. Equally serious objections were raised to other suggestions and, by a process of elimination, the President hit at length on the proposal transmitted to Congress in his message of February 5, 1937.

This message on "judicial reorganization" took as its thesis the necessity for legislative action to quiet complaints over "the complexities, the delays,

Fall in! (By Seibel in the *Richmond Times-Dispatch*.)

and the expense of litigation in United States courts." The overcrowded dockets proved the "need for additional judges" in all ranks of the Federal judiciary. "A part of the problem of obtaining a sufficient number of judges to dispose of cases," the President asserted, "is the capacity of the judges themselves. This brings forward the question of aged or infirm judges—a subject of delicacy and yet one which requires frank discussion." He then alluded to the 1869 voluntary retirement act allowing judges to retire on full pension at the age of seventy. Despite this provision, many continued on the bench long past this age. In exceptional cases they retained their full mental and physical vigor, but the less fortunate ones were "often unable to perceive their own infirmities." The President's solution was embodied in a draft bill accompanying the message. It provided that when any Federal judge reached the age of seventy, had served for at least ten years, and within six months thereafter had not resigned or retired, the President should appoint with Senate consent one additional judge. Not more than fifty judges might be appointed, and no judge might be named to the Supreme Court if the appointment would result in more than fifteen members of that body.

This message was less ably composed than most Roosevelt documents. Its best sentence asserted: "A constant and systematic addition of younger blood will vitalize the courts and better equip them to recognize and apply the essential concepts of justice in the light of the needs and the facts of an ever-changing world." Yet no evidence of the existing Court's failure to adapt itself to new problems was presented. Instead, the principal stress was laid upon the alleged inability of elderly judges to keep up with their work. In later years Roosevelt himself commented: "I made one major mistake when I first presented the plan. I did not place enough emphasis upon the real mischief—the kind of decisions which, as a studied and continued policy, had been coming down from the Supreme Court."

The blunder was serious. Six Supreme Court justices were over seventy; therefore the President could make six new appointments whether the elderly incumbents chose to continue to serve or to retire. The proposal was to pack the Court,[1] and the indirection of the presidential message only made the maneuver appear more Machiavellian than it actually was.

A month later in a radio address, Roosevelt argued for his plan more effectively. He charged the Court itself with violating the spirit of the Constitution by "assuming the power to pass on the wisdom of these Acts of Congress—and to approve or disapprove the public policy written into these laws." Facing squarely the criticism that he would be "packing the Court," he denied that he wanted to appoint justices whom he could control on specific cases and continued:

But if by that phrase the charge is made that I would appoint . . . Justices worthy to sit beside present members of the Court who understand those modern conditions; that I will appoint Justices who will not undertake to override the judgment of Congress on legislative policy; that I will appoint Justices who will act as Justices and not as legislators—if the appointment of such Justices can be called "packing the Courts," then I say that I, and with me the vast majority of the American people, favor doing just that thing—now.

This radio address came too late to overcome the bad impression caused by the deviousness of the first move. Conservatives vigorously denounced the measure both in and out of Congress, warning that Roosevelt was trying to dominate the judiciary and overthrow the Constitution. They now had a tailor-made issue that brought fierce denunciation of the President in newspaper editorials, radio broadcasts, and even sermons.

Insofar as these cries of alarm originated in Republican or Liberty League circles, Roosevelt could shrug them off. Again and again he had seen similar opposition develop, only to be easily overridden when the votes were counted. Even the revolt of conservative Democrats like Senators Carter Glass and

---

[1] Court-packing proposals were not entirely a New Deal innovation. The Federalists were accused of altering the number of Federal judges for party advantage in 1801; the Republicans of doing so after the Civil War.

Harry Byrd of Virginia was not alarming as they had opposed New Deal measures before. What the President had not anticipated was that his proposal would antagonize a dangerously large number of hitherto loyal legislators. Many were at heart conservative and, now with the election over, they were anxious to assert their independence of the White House. They were shocked by the proposal and embittered by the fact Roosevelt had presented it to Congress without previous consultation. The most unexpected blow of all came when the leadership in the antireorganization-bill fight was assumed by Senator Burton Wheeler of Montana, always regarded as spokesman for the extreme liberals. His position was curious. Although bitterly opposed to the Roosevelt plan as a dangerous expansion of executive powers, he himself was the sponsor of a more radical measure—a constitutional amendment permitting a two-thirds congressional vote to overrule any Court decision in which a congressional act was held unconstitutional. Conservative Republicans, having learned the bitter lesson that their prominent participation in a fight against a New Deal proposal was likely to increase its popularity, kept in the background while the Democrats quarreled among themselves.

Public opinion was sharply divided on the issue. At the hearings before the Senate Judiciary Committee, four law school deans opposed the reorganization bill and five supported it. Six New England college presidents condemned the measure, but two of the nation's leading authorities on the Constitution defended it. Had the issue come to a vote shortly after the proposal was presented, it might have passed by a narrow margin. Between March and June, however, developments within the Supreme Court itself profoundly affected the issue.

The New Deal Becomes Constitutional

The President's reorganization proposal gave a new solidarity to the institution under attack. Brandeis, the oldest and most liberal justice, resented the imputation that the age of judges prevented them from keeping up with their business, while liberal and conservative justices alike opposed the creation of new places on the bench. Chief Justice Hughes wrote a letter, in which Justices Van Devanter and Brandeis concurred, defending the Court against the charge it was slow and inefficient. This letter gave a mighty lift to the Wheeler faction, but an even greater one followed when Justice Roberts voted with Hughes, Stone, Cardozo, and Brandeis to uphold the constitutionality of a Washington minimum-wage law (West Coast Hotel Co. v. Parrish), thereby overruling the Adkins decision of 1923 and the New York Minimum Wage case of 1936.

Additional evidence that the Court could reform itself without outside help came on April 12, when a series of five-to-four decisions upheld the National Labor Relations Act (NLRB v. Jones and Laughlin Steel Corporation, Associated Press v. NLRB, and so on). Hughes and Roberts once again sided with the liberals in asserting that the labor practices involved in these cases threatened to obstruct interstate commerce and that the Federal government therefore had the power to act. A third major New Deal victory was gained in a series of decisions upholding the Social Security Act (Helvering *v.* Davis, Carmichael *v.* Southern Coal Company, and so on).

The President felt his attack on the judiciary had already brought results, attributing the new liberalism of Hughes and Roberts largely to their desire to save the Court from unwelcome change. Most commentators have agreed that such a motive was either consciously or unconsciously guiding the judges during the 1937 session. It should be pointed out, however, that Roberts's shift on minimum-wage legislation occurred before the reorganization message was sent to Congress. Other factors influencing the Court may have been the conclusive 1936 election results and a wave of strikes, which gave impressive evidence of the need for labor legislation. Moreover, the laws of the Second New Deal were drafted in less haste than those of the First and thus provided fewer grounds for invalidation.

As a final demonstration that the Roosevelt proposal was unnecessary, Van Devanter retired in June, thus opening the way for the first new appointment in five years. The justice's action was facilitated by the knowledge that under the recently passed Supreme Court Retirement Act, he could leave the bench without resigning, thereby enjoying immunity from certain taxes and being assured that his compensation could never be reduced.

Death of the Court Bill

Legislators supporting the reorganization bill out of loyalty rather than conviction now advised Roosevelt to abandon his project as it had already served the purpose of inducing the Court to take a more charitable view of New Deal legislation. The President refused, however, because the liberal margin in the Court was too narrow and uncertain. If a constitutional "no man's land" had been eliminated, it was only to create a "Roberts's land." Even Van Devanter's retirement did not reassure the President, because he was committed to appointing Senator Joseph Robinson of Arkansas, Democratic leader of the upper house, to fill the vacancy. Though a thoroughly loyal New Deal legislator, Robinson as a judge might revert to a more conservative philosophy.

On June 14 the reorganization bill suffered a staggering blow. Seven Democrats on the Senate Judiciary Committee joined with three Republicans in a majority report against the bill, saying:

We recommend the rejection of this bill as a needless, futile, and utterly dangerous abandonment of constitutional principle. . . .

It is a measure which should be so emphatically rejected that its parallel will never again be presented to the free representatives of the free people of America.

Convinced at last that the original bill could not pass, Roosevelt suggested a modified plan under which he would make two new appointments instead of six, but the opposition was equally determined to defeat this proposal. The Senate became involved in a heated debate, with tempers on all sides worn thin. When Senator Robinson, his strength overtaxed by the battle, fell dead in his apartment, the compromise bill received its final blow. The last chapter was written on July 22, when the Senate, by a vote of 70 to 20, recommitted the measure to committee. Eventually a law providing for procedural reforms in the lower courts, but leaving the Supreme Court strictly alone, was quietly enacted into law.

The New Deal Court

The defeat of the reorganization plan was a great moral victory for the New Deal opponents and equally important were its implications as a revolt against Roosevelt's leadership of his party. Yet it did not prevent his obtaining his ultimate end—liberalization of the Supreme Court. Within the next four years Roosevelt had the opportunity to appoint not six, but seven, justices. Sutherland followed Van Devanter into retirement within seven months; Cardozo died in 1938; Butler and Brandeis both retired in 1939, followed by McReynolds and Hughes in 1941. By the end of the latter year, Roberts and Stone were the only pre-Roosevelt appointees still on the bench.

Roosevelt's first appointment was made in August, 1937, before the excitement of the reorganization-bill controversy had died down. The naming of Senator Hugo Black of Alabama, a most ardent New Dealer, was a bitter dose for conservatives to swallow, but senatorial courtesy led to his confirmation by a vote of 63 to 16. Black quietly took the oath and left for a European vacation before assuming his new duties. At long last the country seemed ready to forget the court issue when suddenly the whole controversy was reopened when newspaper articles charged Black with membership in the Ku Klux Klan and demanded his resignation. So great was the outcry that the new justice cut short his vacation and returned home. In a radio talk he admitted he had once been a Klan member, but insisted he had resigned long ago and did not hold any of the racial or religious prejudices that characterized the organization.

Black's difficulties did not end with his radio statement. An attempt to prevent his taking over his duties through petition to the Supreme Court was rejected, but he then became the victim of a campaign charging him with incompetence. Despite all attacks, Black stuck to his post and gradually won a large measure of respect. The irrelevance of the Klan charge was demonstrated by his strongly worded decisions upholding minority rights.

No subsequent Roosevelt appointment aroused a comparable outcry. There was some opposition to Felix Frankfurter in 1941 because of his reputation for radicalism gained during the Sacco-Vanzetti case, as well as during his behind-the-scenes activities as New Deal adviser. On the bench, however, he proved to be more conservative than most of the other New Deal appointees.[2] Much of the criticism of the President's policy toward the judiciary was quieted when he elevated the widely respected Harlan Stone of New York to the Chief Justiceship when Hughes retired in 1941.

---

[2] The other new judges were Stanley Reed of Kentucky, William Douglas of Connecticut, Frank Murphy of Michigan, Robert Jackson of New York, and Senator James Byrnes of South Carolina. When in 1942 Byrnes accepted a post in the war administration, Wiley Rutledge of Iowa took his place.

As might be expected, the liberal trend in Supreme Court decisions begun in 1937 continued. Such important New Deal laws as the Agricultural Adjustment Act of 1938 (Mulford *v.* Smith) and the Fair Labor Standards Act (United States *v.* Darby) were upheld. The unanimous approval given to the latter was one of the administration's greatest victories because it overruled Hammer *v.* Dagenhart, a barrier to Federal regulation of child labor since 1918.

Executive Reorganization

Ever since Theodore Roosevelt's day the need to reorganize the Federal executive branch had been recognized, and every President thereafter had urged that something be done. Limited steps had been taken, but the task was too complex for detailed congressional legislation. Presidents Taft, Wilson, and Hoover had been in agreement that effective reform could only be obtained through a grant of authority to the President, but the little they had been able to accomplish was no real answer to the problem. The rapid multiplication of government activities, indeed, made the situation increasingly worse.

Consequently, on January 12, 1937, Roosevelt, in a special message, requested congressional legislation to reorganize the executive branch. The charge made against his Supreme Court plan could not be made against this proposal. On the contrary, the President transmitted a proposal carefully formulated by a Committee on Administrative Management consisting of three of the country's leading authorities on public administration: Louis Brownlow and Charles Merriam of Chicago and Luther Gulick of New York. There were five major recommendations: (1) expansion of the White House staff so that the President might have able assistants to keep him in touch with administrative affairs; (2) strengthening the government managerial agencies, particularly those dealing with the budget, with efficiency research, with personnel, and with planning; (3) extension of the merit system "upward, outward, and downward to cover practically all non-policy-determining posts," and reorganization of the civil service system under a single responsible administration; (4) overhauling the hundred independent agencies and commissions and placing them under one or another of twelve executive departments (the ten existing departments plus two new ones—Social Welfare and Public Works); and (5) reform of the government's auditing procedure.

Because of preoccupation with the Supreme Court fight, Congress made little progress in dealing with this proposal until 1938, when a reorganization bill passed the Senate. This included several safeguards and certain departures from the presidential plan: no provision was made for a Department of Public Works; regulatory commissions like the ICC were to be left alone; all executive orders were subject to disapproval by joint resolution of Congress within sixty days. It was difficult to see how such a grant of power to the President could undermine republican government, yet such was the accusation hurled by the anti–New Dealers. The measure was labeled "a dictator bill" and all the propaganda techniques so effective in the Supreme Court fight were once again employed. The House was sufficiently impressed by this clamor to kill the measure, largely through defections in the Democratic ranks.

In 1939, however, a modified bill was passed without serious trouble. It provided for six administrative assistants to the President and directed him to formulate plans either to abolish unnecessary government agencies or to consolidate them for better economy and efficiency. He was to transmit these plans to Congress, after which they would become effective unless the legislature, by concurrent resolutions, disapproved them within sixty days. The powers granted to the President, however, fell short of what he had originally asked by failing to provide for any new executive departments, by exempting from reorganization a number of independent boards and commissions, and by not bringing the civil service system under a single administrator.

The Recession

Meantime, new economic problems were plaguing the administration. For a few months in late 1936 and early 1937 Roosevelt's advisers actually worried about an excess of prosperity, for industrial production was high, the stock market was buoyant, and commodity prices were rising rapidly. It was feared indeed that the country might be entering upon a period of wild speculation like that of the late twenties. Consequently, the administration shifted rather abruptly to deflationary policies. The WPA rolls were greatly reduced, economy was enjoined upon the government departments, and balancing the budget within a year was contemplated.

After August, 1937, however, the situation radically altered. Industrial production declined, prices fell, and unemployment once again became a serious problem. This new depression—or recession as Roosevelt preferred to call it—was short-lived. Recovery began in June, 1938, and by December much of the lost ground had been regained. While it lasted, however, the recession was serious and discouraging, for inevitably it struck a damaging blow at the prestige of the administration.

Many economists attributed the recession to natural factors operating quite independently of government policy. Nevertheless, in the supercharged political atmosphere of 1937 these new economic troubles became the subject of bitter accusations. New Dealers asserted that there was a deliberate "strike of capital," that businessmen were recklessly contributing to economic distress to force a change of government policy. Anti–New Dealers with similar intemperance blamed the whole situation on the administration's hostility to business.

These disagreements as to the causes of the recession led to different proposals for its cure. The conservative prescription called for a halt to government spending, tax relief to the corporations, and a recess on social legislation. Without subscribing to this whole program, right-wing New Dealers advised economy and budget-balancing. On the other hand, more radical advisers attributed the recession to premature reductions in relief expenditures and advocated new spending. Evidently reluctant to commit himself, the President allowed the recession to continue for over eight months before he finally accepted the tenets of the spending school. In a message of April 12, 1938, he attributed the nation's economic troubles to the fact that "production in many important lines of goods outran the ability of the public to purchase them." This led him to assert:

Today's purchasing power—the citizen's income of today—is not sufficient to drive the economic system at higher speed. Responsibility of government requires us at this time to supplement the normal processes. . . .

Let us unanimously recognize that the Federal debt, whether it be twenty-five billions or forty billions, can only be paid if the nation obtains a vastly increased citizen income. I repeat that if this citizen income can be raised to $80 billion a year the national government and the overwhelming majority of state and local governments will be "out of the red."

Congress answered this plea by authorizing more than $5 billion in emergency expenditures. Hopkins again showed himself a master of the art of putting such a program quickly into operation. Monthly WPA expenditures during the final months of 1938 were double what they had been a year before. The PWA also greatly increased its activities, although somewhat more slowly.

Increased government expenditures were paralleled by business recovery, but whether this was cause and effect depended on the point of view. Advocates of compensatory spending said it was and added that, if the government would double or triple expenditures for public projects, the unemployment problem would be completely solved. This reasoning was anathema to conservatives, who insisted that, if the government put its house in order, the resulting wave of confidence would ensure a really sound economic recovery. They regarded deficit spending as evidence that the New Deal could not solve the nation's problems. This acrimonious debate was still raging when World War II completely changed the whole economic picture.

Attempted Purge

Events since the 1936 election had given additional proof of what had long been evident—the complete lack of agreement among Democrats upon basic principles. Some Democrats advocated increased Federal power, others clung to traditional states-rights doctrines; some championed labor's right to organize, others wished to curb labor unions; some sought through government intervention to broaden the opportunities of the underprivileged, others wanted to fortify the position of the dominant economic and social groups.

In 1938 Roosevelt attempted the herculean task of rectifying the situation. He appealed to the Democratic voters to repudiate the party conservatives and elect only liberals. In a radio address of June 24 he asserted: "An election cannot give a country a firm sense of direction if it has two or more national parties which merely have different names but are as alike in their principles and aims as peas in the same pod."

The boldness of the President's effort was best exemplified when he appealed to the Georgia voters in August, to repudiate their Senator, Walter

The New Deal as Don Quixote. (By Berryman in the *Evening Star*, Washington.)

George, while the latter was sitting on the same platform. George, Roosevelt said, was his personal friend and a gentleman and a scholar, but, on most public questions, he and the President did "not speak the same language." With equal directness Roosevelt subsequently sought the defeat of Senator Millard Tydings of Maryland and Representative John O'Connor of New York, while requesting the re-election of Senator Alben Barkley of Kentucky. These were the only contests in which Roosevelt intervened directly, but lesser administration figures became involved in a number of other primaries.

This effort to drive the conservative Democrats out of Congress was promptly labeled "a purge" by the opposition press. Had the term been intended simply in its dictionary meaning of "a cleansing," the President would presumably have been glad to accept it as descriptive of what he was attempting, but in 1938 the word's connotations were far more damaging. Hitler had consolidated his position in Germany by a so-called purge, and Stalin had done the same in the Soviet Union. Hence the use of the term in connection with Roosevelt obviously implied that he too was involved in an undemocratic attempt to crush all who opposed him. Although the President insisted that his objection to certain legislators was their general political philosophy, his critics charged him with taking a mean revenge against Democrats who had opposed the Supreme Court bill. Nor did the President's opponents base their condemnation merely on the motivation of his conduct; they insisted that it was wrong for a chief executive to interfere in such local primary contests.

Only in New York and Kentucky was Roosevelt's intervention effective. O'Connor was defeated in the Democratic primary and then defeated again in the November election when he ran as a Republican, while Barkley won his primary contest. But in Georgia and Maryland the proscribed candidates won decisive victories, as did practically all the other conservative Democrats marked for retirement. The primaries had as their general result the strengthening of the anti–New Deal faction.

Roosevelt's attempt to liberalize his party was bady timed, for the political tide had turned in the opposite direction. This had been demonstrated in the Supreme Court and reorganization fights, and it was given further proof by the November, 1938, elections. In the Senate the Democrats dropped from 75 seats to 69, while the Republicans were climbing from 17 to 23. In the House the Democrats dropped from 333 to 262 seats and the Republicans rose from 89 to 169. Even more impressive were Republican gubernatorial victories in a number of key states.

The Hatch Acts

The revival of the WPA plus the unusual bitterness of the 1938 campaign focused attention on the potentialities of the relief administration for bribing or coercing the voters. Therefore the Senate appointed the Sheppard Committee on Campaign Practices to examine the situation; this Democrat-dominated committee reported in January, 1939, that local WPA agents in Pennsylvania, Kentucky, and Tennessee were using the relief organization to promote the New Deal vote. While it is difficult to say how much actual political manipulation of relief there had been, there was sufficient evidence of irregularities to induce Congress to pass the Hatch Act of August, 1939.

This "act to prevent pernicious activities" made it unlawful for anyone to coerce any other person for the purposing of influencing his vote in any Federal election. Specifically, it was unlawful to deprive anyone of relief on account of race, creed, color, political activity, support of or opposition to any candidate or any political party in any election, or to solicit campaign contributions from relief workers. But the act went beyond prohibition abuses in relief administration to interdict all Federal officers or employees, except policy-making officials, from taking an active part in politics.

A second Hatch Act, passed in July, 1940, applied to state officials receiving any part of their compensation from Federal funds. It also restricted the amount any political committee might spend in a single year to $3 million and limited the amount any single individual or corporation might contribute to $5,000.

New Programs for Agriculture

Even though public attention during the second Roosevelt administration was largely concentrated on a few controversial issues, the New Deal still moved ahead toward some of its other objectives.

In the Hoosac Mills case (United States *v.* Butler, 1936), the Supreme Court had dealt a crippling blow to the first AAA by invalidating the processing tax because it had been levied to regulate agricultural production and not for the general welfare. Although many AAA activities were not affected by this decision, contracts promising government benefit payments in return for the farmers' reduction of acreage were ruled out. AAA officials and farm leaders, convinced that the results might be disastrous, quickly brought forward an alternative policy. On February 29, 1936, the President signed the Soil Conservation and Domestic Allotment Act, an amendment and extension of the less ambitious Soil Erosion Act of 1935. The Secretary of Agriculture could make payments to farmers who maintained and restored the fertility of the soil and prevented erosion. Producers could qualify for these payments by decreasing the acreage planted to soil-depleting crops—cotton, tobacco, corn, wheat, and other grains—and increasing the acreage planted to soil-conserving crops—legumes and perennial grasses, or crops like soybeans and cow peas that were valuable as fertilizer when plowed under. Other conservation practices entitling the user to benefits were the application of fertilizer, the planting of trees, and the terracing and contour furrowing of pastures. The AAA was continued to carry out the provisions of the new law, but some procedures rebuked by the Hoosac Mills decision were abandoned.

Agricultural conservation had much to commend it. The folly of many farming practices of World War I and the postwar period had been dramatically illustrated during the early thirties. Parched by hot sun and scanty rainfall, millions of acreas of Western land were ruined. Great dust storms blew away the thin topsoil, thousands of farms were abandoned, and hundreds of thousands of farmers were reduced to the status of migratory agriculture laborers. Consequently, the conservation program won the cooperation of two thirds of the nation's 16.8 million farmers.

The new law, however, did not prevent agricultural surpluses. The aggregate production of the fifty-three leading crops was larger in 1937 than in any previous year in American history. Huge surpluses of cotton, wheat, and other crops began to accumulate, and the situation threatened to develop a tragedy similar to that of 1932. To meet this situation, a new Agricultural Adjustment Act of February, 1938, provided for a variety of procedures. Underlying the whole was the philosophy Secretary Wallace had been urging for some time. Farm policy, he argued, should try not only to obtain for agriculture its fair share of the national income, but also to guarantee consumers an adequate food supply through years of scarcity and plenty alike. By enabling the farmer to store nonperishable staples, an "ever-normal granary" would be provided.

The 1938 act stressed again the importance of conservation. It required the farmer to plant no more acreage in a particular commodity than his allotment under a national quota large enough to meet normal domestic consumption and export requirements, and also to provide a reserve or carry-over supply of that commodity. If he kept within his acreage allotment and otherwise followed soil-conserving policies, he qualified for benefit payments. Producers of corn, wheat, cotton, tobacco, and rice were granted price-adjustment, or parity, payments if they cooperated with the AAA program. These payments provided the growers with a return as nearly equal to parity price as the funds Congress appropriated would permit.[3]

[3] Parity was defined as "that price for the commodity which will give to the commodity a purchasing power with respect to articles that farmers buy equivalent to the purchasing power of such commodity in the base period. The base period is August, 1909, to July, 1914, except for tobacco where the period is August, 1919, to July, 1929."

Although the Agricultural Adjustment Act of 1938 returned to a system of paying benefits to farmers who restricted their acreage, the processing tax was avoided. The program was financed by annual congressional appropriations of $500 million for benefit payments and about $212 million for parity payments.

Another type of assistance was available through the Commodity Credit Corporation, which could make loans on the security of certain agricultural products. Farmers cooperating in the AAA program might obtain loans ranging from 52 per cent to 75 per cent of parity. These commodity loans not only permitted the storage of grain, but put a floor under agricultural prices. First wheat producers and later corn growers were also given an opportunity to obtain crop insurance against losses due to unavoidable causes, such as drought, flood, and disease. In the case of cotton, wheat, corn, tobacco, and rice, marketing quotas might be imposed under certain conditions. All sales in excess of individual quotas were subjected to heavy penalty. Another method of dealing with the surplus was by expanding the operations already initiated by the Federal Surplus Commodities Corporation, which bought up and distributed such surpluses through relief channels or through sudsidized exports.

Agriculture had obviously joined the ranks of subsidized industries. Many observers regretted this, but no feasible alternative was suggested and Republican counterproposals were notoriously vague. At least it could be said that the taxpayers were now being assured an ample food supply and certain minimum safeguards for the nation's soil resources in return for their annual contribution.

Farm Security Administration

In 1937 the President's Special Committee on Farm Tenancy issued a disquieting report that in the fifty five years between 1880 and 1935, farm tenancy had increased from 25 per cent to 52 per cent. Yet this growth of tenancy was only part of the problem. Agricultural insecurity was the lot not only of tenants and sharecroppers, but of farm laborers, families on submarginal land, families on holdings of inadequate size, owner-families hopelessly in debt, and young people unable to obtain farms. According to another study of 1935, 1.7 million families, representing nearly 8 million men, women, and children, received net income of less than $500 a year.

To this vast company of the agricultural underprivileged, AAA had little to offer. In 1934 a rural rehabilitation division was set up as a branch of the FERA. The next year the Resettlement Administration was established to carry out a more ambitious program under Federal direction, but was replaced in 1937 by the Farm Security Administration (FSA) in the Department of Agriculture.

The FSA fell heir to numerous experimental projects dating back to the early days of the New Deal. About 160 resettlement communities and subsistence homesteads had been laid out in various parts of the country. In some the colonists did full-time farming; in others they did part-time farming and worked the rest of the time either in specially established local industries or in some nearby town. In some, operations were carried on cooperatively, in others individually. These activities were fascinating social experiments, but were extremely vulnerable to criticism. They furnished altogether too much ammunition for those wanting to depict the New Dealers as impractical utopians or as Communists bent on destroying the American economic system. At Congress's insistence, the FSA gradually liquidated the homestead projects, giving the settlers the first opportunity to buy.

Other FSA activities aroused less opposition. In case of flood, drought, or complete impoverishment due to erosion, the agency made outright grants of money, but this was exceptional. The usual procedure was to loan money to the distressed farmer if he accepted guidance in farm and home management intended to make him self-supporting. Under the Bankhead—Jones Act of 1937 selected tenants and laborers might borrow sufficient funds to purchase their farms. Most FSA loans, however, were short-term advances for seed, fertilizers, livestock, farming equipment, clothing, necessary medical care, repairs, and similar purposes. For farmers hopelessly in debt, voluntary adjustments with the creditors might scale down the debt to manageable terms.

Considering the desperate circumstances of its clientele and the fact that its loans were made only to those unable to obtain credit through other channels, FSA was remarkably successful in its financial operation. Up to June 30, 1945, almost 90 per cent of its loans were repaid when they fell due. While a considerable amount of agricultural rehabilitation had been accomplished, vastly more needed to be done. FSA appropriations were always low as compared with those for other agencies, partly because of the suspicion with which larger farmers viewed these efforts to improve the status of tenants and laborers.

Wage and Hour Legislation

For some time after the overthrow of NRA, the minimum-wage and maximum-hour provisions of the codes were maintained in many fields by voluntary agreement. As old abuses reappeared, however, labor insisted on Federal legislation defining labor standards. A beginning was taken in the Walsh-Healy Government Contracts Act of 1936, requiring all producers with Federal government contracts involving $10,000 or more to pay not less than the prevailing local wages, to maintain an eight-hour day and a forty-hour week, and not to employ boys under sixteen or girls under eighteen. The Air Transport Act of 1936 laid down similar requirements for airlines carrying mail or passengers.

The proposal for a general wage-hour law, however, met with strong opposition. Southern legislators were afraid of losing a principal attraction drawing industry to their section. Northern businessmen felt their costs might increase, and farmers feared higher industrial wages would increase their problems with agricultural labor. A wage-hour bill recommended by the President failed to pass in 1937, but in June, 1938, the Fair Labor Standards Act was finally approved. It applied to employees engaged in interstate commerce or in producing goods for interstate commerce, but a number of sizable groups were specifically excluded—among them agricultural laborers, seamen, and domestic servants. Wages were to be not less than 25 cents an hour; this minimum was to be gradually raised until it reached 40 cents an hour in 1945. Similarly, maximum hours were fixed at 44 and were to be reduced by stages until a 40-hour week was established in 1940. When the employee worked more than the maximum, he was entitled to time-and-a-half pay for the overtime. The act also forbade employment of children under sixteen in most occupations and of those under eighteen in occupations found hazardous by the Children's Bureau.

The immediate result was to raise the wages of about 300,000 persons receiving less than the 25-cent minimum and to shorten the working hours of some 1.3 million workers. As the standards were gradually raised, more and more members of the labor force benefited. Since these standards were exceedingly modest, the operation of the law reveals much about the sweating of labor that preceded its enactment.

The New Deal and Business

The Roosevelt administration followed reasonably consistent policies toward agriculture and labor, but its program for dealing with business lacked the same clarity of purpose. Mr. Dooley's famous summary of the trust policy of the first Roosevelt—"On wan hand I wud stamp thim undher fut; on th'other hand not so fast"—might almost as aptly have been applied to that of the second.

The NRA, as has been seen, represented a departure from the philosophy of the antitrust laws toward a policy of permitting industries to protect themselves against the hazards of excessive competition. After the death of NRA, Congress enabled a number of businesses to achieve the same goal through special legislation. The Guffey-Snyder Bituminous Coal Stabilization Act of 1935 established a National Bituminous Coal Commission to promulgate a code for the industry and establish minimum prices. Labor was guaranteed the right of collective bargaining, and maximum-hours and minimum-wage agreements by producers of two thirds of the tonnage and representatives of over half the mine workers bound the whole industry. This little NRA suffered the same fate as its parent, however, when the Supreme Court, in Carter *v.* Carter Coal Company, invalidated it in 1936 because its labor provisions unconstitutionally delegated legislative powers. The following year a new measure, the Guffey-Vinson Act, by omitting the mandatory labor provisions, stabilized the bituminous coal industry and the law was upheld by the Supreme Court (Sunshine Anthracite Coal Company *v.* Adkins, 1941).

Although petroleum refining was concentrated in some twenty corporations, about half of the nation's crude oil came from the wells of small independent producers. During the depression, serious overproduction had ruinous effects on prices. The public interest was involved because chaotic conditions in the industry resulted in serious waste of an essential natural resource. Therefore the legislatures of the oil-producing states established maximum quotas for the individual producers. Two problems subsequently developed: correlating the policies of the various states so that one did not profit unduly through the conservation measures undertaken by another and the curbing of trade in so-called hot oil—that produced in violation of the state quotas. Since Federal assistance was required, Section 9 of NIRA had made special provision for the petroleum industry. But in Panama Refining Company v. Ryan (1935), that section was declared unconstitutional even before the rest of NIRA. A substitute was provided in the Connelly Act of 1935, forbidding interstate commerce in contraband oil produced in excess of state-fixed quotas. Meantime, such quotas had been worked out through interstate compacts of the oil-producing commonwealths.

Independent wholesalers and retailers, facing increasingly serious competition from the chain stores, also demanded protective legislation after NRA's demise. Independent druggists and other interested groups obtained from most of the states fair-trade acts, legalizing contracts under which manufacturers bound retailers not to sell their products at less than a prescribed minimum retail price. Despite Roosevelt's opposition, Congress passed in 1937 the Miller-Tydings Act, exempting such price maintenance agreements from the Sherman Antitrust Act.

New Dealers were sharply divided, however, on legalizing restraints on trade. Many still had faith in the old progressive policy of enforced competition and were supported by a large section of public opinion. One unexpected result of the NRA experiment was to restore to the antitrust laws some of their old-time popularity. Throughout the twenties the laws had been under attack as based upon an outmoded and indefensible philosophy. The eagerness with which many businessmen resorted to price fixing and limiting of production under NRA codes, however, served to educate the consuming public in the Sherman Act's merits.

Early in his administration, Roosevelt tried to restore the FTC to its original functions by removing Chairman William Humphrey, the Coolidge appointee whose conservative policies had been so welcome to big business [4] and by appointing strong men to this and other agency posts. Still more significant efforts to revive the antitrust laws originated in the Department of Justice after the President appointed Thurman Arnold Assistant Attorney General in charge of the Antitrust Division in 1938. Arnold soon began a series of carefully prepared cases against the "bottlenecks of business." Instead of a dissolution order difficult of enforcement, Arnold obtained a "consent decree"—an agreed settlement between the government and the defendants in which the latter promised to abstain from certain practices in restraint of competition. Reform was thus forced upon several automobile finance corporations in 1939 and upon the "block-booking" practices of the motion-picture industry in 1940. Arnold was sufficiently consistent to attack restrictive policies of the building-trade unions as well as those of the contractors.

Meantime, one of the most significant investigations of the workings of American capitalism was undertaken by the Temporary National Economic Committee (TNEC), established by Congress in 1938. Through public hearings and extensive research, a wealth of material was assembled relating to

[4] In Humphrey's Executor v. United States (1935), the Supreme Court ruled that Humphrey's removal was illegal because Congress had specified that commissioners might not be removed except for cause. Since Humphrey had meantime died, however, the decision had no effect on Roosevelt's revitalizing of the agency.

the degree of concentration of control in the American economic system, as well as the methods and effects of that concentration. The TNEC's reports appeared to prepare the ground for new legislation dealing with the abuse of patent laws and other matters, but the coming of war postponed such measures.

The administration's desire to retard the growth of big business and the accumulation of excessive private fortunes was shown in its recommendations for tax revision. Estate-tax and gift-tax rates were increased in 1934 and 1935, making them for the first time a major source of Federal revenue. Also raised were individual surtaxes and corporation income rates, while an excess-profits levy reminiscent of World War I days was restored to the tax structure.

These changes, mostly incorporated in the Revenue Act of 1935, were much resented by businessmen. Even more disliked was the tax on undistributed corporation profits, introduced in the Revenue Act of 1936, to discourage the accumulation of unnecessarily large corporate surpluses, a form of oversaving that, by reducing dividend payments to stockholders, destroyed purchasing power and reduced government revenues from personal income taxes. Spokesmen for business, however, defended these surpluses as needed insurance against hard times and as providing funds for plant expansion.

Conservative Democrats and Republicans mustered enough strength in 1938 to modify the New Deal tax structure. In the Revenue Act of that year Congress radically reduced the undistributed profits tax and otherwise lightened the tax burden of corporations. The conservatives won another victory the next year when the undistributed profits tax was entirely repealed.

Transportation Policy

In dealing with air-transport industry and the merchant marine the New Deal sought certain reforms, yet in the end fell back upon generous subsidies similar to those of preceding Republican administrations.

In 1933 the government's air-mail contracts were vigorously criticized. It was alleged that the Hoover administration had permitted collusive bidding, had favored the big companies, and had made excessive expenditures. Despite the depression, Federal payments to airlines had mounted from $9.4 million in 1929 to $19.5 million in 1933. Therefore early in 1934, Postmaster General Farley canceled the contracts and for some weeks the army flew the mail with unfortunate results. During a severe series of February storms, army pilots and equipment were found inadequate for these abnormal conditions. Ten flyers lost their lives within a month, causing a public outcry that largely diverted attention from the abuses of the old system. The Air Mail Act of 1934 restored contract operations, but with genuinely competitive bidding. The government made such substantial savings that Farley boasted in 1937 that although two and a half times as much air mail was being transported as in 1932, the government's cost was $7 million less.

The airlines claimed, however, that the new contracts were not adequate to maintain the industry on a profitable basis, so in 1938 Congress established the Civil Aeronautical Authority (CAA), not only to regulate aviation but to adjust air-mail payments to the needs of the different classes of carriers.

By 1939 total payments had risen to about $18 million, but this figure was hardly comparable to that of 1933 because of the greatly increased volume of mail.

The merchant marine subsidy program was even more vulnerable to criticism. Despite annual payments of about $29 million, the American merchant marine fleet was rapidly becoming obsolete. By the Merchant Marine Act of 1936 a new United States Maritime Commission was created to grant direct subsidies insead of the discredited mail contracts. Payments were of two kinds: to promote construction and to assist private owners in meeting their operating costs. If the subsidy program proved ineffective, the commission could build ships on its own account, sell or charter them if possible, and operate them itself if necessary.

Toward the railroads the New Deal undertook no radically new policy. The Emergency Transportation Act of 1933 authorized the appointment of a Federal Coordinator of Transportation, a temporary post given to Joseph Eastman of the ICC. His recommendations for economies in operation were opposed by both management and labor, but his advice on future transportation policy had greater influence. "Theoretically and logically," Eastman pointed out, "public ownership and operation meet the known ills of the present situation better than any other remedy." In view of the practical difficulties of such a course, he recommended an extension and improvement of the existing Federal regulation of privately owned and operated carriers. Congress responded by extending the jurisdiction of the ICC to include motor and water carriers, the first by the Motor Carrier Act of 1935, the second by the Transportation Act of 1940.

Government-operated Business

Government competition with private enterprise, the ultimate sin in conservative eyes, advanced somewhat under Roosevelt, but not without encountering strong and bitter opposition.

Because house building was one of the hardest-hit industries of the depression, it was an obvious step in the New Deal recovery program to attempt to stimulate construction. To a large extent, this was done by encouraging private business. In 1934 Congress established a Federal Housing Administration (FHA), with power to insure loans made by private lending institutions for both repairing old dwellings and constructing new ones. In the former case only 20 per cent of the loan was insured, but for new construction fully insured twenty-five-year mortgages might be written up to 90 per cent of the value.

Although FHA stimulated home building for middle-income families, it was no answer to the desperate needs of the low-income group composing more than one third of the entire population. To build decent homes cheaply enough to be sold or rented to such people was apparently beyond the abilities of private enterprise. There was, moreover, a powerful landlord interest in perpetuating a situation where the poor had to live in dilapidated old properties. As early as 1933 low-cost housing and slum-clearance programs had been designated as a desirable PWA expenditure area, but results were inadequate until the United States Housing Administration (USHA) was established in 1937. This body could make long-term low-interest loans to state or local public-housing agencies for slum clearance and low-rent housing construction. As a Federal subsidy for these projects, the USHA might remit the interest and advance an annual sum equivalent to .5 per cent of the construction loan, provided this grant was necessary to maintain low rents and provided the local agency was also contributing. By November, 1939, 296 public-housing projects were in progress, promising better homes for 650,000 persons, but this was only a fraction of the number needed. The administration sought congressional authorization to expand the project, but to no avail.

Business feared New Deal intervention in the power industry even more than it did the public-housing policy. So enthusiastic was the President over the success of TVA that in 1937 he urged similar regional-planning agencies in six other areas: the Atlantic Seaboard, the Great Lakes-Ohio Valley, the Missouri Valley, the Southwest, the Colorado Valley, and the Columbia Valley. Although Congress was not prepared to entertain so bold a proposal, it did provide generous appropriations to build large dams in various parts of the nation. Such projects as Bonneville and Grand Coulee on the Columbia, Fort Peck on the Missouri, Big Thompson on the Colorado, and the Central Valley in California, constructed primarily for navigation, flood control, and irrigation, all contemplated the generation of power. Another favorite Roosevelt project, the St. Lawrence Seaway, failed of realization, however, because of opposition from private power interests and the railroads.

Farmers, to whom electricity was a servant even more useful than to city dwellers, had been largely excluded from its benefits under rugged individualism, for private companies extended service to less than 8 per cent of the nation's farms. In 1936 Roosevelt sought to remedy the situation by setting up the Rural Electrification Administration (REA) and allotting to it $100 million in relief funds. The experiment was given a more secure basis the next year when Congress passed the Rural Electrification Act. Farmers were encouraged to form cooperatives that would erect transmission lines and furnish electricity to persons in rural areas not receiving central-station service. Such associations were assisted by REA with low-interest loans. The administration tried to avoid controversy by not promoting cooperatives in areas already served by private industry and by encouraging farmers' associations to purchase electricity wholesale from the corporations rather than build their own generating plants. Even so, the utility companies did not relish distribution through cooperatives and undertook a rural electrification program of their own. The result of this wholesale competition in good works was gratifying. By 1943 more than 800 cooperatives were providing farmers with electricity, and their activities combined with those of purely private industry were serving the needs of 2.5 million farms, some 26 per cent of the nation's total.

A favorite conservative accusation was that the New Deal was socialistic, but the record shows that this was mostly name-calling. True, there was a measure of socialism in the Roosevelt policies relating to electrical power and public housing, but even in these fields the application was strictly limited. An administration really committed to advancing socialism would certainly have proceeded very differently, particularly in dealing with banks, railroads, coal mines, and the merchant marine—strategic areas of the national economy that were prostrate and dependent on government assistance in 1933. The most characteristic New Deal policies were those designed to pull private enterprise out of the ditch, refuel it with loans, and set it back on the road again with some attempt to add governors to the machinery to prevent it from smashing up again. Roosevelt conceived his mission to be to save capitalism rather than to destroy it. Whether that was a virtue or a defect depended on the point of view. And whether the steps actually taken did in the aggregate strengthen private enterprise or weaken it was a question over which men might honestly differ.

Recess on Reform

Roosevelt had crowded proposal on proposal during his first five years in office because he was convinced the progressive movement runs in cycles. Unless the reforms on which he had set his heart could be speedily achieved, they might be long delayed by the changing public mood. The soundness of this analysis was proved by the anti–New Deal reaction during his second term. The 1938 election results convinced the President that the time had come to go on the defensive as far as his domestic program was concerned, and during the next years no really new campaigns were begun. Some earlier laws, like the Social Security Act, were improved, while a few untenable positions like the tax on undistributed corporation profits were surrendered. On the whole, however, the Roosevelt strategy consisted in holding the ground already won and resisting such conservative counter-attacks as that directed against the National Labor Relations Act. The President's more conservative mood was intensified by his growing pre-occupation with the world situation. Developments in Europe and Asia soon overshadowed every domestic political issue.

18
DEPRESSION AMERICA

From 1929 to 1939 the Great Depression was the most important factor in American social and cultural life. The complacency of the prosperous twenties had been rudely shattered. In 1928 it had been easy to believe that poverty would soon be abolished through the beneficent workings of rugged individualism; two years later poverty's threatening shadow was looming over millions of industrious citizens who had once prided themselves on their ability to provide for their own security.

As faith in the old gods of laissez faire, individual thrift, and welfare capitalism declined, Americans increasingly looked for salvation to collective action and government intervention. The impact of these changing ideas on the political scene has already been described; no less important were the consequences in labor relations, in intellectual trends, and in the conditions under which authors and artists produced their work.

Collapse of Welfare Capitalism

On the eve of the depression, employers could congratulate themselves on the unusual submissiveness of their workers. Not only had labor union membership failed to expand during the prosperous mid-twenties, but many unions had actually lost ground. William Green, who succeeded Gompers as AFL president after the latter's death in 1924, was a mild, friendly man, dedicated to the ideal of a respectable unionism that would not frighten the business community with unseemly tactics. In contrast with the unions' defensive behavior, management was assuming the leadership in labor relations. Although many employers did not hesitate to show the iron hand by using labor spies, black lists, and yellow-dog contracts to combat the unions, their most effective strategy was to convince their employees that strikes and boycotts were old-fashioned weapons and that the utopia of high wages, reasonable hours, wholesome recreational programs, retirement pensions, and other benefits would be speedily achieved through cooperation with enlightened management.

But welfare capitalism, so glittering in appeal during days of prosperity, fell an early victim to the depression. After an initial effort to maintain wages in response to President Hoover's appeal, employers soon found it necessary to cut their labor costs by every possible means. Although statistics

383

might show that hourly wage rates fell more slowly than the cost of living, this afforded little consolation to the average worker. At best, he found employment uncertain and layoffs frequent; at worst, he might spend months without any job at all. In his desperation he might take employment in a small depression-born factory operating under sweatshop conditions.

The other pillars on which welfare capitalism had rested proved as shaky as that of high wages. Health benefits and recreational programs were often considered nonessentials that had to be abandoned as an early step of retrenchment. Particularly unhappy were the situations in which employees had been encouraged to make regular purchases of company stock and now found the value of their investments shrunk to a fraction of what they had paid. Company unions, financed and dominated by management, could not protect the workers against these developments; independent unions could not do much more. Weak and defeatist in temperament, union leaders were in no position to fight against the dark forces unleashed by the depression.

Although revolution seemed a possibility in the imaginations of a few panicky businessmen and a handful of hopeful intellectuals, realistic observers noted that really radical discontent was surprisingly small. Only here and there did demonstrations occur among unemployed workers or veterans seeking payment of the bonus. Instead, the mood was one of stunned disbelief that the depression was real and that the platitudes of prosperity had lost their meaning. At late as 1932, the AFL leadership persisted in its opposition to unemployment insurance and pinned its hopes of recovery on a shorter work week.

Yet if the reaction from the cult of rugged individualism was slow in coming, it was nevertheless irresistible once it started. In politics, Roosevelt's great electoral victories and the whole New Deal program were its manifestations. On the social front, the most dramatic change was the rise of a militant labor movement.

The great expansion of unionism during the 1930's resulted only in part from the new government policy represented by the Norris-La Guardia Act, the NRA, and the National Labor Relations Act. Millions of Americans came to a belated belief in unionism out of disillusionment with welfare capitalism. No longer did the workers trust their destinies to the personnel policies of their employers. They now wanted the terms of their employment spelled out in union contracts. The grim experience of the depression had also taught them to demand more protection from government in the form of old age pensions, unemployment insurance, minimum wages, and limitation of the hours of labor.

Another important factor in the growing labor movement was the almost complete cessation of immigration. The legislation of the twenties, strict administration of the laws, and discouraging job prospects had reduced the influx of foreigners to a mere trickle. Indeed, in some years during the thirties more people left the country than came in. This meant that after 1930 the working force contained an ever-increasing proportion of second- and third-generation Americans, no longer willing to accept the conditions that had satisfied their forebears. Thoroughly Americanized, they demanded what they considered their birthright—not just life and liberty, but security in their jobs and high wages.

Rise of the CIO

For years there had been dissension within AFL ranks over the issue of industrial unionism. An aggressive faction had insisted that the mass-production industries like autos, rubber, steel, and electrical equipment would never be adequately organized except by new unions founded along industrial lines. The established craft unions, however, regarded with great suspicion the creation of more industrial unions than were strictly necessary. When the NRA suddenly opened up an opportunity to invade the unorganized industries, the problem was postponed for the time being by chartering federal locals directly responsible to the AFL officers. This soon proved unsatisfactory. While the craft unions wanted to use such locals as recruiting agencies for their organizations and insisted upon a broad construction of their jurisdictional rights, such groups as the auto and rubber workers were just as insistent that they be brought together in single unions for each industry. Many old-line leaders, their critics charged, were not only too much concerned with protective vested interests, but too cautious and conservative to take full advantage of new conditions.

This dissension reached a crisis at the 1935 AFL convention in Atlantic City. Strongly worded majority and minority reports came from the resolutions committee. Eight members emphasized the duty of protecting the jurisdictional rights of all trade unions organized along craft lines; six contended that "in those industries where the work performed by a majority of the workers is of such a nature that it might fall within the jurisdictional claim of more than one craft union, . . . industrial organization is the only form that will be acceptable to the workers or adequately meet their needs." The AFL, the minority report continued, "must recognize the right of these workers to organize into industrial unions and be granted unrestricted charters which guarantee the right to accept into membership all workers employed in the industry." Sharp debate followed, climaxed by a fist fight in which John L. Lewis of the UMW knocked down William Hutcheson of the Carpenters' Union. Although triumphant in single combat, the burly champion of industrial unionism was short on votes; the majority report was adopted by the convention.

On November 9, 1935, just a few weeks after the tumultuous Atlantic City convention, eight heads of AFL international unions met at Washington and formed the Committee for Industrial Organization (CIO), with Lewis as chairman. The new group announced that its functions would be "educational and advisory" and professed loyalty to the AFL. The AFL executive committee, however, regarded the CIO's activities as rebellious and ordered the group to dissolve. When it failed to do so, the AFL executive council in August, 1936, declared ten unions associated with the CIO guilty of dualism, insurrection, and rebellion, and ordered their suspension. With the insurgent groups unrepresented, the Tampa convention of the AFL voted to uphold this action.

Picketing. (By Kirby in the *New York World-Telegram.*)

Yet the rebels remained unrepentant and all peace efforts failed. Therefore, in 1938, the CIO, keeping its initials but changing its name to the Congress of Industrial Organizations, adopted a constitution and accepted its status as a separate federation of American labor unions. In many ways this was unfortunate because the AFL and the CIO devoted energies to fighting each other that might better have been used to promote the primary interests of labor. Particularly exasperating to employers and the public were the jurisdictional disputes between the two, which frequently led to work stoppages having nothing to do with basic labor-management relations. Despite the split, however, labor usually presented a united front during political campaigns or when antiunion legislation was threatened. The very fact of their rivalry, moreover, led to energetic organizing efforts that greatly increased the membership of both federations. Lewis provided the CIO with pugnacious leadership until 1940, when he resigned after failing to carry the movement with him in support of Willkie in the presidential campaign. He was succeeded by Philip Murray, originally a Mine Workers official but more recently head of the very successful Steel Workers Organizing Committee (SWOC).

Fighting for Recognition

Throughout 1936 and 1937 the country was plagued by strikes. This development was almost inevitable since the workers were now resolved to join trade unions and obtain contracts, while many employers were determined not to put their labor relations on this basis. Despite the prohibitions of the National Labor Relations Act, employers sought to combat unionism by using labor spies, discriminating against trade-union members, and promoting rival company unions. Angered by management's defiance of law, the workers resorted more and more to a technique that, as the courts eventually decided, was itself illegal. This was the sit-down strike in which employees, without quitting the plant, simply refused to work. First tried successfully in 1933 against the Hormel Packing Company in Austin, Minnesota, this weapon was frequently used during the next few years, particularly in the Detroit area.

Another center of sit-down strikes was Akron, Ohio, the home of the rubber industry. Serious trouble developed at the Goodyear plants when management attempted to lower costs by increasing hours, reducing wages, and laying off workers. A five-week strike, beginning in February, 1936, witnessed the longest picket lines in labor history and some disorder. The strike ended without recognition of the United Rubber Workers or dissolution of the company union, yet with substantial concessions to the workers on other issues. The Goodyear workers had been largely unorganized when the strike began, but the CIO, with its prestige at stake, intervened and rendered valuable help. The strike was sufficiently successful to bring the United Rubber Workers thousands of new members during the next few months. In 1935 there had been only 3,000 union members in the rubber industry; the number jumped to 33,000 in 1936 and to 70,000 in 1937.

During 1936 the United Automobile Workers (CIO) also made progress despite the opposition of the large companies—an opposition that led General Motors to spend $994,855 on private detective services between January 1, 1934, and July 31, 1936. A variety of grievances brought increasingly frequent work stoppages until one of the greatest struggles in American industrial history was fought out in January and February, 1937. Two weeks after the strike began, 112,800 of the corporation's 150,000 production workers were idle. The focal point was Flint, Michigan, where the sit-down strategy was employed in its boldest form. For six weeks the strikers held key General Motors plants. An attempt by the local police to prevent food from reaching the strikers precipitated a three-hour battle in which the police used tear gas and buckshot, while the strikers fought back with sticks, metal pipes, nuts and bolts, soda-pop bottles, automobile door hinges, and cold water from the plants' hoses. Thereupon Governor Frank Murphy ordered fifteen hundred Michigan national guardsmen into the city, but he refused to command them to expel the strikers from the plants and he directed that there should be no further attempt to halt the entry of food. The corporation, however, obtained a Federal circuit court order directing the strikers to evacuate the plants under penalty of im-

Sit-down strike at the National Container Corporation in Philadelphia, 1937. (World Wide Photos.)

prisonment for contempt of court and of having a fine of $15 million— the estimated value of the plants—assessed against them. When the workers defied the order, the authorities decided against any effort to carry it out by force.

Governor Murphy, determined to avoid bloodshed, ignored the legal issues involved in the strike and bent all his efforts to obtain a peaceful settlement. The management refused to negotiate until their property was evacuated, but, after a direct appeal from President Roosevelt, it accepted the governor's mediation. On February 11, 1937, the settlement recognized the UAW as the exclusive bargaining agent for the workers in the seventeen strike-bound plants for at least six months. In all other General Motors plants the union would be recognized as the agent of its members. All strikers were to be rehired and there was to be no future discrimination against union members. The company and the union also agreed to settle other outstanding grievances through negotiations leading to a signed contract. It was a CIO triumph, and after brief trials of strength the other auto plants soon fell in line. Ford held out longer than the others, but after a ten-day strike in 1941, it too surrendered and signed a contract granting the UAW for the first time the closed shop, the check-off, and the union label.

The legality of the sit-down strike became a matter of heated controversy. The Roosevelt administration avoided any clear-cut pronouncement on the issue, but in Congress conservatives strongly condemned labor's aggressive tactics, while liberals contended that management's defiance of the National Labor Relations Act had given the workers ample justification. They also called attention to the hearings before the LaFollette Committee on Civil Liberties in which the unsavory tactics of the employers were being revealed. When in 1939 the issue reached the Supreme Court in the case of NLRB *v.* Fansteel Metallurgical Corporation, however, the sit-down strike was finally pronounced illegal.

Meantime, the issue of union recognition was being fought out in the steel industry. The Steel Workers Organizing Committee, with Philip Murray as its head and a substantial portion of its expenses advanced by Lewis's UMW, waged an aggressive campaign. A most successful stratagem was that of winning over the leaders and rank and file of the company unions themselves. So strong was the movement that in March, 1937, the United States Steel Corporation, without risking a strike, recognized the SWOC and permitted the negotiation of contracts with all its subsidiaries.

Several other steel companies followed the lead of the industry's largest unit, but a group of independents elected to resist. The SWOC's struggle with so-called Little Steel precipitated the bloodiest labor battle of the thirties. At the Republic Steel Company's plants at Chicago ten strikers were killed in a fracas with the police on Memorial Day, 1937; similar incidents led to loss of life in the three Ohio cities of Youngstown, Massillon, and Cleveland. In the end the strikes against Little Steel failed—a serious defeat to CIO. Labor's aggressive tactics had brought it into disfavor with most of the American white-collar class. Tom Girdler, president of Republic Steel, was generally acclaimed for his defiance of the CIO, and Lewis was widely denounced. The unpopularity of the CIO was so great in the summer of 1937 that even the President felt its influence. Referring to the bitter struggle between the CIO and Girdler's Republic Steel, he exclaimed: "A plague on both your houses."

A favorite allegation against the CIO was that it was a Communist outfit, but this was certainly untrue so far as its high command was concerned. Neither Lewis, nor Murray, nor Sidney Hillman of the Amalgamated Clothing Workers, nor any other CIO leader of comparable prominence had any connection or sympathy with the Communist party. Among local leaders and local unions there was, to be sure, Communist infiltration, but only because the movement was determined to use any organizing talent offered, without scrutinizing its political coloring too critically. The bitterness of the great strikes of 1936 and 1937 did not result from their Communist character, but rather from the nature of the issue involved. In almost every case this was not primarily wages and hours, but the life or death of the union itself.

In the long run, the CIO withstood all attacks and established itself not only in the rubber, auto, and steel industries, but in the electrical, textile, and canning fields as well. Even white-collar workers like newspaper reporters and store clerks organized. As remarkable as the penetration of unionism into new fields was the growth of the older unions. Between 1933 and 1941 the United Mine Workers (CIO) and the Amalgamated Clothing Workers (CIO) both doubled in membership, while the Teamsters Brotherhood (AFL) had a six fold increase and the Hotel and Restaurant Employees jumped over ninefold. Even Little Steel abandoned its antiunion policy and signed contracts in 1941, after the NLRB ordered the reinstatement of the workers it had discharged in breaking the union in 1937. By 1941 total union membership had risen to 10.5 million—three and a half times that of 1933.

Marx and Other Prophets

The wide prevalence of unemployment and poverty, declining faith in capitalism, and the rise of a militant labor movement appeared to give a golden opportunity to the American Communists. In a score of ways the disciples of Marx and Lenin extended their influence during the thirties, but their efforts to create a formidable mass movement largely failed.

From 1930 until he was dumped in 1946, the leader of the American Communist party was Earl Browder, a colorless Kansan, whose principal asset in Stalin's eyes was probably his unquestioning faithfulness in expounding the current Moscow line. During the worst days of the depression the Communists played a lone hand, in the illusion that an American revolution was just around the corner and that they must monopolize its leadership against all possible rivals. During these years Roosevelt was denounced as a tool of Wall Street, no better than Hoover; Norman Thomas and other Socialists were condemned as "social fascists"; and Lewis and Green were both damned as "labor fakers."

The intransigence of the Communists had curious consequences. Among American workers the party continued to have little support; in 1934—despite unemployment and discontent—the official membership was only about 24,000. Communist contempt for democratic futility did bring a response, however, among many American intellectuals. Serious-minded people, distressed by the sufferings of the depression, exhibited increasing interest in Soviet Russia. They were impressed by the Five-Year Plans, under which the Russians seemed to be moving with giant strides toward a more rational economic system. There was, of course, another side to the picture, but reports of Russian famines, forced labor, and ruthless purges were discounted as reactionary propaganda. Thus was created a growing company of fellow travelers, not willing to go all the way by accepting Communist party membership, but nevertheless wishing success to the Soviet experiment.

In August, 1935, international Communism changed its tactics in a manner that made the path of the fellow traveler much more attractive. At the Seventh Congress of the Comintern, the party officially approved the strategy of the Popular Front. Belatedly recognizing the menace of Nazism and Fascism—a menace that might never have become so great had not the Communists so persistently undermined the democracies, Moscow now ordered the party faithful to cooperate with non-Communists in combatting Fascism on both the domestic and foreign fronts.

Browder and the American Communists shifted gears with obedient promptness. Abruptly halting their attacks on New Dealers, Socialists, labor leaders, and other "social fascists," they presented themselves as zealots for democracy. "Communism is Twentieth Century Americanism," declared a new party slogan. Browder's Midwestern origin from an old-line American family became a party asset; Communist literature glorified George Washington and Thomas Jefferson and depicted Marxists as the legitimate heirs to the Spirit of 1776. Communist orators solemnly renounced any intention of gaining power except through democratic processes.

Although these new tactics did not end the anti-Communist prejudices of most Americans, they did make the party more nearly respectable than it had ever been before. By 1938 it had grown to some 100,000 members. In comparison with the less than 10,000 of predepression days this was an impressive gain; set against a total American population of 130 million it was still very small.

The Communist situation was confused, however, by its many ramifications, as represented by fellow travelers and other conscious and unconscious allies of the party. The fellow travelers were of every hue. Some followed the Moscow line so faithfully that they might as well have been party members, as indeed some of them secretly became. Others prided themselves on their independence, but willingly cooperated with the Communists on issues where they thought the latter were right. Thousands of citizens were innocent of any wish to help the Communists but joined associations devoted to worthy causes, only to discover—sometimes years later—that these associations had been under secret party control.

The success of the Communist front organizations reflected the growing social consciousness of the day. Many college students, eager to demonstrate their hatred of militarism and social injustice, joined the American Student Union. Christian pacifists and other liberals found an outlet for their idealism in the League for Peace and Democracy. A score of fund-gathering committees capitalized on widespread sympathy for the Spanish Loyalists, refugees from Nazi terrorism, black victims of injustice, and mistreated strikers. Non-Communists usually outnumbered Communists in their membership, but the Communist minority was highly successful in worming its way into key positions. One conspicuous result was that these groups usually condemned the evils of Nazi totalitarianism while overlooking those of Soviet Russia.

Communist infiltration extended in many directions. Some of the party faithful occupied government positions, and a few of them were later convicted of spying for the Soviet government. Other Communists bored into the labor movement, gaining particular influence in such CIO unions as the Electrical Workers, the Maritime Union, and the Fur Workers. Individual lawyers, writers, artists, actors, and college professors occasionally fell into the Communist orbit—either as party members, conscious fellow travelers, or innocent members of front organizations.

All in all, the American Communists had pieced together a rather formidable-looking Trojan Horse, but this wooden creature was a jerry-built structure, destined to fall apart at the slightest blow. Among the party leadership itself there was a constant turnover. Some members had been attracted to the conspiratorial atmosphere of the party because of frustrations in their own personalities; these often renounced membership and sought to expiate their guilt by becoming rabid anti-Communists. Other Communist converts were idealists, honestly distressed by the world's ills and hopeful that Marxism would solve all problems. They were likely to become disillusioned and leave the party when confronted by such unpleasant truths as the Moscow purges or the Soviet-Nazi pact of 1939. Members of the front organizations were even less to be depended upon; so long as the Soviet Union appeared to be moving toward a more democratic system and to be sincerely opposing Fascism, these organizations maintained considerable popularity. Once Stalin's duplicity in secretly negotiating with Hitler was revealed, most of them collapsed.

The Communists had in truth failed. In America they never gained the mass following that they did in most European countries. One powerful obstacle was the New Deal. Roosevelt, not Browder, was the savior upon whom most of those who had lost faith in Hoover's brand of rugged individualism now pinned their hopes. Even among the minority for whom the New Deal's program was too moderate, the Communists had too much competition for real success. The armies of discontent were moving under a confusion of separate generals and many different-colored banners. To most volunteers, Marx, Lenin, and Stalin were shadowy figures, less glamorous than the domestic captains who sprang up during the depression years —men like Dr. Townsend, Father Coughlin, and Huey Long.

America Discovers Keynes

Marx's appeal to the intellectuals was further blunted by rising interest in a new body of thought that seemed to give the New Deal what it very much needed—a plausible justification in economic theory. From the viewpoint of classical economics, the New Deal had been all wrong. The older theory had been that the economic system always tended toward healthy equilibrium. Periods of falling demand and apparent overproduction would, therefore, be self-correcting. Nature's cure for depressions was ruthless but sure: liquidation of debts and wage cuts would lead to lower prices; lower prices would increase demand and restore economic activity to a normal level. For the government to intervene by creating more money, spending to help the unemployed, or protecting debtors against their creditors was, from the classical viewpoint, both mischievous and futile.

Whatever the validity of this doctrine, modern democratic governments simply could not steel themselves to follow it to the letter. Even under Hoover the government was committed to helping debtors hold on to their property, trying to prevent the collapse of farm prices, and making funds available for unemployment relief. Under Roosevelt the theory that depressions must run their course was completely abandoned. To the horror of orthodox economists, the New Deal seemed willing to embrace every imaginable heresy: abandonment of the gold standard, curbs on agricultural production, subsidies to farmers, government expenditures to provide work for the unemployed, an unbalanced budget, and the imposition of lower interest rates.

As the actual practice of the day departed farther and farther from classical precepts, two viewpoints were possible. Conservatives naturally argued that the whole tendency of the New Deal must be wrong because it ran counter to the economic wisdom accumulated over many years. Liberals, on the other hand, were quick to apply the standards of pragmatism. When the government did nothing, the depression seemed to go from bad to worse; when the government took action, conditions seemed to improve. Since the theory and the facts had lost contact with each other, might not the theory be wrong?

The need for a new hypothesis gave American economists a lively interest in the writings of John Maynard Keynes, the most brilliant English student of these problems. As a young economist, Keynes had created a great impression by his book *The Economic Consequences of the Peace* (1919), in which he had accurately predicted the financial chaos that would follow the attempt to collect reparations from Germany after World War I. Later in the twenties Keynes directed his attention to the problems created by England's prolonged postwar depression with its loss of export markets and large-scale unemployment. His studies led him to repudiate many assumptions of classical economics. Tentatively in the *Treatise on Money* (1930) and much more confidently in *The General Theory of Employment, Interest and Money* (1936), Keynes laid the basis for what came to be known as the New Economics.

Although Keynes's work was too difficult for any but well-trained economists to understand in detail, something of his viewpoint eventually worked its way into the comprehension of most well-read Americans. "Say's Law," with its assumption that the demand for goods would always automatically equate itself to the production of goods, was the first of the older axioms to fall under Keynes's assault. Demand kept pace with supply, he believed, only so long as all income was spent either in consumption or investment. When either consumption or investment declined and money went into idle savings, depressions and unemployment were inevitable. Since consumption was largely based upon personal habits, it tended to be rather stable. The critical factor in causing depressions and booms was, therefore, investment.

All of this might have seemed to be of merely academic concern had not Keynes drawn startling conclusions as to the proper function of government. The state could no longer be regarded as merely the neutral umpire in the economic game; whether one liked it or not, government was involved as a player. Through taxing and spending it influenced the whole economy. If it drew in more of the national income than it spent, it tended to retard economic activity. If it spent more than it took in, its influence was to accelerate the economy. Keynes declared that a nation should frame its fiscal policies to compensate for the fluctuations in private capitalism. The annually balanced budget was folly. During depression periods the government should deliberately incur a deficit, borrowing money from idle private savings to spend in ways that would compensate for the decline of private investment. During periods of inflation, the opposite policy should prevail.

Keynes also departed from orthodoxy in advocating government policies that might redistribute income. Since the wealthy tended to oversave, their income should be reduced by progressive taxes and lower interest rates. The low-income groups, on the other hand, should benefit through government expenditures for social security and public services. Greater income at the bottom of the economic pyramid would increase the demand for goods and encourage investment.

The relation of the New Economics to the New Deal was largely indirect. When Keynes visited Roosevelt in 1934, the latter found the Englishman's mathematical analysis difficult to understand, while Keynes was disappointed to find out how little the President had read in the field of economics. During the early New Deal days there had been, in truth, very little consistent theory, Keynesian or otherwise, in the administration's feverish attempts to deal simultaneously with a score of practical problems. But if the New Dealers discovered Keynes after rather than before they had formulated their program, they were nonetheless eager to embrace a theory that seemed to justify so much of what they had already done. During the second Roosevelt administration, therefore, the framing of policy along consciously Keynesian lines became more common.

Meanwhile, at the academic level the Keynesian yeast was leavening the whole field of economics. Some scholars, such as Seymour Harris and Alvin Hansen of Harvard, accepted the new theories with enthusiasm; others were critical. In either case, Keynes was far too challenging to be ignored.

Heretical though the New Economics seemed to conservatives, there was little in it to give aid and comfort to the Marxists. A man of great versatility, Keynes was both scholar and practical man of affairs. As adviser to the British Treasury, insurance company executive, and investment counselor, he was deeply committed to the preservation of private capitalism. To American intellectuals, therefore, Keynes served a wholesome function. No longer did the only three rational alternatives seem to be laissez faire, democratic socialism, or communism; impressive academic backing had now been given a fourth possibility—that of a private-enterprise system whose malfunctioning could be corrected by intelligent government policy.

Literature Looks at Society

Many literary trends of the twenties became outmoded during the depression. Before 1930 sensitive authors had been repelled by the smugness and brashness of their prosperous fellow Americans. Many artistic people demonstrated their disapproval by living abroad; others worked off their resentment by savage satire. During the thirties this alienation largely disappeared. The mood of cynical individualism gave way to a growing concern for the problems of contemporary society. The literature of the thirties reflected no consistent philosophy; some of it was unblushingly Marxist; some of it reflected the broadly humanitarian viewpoint of the New Deal; much of it was merely troubled or angry in tone without political implications.

A major literary landmark of the decade was John Dos Passos's trilogy *U.S.A.,* composed of *The 42nd Parallel* (1930), *1919* (1932), and *The Big Money* (1936). Combining such ingenious devices as "The Newsreel" and "The Camera Eye" with sketches of Carnegie, Edison, Debs, Bryan, Theodore Roosevelt, and Wilson, and case histories of a dozen fictional characters, Dos Passos surveyed American life from 1900 to 1930 in its many and varied aspects. What he portrayed was not pleasant; his more unscrupulous characters gained material success, while the few who aspired to improve the world were frustrated. Trade-unionists, IWW agitators, and Communists were more sympathetically depicted than were the figures of the bourgeois world. The novels showed a strong leaning toward Marxism, but one from which the author was in the process of disillusionment even before a first-hand view of the Spanish Civil War completed his disenchantment. Like many others who had put their hands too close to the Marxist stove, Dos Passos in his later writing became not only fervently anti-Communist, but anti–New Deal as well.

Ernest Hemingway also displayed an ambition to outgrow the narrow individualism of the twenties by dealing with some of the basic problems of his generation. In portraying the Spanish Civil War in *For Whom the Bell Tolls* (1940), he combined his old-time facility in describing scenes of bloodshed and violence with a newly displayed talent for telling a love story of unusual tenderness and a new respect for loyalty, idealism, and human decency. Much of the book's success came, no doubt, from its timeliness, since the year of its appearance was one of catastrophic democratic defeats.

Particularly responsive to the new social climate was John Steinbeck, whose *The Grapes of Wrath* (1939) vividly depicted the consequences of the dust storms of the thirties, together with a revelation of the exploitation of itinerant agricultural workers. Despite his grim theme, Steinbeck conveyed a belief in basic human goodness and confidence that in the long run this good would prevail.

The death of Thomas Wolfe in 1938 cut short a career of rich promise. Largely autobiographical, Wolfe's novels, *Look Homeward, Angel* (1929), *Of Time and the River* (1935), *The Web and the Rock* (1939), and *You Can't Go Home Again* (1940) portrayed his Carolina boyhood, his life at Harvard and Oxford, his teaching at New York University, and his residence in France and Germany. They combined graphic realism with passages so lyrical and rhythmic that they have been taken from their context and published as poetry.

American society in its local or regional aspects was dissected by uncompromising realists. In *Young Lonigan: A Boyhood in Chicago Streets* (1932) and its sequels, James T. Farrell drew a savage portrait of the city environment in which he himself was brought up. In *Native Son* (1940), Richard Wright showed how relentless were the forces driving a black boy into crime in the slums of a Northern city. In a more restrained, ironic, and satirical mood, the sterility of the so-called cultured circles in New England was laid bare by John Marquand in *The Late George Apley* (1937) and *H. M. Pulham, Esquire* (1941).

Although the traditionalism of Southern society was still viewed with nostalgic affection by conservative Southern authors, the region was very differently treated in the work of others. Erskine Caldwell depicted the degeneracy of the poor white stock in stories all the more shocking because of the humor of their treatment. The dramatization of his *Tobacco Road* (first published as a novel in 1932) enjoyed a fabulously long run both on Broadway and on tour. The Mississippian William Faulkner was a writer of extraordinary power who intrigued students of style with such boldly constructed novels as *The Sound and the Fury* (1929), a morbid story of decadent aristocracy.

These authors were most discussed by the serious-minded, but larger royalty checks were enjoyed by writers who helped their readers forget contemporary problems. Detective and mystery stories continued to be a popular form of escape literature, but readers with more time derived pleasure from lengthy historical novels, which appeared in large numbers. The most sensationally successful novel of the decade was Margaret Mitchell's *Gone with the Wind* (1936). This set the style for many less able efforts, which appealed to the readers less as vehicles for learning history than for following the escapades of lovely heroines. Of more solid merit were the carefully researched historical novels of Kenneth Roberts and Walter Edmonds.

Americans Learn About Art

During the thirties more Americans than ever before took a serious interest in the fine arts. Training in painting and music gained a more secure place in education, native talent was no longer ignored while the public lionized foreign visitors. Probably little of the artistic production of the period had any claim to greatness, but there were interest and activity, and these offered much promise for the future.

To a greater extent than ever before the Federal government became a patron of the arts. The Great Depression bore down with particular severity upon painters, and by 1935 some four thousand were in serious straits. To relieve this group, the WPA Art Project, directed by Holger Cahill, was organized. During the next five years about 52,000 easel paintings were created by government-paid artists and placed on permanent loan in schools, libraries, and hospitals. Even more remarkable was the stimulus given to mural painting. The WPA program resulted in the installation of over fifteen hundred murals in tax-supported public institutions located in every section of the country. The WPA administration also extensively employed mural painters. Artists as firmly established as George Biddle, Reginald March, and Boardman Robinson contributed to the decoration of the new buildings erected in Washington to house the Justice, Post Office, and Interior departments. Government-sponsored art ranged all the way from the very fine to the worthless. Competent critics found encouragement, however, in the freshness and enthusiasm of much that was produced. Moreover, from the educational point of view, works of art placed in post offices, hospitals, and schools were much more likely to arouse the interest of the general public than pictures purchased by wealthy patrons to be hung in their own homes.

The period was characterized by great variety in style. Some artists worked with a precision of detail that was almost photographic; others painted in a mood so abstract as to bewilder those who inspected their work. Some were traditionalists following the canons of taste well formulated in the past; others were audacious innovators. Combining the thorough technical mastery of the academicians with the force and honesty characteristic of the best of the modernists was Eugene Speicher, acclaimed by many as the country's leading portrait painter. John Marin painted a variety of American scenes ranging from rocky Maine and crowded New York to the barren Southwest in a sensitive style bordering upon the abstract. A stimulating influence was the infinite variety provided by the country's regional differences. Life in the Midwestern prairie country found reflection in the paintings of Thomas Hart Benton, Grant Wood, and John Steuart Curry; New York City's perennial fascination for the artist was captured by Reginald Marsh and Edward Hopper; even Alaska was not beyond the scope of the restless artist, as some of the best of Rockwell Kent's work emphasized.

Radio broadcasts taught many Americans that opera and symphony concerts were less formidable than they had imagined. The moving-picture industry was somewhat more timid in promoting serious music, but it did offer employment to some of the more shapely prima donnas. The most effective medium for broadening the popular interest in music, however, was the phonograph. With better methods of recording and reproduction, recorded music achieved a degree of excellence that provoked genuine enthusiasm. Of course, neither radio nor phonograph offered compensations as rich as personal attendance in the music hall. Opportunities to enjoy this latter experience widened during the thirties and were seized by an increasing number of people. Government sponsorship through WPA orchestras and free concerts not only kept musicians alive during the depression, but served an educational function as well.

The American-born artist became much less of a novelty on the opera and concert stage. Grace Moore, Gladys Swarthout, Lawrence Tibbett, John Charles Thomas, and many others held their own against foreign talent in the operatic field, while Marian Anderson and Albert Spaulding proved prime drawing cards on the concert stage. Top-ranking native conductors were not so common, but Werner Janssen enjoyed considerable success in this field during the thirties. Nor was the country so dependent on European composers as formerly. Deems Taylor repeated his earlier success with the opera *Peter Ibbetson,* produced by the Metropolitan in 1931. Other notable American operas were *The Emperor Jones,* by Louis Gruenberg, and *Merry Mount,* by Howard Hanson, staged by the Metropolitan in 1933 and 1934, respectively. Another interesting work was the folk opera *The Devil and Daniel Webster* (1939), with music by Douglas Moore and libretto by the distinguished poet Stephen Vincent Benét. In the field of symphonic works, John Alden Carpenter's *Sea Drift* (1934) and Daniel Gregory Mason's *A Lincoln Symphony* (1937) combined thoroughly American themes with an orthodox technique. On the other hand, modernistic efforts like the *Third Symphony,* by Roy Harris, and *Music for the Theatre,* by Aaron Copland, represented bold pioneering into new idioms.

It was perhaps the new enthusiasm for art and music that provided the most hopeful symptom for the American future. Such tastes could never, it is true, be the prime driving force for any large percentage of the population, but they pointed to a broadening of interest. The Great Depression had dramatized the flimsiness of a civilization based excessively on material prosperity. There were now hopeful signs that more Americans were perceiving the truth that making a living was not an end in itself but a means and that really rich living depended upon a breadth of culture.

19

GATHERING CLOUDS

President Roosevelt took office during troublesome times. Japan had just successfully defied the League of Nations and the Stimson Doctrine. Benito Mussolini was planning an African empire to renew the power that once was Rome's. Adolf Hitler, recently emerged as the most powerful figure in Germany, was bent on wiping out the stain of the Versailles Treaty. International trade was rapidly declining in the face of growing nationalism and unsettled currencies, and with that decline the war debts and reparations problems were becoming more difficult to solve. The seeds of chaos then being sown threatened a harvest of world-wide discord and strife.

The London Economic Conference

In the 1932 campaign, the Democrats, largely concerned with clearing up troubles at home, said little in their platform about international affairs, and then only in general terms. The platform favored reciprocal trade agreements, an international conference to consider the rehabilitation of silver and promotion of international trade, and peaceful settlement of disputes. Nothing was said about the League of Nations, for even the candidate, a strong Wilsonian in 1920, refused to endanger his party's chances by reviving the League issue. With the exception of advocating reciprocal trade agreements, the Democratic position on international affairs was strikingly similar to the Hoover theses. As the campaign progressed, however, the New Dealers seemed to reject an international economic outlook, under which American farmers and manufacturers would have to fix their prices to compete in a world market, in favor of a planned economy based primarily upon the readjustment of domestic costs and domestic prices.

Following the passage of the Hawley-Smoot Tariff, other nations had raised their own economic barriers in the belief that high import duties would protect their domestic products against the sharp fall of world prices, their gold reserves, and their labor situation. Even Britain, long a champion of free trade, succumbed to this trend in November, 1931.

As a result, international trade fell off sharply in the years immediately preceding Roosevelt's first inauguration. In 1929, the total value of the exports and imports of 110 countries was slightly more than $68 billion; by 1932 it had gradually dropped to $26 billion. A decline of more than

60 per cent in three years was a cause for worry, if for no other reason than that war debt payments were affected; if the debtor nations did not build up their trade, they would never be able to send their semiannual installments to the United States.

Perhaps the solution to the numerous interrelated problems was through an international conference, such as the one proposed by the Lausanne Conference. The invitation reached the United States in time for the Democratic convention to include a plank advocating American participation. President Hoover was also in agreement, and in August, 1932, the United States was represented on a Geneva committee to discuss what would be taken up at the international conference. On the proposed agenda were such problems as world unemployment, the decline of commodity prices, monetary chaos, and debts and reparations.

During April and May, 1933, representatives of Britain, France, and several other countries visited President Roosevelt to discuss the impending meeting. In a "fireside chat" of May 7, the President said: "The international conference that lies before us must succeed. The future of the world demands it and we have each of us pledged ourselves to the best joint efforts to this end." Nine days later he sent the following appeal to the heads of the fifty-four other nations invited:

> The Conference must establish order in place of the present chaos by a stabilization of currencies, by freeing the flow of world trade, and by international action to raise price levels. It must, in short, supplement individual domestic programs for economic recovery, by wise and considered international action.

Despite these glowing statements, the Hoover administration had already taken steps that made the success of the meeting unlikely by ruling off the agenda the questions of tariffs, war debts, and reparations. It is difficult to see how international economics could have been improved and stabilized without a discussion of these matters.

The London Economic Conference opened on June 12, 1933. The American delegation, headed by Secretary of State Cordell Hull, was anxious to achieve accord but was handicapped both by the prohibitions placed upon it and by the changing policy back home. At the beginning, Prime Minister Ramsay MacDonald announced that the question of war debts, although barred from consideration, would have to be discussed eventually. Although his statement was true, it antagonized Congress, which had been largely responsible for the prohibition.

Currency stabilization was the first concrete issue taken up. France, Belgium, Italy, Holland, and Switzerland wanted the basis to be gold, but the American delegation refused to agree because the dollar was declining in international exchange; in turn, American prosperity was beginning to return. Were stabilization on a gold standard adopted internationally, that hoped-for prosperity might prove only an illusion. When the conference threatened to break up, however, the Americans accepted a compromise: the gold countries should continue the gold standard at existing parities; those who had gone off gold should return as soon as possible and in the meantime would try to prevent speculation in currency exchange.

When Roosevelt learned of this compromise, he wired the American delegation on July 3 that he "would regard it as a catastrophe amounting to a world tragedy if the great Conference . . . should . . . be diverted by the proposal of a purely artificial and temporary experiment affecting the monetary exchange of a few Nations only." Although this veto was approved in the United States, where prices had already started to fall as a result of fear of currency stabilization, it was vigorously denounced at the London Conference. The United States was charged with bad faith, for it had shown its willingness to support stabilization during earlier conferences. Roosevelt defended his action by blaming the few gold countries, which, he asserted, were seeking only temporary expedients; but considering that he himself had said that international development should come before domestic economic policies and then had opposed stabilization, his step was not entirely consistent.

With the July 3 "bombshell" telegram, the London Conference really came to an end. While it is true Hull tried to salvage something from the wreckage, his efforts were useless. The British also attempted to effect some stabilization between the pound and the dollar, but the Americans' hands were tied by their country's domestic policy. Regardless of who was to blame, the Economic Conference was a bitter blow to the improvement of international economic accord. Economic nationalism was given additional impetus, and, from the European point of view, the New Deal had started off poorly in international affairs.

The European Nations Default

Closely associated in the European mind with internal economic improvement was the matter of war debts. As has been mentioned, the Lausanne Conference practically canceled German reparations if the European debtors of the United States could satisfactorily decrease their own obligations. Although the United States was unwilling to cancel the war debts, both Hoover and Roosevelt were ready to conduct separate discussions with each debtor nation. By December 15, 1932, the moratorium was over and the semiannual installments were due again. Five nations defaulted; the remainder made their full payments. Britain, in an accompanying note, urged the reopening of the whole debt question as a "contribution . . to world revival."

Roosevelt consistently refused to support cancellation or a general conference to consider lowering the obligations. The latter position was indicated clearly when the United States banned the problem from the London Conference agenda. Three days after that conference opened the next debt payments became due. The nations that had defaulted the previous December once again failed to make any payment. Finland alone paid her full obligation. The remaining countries followed Britain's lead in making partial or token payments "as an acknowledgment of the debt pending a final settlement." The British argument was that full payment would interfere with the success of the London Conference, for in the past when such payments were made world prices went down; the object of the conference was to stabilize them. Thus of the nearly $144 million due the United States, less than $12 million was received.

Roosevelt accepted the token amounts "inasmuch as the payment made is accompanied by a clear acknowledgment of the debt itself . . . I have no personal hesitation in saying that I do not characterize the resultant situation as a default." As to the requests for reconsideration, the President urged the token payers to send their representatives to Congress as soon as possible.

But Congress, representing the current American opinion, was in no mood to review the war-debt issue. The emphasis on domestic recovery, the "poor-sportsmanship"—as Senator Hiram Johnson called it—of the London Conference in alluding to war debts, and the fact that Europe could find money to spend on armaments all combined to develop opposition to lowering these obligations. Consequently, the State Department did not even bother to present the token payers' requests to the legislature. Thus the debtors continued either to default or to make partial payments—with the exception of Finland.

It was in such a mood that Congress considered a bill originally sponsored by the arch-isolationist Hiram Johnson in 1933 to prohibit any American citizen from buying or selling any securities of a nation in arrears or in default of its war debt under penalty of fine or imprisonment. The State Department objected strenuously because it would apply to bonds already sold and thus many Americans would suffer. Therefore the bill was so amended in January, 1934, that no loans could be made to any nation in default or in arrears, nor could such countries sell their securities in the United States. Although there were nearly three months of debate, the Johnson Debt Default Act became law on April 13, 1934.

This act did not achieve its objective of compelling the debtor nations to resume their payments. Instead, on the next installment date (June 15, 1934), the token payers stopped making even partial payment. Moreover, the Johnson Act checkmated any possible conferences for reducing the obligations and it may have thwarted world economic recovery by preventing American loans to foreign nations. Nor did it help America's role in international affairs because Europe regarded it as vindictive.

The Hull Reciprocal Trade Program

Even while it appeared the United States was not helping the international economic situation, Secretary Hull was actually working hard on a reciprocal trade program advocated in the Democratic platform. Hull believed that the Hawley-Smoot Tariff was largely responsible for existing world ills because it suppressed international trade. Reciprocal agreements on the other hand, would not only revive such trade, but would build up international prosperity, help stabilize currencies, and enable European debtors to pay their obligations. Moreover, American economic recovery might be promoted by assisting industry and agriculture in finding broader markets.

On March 2, 1934, Roosevelt asked Congress for permission "to enter into executive commercial agreements with foreign Nations" and "within carefully guarded limits, to modify existing duties and import restrictions in such a way as will benefit American agriculture and industry." He pointed out that world trade had declined 70 per cent since 1929 and that American exports had fallen off 52 per cent during the same period. "This has meant," he continued, "idle hands, still machines, ships tied to their docks, despairing farm households, and hungry industrial families."

Almost immediately a bill was introduced embodying the President's plan. Attacks from numerous quarters were quickly made. Some opposed it because they felt their own special interests would suffer; others believed tariff protection was necessary for national prosperity; still another faction considered it unconstitutional because it delegated both taxing and treaty-making power to the executive branch. Despite this widespread opposition— greater than against any other measure thus far in the New Deal program— it was passed by substantial majorities, mainly Democratic, and signed by the President in June, 1934.

Called "an Act to amend the Tariff Act of 1930," the measure was popularly known as the Hull Trade Agreement Act. First of all, it authorized the President to negotiate trade agreements with other countries to obtain new markets for American products. He could raise or lower the Hawley-Smoot rates up to 50 per cent with the assistance of a special Executive Committee on Commercial Policy. Once arrangements with another country were completed, the President would put the agreement into effect by executive proclamation, no action of Congress being necessary. The act was to have a life of three years.

In negotiating these reciprocal agreements, Hull strove first of all to speed up the exchange of commodities produced by one of the parties and needed by the other. Next, he tried to obtain special concessions for American surplus goods. Finally, he granted similar concessions in American markets for staples of the other signatory, though seldom allowing reductions on imports competing strongly with domestic products.

The first agreement was signed with Cuba in August, 1934, and by the time the three years were up, fifteen other agreements were completed [1] and three were pending. Immediately trade with these nations grew rapidly. For example, during the first year of the treaty with Belgium, American exports jumped $11 million—an increase of 24 per cent; for the first year of the Canadian agreement, the export increase was more than $60 million. And whereas American trade with nonsignatories increased 25 per cent, that with signatories grew by 40 per cent. The administration consistently supported the most-favored-nation principle, and tariff reductions granted under the special agreements with individual countries were automatically extended to all other nations with which the United States had commercial treaties. Thus the Hull program modified greatly the whole tariff structure.

In 1937 the Trade Agreements Act was extended for another three years, during which additional reciprocal pacts were made, principally with Britain and most of the remaining Latin-American countries. Besides helping Ameri-

---

[1] With Belgium, Brazil, Canada, Colombia, Costa Rica, El Salvador, Finland, France, Guatemala, Haiti, Honduras, Netherlands, Nicaragua, Sweden, and Switzerland.

can business, these treaties influenced other countries to conclude similar agreements with their neighbors. Thus the flow of international trade began again and better feeling developed among the signatories. Since 1940 Congress has continued to extend the measure.

The United States also helped American exporters in 1934 by establishing the Export-Import Bank, which loaned money to other countries to stabilize their currencies and their exchange. In addition, many countries received American credit so that they could buy equipment, such as rolling stock, building supplies, and machinery, in the United States.

Recognition of the Soviet Union

The Soviet government was still unrecognized when Roosevelt took office, but American liberals were eager for a change of policy and American exporters were pressing for restoration of diplomatic relations to expand their trade. The initiative leading to recognition was taken by Maxim Litvinov, head of the Russian delegation to the London Economic Conference, when he proposed to Secretary Hull that differences between the two nations might be patched up. As a result, Litvinov was invited to Washington in November, 1933. Meantime, the way was being paved for restoration of friendship when the RFC made a loan to American exporters to facilitate the Russian purchase of American cotton.

After a series of conversations, Roosevelt and Litvinov exchanged notes on November 16, 1933, in which the Soviet emissary promised that his government would not promote propaganda in the United States nor allow any organization to develop in Russia that sought to overthrow the American government. Moreover, Americans in Russia were to be granted freedom of conscience and worship, as well as fair trials if accused of crimes. After diplomatic relations were restored, the Soviet government promised to negotiate the debts contracted under earlier Russian regimes. As these statements were satisfactory to Roosevelt, he recognized the Soviet Union the same day.

In general, this recognition was well received by the American people despite some feeling that the Red menace of post–World War I days was still great. There were high hopes of an immediate increase of exports to Russia. Indeed, one reason for establishing the Export-Import Bank was to speed up commercial relations between the two countries. The failure of the debt negotiations, however, made operative the Johnson Debt Default Act thereby preventing loans to the Soviet. Without loans, the expected trade boom did not materialize. Moreover, as time passed, there was also the feeling that Russia was not living up to her no-propaganda pledge. Yet diplomatic recognition of Russia was in line with the Roosevelt inaugural promise to be a good neighbor, and perhaps behind that recognition was the administration desire to obtain additional support against Japanese aggression.

The Way Toward Philippine Independence

Roosevelt took up the Philippine issue where Hoover left off. Filipino objections to the Hawes-Cutting Act were remedied in the McDuffie-Tydings

Act of March, 1934. During the ten-year probationary period American control of foreign affairs was retained, all insular military forces might be called into American service if danger threatened, immigration differences were worked out to mutual satisfaction, and a special commission would consider the tariff problem. The Philippine Congress approved this act on May 1, 1934.

A special constituent assembly of Filipinos then drew up a constitution, which was approved both by President Roosevelt and the Filipino people by the middle of 1935. Victorious in the first election under this document, Manual Quezon became president of the Commonwealth of the Philippines on November 15, 1935. Before the probationary period was up, however, the safety of the Philippines was dangerously challenged. The occupation of the archipelago by the Japanese from 1942 to 1945 drove Quezon into exile in the United States, where he died. But in the months after V-J Day the United States fulfilled its pledge. On July 4, 1946, the Philippines became an independent republic, with Manuel Roxas serving as president.

The Good Neighbor

The "Good Neighbor" policy of the New Deal, however, is primarily associated with American relations with Latin America. It was foreshadowed by Roosevelt's address to the governing board of the Pan-American union on April 12, 1933. In it he said:

> The essential qualities of a true Pan Americanism must be the same as those which constitute a good neighbor. . . . Friendship among Nations . . . calls for constructive efforts to muster the forces of humanity in order that an atmosphere of close understanding and cooperation may be cultivated. It involves mutual obligations and responsibilities. In this spirit the people of every Republic on our continent are coming to a deep understanding of the fact that the Monroe Doctrine . . . was and is directed at the maintenance of independence by the people of the continent. . . . It is of vital importance to every Nation of this continent that the American Governments, individually, take, without further delay, such action as may be possible to abolish all unnecessary and artificial barriers and restrictions which now hamper the healthy flow of trade between the peoples of the American Republics.

While this speech emphasized increased trade and commerce, Roosevelt quickly showed an interest in maintaining a policy of nonintervention and in ending dollar diplomacy. Fulfillment of these aims was aided immeasurably by Secretary Hull, whose informal dealings with Latin-American leaders accomplished more good than strait-laced diplomacy, and by his assistant, Sumner Welles, whose knowledge of Latin-American problems furnished the basis for many moves in support of the Good Neighbor policy.

One of the first opportunities to act the part of the Good Neighbor was offered during the seventh regular Pan-American Conference held at Montevideo in December, 1933. Hull, head of the American delegation, did not assume a commanding position in open discussions, but used behind-the-scenes diplomacy to achieve his ends. He gained tacit support for reciprocity and prevailed upon the other republics to endorse several commitments to outlaw war. The most important action was to approve Article VIII: "No State has a right to intervene in the internal or external affairs of another." American support of this article showed a definite change of heart since the Havana Conference of 1928. Another step toward peaceful relations provided for permanent bilateral commissions of inquiry and consultation. Moreover, the meeting brought a temporary truce between Bolivia and Paraguay in the Gran Chaco War. A number of cultural and economic questions were also amicably discussed. All in all, the Montevideo Conference ended on a note of great accord; most of the fears and suspicions that Latin Americans had of the United States were erased for the time being.

In putting the Good Neighbor policy into more practical effect in Haiti, Roosevelt found the solution that had evaded his predecessor by concluding an executive "Agreement of August 7, 1933" with Haitian President Stenio Vincent. It provided for complete Haitian control of the national guard by October, 1934, at which time the last American marines would be withdrawn. Actually the marines departed six weeks ahead of schedule.

This still left the somewhat more difficult problem of ending American control over Haitian finances, but by the summer of 1935 the necessary steps had been taken. Among other changes, the Haitian government purchased the controlling interest in the Bank of Haiti from the National City Bank of New York, thus ending the most flagrant example of dollar diplomacy in the West Indies.

Meantime, the United States had signed a reciprocal trade agreement with Haiti in March, 1935. Haiti could now send cocoa, rum, and fruit to the United States at considerably less than the Hawley-Smoot rates, while the insular authorities granted similar reductions on American machinery and automotive equipment.

During the closing days of the Hoover administration, a tense situation had developed in Cuba, where the depression led to political discontent against Dictator Machado. In an effort to end the trouble, Roosevelt named Sumner Welles as ambassador in the early summer of 1933. Welles suggested that Machado take a leave of absence, but the Cuban executive refused. Thereupon the Cubans staged a general strike on August 4, and forced Machado to flee the country. Then followed months of tumult, with no president or *junta* able to remain long in office. Although Roosevelt sent warships to Cuban ports to protect American interests, he asked the ABC powers and Mexico to assist the United States in prevailing upon the Cubans to re-establish orderly government. There was no thought of unilateral action or intervention.

Not until January, 1934, was a semblance of peace restored to the island with the coming into power of Carlos Mendieta, who was recognized promptly by the United States. Additional help was given through Export-Import Bank loans and a reciprocal trade treaty, which granted Cuba concessions on sugar, rum, fruits, tobacco, and numerous other items, while she in turn allowed reductions on more than four hundred imports from the United States.

The most important token of the Good Neighbor policy, however, was the abrogation of the Platt Amendment. As early as November, 1933, Roosevelt had urged this step to show "by deed our intention of playing the part of a good neighbor to the Cuban people." It was not until June, 1934, however, that a treaty was ratified to provide for removal of this amendment from the Cuban constitution and the voiding of the 1903 treaty that incorporated the amendment. For defensive purposes, however, Cuba allowed the United States to continue the lease of Guantanamo Bay.

In somewhat similar fashion the United States ended its protectorate over Panama. For many years Panamanians had disliked the provision of the Hay-Bunau-Varilla Treaty of 1903 giving the United States the right to intervene to preserve order and to ensure independence. They asserted that those rights actually deprived Panama of sovereignty. The situation was complicated still more when the United States went off the gold standard and tried to pay the annual rental for canal rights in fifty-nine-cent dollars instead of gold. Moreover, growing unrest in other parts of the world made the Roosevelt administration realize the need of close accord with Panama to protect the canal.

Consequently, under a treaty of March, 1936, the United States gave up its right to intervene in Panama to protect the waterway, along with its right under eminent domain to obtain additional territories near the terminals. On its part, Panama agreed to cooperate with the United States in defending the canal and the adjacent territory. The United States promised to pay the annual rental in Panama money at the old gold exchange rate.

The Geneva Conference

Thus far the New Deal diplomacy had been trying to promote world economic recovery, which in turn would help the United States fulfill its domestic program. If the rest of the world did not cooperate, then the United States could always rely on the support of the other hemisphere republics that had been wooed with the Good Neighbor policy.

As the early years of the New Deal passed, however, it became increasingly evident that there was more to world unrest than simply monetary and commercial dislocation. A growing spirit of aggression—which may have had behind it economic factors, to be sure—threatened world peace. Despite Roosevelt's wish to complete the domestic recovery program, the growing world tension could not be disregarded.

About a month before Roosevelt's inauguration, the Geneva Disarmament Conference reopened its meetings. Germany, seeking equality of treatment, had been placated and returned to the conference. Once again, however, no agreement was reached during the early weeks. Then in March, 1933, Prime Minister MacDonald offered a new proposition, under which Germany would be allowed to rearm, but only within a tight framework of limited armaments for all powers. To reassure France, MacDonald suggested a meeting of the signers of the Paris Pact to determine how it could be enforced. Germany did not like this British plan and sought fuller rights. When the conference refused, she threatened to build up her armaments anyway.

Roosevelt then tried his hand at a settlement. At the same time that he urged the countries represented at the London Economic Conference to compromise on financial problems (May 16, 1933), he asked the Geneva delegation to "enter into a solemn and definite pact of non-aggression." Six days later, Norman Davis, the new chairman of the American delegation, told the Geneva gathering:

We are ready not only to do our part toward the substantial reduction of armaments, but if this is effected by general international agreement we are also prepared to contribute in other ways to the organization of peace. In particular we are willing to consult the other states in case of a threat to peace with a view to avoiding conflict.

This meant the United States would cooperate with the League of Nations in any action it took to avert war. There was an additional promise the United States would not attempt to restrain collective efforts to bring an aggressor to terms.

While this American position heartened France, it did not bring approval of the British proposal. Germany still refused to admit she was being fairly treated. Although Hitler professed a desire for accord, the actions of the German delegation indicated the opposite. With the meeting still deadlocked in June, an adjournment was called. Just before the conference was to reconvene in October, 1933, Germany stated she would not attend and announced her withdrawal from the League of Nations. Although the Geneva Conference held some abortive sessions in the spring of 1934, to all intents its efforts were fruitless after Germany's departure, and its failure increased Roosevelt's apprehensions about the possibility of new wars.

The Buenos Aires Conference

In line with this apprehension, Roosevelt announced in March, 1936, that all the hemisphere republics had agreed to discuss at Buenos Aires the problem of how to meet the threat of world chaos. The meeting opened on December 1, 1936, and its importance may be gleaned from the fact that the President went to Argentina to deliver the opening address. He said in part:

This is no conference to form alliances, to divide the spoils of war, to partition countries, to deal with human beings as though they were pawns in the game of chance. Our purpose, under happy auspices, is to assure the continuance of the blessings of peace.

After this stirring speech, the conference began its search for greater accord. Secretary Hull gained unanimous approval for his suggestion that all previous treaties for peace and arbitration be ratified once again. It was also agreed that when the peace and safety of the hemisphere were threatened externally or internally, the several republics would meet to find a cooperative solution. Moreover, approval was given to a common policy of neutrality in the event of war outside of the hemisphere or between two or more nations within. Likewise all differences among the republics—territorial or financial —must be submitted to arbitration. The accord reached at Buenos Aires indicated that the Monroe Doctrine had in effect become multilateral.

It was partly as a result of this accord that the United States and five Latin-American republics finally settled the Gran Chaco War after the League of Nations had failed. Yet the policy of nonintervention and the Good Neighbor was sorely tried when Mexico expropriated American, British, and Dutch oil properties valued at nearly $500 million. The American companies appealed to their government for redress and Hull sent vigorous notes to Mexico about seizure without adequate compensation. There was no thought of employing force against Mexico, however, and, after several years of jockeying, a joint commission reached a satisfactory settlement in 1943.

The Growth of Isolation

American public opinion, primarily concerned with domestic recovery, had been apathetic toward the entire Geneva proceedings. That apathy was clearly demonstrated in connection with Hull's request of April 5, 1933, that Congress allow the President to forbid the exportation of arms and munitions of war when such shipments "might promote or encourage the employment of force in a dispute or conflict between nations." The general purpose would be to cooperate with other peace-loving nations in preventing aggressors from obtaining additional military supplies. Hull qualified his request with the assertion the embargo would be used "to the sole end of maintaining the peace of the world and with a due and prudent regard for our national policies and national interests."

Although the House approved a bill incorporating the Secretary's suggestions, the Senate amended it so that the embargo must be applied against all belligerents, aggressor or otherwise. When the House refused to agree, the measure lapsed—for the time being.

Sand. Uncle Sam, ostrichlike, tries not to see the troubles overseas. (By Carlisle in the *New York Herald Tribune.)*

The Senate version reflected a growing spirit of isolation. The feeling was increasing that the country must not be drawn into another world conflict. Norman Davis expressed the views of most Americans when he said in May, 1934, that while the United States would cooperate in an international disarmament program, it would not "participate in European political negotiations and settlements and will not make any commitment whatever to use its armed forces for the settlement of any dispute anywhere."

But why had this spirit developed? It is impossible to place one's finger on any single factor, for there were a number of contributing elements. To many Americans, World War I had been fought in vain; the world had not been made safe for democracy. There was a growing feeling that wars were engineered by munitions makers to make money. In March, 1934, *Fortune* magazine reported the results of an investigation of the munitions industry. Its findings were so damning that Roosevelt asked Hugh Johnson and Bernard Baruch to find a formula for ending wartime profits. The Senate also set up its own investigating committee headed by Gerald Nye of North Dakota, an extreme isolationist. After three years of much publicized hearings, the Nye Committee charged in 1937 that American business leaders had not only profited greatly during World War I, but had evaded the payment of taxes on their gains. Moreover, the Army and Navy departments had been lax to the point of corruption, political connections were important in obtaining contracts, and American bankers were instrumental in bringing the country into war to save their loans to the Allies. Although the report did not prove its points, many Americans were shocked by the findings and completely converted to isolationism.

Another factor in the isolationist trend was the failure of the debtors to repay what they had borrowed during World War I. And what made it worse, Americans felt that this money was being used to build up national armaments that would lead to future wars. The League of Nations was regarded simply as an organization to further the interests of its members, and the World Court as only a League tool. If the United States joined the Court, it might become involved in European entanglements and war. In January, 1935, Roosevelt, following the precedent of Harding, Coolidge, and Hoover, appealed to the Senate to approve the World Court protocol, but the upper house did not provide the necessary two-thirds vote because of isolationist opposition.

Among intellectuals isolationism was also strong. The nation was flooded with literature stressing the futility of war and playing up the need to avoid entanglements with the rest of the world. Charles and Mary Beard developed this thesis in their writings, as did Harry Elmer Barnes, himself a propagandist against the German menace prior to America's entrance into World War I. It became the vogue in college classrooms to teach that the Treaty of Versailles was a harsh peace, responsible for many of the world's troubles during the twenties, and that the Allies were equally guilty with the Germans of starting the conflict. Consequently, the younger generation was imbued with the psychology of isolation; many seemed to act upon the slogan, "Peace at any price."

The Failure of Naval Limitation

This isolationist trend was given added impetus by the results of the London Naval Conference of 1935, provision for which had been made at the 1930 meeting. Preliminary to this session, delegations from the United States, Britain, and Japan had met in London in June, 1934. The Britons urged continuation of the existing ratios, reduction in size of battleships, abolition of the submarine or reduction in its size and number, and an increase in the number of cruisers. The Americans sought a 20 per cent reduction of existing naval armaments and maintenance of existing ratios. On the other hand, the Japanese wanted equality with the other two; they would agree to reduction, but only on their own terms. Since all efforts at compromise failed, Japan announced on December 24, 1934, that it would withdraw from the agreement two years later.

Thus the London Naval Conference of 1935, opening in December, began inauspiciously, with Japan still insisting on equality and the United States continuing to support the existing ratios. When the American delegates took the position that granting equality would be an admission that Japanese actions in the Far East were approved, the Japanese left the conference. The remaining delegations, representing France, Italy, Britain, and the United States, then tried to salvage something from the wreckage. In March, 1936, they agreed to a new London Naval Treaty, under which Britain and the United States were to continue their tonnage parity and not engage in any competitive building. Restrictions on the number of ships in each category were removed, but there were so many escalator and escape clauses that the treaty actually had little significance. Nevertheless, the Senate ratified the treaty without a dissenting vote. To many Americans, Japan's withdrawal and the new naval construction programs of Britain and France meant greater possibility of war. Country after country, large and small, was developing its land armaments. The wise thing to do, therefore, was to insulate the nation from these troubles.

Neutrality Legislation

Meantime, growing tension in two instances had led to actual war. Bolivia and Paraguay had resumed fighting over the Gran Chaco, and Italy, flaunting the League, had attacked Ethiopia in the fall of 1935. Because these wars, especially the Italo-Ethiopian, might broaden to embroil the United States, popular demand for American neutrality grew. Congress answered with the Joint Resolution of August 31, 1935, better known as the "Neutrality Act." This measure, the most sweeping neutrality legislation passed thus far in American history, stipulated that when war broke out between two or more foreign nations, or during the progress of such conflict, the President was directed to proclaim "such fact." Immediately thereafter, an embargo on arms, munitions, and implements of war to any of the belligerents was to become effective, the designation of such commodities to be made by the President. Control and supervision of the manufacture and sale of munitions were placed in the hands of a permanent National Munitions Control Board made up of the Secretaries of State, War, Navy, and Commerce. Also on presidential proclamation, American citizens would travel at their own risk on belligerent-owned ships.

Roosevelt approved this resolution "because it was intended as an expression of the fixed desire of the Government and the people of the United States to avoid any action which might involve us in war." He believed that "the purpose is wholly excellent" but cautioned that some weaknesses in the resolution should be remedied in future legislation.

The resolution expressed the current opinion that the United States had been drawn into World War I because of American traffic in arms. Were that traffic prohibited, there would be less chance of American embroilment in future struggles. Yet to cut off arms to both the aggressor state and the victim of aggression would obviously aid the stronger party.

On October 5, 1935, Roosevelt proclaimed "that a state of war unhappily exists between Ethiopia and the Kingdom of Italy" and declared the Neutrality Act in effect. Implements of war were defined and Americans were warned against traveling on ships of the belligerents.

The new neutrality policy ended America's position as the champion of neutral rights on the high seas. Americans who dealt with either belligerent did so at their own risk; they could not count upon government assistance if, for example, their cargoes were seized. Nor did the act work out as expected. American exporters could and did send to Italy many commodities not on the prohibited list, but which could easily be converted into implements of war. This was not in line with Roosevelt's desire to weaken the aggressor state—and Italy certainly was that.

That the President realized the weaknesses in the measure was shown in his annual message to Congress on January 3, 1936, in which he said:

Nations seeking expansion, seeking the rectification of injustices springing from former wars, or seeking outlets for trade . . . fail to demonstrate that patience necessary to attain reasonable and legitimate objectives by peaceful negotiation or by an appeal to the finer instincts of world justice. They have therefore impatiently reverted to the old belief in the law of the sword. . . .

Consequently, he urged greater cooperation between the legislature and executive in promoting more effective neutrality to avoid war.

Speedy congressional action was required because parts of the Neutrality Act of 1935 would terminate at the end of February, 1936, and the Italo-Ethiopian strife might entangle more countries. Administration leaders in Congress realized that the well-rounded measure the President desired might lead to protracted debate between the isolationists and their opponents. Therefore the Neutrality Act of February, 1936, was a stopgap to keep the original legislation alive until a more inclusive measure could be worked out. The original resolution, with several amendments, was extended to May 1, 1937. No credits or loans could be extended to any belligerent nation; the law was not to apply to other American republics involved in war with a nation outside the hemisphere; and the discretionary right of the President to extend the embargo to other countries that might become belligerents now became a mandatory order to do so.

The Spanish Civil War

This 1936 measure also had its weaknesses—notably the failure to cover civil wars. The issue arose in July, 1936, when an internecine struggle broke out in Spain between those wishing to maintain the existing republic—the so-called Loyalists—and the factions supporting General Francisco Franco and a totalitarian regime. Unfortunately for the cause of peace, Germany and Italy backed the Franco rebels, while Russia aided the Loyalists.

The Spanish Civil War aroused widespread feeling in the United States. Advocates of democracy, sympathizing with the Loyalists, established committees to provide funds, clothing, and medical supplies for them. Hundreds if not thousands of adventurous Americans joined the Loyalist armed forces, and many doctors and nurses went to Spain to help the cause. On the other hand, those who preferred Fascism to Communism countered with similar efforts to assist Franco. Many prominent Catholic prelates swung their influence to his cause. Despite the fact that the civil war quickly became a struggle between two rival ideologies that threatened to break through local barriers, the State Department, voicing the President's wishes, announced in August, 1936, that "this Government will, of course, scrupulously refrain from any interference whatsoever in the unfortunate Spanish situation." At the same time, the Department tried to dissuade American exporters from sending arms to either side, even though there was no specific law to the contrary. In general, the shippers of arms and ammunition followed these wishes, but in December, 1936, a license was sought to export planes and war material to the Loyalist government. This request brought the issue to the fore, and early in January, 1937, Congress almost unanimously approved another Joint Resolution prohibiting the export of arms and implements of war to either side in Spain. Thus the civil war was specifically brought under the 1936 neutrality legislation despite loud objections from those with Loyalist sympathies. These protests were perhaps justified. Germany and Italy were already helping Franco, so the neutrality legislation definitely hurt the Loyalists because it denied them rights customarily enjoyed by *de jure* governments.

When the temporary features of the 1936 acts were about to lapse on May 1, 1937, the troubled international picture had scarcely changed. True, the Italo-Ethiopian War was ended, but only because Italy had overrun all of the enemy territory. The contest in Spain was still being strongly waged, Hitler had defied the Locarno Pact by invading the Rhineland, and hostilities might break out at any moment between Japan and China. Consequently, Congress decided to place a permanent neutrality measure on the statute books.

The debate on the new neutrality bill was long and bitter, showing that while the legislature agreed on the principle, it was at odds on how to achieve it. On May 1, 1937, the measure was finally passed as a compromise between those who believed that an embargo must be proclaimed as soon as a war broke out and those who felt that the President should have some discretion in invoking such an embargo. Much of the previous legislation was kept. The President still had the duty to proclaim when a state of war existed, at which time it would be unlawful to export arms, munitions, and implements of war to any of the belligerents or to "purchase, sell, or exchange" the securities of such contestants. Nor could American ships carry arms or implements of war to belligerents, or be armed. American citizens were forbidden to travel on ships of a country at war. Finally, under the mandatory provisions, belligerency applied as well to civil wars.

The President's discretionary powers included the right to prohibit the use of American ports to armed merchant ships and submarines of belligerents. The chief innovation was the "cash-and-carry" clause: the President could enumerate certain commodities that might not be exported to a warring country "until all right, title, and interest therein shall be transferred to some foreign government"; such goods must not be transported in American ships; in other words, the belligerents must pay for such goods and see that they were then shipped in its own vessels. The National Munitions Control Board was continued, and American republics were exempted from the workings of this measure unless they were "cooperating with a non-American State or States in such a war."

Although the 1937 Neutrality Act contained many more mandatory and discretionary prohibitions than had its predecessors, it actually could provide for what might be called unneutral actions. Undoubtedly the "cash-and-carry" feature would benefit the belligerent with money and shipping. It supposedly warned Germany and Italy that neither could obtain American supplies because they lacked the wherewithal to pay for them. Actually, however, it was not much of a warning. Were either country to go to war, it certainly would be facing a stronger naval power that would prevent it from obtaining any American supplies. All the new law did was to guarantee Germany or Italy that its enemies would also be seriously handicapped in procuring American commodities. The measure also ran contrary to American commitments with Latin-American countries; there were promises not to sell war material to rebels in those republics, yet the measure stipulated that in case of civil war it must be applied to the recognized administration and the challengers alike. In similar fashion, there could be no move to distinguish between the aggressor nation and the one attacked. While international bankers were restricted in their operations, American exporters of goods not on the embargo list were not—provided the belligerent buyer had the cash. As the critical Senator Borah said, "We seek to avoid all risks, all dangers, but we make certain to get all the profits."

Roosevelt proclaimed the Neutrality Act in effect for the Spanish Civil War on May 1, 1937. On the other hand, he did not invoke it after hostilities reopened between Japan and China on July 7, 1937, an event sometimes called the beginning of World War II in the Far East. His excuse was that there had been no formal declaration of war and the institution of the Neutrality Act would make a peaceful and speedy settlement of the strife more difficult. The real reason, however, was that its application would have helped Japan. The administration, wishing to assist China, could not do so were the Neutrality Act applied. Therefore the policy of helping the victim of aggression was placed before the law.

Nevertheless, the publicity attendant upon the contemplated shipment of nineteen planes to China aboard a government ship in August, 1937, caused Roosevelt to proclaim on September 14:

Merchant vessels owned by the Government of the United States will not hereafter, until further notice, be permitted to transport to China or Japan any of the arms, ammunition, or implements of war which were listed in the President's Proclamation of May 1,1937.

Any other merchant vessels flying the American flag, which attempt to transport any of the listed articles to China or Japan will, until further notice, do so at their own risk.

The question of applying the Neutrality Act remains in *statu quo,* the government policy remaining on a 24-hour basis.

As it became increasingly apparent that the Sino-Japanese struggle was more than an incident, Roosevelt still refused to put the Neutrality Act into effect. He left little doubt about which nation he considered the aggressor— even though he did not mention Japan by name—when he addressed a Chicago gathering on October 5, 1937. After reviewing the worsening world political situation, he continued:

If we are to have a world in which we can breathe freely and live in amity without fear—the peace-loving nations must make a concerted effort to uphold laws and principles on which alone peace can rest secure. . . .

When an epidemic of physical disease starts to spread, the community approves and joins in a quarantine of the patients in order to protect the health of the community against the spread of the disease. . . .

America hates war. America hopes for peace. Therefore, America engages in the search for peace.

This so-called quarantine speech indicated that the President was shedding the cloak of isolation forced upon him by the Neutrality Acts. In so doing he was not seeking war, but joint action of peace-loving nations to maintain peace. The speech was probably a trial balloon sent up to test American opinion. If so, the generally hostile response warned him to move cautiously in the face of a public opinion still overwhelmingly isolationist.

The "Panay" Incident

Meantime, American neutrality was severely tested when Japanese planes bombed and strafed the American gunboat *Panay* and three American merchant craft on the Yangtze River on December 12, 1937. The attackers gave no warning, three Americans were killed, seventy-four were wounded, and the *Panay* and two of the other ships were sunk. Possibly to prevent witnesses from describing this unprovoked attack, the planes machine-gunned the boats taking the survivors to shore.

Since the *Panay* was plainly marked with two large American flags and was in the Yangtze on the legitimate business of transferring American refugees and supplies from war-torn areas, the Roosevelt administration was naturally distressed. The following day Hull informed the Japanese ambassador "that the President is deeply shocked and concerned" by this indiscriminate bombing.

The Japanese government, evidently realizing that its forces had gone too far, sent prompt apology, assured the United States that indemnity would be paid, and that it would "deal appropriately with those responsible for the incident." As evidence of good faith, Japan announced ten days later that the chief of the air force had been removed and that all Japanese forces had been ordered to use the utmost caution against similar incidents "even at the sacrifice of a strategic advantage in attacking the Chinese troops." Toward the end of April, 1938, Japan paid more than $2 million for the deaths, injuries, and property losses sustained in the *Panay* incident.

Although there was a flurry of apprehension in the United States over this affair, there was no widespread demand for war after the prompt Japanese apology. Indeed, the average American did not really care what was happening in the Far East; he was primarily concerned with financial problems at home. If too much were made of the incident, war might result—and he did not want war.

This isolationist, antiwar attitude was further shown in December, 1937, when Representative Louis Ludlow of Indiana proposed a constitutional amendment to make mandatory a national referendum before war could be declared, except in case of actual invasion. Early in January, 1968, Roosevelt used all the pressure at his command to defeat this Ludlow Amendment. In a letter to Speaker William Bankhead he stated:

> I must frankly state that I consider the proposed amendment would be impracticable in its application and incompatible with our representative form of government. . . . Such an amendment . . . would cripple any President in his conduct of our foreign relations, and it would encourage other nations to believe that they could violate American rights with impunity. I fully realize that the sponsors of this proposal sincerely believe that it would be helpful in keeping the United States out of war. I am convinced that it would have the opposite effect.

Largely as a result of this administration pressure the amendment was defeated, but only by the close vote of 209 to 188. And the American opposition to involvement in a Far Eastern war was indicated in a popular poll in which 54 per cent desired United States withdrawal from China and only 30 per cent wanted the government to compel respect for American rights there.

Thus, as World War II approached, it became increasingly evident that Americans wanted to avoid any entanglements that might embroil them in conflict. The neutrality measures were based upon a misinterpretation of the reasons for American entrance into World War I and consequently upon a belief that no external danger could possibly touch the United States. Moreover, by trying to maintain a policy of extreme isolation, Congress and the people were indirectly admitting that the nation had no outside interests worth defending. Therefore, the neutrality legislation amounted to a form of appeasement on America's part. To Roosevelt, however, the growing use of force by aggressor states so threatened both American and world security that by the end of 1937 he was fully convinced that a more active policy was needed. With the New Deal at home largely complete, he turned his attention more and more to the international scene.

Troublesome Times

The menace to the world's democracies was clear by the spring of 1938. By that time Hitler had shown his contempt for treaties by denouncing the Treaty of Versailles and by scrapping the Locarno Pact. To promote the German master race and fulfill the theories expressed in *Mein Kampf,* he had marched his troops into the Rhineland in early 1936, and during the Spanish Civil War he had tested the strength of his army, which had grown in defiance of the Versailles Treaty. Moreover, he had persecuted the Jews and other minority groups in Germany. He had arranged an agreement with Italy, known as the Rome-Berlin Axis, which gave him a freer hand in his eventual domination of Austria and in his challenging of France and Britain. He was already casting greedy glances toward neighboring Czechoslovakia. Along with Japan, Germany had resigned from the League.

The new British Prime Minister, Neville Chamberlain, believed in a policy of appeasement toward this German threat to the peace of Europe. He argued that German aggressiveness arose out of dissatisfaction with the Versailles Treaty and the inability to obtain sufficient resources to meet the demands of a growing population. Therefore peace could be preserved by adjusting these complaints. Chamberlain's position had much support in England, where many conservatives felt that the real menace came not from German Nazis, but from Russian Communists. The so-called Cliveden set, in their conservative complacency, did not realize that there was much more to the Hitlerian menace than complaints resulting from World War I.

France, convulsed by hard times and political strife, was deteriorating internally, and thus was in no position to challenge Germany. The League having failed her, she was compelled to follow Britain's lead in appeasing her natural enemy. Russia was more concerned with the progress of her economic experiments than she was with what was happening in the rest of Europe. Furthermore, she realized that she herself was the object of distrust.

In the Far East Japan had once more defied the other powers by attacks on China. Evidently she was attempting to promote the "New Order" there —or the Greater East Asia Co-Prosperity Sphere—under which she would dominate that part of the world, regardless of prior commitments.

In the United States, Roosevelt realized the gravity of the situation and, continuing the stand taken in his "quarantine" speech of the previous October, he took the lead in formulating America foreign policy instead of acquiescing in the prevalent isolationist point of view. In a special message to Congress in January, 1938, he said:

We, as a peaceful Nation, cannot and will not abandon active search for an agreement among the nations to limit armaments and end aggression. But it is clear that until such an agreement is reached—and I have not given up hope of it— we are compelled to think of our own national safety.

To make that safety possible, he asked appropriations for both 1938 and 1939 to build up antiaircraft defenses, modernize field equipment, and increase the enlisted reserve, as well as to construct naval ships of all sizes.

When isolationists in Congress balked at the proposal because it might lead the country into war, Hull defended the plan on February 10. He wrote that the rearmament program was vital for national defense, but was not large enough for the United States to enter an aggressive war. Moreover, said the Secretary, it might help the cause of peace by adding greater weight to American influence in world councils. Hull's appeal, together with the increasing German menace, finally persuaded Congress to pass the rearmament proposals in practically their original form.

Appeasement at Munich

While laying the groundwork for American defense, however, the administration did not relax its efforts to prevent a war in Europe. Convinced that Hitler's next move would be to absorb Austria, Hull told German Ambassador Dieckhoff in January, 1938, that the paramount question facing the world in general and the United States in particular was whether the principles of international law and order should be replaced by the rule of force and aggression. All countries should consistently cooperate to support law and order. This statement could be considered a mild warning to Germany against further aggression.

The gesture was fruitless, for on March 11, 1938, Hitler's legions moved into Austria in defiance of a three-year-old pledge that the Reich would not acquire its neighbor's territory, and two days later the Fuehrer announced the union of the two countries under his control. The American reaction was quickly shown on March 17 when Hull said that the United States must not become "a self-constituted hermit state"; isolation would do no good in the present world. America must maintain its influence in world affairs and work constantly for peace.

Germany paid little attention to the American pronouncements. Instead, during the summer of 1938, Hitler made increasingly serious demands for the Sudetenland of Czechoslovakia. A so-called war of nerves—incessant propaganda and sword-rattling—initiated the move against this territory, which Hitler declared he must have even though he had to go to war for it. The personal trips Chamberlain made to Germany to seek a negotiated peace proved abortive.

Believing the struggle over the Sudetenland might involve Europe in a general war, Roosevelt sent personal messages to the leaders of Czechoslovakia, Germany, Britain, and France on September 26, 1938, in which he said:

> The fabric of peace on the continent of Europe, if not throughout the rest of the world, is in immediate danger. . . . Should hostilities break out the lives of millions of men, women, and children . . . will most certainly be lost under circumstances of unspeakable horror. The economic system of every country involved is certain to be shattered. The social structure of every country involved may well be completely wrecked.

After pointing out that the United States had no political entanglements, he asserted "that there is no problem so difficult or so pressing that it cannot be justly solved by the resort to reason rather than by resort to force." Therefore, on behalf of the American people "and for the sake of humanity everywhere," he asked the disputants to seek a pacific settlement. The replies from three of the countries indicated their desire for peace, but Hitler placed the whole responsibility for the crisis upon Czechoslovakia. If she wanted peace, she could have it by turning the Sudetenland over to Germany without further ado. If she did not, Germany would seize it.

Still Roosevelt did not give up hope. American envoys everywhere were instructed to use their good offices in having the countries to which they were assigned send messages to the potential belligerents stressing the need to preserve peace. The President also sought Mussolini's cooperation in settling the problem and sent another appeal to Hitler.

American opinion overwhelmingly favored any solution that would avoid war. Great was the relief, therefore, at the news that a last-minute conference had been arranged at Munich. There, on September 30, Hitler, Mussolini, Chamberlain, and Edouard Daladier of France signed a Four-Power Accord whereby war was averted at the price of giving the Nazis practically a free hand in taking over the Sudetenland. Chamberlain returned to England declaring: "I believe it is peace for our time," and millions of Englishmen, Frenchmen, and Americans hoped he was right. But this supreme effort to appease Germany soon proved a great mistake. The betrayal of Czechoslovakia destroyed the moral prestige of England and France in the eyes of smaller states. The snubbing of Russia aroused her suspicion and resentment, while Germany and Italy had only contempt for the weakness of the Western democracies. American opinion soon reversed itself and condemned the European appeasers. Illogically, however, few Americans saw that their own country shared in the responsibility. Roosevelt no less than Chamberlain had been desperately anxious to preserve peace, and Congress had insisted on the futile policy represented by the neutrality acts. Hitler could therefore continue his aggressive course convinced that the United States would do nothing to help those who resisted him.

The Munich breathing spell was brief. France and England displayed their growing concern by a great rearmament effort, while as early as October 28, 1938, Roosevelt declared:

It is become increasingly clear that peace by fear has no higher or more enduring quality than peace by the sword.

There can be no peace if the reign of law is to be replaced by a recurrent sanctification of sheer force.

There can be no peace if national policy adopts as a deliberate instrument the threat of war.

And the President was deeply shocked shortly afterward by news of even more violent persecution of the Jews; he said: "I myself could scarcely believe that such things could occur in a twentieth-century civilization." Consequently, on November 15 he ordered Ambassador Hugh Wilson to return from Berlin —an obvious rebuke to the Nazis.

The Lima Conference

While Europe and Asia were facing the possibility of open war at any moment, the Western Hemisphere republics gathered at Lima, Peru, for their regular Pan-American Conference. Naturally they were chiefly concerned with how international law and order could be restored and, if this proved impossible, with how they could prevent external dangers from affecting them.

Secretary Hull, once again the chairman of the American delegation, was the most energetic worker at this December, 1938, meeting and did much to promote the unanimous approval of the so-called Declaration of American Principles, which reaffirmed the doctrine of nonintervention, proscribed the use of force as an instrument of national or international policy, upheld peaceful settlement of disputes, and avowed that "international cooperation is a necessary condition to the maintenance of the aforementioned principles." Perhaps the foremost action was the approval of the Declaration of Lima, affirming "their continental solidarity and their purpose to collaborate in the maintenance of the principles upon which the said solidarity is based." The republics also agreed "to defend them against all foreign intervention or activity that may threaten them"—in answer to the fifth-column menace.[2] Also under that Declaration, "in case the peace, security or territorial integrity of any American Republic is thus threatened by acts of any nature that may impair them, they proclaim their common concern and their determination to make effective their solidarity, coordinating their respective sovereign wills by means of the procedure of consultation. . . ." Such consultation was to take the form of meetings of the several foreign ministers when any republic believed that hemisphere safety was endangered. By this means the diplomats hoped to keep the totalitarian threat from American shores and to use the pressure of a solid hemisphere bloc to avert another world struggle.

The Outbreak of War

Despite the Munich appeasement, the threat of war hung over the world. In his annual message to Congress on January 4, 1939, President Roosevelt said:

All about us rage undeclared wars—military and economic. All about us grow more deadly armaments—military and economic. All about us are threats of new aggression—military and economic.

Then, asserting that the use of force by enemies of democracy made necessary the employment by peace-loving nations of weapons of defense, he called for increased appropriations for the army and navy. Moreover, he criticized

2 The expression "fifth column" was first used during the Spanish Civil War. It refers to subversive agents who go to another country to pave the way, through undermining the confidence of the people and the like, for eventual military invasion.

the existing neutrality legislation because it might conceivably result in the United States helping an aggressor nation at the expense of the one attacked. Shortly after this message, the President sought to build up stockpiles of materials essential to American defense.

Such plans and suggestions were obviously the need of the hour. On March 14, 1939, Hitler invaded the remainder of Czechoslovakia, despite his pre-Munich pledge; the immediate State Department condemnation of this action as "wanton lawlessness" did no good. On April 7 Mussolini, desirous of sharing in the spoils, attacked Albania and soon had that country under his control. Once again the State Department's verbal opposition was useless.

The democratic powers in Europe finally realized the futility of appeasement. Britain and France announced they would go to the aid of Poland, Rumania, and Greece were they attacked. At the same time they sought Russia's support to thwart the Rome-Berlin Axis.

Because the division of Europe into two armed camps boded ill for world peace, Roosevelt sought specific assurance from Hitler and Mussolini that neither would attack or invade the remaining independent countries of Europe and the Middle East, not only for the present, "but also to a future sufficiently long to give every opportunity to work by peaceful means for a more permanent peace." Neither Hitler nor Mussolini saw fit to reply to this plea, although the Fuehrer did tell the German people that he had no thought of attacking any more of the Reich's neighbors. Had he not given them definite pledges to that effect?

How much Hitler's promise meant was shown before April was over. He demanded of Poland the return of Danzig, as well as numerous concessions along the Polish Corridor. To strengthen his demands he mobilized a large army along the Polish border. The worried British and French thereupon announced that an attack upon Poland would mean war.

Remonstrating with the German dictator was obviously futile, for he understood only the language of force—a language Roosevelt was powerless to use. As a minimum contribution to strengthening the anti-Nazi front, the United States needed to repeal the arms embargo, so that in case of hostilities England and France could supplement their inadequate war-production facilities with those of America. But the President's earnest efforts to amend the Neutrality Act before Congress adjourned for the summer failed. Not even a White House conference convinced Senator Borah and his fellow isolationists that war was imminent or that the United States had any responsibility in the situation.

Confidence that America would stand aside, therefore, was one factor encouraging Hitler to pursue his reckless course. The war of nerves against Poland continued, while mutual suspicion frustrated efforts to draw the Soviet Union into an alliance with Britain and France. Instead, the democratic world was stunned when Russia and Germany concluded a nonaggression pact on August 21. Far from being an act of peace, this treaty released Germany from the possibility of a two-front war and revealed that it would probably be but a matter of days before the march into Poland began.

Roosevelt once again tried to effect a peaceful settlement by appealing to King Victor Emmanuel of Italy on August 23 to cooperate with the United States to "advance those ideals of Christianity which of late seem so often to have been obscured." The next day he also sent earnest pleas to both Hilter and President Moszicki of Poland to settle their dispute through diplomacy.

These attempts were fruitless, however, because Hitler wanted no peaceful respite. He placed the blame upon Poland because she refused to accede to all the German demands. On the morning of September 1, 1939, the invasion of Poland started, and two days later France and Britain, living up to their promises, went to her assistance. World War II had begun.

20

THE PRELUDE TO PEARL HARBOR

In many respects American experience in World War II followed the same pattern of World War I days. In both cases there was an attempt to remain neutral; in both cases neutrality became increasingly difficult; in both cases the United States eventually went in on the side of England, France, and Russia against Germany and her allies. Yet there were great differences. During World War II a complete German victory seemed much more likely, and the American people felt a much more serious threat to their own security. Long before hostilities began at Pearl Harbor, the United States had abandoned the pretense of neutrality and committed itself to helping the democracies with shipments of arms and naval patrols. War, when it finally came, was simply the last step, plunging the nation into a conflict in which it had become increasingly involved.

The Impact of War on the United States

The outbreak of World War II did not come unexpectedly to the American people as had World War I. While it is true that many Americans hoped until the actual invasion of Poland that peace efforts would be successful, they had been following events in Europe closely in their newspapers and over their radios for several years. Thus there was not the distinct shock that accompanied the war of 1914.

President Roosevelt was quick to act. After appealing to the participants on September 1, 1939, to refrain from bombing civilians, he delivered a radio talk two evenings later in which he pointed out that European events of the previous four years had "been based on the use of force and the threat of force." America's primary duty should be to seek "for humanity a final peace" that would end "the continued use of force between nations." The President did not ask the people to remain neutral in thought, because "even a neutral has a right to take account of the facts." He believed the United States could stay out of the conflict, but admitted that the war would certainly affect the country in many ways. Yet "as long as it remains within my power to prevent, there will be no blackout of peace in the United States."

On September 5 Roosevelt proclaimed the neutrality laws in effect and prohibited the exportation of arms and munitions to the belligerent nations. The following day the FBI was placed in charge of "matters relating to espionage, sabotage, and violation of the neutrality regulations." Next, Roosevelt declared a limited national emergency to safeguard American neutrality and strengthen national defense.

The Neutrality Act of 1939

Although Roosevelt's official position was one of neutrality, it was clear he favored the democracies. His numerous utterances indicated he desired Britain and France to win, and his efforts during the spring and summer of 1939 to amend the existing neutrality legislation were made so that he could distinguish between the aggressor and the attacked. Moreover, he sought both closer commercial relationships with Britain and France and authority to allow the sale of arms, munitions, and planes to them.

American public opinion (84 per cent according to one poll) undoubtedly desired an Allied victory but also strongly wanted the United States to stay out of the war. These practically contradictory views made it difficult for Roosevelt to put into effect his program to aid the democracies because Americans of the isolationist school, led by Senators Borah and Wheeler, held that anything but strictest neutrality would involve the nation in hostilities.

Nevertheless, on September 21, 1939, Roosevelt called Congress into special session specifically to amend the Neutrality Act because it "so alters the historic foreign policy of the United States that it impairs the peaceful relations of the United States with foreign nations." He continued with the assertion, "I regret that Congress passed the Act. I regret equally that I signed that Act." Specifically he wanted to change the embargo provisions that prevented the sale of completed implements of war but that allowed the selling of uncompleted ones that could be shipped on American vessels. "There in itself . . . lies definite danger to our neutrality and our peace."

Congress immediately became involved in extremely heated debate. Members of the Nye school of thought asserted that repeal of the arms embargo would mean a repetition of World War I days; American munitions makers would sell to the Allies, make a huge profit, and help involve the nation in war. Still another opposition group declared repeal would be an unneutral step; the war had already begun, and a change in policy would aid one side to the detriment of the other. And there were those who still believed that the Neutrality Act of 1937 could best maintain American isolation. Supporters of the administration argued that the existing legislation was in effect unneutral because it helped the aggressors, who knew the countries they invaded could not obtain United States assistance. Moreover, traditional American rights on the high seas had been given up, and the smaller and weaker nations, which had previously looked to the United States for protection, could no longer do so. Some legislators advocated repeal frankly because it was in the best interests of the country for the Allies to win.

Not until November 4, after six weeks of debate, was the Neutrality Act of 1939 finally approved—243 to 172 in the House and 55 to 24 in the Senate. It kept many of the supposed safeguards of earlier legislation and extended the cash-and-carry principle to all commodities. The chief changes were that now Congress, as well as the President, could proclaim that a state of war existed; the embargo on implements of war was dropped; and the President could define danger or combat zones wherein American citizens, ships, and planes could not go.

Roosevelt promptly put this new measure into effect, accompanying it with the definition of combat areas: all belligerent ports, most of the Bay of Biscay, the English Channel and the waters around the British Isles, and the Baltic and North Seas. The closing of the last two seas meant that American vessels could not reach such neutral countries as Belgium, the Netherlands, and Sweden. As a result, it was hoped that there would be no incidents to involve the United States in war.

The Panama Conference

During the debate on the Neutrality Act, steps were taken to safeguard the hemisphere. In line with the decision made at Lima, the several foreign ministers met at Panama in late September to discuss how the war could be kept from the Americas. On October 2 unanimous approval was given to the Declaration of Panama:

The American republics, as long as they maintain their neutrality, have the undisputed right to conserve free from all hostile acts by any belligerent non-American nation those waters adjacent to the American continents which they consider of primordial interest and direct utility of their relations, whether such hostile act is attempted or carried out by land, sea, or air.

The declaration then established a safety, or neutrality, zone roughly two hundred miles wide around the Americas, wherein no belligerent action should take place. Maritime and air patrols would see to it that the zone was maintained as a neutral area.

The foreign ministers also set up an Inter-American Financial and Economic Advisory Committee to furnish the several republics with commercial and financial information in case serious dislocation followed the outbreak of the European war. A General Declaration of Neutrality of the American Republics forbade the use of any American territory as bases for belligerent operations, prohibited belligerent planes from flying over hemisphere territory, established rules for internment of ships, and drew up rules for search.

The United States provided most of the vessels for patroling the safety zone, but the warring countries refused to admit its legality and asserted they would pay no attention to it because their enemies would not. The most notable example of infringement concerned the German pocket battleship *Graf von Spee,* which had been attacking Allied merchantmen in the Atlantic since the war opened. Finally in early December, 1939, she was tracked down by three British cruisers, badly damaged in a running fight off the South American coast, and forced to take refuge in Montevideo. The Uruguayan government insisted she leave after seventy-two hours, but rather than face the awaiting British cruisers, she was scuttled by her crew who were then interned. The American republics protested vigorously against this defiance of hemisphere neutrality, and the following April the Neutrality Committee announced the closing of American ports to ships of those belligerent nations refusing to recognize the safety zone. Because of the British blockade, however, few German ships other than submarines reached American waters after early 1940, so there were only isolated instances thereafter.

The Fall of France

After the initial attacks and the fall of Poland, both sides settled down during the winter of 1939–1940 along their respective western front lines—the Allies behind the Maginot Line, the Germans protected by their ever stronger Siegfried Line. To some this so-called phony war, or *sitzkrieg*, revived hopes of a peaceful settlement. On April 9, 1940, however, Hitler suddenly struck at Denmark, despite a year-old non-aggression pact that he himself had initiated, and at the same time his troops invaded Norway, aided in no small part by the fifth-column work of the Norse traitor, Vidkun Quisling.

May witnessed even more disastrous blows to the Allies as the *blitzkrieg* swept over Holland, Belgium, Luxembourg, and France. With the Maginot Line outflanked, the British forces, pinned against the English Channel, escaped from Dunkirk only through the skill and bravery of the British reserve fleet. The French were subjected to an overwhelming attack, culminating in their surrender on June 22, 1940. Hitler sought to wipe out the stain of November 11, 1918, by staging the armistice conference in the same railroad car used on that occasion in the same forest of Compiègne. Taking advantage of this French disaster, Mussolini had entered the war on June 10 by attacking France from the east.

To Americans the power of the German *blitzkrieg* was astounding. It appeared as though the democracies, now represented solely by the British Empire, could no longer withstand the Axis poundings. Nevertheless, the Roosevelt administration continued to extend moral support, and even more was promised. On the day Mussolini attacked the French rear, Roosevelt, after extending the Neutrality Act provisions to cover the new belligerent, denounced Italy's action as "the hand that held the dagger" that was "stuck into the back of its neighbor." He then announced that the United States "must pursue two obvious and simultaneous courses": the extension of all the material resources of the country to the opponents of force and the promotion of American defense.

More and more Americans supported aid to the democracies and increased preparedness. To them the fall of France meant that the American defense frontier was no longer the Maginot Line as Roosevelt had once intimated. It was now the English Channel and might soon be the Atlantic because the safety of the British Isles was in question after the German air *blitz* of England began in the summer of 1940. None knew whether Britain could hold out against the mounting air attacks and the expected invasion. Were Britain to fall, the United States might be the next object of German attack. But the United States was not prepared; the Atlantic, without the British navy, would no longer be the safeguard that had protected the country for generations. Thus the United States must go all out in providing aid to Britain to withstand the totalitarian blows.

The first step in giving full aid to Britain had already been taken when Roosevelt made his "stab-in-the-back" speech. Using a little-known law of World War I days as authority, the administration resorted to the "trade-in" method. On June 6 the Navy Department started delivery of a hundred "overage" scout bombers to the Curtiss-Wright factory in Buffalo, New York, for eventual trade-in for newer models. The turned-in planes were then sent at once to Britain and France. Subsequently the government by the same means sent indirectly to the democracies 100 armed attack planes, 600,000 British Enfield rifles, and 800 French 75-millimeter guns of World War I vintage, as well as other stockpiles of ammunition, machine guns, and mortars. Although the Federal government did not do the actual selling of these war implements, its neutral position might be open to question because no effort was made to dispose of similar commodities to the Axis. In similar fashion, the United States helped by permitting Canadian fliers to receive training at Florida fields and by allowing British warships to be repaired and refitted in American yards. Moreover, American planes were flown directly across the Canadian border for military use by the neighbor.

The Destroyer-Base Deal

While these supplies were of inestimable assistance to Britain in her lone defense against the Axis, more was deemed necessary to save her from defeat. One way of directly aiding Britain would be to strengthen her navy, and this in turn would diminish the danger of attack on America.

Another menace developing from the fall of France and other countries was that Germany might try to take over their holdings in the New World. The United States had already taken steps at the Havana Conference to prevent this, but additional safeguards were needed. Would it not be possible, therefore, to accomplish both objectives at the same time? The President thought so. Consequently, during the summer of 1940, he opened negotiations with British Ambassador Lord Lothian for the lease of British bases in the Western Hemisphere, the "rental" to take the form of fifty overage destroyers, which could be recommissioned to help strengthen the British navy. The negotiations were secret because of the expected isolationist opposition in Congress, which might hold up the arrangement until too late.

Before Roosevelt made the final commitment, Attorney General Jackson reported that there was no doubt of the President's right to arrange the deal by executive agreement rather than by treaty. Moreover, he found two old laws and a Supreme Court decision to uphold the presidential right to dispose of vessels of the Navy and unneeded naval material." Finally,

Jackson concluded that the transference of the overage destroyers would not run contrary to neutrality laws because they had not been built specifically to be turned over to a belligerent nation.

On September 2, 1940, the negotiations were completed. In exchange for the fifty destroyers, the United States received ninety-nine-year leases for bases in the Bahamas, Jamaica, St. Lucia, Trinidad, Antigua, and British Guiana. In addition, Britain granted the United States similar leases for Newfoundland and Bermuda as "gifts—generously given and gladly received."

The following day the President justified the deal to Congress, saying:

> The value to the Western Hemisphere of these outposts of security is beyond calculation. Their need has long been recognized by our country, and especially by those primarily charged with the duty of charting and organizing our own naval and military defense. They are essential to the protection of the Panama Canal. . . . For these reasons I have taken advantage of the present opportunity to acquire them.

Isolationists throughout the country denounced the action as dictatorial, as a violation of American neutrality, as a step in defiance of traditional American policy, and as contrary to international law. But the majority of the American people, after the initial surprise had worn off, praised the action—although perhaps not the method. They showed thereby that they were ready at last to commit the nation to all-out aid to Britain and to stronger hemisphere defense.

The Havana Conference

Meantime, an actual move to safeguard the hemisphere was taken at the second meeting of foreign ministers, held at Havana, Cuba, in July, 1940 The immediate reason for the session was fear lest Germany try to take over the New World colonies of countries she had occupied. Moreover German fifth-column activities, especially in Chile, Bolivia, and Uruguay appeared to be increasing in a way that would suggest these areas were included in Nazi plans for world domination. Latin-American trade wa badly disorganized by the war, especially in Brazil and Chile—a situatior that made German promises of vast barter deals of raw materials for post war use particularly attractive.

The most important measure of the session was the Act of Havana, which stated that the American republics, jointly or singly, might take over the administration of the threatened territory of non-American nations. A special Inter-American Commission for Territorial Administration wa established to supervise the trusteeships.[1] Further agreements provided for

[1] Eventually the United States, Venezuela, and Brazil assumed the trusteeship of Surinam (the former Dutch Guiana) and the United States alone took over Denmark' Greenland. Guadeloupe and Martinique, both French colonies, were not placed unde this plan, but the American republics kept a watchful eye on the latter because of th presence of part of the French fleet, which they did not want to fall into German hands and because the governor was suspected of being pro-Nazi.

better financial cooperation among the republics, with the United States increasing the lending power of the Export-Import Bank by $500 million. Finally, the completion of the Pan-American Highway was speeded up to improve commercial interchange and hemisphere defense. Secretary Hull concluded the meeting by saying: "The agreements have cleared the decks for effective action whenever such action may become necessary."

The Campaign of 1940

Soon after the fall of France, Americans turned their attention temporarily toward the 1940 election. As in 1916, the world situation played a prominent role as diplomatic issues overshadowed domestic ones for many voters. Many Americans believed it was only a matter of time before their country would be at war with Germany. In the domestic picture, the great problem was whether the New Deal had accomplished its objectives; a growing conservative element believed it had not and that a change to Republicanism would speed the return of prosperity. That element was also worried because the third-term precedent was seriously challenged for the first time.

The Republicans met in Philadelphia in June, with Thomas E. Dewey, the young district attorney of New York City, who had gained national fame as a racket buster, the leading presidential candidate. His major opponent in the early stages of preconvention jockeying was Senator Robert Taft of Ohio, isolationist son of the former President, with Senator Arthur Vandenberg of Michigan, a semi-isolationist, as a potential dark horse. As the convention got under way, however, the tide of popular—rather than political—opinion swung in favor of Wendell Willkie, a Hoosier-born and bred former Democrat, trained as a lawyer, but experienced as well as a teacher and farmer. He gained fame as president of Commonwealth and Southern when he obtained his company's demanded price from the government for subsidiaries taken over by TVA. Although the old-line politicians were cool to Willkie, he received enthusiastic support from a younger and more internationally minded group, some of them amateurs. By clever management the convention galleries were packed with noisy partisans primed to shout, "We Want Willkie." In the early balloting Dewey ran first, Taft second, and Willkie a poor third, but on the sixth ballot the Willkie bandwagon was successful, the politicians finally admitting that Willkie as a liberal conservative would offer the best opposition to the New Deal. Charles McNary of Oregon, the Senate minority leader and active spokesman for the farmers, was selected as his running mate.

The platform denounced the New Deal for its "shifting, contradictory, and overlapping administrations and policies," which had failed "to solve the problem of unemployment and revive opportunity for our youth." The Republicans promised to "put our idle millions back to work," and social security and other New Deal reforms would be amended and be better administered to end the waste, discrimination, and politics for which the New Deal was responsible, especially in the field of relief. In foreign affairs, the Republicans opposed America's entrance into a foreign war but favored "such aid as shall not be in violation of international law or inconsistent with the requirements of our national defense" to be extended to those fighting aggression. Finally, a constitutional amendment was demanded to limit Presidents to a maximum of two terms.

During the spring of 1940 Roosevelt remained silent about a third term, but his name was entered in numerous state primaries, in each of which he gained overwhelming victories. Moreover, his political managers saw to it that no other candidates grew strong enough to challenge his leadership. There were a few, however, whose presidential aspirations were obvious, notably Vice President Garner and Postmaster General Farley, who was vigorously opposed to the third term and subsequently broke with the President over it.

When the Democratic convention opened in Chicago in mid-July, Roosevelt still had not broken his silence, but Harry Hopkins already had a smooth organization working for the President's renomination and the convention was obviously rigged in his favor. After Alben Barkley's keynote speech, Roosevelt did send a message to the delegates that he did not seek the nomination and was releasing his delegates to vote for any candidate

Pinning a tail on the donkey. (By Seibel in the *Richmond Times-Dispatch.*)

they might choose. This cryptic statement did not preclude a draft for himself, so the convention renominated Roosevelt on the first ballot, an action he promptly accepted with the radio answer: "My conscience will not let me turn my back upon a call to serve."

On the other hand, Garner was not named again for the second spot. He was now considered too conservative for the New Dealers, and earlier in the year the President had said that to win and carry on the New Deal program, two liberals would have to be on the Democratic ticket. Consequently, Secretary of Agriculture Wallace was substituted, but without much enthusiasm on the part of the rank-and-file politicians.

The platform declared that "we will not participate in foreign wars, and we will not send our army, naval or air forces to fight in foreign lands outside of the Americas, except in case of attack." Aid to those fighting aggression was promised, along with preparedness. On the domestic scene, promotion of water-power development, enforcement of fair labor standards, defense of "all legitimate business," and expansion of the New Deal were promised.

Willkie did not attack the basic New Deal principles but found fault with the Democratic administration of them, as well as the failure to provide adequate preparedness and sufficient aid to the democracies. Some Republican orators accused the President of dictatorial tendencies, using the destroyer-base deal to prove he was secretly committed to enter the war on Britain's side.

Roosevelt, true to his acceptance promise, did not at first campaign in the usual sense, but devoted his time to domestic and foreign problems. Yet he did tour the country visiting navy yards, factories, and arsenals, thereby making contact with many voters. When it appeared that Willkie was gaining ground, however, Roosevelt made an active and direct appeal for votes. The reason he gave was the necessity for him "to call the attention of the nation to deliberate or unwitting falsifications of fact." On the war issue both candidates became irresponsible. The Republican declared the nation would be involved in war within five months if his opponent won, while Roosevelt rashly assured parents: "I have said this before, but I shall say it again and again and again. Your boys are not going to be sent into any foreign war."

On election day it was the serious world situation that swung the decision to Roosevelt. The electorate decided it would be unwise to change leaders. Nevertheless, the results were much closer than they had been in previous campaigns in which Roosevelt had run. He received 27.3 million popular votes to Willkie's 22.35 million, while in the electoral college the count was 449 to 82. In Congress, the Democrats increased their House seats by 5 (for a total of 268 to the Republicans' 162), but dropped one in the Senate (for a total of 66 to the Republicans' 28).

The Burke-Wadsworth Act

Roosevelt regarded the election as a popular mandate to continue his policies of preparedness, hemisphere defense, and all-out aid to the democracies, and even during the campaign he took steps to further his objectives On August 18, he and Prime Minister Mackenzie King of Canada established a Permanent Joint Board on Defense to consider "sea, land and air problems relating to the "defense of the north half of the Western Hemisphere."

In his July 19 acceptance speech, the President said: "Because of th millions of citizens involved in the conduct of defense, most right-thinkin persons are agreed some form of selection by draft is as necessary and fai today as it was in 1917 and 1918." And while waiting for Congress t approve such a conscription act, he called out the National Guard o August 27 because of "the increasing seriousness of the international situa tion."

The first peacetime draft bill in American history had been introduce into Congress in June, 1940, by Senator Edward Burke, a Nebraska Demc crat, and Representative James Wadsworth, a New York Republicar Extensive discussion and debate in both houses delayed its enactment noninterventionists insisted it would surely lead the nation into war; sup porters declared the army could not wait for voluntary enlistments to buil itself up to needed strength. Differences between the two houses over th age limits also were encountered before a compromise was reached o September 14 and two days later the President signed this so-called Burke Wadsworth Act.

The measure provided that all men between twenty-one and thirty-si must register for an eventual year's military service within the limit of the United States. The maximum number to receive such training i a given year was 900,000. Presidential proclamation fixed October 16 a registration day and President Clarence Dykstra of the University of Wi consin was named as Selective Service Administrator. The first men s drafted began their military training in November, 1940.

Meantime, Roosevelt had made preparedness a bipartisan matter b appointing to his cabinet two Republicans: Henry Stimson as Secretary c War and Frank Knox as Secretary of the Navy. Both men filled these pos with marked ability and efficiency.

Lend-Lease

The President was still not satisfied with what had been done to strengthe the defense of the Americas. He knew that on September 27, 1940, German Italy, and Japan had signed the Tripartite Pact under which they agree to assist one another in case any power then neutral—meaning the Unite States—entered the war against one of them. Consequently, in a nation radio talk on December 29, 1940, Roosevelt described the increasing Ax menace and told of how Hitler had said: "I can beat any other power i the world." Then he told of the need to continue and extend the aid t Britain because:

If Great Britain goes down, the Axis powers will control the continents c Europe, Asia, Africa, Australia, and the high seas—and they will be in a position t bring enormous military and naval resources against this hemisphere. It is n exaggeration to say that all of us, in all the Americas, would be living at the point of a gun—a gun loaded with explosive bullets, economic as well as military.

The President declared that the national policy was "to keep war away from our country and our people." To do this, overall production must be speeded up so that the nations fighting aggression might obtain the supplies they needed. "We must become the arsenal of democracy."

This speech set the stage for further proposals in the President's annual message to Congress of January 6, 1941. He pointed out that while the democracies did not need manpower, they would soon "need billions of dollars' worth of the weapons of defense," for which they would soon be unable to pay "in ready cash." Despite the "cash-and-carry" provision, it would not be right for the United States to say they should surrender. Instead, Roosevelt asked that the democracies be loaned war materials, for which "we shall be repaid within a reasonable time following the close of hostilities, or, at our option, in other goods of many kinds, which they can produce and which we need." If the United States extended these material loans, the democracies would win, thereby making possible a "world founded upon four essential human freedoms"—freedom of speech and expression, freedom of worship, freedom from want, and freedom from fear. This was Roosevelt's first expression of what might be called the victory aims of World War II.

Congress speedily took up the President's request by considering H.R. 1776, a measure "further to promote the defense of the United States." It first defined "defense articles"—weapons, munitions, ships, aircraft, and agricultural and industrial commodities. Then, "notwithstanding the provisions of any other law," the President might authorize the head of any government department or agency "to manufacture in arsenals, factories, and shipyards . . . any defense article for the government of any country whose defense the President deems vital to the defense of the United States." The department or agency might then sell or lease such articles to that government, but they must not be convoyed by American naval vessels, and the President must report to Congress at least once every ninety days about lend-lease activities.

This bill has been called the broadest grant of power ever given to a President, but its supporters asserted it was necessary to assure speed and efficiency in American aid to the democracies. The noninterventionists immediately condemned the measure, declaring it authorized the President to declare war, that it was "monstrous," that it was a "New Deal triple-A foreign policy; it will plow under every fourth American boy," and that it was "a bold attempt to create a dictatorship to govern our future foreign policy." A middle group in Congress approved the aid to Britain but believed it could be done without giving the President so much power. The President, aided by prominent government officials, used his influence on key Congressmen so effectively that the Lend-Lease Act became law on March 11, 1941, in practically its original form. Congress then quickly appropriated $7 billion to put lend-lease into operation, and the President ordered shipments of vital materials to the democracies at once.

The Lend-Lease Act definitely marked an end to American isolationism.

It was the logical step to take to aid opponents of aggression. Britain was naturally thankful; Prime Minister Winston Churchill called the act a "monument of generous, far-seeing statesmanship." Germany, on the other hand, tried to play down its effects by saying that American aid would arrive too late to save Britain, but at the same time she called the measure "the most flagrant North American meddling."

The new policy greatly strengthened the antifascist cause. British dollar credits in the United States were practically exhausted, and American neutrality laws stood as a bar to private loans. Already British purchases in America were being reduced—a most undesirable situation. Lend-lease was based on the sound premise that continued British and Chinese resistance to aggression would give America time to strengthen its defenses, and the further premise that the most sensible thing to do with the major portion of American-made war implements was to place them in the hands of those who would use them against America's potential enemies. Lend lease had the additional merit of making the United States government the sole important customer of the arms industry, giving it complete power over the allocation of weapons.

To be sure, lend-lease marked the end of real neutrality. The nation was now openly trying to help one side to the detriment of the other, but the question had become clearly one of American security. To be neutral in a struggle of this character was to acquiesce in the victory of nations believed by most people at the time to have hostile designs upon the Western Hemisphere.

The Error Must Not Be Repeated

As has been shown, many Americans believed their country's wises policy was to avoid at all costs any act that might lead it into war. These so-called isolationists had been largely responsible for the Johnson Deb Default Act and the subsequent neutrality legislation. They hailed the findings of the Nye Committee as proof that World War I had benefited only a few selfish international bankers and munitions makers. They opposed all efforts to increase the army and navy, to enact the Selective Service Law, and to pass lend-lease because they believed such steps would develop a belligerent spirit and thereby increase the possibility of war As in the period from 1914 to 1917, many isolationists honestly felt that hostilities would be disastrous for America.

Other less idealistic groups within the isolationist camp supported the movement for more selfish reasons. Some anti–New Dealers saw in the preparedness movement a Roosevelt effort to turn attention from the short comings of his domestic policies. Many social reformers regarded the movement as the beginning of the end for the program of social justice Until Germany attacked the Soviet Union, American Communists claimed that war would benefit only the capitalists. American fascists desired neither preparedness nor war because they wanted an Axis victory, with the resulting spread of totalitarianism to the United States. Many German-American and Italo-Americans opposed American entrance into the war because i would spell defeat for their native lands. A few businessmen thought that appeasement of the dictators would bring profitable trade to the country, while Axis agents tried to build up a feeling of security in the United States so that lend-lease would not be granted to Germany's enemies. Normally these diverse elements would have little or nothing in common, but they now rallied in mutual support of their goal—to keep the country out of war.

These strange bedfellows used every means to advance their cause. In Congress there were Senators Johnson, Wheeler, Nye, and LaFollette, together with Representatives Hamilton Fish of New York and Clare Hoffman of Michigan—to mention the most prominent—who constantly spoke and voted against preparedness bills. From public platforms Charles Lindbergh and others severely condemned the Roosevelt foreign policies. Over the radio Father Charles Coughlin preached in a fascist vein. Books, periodicals, and pamphlets such as Elizabeth Dilling's *Red Network,* Father Coughlin's *Social Justice,* and Gerald Winrod's *The Defender* promoted the isolationist viewpoint.

It was through special committees, however, that most isolationist propaganda was disseminated. Some made their appeal chiefly to those of German blood. Under the leadership of Fritz Kuhn, German-American Bund members wore uniforms at their meetings, practiced military drill, and greeted one another with the Nazi salute. Financed in part by the Reich, these pro-German committees [2] tried to dissuade Americans from supporting preparedness measures. They also sang hymns of hate against the British and the Jews.

Many Americans, refusing to join the definitely Nazi organizations, nevertheless did become members of committees that placed their appeal on some different basis. There were more than seven hundred of these isolationist agencies when World War II opened; while most of these were ephemeral, some were strong and vociferous. One of the most publicized was the American Fellowship Forum to promote Nazi ideological warfare, the need for appeasement, and opposition to preparedness. Through *Today's Challenge,* the Forum made its appeal; contributors were Lawrence Dennis, a rank proponent of American fascism, Representative Fish, Senator William Lundeen, and George Sylvester Viereck of World War I notoriety. Another group was William Dudley Pelley's Silver Shirts, using the *Galilean* to urge a purge of Jews and others who Pelley asserted were un-American. The Christian Front, professed admirers of Father Coughlin, claimed a membership of at least 200,000, dedicated to dominating the country by force. More than twenty isolationist Congressmen, wittingly or not, allowed their franking privileges to be used to send out literature detrimental to preparedness and to the Allied cause.

The America First Committee, organized in the fall of 1940 by R. Douglas Stuart, Jr., a wealthy Yale student, tried to consolidate the membership of these numerous groups to fulfill its general purpose of avoiding war at any price. The first national chairman was General Robert Wood, a well-

---

[2] Lesser known agencies were the League of Friends of New Germany, the German Legion, the German Edda Kultur League, the Homeland Regional Group, the League of German-American Writers, and the Hindenburg Youth Association.

Developing a punch. (By Hungerford in the *Pittsburgh Post-Gazette*.)

known Chicago businessman. Prominent among the members or those who cooperated were Charles Lindbergh, Kathleen Norris, Henry Ford, General Hugh Johnson, and Senators Wheeler and Nye. This committee sent out thousands of pamphlets, letters, buttons, and stickers. Hundreds of speeches were delivered, but they showed little contact with reality. For example, on April 7, 1941, Lindbergh asserted that Great Britain was a beaten nation; he concluded, therefore, "that we cannot win this war for England regardless of how much assistance we extend." Six weeks later he and Wheeler sought a negotiated peace because, if the United States entered the war, it would mean the end of democracy on this side of the Atlantic. In September, the eminent flier declared: "The three most important groups which have been pressing this country toward war are the British, the Jewish, and the Roosevelt Administration."

While it is impossible to say how much influence these isolationist organizations had upon the American mind, or to determine accurately their membership, their efforts were not without effect. The debates in Congress showed that opposition to war was strong, and delaying tactics did hold up preparedness measures. The antiwar spirit was also active in the colleges; thousands of students signed the Oxford Pledge not to fight under any circumstances and flooded Washington with petitions not to repeat the mistake of 1917.

The administration did not conceal its bitterness toward these organizations. Roosevelt insisted the isolationists were demanding that he "become a modern Benedict Arnold and betray all that I hold dear—my devotion to our freedom—to our churches—to our country." He referred to Linbergh as an "appeaser and defeatist" in such denunciatory terms that the colonel resigned his commission in the Army Air Force. The President also implied that there was a strong similarity between the writings and speeches of the noninterventionists and propaganda coming from the Reich.

Nor was the opposition to the isolationists limited to the administration. To counteract the efforts of the America First Committee and other such groups, many Americans aligned themselves with the Committee to Defend America by Aiding the Allies and the Fight for Freedom Committee. Pamphlets, speeches, radio talks, and advertisements were used by the internationalists in their fight.

Improving Hemisphere Defense

Despite the attacks of the isolationists, the United States continued to build up American defenses during the spring and summer of 1941, by giving more assistance to Britain, and by cutting down potential Axis influence in the Western Hemisphere. For example, in April, 1941, the United States turned over ten coast-guard cutters to Britain for antisubmarine warfare because of the staggering merchant losses the British were suffering on the seas and because the Neutrality Act prohibited the United States from convoying American supplies to belligerents.

In the same month Roosevelt and Mackenzie King agreed that "in mobilizing the resources of this continent each country should provide the other with the defense articles which it is best able to produce quickly, and that production should be coordinated to this end." Consequently, the United States bought strategic materials—such as aluminum—from Canada, while Canada obtained essential dollar exchange to balance her unfavorable trade and enable her to buy more American goods.

Likewise in April, the United States signed a pact with the Danish minister under which it gained the right to establish military and naval installations in Greenland. Not only was this a move to prevent the island from falling into German hands, but it meant as well that the United States might guard British merchantmen as far east as Greenland.

German protests at these steps were as nothing compared with the cries raised against the seizure of her merchant ships in American ports. On March 30, 1941, the United States Coast Guard, under the Espionage Act of 1917, took over twenty-eight Italian and two German ships lying in American harbors because their crews had wrecked the machinery and engaged in other acts of sabotage, thereby making the vessels a menace to navigation. At the same time thirty-five undamaged Danish ships were brought under American control.

Then arose the question of what to do with the seized ships. The President asked Congress on April 10 to extend his authority to requisition or purchase American vessels to include the recently seized ones. On June 6 Congress did so and on the same day Roosevelt ordered the United States Maritime Commission to take over "any foreign merchant vessel which is lying idle in waters within the jurisdiction of the United States . . . and which is necessary to the national defense." Thus the German, Italian, and

Danish ships, together with subsequently seized French ones—including the *Normandie*—were acquired by the government. Later a number of them carried cargoes to Britain.

Still another blow at the Axis was delivered on June 14 when the President, under the Trading-with-the-Enemy Act of 1917, froze all Axis assets in the United States, thereby diminishing totalitarian propaganda and sabotage in the country. To serve the same end, twenty-four German consulates in the United States, together with the German Library of Information and other propaganda agencies, were closed on July 10 because they were engaging "in activities wholly outside the scope of their legitimate activities." Subsequently, all Italian consulates were also closed.

Nor was the United States finished. Acting under authority obtained through the declaration of the unlimited national emergency of May 27, 1941, the President issued a "Proclaimed List of Certain Blocked Nationals." This consisted of some eighteen hundred persons and firms in the Western Hemisphere "deemed to be acting for the benefit of Germany and Italy"— in other words, undermining American official policy. No American firms were to do business with the black-listed concerns, whose assets in the United States were to be frozen. This was an unusual action for the United States to take while still a neutral, but was further proof of the administration's insistence upon keeping Axis influence at a minimum in the hemisphere.

Meantime, the President pushed the defensive zone closer to Europe by ordering the American occupation of Iceland on July 7, because "the United States cannot permit the occupation by Germany of strategic outposts in the Atlantic . . . to be used for eventual attack against the Western Hemisphere." This pronouncement increased the ire of the isolationists, who asserted it would be only a matter of time before the nation was involved in war. Senator Wheeler declared that American naval ships had already attacked German submarines, a statement bringing quick denial from Secretary Knox.

But if that were not the case, German submarines were attacking American shipping. On May 21, 1941, the *Robin Moor,* clearly marked as an American merchantman, was sunk seven hundred miles off the coast of Brazil while on her way to Cape Town. The submarine commander made no effort to help the passengers and crew, who drifted in lifeboats for nearly three weeks before they were rescued. When the news reached the United States on June 9, an immediate protest was sent to the Reich; but Germany replied she would "continue to sink every ship with contraband for Britain whatever its name."

Consequently, the President, in a special message to Congress on June 20 said:

We must take the sinking of the *Robin Moor* as a warning to the United States not to resist the Nazi movement of world conquest. It is a warning that the United States may use the high seas of the world only with Nazi consent. Were we to yield on this we would inevitably submit to world domination at the hands of the present leaders of the German Reich. We are not yielding and we do not propose to yield

As definite proof that the United States would not yield, the administration condemned Germany's unprovoked attack on Russia in June and announced that lend-lease would be extended to the Soviet.[3] Moreover, at the request of Chief of Staff George Marshall, the President asked Congress in early July to lengthen military service for the draftees because their discharge after a year's training would disrupt plans to enlarge the army. Despite the isolationist opposition, Congress, on August 12, added six months to the military service of conscripted men; the extra service was made more palatable by a $10-a-month pay raise after one year.

The Atlantic Charter

In spite of these preparations, the Axis victories in Europe and Asia, together with continued Allied losses on the high seas, made essential more definite planning by the democracies. Therefore Roosevelt and Churchill met at sea off the coast of Newfoundland August 9–12, 1941. They discussed what aid should be sent to the Soviet, what policy should be followed regarding Japan, and numerous other problems concerning lend-lease and preparedness. Much more important, however, was the agreement on broad aims and principles for the postwar world, known as the "Atlantic Charter," which contained the following eight provisions:

First, their countries seek no aggrandizement, territorial or other;

Second, they desire to see no territorial changes that do not accord with the freely expressed wishes of all the people concerned;

Third, they respect the right of all peoples to choose the form of government under which they will live; and they wish to see sovereign rights restored to those who have been forcibly deprived of them;

Fourth, they will endeavor . . . to further the enjoyment by all States, great and small, victor or vanquished, of access, on equal terms, to the trade and to the raw materials of the world which are needed for their economic prosperity;

Fifth, they desire to bring about the fullest collaboration between all nations in the economic field with the object of securing for all, improved labor standards, economic advancement and social security;

Sixth, after the final destruction of the Nazi tyranny, they hope to see established a peace which will afford assurance that all men in all the lands may live out their lives in freedom from fear and want;

Seventh, such a peace should enable all men to traverse the high seas and oceans without hindrance;

Eighth, they believe that all of the nations of the world . . . must come to the abandonment of the use of force. Since no future peace can be maintained if land, sea, or air armaments continue to be employed by nations which threaten . . . aggression outside of their frontiers, they believe, pending the establishment of a wider and permanent system of general security, that the disarmament of such

[3] This decision also brought vociferous protests from the isolationists. Lindbergh said: I would a hundred times rather see my country ally herself with England, or even Germany with all her faults, than with the cruelty, the godlessness and the barbarism that exist in Soviet Russia. The only sensible thing for us to do is to build an impregnable defense for America and keep this hemisphere at peace."

nations is essential. They will likewise aid and encourage all other practicable measures which will lighten for peace-loving peoples the crushing burden of armaments.

This Atlantic Charter might be called the Fourteen Points of World War II; while the Charter was less detailed than Wilson's statement, it served much the same purpose—that of establishing a postwar goal of peace and collective security. The very indefiniteness of the Charter provided a latitude lacking in the Fourteen Points. Moreover, the Charter had greater weight in that it was sponsored by the heads of the two strongest nations in the world. It gave oppressed peoples a hope for the future and was the beginning of the United Nations.

The Shooting War

American help for Britain was, in truth, coming closer and closer to actual war. During the summer of 1941 American naval vessels were escorting British and American merchant ships as far as Iceland. Although forbidden to shoot unless attacked, they helped protect the sea lanes by reporting to British destroyers and planes the positions of German submarines. In accordance with this policy, the destroyer *Greer* had been tracking an underseas raider for several hours on September 4 when the submarine retaliated by firing two torpedoes at its American follower. Uninjured, the *Greer* dropped several depth charges and pursued the German craft until the latter finally escaped. In a radio talk to the nation Roosevelt condemned the attack upon the *Greer* and made known his future policy:

No act of violence will keep us from maintaining intact two bulwarks of defense: First, our line of supply to the enemies of Hitler, and, second, the freedom of our shipping on the high seas. From now on, if German or Italian vessels of war enter the waters the protection of which is necessary for American defense, they do so at their own peril.

He denied it was an act of war to maintain the American patrol to protect shipping and warned that "American naval vessels and American planes will no longer wait until Axis submarines . . . or raiders . . . strike their deadly blow—first." This amounted to a virtual order to American ships and planes to shoot first.

The isolationists denounced this order as the beginning of a "shooting war," and the Reich called the President a dictatorial aggressor, ready to involve an unwilling nation in war to satisfy his lust for power.

Amending the Neutrality Act

Shortly after the *Greer* incident, the President disclosed his intention to ask Congress for permission to arm American merchantmen; this would mean, of course, a partial repeal of the Neutrality Act of 1939. It is impossible to say what chance of success the request would have had under ordinary circumstances, but it was greatly aided by the actions of Germany herself.

On September 27 the *I. C. White,* an American-owned tanker now under Panama registry (to avoid the prohibitions of the American neutrality laws), was sunk off the Brazilian bulge well within the limits of the neutrality zone. Hull characterized the incident as "another act of lawlessness, piracy, and attempted frightfulness," and, in a special message to Congress on October 9, the President said: "Our merchant vessels are sailing the seas on missions connected with the defense of the United States. It is not just that the crews of these vessels should be denied the means of defending their lives and their ships." Consequently, he asked Congress to repeal the clause prohibiting the arming of American ships, and at the same time intimated he wanted the legislature to remove also the "crippling provisions" banning American vessels from combat zones and belligerent ports.

Debate on amending the Neutrality Act was cut short by the news that on October 17 the destroyer *Kearney* had been hit off Iceland with resulting casualties of ten injured and eleven missing. The incident brought House passage of the bill by an overwhelming vote, but in the Senate three Republicans substituted a measure calling for total repeal of the Neutrality Act because it was "detrimental to the best interests of the United States." The Democratic majority, however, preferred to follow the President's wishes to repeal only three sections: the bans on arming of merchantmen, on entrance into combat zones, and on entering belligerent ports. Rallying their forces, the isolationist Senators threatened a filibuster— like that waged by the willful men of 1917.

This isolationist resistance was quickly overcome, however, after the Germans sank the destroyer *Reuben James,* convoying supplies to Iceland, with the loss of one hundred lives on October 30. Two weeks later Congress approved repeal of the three clauses after fairly close votes.

The order to arm merchantmen was speedily given, and they were thereafter allowed to go to Allied ports with military supplies. Both these merchantmen and American naval vessels could shoot on sight to keep the supply lines open, to maintain freedom of the seas, and to strengthen hemisphere defense. Although the United States was still theoretically neutral, it was neutrality in name only. While the isolationists still demanded that the United States avoid war, war had already come. By November 1 German submarines had taken a toll of eleven American merchant vessels and one destroyer. Two other destroyers and innumerable merchantmen had been attacked, but escaped sinking. To prevent further losses, American ships were now ready to fight. Under the circumstances it could be but a matter of time before all-out hostilities developed. Strangely enough, however, the final steps were taken on the other side of the world.

Mounting Japanese Aggression

Following the *Panay* incident, most Americans turned their backs upon the Far East, while they viewed with increasing apprehension the storm clouds developed over Europe. Nevertheless, from early 1938 until the

Pearl Harbor attack, the Roosevelt administration realized that the Japanese menace was growing, not diminishing. Because of isolationist sentiment, however, that menace was combatted with words rather than deeds during most of these months.

During 1938 the State Department protested Japanese encroachments on American rights in China and the Japanese bombings of Chinese civilians. Moreover, the Western powers worried over reports that Japan was building a larger navy, but when they demanded that Japan reveal her construction program, she refused to answer. There was nothing the other nations could do about this rebuff; France and Britain were too concerned with Hitler's moves, while the United States did not wish to push Japan too far.

Nevertheless, the Roosevelt administration tried to restrain Japan by other means. On July 1, 1938, Hull told manufacturers and exporters of airplanes and aircraft parts that the government strongly opposed the sale of such equipment to any nation using planes to bomb civilians. Although no penalties were threatened, there was general compliance with what might be called a moral embargo. In 1939 the State Department similarly frowned upon the exportation of high-octane gasoline. Even before this moral embargo, the administration persuaded bankers not to extend financial credit to Japan.

Because Roosevelt had never proclaimed that a state of war existed in the Far East, neither the Neutrality Act of 1937 nor that of 1939 was put into effect. At first he withheld the proclamation because he hoped the Sino-Japanese troubles could be settled quickly; later he realized that if the neutrality legislation became effective, China, the victim of aggression, could not obtain American assistance.

These actions had little effect upon Japan, except perhaps to prove the United States was unfriendly. Appeasement at Munich encouraged aggression in Asia as well as in Europe, and on November 3, 1938, Premier Fumimara Konoye for the first time publicly stated his country's ambition:

> What Japan seeks is the establishment of a new order that will ensure the permanent stability of East Asia. . . . This new order has for its foundation a tripartite relationship of mutual aid and co-ordination between Japan, Manchukuo, and China in political, economic, cultural and other fields.

Konoye's pronouncement failed to mention that Japan was forcing the "New Order" upon an unwilling China or to define what East Asia would include. The American State Department called attention to these omissions and protested that Japanese actions were harming American "rights and interests" in China and were "unjust and unwarranted." Nor did the United States consider it just for one party to draw up New Order terms for regions not under its jurisdiction. Hull then concluded with the assertion that his country would not countenance the abrogation of any of its rights through arbitrary methods, but would discuss any new and mutually satisfactory proposals.

By no means impressed by American protests, the Japanese extended their control over Hainan in February, 1939, followed two months later by seizing several islands only seven hundred miles from Singapore. Then in June she blockaded the British and French concessions in Tientsin. As the war spread, more American lives were threatened, American property destroyed, and American rights in the Japanese-occupied sections of China interfered with. Since mere protests were ineffective, Roosevelt decided on more drastic steps.

On July 26, 1939, the United States gave Japan the necessary six months' notification for the termination of the 1911 commercial treaty. The cancellation of this treaty, with its most-favored-nation clause, would remove all obstacles to an actual embargo against Japan. When the six months' period ended, Japanese-American trade relations were maintained on a day-by-day basis, subject to interruption at any time. But even this threat did not cause Japan to change her policies. Her military forces continued to press their advantage, moving into Hunan Province in September, 1939, and capturing Nanning two months later. In this progress Japan was aided by the outbreak of the European war, which prevented Britain and France from assisting their nationals in the Far East or from supporting the American protests.

In early June, 1940, Japan took advantage of France's collapse to move into French Indochina, and simultaneously she demanded that Britain close the Burma Road to all military supplies to China, backing up this demand with the implied threat that if Britain did not comply, Hongkong would be attacked. Britain, now facing the Reich alone and fearing an invasion, had to agree to close the road for three months starting July 18, thereby cutting off China almost completely from the rest of the world.

On September 27, 1940, Japan openly asserted its solidarity with the European Axis by concluding the Tripartite Pact. It provided for mutual recognition and support for each other's objectives; its most important clause was Article 3: "They further undertake to assist one another with all political, economic and military means if one of the three . . . is attacked by a Power at present not involved in the European War or in the Chinese-Japanese conflict."

Although this was certainly intended as a warning to the United States, Roosevelt was not swerved from his position. In a radio address of October 12, 1940, he proclaimed the need for maintaining democracy in the Western Hemisphere. Then he asserted:

The core of our defense is the faith we have in the institutions we defend. The Americas will not be scared or threatened into the ways the dictators want us to follow. . . .

No combination of dictator countries of Europe and Asia will stop the help we are giving to almost the last free people fighting to hold them at bay. . . .

We know now that if we seek to appease them by withholding aid from those who stand in their way, we only hasten the day of their attack on us. . . .

Based on these premises, the President's policy included five main points: the United States should not seek war with Japan; it must insist on respect for American rights in the Far East; it must not withhold aid from the defenders of democracy; all kinds of pressure, diplomatic and economic, should be used to force Japan to cease her aggression; and the United States was willing to confer with Japan and other nations interested in the Far East for a settlement of regional problems.

Additional economic pressure was already being exerted. On December 15, 1938, the first of a series of loans was made to China. On July 2, 1940, the President signed the Export Control Act, empowering him to curtail or stop completely the export of materials considered vital to the American defense program. Almost immediately he announced that no more export licenses would be granted to ship aviation gasoline and machine tools to Japan. This was followed in September by a similar ban on scrap iron and steel. Ambassador Horinouchi denounced these actions as "unfriendly acts" and "discriminatory" measures that might cause "unpredictable results." Hull's answer was sharp and critical. He could not see, he said, how Japan, which had broken so many commitments and had violated so many American rights in China, could object to the embargoes: "Of all the countries with which I have had to deal during the past eight years, the Government of Japan has the least occasion or excuse to accuse this Government of an unfriendly act." Despite Japanese threats, the United States extended the embargo before the spring of 1941 to include arms, ammunition, other implements of war, and many strategic materials.

Mounting Tensions

The opening of 1941 found Japanese-American relations increasingly strained. The Japanese military clique, growing in strength, was taking a more active part in political affairs. Members of jingoistic and terrorist societies were assassinating those advocating peace, and the chauvinistic press was swaying the people in favor of the New Order. If some Japanese wanted to maintain American friendship, others were openly hostile. For example, on October 4, 1940, Foreign Minister Matsuoka is reported to have said: "I fling this challenge to America. If she in her contentment is going to stick blindly and stubbornly to *status quo* in the Pacific, then we will fight America."

Japan was angered by the American refusal to recognize the New Order and by the increasing number of items placed on the American embargo list. Yet there was a feeling that the United States would never risk war with Japan. To this feeling the isolationists in the American Congress contributed when they voted down the presidential request for appropriations to deepen the harbors at Guam and other Pacific islands.

It cannot be said that the United States was not warned of the danger of a Japanese attack. In testimony before the House Foreign Relations Committee on January 15, 1941, Hull pointed out the increasing number of recent statements made by Japanese leaders about plans to dominate the Far East. The Secretary considered these "a program for the subjugation and ruthless exploitation by one country of nearly half the population of the world" and should therefore be a "matter of immense significance, importance and concern" to America. Nine days later, Secretary of the Navy Knox showed his anxiety in his note to War Secretary Stimson:

If war eventuates with Japan, it is believed easily possible that hostilities would be initiated by a surprise attack upon the Fleet or Naval base Pearl Harbor. . .

This remarkable prediction was followed on January 27 with a report from Ambassador Joseph Grew that he had it on reliable authority "that a surprise mass attack on Pearl Harbor was planned by the Japanese military forces, in case of trouble between Japan and the United States; that the attack would involve the use of all Japanese military facilities."

Despite these warnings, American popular attention was concerned chiefly with events in Europe and the debates in Congress over lend-lease. Trouble in the Far East seemed too remote to affect the United States, and the belief persisted that America would not be drawn into the imbroglio unless she herself sought war. Indeed, opinion polls indicated that the primary potential enemy was Germany, not Japan. It was also felt that, if war were to come with Japan, the enemy could be quickly and easily defeated.

Both the United States and Japan wanted to avert an early showdown. The Roosevelt administration did not desire war; if it must come, it would be better late than soon, because the nation was not ready for hostilities either in terms of military preparedness or of national unity. On their side, the Japanese were playing for time in the hope their Axis partners would be victorious in Europe and that Japanese domination over East Asia could thereafter be achieved at a minimum price.

On March 8, 1941, Hull and the new Japanese ambassador, Admiral Kichisaburo Nomura, who had attended the Naval Academy at Annapolis in his youth, began a series of conferences on all outstanding difficulties. The early talks soon indicated Japan had gone so far in her military conquests that she would not consent to stop or to relinquish her gains. To both Hull and the President Japan's course seemed likely to lead to war with the United States, but they hoped to avert hostilities as long as possible. Moreover, the other countries with a stake in the Far East were either too busy with the European struggle or were already occupied by Germany. Under the circumstances it seemed best to continue the peace talks with Nomura as long as possible.

But, even while these talks were going on, the United States was continuing its policy of trying to stem the Japanese advance by economic pressure. With the passage of lend-lease, further credit as well as strategic supplies were extended to China—making a total of more than $100 million since the beginning of 1940. Moreover, lend-lease was granted to the Dutch East Indies and Malaya.

Freezing Japanese Assets

The diplomacy of 1941 cannot be understood without a realization of the extraordinary importance of Malaya and the Dutch East Indies. Most of the world's rubber, tin, and quinine came from this area, and it also had rich supplies of petroleum. Next to the protection of its own territories, the United States held no objective of foreign policy more important than that of keeping this vital area out of hostile hands. Fear that Japan would attack this region had compelled the Roosevelt administration to refrain from a complete embargo—one that would have deprived the Japanese war machine of American gasoline. Japanese occupation of French Indochina in 1940 increased the threat to Malaya and the East Indies and caused Washington to apply more diplomatic pressure against the Asiatic aggressor. A crisis did not arise so long as Japanese forces in French Indochina were small in numbers and concentrated in the northern part, but in July, 1941, the situation was radically altered. The Vichy government gave its assent to full Japanese control over the country, and the Japanese strengthened their forces and moved them into the south. Such steps could hardly be called defensive; Japan was obviously building up French Indochina as an offensive base for an attack upon Malaya and the East Indies.

Since appeasement had failed, the United States resorted to drastic action. On July 25, 1941, the President froze all Japanese assets in the United States, thereby stopping all commercial intercourse between the two countries and imposing at last a complete embargo. To obtain gasoline and other vital supplies, Japan now either had to conquer southeastern Asia, involving herself in war with Britain, or else to induce America to resume trade relations. In such a diplomatic impasse the only outcome could be war—unless one of the countries abandoned its position.

Sumner Welles of the State Department clearly stated the American case. He asserted that the occupation of Indochina was a definite threat to American security because it menaced procurement of raw materials vital to its defense. Moreover, the Japanese advance into southeastern Asia was in direct defiance of the Tokyo promise to respect the Far Eastern *status quo*. Welles concluded: "The Japanese Government is giving clear indication that it is determined to pursue an objective of expansion by force or threat of force." At the same time the United States Navy heads announced that the fleet was virtually ready to back up the national policy in the Pacific.

Japan, however, was not prepared for the showdown. She had partially safeguarded her position, it is true, by signing a nonaggression pact with the Soviet Union on April 13, thereby ensuring that she would not be attacked from the north, but she continued her diplomatic fencing with the United States. American firms in China were merely taken into "protective custody," with the intimation that this policy would be relaxed if America would reciprocate. Another example of her appeasement resulted from the so-called Chung-king incident. Japanese planes dropped bombs near the American gunboat *Tutuila,* anchored in the Yangtze River, causing slight damage. Without waiting for a State Department protest, Toyko sent an apology and said full reparation would be made.

Roosevelt refused to be swerved from his embargo policy by the Japanese actions, largely because Japan had not as yet made satisfactory pledges regarding the future of the Far East. At the Atlantic Charter meeting with Churchill, he opposed a stern ultimatum to Toyko, believing he could "baby them along" for some time to come.

The Failure of Peace Talks

Within the Japanese government there was a significant division of opinion. Emperor Hirohito and Premier Konoye were moderates, hoping for some peaceful settlement with the United States. They had the support of the navy heads, who foresaw that in a long war Japan would probably be defeated, but were strongly opposed by the more fanatical nationalists—a group that included Foreign Minister Matsuoka, War Minister Tojo, and the army leaders. For a time in the summer of 1941 the moderates appeared to have the upper hand when Matsuoka was replaced by Admiral Teijuro Toyada. On August 7 Konoye renewed an earlier proposal that he and Roosevelt meet somewhere in the Pacific to seek a way out of the impasse.

The President was at first inclined to accept this invitation, but Hull advised against the meeting unless the two governments agreed on basic issues. On September 4 Roosevelt personally repeated to Nomura four essential principles developed earlier: (1) both parties should respect the political independence and territorial integrity of all nations: (2) neither should interfere in the other's affairs; (3) the equality of all countries should be upheld; and (4) there should be no change in the Pacific status quo except by peaceful means. The Japanese did not reject these principles, but hedged on how they should be applied in China and other areas.

Diplomatic historians have divided sharply over the President's failure to meet directly with the Japanese premier. Critics argue- that the door was thus slammed shut on America's best opportunity to settle Far Eastern problems through diplomacy and thus avoid a costly war. Roosevelt's defenders doubt that Konoye was in a position to withdraw Japanese forces from China and Indochina and break with the Axis—the only honorable conditions the United States could have accepted in return for aiding Japan in its economic difficulties.

The situation grew worse rather than better. On October 16 Konoye had to resign, and the more aggressive General Tojo became premier. Although less ready than Konoye to make substantial concessions to the United States, Tojo still delayed a final decision on peace or war. On November 5 the Japanese Privy Council decided to make a final offer and then to attack if these terms were rejected. A special envoy, Saburo Kurusu, was sent to Washington to join with Nomura in the final negotiations.

On November 20 Kurusu and Nomura proposed a *modus vivendi,* or temporary agreement, covering the following points: (1) Japan and the United States would not move their armed forces into any region in southeastern Asia or the southern Pacific except those parts of Indochina already occupied by Japan; (2) Japan would evacuate Indochina either upon restoration of peace between Japan and China or upon a general Pacific area settlement; (3) Japan and the United States would cooperate in obtaining needed commodities from the Netherlands East Indies; (4) both countries would restore their commercial relations and the United States would supply Japan with oil; and (5) the United States would refrain from measures prejudicial to the establishment of peace between Japan and China.

The last two points were quite unacceptable to Roosevelt and Hull because they would have required the United States to reverse its support of China and become a partner of Japan. Nevertheless, Roosevelt at first hoped a fairer *modus vivendi* might be arranged. In the end, however, he decided against this procedure, being influenced, on the one hand, by British and Chinese warnings against appeasement, and, on the other, by intercepted code messages from Japan indicating that some warlike move was imminent. On November 26 Hull gave the Japanese envoys a document stating in stronger terms than ever the fundamental American position. Among other things, the United States asked Japan to evacuate China and Indochina, to support only Chiang Kai-shek's government, and to join in a multilateral nonaggression pact to insure peace in the Pacific.

Hull's action reflected his conviction that further negotiations were probably hopeless and all that the United States could do was deal with Japanese aggression in whatever new form it took. For eleven days more the diplomatic stage play continued, but the Japanese war machine was already in action. On November 25 the Japanese fleet had begun to move in utmost secrecy toward Hawaii, and on December 1 the Privy Council made the final decision for war.

Although the Roosevelt administration was certain that Japan was up to something, the general conviction was that she would not want to unify American public opinion by a direct attack on American territory. Alert warnings were sent to American commanders throughout the Pacific, but they were lacking in urgency. The real expectation was that Japan would invade either Siam or Malaya as the first step toward grabbing the oil and rubber she desperately needed. What the United States should do to oppose this was a matter of earnest discussion behind the scenes. To allow Japan to overrun southeastern Asia was dangerous to American economic interests and would expose the Philippines to attack; yet to go to war because Japan invaded some distant territory would bring the full weight of isolationist wrath down on the administration's head. Unable to answer the basic question, Roosevelt decided on three immediate steps: (1) to address a general appeal for peace to the emperor; (2) to explain the situation in a speech to Congress; and (3) to warn Japan against further aggression.

Only the first step was taken before the Pearl Harbor attack. On December 6 Roosevelt cabled a personal appeal to Hirohito to join with him in preventing "further death and destruction in the world." Instead of a reply, the Japanese said their last word when Nomura and Kurusu called on Secretary Hull on December 7 at 2:20 P.M. and handed him their government's arrogant rejection of his November 26 note. Angered both by the note's contents and by the news from Pearl Harbor, which had begun to come into Washington just before this interview, Hull denounced Japanese conduct in sharp terms. "In all my fifty years of public service," he declared, "I have never seen a document that was more crowded with infamous falsehoods and distortions on a scale so huge that I never imagined until today that any government on this planet was capable of uttering them." The two Japanese left in silence.

Pearl Harbor

War had already begun when the envoys presented the Tokyo rejection. At 7:50 A.M. Hawaiian time (1:20 P.M., E.S.T.), on that fateful December 7, 1941, planes from Japanese carriers began dropping bombs on Pearl Harbor. The American military forces under General Walter Short and the fleet under Admiral Husband Kimmel were caught napping, despite the warnings given of a possible surprise attack. The resulting casualties were huge; some

3,500 men were killed, wounded, or missing; the navy had 80 naval planes destroyed and 70 disabled out of 202; the army lost 97 of its 273 planes; either sunk or severely damaged were five battleships—the *Arizona, Oklahoma, California, Nevada,* and *West Virginia,* along with three destroyers, a mine layer, and a target ship; damaged were three battleships, three cruisers, a seaplane tender, and a repair ship.

Several investigations failed to lay the blame conclusively at anyone's door. Early in 1942 the first investigation committee, headed by Justice Roberts, blamed General Short and Admiral Kimmel for not taking necessary precautions in the face of numerous warnings from Washington. In the summer of 1945 the Army and Navy made public their special findings, in which blame was divided between the two Pacific commanders and the authorities in Washington. The longest investigation, made by the joint Congressional Investigating Committee and lasting for ten weeks beginning November 15, 1945, resulted in the following majority report: (1) the responsibility for the well-planned and well-executed attack rested upon Japan; (2) the President and other high government officials in Washington tried their best to avert war with Japan; (3) despite the warnings from Washington, the Pacific commanders failed to have their forces sufficiently alerted; and (4) the War Department erred in not making certain that the Hawaiian defenses were fully prepared. The committee's minority report found: (1) that the Washington messages to Hawaii were so indefinite and conflicting that they failed to impress the need for wartime alert; (2) President Roosevelt did not effect sufficient cooperation among the several branches in evaluating the information gained through cracking the Japanese code.

War Is Declared

That Sunday evening—it was Monday, December 8 in Tokyo—the Japanese government formally notified Ambassador Grew "that there has arisen a state of war between Your Excellency's country and Japan beginning today" and placed the blame on the United States. Roosevelt was quick to reply. Shortly after midday on December 8, he appeared before the specially convened Congress to deliver his war message. He began with these solemn words:

Yesterday, December 7, 1941—a date which will live in infamy—the United States of America was suddenly and deliberately attacked by naval and air forces of the Empire of Japan.

Then he went on to show that peace negotiations were still going on when the Pearl Harbor attack occurred and that the attack must have been planned "many days or even weeks ago." The President also announced that Japan had attacked Malaya, Hongkong, Guam, the Philippines, and Wake and Midway Islands.

No matter how long it may take us to overcome this premeditated invasion, the American people in their righteous might will win through to absolute victory.

I ask the Congress to declare that since the unprovoked and dastardly attack by Japan on Sunday, December seventh, a state of war has existed between the United States and the Japanese Empire.

Congress acted just as speedily. Within four hours the war declaration was approved, first by the Senate 82 to 0, then by the House 388 to 1, authorizing the President to use all the forces and resources of the United States to "bring the conflict to a successful conclusion." And before the day was over, Britain, true to an earlier promise, also declared war against Japan.

Three days later, Germany and Italy, in conformance with the Tripartite Agreement and because of numerous American "provocative" acts, declared war on the United States. On the same day, both houses passed war declarations against Germany and Italy without a dissenting vote.

Meantime, on the evening of December 9, the President, in a radio talk to the nation, gave the general purposes of American participation in the war:

The true goal we seek is far above and beyond the ugly field of battle. When we resort to force, as now we must, we are determined that the force shall be directed toward ultimate good as well as against immediate evil. We Americans are not destroyers—we are builders.

We are now in the midst of a war, not for conquest, not for vengeance, but for a world in which this Nation, and all that this Nation represents, will be safe for our children. . . .

And in the dark of this day—and through dark days that may be yet to come—we will know that the vast majority of the members of the human race are on our side. Many of them are fighting with us. All of them are praying for us. For, in representing our cause, we represent theirs as well—our hope and their hope for liberty under God.

21
THE GLOBAL WAR

World War II was a global war in the truest sense of the war. Rival armed forces faced each other in battle on the continents of Europe, Asia, and Africa, as well as upon hundreds of islands in the Pacific. Naval encounters were fought literally on the seven seas. The number of men involved in actual combat, as well as the number of civilians affected, reached the highest total in world history. The amount of property destroyed reached astronomical figures. Considering the scope of this global contest, the following account of World War II will be primarily concerned with the exploits of the American armed forces.

The Rival Forces

The major countries involved in this epic struggle were, on the Allied side, the United States, Great Britain, France, Russia, and China, with considerable help from the Netherlands East Indies; on the Axis side, Germany, Italy, and Japan, with assistance from Hungary, Finland, Bulgaria, and Rumania. The combined Allied military strength in December, 1941, has been estimated at from 9.7 million men to 15.7 million; that of the Axis, at from 10.6 million to 13.6 million. The Allied air power is said to have been between 12,000 and 15,300 planes to the Axis's 13,200 to 18,400. As for the naval ships in operation or under construction on each side, the estimate for the Allies was 1,394, and for the Axis, 790.

In the beginning, the Axis had numerous advantages. Both in Europe and Asia it was fighting along interior lines and nearer the home front; thus the supply lanes were shorter and the deficit in sea transportation facilities was not too severe a handicap. Moreover, both Germany and Japan opened their attacks unexpectedly and, although they had been preparing for many years, their foes were largely unready. They were both able thereby to overrun large areas from which they obtained supplies needed to continue their war efforts. Their ruthless destruction of people and property tended to cow large sections, and the very speed and daring of their initial onslaughts swept aside all resistance.

The Allies, with their long lines of communication, were at a disadvantage. For example, the United States was about three thousand miles away from the European area and more than twice as far from the Far Eastern front. The problem of logistics had to be solved before the full American weight could be used. Moreover, the speedy Japanese attacks early in the war deprived the Allies of essential materials, such as rubber and tin, while the German advance conquered important agricultural, mineral, and oil areas.

What the Axis did not count upon, however, was the Allied will to win. England was able to withstand the terrible air *blitz* following the fall of France and show the stamina of a bulldog, while Russia survived the initial German attack and was starting to show its immense recuperative power. And the sneak attack on Pearl Harbor, which almost destroyed the American Pacific fleet, did not break American morale. Instead, the United States immediately began to mobilize its fighting and industrial strength to wipe out the stain. Through excellent cooperation, the Allies gradually formulated plans for attack and, aided by the increasing supplies of men, money, and equipment that the United States threw into the struggle, the Axis advantages were slowly but surely wiped away. Indeed, fighting along the interior line in the long run proved a disadvantage, because the Allies directed their full power against the concentrated areas held by the enemy and because Axis supplies ran short in the long and furious contest.

A Black Beginning

In the Pacific theater the six months following Pearl Harbor were indeed dark days for the Allies. Before the end of 1941 the Japanese had taken Thailand, moved into Malaya and seized Hongkong off the Asiatic mainland, captured Guam, Wake, and the northern Gilbert Islands, and made several landings in the Philippines. Moreover, during the Malayan campaign, they dealt another disastrous blow at Allied seapower by sinking the *Prince of Wales* and the *Repulse,* two powerful British warships.

January, 1942, witnessed additional Japanese victories. They moved closer to Burma on the west, pushed deeper into the Philippines where they seized Manila and the important naval base at Cavite, and invaded the rich and strategic Netherlands East Indies. The Allies were beginning to strike back, however, as American troops arrived in Australia and occupied the Fiji Islands to form a ring through which the Japanese could not penetrate. A sharp blow was struck at a Japanese transport fleet in the Strait of Macassar, but without permanently stopping the enemy advance into Borneo.

The following month brought more bad news to the Allies. On February 15 the great British naval base at Singapore fell. Furthermore, the Allied hope of holding the remainder of the Dutch East Indies faded when their fleet lost the battle of the Java Sea (February 27–March 1). Batavia and Java fell before the middle of March and Japanese landings were made in the Solomons. On the continent of Asia the enemy seized Rangoon, thus threatening the vital supply route to China.

Yet the worst news of all was soon to come. Americans had been watching the desperate battles in the Philippines waged by outnumbered American and Filipino troops. The multipronged Japanese invasion could not be stemmed, and their control of the seas prevented reinforcements and supplies from reaching the hard-pressed defenders. On January 2, 1942, the severely bombed city of Manila fell, as well as the nearby naval base of Cavite. The

Americans retreated to the Bataan Peninsula, where they held out until April 9, despite constant pounding from land and air. It was during this heroic defense that Roosevelt ordered General Douglas MacArthur to Australia, leaving General Jonathan Wainwright in command. Those who escaped from Bataan found refuge on Corregidor (the "Rock"), only to be subjected again to round-the-clock bombing. Finally, the defenders, worn out by sleeplessness, suffering from malaria, and weakened by scarcity of food, had to surrender on May 6, thereby bringing organized resistance in the Philippines to an end. Many of the more than thirty thousand troops and a similar number of civilians who were captured perished during the infamous "death march" of Bataan. The heroic defense of both Bataan and Corregidor was not in vain, however, because it upset the Japanese timetable and gave the Allies a valuable breathing spell in which to organize the outer defense ring to check the Japanese advance.

There were a few bright spots in the Allied picture. The American navy, under Admiral Chester Nimitz and Vice Admiral William Halsey, Jr., was striking back. Task forces with carrier planes had already raided the Marshalls, Gilberts, and Wake, as well as numerous Japanese-occupied bases in New Guinea. The army, led by MacArthur, was establishing a base in Australia. Then on April 15, General James Doolittle and his band of daring aviators took off from the deck of the *Hornet*—referred to by Roosevelt as Shangri-La—and bombed Tokyo, thereby boosting Allied morale. Three weeks later, an American squadron prevented Japan from breaking the communication line to Australia by winning the battle of the Coral Sea; the Japanese naval losses far exceeded those of the Americans. And on May 5 British troops landed on Madagascar to end Japanese expansion in that direction.

Nevertheless, up to early June, 1942, Japan maintained the initiative. She had gained control of Thailand, Malaya, Burma, the Dutch East Indies, and the islands of the western Pacific, and was threatening Australia. And in so doing, Japan had gained not only important strategic advantages, but immensely valuable economic resources—petroleum, rubber, and tin. Despite the dark picture, the Allies were confident they could prevent further Japanese advances and, with growing military, naval, and air strength, could start hitting back. Consequently, the Allies concentrated their energies on the European and African theaters in order to crush Hitler and Mussolini.

The Invasion and Conquest of Africa

When Roosevelt and Churchill conferred at the White House at the end of December, 1941, they agreed that the major Anglo-American objective should be the defeat of the European members of the Axis. The first important American troop assignment would be in North Africa, where British and Italo-German forces had been struggling since the summer of 1940.

This African arena was of vast importance to the Allies because control of it was necessary to maintain British domination of the Mediterranean and the life line to India and the Far East. To the United States, German occupation of the African west coast and of Dakar in particular would bring the Axis within sixteen hundred miles of Brazil and threaten the Western Hemisphere. Moreover, an Allied victory would pave the way for an invasion of Europe from the south.

The Allied invasion plans were still in the formative stage when the alarming news arrived in June, 1942, that General Erwin Rommel's Afrika Korps had captured Tobruk and had swept to approximately fifty miles from Alexandria. It seemed nothing could prevent Egypt and the Suez Canal from falling into Axis hands. But the victory-shouting Germans did not count upon the cooperation that followed. General Bernard Montgomery and his British Eighth Army dug in at El Alamein to hold the line until Australian troops, American planes and tanks, and other needed equipment poured in.

In October, 1942, Montgomery opened the counterattack that was to drive the enemy back and eventually destroy the Italian army in Africa. Yet this offensive was but one arm of the pincer movement that Roosevelt and Churchill had planned for an Anglo-American invasion of Africa from the northwest calculated to hem in the Axis troops and force their surrender.

The first step in the invasion plan was taken when American agents in Africa negotiated with several French officers to loosen their Vichy ties. Then in mid-October, 1942, General Mark Clark and a band of commandos landed secretly on the North African coast to complete arrangements for the actual invasion without French interference.

Finally, on November 8, a large British and American armada landed some 400,000 men under General Dwight D. Eisenhower at Casablanca, Oran, and Algiers. The invaders faced some opposition from both Germans and French, but the three towns quickly fell. The surrender of most of the French forces followed speedily, helped by the capture of Admiral Jean Darlan, hitherto of the Vichy regime, who agreed to give the "cease fire" order. Despite much criticism, Eisenhower appointed Darlan as political head of the occupied territories. Dakar surrendered before the end of the month, thereby ending the potential menace against the Western Hemisphere.

Since the primary objective of the invasion was to pinch off the Rommel forces in North Africa, the Allied troops that had landed at Algiers immediately opened their eastward drive into Tunisia to seize naval and air installations at Bizerte and Tunis. They were beaten to these goals by the Germans, however, who sent troops by air from Europe. This German opposition, plus the deep mud, held up the Allied advance for several months. Meantime, Montgomery rolled forward swiftly from the east and finally, in January, 1943, forced the Afrika Korps into Tunisia, which was protected by the Mareth Line. General Henri Giraud, who had succeeded Darlan after the latter's assassination, gave additional help when the Fighting French pushed northward to join the British and Americans.

Yet victory was not easy. In February the Germans forced the Americans through Faid Pass back into Algeria and then won the bloody battle of Kasserine Pass to regain nearly four thousand square miles of territory. Despite these victories, Rommel failed to cut off Americans from the British forces in the north.

The American defeat was partially offset by the fact that the troops had received their first real baptism of fire and, though compelled to retreat, had not broken. Moreover, the leaders now realized that too many men had been trained for mechanized warfare and not enough for the infantry. Throughout February, 1943, the American army was regrouped and reinforcements and additional equipment arrived. Near the end of the month, Kasserine Pass was regained after another fierce struggle, the Mareth Line crumbled to enable the British to seize Sfax and Sousse, and the Afrika Korps was forced into the Tunis-Bizerte pocket where it united with the German troops under General Jurgen von Arnim.

Once in this pocket it was but a question of time before the Germans had to surrender. American bombers pounded the steadily contracting trap and prevented German transports from evacuating many of the beleaguered men. Allied artillery smashed the defenses, while the infantry infiltrated the enemy lines. Finally, on May 7, the British First Army stormed unto Tunis and the American Second Corps under General Omar Bradley captured Bizerte. Those victories, gained through full cooperation among the Allied armies and their respective ground, sea, and air arms, brought German resistance in Africa to an end, and on May 9 what remained of the Axis troops surrendered unconditionally.

The fall of Africa was the first great Allied victory in which Americans participated. Although the cost in men had been high—there were 70,000 casualties, the results justified it. Not only were nearly 350,000 Italians and Germans killed or captured and 200,000 tons of enemy material seized or destroyed, but the Mediterranean life line was rescued from Axis control. Moreover, since from anywhere along the thousands of miles of North Africa coast the Allies might open an assault against southern Europe, German attention was diverted from Russia and the English Channel.

The Invasion of Sicily and Italy

In anticipation of the North African victory, Roosevelt and Churchill mapped out the next move while they were conferring at Casablanca in January, 1943. Eisenhower was informed "that an attack against Sicily will be launched in 1943 with the target date as the period of the favorable July moon." The dual reason for this project was to open the Mediterranean to Allied commerce of all descriptions, thereby saving a twelve-thousand-mile trip around the Cape of Good Hope, and to regain a foothold on the European continent preparatory to the eventual assault on the Reich itself.

Completion of the plan required time, but Eisenhower showed marked administrative ability in supervising the mobilization of men and supplies for the undertaking. The prelude to actual invasion was the bombing, starting in mid-May, of both Sicily and Italy to soften up the enemy possessions. Toward the end of the month Allied aviators concentrated upon the island of Pantelleria and, after twenty days of almost continuous bombing, ten thousand troops there were compelled to surrender—the first time such a victory was achieved through air power alone. Shortly after, the islands of Lampedusa, Linosa, and Lampione were also conquered to end a menace to Allied shipping in the Mediterranean and to provide steppingstones to Sicily.

On July 9, 1943, the invasion of Sicily began with the landing of American airborne troops, followed quickly by the debarkation of more than 150,000 Allied infantry, artillery, and tank corps. The two main forces were Montgomery's British Eighth Army and General George Patton's American Seventh, which had gained fame in the African campaign. Patton, a fearless and rough-tongued leader who was referred to as "Old Blood and Guts," was an expert in tank warfare. In thirty-eight days of vicious fighting, the island was overrun and the enemy forced to surrender. A feature of the victory was Patton's strategy in using his tanks to divide the opposition. Total Allied losses were approximately 25,000, those of the Germans and Italians, more than 150,000—or nearly half the number in Sicily at the time of the original attack.

While the Sicilian campaign was being waged, the Allies were pounding the Italian peninsula from sea and air, directing their bombs and shells toward ports and military installations. Even Rome itself did not escape, for more than 500 American bombers dropped 1,000 tons of missiles on railroad yards and airfields within the city.[1] An Italian appeal to Hitler for more support was turned down. Indeed, the Fuehrer insisted that the Italian boot as far north as the Po River must be evacuated by the Axis. When Mussolini gave in to Hitler's wishes, he was replaced as prime minister by Marshal Pietro Badoglio in July, 1943. Although Badoglio proclaimed that Italy would continue fighting, the populace was now demanding peace.

The continued pounding of Italy brought increased grumbling from the inhabitants. Consequently, Badoglio was secretly arranging with Eisenhower to surrender, which he hoped could be consummated without Hitler's knowledge. During these negotiations, Montgomery and his Eighth Army gained a comparatively easy beachhead at Reggio Calabria on the toe of the Italian boot on September 3, and started northward.

This maneuver speeded the Italian decision to withdraw from the war, an armistice was signed, and Eisenhower announced the unconditional surrender on September 8.[2] Although Allied morale was considerably raised by the elimination of one Axis member, the material advantage was not great because German forces occupied most of Italy and continued to dispute the Allied invasion. On September 9, Mark Clark established a second beachhead at Salerno, near Naples, in order to unite with Montgomery's men pushing through Calabria, thereby cutting off the Germans in southern Italy. This was easier said than done, however, because the enemy took full advantage of the natural fortifications and heavily mined roads to slow the Allied advance. Not until mid-September did the two armies link up, by which time most of the Germans had escaped the trap.

---

[1] Up to this time every effort had been made to spare attacks on Rome because of its religious importance. Now, however, the Allies realized it had become vital as a military and communications center. When the pleas to have it declared an open city were turned down by the Italians and Germans, the fliers were rigidly briefed so that when they did attack they avoided Vatican City and destroyed practically no religious shrines. The Germans raised the cry of vandalism, ignoring what they themselves had done to churches in Allied countries.

[2] When Germany refused to evacuate Italy, the latter declared war on the Reich, October 13, 1943, and was recognized as a cobelligerent by the Allies but was not granted Allied status.

Although a third invasion unit landed at Taranto on the Italian heel, it was not until October 1 that Naples fell.

The surrender of Naples, plus the Allied seizure of Sardinia and Corsica, were bitter blows to the enemy, but the Germans continued to maintain a stiff resistance. They were aided by the very severe winter of 1943–1944 and by the short battle line across the Italian peninsula that enabled them to concentrate their forces. The Reich armies retreated slowly until they reached the Gustav Line, whose main stronghold was Cassino, where they held out for many weeks. During the stalemate Eisenhower was called back to Britain to organize the strategy for the real second front.

In an effort to break the Gustav Line, a combined force under Clark landed to the north of Anzio, only twenty miles below Rome in January, 1944. The Germans apparently expected such a maneuver, however, and the invaders could not break the ring around the beachhead until early May, aided by a coordinated attack on the Gustav Line from the south. That line crumbled when Cassino fell on May 18, and the Allied forces then moved swiftly on Rome, which was taken without serious opposition on June 4.

Starting on the Long Road Back

Meantime, the tide was also turning in the Pacific. Although the Japanese attacked the Aleutians from the air in June, 1942, and subsequently made landings on Kiska, Attu, and Agattu, they never penetrated deeper into North America because of the activity of American naval and air forces.[3]

The temporary loss of the Aleutians was more than offset, however, by the American victory in the Battle of Midway, June 3–6, 1942, helped in no small part by the vital fact that Naval Intelligence had cracked the Japanese code even before Pearl Harbor. Over a hundred Japanese ships, prepared to assault strategic Midway Island, were intercepted and forced to flee after a three-day encounter fought over hundreds of miles of ocean. American land and carrier-based bombers destroyed four Japanese carriers, one cruiser, and 258 planes. The American losses were the carrier *Yorktown,* the destroyer *Hammann,* and 150 planes. This battle was the most crippling defeat inflicted on the Japanese navy up to that time. Combined with previous losses, Midway left the enemy too weak to match the ever-growing American armada in the Pacific. Consequently, plans to start toward Tokyo could be put into operation and, with the Japanese naval threat ended, more American strength could be released to the European theater.

The first blow at Japanese conquests was delivered when the marines, under General Alexander Vandegrift, opened their assaults on the islands of Tulagi, Gavutu, and Guadalcanal of the Solomon group. The first two

[3] In May, 1943, the Americans began their real counterattack by seizing Attu and Agattu after a heavy bombardment. Thus Kiska was by-passed and the Japanese withdrew secretly in August just before the Americans were ready to stage their all-out move to drive the enemy out.

objectives were attained fairly quickly, but on Guadalcanal there was fierce resistance, which was not wiped out until February, 1943. The struggle almost ended in disaster for the Americans at the very outset when the Japanese fleet on August 9 sank four heavy cruisers in the Battle of Savo Island, an encounter temporarily preventing the landing of needed Allied supplies. The marines were not to be denied, however, and they soon controlled the island's main airstrip, thereby enabling the Americans to put their airpower to good use in later phases of the struggle. In addition to the severe land and air fighting, in which casualties on both sides were high, four sea battles were fought, culminating in the Battle of Guadalcanal. In these several encounters, the enemy lost at least forty-seven ships, while they in turn sank the carriers *Wasp* and *Hornet,* together with numerous destroyers and cruisers. By eventually winning Guadalcanal, the Americans gained more than simply a small Pacific island. They learned valuable lessons in jungle fighting that served in good stead later; they learned as well the value of naval and air cooperation with invasion forces; they had a steppingstone for future conquests; and they had dealt grievous losses to the Japanese navy.

During the long struggle over Guadalcanal, MacArthur was striking at the enemy from another direction. The Japanese had gained control of the larger part of New Guinea and were moving uncomfortably close to Port Moresby, a potential jumping-off spot for the invasion of Australia. The Australians checked the advance in September and opened a counterattack with the aid of American air forces, which brought in supplies and prevented the enemy from landing reinforcements. American troops then added their support and by the end of the year Gona and Buna had been recaptured. It required another year of desperate fighting, however, before New Guinea was effectively dominated.

Throughout 1943, American marines, fliers, and fleet put into practice the lessons learned at Guadalcanal. The most important encounters were the mopping up of the rest of the Solomons, the conquest of the Gilberts in November after the bloody battles of Makin and Tarawa (November 21–23), and the invasion of New Britain in December. Several naval battles were fought as well—Bismarck Sea (March 2–6), Kula Gulf (July 5–6, 12–13), and Vella Gulf (August 6–7)—in all of which the Japanese losses far exceeded the American.

By the end of 1943 the Americans had their invasion pattern well worked out. The first move was usually a series of reconnaissance flights to obtain pictures of the objectives. Then followed heavy air bombardments aimed at wrecking airfields and destroying military supplies and installations. Next, a task force would arrive on the scene to set the stage for the actual invasion by attacking from sea and air to prevent the enemy from either escaping or sending in reinforcements and to wreck coastal defenses and sear the beaches. With preparations complete, the invasion forces, usually headed by marines, would be landed from new types of naval craft—such as landing craft infantry and amphibious tractors, to be joined quickly by tanks. The navy stood offshore and planes flew overhead to shell and bomb ahead of the advancing troops.

It was this attack pattern that won for the Americans in 1944 the Marshalls,

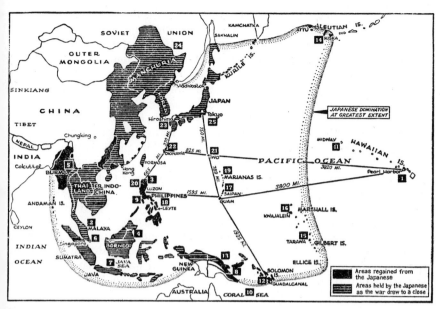

Twenty-five highlights in the history of the war with Japan. (Courtesy of the *New York Times*.)

1941	1	*Dec. 7*—Japanese planes attack Pearl Harbor
	2	*Dec. 8*—Malay campaign launched by Japanese
	3	*Dec. 10*—Landings made on Luzon
	4	*Dec. 22*—Borneo invasion begun
1942	5	*Jan. 19*—Conquest of Burma begun
	6	*Feb. 15*—Singapore falls to Japanese
	7	*Feb. 27*—Allies routed in Battle of Java Sea
	8	*Mar. 8*—First Japanese landings in New Guinea
	9	*May 6*—Surrender of Corregidor
	10	*May 4–8*—Japanese defeated in Battle of Coral Sea
	11	*June 3–6*—Japanese turned back in Battle of Midway
	12	*Aug. 7*—American forces land on Guadalcanal
1943	13	*Mar. 5*—Japanese routed in Battle of Bismarck Sea
	14	*Aug. 15*—Allied forces retake Kiska
	15	*Nov. 20–24*—Tarawa and Makin Islands recaptured
1944	16	*Feb. 1*—First Japanese territory invaded at Kwajalein
	17	*June 14*—Invasion of Marianas begun
	18	*Oct. 20–26*—Landings on Leyte, Battle of Leyte Gulf
	19	*Nov. 24*—First B–29 raids from Marianas bases
1945	20	*Jan. 9*—American forces land on Luzon
	21	*Feb. 17*—Landing on Iwo Jima
	22	*April 1*—Invasion of Okinawa begun
	23	*Aug. 6*—First atomic bomb dropped on Hiroshima
	24	*Aug. 9*—Russia invades Manchuria following war declaration
	25	*Aug. 11*—Tokyo learns Allied answer to surrender offer

where the initial campaign was directed against Kwajalein on January 31, the Admiralty Islands (February), the Mariannas (the struggle for Saipan lasted from June 15 to July 9), Guam (August–September), and Palau and

Halmahera (September), the last Japanese bases in the open Pacific. Moreover, these conquests practically neutralized the important naval base at Truk, which could no longer obtain supplies after the Japanese communication lines were cut. The Japanese navy was being slowly but surely diminished in size, and what remained of it retired to home bases to prepare for the inevitable Allied attack upon Japan proper.[4] At the same time, the Japanese air force was whittled down despite its strong resistance.

One of the most heartening incidents in the Pacific theater came in October, 1944. The attacks on Palau and Halmahera had brought the Americans within several hundred miles of the Philippines. During the rest of September and the first weeks of October American fliers regularly bombed and strafed the archipelago, and the navy swept the sea of Japanese naval and merchant craft. Although the natural initial objective was the island of Mindoro, on October 19 MacArthur struck swiftly at Leyte in the central part of the Philippine chain. Several landings were quickly made, footholds gained, and the principal airstrip seized. The American promise to return had been made good. In a desperate move to isolate the invaders, the Japanese brought up their fleet, only to suffer their greatest naval defeat. In the second Philippine Sea engagement, Admiral Thomas Kinkaid, with his Seventh Fleet, and Admiral William Halsey, with his Third, destroyed or badly damaged some thirty ships during a running two-day battle (October 23–24). American losses were only a fraction of that number.

Mopping up on Leyte was slow because of typhoons, heavy rains, and deep mud. Moreover, ten thousand Japanese reinforcements were brought in by the "Toyko Express"—a large, speedy transport system. Consequently, not until Christmas time did the numerous prongs of the American invaders close in on the enemy and end its opposition. Meantime, additional landings were made on Samar and Mindoro, while planes from Saipan and from carriers blasted at Toyko, Formosa, Okinawa, and Iwo Jima, and the American navy cut deeper into the communications lines between Japan and her outlying conquests.

As 1945 opened, the combined American land, sea, and air arms were poised to complete the destruction of the enemy. On January 5 MacArthur's men landed at Lingayen Gulf on Luzon and started their push toward Manila, only one hundred miles away. Aided by the navy, which thwarted the Tokyo Express, and by fliers who destroyed Japanese installations, the land forces, helped by paratroops, captured the Philippine capital on February 5, followed within two weeks by the seizure of Bataan and Corregidor. Gradually the other islands were brought under American control and on July 5, 1945, MacArthur proclaimed that the Philippines were liberated and his campaign there was "virtually closed."

Other Allied maneuvers, however, endangered the Japanese homeland more directly than did the fall of the Philippines. For example, in the middle of February the invasion of the Bonins opened. Iwo Jima was needed as an airfield for emergency landings of planes bombing Japan from the Mariannas

---

[4] The later conquests were aided by the first Philippine Sea victory (June 19–20), in which four Japanese carriers, three cruisers, three destroyers, one battleship, four tankers, and more than a thousand planes were destroyed. In comparison, American losses under Admiral Spruance were negligible.

and for the planned invasion of Japan itself. The marines gradually overcame the stubborn resistance, captured Mount Suribachi on February 23,
and three weeks later the conquest of the island was completed. The American casualties were high—approximately twenty thousand—grim evidence
of the fury of the opposition. Furthermore, suicidal attacks by kamikaze [5]
fliers damaged or sank many American naval craft.

Still more furious was the struggle for Okinawa in the Ryukyus, about
halfway between Iwo and Japan. After a ten-day bombardment, General
Simon Buckner's Tenth Army and some marine divisions made simultaneous
beachheads to open a contest that was to last ten weeks. Japanese troops were
ordered not to surrender because the home government's hope of escaping
defeat was "anchored solely on Okinawa." In the face of this resistance, the
Americans had to cut the enemy lines into several segments and defeat each
before final victory was achieved on June 21. The losses on both sides were
stupendous: the Japanese dead alone numbered more than 100,000, while
the American casualties neared 80,000. Moreover, kamikaze attacks sank 33
American ships and damaged 45 more; aircraft destruction reached the
astounding figure of at least 3,000 Japanese planes and 1,000 American.
There was, however, a promising note: in spite of indoctrination and orders,
nearly 8,000 Japanese surrendered—a definite sign that the enemy was starting to crack as the homeland was endangered.

On another Far Eastern front—the China-Burma-India theater—the tide
was also turning. After the Americans under General Joseph Stilwell, along
with British, Indian, and Chinese troops, had been driven out of Burma and
into India in 1942, conditions looked very black. Not only was the loss of
territory and prestige great, but the Allies found it difficult to send aid to the
Chinese force under Chiang. Throughout 1943 there were no conclusive
battles and neither side gained material advantage. In 1944, however, the
Allies moved slowly back into Burma. A three-month siege was required
before Myitkina fell in August, and Akyab, Rangoon, and Lashio did not
come into Allied hands until early 1945. The capture of Lashio reopened the
Burma Road and enabled more supplies to be sent to the Chinese, who were
going through periodic reverses and victories.

The turn in the tide also allowed the superfortresses—the B-29's—to open
their attacks on Japan proper from CBI bases. The first raid (June 15, 1944)
was largely a test of the giant bombers, and the test was satisfactory. Despite
the difficulty in obtaining the necessary gas, oil, and other supplies, in the
following autumn the B-29 raids became quite regular, and damage to
Japanese home bases increased when the conquest of the Mariannas gave
the Americans bases from which to launch attacks on Japan from the east
as well. The ruin of Japanese industrial cities mounted with each passing
month of 1945. With her air force largely depleted, her navy forced under
cover, her conquests—except those in China and Manchuria—almost entirely
lost, with her homeland subjected to almost constant bombing, and with

[5] Kamikaze fliers were fanatical Japanese who flew their planes at terrifying speed
directly at an objective, such as a ship, with the hope that in the resulting crash the
objective would be destroyed, even though they themselves were killed. The losses from
these attacks were great for American airmen, and gunners found it difficult to cope with
such tactics.

morale beginning to crack, Japan faced a dismal future, a future made darker on April 5, when Russia gave the necessary one-year notice for the cancellation of her neutrality pact with Japan—a prelude to war. Slightly more than a month later news of the unconditional surrender of Germany reached Tokyo.

Preparations for D Day

Events leading to that German disaster began with the opening of the long-awaited second front in Europe. Since America's entrance into the war, Russia had insisted on such an operation. A second front, she asserted, was the only way to defeat Germany, and the sooner it was opened the better. Churchill urged delay, however, and it was not until Stalin, Roosevelt, and Churchill met at Teheran in December, 1943, that agreement was reached. Then Eisenhower received the following message:

> You will enter the continent of Europe and, in conjunction with the other Allied Nations, undertake operations aimed at the heart of Germany and the destruction of her armed forces.

The task of getting men, supplies, and transportation facilities ready for this gigantic operation was tremendous. Although the first American troops had arrived in North Ireland in January, 1942, most of them, together with those who landed in the ensuing months, had been used in the African and Italian campaigns. Thus, in the midsummer of 1943 there were only about fifteen thousand American troops in the British Isles. From that time on, however, the influx was rapid, helped by the fact that the Mediterranean needs were not so great and the Japanese menace was dwindling. Consequently, transportation facilities concentrated on building up the necessary stockpiles for the continental invasion. By June, 1944, the American army personnel in Britain numbered 1,533,000, and supplies were so abundant that within a month after landing each man was fully equipped.

The softening up of Germany by air bombardment had begun in 1942, but not until July, 1943, when the Royal Air Force swept over Germany at night while the American Eighth Air Force took over during the day, did round-the-clock attacks begin. With the passing months the number of raids, planes included in the raids, and tonnage of missiles dropped increased greatly. For example, on June 6, 1944, the American strength stood at 3,000 heavy bombers and 6,500 planes of other types; and in the 33 months after August, 1942, the Eighth Air Force rained 1.5 million tons of bombs on the continent. The main objectives were communications centers, munitions plants, synthetic-oil factories, submarine pens, dams, and rocket-bomb stations. German industry withstood this rain of destruction remarkably well. Until 1944, indeed, enemy war production continued to rise. In the end, however, the Allied attacks took terrible toll.

Until February, 1944, the German *Luftwaffe* put up a desperate resistance. Then, however, German fliers were ordered to make an all-out attack against the invaders. During a week of raging battle over German industrial centers, a large portion of the German air fleet was destroyed. This setback, added to the dwindling German gasoline and oil reserves, made subsequent Allied air raids less dangerous, although the flak sent up from German ground guns still took its toll. Also contributing to the softening up process was shuttle bombing, in which planes from England continued on to occupied sections of Italy after bombing their objectives, thus avoiding a flight back over the target. A second shuttle run was instituted just before D Day between Italy and Russia, and shortly thereafter a third was begun between England and Russia.

D Day

In addition to getting men, ships, and supplies ready and softening up the enemy, Eisenhower and his staff had to consider where and when the beach-head should be established. After considerable study, Normandy was selected as the site and June 5, 1944, as the most favorable time in terms of tide, wind, and moonlight—an essential for airborne troops. An unexpected storm, however, caused a sudden change in plans and the second front actually opened a day late—on June 6. At 2 A.M. American and British airborne troops were landed to gain control of strategic areas inland from the invasion beaches. An aerial attack started about an hour later, followed at 6 o'clock by a naval bombardment. Then at 6:30 assault troops, carried in a variety of crafts, went ashore in the face of enemy fire, mines, barbed wire, and underwater

United States troops storming a Normandy beach, D-Day, 1944. (Brown Bros.)

entanglements. The American First Army, commanded by General Bradley, eventually gained beachheads in the Carentan-Bayeau area, while the British and Canadians under General Miles Dempsey secured their footholds in the Bayeau-Caen region. Despite determined enemy resistance, reinforcements and supplies piled ashore all day. Within twenty-four hours the beachheads were secure, and the greatest amphibian operation in history was a success.

Again only cooperation could have achieved the result. The credit belongs equally to the staff of experts who planned the maneuver, the weather experts, those who found the proper place to attack, the navies that carried the men to the Normandy beaches and then stood by to protect them, the air forces that had been steadily pounding the interior and that helped prevent the Germans from bringing up supplies, the airborne infantry that led the actual invasion, the divers who removed the undersea obstacles, the sappers who destroyed many of the mines, the supply and ordnance branches that helped to make everything ready, and the regular troops who resolutely carried out their assignments.

The movement into the interior might have been speedy had the invaders gained a large port where additional reinforcements could be landed quickly and easily. But because of stubborn enemy defense of Cherbourg, special docks or breakwaters had to be floated across the Channel as substitutes. Even though Cherbourg finally fell on June 27, it was so badly damaged that it was of little use as a port of debarkation.

On July 5 Eisenhower attributed the slowness of the advances to three factors: the stubborn German defense, the nature of the countryside, and the bad weather that prevented the Allied air arm from attacking and engaging in reconnaissance work. By the end of July, however, conditions were brighter. An average of 30,000 troops were landed daily, along with 30,000 tons of supplies. Bradley was completing the organization of the armies under his command: the American First, headed by General Courtney Hodges, and the Third under General Patton. At the same time Montgomery was consolidating the Canadian First under General Crerar and the British Second commanded by General Dempsey.

After a heavy bombardment, Bradley finally broke out of the beachhead before the end of the month by seizing St. Lo, while Montgomery took the strongly held Caen. Then Patton showed the initiative and daring for which he was famous. In August his tank corps stormed through a breach at Avranches into Brittany and continued on toward Paris. Meantime, the Allies protected his flank by moving deeper inland; a pincers movement developed to form the Falaise pocket, in which about 100,000 of the enemy were captured. The stubborn defense of Panzer units prevented the pocket from closing completely, but the Germans who escaped fled from Normandy in confusion.

The Overrunning of France

The harassed Germans soon faced another front in France when General Alexander Patch's American Seventh Army landed in the south on August 15 against unexpectedly weak resistance. Marseilles, Cannes, and Toulon vere occupied within two weeks and then Patch soon joined up with Patton, vho had run roughshod through Chartres, Tours, Troyes, and numerous other cities to flank Paris.

Meantime, Bradley and Montgomery rushed along the Seine to force the urrender of Paris on August 25, aided by the activities of two underground actions, the French Forces of the Interior (FFI) and the Maquis. Actually he fall of Paris in itself was not important, except to morale, because the Germans were retreating at such a fast pace that the city was soon far behind he lines. Not only were the Germans losing territory, but men and equipment as well. By the end of August, at least 400,000 men had been killed or captured, while 15,000 pieces of artillery, more than 1,000 tanks, and approximately 20,000 motor transports and other mobile equipment either had fallen into Allied hands or had been destroyed.

As September progressed, practically all of France, except some coastal owns, was freed from German control, and Allied armies were moving rapidly through Luxembourg and Belgium. On the eastern flank Patton's Third Army was laying siege to Metz, while Patch's Seventh Army was probing at the Belfort Gap. These rapid maneuvers toward the Reich threatened o isolate the German forces in Italy, thereby aiding the Allied movements north of Rome.

Piercing the Siegfried Line

The first major attack on the Siegfried Line was a flanking movement. In the third week of September, British and American airborne troops attempted to bridge several rivers that made up the Rhine delta in Holland. Despite the fact that this maneuver was the largest airborne effort of the war —2,800 planes and 1,600 gliders were used, the British failed, although the Americans managed to retain control of several crossings of the Waal and the Meuse. Two weeks later came an attack by Hodges on well-defended Aachen. When the request for surrender was rejected, the town was subjected to two days of the most methodical and destructive bombing of the war, followed by a storming that brought capitulation on October 21.

The winter offensive opened early in November, with seven Allied armies moving forward. It might have been more successful had the weather been better and if the supply lines had kept up with the advancing troops. Moreover, Eisenhower had to weaken part of the front line by putting in inexperienced divisions, so that he might continue to hammer against the main points of attack.

The Battle of the Bulge

The Germans under General von Runstedt discovered one of the weak links and, aided by a heavy fog, massed 24 divisions along a 75-mile front between Trier and Monschau. On December 16 his sudden counterattack broke through in an attempt to reach the coast, and for a time it appeared his move would be successful. The enemy overran 700 square miles of

Belgium and Luxembourg and came within 4 miles of the Meuse before the Allies rallied. Montgomery on the north prevented the bulge from widening in that direction, while Patton used his Third Army to hold the southern flank. The 82nd and 101st airborne divisions were speeded from Reims to pinch the bulge.[6] By Christmas the worst danger was over as a change in the weather enabled Allied airmen to cooperate with ground troops in turning the tide. This Battle of Ardennes, better known as the Battle of the Bulge, was the last important German offensive of the war. German reserve strength was ebbing rapidly, the oil supply was dwindling, communications were more and more disrupted by Allied bombing, and the Russians were staging a great drive on their front.

The Surrender of Germany

As 1945 opened, it became apparent that Germany could not hold out much longer. By mid-January most of the Ardennes Bulge had been wiped out, and by the end of the month the Westwall was effectively pierced. In February, Holland was largely in Allied hands and the attack on the Saar Basin opened. By early March four Allied armies were on the bank of the Rhine. Germany was losing her industrial regions—a blow just as telling as the military defeats. Cologne fell to the First Army on March 6, and the following day the Allies enjoyed a bit of unexpected good luck when they captured the undamaged Ludendorff Bridge across the Rhine at Remagen to allow an easy crossing. When the Germans rushed reinforcements to minimize this bridgehead, the Allies spanned the river at other points.

As March progressed, city after city in the Ruhr capitulated; the Allied armies linked up for the final drive, and sent out spearheads to increase the German confusion. Many of the enemy, especially the old men and boys who had been hastily recruited to defend the Fatherland, surrendered—at the rate of more than twenty-five thousand a day. The Western front moved ahead as rapidly as did the Russians from the east. The German pocket grew smaller and smaller as Hanover, Stuttgart, and other key cities fell during April before the Allied *blitzkrieg*. By the middle of the month the Anglo-American forces were not more than fifty miles from Berlin. A week later Patton's speedy tanks reached Czechoslovakia to cut off Austria from contact with the Reich capital, which was already under Russian fire. Another successful cut through the Reich was completed when the Russians and Americans joined at Torgau on the Elbe on April 27.

In Italy, too, the Germans were facing defeat. Although they had held the Gothic Line along the Po for months, they could not stem the coordinated attack that began in April, 1945. Italian partisans, sensing Allied victory, seized and executed Mussolini before he could escape to Switzerland. German troops could not get out through the Brenner Pass, and on May 2 they sur-

---

[6] The 101st gained fame by holding Bastogne against overwhelming odds. General McAuliffe refused to surrender the town, replying to the German request with the answer "Nuts!" The 82nd, less publicized, held open the gap on the west to allow the entrapped First Army divisions to escape.

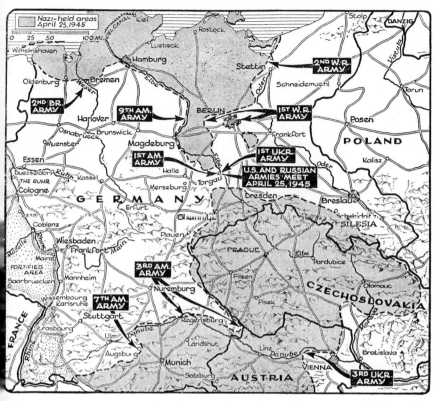

Germany's collapse. (From Francis Brown, *The War in Maps.* By permission of Oxford University Press.)

rendered unconditionally, along with the divisions in Austria trapped by Patton's lunge.

It was the same day, May 2, that Berlin, largely gutted by air attack, fires, and fighting, fell into Russian hands. The day before, the suicide of Adolph Hitler, who had refused to face defeat, was announced. Admiral Karl Doenitz, the new Fuehrer, declared that he would continue the war, but such a promise was futile. On May 4 German forces in Denmark capitulated, northern Germany gave in, and Norway, a potential German refuge, was isolated from the Reich. Moreover, the German forces were cut into smaller segments by the victorious Allies, while the German people showed increasing signs of unrest. Surrender was the only way out.

As the various German army groups continued to lay down their arms, Doenitz realized the folly of continuing. On May 6 he sent a secret delegation to confer with General Walter Bedell Smith, Eisenhower's Chief of Staff, at a little red schoolhouse in Reims. The Germans at first refused the Allied unconditional surrender terms, but when German Chief of Staff Gustav Jodl arrived early on the morning of May 7, they gave in and signed the Act of Military Surrender. The following day formal surrender terms were concluded at Berlin to become effective at 12:01 A.M. (European time) on May 9. The most important clause in the surrender document was:

> We . . . agree to unconditional capitulation of all our armed forces on land, sea, and air, and also all forces at present under German command, to the high command of the Red Army and at the same time to the Allied Expeditionary Forces.

Although some fighting still continued, World War II was at an end as far as Germany was concerned. News of the surrender was followed by celebrations in all parts of the Allied world. Yet there was an undercurrent of sadness because President Roosevelt, who had died on April 12, could not witness the triumph for which he had worked so long and hard.

The End of the Axis: Victory over Japan

By the Potsdam Proclamation of July 26, 1945, the United States, Britain, and China threatened Japan with utter destruction unless she surrendered unconditionally. Although the Japanese cabinet, confronted by increasingly disastrous air attacks and encirclement by Allied naval forces, wanted to bow to this ultimatum, the die-hard army leaders insisted on continuing to fight.

Redoubled Allied attacks by land, sea, and air showed that the warning of destruction was no empty threat. When Japanese resistance continued, the Allies decided to play their ace—a new weapon of revolutionary significance. On August 6 a superfortress dropped an atomic bomb on Hiroshima, virtu-

Devastation of Hiroshima after atomic bombing, 1945. (UPI Photo.)

ally destroying the entire city at a single blow. Scarcely had Japan recovered sufficiently to realize the implications of this event when she faced another sharp blow; on August 8 Russia, in conformity with the Yalta Agreement, informed Japan that the next day war would begin between the two countries. Soviet troops swiftly invaded Manchuria and Korea to remove all possibility that Japanese troops on the Asiatic mainland could hold out. On the same fateful day (August 9) Nagasaki was destroyed by a second and deadlier atomic bomb, while B-29's ravaged the home islands from tip to tip.

Finally comprehending the futility of further resistance, Japan announced on August 10 its willingness to open surrender negotiations, provided Emperor Hirohito were allowed to keep his throne. In answer the Allies asserted that his position could not be guaranteed; he could continue on the throne only until the Allies fully occupied Japan and the unconditional surrender terms were fulfilled. Then there must be a free election under Allied supervision to determine the future leader and type of government. After a three-day delay, Japan accepted the Allied terms at 7 P.M. on August 14. The wild celebration that followed surpassed those of VE Day and Armistice Day. Five days later a Japanese delegation signed the preliminary surrender document at Manila, with MacArthur acting for the victors. Then on September 2, aboard the American battleship *Missouri* anchored in Tokyo Bay, the formal surrender took place.

These terms provided for the surrender of Japanese forces everywhere, with prompt demobilization and the turning over to the Allies of all military supplies and equipment. Moreover, the emperor and the government agreed to obey all orders of the Allied Supreme Command, which, under MacArthur, would supervise the occupation of Japan. Provision was also made for the trial of war criminals, for the establishment of democratic institutions, and for the regulation of the Japanese economy.

Although many Japanese divisions in outlying regions continued fighting for some time, to all intents and purposes World War II had ended. Lasting nearly six years, with the United States participating for three years and nine months, it was the greatest, the most widespread, the most destructive, and the most costly war in history. Victory was gained by the Allies in large part through cooperation, not only among themselves, but among the various branches of their respective services. Naval power played no small part in the triumph, for World War II was the greatest naval war in history; in the struggle for control of the Pacific the American navy was of paramount importance. Logistics also played a prominent role; the Allied ability to transport supplies many thousands of miles gradually offset the shorter lines of the Axis, and the members of the respective merchant marines deserved no less credit for ultimate victory than those in the fighting forces.

It has been estimated that more than 80 million men were under arms at one time or another during the course of the war. Of these, 14 million were killed and millions more were wounded. Civilian populations also suffered greatly from the direct and indirect effects of the struggle. Many communities were wiped out or badly damaged by air assault, long-range missiles, shellfire, fires, and infantry attack. Large industrial and agricultural areas were destroyed in both Europe and Asia. The estimated cost of the war reached nearly the trillion dollar mark.

As for the United States, the casualties were much greater than they had been in World War I. The Army figures revealed that 318,274 were killed and 565,861 wounded. The Navy report, including the marines and coast guard, listed 89,345 killed and 105,953 wounded. The total casualty list was around the 1.1 million mark. Naval ship losses totaled 696 craft in all categories, and merchant ships sunk numbered 538. The monetary cost was around $330 billion. Moreover, the United States was compelled to draw on future reserves of iron, tin, rubber, oil, wood, and numerous other commodities that could have been better used for the peacetime needs of present and future generations. Millions of Americans pondered whether victory was worth the cost. Defeat, they realized, would have cost eternally more; but merely to have escaped defeat was not enough. A just and lasting peace would be the only gain sufficiently precious to balance the great sacrifice.

22

THE HOME FRONT

Pearl Harbor came as a stunning shock to the American people. Nevertheless, that shock was of immediate value in one respect; it effected a unity that had been lacking for years. The attack upon American soil and the possibility of invasion of the United States itself ended the bitter debate that had been raging between the internationalists and the isolationists. Both groups now established common cause, as did Democrats and Republicans, industrialists and labor. Overnight the American people became united in the conviction that they must make a supreme effort to ensure national survival.

Rallying Round the Flag

As concrete proof that partisanship had been put aside, outstanding Republicans like Hoover and Landon, together with the minority leaders in Congress, pledged support to the all-out war effort. Through William Green and Philip Murray, labor quickly promised full cooperation and, with capital, agreed that industrial disputes, especially in essential fields, must be kept at a minimum. John L. Lewis promptly declared: "When the nation is attacked every American must rally to its support. . . . All other considerations become insignificant." Isolationists either abruptly changed their position or became silent. The carping Chicago *Tribune* suddenly ended its criticism of the administration's foreign policy in favor of "our country, right or wrong." The America First Committee ceased its efforts to obstruct the preparedness movement and most of its leaders resigned.

This unity made possible a mobilization program unparalleled in world history. The army, navy, and air forces were quickly expanded; industry, on a round-the-clock schedule, turned out planes, guns, tanks, ammunition, and uniforms in numbers and amounts hitherto undreamed of. The government quickly went on a wartime footing and established agencies to deal with every phase of the emergency. Civilians, both men and women, cheerfully did without many commodities needed primarily for the military.

Raising an Army

Pearl Harbor found the United States still in the preparatory stages of military build-up. Army personnel numbered nearly 1.6 million on December

7, 1941, most of them serving under the Burke-Wadsworth Act and therefore not eligible for overseas service. Many were unacquainted with either the implements or the strategy of modern warfare. Yet less than four years later, on August 15, 1945, the army had an efficient fighting force of 8.3 million, equipped with the finest weapons in the world.

On the day after Pearl Harbor, recruiting offices were literally flooded with men and youths seeking to enlist voluntarily. Although volunteers were accepted for some services throughout the war, army officials could not rely on this unpredictable source. Consequently, the primary dependence was placed upon conscription. On December 13, 1941, Congress removed the ban on using drafted men for overseas service, and a week later the time of such service was extended to the duration and six months. Then in February, 1942, all previously unregistered males within the twenty to forty-four age group were placed in the draft category, and two months later those between the ages of forty-five and sixty-five were ordered to register, not for military service, but as potential draftees for work in essential industries. The final amendment of the Burke-Wadsworth Act in June, 1942, lowered the conscription age for military service to eighteen.

The task of calling up those who had registered was a mighty one. Now under the supervision of General Lewis Hershey, the draft was taken care of by 54 state agencies, 515 boards of appeal, and 6,443 local boards, manned by more than 200,000 workers, mostly volunteer. In general, the local agencies tried to prevent undue hardship. The call of married men with children or other dependents was delayed as long as possible. Naturally, however, the system was not uniform because conditions in each draft area varied. Some had a large pool of young, unmarried men with no dependents; in others the pool was small. In the latter case, married men were called more quickly. Although there were some complaints, the draft on the whole worked well.

In similar fashion the navy complement grew. The number of men in the navy at the time of the first Japanese attack was 325,000; at the conclusion of hostilities there were nearly 3.4 million. The marine forces grew from 28,300 to 477,000 during the same period, while the coast guard expanded from 14,000 to 171,000. The total of combat ships showed the same remarkable increase. For ships of all types under the control of the Navy Department, the number multiplied from 4,500 in 1941 to 91,209 at the end of the war. Of the newer types added, perhaps the most unusual were landing craft for infantry (LCI) and for tanks (LCT). The time needed to construct war vessels was materially reduced as the war progressed: battleships could be built in 32 months as compared with the 39 months of pre–Pearl Harbor days; aircraft carriers in 16 months instead of 32; submarines in $7\frac{1}{2}$ months rather than in 14; and destroyers in $5\frac{1}{2}$ months instead of 13.

Of the specialized branches, the air arms of both army and navy showed the most spectacular improvement. In December, 1941, the number of pilots was pitifully small; by the end of the war the naval branch, including marines, had nearly 50,000 pilots, together with ground crews and other personnel to the number of more than 500,000; for the army, in 1943 alone 65,000 pilots were graduated by the training command, along with nearly 14,000 navigators, 14,000 bombardiers, 82,000 aerial gunners, and approximately 530,000 technicians of various types—indeed, the army air forces ultimately totaled about 3 million. Closely associated with the army air arm were the airborne troops, both parachute and glider battalions, which did such excellent work during the invasions, in the Battle of the Bulge, and in the all-out drive to final victory in Europe. As for planes, in 1941 the combined army and navy air arms included about 8,000, of which many were obsolete. By VJ Day, the navy had nearly 40,000 and the army about twice that number. The planes were constantly being improved in range, fire power, bomb loads, speed, and fighting ability. Perhaps the most notable advances were made in jet propulsion and in size. Radar and the bomb sight were also of inestimable value in American air and bombing progress.

To train this vastly increased armed personnel, 1,200 camps, cantonments, and stations were established throughout the country. An intensive training course lasting from 12 to 17 weeks was given the new men, after which there was a possibility of attending specialized schools in gunnery, mechanized warfare, amphibious operations, radar, communications, and officer training. The various branches of the armed services also used many colleges and universities to train their men in such specialties as air-force training, engineering, radio and radar, meteorology, and language-and-area studies. Moreover, many college graduates were schooled for positions in various phases of military and civilian government in anticipation of the occupation of enemy countries during and after the war.

Beginning in June, 1942, the pay of the various branches was increased. That of the private and the ordinary seaman was raised from $21 a month to $50, with higher ranks increased in proportion. In the same year the Service Men's Allotment Act was passed to provide dependency payments for the servicemen's wives and children. In anticipation of the discharge of military men, the President signed on June 22, 1944, the measure popularly called the GI Bill.[1] First of all, this act provided for 52 weeks of unemployment compensation at $20 a week, together with adjusted compensation for self-employed veterans returning to their old business. Next, the government guaranteed 50 per cent of loans up to $2,000 to veterans who were buying homes or setting themselves up in business. Half a billion dollars was appropriated for the construction of hospitals for veterans and for expansion of the United States Employment Service to help them get jobs. Finally, veterans going to college might obtain $500 a year for four years to be used for tuition and books, plus $50 a month ($75 if married) for subsistence.

An unusual feature of the mobilization was the enlistment of women. In May, 1942, Congress established the Women's Auxiliary Army Corps (WAAC) under the command of Major—later Colonel—Oveta Culp Hobby; on July 1, 1943, members of the WAAC were incorporated into the regular army as the Women's Army Corps (WAC). More than 100,000 Wacs served as clerks, stenographers, weather observers, flying instructors, laboratory technicians, truck drivers, and small-arms repairers. Although most of the Wacs were stationed in the United States, some 15,000 saw service in the various overseas fields of operations. The navy also had its women's branch,

---

[1] The term *GI* first referred to anything issued by the government (Government Issue). Gradually it was applied to the enlisted men themselves and is comparable to the doughboy of World War I. Toward the close of World War II the expression became "GI Joe."

the WAVES (Women Accepted for Volunteer Emergency Service), organized in July, 1942, under Lieutenant Commander Mildred McAfee. A total of 86,000 women joined up. Until the fall of 1944 they did not serve outside of the United States. Thereafter, some 4,000 were on duty in Hawaii, with lesser numbers in Alaska, Puerto Rico, and Bermuda. The United States Marine Corps Women's Reserve, under Colonel Ruth Streeter, organized in February, 1942, had about 19,000 members; after January, 1945, some 5,000 were sent to Hawaii. The SPARS, the women's branch of the Coast Guard, started in November, 1942, under the command of Captain Dorothy Stratton, and eventually numbered 10,000.

Also mobilized were thousands of doctors, dentists, nurses, medical corpsmen, and pharmacists' mates, who performed invaluable service in caring for the sick and wounded.

Civilians and the War

Despite the long hours of regular work that the war entailed, millions of Americans found time to contribute volunteer service. After the Pearl Harbor attack, the possibility that mainland cities might be subjected to air raids no longer seemed fantastic. The Office of Civilan Defense (OCD), established several months earlier, suddenly took on vital significance. Five and a half million persons were trained for special duties as neighborhood air-raid wardens, auxiliary firemen, emergency first aid workers, and aircraft warning personnel. Cities established their own air-raid signals, and practice blackouts educated not only the OCD force but the general public in the grim possibilities of modern warfare. Most OCD activities came to seem unrealistic after the Axis was thrown on the defensive, but the services performed by 77,000 nurses' aides in the dangerously understaffed hospitals were of vital importance.

Other essential work was done under the auspices of the Red Cross. Women sewed or knitted as they had during World War I. Much more significant, however, was the blood-donation service. Techniques had been discovered for extracting the plasma from blood and processing it so that it could be sent to the battlefields throughout the world. There, mixed with sterile water, the plasma gave lifesaving transfusions to wounded servicemen. This procedure more than any other single factor accounted for the cutting down of mortality from wounds.[2]

Local draft and rationing boards required long hours of volunteer work, while the efforts of thousands of unpaid workers in the USO (United Service Organization) centers brightened the off-duty hours of millions of lonely soldiers. Even the housewife in her kitchen helped the war effort by carefully saving waste fats, tin cans, and waste paper for the salvage drives, while the entire family hoed the victory gardens—numbering some twenty million—to be found on virtually every vacant lot.

[2] The chief surgeon of the American forces in Europe announced that 96.1 per cent of the 1,375,000 Americans wounded had been saved. He attributed this achievement to the use of plasma, sulfa, penicillin, and to the fact that the men were bigger and stronger than the soldiers of World War I.

Signs of the times. (By Summers in the *Buffalo Evening News*.)

It proved easier to contribute war work of a positive nature than to accept cheerfully the numerous disruptions that the war made necessary in normal living. Rationing was a nuisance to all concerned, not only because of the need to stand in line to obtain ration books, but because of the added time spent in marketing. Even more annoying was the difficulty in locating such periodically scarce items as butter, sugar, coffee, meat, cigarettes, women's stockings, and men's underwear. These scarcities led to the establishment of black markets where unpatriotic—although they would be the last to admit it—citizens could buy such items without coupons at more than the ceiling price. Such shortages, together with overcrowded transit facilities and crowded housing conditions, were the hardships of the home front over which civilians delighted to grumble, but which did not greatly impress the men in the armed services familiar with conditions in other countries.

Mobilization of Industry

While the country's greatest advantage over the enemy lay in its gigantic industrial potential, the problem of converting factories from peace to war manufacture, of building new plants, and of establishing priorities for the use of raw materials and manpower required central planning and direction to a degree unprecedented in America.

The government profited by the experience of World War I, as well as by several later studies of the war mobilization problem. Nevertheless, many World War I mistakes were repeated, many new ones made, and a long period of trial and error was required before the final organization was evolved and a competent personnel recruited. Impatient critics, emphasizing the President's deficiencies as an administrator, pointed out that the jurisdictions of the various defense agencies overlapped, that jurisdictional and intra-agency feuds were frequent, and that the chief executive was all too prone to resolve such difficulties by creating still another coordinating board instead of simplifying and clarifying the existing lines of authority. All this was true, but in a more important sense Roosevelt did a remarkable job. He challenged the nation with seemingly impossible production goals, he assembled a hard-working team, and achieved the most remarkable record of industrial production in the world's history.

One reason for the unsatisfactory results of earlier defense agencies was that they were established before Pearl Harbor, when the nation was not yet ready to accept the drastic steps required of a war economy.[3] Not until President, Congress, and nation were shocked into drastic action by Pearl Harbor did really effective administrative organization evolve. The First War Powers Act of December, 1941, authorized the President to redistribute the tasks of the several boards and agencies to promote a more efficient prosecution of the war—a counterpart of the Overman Act of World War I. Existing laws were liberalized to facilitate government procurement of essential supplies, while the Trading-with-the-Enemy Act of 1917 was brought up to date to give the President control over all communications and the right to use property confiscated from the enemy.

Under his new authority Roosevelt in January, 1942, placed Donald Nelson, a Sears, Roebuck executive, in charge of the War Production Board (WPB). Occupying a post similar to that of Bernard Baruch in 1918, Nelson was answerable only to the President in his efforts to procure adequate supplies and to increase output. The agency had six major divisions: purchases, production, materials, industry operations, labor, and civilian supply, each under a competent director. Following the Baruch precedent, more than two hundred Industry Advisory Committees were established, and the antitrust laws were tacitly suspended while the concerns in each industry pooled their patents and divided available government contracts. The WPB also sponsored more than five thousand labor-management committees, which considered thousands of workers' suggestions for improving techniques and for saving time.

Both to utilize plant equipment and to conserve vital material, all civilian production of automobiles, radios, mechanical refrigerators, vacuum cleaners, washing machines, and most electrical appliances was halted in the early

[3] Insufficient authority handicapped the activities of the Council of National Defense, established May, 1940, and the Office of Production Management (OPM) and the Office of Emergency Management (OEM), set up early in 1941. Nor did the first attempts to control prices or to settle labor disputes through such overlapping agencies as the Office of Price Administration and Civilian Supply (OPACS), the National Defense Mediation Board (NDMB), the Economic Defense Board (EDB), and the Supply Priorities and Allocations Board (SPAB), prove effective.

months of 1942. Manufacture of hundreds of other metal goods was either stopped entirely or drastically curtailed, while practically all home construction except for defense workers ceased. Many small industries were hard hit by this transition, but the Smaller War Plants Corporation (SWPC) tried to protect their interests by giving them war contracts and assisting them with their engineering problems.

Japanese conquest of 90 per cent of the world's rubber supply created a serious problem. A belated effort at stockpiling rubber had begun in 1941, but less than a year's supply was accumulated before Malaya and the Dutch East Indies fell into enemy hands. Therefore the sale of new tires except on a strict rationing basis was prohibited on January 5, 1942, and a program was adopted for conserving rubber that involved gasoline rationing, a thirty-five-mile-an-hour speed limit, and periodic tire examination. A vast synthetic rubber production was planned, and Roosevelt appointed William Jeffers, a Union Pacific executive, as Rubber Administrator.

Modern war demands global strategy in economic planning as well as in military operations. To preempt vital supplies, to keep them out of enemy hands, to implement foreign policy with rewards and penalties in the form of purchases and sales to particular countries were all important American activities. During the earlier war years numerous agencies were dealing with such problems, and inevitable policy clashes occurred. The most publicized was the feud between Vice President Wallace, the head of the Board of Economic Warfare (BEW), and Secretary of Commerce Jesse Jones, whose RFC advanced the funds for many strategic imports. In July, 1943, the President intervened by abolishing the BEW and transferring its functions to a new Office of Economic Warfare (OEW), headed by Leo Crowley. In turn this agency was later consolidated with others into the Foreign Economic Administration (FEA), which became a key agency for the waging of total war.

Acting under the Anti-Inflation Act of October, 1942, Roosevelt established the Office of Economic Stabilization (OES), under the chairmanship of James Byrnes of South Carolina, who resigned from the Supreme Court to take over this important post. He was given control over "civilian purchasing power, prices, rents, wages, salaries, profits, rationing, subsidies, and all related matters."

Although the OES did some excellent work in improving production and holding the line against inflation, an increasing number of critics asserted Byrnes was loaded down with too much detail, thus impairing OES's efficiency. These critics demanded the establishment of an agency comparable to Wilson's War Cabinet. The presidential answer was to organize on May 28, 1943, the Office of War Mobilization (OWM)—"the nearest thing to an orderly planning committee for the home front that has yet been devised." Heading this new agency was Byrnes, whose powers now became so great that he was popularly referred to as the "Assistant President." Associated with him were Secretary of War Stimson, Secretary of the Navy Knox, Chairman of the Munitions Assignment Board Hopkins, Chairman of the WPB Nelson, and Byrnes's successor as Economic Stabilizer, Judge Fred Vinson of Kentucky.

The economic mobilization machinery often seemed cumbersome. There were terrifying noises emanating from Washington when the gears clashed and angry recriminations were exchanged. As always in wartime, there was much congressional denunciation of the incompetence of the executive departments, but, despite occasional evidences of administrative confusion and profiteering, the task of economic mobilization was magnificently carried through. In 1940 American war production was insignificant; in 1942 it had jumped to a volume equaling that of Germany, Italy, and Japan combined. But this was only the beginning; in 1943 it was one and a half times as great as total Axis war production, and in 1944 twice as great. Stalin himself paid tribute to this record at the Big Three meeting at Teheran when he proposed a toast to this production, without which the enemy could not have been defeated.

The Problem of Price Control

Gigantic government expenditures and full employment, during a time when civilian goods were becoming increasingly scarce, threatened America with the greatest inflation since the War for Independence. Although this danger was recognized on all sides, government price fixing was against American tradition and its imposition was long delayed. The impact of war in Europe had already brought a sharp rise in the cost of living before the United States became directly involved. Only after six months of discussion did Congress approve the Price Control Act on January 30, 1942, which established an Office of Price Administration (OPA), whose administrator could fix maximum prices on commodities whenever they rose unduly. Ceiling prices of farm produce, however, could not be set below 110 per cent of parity and any action must be approved by the Secretary of Agriculture. The administator could also recommend the stabilization or reduction of rents in defense areas, while his rationing power covered all commodities sold for personal needs.

Rationing was gradually extended over the next several months to include sugar, meat, butter and other fats, canned goods, coffee, shoes, gasoline, and fuel oil. The most ambitious step was the General Maximum Price Regulation of April 28, 1942, which imposed wholesale and retail ceiling prices on almost all commodities. The general principle was that prices were not to exceed their highest level during March, 1942. Not until the following October, however, did OPA establish ceilings on most food prices.

OPA became a favorite whipping boy for harassed civilians, both those with things to sell and those with things to buy. Its first two administrators aroused so much opposition both in and out of Congress that in October, 1943, Chester Bowles, a prominent New York advertising executive who had been a successful OPA official at the state level, took over and achieved a very creditable record in one of the war administration's most difficult and unpopular posts.

In May, 1943, more drastic price-control policies were needed because the cost of living had advanced almost 8 per cent in a year. This, combined with earlier increases, meant a 27 per cent rise since 1939. One step to combat the situation was the extension of rent control over the whole nation in October,

1942. Another was the so-called Hold-the-Line order issued by Roosevelt on April 8, 1943—an effort to freeze all items affecting the cost of living. Except in unusual circumstances, wage and salary increases were prohibited, workers could not change jobs for higher pay, and government agencies regulating common carriers and public utilities prevented rate increases. Its hand thus strengthened, OPA successfully restricted the rise of living costs during the next two years to 1.4 per cent. The total increase of less than 29 per cent up to VE Day may be compared with the 63 per cent rise between the outbreak of World War I and the armistice, or the more than 100 per cent increase represented by the prices of 1920.

The validity of the cost-of-living indexes was often challenged, particularly by labor spokesmen seeking pay boosts. This was natural because to the average citizen the increase in living costs seemed much greater. In the first place, high wartime withholding taxes took a very sizable sum. To this should be added the substantial deduction many workers had authorized for war bonds. There was thus a wide gap between what was earned and what was actually received. Moreover, prices had risen in unequal degree and the consumer was most conscious of those that had gone up sharply. He thought very little, for example, about the fact that rents had risen less than 4 per cent since 1939, but he never forgot that food prices had advanced by 50 per cent and clothing prices by 40 per cent.

Statistics were also deceiving because they failed to take into account the very considerable volume of above-ceiling transactions; the OPA itself admitted that some 12 per cent of the items in food stores were sold at higher than ceiling prices. Yet even though the degree of inflation between 1939 and 1945 was larger than government figures indicated, economic controls had saved billions of dollars for both the government and the consuming public. The OPA served as a brake, not entirely stopping inflation, but slowing it down until it no longer endangered the war effort.

The Problem of Transportation

Total mobilization and global war involved enormous strain on railroad and shipping facilities. Instead of bringing the railroads under government operation as in World War I, the lines, left under private management, were closely supervised by the Office of Defense Transportation (ODT) under the experienced Joseph Eastman. Men, material, and supplies were moved around the country in much greater volume and with less confusion than during World War I—a remarkable achievement as the railroads had less equipment and fewer employees. This was not accomplished without paying a price, however, for a number of tragic accidents testified to the strains the war was placing upon both equipment and personnel.

More vital than the coordination of the railroads was the efficient use of every precious unit of shipping. In February, 1942, the War Shipping Administration (WSA), headed by Vice Admiral Emory Land, assumed all the property and powers of the United States Maritime Commission. In addition to the ships thus obtained, the WSA acquired title to or use of practically all the nation's privately owned seagoing vessels, as well as a large proportion of the smaller craft. To this great fleet were added more than 4,000 newly constructed ships. Many World War I building records were beaten, the most remarkable exploit being the construction of a 10,000-ton ship in 78 days, one third of the time required for a similar project during the earlier conflict. This was made possible by radically new techniques, developed particularly in the shipyards of Henry Kaiser.

Although shipping was necessarily more highly regimented than railroad transportation, the actual operation of the merchant marine was through some 130 privately owned companies. An extensive training program provided additional officers and crewmen, the latter composing some of the war's unsung heroes. Enemy submarine and plane attacks resulted in about 6,000 casualties. Several routes like those to Northern Russian ports were particularly arduous and dangerous. Despite many difficulties, however, the merchant marine delivered the weapons of war to every theater.

Transocean air travel and transport, still in their infancy when the war began, were enormously expanded. Presidents, prime ministers, and key personnel hopped from continent to continent with surprisingly few mishaps, while air transport for less dramatic missions became routine.

The Farmers and the War

No individual in World War II played as powerful a role as had Herbert Hoover in World War I. The War Food Administration (WFA), headed by Judge Marvin Jones, was only a pale copy of its famous predecessor. Whereas Hoover had reduced civilian food consumption through a great propaganda campaign, this end was now achieved by extensive OPA-administered rationing. The increased production that Hoover had gained through the incentive of guaranteed high prices was this time achieved through a system of subsidies designed in combination with ceiling prices to protect consumers.

Heated debate raged over the merits of the ceiling price-subsidy system. Farmers argued that subsidies placed a burden on the taxpayer that rightly belonged to the consumer; they demanded that ceilings and subsidies be abandoned and prices be allowed to seek their natural levels. But the administration firmly opposed this proposal. Food prices had already risen sufficiently to make the workers restless; a further jump might precipitate a wholesale outbreak of strikes, a series of pay raises, and an upward spiral of inflation. Subsidies admittedly added to the national debt, but they did not increase it nearly so rapidly as would runaway prices during a period when the government was making huge purchases. Although Congress twice passed bills killing the subsidy program, the President vetoed them.

Farmers had other grievances: livestock raisers and dairy farmers found feed scarce and expensive; agricultural machinery was difficult to obtain; and the armed services and the war industries drew away agricultural manpower and labor costs shot up.

Despite all these handicaps, the farmers achieved a remarkable production record. Favored during most of the war years with good weather, they harvested the largest crops in American history. More than a billion bushels of wheat were produced in 1944, while the corn crop exceeded 3 billion bushels for three years in a row (1942–1944). Meat production kept pace, going over the 20-billion-pound mark in 1942 and 1943 and reaching 25 billion pounds in 1944.

Farm income, including government payments, doubled between 1940 and 1943, exceeding $20 billion in the latter year—a far cry from the 1932 situation when total farm income was less than $5 billion. Income continued to exceed $20 billion in both 1944 and 1945. To be sure, the increasing cost of items the farmers had to buy absorbed much of this rise, yet there was a large net gain and there could be little doubt that agriculture was more prosperous than it had been for a generation. One of the healthiest signs was the shrinking agricultural debt. Total farm-mortgage debt that had risen to almost $8.5 billion in 1920 and to $9.6 billion in 1930 fell to less than $5.3 billion by 1945. Farmers were obviously facing the new postwar era in much sounder financial condition than they had the decade of the twenties.

Labor and the War

Throughout the thirties the nation had struggled with the problem of unemployment, but after Pearl Harbor the situation was transformed. With 12 million men eventually taken into the armed services, who would work in the nation's industries? The answer was found in the entry into factories of millions who had never been wage workers—many of them women. The number of persons gainfully employed rose from 45 million in 1940 to more than 60 million in 1944. A further contribution was provided by millions of hours of overtime work performed in every community.

Less than a week after the United States entered the war a labor-management conference agreed to refrain from strikes and lockouts affecting essential industry during the war, to settle all labor differences by peaceful means, and to accept the jurisdiction of a war labor board. Accordingly, in January, 1942, Roosevelt established the National War Labor Board (NWLB) composed of twelve members giving equal representation to the public, the workers, and the employers, with William Davis of New York as chairman. The board acted only on cases where a dispute had failed of settlement through ordinary channels of collective bargaining and the conciliation services of the Department of Labor.

During the first year the new system worked quite effectively. Although almost 3,000 strikes occurred, they were quickly settled and the number of man-days lost was the smallest since 1930. About 400 of these disputes went to the NWLB; in all but four the parties complied with the findings of the board; the cases of noncompliance in essential plants were handled by government seizure and operation. In July, 1942, the board settled a strike in the lesser steel companies' plants by allowing a 15 per cent pay increase to compensate for the rise in the cost of living since January, 1941. This became known as the Little Steel formula and served as a yardstick for wage scales during the balance of the war.

The strike record was not so good in 1943. Workers were distressed by the increased cost of living, which, despite OPA, continued until the Hold-the-Line order of May, 1943. Jurisdictional disputes increased, as did work stoppages over questions of factory discipline. Many strikes were "wild-catters"—unauthorized by the unions. Employers and employees blamed each other for the situation. The former accused the workers of infringing upon the prerogatives of management; the latter asserted that the employers were trying to discredit unionism with the public by provoking work stop-pages through petty acts of tyranny. In all there were 3,752 strikes in 1943 involving the loss of 13.5 million man-days of labor—three times the amount of time lost the previous year. The most serious trouble came in work stoppages by John L. Lewis's coal miners. The struggle lasted throughout the greater part of the year, during which Lewis defied the NWLB, Fuel Administrator Ickes, and the government generally. Although the adminis-tration refused to admit it, Lewis in effect broke the Little Steel formula by obtaining premium pay and additional overtime work.

Congressional concern led in June, 1943, to the passage of the Smith-Connally War Labor Disputes Act against the opposition of the unions and over the President's veto. Increased powers were granted to the NWLB; thirty days' notice had to be given before a union could take a strike vote; explicit sanction was given to presidential seizure of war industries where production was interrupted by labor disputes; and it was made a criminal offense to instigate, direct, or aid strikes in government operated plants or mines. A final provision, particularly resented by labor, prohibited union contributions to political campaigns. Several states in the South and West passed laws restricting union activities even more stringently.

The strike record of 1944 was somewhat better. While there were more work stoppages—4,956—they were for the most part quickly settled and the number of man-days lost fell to 8.7 million.

The most serious strikes inevitably made the headlines and provoked condemnation of the groups involved. The situation, however, was never actually dangerous, except possibly in connection with the coal strikes. The number of man-days lost was less than 1 per cent of the amount worked. Every time the laborers worked on a legal holiday, as they usually did, the contribution to the war effort was greater than the labor lost through work stoppages. Yet at the same time, the percentage of time lost was not always a true yardstick because the stoppages frequently caused tie-ups in other fields not indicated in the Labor Department statistics.

War Finance

The cost of waging modern warfare has reached figures formerly considered astronomical. By VJ Day, World War II had made necessary United States government expenditures of more than $300 billion—a staggering sum when contrasted with the total American World War I expenditures of some $32 billion.

Despite this huge outlay, the public raised a larger proportion of war costs through taxation than ever before. Between Pearl Harbor and VJ Day the United States collected about $123 billion in revenues, or approximately 40 per cent of its expenditures. This contrasted with the 33 per cent during World War I. The record for the fiscal year ending June 30, 1945, was particularly good. Expenditures for that period reached $100 billion, but net receipts were $46.5 billion or 46.5 per cent of the outlay.

There was general agreement on the necessity of high wartime taxes. They were essential to preserve government solvency, to prevent unjustifiable enrichment of those profiteering from the booming wartime economy, and perhaps most of all to reduce the threat of inflation. The actual rates to be fixed for the various income brackets, however, were matters for heated debate. Months of such controversy were the prelude to the enactment in October, 1942, of "the greatest tax bill in history." The tax base was broadened to require payment of income taxes by all persons receiving more than $1,200 if married and $500 if single. The normal tax rate was increased from 4 to 6 per cent, but this sum was insignificant compared with the imposition of surtaxes ranging from 13 per cent on the first $2,000 of taxable income to 82 per cent on incomes exceeding $200,000. Nor was this all; income exceeding $624 in the case of a single person and a somewhat larger figure for a married individual was subjected to a 5 per cent "Victory tax" withheld by the employer.

These new rates represented a revolution in taxation. The number paying Federal income taxes had been only 4 million in 1939 and 17 million in 1941, but the direct taxes levied under the 1942 legislation reached 50 million persons. Under the 1939 rates a childless couple having $3,000 gross income paid little if any income tax; under the 1941 rates such a couple paid about $109; under the 1942 rates the tax was $340. Corporation taxes were also raised so that the maximum normal and surtax rates on the largest incomes totaled 40 per cent. In addition to this, excess profits were taxed 90 per cent —subject, however, to certain postwar rebates to aid reconversion.

These taxes, plus new or increased excise levies on liquor, beer, telephone service, travel tickets, amusements, and telegraph messages, greatly increased government revenues, but they involved many annoyances and inconveniences. Income-tax forms had become almost impossibly complicated to fill out, the Treasury Department's enforcement problem had become unmanageable, and the system of collecting these huge sums after the completion of the year on which the tax was levied threatened to result in wholesale defaults. In support of a much-needed reform, Beardsley Ruml, a New York financial expert, became the leading proponent of a "pay-as-you-go" plan, under which employers would withhold the Federal income tax from wages and salaries as they were paid. In order to put all taxpayers on a current basis, Ruml insisted that the government forgive the 1942 tax. The latter proposal was unsatisfactory to the Roosevelt administration, but public demand led in June, 1943, to the passage of a Revenue Act that represented a modified version of the Ruml plan. Taxpayers had to file returns for both 1942 and 1943 income, but 75 per cent of their tax for whichever year was smaller was forgiven. Beginning July 1, 1943, income-tax payments were put on a current basis; wage and salary earners had their taxes deducted at the source; those with incomes from other sources had to estimate their income and make quarterly payments to the Treasury.

Despite these large taxes, net corporate income was at record heights, as were many individual incomes. In view of this wartime prosperity, Roosevelt asked early in 1944 for additional taxes to the amount of $10.5 billion. Wendell Willkie also urged higher taxes to curb inflation and lessen the burden of debt to be left for the postwar generation. The majority of Congressmen believed, however, that the current burdens were as heavy as the country could bear. Although they increased the excise levies and raised the excess profits tax to about 95 per cent, the new bill provided only about $2.2 billion in additional revenue, and the net result was considerably less because Congress had frozen the Social Security level at 1 per cent instead of permitting it to jump to 2 per cent as provided by earlier law. To show his strong disapproval, Roosevelt took the unusual step of vetoing a revenue measure with a message so strongly worded that Alben Barkley of Kentucky, the Democratic leader in the Senate, angrily demanded that the veto be overridden—and Congress followed his wishes. The rebellious leader was unanimously re-elected to the post from which he had resigned in protest over the President's message. Roosevelt tried to smooth the ruffled feathers of the legislators with a telegram to Barkley denying his intention of attacking the integrity of Congress.

Even after the pay-as-you-go innovation, the income-tax structure was still so complicated that popular protest led to the passage in May, 1944, of the Individual Income Tax Act, sometimes called the Tax Simplification Act. The new law relieved millions of taxpayers receiving income exclusively from wages or salaries of the necessity of filing returns, it simplified the forms for other taxpayers, and it merged the troublesome Victory tax with the regular levies.

Though the tax burdens laid on the country were as heavy as Congress believed could be borne, there still remained a huge deficit. The public debt, which stood at $49 billion on June 30, 1941, climbed to nearly $259 billion four years later. Every effort was made to borrow as much as possible from individual citizens. This was not essential to raise money, since the banks readily subscribed whatever sums were asked of them, but government borrowing from banks increased the money in circulation, thereby contributing to inflation. Bond purchases by individuals, on the other hand, decreased the volume of money and was one of the best safeguards against inflation.

During the great war-bond drives, thousands of volunteer solicitors conducted house-to-house canvasses; banks, theaters, and department stores set up booths where bonds could be purchased; and newspapers, magazines, radio stations, and movie houses appealed to the public to buy. A particularly effective technique was to induce wage earners and salaried workers to authorize regular deductions from their paychecks for bond purchases—a method that had the special advantage of selling bonds even when special drives were not being conducted. In the single month of April, 1945, 25 million persons bought $485 million in this way. The sale of "E" Bonds, the type particularly designed for the small investor, totaled about $40 billion between May 1, 1941, and December 31, 1945.

A most interesting development of the war years was the vast accumulation of savings of all types. Despite much easy spending of war earnings, the liquid savings of the American public were estimated at $129 billion by the spring of 1945. This helped to keep down prices during the war and created a backlog of purchasing power for the postwar years, but its unusual volume at the same time held future inflationary dangers.

Censorship and Information

By executive order of December 29, 1941, Roosevelt established the Office of Censorship to censor all communications between the United States and foreign countries. The task of censoring mail was a huge one, requiring the services of ten thousand employees who deleted all mention of troop and ship movements, details of war production, descriptions of fortifications, air-raid preparations, and weather reports.

The newspapers and radio also agreed to voluntary censorship. Codes of wartime practices were prepared after consultation between government officials and broadcasting industries. The newspapers and radio stations were asked not to reveal unauthorized information regarding troop and ship movements, air attacks upon the United States, airplanes' characteristics and activities, fortifications, production, weather maps and photographs, and movements of the President or high military and diplomatic officials. The Director of Censorship was Byron Price, a veteran journalist and Associated Press executive, who handled his delicate task in competent fashion, and violations of the letter or spirit of the code were few.

It will be noted that the press had been asked not to publish information involving military security unless cleared with the proper authorities. This made the War and Navy departments the real arbiters in most cases of what might or might not be released. Their tendency, particularly during the early months of the war, was to err on the side of overcaution. Consequently, censorship was sometimes used to shield the public from bad news, like the full truth about Pearl Harbor, or from any mention of military blunders—such as the incident in which American gunfire shot down American paratroopers in the attack on Sicily.

On June 13, 1942, partly as a result of pressure from writers and publishers, the Office of War Information (OWI) was established under the directorship of Elmer Davis, a widely respected essayist and radio commentator. It was authorized to utilize the press, radio, motion pictures, and other facilities to develop an informed and intelligent understanding, both at home and abroad, of the progress of the war and of the government's war aims. Although it was hoped the Davis agency would make accessible larger rations of war news, strict censorship by the War and Navy departments continued to defeat this end. OWI's domestic branch was largely liquidated in 1943 when Congress, suspicious that the agency would serve a political purpose during the presidential campaign the next year, cut its appropriations. But the foreign branch, engaged in propaganda in enemy and neutral countries, survived congressional attacks and conducted an intensive program through all available media. Particularly notable were its short-wave radio activities, which operated 16 transmitters and sent out 2,700 programs weekly in 24 different languages. It discovered the most effective propaganda in a news-starved world was straight factual material about war developments, American war production, and plans for postwar reconstruction. Unquestionably the weapon of psychological warfare undermined the enemy's will to resist and was especially effective in hastening the surrender of Italy.

Dealing with Disloyalty

On the whole, the war period resulted in little interference with freedom of opinion in the United States. The President and the various war administrators were subjected to frequent and at times violent criticism. Some attacks represented mere partisanship, but others revealed honest points of difference. Often freedom of speech proved a source of positive democratic strength since it led to the improvement of weak points in the defense organization and the rectification of mistakes.

There was much less witch-hunting than there had been during World War I, reflecting in part the moderation and good judgment of Attorney General Francis Biddle. It resulted, too, from the fact that Communists and Socialists did not follow the extreme antiwar line that they had in 1917. The former, because of the German attack upon Russia, urged the subordination of every other end to the winning of the war. The Socialists were not so strongly prowar, but after Pearl Harbor they could hardly condemn the struggle as another instance of capitalist imperialism.

The administration did not jail radicals simply because they had unpopular economic or social philosophies; but it did proceed against certain individuals and groups whose activities threatened the war effort by promoting racial hatred, encouraging evasion of military service, or disseminating enemy propaganda. Newspapers such as Father Coughlin's *Social Justice* were barred from the mails, while George Sylvester Viereck, a paid Nazi agent, and various domestic Fascists such as William Dudley Pelley, George Christians, and Ralph Townsend were arrested, some of them receiving prison sentences under the espionage laws. But the government's most ambitious project—a mass sedition trial of twenty-eight pro-Nazis—miscarried. The death of the presiding judge after many weary weeks of court proceedings, enlivened by the antics of the defendants and their lawyers, resulted in a mistrial. Although the whole group never again came to trial on the conspiracy charge, several members were punished on other grounds. Such individuals, however, were few in number and the country supported the war with greater unanimity than in any previous conflict. The enemy made occasional efforts to land agents and saboteurs by submarine, but these were frustrated through the vigilance of the FBI.

The Special Committee to Investigate Un-American Activities, the so-called Dies Committee, first authorized by the House in 1938, was active throughout the war and received generous appropriations. Its supporters claimed it exposed many subversive movements, but the committee was under continual fire from liberals. Its chairman, Martin Dies of Texas, was accused of being much more alive to the dangers of Communism than of Fascism, and of branding recklessly every liberal or labor leader whom he disliked as a Communist.

The most shameful violation of civil liberties was the treatment of Japanese-Americans. Early in 1942 the army removed all persons of Japanese descent from three West Coast states and lodged them in relocation centers farther inland. This drastic step was taken on the contention it was necessary to prevent spy activities and sabotage in an essential military zone, even though two thirds of the 110,000 evacuees were American citizens. The Supreme Court finally held in December, 1944, that the mass evacuation had been legal under presidential war powers but that American citizens against whom no charge had been filed and whose loyalty was not questioned could not be detained after removal from the military zone. Meantime, the War Department repealed its ban against the return of loyal evacuees to the coast, but certain elements of the Western public opposed this. During the next eighteen months, no less than 59 acts of violence terrorized the returning evacuees. Although West Coast opinion in the main condemned such tactics, many Japanese-Americans found new homes elsewhere. This harsh treatment was perhaps inevitable, considering the shock of Pearl Harbor, but it is only just to the Japanese-Americans to stress that 17,600 of them served with the United States armed forces, that Japanese-American battle units had outstanding records in action, and that no Japanese-American was convicted of either sabotage or espionage during the war.

German and Italian groups were dealt with less rigorously. Citizens were not molested unless accused of specific acts of disloyalty, but all enemy aliens were required to register and obtain "certificates of identification." They were barred from vital defense areas and ordered to surrender their firearms, cameras, and short-wave radios. Alien enemies considered dangerous were interned; but only 1,228 Germans and 232 Italians were so treated as compared with 2,151 Japanese. By early 1944, most Italians had been released, but German internees were kept under guard until the end of the war.

Politics as Usual

Unlike the unwritten British Constitution, the American Constitution did not permit postponement of elections during wartime. To many observers this seemed unfortunate; political campaigns were regarded as a dangerous democratic luxury during a national emergency. On the other hand, wartime elections had much to be said for them. They provided an important popular referendum on the civilian direction of the war. More important, freedom of political debate and honest elections gave impressive evidence of the democratic values that America was fighting to preserve.

The congressional election of 1942 came at a dark moment of the war. For eleven months after Pearl Harbor, the United States had been on the defensive and had suffered the humiliation of losing all of her possessions in the western Pacific. On the home front civilians were undergoing the inconveniences of shortages and rationing, of rising prices and increased taxes, and of numerous bottlenecks in industry and transportation. Under the circumstances it was not surprising that the mid-term elections showed a strong antiadministration trend. Democratic strength in the House declined from 267 to 222, while the Republicans were rising from 162 to 209; in the Senate the Democrats fell from 66 seats to 57, while the Republicans increased from 28 to 38. One of the 1942 casualties was Senator George Norris of Nebraska, whose seat was captured by conservative Republican Kenneth Wherry.

The election results were actually more serious for the President than the statistics indicated. The dwindling Democratic majorities in both houses gave the balance of power to conservative Southern Democrats, who often allied with the Republicans. Although this coalition was no less determined than the New Dealers to gain a complete victory over the Axis and to support international peace-keeping machinery, it was rebellious on domestic issues. The attacks upon the OPA and OWI have already been noted, as well as passage of the Smith-Connally Act and rejection of the administration's tax proposals in 1944. Contending that relief was no longer needed, the coalition liquidated such agencies as the CCC, the WPA, and the NYA. A most disturbing conservative victory was the killing of the National Resources Planning Board, an agency trying to formulate a well-coordinated program for the postwar period. In the interests of national unity, Roosevelt announced that "Dr. Win-the-War" had supplanted "Dr. New Deal," but this gesture of appeasement only distressed his liberal supporters without reconciling the conservatives.

The Election of 1944

In November, 1944, the first wartime presidential election since 1864 was held. Wendell Willkie made a spirited fight to win a second Republican nomination. He had become one of the nation's most evangelical advocates of internationalism following a trip around the world by air in 1942. He poured out his convictions in the short but persuasive book, *One World,* which sold two million copies during the next two years. On domestic issues he also did some effective writing, impressing many with the genuineness of his liberalism. But Willkie's frankness and courage were in the end his undoing. He staked everything on winning the Wisconsin primary in April, 1944, hoping to defeat isolationism in a traditional stronghold, but he was badly beaten and retired from the race despite his strong position in public-opinion polls.

Meantime, Dewey's star rose steadily, his greatest asset being his record as a vote getter in the pivotal state of New York. His election as governor in 1942 was the first such Republican victory since 1920 and offered hope he might defeat Roosevelt in the latter's home state. Dewey's other advantages were his youth, his reputation for efficiency, and his wide fame as a prosecutor of racketeers and corrupt politicians. Two other Republican governors, John Bricker of Ohio and Harold Stassen of Minnesota, were prominently mentioned for the nomination, but they could not overtake their New York rival.

At the Chicago National Convention in June, Dewey was nominated on the first ballot, with Bricker as his running mate. The platform incorporated the so-called Mackinac Declaration, calling for "responsible participation by the United States in a postwar organization among sovereign nations to prevent military aggression and to obtain permanent peace with organized justice in the world." The platform pledged the party not only to prosecute the war to total victory, but to bring home as soon as possible after cessation of hostilities all members of the armed forces. The party devoted itself "to reestablishing liberty at home," to ending government competition with private industry, and to terminating rationing, price fixing, and all other emergency powers after the close of the war.

Roosevelt's renomination by the Democrats was inevitable. Millions of citizens regarded his continuance in office necessary to prevent interruption of the war effort and to provide experienced leadership in the postwar period. From the standpoint of party expediency, moreover, it was unlikely any other Democrat could win in November. Serious anti-Roosevelt sentiment in the party was confined to Texas and other parts of the South, where New Deal policies benefiting organized labor, tenant farmers, and Negroes were bitterly resented. Only one man, however, could have prevented Roosevelt's renomination and that was Roosevelt himself. After he announced his willingness to run again on the eve of the Chicago Convention, the only question was how large the anti-Roosevelt vote would be. The answer was given on the first ballot, when Senator Harry Byrd of Virginia received 89 votes and James Farley 1 vote, while the President was rolling up 1,066.

The real fight was waged over the second place on the ticket. Vice President Wallace had not been the inconspicuous figure traditionally associated with that office. Instead, he had become a prominent public character through his championship of the rights of the underprivileged. In the opposition press he was portrayed as the embodiment of all that was most impractical and visionary in the New Deal. Yet the idealism that had aroused conservative hostility won the enthusiastic support of many liberals.

Such was the opposition to Wallace among the Southern Democrats and the machine politicians of the North, however, that his renomination could have been won only if Roosevelt had vigorously insisted upon it. This the President, striving for party harmony, refrained from doing. While he announced that he admired Wallace and that were he a delegate he would vote for Wallace, he disclaimed any intention of dictating to the convention. The first choice of the conservatives would have been War Mobilizer Byrnes, but the CIO's hostility made the choice of some compromise candidate essential. The President suggested either Supreme Court Justice William Douglas or Senator Harry Truman of Missouri. With this help, Truman was named on the second ballot.

The platform preamble read: "The Democratic party stands on its record in peace and war. To speed victory, establish and maintain peace, and guarantee full employment and provide prosperity—this is the platform. We do not detail scores of planks. We cite action." The country was asked to give the President a vote of confidence to continue the international and domestic policies with which he had become identified.

The contest was not lacking in bitterness. The most active workers in the Roosevelt cause were to be found in the Political Action Committee (PAC), organized by the CIO and supported by special contributions from union members, since the Smith-Connally Act forbade the direct use of union funds. Astutely led by the veteran unionist, Sidney Hillman, the PAC waged an energetic campaign, based on effective publicity and house-to-house calls by thousands of enthusiastic amateurs to get out the vote. But these aggressive tactics were bitterly denounced by the Republicans. The fact that Roosevelt had ascertained the attitude of the PAC on Truman before giving the latter his endorsement was twisted to mean that the unionists had captured the Democratic party. "Clear it with Sidney" was the taunt repeatedly hurled at the administration, but the attack upon Hillman boomeranged to a certain extent because many foreign-born and Jewish voters felt the Republicans were playing upon racial prejudice. Dewey toured the country asserting that the government was in the hands of "tired old men" and calling for a thorough "housecleaning." The President responded with much of his old-time fire, lashing out at his critics in particularly aggressive speeches.

The election provided another Democratic triumph. Roosevelt carried 36 states and received 432 electoral votes as against Dewey's 12 states and 99 electoral votes. The popular vote was much closer, with Roosevelt receiving 25.6 million and Dewey 22 million—the closest margin of victory since 1916. The new Senate would have 57 Democrats, 38 Republicans, and 1 independent—the same division as in the old, but the House showed a Democratic gain, 242 of the administration party being elected to 190 Republicans and 2 independents. Isolationism was strongly rebuked by the voters; Senator Gerald Nye of North Dakota, Senator Bennett Clark of Missouri, Representative Hamilton Fish of New York, and Representative Stephen Day of Illinois all failed of relection.

Death of a Warrior

The unprecedented fourth term was brief. On January 20, 1945, a simple inauguration ceremony appropriate to wartime was conducted on the White House grounds. "We have learned that we cannot live alone," Roosevelt asserted in his address. "We have learned to be citizens of the world, members of the human community." Within a few days he embarked for the Crimea, where he participated in the important Yalta Conference with Stalin and Churchill. On his return he appeared before Congress to explain some of the decisions made there and to appeal for strong support for the forthcoming San Francisco Conference at which the United Nations Charter would be drafted.

Meantime, a sharp controversy over domestic issues had been precipitated when the President dismissed the conservative Secretary of Commerce Jones and nominated Henry Wallace to replace him. The whole conservative-liberal battle was reopened in aggravated form, because the post now had connected with it vast powers over the RFC and other Federal lending agencies. Inheritance of the whole kingdom over which Jesse Jones had reigned would give the ex-Vice President a magnificent opportunity to push his own program for full employment in the postwar economy. A bitter struggle in Congress resulted in neither side winning a clear decision. Wallace was confirmed as Secretary, but was divested of all power over the Federal lending agencies.

This, however, was the last important battle of the Rooseveltian period. The strain of war had levied a heavy toll on the President's health. He had spent his energies with characteristic prodigality during the 1944 campaign, even driving in an open car through the rain in New York City as if to answer the charge he was a tired old man. But these exertions, followed by the hard trip to Yalta, exhausted him. Seeking to renew his strength, Roosevelt went to Warm Springs, Georgia, for a spring vacation. There, resting and working in an environment he loved, he was unexpectedly stricken with a cerebral hemorrhage on April 12, 1945, and died within a few hours. Released after his death was a speech on which he had been working during these last days; its closing words afforded an appropriate valedictory from the fallen war leader to the nation:

The only limit to our realization of tomorrow will be our doubts of today. Let us move forward with strong and active faith.

23

THE MIRAGE OF PEACE

During World War II America found strength in the hope that this time a better world would really emerge from the battlefield. The rejection of isolationism after the shock of Pearl Harbor seemed complete. The United States and its allies buried their ideological differences to concentrate on defeating the enemy. Out of this new cooperation there evolved the idea of the United Nations—a new international organization to replace the more or less moribund League of Nations.

Cooperation in wartime proved much easier to maintain, however, than postwar harmony. A hostility developed between the Communist and non-Communist nations that increased in bitterness as time passed. Discouraged Americans had reason to wonder whether the stable world society of which they had dreamed would ever be established.

Comrades in Arms

Under the lash of Axis aggression, Russia, Great Britain, and the United States achieved sufficient cooperation to win the war, with the relationship between Britain and United States being particularly close. Soon after Pearl Harbor, Churchill flew to Washington to confer with Roosevelt upon a plan of action. This direct approach was so successful that the two men conferred on several other occasions—at Washington, at Casablanca, and at Quebec, where the important strategic decisions were made that led to the invasions of North Africa, Sicily, Italy, and France. Also Anglo-American Joint Chiefs of Staff conducted day-to-day planning, while English and American officers cooperated under the command of General Eisenhower on the European front.

With the Soviet Union, however, relations were less cordial. After bearing the brunt of German attacks for many months, the Russians complained of the Anglo-American delay in establishing a second front. Despite such recriminations, a better understanding developed during the latter months of the war. In October, 1943, Secretary Hull conferred in Moscow with Russian Foreign Minister Vyacheslav Molotov and British Foreign Secretary Anthony Eden, and a month later the Big Three—Stalin, Churchill, and Roosevelt—met at Teheran, Persia, to work out plans for a second front.[1]

[1] Churchill and Roosevelt met with Chiang Kai-shek at Cairo just before the Teheran Conference to coordinate action against Japan.

The second Big Three conference was held at Yalta in the Crimea during February, 1945. In the communiqué made public at the time, the leaders announced agreement on such important issues as the postwar occupation of Germany, the fixing of reparations, the right of liberated peoples to establish governments of their own choosing, and the reorganization of provisional governments in Poland and Yugoslavia. These provisions were warmly applauded in America as evidence that Russia and the West had achieved a good understanding. But the Yalta Conference made certain other decisions, kept temporarily secret for military reasons, which provoked sharp controversy when they were eventually revealed. The most important concerned the Far East. The Soviet Union agreed to enter the war against Japan after Germany's surrender in return for the Kurile Islands, the southern half of Sakhalin, and the lease of Port Arthur as a naval base. In addition, the port of Dairen was to be internationalized and the Chinese Eastern and South Manchurian railroads were to be under joint Russo-Chinese operation. Most of these areas and privileges had been lost by Russia as a result of the Russo-Japanese War.

When the full Yalta record became known—months after Roosevelt's death—the wartime President was severely criticized for his "surrender" to Soviet demands. These fatal concessions, so the argument ran, gave Russia control of Manchuria, made the Chinese Reds' victory over Chiang Kai-shek inevitable, and led to Communist aggression in Korea. Roosevelt was also condemned for consenting to Russian occupation of Berlin and Eastern Germany and for acquiescing in Communist-controlled governments in the liberated countries of Eastern Europe. Most of the criticisms appear to be based more upon a desire to find a scapegoat for the nation's postwar troubles than upon an accurate understanding of the military situation in February, 1945. When the Big Three met at Yalta, American troops had neither crossed the Rhine nor completed the conquest of the Philippines, and the feasibility

President Roosevelt arriving in Yalta. To the President's right are Churchill, Molotov, and Secretary of State Stettinius. (UPI Photo.)

of the atom bomb was still to be proved. Decisions at the conference were made upon military estimates that assumed many months of hard fighting still lay ahead. The Chiefs of Staff were particularly eager to bring Russia into the war against Japan, thereby tying up Japanese troops on the continent of Asia and saving the lives of American soldiers when the Japanese home islands were invaded. Whether or not Roosevelt's diplomacy at Yalta was wise, the record seems clear that it was based on what he believed to be a realistic view of the military situation at that time. The belief that the President was senile or pro-Communist when he entered upon these arrangements has little to support it.

The United Nations

At the Yalta Conference the Big Three also agreed upon "the earliest possible establishment . . . of a general international organization to maintain peace and security," and that a meeting for this purpose should be convened at San Francisco on April 25, 1945. Behind this decision lay many months of discussion.

In a sense the seed was planted in August, 1941, when Roosevelt and Churchill expressed in the Atlantic Charter their hope for a postwar "system of general security." The plant began to grow in the United Nations Declaration of January 1, 1942, in which the United States, Britain, China, and Russia promised to employ their full resources against the Axis, cooperate with each other, and make no separate peace. The next day twenty-two more countries ratified the pact, and by January 1, 1945, nine additional nations had done so. At Yalta the Big Three decided that only signatories of this document could be represented at San Francisco, a decision that caused eleven more states to declare war against the Axis and sign the declaration. Argentina signed after the deadline, but a United States plea brought her an invitation to San Francisco.

Most striking was the change in American opinion. Instead of resisting the idea of a new world organization, Congress appeared to be rushing ahead of the Roosevelt administration. In March, 1943, the so-called B_2H_2[2] resolution urged the broadening of the United Nations into a postwar agency to maintain peace. Regarded as premature by Roosevelt, this proposal was not acted upon, but in September, 1943, the House overwhelmingly adopted William Fulbright's resolution to create "appropriate machinery with power adequate to establish and maintain a just and lasting peace among the nations of the world."

The Senate, apparently jealous of its prerogatives in foreign affairs, declined to concur in the Fulbright Resolution, but in November, 1943, it approved the formula agreed upon at the recent Moscow Foreign Ministers Conference:

> That they recognize the necessity of establishing at the earliest practicable date a general international organization, based on the principle of the sovereign equality

[2] It was sponsored by Republican Senators Joseph Ball of Minnesota and Harold Burton of Ohio and Democratic Senators Carl Hatch of New Mexico and Lister Hill of Alabama

of all peace-loving states, and open to membership by all such states, large and small, for the maintenance of international peace and security.

It was evident that the emerging United Nations was being greeted in a very different spirit than had been Wilson's League of Nations.

New Areas of International Cooperation

Advocates of postwar cooperation realized that more was needed than simply an organization to prevent aggression; there must also be cooperation to promote the Four Freedoms and to help the millions of civilians whose property had been ravaged by war. As a first step, forty-four nations, meeting at Hot Springs, Virginia, in May, 1943, established the Food and Agricultural Organization (FAO).

Much more significant were the various problems of relief and rehabilitation, which involved humanitarian as well as military and economic issues. Therefore, the United Nations Relief and Rehabilitation Administration (UNRRA) was organized late in 1943 with funds contributed by the member nations based on their relative national incomes (the United States quota was nearly 75 per cent). First headed by former Governor Herbert Lehman of New York and then by Fiorello La Guardia, former mayor of New York City, UNRRA spent more than $4 billion to send food to destitute countries of Europe and Asia to prevent starvation.[3]

Since war-torn countries would face economic problems when peace came, it was realized that their industries must be rebuilt and their currencies stabilized to prevent a recurrence of the troublesome days of the 1930's. Therefore the Bretton Woods (New Hampshire) Conference in the summer of 1944 established an International Monetary Fund of $8.8 billion (the American quota being $2.75 billion) to stabilize the currencies of the world, as well as an International Bank of Reconstruction, capitalized at $9 billion (the United States quota was about $3 billion) to make loans to member nations to reconstruct their industry and agriculture.

The San Francisco Conference

While these rehabilitation plans were being formulated, the great powers were moving toward a general United Nations organization that had been accepted in principle at the Moscow Conference of Foreign Ministers in October, 1943. The following August, Undersecretary of State Edward Stettinius, Sir Alexander Cadogan of Britain, and Andrei Gromyko of Russia drafted preliminary plans for an association of nations at Dumbarton Oaks (outside of Washington, D.C.). Final arrangements were made, as has been said, at Yalta in February, 1945. Although President Roosevelt died before the San Francisco Conference opened, he contributed substantially to its

---

[3] Unfortunately, there were charges that some of this relief was used for political purposes in several countries, so the United States refused to support UNRRA after 1946.

success. Profiting from Wilson's mistakes, he appointed an American delegation in which Republicans had equal recognition with Democrats and in which Senators and Representatives had important posts.

When the conference opened on April 25, 1945, forty-eight nations were represented. Since the Dumbarton Oaks plan was only a rough outline, there was ample opportunity for disagreement over details. On several issues the Russians took stubborn positions from which they were moved with difficulty, if at all. Indeed, at one point when Soviet intransigence threatened to break up the meeting, President Truman sent Harry Hopkins to Moscow for direct conversations with Stalin. In the end, however, the great powers found acceptable compromises on such troublesome issues as the admission of White Russia and the Ukraine as independent members,[4] admission of Argentina, trusteeships, and the voting and veto rights of the great powers.

According to the preamble of the Charter, the peoples of the United Nations had combined "to save succeeding generations from the scourge of war," "to establish conditions under which justice and respect for the obligations arising from treaties and other sources of international law can be maintained," and to ensure "that armed force shall not be used, save in the common interest." The charter members were the forty-eight nations represented at San Francisco, plus White Russia and the Ukraine, which were admitted during the session, and Poland after its government was organized. Other "peace-loving" states could become members by vote of the General Assembly on recommendation of the Security Council. Members violating the Charter provisions might be suspended or expelled by a similar procedure.

The General Assembly, made up of delegates from each member state, might discuss "any questions or any matters within the scope of the present Charter or relating to the powers and functions of any organs provided for in the present Charter, and . . . make recommendations to the Members of the United Nations or to the Security Council or to both on any such questions or matters." The only restriction concerned disputes already being considered by the Security Council. The Assembly could initiate studies concerning the strengthening and codification of international law, the solution of social, cultural, educational, health, and economic problems, and recommend measures for the peaceful adjustment of any situation likely to cause trouble. On important matters, a two-thirds vote was required.

Much more powerful was the eleven-member Security Council. The United States, Britain, China, France, and Russia held permanent seats, with the other positions filled by General Assembly vote for two-year terms. The vote of seven members was needed to approve any action; on important issues such as the use of military power, the Big Five must be unanimous. It was here that the disputed veto power came in; although a permanent member could not prevent consideration of a dispute in which it was involved, it could use its veto to prevent imposition of economic or military sanction

---

[4] At Yalta, Roosevelt had agreed to support Russia's demand for three votes in the Assembly, with the understanding that the United States might request a similar number. When this agreement became public, the idea of demanding three seats for the United States aroused so much opposition from the American public that it was dropped. The Soviet Union, however, demanded and received separate seats for two of her subordinate republics.

President Truman stands by as Secretary of State Stettinius signs the United Nations charter in San Francisco, 1945. (U.N. Photo.)

Directly under the Security Council was the Military Staff Committee, consisting of the Big Five chiefs of staff. It could call out the UN armed forces when the Security Council deemed it necessary. Another UN agency was the Economic and Social Council, elected by the General Assembly to report on "international economic, social, cultural, educational, health, and related matters." Among the specialized agencies it supervised were the International Bank, the International Stabilization Fund, the International Labor Organization (ILO), the United Nations Educational, Scientific, and Cultural Organization (UNESCO), and the Food and Agricultural Organization (FAO).

A Trusteeship Council was in charge of territories already held under mandate, those lands gained from the Axis in World War II, and the regions voluntarily placed in trusteeship by the nations administering them. The International Court of Justice, to meet at The Hague, consisted of fifteen judges elected by the Assembly. Finally, a permanent Secretariat kept the records and assembled the data needed by the UN.

To maintain peace, the UN was to function in a more or less prescribed manner. When a dispute arose that might endanger international peace, the parties to it were expected to seek a peaceful solution. If such negotiations appeared to be failing, the issue could be presented to either the Assembly or the Council for investigation and recommendations for settlement. In the event of a breach of the peace, the Council could order economic sanctions against the offenders; if these were insufficient, the Military Staff Committee could be called upon to end the disturbance through armed force.

The Charter was criticized on various grounds. The small states deplored the dominating position of the major powers, but the Big Five answered that they would have heavier responsibilities for maintaining peace than their smaller neighbors and must therefore have greater weight in UN councils. For the veto power exercised by the Big Five in the Security Council there was less defense; yet the United States and Britain were no less insistent than Russia upon this safeguard to their interests. It was obvious that the UN would succeed only if the wartime allies maintained a general unity.

This Charter would become effective when the Big Five and a majority of the other members ratified it. Nicaragua was the first to act favorably, but the United States was the initial Big Five member to do so. The Senate, after remarkably little debate, approved of American membership before the end of July, 1945, by the decisive vote of 89 to 2. On October 24, 1945, the ratification of the UN was completed.

The Potsdam Conference

The establishment of the UN was but one phase of the effort to prevent future conflicts. In 1945 the principal danger seemed to lie in the revival of a strong and revengeful Germany. During the war, decisions had already been made for the subjugation of the Reich, and the implementation of these policies was arranged at a Big Three Conference at Potsdam outside of Berlin two months after the German surrender. Representing the victorious power were President Truman, Churchill (who was replaced during the meeting by Clement Attlee, his successor as a result of a British election), and Stalin. The Potsdam Resolution of July 25, 1945, provided for the complete disarming of Germany. This action was to be strengthened by wiping out the entire Nazi organization, by the trial of war criminals, by breaking up cartel and supervising German industry, and by establishing democratic institutions. Germany was divided into four occupation zones, respectively allocated to the Russians, British, French, and Americans. Also East Prussia was divided between Russia and Poland, while larger territories in eastern Germany were allocated to Poland as compensation for land given up to the Soviet Union.

This Potsdam meeting was not a peace conference. Indeed, the procedure laid down was to postpone a general settlement, while clearing the ground through special agreement on specific issues. Treaties for Germany and Austria were not to be considered until those with Italy, Finland, Hungary, Bulgaria, and Rumania had been signed.

Occupation Problems: Germany

Governing vanquished Germany was no easy task. Nazi recruitment of slave labor and imprisonment of potential resistance leaders had torn mi lions of Europeans from their homes and left them at war's end stranded and destitute hundreds of miles from home—if any home still survived. The rehabilitation of these displaced persons was a gigantic problem enormously complicated by the migration of millions of Germans rendered homeless by Allied bombing or expelled from territories allotted to Poland, Czechoslovakia, or Russia. All European economic life was disorganized, and the mobilization of sufficient food to prevent starvation was difficult.

Specially trained military government teams wrestled with these and a thousand other problems. Administration at the local and provincial level had to be entrusted to German personnel, but the selection of individuals both competent and politically reliable was far from easy. Although no Nazi sympathizer was to be employed in any administrative capacity, either in government or industry, this rule was subject to wholesale violation for some time. Military government officers often allowed former Nazis to hold important posts because they were the only ones with the requisite experience, or because some American officers were reluctant to employ trade-unionists or Socialists. This situation led to a showdown in October, 1945, when strict orders brought a thoroughgoing purge of Nazi sympathizers.

The occupying powers tried to inculcate democracy by extending freedom of the press, of speech, and of religion, and schools were reopened with denazified teaching staffs and books. Once again German political parties of various shades of opinion could operate freely. Elections to local councils took place in the American zone in January, 1946, and to higher representative bodies later in the year. But Soviet and French opposition delayed setting up any German-staffed administration for the whole country. The practical effect of the occupation policies was to divide the Reich into four almost completely separate countries, thus adding greatly to the problem of economic reconstruction.

The Potsdam Declaration had called not only for the complete dismantling of the German armament, aircraft, and shipbuilding industries, but for drastic reductions in such potentially dangerous fields as steel and chemicals. It had also been agreed that the Reich's factories and machinery should be available for removal as reparations. Serious controversy arose as to how this should be done. Since Germany with its new boundaries would be unable to feed itself, a minimum of industrial production for export would have to be permitted to pay for essential imports. Russia favored reducing German potential to the lowest possible level, regardless of its effect; Britain, desperately needing a German market, urged a measure of leniency; and the United States supported a middle position.

On one proposition, however, there was substantial agreement: the punishment of German war criminals. Hitler, Himmler, and Goebbels cheated the gallows by committing suicide, but Goering and some twenty other leaders were the defendants in a unique trial opening at Nuremberg in November, 1945. On the bench sat an international military tribunal of distinguished jurists from the Big Four powers (former Attorney General Francis Biddle was the American); the same nations were represented in the corps of prosecutors (Supreme Court Justice Robert Jackson was the chief American prosecutor). This trial established important precedents, both because of its international character and because of the charges included in the indictment. The defendants were accused not only of violating the laws of war and humanity, but of plotting and waging aggressive war. Critics contended this was *ex post facto* procedure—that plotting aggression had been defined as a crime after the deed was done. Justice Jackson argued, however, that since the Paris Pact of 1928 and other treaties had condemned recourse to war, the actions of German leaders had been clearly illegal. The trial, lasting more than ten months, resulted in conviction of all but three defendants. Eleven were sentenced to be hanged and eight were given prison terms. Although Goering escaped execution by a last-minute suicide, the other death sentences were carried out on October 16, 1946.

Lesser criminals were also tried and punished. Thirty-six officials and guards from the infamous Dachau concentration camp were condemned to death by an American military tribunal, while several German civilians who had participated in the murder of American aviators met a similar fate. In the end, nearly three hundred Germans were executed for war crimes by United States authorities.

Occupation Problems: Japan

The postwar situation in Japan differed from that in Germany in certain important respects. First, the surrender negotiations had resulted in an Allied agreement to retain the emperor and govern through him, with the eventual decision regarding his status being left to the Japanese people. Second, Japan was occupied for the most part by American forces, giving American officials the principal authority in formulating occupation policy.

Supreme Allied Commander MacArthur exercised enormous powers over the defeated enemy. During the crucial first weeks of the occupation, this authority was controlled only by his superiors in Washington. Russian and other Allied protests brought some modification by the end of 1945, when the Big Three foreign ministers meeting in Moscow established a Far Eastern Commission representing eleven nations. This body, with its headquarters in Washington, formulated principles to govern the control of Japan, and the Allied Council, representing the United States, the Soviet Union, China, and the British Commonwealth, sat in Tokyo to advise MacArthur on the spot; but the terms of the Moscow agreement still left most power in American hands.

No elaborate system of military government comparable to that in Germany was set up. MacArthur with a small corps of advisers operated through directives to the emperor and the Japanese cabinet. The Imperial General Staff was quickly dissolved and the army demobilized, while the secret police and the jingoistic Black Dragon society were liquidated. The Japanese press was freed from Japanese censorship, though subjected to American control, political prisoners were released, and civil liberties proclaimed.

Political institutions were substantially altered by a new constitution drafted with MacArthur's approval in March, 1946. This defined the emperor's power as derived from "the sovereign will of the people" and required cabinet approval for all his acts in state matters. The Diet, elected by universal suffrage, exercised supreme legislative power and appointed the premier and the supreme court. This constitution renounced war and the use of force and forbade the maintenance of an army, navy, or air force.

In other particulars, the treatment of Japan followed the German precedent more closely. Similar provision was made for collecting reparations by confiscating external assets and removing factories and machinery. The arrest and trial of war criminals were likewise stipulated. American tribunals ordered the execution of Generals Yamashita and Homa after hearing testimony of Japanese atrocities in the Philippines under the defendants' commands. Former Premier Tojo and othe major leaders were tried and sentenced to death by a special international tribunal like that at Nuremberg.

The Iron Curtain

The Axis defeat for the time being ended all threat of aggression from Germany and Japan, but grave new problems arose out of the power vacuum left by these two great nations. With France and Britain too weakened by the war to play an important role in world politics, only two major powers remained: Soviet Russia and the United States.

Neither the American people nor their government at first realized the full implications of the new situation. They had renounced isolation to be sure, but they were thinking of American participation in world affairs as confined largely to temporary occupation duties in the defeated countries and long-range cooperation with the UN. Under clamorous pressure to "Bring Daddy Home," American forces were withdrawn from distant bases and demobilized at a rapid rate. The army and navy that totaled over twelve million in June, 1945, had shrunk to two million a year later.

As the American turtle withdrew into its shell, its Russian counterpart stretched out its neck more and more boldly. Even before Roosevelt died, he and Churchill protested to Stalin that a Communist government in Poland violated the Yalta pledge of "free and unfettered elections." And what happened in Poland was only one in a chain of similar episodes. Taking full advantage of European chaos, the Soviet Union steadily expanded its influence by incorporating the prewar Baltic states and part of Poland within its own boundaries and by supporting Communist or pro-Russian regimes in the neighboring states of eastern Europe and the Balkans. The United States protested repeatedly against the undemocratic character of these governments and their violation of American property rights.

Similar concern was aroused over Soviet policy in other parts of the world. The Russians were accused of promoting the interest of local Communist parties in Germany and Austria, of seeking to coerce Turkey into surrendering control of the Dardenelles, and of intriguing in the politices of Iran and other Middle Eastern countries. Suspicion extended to the Far East, where the Soviet shadow fell menacingly over China, Manchuria, and Korea.

Many Americans were reluctant to believe that their recent ally was engaged in anything more sinister than defensive steps based upon an exaggerated estimate of her security needs. American public opinion at first gave a rather tepid response to Churchill's grim warning during a speech at Fulton, Missouri, in March, 1946, when he declared, "From Stettin in the

Baltic to Trieste in the Adriatic, an iron curtain has descended across the continent." Condemning the "police governments" of the Russian sphere, he called for Anglo-American cooperation against the growing menace.

President Truman, on the other hand, needed little convincing of the need for stronger resistance to Communist expansion. His attempts to negotiate with the Soviet Union on a variety of issues had been a continuing disillusionment. Throughout 1946 and early 1947 events moved relentlessly toward the formation of two hostile camps in world politics; one centered around the Soviet Union, the other around the United States.

Diplomatic Bickering

Drafting peace treaties in this atmosphere was a long, arduous task. Throughout 1946 the foreign ministers of the victorious powers struggled with those for Italy, Bulgaria, Rumania, Hungary, and Finland. Three questions aroused particular controversy. The first, regarding disposition of the Italian colonial empire, was compromised fairly early by agreement that it should continue under British administration for one year and then the final status would be determined by the Big Four or by the UN Assembly were the Big Four unable to agree. The second concerned the rival claims of Italy and Yugoslavia to Trieste and provoked the greatest bitterness because control over this strategic port was regarded as vital to both blocs. Final agreement was the establishment of the Free Territory of Trieste under a governor responsible to the UN Security Council; in 1954, however, Trieste was partitioned between Italy and Yugoslavia. The third battle was over the navigation of the Danube; the United States wanted free navigation, which the Russians opposed as a covert form of economic imperialism. The United States finally won out.

In his long struggle with the Russian diplomats, Secretary of State Byrnes relied heavily on the support of Democratic Senator Connally and Republican Senator Vandenberg, who accompanied him to all the important conferences. Thus did the Truman administration seek to prevent any repetition of Wilson's unhappy experiences with the upper house. But this bipartisan support did not mean that Byrnes escaped criticism. In a September, 1946, speech, Secretary of Commerce Wallace condemned America's "get tough" policy toward Russia, declaring that the United States had no more business in Eastern Europe political affairs than Russia had in the West. Faced with the unhappy alternative of choosing between Byrnes and Wallace, Truman asked for Wallace's resignation—despite the embarrassing fact that he had previously approved Wallace's speech.

Completion of the satellite treaties cleared the way for consideration of the future of Germany and Austria. The Big Four ministers met for this purpose in Moscow in March, 1947, with Secretary of State George Marshall now the American representative (Byrnes had resigned because of ill health). After a month and a half the conference broke up without agreeing on either a German or Austrian treaty. Among the controversies that led to this deadlock, the reparations issue was the most important. The Russians demanded $10 billion in goods produced by German industry. The Americans and

Britons declared this would so burden German economy that the population would be unable to pay for essential food imports. The form of government for Germany also led to controversy; the Western ministers wanted a federal republic with a weak central government; the Soviet demanded a strongly centralized government, about which Marshall voiced his suspicions in a radio address to the American people:

> Agreement was made impossible because the Soviet Union insisted upon proposals which would have established in Germany a centralized government, adapted to the seizure of absolute control of a country which would be doomed economically through inadequate area and excessive population and would be mortgaged to turn over a large part of its production as reparations.

This mutual suspicion made it impossible to map out the future of Germany. Yet until a German treaty was completed, order and security could hardly be restored in Europe.

Frustrations in the United Nations

When the UN operations began, most Americans still hoped that the One World ideal of World War II days could be achieved. To the organization meeting at London in January, 1946, the United States sent a distinguished delegation headed by Secretary Byrnes. American interest in the new experiment was intensified when the Security Council began the continuous functioning for which the Charter provided. First in temporary New York quarters and later in the beautiful buildings constructed in New York City on an East River site contributed by John D. Rockefeller, Jr., the UN sessions became a favorite attraction for sightseers.

Despite the hopeful beginning, the UN was at once dangerously involved in the great contest for power between the Soviet Union and the United States. Russian diplomats condemned what they claimed was British imperialism in Syria, Indonesia, and Greece, while Britain and the United States denounced Soviet conduct in Iran, which they said must be evacuated by Soviet troops by the beginning of March, 1946, if earlier treaties were to be respected. Gromyko insisted, however, that this was a matter for direct settlement between the two parties. When the other members of the Security Council refused to change their position, he walked out and refused to attend subsequent sessions in which the issue was discussed. Tension subsided, however, when Soviet troops were finally withdrawn and outstanding controversies between Russia and Iran were compromised through direct negotiations by the two countries.

The UN did help settle other troublesome issues. When the newly founded Israel became involved in war with her Arab neighbors in 1948, hostilities were ended through the skillful efforts of the UN mediator, Ralph Bunche, an American black. In similar fashion, the controversy between the Netherlands and its recently emancipated colony, the Republic of Indonesia, was satisfactorily mediated. Optimists could also be comforted by the progress made in many nonpolitical UN activities: the negotiation of international agreements outlawing genocide (race murder) and defining basic human rights, the study of international economic problems, the promotion of cultural exchange, the control of trade in narcotics, and the provision for emergency aid for afflicted children in backward nations.

All such UN success was overshadowed, however, by increasing conflict between the Communist bloc and the Western powers. Russian obstructionism prevented organization of the UN military forces provided for in the Charter. By the end of 1950, the Soviet Union had used its Security Council veto fifty times; when the Council instituted discussions that could not be vetoed, Soviet delegates resorted to boycotts, sometimes absenting themselves for many weeks. Russia also refused to participate in the FAO, the International Bank, and several other UN agencies.

The Problem of Disarmament

Among the problems the UN faced, none was more significant than that of mounting armaments. Heavy military expenditures were a burden on the world economy, and the development of new weapons monopolized the efforts of scientists and engineers to the exclusion of more constructive tasks. Most serious of all, the atomic bomb development was a warning that, unless controlled, the human race might be wiped out.

The United States earnestly tried to safeguard the world from the horrors of nuclear warfare. At the opening session of the UN Atomic Energy Commission in June, 1946, Bernard Baruch proposed to establish an international authority to control all potentially dangerous atomic-energy activities. The bomb itself should be outlawed, and the international authority should be able to punish violators. The United States promised to stop manufacturing bombs, dispose of its stock of bombs, and make available its scientific information after the international authority was effectively operating. As Baruch grimly said, the choice was between "World Peace or World Destruction."

Although the American proposal seemed generous to most nations, the Soviet Union viewed it with suspicion. She opposed broad international control and particularly the stipulation that acts of the new atomic authority could not be vetoed. The first Russian counterproposal was for a simple renunciation of atomic weapons without provision for international control or inspection. In subsequent UN debates she changed her position somewhat: the need of an international authority and some form of inspection was conceded, but fundamental differences remained. Russia insisted that, as a prerequisite to international control, atomic bombs be prohibited and all atomic energy plants turned over to international management. The United States refused to agree until the international control was made effective. She wanted the power of inspection to be broad and exempt from veto; the Russians wanted to define the control more narrowly. Finally, and most important, the United States asserted that once a treaty had been approved, there should be no legal right, by veto or otherwise, whereby a willful violator could escape punishment. The Soviets wanted to retain enforcement within the Security Council, where each of the Big Five had a veto.

Meantime, negotiations for general disarmament marked time. By unanimous agreement in December, 1946, the UN Assembly approved a sweeping resolution to formulate   practical disarmament measures that would be presented to a special Assembly session, for the elimination of weapons of mass destruction, for international inspection and safeguards against violators, for the establishment of an international police force, for balanced withdrawal of troops from ex-enemy countries, and for gradual reduction of national armed forces. But the Soviets wanted to consider the atomic energy problem as one phase of the whole disarmament problem; the United States insisted that this issue must have priority. Whatever the relative merits of these two lines of procedure, it was obvious that no realistic disarmament could be achieved until Russia and America worked out their differences.

The Truman Doctrine

Britain and America felt growing concern as more and more of Europe fell under control of pro-Russian governments. By early 1947 these included Finland, Poland, Hungary, Yugoslavia, Rumania, and Bulgaria, as well as Soviet occupation zones in Germany and Austria. In Italy and France, moreover, there were powerful Communist parties.

Greece had an anti-Communist government, but its hold on the country was insecure because of desperate economic conditions and the threats against it from guerrillas in the north. It was feared that a rebel victory would extend Russian influence over yet another country and one of critical importance because it was near the strategic Dardenelles and the oil-rich Middle East.

For some time Britain had provided the threatened regime with military and economic support, but in March, 1947, England's own economic position was so precarious that she would have to withdraw her help from Greece at the end of the month. Truman, having decided to take over this responsibility, asked Congress on March 12 to approve a $400 million program of economic and military aid not only for Greece, but for Turkey as well. In what was promptly dubbed the Truman Doctrine, he said:

I believe that it must be the policy of the United States to support free peoples who are resisting attempted subjugation by armed minorities or by outside pressures.

I believe that we must assist free peoples to work out their own destinies in their own way.

I believe that our help should be primarily through economic and financial aid which is essential to economic stability and orderly political processes.

Not since Pearl Harbor had there been such widespread controversy over foreign policy as the Truman Doctrine provoked. Many Americans supported it to check Soviet influence. Others criticized it as a form of economic imperialism, an interference with the domestic affairs of other nations, and the beginning of a dangerous adventure in power politics that might end in war. Henry Wallace was its sharpest critic.

Many who did not go as far as Wallace did regretted that America had taken unilateral action without trying to use UN machinery. Truman defended himself by saying the UN was not yet equipped to deal with such problems, and Warren Austin, the American representative on the Security Council, argued that the Doctrine was intended to strengthen, not weaken, collective security. Nevertheless, the supporters thought it best to accept the so-called Vandenberg amendment, under which Congress directed the President to withdraw any or all aid if the Security Council found its continuance unnecessary or undesirable. The United States waived its veto right on this issue.

After hot debate, Congress in May, 1947, approved spending $400 million on Greek and Turkish aid, and later appropriations made it possible to continue the policy. In many ways the Truman program was a striking success. The Greek government was sufficiently strengthened to defeat its enemies. In October, 1949, the long civil war was ended, not only as a result of American aid, but of Marshal Tito's action in closing the Yugoslav frontier to Communist guerrillas after his break with Stalin. Economic rehabilitation also made good progress with the repair of highways, bridges, and railroads, the resettlement of refugees, the expansion of agriculture, and a health program that reduced greatly malaria.

The European Recovery Program

Greece and Turkey were not the only nations needing economic aid. Therefore in the spring of 1947 Congress appropriated $350 million for relief supplies for Italy, Austria, Poland, China, Trieste, and Greece. Somewhat earlier, Britain, France, and Italy had successfully obtained American postwar loans. The Soviet Union had also sought American credit to finance exports, but strained relations had delayed the negotiations.

By June, 1947, it was clear that the whole question of American financial assistance to the rest of the world required review and clarification. How much would the United States need to spend? Should its aid be available to all European countries or only to those shunning Communism? On June 5, in an address at Harvard, Secretary of State Marshall announced a healthy new approach to the problem:

Our policy is not directed against any country or doctrine, but against hunger, poverty, desperation and chaos. Its purpose should be the revival of a working economy in the world so as to permit the emergence of political and social conditions in which free institutions can exist. Such assistance I am convinced must not be on a piecemeal basis as various crises develop. . . . The initiative I think must come from Europe. . . . The program should be a joint one, agreed to by a number of, if not all, the European nations.

Britain and France accepted this suggestion with alacrity by promptly initiating steps to formulate a broad European rehabilitation program and urging the Soviet Union to join in the enterprise. But Russia, unwilling to cooperate in a project requiring exchange of statistical information and giving American capitalism a dominant position in the European economy, refused to attend a general conference, as did eight of its satellites. Representatives of sixteen other nations, however, met in Paris from July to September, 1947, where they promised to help themselves as much as possible and formulated a four-year recovery program that would require some $15 billion in American aid.

The Marshall Plan was subjected to careful scrutiny in the United States. Senator Taft was among those who questioned whether his country could do what was asked without weakening its own economy, but congressional misgivings were largely forgotten after the Communists seized control of Czechoslovakia in February, 1948, in a coup that shocked Americans. On April 3, Truman signed the Foreign Assistance Act of 1948, which appropriated $5.3 billion for the first year of Marshall plan aid.[5]

Truman appointed Paul Hoffman, president of the Studebacker Corporation, to head the Economic Cooperation Administration (ECA), responsible for making grants and loans under the European Recovery Program (ERP). Into Europe now flowed grain to alleviate hunger, coal, petroleum products, cotton, and other raw materials to feed lagging industries, and machinery to increase future production. This flood of exports had, of course, a highly stimulating influence on the American economy as well.

The European economic problems were serious, for to the devastations of war were added exasperating postwar difficulties. The continuing "cold war" between western and eastern Europe disrupted normal trade between the industrialized and the agricultural regions of the continent. The continued partition of Germany was an especially disrupting factor, while the independence movements in the colonial empires of western European states reduced the flow of badly needed raw materials and revenue. All these conditions contributed to Europe's dependence on imports from the Western Hemisphere. Since the war-ravaged continent could produce little for export and since American tariffs still restricted the sale of foreign goods in the United States, the problem of finding dollars to pay for imports was perplexing. American aid under ERP permitted the temporary bridging of this "dollar gap," but the solution depended on increasing European exports and decreasing imports until trade was in reasonable balance. This was the long-range objective of the European Recovery Program.

Optimistic Americans hoped that western European nations might merge their economies by eliminating tariff barriers and trade quotas and adopting a uniform currency. Economic nationalism, however, proved too deep to permit such immediate reforms. The various countries still followed policies that sometimes conflicted with the interests of their neighbors and those of western Europe as a whole.

Despite such disappointments, ERP was on the whole a distinct success. Congress appropriated some $11 billion during its first three years. An ECA report in 1951 stressed such impressive gains as the following: overall industrial production in western European was running 40 per cent higher than it had been in 1938; harvests were about 10 per cent above their prewar

---

[5] Economic aid was granted to Britain, France, Italy, Belgium, the Netherlands, Luxembourg, Norway, Sweden, Denmark, Austria, Greece, Portugal, Switzerland, Turkey, Ireland, Iceland, and Nationalist China. Military assistance to Greece and Turkey was also extended.

levels; economic recovery in Britain and Ireland had advanced to a point where those two nations were able to get along without further aid.

A principal objective of American economic aid was to strengthen democratic regimes and to halt the spread of Communism. This aspect of ERP also appeared to succeed. The turning point was the Italian election of April, 1948. Backed by a militant party membership of 2.3 million—probably the largest Communist group outside of Russia—the Italian Reds threatened to gain control of the Chamber of Deputies. To prevent this, Secretary Marshall warned that a Communist Italy would receive no ERP help; Italo-Americans wrote thousands of letters to relatives and friends in the old country to influence their votes. This pressure, together with the active intervention of Roman Catholic bishops and priests, brought victory to the conservative De Gasperi government and a setback for the Communists. Subsequent elections in France and West Germany marked similar checks to Communist voting strength.

Struggle for Germany

As the cold war became increasingly bitter, the importance of Germany became obvious. With its large population, heavy industry, and scientific knowledge, a reunited Germany would give an overwhelming preponderance to whichever side gained its support. Throughout 1948 and early 1949 a dangerous contest to win the upper hand was in progress.

Unable to reach agreement with Russia, statesmen from Britain, France, and the United States, together with those from the Benelux countries (Belgium, the Netherlands, and Luxembourg), met in London from February to June, 1948, to break the stalemate on German policy. They decided to merge their occupation zones in a new West German state. To minimize the danger of future German aggression, they planned a federal rather than a centralized government and agreed that the strategic Ruhr industries be controlled by an International Authority. With these safeguards, West Germany's economic revival would be encouraged as a necessary condition to Marshall Plan success. As a first step, new "West marks" were to be substituted for the worthless reichsmarks then flooding the country.

Russia denounced these measures as contrary to the Potsdam Agreement. To counter the new currency, the Soviets issued their own East marks. Then, under the pretext that the West marks in Berlin made drastic control measures necessary, Russia in April, 1948, began interfering with railroad, highway, and canal traffic from the Western occupation zones across the hundred-mile Soviet-controlled corridor to Berlin. Finally, on June 24, all traffic over that route was stopped—probably to prevent the Western powers from putting into effect their own plans for a West German state and to force unification on Russian terms. Failing this, the Soviets hoped to force their rivals out of Berlin—giving Russia a great psychological advantage in the struggle for all of Germany.

Within the three Western sectors of Berlin, more than two million persons, now deprived of essential food and fuel, looked to the Western powers for help. First, a counterblockade of the Soviet zone was promptly imposed. Much more spectacular, however, was the gigantic effort to supply Berlin by air. Pressing into use every available cargo plane, daring pilots carried into the city some four thousand tons of food and other necessities each day.

At first few observers believed that this airlift could succeed, regarding it as a makeshift, pending some diplomatic solution. A few impatient Americans called for military action to convoy trains and highway caravans into the city, but responsible statesmen ruled out any step that might plunge the world into war. Instead, the airlift was continued week after week with increasing effectiveness. Despite predictions that bad flying weather and heavy coal loads would defeat the operation during the winter, the flights continued successfully.

The arduous service of the airlift pilots won an important victory for the Western powers. Instead of demonstrating to the hapless Berliners their dependence on Russia, the blockade intensified the anti-Communist feeling of all Germans not under Soviet control. Finally recognizing the failure of its policy, the Soviet government lifted the blockade on May 12, ~~1946~~.[6] The *1949* Western powers thereupon agreed to another Big Four foreign ministers' conference on the whole German problem, but this meeting was no more successful than earlier ones had been.

From September, 1948, to May, 1949, delegates from the three Western zones met at Bonn to frame a constitution for the West German State, officially known as the Federal Republic of Germany. The original members were to be the eleven states included within the British, French, and American zones, but provision was made for the admission of others in the hope that the five states of the Soviet zone would eventually join. The relations of the Federal Republic with the three Western powers were defined in an Occupation Statute. Occupation troops remained in their three respective zones, but Allied military government was replaced by an Allied High Commission, composed of civilians.

In a countermove, the Communists of the Soviet zone proclaimed a German Democratic Republic, with its capital at Berlin. The effect of four years of military occupation was thus to divide Germany into two nations, each desirous of absorbing the other on its own terms. Although West Germany had more than twice the population, as well as much greater resources in coal, steel plants, and other industries, East Germany was not without its own advantages. More than half of the prewar German food production came from this area. Moreover, a government with its capital at Berlin would appeal to German nationalism.

The longer tension persisted between the Soviet Union and the Western democracies, the more each side modified its German policy. No longer was the principal objective that of keeping the former enemy weak and incapable of military action. Instead, the major consideration was how German resources and manpower might be brought to bear in a future conflict between the East and the West. In this dangerous game, the Soviet occupation authorities played one card by granting a general amnesty to former

---

[6] During the course of the airlift, pilots made 277,264 flights to Berlin and carried 2,343,315 tons of necessities to the inhabitants.

Nazis and officers of Hitler's army, while the Western policymakers played another by curtailing their program for dismantling German war industries. In the Soviet zone the core of a future East German army was created by organizing an efficient, well-armed, and thoroughly loyal Communist police force of some fifty thousand. This stimulated American officials to consider the rearming of West Germany.

Defense in the West

Believing that democratic failure to make a united stand had been an important cause of World War II, Western leaders tried to avoid the same error in dealing with the new Communist threat. In January, 1948, Britain offered to enter a defensive union with its neighbors across the Channel. The February coup of the Communists in Czechoslovakia added urgency to the British overture, and in March, 1948, Britain, France, and the Benelux countries signed a fifty-year military and economic assistance treaty at Brussels.

This Brussels Pact was only the first step toward adequate security. Whether united or divided, western Europe was indefensible against Soviet armed attack without strong help from America. Would the United States complete its renunciation of isolationism by promising to aid foreign nations resisting aggression? To be sure, a general obligation of this nature had been undertaken in the UN Charter, but Soviet obstructionism had made the UN an uncertain factor in international affairs. The Senate acknowledged that something more was needed when, on June 11, 1948, it adopted the Vandenberg Resolution, authorizing the government to develop collective defense arrangements within the UN Charter and to associate the United States with them. Although the issue was overshadowed by the presidential campaign of 1948, the Berlin blockade and other Communist actions made a Western defense system more and more necessary. Truman, in his inaugural address, pledged his second administration to this objective.

Such were the circumstances behind the North Atlantic Treaty, signed at Washington on April 4, 1949, in which the twelve signatories [7] agreed

that an armed attack against one or more of them in Europe or North America shall be considered an attack against all of them and that in the exercise of the right of individual or collective self-defense, recognized by Article 51 of the United Nations Charter, they will take such action as deemed necessary, including the use of armed force, to restore and maintain the security of the North Atlantic area. The attack and counter-measures shall immediately be reported to the United Nations Security Council, and action shall be terminated when the Council has taken measures to restore international peace.

Although care had been taken to reconcile the new pact with the UN Charter, many Americans regretted the treaty as a step toward substituting regional defense arrangements for the general security of a world organiza-

[7] The United States, Canada, Britain, France, Belgium, the Netherlands, Luxembourg, Norway, Denmark, Iceland, Italy, and Portugal.

tion. Senator Taft and other Republicans criticized the implied obligation to supply arms to the new allies. But ratification was so strongly urged by such Republican Senators as Vandenberg and Dulles that on July 21, 1949, the upper house approved the treaty, 82 to 13.

As predicted, the next urgent question was that of supplying arms to the other members of the North Atlantic Treaty Organization (NATO). Although many legislators were dismayed by the prospect of new expenditures and enlarged power for the President, world events crumpled the opposition. Truman's announcement on September 23, 1949, that Russia also had the secret of the atomic bomb shattered any illusion that American monopoly of this weapon was a sufficient guarantee against Soviet attack. On September 27 Congress overwhelmingly passed the Mutual Defense Assistance Act, approving $1 billion for arming western Europe and $314 million for threatened areas elsewhere.

The first American arms shipments reached France and Italy in April, 1950, without serious incident, despite Communist threats to halt their movement by strikes and sabotage. Throughout 1950 Communist tactics featured "peace congresses" and "peace petitions" to convince western Europeans that Russia had no aggressive designs and that "capitalist warmongers" in America were the real world threat. Such propaganda was not without its appeal to war-weary peoples.

Despite these obstacles, plans for western Europe defense became more definite in 1950 and 1951. In September, 1950, the North Atlantic Council decided to create "in the shortest possible time, an integrated military force adequate for the defense of the freedom of Europe," and two months later Eisenhower was appointed NATO Supreme Commander.

These plans largely hinged on the extent the resources and manpower of West Germany could be utilized. Secretary Acheson wanted ten German divisions for the Atlantic Pact army, but France opposed this because of vivid memories of three German invasions within seventy years. Other plans that would have dispersed German combat units through the NATO army were rejected by the Adenauer government, which was reluctant to rearm unless German nationalism was satisfied by the creation of German divisions. This problem was still unsolved when the Truman administration ended, but certain intermediate steps had been taken. In October, 1951, Congress declared the war with Germany at an end, and in 1952 the Bonn government was granted almost complete sovereignty. Formal military occupation by American, British, and French troops was ended, but the Western powers, with Bonn's consent, kept troops at German bases as a deterrent to Russian aggression.

Strange Bedfellows

American efforts to check Soviet imperialism brought a change of policy toward two other European countries. Although Communists seized power in Yugoslavia after World War II, Marshal Tito proved much less manageable than puppet heads in other Soviet-dominated countries. The Cominform—the Communist International in its postwar reincarnation—

denounced Tito in an attempt to overthrow his leadership, but he clung to power and maintained his country's independence. America encouraged his defiance through trade deals and relief to prevent famine. Although aid to Yugoslavia prevented complete Russian domination of the Balkans and encouraged defiance of Moscow by other Communist regimes, the policy was criticized by Americans who condemned the Tito government as both totalitarian and antireligious. Even more sharply attacked was the closer American relations with Spain, where Franco, once the protégé of Mussolini and Hitler, still maintained a dictatorial regime.

In Latin America, too, the United States had to choose between greater and lesser evils. During World War II Argentina, from the United States point of view, behaved very badly. While the other Latin-American states gave moral and material support to the UN cause by declaring war, curbing Axis activities, and supplying strategic materials, Argentina refused to cooperate. A fierce competitor with the United States in agricultural exports and jealous of the North American nation's leading role in hemisphere affairs, she had become strongly nationalistic. Many of her wealthy leaders believed in totalitarian government and sympathized with the Axis.

Fear of economic sanctions by the United States and Britain induced President Pedro Ramirez to sever relations with Germany in January, 1944, but this step was unpopular with the Argentine military. Toward the end of February, the so-called Colonels' Clique overthrew Ramirez and placed Edelmiro Farrell in the presidency, with the real power in the hands of Colonel Juan Perón. The United States refused to recognize the new regime and later withdrew its ambassador, froze Argentine credits, and barred American ships from Argentine ports.

All the republics except Argentina were represented at a Mexico City conference held in anticipation of the end of the war in February and March, 1945. There was framed the Act of Chapultepec, which read in part:

That every attack of a State against the integrity or the inviolability of the territory or against the sovereignty or political independence of an American State, shall . . . be considered as an act of aggression against the other States which sign this act. . . .

That in case acts of aggression occur, or there may be reasons to believe that an aggression is being prepared by any other State against . . . an American State, the States signatory to this act will consult amongst themselves in order to agree upon the measures it may be advisable to take.

Because the act covered aggression both from without and within the hemisphere, it was interpreted as being largely directed against Argentina. Moreover, the willingness of other American states to rely upon the armed forces of the United States showed that the old fear of *Yanqui* imperialism was largely gone.

The Mexico City conference also provided for cooperation in the postwar period and support of the proposed UN. Although Argentina's recent pro-Axis leanings were deplored, the door was left open for her to resume her place in the hemisphere family by declaring war against the Axis and approving the conference resolutions. These steps the Farrell-Perón government took in a last-minute effort to escape its isolated position. Despite Soviet objections, Argentina obtained a place among the UN charter members.

Events of the succeeding months gave the United States reason to doubt the sincerity of Argentina's conversion. The Perón regime continued its undemocratic policies and allowed Axis exiles a haven on Argentine soil. Therefore the United States threw its weight against the dominant faction, especially in February, 1946, when a "Blue Book" was released by the State Department that provided damning evidence of the pro-Axis course Perón and his associates had followed. Nevertheless Perón won the presidency by a decisive margin.

In a long debate as to the course the United States should follow, one State Department faction wanted to continue the anti-Perón policy; another favored accepting Perón to bring Argentina again into full participation in inter-American affairs. The latter position prevailed and in June, 1947, Truman was ready to include her in discussions for a hemisphere defense pact.

On September 2, 1947, all the hemisphere republics signed the Treaty of Rio de Janeiro, which stated that an armed attack on any American nation would be considered an attack on all American states. The signatories agreed to go to the assistance of the victim of aggression in conformity with Article 51 of the UN Charter, which recognized the right of individual or collective self-defense.

In a further step, the Inter-American Conference at Bogotá in the spring of 1948 established the Organization of American States (OAS), which provided for regular Inter-American conferences and consultations of foreign ministers, for an Advisory Committee, and for a Council of the Organization, made up of one representative of each member state, with headquarters in Washington. The OAS was considered one of the regional associations provided for in the UN Charter. Thus American foreign policy had undergone a significant reorientation, being primarily shaped now by fear of Communism rather than of Fascism.

Troubles in Asia

The policy of "containment," upon which the Truman administration had based its policy toward the Soviet Union was much more difficult to apply in Asia than in Europe. In the West the old established democratic states, even though weakened by war, could be used as bastions of a defense system, but in the Orient all was in flux. Militaristic Japan had been destroyed, but none knew what the new Japan would be like. China was now tragically involved in a renewal of the civil war between the Nationalists and the Communists. Elsewhere the vast populations that had been under colonial rule were demanding and achieving independence.

Fortunately for the United States, the decision to grant Philippine independence had been made before World War II, and it was possible to carry the policy through with a minimum of the bad feeling that accompanied the separation of the European nations from their Asiatic colonies. On July 4,

1946, Truman formally recognized the independence of the Philippines, and the new republic readily agreed to maintain close relations with the United States. Under a ninety-nine-year pact made in 1947, the Filipinos allowed American military and naval bases in the islands.

Most of the other Asiatic nations, however, followed India's example in resisting close ties with either the Communist or anti-Communist blocs. Jealous of their new independence and fearing a revival of Western imperialism as much as they did Soviet aggression, they clung to a policy of neutrality.

What happened in China was particularly unwelcome to American opinion. Under the Yalta agreement, the Soviet Union entered the war against Japan and took over certain Japanese privileges in Manchuria as compensation. As a result, the Russians were able to arrange that most captured Japanese war material fell into Chinese Communist hands. This was only one of many factors strengthening the Reds and weakening Chiang Kai-shek in the months following World War II.

Truman believed that continued civil war would not only be a tragedy for the Chinese, but threaten world peace if the United States and the Soviet Union became involved in aiding the two factions. In December, 1945, he sent General Marshall as a special envoy to China to mediate between the warring factions, but in the end compromise proved unacceptable to the extremists in both camps.

In January, 1947, America terminated its mediation efforts and withdrew virtually all the twelve thousand American military personnel that had been in China since VJ day. Although determined not to risk American troops in the Chinese caldron, Truman still helped the battered Nationalist forces with arms and supplies.

Yet the war continued to go badly for the Nationalists, and in 1949 their whole front collapsed. Driven from one temporary capital after another, the Chiang regime finally abandoned the mainland in December, 1949, and established itself on Formosa. Virtually all of China thus fell under the rule of Mao Tse-tung.

Nationalist China's collapse posed problems of fundamental importance to the Truman administration. Should the United States increase its aid to Chiang, supply more arms and technical assistance, and even send American troops to defend Formosa and help reconquer the mainland? Such was the policy advocated by certain influential Congressmen and publishers, backed by the so-called China lobby—a somewhat mysterious, but apparently well-financed, pressure group. Or should the United States recognize Mao's government, let it represent China in the UN, and hope that Chinese nationalism would prevent China from becoming completely subservient to Moscow? This was the policy favored by Britain, which recognized the Communists soon after Mao completed his conquest of the mainland.

The Truman administration finally decided against both alternatives. A voluminous White Paper, issued by the State Department in August, 1949, revealed the discouraging efforts to aid Chiang and end the civil war. Between 1945 and 1949 the United States had given $3 billion in aid to the Chinese Nationalists, but this had been largely wasted through the inefficiency and corruption of the Nationalist government. A major share of the American arms was easily captured by the Communists. Also the Chiang regime had stubbornly resisted American political and military advice and suggestions for reform. As a result, Truman opposed further aid to the Nationalists and rejected Republican proposals that American troops help defend Formosa. On the other hand, the administration refused to recognize the Chinese Communist government, which had seized American consular property and signed a treaty of alliance with the Soviet Union. Persisting in this policy of nonrecognition, the United States took the lead in opposing the transference of China's seat in the UN to the Communist government.

The Chinese Communist victory was a staggering setback for the anti-Communist cause. Was the disaster inevitable, or could it have been prevented by greater foresight and wisdom? The Republicans blamed the Democrats for what had happened. The mischief, they alleged, had begun with Roosevelt's folly at Yalta; it had been continued by the blindness of Truman, Marshall, and Acheson in failing to recognize the seriousness of the Communist threat and withholding from Chiang full American support. The Democrats, while deploring what had happened, argued that the United States had given Chiang as much aid as it could, short of an all-out military effort that the American people would not have supported, and insisted that the Nationalists were largely responsible for their own defeat.

War in Korea

On June 25, 1950, the most serious international crisis since World War II suddenly developed when the Communist armies of North Korea invaded South Korea. The existence of these two states was another unfortunate result of Soviet-American hostility. Korea, liberated in 1945 after thirty-five years of Japanese rule, had been divided into two occupation zones: Soviet troops were in control north of the thirty-eighth parallel and American forces south of that line. As in Germany, mutual suspicion led to the establishment of two governments, each claiming to be the legal authority for the whole nation. The South Korean government, headed by Syngman Rhee, was set up under the observation of a UN committee and therefore possessed superior credentials in all but Communist eyes. By July, 1949, the Soviet Union and the United States had both withdrawn their troops, but they continued to give aid and advice to the two Korean regimes.

Under these circumstances, the North Korean invasion seemed a particularly flagrant defiance of the UN. Truman had to decide quickly whether the United States should allow South Korea to defend itself as best it could, or take the lead in proposing strong UN countermeasures. On the very day of the invasion, the Security Council, by a vote of 9 to 0—with Yugoslavia abstaining, condemned the North Korean action and called for withdrawal of its forces. Ironically, a Soviet boycott of the Council on the China issue made it possible for this important action to be taken without a Russian veto.

News from the Korean battlefields soon revealed that no paper declaration could save the South Korean Republic. Well-disciplined and well-equipped with Russian guns and tanks, the Communist armies rapidly overran the enemy defenses. If aggression were to be repelled, American arms would be required. Therefore, on June 27, 1950, Truman ordered the United States air and sea forces to support the hard-pressed South Korean armies. He also announced a significant policy change toward Formosa: since Communist seizure of that island would threaten American forces in Korea, he ordered the Seventh Fleet to neutralize the area by preventing both Communist attacks on the island and Nationalist forays against the mainland. Once again the United States was firmly supported by the UN Security Council, which voted seven to one to call upon UN members to give military assistance in repelling the North Korean invasion. Hope that aid could be restricted to air and naval support soon ended with the news of further South Korean defeats; on June 30 American ground troops were flown into Korea from Japan.

Truman's prompt measures had the support of almost all Americans except the Communists and their fellow travelers. Republicans who had been sharply critical of the Truman-Acheson China policy applauded this stiffer position and Henry Wallace, long an administration critic, announced his support of the UN action.

Within the UN itself the situation became more difficult in August, 1950, when the Soviets ended their boycott and returned to a policy of obstructionism in the Security Council. Acheson, however, obtained enlarged Assembly powers that largely circumvented the Soviet's ability to prevent UN action through the veto.

Although this decision to combat aggression in Korea had strong national and international support, the military problems were serious. The UN army, commanded by Douglas MacArthur, eventually included units from a dozen or more countries, but the major burden was borne by the United States. American occupation troops from Japan were poorly equipped for savage mountain fighting and reinforcements drawn from the American homeland were ill prepared for war. Therefore, South Korean and American forces suffered a series of defeats that threatened disaster. In August, 1950, the UN army held only a small bridgehead around the South Korean port of Pusan.

On September 15, however, MacArthur suddenly seized the offensive with an amphibious landing at Inchon on the west coast, near the former capital of Seoul. This bold maneuver was followed by rapid UN advances that soon cleared South Korea up to the thirty-eighth parallel. Although South Korean troops pushed into enemy territory as early as October 1, the main forces halted temporarily to await a clear mandate for the UN. There was some opposition to authorizing MacArthur to cross the parallel. India warned that an invasion of North Korea might bring Communist China into the war; but spokesmen for the United States and other Western nations minimized this possibility. On October 7 the UN Assembly overwhelmingly recommended that "all appropriate steps be taken to ensure conditions of stability throughout Korea."

MacArthur made the most of his new authority. As North Korean resistance largely collapsed, UN forces swept northward, captured the Communist capital, Pyongyang, on October 20, 1950. This period of easy victories ended six days later when, for the first time, the UN army was

Assault on a Communist-held hill in Korea, 1951. (U.S. Army Photo.)

opposed by Chinese Communist "volunteer" units. After sharp fighting with this new enemy, the UN forces fell back some one hundred miles. The Chinese did not then press their offensive, but withdrew to the north, arousing hope that their intervention was of limited character.

The question of what to do next aroused serious disagreement. The Europeans, alarmed by the Chinese intervention and fearing that the war might broaden into general hostilities, wanted no further UN advance until a serious effort was made to settle the issue by diplomacy. Although Communist China rejected an invitation to explain its action in Korea, it sent a delegation to the UN to charge the United States with aggression against Formosa. Diplomats hoped that this contact with the Mao regime might open the way to a Korean settlement.

But events took a turn that ended all hopes for a quick peace. On November 24, 1950—the very day the Chinese delegation arrived in New York, MacArthur ordered a full-scale offensive north to the Yalu River, the boundary between Korea and Manchuria. This, the general declared, would end the war and allow the withdrawal of UN forces, with hostilities over before Christmas.

MacArthur's "end-the-war" offensive, instead, brought near-disaster to his army. Instead of the 100,000 Chinese troops estimated in UN intelligence reports, nearly 300,000 had secretly massed in the North Korean mountains. They allowed the UN forces to press forward to within fifty miles of the frontier before springing the trap in a huge counteroffensive that split the Tenth Corps in the northeast from the Eighth Army in the west. The Tenth Corps, after a desperate struggle to avoid encirclement, was finally evacuated from Hungnam, where it was incorporated with the Eighth Army, which had retreated to the thirty-eighth parallel.

China's full scale intervention and the great UN defeat plunged America and Europe into the bleakest pessimism. MacArthur was bitterly criticized for his advance so near the Chinese frontier, for proceeding on faulty intelligence, and for deploying his men so that they were easily split. The Peiping radio boasted of the Chinese intention to drive the UN troops into the sea—and such seemed to be a possibility when 1951 opened. Plans were openly discussed for an evacuation to Japan if worst came to worst.

On the diplomatic front matters were just as bad. The Chinese Communist delegation to the UN denounced American imperialism, demanded

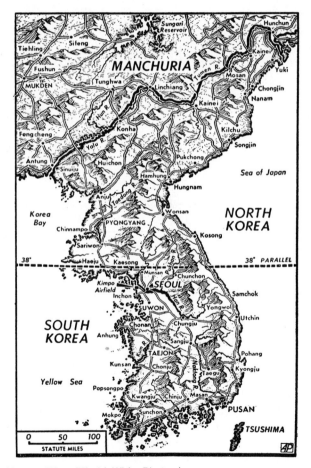

Map of the Korean War. (World Wide Photos.)

UN evacuation of Korea, Communist control of Formosa, and representation for their country in the UN. Still hoping for peace, the UN Assembly appointed a truce commission, but all overtures were defeated. After long debate, the Assembly on February 2, 1951, finally found Communist China guilty of aggression in Korea.

By the end of January, danger that the Communist armies could push the UN forces into the sea largely disappeared. Passing again to the offensive, the UN army, aided by Sabrejet planes and long-range bombers, recaptured Inchon and Seoul in a campaign to wear down the enemy. But if fear of disastrous UN defeat lessened, belief in a possible decisive victory did not revive.

Truman Versus MacArthur

The recess on domestic politics that followed the outbreak of the war did not last long. As the conflict dragged on with lengthening casualty lists, the public found an outlet for its frustrations in blaming the Truman administration. Republicans charged the Communist attack had been invited by the weak American policy toward Asia. Truman and Acheson were further blamed for fighting a limited "police action," instead of the full-scale war that might bring decisive victory.

The controversy over strategy became dramatized as a personal struggle between Truman and MacArthur, a struggle that had been building for many months. Truman had emphasized that the neutralization of Formosa was a temporary policy and that the final disposition of the island would be left to the UN. MacArthur expressed disapproval in a message prepared in August, 1950, for a meeting of the Veterans of Foreign Wars. Learning of this message shortly before it was to be delivered, the President ordered its withdrawal, but it was too late to prevent wide publication of the general's views. Describing the Truman position as "the threadbare argument by those who advocate appeasement and defeatism in the Pacific," MacArthur implied that Formosa should be permanently held by the United States or some friendly ally as an essential link in the nation's Pacific defenses. To improve relations with the strong-willed commander, Truman flew to Wake Island for a personal conference in October.

The reconciliation was short-lived. MacArthur's refusal to confine himself to military matters caused the Asiastics to regard him as a symbol of American imperialism, while Europeans feared his impetuous statements and actions might involve the United States in a full-scale war against Communist China and the Soviet Union, thereby committing American forces to Asia while Europe was left defenseless. On December 6, 1950, MacArthur was sternly ordered to clear all foreign or military policy statements with Washington before making them public.

The final break came in the spring of 1951. On March 20 the Joint Chiefs of Staff informed MacArthur that a new Korean policy statement was being prepared. Instead of waiting for this, the general issued another unauthorized statement announcing that he was ready to arrange a truce with the

Chinese commander and warning that an expansion of military operations against Chinese coastal areas and interior bases would doom the Chinese government. Angered by MacArthur's act in transforming a proposed peace gesture into a kind of ultimatum, Truman again warned the general against making uncleared policy statements. MacArthur defied the new order with audacious promptness. On April 5, Representative Joseph Martin, Republican House leader, read a message from the general, calling for a completely new foreign policy: landing Chiang's Formosa-based troops on the mainland to open a second front against the Communists and the concentration of American power in Asia, not Europe.

On April 11, 1951, the nation was stunned to learn that Truman had relieved MacArthur of his command and named General Matthew Ridgway to succeed him. Although at UN headquarters and in European capitals Truman's decision was received with elation, the American reaction was very different. For millions MacArthur was the greatest World War II hero, who had added to his laurels by brilliant feats during the occupation of Japan and the Korean War. City after city arranged triumphal welcomes for the homecoming general, while a few Republicans talked of impeaching the President. Excitement reached its peak on April 19, when MacArthur addressed a joint session of Congress. Asserting that "in war there is no substitute for victory," he presented his formula for bringing the conflict to a victorious conclusion: an intensified economic blockade of Communist China; a naval blockade of the China coast; air reconnaissance over China's coastal areas and Manchuria; and removal of restrictions on Chiang's forces on Formosa, "with logistical support to contribute to their effective operation." Recalling the line from an old West Point ballad that "old soldiers never die, they just fade away," the general ended on a strongly emotional note.

The old soldier faded rather slowly, however, for three months later he was still making triumphal visits to various cities and delivering impassioned attacks on the Truman foreign policy. Meantime, the general's dismissal was investigated by a Senate committee. MacArthur developed his views with his usual vigor, while the case against him was clarified by Secretary of Defense Marshall, Secretary Acheson, and other witnesses. Although the general still had strong emotional support, not many politicians were ready to commit themselves wholly to his policy. The real issue was whether the United States should bomb Chinese territory and support Chinese Nationalist attacks on the mainland despite the risk of precipitating World War III, or whether it should try to limit the war in Korea while building up its own armed strength and that of its allies so that Communist aggression need no longer be feared. In the heated political atmosphere, Democrats and Republicans did not agree on whether MacArthur's dismissal had been justified, but the hearings hardened American policy. Secretary Marshall and other administration spokesmen promised to keep Formosa out of Communist control and to oppose Red China's "shooting her way" into UN membership. In addition, the United States increased its aid to the Nationalist government, thus moving closer to the policy advocated by the Republicans.

Diplomatic Tug of War

On June 23, 1951, Jacob Malik, Soviet delegate to the UN, suggested an armistice providing for the mutual withdrawal of forces from the thirty-eighth parallel. This unexpected overture was followed by an exchange of cease-fire suggestions between General Ridgway and Communist headquarters in North Korea. On July 10 truce neogotiations began at Kaesong, near the battle front in western Korea. The talks soon developed into a succession of tedious wrangles, some genuine, others for mere propaganda advantage. Charges and countercharges of violations of the neutral zone led to suspension of talks from August 23 to October 25, 1951, when they were resumed at Panmunjom, six miles to the southeast of Kaesong.

The Communists at first demanded a buffer zone at the thirty-eighth parallel, but the UN delegation opposed this because the earlier invasion had proved this line indefensible. Instead, they wanted the armistice line to follow the actual battle front, lying for the most part some distance north of that parallel. Eventually the Communists conceded this point, but they were more persistent in their stand on the exchange of prisoners and policing the armistice. The prisoner question involved an issue of grave moral significance. The Communists demanded the repatriation of all prisoners of war; the UN negotiators insisted it be voluntary because many Chinese and North Korean prisoners were non-Communists who feared death or torture if they returned home. After months of futile debate on this point, the truce talks broke down completely in October, 1952.

The Truman administration's inability to bring these negotiations to a satisfactory conclusion was a heavy burden to the Democrats in the presidential election of 1952, for Republican denunciations of Truman and Acheson naturally reached a crescendo during the political campaign.

Just as the change of policy toward Germany had been forced by the Soviet threat to the West, so an altered policy toward Japan was hastened by Communist aggression. On September 8, 1951, the United States and forty-seven other nations signed a peace treaty with Japan. During the year of delicate negotiations that preceded this event, John Foster Dulles, a Republican foreign affairs expert, acted as special representative of President Truman. Warned by the difficulties that had embarrassed conferences on European problems, the State Department ignored Russian demands that the Japanese treaty be prepared by Britain, the United States, China, and the Soviet Union. Instead, Dulles conferred separately with the various governments concerned. Since neither the Communist nor the Nationalist regime had an undisputed right to speak for China, that country was left out of the negotiations with the understanding that Japan would eventually make a separate treaty with its neighbor. Although consulted in the preliminary discussions, the Soviet Union would have nothing to do with the negotiations.

Having won the support of forty-nine nations for its program of action, the United States hosted the formal peace conference in San Francisco in September, 1951. Gromyko tried to disrupt the proceedings by insisting that

Red China be invited and by denouncing the draft treaty as an instrument of American imperialism. Under Acheson's skillful presidency, however, Russian obstructionism was squelched, and the conference approved and signed the treaty.

Under this document, Japan was compelled to recognize Korean independence, to renounce all claim to Formosa, the Kurile Islands, and South Sakhalin, and to concur in an American-administered UN trusteeship over the Ryukyus, the Bonins, and the other Pacific islands. Japan agreed to abide by the UN provisions for the peaceful solution of international disputes and to assist the UN in any action it might undertake; in return, Japan gained the sovereign right to "individual or collective self-defense," a stipulation that would permit her to rearm and to seek allies. Occupation troops were withdrawn, but foreign armed forces might be stationed on Japanese territory under special agreement with the Japanese government. Although it was recognized that Japan ought to pay for the extensive damages her aggressions had caused, it was also realized that her resources were insufficient to make complete reparation. Some provision was made for confiscation of Japanese assets in foreign countries, and a plan was outlined for the payment of partial reparations through Japanese manufacture of consumer goods and industrial equipment out of raw material supplied by claimant states. On the whole, the treaty was a generous one—at least in comparison with the harsh terms that had become traditional in dealing with vanquished countries during the twentieth century.

Although the United States had achieved a major victory in gaining the support of so many nations for the Japanese peace settlement, its policy did not escape sharp criticism. In refusing to sign the treaty, the Soviet Union had the support of its satellites, Poland and Czechoslovakia. India and Burma, professing fear that American bases in Japan and in the trusteeships would cause future trouble, refused to participate in the San Francisco Conference. Both rival governments of China protested against exclusion from the negotiations. Even among the signatories there were misgivings. The Philippine government criticized the inadequacy of the reparations clauses and feared a revival of Japanese imperialism. To quiet these apprehensions and also to strengthen the defenses against international Communism, the United States signed mutual defense pacts with the Philippines, Australia, and New Zealand. To complete this security system, the United States concluded a security treaty with Japan immediately after signing the peace treaty. This authorized the maintenance of American land, air, and sea forces in and around Japan "so as to deter armed attack upon Japan."

Partisan criticism of the Truman-Acheson foreign policy as being "soft on Communism" had little basis in fact. By the Truman Doctrine, the Marshall Plan, the Berlin airlift, NATO, the defense of South Korea, and the Japanese peace treaty the administration had again and again taken strong action to curb Communist expansion. Indeed, critics of a later generation would ask whether such a militantly anti-Communist foreign policy had been either wise or necessary. The United States, confident at first of having an invincible weapon in the atomic bomb, had followed a course that even less suspicious leaders than Stalin or Mao Tse-tung might have considered menacing. It had intervened in western European politics to injure Communist electoral chances; it had helped West Germany and Japan to regain much of their power; it had built up hostile alliances and encircled the Communist states with military and naval bases. To make these criticisms of the Truman foreign policy is not to exonerate the Russians and Chinese of all responsibility for the cold war. The sad truth is that spiraling suspicion on both sides of the Iron Curtain led to a succession of steps and countersteps. In an age when policy needed to be flexible, it became increasingly rigid.

24

TRIBULATIONS OF TRUMAN

In domestic affairs as well as in foreign relations, troubled seas prevailed during the years of the Truman presidency. To convert the national economy from a wartime to a peacetime basis involved vexing problems, for whose solution advocates of national planning counseled one course of action and champions of rugged individualism another. Labor-management relations went through a succession of crises, in which the aggressive tactics of labor leaders played into the hands of those wishing to place legal curbs on union activities. Even more persistent was the loyalty issue. The Soviet threat aroused fear of subversion at home, and the Truman administration came under attack both from those who charged that it was coddling Communists and from those who complained that it was persecuting them. In 1948 Truman rode out the storm to win unexpected re-election, but he found no calm waters ahead. On the contrary, the frustrations of the Korean War and revelations of wrongdoing among lesser officeholders intensified the lightning flashing around the presidential shoulders.

The New Team

Roosevelt's death brought to the White House a man of very different background. Born on a Missouri farm in 1884, Harry S. Truman received no more than a high-school education. After holding unimportant clerical jobs in Kansas City, he returned to the farm until the United States entered World War I. Then he achieved his first minor distinction; his long Missouri National Guard service enabled him to gain a captaincy in the field artillery. He won commendation for his coolness under fire and returned from France a major. A postwar adventure in the haberdashery business failed, but a modest start in politics came in 1922 when he was elected judge of the Jackson County Court, an administrative board. He was defeated for re-election, but in 1926 returned to the court as presiding judge. Then in 1934 Tom Pendergast, the Kansas City boss, engineered Truman's election as United States Senator. Despite an undistinguished beginning, Truman emerged as a respected member of Congress—largely because of his energetic chairmanship of the special committee to investigate the national defense program.

Like most vice-presidential candidates, Truman was selected more for the political strength he would give the ticket than for his qualifications for chief executive. When he suddenly assumed the highest position in the government, the country had to appraise his qualities in a new perspective. There were some misgivings. Truman's early connection with Pendergast was disturbing, as were his provincial background and limited acquaintance with broad issues. Yet friends pointed out that Truman's integrity had never been challenged, that he was a hard and earnest worker, and that he desired to do the right thing. Perhaps his most impressive asset was his friendships in Congress, which it was hoped would lead to closer cooperation between the executive and legislative branches than had been the case during Roosevelt's later years.

As was customary, the new President promised to carry out the policies of his predecessor and asked the cabinet members to remain at their posts. Anti–New Dealers hoped that Truman would soon move sharply to the right, but in this they were doomed to disappointment. Indeed, Truman's legislative recommendations followed closely his predecessor's program. In the personnel of government, however, important shifts were made. One cabinet change followed another until by the end of 1945 Secretary of the Navy Forrestal, Secretary of the Interior Ickes, and Secretary of Commerce Wallace were the only holdovers. The most trusted advisers of the new President were Secretary of State James Byrnes, Secretary of the Treasury Fred Vinson, and John Snyder, a St. Louis Banker, who headed the important Office of War Mobilization and Reconversion (OWMR), the successor to OWM. Vinson and Snyder achieved additional prestige in June, 1946, when the former became Chief Justice of the United States after the death of Harlan Stone and the latter succeeded to the Secretaryship of the Treasury.

Although the initial changes were well received, some later appointments encountered sharp criticism. This came to a head early in 1946, when Truman asked the Senate to confirm Edwin Pauley, a wealthy California oil operator, as Undersecretary of the Navy. Pauley had been treasurer of the Democratic National Committee during the 1944 campaign, and opponents of his nomination accused him of using his influence in the interests of California oil magnates. The star witness for the opposition was Secretary Ickes. When Truman suggested that Ickes had been mistaken in his allegations, the veteran Secretary resigned. Convinced at last that Pauley could not be confirmed, Truman withdrew the nomination. Ickes's retirement under these circumstances was a damaging blow to the administration, but Truman retrieved some lost ground by appointing to the Interior post Julius Krug of Wisconsin, who had won respect for his effective work on the WPB.

Demobilization

The American soldier had fought with determination and courage not because he loved war, but because he hated it. His greatest desire was to do the disagreeable job as quickly as possible so that he might return home. Inevitably the defeat of the enemy first in Europe and then in the Pacific brought an overwhelming demand for rapid demobilization.

The first step was taken just after VE Day, when a point system for the discharge of enlisted men was announced, under which length of service, time overseas, decorations and battle stars, and number of children were counted. The rapid collapse of Japan made it possible to liberalize the system in September, 1945. Under pressure from Congress and the public, the services speeded up demobilization; by the end of the year, 5 million had been discharged from the army and 1.5 million from the navy.

In January, 1946, however, the occupation of conquered countries and garrisoning of bases throughout the world required large forces. With new enlistments lagging and draft boards following more lenient policies, the army announced that the number of monthly discharges would be sharply curtailed. This order brought serious demonstrations by bored and homesick soldiers in places as far removed as Manila, Yokohama, Vienna, and Frankfurt, and Congress was flooded with letters and deputations from "Bring Daddy Back Home" clubs. The uproar quieted down after Eisenhower, now Chief of Staff, clarified army policy, and demobilization proceeded with reasonable smoothness. Plans called for an army of 1.5 million and a navy of 700,000 by July 1, 1946.

A continuing policy of discharging soldiers after twenty-four months of service would reduce the army by December, 1946, to half a million less than the 1.5 million necessary for America's immediate postwar commitments. Therefore Truman asked that the draft be continued beyond its scheduled expiration date of May 15, 1946. Congress was sensitive to the hostility of millions of voters to peacetime conscription, so extensions to the draft were provided grudgingly until March 31, 1947, when selective service was terminated for the time being.

Growing tension between the United States and Russia eventually required a new conscription law. The Selective Service Act of June, 1948, made those nineteen through twenty-five eligible for induction for a maximum of twenty-one months, but most World War II veterans were exempted.

Reconversion

The soaring national debt and the demand for civilian goods dictated the rapid reconversion of American industry from war to peace production. Victory in Europe permitted the first cutbacks, but wholesale reconversion did not commence until shortly after Japan's surrender. Then the Army and Navy promptly cancelled $35 billion in war contracts, while 229 WPB controls were removed. The 150 still retained dealt with critically scarce commodities such as tin and rubber. Sale of surplus government property was speedily begun; 252 plants and factories built by the government at a cost of nearly $1.5 billion were put up for sale, along with a tremendous quantity of machine tools, trucks, jeeps, and miscellaneous equipment of all types.

Both harassed businessmen and individual wage earners eagerly sought relief from wartime tax burdens. In November, 1945, a new revenue act reduced taxes by an estimated $6 billion, all excess-profit levies were eliminated, and corporation income-tax rates were reduced from 6 to 4 per cent. Extending the $500 exemption for taxpayers and dependents to normal as well as surtaxes freed about 12 million individuals from paying any income tax whatsoever. For 36 million others the tax burden, though still heavy, was reduced by scaling down surtax rates and granting a 5 per cent overall reduction.

Although Director Snyder had predicted in October, 1945, many serious reconversion problems, including 8 million persons out of work by the following spring, he was being unnecessarily gloomy. By April, 1946, he reported that unemployment had passed its peak and was down to about 3 million, while production of civilian goods had reached the rate of $150 billion a year—18 per cent more than on VJ Day and 26 per cent more than in 1939. Wartime savings of about $140 billion were available for new homes, new cars, new radios, more clothing, and more food. The principal grievance was that production still fell short of demand, causing black markets to flourish in the scarce fields.

Particularly acute was the need for housing, as new construction languished, in part because of an acute lumber shortage. Consequently, millions had to pay inflated prices for real estate to obtain shelter. Named as Housing Expediter was Wilson Wyatt, former mayor of Louisville, Kentucky, whose suggestions to build 1.2 million homes in 1946 and 1.5 million in 1947 were embodied in the Patman Act of April, 1946. Congress also passed an emergency appropriation of $254 million for temporary homes—trailers and converted military barracks and war housing—to meet the immediate needs of veterans and the families of men still in service. Many of these were located near colleges and universities to house veterans who had resumed their education under the GI Bill of Rights.

Strikes

The greatest reconversion problem proved to be labor unrest, for unions were stronger than ever before. In 1935 there had been fewer than 4 million union members; there were 14.5 million by 1945. The workers had enjoyed high earnings during the war, largely through overtime pay and bonuses. The national weekly average for factory employees increased from $23.19 in 1939 to $47.16 in 1945. With the coming of peace, labor feared its income would be sharply reduced unless it could obtain raises to compensate for the loss of overtime. Such a reduction would be a serious blow at a time when prices were 33 per cent higher than they had been in 1941. Throughout the country workers began to demand raises of 30 per cent—which would give as much pay for 40 hours of work as had been received for 48 hours during the war. Management pronounced this unreasonable and inflationary, because pay raises would throw business into the red unless there were price increases—and these were forbidden by OPA.

On November 21, 1945, some 180,000 workers walked out of General Motors plants in twenty states. The strike was fought along far different lines than the conflict of 1937. On labor's side there was no attempt to take possession of corporate property; on management's side there was no aggressive strikebreaking. Walter Reuther, UAW vice president and spokesman for the workers, employed ingenious tactics. The workers' demand for a 30 per cent raise was accompanied by an elaborate brief, which argued that the corporation could make this concession without increasing prices on its products and still earn almost double the annual profit it had made during the 1935–1939 period. The company, refusing to allow examination of its accounts, countered with an offer of a 10 per cent raise with a 45-hour week—to increase the employees' take-home pay to 6 per cent above war-time levels. Pickets of the UAW stressed the failure of General Motors to open its books, while the company in paid advertisements denounced Reuther's challenge to private enterprise.

The President's fact-finding commission recommended a wage increase of 19.5 cents an hour (a little over 17 per cent), which was refused by the company. Not until March, 1946, did a settlement finally provide an 18.5-cent pay raise and liberal vacation allowances. Ford and Chrysler had already granted comparable concessions without strikes.

The Bulge in the Line

The General Motors strike was only one of the major struggles early in 1946. By the end of January about 1.6 million men were on strike and the whole reconversion effort was threatened with paralysis. Congress began to talk of drastic legislative remedies, while the Truman administration hunted feverishly for some magic formula to dispel the conflict.

Greatest in size and seriousness was the tie-up in steel, which reduced output to 89,000 tons a week as compared with the 88-million-ton rate during the war. The issue had been defined early the preceding fall when Philip Murray demanded a 25-cent-an-hour increase to hold pay at its wartime level. Benjamin Fairless, president of United States Steel and spokesman for the entire industry, would not discuss wage adjustments unless the government agreed to a $7.00-a-ton rise in the price of steel. Truman sought to avert the strike by announcing the government would permit a $4.00-a-ton price increase if the industry settled its labor controversy. When Murray and Fairless failed to come to terms, the President then suggested an 18.5-cent-an-hour raise as a reasonable compromise. This Fairless rejected, making a strike inevitable. Although some 800 plants in 250 cities and 25 states were involved, there was very little violence; as in the General Motors strike, both sides appealed for public support.

Government price policy was central to the controversy. To what extent should prices be allowed to rise to enable management to pay higher wages and still make a fair profit? Chester Bowles, head of OPA, opposed any major price change, contending that wages could be raised and industry still could make a profit because of the repeal of the excess-profits tax and the assured market for a large volume of goods. Price increases, he said, would cause a disastrous inflation spiral. But Reconversion Director Snyder argued that the best weapon against inflation would be to stimulate production by relaxing the price line. A compromise was embodied in the "bulge in the line" policy announced by Truman on February 14, 1946; labor was entitled to wage increases to match the 33 per cent rise in the cost of living since January, 1941. If such raises brought company earnings below their prewar averages, prices increases would be permitted, but the wage raises would require approval of the WSB.

The new formula was first used to settle the steel strike. The government granted a $5.00-a-ton price raise, while the industry conceded the 18.5-cent pay increase. This pattern was widely copied. Strikes in the electrical industry and elsewhere were settled, and wage increases of 18 to 20 cents an hour were made by many other companies after peaceful negotiation. Combined with the 15 per cent that most workers had received during the war under the Little Steel formula, the total raise since 1941 approximated the 33 per cent increase in living costs.

The May Crisis

The improved situation of March, 1946, was a false dawn, for the most difficult labor problems still lay ahead. The first new challenge came from John L. Lewis. Enemies asserted that the miners' chieftain, piqued by the gains Murray had won for the steelworkers, wanted to capture the center of the stage again for himself. But whatever part personal ambition may have played, Lewis sincerely desired to obtain better working conditions for one of the nation's most hazardous occupations.

Negotiations for a new bituminous contract to replace the one expiring on March 31, 1946, broke down completely. Lewis postponed discussion of wage rates while he fought to win from the operators stricter safety rules and contributions to a huge health and welfare fund to be administered by the union. He quoted impressive statistics to support his

ohn L. Lewis leaving court in Washington, 1946. (UPI Photo.)

demands: according to the United States Bureau of Mines, 17,626 persons had been killed and 855,056 injured in mine accidents in fourteen years, while insurance rates for miners were 277 per cent above standard. The fund, he said, would permit modern medical service, standardized hospitalization, and insurance at reasonable premiums. The operators objected to turning over money that might run as high as $70 million annually to Lewis's exclusive control.

The deadlock caused 400,000 bituminous miners to strike on April 1. During the next six weeks the situation became steadily more serious. By early May steel output dropped to 57 per cent of capacity; Detroit's auto factories closed down, throwing 350,000 out of work; Chicago and other cities adopted "brown-out" restrictions to conserve electricity; railroads curtailed passenger service by 25 per cent; and the ODT imposed a drastic freight embargo allowing only the most vital commodities to move. When a complete industrial shutdown threatened, however, Lewis sent the miners back to work on May 13 for a twelve-day truce.

Thus Lewis adroitly sidestepped an avalanche of public resentment and allowed its impact to be taken by the Brotherhoods of Locomotive Engineers and Railroad Trainmen, who took the unprecedented step of tying up the nation's railroads on May 23. The dispute leading to this crisis began in July, 1945, when all twenty brotherhoods demanded increases averaging $2.50 a day and changes in the working rules. When no settlement was reached with the carriers, eighteen brotherhoods agreed to arbitrate, but the trainmen and engineers refused. Truman averted an immediate showdown by appointing a fact-finding board as provided in the Railroad Labor Act of 1926. On April 18, 1946, the board recommended a wage increase of $1.28 a day and seven rule changes. The two brotherhoods found these proposals unsatisfactory and issued a strike call.

On May 17 the President ordered government seizure of the lines, and five days later suggested a wage increase of 18.5 cents an hour with no change in working rules for a year. The compromise was accepted and incorporated in a contract between the carriers and all the other brotherhoods, but the trainmen and engineers continued to demand rule changes.

On May 23, these two unions went out on strike, handling only milk, army hospital, and troop trains. Supervisory personnel ran a few other special trains, but otherwise the tie-up was complete, with neither passengers nor freight able to move except through the overstrained facilities of buses, taxis, trucks, and planes. Improvised relays of mail trucks delivered first class mail, but an embargo on all other mail became necessary.

Because such a complete paralysis of the nation's economic life was intolerable, Truman resorted to vigorous action. In a radio address on May 24, he declared he would use every power at his disposal to get the trains running unless the strike were ended by the next afternoon. His greatest weapon was public opinion, now thoroughly aroused. A few minutes before the deadline on the 25th, A. F. Whitney and Alvaney Johnson, the heads of the striking brotherhoods, accepted the presidential recommendations and the strike was over.

On the other hand, Lewis, a better strategist than the inept Whitney and Johnson, won a substantial victory. On May 22, near the end of the twelve-day truce, the government took over the mines; a week later Interior

Secretary Krug and Lewis signed a contract providing for an 18.5-cent-an-hour wage rise, increased vacation pay, and much stricter safety rules. The controversial welfare-fund issue was compromised: 5 cents on each ton of bituminous coal mined was to be assigned to a "welfare and retirement" fund administered by a board representing both operators and the union, but a special medical fund was to be managed by the union alone.

Congress and the Labor Issue

Inevitably these strikes strengthened the hand of the those wanting to regulate the unions. In December, 1945, Truman proposed that the principle of the Railroad Act of 1926 be extended to other important industries: there should be a thirty-day cooling-off period between a breakdown in collective bargaining and the beginning of a strike or lockout; and during this period a fact-finding commission should consider the issues. On May 25, 1946—the day the railroad strike reached its climax—Truman asked Congress for drastic legislation: if the workers in any essential industry taken over by the government under its wartime powers ignored the President's appeal to return to work, their union leaders might be subjected to injunction proceedings, recalcitrant union leaders and employers might be subjected to criminal penalties, strikers might be deprived of seniority rights and drafted into the armed forces, and the net profits of an industry being operated by the government during such an emergency would go to the United States Treasury. The House overwhelmingly passed a bill embodying these emergency powers within an hour after the presidential message, but the Senate was more cautious. It amended the bill radically and sent it back to the House, which allowed it to languish.

Congress finally determined on an independent course of action by passing in May, 1946, the Case Federal Mediation Bill. In a long veto message, Truman declared the measure struck at symptoms rather than causes and would have prevented none of the big strikes of 1946. An attempt to override the veto failed, so the effort to write major labor legislation was over for the moment, although in July the Hobbs Act provided penalties up to a $10,000 fine and twenty-years' imprisonment for interference by threats of violence or by robbery or extortion with the movement of goods in interstate commerce.

Truman and Congress

The deadlock between Congress and the President on strike legislation was paralleled by disagreements on many other issues. Truman's honeymoon was of short duration, and he soon found himself involved in conflicts with the legislative branch so characteristic of the American governmental system. His recent graduation from the Senate seemed to encourage his former colleagues to match their judgments against his.

On September 6, 1945, Truman sent his first fully articulated program to the Capitol. It was a distinctly New Deal document, calling for an increase in the legal minimum wage from 40 to 65 cents an hour, an expanded

"Are you sure you didn't miss anything?" (By Herblock in the *Washington Post.*)

and liberalized social security plan to include health insurance, a national housing and slum clearance program, long-range planning to develop natural resources and to carry on essential public works, aid for the farmer and small businessman, a permanent Fair Employment Practices Act, and government assistance for scientific research. For the transitional period he requested a continuance of his war powers, of price and wage control, and also of selective service.

In seeking to achieve his so-called Fair Deal, Truman soon discovered what Roosevelt had had to contend with during his later years. The Democratic majority in Congress was deceptive, for conservative Southern Democrats—many of them holding strategic committee posts—were ready to cooperate with Republicans in blocking the presidential program. When they lacked votes for a frontal attack, they amended bills until they bore little resemblance to the administration proposals. The President found it hard to overcome the coalition, even though he had the support of liberal Republicans on some issues.

Full-Employment Bill

America's impressive wartime economy had achieved huge production goals, plant expansion, and the virtual disappearance of unemployment

Why could not the peacetime economy make full use of the nation's enormous productive capacity and assure employment to all able and willing to work? Practical men as well as idealists were forced to think along these lines. As a matter of realistic finances, how could a national debt of $270 billion be carried unless the national income were raised to a figure that would have been considered fantastic in 1939?

Before the war was over, Alvin Hansen, Seymour Harris, and Stuart Chase had written extensively about full employment. Although private enterprise must bear the major responsibility for postwar prosperity, these economists emphasized the need of government controls until the danger of inflation was past, and urged government spending to take up the slack if private investment declined and unemployment threatened. These Keynesian ideas influenced the politicians. During the 1944 election, the Democratic platform, Roosevelt's speeches, and CIO Political Action Committee literature all stressed the full-employment theme, and the Truman administration gladly accepted this legacy.

Many Americans hoped for full employment without accepting the need of government planning to achieve it. Dewey and the Republicans contended in 1944 that the principal danger to peacetime prosperity was excessive government interference. The anti–New Deal Bible became *The Road to Serfdom*, in which Friedrich Hayek, a distinguished Austrian émigré economist, warned that governmental planning and economic intervention led inevitably to totalitarianism. The NAM wanted to remove wartime controls as speedily as possible in order to achieve full production and maximum employment.

The Fair Deal postwar plans were incorporated in the Murray-Wagner Full Employment Bill. As originally drafted, this was a far-reaching proposal, which recognized the Federal government's obligation to maintain full employment, provided for a board of economists to draw up a national production and employment budget showing how much governmental spending would be required, and assigned to Congress the duty of appropriating adequate Federal funds.

In this form the bill was highly unpalatable to conservatives of both parties. Federal spending to prevent unemployment raised specters of deficit spending, while the production budget spoke in the hateful language of economic planning. On the other hand, conservatives could not afford to go on record as opposing the measure's basic purpose. Attack therefore took the form of weakening amendments.

As finally passed in February, 1946, the Maximum Employment Act was a compromise. It set a goal of "maximum" rather than "full" employment; it substituted for the national production budget an annual "economic report" prepared by three economists; instead of committing Congress "to provide Federal expenditure" to maintain full employment, the Federal government was to "coordinate and utilize all its plans, functions, and resources" for this purpose. Conservatives considered it a harmless "New Year's resolution" that left Congress free to do what it pleased, while liberals hailed it as a basic new government responsibility.

Price Control

The debate over economic policy assumed a more acute form in the controversy over the continuance of price control. Chester Bowles, first as head of OPA and then as Economic Stabilizer, argued that only price control stood between the country and a repetition of the economic pattern of 1919 and 1920—runaway inflation followed by depression. So long as the demand for goods ran far in advance of supply, OPA was necessary. As always, however, consumers' interests were pressed upon the government with less effectiveness than were those of special interest groups. The NAM engaged in a huge advertising campaign to convince the public that the removal of price controls was the best way to combat inflation. Higher prices, so the argument ran, would stimulate higher production; the law of supply and demand would soon correct unreasonably high prices. Price ceilings, on the contrary, denied the manufacturer a reasonable profit and either deterred production or diverted it to the black market, thereby contributing to inflation. The argument was persuasive, but OPA defenders denied that businessmen were being required to operate at a loss or that price control deterred production.

Other groups also attacked OPA. Agricultural spokesmen contended that the high cost of farm labor, of feed, and of other necessities made price increases imperative. They wished to end the subsidy system and remove price controls on agricultural commodities. If not, they wanted new legal definitions of parity that would compel a substantial increase in price ceilings. Congressmen were particularly impressed by these farm demands because of shortages of meat, butter, and cooking fats, and the growing black market in these items.

The OPA would expire on June 30, 1946, unless Congress gave it a new lease on life. For six months before this date Truman urged prompt action to end uncertainty and the withholding of goods in hope of higher prices, but the debate in Congress was long and bitter. Legislators hoping to continue the agency with full powers and legislators wishing to kill it were both in a minority; the majority favored extension—but with provisions limiting the agency's authority. Not until three days before the June 30 deadline did Congress finally extend the Price Control Act for another year, but with a number of "booby-trap" amendments.

The President was under great pressure to sign this measure, but the government officials most concerned with the battle against inflation urged a veto. To emphasize his disapproval of the measure, Bowles resigned. Truman's final decision caught the country by surprise. On June 29 he vetoed the bill because it was an "impossible" measure that provided "a sure formula for inflation."

The result was a three-week period during which OPA had no legal powers while the legislators debated their next step. Despite appeals to hold the line on a voluntary basis, sharp price increases occurred all over the country. Some were inevitable because Federal subsidies had been ended along with price control. But soaring prices for steak and butter reflected a shrewd estimate of what the market would bear rather than

Political dilemma. (By Berryman in the .*Evening Star*, Washington.)

minimum raise to cover increased production cost. Consumer resistance brought down some unreasonable prices, and the restraint of manufacturers who did not want to strengthen the arguments of the price control advocates held down others. Yet the danger of runaway inflation was enough to induce Congress to pass a compromise measure extending OPA until June 30, 1947, and restoring controls over rents and most commodities. It also required price ceiling adjustments to permit the same margin of profits enjoyed by manufacturers in 1940; meat, poultry, grains, dairy products, and a number of other key commodities were exempted from control until August 20; and a three-man "decontrol" board could lift ceilings and recontrol commodities when necessary. This new act was scarcely more workable than the measure Truman had vetoed earlier.

A worse formula for dealing with the meat situation could hardly have been devised. For almost two months livestock raisers hurried their product to market, impelled by high prices and uncertainty as to what the decontrol board would do on August 20. The board decided that since prices had risen unreasonably and meat was in short supply, controls should be restored. With their reimposition, meat practically disappeared from the market as producers simply held their stock, fattening them up against the day when they might force a relaxation of government policy.

The President's first inclination was to stand firm, but Democratic politicians, nervous at the impending congressional elections, begged him to give the voters meat. On October 14, Truman gave up. In a national radio address, he announced not only the immediate termination of meat controls, but abandonment of all price ceilings except on rents as rapidly as was "compatible with economic security." The step was inevitable be-cause events had proved the near impossibility of holding some prices down and not others. Premature relaxation of rationing after VJ Day, the "bulge in the line" policy, congressional failure to pass adequate legislation, and contradictions in executive policy had all contributed to this vexatious situation.

Republican Landslide

Truman's retreat on price control did not save his party from a bad mauling in the November, 1946, elections. Ever since 1938 the Republicans had shown increasing strength; only the war emergency and Roosevelt's great personal appeal had prevented more decisive opposition gains. With the termination of both these influences, a strong swing to the Republicans was to be expected. The Democrats were blamed—sometimes with reason, sometimes without—for every postwar annoyance: shortages of housing and civilian goods, the unbalanced Federal budget and heavy taxes, Communist activities, and, above all, the labor troubles. To sum up the whole opposi-tion case, some inspired partisan coined the slogan: "Had enough? Vote Republican."

When the votes were counted, the full extent of the Republican swing was revealed. Democratic strength in the House was cut from 241 to 188, while the Republicans increased their representation from 192 to 246. The new Senate contained 51 Republicans and 45 Democrats as compared with 39 Republicans and 56 Democrats in the old. The Republicans now controlled both legislative branches for the first time since 1930. Dewey gained new prestige by rolling up an extraordinary 680,000 vote majority in the New York gubernatorial contest.

Revival of Laissez Faire

Truman accepted the election returns as evidence that the country had "had enough" of wartime regulation. Four days after the election he dropped all controls on prices and wages but continued rent control and the rationing of sugar and rice. The OPA began a process of gradual liquidation. Meantime, because of inadequate presidential support, Wyatt resigned as National Housing Expediter. On December 14 Truman swept away the priorities system and removed the $10,000 sales ceiling for new homes, as well as the $80 maximum rental, thereby virtually abandoning any effort to compel the construction industry to concentrate on building modest homes at prices the veterans could afford. Additional steps in lifting controls were the presidential proclamation of December 31, 1946, announc-ing the end of hostilities, and the executive order of June 11, 1947, terminat-ing sugar rationing. Although Congress continued rent control, landlords and tenants might agree upon leases 15 per cent higher than the previous ceiling.

The nation paid heavily for the return to laissez faire. Effective price control had broken down on June 30, 1946, and in the next ten months wholesale prices rose 31 per cent—nearly four times the rise of the preceding thirty-seven months of stringent control. Finding its 18.5-cent wage increase of 1946 canceled by the soaring cost of living, labor pressed new wage demands. A "second round" of raises became necessary in 1947 and a third in 1948 as prices continued to rise. The spiral of inflation seemed inexorable. Wage raises led in their turn to higher prices. Managers, workers, and farmers each laid the blame on the other groups. As in all periods of inflation, those able to speculate often reaped fortunes, while recipients of pensions or fixed incomes suffered seriously.

Curbs on Labor

The November, 1946, Republican victory was generally interpreted as a rebuke to the labor unions, whose aggressiveness had alarmed many sections of the public. That the Truman administration shared this impatience was evident from its handling of the coal crisis after the election. Nominal government control of the bituminous mines had been retained since May, 1946, because of the unwillingness of some operators to accept the terms negotiated by Secretary Krug with the UMW. In November Lewis tried to reopen the contract and, when the government refused, the Mine Workers declared it terminated, thus giving the signal for a new walkout. Lewis's action was in defiance of the government's temporary injunction obtained from Federal District Court Justice T. Alan Goldsborough. After a stormy trial, Lewis and the UMW were found guilty of contempt of court, and on December 4 Goldsborough fined the former $10,000 and the latter $3.5 million.

While the government wrestled with the union, economic activity throughout the country slowed down alarmingly. Factories closed for lack of coal, blast furnaces were shut down, railroad passenger service was sharply curtailed, a rigid freight embargo was ordered, and communities reverted to the "brown-outs" of wartime. Great was the nation's relief, therefore, when on December 7 Lewis suddenly ordered the miners to resume work, while the legal issues were considered by the Supreme Court.

On March 6, 1947, the Supreme Court, by a seven-to-two vote, upheld Goldsborough's verdict that Lewis and the Union were guilty of contempt; by a narrower margin, five-to-four, it ruled that the Norris–La Guardia Act did not apply to labor disputes between the government and its employees. The gargantuan $3.5 million fine against the union, however, was reduced to $700,000, with the proviso that the full amount would have to be paid if the union failed to comply with the lower court's restraining order.

This protracted struggle strengthened the case of those demanding drastic legislation regulating labor unions. A bill passed in the House under the leadership of Fred Hartley, Jr., of New Jersey went too far to win the support of the Senate, which drafted a somewhat more moderate plan.

Senator Taft took the most prominent role in the upper house and in the conferences where the two legislative branches reached a compromise.

As finally passed on June 9, 1947, the Taft-Hartley Labor-Management Relations Bill amended the Wagner Act in many particulars. It prohibited such unfair union practices as coercing nonmembers, refusing to bargain collectively, and engaging in secondary boycotts or jurisdictional strikes. The closed shop in which employers agreed to hire only union members was banned; the union shop, wherein employees might be compelled to join a union after they were hired, was permitted—but only under rigid safeguards. Unions might be sued by employers for breach of contract, or by third parties for injuries suffered through secondary boycotts or jurisdictional strikes. Unions must publish financial statements and were debarred from making contributions for political purposes. Union officers were required to sign affidavits that they were not members of the Communist party and did not support any organization advocating overthrow of the United States government. Employers or unions wishing to terminate or modify a contract must give sixty-days' notice; employees striking during this "cooling-off" period lost their rights under the act. The government could obtain injunctions prohibiting for eighty days strikes or lockouts that threatened national health or safety.

President Truman vetoed this bill in a long and caustic message:

The bill taken as a whole would reverse the basic direction of our national labor policy, inject the Government into private economic affairs on an unprecedented scale, and conflict with important principles of our democratic society. Its provisions would cause more strikes, not fewer. It would contribute neither to industrial peace nor to economic stability and progress. It would be a dangerous stride in the direction of a totally managed economy. It contains seeds of discord which would plague this nation for years to come.

But Congress was unimpressed, and both Houses overrode the veto by impressive majorities.

Labor leaders refused to concede the battle was lost. Although divided in other matters, the AFL, the CIO, the Railroad Brotherhoods, and many unaffiliated unions combined in condemning the new law and calling for its repeal. The non-Communist affidavit, considered an insult to labor since no comparable pledge was exacted from employers, provided an issue on which it was thought advisable to make the first stand. Lewis, who had led the UMW out of the CIO after his unsuccessful support of Willkie and back into the AFL in 1946, now tried to persuade other Federation officials to join him in refusing to file the non-Communist statements. Outvoted on the issue, Lewis, with characteristic stubbornness, again withdrew his union from the AFL to resume independent status. Within the CIO there was a similar division of opinion over signing this affidavit. In the end, however, most union officials complied because refusal meant forfeiture of rights before the NLRB—a very serious matter now that government played so important a role in labor-management relations.

Eventually labor leaders obeyed the new law but continued to demand its repeal. In practice the measure proved less damaging to the unions than they had feared. Most employers hesitated to provoke serious strife by using the law to harass the unions during a period of prosperity. But the unions feared that the act might weaken their bargaining power in a future depression and handicap their organizing campaigns in the South.

The Eightieth Congress

The Taft-Hartley Act was the major legislative achievement of the Republican Congress elected in 1946. Even less than its predecessor was this Congress disposed to enact any substantial portion of Truman's proposed Fair Deal. Instead of broadening the coverage and increasing the benefits of social security, Congress excluded certain salesmen and other groups hitherto covered. Proposals for national health insurance and Federal aid to education were rejected, together with recommendations for raising the minimum hourly wage from 40 to 75 cents. Truman's request for a long-range housing program was answered by legislation granting limited government aid to private construction, but no funds for public housing and slum clearance.

Republican leaders in Congress devoted major attention to cutting government expenditures and reducing taxes. Truman's budget for the year ending June 30, 1948, fell under speedy attack. Although it contemplated lower expenditures than had been possible during the six previous years, the total of $37.5 billion was still huge by prewar standards; even the largest pre–World War II budgets had not exceeded $9 billion. The House resolved to cut the President's recommendations by $6 billion; the Senate more realistically proposed a $4.5 billion reduction. Even this latter cut was difficult to achieve when Congress began consideration of specific items. The largest ones were for national defense, veterans' services, and interest on the public debt, which even the thriftiest legislators were reluctant to attack. In the end, less than $3 billion was slashed from the Truman budget.

Although the budget cuts were not as great as were first promised, the Republicans believed it was feasible to reduce taxes. Postwar prosperity brought into the Treasury so much revenue that it seemed possible to repeat the Republican financial formula of the twenties—balance the budget, reduce the public debt, and still cut taxes. Congress and the President could not agree, however, on a tax reduction measure. In June, 1947, a bill was passed to cut income tax rates in all brackets, but Truman vetoed it, saying: "The right kind of tax reduction, at the right time, is an objective to which I am deeply committed. But I have reached the conclusion that this bill represents the wrong kind of tax reduction, at the wrong time." It was the wrong time, he believed, because of inflation; it was the wrong kind because it failed to give major relief to the small taxpayers who needed it most. The effort to override the veto failed in the House by two votes. In July another tax reduction bill was also vetoed by Truman.

The Republican majority finally had its way in April, 1948. Although his third attempt at tax reduction was also vetoed, this time Congress overrode the President. Under the new law personal exemptions were increased from $500 to $600, married couples were permitted to split their incomes for tax-filing purposes, and levies were reduced on a sliding scale from 12.6 per cent in the low brackets to 5 per cent in the high.

On foreign policy issues there was less partisanship than on domestic ones. Through the assistance of Senator Vandenberg, the Truman administration could count on enough Republican votes to carry through aid to Greece and Turkey and the European Recovery Program. The Eightieth Congress also extended the Reciprocal Trade Agreements Act, revived the draft, and passed adequate appropriations for national defense.

The Election of 1948

Rarely in their history had the Republicans more confidently prepared for a presidential election than they did for that of 1948. The 1946 election indicated an apparent Republican trend, while events of the next two years seemed to increase the likelihood of Democratic defeat. Growing fear of Communism favored the Republicans, who charged their opponents with softness on the issue. The Democrats, moreover, appeared to be badly divided. Former Vice President Wallace condemned the Truman Doctrine and the European Recovery Program as forms of American imperialism, advocated better relations with Russia, and urged bolder domestic reforms. Thousands of Americans with similar views organized the Progressive Citizens of America to launch a third-party movement, with Wallace as the presidential candidate. While this movement threatened to attract a wide Democratic left wing following, conservative Southern Democrats were preparing a rebellion of their own. Angered by the President's support of a civil rights program to promote Negro equality in employment, education, and voting, Southern leaders threatened to desert the party if Truman were renominated.

Cheered by these favorable omens, several Republican hopefuls sought the party nomination: Senator Taft of Ohio, the most conspicuous legislator in the Eightieth Congress; Governor Dewey of New York; and Harold Stassen, former governor of Minnesota and an advanced internationalist. A grass roots movement to draft General Eisenhower gained ground until the World War II hero firmly eliminated himself.

When the Republican Convention met in Philadelphia in June, Dewey had more committed delegates than any other candidate. Taft and Stassen made a belated effort to stop the New York governor, but neither was willing to step aside in favor of the other. Thus on the third ballot Dewey's nomination was made unanimous, with Governor Earl Warren of California as his running mate. In its platform the party promised to continue support for the UN and the European Recovery Program but urged reduction of government expenses and taxes, as well as new legislation to root out domestic Communism.

Within the Democratic party there was some talk of shelving Truman in favor of a less controversial figure. Despite Eisenhower's disavowal of presidential aspirations, a number of Democratic leaders, both liberal and conservative, urged his nomination, but again the general unequivocally refused to allow his name to be considered. Some party progressives then tried to shift support to Justice William Douglas, but he said he would refuse the nomination. Without any outstanding rival, Truman was nominated on the first ballot, with Alben Barkley, veteran Senator from Kentucky, chosen as his running mate.

Much of the excitement of the Philadelphia convention centered on the framing of the platform. To appease the Southern wing, a weak civil rights platform was first drafted, but it was rejected in favor of a strong resolution, championed by Mayor Hubert Humphrey of Minneapolis and other liberals, many of them associated with the Americans for Democratic Action (ADA), a progressive pressure group of former New Dealers. In its fight for a strong civil rights plank the ADA had the support of several city bosses anxious to win the black vote. The close liberal victory was followed by an ominous withdrawal of thirty-five delegates from Mississippi and Alabama. In its other planks, the platform called for support of the Truman foreign policy and a consummation of his Fair Deal.

The new protest parties quickly took the field. On July 17, just two days after the end of the Democratic Convention, the Southern rebels, popularly dubbed the Dixiecrats, held a States Rights Convention at Birmingham, where they condemned the civil rights program and called for continued segregation of blacks. They nominated Governor J. Strom Thurmond of South Carolina for President and Governor Fielding Wright of Mississippi for Vice President. Later in the month the new Progressive party [1] named Henry Wallace for President and Senator Glen Taylor, radical Democrat from Idaho, for Vice President. The platform called for peace with Russia, destruction of all atom bombs, repeal of conscription, and far-reaching domestic reforms.

All these events convinced the Republicans that victory was certain. Much of the Southern electoral vote was expected to go to Thurmond; the anticipated Wallace vote of five or six million would so diminish the Truman large city vote that the pivotal states would go to Dewey. Confident in this analysis and relying on public opinion polls, Dewey conducted a quiet campaign, avoiding controversial issues and stressing such safe principles as the need for national unity.

Truman refused to concede that his cause was hopeless. To demonstrate that Republican pledges were hollow, he called the Eightieth Congress into special session on July 26 to deal with inflation, housing, and civil rights. The Republican majority, denouncing this maneuver as a political trick, passed only a few measures before adjourning on August 7. This provided ammunition for Truman's most effective argument—the Eightieth Congress had been a "do-nothing" body, refusing to enact laws to curb inflation and advance the welfare of the people. The President proved an indefatigable campaigner, visiting every section of the country and arguing his case in informal speeches from station platforms.

Following many hours of uncertainty, the election results finally became

---

[1] This is not to be confused with earlier parties bearing the same name. The first Progressive party lasted from 1912 to 1916, the second existed as a national party for only the 1924 campaign, although the LaFollette family led a local Progressive party for many years in Wisconsin state politics.

President Truman has the last laugh, 1948. (UPI Photo.)

clear. Truman received 304 electoral votes; Dewey, 115; Thurmond, 38. In the popular vote, Truman had over 24 million; Dewey, not quite 22 million; Thurmond, 1,176,000; and Wallace, 1,157,000. In the new Congress, the Democrats won 262 House seats to the Republicans' 171 and the American Labor party's 1; in the Senate there were 53 Democrats and 43 Republicans.

A number of factors contributed to Truman's unexpected victory. Republican overconfidence played a major part; since Dewey's total vote in 1948 was less than it had been in 1944, it was obvious that many Republicans failed to vote. A decline in farm prices and fear that Republicans would not give adequate aid cost Dewey the electoral vote of such farm states as Iowa, Wisconsin, and Minnesota. In several states the Truman candidacy was strengthened by excellent Democratic nominations for congressional and state offices. Of crucial importance was the relative failure of the Wallace candidacy; although willing to concede his loyalty and idealism, most voters were disgusted by the noisy Communist activity in Wallace's behalf. Key labor leaders were particularly careful to avoid commitment to the new party. In the end Truman made a major contribution to his own victory: thousands of doubtful voters were won over to his courageous campaign and willingness to debate issues Dewey appeared to be avoiding.

The Second Administration

In his inaugural speech on January 20, 1949, President Truman prophetically declared: "Today marks the beginning of a period that will be eventful, perhaps decisive, for us and the world." He strongly condemned Communism and outlined a four-point program to combat this "false philosophy" on a world-wide scale. The first three points were support of the UN, new appropriations for the European Recovery Program, and negotiation of a North Atlantic Security Pact—all familiar ideas to the nation. Point Four, however, incorporated an important new proposal. "We must," he asserted, "embark on a bold new program for making the benefits of our scientific advances and industrial progress available for the improvement and growth of undeveloped areas." Despite wide agreement that Truman had pointed out one of the major world needs—that of extending American technical and financial assistance to underdeveloped areas in Asia, Africa, and Latin America—the actual implementation of the idea progressed slowly.

To direct American policy through this troublesome period, Truman had to choose a new Secretary of State because George Marshall, whose great prestige had strengthened the administration for two critical years, had to resign because of ill health. In his place was appointed Dean Acheson, who had served earlier as Under Secretary of State. With an intimate knowledge of foreign affairs and wide experience in government, Acheson appeared to be an excellent choice, but many critics accused him of being soft on Communism. This was ironical since he was on the contrary probably too rigid in his anti-Communism.

Government Reorganization

Democrats and Republicans both agreed that greater government efficiency was necessary to deal with increasingly complex problems in the foreign and domestic fields. In December, 1945, Congress granted Truman more extensive powers than had been given previous Presidents to reorganize the executive departments, with only the ICC, the FTC, and SEC, and a few other independent boards exempted. The need to improve the government machinery was recognized in another form when, in August, 1946, the Legislative Reorganization Act raised the salaries of Congressmen, provided for more regular consultation between the executive and legislative branches, and simplified the complex and overlapping congressional committee system.

After the experiences of World War II, there was also wide recognition of the need to unify the armed services. A new law of July, 1947, set up the National Military Establishment, headed by a Secretary of Defense with Cabinet rank, supported by three subsidiary Secretaries of the Army, Navy, and Air Force. Integrated defense plans were to be prepared by the Joint Chiefs of Staff composed of the Army Chief of Staff, the Chief of Naval Operations, the Chief of Staff of the Air Force, and the Chief of Staff assigned to the President. This act also provided for such important coordinating agencies as the National Security Council, the National Security Resources Board, and the Central Intelligence Agency (CIA).

The first Secretary of Defense, James Forrestal, who had been Secretary of the Navy, found his new position a difficult one. The various services could not forget their traditional jealousies, and genuine unification was hampered by constant bickering between officials trying to obtain maximum appropriations for their particular branches. Forrestal's difficulties were increased because the new law granted too much authority to the subsidiary secretaries and provided no single Chief of Staff. His health broken by nerve-racking overwork, he resigned in March, 1949. His suicide two months later underlined the need to enlarge the powers of his successor, Louis Johnson. Therefore, in August, 1949, Congress did so and also provided for a non-voting chairman, General Omar Bradley, for the Joint Chiefs of Staff to help break stalemates in their discussions. Johnson's vigorous personality soon made enemies. Navy spokesmen bitterly complained that their plans to expand the naval air force were overridden, while all the services objected to the economy imposed upon them. Under these attacks Johnson resigned in September, 1950, to be succeeded by George Marshall.

Meantime, government reorganization was proceeding in other departments. In 1947 Congress had unanimously authorized a Commission on Organization of the Executive Branch of the Government under the chairmanship of Herbert Hoover. Most of the detailed work was done by three hundred experts who made exhaustive studies of the actual functioning of the government. The Hoover Commission issued eighteen reports between February 7 and April 1, 1949, which recommended a reduction in the number of government departments and agencies, the introduction of uniform budgeting and accounting systems, greater State Department authority over other units engaged in foreign affairs, the operation of the Post Office on a business basis to eliminate its chronic deficit, and the establishment of a cabinet rank department to deal with social security and education. It was estimated that annual savings of some $3 billion could be achieved by adopting these reforms.

In June, 1949, Congress passed a Reorganization Act generally approving the Hoover Commission reports and authorizing the President to prepare specific proposals to carry them out. These plans would go into effect unless either house disapproved within sixty days after the President submitted them. Of the first seven plans submitted, only one was disallowed. Fearing that a Department of Welfare would strengthen the demand for national health insurance, a Senate coalition of Republicans and Southern Democrats killed this proposal.

Truman also obtained legislation dealing with the important matter of presidential succession. An act of July 18, 1947, provided that if, by reason of death or other cause, there was neither a President nor Vice President to discharge the duties of the chief executive, the Speaker of the House should act as President. Thereafter the succession passed through the President *pro tempore* of the Senate and the cabinet officers in order of rank. Truman advocated this plan in place of the older provision under which the Vice President was followed by the Secretary of State because he believed the Presidency should pass to elective officers before it passed to the purely appointive officers of the cabinet.

Another major step pleased the President much less. In 1947 the Eightieth Congress mustered the two-third majority necessary to approve the following Constitutional amendment:

No person shall be elected to the office of the President more than twice, and no person who has held the office of President, or acted as President for more than two years of a term to which some other person was elected President shall be elected to the office of the President more than once. . . .

Widely regarded as little more than a futile rebuke to the late Franklin Roosevelt, it received much less attention than it deserved in view of the fact that it might tie the hands of the electorate in some future emergency. With little debate or public discussion, the necessary number of states approved the Twenty-second Amendment by February, 1951. At first its support was primarily Republican, but the final push came largely from Southern Democrats as a gesture of defiance to Truman. Although he was specifically exempted, it was believed the amendment would greatly diminish his chances for a third term.

Progress of the Fair Deal

Many Truman supporters believed that the Democratic triumph in 1948 would bring speedy enactment of the Fair Deal Program, but events soon proved that the situation of earlier years had not materially changed. Much of the Truman domestic program was unacceptable to the Dixiecrat faction of his own party. By loose alliance with the Republicans, the Southern Democrats were able to obstruct many proposals. Their position was particularly strong because they headed key committees through seniority.

Illustrative of the situation was the fate of the civil rights program, which had become increasingly important during the first Truman administration. In 1947 a distinguished Committee on Civil Rights had recommended measures to protect the rights of blacks and other minorities. These included legislation to make lynching a Federal crime, to end poll tax requirements for voting, to enforce fair employment practices, to prohibit discrimination or segregation on interstate trains, buses, and other means of tranportation, and to make nondiscrimination a condition for all Federal grants-in-aid for housing, education, and the like. Truman had accepted the committee's major recommendations and urged Congress to pass the necessary measures— thereby precipitating the Dixiecrat revolt of 1948.

Because the Republican platform had advocated similar legislation, the outlook for enactment of such measures seemed bright, but Southern legislators still had a potent weapon of opposition. Senate rules permitted unlimited debate except when cloture was imposed by a two-thirds vote. Through filibusters, therefore, Southern Senators could not only block all civil rights bills, but hold up all other business as long as such proposals were being considered. In March, 1949, when the Truman administration tried to reform the cloture rules to make it easier to limit debate, it was opposed by a Republican–Southern Democrat alliance. A new rule was adopted, but it merely clarified certain ambiguities in the old. Defeat on this issue placed an almost insuperable obstacle in the path of the Truman civil rights proposals. On a test vote in May, 1950, supporters of the Fair Employment

Practices Bill were twelve votes short of the necessary two thirds needed to impose cloture.

Efforts to carry out the Democratic pledge to repeal the Taft-Hartley Act were similarly unsuccessful. An administration bill failed by close votes in both houses during the spring of 1949. Then Senator Taft proposed to modify the injunction provisions and make a few other concessions, but his bill died in the House. In 1951, however, the act was amended to permit the negotiation of union-shop agreements without special vote of the workers.

Other Fair Deal failures followed. Most doctors opposed a national health insurance system; condemning it as "socialized medicine," the AMA raised $3 million to defeat it. Congress did vote increased appropriations for hospital construction, medical research, and medical education. Despite wide demand for Federal aid to the states to equalize educational opportunities, all such measures failed, largely because of disagreement on whether such aid should be restricted to public schools or should include funds for bus transportation and other services for parochial school children.

The problem of devising an agricultural program was not easily solved, for the administration felt two conflicting obligations: one to the farmers to prevent any such drop in farm income as had followed World War I, and a second to the consumers who resented soaring food prices. Secretary of Agriculture Charles Brannan tried to reconcile this conflict of interests with a plan to change the parity formula for storable staples and allow the prices of perishable commodities to be determined by supply and demand, with government subsidies to guarantee minimum returns to producers. The American Farm Bureau and other major farm organizations opposed the Brannan Plan because it seemed to favor the small farmers over the large. Consequently, Congress rejected it in favor of continuing the existing price support system. The Commodity Credit Corporation continued to make extensive crop loans to protect producers against falling prices. Under the Agricultural Act of 1949, prices on such basic commodities as corn, wheat, cotton, tobacco, rice, and peanuts were supported on a sliding scale: 90 per cent of parity through 1950, not less than 80 per cent in 1951, and thereafter 75 and 90 per cent as needed. Flexible price supports were provided for butter, milk, and other perishable items. Since industrial prices continued to mount, the prices guaranteed to the farmers went up with them.

Despite these setbacks, the Fair Deal achieved some legislative goals. In 1949 over a million workers benefited through the raise in the minimum wage from 40 to 75 cents an hour. The Reciprocal Trade Agreements Act was extended another three years without the restricting amendments that had been voted by the Republican Congress in 1948. And in July, 1949, a National Housing Act authorized construction of 810,000 units of public housing over the next six years.

Truman also achieved a liberalization of the Displaced Persons legislation passed by the Eightieth Congress. Since World War II, much sympathy had been aroused by the plight of some 850,000 Europeans who had lost their homes. Many were Jews who had lost everything through Nazi and Polish persecution; others were Germans expelled from Czechoslovakia and Poland in reprisal for indignities suffered by the nationals of those countries; still a third group consisted of Poles, Lithuanians, and other Baltic peoples unwilling to return to homelands now annexed by the Soviet Union. Since immigration quotas assigned to these European countries had not been filled during the war years, there was wide support for temporarily relaxing the annual quotas to permit a portion of these displaced persons to find American homes. In June, 1948, a measure was enacted to admit 205,000 of them. Although Truman signed the bill, he vigorously condemned certain provisions as discriminatory against Jews and Catholics. The law's deficiencies became more apparent as time went on. Because of its restrictive provisions, only 140,000 displaced persons were actually admitted during the next two years. In June, 1950, Congress finally liberalized its policy to admit 415,000 without discrimination.

Impact of the Korean War

The Korean War multiplied the administration's problems. Although the new situation demanded a return of World War II policies, the nation was reluctant to suffer again the inconveniencies of large-scale conscription, economic mobilization, price controls, and the like. The conflict's unpopularity was reflected in an unwillingness to give full cooperation to national policy.

Even before North Korea began its invasion, Truman's budget requests had reflected the world's worsening situation. In January, 1950, he asked Congress for $40.4 billion, of which $12.8 was for defense and $5 billion for foreign aid, but even these large amounts appeared inadequate after war broke out. By the time Congress adjourned in September, 1950, it had appropriated over $53.2 billion—almost $25 billion for defense and over $10 billion for foreign aid. Still larger budgets followed in 1951 and 1952, as defense production shifted into high gear.

Chinese intervention in Korea and subsequent UN defeats created an atmosphere of crisis. On December 16, 1950, Truman declared a national emergency and announced an increase in the armed forces to 3.5 million men, with a rapid speed-up in production of military equipment. To direct the new Office of Defense Mobilization, the President appointed Charles E. Wilson, a former GE president and vice-chairman of the WPB during World War II. To supply the manpower needs of the armed forces, Congress extended and revised the Selective Service Act in June, 1951.

War orders greatly increased the inflationary pressures that had been forcing prices up since the end of World War II. The need for economic controls had been recognized in the passage of the Defense Production Act in September, 1950, which authorized the President to encourage voluntary action to prevent inflation and to place ceilings on prices and wages where necessary. Reluctant to impose full price control, the administration tried to rely on voluntary cooperation. By December, 1950, there was a need for stronger measures, but the imposition of controls proved difficult. Manufacturers strenuously objected to ceilings on their prices unless wages were controlled, while union leaders insisted it was unjust to freeze wages unless the cost of living were stabilized through general price control. On January 26, 1951, the administration imposed a general price ceiling at the highest level charged between December 19, 1950, and January 25, 1951, and wages were not to be raised beyond their January 25 level without authorization of the Wage Stabilization Board.

Despite Truman's early request, it was not until July 31, 1951, that Congress amended and extended the Defense Production Act for eleven months. Price control was weakened by provisions prohibiting the establishment of slaughtering quotas for livestock and limiting the imposition of rollbacks. By the controversial Capehart amendment, manufacturers could apply for price increases to cover increased expenses since the outbreak of the Korean War. The bulwarks against inflation were further weakened by relaxing the strict terms required for installment purchases. Truman described the bill as the "worst I ever had to sign" because it would push prices up and lead to new wage demands.

Resistance to strict economic controls and higher taxes resulted in large part from the fact that the nation did not feel the same urgency to close ranks and to accept sacrifice that a full state of war would have brought forth. Perhaps by design, Communist leaders alternated menacing actions with gestures toward conciliation. Although Soviet peace moves did not divert the nation from rearmament, they did perceptibly ease tension and stiffen opposition to full mobilization.

The Question of Loyalty

War in Korea and the threat of war with the Soviet Union heightened concern over the problem of internal security. Under such circumstances, American Communists could hardly be regarded merely as members of a political faction; most Communists appeared to place loyalty to party above all other loyalties and to follow orders from Moscow. There was danger that they might infiltrate government bureaus and pass secret information to Russian agents, or cause trouble in defense industries through control of key labor unions. In 1947 Truman had ordered a loyalty check of all government employees and dismissal of any with subversive affiliations, and, under the leadership of Philip Murray and Walter Reuther, the CIO expelled Communist-dominated unions and organized new ones.

A powerful faction in Congress believed these measures did not go far enough. Through sensational investigations they tried to convince the country that the government was honeycombed with Reds and that subversive influences were dangerously at work, not only in the labor unions but in the entertainment world and in schools and colleges. The leading Red-hunter in the Eightieth Congress was Representative J. Parnell Thomas of New Jersey, chairman of the House Committee to Investigate Un-American Activities. Like Martin Dies, who had won earlier notoriety in this post, Thomas kept his name in the headlines through reckless charges. Many citizens regarded the committee's dictatorial methods as themselves un-American.

When Thomas was sentenced to prison for graft, there was some hope that the loyalty issue would be handled more judiciously, but a number of incidents soon combined to alarm the public and lend color to the wildest charges of Communist infiltration. In June, 1949, Judith Coplon, a Justice Department employee, was convicted of taking secret documents to pass on to a Russian agent.[2]

This was a minor sensation, however, compared with the case of Alger Hiss. Slender and handsome, Hiss seemed to represent the finest type of young intellectual drawn into government service during the New Deal era. A graduate of Johns Hopkins and Harvard Law School, he had once been secretary to the famous Justice Oliver Wendell Holmes. Given a position in the State Department in 1936, he subsequently held a minor post in the delegation sent to the Yalta Conference and was secretary general of the UN Charter Conference in San Francisco. After leaving government service in 1946, he became president of the Carnegie Endowment for International Peace.

The first public charge that Hiss was a Communist was made in testimony before the Un-American Activities Committee by Whittaker Chambers, a confessed former Communist who had left the party in 1938. To prove his contention, Chambers produced copies of secret State Department documents that, he alleged, had been given him by Hiss in 1937 and 1938. When Hiss denied before a Federal Grand Jury that he had given Chambers any documents or that he had even met him after early January, 1937, he was indicted for perjury. Statutory limitations prevented his indictment on a direct charge of espionage. In the first Hiss trial the defendant had impressive character witnesses, including Justices Frankfurter and Reed, but there was disturbing evidence that some key documents were in his handwriting and others were written on the same kind of typewriter as his. The first jury failed to reach a verdict, but in a second trial, Hiss was found guilty in January, 1950, and sentenced to five-years' imprisonment.

As fear of Communists increased, there was sharp division of opinion on whether the party itself should be outlawed. Proponents argued that the Communist party was not a party in the American sense of the term, but a conspiracy controlled by a foreign power and committed to the overthrow of the government. Opponents contended that to outlaw a political party grossly violated American civil liberties and that such a measure would be ineffective since it would simply drive Communist activity undercover.

The outbreak of the Korean War intensified the demand for anti-Communist legislation. In September, 1950, Congress passed the McCarran Internal Security Bill, which required registration with the Attorney General of all Communist and Communist-front organizations and all their individual members. Such members were prohibited from obtaining passports or from working for the government or for any defense industry. Aliens who had ever belonged to the Communist party or to other totalitarian parties were forbidden to enter the country as immigrants, while similar safeguards were established for naturalization. Finally, the bill empowered the government in case of war to hold Communists and other potential saboteurs in detention camps. Truman vetoed the bill, saying, "In a free

---

2 Miss Coplon's conviction was eventually reversed on technical grounds.

country we punish men for the crimes they commit, but never for the opinions they have." Both houses, however, overrode the veto by large majorities, and the Internal Security Bill became law.

Meantime, the Communist party had been strongly attacked from a different quarter. In July, 1948, a Federal Grand Jury indicted William Z. Foster, Eugene Dennis, and ten other leading American Communists for violating the Smith Alien Registration Act of 1940, a little-known statute that made it unlawful to teach the desirability of overthrowing the United States government by force or violence, to print or circulate written matter aimed at causing such an overthrow, or to help organize or have membership in any group that advocated violent overthrow. Foster's poor health caused his trial to be deferred, but the eleven others were the principals in a court battle lasting from January to October, 1949. In the end the jury found them guilty and Judge Harold Medina imposed prison terms ranging from three to five years.

Not until June 4, 1951, did the Supreme Court by a six-to-three decision uphold the constitutionality of the Smith Act as applied in this case. According to Chief Justice Vinson, the act did not violate the guarantee of free speech in the First Amendment because of the clear and present danger involved in Communist activities. "Overthrow of the Government by force and violence is certainly a substantial enough interest for the Government to limit speech." Strong dissents were written by Black and Douglas, who saw no clear and present danger that Communist advocacy might succeed. "There is hope," wrote Black, "that in calmer times, when the present pressures, passions, and fears subside, this or some later court will restore the First Amendment liberties to the high preferred place where they belong in a free society." The effect of the Smith Act was to outlaw practically all Communist activity. The decision was followed by arrests of many other party leaders on charges of conspiring to advocate the overthrow of the government.

The most serious case of actual espionage involved the development of the atomic bomb. In February, 1950, Dr. Klaus Fuchs, a scientist employed on atomic research by the British during World War II, was arrested in England and confessed to supplying Soviet agents with vital data. Interrogation of Fuchs led to the arrest of several Americans who had also spied for Russia, providing information about the atomic bomb. Convicted of espionage in April, 1951, Julius and Ethel Rosenberg were sentenced to death, while Morton Sobell and David Greenglass were given long prison sentences.

Not to be outdone by Federal Congressmen, many state legislators worked the loyalty issue for all it was worth. Committees investigated alleged subversive activities, and laws forbade state employment of Communists. A number of states required special loyalty oaths from state employees.

Among the politicians who sought to ride the anti-Communist wave, none was more extravagant in his accusations that Republican Senator Joseph McCarthy of Wisconsin. In a speech in February, 1950, he charged that there were "at least fifty-seven" Communists in the State Department. Later, he described eighty-one State Department officials, past or present, as bad security risks. In March, a subcommittee of the Senate Foreign Relations Committee, chaired by Democratic Senator Millard Tydings of Maryland, opened hearings on these charges. It soon became apparent that McCarthy could not name a single Communist party member in the Department. His most vigorous attack was upon Professor Owen Lattimore of Johns Hopkins, whom he described as Russia's "top espionage agent in America" and the "architect" of America's Far Eastern policy that had led to the "betrayal" of Nationalist China. After four months of hearing, the Democratic majority on the committee reported that McCarthy had failed to prove a case against anyone in the State Department and that his charges constituted "the most nefarious campaign of half-truths and untruth in the history of the Republic." In a minority report, Senator Henry Cabot Lodge, a Massachusetts Republican, conceded that McCarthy had not proved his charges, but criticized the investigation as superficial and inconclusive. Senator Bourke Hickenlooper of Iowa, the other Republican on the committee, refused to sign the report, but left little doubt that his sympathies were with McCarthy.

Fear of subversion was readily translated into fear of aliens. In June, 1952, Congress passed over Truman's veto the McCarran-Walter Act, a codification and revision of Federal immigration laws. Although it repealed the Asiatic exclusion clause that had damaged American prestige in the Far East since 1924, it was the reverse of liberal in most other provisions. The discriminatory national origins quotas were retained, and strict new barriers were added to exclude aliens who at any time had been affiliated with Communist or Communist-front groups or with any other totalitarian party.

Republican Upsurge

The heavy atmosphere of party politics hanging over the loyalty issue pervaded an even larger area of public discussion. The congressional election of 1950 was bitterly contested, with the Democrats claiming exclusive credit for saving the world from Communist domination and the Republicans charging their opponents were leading the nation into disaster by domestic "socialism" and foreign appeasement. "Acheson Must Go" was a favorite Republican slogan. This attack probably derived in part from his aloofness and unpopularity with politicians, but primarily because his Far Eastern policy was blamed for the Communist victory in China and American involvement in Korea.

The election resulted in heavy Republican gains. Although failing to win control of Congress, Republican representation in the Senate rose from 42 to 47 seats and in the House from 171 to 199. Two contests had particular significance. Senator Taft's prestige was much increased by his great majority in the Ohio senatorial election, despite organized labor's all-out efforts to defeat him. In a bitter Maryland contest, Republican John Butler defeated the veteran Senator Tydings who was charged as chairman of the committee investigating Senator McCarthy's accusations with "whitewashing" the Truman administration and protecting the "Reds." Considering that Tydings was a well-known conservative whom Roosevelt had tried to "purge" in 1938, these charges appeared absurd, but they apparently counted with many Maryland voters.

These and other striking Republican victories in 1950 aroused party hopes for the presidential election of 1952. Although determined never again to underestimate Truman, the Republicans gained confidence when numerous episodes diminished the administration's prestige. Men close to the White House were accused of accepting gifts for influencing government decisions on contracts and loans. In 1949 an investigation of the so-called 5 per centers—politicial fixers who undertook to obtain government contracts for small businessmen for a fee—resulted in a jail sentence for John Maragon, a crony of General Harry Vaughan, the President's military aide. In 1951, Senator Fulbright of Arkansas, himself a Democrat, charged that the RFC had been influenced in making loans by a ring of fixers with connections in the White House and in the RFC itself. Seeking to restore public confidence in the integrity of the RFC, Truman reorganized the agency under a single administrator. Despite strong opposition by Republicans, who believed the RFC should be entirely liquidated because its original objective had been fulfilled, the President's plan was allowed to stand.

The Truman administration was further weakened by widespread irregularities in the Internal Revenue Bureau. Prosecutions for income-tax frauds had been squelched through bribes and "gifts" to bureau officials who had extorted money from taxpayers fearing investigation. When the President ordered a belated housecleaning, dismissals and sudden resignations swept the country. Seven out of 64 collectors gave up their posts, and almost 200 other subordinates resigned or were dismissed. The scandal even touched the Justice Department when Assistant Attorney General T. Lamar Caudle was fired for accepting favors from tax delinquents.[3] Truman submitted to Congress a plan for complete reorganization of the Bureau, but his reform steps were too faltering to save his prestige.

The Republicans also found campaign ammunition in the widely publicized hearings of the Senate Special Crime Investigation Committee, headed by Estes Kefauver of Tennessee. These revealed a close tie between underworld elements and local politicians in many Democrat-controlled cities.

Scandal-besmirched Republican administrations like those of Grant and Harding had been able to brazen out the situation and hold on to power. The sterner punishment imposed by the voters on the Democrats did not mean that their misdeeds were more heinous than the Republicans' had been or that the country was more virtuous. The revelations of wrongdoing came at just the opportune moment to accentuate the swing to the Republicans, a swing already strongly apparent because of popular discontent over the Korean War, over the bad relations with Russia, and over real or imagined Communist infiltration of government. Under the circumstances, any Republican candidate for President would have been a strong contender in 1952, and the popular hero, Dwight D. Eisenhower, was a sure winner.

---

[3] In 1956 Caudle and Matthew Connelly, who had been Truman's appointments secretary, were convicted in Federal court of having conspired to help a defendant accused of tax evasion.

25

CHANGING AMERICA

After the end of World War II the conditions of American life were strikingly different from those that had prevailed during the thirties. To a new generation, stories of collapsing prices, wholesale foreclosures, and mass unemployment seemed as remote and unreal as though these comparatively recent misfortunes had been suffered on another planet. War and the threat of war kept industrial activity at a high peak; nearly full employment and good wages laid the basis for a high standard of living despite high prices. And yet, although it was an age of prosperity, the post–World War II era was not one of complacency like the twenties. The possibility of nuclear war hung over life like a threatening shadow, interdicting the kind of irresponsible individualism that had prevailed in the decade after World War I. Because it was an age of anxiety, it was an age that feared the unfamiliar. The man who got ahead was the man who avoided eccentricities of opinion and behavior and conformed to established patterns.

The New American Capitalism

The American economic system was still in the process of evolution, but the form it was taking was not easy to describe. It bore little resemblance to the stereotype of capitalism denounced in Marxist propaganda, but it was not much like the free competitive system described in the older American textbooks either.

The tendency toward what the economists called oligopoly, already evident during the twenties, continued. In most leading industries a few major corporations dominated the field. The general situation was neatly illustrated in the automobile industry. During World War II, when the manufacture of all pleasure vehicles was halted, magazines and newspapers contained frequent articles about the new automobile companies to be expected after the return of peace. In the cold postwar dawn, however, all these dreams evaporated. Despite the sale of millions of dollars of stock to hopeful investors, the Tucker—heralded as a marvel of advanced design—never went into production at all. The Kaiser and the Henry J. survived the perils of birth, but succumbed during infancy despite the backing of Henry J. Kaiser, who had made an outstanding success in wartime shipbuilding.

Even the older independents held on with difficulty. In 1954 the American

Motors Company was organized to merge the Hudson and Nash companies, and later in the same year the remaining two independents united forces in the Studebaker-Packard Corporation. But these reorganizations could not alter the basic elements in the situation: the big three—General Motors, Ford, and Chrysler—continued to enjoy overwhelming advantages in acquiring the best plants and machinery, the ablest personnel, the best contracts with suppliers, and ample working capital. Particularly in the field of distribution, the older independents competed only with difficulty, and the newer ones found the situation impossible. The mass sale of cars depended upon a nation-wide network of enterprising dealers and a loyal following among the buying public.

In 1963, when the total number of passenger car sales reached an unprecedented 7.5 million, General Motors commanded 54.5 per cent of the market, Ford, 26.4 per cent, Chrysler, 12.8 per cent, and American, 6 per cent. This left for the other struggling independents less than 1 per cent of the market. Faced with this competition, Studebaker, which had previously dropped its Packard line, decided in December, 1963, to move its plants from Indiana to Canada. Foreign competition was furnished chiefly in the form of the so-called compact cars, with the Volkswagen in the lead in 1963 with 233,000 imports; Renault was a very poor second with only 22,500.

The automobile situation was by no means unique. In the manufacture of steel, chemicals, gasoline, cigarettes, and a score of other products, a few firms were the leaders, and the smaller companies survived as best they could. According to one authority, 135 corporations owned 45 per cent of the indus-

A Cadillac sedan of 1951. (Courtesy General Motors.)

trial assets of the United States: this was almost one quarter of those of the entire world. Some experts believed that the situation had now stabilized and big and small business would henceforth continue to exist in the same ratio, although the aggregate of production, of course, would continue to grow.

Aggressive price competition was not characteristic of the new capitalism. The standard brands of cigarettes always sold for the same price; the price per ton of steel was customarily the same, from whatever company it was purchased; the price differential among Chevrolets, Fords, and Plymouths was never large. Obviously, some force other than conventional supply and demand was at work. The large corporations administered their prices on the basis of careful calculations of costs at given levels of production, desired margins of profit, potential markets, public relations, and other highly sophisticated considerations.

This did not mean that competition had disappeared. The rivalry between Chevrolet and Ford, or between Camels and Luckies, was obviously acute, but it emphasized supposed differences in quality rather than price. In the automobile market the struggle to a large extent was fought out on the drafting boards, where the annual models were designed. To anticipate the trends in popular taste, to gain an advantage in placement of headlights, curvature of windshield, or shape of fenders was worth millions of dollars. Out of this competition the postwar car evolved as a longer, wider, shinier, and faster model than its prewar predecessors. Most of the public apparently loved the illusion of luxury provided by 120-inch wheelbases and 200-plus-horsepower engines, but a rebellious minority expressed disapproval by buying smaller and more economical cars imported from Europe. This forced the major companies in the late fifties and early sixties to come out with compact cars of their own. In the cigarette industry, the competition also broadened to include king-size, filter-tip, and mentholated brands.

If female purchasers in particular seemed more interested in car bodies than engines, the same tendency could be seen throughout the merchandising world. As self-service drugstores, hardware emporiums, and other wait-on-yourself establishments followed in the path of the already triumphant supermarkets, attractive packaging often seemed the most important advantage a produce could have.

An even greater asset, however, was a familiar brand name that customers would ask for instinctively. To implant these desired responses, industry spent increasing sums that reached a total of well over $10 billion in 1963. The writing and placing of this advertising became a highly specialized business, centering on Madison Avenue, New York. In planning their sales strategies, the experts conducted ambitious market surveys and even experimented with appeals suggested by Freudian psychology.

The Managers

The death of Henry Ford in 1947 was a symbolic event. Even during his lifetime Ford had become an anachronism, and after his passing this species of industrial tycoon became almost extinct. The poorly educated, erratic genuis, who made millions through native shrewdness and flashes of intuition, was well equipped to build an economic empire, but not to administer it. Business leaders were now usually college-educated men who had spent many years gradually making their way up the managerial ladder. The new managerial class looked for its financial rewards not through appropriating a lion's share of the profits, but through substantial salaries and retirement benefits. Its most important incentive was perhaps not financial at all, but professional pride in the progress of the corporation. The successful business executive was no longer a man of dictatorial temperament who handed down commands to his subservient lieutenants. He was more likely to have the qualities of a good team captain, able to inspire the loyalty of his fellow executives and keep a complex organization running smoothly. Not one man, but groups of men, generally worked out the key company policies. To supply the data for these decisions, the corporations employed large research departments as well as efficient squads of accountants, lawyers, and engineers.

The result of these changes was paradoxical. In the old days everyone had known about John D. Rockefeller or Andrew Carnegie; now relatively few people could identify the men who were managing General Motors, Standard Oil of New Jersey, or U. S. Steel. Yet the new corporations were much more powerful than the old ones had been. Management decisions might affect the welfare of whole communities; they might tip the sensitive balance of the national economy; they might involve American foreign relations in remote sections of the world. Almost any management policy of a billion-dollar corporation had limitless ramifications.

Who chose these men of power? In theory, the corporation stockholders elected the board of directors; and the board in turn fixed the major policies and hired the managers to run the company. In practice, however, the stockholders had little influence. The large corporations had so many stockholders, and even large stockholders held so small a proportion of the entire stock, that ownership meant little more than a right to receive whatever share in the profits the directors voted to distribute. In the election of directors and other matters the vote was by proxy, and under normal circumstances only the existing management had the necessary facilities for collecting these. This meant that, except in the case of a major revolt, the management was self-perpetuating.

At least in the case of the largest corporations, finance capitalism, which had seemed so powerful in 1900, exerted much less influence half a century later. The vast sums needed for business expansion were largely raised through channels independent of the investment banker. According to one study, 64 per cent of the $150 billion spent in capital expenditure in the United States between 1946 and 1953 came from "internal sources"—that is, by plowing back a share of the profits of the corporations themselves. Of the remainder, 36 per cent was raised by current borrowing, 12 per cent by the issue of bonds, and 6 per cent by the issue of stock. Even in the cases where bonds and stock were issued to raise capital, the corporations were sometimes strong enough to sell the new securities directly to their own stockholders without depending upon Wall Street syndicates. This ability to find their own money was another bulwark of management strength.

Management control encountered some criticism from stockholders who grumbled because more of the corporate profits were not distributed as dividends or accused the company executives of rewarding themselves too generously with high salaries, retirement benefits, and stock option plans. The shrewder managements were able to keep such discontent at a minimum and to instill in their stockholders a sense of pride in the accomplishments of the company. The annual report, once a dreary compilation of unexplained statistics, now blossomed forth as an attractively printed brochure with glossy covers, pictures, and down-to-earth explanations of company policies. By serving refreshments and instituting question-and-answer periods, many corporations transformed the annual stockholders' meeting from an anachronistic formality into a happy gathering combining the spirit of the family reunion and the college pep fest.

This urgent need to humanize the corporations extended far beyond the relationship of the managers with their own stockholders. Each company had its public relations officers alert to obtain favorable publicity. Schoolteachers were provided with educational movies and other free teaching material. Rotary clubs and other luncheon groups found a convenient source of free speakers. Community chest drives and other local charities received enthusiastic support. Just how far corporate responsibility extended in the direction of philanthropy was a serious question. Many progressive industrialists believed that the corporations should make generous annual gifts to colleges, hospitals, and research organizations; conservative businessmen feared that such a policy would subject them to stockholder criticism and involve them in controversial issues.

Whether or not the corporations had a direct obligation to practice philanthropy, wealthy men did feel increasing responsibility to make personal gifts. The earlier examples of Carnegie and Rockefeller were followed by the establishment of a long list of charitable foundations. Greatest of all these public trusts was the Ford Foundation, established in 1936 but receiving most of its assets after the death of Henry Ford in 1947. Endowed with over three million shares of stock in the Ford Motor Company, the new foundation was in a position to distribute princely sums, particularly in the field of education. In part, the rise of the great foundations was to be explained in terms of the greater responsibility toward society felt by wealthy families; in part, the gifts reflected the influence of heavy taxes on income and inheritance. The choice confronting rich men was not between keeping or giving away their money, but between redistributing their fortunes through the agency of government or doing the same thing through private trustees.

Labor Seeks Security

Despite labor's dislike for the Taft-Hartley Act and state right-to-work laws, the unions suffered no real diminution of power, at least in the economic sphere. The American public now accepted it as part of the normal course of events that union contracts with management would periodically run out and have to be renewed. This set the stage for feverish bargaining and sometimes for strikes—although after 1946 these were seldom as serious as the immediate postwar strikes had been. The principal reason was the prevailing prosperity, which encouraged employers to grant much of what labor demanded in order to keep production rolling. The relation of these successive wage increases to inflation was a matter of dispute. The workers claimed they were demanding no more than they needed to meet rising prices; management retorted that the increased cost of labor was one of the principal causes of these higher prices.

As much of the old-time blood and thunder passed out of labor-management relations, hopeful new formulas were evolved to make strikes less frequent. In 1948 General Motors and the United Automobile Workers (UAW) signed a contract containing a so-called escalator clause, under which wage rates were tied to the Bureau of Labor Standards cost-of-living index. Many other companies accepted the escalator clause—to the general satisfaction of the workers in a period of rising prices. A contract signed by GM and the UAW in 1950 provided an even more important precedent. Instead of the usual one-year term, the new agreement was to run for five years with annual wage increases, cost-of-living adjustments, and a variety of fringe benefits. Once again the example of GM was followed by other companies, and the one-year contract, with its unsettling effects, became less common.

By this time the general public had become accustomed to the idea that the automobile industry was likely to be the testing ground for new strategies on the part of both management and labor. Therefore, it was no surprise when Walter Reuther of the UAW began to push a demand for what was called the guaranteed annual wage. Intended as security against unemployment and seasonal layoffs, this would have obligated the automobile companies to supplement state unemployment benefits so that unemployed workers would be guaranteed 80 per cent of their pay for 52 weeks. In its original form the guaranteed annual wage was unacceptable to management, but in 1955 first Ford and then the other companies granted a modified version called Supplementary Unemployment Benefits (SUB). This provided that the companies would set up funds out of which state unemployment benefits would be supplemented, so that laid-off workers would receive 65 per cent of their take-home pay for 4 weeks and 60 per cent for 22 more weeks. Labor hoped that the new policy would not only ensure greater justice to the unemployed, but would spur management to plan its production schedules so that the seasonal layoffs would be reduced to a minimum.

All labor contracts showed an increasing emphasis on the so-called fringe benefits—retirement pensions, vacation with pay, group life insurance, accidental death payments, and hospitalization and medical plans. Sometimes these benefits were administered through union welfare funds, to which the employers agreed to make regular contributions. In 1946, for example, the United Mine Workers under John L. Lewis's aggressive leadership won a royalty on each ton of bituminous coal to be paid into a welfare and retirement fund. Although there were occasional charges of mismanagement, the miners' fund provided for the building of hospitals and the provision of medical care in communities that had never had such services before.

The two main branches of the labor movement had been discussing the possibility of ending their twenty-year quarrel and reuniting for some time. Both had come under new leadership in November, 1952, when by coincidence Philip Murray of the CIO and William Green of the AFL died within two weeks of each other. Walter Reuther, the new CIO executive, and George Meany, now head of AFL, laid the groundwork for reconciliation. In 1954 the two federations agreed to a "no-raiding" pact, and in December, 1955, the merger was finally consummated at a New York City convention. Total membership of the new AFL-CIO was about fifteen million—ten million contributed by the old AFL and the rest by the CIO. Meany was elected president; Reuther became vice president in charge of the Industrial Department.

Many serious problems confronted Meany and Reuther. The old quarrel had left many unhealed wounds. Moreover, the labor movement was not yet completely unified. Some two million workers belonged to independent unions like the United Mine Workers and the Railroad Brotherhoods. Since three quarters of American wage earners still did not belong to any union, the new federation pledged itself to a vigorous organizing campaign, but workers in the 1950's and 1960's proved much more difficult to recruit than they had been in the 1930's and 1940's. Prosperity had brought so much improvement in working conditions that the gnawing discontent that makes for swift unionization was no longer prevalent.

Automation offered a particularly troublesome problem. Throughout

George Meany of the AFL and Walter Reuther of the CIO as the two organizations were merged, New York, 1955. (UPI Photo.)

industry ingenious new devices were automatically monitoring machinery that once had been tended by workers, and new equipment was performing many arduous tasks that once required human brawn. To produce 1,000 tons of coal in 1947 had required 1,300 man-hours of labor; to produce the same amount in 1963 required less than 500. To produce an automobile in 1947 had required 310.5 man-hours; in 1963 the man-hours required were only about 150. To try to block this technological change was obviously folly, since increased productivity made it possible to pay high wages. Yet the union leaders had to do what they could to protect the jobs of their members, and in this worrisome tug-of-war lay the threat of new labor troubles. The most serious involved the railroads, which in 1959 sought to discharge nearly 40,000 firemen no longer needed on modern diesel locomotives. When the brotherhoods objected and threatened to go out on strike, it took three presidential fact-finding commissions, the United States Supreme Court, congressional imposition of compulsory arbitration, and personal intervention by President Johnson in the spring of 1964 to reach a satisfactory settlement of the issue. The unions were worried during this four-and-a-half-year controversy lest Congress extend compulsory arbitration to other fields, thus marking the beginning of the end of collective bargaining.

Labor's Bad Boys

Although Meany and Reuther believed in aggressive unionism, they wanted to keep the labor movement free from infiltration by Communists and tie-ins with racketeers and criminals. Before the merger the leaders had largely won their battle to throw out the Communists, but the struggle against union corruption was just beginning.

The situation along the waterfronts of New York City and other Eastern ports well illustrated the dangers of corrupt unionism. The rough workers upon whom the ports depended to load and unload ships belonged to the International Longshoremen's Association (ILA). In December, 1952, an investigation by a special New York Crime Commission revealed that racketeers were using the ILA to terrorize the waterfront. By controlling the hiring halls they arbitrarily decided which longshoremen would have jobs. By threatening strikes and slowdowns they forced shipping lines to pay tribute that went directly into their own pockets. So long as these extortions were not too outrageous, the companies found it more advantageous to go along with the system than to try to buck it. The New York investigation also revealed that the waterfront racketeers had gained protection by tying in with corrupt politicians in New York City and Jersey City. The prize-winning movie *On the Waterfront* gave wide publicity to the situation.

Despite all this adverse publicity, the ILA defended itself successfully against all who tried to destroy it. The state governments of New York and New Jersey established a Waterfront Commission to attack the abuses, and the AFL cooperated by expelling the ILA and sponsoring a new union. But when NLRB elections were held in 1953, 1954, and 1955, the independent ILA defeated its AFL-chartered rival on each occasion—either because the longshoremen actually preferred the old union or because they dared not vote against it. During the long struggle the ILA weathered major strikes, Taft-Hartley injunctions, and convictions for contempt of court. But if this tough union refused to die, it did at least submit to face-washing. Under pressure from the Waterfront Commission it corrected the worst abuses in the hiring system and began to deal somewhat more fairly with its own membership.

The ILA was a relatively small union, with only 60,000 members. Its greatest importance lay in its ability to tie up shipping in Eastern ports. To the honest labor movement the International Brotherhood of Teamsters posed a much more formidable challenge. With its 1.4 million members, this giant now had the distinction of being the largest American union. Controlling practically all the truckdrivers of the nation, the union was in a position to tie up the business of almost any city or region. The success or failure of other unions' strikes often depended on whether or not the Teamsters would respect their picket lines. Yet a series of revelation beginning in 1957 showed that the leadership of the Teamsters was shockingly corrupt.

A special Senate Committee on Improper Activities in the Labor or Management Field, with Senator John McClellan, an Arkansas Democrat, as chairman and Robert Kennedy as special counsel, dug into the Teamsters' tangled affairs. Despite mysterious disappearances of key witnesses, burning of records, lapses of memory, and refusals to answer incriminating questions, the committee discovered that union officials had controlled a string of taverns, gambling joints, and houses of prostitution in Portland,

Senate Investigating Subcommittee, 1955. Senators Ervin, Jackson, McClellan, and McCarthy with Chief Counsel Robert Kennedy. (UPI Photo.)

Oregon. Dave Beck, the portly president, had become wealthy by exploiting his position. Not content with a princely salary and the privilege of living rent-free in a Seattle mansion purchased with union funds, Beck had made highly profitable investments with money improperly "borrowed" from the union welfare fund. Beck's practice of borrowing money from companies with which the union had labor contracts was particularly unethical.

To the AFL-CIO leadership, Dave Beck was a serious problem. Unless energetic steps were taken to clean house, the whole labor movement might be injured through public resentment and demands for antiunion legislation. Yet the constitution of the federation provided unions with almost complete autonomy. Unless the Teamsters themselves elected new leaders, Meany and his associates could only reprimand the wrongdoers and threaten the union with expulsion. In February, 1957, the AFL-CIO executive council adopted a strict code of ethics, condemning such abuses as those that had developed in the Teamsters union. In May the council removed Beck from his AFL-CIO vice-presidency after a hearing in which he was found guilty of gross misuse of union funds.

The convergence of heat from congressional investigation, AFL-CIO condemnation, and Federal indictment for income tax evasion convinced Beck that he should not run for re-election to the Teamster presidency. But the heir-apparent to Beck's crown, Jimmy Hoffa, was, in the opinion of many observers, an even more sinister figure than Beck himself. Hoffa had the same reputation for using union funds for business speculations and was alleged to have close ties with the gangsters of many cities. In what appeared to be a coordinated drive to prevent Hoffa's election, the Mc-Clellan Committee subpoenaed him to testify concerning his activities, the AFL-CIO gave the union an ultimatum to clean up, and a rival faction within the Teamsters appealed to the Federal courts to halt the union election on the ground that Hoffa had rigged it through the chartering of "paper" locals and other irregularities. But at their October, 1957, convention, the defiant Teamsters resisted all these pressures and gave the presidency to Hoffa by an overwhelming vote.

In December, 1957, the AFL-CIO voted to expel the Teamsters and several other smaller unions where corruption had been uncovered. But this attempt to punish misbehavior appeared to hurt the parent more than the child. Between 1957 and 1961, total membership in the AFL-CIO shrank from 15 million to 12.5 million, while the Teamsters grew from 1.4 million to 1.7 million. In 1961, Hoffa was triumphantly re-elected president of the union, had his salary raised to $75,000 a year—the highest of any union official, and obtained an amended charter allowing him to organize workers in any field. Unless the AFL-CIO took the Teamsters back in, Hoffa threatened to destroy it with a rival federation. Some AFL-CIO leaders favored compromise, but Meany continued to oppose readmission to the unrepentant union.

Although Dave Beck ended his career in a Federal prison, Jimmy Hoffa for a long time avoided a similar fate. In 1957 and 1958 he was acquitted on separate charges of bribery and wiretapping. When Robert Kennedy, Hoffa's would-be nemesis, became Attorney General, the Department of Justice began a new campaign to break the defiant union leader. It was not until March, 1964, however, that a Federal court in Tennessee found him guilty of tampering with the jury in one of his earlier trials. The judge sentenced him to eight years in prison and a fine of $10,000. Three months later he was convicted and sentenced on a charge of diverting $1.7 million of union funds. Legal maneuvers still kept Hoffa out of prison until March, 1967, when he finally began serving his sentences after the Supreme Court upheld the convictions. Under its new president, Frank Fitzsimmons, the Teamsters continued in defiant independence of the AFL-CIO.

Meantime, however, the McClellan Committee's investigations had paved the way for new legislation. In 1959, Congress passed the Landrum-Griffin Labor-Management Reporting and Disclosure Act, which laid down a bill of rights for union members, required the unions to file full public reports of their financial affairs and other activities, insisted upon regular elections and bonding of union officers, and prohibited extortion and blackmail picketing.

Radicals of the Left and Right

During the 1950's the American Communist movement was in partial eclipse. In part, this was the result of official and unofficial harassment. The leaders were in prison, and many of the rank and file found it difficult to find jobs. But in large part, the party's decline reflected the impact of world events. Unable to stomach harsh resort to force by the Soviet Union and Red China, the more idealistic party members and fellow travelers cut their ties. This loss still left, however, a hard core of Communists, relatively few in numbers but highly dedicated and strongly disciplined. Although liberals were now more alert to Communist meddling, the radicals of the left found some opportunity to infiltrate organized efforts for such good causes as world peace, ban-the-bomb, and civil rights.

Most American liberals were as firmly anti-Communist as were American conservatives, but it was difficult for the latter to concede this fact. As the rightists read the political question, it ran: welfare state = Socialism = Communism. So long as Senator McCarthy remained a powerful force in American politics, any critic of the status quo stood in danger of senatorial inquisition. After McCarthy's death in 1957, the rightists carried on their vendetta against liberalism with other weapons.

Among numerous rightist groups, the most controversial was the John Birch Society, organized in 1958 and named for an American officer killed in 1945 by the Chinese Communists—the first victim of the cold war. Robert Welch, the society's founder, was a retired Massachusetts candy manufacturer, who had once characterized President Eisenhower as "a dedicated, conscious agent of the Communist conspiracy." Although Welch later soft-pedaled his attacks on the hero-President, he continued to blister others whom he branded as "Comsymps" (Communist sympathizers). In 1961, Welch offered $2,300 in prizes to college students for the best essays on grounds for impeachment of Chief Justice Warren—a prime target for the ultraconservatives because of recent Supreme Court decisions restraining the powers of congressional investigating committees and upholding the civil rights of blacks. As chapters of the John Birch Society spread across the country, local patriots found an outlet for their energies in attacking teachers and textbooks that gave favorable mention to the United Nations.

In 1961, Major General Edwin A. Walker was relieved of his command in West Germany after an Army investigation disclosed that he had been indoctrinating his troops with Birch-like propaganda and attempting to mobilize absentee ballots for conservative candidates to Congress. Rightists made a martyr of Walker and protested bitterly against the "muzzling" of the military, but a senatorial investigating committee soon dropped the matter when it became clear that Walker's activities had been in violation of both Army regulations and Federal statutes. The Walker episode dramatized the attraction that the radical right possessed for a certain type of military mind. Retired army and navy officers took a prominent part in conservative organizations, and officers on active service sometimes sponsored "schools" or "seminars" in which self-appointed "experts" on Communism branded as dangerously radical everything from foreign aid to fluoridated water. Also fascinated by the rightist cause were certain millionaire businessmen—particularly those of Texas and southern California—who gave large sums of money for conservative "educational" activities.

Disappointed by Eisenhower's moderation and Kennedy's liberalism, the ultraconservatives pinned their hopes for national salvation on Senator Barry Goldwater of Arizona. Although Goldwater did not countenance the more extreme forms of Birchism, his doggedly conservative position on both domestic and foreign affairs attracted a wide following not only among the radical right, but among more moderate and responsible conservatives as well.

Women and the Family

During World War II, more than three million women who would not ordinarily have been wage earners took jobs. In addition, millions of farm wives did outside chores that had always been considered men's work. A quarter of a million women enlisted in the WACS, the WAVES, or some other service. It was convincing proof of women's ability to perform any task not involving extraordinary physical strength. The effect of the war was not so much to institute a new trend as to accelerate one already strongly established. In 1880, 2.5 million women had worked; the number had increased to 5 million by 1920 and to 11 million by 1940.

After the war it became even more common for women to become wage and salary earners. By 1963 the number of females over the age of fourteen gainfully employed had risen to over 23.5 million. Prosperity opened up the jobs; electric appliances lightened the housework that had bound wives to the home; and inflation provided the spur to seek extra income for the family.

Women found inspiration in the career of Eleanor Roosevelt. Impatient with the purely social duties traditionally imposed upon the First Lady, Mrs. Roosevelt carried on an extraordinary number of activities. At various

Mrs. Eleanor Roosevelt at a meeting of Democrats, 1953. (UPI Photo.)

times she accepted employment as a teacher, lecturer, radio commentator, magazine feature writer, and columnist for the daily press. Her unpaid activities were even more extensive. The First Lady's zeal made her a figure scarcely less controversial than her husband. Many Americans asserted that Mrs. Roosevelt's activities should be confined to the White House, that her restless traveling was undignified and meddlesome. But to her millions of admirers, she was a great person in her own right, giving herself without stint to causes in which she believed. After her husband's death, Mrs. Roosevelt gained new respect as a courageous advocate of human rights at the United Nations.

Women gained distinction in many different lines of endeavor. Within the field of government they achieved administrative posts, seats in the Senate and House, governorships, and important diplomatic missions. Few journalists commanded more respect than Dorothy Thompson, Anne O'Hare McCormick, Marguerite Higgins, and Freda Kirchwey. Nevertheless, ambitious women still encountered many obstacles. In most fields of endeavor, males monopolized the most powerful and prestigious positions.

The extent to which women's ambition for a career undermined the stability of the family was a matter of dispute. An increasing number of women confronted with the choice of marriage or a job, elected to take both. Critics connected the practice with the rising divorce rate and increasing juvenile delinquency, but it was difficult to prove that the woman who worked was necessarily a worse wife and mother than the woman who stayed home.

Whatever its perils, marriage was hardly declining in popularity. In 1910, 60 per cent of all women over the age of fourteen were married, while 25 per cent were single; in 1960, 66 per cent were married, while only 19 per cent were single. The war years were charactrized by an unusually large number of youthful marriages. The depression of the early thirties had caused the marriage rate to drop to 7.9 per thousand population in 1932, but it climbed to 13.2 by 1942, the highest rate since 1920. For the next three years the rate was lower, but in the first postwar year, 1946, the marriage rate jumped to 16.4, the highest in the twentieth century. Many war marriages were entered upon in haste and were strained by separation and the tensions of wartime living. The divorce rate, which had climbed from 0.73 per thousand population in 1900 to 2.0 in 1940, jumped to an abnormal 4.3 in 1946 and then fell back to about 2.5 per thousand in 1950 and to 2.2 in 1960.

The decline in the birth rate, which had disturbed some observers during the twenties and early thirties, was temporarily arrested. In the depression year of 1933 the rate had fallen to 16.6 per thousand population; better times brought it up to 17.9 in 1940, while the war resulted in its rising to 21.5 in 1943—the highest since 1925. Youth's eagerness to marry and have children during the darkest period of the war seemed to indicate that it had little fear of the future. The trend continued during the postwar years with a birth rate of 25.8 in 1947 and 22.4 in 1962.

Wartime conditions brought many parental problems. The juvenile delinquency rate, which had shown a gratifying decline during the thirties, jumped up sharply. In 1944 there were 56 per cent more court cases than there had been in 1939. The increase in the delinquency rate was greater for girls than for boys, although the actual number of delinquent boys continued to be larger than the number of girls. During the 1950's the rate of delinquency in proportion to population declined somewhat, but evidences of serious maladjustment still continued. Newspaper accounts and periodic legislative investigations described city schools transformed into "blackboard jungles," youthful gang wars involving killings and mutilations, and teen-age drug addiction and sex orgies. Less publicized were the earnest efforts being made in many communities to get to the root of the problem and provide facilities for extending psychiatric care to the worst-adjusted youngsters, as well as wholesome activities for those whose principal trouble appeared to be a combination of high spirits with too much idle time.

Churches on the Move

The troubles of the depression, the long agony of war, and the anxieties of the postwar period caused many Americans to return to the shelter of the church. Books from the warfronts testified to the comfort that religion had provided for men adrift on the Pacific or flying on dangerous missions. Many servicemen were impressed by the sacrificial spirit and the fine teamwork of Catholic, Protestant, and Jewish chaplains. The greater interest in religion continued into the postwar period, as evidenced by the extraordinary popularity of such inspirational books as Lloyd Douglas's *The*

Robe (1943), Thomas Merton's *Seven-Storey Mountain* (1948), and Norman Vincent Peale's *The Power of Positive Thinking* (1952).

The Roman Catholic Church appeared to be vigorously alive. Bishop Fulton J. Sheen exerted an extraordinary influence. Through his personal contacts the church won a number of prominent converts, including the journalist Heywood Broun, the industrialist Henry Ford II, and the playwright-politician Claire Booth Luce, while his TV appearances touched the lives of millions of other Americans. The membership of the church grew rapidly, largely through births but with a substantial flow of conversions as well. Catholic strength was manifest in the increasing enrollment in parochial schools, in the building of churches, and in the organization of new suburban parishes.

The Protestant churches also seemed to be advancing. Some of the excessive denominationalism that had characterized the nineteenth century disappeared. Three separate Methodist bodies merged in 1939 to form the Methodist Church. The number of Lutheran bodies was reduced by the organization of the American Lutheran Church in 1960 and the Lutheran Church of America in 1962. A similar impulse led to the establishment of the United Presbyterian Church in the U.S.A. in 1958. Meanwhile a series of denominational mergers involving the Congregational, Christian, Evangelical, and Reformed churches was culminated in 1957 by the formation of the United Church of Christ. Churches not formally united showed an increasing degree of cooperative enterprise. Interdenomination cooperation was carried further than ever before with the organization in 1950 of the National Council of the Churches of Christ in the United States. This body, supported by 26 Protestant denominations and 4 Eastern Orthodox groups, represented nearly 32 million church members and brought within a common framework such hitherto separate agencies as the Federal Council of Churches, the Foreign Missions Conference, and the International Council of Religious Education.

Many Protestant clergymen, ashamed of the church's excessive zeal in whipping up war fever during World War I, swung over to radical pacifism. Of nineteen thousand ministers polled in 1931, 62 per cent expressed a conviction that the church should refuse to sanction or support any future war. Such sentiment became particularly characteristic of Christian young people and students, thus contributing materially to the isolationism of the thirties. When war finally came, a sizable group stuck to these convictions and suffered internment in conscientious objectors' camps rather than submit to conscription into the armed services. The great majority, however, considered the moral issues of the conflict important enough to override all other considerations. They pinned their hopes for the future upon victory in a just war and the promotion of good will in the postwar world. The cold war was a cruel disappointment to these hopes. Many religious leaders regretfully accepted the necessity of the government's anti-Communist foreign policy, but events in the sixties strongly revived the cause of Christian pacifism.

The Billy Sunday type of evangelism was no longer in vogue among the older Protestant bodies, which preferred to expand their membership by less bombastic means. To many more emotional Christians this conservatism of method seemed defeatist. One of the phenomena of the war years was a series of massive Youth-for-Christ rallies in various parts of the country. During the postwar years revivalism had a strong resurgence, particularly in the person of Billy Graham, a handsome young Southerner, whose earnest eloquence drew huge crowds to his meetings, whether they were held in Scotland, in India, or in supposedly blasé New York City. Another evidence of the revolt against religious intellectualism was the remarkable growth of such groups as the Pentecostal and Holiness sects, the Assemblies of God, the Church of the Nazarene, and Jehovah's Witnesses. Entirely different in its appeal was the Oxford Group, or Moral Re-Armament, movement, which stimulated many rich and well-educated people to a new interest in religion.

Religious statistics for 1963 recorded church membership at nearly 119 million. This included 64.9 per cent Protestants, 44.8 Catholics, and 5.5 million Jews. Only 36 per cent of the population were nonmembers, as compared with 65 per cent in 1900.

Despite this impressive evidence of church growth, many observers believed that church membership meant less than it had in earlier days and that fewer people were deeply motivated by religion. At all events, evidence in dismaying abundance demonstrated that many Americans had foggy ideas of right and wrong. Early in 1951 millions of Americans watched by television the hearings of a special Senate crime investigating committee under the chairmanship of Estes Kefauver of Tennessee. The testimony revealed the existence of great crime syndicates controlling gambling resorts, houses of prostitution, and other illegal establishments in cities across the country. Even more shocking than this demonstration that American crime was still big business was the realization that these conditions could not exist without the protection of complaisant politicians. Much of the ultimate responsibility rested upon ordinary citizens who gave their patronage to bookies and horse parlors and voted for corrupt political machines.

The Challenge of Science

The atomic bomb dropped on Hiroshima on August 6, 1945, had intellectual repercussions not less impressive than its material destruction Intelligent Americans suddenly realized that the advance of science had been so rapid and revolutionary as to require fundamental readjustment in all political and social relationships. Yet the bomb represented the culmination of merely one line of recent research. Science had made less dramatic but scarcely less significant progress in the fields of aviation, electronics chemicals, and medicine.

Even before the war it was obvious that America was becoming increasingly science-minded. The number of industrial research laboratories in the country increased from around 400 in the early twenties to approximately 2,400 in the late thirties. During the latter decade, $300 million was being expended for industrial research each year. The National Research Coun

The mushroom cloud over Nagasaki after an atomic bomb was dropped, August 9, 1945. (Official U.S. Air Force photograph.)

cil, organized in 1916, gave valuable support and direction to scientific work throughout the country.

The general public accepted as a matter of course the assumption that science would more and more transform daily life. Women wore clothing made of synthetic fabrics and used innumerable plastic gadgets around the home. Newspapers printed photographs flashed through space, and householders eagerly purchased television sets. Each year saw new knowledge in the field of nutrition, and the manufacture and sale of vitamins became big business. Many serious diseases lost much of their terror when treated with sulfa drugs or other new miracle workers like penicillin, aureomycin, and cortisone. Meanwhile, preventive medicine continued to advance— quietly as a rule, but sometimes with extraordinary fanfare as in the 1955 announcement of the successful testing of the Salk polio vaccine.

The necessities of war telescoped into a few years developments that might have been expected over a generation. Not only did the use of blood plasma transform the treatment of the wounded, but it led to an intensified study of the proteins contained in the plasma. From these investigations came the discovery of serum albumin for the treatment of shock, fibrinogen to combat excessive bleeding, and globulins for the treatment of measles and jaundice. Another line of research led to the production of DDT, an insecticide whose use during the war cut down malaria during the Pacific island campaigns and checked the spread of typhus in Italy. Not for many years did sobering evidence accumulate that overuse of DDT was seriously upsetting the balance of nature.

No less impressive was progress in electronics and aviation. Radar permitted antiaircraft guns to detect the approach of planes in the darkest night one hundred miles away, enabled plane crews to observe the nature of the terrain beneath them through darkness or fog, and made marine navigation safer. Aeronautical engineering more than doubled the speed of aircraft and made it possible to fly at much higher ceilings. Turbine and jet engines destined to revolutionize transportation were developed.

The government recognized the great importance of wartime science by establishing the Office of Scientific Research and Development (OSRD) under the direction of Dr. Vannevar Bush of the Carnegie Institution. The activities of this agency probably shortened the war by many months; indeed, if the enemy had been allowed to preempt the field of scientific research, United Nations victory might not have been achieved.

A listing of the key discoveries that laid the theoretical groundwork for the atomic bomb demonstrates the international character of science under normal circumstances. In 1905, Albert Einstein, a German by birth but residing in Switzerland, opened up a new line of scientific thought with his hypothesis that matter might be converted into energy. Some five years later, Lord Rutherford in England and Professor Nagaoka in Japan theorized that the chemical atom was not a hard massy particle, ultimate and indivisible, but had a nucleus at the center containing concentrated matter and energy. Rutherford later demonstrated that bombardment with rays of radium could convert atoms of one element into atoms of other elements. Dr. Enrico Fermi in Rome showed that such conversion could be effectively obtained by using small atomic fragments called neutrons. This line of research culminated in an epochal experiment in 1939 when Dr. Otto Hahn and Miss Lise Meitner of Berlin, working at the Kaiser Wilhelm Institute, bombarded atoms with neutrons and caused them to fly apart with a velocity of 200 million electron volts. However little this news might mean to the man in the street, it was of world-shaking significance to the world's physicists. The great experiment had transformed nuclear matter into nuclear energy, energy higher than man had ever attained before.

The absence of American names in the foregoing list does not mean that the study of the new physics had been neglected in the United States. On the contrary, the invention of the cyclotron or atom-smasher by Dr. Ernest O. Lawrence of the University of California won him the Nobel Prize in Physics in 1939, while equally important landmarks were the discovery of deuterium, or heavy hydrogen, by Dr. Harold C. Urey of Columbia University and that of U-235, a rare form of uranium, by Professor Arthur J. Dempster of the University of Chicago. The onset of the war found the country with a company of brilliant scientists already well grounded in the fundamentals of nuclear physics. American science also gained important reenforcement when four of the world's greatest physicists—Albert Einstein, Lise Meitner, Niels Bohr, and Enrico Fermi—found refuge in the United States after being forced out of Germany and Italy.

The possibility of using atomic power for military purposes was brough to President Roosevelt's attention late in 1939 and resulted in the appointment of a committee to survey the problem. Two years later it was decided to expand the research program. At Roosevelt's suggestion, British and Canadian scientists came to the United States and joined forces with the Americans, directed by Dr. Bush in the OSRD. Military security needs led to the transfer of a major part of the program to the War Department in June, 1942, and Major General Leslie R. Groves was placed in charge.

Extraordinary secrecy shrouded the so-called Manhattan Project. It employed thousands of persons but kept its work so compartmentalized that only a few highly placed men in government and science knew the whole story. Congress cooperated by making almost $2 billion available without asking embarrassing questions. The Project erected key plants in areas as remote from each other as Tennessee and Washington and built the country's best-equipped physics laboratory at Los Alamos, New Mexico. Dr. J. Robert Oppenheimer of the University of California was in charge of the Los Alamos project, and the émigrés Bohr and Fermi gave valuable technical assistance. Near there, on June 16, 1945, the experimenters detonated the first atomic bomb, causing an explosion felt two hundred miles away and seen for over one hundred miles. Two months later the destruction of Hiroshima and Nagasaki hastened Japanese surrender.

These highly publicized events brought problems of the utmost gravity to American statesmen. Should the technology of the bomb be kept secret, or shared with the Soviet Union and other allies? Should the bomb's use be outlawed, or should it be entrusted to the UN? Should the control of atomic power remain in military hands, or should it be transferred to civilians? What peacetime uses had this new source of energy? Should this energy be exploited under private ownership, or should it be socialized? Despite much discussion, it was doubtful whether Americans generally realized the urgency of the new problems posed by scientific progress.

Failure to achieve effective international control of atomic power resulted in an expensive and dangerous race in developing new weapons. Early in 1950 President Truman ordered American scientists to try to develop a much more powerful hydrogen bomb. Thereafter, the United States and Russia matched strides. In November, 1952, the United States exploded what it described as an H-bomb prototype; in August, 1953, Russia countered with the testing of what may have been the first true H-bomb. Subsequently both powers undertook periodic trials of their newest nuclear weapons, and in 1957 Britain joined the race by testing its first H-bomb. Scientists warned that continuance of the contaminating tests was likely to prove injurious to the whole human race.

The rival powers also enlisted their scientists in an effort to develop long-range missiles. During the closing months of World War II the Nazis had caused substantial damage by bombarding the English coast with V-2 rockets. Although inaccurate, these weapons were of such potentially great importance that Soviet and Western armies competed in trying to capture as many German scientists as possible. Among the prisoners taken by the United States was Professor Werner von Braun, who eventually became an American citizen and a key figure in the American missiles program. Braun dreamed not only of developing super-weapons capable of destroying targets thousands of miles away, but of rocket-propelled space vehicles that might travel to the moon and the planets.

During the early 1950's the United States gave rather low priority to its missiles and space program, but American complacency received a rude jolt in October, 1957, when the Russians orbited *Sputnik I,* the first artificial satellite. The Soviets followed this triumph with a succession of other space exploits. The envious American public had to take what satisfaction it could in the orbiting of *Explorer I* in January, 1958, and other satellites in succeeding months.

The Russians' dramatic success in space aroused grave concern about national security. The rocket power evidenced in these exploits was interpreted to mean that the Soviet Union had jumped ahead of the United States in the development of ICBMs (intercontinental ballistic missiles)—weapons that might outmode manned aircraft and destroy the value of American overseas bases. During the election campaign of 1960, Democratic orators made much of this alleged "missiles gap."

Boom in Education

During World War II thousands of young Americans came to a new realization of the utility of higher learning. The most desirable branches of the services were open only to those who had been to high school or college. Many bright soldiers and sailors were sent to college for short terms; some received a complete training in medicine or engineering. This taste of college life, together with the benefits of the GI Bill, contributed to the extraordinary situation that prevailed six months after VJ Day when almost every college in the country was overflowing with returned veterans. In the fall of 1949 college enrollments exceeded 2.4 million as compared with 1.4 million in 1939. Once again the result of war was to accentuate a trend already well established. In 1900 only 11 per cent of American young people between the ages of fourteen and seventeen were to be found in full-time high schools. The percentage had risen to 73 by 1940. During that same period the number of American colleges had risen from about five hundred to three times that number, while college enrollment had increased eightfold.

During the 1950's these educational trends continued. The Korean War reduced college attendance for a year or two, but the campus flood soon began again. The prospect for the future seemed to be still more rapid expansion. With the higher birth rate and the larger proportion of young people seeking higher education, the colleges were confronted with challenging questions. How were the new buildings needed for swollen enrollment to be provided? Would alumni and other individuals provide the fund for the capital expansion? Would business corporations accept this as one of their new responsibilities? Or must the funds come from the state and Federal governments?

A particularly critical problem arose out of the faculty salary situation. Postwar inflation tended to increase the cost of living faster than the college could adjust professors' salaries, even with frequent tuition raises. In some fields a drift from teaching into better paid professions was already taking place. How then could the additional teachers needed for anticipated enrollments be found? In December, 1955, the Ford Foundation showed its concern both with this problem and with the nation's growing shortage of medical facilities by granting $500 million, the largest gift in the history of philanthropy, to colleges and hospitals. The grant to the colleges was especially earmarked for the improvement of salaries. Even with this help, however, the faculty salary problem was far from solved.

Along with the rapidly expanding university enrollment went a bewildering growth in course offerings. An attempt was made to prepare students for more and more special vocations, while the elective system made it possible to obtain an A.B. degree with almost any combination of courses. Many authorities became alarmed. As early as 1930, Abraham Flexner had asserted that there was in the United States no university in the real sense of the term—"no institution, no seat of learning devoted to higher teaching and research. Everywhere the pressure of undergraduates and vocational activities hampers the serious object for which universities exist."

President Robert Maynard Hutchins of the University of Chicago urged that the liberal arts college be restricted to general education based upon the study of the greatest books of the Western world and the arts of reading, writing, thinking, and speaking, together with mathematics. He called for a reorganization of American education so that the last two years of high school and the first two years of college might be combined in a well-integrated course of studies leading to the A.B. degree at about the age of 20. Thereafter, the more competent students would be accepted in the university proper, where they would study metaphysics, social science, and natural science. Hutchins's ideas were hotly debated both at the University of Chicago and in the educational world generally. At his own institution he succeeded in having some, although by no means all, of his principles carried out. A more radical experiment based upon his philosophy was undertaken at St. John's College in Annapolis, Maryland, in which all the students were required to read in their entirety a long list of important books ranging from Homer's *Iliad* to Veblen and Young's *Projective Geometry*.

Most educators rejected the idea of directing education back to the so-called Great Tradition. In fact, such new colleges as Bennington and Sarah Lawrence, with their emphasis on the cultivation of the fine arts and their highly individualized programs, were experiments in the opposite direction. Most institutions avoided the two extremes. There was much modification of the curriculum, with an increasing emphasis on broad survey or general-education courses during the freshman and sophomore years and some departure from narrow departmental majors. Obviously, the complexity of contemporary political and social problems had compelled much hard thinking about the objectives of education, and most institutions tried to reorganize their programs to meet these new conditions. Russian space triumphs focused attention on the need for stronger work in science at all levels of American education.

Newspapers, Magazines, Radio, and Television

In the financial organization of the newspaper field, trends already noted continued. No new national chains as extensive as the Hearst or Scripps-Howard developed—and the Hearst empire had begun to break up. But smaller chains flourished, and consolidation reduced the number of papers published in most cities. Newspapers became increasingly dependent on the Associated Press and the United Press for their news; recognizing this, the Supreme Court ruled in 1945 that it was a violation of the antitrust laws for the Associated Press to reject arbitrarily an application for membership because of the veto of a rival journal. The amount of space devoted to syndicated features also continued to increase. The thirties and forties witnessed a great rise in the popularity of the columnists. The widely printed opinions of Walter Lippmann, Westbrook Pegler, and Drew Pearson had an influence far greater than the ideas expressed in the editorials of the individual newspapers.

American newspapers of the forties and fifties differed from those of earlier days in the much larger coverage given to foreign affairs. From being poorly informed on such matters, the American public had become perhaps the best informed of all peoples. A generation of intelligent reporting of world affairs did much to educate Americans for new responsibilities in the postwar world.

Growing interest in the news led to the establishment in 1923 of the magazine *Time*. The enormous success of this weekly venture encouraged the founding of *Newsweek* and other periodicals devoted to briskly written summaries of current events. The same Henry Luce who made a fortune out of *Time* hit upon another winning formula in 1936 when he developed *Life* as a magazine featuring interesting pictures so arranged as to tell a story. This also brought a large number of imitators and competitors into the field, the most successful of which was *Look*. The greatest moneymaker of all was the *Reader's Digest*; guided by the intuition of DeWitt Wallace, this pocket-sized magazine was so perfectly tailored to suit the taste of the average middle-class American that it achieved a monthly circulation of around eight million at the end of World War II.

Meantime, the radio became increasingly important as a medium through which history was both made and witnessed. Roosevelt often seemed to exercise political magic by speaking directly to the voters over the radio. Through the same medium, the American people gained a sense of direct participation in events when they listened to the ranting speeches of Hitler, the magnificent oratory of Churchill, or the solemn voice of MacArthur presiding over the Japanese surrender ceremony. During the most critical periods of the war, listeners turned to their radios almost hourly for the latest reports. Of the total broadcasting time on NBC, only 3.6 per cent was devoted to news in 1939, but by 1944 it was 20.4 per cent.

Television was developed as a medium for mass communication much more rapidly than had been anticipated. Although receivers were expensive, high postwar earnings enabled large numbers of people to buy sets as soon as broadcasting began in any section of the country. Rather than being a luxury monopolized by the rich, television became the proud possession of thousands of families that would have been considered underprivileged during the thirties. In 1963, more than fifty-six million television sets were to be found in the country. Even more than radio, television became a matter of sharp controversy. Critics decried the large number of programs devoted to Western and crime stories regarded as a bad influence on children, for whom television had a particular fascination; they also denounced the "fixed" quiz shows. Book publishers complained that TV addicts were forgetting how to read; film producers and exhibitors were hard hit by reduced attendance at movies. Because the medium was an expensive one, the time devoted to advertising was even greater than on radio, while the proportion of programs devoted to good music or education was smaller. But the cultural results were not all bad. The eagerness with which TV audiences followed the deliberations of the United Nations, the presidential news conferences, and congressional investigations demonstrated that the new invention might give Americans a new sense of direct participation in important events.

Literature and the Arts

From the standpoint of the serious reader, the literary production of the post–World War II years was disappointing. Most of the bright young authors of the twenties and thirties failed to sustain their earlier reputation. Sinclair Lewis died in 1951, his prestige sadly damaged by the mediocrity of his later books, while John Dos Passos seemed to be doing some kind of painful penance for his earlier radicalism. To be sure, three American novelists received Nobel prizes during these years: William Faulkner in 1949, Ernest Hemingway in 1954, and John Steinbeck in 1962, but this appeared to be belated recognition for their earlier work rather than for their more recent achievements. Faulkner was the only one of the three whom the critics seemed to rate more highly at the end of his career than they had twenty years earlier.

The younger generation of writers included many men of talent, but few, if any, who appeared destined for permanent fame. In short stories and novels John O'Hara described with sharp penetration the political, social, and sexual activities of the well-to-do set in small-city Pennsylvania. A realism even more brutal characterized the two most widely read novels dealing with World War II: Norman Mailer's *The Naked and the Dead* (1948) and James Jones's *From Here to Eternity* (1951). Several brilliant black novelists explored the meaning of the black experience in America; Ralph Ellison's *Invisible Man* (1952) and James Baldwin's *Go Tell It on the Mountain* (1953) were particularly powerful works.

Although most authors wrote in a spirit of protest against cruel or stupid aspects of American life, others strongly reasserted traditional values. Herman Wouk's *The Caine Mutiny* (1951) dealt with the navy with a respect for authority that contrasted sharply with the cynicism of Mailer and Jones. An impressive vein of idealism also ran through the works of John Hersey, particularly in *The Wall* (1950), a novel depicting the stubborn heroism of the Warsaw Jews during World War II. This increased respect for man's basic decency was reflected in Saul Bellow's *The Adventures of Augie March* (1953), Robert Penn Warren's *Band of Angels* (1955), and James Gould Cozzens's *By Love Possessed* (1957).

Still another tendency was reflected by sensitive young authors who avoided the issues of the wider world to concentrate on the personal problems of individuals. J. D. Salinger's *Catcher in the Rye* (1951) was a skillful probing of the world of an adolescent schoolboy. With similar psychological insight John Updike's *Rabbit, Run* (1960) described the disintegration of a young couple too immature for marriage and family responsibilities. John Cheever, author of *The Wapshot Chronicle* (1957), entertained his readers with rare comic writing, while chilling them with his unsparing revelation of the sterility of contemporary American life.

The most exciting trend in the world of books was the rise of the paperbacks. Enterprising promoters discovered that they could reach a vast new market by publishing books in cheap editions and selling them through drugstores and newsstands. At first the paperbacks were mostly mystery stories or sensational novels whose sales appeal depended upon provocative titles and sexy pictures on the covers. Further experimentation demonstrated that although good books might not sell as well as bad they would often do well enough to justify republication. Thrifty readers with serious tastes could now afford to own not only the writing of contemporary authors but older classics as well.

If the popularity of the high-class paperbacks seemed inconsistent with the low level of taste reflected in other newsstand literature, it simply provided one more proof of the variety of American society. Despite the tendency toward conformity, a nation of 190 million people and continental size could provide a market for many different levels of taste. The phonograph industry that could give a princely income to the swivel-hipped Elvis Presley could also supply to thousands of music lovers the symphonic interpretations of Arturo Toscanini.

In architecture and the arts there was a similar broad spectrum of taste. The new homes that filled thousands of suburban housing developments were attractive and comfortable with their picture windows, glassed-in shower stalls, and built-in ovens, but there was a certain monotony about them. A similar lack of individuality characterized the new office buildings of New York and other cities with their boxlike shapes and extensive use of glass. A rebel to the day of his death in 1959, Frank Lloyd Wright combatted the smooth uniformities of modern architecture and kept alive a tradition of romanticism. Similarly imaginative were the decorative designs of Edward Durrell Stone and the sweeping curves of Eero Saarinen's buildings.

Inspired by the well-known example of Winston Churchill, thousands of Americans now dabbled with paint and brush—sometimes assisted by kits that could be purchased in variety stores. Among the amateur painters of the 1950's was President Eisenhower himself. But the pretty landscapes and stiff portraits of these Sunday painters had little in common with the savage swirls and blotches of color that constituted the work of artists like Jackson Pollock and William de Kooning. Scorning the regionalism and social realism of the thirties, the exponents of "abstract expressionism" applied paint to canvas almost at random—or so it seemed to a bewildered public accustomed to look for composition and design, if not exact representation, in works of art.

The world of music had a similar profusion of standards. Broadway musicals reached a new height of excellence after World War II with the work of talented melodists like Richard Rodgers and Frederick Loewe. Even simpler was the folk and country music being performed by scores of long-haired, guitar-strumming trios and quartets. On the other hand, many serious composers turned their backs on conventional melody and harmony to experiment with twelve-tone scales, dissonance, and other innovations that outraged the ears of the uninitiated. Less radical than many of their contemporaries, Aaron Copland and Samuel Barber continued to produce works eligible for inclusion in the standard symphonic repertoire.

America was changing—but it was changing in more than one direction. Pessimists, convinced that things were getting worse and worse, could wring their hands over the decline of economic individualism, the blatancy of advertising, the racketeering labor unions, race prejudice, and schools where no one learned to spell. But optimists could nourish their faith by noting the rising standard of living, the greater security of workingmen, the improved status of minority groups, the progress of medicine and science, and the proliferation of community projects in art and music.

26
EISENHOWER REPUBLICANISM

On one occasion Dwight D. Eisenhower asserted that Republicans should be "progressive moderates"; another time he defined the party goal as "dynamic conservatism." By such verbal combinations the man who entered the White House in January, 1953, tried to stake out a political position that would borrow from the New Deal and the Fair Deal a concern for human welfare, but would temper this with deference to states' rights and economic individualism. In avoiding the extremes of either right or left, Eisenhower had the support of most Americans. Although not exciting, the middle of the road appeared to be quiet and safe.

Eisenhower Versus Taft

Although Truman's surprise victory in 1948 warned the Republicans against overconfidence, their party's prospects for 1952 looked sufficiently bright to inspire a vigorous struggle for the presidential nomination. Despite the efforts of such hopefuls as Earl Warren, Harold Stassen, and Douglas MacArthur, the battle quickly narrowed down to one between Eisenhower and Taft.

With customary candor, Taft made no mystery of his desire for the nomination. Supporting his candidacy were thousands of conservative Republicans who admired his stubborn opposition to the New Deal and the Fair Deal. The Taftites bitterly remembered how their hero had been passed over for Willkie in 1940 and for Dewey in 1944 and 1948. Blaming "me-tooism"—that is, Republican acceptance of New Deal social welfare goals—for the recent party defeats, they demanded a return to old-fashioned Republicanism. On foreign policy, they tended toward isolationism. They regarded the UN and NATO with suspicion, distrusted England and France, and wanted to give priority to Asia in the struggle against Communism. Already strong in the Midwest, the conservatives hoped to pick up many delegates from the South, where the Republican rank and file was negligible and party hacks controlled the state organizations.

Although Taft had many backers in the East, Governor Dewey of New York and Senators Henry Cabot Lodge of Massachusetts and James Duff of Pennsylvania were not among them. They and other Eastern leaders believed that Taft's nomination would doom the party to defeat. They wished to retain the New Deal's social gains, but with greater economy and efficiency of administration; even more did they want to preserve continuity of foreign policy by renouncing isolationism and giving strong support to the UN and NATO. Here again their complaint was not so much that the Democrats were doing the wrong things as that they were doing the right things badly. This moderate Republicanism had wide support among party amateurs, especially among business executives.

The anti-Taft Republicans found an ideal candidate in General Eisenhowever. As NATO commander, he knew the realities of the world situation; on domestic issues, he was for the most part open-minded. Most important of all, his military fame and affable personality made him enormously popular among all sectors of the American public. It was not until January, 1952, however, that he announced he would accept the Republican nomination if proffered, but would remain at his NATO post and not actively participate in the scramble for delegates. When it became clear, however, that Taft could be beaten only if Eisenhower fought for the nomination, the general returned from Europe in June, took off his uniform, and plunged actively into politics.

The Taft-Eisenhower fight was strongly reminiscent of the 1912 struggle between the Senator's father and Theodore Roosevelt. In both instances the Taft conservatives were accused of trying to steal the nomination by manipulating the Southern delegates. Yet there was a significant difference: in 1912 the older Taft controlled the convention machinery and seated his challenged delegates; in 1952 the conservatives tried similar tactics but were defeated. When the Republican National Committee awarded temporary seats to the challenged Taft delegates, twenty-three out of twenty-five Republican governors attending a Houston conference protested the decision. Charges and countercharges were intensified when the National Convention opened at Chicago in July. The Eisenhower faction demanded that the contested delegates be excluded from voting not only on their own cases but on all others as well. The Taft compromise was voted down. This fight was only a warm-up for the decisive struggle over seating the Georgia delegation; Eisenhower supporters won by a vote of 607 to 531.

The rest of the convention was anticlimactic. On the first ballot the initial standing was Eisenhower 595 and Taft 500, but subsequent switches gave the general 845 votes and the nomination. Eisenhower chose as his running mate Senator Richard Nixon of California, whose prominence in the Alger Hiss investigation made him popular with the more nationalistic elements. The platform took a middle ground between the Europe-first and Asia-first partisans by pledging vigilance in both areas and condemning Democratic failures. Reciprocal trade agreements were favored if they protected "our domestic enterprises." Amendments to the Taft-Hartley Act were promised to meet labor criticism. On civil rights the party took a weaker position than it had in 1948; on farm policy the pledges were more specific: "full parity prices for all farm products," adequate storage and credit facilities, and farm loans.

Although the Taft-Eisenhower feud left deep party wounds, it by no means injured Republican prospects in the ensuing campaign. For most of the vast TV audience watching the convention, Eisenhower was cast in the role of hero and Taft as villain. When virtue triumphed, the viewers were delighted, and the Republicans were off to a magnificent start before the Democrats had even chosen their candidate.

Eisenhower Versus Stevenson

When the Democratic Convention opened in Chicago there was still confusion over who would be the candidate. All talk of a third term for Truman ended in March when the President removed himself from the running. His first choice for the succession was reported to be Governor Adlai Stevenson of Illinois, who insisted, however, that he still had important work to do in his state administration. Truman then transferred his backing to Vice President Barkley, but the CIO vetoed this suggestion because Barkley at seventy-four was too old. In the primaries Senator Kefauver gained many victories, but he was disliked by Truman and most party leaders because of the embarrassing disclosures of his highly publicized crime investigation. Each of the other potential candidates had some fatal weakness.

Kefauver led on the first two ballots, but on the third the delegates turned to Stevenson, who had indicated he would not resist a genuine draft. To balance the ticket, Senator John Sparkman of Alabama was nominated for Vice President. The platform pledged the party to the ideals of the Fair Deal: high prices supports for agriculture, strong civil rights legisla-

Democratic presidential candidate Adlai Stevenson flanked by Massachusetts Governor Dever and Congressman John F. Kennedy, 1952. (UPI Photo.)

tion, repeal of the Taft-Hartley Act, and international cooperation to resist Communism and to preserve peace.

Once nominated, Stevenson staged an aggressive campaign. His speeches were eloquent and witty, but they did not win the enthusiastic following that a relatively little known man needed to deflect the spotlight from a great national hero. Meantime, Eisenhower was proving a better campaigner than might have been expected. Wherever he went, huge crowds turned out to greet him. His speeches were impressive for their vigor and dignity.

Except for Truman, who criticized Eisenhower with characteristic sharpness, the Democrats avoided attacking the popular general directly. Instead, they concentrated their attention on Nixon, whom they expected to find vulnerable because of his allegedly unfair tactics in defeating New Deal rivals in earlier California elections. Great was their jubilation, therefore, when a newspaper uncovered the fact that California businessmen had contributed $18,000 to help Nixon pay expenses incidental to a political career. These revelations threatened to be so damaging that a few timid leaders urged Nixon to yield his place on the ticket, but the high party command turned back the Democratic attack with an adroit counteroffensive: they charged that Stevenson's subordinates in Illinois had been aided by similar funds. Even more effective was a nationwide TV broadcast in which Nixon defended the purity of his conduct in highly emotional fashion.

Democratic efforts to stem the Republican tide were fruitless. The returns gave Eisenhower 34 million popular votes and 442 electoral votes to Stevenson's 27.3 million and 89, respectively. Stevenson carried no state outside of the South, and even in that traditionally Democratic region he lost Florida, Oklahoma, Tennessee, Texas, and Virginia. The election was more of a personal triumph for Eisenhower, however, than a vote of confidence in his party. Indeed, the Republicans won control of Congress by the slimmest of margins: in the new House there were 221 Republicans, 213 Democrats, and 1 independent; in the Senate there was a razor-thin balance of 48 Republicans, 47 Democrats, and 1 independent.

While Eisenhower's victory resulted in large part from the overwhelming sentiment summed up in the slogan "I Like Ike," he also benefited from other factors. There was widespread belief that the Democrats had been too long in power and that the nation would benefit from a change. This was closely related to popular resentment over recently revealed scandals in the Truman administration. Particularly damaging to the Democrats were the Korean War and the stalemated peace talks. One of Eisenhower's most effective promises was that he would go to the Far East to investigate the situation.

New Faces in Washington

On January 20, 1953, the capital city was jammed with joyful Republicans eager to celebrate the end of twenty black years of Democratic rule. Eisenhower's inaugural address, dealing largely with foreign affairs, was solemn

Republican and Democratic campaign headquarters, Williamstown, Massachusetts, 1952. (UPI Photo.)

in spirit and moderate in tone. It promised no abrupt policy changes, and, for the most part, there were none. The Democrats found little in it to criticize, and the only disapproval came from the extreme nationalist Republican right wing.

The new President came from a background far different from that of any twentieth-century predecessor. Born in Denison, Texas, in 1890, Eisenhower spent his formative years in Abilene, Kansas, where his family moved when he was a year old. After graduating from high school, Dwight received an appointment to West Point. In 1915 he began his military career with the usual second lieutenant's commission and made his way up the hierarchy of rank until the eve of American entrance into World War II, when he was a major general and Chief of Staff of the Third Army. Up to this time his record had been good but not extraordinary. He was brought to Washington as trusted subordinate of Chief of Staff General Marshall. Eisenhower's first major opportunity came when he commanded the American invasion forces in North Africa in 1942; success in this campaign and in the conquest of Sicily and southern Italy led to his transfer to England to direct the triumphant second-front invasion. After the war he served for three years as Army Chief of Staff, for two more as president of Columbia University—a strange and not altogether happy interlude—and finally from late 1950 to June, 1952, he was supreme commander of the new NATO army.

Eisenhower's great military success was based upon certain traits of personality. He was not a brilliant general after the fashion of Napoleon or MacArthur. The grand strategy of the Allied campaigns was devised far from the battle fronts and Eisenhower merely carried it out. Nor was he a hard-driving field commander like Patton. Eisenhower's talents were those of a team captain. In coalition warfare, it was a difficult task to reconcile the conflicting ideas and clashing temperaments of high-ranking officers from different services and different countries. Simple and direct in manner and with an unusual ability to listen patiently to every shade of opinion, Eisenhower inspired trust and affection and was therefore able to coordinate the vast war effort.

As President, Eisenhower directed the government in similar fashion. He sought to recruit a competent team of administrators and trust them with the task of formulating policy and carrying it out. He kept himself as free as possible from the day-to-day routine of government so that he could concentrate on major issues. He conducted his relations with Congress on the same basis, making recommendations and signing or disapproving bills that came to his desk, but leaving the legislators free from constant pressure from the White House.

Eisenhower's reluctance to play the role of strong executive made his cabinet appointments highly important, and his administration differed from the old most strikingly in personnel. Under Truman the key offices were usually held by men who had gained their experience in politics and government; under Eisenhower the posts were more likely to go to businessmen. John Foster Dulles, the new Secretary of State, was a corporation lawyer and specialist in international affairs who had been a State Department consultant during the Truman administration. George Humphrey, the Secretary of the Treasury, was a highly successful Ohio industrialist with extensive coal and steel interests. Charles E. Wilson, the Secretary of Defense, had been president of General Motors. These three men became the most influential figures in the administration; their cabinet colleagues came mostly from the same kind of business or legal background.

Even Taft was troubled by the economic complexion of the administration. "I'm not at all sure," he said, "that all these businessmen are going to work out. I don't know of any reason why success in business should mean success in public service." Reluctant to sell his GM stock in conformity with conflict-of-interest laws, Wilson assured a congressional committee that "what is good for the country is good for General Motors and vice versa." For this and subsequent blunt statements, he became a frequent center of controversy. Other businessmen-in-government behaved more discreetly, but a succession of minor incidents illustrated the pitfalls inherent in the situation. Air Force Secretary Harold Talbott resigned under fire in 1955 after disclosures that he had used his position to promote personal business interests. Two or three less prominent officials encountered the same kind of trouble.

Eisenhower's policy of saving his energies for major concerns required heavy reliance on his White House assistants. The post of Assistant to the President was entrusted to Sherman Adams, a taciturn, hard-working former governor of New Hampshire, who acted as a chief of staff, mediating between feuding administrators, assuming personal reposibility for many matters, and organizing the data the President needed for final decisions. Not the least of his functions was to divert criticism from Eisenhower;

when conservative Republicans disliked the presidential policies, they usually found it more discreet to attack the king's minister rather than the king himself. And these conservatives had more definite reasons to attack in 1958 when it was discovered that Adams had accepted a vicuna coat and other gifts from Bernard Goldfine, a wealthy Boston manufacturer, in supposed return for special favors with the SEC and the FTC. Although Adams was cleared of any wrongdoing and Eisenhower wanted him to stay on, Adams resigned in September, 1958, to weaken any Democratic charge about a Republican "mess" in Washington.

One of Eisenhower's greatest needs was congressional leadership thoroughly committed to his brand of Republicanism. Instead, he had to work with right-wing leaders unsympathetic to many aspects of his program. Fortunately, Taft, despite his disappointments, cooperated to achieve a good record for the administration, but his sudden death in July, 1953, made William Knowland of California the new Republican leader. An honest but opinionated man, Knowland did not hesitate to oppose the President when he thought him wrong, particularly in foreign policy. Eisenhower found much more consistent support from Eastern legislators like Senators Clifford Case of New Jersey and Irving Ives of New York, but these liberals had less influence in party circles than the conservatives. Consequently, the administration's success often hinged on its ability to gain Democratic votes.

Balancing the Budget

A businessman's administration naturally felt that its first responsibilities were to balance the budget and halt inflation. Eager to impose efficiency, new department heads warned their subordinates against tardiness, coffee breaks, and all other time-wasting artifices familiar to office workers. Meanwhile, the administration leaders took up the more serious business of cutting the budget Truman had submitted just before leaving office. With proposed expenditures of $78.6 billion—about $10 billion more than anticipated revenues—the Truman estimates seemed final proof of Democratic recklessness.

The Republicans soon discovered, however, that a balanced budget could not be achieved overnight. Many items like interest on the public debt and veterans' benefits were required under earlier laws. Of the other items, the amount to be saved through greater efficiency never proved to be as large as they had seemed to enthusiastic campaigners. Between 1952 and 1956 the Republicans reduced the number of Federal employees from 2.4 million to less than 2.2 million, but the limit of such economies was soon reached.

The hard truth was that two thirds of the budget was for security items—defense and foreign aid—and it was here that cuts must be made if major savings were to result. Secretary Wilson made a significant overhaul of defense policy. Instead of continuing a herculean effort to bring the nation to a high state of readiness by 1954—likely to be a crucial year according to Truman's advisers—he advocated a stretch-out over a longer period. Wilson also believed it possible to get "a bigger bang for a buck"—that is, to save money by concentrating on nuclear weapons at the expense of conventional armaments. Despite Democratic charges that this involved a gamble with national security, defense appropriations were reduced considerably. Total expenditures for fiscal 1954 were $67.8 billion—almost $11 billion less than Truman had recommended—and the deficit was only $3 billion instead of the estimated $10 billion. The Korean armistice in July, 1953, undoubtedly helped Republican finances substantially.

Eisenhower hoped to balance the budget before fulfilling his campaign pledge to cut taxes. During his first year he even induced a reluctant Congress to continue for six months the excess-profits tax due to expire on June 30, 1953. In 1954, with the congressional elections approaching, however, the demand for tax reduction was too strong to be resisted. Therefore Congress gladly allowed the excess-profits tax to die and a previously authorized income tax cut to go into effect. More important, it thoroughly revised the income tax laws, allowing large deductions to heads of households, widows and retired persons, farmers, and businessmen. The Democrats charged the measure with unduly favoring the higher income groups, particularly stockholders, by exempting the first $50 in dividends from taxation and reducing the rate on dividends above that figure. The Republicans retorted that the exemption would benefit small stockholders more than the large and was an act of justice to relieve investors from a form of double taxation.

By these actions Congress reduced taxes by $7.4 billion—a larger cut than ever before provided in a single year. Welcome though it was, it delayed balancing the budget. For fiscal 1955 there was a deficit of over $4 billion despite further reduction in expenditure, but a year later the picture was quite different. For the twelve months ending June 30, 1956, the government took in $1.75 billion more than it paid out—the first surplus since 1948. This was achieved not by new economies, but by larger revenues—the by-product of a new wave of prosperity. Indeed, after 1955 the Eisenhower administration spent more freely, for both defense and social welfare.

During the second administration the budget problem provoked serious controversy. On one side were the conservatives, insistent on holding down expenditures and providing further tax cuts; on the other were the liberals, acutely conscious of the need for continued foreign aid, rapid development of new weapons, and increasing Federal activity in such fields as health and education. For the first eight months of 1957 the problem was hotly debated. Eisenhower's proposed expenditures for fiscal 1958 were $71.8 billion, larger than any previous peacetime budget. Secretary Humphrey took the unusual step of criticizing this budget in a press conference; unless government expenditures were curtailed and taxes cut, he predicted a depression "that will curl your hair." A bipartisan economy bloc began cutting away at the budget and Congress appropriated $5 billion less than Eisenhower had originally asked.

Despite this budget battle in 1957 and an economic recession that began in the fall of that year, Eisenhower sought $73.9 billion in his budget request in January, 1958, which anticipated a deficit of about $12 billion. Nearly 65 per cent was earmarked for national defense and foreign aid, and Congress, despite the fact it was an election year, could not vote tax cuts that might weaken national security. And when "Eisenhower prosperity" returned in the fall of 1958 and continued until the spring of 1960, the President persuaded Congress not to change the income tax levies because of the increasing national debt, now fast reaching the $300 billion mark. Yet the Democrat-controlled legislature frequently took the bit in its teeth in the last two years of the Eisenhower regime by cutting certain taxes and by passing over the President's veto a 7.5 per cent wage increase for government employees. Nevertheless, in three of his eight years in office, Eisenhower attained a balanced budget without weakening national defense or materially cutting foreign aid. On the other hand, income tax cuts were not as great as he undoubtedly wished and the national debt continued to rocket.

The Fight Against Inflation

Secretary Humphrey, it may safely be assumed, did not consider John Maynard Keynes his patron saint. He would not have conceded that the government should adjust its spending and taxes policies to the ups and downs of the economic cycle, or that it had to provide massive public investment when private investment failed. Yet Humphrey was not afraid to use government weapons of a more conservative type.

When Eisenhower took office, inflation, fed by the Korean War and rearmament, was a serious problem. The President and his advisers fought the fire, not with more regulation, but with less. Price and wage controls were terminated, and the economy was left largely free in accordance with conservative doctrine. On the other hand, Humphrey believed that to tighten credit was a legitimate anti-inflation policy. By raising the interest rate on new issues of government bonds, the Treasury deliberately undertook to attract investment funds and make it harder for private borrowers to obtain loans. Thus was initiated the administration's "tight money" policy, in which the Treasury and the Federal Reserve Board were close allies.

During the fall of 1953 and the spring of 1954 concern over inflation gave way to fear of another depression. Industrial production declined 10 per cent and the number of unemployed grew to a disturbing 3.75 million. The Eisenhower administration met the situation by relaxing its tight-money policy, allowing tax cuts, and postponing its efforts to balance the budget.

Whether these moderate steps would be enough to stem the depression was by no means certain. Both the CIO and the AFL criticized Eisenhower for inaction, and Truman urged spending $3 billion for emergency public works and welfare. Within the Cabinet, counsels were divided: the more politically minded advisers wanted to expand government spending, but Humphrey and the conservatives opposed hasty action. Taking his characteristic middle position, the President moved slowly, but ordered plans for highway construction and other public works to be ready in case the situation worsened.

To the Republicans' great relief, the economic picture brightened in the spring of 1954, and by mid-year the recovery was almost complete. With the passing of these economic clouds the country entered a period of impressive prosperity. Between 1953 and 1956 the gross national product increased from $363.2 billion to $412.4 billion, and employment in 1956 reached a new high of 65 million—a rise of 3.7 million over 1953. Although the farmer failed to share in this prosperity, most other groups enjoyed a substantial increase in income.

Despite this boom, the Eisenhower administration was able to boast during its first three years in office that inflation had been halted and that the consumers' price index had remained relatively stable. Thereafter, however, prices started to push up again. During 1956 the cost of living rose 3 per cent, and this upward trend continued through most of 1957. Management blamed labor for pushing up wages faster than productivity, thus increasing industrial costs and making higher prices necessary. Labor denied this and attributed the higher living costs to excessive corporate prices.

Undoubtedly Humphrey believed that heavy government spending and high taxes were major factors in this inflation, but he could do little about them so long as the world situation remained critical. The administration's principal anti-inflation weapon had to be its tight-money policy. The Federal Reserve Board, with Treasury blessing, applied the brakes with increasing pressure so that borrowers, both large and small, found it harder to obtain money and were charged higher interest rates. Hostile critics blamed this policy for hampering small business and home construction and for adding to the difficulties of states and municipalities in building new schools. Despite such criticism, the administration continued this policy until the fall of 1957, when declining business activity and falling stock prices brought a relaxation.

The 1958 Recession

The economic recession, even though it lasted until mid-1958, was not of the hair-curling variety that Humphrey had warned about. Economists generally attributed it to a decrease in consumer purchases of durable goods, to a $6 billion cut in defense spending, and to a decline in exports. During the nine months of this recession, unemployment increased to 5.3 million in July, 1958, and industrial production declined about 15 per cent, but there were several unusual features: the gross national product rose from $442 billion in 1957 to $444 billion in 1958; the lot of the farmer improved; and the cost of living increased 3 per cent.

Despite demands by such diverse elements as the AFL-CIO and the J. P. Morgan Company for tax cuts, Eisenhower refused to support them; to him the "moderate" recession did not warrant "any tax reduction that will create greater deficits." And both Speaker Rayburn and Senate Majority Leader Johnson agreed they would oppose any material tax changes for political advantage. The President, however, used other means to stimulate the economy: interstate highway building was speeded; Federal aid to housing, college dormitory construction, and urban renewal was increased; more defense contracts were awarded to areas where unemployment exceeded 6 per cent; and states were helped to take care of their unemployment compensation problems. Eisenhower also successfully appealed to the American public to dip into their savings to buy articles they did not necessarily require at that time; the people responded to an estimated $100 billion. Thus prosperity returned without resort to inflationary methods, tax cuts, or large deficit spending.

The restored "Eisenhower prosperity" did not last as long as the President anticipated. By the spring of 1960 there were signs of trouble ahead. Unemployment rose once more to five million, industrial production started to decline again, and foreign sales fell off. Yet concentration on the presidential election and the fact that the gross national product reached the $500 billion level for the first time put off any remedial measures, thereby leaving the problem for President Kennedy to try to solve.

Governmental Reorganization

The Eisenhower administration believed that another method of trying to balance the budget was to continue the movement for more efficient government. In addition to saving money, it might prevent scandals similar to those in the latter months of his predecessor's administration. In March, 1953, the first step provided for ending the RFC in June, 1954; in the interim its loans were limited to $1 million and the Treasury Department gradually took over its assets. Next, Congress continued the life of the Reorganization Act of 1949, thereby giving Eisenhower authority to make changes in the executive branch—unless either house disapproved within two months. Another Eisenhower victory was achieved in the spring of 1953 when the Department of Health, Education and Welfare was established.

One of the most controversial proposals grew out of the so-called Battle of the Pentagon that began in 1956 when the Air Force challenged the effectiveness of the Army's Nike missile as a defensive weapon; the Army questioned whether the nation should rely primarily on air power; and the Navy denied that its supercarriers were obsolete. Since this bickering was detrimental to national defense, Eisenhower proposed a major reorganization plan in April, 1958, under which the Secretary of Defense, a civilian, would be given practically full control over military planning and the spending of defense appropriations. The Joint Chiefs of Staff would work directly with the Secretary to promote unified control, rather than to concentrate on the particular service they represented. Thus if the United States were involved in war, "one single concentrated effort" could be achieved among the three branches. Although Congressmen tried to weaken the Defense Department Reorganization Bill, the measure was passed in July in virtually its original form—the greatest step thus far taken toward unification of the armed forces.

About the same time Congress also approved the establishment of the National Aeronautics and Space Administration (NASA), responsible to the Secretary of Defense, to centralize all military research, as well as to promote space exploration technology, in which many believed Russia held the lead as a result of her recent launching of the first *Sputnik*. The Office of Defense Mobilization was likewise established to take over the management of manpower and production from the National Security Resources and Munitions Boards. Furthermore, the Foreign Operations Administration (FOA) assumed the responsibilities previously administered by a number of separate agencies, notably the Mutual Security Administration, and the United States Information Agency (USIA) was set up to coordinate all foreign information programs.

Middle-of-the-Road Politics

Two facts dominated the politics of the Eisenhower age: the extraordinary popularity of the President himself and the strange inability of the Republicans to derive full political advantage from this popularity. In the four congressional elections held during Eisenhower's time, only the Eighty-third Congress was Republican—and by only a narrow margin.

The Republicans suffered their first disappointment in the congressional election of 1954. Throughout the campaign Nixon warned the country that a Democratic victory might restore "Trumanism," which he identified with "Korea, Communism, corruption, and controls"—language the opposition party deeply resented. Eisenhower also took to the road, campaigning more actively than any previous President in a midterm election. The Democrats retaliated with charges that the administration favored big business, was unsympathetic to the plight of the farmers and the unemployed, and was giving away national resources. The election showed no strong trend for either party. The new Senate line-up was Democrats 49, Republicans 47; the House division was Democrats 232, Republicans 203. The Republicans' only consolation was that their losses were smaller than those commonly suffered in midterm elections by the party in power.

Despite predictions that the election would result in a deadlock, the executive and legislative branches did not indulge in much open feuding. Senate Majority Leader Lyndon Johnson advocated a policy of moderation, and his fellow-Texan, Speaker Sam Rayburn, exercised a similar restraint upon the House. On issues involving international cooperation, Eisenhower often gained stronger support from the Democrats than from the Republicans; on domestic issues he was less fortunate, but here party lines were frequently crossed and the President achieved at least some of his goals.

With Taft's death and the eclipse of McCarthy, Eisenhower's leadership of the Republican party was now unchallenged. The lesson of the 1954 election was clear even to right-wing Republicans: Eisenhower's renomination was absolutely vital to party success in 1956. Great was the consternation, therefore, when the President suffered a "moderate" heart attack on September 24, 1955. Most Americans assumed that even if he recovered, this serious illness would end his political career. Reflecting the alarm of the business community, the stock market suffered its sharpest decline since 1929.

Fortunately, the crisis came at a quiet moment in national affairs, and routine business continued under the informal direction of Nixon and Adams. For seven weeks the President remained in a Denver hospital, followed by five weeks of further convalescence at his Gettysburg farm. Then in February, 1956, his doctors delighted the Republican leaders with the diagnosis that he was probably good for "five to ten years" more of active service. At the end of the month he announced his willingness to run for re-election.

The possibility that Eisenhower might have to reverse this decision was ,raised when he once again became a hospital patient in June—this time because of an intestinal obstruction caused by ileitis. An emergency operation was successful, however, and on July 10 he reaffirmed his intention to run again.[1]

The Election of 1956

Contrary to custom, the Democratic National Convention of 1956 was held earlier than the Republican. When it opened at Chicago, Adlai Stevenson's renomination appeared certain. Showing none of his 1952 reluctance, he had entered actively into the preconvention campaign and had gained the pledges of more delegates than any of his rivals. His reputation for moderation was particularly valuable because the party leaders were seeking a standard-bearer who could hold the party together. Neither of the other leading candidates was acceptable to the South: Governor Averell Harriman of New York was strongly New Deal in background; Senator Estes Kefauver of Tennessee was distrusted for his liberalism on civil rights and other matters. Stevenson's chances were further improved just before the convention when Kefauver withdrew from the race. Although Harriman remained in the contest with strong support from Truman, the outcome was never seriously in doubt. Stevenson was nominated on the first ballot by a one-sided majority.

A much more exciting contest developed for second place on the ticket. Stevenson broke precedent by expressing no preference and allowing the delegates a free hand. The leading candidates on the first ballot were Senator Kefauver and Senator John F. Kennedy of Massachusetts. Although a Catholic, young Kennedy won considerable support from Southern delegates. For most of the second roll call he appeared to be ahead, but a few strategic shifts from favorite sons to Kefauver gave the nomination to the man from Tennessee.

The platform condemned Republican farm policy and advocated a return to 90 per cent of parity supports, accused the Eisenhower administration of allowing private interests to pillage national resources, and criticized the State Department's conduct of foreign affairs as "inept and vacillating." On civil rights the Democrats took a cautious position to avoid a party split.

When the Republicans met at San Francisco, Eisenhower had no opposition for the first place on the ticket, but sentiment for Nixon was not equally unanimous. Some Republicans hoped the nomination would go to someone else. A month before the convention Harold Stassen announced that private polls showed that a ticket of Eisenhower and Governor Christian Herter of Massachusetts would run much better than an Eisenhower-Nixon one. Conservative Republicans denounced this maneuver, Eisenhower said he would be "delighted" to have Nixon again, and Herter disavowed the move-

---

[1] These two illnesses, plus a mild stroke in November, 1957, again raised the question of when a President's disability warranted the succession of the Vice President. The related question was who should determine the problem. Although there was much discussion of this important issue, nothing was done to solve it.

Vice President and Mrs. Nixon and President and Mrs. Eisenhower at the Republican convention, San Francisco, 1956. (UPI Photo.)

ment by agreeing to put Nixon's name in nomination at the convention. Yet Stassen continued to boost Herter until just before the convention opened, when he finally gave up and promised to make a seconding speech for Nixon.

With this issue settled, the convention took on the aspect of a monster Eisenhower rally. The drama reached its high point when the President accepted the nomination in a speech that avoided bitter partisanship. "Let us quit fighting the battles of the past," he urged, "and let us turn our attention to these problems of the present and the future, on which long-term well-being of our people so urgently depends." The platform praised the administration for having achieved prosperity and peace and commended the "partnership" policy on natural resources. On civil rights the Republicans accepted the Supreme Court's decision that segregation must be "progressively eliminated."

Stevenson and Kefauver campaigned vigorously, criticizing the Eisenhower record in both domestic and foreign affairs. Stevenson's boldest move was to advocate that further testing of hydrogen bombs be banned by international agreement to save mankind from the injurious effects of radioactive fallout. Such a ban would ease dangerous world tensions and would involve no risk to the United States because any violation could be easily detected. Eisenhower condemned the proposal as dangerous to national security in the absence of an adequate inspection system. Since the scientists themselves were divided on whether the tests involved a threat to health, most voters found the issue completely confusing.

Actually, the Democrats could do little to halt the Eisenhower sweep. The President's health was an important issue, but Stevenson's few attempts to discuss the matter were condemned as unsportsmanlike. For most voters the President's vigorous campaigning was the best answer to suggestions that he might not survive four more years in the White House.

A week before the election a sudden threat to world peace developed when first Israel and then England and France invaded Egyptian territory. Stevenson charged that this Middle East crisis demonstrated the bankruptcy of Republican foreign policy, but this last attempt to win votes failed. The gathering war clouds only increased the voters' determination to entrust the nation's safety to Eisenhower for another term.

Eisenhower's victory was more sweeping than it had been in 1952. His popular vote was 35.6 million to Stevenson's 26 million. By carrying 41 states Eisenhower won 457 electoral votes to Stevenson's 73. Florida, Louisiana, Oklahoma, Tennessee, Texas, and Virginia were all in the Republican column. Not since Franklin Roosevelt defeated Landon in 1936 had a presidential candidate won so decisively.

But even the President's coattails could not carry the Republicans back into control of Congress. In the Senate the Democrats exactly held their own with 49 seats to the Republican 47; in the House they increased their margin by winning 235 seats to the Republican 200. The Republican defeat that rankled most occurred in Oregon, where former Secretary of the Interior Douglas McKay was beaten by Senator Wayne Morse, the former Republican who had shifted to the Democratic party because of disillusionment with Eisenhower.

While Eisenhower continued a hero in the eyes of the American majority during his second administration and his relationship with the Democratic Congress was good, criticism of him increased. Some of this arose from his growing conservatism; some developed from his longer absences from Washington on hunting and golfing trips; some undoubtedly was because he could not run again; and some resulted from his continued insistence on trying to balance the budget, with the accompanying refusal to approve what he considered unnecessary spending, even for welfare purposes.

These factors, plus the 1958 recession, contributed to widespread Democratic gains in the 1958 elections. In the House, the Democrats picked up 48 additional seats; in the Senate their gain was 15 seats; thus they had the greatest control since 1936. To some political observers, the success of so many liberal candidates was basically a rebuke to the "standpat" position of the administration. But the Eighty-sixth Congress did not heed the trend and cooperated, as had its two predecessors, with President Eisenhower in continuing in the middle of the road.

Although both major party platforms had demanded Alaskan and Hawaiian statehood since 1948, partisanship in Congress had prevented any action. Republicans feared Alaska would be Democratic, and Democrats opposed the admission of Hawaii because it would be Republican. Business leaders added their pressure against either admission, believing they could obtain larger profits under territorial government. On the other hand, powerful factors were working in favor of statehood. Eisenhower continued to urge Congress to admit both territories; territorial lobbies became increasingly active; and, perhaps, most effective of all, increasing interest in civil rights made it seem unjust that the inhabitants of Alaska and Hawaii did not enjoy all of the rights and privileges of the residents of the forty-eight states. Therefore Congress relented and approved the admission of Alaska in June, 1958, and of Hawaii in March, 1959, for another middle-of-the-road victory for the administration.

The Changing Farm Problem

Secretary of Agriculture Ezra Taft Benson of Utah, a high dignitary of the Mormon Church and a leader in the farmers' cooperative movement, inherited a disturbing farm situation. During the year before Eisenhower took office, both agricultural prices and total farm income had been falling. Benson blamed the trouble on bad government policy. Although the Agricultural Act of 1949 had provided for a transition from rigid price support to flexible ones, farm belt pressure resulted in an extension of rigid supports at 90 per cent of parity through 1954. This government guarantee, Benson believed, encouraged farmers to overproduce, necessitated large government expenditures, and piled up unsalable surpluses in government warehouses. Therefore he urged that rigid price supports be replaced with flexible ones; thus the law of supply and demand would have a chance to operate, and farmers would divert acreage from unprofitable staples to other crops.

The Benson program involved some change of position for Eisenhower, who had favored full parity during the 1952 campaign, but the lessening of government regulation appealed to him and he gave his Secretary full support. As a result, the Agricultural Act of 1954, forced through Congress after a sharp battle, established flexible supports—from 82.5 per cent to 90 per cent in 1955, and from 75 to 90 per cent thereafter—on five basic crops: corn, cotton, peanuts, rice, and wheat. The measure also revised the parity formula, offered incentives for expanding wool production, and provided modified supports for milk, tobacco, and certain other commodities.

While Benson's victory was impressive, it involved political risks if the farm situation continued to deteriorate. After winning in the 1954 congressional elections, the Democrats sought to gain favor with the farmers by restoring rigid 90 per cent supports. Congress passed such a bill in the spring of 1956, only to have Eisenhower veto it. To soften the blow, the administration fixed supports for corn, cotton, and wheat at 82.5 per cent for another year instead of cutting them to 75 per cent as the law permitted. The President also obtained bipartisan backing for the so-called soil-bank plan, a scheme to reduce the surplus by paying farmers to take acreage out of production and convert it into pasturage or forest. In May, 1956, Congress appropriated $1.2 billion for this program, under which some twelve million acres were put in the soil bank.

Other means of diminishing the ever-mounting surpluses in government storage were the Agricultural Trade and Development Act of 1954, under which surpluses could be used for school lunches, to alleviate conditions in disaster areas, and to exchange abroad for strategic materials; and the Foreign Aid Act of 1955, aimed at exchanging surpluses for foreign currencies.

Nevertheless, as the second Eisenhower administration began, the farm situation continued to be unsatisfactory. Farm prices pushed upward a little—although not as much as other prices, so that the parity index continued to fall. Despite his distaste for regimentation, Benson insisted that farmers accept acreage allotments on staple crops before they could qualify for price supports. Thus everyone was unhappy: the Republican administration because it found itself continuing policies for which it had criticized the Democrats; the Midwestern farmers because they resented Benson's lower support prices and production restrictions; and consumers because they had to pay higher food prices and higher taxes.

Strange to say, the 1957–1958 recession brought an increase of 10 per cent in farm income while the rest of the national economy suffered. Secretary Benson claimed full credit for this upturn, but most economists insisted that a poor 1957 growing season and increased grain and cotton exports were more responsible.

When overproduction in 1958 again resulted in surpluses with the inevitable taxpayers' plaints, Benson sought another solution which, after many congressional amendments, was passed as the Agricultural Act of 1958. Growers of most staples except wheat had their choice of lower parity with no controls or a higher parity with production regulated. This measure was no more acceptable to the farmer or the taxpayer than previous plans had been. Ironically, neither the shift to flexible supports nor acreage restrictions eliminated the agricultural surplus. Better methods had so increased the farmer's efficiency that government efforts to reduce production were largely nullified. Indeed, the harried Commodity Credit Corporation found itself loaded with greater surpluses than ever.

Straws in the political wind indicated that Benson's policies were a serious liability to the party in the Midwest. When traditionally Republican Wisconsin elected a Democrat, William Proxmire, to fill the vacancy left by Senator McCarthy's death in 1957, the upset was generally attributed to the discontent of the dairy farmers. Despite such incidents, however, there was evidence that the farm bloc was no longer a potent force. The number of farmers in proportion to the total population was decreasing and the farmers themselves were divided. The big competition for votes was now in the fast-growing urban suburbs, where high price supports for agriculture were unpopular. Eastern farmers who had to buy feed for chickens and livestock obviously had different interests than the Western wheat and corn growers. And even among the latter there was more grumbling than open revolt over the Benson program. Though farm profits were not what they had been during World War II days, the more efficient producers were able to make a respectable living. Some authorities believed that the most helpful policy would be to cut marketing costs in the interests of both farmers and consumers and to induce marginal producers to move off the land.

Power and Natural Resources

One of the few issues on which there was a clear-cut conflict of philosophy between Eisenhower Republicanism and New Deal Democracy was that of public versus private power. Under Roosevelt and Truman vast Federal power projects had been built in the Tennessee Valley and in the Pacific Northwest, and plans had been pushed for similar developments elsewhere. Eisenhower and his Secretary of the Interior, Douglas McKay, advocated the so-called partnership principle, under which the primary responsibility for power would rest upon "the people locally"—that is, upon the states, municipalities, and private companies. The Federal government would act only in exceptional cases where the necessary projects were too large for local action.

The new approach to the power issue was illustrated by Eisenhower's policy toward Hell's Canyon, a deep gorge on the Snake River at the Idaho-Oregon boundary that was one of the best remaining power sites in the country. The Truman administration had planned to build a high multipurpose dam as a Federal project; the Idaho Power Company had offered an alternative plan for constructing three small dams with private capital. The Eisenhower administration rejected the high-dam plan, and the FPC granted a license to the private utility company. The public-power advocates then made a determined fight to upset this decision. In 1956 most congressional Democrats supported a bill to substitute the Federal project, but Eisenhower marshaled enough support to defeat the measure. Still unwilling to give up the fight, the public-power faction attempted to persuade the Supreme Court to annul the FPC license for the private development, but this effort also failed.

A major struggle developed over TVA—an enterprise that Eisenhower had once characterized as "creeping socialism." This great public agency had attracted so much industry to the region that it had to supplement its hydroelectric generating facilities with steam plants. Private power advocates were opposed to further expansion of this kind, claiming that the growing proportion of steam-generated power showed how far TVA had moved from its original purposes. They argued that TVA competition was unfair because the public agency's payments in lieu of taxes fell far short of the taxes imposed upon private utilities. The Republican Eighty-third Congress refused to appropriate funds for TVA expansion.

This unwillingness to build new TVA steam-generating plants involved the Eisenhower administration in a hornet's nest. By a complicated arrangement, the Atomic Energy Commission contracted with Edgar Dixon and Eugene Yates, the executives of two private utility companies, to build a private generating plant in Arkansas, across the Mississippi River from Memphis, Tennessee. The AEC would then supply the city of Memphis with power from the Dixon-Yates plant, and the TVA, relieved of responsibilities at Memphis, would continue to deliver power to various atomic energy plants.

Public power advocates denounced the Dixon-Yates contract as a conspiracy to weaken the TVA. They charged the deal had been secretly made by the AEC on terms unfavorable to the government. Disliking an arrangement that might mean higher electric rates, Memphis decided to build its own municipal generating plant. The Eisenhower administration accepted this solution as being consistent with its partnership policy and canceled the Dixon-Yates contract.

But the last had not been heard of the affair. The Democrats, scenting campaign material, demanded a congressional investigation, which revealed that a vice president of the First Boston Corporation had been employed by the government as a consultant in negotiating the Dixon-Yates contract, and that the Corporation had subsequently acted as financial agent for the Dixon-Yates group. The AEC declared that this conflict of interest voided the contract and refused to compensate Dixon-Yates for expenditures already made when the project was canceled.

Although the administration continued to oppose TVA expansion, it did demonstrate the other side of its partnership policy. On the grounds that the projects were too costly and complex for local enterprise, the Republicans supported plans to produce public power by a dam on the upper Colorado River and by a tunnel between the Fryingpan and Arkansas rivers.

While the nation's water power, coal, and oil resources made it unlikely that atomic power would be needed for generating electricity in the near future, a jockeying for advantage between the public and private power factions developed in this field as well. The Atomic Energy Act of 1946 had vested full control of atomic power in the AEC. Eisenhower asked Congress to allow the AEC to license private agencies to develop nuclear energy for peaceful uses. Most of the President's recommendations were incorporated in the Atomic Energy Act of 1954, but the public power advocates added safeguards to prevent private monopoly of atomic patents and nuclear-generated electricity.

Offshore Oil

Paralleling the controversies between the public and private power factions was a series of disputes involving conservation policy. Roosevelt and Truman had been jealous guardians of the national domain; Eisenhower favored turning over much of the responsibility to the states.

This issue came to focus early in the administration over the question of the offshore oil resources. In 1946 Congress had attempted to give the states full control over the underseas resources lying off their coasts, but Truman, believing in Federal control, vetoed the bill. In 1947 and 1950 the Supreme Court upheld the paramount right of the Federal government over the submerged lands. Congress countered with a bill to transfer title to the states, but Truman once again interposed with a veto.

During the 1952 campaign Eisenhower came out in favor of state control, and early in his administration this pledge was fulfilled. On May 22, 1953, he signed an act transferring to the coastal states all rights to the oil, natural gas, and other resources lying within their historic limits—three miles in most instances, and ten and a half miles in the cases of Texas and Florida. Upon the President's recommendation a second law retained Federal control over the continental shelf beyond those limits. Particularly in the Gulf of Mexico the potential wealth to be drawn from this outer rim was enormous.

The transfer of offshore rights to the states was supported by a coalition of Democrats and Republicans—some because their states had an immediate interest, others because of a desire to defend states' rights; the opposition came from Northern Democrats eager to extend the Federal conservation policy. Senator Wayne Morse, a former Republican who had become a Democrat, led the conservation faction not only on the public power issue, but upon numerous other matters. He charged that subordinate officials in the Interior Department had sacrificed the national domain by awarding timber contracts to privileged operators and allowing the exploitation of oil deposits within national wild life preserves.

The St. Lawrence Seaway

Democratic attacks on the Republican "giveaways" tended to be ineffective because, for one thing, Southern Democrats had been so prominent in the offshore oil bill fight. Moreover, the Republicans' record on development of national resources had its bright, as well as dark, spots. Particularly impressive was Eisenhower's victory in obtaining congressional approval for the St. Lawrence Seaway—a proposal five previous Presidents had unsuccessfully advocated. Earlier attempts to link the Great Lakes to the Atlantic Ocean had been blocked by the railroads, the Eastern seaports, and the coal miners, but compelling new reasons for the waterway had arisen. Rapidly depleting American ore deposits made it imperative that Midwestern steel mills gain access to new sources of supply in Labrador and elsewhere. For

President Eisenhower and Queen Elizabeth at the opening of the St. Lawrence Seaway, 1959. (Courtesy NFB.)

this and other reasons connected with national defense, the Eisenhower administration gave the Seaway strong backing. Moreover, Canada, weary of the long delay, indicated it would build the project alone if the United States did not act promptly. On May 13, 1954, the President signed a bill authorizing joint construction by Canada and the United States. The American share was to be built by a government corporation, which would raise $105 million by selling its bonds to the Treasury. Construction and control of hydroelectric installation were entrusted to the New York State Power Authority and the Ontario Hydro-Electric Commission—in conformity with Eisenhower's "partnership policy."

Labor and Welfare

When Eisenhower chose as his Secretary of Labor Martin Durkin, president of the Plumbers' Union and a Stevenson supporter, most Republicans disapproved. With characteristic bluntness, Taft called the appointment "incredible." Yet Eisenhower's good intentions were obvious. By appointing a prominent union leader, he wanted to assure organized labor that he was no enemy to its legitimate rights. Durkin, with equal good faith, accepted the post in the hope he could revise the Taft-Hartley Act. He worked out nineteen Taft-Hartley amendments that he hoped the President would recommend to Congress. Republican conservatives opposed his program, however, and Eisenhower withheld his approval. In September, 1953, Durkin resigned, charging that the President had broken his word—a contention the White House emphatically denied.

To succeed Durkin, Eisenhower appointed James Mitchell, a man of very different background, whose knowledge of the labor problem came from management rather than union experience. Respected by labor as honest and fair, Mitchell salved the wounds left by the Durkin resignation. He enforced the Federal minimum wage vigorously and called for higher standards. In 1956 Eisenhower recommended raising the minimum to 90 cents an hour; the Democratic Congress went the administration one better by fixing the standard at $1.00 an hour. On the whole, the Eisenhower administration and organized labor got along better than had been expected. Despite union complaints that the NLRB had been packed in favor of management and that the President did little to change the Taft-Hartley Act, labor resentment remained moderate, especially during Eisenhower's first term.

The major strike during the Eisenhower years occurred during 1959. In June, the United Steel Workers demanded an hourly increase of 15 cents (to make a total of $3.25) and a continued escalator cost-of-living clause in their contract. The steel companies would offer only increased fringe benefits at the time, with a promise of a "modest" wage increase in 1960 if steel output increased. When collective bargaining failed, about 500,000 union members on July 15 began the longest strike—116 days—in steel history. Because this walkout threatened the national economy, Eisenhower finally invoked the injunction provision of the Taft-Hartley Act, which the Supreme Court upheld despite union charges that it was unconstitutional, and on November

7 the strike ended. Yet in the contracts the USWA subsequently signed, the members obtained most of their original demands.

In April, 1953, Congress created a Department of Health, Education and Welfare. Mrs. Oveta Culp Hobby, the first Secretary, was a Texas Democrat, well known both through her command of the Women's Army Corps in World War II and her career as publisher of the *Houston Post*. She followed a cautious course, partly because of personal conservatism, partly to allay the suspicion that the new department meant Federal encroachment in the field of medicine and education. In the spring of 1955, Mrs. Hobby was sharply criticized for not having made adequate plans to distribute the new Salk polio vaccine. When some fifty-six cases of polio were traced to the faulty vaccine produced by a particular manufacturer, the department was further condemned for an unsatisfactory testing program. In July, 1955, Mrs. Hobby resigned, giving her husband's illness as her reason.

Her successor was Marion Folsom, an Eastman Kodak Company executive with extensive business and government experience in the welfare field. He did much to extend social security, facilitate medical care, and broaden the nation's educational plant.

Without going as far as Truman had in his Fair Deal, Eisenhower nevertheless sponsored a variety of welfare proposals. In August, 1954, Congress extended the Social Security Act to cover one million more persons, including farmers, state and local government workers, and clergymen. Old-age pensions were also raised and more liberal rules for pensioners were adopted. In 1956 the system was made still more generous by lowering the eligibility age for women to sixty-two and that for disabled workers to fifty, and by bringing under Social Security some 600,000 more farmers, 225,000 doctors and self-employed professional men and women, and those in the armed services. Despite some Eisenhower opposition based on a desire not to increase the national debt, Congress overwhelmingly approved in 1958 a substantial increase in security benefits.

The Housing Act of 1954 was intended to promote home building, not only as a desirable goal in itself but as a stimulus to drooping business activity. Private construction was encouraged by reducing down payments and extending the amortization period of FHA-insured loans. In support of the "urban renewal" movement, the FHA could insure loans for renovating older dwellings. Eisenhower had recommended that the government be authorized to build 140,000 public housing units over a four-year period, but on this Congress balked, limiting this number to 35,000 units for one year. The next Congress was more favorable to public housing but was unable to do much more than keep the program alive in subsequent legislation. By steering between those who demanded a bold public housing policy and those who wanted none at all, Eisenhower once more demonstrated his preference for the middle course.

The Republicans displayed much more enthusiasm for road building, where the need of action was obvious. Because of depression and war, highway construction had fallen far behind the multiplying motor traffic of the nation. In 1956 Congress, on Eisenhower's recommendation, authorized $33.5 billion to construct 41,000 miles of modern superhighways over a period of sixteen years. The states were to do the building, but the Federal government would pay 90 per cent of the costs. Federal excise taxes on gasoline and tires were raised to provide the necessary funds.

Eisenhower also recommended additional Federal expenditure for hospital construction and public health research. His proposal for a $25 million reinsurance fund to encourage private and nonprofit health insurance organizations to offer broader protection fell under attack from both left and right. Those who believed in national health insurance said it was hopelessly inadequate; the AMA opposed it as a dangerous step toward "socialized medicine." Consequently, Congress enacted only the noncontroversial recommendations and left the reinsurance proposal strictly alone until 1960, when liberal Democrats introduced several bills to increase the Social Security tax to provide medical, surgical, and hospital care for the twelve million aged persons who had Social Security protection. The administration, however, preferred the proposal introduced by the conservatives to increase Federal aid for state "medicare" programs. Despite the protests of the liberals and labor, the Kerr-Mills Act became law in September, 1960, as the first Federal measure in the field of medical help for the aged.

Aid for Education

Similar frustrations resulted from the President's attempts to aid education. Eisenhower was torn between a desire to act and a fear of Federal interference with local affairs. A first step was taken in 1953 when Congress authorized Federal grants to help build schools in districts where defense industry had resulted in an abnormal population growth. Two years later, the President proposed outright grants of $200 million to construct schools in hardship areas and authority for the Federal government to purchase local district school bonds up to $750 million. Since Northern Democrats criticized the measure as a "do-it-yourself" program and Southern Democrats feared any action that might undermine racial segregation in the schools, Congress did nothing.

In November, 1955, a White House Conference on Education, attended by two thousand educational and community leaders, concluded that national expenditures for education would have to be doubled within ten years and that Federal aid for school construction was necessary. Using these findings, the President recommended a program under which the Federal government would make outright grants of $1.25 billion over a five-year period and would provide $750 million more through the purchase of local school construction bonds. This proposal, however, was killed in the House by a complicated series of maneuvers involving both Republicans and Democrats. The President's failure to hold the support of his own party was also illustrated in 1957, when the House again voted down the school construction program with most of the Republicans and Southern Democrats in opposition. Three years later Eisenhower tried once more to persuade Congress to pass the School Assistance Bill, but the segregationists, this time aided by Catholics who objected to the bill's failure to include Federal aid to parochial schools, were able to defeat the measure.

The Eisenhower administration had better success in obtaining Federal assistance for higher education. Although more and more high school graduates were going to college, reports of several committees between 1953 and 1957 indicated that the nation was lagging far behind the Soviet Union in training students in science and technology. Unless something were done, the gap would widen and national security would be endangered. These reports suggested that the Federal government, the states, industry, and foundations cooperate in sponsoring scientific research in the colleges and that college students in good standing continue to be draft exempt.

As a result, Eisenhower successfully persuaded Congress to pass the National Defense Education Act in September, 1958, which established a $300 million fund from which college students could borrow on easy terms to complete their education. A similar amount was granted to public schools for laboratories and textbooks to improve the teaching of mathematics, science, and modern languages provided the states made matching giants. An $80 million fellowship fund was set up for students who agreed to go into college teaching, and lesser amounts were made available to improve college and vocational school techniques in language and scientific areas.

Challenge from McCarthy

Although the Truman administration had undertaken to purge disloyal persons from sensitive government posts, the Republicans were convinced that not enough had been done. Consequently, in April, 1953, Eisenhower ordered a far-reaching revision of the security system: government employees were now to be dismissed not merely for disloyalty, but for alcoholism, drug addition, immoral conduct, or any other cause that might make them security risks. The Loyalty Review Board was abolished, each agency head was made responsible for his own personnel, and the right of arbitrary dismissal was extended to nonsensitive posts.

Under this new directive there were 6,926 "security separations" between May, 1953, and October, 1954, a fact Nixon and other Republican orators emphasized during the congressional elections of 1954. The Democrats indignantly charged their opponents were playing a "numbers game," in which dismissals and voluntary resignations were lumped together, with no indication of how many employees had been found guilty of disloyalty and how many were fired merely for drinking or talking too much, or even of how many were Truman holdovers and how many were Eisenhower appointees.

The difficulties inherent in the security problem were dramatized by the case of Dr. J. Robert Oppenheimer, who had directed the manufacture of the first atomic bombs at Los Alamos and was now employed as an AEC adviser. After considering charges that Oppenheimer had associated with Communists and had obstructed the development of the hydrogen bomb, a special investigating board recommended by a three-to-two vote that his security clearance be withdrawn. Upholding this decision by four to one, the AEC ruled that although the famous scientist was not disloyal, he had 'fundamental defects" of character and had associated with Communists "far beyond the tolerable limits of prudence and restraint." Many Americans were distressed that in a time when scientific knowledge was at a premium, the government had deprived itself of the services of such a brilliant mind.

By vigorous action on government security risks and by further prosecutions under the Smith Act, Eisenhower hoped to make unnecessary the blunderbuss tactics used by congressional investigating committees. Senator McCarthy showed no disposition, however, to turn over his Red-hunting mission to the President. As a result of Republican control of the Eighty-third Congress, McCarthy became chairman of the Government Operations Committee and its strategic Permanent Subcommittee on Investigations. Determined to keep his name in the headlines, he directed sensational assaults upon the Voice of America overseas radio program, American libraries in foreign countries, and the CIA—in all of which he professed to see evidence of Communist infiltration.

McCarthy's ruthless tactics were condemned not only by the Democrats, but by many Republicans who feared that he was trying to seize the party leadership. Despite these warnings, Eisenhower followed a cautious policy. Although he occasionally criticized McCarthy, as at Dartmouth College in 1953 when he admonished the graduating class not to join the "book-burners," he shrank from an open fight and directed his subordinates to cooperate in the McCarthy investigations.

Such cooperation had its risks, however, as Secretary to the Army Robert Stevens discovered. When Stevens volunteered to help an investigation of alleged Communist infiltration into the Army, McCarthy exploited the honorable discharge of Major Irving Peress, who had been accused of harboring Communist sympathies. Then when General Ralph Zwicker, a much decorated World War II hero, refused, on orders from his superiors, to reveal the names of those who had authorized the discharge, McCarthy denounced him as not having the brains of a five-year-old and being unfit to wear his uniform. Stevens did not help the situation when he first directed Zwicker not to appear before the committee but later retreated ignominiously when McCarthy pressed the issue.

The Army retaliated by alleging that McCarthy and his two chief assistants —Roy Cohn, the committee counsel, and Francis Carr, the executive director—used the threat of hostile investigation to obtain special privileges for Cohn's close friend, David Schine, a former committee consultant who had been drafted as a private.[2] McCarthy and his aides in turn charged the Army was using the unhappy Schine as "a hostage" to compel the committee to halt its probe.

Some neutral group should have determined the truth or falsity of these conflicting charges, but the Permanent Subcommittee on Investigations insisted on doing the job itself, under the temporary chairmanship of Republican Senator Karl Mundt of South Dakota. For thirty-six days in the spring of 1954 millions of Americans watched the televised hearings that were marked by McCarthy's arrogance, wranglings between the Republican

___

[2] Cohn and Schine had been sent to Europe earlier by McCarthy. They had made themselves thoroughly obnoxious and were largely responsible for the recommendation that resulted in the removal of books from American libraries overseas.

and Democratic committee members, and the cold castigation of McCarthy by Army Counsel Joseph Welch. The subcommittee's findings reflected its initial prejudices: the Republican majority exonerated McCarthy of serious misconduct; the Democrats condemned him for condoning Cohn's improper activities on behalf of Schine. Both sides were severely critical of Stevens and his Army associates. Cohn resigned immediately after the hearings; Stevens held on for a decent interval but retired to private life a year later.

If the Army-McCarthy hearings appeared to have ended in a draw, the outcome was deceptive. McCarthy had gone too far. Senators Ralph Flanders, Vermont Republican, William Fulbright, Arkansas Democrat, and Wayne Morse, Oregon independent, preferred formal charges of misconduct against him, and a special committee of three Republicans and three Democrats conducted hearings. In sharp contrast to the Army-McCarthy soap opera, Chairman Arthur Watkins, a conservative Utah Republican and former Federal judge, insisted upon orderly proceedings without irrelevant appeals to the galleries, and the committee recommended formal Senate censure of McCarthy.

Although McCarthy characteristically fought back by calling Watkins cowardly and stupid and denouncing the hearings as a "lynch party," the tide was now running strongly against him. By a vote of 67 to 22 the Upper House "condemned" McCarthy both for his earlier conduct and for his more recent slurs upon the Watkins Committee. The President added his vote against McCarthy by publicly complimenting Watkins for a "splendid job." The Wisconsin Senator tried to get in the last word by apologizing to the American people for having urged Eisenhower's election. After this defeat McCarthy's star sank quickly. When the Democrats gained control of Congress, he lost his committee chairmanships, and in 1957 he died, a bitter and frustrated man of forty-eight.

Repudiation of McCarthy did not mean Congress was relaxing its hostility toward the Communists. On the contrary, antisubversion laws continued to be added to the statute books. Persons convicted of conspiring to overthrow the government by force now lost their citizenship, and peacetime espionage was made punishable by death. In 1954 the Democrats, eager to prove they were just as patriotic as the Republicans, pushed through the Communist Control Act, formally outlawing the Communist party.

All this zeal to annihilate the Communist conspiracy involved a danger that the government would jeopardize constitutional guarantees of fair trial and orderly procedure. In a number of significant cases during 1956 and 1957 the Supreme Court tried to prevent this. In the Jencks case, the Court ruled that when the government used the testimony of witnesses interrogated by the FBI, the defense was entitled to examine the FBI files to see whether what the witness had said on earlier occasions was consistent with his testimony in open court. In the Watkins case, the Court overruled the conviction of a witness who had refused to answer certain questions put to him by the House Un-American Activities Committee. The Court asserted that Congress must delineate the area a committee was authorized to investigate and that the questions must be pertinent to this area of inquiry. By other decisions the Court restricted the government's security-risk program to sensitive posts and placed a strict interpretation upon that clause in the Smith Act making it a crime to "organize" any group that advocated the violent overthrow of the government.

The Court, already under attack in the South for its antidesegregation decisions, was bitterly denounced in many conservative quarters for seeming to hamper the anti-Communist program. Several bills to nullify the decisions were introduced into Congress in 1957, but only one—a measure requested by the Justice Department—to limit the application of the Jencks decision and to safeguard, as much as possible, the confidential character of the FBI files was passed. Congressional acquiescence in the other rulings gave further evidence that McCarthyism was on the wane.

Another sign of this decline was indicated in the immigration issue. The controversial McCarran-Walter Immigration Act of 1952 was just becoming effective when Eisenhower took office, and the new chief executive was highly critical of its discriminatory features. In consequence, Congress passed the Refugee Relief Act in the summer of 1953, to allow some 215,000 escapees from Communist persecution and certain displaced persons to enter the United States over the next three years over and above the McCarran-Walter quotas.

The next move to lower the immigration bars was made in 1956, when the President learned that immigration from the countries with the largest quotas had fallen, while those nations with smaller quotas were piling up waiting lists. Unfortunately, he failed to persuade Congress to allow the smaller quota countries to take advantage of the unused quotas of the larger and to change the base year from 1920 to 1950.

In the fall of 1956, however, the unsuccessful revolt in Hungary led to an executive order permitting more than twenty thousand refugees from that Communist-suppressed country to enter the United States. And in 1957, when Eisenhower asked that the yearly immigration admissions be doubled, Congress embodied most of the President's proposals in amendments to the McCarren-Walter Act.

During Eisenhower's eight years in the White House not much happened in the way of important new programs or legislation. This lack of activity did not displease the majority of voters, who seemed glad of a respite after the excitement of the Roosevelt presidency and the turmoil of the Truman period. Yet grave national problems were piling up, and the pressure for more action mounted during the general's second term. The sixties were destined to be another period of clashing social forces, particularly in the field of white-black relations—an issue that Eisenhower tried to avoid but was forced to deal with, as will be discussed in Chapter 29.

THE UNITED STATES IN A TROUBLED WORLD

Although Republicans had severely criticized Democratic handling of foreign affairs, they found no easy path of their own through the jungle of world politics. Secretary of State Dulles tried to impress upon both the Soviet rival and the NATO allies in speeches and diplomatic notes that the American government was now in more vigorous hands. Yet the difference between Acheson and Dulles was largely in the area of words, for, as a matter of practical necessity, the Eisenhower foreign policy had to be built upon the Truman foundations. The United States continued to oppose the extension of Soviet power by granting aid to the nations that resisted Communist threats and blandishments and by building a ring of defensive alliances and bases around the periphery of the Communist world. Although the Soviet Union and the United States both professed a desire to ease tensions and to negotiate a disarmament treaty, they failed to agree except on minor issues, and the alarming race to develop even more destructive weapons continued.

Internationalists Versus Nationalists

The struggle between the internationalist and the nationalist wings of the Republican party was sharply waged during Eisenhower's early months in office. Many Republicans were eager to reverse the Roosevelt and Truman policies, but the President, fresh from his NATO experience, proceeded cautiously.

The Republican platform of 1952 had promised that their administration "will repudiate all commitments contained in secret understandings such as those of Yalta, which aid Communist enslavements." Eisenhower tried to soften this plank by suggesting to Congress in February, 1953, a resolution to reject "any interpretations or applications" of secret agreements "which have been perverted to bring about the subjugation of free peoples." Since this did not repudiate the Yalta agreement itself, but only its perversion by Russia, and implied no condemnation of Roosevelt, the Republican nationalists were unhappy. Therefore the Senate Foreign Relations Committee added a clause stipulating that the resolution did not constitute "any determination by Congress as to the validity or invalidity" of the agreement. Resenting the intended slap at Roosevelt in the word "invalidity," the Democrats opposed the resolution, and the whole matter was dropped—to the President's great relief.

Eisenhower had two strong reasons for refusing to repudiate the Yalta agreement outright. By assuming that such agreements could be repudiated at will by one of the parties, the United States would lose its right to insist that Russia fulfill her promises, both at Yalta and elsewhere. Moreover, because of divisions within his own party, he had to depend on Democratic support to carry out many aspects of his foreign policy. The President could not expect the Democrats to cooperate if he collaborated in partisan moves to impugn the patriotism of his Democratic predecessors.

The Bricker Amendment

The so-called Bricker Amendment involved more complex issues. Ostensibly it was intended to deal with two alleged dangers to the American constitutional system: the secret executive agreement, like Yalta, under which a President committed the nation without congressional approval, and any treaty involving Federal regulation of matters ordinarily reserved to the states. The latter problem had been recognized as early as 1920 when the Supreme Court (Missouri v. Holland) upheld a Federal migratory bird law, passed in conformity with an Anglo-American treaty, despite the fact that such legislation would have been invalid under other circumstances. To meet the first danger, the constitutional amendment proposed by Senator Bricker would give Congress power to regulate all executive agreements; to meet the second, a treaty should become "effective as internal law in the United States only through legislation which would be valid in the absence of a treaty."

This amendment gained strong support from such diverse organizations as the AMA, the DAR, and the Vigilant Women for the Bricker Amendment —a "volunteer organization of housewives and mothers of boys overseas." In a revival of isolationism, alarmists warned that the United States might sign UN-sponsored treaties that would invade national sovereignty. On the other hand, the League of Women Voters and many other groups opposed the amendment.

Although Eisenhower at first sympathized with its broad objectives, he was soon convinced that the proposal would dangerously limit the executive. In a January, 1954, letter to Senate Majority Leader Knowland, he warned that it would

so restrict the conduct of foreign affairs that our country could not negotiate the agreements necessary for the handling of our business with the rest of the world. . . . Adoption of the Bricker amendment in its present form . . . would be notice to our friends as well as our enemies that our country intends to withdraw from its leadership in world affairs.

While the President's opposition decisively killed the original Bricker Amendment, Senator Walter George of Georgia introduced a slightly amended version. Despite Eisenhower's continued criticism, the George proposal came within one vote of receiving the necessary two-thirds majority needed for passage on February 26, 1954.

Although several other similar amendments were introduced by various Senators, the Bricker-George efforts represented high tide for the nationalists; thereafter Eisenhower's leadership in foreign affairs was not seriously challenged on major issues. On smaller matters, however, nationalist hostility continued. Among both Republicans and Democrats there was much opposition to foreign aid, and a battle developed each year over these items in the budget. The recommended amounts were often whittled down—particularly economic aid, which was much more vulnerable than military. The administration supported the reciprocal trade agreements program, but Congress tended to load the extension bills with restrictive amendments. This was no longer strictly a party issue; within the Republican party, the traditional protectionists were now balanced by many large exporting corporations favoring a liberal trade policy, while within the Democratic party the older free-trade tendencies had been greatly modified by recent industrialization in the South. The President followed his favorite middle-of-the-road tactics; in the interest of international good will and economic prosperity he maintained a generally liberal position on foreign trade, but he permitted such concessions to protectionism as increased duties on foreign watches and bicycles.

Korean Armistice

Although the Republican right wing hoped Eisenhower would support the MacArthur program for winning total victory in Korea, the President soon decided against this because it would require the use of large forces, involve huge expenditures, antagonize America's European allies, and risk war with Russia. After discussing the situation with Dulles and other advisers after his postelection trip to the Far East, Eisenhower decided to continue Truman's effort to obtain an armistice.

Even though wanting peace, the administration made a few big-stick gestures to jolt the stalled negotiations back into motion again. The Seventh Fleet was ordered not to continue to "shield Communist China" from attack by Nationalist Formosa. Actually this order had little meaning because Chiang Kai-shek was too weak to do more than make pin-prick raids against the mainland and these the Seventh Fleet had been permitting for many months. It was hoped, however, that Formosa's "deneutralization" would stir Communist fears that American troops might be sent to aid Chiang in a real offensive.

As additional measures to pressure the Communists, the United States dispatched more Sabrejet fighter planes to the Korean front, otherwise strengthened the UN forces, and sent atomic missiles to Okinawa. During a visit to India in May, 1953, Dulles told Premier Nehru that the United States wanted an honorable Korean peace, but that if the Communists continued to stall, American planes would bomb the Chinese Manchurian bases north of the Yalu River. No doubt this warning reached Peiping—as it was intended to.

Meanwhile, the world wondered if the death of Stalin on March 5, 1953, would change Communist policy. His successor, Georgi Malenkov, appeared to favor some softening of tactics. On March 28 the Chinese and North Korean commanders accepted an earlier American proposal for the exchange of sick and injured prisoners and suggested that the general armistice negotiations, suspended since the previous September, be resumed.

The UN accepted the Communist overture, and on April 11 negotiators at Panmunjom agreed on terms for the injured prisoner exchange, but it still required three months of wrangling to hammer out a general armistice. Although the Communists had abandoned their earlier insistence upon the repatriation of all prisoners, it was difficult to decide just what should be done with those refusing to go home. Early in June, the two sides agreed to turn this group over to a Neutral Nations Repatriation Commission, under whose supervision Communist and UN representatives would have ninety days in which to "explain" to the prisoners why they should go home. If they still refused, they would be held for thirty days more while a political conference considered what to do with them. Were no decision reached, the prisoners would be released and helped to find sanctuary.

With this agreement it was hoped that all remaining problems might soon be solved. At this point, however, South Korean President Syngman Rhee almost torpedoed the negotiations. Angry because the proposed truce would end the war without unifying his country, he secretly ordered the release of some twenty-seven thousand North Korean prisoners and threatened to reopen hostilities unless his terms were met. Walter Robinson, an Assistant Secretary of State, flew to Seoul, where he spent two weeks bringing Rhee into line. At last the South Korean government agreed to respect the proposed armistice in return for assurances that the United States would go to South Korea's assistance were she again attacked by the Communists.

Although the enemy had at first demanded the recapture of all the released prisoners, it fortunately did not insist upon this impossible condition, and on July 27, 1953, the armistice was finally signed. Besides incorporating the agreement on prisoner exchange, it provided for a demilitarized zone two and a half miles wide running along a truce line somewhat north of the thirty-eighth parallel for most of its distance, but dropping to the south of the parallel at its western end. Each side promised not to use the armistice, to strengthen its armed forces within Korea. A Neutral Nations Supervisory Commission was to see that these pledges were kept.

This armistice had a somewhat chilly reception in America. Despite Republican criticism of Democratic softness toward the Communists, Eisenhower had accepted terms less favorable than Truman had been demanding. Senator Knowland declared this was not a "truce with honor." Yet if the armistice fell short of the decisive victory that American nationalists had demanded, it did end the bloodshed. True, the Communist tide had not been rolled back, but it had been halted at a strategic point. Most Americans were sufficiently grateful not to criticize the terms; and, in the long run, his ending of the Korean War became one of Eisenhower's greatest political assets.

When "Operation Big Switch" for voluntary repatriation was completed early in September, 1953, attention was focused on those who declined to return. About 22,500 or some 23 per cent of the total, refused to go back to North Korea or Red China, as compared with only 359, or less than 3 per cent, on the UN side who did not go home. Despite feverish Communist efforts during the "explanation" period, only 333 of their nationals changed their minds, while 8 on the other side did so. Most of the 22 Americans who elected to stay behind the Iron Curtain probably feared to return because of collaboration with the enemy or other misconduct that might subject them to punishment. In time, however, most of these became disillusioned with the Communist Utopia and returned to America reconciled to accepting whatever penalties might await them.

The armistice still left unsettled the basic divisions that had caused the war. Subsequent efforts to negotiate a real peace treaty failed, and Korea, like Germany, continued to be a divided country. The rival armed forces along the truce line warned that a renewal of the war was by no means impossible. Therefore, on August 8, 1953, the United States and South Korea signed a mutual defense treaty.

The China Problem

What to do about Red China proved to be as difficult a problem for Eisenhower as it had been for Truman. The naive hope of earlier days that the Chinese Communists were not Communists at all but simply agrarian radicals was no longer tenable. Mao Tse-tung proved himself a true Communist by maintaining close ties with Moscow, ruthlessly imposing social and economic change upon China, and liquidating all opposition. Substantial progress was made in industrializing this vast, backward nation with the aid of Soviet technicians. And as China became increasingly stronger and more unified, it cast an increasingly ominous shadow across the Far East.

To most Europeans the realistic thing to do would be to recognize the Communist regime as the true government of China and admit it to the UN. With this done, Chinese nationalism might assert itself and Mao might follow Tito's example and refuse slavishly to follow the Moscow line. But the Eisenhower administration could not have adopted such a policy even if had so desired. American nationalists strenuously opposed any change of policy toward Red China, and in this they were supported by general American opinion, embittered by Red China's role in the Korean War and her continued imprisonment of American airmen and other citizens. Whenever the question of Red China's admission was raised in the UN, the United States insisted that its friends vote against it. Meantime, it continued the military and economic aid to the Nationalist regime on Formosa.

Although the United States was clearly determined to resist any Communist attempt to capture Formosa, would it also help the Nationalists hold certain other islands close to the China mainland? This issue became suddenly important in September, 1954, when the Communists heavily bombarded Quemoy, only five miles off the coast. Fearing an invasion attempt, some American military and naval leaders proposed that American planes join with Chiang's in bombing the Communist mainland bases.

Army Chief of Staff General Ridgway opposed this as likely to involve the United States in a futile war. Beset by conflicting counsels, Eisenhower sided with the moderates in opposing air attacks and a proposed blockade of the China mainland.

On December 1, 1954, the United States and Nationalist China clarified their relations in a mutual defense treaty, in which the former explicitly pledged to go to Chiang's assistance in case of a Communist attack on Formosa and the Pescadores. No such assurance was given concerning the offshore islands, although the door was left ajar with a provision that additional territories might be brought under the treaty with mutual consent. In an accompanying exchange of notes, the State Department obtained Chiang's promise not to attack the mainland without prior consultation with Washington. In effect, therefore, Formosa, which had been "unleashed" with such a flourish in 1953, was now "released."

Communist China denounced this defense pact and in January, 1955, moved into the Tachens, the northernmost of the Nationalist-held offshore islands. Although this region was of little strategic value, it raised anew the problem of where the United States would draw the line. Once again the administration was caught in the cross fire of the nationalists, who demanded strong support for Chiang, and moderates, who wanted strictly limited American commitments in the Far Eastern trouble spot. In the end, the middle path was chosen. Eisenhower limited immediate aid to helping Nationalist troops evacuate the Tachens. At the same time, a congressional resolution of January 28, 1955, authorized the President to employ armed forces "as he deems necessary for the specific purpose of securing and protecting Formosa and the Pescadores against armed attack, this authority to include the securing and protection of such related positions . . . as he judges to be required or appropriate to assuring the defense of Formosa and the Pescadores." Although purposely vague, the resolution apparently left it in the President's discretion to defend the major offshore islands of Quemoy and Matsu.

According to a subsequent statement by Dulles, this so-called Formosa Resolution prevented Red China from trying to invade Formosa by way of the offshore islands. Dulles admitted that this strong position, with the threat of "massive retaliation" against Red China, had brought the United States to the brink of war, but it had accomplished its objective. Although critics denied that the diplomacy of "brinkmanship" saved the day for Formosa at that time, Eisenhower subsequently showed that the resolution could be effective. In mid-1958, the Red Chinese opened a six-week bombardment of Quemoy and Matsu as a preliminary invasion step. The President quickly sent the Seventh Fleet to the scene, along with huge supplies of military equipment to Chiang. Undoubtedly this show of force prevented the invasion attempt. Yet Formosa, like Korea, continued to be a pivotal point in the world balance of power. For the moment it had acquired an uneasy equilibrium that might be joggled into violent action at any moment.

So important in the history of Far Eastern diplomacy and in American politics was the contest over Indochina and especially of Vietnam, that it will be treated at much greater length in Chapter 30.

Strengthening the Japanese Ties

Red China's failure to invade the offshore islands in 1958 was still regarded in administration circles as but a temporary respite for the dangerous Far Eastern situation. Furthermore, Eisenhower was worried about the ineffectiveness of SEATO in preventing the spread of Communism in Southeast Asia; it was regarded as nothing more than a "paper tiger." Under the circumstances, would it not be wise to strengthen the ties with Japan, which had grown steadily both economically and politically during the 1950's and which had become an ardent foe of Communism? Yet Japan was unhappy with her 1951 security treaty with the United States, which failed to provide for American defense of Japan and only provided for joint consultation in case Japan were attacked.

Consequently, Secretary of State Christian Herter, who had taken over from the seriously ill Dulles in the spring of 1959, and Premier Nobusuke Kishi completed a new mutual cooperation and security pact in January, 1960. It provided for joint action in case of armed attack, as well as for United States bases in Japan to safeguard the peace and security of both Japan and the Far East. To Eisenhower this agreement set up "an indestructible partnership . . . based on complete equality and mutual understanding" between the two nations. In Japan, however, this treaty brought loud protests from the Socialists, who worried lest it involve their country in war again, and from Communists, who incited widespread rioting in Tokyo and other large cities.

The President, about to start on a goodwill mission to the Far East, had to give up his plans to visit Japan because of this opposition, and Kishi's cabinet was turned out of office. The United States Senate nevertheless ratified this treaty by a vote of 90 to 2 in June, 1960, while the Japanese electorate supported the pact by a large majority the following November. In consequence, the United States found Japan its strongest backer in the Orient.

Problems in NATO

In the West, the attempt to build an anti-Communist front still hinged on Germany. If the former enemy were remilitarized and admitted into NATO, there would be a fair chance to restrain Soviet expansion. Otherwise the NATO army would be no match for Russian power. The need was increased by the weakening of France because of colonial troubles and domestic financial problems.

Yet to France and other nations that had undergone Nazi invasion, the remilitarization of Germany seemed a dangerous remedy for Europe's maladies. Were it accepted, it must be hedged with careful safeguards. Such had been the French intention in the so-called Pleven Plan, in which the European Defense Community (EDC) had been first proposed. By incorporating national combat units from West Germany, France, Italy, and the Benelux countries in a multinational army, it was hoped to gain the strength of German manpower without creating a German national force. In May, 1952, an EDC treaty had conceded much more to German nationalism than the French had wanted.

For many months the Eisenhower administration based its European policy on the premise that EDC must be ratified. When France delayed doing so, Secretary Dulles asserted in December, 1953, that its rejection would compel "an agonizing reappraisal" of American policy, but this threat to cut off military aid only antagonized the French still further. In August, 1954, the French Assembly turned down the treaty by a 319-to-264 vote.

At first the death of EDC seemed to imperil the whole policy of Western defense under which both Truman and Eisenhower had operated. Fortunately, a solution was discovered by British Foreign Secretary Anthony Eden. French fear of Germany was reduced by a new British pledge to keep four divisions and a tactical air force in Europe as long as the allies wanted them. Britain also agreed to defend these allies not only against Russia, but against other aggressors as well. The United States, however, promised only to maintain troops in Europe for the time being.

With these matters clarified, the various nations agreed on October 3, 1954, to a Paris Pact with far-reaching provisions. West Germany was granted full sovereignty and was linked with France, Italy, and the Benelux countries in a Western European Union (WEU). Through this agency West Germany would provide twelve divisions to the NATO army, but she could not remilitarize further without the consent of her WEU partners. At the same time, West Germany and France took the first step toward an amicable settlement of the Saar Basin dispute—a hopeful augury of genuine reconciliation between the ancient enemies.

Despite the admission of Germany and the generally improved political relations of 1954, NATO's military strength grew less rapidly than its proponents had hoped. Troubles in her North African dependencies drained off so much of France's military and financial strength that she had to reduce her NATO contributions. In West Germany, meanwhile, remilitarization was not particularly popular and proceeded slowly. Britain found her defense expenditures had a serious effect on her struggling economy, and even the United States, under the budget-conscious Republicans, was ready to cut back military programs.

The Summit Conference

Many Europeans continued to believe that the cold war tensions could be reduced only if the rival heads of state met face to face. Prime Minister Churchill deeply desired to round out his historic career with such a "summit conference," but finally retired in April, 1955, without having achieved it. Eisenhower and Dulles feared that the Russians were more likely to turn a summit meeting into a propaganda battle than to make an honest effort to settle outstanding issues. Moreover, exaggerated charges that Roosevelt had sacrificed American interests at Yalta had conditioned the American public to distrust all such high-level diplomatic bargaining.

Despite these misgivings, Eisenhower was forced by circumstances to change his position. After Stalin's death in 1953, Soviet diplomacy became more flexible, fluctuating between a tough and a moderate line. One result was the signing of an Austrian peace treaty in May, 1955, under which foreign forces were evacuated and Austria was restored to her pre-1938 boundaries in return for her promise to follow a neutral policy and not permit foreign bases upon her soil. This settlement revived hopes that the much more complex German problem might be solved. Political leaders in both England and France came out strongly in favor of a summit meeting, and even in the United States, Senator Walter George, Democratic chairman of the Foreign Relations Committee, urged such a conference.

Consequently, on May 10, 1955, the British, French, and American governments jointly invited the Soviet Union to a meeting of heads of state, and the Russians promptly accepted. Although Eisenhower warned against pinning too much hope on the conference, he himself showed rising optimism as the session approached. An attempt by Senator McCarthy to tie the President's hands was decisively defeated in the upper house.

The much-publicized Summit Conference, attended by Eisenhower, Eden, French Premier Edgar Faure, and Russian Premier Nikolai Bulganin, opened at Geneva on July 18, 1955. In the early sessions, the President's sincere pleas for peace made a deep impression. To assure Russia that NATO was purely defensive in nature, he declared: "The United States is a fairly important member of NATO, and I can assure you that under no circumstances is the United States ever going to be a party to aggressive war—against any nation." Bulganin's simple and direct reply was: "We believe you." By this and other friendly exchanges the Geneva Conference lowered international tension.

But the Big Four were unable to translate these peaceful professions into solutions to concrete problems. Bulganin urged a collective security pact that would obviate the need for NATO and WEU on the one side and for the Warsaw Pact between Russia and her satellites on the other. Eisenhower, however, contended that such an agreement would be futile unless the German question were first settled by reunification of the country and free elections.

Both sides professed to want disarmament. Bulganin revived an earlier Russian proposal to limit the armed forces of all the powers and abolish nuclear weapons. Eisenhower fell back on the familiar American position that a foolproof inspection system must be established before the West could afford to give up its new weapons, but he contributed the most important new suggestion in his so-called open-skies plan: the two sides should exchange complete blueprints of all their military establishments and provide each other with ample opportunities for aerial reconnaissance to assure that neither was preparing a surprise attack.

Because the Summit Conference plans had emphasized that the Big Four would limit themselves to an exchange of views and leave final settlements to a later conference of foreign ministers, the general reaction to the Geneva meeting was enthusiastic. In impressing the world with the American desire for peace and disproving Communist charges of capitalist warmongering, Eisenhower seemed to have achieved an outstanding triumph.

Unfortunately, however, the aftermath brought a large measure of disillusionment. When the foreign ministers met in Geneva in the fall, the Soviet Union seemed to revert to its earlier suspicion and obstructionism. Although the West offered a security pact pledging NATO to go to Russia's defense were she attacked by a reunited Germany, even this assurance failed to end Communist objections to free elections in East Germany. Thus the cold war continued—but with somewhat less vituperation.

Middle East Storm Clouds

In the post–Summit Conference period both the Communist and non-Communist blocs made stronger efforts to win over the uncommitted nations. In this category were not only the South Asian states like India and Burma, but the Arab countries of the Middle East. This region was vital because of its strategic relation to the Suez Canal and air routes between Europe and Asia and even more because of its tremendous oil resources—almost 65 per cent of the world's known reserves. Between 1938 and 1955, Middle East oil production rose from 6 million to 163 million tons a year. All western Europe was dependent on this source; in the future even the United States might need it.

Eager to win Arab support in the power struggle with Russia, Dulles took a benevolent attitude toward Colonel Abdul Gamel Nasser, the Egyptian strong man who master-minded the deposition of King Farouk in 1952 and became premier in 1954. The State Department encouraged the British to bid for Nasser's friendship by hastening the withdrawal of British troops from the Suez Canal Zone. As a further friendly gesture, Britain and the United States promised to contribute $70 million toward building a high dam and hydroelectric plant at Aswan on the Nile—a project for which the World Bank was to advance $200 million more and Egypt itself was to provide $900 million in services and materials.

But the effort to win Egyptian friendship failed. Nasser's ambition to revenge the Arab world against Israel and perhaps ultimately to be· the Bismarck who would create a united Arab state caused him to play the West against the East, getting what he could from both sides.

When Egypt and other Arab countries declined Dulles's invitation to join in a Middle Eastern Defense Organization, the Secretary of State encouraged the formation of the so-called Baghdad Pact. This agreement of November, 1955, linked Iran, Iraq, Pakistan, and Turkey—the so-called northern tier states—with Britain in a defensive alliance, which Nasser bitterly opposed. For one thing, it increased the prestige of Iraq, Egypt's chief rival for Arab leadership; for another, it included Turkey and other non-Arab countries; for a third, by including Britain and indirectly the United States, the Pact appeared to be an instrument of Western imperialism. Syria, Jordan, and Saudi Arabia joined Egypt in hostility to the alliance.

The Baghdad Pact also provoked Russia into a much more active Middle Eastern policy. The Communists found their opportunity in Egypt's rising enmity to Israel, evidenced by reprisals and counterreprisals along the armistice line. Egypt wanted to purchase modern arms, but the West stuck to its 1950 decision not to sell offensive weapons to either Israel or her Arab neighbors. Great was Western indignation, therefore, when in September, 1955, Nasser announced that his country would get weapons from Czechoslovakia in exchange for cotton. By this and direct agreements with Russia herself, Egypt over the next year obtained substantial deliveries of planes and tanks, and Syria also received Communist munitions. Alarmed by these events, Israel too sought more weapons, but, except for small deliveries from France, the Western powers refused to sell, believing that to do so would intensify the threat of war.

During 1956 Nasser continued to flirt with the Communists and to make trouble for England and France, Apparently determined to discipline the Egyptian leader, the United States withdrew on July 19, 1956, its offer to help finance the Aswan Dam, and the next day Britain took similar action. Since the World Bank loan was contingent upon Anglo-American participation, this too was nullified.

This abrupt change of policy was intended as a lesson to Nasser in the limitations of Soviet aid, and Russia, as expected, made no move to finance the dam. The American and British leaders probably also hoped that by killing the project they could speed Nasser's overthrow. If so, this was the most serious of their many miscalculations in dealing with the Middle Eastern hornet's nest.

On July 26, Nasser, recently elected president, announced Egyptian nationalization of the Suez Canal, whose revenues were now to be used to build the Aswan project. He promised to compensate the old Suez Canal Company's stockholders and to operate the canal in conformity with the Constantinople Convention of 1888, which stipulated the waterway would remain open to the ships of all nations. Placing no confidence in the wily Nasser's promises and bitterly opposed to exclusive Egyptian control of an artery so vital to their economic health, Britain and France denounced the nationalization order as a breach of international law.

Next, eighteen out of the twenty-two nations represented at a London conference in August backed a Dulles proposal for an international operating board, but Nasser rejected this. Then Dulles came up with a scheme for a Suez Canal Users Association. Fifteen nations joined this project, but it was still a matter of dispute as to how the Association should function—whether it should impose its will on Egypt by force or try to induce Egyptian concessions by diverting traffic around the Cape of Good Hope. Early in October the UN Security Council, with Egypt's approval, unanimously adopted a set of principles, which included open transit of the canal, Egyptian sovereignty, fair tolls, and other safeguards. The negative votes of Russia and Yugoslavia, however, killed a resolution for international control.

The Suez Fiasco

Meantime, border incidents between Israel and the Arab states had been multiplying, especially on the Jordanian frontier. On October 29, 1956, Israel struck, not against Jordan, but against Egypt, her most dangerous enemy. Advancing rapidly, the Israelis easily defeated the Egyptian armies in the Sinai Peninsula, taking a large bag of prisoners and equipment, much of it Russian and Czech in origin.

On October 30, Britain and France demanded that Israel and Egypt withdraw their forces from the Suez Canal area and allow French and British troops to occupy key positions along the waterway. When Nasser rejected these demands, British and French air attacks on Egypt began the next day.

Deeply shocked by these attacks, taken without consultation with Washington, Eisenhower used UN machinery to oppose the aggression. Two Security Council resolutions, one offered by the United States and the other by Russia, were vetoed by France and England, but in the Assembly, where the veto did not apply, the outcome was different. On November 1, the UN members approved an American-proposed immediate cease-fire and the withdrawal of Israeli and Egyptian forces behind the 1948 armistice lines. Only Australia and New Zealand lined up with Britain, France, and Israel in opposition.

Britain and France refused to abide by this resolution unless the UN itself policed the canal zone. By thus defying world opinion, antagonizing their powerful American ally, and uniting the Arabs against them, they were obviously choosing a perilous course in order to overthrow Nasser and internationalize the canal. They might have succeeded had their invasion and conquest been carried out with lightning speed. Instead, the invasion was a cumbersome operation in which the first troops did not land at Port Said until November 5. Not only did the Egyptians have ample time to block the canal by blowing up bridges and scuttling ships, but so much pressure was mobilized against Britain and France that they had to back down and agree to the cease-fire the next day. Egypt and Israel had already promised to abide by the UN order.

The humiliation of Britain and France was the result of many forces. In the Arab world even Iraq and other anti-Nasser governments rallied to Egypt's cause, sabotaging British-owned pipelines within their borders and threatening to expel Britain from the Baghdad Pact. Except for Australia and New Zealand, British policy found no support within the British Commonwealth: India's condemnation was expected, but Canada's disapproval was almost as strong. In England Prime Minister Eden's position was bitterly opposed by the Laborites and even by some of his own Conservative party. The most decisive steps were taken, however, by the United States and Russia. American disapproval was expressed not only within the UN, but behind the scenes where the recalcitrant allies were threatened with economic reprisals. For Russia, the Suez crisis provided a golden opportunity to pose as the champion of peace, to win favor among the Arabs, and to counteract the bad publicity resulting from its ruthless suppression of Hungary.

To Britain, France, and Israel, Bulganin sent stern warnings on November 5, and at the same time he proposed joint Soviet-American action to halt the invasion. Eisenhower replied immediately, calling the suggestion unthinkable and warning that the United States would oppose "the introduction of new forces" into the Middle East. He accused Bulganin of trying to divert attention from the Russian army, which was "brutally repressing the human rights of the Hungarian people." The Anglo-French decision to halt their campaign was probably more the result of American disapproval than of Soviet threats, but the Communists obtained enormous propaganda advantage from the widespread Arab conviction that Russia had played the decisive part.

Although the November 6 decision quieted the guns along the Egyptian front, Israeli troops still occupied the Sinai Peninsula and the Anglo-French forces controlled about one quarter of the Suez Canal. Israel wanted Egypt to allow Israeli ships to use the canal, to end the blockade of Israeli ports on the Gulf of Aqaba, and to recognize Israel's legal existence. Britain and France still hoped Egypt would accept international control over the canal. These demands might have been legitimate enough under other circumstances, but world opinion opposed allowing the aggressors to reap any dividends from their venture. Therefore the United States backed UN demands for the complete withdrawal of the invading forces without preconditions, and the UN organized a police force of units from the smaller countries to patrol the Israeli-Egyptian border and prevent further clashes.

It was several months before the situation became as near normal as that troubled area could be. The British and French forces evacuated the canal zone by Christmas, 1956, but the Israelis held on in the Gaza Strip and along the Gulf of Aqaba until March, 1957. The Israelis coupled their promise to withdraw with a threat to take action again unless UN police prevented raids on their territory and unless their ships could use the Gulf of Aqaba—and the United States supported them on these issues.

The Suez episode was a severe blow to the Western alliance. Even though the United States had stood by Britain and France by warning Russia not to intervene, the Americans bitterly condemned the aggressors. Eisenhower and Dulles were distressed because the Anglo-French resort to force made Western objections to Soviet aggression seem insincere and because the allies had not informed the American government of their intentions. But if the British and French had behaved badly, they in turn felt that Dulles had bungled. By encouraging the Baghdad Pact and then failing to join it, by professing friendship for both Israel and Israel's enemies, by building up Nasser and then slapping him down, and by blowing hot and cold on proposals to internationalize the Suez Canal, the United States had followed such a vacillating course that no one knew just where it stood.

The Eisenhower Doctrine

When Anglo-French troops pulled out of Egypt in December, 1956, their withdrawal symbolized the almost complete collapse of British and French influence in the Middle East. Unless the United States assumed far greater responsibilities there, Russia might fill the vacuum of power.

To forestall such a possibility, Eisenhower asked Congress on January 5, 1957, for authority to extend economic and military aid to any Middle Eastern country that desired it and to employ American armed forces "to secure and protect the territorial independence of such nations . . . against overt armed aggression from any nation controlled by international communism." This Eisenhower Doctrine provoked a long discussion in Congress—not so much over its purpose as over its form. Believing that the President was trying to force Congress to share a responsibility that was primarily his, the Democrats amended it to show general congressional backing for the Doctrine, but leaving it to the President to decide when to use American forces. In the same resolution of March 9, 1957, Congress authorized $200 million for economic and military aid in the Middle East. Moscow naturally denounced this as additional evidence of an "imperialistic" attempt to interfere in the internal polity of weaker countries.

The initial reception of the Eisenhower Doctrine in the Middle East was varied. In the Arab countries that had signed the Baghdad Pact because of fear of Communism, it won considerable support. In March, 1957, King Hussein of Jordan crushed an attempted coup by a pro-Nasser faction with the help of $10 million in American aid and the presence of the Sixth Fleet along the coast. King Saud of Saudi Arabia also remained in the Western fold because of his enthusiastic reception in the United States and the promise of American financial assistance. On the other hand, Egypt, showing little gratitude for American policy during the Suez crisis, continued to incline toward Moscow. In Syria, too, the anti-Western controlled government accepted monetary aid and arms from the Soviet Union. Then, in the spring of 1958, Nasser persuaded Syria and Yemen to join Egypt in establishing the United Arab Republic.

Apparently the American policy had many weaknesses. It depended too much on the support of narrow governing cliques and offered too little to the Arab masses. It was aimed at a threat of external aggression, whereas the real problem seemed to be the internal danger of growing anti-Western sentiment. Finally, it left unhealed the major sore spot in the Middle East—the continued hostility between Israel and her Arab neighbors.

The summer of 1958 witnessed continued turmoil in the Middle East. On July 14, General Abdul Karim el-Kassem led an Arab nationalist revolt in Iraq, during which King Faisal and his prime minister were brutally slain by the rebels. This Pan-Arab victory threatened to spill over into Lebanon and Jordan, both favorably disposed to the West. The following day, President Camille Chamoun of Lebanon and Jordan King Hussein asked for United States assistance under the Eisenhower Doctrine. Eisenhower immediately ordered the landing of thirty-five hundred marines from the Sixth Fleet, together with additional troops from West Germany because the independence of Lebanon was "vital to United States national interests and world peace." If the UN intervened to maintain Lebanese independence, the United States would withdraw its armed forces. About the same time, Britain sent paratroopers to safeguard Jordan.

When the Soviet Union threatened to retaliate against the "grave menace" to her borders by Western "aggressors" and when India, Japan, and Sweden criticized the Anglo-American intervention, many foreign observers feared this might be more serious than the Suez crisis. Yet though both sides had approached to the brink of war, neither wished to commit the first hostile act. Instead, they sought a compromise. Khrushchev suggested another summit conference, but changed his tune when the Western leaders demanded such a meeting be under UN auspices. Then, when the matter reached the Security Council, Ambassador Lodge insisted that unless the UN ensured the independence of Lebanon and Jordan, the Anglo-American forces would stay on. The Soviet Union vetoed this suggestion, but in turn its proposal for the immediate withdrawal of the Western troops was turned down.

Fortunately, when the issue came before the General Assembly, the Arab nations unexpectedly proposed a compromise that was overwhelmingly endorsed: the Arab League would not interfere in each other's internal affairs and a UN observation team would protect the independence of Jordan and Lebanon. This action, together with the ending of the civil strife in Lebanon after the election of a new president, resulted in the complete evacuation of the Anglo-American troops by the end of October, 1958.

Although Eisenhower had successfully defended the independence of Lebanon and indirectly of Jordan, the Middle East was still a cause of concern in Washington. Indeed, Dulles, worried about the revolt in Iraq and the possible loss of oil supplies, was already trying to strengthen the Middle East Treaty Organization (METO), which had grown out of the Baghdad Pact. In July, 1958, he promised more American military aid to the METO members, as well as closer American cooperation "for their security and defense." Then in March, 1959, the United States, in executive agreements with Iran, Pakistan, and Turkey,[1] promised to "take such appropriate action, including the use of armed force to defend them against aggression." Encouraged by this promise, the remaining METO members renamed their alliance the Central Treaty Organization (CENTO) in the summer of 1959 and agreed to cooperate "for mutual defense and economic development." Although the United States did not join CENTO, its members could be assured of hearty American support.

Despite the Eisenhower Doctrine and the establishment of CENTO, Middle East problems were by no means settled when Eisenhower left office. Egypt was drawing closer to the Soviet Union as a result of a $100 million contribution toward construction of the controversial Aswan Dam. Rival factions struggled for control of the different Arab countries. The border raids between Israel and the neighboring Arab nations were unceasing. The major bright spot was the discovery of oil in the Sahara, thereby lessening Western dependence on the still turbulent Middle East.

---

[1] At this time Iraq resigned from METO, whose meetings she had not attended since the pro-Arab coup the previous July. Despite the United States concern lest Iraq fall under the spell of Nasser or the Kremlin and thus end any oil agreements with Washington, Premier Kassem pursued an independent policy. Therefore the United States soon recognized his regime and Iraq theoretically continued to be considered pro-West.

Promoting Latin-American Partnership

While the Truman administration was primarily concerned about the cold war in other parts of the world, Latin America had become increasingly fertile ground for the growth of Communism. Dictatorships in Argentina, Bolivia, Chile, Cuba, the Dominican Republic, and Ecuador meant the stifling of democracy in those countries. Little was done to end the illiteracy and poverty rampant in most of Latin America, a situation made steadily worse by the rapid population explosion. Yet the growing masses, emulating those in Asia and Africa, were now demanding essential benefits; if their governments did not provide the reforms, they might easily turn to Communism. Furthermore, the United States seemed to be forgetting Latin America. Of the billions spent under the Mutual Security Program, only about $75 million in United States aid trickled into Latin America in 1952. At the same time, moreover, there was a revival of the old fear of *Yanqui* imperialism. Although Truman recognized the danger, he did little to avert it, except for his effort to defeat Perón in Argentina and to promote the OAS.

Eisenhower took note of what was taking place in the rest of the hemisphere. He talked about the need of a hemisphere partnership—something closer and more equal than good-neighborliness. In line with this approach, he sent his brother Milton as head of an exploratory mission in the summer of 1953. In its report of the following November, this mission concluded that economic and technical aid was of primary importance for Latin America to provide modern farm equipment, to develop the natural resources, to improve transportation, and increase technical skills. Private foreign investment would be better than public loans in speeding Latin American development, but such investments could not be obtained as long as Latin-American governments expropriated investment property without proper compensation or fell into Communist hands. Consequently, the first step must be the establishment of orderly, responsible governments. The United States could contribute to Latin-American improvement by purchasing Latin-American products, by more Point Four technical aid, by encouraging private American investors, and by public loans through the World and Export-Import Banks to take care of projects not appealing to private investors.

To obtain hemisphere support for these proposals, a meeting of finance ministers was held at Petropolis (near Rio), Brazil, in November, 1954. While there was much discussion on ways and means of developing an economic partnership, little of a tangible nature was accomplished. One reason for this comparative failure was the appearance of a more obvious Communist threat. President Jacobo Arbenz Guzmán of Guatemala was alleged to be under the influence of Communist advisers. Rumor had it that arms were on their way from Czechoslovakia to help keep the dictator in office and to spread the Kremlin ideology by force into neighboring countries. In accordance with the partnership theory, Dulles believed that the OAS should combat this menace. Therefore, at the Tenth International Conference of American States at Caracas in the spring of 1954, the delegates approved the Act of Caracas: "That the domination or control of any American state by the International Communist movement . . . would constitute a threat to the sovereignty and political independence of the American states. . . ."

But the Eisenhower administration did not depend on high-sounding resolutions to rid itself of the Arbenz annoyance. The Central Intelligence Agency (CIA) gave secret backing to an invading force of Guatemalan exiles that seized the capital and installed the militantly anti-Communist Carlos Castillo Armas in the presidency. Many Latin Americans were unhappy about this covert American intervention, charging the United States with unilateral action that violated the spirit of the recent Caracas agreement. And if the United States were so eager to establish democratic governments in Latin America, why did it not oppose dictatorial regimes in Cuba and the Dominican Republic?

But if the United States did nothing, the same was not true of some Latin Americans themselves. Perón was turned out of office in Argentina in 1955, Colombians ousted Gustavo Rojas two years later, and Venezuelans overthrew Dictator Marcos Pérez Jiménez in 1958. Haiti experienced several presidential changes in 1957 as a result of popular unrest, and economic turbulence was shown by riots in Chile and strikes in several other republics. Honduras and Nicaragua exchanged frequent blows along their frontier, while the United States had to quiet Panama in 1955 by increasing the annual canal rental to $1.9 million and by agreeing to a more equitable share of the economic benefits.

Because of these rumblings of discontent, Eisenhower sent Vice President Nixon on a so-called goodwill tour of several Latin American countries early in 1958, but his reception was anything but friendly. Hecklers greeted his speeches with: "Get out, Nixon"; elsewhere he was the victim of thrown eggs, fruit, and even stones, and some demonstrators spat on him. Eisenhower considered the situation so tense that he sent more troops to American bases in the vicinity. In his report on his trip, Nixon reiterated the need to pay greater heed to Latin America's economic difficulties, which were becoming worse with increasing inflation. He concluded that the anti-American displays were brought on by economic matters, and that Communists were taking full advantage of the local unrest.

Both the administration and Congress went along with the Nixon diagnosis by paying more attention to Latin America's problems. In the last two years of the Eisenhower presidency, the various loan agencies extended credit of more than $2 billion to the republics to the South; American private investors poured in more than $9 billion and were paying about 14 per cent of the taxes collected by Latin-American governments; and the United States was the largest stockholder in the Inter-American Development Bank, capitalized at $1 billion. This bank had been established as a result of a hemisphere economic conference at Bogotá in the fall of 1960. The outstanding accomplishment of this meeting was the Act of Bogotá, under which the republics, with United States aid, would cooperate in improving agriculture, educational facilities, health, and long-range economic development. This partnership scheme was the immediate forerunner of the Alliance for Progress during the Kennedy administration. That the open-handed policy of the United States had brought a change in Latin-American attitude was shown by the tumultuous reception given President Eisenhower on his mission in February, 1960—a far cry from the rude treatment accorded Nixon just two years before.

Vice President Nixon in Venezuela, 1958. (UPI Photo.)

These efforts to improve the economic and social lot of the Latin Americans by no means brought an end to the problem. As the Eisenhower administration came to a close, Cuba became the sore spot. Throughout the 1950's, the island was in almost constant turmoil, first over the dictatorial regime of Fulgencio Batista and then because of Fidel Castro's attempts to overthrow him. On January 1, 1959, Castro finally gained the upper hand and promised the Cubans a constitutional and democratic government that would enact economic reforms for the poverty-stricken masses.

The Eisenhower administration at first welcomed the advent of Castro, but with the passing months the Cuban premier's actions indicated increasing Communist tendencies, closer ties with the Soviet Union, and growing enmity toward the United States. The latter trend was shown by his seizure of American property without adequate compensation and his attempts to spread Communism to other hemisphere republics. So bad did the situation become that Eisenhower severed diplomatic ties with Cuba about two weeks before he left office, thereby leaving to his successor the major responsibility of dealing with this perplexing situation.

Beyond the Iron Curtain

American diplomacy would have been easier had it been possible to make a firm estimate of the Communist world's strength and weaknesses, but all efforts to measure the opponents' muscle seemed futile. Again and again news of feuds within the Soviet ruling clique, economic failures, or uprisings in the satellite states would lead to optimistic predictions of Communist collapse; the next month the crisis would be over and the free world would enter a new period of pessimism.

After Stalin's death in March, 1953, Georgi Malenkov was for a time dominant in the Kremlin hierarchy, but in February, 1955, he resigned and Nikolai Bulganin became premier. From the first, however, the real strong man was the shrewd and tough Nikita Khrushchev, the boss of the Russian Communist party. In February, 1956, he astounded the world with a four-hour tirade to a Communist party congress denouncing the hitherto venerated Stalin as a vain and power-thirsty ruler who had sent to death thousands of "honest and innocent Communists."

Under the guise of "de-Stalinization," Bulganin and Khrushchev made bewildering shifts in both domestic and foreign policy. In little matters such as permitting more foreigners to enter Russia and relaxing some of the internal regimentation, the new regime seemed less tyrannical than the old; yet the iron hand was still ready to crack down upon any opposition. In 1957, the veteran Foreign Minister Vyacheslav Molotov and Defense Minister Georgi Zhukov, a friend of Eisenhower from World War II days, were both demoted, and in March, 1958, Bulganin himself was pushed aside and Khrushchev assumed the premiership.

Part of the Bulganin-Khrushchev line was to allow more liberty to the satellites. Yugoslavia was welcomed back into the fold, and Poland, where Wladyslaw Gomulka had established a Tito-like regime against Moscow's wishes in 1956, went unpunished. In Hungary, however, events took a different and tragic course. Inspired by the examples of Yugoslavia and Poland, the Hungarians revolted against Soviet domination. Once started, however, the movement could not be kept within the limits of so-called national Communism. Liberty-intoxicated crowds roamed the streets of Budapest, burning Communist literature, destroying Red Army monuments, killing members of the hated secret police, and otherwise showing their determination to stamp out Communism, root and branch. Confronted with such a challenge, Bulganin and Khrushchev quickly ordered the Soviet army to put down the rebellion with ruthless thoroughness.

The suppression of the Hungarian insurrection horrified the West, but nothing could be done to help the patriots except to offer asylum to almost twenty thousand refugees who fled to Austria. There was little likelihood that the Western nations would have attempted to intervene under any circumstances, but the revolt broke out when the Western alliance was at odds over the Suez crisis. The UN condemned Soviet action and called for the withdrawal of Russian troops from Hungarian soil but was powerless to enforce its orders. Nevertheless, the Communists suffered seriously in world opinion as Nehru and other neutralist leaders criticized the Soviet conduct in Hungary.

The Hungarian tragedy was a sobering lesson for the American people in the realities of world politics. During the 1952 campaign Republican orators had denounced Truman for basing his foreign policy on "containment" of the Soviet threat; the true goal should be the "liberation" of captive peoples. While Eisenhower and Dulles had been careful not to make explicit pledges to the satellite populations, the propaganda broadcasts across the Iron Curtain nonetheless encouraged resistance to and revolt against Communist rule. It was understandable, therefore, that the Hungarian rebels felt bitter toward the West when their frantic appeals for help were answered only with resolutions of sympathy. Obviously if subject peoples made a bid for freedom, they did so at their own risk.

The Arms Race

The United States and the Soviet Union continued to deplore the development and stockpiling of ever more deadly weapons and the expenditure of vast sums for military preparations. Both claimed to desire disarmament, but repeated efforts to agree upon practical measures brought no result.

Stymied on the major problem, Eisenhower sought more modest goals with his atoms-for-peace plan, proposed in an address before the UN Assembly on December 8, 1953. After painting an horrendous picture of the dangers of atomic warfare, he again emphasized America's willingness to cooperate in effective international control of the new weapons. He proposed that the various nations contribute uranium and other fissionable materials to an international atomic agency, which would make them available for electric power, medicine, and other peaceful activities.

Although the atoms-for-peace plan was enthusiastically applauded by most of the world, it was regarded with the usual suspicion both by Russian spokesmen and by the Republican nationalist wing. Eventually, however, the American project won general acceptance. In April, 1956, the United States, the Soviet Union, and ten other nations drafted the charter of the International Atomic Energy Agency, which was unanimously approved by representatives of eighty-two countries the following October. By the summer of 1957, both Russia and the United States had ratified, and the latter had already made fissionable materials and technical knowledge available for power projects and other peaceful atomic energy uses by other nations.

However commendable atoms-for-peace might be, the threat of atoms-for-war increased in seriousness. A UN Disarmament Commission, intermittently at work since 1951, found the Soviet Union and the United States still far apart on fundamental issues. Eisenhower's "open-skies" proposal of 1955 provided a new basis for discussion, but Russia would accept only a limited version. During 1956 many suggestions that the powers should at least agree to ban further testing of nuclear weapons failed because Britain and the United States were not satisfied with the limited control the Soviet Union was willing to accept.

During the summer of 1957, Harold Stassen, the President's Disarmament

Adviser, was involved in long UN negotiations at London, where it was hoped to achieve arms limitation by a succession of stages. Since a compromise could not be reached, the conference broke up in failure. Next, Russia, after staging a series of successful and spectacular nuclear tests, declared it was suspending further trials in March, 1958. This decision placed the United States on the defensive; to quiet critics at home and to try to prevent neutralist nations from swinging over to the Soviet side, it followed suit in the fall of the year. When Eisenhower left office, this unwritten moratorium on nuclear tests was still in effect.

Russia's inflexibility in disarmament negotiations probably reflected Communist confidence that they were forging ahead in the arms race and had more to lose than to gain by accepting limitation. The speed with which Russia progressed in the field upset all the premises upon which the Eisenhower administration had been proceeding. The New Look in defense policy had been based upon the assumption that American scientific and technological superiority made it feasible to economize on ground troops and conventional armaments, while concentrating on air power and nuclear weapons.

In January, 1954, when American confidence in the superiority of its weapons was at a peak, Secretary Dulles said in a public speech:

> Local defense will always be important. But there is no local defense which alone will contain the mighty land power of the Communist world. Local defenses must be reinforced by the further deterrent of massive retaliatory power. A potential aggressor must know that he cannot always prescribe battle conditions that suit him. . . .
>
> The basic decision is to depend primarily upon a great capacity to retaliate, instantly, by means and at places of our choosing. . . .

This policy of "massive retaliation" caused great concern to America's allies, who interpreted it as meaning that the United States had decided not to fight any more limited, or "brush-fire," wars like that in Korea. Instead, a Communist attack against Formosa or some other free world outpost might be countered by dropping hydrogen bombs on Moscow or Peiping. Since the Russians were in a position to retaliate, the American policy seemed to threaten to turn every small conflict into a major war of terror. The allies also feared that massive retaliation might mean a drastic reduction in the American contribution to NATO ground forces.

As frequently happened, Dulles's actual policies proved less rash than his language. He sought to reassure world opinion that the United States meant no more than that it would retaliate in kind. In dealing with the actual situations in Indochina and the Formosa Strait, moreover, the United States made no move toward putting "massive retaliation" into effect.

Actually, the rapid development of new weapons made military planning very difficult. Were future wars to be fought with nuclear weapons, the maintenance of vast ground forces, armed with conventional weapons, would be a waste of money. Yet there was danger in the other alternative; if ground forces were neglected and the nation prepared only for nuclear war, the enemy might nibble away at neighboring territory under such circumstances that world opinion would not tolerate retaliation with total war. Many observers believed that the two sides were moving toward a balance of terror, or atomic stalemate, in which neither would dare to risk hostilities.

Even in prosperous America the cost of maintaining both nuclear and conventional armaments was so great that the United States was continually having to get along with less of one or the other than extreme advocates of preparedness approved. For the poorer NATO allies, the necessity of sacrificing one military arm to support the other became imperative. In April, 1957, Britain began concentrating on nuclear weapons and cutting back her air and ground forces, and even her naval strength. This decision was hastened by the Suez fiasco, which served both to illustrate the weakening of the older forms of military power and to injure the British economy.

It was this increasing dependence of the West upon new weapons that caused such great dismay when Russia launched two *Sputniks* in October and November, 1957. Although these satellites posed no threat to the free world, they completely exploded the American assumption that the United States was superior to all other nations in scientific and engineering ability and that the Russians had developed atom and hydrogen bombs only by stealing American secrets. Particularly after an American attempt to launch a much smaller satellite ended in humiliating failure in December, 1957, it became clear that in the field of rocketry, at least, the Soviet Union was ahead.[2]

The *Sputnik* crisis brought about a sober reappraisal of the whole military situation. The Russians' success in launching a satellite was convincing proof that their earlier boast of possessing an intercontinental ballistic missile (ICBM) was not mere propaganda. However, there was still hope that the United States could catch up. The more immediate problem was the intermediate range ballistic missile (IRBM). Here, too, the Russians appeared to be ahead of the United States and were already probably in a position to destroy London and Paris, while the American IRBM's, although successfully tested, were not yet being produced in quantity.

Yet the situation was not quite as desperate as the more pessimistic commentators made it appear. The United States Strategic Air Command (SAC), with bases in England, western Europe, and North Africa, was prepared to drop hydrogen bombs on Russian targets on a moment's notice. Despite the rapid progress of Communist armament, the West retained its power of massive retaliation.

Even so, the United States felt it imperative to establish missile bases in the NATO countries. The best deterrent to Soviet ICBM attacks on New York or Detroit would be an ability to retaliate with IRBM's against the industrial centers of Russia. On the diplomatic front, therefore, Eisenhower's most important move in the *Sputnik* crisis was to join with Prime Minister Harold Macmillan of England in arranging a December meeting in Paris of the NATO heads of state to discuss the new defense problem. There the American proposals for missile bases in the NATO countries encountered opposition. Communist warnings to nations permitting anti-Russian bases to be constructed were not to be taken lightly in view of the Soviet's apparent

---

2 American success in orbiting three small satellites early in 1958 did much to salve American pride, but did not alter the basic factors in the rocketry situation.

superiority in the newest weapons. With characteristic carrot-and-stick tactics, Bulganin and Khrushchev linked grim threats with tempting offers to negotiate. The Russians promised not to station missiles and other atomic weapons in East Germany, Poland, and Czechoslovakia if the United States agreed to the same restrictions in West Germany; they suggested stabilization of the Middle East by mutual pledges of noninterference; and they proposed a ban on nuclear testing and a new summit conference to discuss other issues.

Although the United States condemned the Russian overture as a propaganda attempt to divide the Western allies with a rehash of old proposals, most NATO countries wanted to leave the door open to negotiations. In the end, therefore, the Paris meeting ended in compromise. The United States would give intermediate-range missiles to those NATO nations willing to accept them, but an effort would be made to negotiate a disarmament agreement with the Soviet Union.

On the domestic front, Republicans and Democrats engaged in minor recriminations, each side blaming the other for the American delay in the missiles race, but the situation was too serious for a major political battle. By spending more money on missiles research and development and by long-range steps to encourage education in science and technology, the nation hoped to preserve the balance of power upon which the peace of the world seemed to depend.

The Berlin Issue Again

The Soviet Union, encouraged by its apparent leadership in the space race, pursued its advantage by pressing again the issue of Berlin and Germany. In November, 1958, Khrushchev offered the Western powers two alternatives: either Berlin should be unified under East German control or the Western zones must be neutralized. If the West accepted neither proposal within six months, Russia would give its Berlin zone to East Germany, with whom the other powers would then have to deal for access routes to the city. The West refused to yield to Khrushchev's demands, regarding them as an effort to force recognition of East Germany and its complete control over Berlin.

Early in 1959 Khrushchev next proposed that if the Western powers evacuated their troops from Berlin, East Germany would allow free access to the city. Otherwise, he threatened to make a separate treaty with East Germany and give it control over access to Berlin. But once again the West refused to be intimidated. Indeed, Britain, France, and the United States countered with the promise to use force if necessary to protect their rights in Berlin and to safeguard the West Berliners from "hostile domination."

After considerable discussion, the Western leaders finally agreed that the only way to ease the tension was to hold a Big Four foreign ministers conference at Geneva in May, 1959. There the Western statesmen (with the new Secretary of State, Christian Herter, representing the United States) submitted to Gromyko three proposals for ending the cold war in Europe: a Berlin settlement that would protect those in the Western zones; the reunification of Germany; and the drafting of a security treaty for all of Europe. Just as Eisenhower had predicted, however, nothing came of this session.

Gromyko refused to consider any of these suggestions; he was especially against any Berlin settlement not initiated by the German people themselves.

By the time this abortive meeting was over, the Khrushchev six-month deadline had been reached; yet the Soviet premier made no effort to carry out his threats. Instead, he admitted the West was justified in remaining in Berlin. Tensions were further eased by a series of cultural exchanges: the Russians staged an exhibition in New York City in the spring of 1959, and the United States reciprocated with a showing of American wares in Moscow the following summer; American symphony orchestras were enthusiastically received in the Soviet Union, while Americans viewed performances by Russian ballet companies with equal pleasure.

Capping this "era of good feeling" was Khrushchev's acceptance of Eisenhower's invitation to visit the United States in September. In his cross-country tour, the Soviet leader saw Midwest farms, huge factories, and modern supermarkets. Although American hosts and Russian guests indulged in a few sharp gibes about their rival ideologies, on the whole the trip went well. It culminated in a meeting at Camp David, Maryland, between Khrushchev and Eisenhower, where they agreed they would do their best to settle East-West differences peaceably, possibly at a Big Four summit session in the immediate future. Clearing the way for such a settlement, Khrushchev withdrew his ultimatum on Berlin.

To pave the route further for a summit conference, Eisenhower, who took a more personal interest in diplomacy after the death of Dulles in 1959, visited a number of countries of the Middle East, southern Asia, and Europe, where his speeches on the need for world peace were enthusiastically greeted by literally millions of listeners. In Paris, he conferred with Adenauer, De Gaulle, and Macmillan; the four heads of state then invited Khrushchev to a summit meeting in the French capital in May, 1960.

Failure at the Summit

The optimism that this top-level session might end East-West tensions was largely unfounded. Khrushchev, in a number of speeches, continued to stress the Soviet objective of making peace with an independent East Germany, which would have complete jurisdiction over Berlin. The Western allies, on the other hand, repeated their stand on the defense of their rights in the city and did their best to strengthen the Soviet-hated NATO. Thus it was apparent that neither side was ready to yield sufficiently to reach an acceptable compromise.

Nevertheless, what little chance the meeting had was ended on May 1, when an American U-2 reconnaissance plane was shot down more than a thousand miles inside Soviet territory. This was bad enough, but making it worse was Washington's inept handling of the affair. When the Soviet Union first revealed the incident on May 5, NASA merely replied that a weather research craft was missing and the State Department insisted that the United States had never violated Russian air space. These cover-up efforts were shown to be untrue when Moscow announced on May 7 that Francis Gary Powers, the U-2 pilot, had confessed he was on a spying flight; furthermore, the Soviet authorities had found cameras in the captured plane containing films of Russian military installations. Secretary Herter then had to admit the falsity of his Department's earlier statement; he justified this and preceding flights over Soviet territory on the West's need to prevent Soviet surprise attacks and implied that reconnaissance flights would continue. Khrushchev, still trying to make the rest of the world believe he was interested in the success of the summit meeting, gave Eisenhower the opportunity to say that he had not given the orders for the spying expeditions. On May 11, however, the President admitted that he was fully responsible. He asserted that since Moscow had often threatened to "bury" the West, the United States had to know what was going on in the Soviet Union to prevent "another Pearl Harbor."

Possibly confused by Eisenhower's admission of responsibility—something most unusual in diplomatic circles, Khrushchev severely denounced the "aggressive acts" of the United States against his peace-loving country. He called upon the President to apologize for his shameful orders and threatened to retaliate against those nations allowing their soil to be used as bases for American espionage activities. Although the President did cancel future

Soviet Premier Khrushchev in New York, 1960. (UPI Photo.)

U-2 flights, he refused to apologize. Furthermore, he assured the countries with American bases that the United States would come to their aid if Russia attacked them.

Such was the atmosphere at the time the Paris conference was scheduled to open. On his arrival, Khrushchev still asserted he would do all in his power to work for world peace and security, but at the initial session he was unyielding in his demands. Further proof of his unwillingness to compromise was indicated when he withdrew the invitation to Eisenhower to visit Russia later in the year. Under the circumstances, the Western Big Three ruefully adjourned the conference. While the U-2 incident was regarded at the time as the immediate cause for the failure of the summit meeting, subsequent evidence indicated that the Soviet hierarchy would have come up with some other excuse for sabotaging the meeting had that incident not occurred.[3] Moscow officials apparently lost interest in the Paris summit because of Western firmness on the issues of Berlin and nuclear tests.

The bitterness shown by Khrushchev in Paris had not worn off by the time he addressed a UN meeting in New York City in September, 1960. He declared he would have no dealings with the United States as long as Eisenhower was President. He also warned the West that the Soviet Union was widening the missile gap with America and its allies and accentuated his boasting by pounding on the lectern with one of his shoes. It was with this intemperate display that the Eisenhower administration's efforts to solve the issues of Berlin, a united Germany, and a European security treaty ended in failure. But at least the administration had prevented the cold war from erupting into a shooting contest.

---

[3] There is proof that the Russians were aware of the American espionage flights over their territory from the time they began in 1956. Thus they merely used the May 1, 1960, incident as an excuse. On the other hand, many Americans criticized the Eisenhower administration for ordering the Powers flight on the eve of such an important conference. Powers was subsequently found guilty by the Russians and sentenced to a ten-year prison term. Early in 1962, however, he was exchanged for a Russian found guilty of spying against the United States.

28

A NEW AGE OF REFORM

In January, 1961, the fatherly image of President Eisenhower was replaced by the youthful figure of John F. Kennedy, whose emphasis on vigor delighted the country. Challenging the nation to venture out to what he called "the new frontiers," Kennedy advocated ambitious programs to provide medical care for the aged, improved education for the young, and fresh approaches to the problems of the city. But if the new President was full of youthful vigor, Congress still contained a preponderance of elderly skepticism. The administration programs were slow to obtain approval, and the President soon found that the pressure of other problems left him relatively little time and energy to fight for his welfare goals. During the crowded thirty-four months of his presidency, he had to deal with a succession of crises that ranged from Germany and Cuba to Mississippi and Alabama. When sudden death cut Kennedy down, Lyndon Johnson took over the struggle to reach the New Frontier. An experienced manager of Congress, Johnson achieved an extraordinarily broad program of reform. Yet he never won the trust of the liberals. Increasing opposition to his Vietnam policy made Johnson so unpopular that he decided not to run for a second elected term.

The Election of 1960

After the 1956 Democratic convention, when the thirty-nine-year-old John F. Kennedy almost won the vice-presidential nomination, it was obvious that the Massachusetts Senator would sooner or later be a serious contender for the presidency. But would Kennedy be able to capture the top prize in 1960? One possible handicap was his youth—especially since such experienced Democrats as Senator Hubert Humphrey of Minnesota, Senator Lyndon Johnson of Texas, and Adlai Stevenson were available. A greater obstacle was Kennedy's religion. Would the Democratic party, remembering the bitterness of Al Smith's 1928 campaign, run the risk of nominating another Roman Catholic?

A realist in politics, Kennedy knew that his best chance for the nomination lay in demonstrating an ability to win votes in the presidential primaries. Most of his rivals avoided these grueling contests in the hope that they could line up delegates by other means. But Senator Humphrey's case was more like Kennedy's own. The Minnesota Senator was a highly popular figure in his own section, particularly among farmers and labor unionists, but he needed to prove that he could campaign successfully in other states. Kennedy's narrow victory in Wisconsin was impressive because it was in Humphrey's own back yard, but the Kennedy margin was largely built up in election districts where there was a heavy concentration of Catholics. Much more decisive was the Kennedy victory in West Virginia, where Catholics were few but economic distress was great.

After the West Virginia primary, Humphrey withdrew from the contest, and Kennedy took advantage of the growing momentum of his campaign to obtain impressive support from other states. When the Democratic National Convention opened at Los Angeles in July, Kennedy-pledged delegates numbered over six hundred. Since this was less than a majority, there was still the possibility that a "Stop Kennedy" coalition might upset the bandwagon. The candidate with the second largest number of pledged delegates was Lyndon Johnson, but his efforts to win support in the West as well as the South had only limited success. Kennedy's true rival at the convention was the unannounced candidate, Adlai Stevenson. Stevenson strength was particularly strong in California, and it appeared possible that the Stevenson-packed galleries might stampede the delegates as the Willkie partisans had done in the Republican convention of 1940. But the Kennedy forces were too well organized to be defeated by any last-minute maneuver. The desire to be on the winner's side converted enough wavering delegates to give Kennedy a decisive victory on the first ballot.[1] Aware that his big-city, Catholic background might fatally handicap his candidacy in the South, Kennedy chose Johnson for the vice-presidential nomination, and the convention acceded to his wishes.

The platform pledged the party to work for "an enduring peace." To achieve this goal, the Democrats declared, "we must first restore our national strength—military, political, economic, and moral." As for specifics, they pledged themselves to policies that would result in an average rate of economic growth of 5 per cent a year—almost twice that maintained under Eisenhower, diversify the defense establishment, and extend the social security system to include medical care for older citizens. Overriding Southern opposition, the party adopted a strong civil rights plank pledging prompt action on school desegregation, abolition of poll tax and literacy qualifications for voting, and establishment of a Federal fair employment practices commission. It upheld the right of black people to conduct "peaceful demonstrations for first-class citizenship."

Vice President Richard M. Nixon was the leading candidate for the Republican nomination. During his second term President Eisenhower had given the Vice President frequent opportunities to build up his prestige through goodwill missions abroad and mediating roles at home. Nixon's only aggressive rival was Governor Nelson A. Rockefeller of New York. After an on-again, off-again preconvention campaign, Rockefeller made one final effort in June, 1960, when he issued a public statement condemning the Republican leadership for having "failed to make clear where this party is heading and where it proposes to lead the nation." He then offered his own

---

[1] The vote was Kennedy, 806; Johnson, 409; Symington, 86; Stevenson, 79½; with 140½ scattered.

program, which contrasted sharply with that of the administration. Although the "Draft Rockefeller" movement was too small to challenge Nixon's control of the July convention, it did convince the cautious Vice President that he should accept some of Rockefeller's ideas for the party platform. Meeting in New York City, the two men agreed to what the newspapers called the Fourteen Point Compact of Fifth Avenue. This pressure caused the Republican platform committee to rewrite its original draft to take more advanced positions, particularly on civil rights and defense. The Republicans defended the right to peaceful protest against discrimination and pledged "intensified efforts" in providing for national defense. On other points, the platform was less bold, emphasizing the need for "responsible and mature" leadership and defending the record of the Eisenhower administration.

With the platform at last settled, the convention delegates ratified enthusiastically the decisions already made by the party leadership. Nixon was nominated on the first ballot—unanimously except for ten conservative protest votes cast for Senator Barry Goldwater of Arizona. The convention then named Henry Cabot Lodge of Massachusetts as vice-presidential candidate. Since Lodge had gained respect as an eloquent United States ambassador to the United Nations, this decision underlined Nixon's intention to emphasize foreign affairs and experienced leadership.

Kennedy's first objective in the campaign was to combat anti-Catholic prejudice. He found his opportunity by accepting an invitation to speak before a Protestant ministerial association in Houston, Texas. There in the strongest terms, he stated his belief in the absolute separation of church and state. Whatever issue might come before him if he were elected, he would make his decision in accordance with what his conscience told him to be in the national interest "and without regard to outside religious pressure or dictate." Recorded on film and subsequently shown at rallies in all sections of the country, Kennedy's Houston speech became one of the most effective Democratic campaign documents. Nixon left the religious issue strictly alone, as did Kennedy for the rest of the campaign. Although both Protestant and Catholic bigotry was undoubtedly at work beneath the surface, religious prejudice played a much smaller role than it had in 1928.

The major innovation of the Kennedy-Nixon contest was the so-called Great Debates—a series of four joint appearances on television. In the opinion of most viewers, Kennedy gained an advantage in these TV encounters. Appearing more poised and confident than Nixon, he managed to erase the image of being an "inexperienced youth." The candidates carried their appeal in person to as many localities as possible. Nixon fulfilled a pledge to visit every state; Kennedy traveled almost as widely, although shrewdly concentrating his major efforts on the nine most populous states.

When the ballots were counted in November, it was discovered that Kennedy had carried 23 states with 303 electoral votes, while Nixon had taken 26 states with 219 electoral votes. Decisive though this appeared, the popular vote was extraordinarily close: Kennedy received 34,277,096 (49.7 per cent) to Nixon's 34,108,546 (49.6 per cent). A shift of fewer than 33,000 votes in Illinois and Texas would have brought a Nixon victory. It was generally agreed that Kennedy had acted shrewdly in selecting Johnson as his running mate. Although Nixon did well in the South, carrying Florida,

Kentucky, Oklahoma, Tennessee, and Virginia, Johnson's influence was probably decisive in holding the rest of the section for the Democrats. Kennedy had also shown good judgment in concentrating on the more populous states; he carried seven out of nine of these, losing only California and Ohio. In these states his religion proved an asset, since he apparently won back many Catholic voters who had supported Eisenhower in the last two elections. Of great importance also was the black vote cast overwhelmingly for Kennedy in response to his vigorous stand on civil rights and his intervention on behalf of Martin Luther King when the black leader was incarcerated in a Georgia jail on trivial charges.

New Frontiers at Home and in World Affairs

In his speech accepting the Democratic nomination, Kennedy had declared that the nation stood on the edge of a "New Frontier—the frontier of the 1960's—a frontier of unknown opportunities and perils—a frontier of unfilled hopes and threats." In an eloquent inaugural address, the new President said:

Let the word go forth from this time and place, to friend and foe alike, that the torch has been passed to a new generation of Americans—born in this century, tempered by war, disciplined by a hard and bitter peace, proud of our ancient heritage—and unwilling to witness or permit the slow undoing of those human rights to which we are committed today at home and around the world.

Appealing for national dedication to the goal of achieving "a more fruitful life for all mankind," he solemnly declared: "And so, my fellow-Americans: ask not what your country can do for you—ask what you can do for your country."

As leader of the "new generations of Americans," Kennedy possessed many assets. His family background was unusual. His maternal grandfather had been a famous Boston politician, Mayor John F. ("Honey Fitz") Fitzgerald; his father, Joseph P. Kennedy, had amassed a huge fortune through shrewd investment and then served the New Deal as chairman of the Securities and Exchange Commission and as Ambassador to Great Britain. Patriotic and ambitious, the senior Kennedy had consciously groomed his sons—first Joseph, Jr., killed in service during World War II, and then John—for the presidency. John strode toward this White House goal with giant steps. He graduated with honors from Harvard, was decorated for bravery during World War II, was a Congressman at twenty-nine, and a Senator at thirty-five. Particularly impressive had been the campaigning ability he displayed in defeating the incumbent Massachusetts Senator Henry Cabot Lodge in 1952—the year of the first Eisenhower landslide.

In choosing his cabinet, Kennedy surprised many people by appointing two Republican businessmen to important posts. Robert S. McNamara, president of the Ford Motor Company, became Secretary of Defense, and Douglas Dillon, a Wall Street banker who had served in the Eisenhower State Department, was named Secretary of the Treasury. Most of the other cabinet appointees were relatively young men, whose testing had been in the field of public affairs. Dean Rusk, little known to the general public but experienced in subordinate State Department posts, became Secretary of State, Arthur Goldberg, counsel for the AFL-CIO, headed the Labor Department. Youngest of all was Robert F. Kennedy, the President's thirty-five-year-old brother and campaign manager who was appointed Attorney General. For the most important diplomatic post, Ambassador to the United Nations, Kennedy called upon the veteran Adlai Stevenson.

Despite considerable criticism, President Kennedy gave major responsibilities to members of his own family. Although Robert ("Bobby") Kennedy did not have the legal experience usual in an Attorney General, he became an unusually vigorous cabinet member and the President's most trusted adviser. The chief executive also entrusted important duties to Sargent Shriver, his brother-in-law, appointed director of the newly created Peace Corps. When Edward ("Teddy") Kennedy, the President's younger brother, announced his candidacy for a United States Senate seat in 1962, many Democrats as well as Republicans complained that he lacked experience. But the Kennedy magic overrode all obstacles and "Teddy" won an easy victory.

Kennedy's hope to infuse a fresh spirit of dedication and service found its most appealing symbol in the Peace Corps. Carrying out an idea suggested in one of his campaign speeches, the President issued an executive order on March 1, 1961, creating a small experimental Peace Corps to be composed of young men and women who would volunteer to serve, for expenses only, in helping the undeveloped nations deal with their problems of education, sanitation, and agriculture. Cynics who ridiculed the Peace Corps experiment as a global boondoggle were amazed at the enthusiastic response it drew from the nation. Hundreds of volunteers, not all of them young, offered their services in a spontaneous outburst of idealism. Impressed by this response, Congress provided the funds in September, 1961, to put the Peace Corps on a permanent basis.

The Peace Corps continued to enjoy an excellent reputation. Carefully selected for special skills and emotional stability, the participants were given short periods of intensive training. Then they were sent to distant countries to work side by side with native teachers, nurses, and other technicians. In the new nations of Africa and Asia these earnest young volunteers created a more favorable image of America than any propaganda could have shaped. Congress voted funds for a gradual enlargement of the Peace Corps to reach ten thousand members by the fall of 1963.

Kennedy attempted another initiative in promoting the Alliance for Progress. Throughout most of Latin America the masses lived in appalling poverty, while a small privileged class enjoyed wealth and luxury without bearing any significant proportion of taxes. To the discontented majority and particularly to university students, Castroism possessed a strong appeal —even though the Castro regime in Cuba was having its own desperate economic difficulties. Remembering how the Marshall Plan had saved western Europe from Communism, President Kennedy sought to develop a

A Peace Corps representative at work in Malaysia. (Courtesy Peace Corps.)

Another kind of Peace Corps work. (Courtesy Peace Corps.)

similar program for Latin America. Yet the obstacles to success were much greater, because in Europe American dollars could be used to revitalize an already highly developed industrial society, while in Latin America a healthy basic economy had never existed. Despite these obvious difficulties, Kennedy proposed in March, 1961, a ten-year program in which the Latin-American nations, aided by the United States, would make a major attack upon their economic and social problems. The President's initiative resulted in a conference attended by representatives of the United States and all the Latin-American republics except Cuba at Punta del Este, Uruguay. There on August 17, 1961, the Alliance for Progress was officially launched. Latin-American nations were to receive a minimum of $20 billion over a ten-year period; the United States would advance more than half of this; international agencies, western European countries, and private sources would supply the balance. The Alliance countries set a number of important economic and social goals, such as six years of free schooling for all children, the reduction of infant mortality and endemic disease, agrarian reform, and industrialization.

At the end of its first two years, the Alliance for Progress could list modest accomplishments. It had provided 140,000 new homes, 8,200 additional classrooms, 900 hospitals and health centers, and 700 community water systems. Some 10 million children were receiving daily servings of United States surplus food—often their only hot meal of the day. Ironically, however, these achievements only dramatized the size of the basic problem. The Alliance projects were scarcely making a dent upon the region's massive poverty. The high Latin-American birth rate, for example, was creating a housing shortage twelve times as fast as the Alliance could build new units. Obviously there were strict limits on what American dollars could do. The first and greatest need was for enlightened political leadership in the Latin American nations themselves. Yet this was hard to achieve. In some countries the privileged classes clung to power, greedy for dollars but slow to make needed social reforms. In other countries military juntas overrode the constitutional system to seize control, thereby creating problems for Washington as to whether or not to cut off American aid. In a few countries democratic governments struggled earnestly to rule in accordance with the Alliance ideals only to find themselves under savage attack from both left and right.

The Kennedy administration tried to play a role of friendship toward the newly independent African nations, but this proved at times extremely difficult. Particularly frustrating was the bitter civil war in the Congo, where the Soviet Union backed Patrice Lumumba and various rightist groups supported Moise Tshombe. The United Nations, guided by Secretary General Dag Hammarskjold, threw its support behind a central Congolese government that would be free of foreign domination. After Hammarskjold was killed in an airplane crash in the Congo, his successor, U Thant, continued this policy. UN troops helped the central government to survive, but the costs were heavy. Disapproving of UN policy, the Soviet Union refused to share in the costs of the Congo operation, which made it necessary for the United States to advance special funds to the UN to keep it from going bankrupt.

Kennedy and Khrushchev

On June 3 and 4, 1961, President Kennedy and Premier Khrushchev met in Vienna, Austria, for their only face-to-face encounter. It was, as Kennedy later reported to the nation by television, "a very sober two days." Except for a minor agreement on the principle of a neutral and independent Laos, the two leaders decided nothing. On the major issues confronting them—Berlin and nuclear testing—they found themselves far apart. By stressing the Berlin problem, Khrushchev renewed the vague ultimatum first given to the Eisenhower administration. But the Western allies refused to take any step that would involve recognition of Communist East Germany. On July 17, France, Britain, and the United States sent similar notes to the Soviet Union emphasizing their determination to defend their legal rights in Berlin. Reemphasizing American determination in a television speech a week later, President Kennedy asked Congress for new defense appropriations and an enlargement of the armed forces.

As a new Berlin crisis seemed in the making, more and more residents of East Berlin streamed across the border seeking greater liberty and economic opportunity in West Germany. Resorting to drastic measures on

President Kennedy, Mrs. Khrushchev, President Schaerf of Austria, Premier Khrushchev, and Mrs. Kennedy in Vienna, 1961. (UPI Photo.)

August 13, 1961, the East German government closed the border between East and West Berlin. Within the next several weeks the Communists built a cement-block wall twenty-five miles long to separate the two sectors of the city. Some eighty thousand East Berliners were cut off from their jobs in West Berlin, and many families were separated from their relatives. So great was the yearning to escape that many East Berliners risked their lives to climb over the wall, tunnel under it, or smash through some check point.

Although the Western allies protested the building of the wall as a violation of Soviet pledges to permit free movement within the city of Berlin, they made no attempt to tear down the barrier. But President Kennedy did take steps to warn the Russians against any effort to renew the blockade. He ordered 1,500 American troops into West Berlin to join the 5,000 already there, and for several weeks Allied tanks and guns faced their Soviet counterparts across the tense Berlin border. Since the Russians could have destroyed these forces at any time, the Allied show of strength was more symbolic than real. Yet to face up to the Soviets without flinching appeared essential not only to Allied morale, but to that of the menaced West Berliners. Although the Russians occasionally tested Allied nerves by holding up traffic on the highways leading to Berlin and by other harassments, they avoided any decisive showdown. Nor did they go through with their often-repeated threat to make a separate treaty with East Germany. In 1961 Vice President Johnson made a symbolic visit to West Berlin, and in the summer of 1963 President Kennedy went there himself. "All free men, wherever they may live, are citizens of Berlin," he declared. "And therefore, as a free man, I take pride in the words 'Ich bin ein Berliner.' "

Even before the Berlin scare President Kennedy had laid heavy emphasis on strengthening national defenses. He believed that too much reliance on nuclear weapons had tied the hands of American diplomacy, since it offered no middle road between all-out war and no war at all. Therefore the Defense Department now built up a more diversified arsenal of large and small nuclear weapons, speeded the construction of Polaris submarines, rehabilitated the ground forces, and developed special units to combat guerrillas. The "missiles gap," the supposed Soviet superiority in intercontinental ballistic missiles (ICBM), was now disclosed to have been pretty much a myth, originated by Pentagon propagandists and blown up by Democratic orators, including Kennedy himself, during the 1960 campaign. The United States, in sober fact, appeared to have a decisive superiority in nuclear weapons.

The Kennedy administration continued to abide by the unwritten moratorium on nuclear testing that the Soviet Union, Great Britain, and the United States had been observing since October, 1958. Eager to make the moratorium official, the President pressed for a test-ban treaty, only to encounter the same Soviet obstructions that had thwarted similar efforts during the Eisenhower administration. The recess on testing was terminated during the summer of 1961 when the Russians began a series of over 40 tests, including one massive blast of over 50 megatons of force—more than 2,500 times the power of the bomb that had destroyed Hiroshima. The United States, in turn, resumed testing during the spring of 1962.

On June 10, 1963, President Kennedy announced a new effort to halt this deplorable poisoning of the air. In a speech at American University, he proposed a "strategy of peace." The Soviet Union and the United States, he said, had their differences, "but let us also direct attention to our common interests and the means by which those differences can be resolved." He made two important announcements: representatives of the United States, Great Britain, and the Soviet Union would soon meet in Moscow to renew negotiations for a test-ban treaty; and the United States would not conduct further nuclear tests in the atmosphere "so long as other states do not do so." Kennedy's overture had a favorable reception in the Soviet Union, and a few weeks later Khrushchev gave a significant interview indicating that he might now be willing to consider a limited test-ban treaty.

Thus when the veteran American diplomat Averell Harriman and the British negotiator Lord Hailsham met with Foreign Minister Gromyko on July 15, the atmosphere was one of uncommon geniality. The Russians were indeed prepared to accept the limited test-ban treaty they had so long rejected. On July 25, such an agreement was initialed, and on August 5, 1963, it was formally signed by Secretary Rusk and the other foreign ministers at a ceremony in Moscow. Simple in its provisions, the treaty banned all nuclear tests in the atmosphere, in outer space, and under water. The contracting parties promised to continue negotiations on the problem of underground tests and agreed not to encourage nuclear tests by other nations. Other nations were invited to subscribe to the treaty, and 99 of them did so by the end of 1963. The principal abstainers were France and Red China—each eager to achieve a nuclear arsenal of its own. Despite the opposition of Senator Barry Goldwater of Arizona and other ultranationalists, the Senate approved the test-ban treaty on September 24 by an 80-to-19 vote.

Achilles' Heel—Cuba

On January 3, 1961—less than three weeks before Kennedy's inauguration —the Eisenhower administration broke off diplomatic relations with the Communist-dominated Castro government, thus retaliating for a long series of provocations. The new Democratic President was destined to find the Cuban situation even more worrisome than had his Republican predecessor. Kennedy had first to decide whether to continue a secret policy adopted by the Eisenhower administration in the spring of 1960. At that time the Central Intelligence Agency (CIA) had received permission to equip and train an armed force of anti-Castro Cuban exiles in preparation for a possible invasion of the island. When Kennedy became President, a Cuban exile army had been assembling for several months in Guatemala and elsewhere. Although the project was none too sharply defined, its apparent assumption was that a well-timed invasion of Cuba might spark an internal revolt on the island and overthrow Castro.

The whole scheme was badly conceived. Unless strongly supported by United States air and naval power, no invasion was likely to succeed, yet the use of American forces in this way would be exactly the kind of intervention forbidden under the Charter of the United Nations and the Bogotá

Charter of the Organization of American States. Even if successful, an overthrow of Castro thus achieved would have exposed the United States to all the criticism that had followed earlier interventions under Theodore Roosevelt and Woodrow Wilson. Despite warnings by some of his advisers and his own misgivings, Kennedy did not cancel the invasion plans. Trusting too much the supposed expert advice of the CIA, the President approved the project with minor modifications to reduce the American involvement.

When the invasion was finally attempted on April 17, 1961, there was little or no surprise. American newspapers had been full of invasion rumors, and forty-eight hours before the invasion, three American bombers, unconvincingly disguised as Cuban, had taken off from Guatemalan bases for an air strike against Castro bases in Cuba. When the Cuban ambassador to the UN charged an act of American aggression, Ambassador Stevenson, apparently himself unaware of the truth, denied that the planes were American and described them as deserters from Castro's air force. Thus the air strike, ineffective in a military sense, hurt the American cause by giving a new warning to Castro and suggesting an American policy more aggressive than it actually was.

The invasion itself was a sickening failure. Convoyed by United States naval vessels and landed at the Bay of Pigs on the southern coast of Cuba, the exile army—some fifteen hundred strong—did not have the planes or equipment to oppose the waiting Castro forces. Nor did the hope of internal revolt materialize. Within seventy-two hours the last of the invaders had been forced to surrender, and Castro was taking advantage of his triumph to arrest thousands of suspected opponents on the island.

While the battle still raged in Cuba, Khrushchev brusquely demanded a halt to the American aggression. Kennedy replied that in the event of any military intervention by outside force the United States would immediately honor its obligation to protect the hemisphere from external aggression. Despite these threats, the Soviet Union took no steps to intervene, and the United States held back the massive air and naval support that might have given victory to the invaders.

Inevitably, the Kennedy administration found itself under severe attack from two directions. Liberals were shocked that the nation should have violated the Good Neighbor tradition by aiding the invasion attempt, while conservatives condemned the President for not providing enough air and naval support to ensure victory. Sharp though the criticisms were, they appeared to damage Kennedy's personal popularity less than might have been expected. Republican attacks were blunted by the support given to the President by former President Eisenhower. Kennedy also helped himself by shouldering without complaint primary responsibility for the fateful decisions on whether to permit the invasion and how much assistance to give.

In October, 1962, the Kennedy administration passed through a second and much more serious Cuban crisis. For weeks there had been charges that the Russians were transforming Cuba into a hostile base, but the administration—relying on Soviet assurances that they were supplying the Cubans with defensive weapons only—denied these charges as Republican election material. But aerial surveillance at length provided photographic evidence that the threat was all too real: a string of bases was being built in Cuba, from which the Soviets might launch nuclear attacks against cities throughout the Western Hemisphere. For several days a special committee of high military and civilian officials secretly debated what the American response should be. At first most of the participants urged a massive Pearl Harbor–type attack to wipe out the offending bases without warning, but Attorney General Robert Kennedy and a few others argued against a policy that might result in thousands of deaths, both Cuban and American, and would be condemned throughout the world as a brutal act of aggression. The Soviets might retaliate against Berlin; indeed, an American attack upon Cuba might trigger an all-out nuclear war between the great powers. Instead, Robert Kennedy favored the less drastic response that President Kennedy announced to the nation in a somber television speech on October 22. Revealing what had been learned about the missile bases and condemning the Russians for their deception in the matter, the President announced that he had ordered "a strict quarantine" on all offensive military equipment under shipment to Cuba. All vessels bearing offensive weapons were to be turned back. The quarantine would be continued until all offensive weapons in Cuba were dismantled and withdrawn under the supervision of UN observers. The President called upon Khrushchev "to halt and eliminate this clandestine, reckless and provocative threat to world peace."

The naval quarantine involved, in Kennedy's words, "a difficult and dangerous effort." Never before in American history had the threat of nuclear destruction seemed so imminent. If Russian cargo ships defied the American quarantine and were fired upon, would not this be the signal for all-out war? The President ordered the armed forces to maintain a state of readiness, and the nation waited with fatalistic calm for Russia's next move. If Khrushchev's principal purpose had been to test American reflexes, the strong reaction convinced the Russian leader of the need for caution. Although he denounced the blockade of Cuba as "piracy," he avoided any direct challenge. The threatened war of nuclear bombs became instead a diplomatic debate, as Stevenson and Valerian Zorin exchanged bitter charges in the UN Security Council.

In the end, the Cuban storm subsided almost as suddenly as it had blown up. On October 28, Khrushchev agreed that the Russians would halt their building of bases, dismantle offensive weapons already in Cuba, and desist from further shipments—all under UN verification; President Kennedy promised in turn to lift the blockade and give a pledge against any United States invasion of Cuba. Castro's refusal to allow on-site UN inspection threatened to disrupt these plans, but in the end the settlement held up. Checks from the air and sea convinced the Kennedy administration that the Soviet weapons had in fact been removed from Cuba, and the naval blockade was therefore lifted, although the promised no-invasion pledge was withheld in view of Cuban intransigence. If the Bay of Pigs affair was Kennedy's greatest humiliation, the facing-down of Khrushchev on the missiles issue was his greatest triumph. In the weeks following the Soviet retreat the President achieved a new height of popularity.

Soviet missile material awaiting withdrawal from Cuba, 1962. (UPI Photo.)

Kennedy and Congress

Despite the young President's growing prestige, Congress enacted relatively little of his domestic New Frontier into law before his death. There were several reasons for this congressional foot dragging. The leap from junior Senator from Massachusetts to President had been so rapid that Kennedy's older colleagues demonstrated an understandable tendency to match their own judgments against his. Moreover, his razor-thin margin in the popular vote gave the New Frontier a rather dubious mandate. Although the elections of 1960 seemed to give the President's party substantial majorities with 64 Democrats to 36 Republicans in the Senate and 262 Democrats to 175 Republicans in the House, these figures were highly misleading. Actually the Democrats had lost more than 20 House seats that they had held during the last two Eisenhower years, and these were mostly seats held by liberals and moderates. Thus the new Eighty-seventh Congress was even more strongly controlled than the old by a conservative coalition composed of Republicans and Southern Democrats. A further blow to Democratic solidarity was the loss of the two masterful Texans who had managed Congress during the Eisenhower years. Vice President Johnson was succeeded as Senate majority leader by the mild-mannered Mike Mansfield of Montana, and Speaker of the House Sam Rayburn died in 1961, leaving John W. McCormack of Massachusetts, a man of far less prestige, to take his place.

Overrepresentation of the rural districts at the expense of the cities facilitated conservative control of the House of Representatives. Although inequities in apportionment existed in almost every state, there seemed little chance for reform as long as the state legislatures enjoyed sole power over districting. Earlier attempts to have state apportionment laws reviewed by the Supreme Court had failed; the Court had ruled that apportionment was a political question entirely within the power of the legislative branches of government. But in March, 1962, the Court reversed itself in an historic six-to-two decision (Baker v. Carr). Accepting the contention of a group of Tennessee voters that unequal representation in the state legislature denied them the equal protection of the laws, the Court ruled that these citizens had an arguable claim under the Fourteenth Amendment and that the Federal courts should hear their case. The decision opened the door for a flood of litigation that forced the state legislatures to redistrict the states. Yet this liberalizing influence manifested itself only slowly—too late to help the New Frontier program.

On paper, the Kennedy administration successfully withstood the traditional midterm reaction against the party in power in the congressional election of 1962. In the Senate the Democrats gained four seats; in the House they lost only six. Yet the heavy Democratic majorities in the Eighty-eighth Congress did not necessarily reflect voter support for the domestic New Frontier program. Local issues and the firm administration stand in the Cuban crisis—Republican leaders estimated that the Cuban issue lost twenty seats for their candidates—were mainly responsible for the results. Thus the composition of the new Congress was little different from that of its predecessor; the coalition of Southern Democrats and conservative Republicans was still in control.

In his first year in office President Kennedy received strong congressional support on most issues relating to national defense and foreign policy. He also had substantial success in consolidating the older New Deal objectives. Congress raised the Federal minimum wage from $1 to $1.15, with another hike to $1.25 for 1963, and extended its coverage to some four million workers in the retail trade, construction, and service industries. The Housing Act of 1961 authorized grants of $5.6 billion, the most liberal measure of its kind in more than a decade. The new law made much greater provision than predecessor acts for housing the elderly and the moderate-income groups and for encouraging urban renewal and mass transportation. A third major measure, the Area Redevelopment Act of 1961, sought to ease the problems of distressed regions by loans for new businesses and grants for retraining the technologically unemployed. In gaining approval for these measures as well as for the liberalization of Social Security benefits, the President often had the help of Republicans with urban constituencies.

The New Deal still lived, but could the more ambitious goals of the New Frontier be achieved? In this area Kennedy suffered many frustrations. His proposals for massive Federal aid to education were shipwrecked on the treacherous rocks of church and state. Although Kennedy requested aid for all levels of education, he carefully stipulated that at the elementary and secondary level assistance should be granted to public schools only. But in this matter the hierarchy of his own church opposed him. A spokesman for the American bishops warned that to exclude children in private schools from the bill's benefits would be discriminatory. With the President and the bishops at odds in their interpretation of the Federal Constitution and economy-minded Republicans and Southern Democrats opposed to the whole idea, any broad program of Federal aid was for the time being doomed.

Kennedy encountered even less success in his efforts to extend the Social Security system to provide medical care for the elderly. In 1962 he made a vigorous fight for the King-Anderson Bill, under which Social Security pensioners would receive hospital care for ninety days and certain other benefits, but the American Medical Association persisted in regarding any provision for health insurance under Social Security as the opening wedge for "socialized medicine." The AMA found willing allies for its fight in the private health insurance companies, the United States Chamber of Commerce, and conservative politicians of both parties. The debate over "medicare" reached a climax in May, 1962, when President Kennedy appealed for passage of the bill before an overflow crowd in New York's Madison Square Garden. The next day Dr. Edward R. Annis, a spokesman for the AMA, denounced the President's program as "a cruel hoax and delusion."

Although Kennedy was unable to get what he wanted, Congress did pass three important acts involving the nation's health. The Drug Industry Act of October, 1962, gave the government greater control, especially over experimental drugs such as thalidomide, which had resulted in pathetic malformations at birth. Almost a year later Congress provided $175 million to help medical schools expand their facilities and at the same time set up a loan fund to enable medical students to complete their education; this measure was aimed at correcting the shortage of doctors. At about the same time Kennedy signed an act under which the Federal government would grant funds to the states for the care of the mentally ill and mentally retarded.

Fuel for the Economy

During the fifties the national economy had not grown fast enough to furnish employment for the increasing number of young people entering the job market. Both in his electoral campaign and in his presidential messages, Kennedy gave high priority to the need for a more dynamic economy. Adding urgency to the problem was the fact that when he took office in January, 1961, the nation had been in a recession for about seven months. Almost 5.5 million persons—some 7 per cent of the labor force—were out of work. Government action seemed to be called for—but what kind of action?

Despite liberal pressure for massive public works and increased Federal spending, the President at first followed a relatively cautious course. He advocated temporary extension of unemployment insurance, liberalization of Social Security, a higher minimum wage, and aid to depressed areas—

mild antidepression remedies that Congress with some modification provided. Why was Kennedy reluctant to advocate stronger medicine? The most obvious reason was the precarious foreign payments situation inherited from the Eisenhower administration. With the revival of the European economy, American exports were not in such heavy demand. Indeed American capital was being poured into foreign factories and other facilities. At the same time, American dollars were flowing abroad for the maintenance of American armed forces and for economic and military aid to foreign governments. The result of all these factors had been an adverse balance of payments and an outward flow of gold. Committed to safeguard the dollar, President Kennedy had to listen to conservative advisers who opposed any large-scale spending program that might set off a new spiral of inflation and a further flight of gold to foreign havens.

Kennedy's middle-of-the-road economic policy achieved a modest success. Recovery from the recession began in the early spring of 1961 and continued without serious interruption. By August, 1962, the President could report that since he took office, industrial production had increased 15 per cent and unemployment had decreased 23 per cent. But a recovery of this character fell far short of Kennedy's ambition for national economic growth.

Hampering the President's efforts was a lack of trust between the admin-

How to succeed in business—and labor—without really trying. (By Haynie in the *Louisville Courier-Journal.*)

istration and the business community. Anxious to maintain price stability, Kennedy had asked Secretary of Labor Goldberg to use his influence with the unions to moderate their demands. The Secretary had done so in several cases, and most significantly in March, 1962, when the steelworkers union signed a two-year contract with the first-year gains limited to increased fringe benefits. Confident that the steel industry would reciprocate by holding the price line, Kennedy was vexed when, on April 10, 1962, United States Steel announced a 3.5 per cent increase in its prices—a step soon followed by five other major steel companies. In a dramatic display of presidential wrath, he denounced the industry's action as "a wholly unjustifiable and irresponsible defiance of the public interest." Roger M. Blough, board chairman of United States Steel, defended higher prices as necessary to enable the industry to modernize its plants and equipment. But the President brandished all the weapons at his command. Threatened with antitrust prosecutions and a shift of defense orders to rival companies, the industry front soon began to crack. Inland Steel and Bethlehem Steel rejected the increase, and finally on April 13 United States Steel capitulated, with the other companies soon falling into line. But Kennedy's resounding victory antagonized many businessmen. Unless they could be assured an adequate margin of profit, they threatened to cancel their plans for expansion.

Insisting that he was a friend and not a foe, Kennedy took steps to appease the business community. In July, 1962, the Treasury Department liberalized depreciation allowances in a way estimated to save businessmen $1.5 billion in corporate income taxes. The idea of refueling the economy through major tax cuts—long advocated by Chairman Walter Heller of the President's Council of Economic Advisers, gained increasing support during the summer of 1962. As finally proposed to Congress in January, 1963, Kennedy's program called for gradual tax cuts amounting to $13.6 billion over three years. To offset some $3.4 billion of loss of revenue, he asked for reforms to plug notorious loophopes in the tax laws. Although the immediate result of a tax cut would be to increase the deficit, the President argued that the release of these funds for private investment would give the economy an enormous lift, thus making it easier to balance future budgets.

The Kennedy tax program encountered much criticism. Both businessmen and labor leaders complained that the cuts were unfairly distributed, and every group with a stake in existing tax exemptions beseeched Congress to protect its special interests. When it became apparent that he might not be able to get both a tax cut and tax reforms, the President gave priority to the cut. But even with this concession he could not get his bill through Congress. In September, 1963, House Democrats closed ranks to push through an $11 billion tax cut, but the Senate continued its dilatory tactics.

Death in Dallas

In November, 1963, the prospects for Kennedy's re-election looked excellent. To be sure, he had made enemies, particularly in the South where his strong civil rights program was intensely resented. Although some of his supporters were disappointed that he had been unable to get more of the

President and Mrs. Kennedy in Texas a few hours before the President's assassination, November 22, 1963. (UPI Photo.)

New Frontier program enacted into law, they placed the blame more on Congress than on the President. Most citizens admired the courage Kennedy displayed in dealing with the steel price issue, the integration crises in the South,[2] and the Cuban missiles showdown. The recent test-ban treaty had also contributed greatly to the President's popularity. Intellectuals found other things to praise; they liked the literary quality of his state papers, the flashes of wit that brightened his press conferences, and the unusual recognition awarded to poets, musicians, and artists by the President and his wife.

On November 21, 1963, President Kennedy flew out of Washington for a three-day speaking tour of Texas. This was a state that he had carried by a very slim margin in 1960; it was a state where conservative opposition to the New Frontier was very strong. What better place to do some political fence-mending in preparation for next year's election? Accompanied by his wife and by Vice President and Mrs. Johnson, the President received an enthusiastic reception at San Antonio, Houston, and Forth Worth. On November 22, the presidential party flew to Dallas, where Kennedy was scheduled to address a luncheon meeting. But the motorcade, proceeding from the Dallas airport to the Trade Mart, never reached its destination. As the open car bearing the President and Mrs. Kennedy, together with

[2] See Chap. 29.

Texas Governor John Connally and his wife, approached the end of the route, three shots rang out in quick succession. The President was struck in the throat and head; Connally received a bullet in his shoulder. The victims were rushed to the nearest hospital, where the governor's wound was satisfactorily treated. The President was beyond help and died within half an hour of the shooting.

Air Force One, the presidential plane, brought the fallen leader's body back to Washington. There under the steady gaze of television cameras, three days of national mourning were observed, culminating in a funeral ceremony in the city's Roman Catholic cathedral and burial in the Arlington National Cemetery.

A few hours after Kennedy's death, the Dallas police arrested Lee Harvey Oswald and charged him with the crime. Born in New Orleans, Oswald had long shown symptoms of instability. His strange life had included a troubled boyhood, an "undesirable" discharge from the Marines, two and a half years of voluntary exile in the Soviet Union, marriage to a Russian girl, and a succession of short-term jobs. He finally ended up working at the Texas School Book Depository, from whose building the fatal shots that had killed the President were alleged to have come. The evidence against Oswald was circumstantial, but damning. An Italian carbine found near a sixth-story window in the Depository building bore his fingerprints and was identified as a weapon he had purchased under an assumed name from a mail order house.

But Oswald never came to trial. Two days after his arrest, while he was being transferred from one jail to another, he was shot and fatally wounded by Jack Ruby, a Dallas night club operator. This fantastic crime, seen by millions on TV as it happened, brought wide condemnation upon the bungling Dallas police and raised a whole crop of questions about the assassination and its aftermath. Did Oswald really kill the President? Did he act alone, or was there a conspiracy? Why did Ruby kill Oswald? How did he get the chance? To answer these and other questions, President Johnson appointed a special commission of investigation headed by Chief Justice Warren. The Commission's major findings, submitted in September, 1964, were that Oswald was the President's killer beyond reasonable doubt; that Oswald acted alone and not as part of any conspiracy; that Ruby acted on his own in murdering Oswald; and that the Secret Service and FBI were delinquent in their efforts to protect President Kennedy. A Dallas jury found Ruby "guilty with malice" and sentenced him to death, but he died in prison of natural causes in 1967 while his case was still under litigation. The two killings made so little sense that many Americans refused to believe the prosaic findings of the Warren Commission. This provided a boom market for publicity-seeking authors and willing publishers who garnered huge profits on books purporting to reveal "the real truth" behind the slayings.

President Johnson

Just before the plane bearing Kennedy's body left the Dallas airport on November 22, 1963, Lyndon B. Johnson took the presidential oath of office

President Johnson taking the oath of office in the presidential plane in Dallas shortly after President Kennedy's assassination: Mrs. Johnson and Mrs. Kennedy look on. (Wide World Photos.)

in a somber ceremony. The new President was a thorough Texan, whose grandfather and father had served in the Texas legislature. As a boy, he knew the grinding hardship of rural poverty and had to work at a variety of jobs before he could enroll at Southwest State Teachers College at San Marcos, Texas. Supporting himself with stints as janitor, part-time teacher, and secretary, he completed his college course and taught briefly in a Houston high school. In 1931 young Johnson went to Washington as secretary to a Texas Congressman, and in 1935 he was appointed state administrator of the National Youth Administration. Two years later he won election to the United States House of Representatives. He saw a year of active duty as a Navy aviator during World War II and was elected Senator from Texas in 1948.

In 1952, despite his lack of seniority, he became Democratic leader in the Senate. Few men have made so much of this post. In part, this resulted from the unusual situation that prevailed from 1955 to 1961 when a Republican President had to deal with a Senate and House controlled by Democrats. To Senator Johnson and House Speaker Sam Rayburn went the responsibility of pushing through legislation needed to support a bipartisan foreign policy and deal with the more pressing domestic problems. But Johnson's success also testified to his unusual flair for practical politics. Affable and shrewd, he knew when to appeal to his fellow Senators' sense of patriotism and when to wheel and deal in political compromise. Johnson's evident abilities had made him a Texas favorite son for the presidential nomination in 1956 and a more serious contender in 1960.

Despite the profound shock of Kennedy's assassination, the transfer of power to President Johnson was impressively smooth. His pledge to continue his predecessor's policies and his request for all the Kennedy cabinet and staff to stay in their posts did no more than to follow precedents established by men like Coolidge and Truman, yet his first address to Congress on November 27 was delivered with special fervor. Speaking of Kennedy, he said: "No words are strong enough to express our determination to continue the forward thrust of America that he began." The new chief executive laid particular stress on the importance of congressional action on the Kennedy-proposed tax cut and the civil rights bill.

Johnson clearly understood the pressure of time. With less than a year to make a record of his own before the 1964 election, he took immediate steps to cement an alliance with spokesmen for the blacks and labor union leaders who might have serious doubts about a Southerner in the White House. But at the same time he began a shrewd maneuver to reassure the nation's moderates. Emphasizing the need for economy, he pared his budget requests down to $97.9 billion, considerably less than Kennedy had been expected to ask. This mollified the conservative Democrats enough to facilitate passage of the long-delayed tax bill in February, 1964. In its final form, it provided for a $9.1 billion cut in individual income taxes and $2.4 billion in corporation taxes, two thirds of which would become effective in 1964 and the rest the following year. The tax cut resulted in increased take-home pay, increased consumer spending, and increased industrial production. Both industrialists and workers were delighted with this lesson in the New Economics. But in later years of the Johnson administration, when accelerating inflation called for higher taxes instead of lower, the teachings of the New Economics proved much more difficult to sell.

The new President's success with the tax bill was followed by several other striking victories. Johnson's accomplishments resulted in part from the unusual situation of these months. Sobered by the Dallas tragedy, the legislators seemed to feel that the finest tribute to the fallen leader would be to act upon his key proposals without the usual petty partisanship. Moreover, the impending 1964 election warned the Democrats of the need to close ranks and establish a positive record of action. Many Republicans also felt it wise to avoid the appearance of being against all reform proposals. Yet quite apart from these favoring circumstances, President Johnson gave impressive evidence that he had lost none of the political skill gained in twelve years as a Congressman and Senator.

The administration's second major landmark was achieved on July 12 when President Johnson signed the Civil Rights Act of 1964. Southern Senators had sought to block the bill through their usual filibustering tactics, but a coalition of Democrats and Republicans provided the votes to impose cloture. This bipartisan effort had the support of Senator Everett Dirkson, the minority leader, who contented himself with obtaining certain clarifying amendments in the strong bill passed by the House.[3]

---

[3] For further details, see Chap. 29.

Before the November election Congress had given the President a cluster of other significant laws—the so-called War on Poverty Act, the Urban Mass Transportation Act, the Housing Act, and the Wilderness Areas Act. On most of these Kennedy had sown the seed, and Johnson proudly gathered in the harvest.

The Election of 1964

Meantime, the moratorium on partisan politics that the Kennedy tragedy had brought about ended soon after New Year's Day, 1964. First to declare himself in the race for the Republican presidential nomination was Nelson Rockefeller, who had been re-elected governor of New York in 1962. A strong internationalist and an advocate of health insurance for the elderly, he had a large following among the liberal wing of the Republican party, but his recent divorce and remarriage had dimmed his popularity somewhat. A second declared candidate was Senator Barry Goldwater of Arizona, the hero of the Republican conservatives, who admired his demands for returning regulatory powers to the states, reducing the operations of TVA, taking a tougher stand with the Soviet Union, forcing Castro out of Cuba, and increasing military aid to South Vietnam. Eastern Republicans who favored a strongly internationalist foreign policy and cautiously liberal domestic measures badly misjudged the strength of the Goldwater movement. Long accustomed to controlling the party nomination and platform, these moderates paid scant attention to the tireless activity by which the Arizona Senator had been gaining control of the party. Since the election of 1960, Goldwater had been the most sought-after speaker at local Republican fund-raising affairs, and he had won a legion of followers among minor political leaders. Before the Eastern press realized what had happened, Goldwater had lined up enough strength in the South and West to bring the nomination almost within his grasp.

When the Republican National Convention opened at San Francisco in July, the Goldwater forces were in firm control. Not only did they vote down the moderates' attempts to condemn the John Birch Society and make other changes in the proposed platform, but they subjected Rockefeller to severe heckling during the debate. As adopted, the platform echoed the Goldwater line in foreign policy by advocating "a dynamic strategy aimed at victory" and promising stronger measures on the Berlin Wall, Cuba, and Vietnam. The party condemned huge Federal expenditures, high taxes, and government controls as detriments to business. It promised to strengthen the Social Security system, but opposed its extension into the field of medical care.

The victorious faction achieved the nomination of Goldwater on the first ballot.[4] Making no effort to conciliate the vanquished moderates, Goldwater chose as his running mate another conservative, Representative William Miller of New York. In a militant acceptance speech, Goldwater

---

[4] Goldwater received 883 votes; Governor William Scranton of Pennsylvania, 214; and others, 211.

declared: "Extremism in defense of liberty is no vice . . . moderation in the pursuit of justice is no virtue."

There was no doubt that President Johnson would receive the Democratic nomination. Governor George Wallace of Alabama opposed him in three Northern primaries and won a surprisingly large vote ranging from 30 per cent in Indiana to 43 per cent in Maryland. This warned of a disturbing "white backlash" of resentment against the administration's civil rights program but did not challenge the President's firm control of the party. Among Democrats the chief speculation was over the vice-presidential nomination, considered unusually important after the Dallas tragedy. After keeping the country in suspense throughout the summer, President Johnson finally announced his preference for Senator Hubert Humphrey of Minnesota in a dramatic appearance at the Democratic National Convention in Atlantic City in August.

Except for this bit of stage management, the Democratic Convention was a rather tame affair. The platform praised the Kennedy-Johnson policies and promised their continuance. In pointed reference to Goldwater's more rabid supporters, the Democrats condemned "the extreme tactics of such organizations as the Communist party, the Ku Klux Klan, and the John Birch Society."

During the fall campaign both major candidates engaged in extensive speaking tours. The rift within Republican ranks was evident by the failure of such prominent moderates and liberals as Rockefeller, Governor William Scranton of Pennsylvania, and Senator Jacob Javits of New York to support the national ticket. Goldwater tried to prove that he was neither "trigger happy" nor opposed to desegregation; he insisted that his vote against the Civil Rights Act was based upon constitutional scruples and not prejudice. He avoided any direct bid for the white backlash vote, although his condemnation of violence in the city streets seemed to imply that this was largely black violence, encouraged by the administration's civil rights program. President Johnson concentrated his speeches on the need to promote the "Great Society"—an extended version of the New Frontier.

On November 3, some 43 million Americans cast their ballots for Johnson, and slightly more than 27 million for Goldwater. The Democratic majority of about 15 million votes was the largest in American history, and the Democratic percentage of the popular total was close to 62, the highest in the twentieth century, exceeding that of Franklin Roosevelt in 1936 (60.8 per cent), the previous high. In the electoral college, Johnson received 486 votes to Goldwater's 52; the only states in the Republican column were Arizona and the five Southern states of Alabama, Georgia, Louisiana, Mississippi, and South Carolina. Those Southern states furnished the only concrete evidence of a white backlash, for several of them had not gone Republican since Reconstruction days. In the congressional elections the Democratic sweep, while strong, was not so great, because of split voting. In the new Congress there were two more Democrats in the Senate and approximately 40 more in the House.

The Great Society

On October 31, 1964, at New York's Madison Square Garden—the setting for so many great political speeches—President Johnson had said:

This nation, this people, this generation has man's first opportunity to create the Great Society. It can be a society of success without squalor—beauty without barrenness—works of genius without the wretchedness of poverty. We can open the doors of learning, of fruitful labor, and rewarding leisure—not just to the privileged few, but to everyone.

In his first message to Congress after the election, the President elaborated a broad program to achieve these goals.

Johnson gave highest priority to the Medicare Bill—significantly given the numbers S 1 and HR 1 in the two houses of Congress. To avoid charges of promoting socialized medicine, the administration plan covered hospital charges but not doctors' bills. But the AMA used this omission as a basis for asserting that the coverage was inadequate. The association threw its support behind a Republican alternative sponsored by Representative John Byrnes of Wisconsin. This would extend voluntary insurance to cover both hospital and doctors' bills. The administration believed that a voluntary system would not reach the people most in need of coverage, yet it saw an opportunity to weaken AMA opposition by incorporating some features of the Byrnes bill in its own. The eventual package was in large part the work of Wilbur Mills of Arkansas, the powerful chairman of the House Ways and Means Committee. Hitherto an obstructionist in the path of health insurance, Mills now put together a bill that gained wide acceptance. In April the House passed the Mills bill by a vote of 313 to 115; in July the Senate approved it by the overwhelming vote of 68 to 21. President Johnson signed the measure in the Harry S. Truman Library in Independence, Missouri, in a generous tribute to the former President's foresight in first proposing such legislation twenty years earlier.

Actually the legislation of 1965 was only a cautious beginning, falling far short of what Truman had proposed in 1945. In the description of one of its drafters, it was a three-layer cake. The first layer extended the Social Security system to provide retired workers with 90 days of hospital care and 100 days of nursing home care with only minimal payments by the patient. The second layer offered persons over the age of sixty-five an opportunity to purchase for $3 a month medical insurance coverage that would pay 80 per cent after the first $50 of their doctors' bills. The third layer—potentially the most far-reaching in its implications—offered grants-in-aid to states that set up systems of "medicaid," that is, systems for paying the doctors' bills and drugs for poor people of all ages.

Despite considerable grumbling at the paperwork involved, almost all doctors cooperated in the Medicare and Medicaid programs. However, with millions of people getting adequate medical care for the first time in their lives, serious shortages of hospitals, nursing homes, doctors, and other personnel soon developed. During the years of the Johnson presidency Congress passed some forty laws dealing with health problems, and annual Federal expenditures in this field increased from $4 billion to $14 billion.

Johnson's second legislative goal for 1965 was to provide a massive program of Federal aid for education—something desperately needed by hard-pressed cities and states as well as by private institutions. As a Protestant, he discovered more leeway for dealing with Catholic needs than the Catholic Kennedy had found. In April Congress passed the Elementary and Secondary Education Act providing aid to the amount of $1.1 billion. By apportioning the grants to accord with the number of poor pupils in each school district, many objections that had blocked Federal aid in the past were overcome. Although only public schools were to benefit from the direct grants, pupils in private schools as well as public would benefit from special programs in art, science, foreign languages, and technical skills and would be able to borrow certain textbooks and library materials purchased with Federal funds. To dramatize the fact that he had himself risen out of poverty, the President signed the act in the one-room Texas schoolhouse where he had begun his education. His first schoolteacher witnessed the ceremony.

The President also gained congressional authorization in 1965 for a three-year program to aid higher education, in part through scholarships and loans to individual college students, in part through grants for the purchase of equipment and the construction of buildings. In all, Congress passed sixty education bills during the Johnson administration. "When I left office," Johnson wrote in his memoirs, "millions of young boys and girls were receiving better grade school education than they once could have acquired. A million and a half students were in college who otherwise could not have afforded it." [5]

In the historic 1965 session of Congress, Johnson obtained increased appropriations for the War on Poverty, which had been initiated by the Economic Opportunity Act of 1964. To head the Office of Economic Opportunity (OEO), the President appointed Sargent Shriver, widely respected for his leadership of the Peace Corps. Shriver found the OEO assignment much more difficult. He had to administer a complex of different programs—among them the Job Corps to engage in conservation work and develop elementary skills, VISTA to function as a domestic Peace Corps, vocational training programs, Community Action programs to permit the poor to institute their own projects, and Head Start to prepare disadvantaged children for school. With so many different projects in motion at once, critics had little difficulty in finding horrible examples of ill-considered experiments, wasted and stolen money, and feuding factions. Especially bitter was the struggle for power between militant practitioners of community action and local politicians. Conservative attacks upon the agency reached a peak in 1967, but by making concessions to the opponents of community action, the administration was able to save the program. Although admitting that the War on Poverty had not

[5] Lyndon Baines Johnson, *The Vantage Point: Perspectives of the Presidency* (New York: Holt, Rinehart & Winston, 1971), p. 219.

been fully successful, Johnson claimed that between 1964 and 1969 the number of poverty-stricken Americans had dropped from 35 million to 22.5 million—a reduction of 36 per cent. Not all of this decrease, however, could be attributed to the antipoverty measures; the booming economy of these years was probably the most potent factor.

Rounding out the legislative record of the early Johnson administration—an age of reform comparable to the early Woodrow Wilson and Franklin Roosevelt periods—was a new immigration act in 1965 repealing the national origins quotas and establishing more humane and rational standards, a Civil Rights Act of 1965 protecting the right to vote, and laws to combat water and air pollution and to preserve beauty along the highways. In recognition of the desperate needs of the cities, Congress created the Department of Housing and Urban Development, and the President appointed as Secretary Robert C. Weaver—the first black Cabinet member. Other pressing problems led to the establishment of a Department of Transportation, with Alan S. Boyd as its first Secretary.

Storm Clouds on the Johnson Horizon

With such an outstanding record of leadership on domestic issues, why did President Johnson fail to win the loyalty of the nation's liberals? The major reason for this was, of course, the Vietnam war, an issue so troublesome that it will require its own separate chapter. But other episodes in the area of foreign affairs also injured Johnson's standing in liberal circles.

The Cuban situation, which had caused so much trouble for Kennedy, remained relatively quiet under Johnson. In February, 1964, Castro cut off the water line to the United States naval base at Guantanamo, ostensibly in retaliation for American seizure of some Cuban fishing boats alleged to be operating illegally within American waters. But prompt action to bring in temporary supplies of water and to build a permanent desalination plant protected the base without directly confronting Castro.

Much more serious was a crisis that developed in the Dominican Republic. Thirty years of strong-arm government had ended with the assassination of the dictator Leonidas Trujillo in 1961. The next year the Dominicans had elected the liberal Juan Bosch to the presidency, but a military junta had overthrown him in 1963. Tensions mounted as the succeeding moderate government encountered hostility from both left and right. In April, 1964, a rebel force captured the presidential palace and installed José Rafael Molina y Ureña as temporary president to await the return of Bosch from exile. But military elements opposed the Molina-Bosch faction, and the forces of the right and left began a bloody struggle in the streets of the Dominican capital.

Announcing that it was necessary to protect American lives and property, Johnson ordered marines to the scene on April 28. Only 400 men were landed at first, but within a few weeks there were 22,000 American troops enforcing a neutral zone between the rebel forces and those attached to the military junta headed by Colonel Pedro Benoit. Johnson defended his action on the ground that the Dominican Republic must not be permitted to become another Cuba. Although he did not accuse either Molina or Bosch of being Communists, he asserted that Communist cadres within the rebel force were strong enough to create a real danger of Communist take-over.

The Johnson administration attempted to broaden the basis of American intervention by gaining the support of the Organization of American States. At first, the Latin-American governments were upset by the unilateral action of the United States, but fear of Castro had enough unifying influence to induce the OAS to help mediate in the situation. Eventually, the parties accepted a cease-fire and agreed upon an interim government. In a peaceful election during June, 1966, the Dominican voters chose the moderate Joaquin Balaguer over the controversial Juan Bosch and a third candidate. From Johnson's point of view, his policy had been entirely successful. He had prevented the spread of Communism and supported the cause of free elections. But most American liberals were severely shaken. As they saw the matter, the United States had reverted to the policeman role renounced thirty years earlier in the Good Neighbor policy. Charging that the Communist threat had been grossly exaggerated, they regarded Johnson's anti-Bosch policy as reactionary.

The rigid anti-Communist line followed in Vietnam and the Caribbean did not prevent the Johnson administration from showing more flexible policies in other parts of the world. With Berlin and the rest of Europe relatively quiet, the area of greatest threat to peace shifted to the Middle East. Here the Soviet Union was seeking to expand its influence by providing arms and advisers to the various Arab states, while the United States tried to maintain the status quo by selling arms to the Israelis without further estranging the Arabs. Russian aid proved intoxicating to Arab nationalists who hated Israel and wanted revenge for earlier defeats. In 1967 there was rising tension along the Israeli borders. Arab nationalists, based especially in Syria, shelled and raided Israeli villages, provoking Israeli retaliations. President Gamal Abdel Nasser of Egypt, the would-be strong man of the Arab world, took steps to overturn the peace-keeping arrangements made after the Suez war of 1956. Upon his demand, UN Secretary General U Thant ordered the withdrawal of UN forces from the Sinai Peninsula, and Egyptian forces moved menacingly close to the border of Israel. Nasser also closed the Gulf of Aqaba to Israeli shipping, thus posing a serious problem for the United States, which had promised along with other nations in 1956 to keep the Gulf open.

Realizing that Israel could not accept these threats to her security, the Johnson administration sought to prevent war, either by UN action or by cooperation with Britain and other naval powers to reopen Aqaba. For a few days Israel accepted American restraint, but the processes of diplomacy were too slow for a nation that felt its very existence was at stake. On June 5 the Israelis attacked the Egyptian forces in the Sinai, thus beginning the lightning war that ended six days later with the Israelis in military control not only of the Sinai Peninsula and the Gulf of Aqaba, but of all of Jerusalem and other strategic Jordanian and Syrian territory.

Fortunately the Soviet Union no more wanted to become involved in war on behalf of its Arab clients than did the United States in defense of Israel. Premier Kosygin and President Johnson were in frequent communication over the "hot line"—the special teletype circuit linking Moscow and Washington established after the Cuban missiles crisis. Johnson kept Kosygin informed during a confusing incident in which Israeli gun boats mistook the identity of an American communications ship and attacked it, killing ten Americans. Only once did the Soviet Union and the United States resort to dangerous brinkmanship. On June 10, when the Russians threatened "necessary actions—including military" unless Israel accepted an immediate cease-fire, Johnson ordered the United States Mediterranean fleet to move closer to the Syrian coast. But this moment of crisis soon passed. As early as June 6, the UN Security Council with United States and Soviet support had called for a cease-fire, and on June 10 all fighting finally stopped.

During the Six Days War the United States and the Soviet Union demonstrated their determination to avoid direct hostilities. Unfortunately, however, they could not agree on the principles of a just Middle East peace. The Russians backed the Arabs in their demand for complete Israeli withdrawal from all territory occupied during the latest fighting, while the United States supported Israel in its demands for secure boundaries and recognition of its right to exist. The American government made occasional attempts to mediate the dispute, but neither party would budge, and periodic outbreaks of fighting along the Suez Canal gave grim reminders that the Middle East was still a tinder box.

Less than two weeks after Kosygin and Johnson exchanged muted threats over the hot line, they met face to face in Glassboro, New Jersey, in the home of the president of Glassboro State College. This unlikely meeting place was selected because it was halfway between Washington and New York City, where the Russian leader was attending a meeting of the UN. Although nothing of importance was decided in these Glassboro meetings running from June 23 to 25, 1967, they did have a warming influence on the relations of the two countries.

Johnson hoped to reach two key agreements with the Russians; one was for a nonproliferation treaty to prevent the spread of nuclear armaments to other countries, the second for a strategic arms agreement to limit the costly and dangerous missiles race between the Soviet Union and the United States. In time he achieved the first, but the second escaped him. On July 1, 1968, representatives of the Soviet Union, the United Kingdom, and the United States, as well as from more than fifty other nations, signed a UN-sponsored Non-Proliferation Treaty. Countries without nuclear weapons promised not to make them or receive them from other powers and were in turn assured full opportunity to develop the peaceful uses of atomic energy. The countries possessing nuclear weapons—with the significant exceptions of France and China—promised to work toward effective arms control and disarmament.

The Senate did not approve the Non-Proliferation Treaty until March,

Secretary of Defense McNamara, Secretary of State Rusk, Soviet Premier Kosygin, President Johnson, and Soviet Foreign Minister Gromyko at Glassboro, N.J., 1967. (UPI Photo.)

1969—two months after Johnson left office. The strategic arms negotiations did not begin until November, 1969—eleven months after Johnson's departure from the White House. The first visit of an American President to Moscow, which Johnson had hoped to make, did not occur until Nixon went there in 1972. Thus was Johnson frustrated in his dream of rounding out his presidency with a dramatic bit of summitry. Two developments dashed his hopes: the first was the brutal Soviet intervention to suppress the Dubček regime in Czechoslovakia, which chilled Soviet-American relations anew; the second was the Republican victory in the presidential election.

In domestic affairs, also, the tide that had run so strongly in Johnson's favor during the years between 1963 and 1966 was beginning to turn. He found it much more difficult to get what he wanted from Congress in the way of new laws and appropriations to advance the goals of the Great Society. In the congressional elections of 1966 the Republicans gained 47 seats in the House and 3 in the Senate. Especially damaging to Johnson's position was the defeat of 30 or more congressional liberals. Nominally, the Democrats still controlled both houses, but the old coalition of Southern Democrats and Republicans had regained much of its power. At the state level, the Republican resurgence was even more significant: the handsome conservative Ronald Reagan became governor of California and seven other new Republican governors were chosen. Thus Johnson moved into the last two years of his presidency under threat from two directions— from Republicans eager to regain the White House and from dissident Democrats strongly opposed to the Vietnam war and determined to prevent Johnson's renomination in 1968.

29
STRUGGLE OF THE BLACKS

During the 1950's and 1960's, the black people of the nation made a powerful demand for improvement in their status. Casting off with increasing impatience the shackles by which white society had bound them into an inferior position, the blacks demanded an end to inferior schooling, job discrimination, segregated housing, denial of the right to vote, and unequal justice in the courts. In their rebellion against these injustices, the blacks presented an united front, but they disagreed among themselves about strategies to be adopted and ultimate goals to be sought. The older leadership worked for integration; their ideal was a color-blind society where each man would be judged on his own merit and blacks and whites would participate in full equality in the same institutions. Many younger blacks rejected, however, the goal of integration; they urged black people to be proud of their own color, to cherish their own institutions, and to develop a structure of power with which they could deal on a basis of strength with their white counterparts. Many of them hoped to create a largely autonomous black nation within the greater nation.

The New Factors

In Booker T. Washington's day, a militant movement of black protest was hardly possible. The great mass of blacks were living in rural poverty in the South. As sharecroppers and agricultural workers, they did obeisance to the authority of white landlords, employers, sheriffs, and deputies. But the situation in 1950 was far different. Two world wars and other historical factors had resulted in a dual migration of blacks: (1) they had in large numbers moved off the land and into Southern cities such as Atlanta, Birmingham, Memphis, and New Orleans; (2) they had also in large numbers moved out of the South into industrial states such as New York, Pennsylvania, New Jersey, Illinois, Michigan, Ohio, and California.

Heavy concentrations of black voters in Northern and Middle Western states gave them increasing political leverage. Politicians could no longer safely ignore the wishes of groups that might hold the balance of power in close elections. In the South the blacks had much less political clout, but they sought to change this by establishing their right to vote and getting their people registered.

Despite the obstacles that had hampered the schooling of blacks, the new generation was much better educated than the older ones had been. In 1910, 30 per cent of the black population had been illiterate; by 1940, only 8 per cent were thus handicapped. As late as 1915 there had been only 64 black high schools in the country; by 1940 the number had risen to 2,500. Almost 20,000 blacks graduated from college during the thirties—more than twice the number of the more prosperous twenties. After World War II these educational trends were accelerated. Increasing education produced the black lawyers, ministers, and other spokesmen equipped to provide the protest movement with effective leadership.

During these years the blacks could take pride in the achievements of many talented individuals. Marian Anderson's superb musicianship paved the way for other remarkable black singers. As the Jim Crow lines were erased in one field after another, a whole generation of black sports heroes emerged—Jesse Owens in track, Jackie Robinson in baseball, Joe Louis in boxing, and Jim Brown in football. And to refute whites who conceded black prowess in vocal and muscular exploits but doubted their mental powers, there were many outstanding careers in other fields. George Washington Carver benefited the whole South through his development of industrial uses for the peanut, the sweet potato, and the soybean. Richard Wright, Ralph Ellison, and James Baldwin wrote fine novels; Ralph Bunche became one of the key administrators of the United Nations; Thurgood Marshall reached the peak of the legal profession when President Johnson appointed him a justice of the Supreme Court in 1967. Clearly the exceptional black could now rise to the very top in fields like athletics and the arts and close to the top in politics. Yet for the black of average or less than average ability the social and legal barriers to advancement were still frustratingly high.

Black men asserting their rights during these years had the benefit of a favorable ideological climate. After the excesses of the Nazis, all theories of racial superiority stood condemned. Large numbers of black servicemen fought bravely in World War II and subsequent conflicts. By what conceivable logic could men who had fought for their country be treated like second-class citizens? Moreover, during the years of the cold war, the United States was competing with the Soviet Union and Communist China for influence in the new nations of Asia and Africa. How could black and brown men in foreign countries have any respect for a nation that treated its own black people unfairly? Many whites were shamed into shedding the racial prejudices they had absorbed in their earlier years and supporting more liberal measures. Notable among the new converts were Harry Truman of Missouri and Lyndon Johnson of Texas.

Many young whites passed beyond mere sympathy for the blacks. Not since the days of the abolitionists had there been so many whites passionately committed to helping their black brothers. Thousands of college students literally risked their lives to travel to the South and participate in the great civil rights demonstrations of the early sixties. Indeed white workers in the crusade were so zealous that they eventually aroused some black hostility. Black nationalists began to demand for blacks the dignity of leading their own protest movements. Consequently, white participation in the struggle for racial justice was a tide that crested in 1963 and then began to ebb. Yet while it lasted, it helped the blacks to achieve new civil rights laws at the Federal level and the abandonment of many discriminatory practices at the local level.

Victories in the Courts

During the forties and fifties the National Association for the Advancement of Colored People led the battle for advancement. Black leaders like Walter White and Roy Wilkins headed the NAACP, but many whites participated in the local chapters. Middle class in its goals and strategies, the organization sought to improve the status of black people primarily through getting new legislation and favorable decisions from the courts.

Although Eleanor Roosevelt was an outspoken champion of the blacks, Franklin Roosevelt was too dependent on Southern politicians to push very hard for the Federal legislation that the NAACP advocated. Some New Deal policies actually injured the blacks; AAA restrictions on acreage often favored the large holders at the expense of small farmers and sharecroppers and NRA minimum wage provisions sometimes resulted in black workers losing their jobs. But in the experience of most blacks, their profits in the New Deal ledger far exceeded their losses. As the group most devastated by the depression, the blacks welcomed the WPA and other benefits to the unemployed as truly life saving. They were similarly grateful for government housing projects, Social Security protection, and the rehabilitation loans made available by the Farm Security Administration. So appreciative were the blacks that Roosevelt won an estimated 70 to 80 per cent of the black vote in his later elections. Since this vote had hitherto been largely Republican, the shift in allegiance had a profound and lasting effect on American politics.

During the months before Pearl Harbor, black leaders determined not to repeat the mistake of World War I, when they had given loyal support to the war effort without receiving any guarantee of better treatment for their people. To forestall the embarrassment of a threatened march on Washington of thousands of blacks, President Roosevelt issued an important executive order on June 25, 1941, declaring:

the policy of the United States is to encourage full participation in the national defense program by all citizens of the United States, regardless of race, creed, color, or national origin, in the firm belief that the democratic way of life within the Nation can be defended successfully only with the help and support of all groups within its borders.

Such affirmations of principle had been made before; what made this one more than mere words was the appointment of a Fair Employment Practices Committee (FEPC) to investigate complaints and to take steps to redress grievances. The effort to open up new areas of employment for blacks was well timed because war production provided an almost unlimited demand for labor of all kinds. Between 1940 and 1944, the number of blacks employed in manufacturing and processing increased from 500,000 to around 1.2 million; in government service from 60,000 to 200,000.

After the war, President Truman took up the cause of black rights more vigorously than Roosevelt had ever done. Acting upon the recommendation of a distinguished committee, he proposed a permanent FEPC and a broad program of new laws to protect the civil rights of minorities. But Southern Democrats with the help of conservative Republicans used all their legislative skill to prevent such bills from even coming to a vote. Blocked in Congress, Truman took what action he could under his own executive power. He imposed nondiscriminatory hiring practices within the governmental establishment and began the desegregation of the armed forces.

During these years the blacks won their most important victories, however, in the courts. Long reactionary in defining the rights claimed by black people under the Fourteenth and Fifteenth Amendments, the Supreme Court began to modify its position during the 1930's. As was perhaps natural for the nation's highest judicial body, it demonstrated its earliest concern for the right to fair trial. In the so-called Scottsboro cases (1932, 1935) in which Alabama courts acting on very flimsy evidence had sentenced nine black youths to death on charges of rape, the Supreme Court twice set aside the verdicts and ordered new trials—in the first case because the state had not provided the defendants with adequate counsel; in the second because the Alabama authorities had systematically excluded blacks from the jury lists. The Court also protected the right to vote. In Smith v. Allwright (1943) and subsequent cases, it declared unconstitutional the various devices by which Southern states tried to prevent blacks from voting in the Democratic primaries. In 1948 the Court took a partial step toward protecting the individual's right to buy a house wherever he pleased; it ruled that courts might not enforce restrictive covenants under which homeowners promised not to sell them to blacks or Orientals.

Most important were the Supreme Court decisions undermining the whole system of segregation in schools and colleges. Earlier interpretations of the Fourteenth Amendment had permitted segregation, provided the facilities for blacks were "separate but equal" to those for whites. The new decisions placed much stronger stress on equality. Blacks, it was ruled, did not enjoy equal educational facilities if the state paid their tuition at out-of-state schools while it provided white students with higher education in state-supported institutions within the state. The issue was particularly acute in law, medicine, and other expensive forms of graduate education. The Court also ruled that equal facilities were not provided when special graduate schools for blacks were demonstrably inferior to state-supported white institutions and when blacks were permitted to attend classes along with whites but were required to sit apart in classroom and library. Confronted by these decisions, a number of Southern state universities abandoned segregation at the graduate level. Intelligent Southerners now recognized that segregation in education could be retained, if at all, only through such radical improvements in the black schools that their "separate but equal status" would be an actuality.

The final overthrow of the "separate but equal" doctrine came in a Supreme Court decision of May 17, 1954 (Brown v. Topeka). Chief Justice

Earl Warren, speaking for an unanimous court, ruled that separate facilities were inherently unequal and laws requiring blacks to attend separate public schools violated the Fourteenth Amendment by denying to persons "the equal protection of the laws." Thus at one stroke the Supreme Court destroyed the whole legal structure by which seventeen states required and four others permitted segregated education.

Unequivocal though the decision was, the tribunal recognized that school segregation could not be eliminated overnight. Not until a year later, in May, 1955, did the Court lay down the principles that should guide compliance. It placed responsibility for integrating schools upon the shoulders of local school authorities, but ordered the Federal district courts to see that the task was done. The elimination of segregation should proceed with what the Court called "deliberate speed."

The way in which the various states responded to the Supreme Court's directive differed greatly. The District of Columbia integrated its schools promptly, and such border states as Maryland, Delaware, Kentucky, Missouri, and Oklahoma at once began the gradual process the Court had recommended. In a second ring of states including Tennessee, Arkansas, Texas, and North Carolina, integration went forward much more slowly. In the remainder of the South—in Virginia, South Carolina, Florida, Alabama, Louisiana, Mississippi, and Georgia—the attitude was one of stubborn noncompliance. The politicians sought to prevent integration by a network of legal obstacles. Some state legislatures declared the Supreme Court's decision to be itself unconstitutional and affirmed their right to "interpose" —whatever this vague term might mean—to prevent enforcement of the ruling. Other states passed laws authorizing officials to abolish the public school system if segregation were required, to cut off state funds from any district that integrated its schools, and to use state funds for the support of private segregated schools. Even more serious was the increasing resort to racial hatred and mob action. In some communities the Ku Klux Klan reappeared; in others, so-called Citizens Councils encouraged economic reprisals and mass demonstrations against blacks who tried to assert their rights.

Eisenhower and the Blacks

The Eisenhower administration found it difficult to deal with the dual problems of growing black demands and bitter white resistance. The President was a decent man without strong convictions of his own on racial issues and eager to please as many people as he could without antagonizing others.

Republicans in the great industrial states were not ready to surrender all the black vote to the Democrats. Republican Governor Thomas E. Dewey of New York had induced the legislature to pass a strong anti-discrimination law in 1945, and Republican lawmakers in other states and cities had supported similar legislation. When the Republicans gained control of the Federal government in 1953, these liberal elements hoped to establish a record that would appeal to the black voters. They sensed a real opportunity because of black disillusionment with the obstructionist tactics of the Southern Democrats. Without much fanfare President Eisenhower took steps to reduce discrimination. He appointed blacks to a number of important positions and completed the integration of the armed forces. He ended segregation in schools serving military bases, in veterans' hospitals, and naval installations. The President's Committee on Government Contracts succeeded through persuasion in largely eliminating job discrimination in firms working on government orders. And in the city of Washington itself Eisenhower's influence was extended toward ending discrimination in restaurants and places of amusement. Many black leaders credited the President with having made a good record. In the 1956 election Representative Adam Clayton Powell, one of the most influential black Democrats, supported Eisenhower.

While Eisenhower did not show enthusiasm for the kind of sweeping civil rights legislation that Truman had recommended, he did send to Congress in 1956 a moderate program formulated by Attorney General Herbert Brownell. In its first encounter with Congress, the Eisenhower civil rights program met the fate of so many of its predecessors: it passed the House but never came to a vote in the Senate. A year later, however, events developed quite differently. For one thing, many more Americans now believed that the cold war made it imperative for the nation to move more strongly against racial discrimination. For another, the 1956 election returns had quickened Republican interest in the black vote and warned the Democrats that they could not rest upon their past achievements. When Majority Leader Lyndon Johnson convinced the Southern Senators that it would be a mistake to resort to the usual filibuster, they allowed the bill to come to a vote, but only after weakening it by amendments. As finally passed, the Civil Rights Act of 1957 provided for a Civil Rights Commission to investigate and make recommendations and for a new Assistant Attorney General to handle civil rights cases. In instances where there had been a denial of the right to vote, the Federal government could appeal to the Federal courts for an injunction.

Although the measure represented only a modest victory for civil rights, it was the first act of its kind passed since Reconstruction days. The first report of the Civil Rights Commission in September, 1958, showed that at least 75 per cent of the six million blacks in the eleven states of the South did not vote. Although many of them did not do so because of a lack of interest, even more were prevented from exercising the franchise because of "the creation of legal impediments, administrative obstacles, and positive discouragement engendered by fears of economic reprisal and physical harm." As a result of these findings, the Eisenhower administration pressed for the passage of a broader civil rights measure in 1960. Despite a long Southern filibuster, Congress put the measure through in May. Under the Civil Rights Act of 1960, persons found guilty of using threats or force to prevent blacks from voting in defiance of Federal court orders were liable to fines and prison sentences. Furthermore, if a Federal court found that a person was denied the right to vote because of his race or color, it could appoint referees to examine the voting requirements and grant provisional enrollment to the petitioner.

On issues involving Federal hiring policies and on matters as basic as the right to vote, Eisenhower's characteristic moderation and fairness were adequate to the situation, but the issue of school desegregation was too explosive for him to defuse. A President of stronger commitment might have placed the great prestige of his office on the line. He might have praised the justice of the Supreme Court decision and initiated policies to help local authorities comply with the new principle. Instead of this, Eisenhower's comments were so noncommittal that Southern politicians felt safe in their obstructionism.

Not until 1957 did a Southern governor defy the Federal authority so directly that Eisenhower had to take firm action. In September, 1957, nine black students were scheduled to enter the hitherto all-white Central High School in Little Rock, Arkansas, in compliance with a Federal district court order. Governor Orville Faubus attempted to prevent this by a series of countermoves. First, he obtained a state court injunction forbidding the integration of the school. When the Federal judge overruled this, Faubus used the National Guard to keep the pupils out. After a court order and a request from the President, the governor removed the

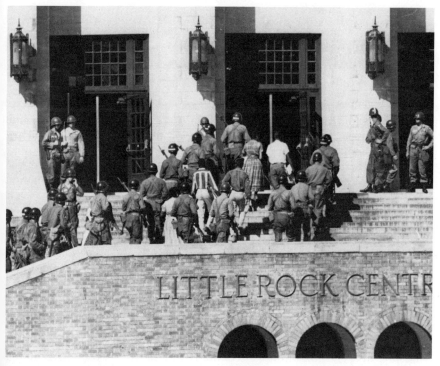

Federal troops escorting black students at Little Rock, Arkansas, 1957. (UPI Photo.)

Black student and white reaction at Little Rock, 1957. (UPI Photo.)

guard, but when the young blacks attempted to attend the school, a mob of white segregationists became so threatening that the black children had to be sent home.

With the Little Rock challenge to Federal law now flagrant, the President denounced "the disgraceful occurrence" and issued a proclamation commanding all persons obstructing Federal law and Federal court orders to desist and disperse. When a mob defied this proclamation by reappearing at the school, Eisenhower ordered a thousand Army paratroopers to the scene and federalized the state National Guard, thereby removing it from Faubus's control. With this military support, the nine black pupils returned to school, and the full authority of the Federal government was finally exercised to protect them in their constitutional right to attend a nonsegregated school. Faubus protested the "military occupation of his state." In 1958 and 1959 Arkansas again challenged the Federal courts, and it was not until August, 1959, that the schools of Little Rock were widely integrated.

Despite his good intentions, Eisenhower thus ended his presidency under attack from both sides. Blacks accused him of not having done enough to hasten the integration of the schools; Southern whites criticized him for having done too much.

The Emergence of Martin Luther King

Hitherto the dominant black strategy had been to get Congress and the President to take official action on behalf of equal rights and to obtain favorable decisions from the Federal courts. Such means, however, had proved exasperatingly slow. Moreover, conventional legal remedies were ineffective in dealing with many frustrating local restraints. An early resort to a different strategy began in Montgomery, Alabama, in December, 1955. Angered by the arrest and fining of a black seamstress for refusing to give up her bus seat to a white person, the blacks of the city refused to use the buses. Originally intended for a single day, the boycott continued for 385 days until the bus company and the local authorities finally gave up the requirement for segregated seating.

Dr. Martin Luther King, Jr., pastor of a Baptist church in the city, emerged as the inspired leader of the Montgomery bus boycott. Only twenty-six years old, King was richly endowed for his historic role. The son of a well-known minister in Atlanta, Georgia, he had received an excellent education at Morehouse College, Crozer Theological Seminary, and Boston University. Handsome and eloquent, King infused the black rights movement with an unique moral fervor. In teaching his followers to use the weapons of civil disobedience and nonviolence in their struggle for justice, he drew upon the example not only of Jesus but of Mahatma Gandhi. To spread this philosophy, he assumed leadership of the Southern Christian Leadership Conference (SCLC), largely composed at first of preachers.

The SCLC was not the only new organization to offer an alternative strategy to the legalistic approach of the NAACP. As early as 1942, James Farmer had helped organize the Congress of Racial Equality (CORE), a group that had pioneered in the use of nonviolent demonstrations to combat discrimination in Northern and border-state restaurants.

In February, 1960, black college students at Greensboro, North Carolina, began a spontaneous "sit-in" to protest the practice of Southern department and variety stores in reserving lunch-counter seats for whites only, thus forcing their black customers to eat standing up. These demonstrations spread rapidly from one city to another. Blacks would sit at the lunch counters by the hour despite refusals to serve them, police arrests for trespass, and beatings by pugnacious whites. Both Martin Luther King's SCLC and Farmer's CORE moved in to encourage and support the students, and the NAACP defended those who were arrested. Although not always successful, the sit-ins did open lunch counters in many Southern cities. The enthusiasm of the movement also gave birth to still another organization, the Student Nonviolent Coordinating Committee (SNCC).

Encouraged by these examples of fortitude, CORE prepared an assault upon the "White Only" signs confronting black travelers in waiting rooms, rest rooms, and restaurants of Southern bus terminals. In May, 1961, a biracial group of thirteen "Freedom Riders" left Washington by bus with New Orleans as their destination. Insisting upon the right of blacks and whites to use the same facilities, the Riders traveled through the Upper

South with only minor harassments, but in Anniston, Alabama, a mob set fire to one of their buses and assaulted the demonstrators. In Birmingham the Riders were again manhandled. Since the Alabama state officials would not guarantee effective police protection, the bus drivers refused to take further risks, and the original Riders had to complete the trip to New Orleans by plane. But this dramatic episode drew many more Freedom Riders to the South, thus presenting the Kennedy administration with the difficult task of trying either to get the state authorities to protect these interstate travelers or to use Federal force to do so.

King and the Kennedy Brothers

The converging forces of history brought Martin Luther King to leadership of the nation's protesting blacks during the same years that John Kennedy was taking over the responsibilities of the White House and Robert Kennedy was charged with the duty of enforcing Federal law as Attorney General. Each of these three men was idolized by millions of youthful admirers; each would die as the victim of senseless assassination before the decade was over.

In dealing with the demands of the blacks, President Kennedy attempted to maintain a delicate balance between moral idealism and political realism. Needing Southern Democratic votes to push through his congressional program, he did not at first press for new civil rights legislation. Yet realizing the decisive weight of the black vote, he endeavored to do as much as he could by executive action. He appointed more blacks to important posts than had any President before him. Robert C. Weaver headed the Housing and Home Finance Agency, and Thurgood Marshall, famous for his court victories as counsel for the NAACP, became a judge on the United States Circuit Court of Appeals. Kennedy also appointed blacks as district judges in Michigan and Illinois and as United States attorneys in California and Ohio. As head of a Committee on Equal Employment Opportunity, Vice President Johnson did much to open up jobs for blacks with companies working on government contracts. Firmest friend of the black movement within the administration was Attorney General Robert Kennedy, who ordered his subordinates to enforce vigorously the civil rights legislation already on the books—particularly the laws guaranteeing the right to vote.

In dealing with the Freedom Riders, Robert Kennedy prodded reluctant Alabama officials into providing police protection and, when that protection proved inadequate, he sent a force of four hundred armed Federal marshals and deputies to Montgomery to save the Riders from further mob attacks. Although the Attorney General caused some black unhappiness by counseling a "cooling-off" period in the Freedom Rides, he continued to show himself a friend of the movement. Acting upon a Department of Justice request, the ICC issued a sweeping order prohibiting all segregation in interstate bus travel, both on the buses themselves and in the terminals. The blacks' victory on this issue was completed when the Southern rail-

A 1963 White House conference of civil rights leaders sponsored by President Kennedy. *Front row, from left:* Dr. Martin Luther King, Attorney General Kennedy, Executive Secretary of NAACP Roy Wilkins, and Vice President Johnson. (UPI Photo.)

roads voluntarily desegregated their stations, and the airlines took similar steps under the threat of Federal court action.

Behind the scenes, the Kennedy administration was urging the black leaders to concentrate their energies on the right to vote. Because of laws already on the books, the Federal government could act more vigorously in this matter than in any other. Moreover, any large increase in the black vote might alter the whole complexion of Southern politics. Northern philanthropic foundations financed black registration drives, while the Department of Justice pushed to a successful conclusion a number of cases involving voting rights. Thousands of white and black college students spent their summer vacations helping Southern blacks to meet the voting requirements. In 1962 the administration pressed for laws banning discriminatory literacy and poll tax requirements. A Senate filibuster defeated a bill relating to literacy tests, but Congress passed a constitutional amendment providing that in Federal elections the right to vote should not be denied "by reason of failure to pay any poll tax or other tax." This became the Twenty-fourth Amendment to the Constitution in January, 1964, when South Dakota, the thirty-eighth state, ratified it.[1]

[1] The Twenty-third Amendment, granting residents of the District of Columbia the right to vote for presidential candidates, became part of the Constitution in April, 1961.

Sharply criticized for delay in fulfilling one of his campaign pledges, President Kennedy finally braved the wrath of Southern legislators to issue an executive order on November 20, 1962, banning discrimination in housing built or purchased with Federal aid.

Meanwhile, the integration of Southern schools was proceeding far too slowly to satisfy black aspirations. In September, 1962, James Meredith, an Air Force veteran, obtained a Federal court decree ordering his admission to the University of Mississippi, but Governor Ross Barnett, with the support of the state legislature, opposed any breach in the wall of school segregation. On three occasions when Meredith tried to register, he found his way barred, twice by the governor in person and once by the lieutenant governor. The United States Circuit Court in New Orleans found Barnett guilty of contempt of court and ordered him to purge himself within three days under threat of heavy penalties. This confrontation between Federal and state power reached its unhappy climax on Sunday night, September 30. Given a qualified promise from Barnett that law and order would be preserved, the Justice Department brought Meredith to the university campus at Oxford under the protection of several hundred armed Federal marshals. In a television address, President Kennedy urged the Mississippians to comply peacefully with the law, but his appeal was ignored by a mob of students and outsiders who attacked the marshals with a barrage of rocks, pipe, acid, and bullets. The marshals defended themselves with tear gas, but the rioting continued for some fifteen hours until three thousand Federal troops and federalized National Guardsmen arrived in Oxford the next day. A man of steely courage, Meredith finally completed his registration and continued his studies under Federal protection until he graduated the following year.

In June, 1963, history threatened to repeat itself when two blacks obtained a court order upholding them in their application for admission to the University of Alabama. Governor George Wallace, who had campaigned on a pledge to stand "in the schoolhouse door" to prevent integration, was on hand to bar the black students when they arrived in Tuscaloosa to register for the summer session. But this time the attempt at state interposition was more symbolic than real. When President Kennedy federalized part of the Alabama National Guard and ordered it to the university campus, the governor allowed the registration to proceed peacefully. Wallace again challenged Federal authority in September when he attempted to prevent public school integration in Birmingham and two other Alabama cities, but once again he submitted after President Kennedy federalized the National Guard.

With their reckless playing for segregationist votes, politicians like Barnett and Wallace fanned the flames of hatred already burning dangerously in many parts of the South. In April, 1963, William Moore, an eccentric white bearing prointegration placards on a walking tour through the South, was murdered in northern Alabama; in June, Medgar Evers, Mississippi field secretary for the NAACP, was ambushed and killed in Jackson, Mississippi. And for many weeks Birmingham was wracked by violence as local police resorted to the use of fire hoses and police dogs to combat

Dr. Martin Luther King leading a civil rights march in Detroit, 1963. Walter Reuther, president of the United Automobile Workers, is at the far left. (UPI Photo.)

Martin Luther King's adroitly organized campaign to overturn the city's highly repressive system of segregation and job discrimination. In May, 1963, the Birmingham skies brightened after white and black leaders agreed on a program of amelioration, but in September came the most shocking incident of all, in which a bomb explosion destroyed a black church and killed four little girls attending Sunday School.

Long before the Birmingham atrocity, President Kennedy had announced a major new campaign. In a television address on June 11, 1963, he declared: "We face . . . a moral crisis as a country and a people . . . . It is time to act in the Congress, in your state and legislative bodies, and, above all, in all of our daily lives." A week later he sent to Congress the strongest civil rights program ever proposed by an American President.

By prompt congressional action the President hoped to bring a lull in the storm of black protest now sweeping cities in the North as well as the South. He did not discourage, however, the most impressive demonstration of them all, a gigantic "March on Washington." On August 28, 1963, some 200,000 persons—blacks and white sympathizers—converged on the capital from all sections of the country. After parading through the streets bearing signs demanding "Freedom—Now," the vast throng crowded around the Lincoln Memorial to hear speeches by leaders of both races. Martin Luther King raised the crowd to a peak of exaltation. Reiterating the hypnotic phrase "I have a dream," the great preacher painted a glowing picture of an America where black children and white children would walk together as brothers and sisters. He hailed the day

Part of the crowd between the Lincoln Memorial and the Washington Monument at the 1963 civil rights march on Washington. (UPI Photo.)

when all of God's children, black and white men, Jews and Gentiles, Protestants and Catholics, will be able to join hands and sing in the words of that old Negro spiritual, "Free at last! Free at last! Thank God almighty, we are free at last!"

Well-disciplined and completely free of violence, the March on Washington constituted a powerful plea for the enactment of the President's civil rights program. But Congress, still dominated by Southern committee chairmen, would not be hurried. Three months later, when the Kennedy administration ended in tragedy, the lawmakers had still not acted.

Johnson and the Blacks

In his earlier years as Congressman and Senator, Lyndon Johnson had demonstrated the usual Southern resentment to outside interference by voting against six civil rights bills. Yet he became the key figure in the eventual enactment of five civil rights laws—the two weak ones that he helped pass as Senate Majority leader under Eisenhower and the three strong ones of his own presidency. Two facts explain the shift in his position: as he graduated from sectional politics and became a national leader, he saw the issue from a national point of view; moreover, as he began to think the matter through, he had a genuine change of heart. Political expediency might explain some of his effort to get civil rights legislation, but sincere concern for the plight of black people seemed to endow him with more than ordinary eloquence in urging Congress to take action.

Arguing that passage of the Kennedy civil rights program would provide a most fitting memorial to the slain leader, President Johnson succeeded in getting the bill passed without the usual crippling amendments. Senator Dirksen, the Republican Minority Leader who had his own black constituency in Illinois, cooperated by delivering the essential votes to impose cloture. The Civil Rights Act of 1964 went far beyond earlier laws because it prohibited discrimination in its most pervasive form, the form that kept blacks out of motels, restaurants, theaters, and filling stations. In addition to this public accommodations section, the new law created a bipartisan Equal Employment Opportunity Commission with extensive powers to prevent discriminatory practices by employers and labor unions. It also permitted government agencies to cut off funds to any federally aided program in which racial discrimination was allowed to persist—thus providing a major prod to speed up school integration.

Strong though it was, the Civil Rights Act of 1964 did not prevent brutal repression of the effort to register black voters. In Philadelphia, Mississippi, the local sheriff and his deputy as well as Ku Klux Klan leaders were alleged to have savagely murdered three young civil rights workers—two whites and one black. In 1965 the voter registration struggle came to focus on Selma, Alabama. Martin Luther King chose this Black Belt city of 28,000 inhabitants because it symbolized the whole issue. Although about half the population was black, only 335 of them were voters and the effort to register more encountered paralyzing rebuffs and delays. After local protest marches had proved ineffective, some 500 blacks set off on March 7 for Montgomery, the state capital fifty-two miles away. But a force of state troopers, acting under orders from Governor Wallace, ordered them to turn back, and, when the blacks refused, the troopers clubbed and tear-gassed them so violently that seventeen had to be hospitalized. Two days later a white mob assaulted three white ministers from the North, and one of them, the Reverend James Reeb of Boston, died from his injuries.

Shocked by the Selma violence, President Johnson went before Congress on March 15 to make a highly emotional appeal for a new civil rights act. He called Selma a turning point in "man's unending search for freedom"—a place of destiny like Lexington and Concord. Raising his arms in the familiar gesture of black protestors, he declared: "Their cause must be our cause too. Because it is not just Negroes, but really it is all of us who must overcome the crippling legacy of bigotry and injustice. And we shall overcome."

A week later the Selma demonstrators celebrated a symbolic victory when King led a peaceful march from Selma to Montgomery, in which thousands of blacks and whites—among them ministers, priests, and nuns—participated. Federalized National Guard and Federal troops protected the marchers after Governor Wallace complained that the state was too poor to pay the expense. King addressed the great crowd from the steps of the state capitol building—once the heart of the Confederacy—in one of the climactic moments of his career. But the day of triumph was also a day of tragedy because that night shots from a passing car killed Mrs. Viola Liuzzo, a white woman from Detroit who was helping King's campaign.

In this year of bitterness, Congress passed the Civil Rights Act of 1965, which suspended all literacy, knowledge, and character tests for voters in districts where less than 50 per cent of those old enough to vote were registered or voted in November, 1964. It authorized the appointment of Federal registrars where necessary to guarantee the right to vote. Despite complaints of unfairness, the law was obviously so drawn that it would apply only to the Deep South, which had systematically deprived black people of the ballot.

But the blacks of the South were not the only ones with pent-up feelings of bitterness and anger. On the contrary, millions of Northern blacks crowded into ramshackle tenements in the great cities, attending inferior schools, getting only inferior jobs and often unemployed built up explosive pressures that erupted again and again during the sixties. Riots were particularly likely to start on hot summer evenings when the arrest of a young black on some minor charge drew a hostile crowd. In August, 1965, such an incident triggered several days of wild disorder in the Watts district of Los Angeles, during which 34 lives were lost and $35 million worth of property was destroyed. In the summer of 1967, riots in Newark, New Jersey, resulted in 25 deaths and those in Detroit in 43 deaths. Not until President Johnson sent in Federal troops did the Detroit nightmare end.

Frightened whites were quick to suspect that Communist intrigue or some other sinister activity lay behind these and scores of lesser outbreaks,

Rural Alabama blacks waiting to vote in 1966. (UPI Photo.)

A devastated corner after the second day of rioting in Detroit in 1967. (UPI Photo.)

but a National Advisory Commission on Civil Disorders, appointed by the President and headed by Governor Otto Kerner of Illinois, rejected the conspiracy theory. The riots were unplanned; their cause was "white racism"—the stifling system of discrimination, segregation, and poverty that was so embittering to black youth. The commission recommended a major national effort in the fields of employment, education, welfare, and housing.

The Kerner Commission's recommendations carried too high a price tag for Johnson to accept in full, although he did press his requests for more funds for the War on Poverty. The urban riots contributed, however, to a hardening of the mood of the country. In many sectors of Northern society—particularly in workmen's neighborhoods—white prejudice against the blacks was mounting, and Martin Luther King encountered a discouraging situation when he tried to combat housing discrimination in the Chicago suburbs.

As additional victories for nonviolent protest became more difficult to achieve, King's leadership came under increasing attack from more radical blacks. Although he continued to warn against any resort to violence as suicidal, King began to advocate a somewhat more radical program himself. He became a bitter critic of the Vietnam war and an advocate of mobilizing all the poor, both black and white, to demand a decent livelihood. On the night of April 4, 1968, he was in Memphis, Tennessee, preparing to help the city's striking garbagemen. When he stepped out on the motel balcony for a breath of air, James Earl Ray, a white escaped convict, shot him from the window of a neighboring rooming house.

News of the black leader's death set off a wild night of rioting in Washington and forty other cities. Once again President Johnson used the chastened mood that followed a national tragedy to get action from Congress. This time the result was the Civil Rights Act of 1968, an open-housing measure intended to ban discrimination in the sale and renting of some 80 per cent of the country's homes.

The Johnson record in the field of civil rights was a remarkable one. Yet despite his longing to be remembered as a second Lincoln, the plight of the blacks had in some respects grown worse rather than better during his presidency. The urban ghettos were still enclaves of demoralizing poverty; the Vietnam war and the military budget were making inordinate demands upon the Federal revenues; King was dead and there was no leader of comparable stature to take his place; and white taxpayers were becoming increasingly resentful of paying for welfare, medicaid, and other social benefits. The assassination of Robert Kennedy on June 5, 1968, had nothing directly to do with the racial situation, but it removed from public life a beloved figure whom many blacks had hoped to see in the White House.

Black Nationalism

Long before King's death, leaders with a radically different viewpoint had been challenging his basic philosophy. Even in the nineteenth century a few prominent blacks had argued that the racial goal should not be integration into white society, but the building of a separate black society proud to be different. During the 1920's, Marcus Garvey, an immigrant from Jamaica, built up a large following for his ambitious plans to unite black people of all countries into one great racial movement. Charged with using the mails to defraud, Garvey was imprisoned and later deported, but the racial pride he had inspired continued to have strong appeal.

Although Elijah Poole, a black from Georgia, did not found the Nation of Islam, or so-called Black Muslim, movement, it was he who transformed it from a small local cult in Detroit to a national organization with its headquarters at Chicago. Adopting the name Elijah Muhammed, he preached a welcome doctrine to impoverished residents of the urban ghettos. All that was beautiful and good, he taught, originated with black people. The evil white race had enslaved the blacks and destroyed their culture, but the days of white oppression would soon be over. Allah had sent Elijah Muhammed to deliver his people. Highly puritanical in his teachings, the Muslim leader admonished his followers to abstain from the use of alcohol, tobacco, and drugs and to shun adultery and other forms of sexual impurity. Since white society was evil, Muslims were to avoid it as much as possible by working hard, practicing thrift, and establishing their own stores and industries.

The Muslims were particularly successful in converting and rehabilitating black convicts. Malcolm Little, renamed Malcolm X, provided an extraordinary example of this. Brought up in Michigan, Malcolm had peddled drugs, solicited customers for prostitutes, and robbed apartments in New York City and Boston. Sent to prison for burglary, he became a zealous Muslim convert. A man of brilliant intellectual power and natural eloquence, Malcolm X proved to be a highly successful evangelist for the cult, founding new temples in several cities and making his own Temple No. 7 in Harlem a citadel of Muslim power. In 1963 Elijah Muhammed expelled Malcolm from his movement, but Malcolm then set up his own Organization for Afro-American Unity and made well-publicized pilgrimages to Mecca and Africa. In 1965 fanatical followers of Elijah Muhammed shot Malcolm to death, but his influence continued to be great. *The Autobiography of Malcolm X* and *Malcolm X Speaks* provided inspiration to white youths as well as black.

Only a few thousand blacks actually adopted the rigorous Muslim faith, but many more embraced black nationalism in some other form. In part, the new mood arose out of disillusionment with the American political process. In its 1964 convention, the Democratic party avoided the issue presented by the Mississippi Freedom Democrats—a biracial delegation contesting the credentials of the delegation chosen through the traditional discriminatory procedures. Many blacks drew the conclusion that they could never exercise political influence unless they conquered the local bases of power. Disillusionment with the politicians soon widened to include a general disenchantment with white liberals. Blacks accused white civil rights workers of timidity and a willingness to compromise at the blacks' expense. The younger blacks had equal scorn for their own older leaders, among whom they were now beginning to include Martin Luther King. King's preaching of nonviolence seemed visionary to many blacks embittered by innumerable acts of white violence during these years. Must the blacks forever turn the other cheek? Had the time not come when they must assert the right of self-defense—of meeting violence with violence? In 1966 Stokely Carmichael of the SNCC directly challenged King's leadership during a freedom march across Mississippi. Hundreds of marchers and bystanders cheered Carmichael's defiant slogan, Black Power!

Although the expounders of black power did not plot the urban riots, they defended these outbursts of violence. They argued that conditions in the urban ghettos were intolerable, and only mass action could frighten the white establishment into making changes. Although in some sectors such as Watts, the riots did result in remedial programs, most observers believed that the riots were counterproductive, making it even more difficult to get the huge expenditures necessary to create employment and provide decent living conditions. A number of other forms of black radicalism also seemed to injure rather than help the majority of blacks. Although Black Panther groups in various cities did good work in providing food and other assistance to the poor, they antagonized white opinion by storing arms and allegedly shooting policemen—forms of violence and threatened violence that sometimes brought harsh counterviolence from the police. Ineffective though the Black Panthers seemed to be, they provided defiant leaders—men such as Eldridge Cleaver and Bobby Seale—who became heroes to young radicals, both black and white.

TV cameramen and newspaper reporters naturally featured black na-

Rally sponsored by the Black Panthers at the Lincoln Memorial in Washington in 1970 in support of a new constitution. (UPI Photo.)

tionalism in its most controversial forms, but the effort to achieve black power took many quieter courses. Some struggles took place on university campuses. Seeking an opportunity to learn about their own culture, black students demanded black studies programs made up of courses in Afro-American and African history, in the art and music of black people, and in literature written by black authors. They also insisted upon black administrators and black professors to staff these programs and separate dormitories for their students. White liberals and black moderates deplored this trend toward self-segregation, but at least for the time being most black students seemed committed to the goal of developing race consciousness.

Within many cities the anti-integrationists also had a strong voice. Rejecting school integration as no longer a feasible or even a desirable goal, nationalist elements advocated decentralization of education and control of school districts by their residents. In other fields as well, particularly in projects associated with the War on Poverty, there were insistent demands for community control. Blacks often competed with blacks in local power struggles.

Although black nationalists frequently seemed to shout down the more moderate black leaders, there was some evidence that this was a passing phase. When Whitney Young, the widely-respected director of the Urban League, died in 1971, there were impressive expressions of grief for this able man who had avoided showy rhetoric while working ceaselessly to open up employment opportunities for blacks. Moreover, a new generation of black politicians—men such as Julian Bond of Georgia, Charles Evers of Mississippi, John Conyers of Michigan, and Andrew Hacker of Indiana— began to exercise increasing power within the Democratic party, especially after reforms in the party's structure between 1968 and 1972. Blacks had some reason for new hope that black power could operate effectively within the traditional institutions of American society.

30
THE VIETNAM TRAGEDY

The involvement of the United States in the affairs of Vietnam began with grants of money and military equipment, grew with the dispatch of military advisers and maintenance personnel, and mushroomed with the commitment of ships, planes, tanks, and 550,000 troops. Dragging out into the longest conflict in the nation's history, the war became an issue in three presidential campaigns. It divided the country more sharply than any controversy since the conflict over slavery. The war's tragic harvest included thousands of Vietnamese and American lives lost, thousands more crippled and blinded, thousands of American youths alienated—many of them living in exile in Canada or Sweden to avoid military service, and millions of poor, ill, undereducated, and unemployed Americans deprived of aid that might have been provided through a more rational division of Federal revenues between the purposes of peace and those of war.

France Loses a Colony

The Vietnamese people had a long tradition of struggling to assert their independence against powerful outside nations. In their original homeland, the Red River delta, they fell for centuries under the rule of China. They borrowed extensively from Chinese civilization—notably the mandarin tradition of government, Confucian philosophy, and Buddhist religious cults, yet they resented alien rule and eventually won their independence. In the nineteenth century they were again conquered when France added Vietnam to her empire as part of French Indochina. During World War II, Japanese military forces occupied this region, but they allowed the civil administration to continue under collaborationist Vichy French officials. Before the war was over, a powerful Vietnamese underground was resisting the authority of both the French and the Japanese.

Ho Chi Minh provided the Vietnamese nationalists with bold and adroit leadership. Born the son of a mandarin official in central Vietnam, Ho left his homeland at the age of nineteen and lived for the next twelve years in London and Paris. In 1920 he joined the French Communist party and in 1923 he spent some time in Moscow. Two years later he went to China as part of the Russian team of advisers aiding Chiang Kai-shek during those days of cooperation between the Chinese Nationalists and the Communists. As part of the anti-imperialist campaign, Ho helped to organize a Vietnamese

Communist party. During the thirties he again lived in Moscow, but after the start of World War II he returned to southeastern China where he could direct underground resistance to the Japanese and the French in Vietnam.

Ho Chi Minh was clearly a dedicated Communist, trained in Moscow in in revolutionary tactics, but he was also a strong nationalist eager to lead the Vietnamese people in regaining their independence. In organizing the Vietnamese Independence League, or Vietminh, he had wide support from non-Communists as well as Communists. In the confused situation caused by the Japanese surrender and the collapse of Vichy France, Ho had a unique opportunity. The Vietminh gained control of most of northern and central Vietnam, and on September 2, 1945, Ho formally proclaimed the independence of the Democratic Republic of Vietnam.

France's postwar government at first dealt cautiously with the Vietminh. In the southern part of Vietnam it maintained its own puppet regime, but it negotiated an armistice recognizing a degree of independence to the Ho Chi Minh government. In 1946, however, the shaky peace collapsed, and the French began an eight-year effort to reestablish their authority over the entire country.

In the beginning Ho Chi Minh was not anti-American. Appealing to the pledges of the Four Freedoms, Ho asked that the anti-Axis powers recognize the Vietnamese right to independence. Between October, 1945, and February, 1946, he addressed eight different messages to President Truman or the American Secretary of State appealing for recognition and support. It is not clear how many of these appeals reached their destination; in any case the United States government did not clasp the proffered hand.

At first the Truman administration did not support the French either. Reluctant to prolong colonialism, the President did nothing for many months. In December, 1949, however, he decided upon a fateful change of policy by approving a National Security Council recommendation for support to governments resisting Communist aggression in countries like Vietnam. On February 7, 1950, the United States recognized the French puppet regime of Emperor Bao Dai, and some three months later it granted $10 million in economic and military aid to the French for their Vietnamese operations.

Why had the United States abandoned its prudent policy of neutrality? Undoubtedly, the decisive event had been the defeat of Chiang Kai-shek and his withdrawal to Formosa in December, 1949. Stung by Republican charges that it had "lost" China, the Truman administration hastily decided that it must not lose Vietnam as well. This was an unfortunate decision. In the first place, no substantial American interest was at stake. Whether the Vietminh or the French ruled Vietnam counted very little in the global balance of power. Indeed, in the contest for respect among the small nations, the United States was likely to lose more by supporting French colonialism than she would gain by preventing a Communist take-over. Even if the American goal had been desirable, it was next to impossible to achieve. In the existing situation, attempting to contain Communism in Vietnam was like building a dam with sand and no cement. Neither the French troops nor their native auxiliaries had the morale and endurance to withstand a broadly based movement linking the dynamic faiths of Communism and nationalism.

The initial $10 million American investment in Vietnam was only a tiny beginning. The French needed more and more. American grants for the anti-Vietnam campaign amounted to $150 million in the fiscal year 1950 and climbed to over $1 billion in 1954. By this time the United States was bearing 80 per cent of the cost of the war. American planes were carrying French troops to the fighting fronts, and the United States was providing the French with fighter planes and American mechanics to service them. Despite this vast investment in money and arms, the Vietminh were taking over most of the country, oftentimes arming themselves with American weapons seized from their opponents. Except for a few regions around Hanoi, Saigon, and other cities, the anti-French forces controlled the whole country both north and south. In the spring of 1954 the struggle between the French and the Vietminh reached its climax in the siege of Dienbienphu, the great fortress in northern Vietnam that was the key to the whole French position in Indochina. When the Vietminh, adroitly led by General Vo Nguyen Giap, overran Dienbienphu in May, the whole game was up, leaving France to get out of its costly predicament as best she could.

Eisenhower Makes a Pledge

What should the United States do next? The Eisenhower administration, which had come to power in 1953, was even more strongly opposed than the Truman administration to permitting a Vietminh take-over of the whole country. Indeed, during the spring of 1954 a momentous debate was in progress within administration circles. One group, including Admiral Arthur Radford, Chairman of the Joint Chiefs of Staff, and Vice President Nixon, wanted to commit American forces, if necessary, to prevent a Vietminh victory; a more cautious group, headed by Army Chief of Staff General Matthew Ridgway, opposed any step that might involve American ground forces in a Korea-like struggle. Secretary of State Dulles sympathized with the hard-liners, but hoped he could obtain the support of other governments in a joint intervention. Early in April, 1954, the internal dispute focused on a specific proposal. With Radford's encouragement, the French asked for a massive air strike by carrier-based American planes as a means of saving Dienbienphu. The interventionists urged acceptance, but Eisenhower drew back. From his own military experience he appreciated the misgivings of General Ridgway. Moreover, the President knew how little support the French regime had among the Vietnamese people and how strongly opposed most of Congress and the American public would be to a warlike course.

Even after Dienbienphu fell, the American hard-liners persisted in their determination to prevent a Vietminh take-over of the country. From April to July, 1954, an international conference was in progress at Geneva, called by the Big Four foreign ministers to discuss both Korea and Indochina, to which Communist China and other interested nations had been invited. Yet although the United States was one of the original sponsors of this Geneva Conference, it regarded the whole proceeding with suspicion, fearing that in its desperation to get out of Indochina, France would leave the region wide open to Communist control. Still attempting to prevent France from agreeing to a cease-fire, Dulles kept trying to organize a joint intervention, and the more militant elements of the administration laid plans for America to go it alone if necessary.

The new French premier, Pierre Mendès-France, kept his pledge, however, to end the hopeless Vietnam struggle. On July 20, the Ho Chi Minh government and the French signed an armistice, agreeing to a provisional demarcation line at the seventeenth parallel. The Vietminh would withdraw their forces to the north of this line, the French to the south. The armistice, however, did not establish a permanent division of the country. On the contrary, the Vietminh and the French promised to administer their separate zones only until general elections should bring about unification of the entire nation. The two parties also agreed to permit a voluntary relocation of the population north and south of the demarcation line, to forbid the introduction of any fresh troops or arms into the area, and to entrust supervision of the armistice to an international commission representing Canada, India, and Poland. The Geneva Conference also resulted in a declaration by the various powers promising to respect the independence of the other Indochina states of Laos and Cambodia and to cooperate in supporting the Vietnam armistice, pledging among other things that the crucial general elections should be held in July, 1956.

In accepting an armistice that left the French in control of southern Vietnam, Ho Chi Minh seemed to be giving up more than he gained. The Vietminh forces controlled most of the country and their prospects for complete victory seemed excellent. Why then did Ho make peace? One probable reason was the very real danger of an American intervention that might protract the struggle for many years. Indeed, there is evidence that the Soviet Union and Communist China, reluctant to be drawn into a major confrontation with the United States, strongly urged Ho to accept the armistice. Yet even more important, it seems certain that the shrewd Vietminh leader believed the settlement would enable him to gain control of the whole country within a few years. Confident that the French regime had very little popular support, Ho could well afford to wait for the promised elections in 1956.

Secretary Dulles left no doubt of his dislike for the Geneva settlement. He refused to attend in person, sending Under Secretary Walter Bedell Smith instead. In the end, Smith neither approved nor disapproved the settlement, but he did make an official statement in which the United States promised to refrain from using or threatening to use force to disturb the agreements and also approved internationally supervised Vietnamese elections in 1956.

The Eisenhower administration immediately embarked upon a policy designed to prevent the Communists from gaining any advantage from the Geneva agreements. On September 8, 1954, the South East Asia Treaty Organization (SEATO) came into being with the United States, Britain, France, the Philippines, Australia, New Zealand, Thailand, and Pakistan as charter members. They bound themselves to regard any attack upon the territory of one of them as a threat to all and to "act to meet the common danger in accordance with its constitutional processes." By a separate protocol this guarantee was also extended to Laos, Cambodia, and "the free territory under the jurisdiction of the State of Vietnam." As a Pacific counterpart to NATO, the new SEATO was anemic. Not only did it lack the military power that made the North Atlantic organization formidable, but it failed to win the support of the major independent nations of the region—India, Burma, Ceylon, and Indonesia.

Although SEATO sought to protect the independence of a nation of South Vietnam that did not yet exist, cloak-and-dagger experts like Colonel Edward Lansdale of the American Military Mission worked secretly to bring such a nation to birth. They wanted a Saigon regime that would throw off the unpopular link with France, but at the same time follow a strongly anti-Communist policy. The Americans found a promising leader for such a government in Ngo Dinh Diem, a prominent Roman Catholic from central Vietnam. Because of a disagreement with the French in 1933, Diem had resigned his government post and retired to live the life of a scholar for ten years. In 1946 Ho invited Diem to take an important post in a popular front government, but Diem refused because of his dislike for the Communists. From 1950 to 1954 he spent much of his time in the United States, where he made a strong impression on New York's Cardinal Spellman and on many politicians—Senator John Kennedy of Massachusetts among them.

In July, 1954, Emperor Bao Dai appointed Diem his premier. The situation confronting the new minister was grim; the French forces were shattered, the Geneva agreements were about to be signed, and many rival Vietnamese factions were struggling for power. Nevertheless, Lansdale helped Diem consolidate his position. American naval vessels transported Vietnamese who wanted to get out of the North under the terms of the armistice. Many of these refugees were former officials and soldiers; many were Catholics; and both elements gave Diem strong support.

On October 1, 1954, Eisenhower sent a significant letter to Premier Diem, promising direct financial aid to his government. "The purpose of this offer," the President wrote, "is to assist the Government of Vietnam in developing and maintaining a strong, viable state capable of resisting attempted subversion or aggression through military means." Firm though this commitment was, the President did attach the condition that Diem should undertake "needed reforms."

Events were soon to prove, however, that Diem was much more interested in extending his own power than he was in reforming political and social conditions. During a protracted struggle in 1955, he overcame the opposition of rival leaders and challenged the authority of Emperor Bao Dai himself. In October, 1955, he conducted a plebiscite on the question of whether the people wanted a continuance of the monarchy or a republic with himself as President. With the support of a suspiciously large majority—announced as 98.2 per cent, Diem proclaimed the establishment of the Republic of Vietnam.

Diem's success in this balloting did not mean that he wanted the internationally supervised elections promised in the Geneva agreements. The Hanoi government invited the Saigon regime to confer on making the necessary arrangements, but Diem repeatedly refused, using as his excuse the fact that the government of South Vietnam had never accepted the Geneva settlement. Although the Eisenhower administration would have preferred to have Diem stall off the elections by delays and diplomatic quibbling rather than by open defiance, there is little doubt that it approved the end result. Determined to prevent the Vietminh from taking over the entire country, the United States government was not disposed to be fastidious about the means.

President Diem was hardly the man to transform South Vietnam into a showcase of democracy. Essentially a secretive man and a traditionalist, he trusted few people and gave the most important posts to members of his own family. Especially powerful were his brother Ngo Dinh Nhu, the "Political Counsellor," and the beautiful and sinister Madame Nhu. Although the republic had adopted a constitution and elected a national assembly, the ruling family would tolerate no opposition. They ordered the imprisonment of between 50,000 and 100,000 persons. The political prisoners were accused of being Communists, but many non-Communists were arrested as well. Diem also alienated much of the peasantry by his policies. The Vietminh had allowed poor farmers to take over the land of absentee landlords, but Diem tried to restore the landlords' rights to collect at least a portion of their former rents. Urged by the Americans to follow a more liberal policy, the Diem government offered land to the peasants on terms that they considered burdensome. Diem also created wide resentment by appointing local officials instead of allowing the villagers to elect their own councils—a right that even the French had respected.

Diem's harsh and unpopular rule provoked sporadic bombings and assassinations in 1957 and 1958. At first these insurrectionary acts received no open encouragement from the North Vietnamese government. Still hoping to unite the country by political means, Ho Chi Minh advised against revolutionary acts that might arouse middle-class fears. Moreover, he had problems enough in reorganizing the economy of the North to keep him from inviting trouble in the South. Although there was undoubtedly a Communist underground in the South and some infiltration from the North, Hanoi did not begin giving major aid to Diem's enemies until about December, 1958. During the next two years the National Liberation Front (NLF)—called by Saigon the Vietcong or Vietnamese Communists—attempted to unite all the Communist and non-Communist factions opposed to Diem, and the North Vietnam government began to develop the Ho Chi Minh trail, over which it could send arms to the rebels.

Diem's difficulties with the Vietcong only stiffened Eisenhower's determination to support him. Explaining at a press conference why it was so important to prevent a Communist take-over of South Vietnam, he used the analogy of a row of dominoes; if you knocked over the first one, all the others would fall over too. In other words, if South Vietnam fell to the Communists, the other countries of the region—Laos, Cambodia, Thailand, Burma, Malaysia, Indonesia—would soon topple into Communist hands also. Despite the dubious logic of the "domino theory," it gained a tenacious grip not only on President Eisenhower, but on the next three occupants of the White House as well.

Kennedy Raises the Stakes

One of the values of a two-party system ought to be the opportunity to review policy and change direction when a new administration takes office. Yet key Republicans and key Democrats shared so many assumptions about the cold war that a fundamental shift in foreign policy was almost impossible during these years. Indeed, the political leaders were so afraid of being branded "soft on Communism," that they tried to outdo each other in rigorous policies. Instead of reversing Eisenhower's Vietnam policy, therefore, President Kennedy committed more men and money to the gamble.

The new President did exhibit some caution on a related issue. When Kennedy came into office, the situation in Laos demanded immediate attention. Although the Laotians were a singularly unwarlike people, wanting only to be left alone, rival outside powers were engaging in dangerous intrigue with Laotian leaders and aiding their rival factions. The Eisenhower administration had backed a rightist regime, while the Russians, Chinese, and North Vietnamese were aiding a leftist force called the Pathet Lao. Some of Kennedy's advisers wanted an armed American intervention to prevent a Communist victory, but the President chose a less militant course. Meeting Khrushchev in Vienna in June, 1961, Kennedy found that Laos was one of the few issues on which they could agree. The two subscribed to the principle of "a neutral and independent Laos under a government chosen by the Laotians themselves." A conference at Geneva worked many months trying to fill this prescription. The results were not altogether satisfactory: the new ruler, Prince Souvanna Phouma, tried to follow a neutralist course, but still had to contend with Communist rebels and infiltrators from North Vietnam. Yet Kennedy had at least defused a highly explosive situation.

But Kennedy's willingness to compromise on Laos seemed only to strengthen his determination to take a firm stand on Vietnam. He felt that the Russians would interpret any backdown as a sign of weakness—a weakness Kennedy could not afford to permit after the Bay of Pigs affair and the confrontation in Berlin. So in the summer of 1961 the President sent Vice President Johnson on a mission of encouragement, not only to Saigon, but to other Asiatic capitals as well. After his return to Washington Johnson carried the domino theory to its ultimate absurdity. "We must decide," he wrote, "either to help these countries to the best of our ability or throw in the towel in the area and pull back our defenses to San Francisco and a 'Fortress America' concept." He also stressed the contention that unless the United States gave a strong hand to South Vietnam, other countries would not trust it to live up to its treaties and stand by its friends. Firmly though Johnson supported Diem, he was not blind to his faults. "He has admirable qualities," Johnson wrote, "but he is remote from the people, is surrounded by persons less admirable and capable than he."

For more specific advice on what he should do, Kennedy turned to General Maxwell Taylor, his special military adviser whom he sent to Vietnam in the fall of 1961. Taylor recommended among other forms of military aid an American force of some eight thousand men, ostensibly to aid in flood relief, but actually to strengthen sagging morale in Diem's army. Although he proposed their use primarily for advisory and logistical purposes, he recognized that they were likely to be drawn into combat and that increasing American involvement might result. Secretary of Defense Robert McNamara gave qualified support to Taylor's recommendations, as did Secretary of State Dean Rusk. Rusk, however, also emphasized the urgent need for reform of Diem's civilian government.

In earlier years a stern critic of French mistakes, Kennedy had no wish to repeat these errors in his own handling of the Vietnam situation. Therefore, he declined at first to commit as large a force as Taylor advised, although he did substantially increase the "Special Force" personnel that became engaged not only in training and transporting the South Vietnamese army, but in clandestine operations in North Vietnam as well. Since the Geneva agreements had limited the number of American military personnel to 685—the number there in 1954, the United States was now clearly ignoring that settlement. It justified its actions on the grounds that it had never formally accepted the Geneva agreements and that, in any case, North Vietnam had violated them first by infiltrating men and arms to help the Vietcong. As yet, however, North Vietnamese intervention was still minor; the Vietcong were residents of the South who armed themselves largely with American-made equipment captured from Diem's army.

The hard truth was that the Vietcong were proving increasingly formidable foes for the Saigon government. Much of the peasantry sympathized with the rebels and gave them food and shelter. With this support the Vietcong actually governed large areas of the countryside. Even in the villages that government officials ruled by day, the Vietcong often returned to control each night. It was a cruel war in which the government tortured and summarily executed alleged Vietcong, and the rebels retaliated with assassinations and other acts of terror. When the Vietcong captured a village, they sometimes beheaded the Saigon-appointed officials in the public market place for the education of the peasants.

Unwilling to permit a Vietcong victory, the Kennedy administration sent more and more special forces to the country. Although the Vietnamese were still supposed to be doing all the fighting, the line between combat and noncombat roles was easily crossed. American helicopters transported Vietnamese troops to the trouble spots; American trainer-pilots accompanied their Vietnamese pupils on combat missions; and unquestionably American pilots and gunners sometimes actually strafed and bombarded the enemy. By the fall of 1963, more than 16,500 United States military personnel were in South Vietnam, and they had already suffered over 600 casualties.

Originally an admirer of President Diem, President Kennedy became increasingly disillusioned with him. Now confident of American military support, Diem became more and more callous in resisting American suggestions for reform. Or if he did adopt a proposal, he twisted it to serve his own purposes. Such was the case with the "strategic hamlet" program. Jumping to the conclusion that a strategy the British had successfully employed in Malaya would work in Vietnam, American advisers suggested a resettlement of many of the peasants in protected villages where they would enjoy such satisfactory economic and social conditions that they would become immune to Vietcong propaganda. Diem's government took up the idea with enthusiasm and forced the resettlement of several million peasants. But Diem's motives were purely political; he used the strategic hamlets as a device for controlling the population. There was widespread corruption and little of the American aid intended for the villagers actually reached them. Instead, the program further embittered the peasants by forcing them out of their traditional homes.

Thus by the summer of 1963 Diem had aroused the hatred of a dangerously large proportion of the population, ranging all the way from the peasants to intellectuals and university students. Still more serious was his alienation of the Buddhists. Diem's favoritism toward the Catholics was bound to be resented in a country where Buddhists outnumbered Catholics by something like 13 to 1. Many Vietnamese were not particularly religious, yet the Buddhist monks, or bonzes, had great influence. Clashes between government suporters and Buddhists culminated in a major crackdown in August, 1963. Alleging a Buddhist conspiracy against the government, Diem's special police force raided pagodas and arrested over a thousand monks and other devotees. In startling acts of protest, first one and later some five other Buddhist monks committed suicide by self-immolation—dousing themselves with gasoline and then setting themselves on fire.

Even before these tragic events deeply shocked American public opinion, President Kennedy had decided that he must take a much sterner line with Diem. He accepted the resignation of the pro-Diem American Ambassador to Saigon and appointed in his place Henry Cabot Lodge, his old-time Republican rival in Massachusetts politics. Immediately after his arrival in Vietnam, Lodge became involved in intrigue of a most serious nature. Some high officers in the South Vietnamese army were considering a coup against Diem and cautiously sounded out Lodge. The ambassador cabled Washington and received a highly significant reply signed by Acting Secretary of State George Ball. Diem was to be given a reasonable opportunity to remove his notorious brothers from power, "but if he remains obdurate, then we are prepared to accept the obvious implication that we can no longer support Diem." Lodge soon concluded that it was impossible to deal with him, and confidential American agents kept in contact with the plotting generals.

Kennedy wrote directly to Lodge, assuring him that the United States would not act to save Diem were a coup attempted. Yet determined to avoid another Bay of Pigs, he warned Lodge not to encourage the coup unless success were certain. Meantime, the President publicly expressed his disapproval of Diem's recent actions and began to withhold certain forms of financial aid.

Thus with substantial American complicity, the Vietnamese generals made their move on November 1, 1963. They turned their American-made tanks and artillery against the presidential palace and forced the surrender of Diem and his supporters. Both the president and his hated brother, Ngo Dinh Nhu, were killed, and a military caretaker government under General Duong Van Minh took over the country. Before President Kennedy could formulate a policy to deal with the new situation, he came to his own bloody death in Dallas.

The Tonkin Gulf Affair

The overthrow of Diem might have provided an opportunity to work out a peaceful solution of the tangled Vietnam situation. France's president Charles de Gaulle had suggested earlier in the year a reconvening of the Geneva Conference and an attempt to re-establish the principle of neutralization. South Vietnam's National Liberation Front offered to negotiate with General Minh for a cease-fire and a coalition government, and UN Secretary General U Thant supported the idea. But the new American President was even more opposed than Kennedy had been to such proposals. In a New Year's message to General Minh, Johnson said: "Neutralization of South Vietnam would only be another name for a Communist take-over." He promised Minh "American personnel and material as needed to assist you in achieving victory."

But was victory possible? Alarmed by neutralization talk and accusing Minh of indecision, a new military junta under General Nguyen Khanh seized power on January 30, 1964. Despite the changing cast of characters, however, the drama's plot unrolled with monotonous sameness. In April, 1964, American observers reported that the government controlled only about one third of the villages; the rest were either under outright Vietcong control or were trying to avoid involvement on either side.

As Johnson's advisers studied the problem, they convinced themselves that the core of the problem was Hanoi. It was Ho's government, they believed, that directed the operations of the Vietcong. Without the men and arms that North Vietnam smuggled into the South, the Vietcong would have to surrender. This theory, on which the Johnson policy was increasingly based, had at first relatively little evidence to support it. No North Vietnamese soldiers had yet been sent to the South, and the infiltrators consisted mostly of former Vietminh who were returning to their homes to continue the struggle for their idea of freedom. There were only a few thousand of these in any case. Nor was there much evidence that the North Vietnamese were providing the rebels with arms. For the most part, the Vietcong were still using what French or American weapons they could capture or purchase. The Johnson administration refused, however, to concede that it was intervening in what was essentially a civil war; instead it chose to believe it was combatting a Communist conspiracy, involving not only Hanoi, but Moscow and Peking.

The solution, Johnson's advisers believed, was to bring enough pressure to bear upon Ho Chi Minh to make him stop helping the Vietcong. During the first six months of 1964 the brain-trusters, both military and civilian, discussed alternatives ranging all the way from all-out bombing of the North to minor harassments. Complicating the American deliberations were the rash pronouncements of South Vietnam's new ruler. To strengthen his shaky position, General Khanh was urging a "March North" strategy—a South Vietnamese invasion of North Vietnam. Unwilling to risk Khanh's drawing the United States into a deeper involvement, General Maxwell Taylor, the new Ambassador to Saigon, advised Washington to speed up contingency planning for its own operations. Contingency plans of a most serious character were, in fact, being drawn. In May, 1964, a planning team headed by

William Bundy of the State Department prepared a thirty-day timetable that would start with a presidential message condemning Hanoi's aggressive actions, continue with a congressional resolution authorizing the President to use force to repel this aggression, and culminate on D-day with bombing attacks on strategic targets in North Vietnam. Happily cooperating in this business, the military prepared a list of ninety-four key targets, while Bundy drafted the proposed congressional resolution.

The planners were ready to move much faster than was the President himself. With the November election and Barry Goldwater, his probable Republican opponent, very much on his mind, Johnson hoped to postpone any drastic new step in Vietnam. Goldwater, a notorious hawk, was an early advocate of bombing North Vietnam and of using nuclear weapons if necessary. Knowing that much of the electorate would be frightened by such bellicosity, Johnson wanted to present himself, by contrast, as a moderate man, opposed to any course that might involve the United States in full-scale war. Plans for a congressional resolution and for bombing the North were therefore shelved—at least until after the election.

This cautious policy did not mean that Johnson abstained from lesser harassments of the Communists. In June, when the Pathet Lao fired upon American planes making reconnaissance flights over Laos—missions in which they had been secretly engaged since 1962, Johnson ordered retaliatory air strikes against the rebel positions. American advisers also continued to help the South Vietnamese carry out raids and acts of sabotage in the North. They provided their protégés with speedy patrol boats and trained them for hit-and-run raids against North Vietnamese ships and shore points —34A operations, as they were called. As an entirely separate program, the United States Navy began to send destroyers on reconnaissance missions off the coast of North Vietnam to gather information about North Vietnam radar installations and to monitor their radio communications, as well as to convey still another warning to Hanoi that it should stop helping the Vietcong.

On August 2, 1964, the destroyer *Maddox* was cruising in the Bay of Tonkin on one of these missions when it encountered three North Vietnamese PT (patrol torpedo) boats. Convinced that the PT boats were about to attack it, the *Maddox* opened fire and a brief battle ensued, with planes from a nearby American carrier joining in. The Vietnamese scored only one harmless hit on the *Maddox,* which apparently sank one PT boat and damaged the other two. Why had the little ships undertaken so foolhardy a conflict? Their rashness is probably to be explained by the fact that South Vietnamese patrol boats had staged one of their 34A raids on nearby islands the previous night. The North Vietnamese apparently made the mistake of believing that the American vessel was part of this hostile force.

Because of the possibility of such a mistake and also because Johnson wanted to continue his moderate pre-election stance, the United States reaction was relatively mild. It sent a protest to Hanoi against "an unprovoked attack" on an American vessel operating on "the high seas" and a warning against "any further unprovoked offensive military action against United States forces."

To prove to the North Vietnamese—and, perhaps also to the Republicans

A damaged patrol boat under fire in Vietnam, 1968. (Official U.S. Navy photograph.)

—that he could not be intimidated, Johnson ordered the Bay of Tonkin maneuvers to continue—this time with two destroyers instead of one. Two days later a second battle occurred—or was imagined to have occurred, as critics of the administration later charged. The action came on a night so dark and rainy that the two American ships could not see each other, to say nothing of any enemy vessels that might have been stalking them. Convinced by mysterious blips on their radar screens and noises detected by the sonar equipment that they were being ambushed, the *Maddox* and the *Turner Joy* fired round after round against unseen targets and called upon carrier planes to help them. In the aftermath, the North Vietnam government denied that their boats had been anywhere near the scene, but the American commanders continued to insist that they had been under attack—although their earliest reports were admittedly based on dubious evidence.

Whether or not the attack of August 4 ever occurred, it had most serious results. In a somber late-evening TV speech President Johnson announced that he had ordered retaliatory air strikes against North Vietnamese targets and was asking Congress to support his action. The timetable prepared in earlier months was thus put into effect to take advantage of this unexpected opportunity. While Johnson spoke, planes from American carriers were taking off for strikes against three North Vietnamese torpedo boat bases and an oil storage depot, four appropriate targets selected from the earlier list of ninety-four.

Congress accepted with scarcely a doubting voice the administration claim that the United States had suffered two unprovoked attacks. The House passed the so-called Tonkin Gulf resolution—based in part on the Bundy draft written two and a half months earlier—by a vote of 466 to 0; the Senate approved by a vote of 88 to 2. Congress thus approved "the determination" of the President "to take all necessary measures to repel any armed attack against the forces of the United States and to prevent further aggression"; in another section, the resolution asserted that the United States was prepared, "as the President determines, to take all necessary steps, including the use of armed force, to assist any member or protocol state of the Southeast Asia Collective Defense Treaty requesting assistance in defense of its freedom." In a rally-round-the-flag mood Congress had given the President a blank check, little realizing how much he would draw upon it. Only Senators Wayne Morse of Oregon and Ernest Gruening of Alaska voted no. Senator J. William Fulbright, chairman of the Foreign Relations Committee, sponsored the resolution, and other future Senate doves like George McGovern and Jacob Javits voted for it.

The Great Escalation

Still emphasizing his own moderation as contrasted with Goldwater's rashness, Johnson took no further drastic step during the pre-election period. In a campaign speech late in August he condemned the idea that the United States should resort to bombing that would escalate the war and "result in our committing a good many American boys to fighting a war that I think ought to be fought by the boys of Asia to help protect their own land."

Yet at the very time when the President was promising not to enlarge the war, Ambassador Taylor in Saigon was urging a "carefully orchestrated bombing attack" on North Vietnam, and the Joint Chiefs of Staff in Washington were warning that an air war against the North was now "essential to prevent a complete collapse of the United States position in Southeast Asia." Confronted with this conflict between the demands of his military advisers and those of domestic politics, Johnson stalled for time. He allowed the generals to continue making plans for bombing the North, but for the time being he authorized only covert measures—American bombing of Communist infiltration routes in Laos, South Vietnamese raids on the coasts of North Vietnam, and more American reconnoitering in the Bay of Tonkin. Without provoking any outcry in the newspapers and other media, he hoped to harass Ho's government enough to make it stop helping the Vietcong. At the same time he wanted to take enough action to improve sagging morale in South Vietnam.

Any hope that Johnson may have had for a quick and easy resolution of the Vietnam problem soon evaporated. American pin pricks only incited the Communists to more belligerent moves of their own. The Vietcong became bolder and more successful in their operations, and in the spring of 1965 American intelligence officers for the first time confirmed reports of North Vietnamese units operating south of the DMZ (the demilitarized zone along the border). And as the Vietcong grew stronger, the political situation in Saigon became more and more chaotic. South Vietnamese generals struggled for power with civilian politicians, and the generals themselves divided into rival factions. Despite Ambassador Taylor's optimistic predictions that things would soon be better, there was a monotonous succession of coups, attempted coups, student demonstrations, and Buddhist protests. Suspected of inclining toward neutralism, General Khan was forced into exile in February, 1965, leaving the hard-liners, General Nguyen Van Thieu and Air Marshall Nguyen Cao Ky, as the most powerful figures on the scene.

To American policymakers, obsessed with the necessity of keeping an anti-Communist government in power in South Vietnam, the situation in the early months of 1965 seemed desperate. It was impossible to wait for the bickering Saigon generals and politicians to pull the country together. On February 6, 1965, Vietcong guerrillas raided an American military advisers' compound at Pleiku in the Central Highlands and also a nearby American helicopter base. Nine Americans were killed, and seventy-six were wounded. This triggered the decision to proceed with the long-planned bombing. The day after the Pleiku raid forty-nine navy jets made a reprisal attack on a North Vietnamese barracks forty miles north of the border. New incidents provoked similar reprisals later in the month. Then on March 2, something new was added. No longer pretending that the American raids were special events, a systematic regular bombing campaign against the North began— Operation Rolling Thunder, as the planners had already named it. Within a week the American planes began using incendiary bombs containing napalm, spreading destruction on villages and forests and cruelly burning both animals and human beings. What did the policymakers hope to achieve by these waves of destruction? Although the advocates of air power hoped to interdict the lines of supply between North Vietnam and the Vietcong, realists knew that this was almost impossible to achieve. The more realistic goal was to cause so much destruction to factories, storage tanks, railroads, and bridges that the North Vietnamese would have to accept American terms of peace— an end to their support for the Vietcong and a recognition of the independence of South Vietnam under an anti-Communist government. Until Ho was ready to agree to these terms, the Johnson administration was opposed to negotiations. Indeed, it declined various offers of mediation from Russia, France, and UN Secretary General U Thant.

But Operation Rolling Thunder had no perceptible impact on Communist determination. With the Vietcong still holding the upper hand in the South, American military planners soon decided to change the mission of American ground forces from defense to offense. On April 1, 1965, the President sent 20,000 more men to Vietnam to join the 27,000 American soldiers already there and at the same time authorized "the more active use" of the marines. From this time on, the escalation of the war proceeded rapidly. In June, General William Westmoreland, the American commander in Vietnam, requested additional forces to bring the total to almost 194,000 men. Some of the President's advisers warned of danger ahead. Under Secretary of State George Ball pointed out in a July 1 memorandum that once large numbers of American troops were committed to direct combat they would take heavy casualties "in a war they are ill-equipped to fight in a non-cooperative if not downright hostile countryside." Once the Americans suffered these heavy casualties, it would be almost impossible to go back. Either the United States would have to push on to a clearcut victory or suffer national humiliation. *"And of these two possibilities,"* Ball wrote, *"I think humiliation would be*

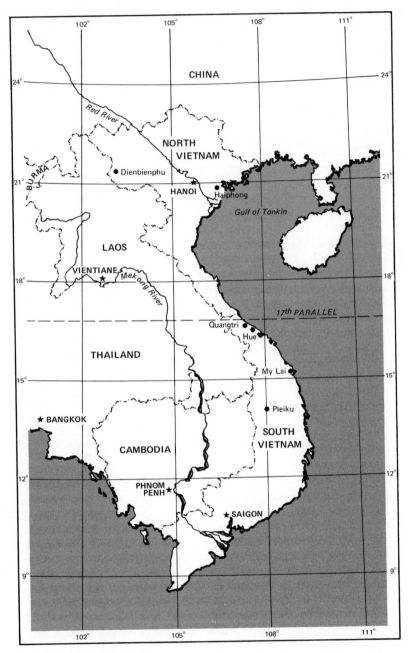

Sketch map of Southeast Asia.

more likely than the achievement of our objectives—even after we have paid terrible costs." He advised cutting American losses and seeking a compromise settlement.

President Johnson was truly at a fork in the road—and he chose the path of war. Before July was over he had authorized the full 194,000 force that Westmoreland had requested and had given the general sweeping powers to use the men in "search-and-destroy" missions—that is, to seek out and kill the Vietcong wherever they might be hiding in the jungles and mountains of South Vietnam. To dress up the American intervention with more flags, the United States induced some SEATO countries—Australia, New Zealand, South Korea, the Philippines, and Thailand—to send small forces to join in fighting the Communists.

Unfortunately, escalation was a game that two could play. North Vietnam kept matching the American build-up by sending additional forces to the South, and General Westmoreland, in turn, beseiged Washington with demands for more and more troops. By October, 1967, 40 per cent of the combat-ready divisions of the United States, half of its tactical air power, and a third of its naval strength—some 480,000 men in all—were involved in the Vietnam war. Was this massive concentration of power achieving its goals? The American and South Vietnamese troops undoubtedly killed thousands of the Vietcong and North Vietnamese, although the reported count of enemy dead was always suspiciously high. By the fall of 1966 Secretary McNamara reported that the American operations "had blunted the communist military initiative," but the situation more nearly approached stalemate than American victory. "Enemy morale has not broken," McNamara wrote; "he apparently has adjusted to our stopping his drive for military victory and has adopted a strategy of keeping us busy and waiting us out (a strategy of attriting our national will)." Even more serious was the failure to win the support of the peasantry. McNamara reported that as compared with two or four years earlier, "we control little, if any, more of the population; the political infrastructure thrives in most of the country, continuing to give the enemy his enormous intelligence advantage; full security exists nowhere . . .; in the countryside, the enemy almost completely controls the night."

In 1967 the Thieu-Ky regime appealed to the people in an unconvincing show of democracy. The constituent assembly approved a new constitution, and the voters elected Thieu president and Ky vice president. Skeptical observers noted, however, that the constitution specifically barred Communists from all offices, and the government also disallowed the candidacy of non-Communist advocates of peace and militant Buddhists.

In their effort to "save" South Vietnam, the American themselves were bringing death and suffering to the South Vietnamese people. In March, 1968, an American platoon under Lieutenant William Calley, Jr., slaughtered more than one hundred unarmed men, women, and children in the South Vietnamese hamlet of Mylai. Hushed up at the time, the massacre was revealed two years later and resulted in Calley's court-martial and conviction. For a few uncomfortable weeks the American public was compelled to face the truth about its government's actions in Vietnam. Doves and other critics of the war insisted that the Mylai incident was recognized as a crime only because the ground troops could see what they were doing. Never charged with murder, they declared, were the crews of American planes and the artillery units that killed thousands of helpless women and children in the ruthless bombings and shellings of the search-and-destroy missions. Moreover, these opponents of the war avowed, the American operations forced almost a million peasants from their homes and into the squalor of refugee camps. While many South Vietnamese were losing everything they possessed, others were gaining sudden affluence from lavish American spending and black market operations. There was widespread corruption in the handling of aid funds, and thousands of prostitutes and drug peddlers prospered at the expense of lonesome and bored GIs. American money, flooding into the country, completely disorganized the native economy, resulting in a runaway inflation. Why not bring the useless war to a speedy conclusion? was the growing question of the increasing number of war critics.

Despite these revelations, Operation Rolling Thunder continued the bombing of the North. Unlike the situation in the South where General Westmoreland had been given a free hand, President Johnson personally directed the air war, approving all targets and carefully studying the reported results. Hoping to reduce criticism both at home and in foreign countries, Johnson at first limited the bombing to the southern part of North Vietnam, sparing Hanoi, the heavily populated capital, and Haiphong, the principal port. Despite anxiety over the increasing quantities of Russian and Chinese equipment arriving in North Vietnam, the President would not approve harbor bombings that might injure Soviet ships or attacks close to the

United States soldiers and a wounded Vietnamese girl during action in 1967. (UPI Photo.)

northern border that might alarm the Chinese. Besides limiting the war in this fashion, the President resorted to occasional bombing halts in an effort to encourage peace overtures from the enemy. Since each party was still demanding a complete reversal of the other's basic policy, however, no negotiations resulted, and the bombing was resumed with more ferocity than ever. In the end, Johnson lifted many of the earlier limitations and ordered the bombing of oil storage facilities in the Haiphong area and other tempting targets close to Hanoi. But Rolling Thunder was no more successful than the ground war in the South. The North Vietnamese stoically dispersed their industry and storage facilities, rebuilt roads and bridges, and kept men and supplies moving almost without interruption toward the battlefields of South Vietnam. In May, 1967, McGeorge Bundy, one of Johnson's more hawkish advisers, wrote frankly to the President: "Ho Chi Minh and his colleagues simply are not going to change their policy on the basis of losses from the air in North Vietnam."

Doves Versus Hawks

From the beginning of the American involvement in Vietnam a vocal minority had sharply criticized government policy. In voting for Johnson instead of Goldwater in 1964, they had intended to register their strong opposition to any enlargement of the conflict. They felt, therefore, a profound sense of outrage when the President began bombing North Vietnam only three months after the election. Angry protest demonstrations against the war began in 1965 and mounted in seriousness until they reached their high point following President Nixon's order for the invasion of Cambodia in the spring of 1970.

University professors and students were among the earliest critics of the American intervention. The protestors conducted "sit-ins" and "teach-ins," during which they studied the background of the Vietnam situation and condemned government policy. In August, 1965, representatives of various civil rights, peace, and church groups organized a National Coordinating Committee to End the War. The following October this Committee sponsored a series of mass meetings and marches in cities across the nation. Some ten thousand antiwar demonstrators marched down Fifth Avenue in New York, while in Berkeley, California, the police halted an attempted march on the Oakland Army Terminal. One New York demonstrator publicly burned his draft card, and efforts to evade and disrupt the selective service system became a favorite form of protest for young men determined not to fight in what they regarded as an immoral war. Eventually many of them chose exile in Canada or Sweden. Highly visible though the protestors were, they constituted only a small minority in the early days. Unfriendly bystanders heckled the peace marchers and sometimes pelted them with eggs; self-styled patriots conducted counterdemonstrations demanding still stronger anti-Communist measures.

As the war dragged on, the antiwar demonstrators became more passionate. Convinced that the war was demoralizing the nation and crippling the progress of black people, Martin Luther King now took a prominent part in

Demonstrators and military police during an antiwar protest at the Pentagon, 1967. (UPI Photo.)

the movement. In April, 1967, he led a march of over 100,000 people from New York's Central Park to the UN headquarters, while more than 50,000 persons attended an antiwar meeting in San Francisco. In October, 1967, police arrested 647 protestors during a two-day demonstration in Washington that culminated in a march on the Pentagon, hated symbol of the American war machine. Opposition to the war was by no means confined to long-haired youths. Prominent reporters and TV commentators revealed their distate for the American policy, and the highly respected *New York Times* began during 1967 to call for a halt in the bombing and the beginning of peace negotiations.

In Congress the first doves—Senators Wayne Morse of Oregon, Ernest Gruening of Alaska, and Gaylord Nelson of Wisconsin—were a brave little group, risking their political future by opposing government policy, but the great escalation of 1965 soon increased the antiwar faction. Because of his chairmanship of the Foreign Relations Committee, the position of Senator Fulbright was particularly important. In 1964 he had been Johnson's most valuable supporter during the Tonkin Gulf crisis; two years later he was demonstrating his unhappiness with the President's policies by sharp questioning of administration leaders. Particularly damaging were the hearings of February, 1968, when Fulbright explored the Tonkin Gulf affair and found that the August 4 attack had perhaps never occurred. Referring to his

Dr. Benjamin Spock reading a statement at the White House gates during the Mobilization to End the War in Vietnam, 1967. Mrs. Martin Luther King is to the right of Dr. Spock. (UPI Photo.)

own role in pushing through the Tonkin Gulf Resolution, Fulbright said he regretted this "more than anything I have ever done in my life."

Although Fulbright was the most prestigious figure among the Senate doves, his Hamlet-like character—publicly agonizing over his decisions—made him less willing to lead vigorous attacks upon the Vietnam policy than were younger and more ambitious men like Senators Eugene McCarthy of Minnesota and George McGovern of South Dakota. Potentially the most important dove of all was Robert Kennedy, who had been elected Senator from New York in 1964. Despite President John Kennedy's part in the American involvement, his brother became an outspoken critic of Johnson's escalation of the war.

Within the Johnson administration itself there was a rising undercurrent of doubt. At first Under Secretary of State Ball seemed only to be playing the lonely role of devil's advocate to test the faith of the true believers. By the fall of 1967, however, his misgivings were shared by such men as Deputy Secretary of Defense Paul Nitze and Under Secretary of the Air Force Townsend Hoopes. These moderates found it hard to reach the President's ear because his most trusted advisers—Walt Rostow of the White House staff and Secretary Rusk—were persistent hard-liners. A key man in the behind-the-scenes struggle was Secretary of Defense McNamara, an expert in business management, who had long believed that the efficient application of adequate force would solve the Vietnam problem. As early as the fall of 1966, however, he was beginning to question the recommendations of the Joint Chiefs of Staff, and a year later he was advising the President to cut back the bombing of North Vietnam and to refuse General Westmoreland's request for 200,000 more troops to add to the 500,000 already there. Unhappy with McNamara's change of position, Johnson found a different post for him as president of the World Bank. Clark Clifford, who became Secretary of Defense on March 1, 1968, was presumed to be a hawk since he had been one of Truman's most trusted advisers when the containment policy originated, but, as a keen lawyer, he insisted on studying the whole Vietnam problem for himself. Before his first month in office was over, Secretary Clifford threw his weight to the side of the doves.

Johnson Changes Gears

Several events early in 1968 forced President Johnson to a painful re-appraisal of his Vietnam policy. On January 1—the beginning of Tet, the lunar New Year—the Vietcong and North Vietnamese launched their heaviest offensive of the war. Vietcong commandos seized several buildings within the United States Embassy compound in Saigon and held them for six hours until American forces wiped them out. A more formidable unit captured Hue, ancient capital of central Vietnam, liquidated some three thousand residents, and remained in occupation for twenty-six days. Most of the major cities also underwent attack during the crucial days of early February. United States military spokesmen were quick to interpret the Tet battle as a major disaster for the enemy: facing defeat, the Communists had made one last desperate gamble and lost, suffering enormous casualties in the process. But other observers drew different lessons from the battle. The ferocity of the enemy attacks demonstrated how little had really been accomplished by three years of American ground and air operations. The enemy still appeared dangerously strong in the ability and will to fight. Moreover, the redeployment of South Vietnamese forces to defend the cities had stripped the countryside and set back the pacification campaign many months. What should the United States do next? Should it pour 200,000 more troops into the quicksand of Vietnam fighting, or should it seek some other way out of its predicament?

Through UN Secretary General U Thant and other channels came hints from Hanoi that Ho's government would be willing to begin peace negotiations if the United States would halt the bombing. In order to test out these possibilities, Secretary Rusk, usually a hawk, was now advising a curtailment of the bombing. Yet the advice streaming into the White House was not all in one direction; some high officials and a strong faction of congressional hawks wanted not less but more bombing on the argument that North Vietnam was near defeat.

Johnson's decision was made more painful by storm clouds on the political horizon. On March 12, Democratic voters gave him only 49 per cent of their ballots in the New Hampshire presidential primary, as compared with 42 per cent for Senator Eugene McCarthy, the candidate of the doves. Since the President had not authorized the printing of his name on the ballot and his supporters had had to write it in, he had not really done very badly. Nevertheless, the enthusiasm of hundreds of college students who had converged on New Hampshire and their success in winning votes for McCarthy gave the antiwar cause a shot of adrenalin. Perhaps the doves could indeed capture the Democratic convention and deny renomination to Johnson. A second formidable rival took the field against the President on March 16 when Senator Robert Kennedy announced his candidacy.

All these converging lines of force made President Johnson's TV speech of March 31 an event of extraordinary interest. Stressing his desire for peace, he announced that he was ordering American aircraft and naval vessels "to make no attacks on North Vietnam, except in the area north of the Demilitarized Zone where the continuing enemy buildup directly threatens allied forward positions." This meant a stop to the bombing of areas inhabited by almost 90 per cent of the North Vietnamese population. "I call upon President Ho Chi Minh," Johnson said, "to respond positively, and favorably, to this new step toward peace." Qualifying this appeal with the assertion that the United States would not accept any "fake solution," he announced minor troop additions and efforts to strengthen the South Vietnamese army. Johnson cagily reserved his greatest surprise to the very end of his speech. After emphasizing the need to heal political divisions, he said: "Accordingly, I shall not seek, and I will not accept, the nomination of my party for another term as your President."

Ho Chi Minh responded with unexpected promptness to the President's peace overture. On April 3 the Hanoi government announced its willingness to establish contacts and explore the possibilities of formal negotiations. Since there was deep suspicion on both sides, however, each subsequent step was a painful one. For a month the two governments wrangled over a meeting site with each side trying to choose one likely to have a favorable atmosphere for its own case; at long last they decided on Paris. It was in that city, accordingly, that on May 10 an American delegation headed by the veteran diplomat Averell Harriman began face-to-face talks with a North Vietnamese group headed by Xuan Thuy, former foreign minister of the Hanoi government. But even then the talks were considered to be exploratory discussions rather than formal peace negotiations. Each side stipulated conditions that must be met before serious parleying could begin. The North Vietnamese insisted that there must be a complete rather than a partial halt to the bombing of their country; the United States refused to consider any further step until North Vietnam reduced the level of its own military operations. Equally serious was the dispute over who should participate in the formal peace talks: North Vietnam refused to sit down with representatives from Hanoi; the United States would not admit the NFL, or Vietcong, as a party.

This stalemate at Paris seriously hampered the Democratic presidential campaign. In a tumultuous convention at Chicago, Vice President Hubert Humphrey had gained the presidential nomination, but the bitterness of the defeated doves made his election doubtful unless there were a speedy turn for the better in the Paris talks. On the other hand, Johnson could not afford to make too many concessions to the Communists. If he accepted terms that seemed humiliating to the national honor, the Republican candidate, Richard Nixon, would be certain to make this a major issue.

On October 31—just before the election, when Presidents like to time their dramatic announcements—Johnson ordered a complete halt to the bombing of North Vietnam. As its contribution to the new peace effort, the Hanoi government consented to the participation of the Saigon government in future negotiations. Besides these public commitments, there was apparently some kind of tacit understanding between Washington and Hanoi. The bombing halt would continue only if North Vietnam respected the demilitarized zone and refrained from attacks on the South Vietnamese cities. Although the bombing halt made the election closer than had been expected, it came too late to save the presidency for the Democrats.

Johnson would still have liked to bring the peace negotiations to a successful conclusion before he turned over the White House to Nixon on January 20, 1969. But at Paris one wrangle followed another. A dispute over the shape of the conference table seemed the most absurd quibble of all. Involved in such debates, however, were symbolic issues of real significance, involving the rival claims of the Saigon regime and the NFL to be the rightful government of South Vietnam. By the time Johnson left office, the conferees had compromised on a round table, but nothing else had been settled and the ground war in Vietnam was still taking sickening toll of American and Vietnamese lives.

Vietnamizing the War

In February, 1968, in one of his earliest campaign speeches, Richard Nixon promised to "end the war and win the peace in Vietnam." Thereafter he continued to insist that he had a plan for achieving this dual goal but refused to reveal its details. After he became President, he was confronted with the usual problem of choosing between radically different alternatives. The Joint Chiefs of Staff and General Creighton Abrams, the American commander in Vietnam, continued to urge strong measures to force the enemy to surrender; the new Secretary of State, William Rogers, hoped to end the war through diplomacy; the new Secretary of Defense, Melvin Laird, wanted to reduce the number of American troops in Vietnam to quiet public opinion at home. More powerful than any of these officials was Professor Henry Kissinger of Harvard, a brilliant analyst of international relations, whom Nixon installed in the White House as his chief adviser on foreign policy. Neither hawk nor dove, Kissinger was a skillful technician, adept at both clarifying the options for Nixon and implementing the President's decisions.

At first, Nixon had some hope of an early breakthrough in the peace negotiations. He replaced Harriman as chief negotiator at Paris with Henry Cabot Lodge, who had served two separate stints as Ambassador to Saigon. But the two sides speedily took up positions from which neither would budge. On May 14, 1969, Nixon stated his terms in a TV speech: the United

States and North Vietnam should agree on a policy of mutual withdrawal of their forces from South Vietnam, and the voters of that country should select their future government in internationally supervised elections. To most Americans, the Nixon plan sounded democratic and fair; to the Communists, however, it must have seemed a replay of the Geneva agreement of 1954 that had been sabotaged by American agents and South Vietnamese politicians and generals. The Communists insisted upon a complete withdrawal of American forces and the installation at Saigon of a coalition government that would include the NLF.

Nixon had hoped to use the reduction of American troop strength in Vietnam as a bargaining point in the Paris negotiations, but the domestic political situation would not permit delay. In the spring of 1969 there was a force of 543,000 men in South Vietnam, and almost 34,000 Americans had already lost their lives with a continuing casualty rate of almost 200 deaths a week. Whatever transpired at Paris, the Nixon administration had determined on a policy of "Vietnamization"—that is, of building up the South Vietnamese army and handing over to it more and more of the fighting, while Nixon gradually withdrew American combat troops. After meeting with President Thieu on the island of Midway, Nixon announced that he would withdraw the first 25,000 American troops by August 31, 1969.

By this gesture the President hoped both to blunt antiwar criticism at home and to induce concessions from Hanoi. On neither front did he win any measurable ground. Even after the death of Ho Chi Minh on September

Midway Island meeting between President Nixon and President Thieu of South Vietnam, 1969. (UPI Photo.)

3, 1969, the North Vietnamese government stuck to its course. Meanwhile, demonstrations against the war mounted in size and fervor. On October 15, 1969, hundreds of thousands participated in the first "moratorium" day. University students cut classes, and older protestors joined with them in marches and meetings, calling for an immediate cease-fire and withdrawal of American forces. A second moratorium on November 15 drew still larger crowds. Some 250,000 persons went to Washington for a massive demonstration, culminating in a three-day march from Arlington National Cemetery to Capitol Hill.

On November 3, 1969, President Nixon denounced the demonstrators in an angry TV speech. Appealing for support from what he called "the great Silent Majority," he declared that he would be untrue to his oath of office if he allowed his policy to be dictated by the minority who were mounting demonstrations in the streets. Vice President Spiro Agnew went still further in condemning the antiwar students as "effete snobs" and "rotten apples." Although the Nixon-Agnew rhetoric angered the liberals, it undoubtedly pleased many other people in the country. Whether or not there was a silent majority supporting the President, millions of Americans—not only business people but construction and factory workers—visibly resented the antiwar demonstrators. Public opinion in the country was becoming dangerously polarized, with still more serious confrontations to come.

Despite the President's disdain for the antiwar faction, he persisted in his Vietnamization policy. Every few months he would announce a further reduction in American troop strength in Vietnam. Not really trusting the President but awaiting further developments, the antiwar faction slackened off its activities until a new surprise from the White House triggered the most serious protests of the entire war. On April 30, 1970, Nixon announced that he had ordered American troops into eastern Cambodia to destroy the sanctuaries long used by the North Vietnamese to build up forces and equipment for incursions into South Vietnam. Although the President promised that the American forces would withdraw as soon as their mission was accomplished, he seemed to be deliberately fanning the flames of war by his speech. "We will not be humiliated," he declared. "We will not be defeated. If when the chips are down the United States acts like a pitiful helpless giant, the forces of totalitarianism and anarchy will threaten free nations and free institutions throughout the world." He would rather be a one-term President, he said, than see America become a "second-rate power" and accept "the first defeat in its proud 190-year history."

On military grounds, the campaign in Cambodia had some plausible justification. Rather than being inconsistent with Vietnamization, it was intended to reduce the risk of Communist attack during the crucial period when American forces were being withdrawn and the burden of defense was being transferred to the South Vietnamese army. Moreover, some action seemed to be necessary to keep the Communists from taking over all of Cambodia. A recent right-wing coup had overthrown the government of Prince Sihanouk, who had purchased a precarious neutrality by closing his eyes to Communist operations along the Vietnamese border and to American bombing raids—unreported at the time. Now the anti-Communist Lon Nol was in power, but the Communists were threatening to drive him out.

Whatever military justification the Cambodian venture had, it was a slap in the face to all opponents of the war. Just when Nixon was supposedly winding down the conflict, he had extended it to another country. In the subsequent wave of protests, the National Guard killed four students at Kent State University in northeastern Ohio. By the end of the week student protests had forced the closing of 426 colleges and universities. Many of them did not resume normal classes or examinations for the rest of the semester. Once again thousands of demonstrators traveled to Washington to express their condemnation of the President's policy.

On May 30, 1970, with its mission at least partially accomplished, the last United States ground troops withdrew from Cambodia, leaving anti-Communist operations in the uncertain hands of Lon Nol's forces and the South Vietnamese, supported by American helicopters and planes. Thereafter, Vietnamization continued—very much to Nixon's political advantage at home. By the fall of 1971 American forces in Vietnam were down to around 200,000 and weekly casualty figures were sometimes as low as eight deaths. But what of the other half of the Vietnamization policy? Was the South Vietnamese army getting strong enough to "hack it alone"—in Nixon's phrase? A test came in February, 1971, when it invaded eastern Laos in an attempt to cut off the Ho Chi Minh trail, the vital supply route for the North Vietnamese troops in South Vietnam. Despite support by American helicopters and planes, the South Vietnamese forces suffered heavy losses and withdrew at the end of six weeks. And if South Vietnamese progress in

A casualty of the confrontation of antiwar protesters and National Guardsmen at Kent State University, 1970. (UPI Photo.)

military affairs was unimpressive, its advance in democracy was even less so. In October, 1971, President Thieu was re-elected without opposition, when all potential rivals withdrew from the contest in desperation.

Events in Vietnam soured American opinion still further. Within Congress the moderates began to vote with the doves on significant issues. In a classic example of locking the barn door after the horse was stolen, Congress late in 1970 voted to deny funds for any further American ground operations in Cambodia and repealed the Tonkin Gulf resolution. Outside of Congress the mood was one of frustration and anger. In March, 1971, a military court-martial found Lieutenant William Calley guilty of premeditated murder of twenty-two South Vietnamese men, women, and children at Mylai and sentenced him to life imprisonment. Although the evidence against Calley was damning, both hawks and doves attacked the decision. To the hawks, Calley was a war hero, being punished for his zeal in wiping out probable and potential Communists; to the doves, he was a scapegoat, being punished for his minor part in the much larger crimes being committed by Presidents and generals. President Nixon intervened in the case by ordering Calley to be confined in comfortable quarters rather than in military prison while his case was being appealed and by promising to make the final review in person. To many critics, Nixon seemed to be playing politics at the expense of the whole system of military justice.

As the 1972 election approached, Nixon needed a Vietnam settlement more and more. But the Paris peace talks remained deadlocked, and in the spring of 1972 the Communists launched their most powerful offensive since the Tet drive of 1968. With most of the American ground troops now withdrawn and the burden of defense upon the South Vietnamese, the Communists quickly overran Quangtri province in the northern part of the country and made serious advances in the central and southern parts as well. Some South Vietnamese units broke in panicky flight from the enemy. Only with the help of intensive bombing by American planes did the defenders finally stabilize the situation and win back some of the lost territory.

With the whole Vietnamization program in jeopardy, President Nixon once again resorted to drastic action. Claiming that Communist escalation of the war had violated the implicit understanding under which Johnson had halted the bombing of North Vietnam, American planes resumed attacks north of the DMZ, first with sporadic retaliatory raids, then with sustained bombing. In a TV speech on May 8, 1972, Nixon announced still more serious steps. To cut off Soviet and Chinese arms reaching the enemy by sea, he ordered the mining of Haiphong and other North Vietnamese ports; to cut off the land routes from China he sent planes on massive attacks against railroads, highways, and bridges. Tough though these measures were, the President offered more lenient peace terms than ever before. If the Communists would release American prisoners of war and agree to an internationally supervised cease-fire, the United States would halt all acts of war and withdraw all American forces within four months.

Nixon's new measures involved serious risks since they challenged Russia and China more directly than had any previous American action in the war. But the two great Communist nations—each for its own sake courting American favor that spring—did nothing more than grumble at American attempts to cut off their help to North Vietnam. And American public opinion accepted with only minor protests this re-escalation of the war. Although the new bombing attacks subjected a small nation to even more devastating attacks than the Johnson-ordered raids, most Americans seemed so hardened to the horror that they shrugged off the news. At least, the killing and wounding of Americans had been checked. In August, 1972, the last American ground combat unit in Vietnam was deactivated, leaving some 39,000 other American troops in the country as well as a vast array of air power based on Thailand and on navy carriers. Only in Hanoi did Nixon's policy seem of dubious effectiveness. Despite the terrible costs and the hardening attitude of Russia and China, the North Vietnamese government still fought on, insisting that there could be no cease-fire or freeing of American prisoners of war until a new government was installed in Saigon.

Cease-Fire

Even while the American bombing of North Vietnam and heavy fighting in South Vietnam continued, Henry Kissinger met frequently in Paris with Le Duc Tho, a high-ranking emissary of the Hanoi government. On October 8, 1972, Tho broke the diplomatic stalemate by a significant concession. No longer insisting on a new government in Saigon, he offered to accept an internationally supervised cease-fire and promised the release of American prisoners of war in return for the withdrawal of American forces from Vietnam. Since these terms were roughly in line with those that President Nixon had outlined in his speech of May 8, Kissinger quickly accepted them. Why had the Communists modified their position? It was widely assumed that the approaching American election influenced their decision. Convinced that Nixon would be returned to office, they had reason to believe that it would be easier to deal with him before the election than after. Moscow and Peking probably used their influence to support this reasoning. Moreover, under the terms of the proposed settlement, the Communists would remain in a fairly strong position since they would be in occupation of large areas of the South Vietnamese countryside. Indeed this and other terms were so little to President Thieu's liking that he was very reluctant to go along with the proposed settlement.

Although negotiations among the parties had hitherto been secret, the Hanoi government tried to hasten events by announcing the terms of a nine-point agreement. According to the Communists, the United States had promised to sign this on October 31. In a Washington press conference on October 26 Kissinger warned that some further negotiations would be required to discuss points raised by Thieu and to clarify other details. But Kissinger did not dispute the Communist claim that a settlement was near. "We believe that peace is at hand," he said. Peace was "within reach in a matter of weeks or less." Bathed in the euphoria resulting from this statement, the American voters went to the polls twelve days later. The role of peacemaker which McGovern was so eagerly seeking fell more firmly than ever into the hands of Nixon instead.

However, the American public had still another two months of frustration ahead of it. Going back into conference supposedly only to work out a few final details, Kissinger and Tho became involved in several weeks of haggling instead. Each side blamed the other for reneging on the earlier terms and seeking unacceptable changes. On December 16 Kissinger announced that the negotiations had been broken off, and two days later the United States resumed massive bombing in the Hanoi-Haiphong area. Even though the objectives were supposed to be transportation centers and military installations, the newspapers were filled with harrowing descriptions of the heaviest raids of the war resulting in many civilian casualties and the destruction of a hospital. Nor were the victims of the intensified hostilities all Vietnamese; the Air Force announced the loss of 15 giant B-52 bombers with 93 airmen killed, captured, or wounded during 12 days of heavy bombing.

In January Nixon again halted air raids north of the twentieth parallel and Kissinger and Tho resumed their talks in Paris. This time the negotiators found the necessary words to settle or paper over their differences. In a TV address on the evening of January 23, 1973, the President announced that an agreement had been initialed. Secretary of State Rogers emerged from off stage along with other dignitaries to participate in the formal signing ceremony on January 27. This was an absurdly complicated affair because it involved four parties—the United States, North Vietnam, the Thieu government, and the Vietcong, with the last two of these each claiming to be a legal government and refusing to recognize the credentials of the other.

Except in face-saving verbal formulas the Paris Accord differed very little from the abortive agreement announced in October. Fighting was to cease throughout Vietnam at 7 P.M., Eastern Standard Time, on January 27. Two supervisory bodies were to facilitate the truce: a Joint Military Commission composed of representatives of the four belligerents—the United States, North Vietnam, Saigon government, Vietcong—and an International Commission for Control and Supervision with personnel sent in by four outside powers—Canada, Hungary, Indonesia, and Poland. The United States promised to withdraw all military forces from Vietnam within sixty days and to remove or deactivate all its mines off the coasts. All parties agreed to release their prisoners of war; the Communists were to return the first group of American POWs within fifteen days and all the rest within sixty days. Carefully phrased pieties provided for the political future of Vietnam: the United States recognized "the unity and territorial integrity of Vietnam"; nevertheless, the demilitarized zone was to be retained as a provisional military demarcation line. The United States and North Vietnam both recognized "the South Vietnamese people's right to self-determination." The Saigon government was to remain in power pending an election to be organized by a "National Council of National Reconciliation and Concord" made up of representatives of three groups: the Saigon government, the Vietcong, and neutralists.

Would the truce bring true peace or only new forms of conflict to the tortured country? Although the accord provided for the presence of some four thousand supervisory personnel, these would have neither the legal authority nor adequate force to compel the rival Vietnamese factions to lay down their arms unless they wanted to. Indeed, the first weeks of the cease-fire witnessed much loss of life in a bitter struggle for control of strategic hamlets. It was equally doubtful whether the South Vietnamese people would really get the opportunity to decide their own future in free and honest elections. But at least the truce permitted the United States to withdraw its forces—"with honor," as the President never tired of announcing to the country—and to get back its prisoners of war. The first group of 142 released POWs were flown to Clark Air Base in the Philippines in February. Found to be in generally good physical and mental condition, the men were rapidly returned to the United States for reunion with their families. Release of a second group of prisoners was slightly delayed because of Hanoi's accusations of truce violations but finally took place the first week in March. Still another shaky step toward peace was provided at an international conference in Paris, where twelve nations, including the Soviet Union, France, Britain, Communist China, Poland, Hungary, Canada, Indonesia, and the four belligerents gave their approval to the cease-fire.

These events gave President Nixon a welcome opportunity to dramatize his role as peacemaker. Just as President Theodore Roosevelt had spoken softly and waved a big stick, Nixon had combined offers to negotiate with decisive acts of force—the invasion of Cambodia, the mining of the harbors, and the massive bombing raids. Although the Communists remained in control of large parts of South Vietnam, Nixon had provided the Thieu government with a chance of survival—a chance increased by very large deliveries of aircraft and other military equipment just before the cease-fire went into effect.

Nixon's many critics, however, were not convinced that the agreements at Paris and the return of the prisoners proved that his policies had been right all along and that those who had opposed them had been wrong. Critics charged that with more flexibility Nixon might have achieved peace in 1969 on terms not much different from those of 1973. They believed that the President's stubbornness had extended the war and kept the American prisoners in captivity for four years, cost thousands of American lives, and prolonged the agony for the people of both North and South Vietnam.

Obviously the psychic wounds left by the Vietnam conflict would remain painful for many years to come. But at least the sad drama seemed to be coming to a close. When Lyndon Johnson, so central a figure in the tragedy, died the day before the truce was announced, it seemed an event of symbolic fitness.

An Uncertain Future

As all students of the area had predicted, the cease-fire did not really end the struggle for control of Indochina. Although American forces left South Vietnam, the rival factions continued to jostle for advantage. Thieu's army was strong enough to retain or retake most of the disputed hamlets, but the Communists not only continued to hold large sections of the country but moved in additional troops and arms from North Vietnam. The International Control Commission proved helpless to prevent violations of the truce, and the Communists justified their actions on the ground that the Americans had rushed in large quantities of armaments to the Thieu government just before the cease-fire. One side's disregard of the truce provided the excuse for the other side to avoid compliance; accordingly, the Americans procrastinated in clearing their mines from North Vietnamese waters.

In such an atmosphere the promised negotiations among the South Vietnamese factions to arrange for new elections amounted to nothing. It seemed more probable that the future of the country would sooner or later be decided by a renewal of hostilities. Nevertheless, the tireless Kissinger continued to try through diplomacy to make the truce work. In June, 1973, he and Le Duc Tho signed a new accord in Paris, under which North Vietnam pledged once again to co-operate in carrying out the cease-fire; for its part, the United States promised to stop reconnaissance flights over North Vietnam and to complete the clearing of the mines.

The January cease-fire had contained no more than pious hopes in its references to Laos and Cambodia. In both these countries civil war continued, with North Vietnam providing help for the Communists and the United States flying bombing missions for the government forces. In Laos serious negotiations among the various factions finally brought the fighting to at least a temporary halt, but in Cambodia the situation continued to be chaotic. The Lon Nol government was weak and corrupt; its army lacked the will to fight. The Communists already held a large portion of the country, and only the efforts of the American air force seemed to prevent their gaining control of the rest. Heavy American bombing continued day after day. Confident of public support in the afterglow of the prisoner-of-war return, the Nixon administration brushed aside criticism and continued its attacks in an effort to force the Cambodian Communists to accept a Vietnam-type truce.

But the longer the bombing continued, the greater became the danger that the United States would become ever more deeply involved in trying to save Lon Nol. Determined not to permit a rerun of the Vietnam horror story, Congressional opponents of the administration policy eventually forced Nixon to modify his course. Weakened by the revelations about the Watergate affair and losing the support of several prominent Republican legislators, the Nixon faithfuls could not round up enough votes to prevent the passage of anti-bombing bills during May and June, 1973. The House of Representatives, in the past more hawkish than the Senate, now joined the Upper House in attaching to general appropriation measures prohibitions against using funds for bombing in Cambodia. With the President determined to veto all such curbs and Congress promising to attach them to one proposed law after another, the issue threatened to paralyze the government. To escape from this impasse, Nixon and his opponents worked out a compromise under which the President promised to end all such bombing after August 15, 1973. Apparently, the day when American Presidents could call the tune in Indochina was drawing to a close. For better or worse, the people of this troubled area were to be left alone to work out their own destiny.

The Nixon administration had to concentrate its hopes on continued betterment of American relations with Russia and China. Since both Communist nations were eager to improve their trade relations with the United States, American policy-makers obviously hoped that they would exert a restraining influence on the Communists of Indochina. Beset by domestic difficulties in June, 1973, President Nixon eagerly welcomed Leonid Brezhnev when the Russian leader visited Washington and California. The agreements announced between the two governments amounted to little more than promises to continue disarmament negotiations and to seek increased trade and cultural contacts. Although neither side made any public commitments about Indochina, there was hope that both now perceived mutual advantage in damping down explosive forces not only in this troublesome spot but in the much more dangerous region of the Middle East.

31

THE COMPUTER AGE AND ITS CRITICS

To California residents still planning to vote, it was sometimes a minor annoyance to watch NBC or CBS television confidently announce that the final results of the election could already be predicted on the basis of scattered early returns from other parts of the country. The race between the computers of the rival networks often seemed more frantic than that between the politicians themselves. But presidential elections were only one of many areas of American life now being computerized. Computers guided spacemen to the moon, checked income tax returns, compounded bank interest, compiled student records, dispatched trains, and processed research. data.

Many sensitive people, especially college students, saw in the computer a hateful symbol of modern technology. To them, the modern compulsion to express everything in numbers to be fed into machines seemed a destruction of precious human values—values such as love, compassion, beauty, dignity, and freedom. Refusing to allow their lives to be programmed, the rebels sought ways to dramatize their independence and autonomy.

Rise of the Smart Machines

Although generally a destructive force in history, war undoubtedly accelerates the progress of science and technology. During World War II, mathematicians slaving over ballistic tables for new weapons demanded faster and more sophisticated electronic calculators than the simple ones then in use. To meet this need, Harvard scientists cooperated with engineers from the International Business Machines Corporation (IBM) to construct the pioneer Mark I Calculator at Harvard in 1944. Although this huge machine was cumbersome in operation and subject to frequent breakdowns, it inspired efforts to develop better machines in the postwar years. Professor John von Neumann of the Institute for Advanced Study at Princeton made particularly important contributions. At first each computer was specially built for some defense agency or major research center, but during the 1950's IBM and other companies began to produce standard models that they sold, or more often leased, to government agencies, insurance companies, business firms, and universities.

Although still very expensive to operate, the computers were so speedy and so ingenious in their ability to store data and carry through complicated programs that they went into rapid use. Computers made possible the split-second precision with which rockets projected space vehicles into flight, landed them on the moon at a specific time and place, and returned them safely to earth. And—a far less comforting thought—computers made it certain that intercontinental ballistic missiles could destroy Moscow or Washington any time that the ruling authorities issued the orders. Yet however grim the computers' capacity for destruction, their peacetime utility was undeniable. In the field of medicine, for example, the great machines speedily processed data important for tracing the causes of disease, the efficacy and safety of new drugs, and the diagnosis of ailments. Hospitals and medical centers too small to have computers of their own could feed data into research centers hundreds of miles away and get back almost instantaneous answers.

World War II also speeded up the use of so-called cybernetic controls. These involved instruments that registered information and transmitted appropriate orders. (The simple thermostat maintaining a constant temperature by calling for more or less heat provides an example.) By using the "feedback" principle, these instruments continually adjusted the process to incoming information. Such cybernetic controls made possible highly accurate antiaircraft guns, rocket-fired missiles that changed course in flight, and much more effective torpedoes for submarines and destroyers. Cybernetic control also had many important peacetime uses. Machines that could inspect their own output and adjust themselves pointed toward the increasing automation of industry.

Another highly significant development was "systems analysis." This involved breaking down a major project like sending spacemen to the moon into the hundreds of component projects that were necessary to achieve the ultimate goal. Each "system," in turn, could be analyzed into its "sub-

A model computer installation. (Courtesy IBM.)

systems." Systems analysis made it possible not only to accomplish enormously difficult new tasks, but to administer more effectively many older enterprises. Business executives radically reformed the operations of their companies, and Robert McNamara, as Secretary of Defense, used systems analysis in an attempt to impose order on the whole vast military establishment.

The Space Race

When President Kennedy coined the campaign slogan "New Frontier," it was obvious that it might refer to many different areas of effort. Not least among these was the frontier of outer space. Challenged by Russia's dramatic launching of *Sputnik* in 1957, the Eisenhower administration had taken steps to accelerate American missile development. In 1958 Congress had created a National Aeronautics and Space Administration (NASA), and during the last three years of the Eisenhower administration a score of American satellites had been hurled into orbit bearing ingenious electronic equipment that transmitted back to earth a great variety of scientific information.

Yet American opinion was far from satisfied with the progress of the space program. All too frequently reporters drawn to Florida's Cape Canaveral (now Cape Kennedy) to witness a missile launching had only a disappointing failure to report. And the modest achievements of the American program compared poorly with the dramatic accomplishments announced from Russia. In 1959, a Soviet space vehicle hit the moon, and another passed around the moon in orbit, sending back photographs of the dark side. The most startling Soviet triumph of all was the first manned space flight in April, 1961, when Major Yuri Gagarin was hurled into orbit and returned safely to the ground after circling the earth.

Even before the Gagarin flight, President Kennedy had attempted to accelerate the space program by appointing the energetic James E. Webb as director of NASA and delegating Vice President Johnson to head a Space Council with broad supervisory powers. On May 25, 1961, the President took much more challenging action. Appearing before Congress to discuss several urgent problems, he said:

I believe that this nation should commit itself to achieving the goal before this decade is out, of landing a man on the moon and returning him safely to earth. No single space project in this period will be more impressive to mankind or more important to the long-range exploration of space; and none will be so difficult or expensive to accomplish.

Accepting with little debate the idea of racing the Russians to the moon, Congress passed greatly increased appropriations for NASA, and the nation soon had evidence of progress. On May 5, 1961—three weeks before the Kennedy appeal—Commander Alan B. Shepard, Jr., made the first American manned space flight of some three hundred miles. Nine months later, on February 20, 1962, Lieutenant Colonel John H. Glenn became the first American to be hurled into orbit. Safely completing three circuits around the earth, Glenn became a hero to the nationwide audience which followed his venture on TV. Several other successful flights soon followed with the 22-orbit mission of Major Gordon Cooper on May 15–16, 1963, being particularly impressive in its competence and precision.

Yet American satisfaction with these achievements was tempered by the evidence that the Russians still led in many aspects of the space race. Before Glenn made his 3-orbit flight, a Russian cosmonaut had made a 17-orbit one. Before Cooper made his 22-orbit flight, the Russians had succeeded in placing two space vehicles in orbit at the same time, with one of them completing 64 orbits. And most colorful of all was the Russian extravaganza of June, 1963—a few weeks after the Cooper flight—when the world's first woman astronaut circled the earth 48 times, while her male counterpart was completing a fantastic 81 orbits.

Watching these developments, Americans took what comfort they could from the fable of the tortoise and the hare. They could only hope that behind the scenes American scientists were doing the necessary homework to bring about a breakthrough in the staggering problems involved in an actual expedition to the moon. Meantime, some Americans began to have misgivings about the whole idea. Was victory in the moon race important enough to justify so large an expenditure of money and time? Would not a similar effort in the fields of education, urban renewal, and health bring greater benefits to the nation? Even President Kennedy appeared to have moments of hesitation. Addressing the UN General Assembly on September 20, 1963, he asked: "Why . . . should man's first trip to the moon be a matter of national competition?" Instead of wasteful. Soviet-American rivalry, he urged a cooperative conquest of space, "sending some day in this decade to the moon, not the representative of a single nation, but the representatives of all humanity." Timed to take advantage of a thaw in the cold war following the signing of the test-ban treaty, the President's suggestion was highly logical but had no significant results.

Whether it was rational or not, the United States and the Soviet Union continued their space efforts in a spirit of rivalry. Undoubtedly this competitive spirit reflected the expansive foreign policies of the two nations. Each sought to prove to the world the superiority of its political and social system. And the American people themselves seemed to crave this reassurance—however dubious might be the evidence of moral worth to be provided by landing the first man on the moon. In 1965 the American taxpayers began to get the first returns on their investment in a series of two-man Gemini flights. Every few months American astronauts captured the headlines with some new exploit, while Russian efforts seemed to be bogging down in unexplained difficulties. Tragedy hit both nations in 1967: three American spacemen lost their lives in a flash fire that destroyed a new spacecraft being tested on its launching pad; and a Russian cosmonaut crashed to his death when his vehicle's re-entry parachute snarled.

The American accident delayed work on the Apollo, the ingenious craft composed of multistaged rockets, space vehicle, and landing module being developed for the actual flight to the moon. But 1968 was another year of triumphs. In October Captain Walter Schirra, Jr., and two other men circled the earth 163 times in the first manned Apollo flight. This was so successful that in December—earlier than had been originally planned—Colonel Frank Borman led the memorable Apollo 9 flight that orbited around the moon ten times, taking pictures of extraordinary beauty and radioing a Christmas Eve message back to earth.

After two more successful trial flights, the Apollo 11 expedition actually landed men on the moon on July 20, 1969. Neil Armstrong, the civilian commander, was the first to set foot on the strange new soil, and he was soon joined by Colonel Edwin Aldrin, Jr. Millions of people in all parts of the world watched the triumphant moment on television and listened to the messages exchanged between the astronauts and President Nixon. The return trip was successfully performed: the landing module safely rejoined the command module in which the third member of the crew, Colonel Michael Collins, had been orbiting, and the parachute-supported capsule finally splashed down in the Pacific close to a waiting aircraft carrier.

This impressive victory for American science and technology led to several subsequent expeditions. The second trip to the moon in November, 1969, went with the same smoothness as the first, but a third attempt in April, 1970, gave the nation several anxious days when serious mechanical difficulties developed. Although they orbited the moon, the astronauts had to give up their plan for a landing and return to earth. The safe recovery of the crew after this mishap demonstrated the ability of NASA to meet an

Man's first visit to the moon, 1969. (Courtesy NASA.)

unexpected crisis, but the American public nevertheless lost much of its relish for this dangerous and expensive game. Congress made drastic cuts in appropriations, and NASA had to sharply reduce the force of scientists, engineers, and workmen who had found employment in this boom industry of the 1960's.

Space exploration regained some of its prestige with two successful trips to the moon in 1971 and another in 1972. By using an electric vehicle the astronauts were able to extend the range of their explorations and to collect a great variety of rock samples. Through studying these moon rocks geologists hoped to answer important questions about the early history of this earth satellite. The space program also contributed to many other aspects of science, such as the study of cloud formations, cosmic energy, and radiation belts and the mapping of geological formations and ocean currents. As the moon missions drew to a close, NASA had to define new goals. Should it press for its more exotic agenda—sending men to Mars or other planets? Or would it confine itself to more modest proposals for exploring distant goals through unmanned, instrument-transmitting vehicles and for designing permanent space stations to serve as orbiting laboratories?

Crisis in Education

During the 1960's all levels of education continued their rapid growth. Between 1961 and 1971 elementary school enrollment climbed from 33 million to 36.4 million, high school enrollment from 11 million to 15.2 million, and college enrollment from 3.7 million to 8.5 million—more than double. Since the birth rate fell during the decade—from 23.7 per 1,000 population in 1960 to 17.5 in 1968—it was predictable that during the seventies school enrollment would not continue to grow at anything like the same rate. Indeed, in the fall of 1972, the elementary schools had 500,000 fewer pupils than they had had in 1971—thus beginning a shrinkage that would undoubtedly be reflected within a few years in lower high school and college enrollments.

While it lasted, however, this gigantic demand for education created gigantic problems for the suppliers—school districts, state colleges and universities, and private institutions. In the cities many schoolhouses were grim factory-like structures built half a century earlier and now marred by broken windows, scarred desks, and crumbling plaster. In the suburbs school construction could scarcely keep up with the rapidly increasing population of the villages and towns. From every direction came pressing demands for new buildings. And the price of these soared—partly because of rapidly increasing construction costs, partly because educators were recommending more attractive and better-equipped buildings.

Expenditures for salaries also increased greatly. Historically an underpaid group, teachers became much more assertive in their demands for better pay and lighter work loads. Many of them joined unions and insisted on their right to collective bargaining. Teachers' strikes—unheard of in earlier years—became relatively common in the late sixties and early seventies, despite the efforts of some state legislatures to make them illegal.

Sometimes teachers' unions encountered the hostility of black community groups seeking to institute their own educational programs and to control the hiring and firing of teachers.

The rising cost of education created critical political problems. Although most states provided some measure of aid to the local school districts, the major burden remained upon the shoulders of the local taxpayers. Mayors and city councils struggled with the almost impossible task of finding the money in their budgets, not only for the urgent needs of education, but also for rising welfare costs and the demands of policemen and firemen for fairer pay schedules. The cities not only raised real estate taxes to their legal limits—often driving more property owners to the suburbs in the process—but levied high sales taxes and other local excises. Even to stand still in the face of these needs the cities desperately needed more help from the state legislatures and Congress, but it was dangerously slow in coming, in part because of continuing rural hostility and suspicion. Even in the suburbs and country places the rising costs of education created serious problems. Frightened property owners were particularly likely to focus their frustrations on the district school budget. Sometimes rejecting one revised budget after another, local taxpayers forced cutbacks in school construction and the elimination of special programs. Many local groups were eager to apply the hatchet to what they considered "frills" in the schools.

Meanwhile, Catholic parochial schools were going through their own crisis. They confronted all the problems of the public schools—antiquated and overcrowded buildings, new communities, high costs—and some others peculiarly their own. Hitherto they had depended on nuns and brothers in the various religious orders to do most of their teaching. Now fewer young people were choosing religious vocations, and the Catholic schools had to employ more lay teachers. Although salary scales in the parochial schools were usually lower than in the public ones, the shift from clerical to lay teachers greatly increased school expenses. Catholic administrators could not greatly increase the tuition charges being paid by working class parents, nor could they risk bankrupting other diocesan resources. Increasingly, therefore, they turned to the state and federal governments for help, despite constitutional and traditional bans on such use of tax funds. Mindful of the Catholic vote, politicians showed increasing ingenuity in devising formulas for indirect aid, but the help was not enough to save some of the parochial schools. Facing insoluble problems, Catholic bishops had to close certain institutions, simply transferring responsibility for their pupils to the public schools.

Public expenditures for higher education also went up sharply during the 1960's. Throughout the country the states were enlarging their state universities, transforming older teacher preparatory institutions into standard four-year colleges, and founding scores of new two-year community colleges. For a few years new campuses and new buildings sprang up almost overnight. Yet here too rebellious taxpayers were in a mood to call a halt by the end of the decade. Not daring to vote further tax increases, the state legislatures began to be much more resistant to the budget requests of the college administrations.

Private colleges and universities had still greater financial problems. They too felt the need for new dormitories, classroom buildings, and libraries to meet the extraordinary educational demands of the day. They had to make a major effort in raising faculty salaries. And all their other costs were soaring too—for student services, for custodial and secretarial help, for the rental of computers and the purchase of other expensive equipment, for more and more administrators. The private institutions raised tuition almost every year, beseeched their alumni for gifts, sought out wealthy donors—both individual and corporate, and applied to the Ford Foundation and similar philanthropic funds for grants.

Both public and private universities found a welcome resource in "sponsored research." In a technological society, the processing of knowledge was a valuable commodity. Various government agencies needed to have data collected and analyzed; many business corporations had similar needs. Sponsors in the market for such research signed contracts with "research corporations," legally separate from the universities but closely associated with them. The research corporations employed university professors and graduate students, usually on a part-time basis. Sponsored research, therefore, provided a direct subsidy to graduate education in certain fields and additionally provided "overhead"—or profit—that could be utilized for other university needs. Despite the life-saving blood transfusion thus given to university budgets, many educators deplored the growth of so much sponsored research as a kind of cancerous growth. They felt that it built up the physical sciences, medicine, engineering, and other "practical" fields at the expense of the humanities and the social sciences and encouraged the formulation of research proposals designed to attract financial support rather than to serve the advancement of knowledge.

Even with sponsored research, university administrators found their financial problems increasingly oppressive. By the early seventies many prestigious private institutions were operating with an annual deficit and were cutting down staff and faculty. In this field as in other areas of education, only the federal government seemed to have the potential resources adequate to meet the emergency. Yet with the Republicans in charge of the executive branch and with the Democratic majority in Congress divided on the form and amount that aid to education should take, prospects for a bold and imaginative attack upon the problems of education seemed dim in the early seventies.

Campus Protests

In addition to all their other troubles, college administrators had to contend with "nonnegotiable" student demands and accompanying pressure mobilized through picket lines, marches, mass meetings, boycotted classes, the seizure of campus buildings, and even the capture of deans. The student protest movement first exploded on the Berkeley campus of the University of California in December, 1964, spread to more and more institutions, and finally culminated in the widespread student strikes of the spring of 1970.

The student rebellion had highly complex causes—some arising out of conditions within the universities themselves, others rooted in the Vietnam war and other critical problems of the sixties. Many students objected bitterly to the factory-like methods of higher education—large classes, inaccessible professors, archaic course requirements, irrelevant subject matter. Still more frequently they complained about their living conditions—barracks-like dormitories, tasteless food, and rules that cramped their desire for independence and autonomy. The students demanded a greater say in all matters that concerned them.

Students and professors were the first groups to demand an end to United States involvement in Vietnam. Students were particularly upset by the prospect of being conscripted to fight in what they regarded as an immoral war. During most of these years they constituted a special group protected by the prevailing system of draft deferments. This often kept boys in college who would have preferred not to have gone or to have dropped out. Indeed, graduate students sometimes seemed to drag out their studies year after year, just to avoid the draft. Yet conscription still hung over student heads like a threatening sword; for many of them deferment simply postponed an obligation they ultimately had to meet; even those who entirely escaped often had a feeling of guilt and a desire to demonstrate against local draft boards. Since the students hated everything connected with the military, they found a particularly vulnerable target in the Reserve Officers Training Corps. At many colleges, students had the support of a majority of the faculty in either driving ROTC completely off campus or in reducing its operations. Student pickets often tried to halt the activities of army and navy recruiters or recruiters for corporations such as the Dow Chemical Company, known to be manufacturing lethal materials for the military. Student rebels also focused their displeasure on the affiliates of their own universities accused of complicity in American imperialism through their research contracts with government agencies.

Many of the student activists had learned the techniques of mass demonstration during the civil rights campaigns of the early sixties. They had participated in voter registration drives and other black protest movements of the day. This interrelation influenced both the methods and the objectives of the student protests. For example, the great Columbia demonstration of April, 1968, in which rebellious students held five campus buildings for six days until the police finally drove them out, involved opposition both to university-connected research for the Defense Department and to the building of a new gymnasium on land that students thought should be reserved for the use of the black Harlem community. Although white radicals were as eager to demonstrate for black causes as for white, the black students soon developed a determination to do their own independent things, boycotting athletic teams and occupying administrative offices in support of demands for admission of more black students and the establishment of black studies programs to be staffed and administered by the blacks themselves.

Dissident students across the country were loosely affiliated through the Students for a Democratic Society (SDS), founded in June, 1962, with Tom Hayden, a graduate of the University of Michigan, as one of its most important leaders. The Port Huron Statement, adopted at the organizing convention, emphasized student resistance to the computerized society, described as one based on the idea that man was "a thing to be manipulated." In contrast to this, SDS held that "men have unrealized potential for self-cultivation, self-direction, and creativity."

Because it was committed to the ideal of "participatory democracy," in which people at all levels of life would share in the decision-making process, SDS could not impose any single party line on its hundreds of local chapters. Instead, the young members debated the merits of every political philosophy—liberal, socialist, anarchist, pro-Soviet Communist, pro-Mao Communist, nonideological. Thus divided, the student radicals had more negative than positive power. They could raise issues, formulate demands, and organize the demonstrations that created crisis situations. Yet once they had won a place for students on university committees and governing bodies, they found it difficult to agree on programs of reform.

Sociologists studied the youth movement with intense interest. Although black student rebels usually came from backgrounds of poverty and deprivation, this was far from the case with the white protestors. They usually came from relatively privileged backgrounds. The more prestigious the institution the more likely it appeared to encounter trouble. There were serious disruptions at Berkeley, Columbia, Cornell, Harvard, Chicago, Wisconsin, and Michigan—all preeminent for scholarship. Not only did the rebels usually come from good homes, most of them were relatively good students, particularly interested in the humanities and social sciences. To say that they were revolting against their parents was too simple an explanation. Usually the parents were not particularly conservative people; very often they had been New Deal liberals. What drove the students into protest seemed to be the contrast between the humane values they had learned to respect and the computerized society in which they found themselves—a society to which they accused their parents of selling out.

By the fall of 1972, the student protest movement seemed to have spent most of its force. Although the Nixon administration had not yet ended the Vietnam war, it had terminated the American ground combat role, stopped sending men to the war theater unless they wanted to go, and announced plans for an all-volunteer army and an end to conscription. Student dissidents still had many other grievances, but for the time being the campuses were quiet. What had the protests accomplished? Within the colleges, substantial changes had resulted. Most institutions had given up their parental role: no longer did they attempt to ban the use of alcoholic beverages or visits by the opposite sex in the dormitories; indeed the newer dormitories sometimes housed both men and women. Many colleges and universities had reorganized their governing structures to include student representatives. Many had opened up their curriculums to a wide variety of new "relevant" courses. Beyond the campuses the students could claim to have had an important role in speeding up Lyndon Johnson's retirement from politics, in modifying Richard Nixon's Vietnam policy, and in winning the Democratic presidential nomination for George McGovern.

Yet student protests were, to some extent, counterproductive. Many Americans, both middle class and working people, regarded the long-haired,

Scuffle between "hard hat" construction workers and participants in an antiwar rally in New York's Wall Street, 1970. (UPI Photo.)

bearded, blue-jeaned students with extreme dislike. President Nixon and Vice President Agnew both played upon this feeling, attempting to differentiate between the "good kids"—the complacent ones—and the "bad kids"—those who protested. It was by no means clear whether the student protestors had helped or hindered the achievement of the better world to which they aspired.

Women's Liberation

The spirit of revolt, first evident among the blacks, then among college students, flared up also among women during the later sixties. Although adoption of the woman's suffrage amendment in 1920 had seemed at the time to be a final triumph for the cause of equal rights, it became obvious half a century later that women still encountered widespread discrimination. In contrast to countries like India or Israel where women headed the government, American women had risen no higher in politics than an occasional cabinet post, governorship, or Senate seat. In contrast to the Soviet Union where three quarters of the physicians and one third of the engineers were women, in the United States only 7 per cent of the physicians and 1 per cent of the engineers were women. Far from being in the forefront of the equal rights movement, American women seemed to be lagging behind.

What was holding the women back? Undoubtedly, male selfishness was a major factor. Professional politicians arranging nominations for public office usually threw a few goodies to the ladies, but reserved the positions of real power for the men. The same kind of tokenism was widespread. Medical schools admitted a few women to each class; even engineering schools good naturedly let in an occasional woman—although they thought it was eccentric for the girls to apply. In many fields women had wide opportunities for employment, but found it difficult to rise above a certain level. Thus there were many women teachers, but few women school superintendents; many women secretaries, but few corporation executives. Unquestionably there was a male power structure in control of the whole society, and the men were not eager to make room at the top for the women—even though most men indignantly denied having any prejudices in the matter.

Yet male obstructionism was only half the story. During the post–World War II years the vast majority of girls seemed to be choosing the role of wife and mother over that of business or professional woman. Many girls could not wait to get out of high school or college before getting married, and they often had four or five children. A typical suburban housewife might drive her husband to the railroad station early in the morning, then get the children off to school before taking off on a variety of household errands. After school she transported the children to dancing classes, music lessons, scout meetings, and Little League practice fields. Somehow she managed almost simultaneously to prepare dinner and pick up her husband at the railroad station. Often she spent the evening at a parent-teacher meeting or some other civil event. Many women experienced genuine happiness in the busy vocation of homemaker. Other women, however, failed to find contentment in this hectic domesticity. Their chores became meaningless drudgery, and they complained that they had become slaves to their families.

Either through choice or necessity, many married women took jobs and delayed child-bearing; often they returned to outside employment when their children became old enough to take care of themselves. Yet women who put their homes first and were in and out of the job market seldom advanced into good-paying and responsible positions. On the other hand, women who put their careers first, either not marrying at all or having no children, often paid a heavy price. Other people considered them mannish and unfeminine; and often they condemned themselves on the same grounds. Popularized Freudianism gave a new lease on life to the ancient prejudice against women who were too ambitious to achieve success in activities usually performed by men; they were accused of "penis-envy."

In *The Feminine Mystique* (1963) Betty Friedan argued that women had fallen into a trap by defining their happiness in terms of finding a husband and having babies. She urged her sisters to educate themselves for meaningful careers and insist on their right to rise as high as their abilities would permit. She believed that women should be able to have both marriage and a career without sacrificing one for the other.

In 1966 Betty Friedan and other women of similar determination founded the National Organization of Women (NOW) to press for new government policies and new social arrangements that would liberate women. NOW demanded vigorous enforcement of the Civil Rights Act of 1964, which had prohibited job discrimination not only on the basis of race and religion but of sex as well. As an additional safeguard, NOW advocated an amendment to the Federal Constitution reading: "Equality of rights under the law shall not be denied or abridged by the United States or by any state on account of sex." Not all women favored the Equal Rights Amendment. Groups long active in the trade union movement warned that it would invalidate scores of state laws providing special protection to women workers. But spokesmen for NOW argued that the protective laws had become a device for keeping women out of many good-paying jobs. Throw all jobs open, the feminists argued, then let individual women compete wherever they could demonstrate the necessary strength and skill. Since women now constituted some 52 per cent of the population, the lawmakers were not disposed to antagonize them as soon as concerted pressure for the Equal Rights Amendment developed. The House of Representatives approved it by a vote of 354 to 24 in October, 1971, and the Senate by 84 to 8 in March, 1972. In the state legislatures, however, the amendment encountered increasing opposition.

Yet, as the struggle of the blacks had shown, it was one thing to have a constitutional guarantee of equal rights and quite another thing to gain actual equality. NOW and other groups of organized women engaged in hundreds of local skirmishes. They picketed the *New York Times* and other newspapers to get rid of the separate classification of jobs by the designations: "Help Wanted: Male" and "Help Wanted: Female." By picketing and court action women established their right to drink in bars and clubs hitherto reserved for males. Washington's important National Press Club admitted women reporters to membership. Colleges and universities employed more women on their faculties—partly out of a belated sense of fairness, partly out of fear of losing Federal funds unless they took "affirmative action" to recruit not only more women, but more blacks and other minority people.

On August 26, 1970—the fiftieth anniversary of the ratification of the Woman Suffrage Amendment—the feminists conducted a "Strike for Equality." Some of them took the day off to prove to their employers and husbands how much their services were needed; many more simply took a long lunch hour to march and cheer in mass meetings. Some ten thousand women paraded down New York's Fifth Avenue; and similar, if smaller, demonstrations took place in scores of other cities. The women emphasized three major demands: equal opportunity in jobs and education; free twenty-four hour child-care centers; and free abortions on demand. The first demand for equality was, of course, nothing new, but the second and third were more controversial. The plea for child-care centers emphasized the conviction of many women that they could only really enjoy their right to both marriage and a career if society provided fundamentally

Women's March on the Pentagon, 1971: (UPI Photo.)

different arrangements for the care of the young. Most challenging of all was the demand for free abortion, a surgical procedure prohibited in all the states except when necessary to save the woman's life. Critics of these antiabortion laws made two powerful arguments. They said that abortions ought at least to be the right of women whose pregnancy resulted from rape or who might expect to have malformed children because of accidents or illness during pregnancy. In any case, they added, abortion was a fact of modern life. Thousands of desperate women were undergoing illegal operations performed under unsanitary and dangerous conditions at extortionate fees. It would be much better, they argued, to allow the woman to have the operation performed under proper clinical conditions whenever she wanted it and her doctor agreed to do it. The proabortion faction won a major victory in the liberal abortion law passed by the New York legislature in 1970 and lesser victories in the modified laws of several other states. But the issue aroused strong passions. Roman Catholics—both priests and laymen—vigorously condemned abortion as a violation of the unborn child's right to life; the liberation groups retorted that a woman should have sovereignty over her own body and the right to decide whether or not she would bear a child.

Labor's Vested Interests

The labor unions which had led the battle for change and reform in earlier decades followed an ambivalent course in the sixties and seventies.

Having won their own great battles, many members became suspicious of newer forms of radicalism as evidenced by the blacks, the students, and the women.

After the minor recession of 1960, the country enjoyed a period of substantial prosperity for the rest of the decade. The gross national product rose from $504 billion in 1960 to $974 billion in 1970. And a good proportion of this represented increases in wages and salaries, which doubled from $271 billion in 1960 to $541 billion in 1970. Wage earners seemed to be making visible improvements in their standard of living. Many of them moved out of their rented flats in the cities to modest homes of their own in the suburbs; many bought second cars so that their wives could do the family errands while they commuted to work; many bought expensive color-TV sets, boats, and snowmobiles. Yet paradoxically many blue-collar workers felt a rising sense of frustration and injustice. They complained bitterly over rising taxes and found an outlet for their discontent by voting down local school budgets. They resented the efforts of the blacks to get better jobs and move into better neighborhoods. They protested when local school boards tried to achieve a better racial balance in the schools by busing. They complained about the increasing number of people on welfare.

Despite all that had been done in the name of social security, the worker still felt insecure about his position in a rapidly changing society. For one thing, the blue-collar group was no longer increasing in size. Between 1960 and 1970 the number of people employed in manufacturing grew by only 12 per cent—less than the 13 per cent growth of the entire population. Even more striking was the fact that the number of miners actually declined 11 per cent during the decade as a result of strip mining, mechanization, and the dwindling use of coal. Only in the construction industry was there a modest—18 per cent—increase in employment during the sixties. But white-collar employment was meanwhile increasing dramatically. Between 1960 and 1970 the number of people employed in finance, insurance, and real estate went up by 81 per cent; those in the service industries by 61 per cent; those in government service by 56 per cent; and those in wholesale and retail trade by 33 per cent.

These changing patterns of employment altered the prospects of the labor unions, which found it difficult to recruit new members, either in antiunion sections of the country or among the increasing army of white-collar workers. More and more, union tactics became essentially defensive—to win better contracts for their existing membership and protect their interests against the threats of automation and newcomers to the labor force. George Meany, the aging president of the AFL-CIO, acknowledged this: "When you have no property, you don't have anything, you have nothing to lose by these radical actions. But when you become a person who has a home and has property, to some extent you become conservative. And I would say to that extent labor has become conservative."

Walter Reuther, veteran head of the United Automobile Workers, severely criticized Meany's conservatism. In 1967, he wrote: "It is sad but nevertheless true that the AFL-CIO is becoming increasingly the comfortable, complacent custodian of the status quo." Reuther demanded a more democratic governing structure for the federation, a massive organizing campaign to unionize such groups as sales clerks, office workers, government employees, and teachers as well as millions of agricultural workers and the working poor of the cities and rural areas. He also wanted the federation to take an active political role in support of urban renewal, low-cost housing, improved education, national health care, and minority rights. Unable to remake the AFL-CIO in this fashion, Reuther took the UAW in effect out of the federation. In 1970 Reuther died in an airplane crash, but Leonard Woodcock, the new UAW president, continued the schism with the AFL-CIO. Yet his effort to ally the UAW with other progressive groups encountered serious resistance from the union's own rank and file. By casting their votes for George Wallace in the political battles of 1968 and 1972, thousands of auto workers in the Detroit suburbs expressed fears and frustrations that they shared with many other blue-collar workers.

Cesar Chavez of the United Farm Workers. (UPI Photo.)

Meanwhile, millions of underprivileged Americans—especially urban blacks and rural farm workers—found themselves outside the protected area of unionism. In scores of cities blacks struggled to get into the almost all-white construction unions. Federal policy and other forms of pressure helped some blacks to achieve this goal, but union foot-dragging made progress slow. In California and the Southwest, Cesar Chavez became an effective leader for thousands of harvest workers—most of them Chicanos (Mexican-Americans). In organizing the grape pickers he gained powerful support from millions of progressive sympathizers who boycotted grapes until the union was recognized. Strengthened by this success. Chavez undertook to use the same combination of strike and boycott to organize the lettuce workers.

Religion and the New Morality

In many ways, the young people of the sixties were highly moral. They had an acute sense of right and wrong that made them indignant at the slaughter of Vienamese villagers, the mistreatment of blacks, the exploitation of Chicanos, and the pollution of the atmosphere. Yet in their personal lives many youths adopted behavior strikingly at odds with older ideas of morality. Despite laws forbidding the sale and possession of marijuana, millions of Americans, not all of them young, smoked "pot," as it was called. They denied that the practice was injurious to health and denounced attempts to enforce the antimarijuana laws as irrational. To smoke pot thus became a symbolic gesture of protest reminiscent of the flaunting of Prohibition during the twenties.

But experimentation with drugs took many other, much more dangerous, forms. Many youths took "pep" pills or "speed," even though an overdose might be fatal. Others tried out LSD, whose unpredictable qualities provided ecstatic visions for some users and terrifying delusions for others. Most pathetic of all were the many—both white and black—who became addicted to heroin, often resorting to crime to get the money to support their expensive habit.

Changes in sexual behavior were even more challenging to older ideas. Many students preferred not to live in college dormitories despite the greatly relaxed rules. Instead, they found rooms or apartments, which they shared with roommates—sometimes of their own sex, sometimes of the other. Communal and quasi-communal living was common, and an exchange of bedmates was sometimes, although not always, a part of the arrangement. The behavior of many married couples was equally unconventional, with husband and wife openly carrying on affairs with other people and even going together to "swinging," or wife-swapping, parties. Many homosexuals no longer lived clandestine lives; they boasted of their preferences and supported the cause of "gay liberation."

Young people who carried their defiance of conventional society to an extreme in matters of hair style, clothing, drug use, and casual sexual behavior became known as "hippies." There were hundreds of these living a precarious existence in New York's Greenwich Village, San Francisco's Haight-Ashbury section, and on the fringes of many college campuses. But these hippies who "dropped out" were a minority of youth; much more numerous were the people, both young and middle-aged, who continued to study or to work while holding out. against traditional patterns of family life and personal conduct. Some social observers saw in this the growth of a counterculture with its own set of values.

Although members of the counterculture usually scorned traditional religion, they often embraced exotic cults like Zen Buddhism or Yoga. Indeed, some of the popularity of the mind-expanding drugs seemed to be their contribution to mystic religious experience. Rock music often carried a religious message. The earnestness of "Jesus freaks" and "Jesus people" sometimes seemed a throwback to old-time revivalism.

Religion in its new modes by no means extinguished religion in the more traditional forms. Many ministers and laymen clung to Protestant fundamentalism as a rock of safety in the turbulent seas of contemporary immorality and sacrilege. The Reverend Billy Graham and President Nixon maintained a highly public friendship—advantageous to both of them. Yet not all religious leaders threw their influence on the side of the status quo. Many of them played roles of courageous leadership in both the civil rights and the anti–Vietnam war movements.

During the sixties the Roman Catholic Church went through a period of stress and strain. The short pontificate of the beloved John XXIII and the Second Vatican Council, summoned at his call and concluded under Paul VI, made many significant changes in the worship and government of the church. Encouraged by this liberalization, many Catholics hoped for a modification of the church's position on birth control and on marriage for the clergy. But Pope Paul placed a stern limit on the extent of change and refused to relax traditional Catholic teachings on issues of sexual morality. Despite the conservatism of the hierarchy, many Catholic priests and nuns took a prominent part in the radical politics of the sixties. The Berrigan brothers, Father Daniel and Father Philip, both served terms in Federal prison for destroying draft board records—highly dramatic acts of symbolic opposition to the Vietnam war.

Conflict in Literature and the Arts

Sensitive authors found themes in the conflicting forces of American life during the sixties. Saul Bellow, probably the most widely respected novelist of the day, wrote about troubled Jews, baffled by the perplexities of the American situation, yet able to survive by clinging to fundamental human values. *Herzog* (1964) described with humor and compassion the emotional travail and near breakdown of a middle-aged professor. *Mr. Sammler's Planet* (1970) confronted an émigré Jew, who had seen the best and worst of European culture, with the grasping and violent life of contemporary New York City. Despite disillusioning experience, old Sammler remained convinced that the ultimate value was "to do what was required"—required, that is, by decency and self-respect. Bernard Malamud, in *The Fixer* (1966), also found a symbol of human courage in the Jew's ability to survive despite hardship and persecution.

Several novelists explored the life of America's new suburbanites—people who had escaped from the depressing decay and violence of the cities to live in split-level comfort in small communities. In *Couples* (1968), John Updike combined a comic account of the casual infidelities of these sophisticates with a brooding overview of religious judgment upon their sins. In *Bullet Park* (1969), John Cheever cut through the commonplace conformity and busy neighborliness of suburban life and found dangerous undercurrents of madness and violence.

The violence lying latent in the suburbs was part of a more general violence that seemed to hang over all sectors of American life during the sixties. Especially suited by temperament and experience to depict this threatening atmosphere were two authors who had first won fame by their

World War II novels, Norman Mailer and James Jones. Mailer's *The American Dream* (1964) described with frightening power brutal murder and loveless sex. It was a commentary on the harsh reality of the day that Mailer turned from fiction to nonfiction to write *Armies of the Night* (1968), a brilliant account of his own participation in the antiwar March on the Pentagon. Jones's *The Merry Month of May* (1971) portrayed the disintegration of a group of Americans living in Paris who became involved in the great confrontation between the French students and the De Gaulle government. Even the most notable historical novel of the decade, William Styron's *The Confessions of Nat Turner* (1967), was a frightening recognition of the bloody pattern of violence underlying the relations of whites and blacks in America.

While male novelists seemed to have a special interest in the harsh and brutal aspects of contemporary American life, the woman authors of the period showed greater subtlety in exploring people's inner conflicts—their fears and anxieties, their moments of courage and cowardice, the comedy and tragedy of everyday experience. Often the short story provided the best medium for literary artistry of this kind. Critics particularly admired the work of Eudora Welty, Jean Stafford, and Joyce Carol Oates.

Popular taste, as reflected in the best seller lists, ran in channels of its own, largely uninfluenced by the approval or disapproval of the literary critics. During the sixties there was a plethora of titillating sex novels, the work of such literary entrepreneurs as Jacqueline Susann, Harold Robbins, and Irving Wallace. Better written and more amusing was Philip Roth's Freudian romp, *Portnoy's Complaint* (1969). Allen Drury's political novels, Helen MacInnes's stories of international intrigue, and Victoria Holt's gothic thrillers had great popularity. The public's fascination with the cold-blooded violence of the Mafia gave an enormous sale to Mario Puzo's *The Godfather* (1969). Yet tear-jerking romance was not dead, as Erich Segal proved with his highly successful *Love Story* (1970).

Although the general level of television programming remained mediocre or worse, TV journalism gave millions of families an unhappy proximity to disturbing events. Watching every night scenes of death and destruction from Vietnam shook many viewers out of their complacency and added greatly to antiwar sentiment. Television provided a similar vividness to the various domestic protest movements of the sixties. Indeed, the protestors sometimes confessed to staging a bit of "street theater" for the benefit of the TV cameras. The effect of all this on the general public was far from clear. Demonstrating groups—blacks, students, women—succeeded in conveying their message to a wider public. Yet many viewers reacted with fear and anger to what they saw. Politicians such as George Wallace and Spiro Agnew gained a following in part by playing upon the resentment that many middle-class and working-class TV watchers felt for the protestors.

Since children constituted a large part of the television audience, many people regretted that so many programs featured gun battles between sheriffs and bad guys, or between cops and robbers. Psychiatrists differed in their view of whether such daily diets of lurid violence were dangerous or harmless to viewers of tender age. Periodically the networks promised to purge the airwaves of excessive gunplay, but little change was to be observed. On the other hand, TV executives did rule out nudity and explicit sex as unsuitable for transmission.

Moviemakers had largely freed themselves of such restraints. Although in earlier years, movie censors and industry review boards had refused to approve pictures unsuitable for children, the industry opened the way for freer expression by instituting a classification system in 1968. Motion pictures were now divided into four categories, ranging from "G"—presumably 100 per cent pure and suitable for children of all ages—and "X"—presumably impure and banned for youths under the age of seventeen. Particularly in the pictures approved for adults only, the moviemakers exploited nudity to the limit and catered to sexual curiosity by working highly erotic scenes into their pictures and by producing supposedly educational pictures on the art of lovemaking. Although the production of X-rated films might be profitable, the big money was still in pictures to which a wider audience could be admitted. It therefore became a fine art to include just enough nudity and sex to whet the appetite, yet not enough to get an undesirable classification.

But the motion pictures of the sixties were characterized by an emphasis on violence—which appeared to have little influence on a picture's rating—even more than they were by the exploitation of sex. Millions of cinema-goers shuddered with delicious horror at the mutilations and killings of pictures like *The Boston Strangler, In Cold Blood, The French Connection,* and *The Godfather.*

Hollywood was experiencing hard times. Many families who had been regular patrons of the movie theaters now sat glued to their TV sets, content to see warmed-over movies on the late show. With declining attendance many big companies sold their expensive studios and distributed the pictures made by smaller independent producers who cut costs by using no-star casts, improvising their scripts, and shooting their stories in foreign countries or on the streets of American cities and villages. Yet movies were still popular with college students and young people. To appeal to them, theaters showed pictures particularly expressive of their point of view. Especially successful were *Easy Rider, Alice's Restaurant, Midnight Cowboy,* and *The Graduate.* Another huge audience opened up when blacks began to throng to pictures with blacks in the principal roles—pictures like *In the Heat of the Night, Shaft,* and *Sounder.* The last two of these were all-black productions—written, directed, and acted by black people.

The popular art most loved by youth was music in such various forms as rock, pop, country, and folk. Individual performers such as Bobby Darin, James Brown, Janis Joplin, and Aretha Franklin drew tremendous audiences of screaming teen-agers, and the fabulous success of the Beatles, an English group, led to the formation of highly popular American groups like the Supremes, the Fifth Dimension, and the Jefferson Airplane. Great crowds of young people thronged to summer rock festivals at such places as Newport, Rhode Island; Woodstock, New York; and Monterey, California. The highly successful stage show *Hair* combined the new music with moments of nudity and eroticism to provide a major expression for the counterculture.

"Pop art" (popular art) served as still another commentary on the Age of the Computer. Innovators such as Andy Warhol and Roy Lichtenstein shook up the art world with paintings of Coca-Cola bottles, Campbell Soup cans, movie goddesses, and comic-strip characters. Accepting the banal and the commonplace as the American reality, they transferred it to canvas—to be contrasted with the Madonnas and serene landscapes that had symbolized the spirit of earlier ages.

In his acceptance speech at the 1968 Republican National Convention, Richard Nixon condemned the noisy turbulence of the country and contrasted this with what he defined as the "quiet voice" of the true America. "It is the voice," he said, "of the great majority of Americans, the forgotten Americans, the non-shouters, the non-demonstrators. . . . They work in American factories, they run American business. They serve in government; they provide most of the soldiers who die to keep it free."

A shrewd politician, Nixon worked tirelessly to bind this quiet majority to his leadership. In his 1968 campaign he did not win an absolute majority: only 43.4 per cent of the electorate voted for him, as against 42.8 per cent who voted for Hubert Humphrey and 13.5 for George Wallace. Once in the White House Nixon made skillful use of the power of the office to nail together a genuine majority that would supplant the old New Deal coalition that had controlled American politics for most of the years since 1932. The election of 1972 provided the best measure of his success. About 61 per cent voted for Nixon and his middle-of-the-road program; about 38 per cent voted for George McGovern and his appeal for a new progressivism.

The Resurrection of Richard Nixon

So narrow was John Kennedy's victory in the presidential election of 1960 that it was not seriously damaging to Richard Nixon, the defeated candidate. But two years later the former Vice President suffered an apparently fatal political wound when he could not even get elected governor of California, his home state. He was decisively defeated by the Democratic governor, Edmund ("Pat") Brown running for re-election. Reacting angrily in a press conference, Nixon told the reporters that they would not have him "to kick around any more." In this graceless way Nixon appeared to retire from politics, and he soon after became a senior partner in one of the most prosperous law firms in New York City.

But Nixon was too ambitious a man to be satisfied for long with mere money. During the period when the Republican party was licking the wounds suffered in the course of the disastrous Goldwater campaign, Nixon quietly began to rebuild his organization. He won the gratitude of hundreds of local candidates during the election of 1966 by helping them raise money and by making speeches in their behalf. The election results were encouraging to the Nixon faction. The Republicans reduced the Democratic majorities in Congress and elected or re-elected governors in key states. President Johnson was running into increasing trouble in Vietnam, and prospects for Republican success in 1968 brightened rapidly.

But would the Republicans give the presidential nomination to a man who had run once and been defeated? In Nixon's path stood three ambitious Republican governors—George Romney of Michigan, Nelson Rockefeller of New York, and Ronald Reagan of California. Romney, a remarkable businessman who had built the struggling American Motors Company into a going concern, had served three eventful terms as governor of Michigan. As a potential presidential candidate, he enjoyed high ratings in the public opinion polls early in 1967, but then lost popularity rapidly, largely because of a series of blundering and contradictory statements about the Vietnam war. Shortly before the New Hampshire primary in March, 1968, Romney withdrew from the race. Without effective competition Nixon won the primary over Rockefeller, a write-in candidate, by a margin of seven to one.

Governor Rockefeller had supported Romney until the latter's candidacy collapsed. Then the New York governor hesitated until April 30 before finally announcing his own candidacy. Despite energetic campaigning Rockefeller was so far behind in the contest for delegates that his only chance for the nomination lay in Reagan gaining enough strength to deprive Nixon of a majority on the early ballots.

If Rockefeller was the hope of Republican liberals, Governor Reagan was the darling of Republican conservatives. A handsome former movie star, Reagan had delighted the Goldwater wing of the party by trouncing Governor Brown in 1966—thus achieving the victory that had eluded Nixon. If Reagan could gather a substantial body of delegates from the South— good Goldwater territory—he might become a dangerous rival for the nomination. On June 1 Nixon cooly ended this threat by a meeting at Atlanta with Senators Strom Thurmond of South Carolina and John Tower of Texas along with other influential Southern Republicans. Nixon promised to nominate strict-constructionist justices to the Supreme Court and to consider Southern white wishes on school busing and other civil rights issues; and the Southerners pledged him their support at the convention. This political bargain guaranteed Nixon the Republican nomination, helped him win the November election, and laid the basis for the subsequent "Southern strategy" of the Nixon administration.

At the Miami convention early in August, Nixon was firmly in command. He received 692 votes to 277 for Rockefeller and 182 for Reagan—thus winning the nomination on the first ballot. He made a somewhat unexpected choice of Governor Spiro Agnew of Maryland for the vice-presidential nomination. Since Agnew came from a border state and had rebuked militant black nationalism, Nixon's choice pleased Southern conservatives much more than Northern liberals who had hoped that the nomination would go to Mayor John Lindsay of New York City. The party platform emphasized such popular issues as an "all-out" crusade against crime, reform of the welfare laws, efficiency in government, an end to inflation, and strengthened national defense. On Vietnam, the Republicans promised to "de-Americanize" the war, to engage in "clear and purposeful negotiations," but not to accept a camouflaged surrender.

Democratic Disarray

Lyndon Johnson says in his memoirs that reasons of health dictated his decision not to run in 1968. Shortly after the 1964 election he confided his intention to his family and a few close friends, but he did not find an appropriate occasion for a public announcement until March 31, 1968. Under the circumstances, however, a surprised nation could scarcely be blamed for assuming that setbacks in Vietnam, rising discontent at home, and the warning of the New Hampshire primary were the decisive factors in the President's final decision not to run. Indeed, one of the unanswerable questions of history must be this: If March, 1968, had been a good instead of a bad month for Johnson, might he not have run again despite his reluctance?

Johnson's withdrawal left the field open to three major rivals for the Democratic nomination—Senator Eugene McCarthy of Minnesota, Senator Robert Kennedy of New York, and Vice President Hubert Humphrey. McCarthy and Kennedy had already announced their candidacy before Johnson took himself out; Humphrey did not formally enter the race until April 27, although he was the obvious heir to the Johnson legacy. McCarthy and Kennedy were both vigorous opponents of the administration's Vietnam policy; Humphrey was cast—somewhat reluctantly—in the role of defender of the Johnson record in both domestic and foreign affairs.

Although professional politicians might ridicule McCarthy's "Kiddie Korps," his college-student volunteers, they proved to be a formidable force in the preconvention campaign. Their energetic door-to-door campaigning gave McCarthy 42 per cent of the vote in the New Hampshire primary and 56 per cent in the Wisconsin primary on April 2. But in both of these contests McCarthy had been running against a noncampaigning Johnson rather than against Kennedy or Humphrey. The Indiana primary on May 7 was the first one in which McCarthy's and Kennedy's names both appeared on the ballot; and this time McCarthy received only 27 per cent of the vote as against 42 per cent for Kennedy.

Confident of his ability to win a majority of the delegates in the states that had no primaries, Humphrey allowed McCarthy and Kennedy to slug it out in these grueling campaigns. Since the latter two were so similar in their opposition to the Vietnam war and their liberalism on domestic issues, it was deplorable that they fought each other so bitterly. But each man was surrounded by fervent admirers, deeply suspicious of the rival candidate. McCarthy made his greatest appeal to intellectuals and students who regarded Kennedy as a ruthless politician attempting to steal the leadership of their movement. The Kennedy entourage, on the other hand, believed that their man could appeal to a much wider public composed of those who venerated the memory of the murdered President and the blacks and urban ethnic groups who regarded "Bobby" himself as their friend and champion; the Kennedy camp put down McCarthy as a lazy intellectual unsuited for the presidency.

After Kennedy beat McCarthy in Nebraska and McCarthy beat Kennedy in Oregon the struggle came to its climax in the California primary of June 5. This time 46 per cent of the Democratic voters chose Kennedy as against 42 per cent for McCarthy. Kennedy's victory was a narrow one, but it might have turned the tide had he lived until convention time. Instead, the decade's third shocking assassination removed Kennedy from the contest. As the candidate was walking through the kitchen of a Los Angeles hotel during the victory celebration, a young Jordanian, Sirhan Sirhan, angered by Kennedy' pro-Israel position, shot and fatally wounded him. For the next few days politics were adjourned while thousands paid tribute to the fallen leader in New York City and Washington.

Before his death Kennedy had won over three hundred delegates. What would they do now? Many went over to McCarthy, but others were too bitter to do so. Some gave their support to Humphrey; others remained uncommitted, hoping that the surviving brother, Senator Edward Kennedy of Massachusetts, would accept a draft. Just two weeks before the convention Senator George McGovern of South Dakota, an outspoken dove, announced his candidacy and gained the backing of a bloc of Kennedy loyalists.

The Democratic National Convention, which met in Chicago the last week of August, was a tumultuous affair both outside and inside the convention hall. For months youthful opponents of the Vietnam war had been planning to converge on Chicago and conduct mass demonstrations during the conven-

Struggle between police and antiwar protesters during the Democratic convention in Chicago, 1968. (UPI Photo.)

tion. Most of the several thousand who came were committed to nonviolent forms of protest, but a militant minority was not. Mayor Richard Daley, Chicago's powerful Democratic boss, took a hard line that played into the hands of the troublemakers. Attempting to enforce prohibitions against sleeping in public parks and holding unauthorized meetings and marches, the Chicago police became involved in violent confrontations with the demonstrators. Some of the protestors taunted the police with obscenities and threw stones at them; the police used tear gas, mace, and clubs not only against their tormenters but against scores of peaceful marchers and by-standers. Millions of Americans watched these brutal events on television—a kind of publicity that the harried Democratic party could scarcely afford.

The convention itself was a bitter one. The Humphrey delegates were in control, but the anti-Humphrey factions challenged them every step of the way—credentials, rules, platform, balloting. After angry debate the delegates voted down a minority report calling for a total end to the bombing and speedy withdrawal from Vietnam and adopted the majority plank supporting the President's efforts to achieve "an honorable and lasting settlement." Less controversial were the planks promising an extension of the Johnson domestic policies. With the disciplined support of Southern stalwarts, Northern professionals, and the leadership of the AFL-CIO, Humphrey rolled through to a first ballot nomination. He received 1760¼ votes to McCarthy's 601, and McGovern's 146½. The delegates willingly accepted Humphrey's choice for the vice-presidential nomination, Senator Edmund Muskie of Maine, a quiet and respected legislator likely to win some votes for the ticket as a Catholic of Polish extraction.

After the excitement of the preconvention politicking, the fall campaign came almost as an anticlimax. Nixon had a comfortable lead in the early public opinion polls, but Humphrey managed to pull close in the final weeks, especially after he broke away from Johnson's leash long enough to promise a complete bombing halt in Vietnam in the hope of getting reciprocal concessions from the Communists. The President helped out by actually ordering such a halt on October 31. This permitted many McCarthy followers to swallow their misgivings about Humphrey and swing to his support.

The activities of the American Independence Party, headed by Governor George Wallace of Alabama, complicated the situation. Long a hero to those who resented Federal intervention on behalf of the blacks, Wallace won additional followers by promising a policy of victory in Vietnam and tough measures at home against criminals, dope-users, hippies, and Communists. In the anxiety-wracked 1960's Wallace's angry rhetoric appealed not only to voters in the Deep South but to many ethnic communities in the North as well. If Wallace could carry enough states, he might prevent either Nixon or Humphrey from winning in the electoral college. And if the election were thrown into the House of Representatives, Wallace might manipulate his role as king-maker to gain major concessions for the ultraright.

In the end, this Wallace strategy failed. Although he carried five states (Alabama, Arkansas, Georgia, Louisiana, and Mississippi), this did not prevent Nixon from winning an electoral majority. The breakdown was Nixon, 301; Humphrey, 191; Wallace, 46. The 32 states carried by Nixon included such Southern states as Virginia, North and South Carolina, and

Florida, as well as most of the states in the Middle and Far West. Humphrey carried only 13 states, but these included several of the most populous ones like New York, Pennsylvania, Michigan, and Texas. The popular vote was very close: Nixon, 31.8 million; Humphrey, 31.3 million; Wallace, 9.9 million. In the congressional elections the Republicans made only slight gains. In the new Senate there were 57 Democrats and 43 Republicans—a Republican gain of five; in the House there were 243 Democrats and 192 Republicans—a Republican gain of only four. The election had given Nixon a clear mandate to see whether he could do better than Johnson in dealing with the distressing Vietnam situation, but it left unresolved the question of what direction domestic policy should take.

Nixon Organizes for Power

The second of five sons born to hard-working Quaker parents, Richard Nixon began life in Yorba Linda, California, a small farming community, on January 9, 1913. When he was nine, the family moved to Whittier, California, where Nixon graduated from Whittier College in 1934. After completing a three-year course at Duke University Law School with high grades, he returned to Whittier to practice law. During World War II he worked briefly as a lawyer in the Office of Price Administration and then entered the navy, where he served in the South Pacific and attained the rank of lieutenant commander. In 1946 he broke into politics, winning two terms in the United States House of Representatives and then advancing to the Senate in 1950. These were the years of rising alarm against Communism, and Nixon rode the tide by branding rival candidates as dangerously radical and exposing the spy activities attributed to Alger Hiss. A hero to Republican conservatives and a thorn in the side of liberal Democrats such as Harry Truman and Adlai Stevenson, Nixon continued to be a figure of controversy during the eight Eisenhower years when he served as Vice President.

To many who had followed him during these years of bitter partisanship, he seemed a somewhat changed person when he finally entered the White House on January 20, 1969. The "new Nixon," as he was sometimes described, seemed a more relaxed and confident man, more open to new ideas and less harsh in his rhetoric. Indeed, the closest thing to the "old Nixon" now seemed to be Vice President Agnew, with his bitter speeches loaded with multisyllabled epithets denouncing radical students and professors and such seditious media as the *New York Times,* the *Washington Post,* and the Columbia Broadcasting System. While Agnew sallied forth to assail the liberals, President Nixon divided most of his time between his several "White Houses"—in Washington, in Florida, and in California. Still a somewhat shy and introspective man, he avoided press conferences and other situations he could not control, preferring to appear at carefully staged public events. Yet he welcomed opportunities to polish his new image of high-minded public servant. He particularly cherished the friendship of the popular evangelist Billy Graham and invited the whole range of American clergymen—Catholic priests, Jewish rabbis, and Protestant ministers—to speak at newly instituted Sunday services at the White House.

Nixon's cabinet was undistinguished. The new Secretary of State, William P. Rogers, was an able New York lawyer who had been Eisenhower's Attorney General, but he had had very little diplomatic experience; obviously Nixon intended to be his own foreign minister. The new Secretary of the Treasury was David Kennedy, a respected Chicago banker but without political experience. On the other hand, the powerful post of Secretary of Defense went to Melvin Laird, a veteran Congressman from Wisconsin. Nixon's recent rival for the presidential nomination, George Romney, became Secretary of Housing and Urban Development. Two other cabinet posts went to close friends of the President: his New York law partner John Mitchell became Attorney General and his California confidant Robert Finch became Secretary of Health, Education, and Welfare.

It was characteristic of Nixon's presidency, however, that several members of his White House staff exerted more real power than most of the cabinet members. During the early months of the administration one key man was Professor Daniel P. Moynihan of Harvard, a Democrat who had held administrative posts under Governor Averell Harriman of New York and Presidents Kennedy and Johnson. Disillusioned with what he regarded as the growing irresponsibility of the liberals, Moynihan gladly accepted the invitation to serve under a man who he hoped would prove to be an intelligent moderate. Vaguely described as an Assistant to the President in the field of urban affairs, Moynihan was Nixon's principal idea man for domestic policy. Much more important in the long run was another presidential assistant, Henry Kissinger, also a Harvard professor. Brought to America as

President Nixon with Dr. Henry Kissinger, 1972. (UPI Photo.)

a boy by German-Jewish parents fleeing the Nazi terror, Kissinger still retained a pronounced German accent and bearing. In 1957 he had established his reputation as a brilliant student of world affairs with his widely read book, *Nuclear Weapons and Foreign Policy.* He had performed advisory assignments for Presidents Kennedy and Johnson and had been a leading figure in the brain trust assembled by Nelson Rockefeller during his pursuit of the White House. Despite these earlier affiliations with Nixon's rivals, Kissinger found his new White House post highly congenial. A superb technician, he was ideally suited to serve as the President's confidential agent in a series of increasingly bold diplomatic adventures. Not since the days of Colonel House had a presidential confidant traveled so widely and mysteriously from one foreign capital to another. And since jet aircraft had now displaced ocean liners, Kissinger went faster and farther than House ever could.

Nixon and the Supreme Court

When Nixon promised his Southern supporters in 1968 that he would appoint "strict-constructionist" judges to the Supreme Court, he was acting in accordance with his own wishes. For almost two decades conservatives had been deploring the Court's activist philosophy. Ironically, their anger was particularly focused on Earl Warren, appointed Chief Justice by President Eisenhower in 1953. Warren was a highly respected Republican who had been one of California's most popular governors and his party's candidate for Vice President in 1948. Despite these political antecedents Warren turned out to be one of the most consistent and effective liberals in Supreme Court history. Moreover, a majority of the justices who served under him shared his humane philosophy. In 1968 the oldest and most liberal members of the court were Hugo Black and William O. Douglas, durable holdovers from New Deal days; their fellow liberals included William Brennan, another Eisenhower appointee, and Abe Fortas and Thurgood Marshall, chosen by Johnson. The conservative wing of the court included John M. Harlan and Potter Stewart, appointed by Eisenhower, and Byron White, chosen by Kennedy.

Conservatives condemned the Warren Court for its decisions in many different areas. Southern whites particularly disliked the Court's consistent record in protecting the constitutional rights of black people by overruling all local efforts to circumvent desegregation and by upholding the validity of the various civil rights acts passed by Congress. Right-wingers eager to stamp out domestic Communism by any means found it disgusting that the Court insisted upon safeguarding the constitutional rights of accused radicals. Conservatives were also shocked by a series of decisions in which the Court declared that such public school practices as the recitation of prayers or reading from the Bible were a violation of the First Amendment. In a flurry of indignation, certain members of Congress proposed a constitutional amendment to permit school prayers, but the movement soon collapsed. Moralists were even more upset by the Court's decisions in obscenity cases, which sharply curtailed the power of movie censors to rule out scenes depicting the nude human body or explicitly erotic behavior. The Court had also overruled the convictions of certain defendants charged with selling obscene books and magazines. Although the justices did not protect blatantly pornographic materials, they laid down standards too vague to be of much help in guiding legislators and local police.

Since earlier state apportionment laws had almost always overrepresented the rural counties at the expense of the cities, conservatives deeply resented the decisions by which the Warren Court insisted upon fair and equal electoral districts for both Congress and the state legislatures. As Justice Douglas summarized the principle, political equality required "one person, one vote." Senator Dirkson had led an unsuccessful attempt to overturn the Court's reapportionment orders by constitutional amendment.

But by 1968 the charge that the justices were shielding criminals and hampering the police overshadowed all the other conservative grievances against the Warren Court. Resentment on this issue had been building up since the 1950's when the Court had ruled that the defense might under certain circumstances examine confidential FBI reports. In Gideon v. Wainwright (1963), the justices had extended the defendant's right to counsel to all criminal cases. But how soon did this right begin? Was it enough to have a lawyer at the actual trial, or must one be permitted immediately after arrest? In Escobedo v. Illinois (1964) the Court overruled a conviction based upon a confession that the defendant had made to the police after his request to consult his lawyer had been denied. Speaking for the majority in a five-to-four decision, Justice Black said: "Our Constitution, unlike some others, strikes the balance in favor of the right of the accused." Chief Justice Warren spelled out the rights of defendants still further in Miranda v. Arizona (1966)—another five-to-four decision. Before the police questioned a person suspected of crime, they must inform him of his constitutional right to remain silent and to have counsel and they must warn him that any statement might be used against him. Some police authorities, already insisting upon the painstaking collection of evidence rather than extracting confessions, accepted the Miranda decision without much protest. But other police chiefs were indignant. "Damnedest thing I ever heard of," fumed one Texas officer. "We may as well close up shop."

In 1968 Americans were legitimately worried about crime. In that year there were 13,650 murders in the United States—almost twice as many as in 1953. Even more shocking was the increase in other serious crimes—over four times as many robberies and three times as many aggravated assaults in 1968 as in 1953. The causes for this wave of violence were complex: lax gun control laws, undermanned and poorly trained police forces, overworked criminal courts, brutalizing prisons, overcrowded ghettoes, broken families, youthful unemployment, drug addiction, overemphasis on violence in movies and TV. Obviously, therefore, it was an absurd oversimplification to blame the crime statistics on the leniency of the Warren Court. Yet conservatives, eager in any case to change the philosophy of the Court, made the most of the law-and-order issue.

Even before Nixon gained the White House, a bitter struggle over control of the Court had begun. In an effort to prolong the liberal preponderance, Chief Justice Warren had resigned in June, 1968, thus giving President Johnson an opportunity to nominate Associate Justice Abe Fortas to become Chief Justice and Judge Homer Thornberry of the Federal Appeals Court to fill Fortas's place. Since Fortas had the reputation of being both a brillant lawyer and a distinguished judge, he seemed to have excellent qualifications for succeeding Warren. But Senate Republicans and Southern Democrats attacked the appointment bitterly, charging that Fortas was a "crony" of the President and had violated judicial ethics by continuing his role as White House adviser. The conservatives filibustered so stubbornly that Fortas asked the President to withdraw his nomination. In consequence, when Nixon became President, Warren was still holding on as Chief Justice, Fortas was still an associate justice, and the Thornberry nomination to the Supreme Court was dead.

Round 2 of the Fortas affair was much more sensational. A story in *Life* magazine charged that a family foundation established by Louis Wolfson had agreed to pay an annual stipend of $20,000 to Justice Fortas, presumably to subsidize him after he had given up the high earnings of a Washington lawyer for the modest salary of a Supreme Court justice. Highly questionable in any circumstances, Fortas's connection with the Wolfson foundation became scandalous when Wolfson was sentenced to prison for stock manipulations. Although Fortas had given the money back before Wolfson's conviction and denied that he had done anything wrong, widespread condemnation of his conduct forced him to resign on May 14, 1969. This bombshell injured the prestige of the Supreme Court generally and hurt the reputation of the liberal wing in particular.

Taking swift advantage of the new situation, President Nixon accepted the resignation of Earl Warren and nominated Warren Burger for the Chief Justiceship. A former Assistant Attorney General under Eisenhower and more recently Chief Judge of the Court of Appeals for the District of Columbia, Burger was known as a law-and-order judge and a critic of the Supreme Court's Miranda decision. The Senate approved the new Chief Justice by a vote of 74 to 3, and he took his seat on June 23, 1969.

To fill the Fortas vacancy, the President nominated Clement Haynsworth, Jr., of South Carolina, Chief Judge of the Fourth Circuit Court of Appeals. Despite Haynsworth's known conservatism, he was a widely respected judge, and no serious opposition was anticipated. But some of Haynsworth's acts on the bench had bitterly antagonized two powerful groups—the black civil rights organizations and the AFL-CIO. To strengthen their case against him, they revived an old charge that he had owned stock in a company involved in litigation before his court. The evidence of conflict of interest was not very strong, but so great was Senate sensitivity to charges of judicial impropriety after the Fortas affair that the Haynsworth nomination was rejected, 45 to 55.

In his annoyance at this rebuff, Nixon now submitted the name of a judge much less qualified than Haynsworth. Senate liberals revealed that the nominee, G. Harrold Carswell of Florida, a judge on the Fifth Circuit Court of Appeals, had been a racist in his earlier political career and had treated black litigants in his court with disdain. Moreover, he had been a mediocre judge, frequently overruled on appeal. Seven of his fellow judges on an eighteen-man court declined to recommend him, and many law school deans and prominent lawyers protested against the appointment. In the end, the Senate rejected him 45 to 51, with such respected Republicans as Kentucky's Marlow Cook and Maine's Margaret Chase Smith voting with the majority. In a bitter statement to the press, the "old Nixon" suddenly reappeared:

> With yesterday's action, the Senate has said that no Southern federal appellate judge who believes in a strict interpretation of the Constitution can be elevated to the Supreme Court. As long as the Senate is constituted the way it is today, I will not nominate another Southerner and let him be subjected to the kind of malicious character assassination accorded both Judges Haynsworth and Carswell.

This rebuke did not endear the President to the Senate, but it gained him wide applause in the South.

Nixon's ambition to reshape the Court was thwarted only briefly. In May, 1970, the Senate unanimously approved Judge Harry Blackmun of Minnesota, thus filling the Fortas seat that had been vacant for a year. The Burger Court was now composed of five conservatives and four liberals. In September, 1971, the death of Hugo Black and the resignation of John Harlan gave the President an opportunity to make two new appointments. The President first asked the American Bar Association to evaluate six possible candidates whose credentials were so unimpressive that he was accused of trying to downgrade the Supreme Court by staffing it with mediocrities. This sleight of hand made his eventual conservative nominees, Lewis F. Powell, a respected lawyer from Richmond, Virginia, and Assistant Attorney General William Rehnquist look good enough to win Senate approval.

By other means as well, Nixon sought to establish himself as the champion of law and order. The new Attorney General toughened up the administration of the Justice Department and obtained new anticrime legislation. To combat notoriously unsafe conditions in the national capital, Congress passed a special act for the District of Columbia with controversial provisions authorizing the police to enter homes without knocking under certain warrants, permitting pretrial detention without bail for allegedly dangerous suspects, and authorizing wiretaps under court orders. Other new laws provided the death penalty for bombings involving loss of life and made bombings and arson at federally aided colleges Federal crimes. Congress strengthened the administration's hand in its antidrug campaign by tougher penalties for sellers and no-knock authority for the police in raids on suspected premises. Although the Burger Court interpreted the rights of accused more strictly, it did not entirely reverse the humane precedents of the Warren Court. Indeed, in Furman *v.* Georgia (1972), the Court broke new ground by holding capital punishment unconstitutional as "cruel and unusual," except when the law made it mandatory.

Civil Rights

In cracking down on murderers and dope peddlers, Nixon was an earnest champion of law and order, but in dealing with violations of the rights of black people he was far less zealous in upholding the law. Fifteen years before he became President the Supreme Court had ruled that all laws requiring segregation of school children were unconstitutional, but most school districts in the Deep South had continued to maintain their dual systems. In the Civil Rights Act of 1964, Congress had empowered the Justice Department to initiate suits against school districts where parents or children complained of denial of equal opportunity. The same law provided the Federal government with a powerful weapon by prohibiting the grant of Federal funds to any activity in which there was discrimination. Under President Johnson vigorous Attorneys General and Secretaries of Health, Education and Welfare (HEW) had kept the heat under Southern school districts and forced most of them into programs of desegregation, but a recalcitrant minority were still defying Federal law and were looking to President-elect Nixon for a change of policy.

Nixon's Southern strategy involved wooing Southern white politicians and voters away from George Wallace and into the Republican camp in preparation for the 1972 election. At first, there seemed to be relatively little that the President could do for his Southern clients. During the campaign he had given his blessing to "freedom of choice"—an euphemism for allowing dual schools to continue except for those few black children whose parents were courageous enough to request transfers. The Supreme Court, however, had shut this door even before the election. In Green v. County School Board (1968), it had ruled that the goal was to achieve "a unitary, nonracial school system" and, unless it helped to speed that end, " 'freedom of choice' must be held unacceptable." This left the Nixon administration only the limited alternatives of vigorous enforcement of existing civil rights law or flaccid complicity with Southern requests for delay. As one of the masterminds of the Southern strategy, Attorney General Mitchell was in a good position to dampen Justice Department ardor in the civil rights field. The role of HEW Secretary Finch was much more ambivalent. As a member of the more liberal wing of the Republican party, he appointed Leon Panetta, an energetic young lawyer, to heard the HEW Office for Civil Rights and supported many of the latter's recommendations. At the same time, however, Finch was too ambitious a politician to withstand conservative pressure from the White House. As a result, he fluctuated between firm enforcement by cutting off funds to noncomplying Southern school districts and weak grants of delay. In the very first month of the administration Finch relaxed HEW policy against five school districts in South Carolina, the home state of Senator Thurmond, "Mr. Southern Republican." Finch's vulnerability to political influence was even more painfully evident in August, 1969, when the administration changed gears in the midst of litigation involving thirty-three Mississippi school districts. Although HEW experts had already approved desegregation plans for the fall school opening, Finch wrote a letter to the Federal judge warning that speedy action would cause "chaos, confusion and a catastrophic educational setback." The Secretary sent different experts into court to disavow the findings of the first group, and Justice Department lawyers joined those for the state of Mississippi in requesting delay.

What lay behind this flip-flop? Apparently it was the desperate eagerness of the Nixon administration to mollify Mississippi's powerful Democrat, Senator John Stennis, then leading a fight for the Pentagon's Antiballistic Missile (ABM) program. Although the circuit court granted the requested delay, the Supreme Court overruled it in a sweeping action (Alexander *v.* Holmes County, 1969). In a unanimous decision that included Chief Justice Burger, Nixon's appointee, the Court declared that "the obligation of every school district is to terminate dual school systems at once and to operate now and hereafter only unitary schools."

This Mississippi case still further restricted the President's options. In February, 1970, he pleased his Southern constituency by abruptly firing Panetta. On March 24, 1970, the President issued his most comprehensive statement on civil rights policy. Defending himself against liberal criticism, he declared: "We are not backing away. The Constitutional mandate will be enforced." He promised not only to compel compliance with the laws against discrimination, but to work for more jobs and better housing for blacks. He would ask Congress for $1.5 billion to improve education in racially impacted areas, North and South, and to help school districts meet the problems caused by court-ordered desegregation. But Nixon's proposals to help the blacks were carefully qualified. Emphasizing the distinction between *de jure* segregation based on discriminatory laws and *de facto* segregation based on residential patterns, he made it clear that his administration did not intend to move against the latter. Most significantly, the President promised that "transportation beyond normal geographical school zones for the purpose of achieving a racial balance will not be required." In other words, the administration would oppose forced busing as a means of changing the complexion of predominantly white or black schools.

Politically, Nixon played a winning card with his antibusing stand. By stealing Wallace's most potent slogan the President won widespread support, not only in the South, but in the Northern suburbs as well. Fearing that the courts would order extensive busing to desegregate the urban ghettoes, the suburbanites were rallying in increasing numbers to politicians who would promise to save their all-white schools from so dire a fate. Lower court orders in 1972 requiring busing across suburban lines in Richmond, Detroit, and other metropolitan areas brought the issue into sharp focus. Especially feared was so-called reverse busing—the busing of white pupils into schools located in black neighborhoods.

The President pushed his advantage relentlessly. On March 16, 1972, he made an appearance on television to describe two proposals he was sending to Congress. One bill would impose a "moratorium" on court orders requiring new busing until June 1, 1973, or until Congress passed the second of his proposed bills, an "equal educational opportunities act." By asking $2.5 billion for the improvement of education in the ghettoes, the President seemed to be offering a generous bribe to the blacks to accept the continuance of all-black schools. Actually, he was playing a numbers game, combining $1 billion already authorized under earlier legislation and $1.5 billion that he had requested on earlier occasions. Critics of the Nixon proposals argued that the moratorium on court orders was probably unconstitutional and that aid to the ghetto schools relied upon a concept of compensatory education that had already been tried and found ineffective.

Many members of Congress were even more eager than Nixon to go on record as opposed to "forced busing." Northern legislators, some of them with strong civil rights records, now sought to appease their suburban constituents before the 1972 election. Despite this situation there was no clear majority for the Nixon proposals. Some legislators wanted to outdo the President by enacting much more drastic legislation than he had asked; some wanted to undercut him by consenting to mild measures that would still leave the courts with authority to require busing if this were necessary to achieve desegregation. By a rider added to an educational aid bill in June, 1972, Congress attempted to stay lower court orders requiring busing "for the purpose of achieving a balance among students with respect to race" until all appeals had been exhausted or until January 1, 1974. Since this did not ban busing as a remedy for actual segregation, the conservatives pushed for more drastic legislation and a constitutional amendment that would curb the power of the courts. In order to stall off a tough antibusing bill in October, 1972, Senate liberals had to resort to a filibuster—the favorite weapon of harassed Southern conservatives in the past.

From the moral point of view, Nixon's championship of the antibusing cause left much to be desired. It appealed to emotion and prejudice in an area where reason and good will were imperative. It betrayed thousands of Southern moderates who had accepted the inevitability and justice of desegregating the schools. It helped to prove that Southern conservatives had been right in charging that Northern liberals were hypocritical and would never integrate their own all-white schools. The Nixon policy also damaged the prestige of black moderates who had encouraged legal action instead of violence; it pleased only a minority of black militants who scorned the goal of integration.

But the Nixon administration record in dealing with minority groups was not all negative. It did its best work in opening up new opportunities for employment. With commendable courage, Secretary of Labor George Shultz pushed the so-called Philadelphia Plan that sought to provide jobs for blacks on Federal construction. Since most local construction unions had notoriously discriminated against blacks, the government now required that contractors and unions working on government buildings accept certain numbers of black apprentices for training and eventual union membership. By a somewhat similar use of the Federal power to award contracts and grants, HEW nudged colleges and universities into "affirmative action" programs that would result in the recruitment of more teachers and employees from the several groups that had suffered from discrimination—blacks, Chicanos, and women.

Nixon the Reformer

"We intend to begin a decade of government reform such as this nation has not witnessed in half a century," declared President Nixon in a message to Congress on October 13, 1969. "That is the watchword of this Administration: *Reform*." In rhetoric still more soaring, he called upon Congress in January, 1971 to open the way to "a New American Revolution." Journalists with sources of information in the White House attributed much of this fervor to the influence of Patrick Moynihan, who encouraged the President to emulate the strategy of Benjamin Disraeli, the great British conservative, in winning working-class support by prudent programs of reform.

There was, however, one great difference between Disraeli and Nixon. The former led a Tory majority in Parliament; the latter had to deal with a Democratic Congress. Actually, the President could not even count on solid Republican support for his reform proposals. Moynihan projects had first to overcome the suspicion of Attorney General Mitchell and other conservative advisers; then in Congress they encountered opposition from both conservative Republicans and conservative Democrats. On the other hand, liberal Democrats always looked upon Nixon's proposals with suspicion and sought to go farther and faster than he wanted. Consequently, his program had to enlist most of its support from liberal and moderate Republicans and moderate Democrats. Sometimes this was enough to result in legislation; more often it was not.

Boldest of the Moynihan-Nixon proposals was the Family Assistance Plan (FAP), which Nixon presented in a TV speech in August, 1969. Instead of the confused system of Federal welfare grants, the government would make a cash payment to maintain a prescribed minimum income level—$1,600 a year in the case of a family of four where there was no wage earner. To assist families where someone was working in a low-income job, the government would make graduated grants until the family income reached $3,920. Attempting to make FAP more palatable to conservatives, the President emphasized provisions designed to force the beneficiaries to work. All unemployed heads of families receiving assistance, except the disabled and mothers of preschool children, would be required to take job training.

The Nixon proposals drew fire from both right and left. Conservatives protested that FAP would be far too expensive; liberals complained that the prescribed minimum income was too niggardly for decent subsistence and that it was heartless to require work in an economy where there were not enough jobs. Yet moderate opinion welcomed a fresh approach to the existing welfare system, which was both burdensome to the taxpayers and demeaning to the poor. Wilbur Mills, the powerful Democratic chairman of the House Ways and Means Committee, guided a bill containing the essence of the Nixon program through the lower house in 1970. In the Senate, however, the welfare reform bill encountered so much crossfire that it failed to emerge from the Finance Committee. In the Ninty-second Congress this pattern of events was more or less repeated. The House passed a bill in line with the President's request, but the Senate was still so divided on the issue that it took no action before adjournment in 1972. Critics accused Nixon of complicity in this outcome; he seemed to have less and less enthusiasm for FAP as he sensed the depth of middle-class resentment against the welfare recipients.

Revenue sharing, a second major Nixon proposal, had a happier history. As presented in his State of the Union Message in January, 1971, the plan called for eliminating a number of specific Federal programs and substituting $16 billion in general purpose grants to the states and cities to administer as they thought best. This would promote what the President called "the New

Federalism" by halting the steady enlargement of the central government and returning more responsibility to local communities. Since most Senators and Congressmen looked with suspicion upon a policy that would sharply reduce their power of specific appropriation, prospects for revenue sharing did not at first look bright. But governors and mayors of both parties, desperate for more money to meet a wide variety of needs, brought strong pressure to bear, and in October, 1972, Congress approved a revenue-sharing program that would funnel $30.1 billion of Federal money to state and local governments over a five-year period.

Closely linked to the revenue-sharing plan in Nixon's 1971 message was a proposal to reorganize the Federal departments. Accepting the recommendations of an Advisory Committee on Executive Organization headed by Roy Ash, a prominent businessman, the President sought to reduce the number of cabinet officers from eleven to eight. Of the old departments only State, Treasury, Defense, and Justice would continue; the others would be consolidated into four new departments: Human Resources, Community Development, Natural Resources, and Economic Development. Congressional fear of increasing executive power and decreasing legislative control, however, prevented legislation. Instead, Nixon continued the process of undercutting the cabinet and consolidating power in the White House. Moynihan went back to Harvard in 1971, but other White House aides, especially John Ehrlichman and H. R. ("Bob") Haldeman, became men of extraordinary power sometimes accused of maintaining a Berlin Wall around the President.

In calling for legislation to protect the environment, Nixon was taking up a problem of great concern, particularly to young people. By an ironic turn of events, Secretary of the Interior Walter Hickel became a focus of controversy. When his appointment was first announced, environmentalists denounced him as a millionaire businessman who had been hostile to conservation while governor of Alaska. But Hickel soon won over his critics by taking firm action to protect the Florida Everglades from a proposed jetport and to penalize oil companies responsible for leakage from drilling operations off the California and Gulf coasts. Young people admired Hickel even more when he spoke out in their defense in a letter to the President after the Kent State affair. Apparently festering resentment over this criticism motivated Nixon in firing Hickel in November, 1970, and naming in his place Rogers Morton, chairman of the Republican National Committee and a man not likely to carry the environmentalist cause to impractical lengths. This indeed was the problem with environmentalism. The principal polluters were the huge corporations such as the auto manufacturers, the aviation industry, and the oil companies. The probusiness Nixon administration sought moderate legislation that would improve conditions without placing expensive burdens on industry. Some congressional champions of the environment, prodded by reformers like Ralph Nader, wanted more drastic action. Despite these differences, Congress and the President were able to agree on some positive measures to protect lakes and rivers, aid local sewage and waste disposal projects, and cut down on noxious fumes from automobiles.

In August, 1970, Congress responded to a presidential initiative by establishing the United States Postal Service, intended to take this deficit-ridden agency out of politics and place it under a Board of Governors who would appoint the Postmaster General and operate the service on a business basis. But the increase in revenues and improvement in service promised by the advocates of postal reform were slow in coming.

Struggle Against Inflation

During Johnson's second term, inflationary pressures—endemic to the American economy since World War II—intensified. Between 1965 and 1968 the consumer price index went up over 10 per cent. Economists attributed this to a variety of forces: overstimulation of investment by the tax cut of 1964, the expenses of the Vietnam war, and heavy Federal spending for the social programs of the Great Society. In a belated effort to apply the brakes Congress had enacted a 10 per cent income tax surcharge in 1968.

Although Nixon considered the halting of inflation to be one of his most important tasks, he was limited in his choice of weapons by his conservative philosophy. Convinced by his own brief service in the World War II OPA that price control led to black markets and regimentation, he at first ruled out any step in this direction. He even rejected "jawboning"—the verbal rebukes by which Kennedy and Johnson had exerted pressure against price raises in key industries. Instead, he sought to use the favorite conservative remedies: tightening credit and cutting government spending. During the first six months of 1969 the Federal Reserve Board raised interest rates so sharply that businessmen and real estate dealers began to take alarm. Unwilling to risk throwing the nation into a depression, the Board relaxed its tight money policy during the fall.

Nixon was no more successful in trying to combat inflation by cutting government expenditures. Instead of spending less, the Federal government spent more each year: in fiscal 1968–1969 the budget totaled $194.6 billion; for fiscal 1972–1973 the President fought a losing fight to hold expenditures to $250 billion. Meanwhile, revenues were lagging farther and farther behind so that Nixon's first four years in office accumulated a deficit of more than $100 billion. Who was responsible for this shocking departure from principles laid down by such Republican saints as Calvin Coolidge and Andrew Mellon? The President blamed free-spending Democratic Congresses, which often appropriated more than he asked for existing agencies and were still mandating new programs. He publicized his disapproval by several vetoes— of HEW appropriation and hospital aid bills in 1970, a child-care center bill in 1971, and a water pollution bill in 1972. Sometimes Congress sustained these vetoes; sometimes it did not. Whereas Nixon wanted to save money in social services, liberal Democrats found more congenial targets in appropriations for the armed services or subsidies to industry. The liberals failed to prevent authorization of the expensive ABM system, but they did kill Federal sponsorship for developing a supersonic transport plane (SST)—a victory both for economy and ecology.

A President and Congress seriously concerned about inflation would have closed the budgetary gap by higher taxes, but neither party wanted to risk such a step. Better still, President and Congress could have cooperated in plugging the notorious loopholes—oil depletion allowances, capital gains deduction, investment credit, municipal bond exemptions, and the like—by which individuals and corporations were reducing their income tax obligations at an expense to the Treasury estimated as high as $50 billion a year. But reform efforts in 1969 had puny results: the oil depletion allowance was cut from 27.5 per cent to 22 per cent; the investment credit was dropped; and personal exemptions were raised. Instead of increasing government revenues, however, the new revenue act reduced them by $2.5 billion a year. The struggle over the bill had demonstrated that the President would not support any drastic attack on the tax shelters of his business backers and that Congress was still under the influence of powerful lobbies.

Nixon was not really a budget-balancer. He had to worry not only about inflation, but about unemployment. Believing that Eisenhower's conservatism on economic policy had led to Kennedy's victory in the 1960 election, Nixon was determined not to let a lagging economy sink into a full recession. Now a professed Keynesian, the President began to talk in terms of a full-employment budget—that is, a budget temporarily out of balance, but which would be balanced when increased production and employment produced expected revenues. Although Nixon was sincere in wanting to reduce the alarming gap between expenditures and revenues, he accepted the necessity of a moderate deficit to feed money into the economy.

Although the President was already a heretic on the doctrine of balanced budget, he continued to insist that the government should not intervene directly to control wages and prices. In August, 1971, however, he found it necessary to change his mind. The economic skies were filling with thunder clouds. Instead of slowing down, inflation was accelerating. The consumer price index had risen 5.6 in 1969, 6.5 in 1970, and almost 4.0 in the first six months of 1971. Yet inflation was not linked to any accompanying prosperity: industrial production was lagging and 6.1 per cent of the labor force was unemployed. Moreover, American exports had leveled off, imports were increasing, and a critical balance of payments problem was developing. Under existing exchange ratios the American dollar was overvalued in relation to the German mark, the Japanese yen, and other foreign currencies. This was great for American tourists abroad, but damaging to American exporters.

In a TV address on August 15, 1971, President Nixon announced a radically different economic game plan. Under authority voted to him by Congress a year earlier that he had said that he would never use, the President now froze all wages, prices, and rents for ninety days. To improve the position of the dollar abroad, he cut its tie with gold and allowed it to float freely in foreign exchange. To reduce imports, he imposed a 10 per cent surtax on a wide list of goods. To stimulate industry and reduce unemployment, he asked Congress for changes in the tax laws: repeal of a 7 per cent excise tax on automobiles, granting of a 10 per cent tax cut for new investments, and more generous personal exemptions. The President appointed a Cost of Living Council headed by Secretary of the Treasury John Connally to administer the new program.

Nixon's price-wage freeze—the boldest Presidential initiative in economic policy since New Deal days—encountered bitter criticism. AFL-CIO President George Meany denounced a policy that froze wages but not corporate profits, dividends, or interest, calling it "Robin Hood in reverse because it robs from the poor and gives to the rich." Foreign statesmen denounced the tariff surcharge and the floating dollar as threatening a world trade war. But Nixon could afford to shrug off such criticism in view of the general popular approval of his action. Despite some Democratic fault-finding, Congress cooperated by giving the President the changes in the tax laws that he wanted.

Secretary Connally, a Democrat and former governor of Texas, was the dominant figure over the next few weeks. Breezy and confident, Connally out-talked all critics at home and played his hand like a Western poker-player in international negotiations. At a monetary conference in December, the United States agreed to reduce the exchange value of the dollar by about 12 per cent and to drop the 10 per cent import surtax in return for raises in the exchange rate of foreign currencies and other trade concessions.

What would come next after the wage-price freeze expired on November 13, 1972? Well in advance of that date, the President announced his plans for "Phase 2," which would continue controls but introduce a measure of flexibility. He appointed a Price Commission of seven members headed by Dean C. Jackson Grayson, Jr., of Southern Methodist University's business school, with authority to pass on requests for higher prices, and a Pay Board with five representatives each from labor, industry, and the public, headed by Federal District Judge George Boldt, to consider proposed wage hikes. The Cost of Living Council under Connally would have general supervisory powers. The new economic high command soon laid down its general guide lines. The overall goal was to reduce the rate of inflation to between 2 and 3 per cent annually: to achieve this the Price Commission would permit price raises of no more than 2.5 per cent and the Wage Board would hold pay increases to 5.5 per cent. In support of Nixon's policy Congress extended his control authority to April 30, 1973.

The new machinery—kept purposely simple by Nixon—did not operate without occasional clashing of gears. In March, 1972, Meany and three other labor members resigned from the Pay Board. The AFL-CIO president denounced the failure of Phase 2 to control rising food prices and corporate profits. "There is no fairness, no equity, no justice in the Administration's economic policy," he said. Nixon retaliated by calling the Meany group "totally selfish and irresponsible" and by reorganizing the Pay Board to include five public members, one industry member, and one labor member— Frank Fitzsimmons of the Teamsters' Union, an anti–AFL-CIO body.

During its first year Nixon's new economic policy was neither a great success nor a great failure. The rate of inflation declined to 3.2 per cent, within sight of the 2 to 3 per cent target. Uncontrolled food prices, however, were meanwhile rising at a 4.2 per cent rate. Wages were, for the most part, held within the 5.5 per cent raise guide line. Industrial production, aided by the new incentives, rose about 9 per cent during the year with an even faster growth in business profits. But the good news was balanced by bad. In the fall of 1972 there were still about five million unemployed—5.5 per cent of labor force—and the deficit in foreign trade was still running almost $500 million a month. Politically, however, Nixon had scored impressive gains by erasing the image of a do-nothing President and substituting that of a bold and imaginative leader.

Adventures in Diplomacy

The activist role, which Nixon first avoided and then assumed in economic affairs, characterized his foreign policy from the start. His close associates described the President as bored by domestic problems but fascinated by world politics. He dramatized his role by frequent trips to foreign capitals. On the first of these, undertaken just a month after his inauguration, Nixon visited Belgium, England, West Germany, Italy, and France. He sought no new agreements; his purpose, he said, was the "strengthening and revitalizing" of the North Atlantic Alliance. Beyond this, he was trying to lay the groundwork for an ultimate understanding with the Soviet Union. He wanted, he said, to end the era of confrontations and enter that of negotiations.

In July, 1969, Nixon embarked on a much more extensive tour. After greeting the first astronauts to land on the moon on an aircraft carrier in the Pacific, he flew on to Guam where he outlined the principles that would guide his policy in Asia. The United States, he said, would continue to be a "Pacific power," ready to protect its vital interests and support both its allies and other nations in case of external Communist attack. However, he wanted no more Vietnams. He opposed the use of American ground troops to put down domestic rebellions. In the future, the United States would concentrate on economic and technical help and encourage the Asiatic nations to take over their own defense. Sometimes called the Nixon Doctrine, this policy statement might be more accurately described as a characteristically Nixon balancing act, promising American help to threatened nations but avoiding the interventionist quagmire that had sucked in the Johnson administration.

From Guam, Nixon flew on around the world making brief stops in the capitals of the Philippines, Indonesia, Thailand, South Vietnam, India, Pakistan, and Rumania. By accepting the invitation to visit Bucharest, the President made a significant breakthrough. Not since Roosevelt's fateful trip to Yalta had an American President visited a Communist country. Nixon's choice of Rumania was significant. In the intricate politics of the Communist world, the Bucharest government had been leaning away from the leadership of Moscow and toward that of Peking. The President was thus beginning his game of courting better relations with China as a means of moving the Russians toward a more helpful attitude—helpful in negotiating a settlement of the Vietnam war, in damping down the explosive Middle Eastern situation, in reducing friction over Berlin, and in putting limits on the dangerous race in nuclear weapons.

Nixon had good reason to worry about the Middle East, where the Soviet Union was capitalizing on Arab anger over Israel's triumph in the Six Days War of 1967 and occupation of Arab territory. By supplying arms and advisers to Egypt, Syria, and Iraq, the Russians were bringing these countries under their influence. At the same time they were building up a strong fleet in the eastern Mediterranean to challenge the naval power of the United States and its NATO allies. In an effort to defuse this explosive situation, the Nixon administration at first modified what it considered to be the excessively pro-Israel policy of the Johnson administration. It delayed supplying additional arms to the Israelis, while it tried to negotiate with the Soviet Union and Egypt on a plan calling for Israeli withdrawal from the occupied territories in return for a recognition of Israel's right to exist and to use the Suez Canal and other waterways. Although the Nixon administration did help to obtain an Israeli-Egyptian cease-fire along the Suez Canal, it did not have much success with its other attempts at mediation. The Israelis complained bitterly that their American friends were deserting them, while the Soviet Union and Egypt would not agree on any terms reasonable enough for the Americans to urge the Israelis to accept.

In the summer of 1970, the Middle East seemed about to explode again. Angry because King Hussein of Jordan would not allow his territory to be used for raids on Israel—raids that always provoked severe Israeli reprisals— Palestinian commandos attacked the king's army. Syria intervened in this civil war by sending tanks to help the rebels. The Nixon administration was greatly alarmed by the peril of the situation. To prevent Hussein's overthrow, the Israelis might use their air force against both the Syrians and the Egyptians. The Russians might then intervene to protect their clients; the United States might have to take countermeasures, and the long-feared World War III would have started. To forestall this disaster, Nixon appealed to the Russians to restrain the Syrians and at the same time strengthened the Sixth Fleet in the Mediterranean. Fortunately, Hussein's air force proved stronger than expected and mauled the Syrian tank force enough to hasten its withdrawal from Jordanian territory. As tension relaxed, the President underscored American interest in the Mediterranean by visiting the Sixth Fleet as well as Italy, the Vatican, and Spain. Once again he courted one of Moscow's rivals in the Communist world by stopping in Yugoslavia to confer with Marshal Tito. He returned to the United States by way of Ireland—the homeland of some of his ancestors, politician Nixon announced.

Meanwhile, the sudden death of President Nasser posed new problems. When his successor, Anwar Sadat, professed himself no less determined to crush Israel and no less loyal to the Russian alliance, Nixon resumed the policy of selling enough arms to Israel to preserve her military supremacy in the area. Eventually Sadat rebelled against Russian intrigue in Egyptian affairs and expelled the Russian advisers—a step that somewhat reduced American anxieties about the Middle East.

Ever since the Communists overran mainland China in 1949, the United States had followed an unfriendly policy toward the new regime. It had refused to recognize the People's Republic of China as the official government, had led the fight to keep it out of the United Nations, and had made a defense treaty and given massive military aid to the rival Chiang Kai-shek government on Taiwan.

Ironically, it was Nixon, one of the old hard-liners against Communist China, who initiated a significant change of policy. Seeing in the rivalry of Moscow and Peking an opportunity to play one against the other, the President began early in his first term to drop hints that he wished to set up some kind of dialogue with the People's Republic. On China's side,

Chairman Mao Tse-tung and Premier Chou En-lai feared Russian attack and were in a mood to respond to Nixon's signals. In their aid to North Vietnam the Chinese Communists carefully avoided any step that would involve them in direct hostilities with the Americans. In April, 1971, Premier Chou made a friendly overture by inviting a touring American ping-pong team to play in Peking. The invitation was accepted, and American journalists—permitted to visit mainland China for the first time since the Communist take-over—sent back reports not only of Chinese mastery in the game of ping-pong but of everyday life behind the bamboo curtain. Nixon promptly responded to this Chinese hospitality by relaxing the American trade embargo to allow trade with China in nonstrategic goods.

Three months later, in July, 1971, the American public received a still greater surprise when the President announced that Henry Kissinger, while on an Asian fact-finding tour, had eluded reporters in Pakistan by feigning a stomach upset and made a secret trip to Peking. As a result of two days of discussion between Chou and Kissinger, Nixon was able to inform his TV audience that he had accepted an invitation to visit China himself sometime before May, 1972.

Although the President tried to reassure Chiang Kai-shek that he would not pursue his new China policy "at the expense of our old friends," the Taiwan government had good reason to be alarmed. At the UN General Assembly in October, 1971, the United States proposed a "two-China" policy—that is, of admitting Communist China to membership but allowing Nationalist China to remain a member also. But the small nations, resentful of the earlier stubbornness of the United States on the China question, were in no mood to compromise. Rejecting the two-China idea, the required majority voted to admit Communist China and expel Nationalist China.

On February 21, 1972, President and Mrs. Nixon, accompanied by a large entourage of officials, advisers, and journalists, landed in the Peking airport to begin a hectic week of ceremonial functions, high-level talks, and sightseeing. The visit was the year's best television show, but what did it accomplish? Not much, in the way of explicit agreement. In the carefully phrased communiqué issued at the time of Nixon's departure, the emphasis was on peaceful coexistence. China reasserted its right of sovereignty over Taiwan but refrained from any threat of force. The United States conceded the principle that there should be one China and promised to withdraw its forces from the area whenever Peking and Taipei could settle the question peacefully. The Nixon visit had much more importance as a symbolic event than as a diplomatic conference. By clicking glasses in toast after toast, President Nixon and Premier Chou publicly acknowledged the futility of a policy of not talking to each other. What they would actually say would depend on future events. Moreover, since no agreement to restore normal diplomatic relations was announced, communication would presumably continue through Kissinger-like agents.

By his dramatic trip to China, Nixon had captured the headlines during an election year. In May, 1972, he gained still further publicity by making a trip to Moscow. Superficially similar in their rounds of banqueting, sightseeing, and negotiating, the China and Russia missions differed greatly in

President and Mrs. Nixon and Secretary of State Rogers on the Great Wall of
China, 1972. (UPI Photo.)

their immediate results. Because of many months of patient exploration,
the American and Soviet leaders were able to cap off the Moscow visit by
signing two highly significant agreements and several lesser ones. Ambitious
to win a place in history as a great peacemaker, Nixon had begun early
in his presidency to push for a Soviet-American agreement limiting the
deployment of nuclear weapons. Preliminary SALT (Strategic Arms Limitation Talks) negotiations had been conducted in Helsinki, Finland, during
December and November, 1969. This had led the way to several rounds
of formal talks at Vienna and Helsinki. The problems of nuclear disarmament were extraordinarily technical and difficult. Because of the danger
and expense of the arms race, each side wanted some kind of limitation,
but progress in the negotiations was slow. A breakthrough became possible
when the two parties consented to make agreements on some of the problems while continuing to negotiate on the rest. During his Moscow visit,
therefore, the President was able to join in the signing of a treaty on
defensive weapons limiting the building of antiballistic missile systems
(ABMs) to two sites in each country—in the case of the United States
around Washington, D.C., and an IBM site in North Dakota. On the issue
of offensive weapons—much more difficult because of the extensive deployment already carried out—the two countries agreed to freeze for a period
of five years missiles at their current levels—1,054 land-based and 635 sea-
based for the Americans, 1,550 land-based and 740 sea-based for the Rus-

sians. The apparent Soviet superiority was misleading. Because of multiple, separately targetable warheads (MIRVs) the United States had a substantial, if perhaps temporary, advantage. Because of possible difficulties in obtaining Senate ratification for this offensive weapon freeze, this agreement was in a form requiring only concurrent action by the two houses of Congress. Besides these major accords, the American and Russian leaders agreed to establish a joint commission to study environmental problems, to accept rules to prevent collisions at sea between both ships and planes, to carry out joint space projects, to cooperate in science and technology, and to resolve trade problems through a special commission.

The American public appeared to greet the thaw in Soviet-American relations with relief and approval. In the Senate, Henry Jackson, the Democratic hawk of Washington, criticized the SALT agreements as conceding too much to the Russians and succeeded in getting congressional approval for a proviso that in any future accords the United States would not accept any inferiority to the Soviet Union. Except for this reservation the Nixon agreements won overwhelming support. On August 3 the Senate approved the treaty on ABM systems by a vote of 88 to 2, and in September the two houses passed a resolution approving the five-year freeze on offensive weapons. Meanwhile, the Soviet Union had met a harvest shortage at home by making a large purchase of American wheat. Although the Democrats charged that Nixon administration mismanagement and favoritism had resulted in too much profit for the middleman and not enough for the farmer, the wheat deal opened exciting possibilities for widely expanded Russian-American trade. All in all, Nixon's adventures in diplomacy were successful enough—particularly in 1972—to give him a powerful advantage in his re-election campaign.

The Nixon Tide

The congressional elections of 1970 gave no reason to predict that Nixon would win re-election by a landslide two years later. Both the President and the Vice President had made tough speeches denouncing the Democrats, but these tactics had seemed to boomerang. The Republicans lost 9 seats in the House, which now had 254 Democrats to 181 Republicans. In the Senate they did slightly better by winning 2 seats, but the Democrats still had 54 seats to 44 for the Republicans, and 2 for independents. In state contests the Republican record was even poorer: they lost 9 governorships so that there were now 29 Democratic governors to 21 Republicans. As a shrewd politician, Nixon apparently decided that the policies of his first two years had been too cautious and conservative. During 1971 he struck out boldly in new directions, as evidenced by his acceptance of the Keynesian budget, wage-price controls, and friendlier relations with Communist China and the Soviet Union.

During the early months of 1969 it seemed probable that the Democratic party would bestow its next presidential nomination on Senator Edward Kennedy, whether he wanted it or not. Millions loved him as the political heir of his popular brothers. Moreover, he had great assets for a presidential candidate: he was handsome, eloquent, and liberal—a master campaigner with a warm, outgoing personality. But Kennedy's career suffered a major setback because of a tragic accident on the night of July 18, 1969. A car that he was driving back from a party on Chappaquiddick Island off Martha's Vineyard careened off a primitive bridge into the water below. The Senator escaped from the submerged vehicle but was unable to rescue the girl who was with him. In a TV speech the Massachusetts Senator denied that he had been drinking or was involved in an illicit love affair. He explained his ten-hour delay in reporting the accident as the result of shock and confusion. Although many admirers, especially those in Massachusetts, rushed to his support, he suffered a sharp decline in popularity with the general public. Whether or not he had been guilty of any moral transgression, he had not handled this personal crisis in a way to create confidence in his ability to withstand the pressures and tensions of the presidency. Unwilling to put his family through further unpleasantness, Kennedy resisted all efforts to make him the 1972 Democratic candidate.

The next front-runner was Senator Edmund Muskie of Maine. He had won respect by his effective campaigning as vice-presidential candidate in 1968 and made a particularly impressive presentation of the Democratic case on the eve of the 1970 congressional elections. He gained so many endorsements from local Democratic leaders that he seemed in a very strong position early in 1972. He ran poorly, however, in the early Democratic primaries, seemingly unable to arouse any genuine enthusiasm among the voters. Discouraged and short of money, he gave up his active campaign at the end of April.

This reduced the Democratic field to three major contenders—Hubert Humphrey, once again Senator from Minnesota as a result of the election of 1970, Governor George Wallace of Alabama, and Senator George McGovern of South Dakota. Once considered an advanced liberal, Senator Humphrey was now regarded as a middle-of-the-roader. Many of the old professionals in the party supported him strongly for this very reason, as did George Meany of the AFL-CIO. But in the political climate of 1972, the middle position did not have as many advantages as usual. Humphrey and Muskie tended to divide the moderate vote so long as Muskie remained in the race. After he dropped out, Humphrey suffered because many Democratic voters still associated him with the Lyndon Johnson policies. Democratic dissidents of the right voted for Wallace; dissidents of the left for McGovern. As a result, Humphrey did poorly in the primaries, winning only in a few states such as Pennsylvania and Minnesota.

Governor Wallace capitalized not only on widespread dislike for court-ordered busing of school children, but on middle-class resentment against all persons regarded as troublemakers—blacks, welfare recipients, anti-Vietnam demonstrators, college radicals, and feminists. Wallace's strong appeal to Southern Democrats was confirmed when he swept the Florida primary in March. If he could also capture a few Northern delegations, he would make himself a force to be reckoned with at the National Convention. Although it would probably be impossible for him to win the nomination, he might be able to swing his delegates to some acceptable candidate and gain concessions in the party platform. Once again, however, an act of violence disrupted the political process. A jobless young man, Arthur Bremer, shot Wallace during a campaign appearance in a Maryland shopping center on May 15—just one day before he won striking victories in the Michigan and Maryland primaries. Wallace's injuries paralyzed him from the waist down, and he was able to play only a minor role in the events of the next few months.

Not very well known in the country as a whole, Senator McGovern captured the Democratic nomination because of the tireless efforts of his young workers. In state after state these newcomers to politics made thousands of telephone calls and house-to-house visitations, delivering every possible McGovern vote to the polls on primary day. In this way McGovern won primary victories in Wisconsin, Massachusetts, California, New York, and six other states. Meanwhile, he had also been unexpectedly successful in picking up delegates in the states that had no primaries. Under new rules, formulated by a committee that McGovern himself had headed, the Democratic party had democratized itself, making it impossible for a few local leaders to pick the delegates. The new rules required that delegations contain substantial percentages of women, blacks, Chicanos, and young people—all groups with whom McGovern was strong.

The Democratic National Convention, which opened in Miami on July 10, differed strikingly from all its predecessors. Some 80 per cent of the delegates had never attended a convention before. All the hitherto underrepresented groups—especially women, young people and blacks—were present in force. On the other hand, many powerful figures of other years were not even present. Mayor Daley of Chicago and his hand-picked Illinois delegation were denied seats under the new rules. In a desperate effort to deprive McGovern of the nomination, his opponents challenged the seats of 271 delegates won by McGovern in a winner-take-all California primary. Humphrey and other candidates demanded that the delegates be split in proportion to the votes they had received in the primary. The Credentials Committee upheld the challenge, but the full convention overruled this decision by a vote of 1,618 to 1,238, thus allowing the full McGovern delegation to keep its seats.

This victory on the California challenge put the reform faction in full control of the convention. Despite the strong dissent of Governor Wallace, delivered from a wheelchair, the delegates approved a platform calling for "immediate and complete withdrawal" from Vietnam, amnesty for those who had resisted the draft on grounds of conscience, reduced military spending, national health insurance, an "income-security" program to aid the poor, and retention of busing as "another tool" to achieve school integration. McGovern gained the presidential nomination on the first ballot, receiving 1,715 votes to 534 for Senator Henry Jackson of Washington, candidate of the hawks, 386 for Wallace, 152 for Shirley Chisholm, dynamic black Congresswoman from New York City, and 77 for Terry Sanford, former governor of North Carolina. Humphrey and Muskie withdrew before the balloting but received 66 and 24 votes, respectively.

Exercising the right usually accorded to a presidential nominee, McGovern proposed and the convention voted the nomination of Senator Thomas Eagleton of Missouri, a big-city Catholic who would balance the ticket headed by a rural Protestant. Although not well-known, Eagleton was a promising young leader—good-looking, articulate, and dynamic. Less than two weeks after his nomination, however, Eagleton found it necessary to explain that on three occasions between 1960 and 1966 he had undergone voluntary treatment in mental hospitals. Claiming that his mental health was now excellent, Eagleton sought to remain on the ticket, and McGovern at first supported him—even asserting that he backed him 1,000 per cent. But some of the country's leading newspapers and many local Democratic leaders demanded Eagleton's withdrawal. Some argued that the office was too important to be held by anyone with a history of instability; others conceded that Eagleton appeared to be a well man but criticized him for not disclosing all the facts before his nomination. Yielding to these criticisms, McGovern finally asked Eagleton to withdraw, and after several other prominent Democrats had refused to take the place, he finally chose Sargent Shriver, another Catholic and well known as President Kennedy's brother-in-law and first director of the Peace Corps. On August 8 the Democratic National Committee formally nominated Shriver for Vice President. The Eagleton affair hurt McGovern very seriously. Not only did it delay effective campaigning, but it permanently alienated many voters. Some of these sympathized with Eagleton and condemned McGovern for dumping him; others recognized that McGovern could not

At the conclusion of the 1972 Democratic convention in Miami Beach. *From left:* Vice Presidential nominee Eagleton, Senator Humphrey, Representative Chisholm, Presidential nominee McGovern, Senator Jackson, Senator Muskie, and former Governor Sanford of North Carolina. (UPI Photo.)

stick with so vulnerable a candidate but criticized the inefficient staff work that had not discovered the full facts about the Missouri Senator in the first place.

Meanwhile, Nixon was demonstrating complete control of the Republican party. Two Congressmen did attempt to challenge him in the primaries: Paul McCloskey, a liberal who opposed the Vietnam war, and John Ashbrook of Ohio, a conservative who disliked Nixon's economic policies and his overtures to the Communist nations. But these dissidents received only a scattering of votes, and there was more pageantry than conflict at the Republican National Convention, which opened at Miami on August 23. Carefully planned to present to TV viewers the image of a happy united party in contrast to the factionalized Democrats, the Republican assemblage approved without serious dissent a platform praising the Nixon administration as "a saga of exhilarating progress" and pledging the party to an honorable peace in Vietnam, no amnesty for draft evaders, no busing to achieve racial balance, no "meat-ax" cuts in the defense budget, and no government-guaranteed income for the poor. The delegates renominated Nixon by a vote of 1,347 to 1 for McCloskey, and Agnew by an almost identical margin. A few thousand anti-Vietnam demonstrators harassed the delegates on route to the convention hall, but they achieved little except to get themselves arrested and to provide TV cameramen with unkempt subjects to contrast with the well-groomed youths planted in the galleries to cheer for Nixon.

The President adroitly campaigned by not campaigning. Wealthy backers provided him with a huge campaign fund, which his workers used to contact by mail and telephone as many individual voters as possible. But the President avoided the customary campaign trips and political rallies, confining his activities to a few radio talks and motorcades through friendly suburbs. Most of the time he kept in seclusion, preserving the image of a chief executive too occupied with the public business for politicking. Instead he campaigned by surrogate, sending his wife, his daughters and their husbands, and various cabinet officers to make appearances at Republican functions.

All this was exasperating to Senator McGovern, who continued to challenge the President to debate him. McGovern and Shriver both campaigned energetically, concentrating their efforts on the most populous states, but their cheering crowds were almost all made up of those already dedicated to their cause. McGovern's capture of the nomination had antagonized a dangerously large number of Democrats. John Connally, who had resigned as Secretary of the Treasury, headed a "Democrats for Nixon" committee that included two sons of Franklin D. Roosevelt, as well as other well-known names. Even more injurious to McGovern's cause was the unfriendly neutrality maintained by Governor Wallace and George Meany of the AFL-CIO. The Senator did obtain the grudging endorsement of Mayor Daley and other old-line political leaders, but his efforts to appease this group by moving toward the center somewhat dampened the ardor of the reform faction.

McGovern had similar difficulty in finding an issue that would stir the voters from their apathy. He had made his reputation and gained his most loyal supporters by his strong demand for withdrawal from Vietnam, but Nixon's withdrawal of ground forces had reduced public concern over the war. The President gained a new advantage on October 27 when Kissinger assured the press that peace was "within reach in a matter of weeks or less" as a result of his secret talks with the North Vietnamese at Paris. With negotiations at this critical point, a majority of the voters appeared to be willing to leave the matter in Nixon's hands. McGovern stressed the need to reform the tax laws to distribute the burden more justly between rich and poor, to cut the huge expenditures for defense, and to develop better programs in the fields of education, health, and welfare. Although such proposals were far from radical, Republican spokesmen succeeded in convincing many voters that McGovern was an "extremist" —as far out of the American consensus on the left as Goldwater had been on the right.

McGovern did make damaging charges of corruptions and criminal eavesdropping against the Nixon administration. In March, 1972, columnist Jack Anderson published a secret memo from the files of the International Telephone and Telegraph Company (ITT) indicating a connection between a promise to underwrite expenses of the Republican National Convention (originally scheduled at San Diego) and a favorable settlement in an antitrust suit. Even more sensational was an episode on June 17 when the police arrested five men in the act of searching the files and arranging wiretaps in the offices of the Democratic National Committee in Washington's Watergate Building. Despite the fact that the arrested men appeared to be in the pay of the Committee to Re-elect the President and even to have ties with persons on the White House staff, the general public displayed more curiosity than indignation at this so-called Watergate Caper.

The election returns on November 7 confirmed the predictions of an overwhelming Nixon victory. McGovern carried only Massachusetts and the District of Columbia; Nixon took the other forty-nine states. The electoral vote was 520 to 17 [1]—the largest margin since Franklin Roosevelt's 523 to 8 triumph in 1936. The popular vote was 47.1 million (61 per cent) for Nixon, 29.1 million (38 per cent) for McGovern. Although Johnson had had a slightly higher proportion of the total vote (62 per cent) in 1964, Nixon's plurality of nearly 18 million was larger than Johnson's of 16 million. A Gallup survey taken after the election indicated that almost one third of the Democratic voters cast their ballots for Nixon. McGovern suffered especially heavy defections among manual workers and labor union members. Within the old Democratic coalition only the nonwhites remained loyal, casting about 87 per cent of their votes for McGovern. Voters in the eighteen–twenty-nine age group split about 50–50 between Nixon and McGovern. This result was of particular interest because in 1970, when Congress passed and Nixon approved a bill extending the franchise to the eighteen–twenty-one age group, many Republicans had feared that the new voters would be predominantly Democratic. Yet even with this

---

[1] One Republican elector from Virginia cast his ballot for John Hospers of California, a Libertarian.

group McGovern had received only about half the votes; the liberalism of the college students was balanced by the conservatism of the noncollege young people.

Democratic factionalism that had been so disastrous to their presidential candidate did not much injure their congressional and gubernatorial nominees. In the Senate the Democrats actually gained 2 seats, giving them a 57–43 margin; in the House they lost 13 seats but still retained a 241–190 advantage; in the governorships they gained 1, so that there were now 30 Democrats to 20 Republicans. Some disgruntled Republicans blamed Nixon for this unsatisfactory showing; his noncampaign had paid off handsomely for him but had provided no surplus of enthusiasm to help Republicans on local tickets.

Downhill with Nixon

Shortly after Nixon's re-election he commented that second terms of American Presidents "almost inevitably are downhill," but that he was determined to "change that historical pattern." To help prevent any loss of ground, he announced changes in personnel. He chose Elliot Richardson to succeed Melvin Laird as Secretary of Defense and Caspar Weinberger to succeed Richardson as Secretary of Health, Education, and Welfare. Since Weinberger had been director of the White House Office of Management and Budget, it was apparent that the new team was largely a reshuffling of the old. Only a few faces were really new, belonging to such men as Roy Ash, president of Litton Industries, who took over the Office of Management and Budget, and Peter Brennan, president of the Building and Trades Council of New York City—a pro-Nixon "hard-hat"— who became Secretary of Labor. Actually, Nixon's second term began with the small group who had dominated the first term more firmly in control than ever. Henry Kissinger was at the height of his prestige and power in the field of foreign relations; H. R. Haldeman and John Ehrlichman supervised all domestic affairs and political activities; George Shultz, the Secretary of the Treasury, formulated economic and fiscal policy.

What were Nixon's goals for his second term? For foreign relations, the answer was relatively simple. He hoped to consolidate his earlier achievements by preserving the precarious peace in Vietnam and by building closer relations with the Chinese People's Republic and the Soviet Union. He wanted to negotiate further limitations on nuclear armaments and to help the Western and Eastern European power blocs achieve a mutual reduction of forces. Eager to reassure the NATO allies and aid American trade, he hoped to make 1973 the "year of Europe." In domestic affairs, Nixon's objectives were much less clearly stated—probably because they were more negative than positive. He lectured the nation on the dangers of government programs that would "pamper" child-like Americans and make them "completely dependent" on the government. Too shrewd to attempt a frontal attack on the whole structure of social legislation, he weakened the various programs by putting them under unsympathetic administrators, cutting their budgets, and turning problems whenever possible back to the states and cities. In attempting to hold down expenditures for education, health, and welfare, he found his most persuasive arguments in the need to combat inflation.

The Democratic majority in Congress professed to be equally anxious to prevent a runaway budget, but it differed from the President on where cuts could best be made. Liberal Democrats would have spent less than Nixon requested on such items as defense and military assistance and more on social services. Congress and the President locked horns on the issue repeatedly. At first Nixon won most of the skirmishes: when he vetoed bills in the interests of economy his liberal opponents usually failed to get the two-thirds vote necessary to override. More irritating still to the liberals was the President's increasing boldness in "impounding" funds— that is, simply refusing to spend Congressional appropriations that were larger than he wanted.

So long as most things continued to go well, Nixon could count on substantial public support for his challenges to Congress. But the slide downhill that he had hoped to prevent began with sickening abruptness during the spring and summer of 1973. The economy performed erratically with consumers' prices soaring, stock market prices declining, and the American dollar dropping to unprecedented lows on foreign markets. And the Watergate affair—earlier dismissed by most voters as no more than an amusing "caper"—suddenly mushroomed into one of the major scandals of American political history.

Serious economic problems began soon after January 11, 1973, when the President surprised the country by announcing Phase 3 in his wage-price policy. Instead of continuing the mandatory controls that had brought the annual rate of inflation down to 3.4 per cent, he removed all restraints except in the processing and retailing of food, construction, and health care. He abolished the Price Commission and the Pay Board and retained only a Cost of Living Council with feeble powers. Once more in a comfortable role, Nixon was placing his bets on the voluntary cooperation of businessmen and union leaders.

Phase 3 worked very badly. Each month the price indexes jumped upward until by June, 1973, inflation was increasing at an annual rate of over 9 per cent—a shocking contrast to the administration's announced goal of a 2.5 per cent rise for the year. Although the rising cost of living was evident on many items—rents, fuel, manufactured goods—housewives found most to alarm them in their skyrocketing food bills. Meat prices jumped rapidly, and consumers found little relief in turning to substitutes, since chicken, fish, cheese, and eggs were also becoming more expensive. Late in March, 1973, the President responded to consumer protests by placing a ceiling on the retail prices of beef, pork, and lamb. Believing that prices should be rolled back rather than frozen at unprecedently high levels, housewives participated in a week-long meat boycott in April. As a nationwide gesture of protest, the boycott was impressive, but meat prices did not come down. Indeed, farmers and cattle raisers argued that they needed still higher prices to make their activities pay in view of the high price of feed and other costs. On June 13 Nixon acknowledged the failure of Phase 3 by imposing a 60-day freeze on all price increases except for food products at the farm level. Once again, however, he sought to preserve his precarious alliance with the labor union leaders by exempting wages.

The freeze, ridiculed by some reporters as Phase 2½, lasted only until the Cost of Living Council could shape a new policy. In mid-July Secretary Shultz announced that Phase 4, a system of moderate controls allowing price adjustments would begin on August 12.

These floundering efforts to control inflation seriously weakened confidence in the American economy. In many ways industry and agriculture were booming: industrial production was high; corporate profits were increasing; unemployment was decreasing; and farmers had an eager market for their products in Russia and other foreign countries. Nevertheless, everyone was complaining: workers claimed that their real wages were going down because of the high cost of living; would-be homeowners and industrialists seeking to expand lamented high interest rates; purchasers of stocks found their uncertainties reflected in declining Wall Street prices; farmers drowned their baby chicks and slaughtered pregnant sows because they could not afford to raise them; purchasers of gasoline, fuel oil, and electricity read with alarm of a threatened "energy crisis."

On foreign money markets the American dollar suffered a series of humiliations. In December, 1971, the United States had agreed to a devaluation of about 12 per cent in relation to foreign currencies; in February, 1973, it swallowed another dose of the same medicine—a devaluation of a further 10 per cent. But the stabilization attempts failed. Traders continued to push the price of the dollar down, thereby causing extreme unhappiness to Americans touring abroad or compelled by their work or military assignments to live in foreign countries. The causes of the dollar crisis were in part economic—the continuing unfavorable balance of payments. But psychological factors were probably more important. Foreign traders doubted the will and ability of the American government to control inflation. More familiar with the instability of parliamentary governments than with the rigidity of the American constitutional system, they asked whether the Nixon administration could continue in office.

The cloud of doubt hanging over Nixon's future resulted especially from growing concern over the ramifications of the Watergate affair. During the campaign the President had assured the voters that no one then employed at the White House had foreknowledge or complicity in the break-in of the Democratic National Headquarters. Five of the men arrested for the crime pleaded guilty; two—G. Gordon Liddy, counsel for the Nixon campaign fund committee, and James McCord, security officer for the re-election committee—came to trial in January, 1973, and were convicted. Although the evidence did not implicate any higher-ups in the crime, the presiding jurist, Judge John J. Sirica, made it evident that he was not satisfied the witnesses were telling the full truth.

Persistent journalists—particularly those employed by the *Washington Post* and the *New York Times*—continued to dig into the story, and during March and April a succession of revelations tore down the false front behind which the facts had been concealed. A Senate committee considering the nomination of L. Patrick Gray to be director of the FBI heard evidence implicating officials in the White House with the Watergate affair. After admitting that he himself had destroyed certain documents, Gray asked to have his name withdrawn. Meanwhile, McCord, one of the convicted men, had written an extraordinary letter to Judge Sirica asserting that there had been perjury in the trial and that political pressure had been exerted on the defendants to get them to plead guilty and remain silent. Postponing the final sentencing, Judge Sirica admonished the defendants to tell all they knew both to the grand jury and to a special Senate committee that had been authorized to investigate both the Watergate affair and other illegal campaign activities. Only McCord, however, did so.

Although the ensuing testimony before these bodies was supposed to be secret, reporters had little difficulty in finding out what various suspects were saying. Officials accused of guilty knowledge sought to gain immunity or lighten their punishment by implicating others. In this way, Jeb Magruder, one-time White House assistant and deputy director of the Committee to Re-elect the President, pointed to John W. Dean, special counsel to the President. And Dean, in turn, related illegal activities involving some of the most powerful figures in the government—Haldeman, Ehrlichman, and John Mitchell, former Attorney General and former director of the Re-election Committee.

Threatened by shipwreck, President Nixon made his first public admission that White House officials might be involved on April 17 when he told reporters that he was now making "intensive new inquiries." In a somber television address on April 30, he announced the resignation of four high officials—Haldeman, Ehrlichman, Dean, and Attorney General Richard Kleindienst. By praising Haldeman and Ehrlichman and dealing coldly with Dean, Nixon implied that Dean was the principal culprit and that Haldeman's and Ehrlichman's roles were insignificant. Kleindienst's resignation appeared to be necessary, not because he was involved in the scandal, but because he had been so closely associated with Mitchell and other suspects that the public would not believe he was vigorously prosecuting the cases. In his place the President appointed Elliot Richardson, who had scarcely begun his duties as Secretary of Defense. But this was not enough to reassure the public. Even the conservative Republican Senator Barry Goldwater was now urging the selection of an independent special prosecutor. Richardson bowed to these demands and gave broad powers to Archibald Cox, a professor at the Harvard Law School and a former Justice Department official under Democratic administrations.

Although Nixon appealed to the nation to transfer its interest to more important concerns and trust his new team to clear up the Watergate mess, the public was in no mood to do so. From May to August, 1973, the Senate special investigating committee under the chairmanship of Senator Sam Ervin of North Carolina held its first round of public hearings. A nationwide television audience heard day after day of testimony highly damaging to the administration. Particularly shocking was the testimony of John Dean, who frankly admitted his own role in trying to suppress the facts about Watergate and claimed that the President himself had been aware of the cover-up. Subsequent testimony in part supported and in part dis-

The Senate committee investigating the 1972 presidential election (the "Watergate Committee") hears testimony from former presidential counsel John W. Dean III (foreground) in June 1973. Committee members and staff at table are (from left) Senator Gurney, minority counsel Thompson, Senators Baker and Ervin, chief counsel Dash, assistant counsel Hamilton, Senators Talmadge, Inouye, and Montoya. Senator Weicker is not shown. (UPI Photo.)

puted Dean's story. Other witnesses related details seriously implicating former Attorney General Mitchell and various members of the Committee to Re-Elect the President and the White House staff. Money from secret campaign funds had been used to pay Liddy for political espionage; an attempt had been made after the initial arrests to put the FBI off the trail by implying that secret CIA activities might be uncovered; large sums of money had been surreptitiously paid to buy the silence of the defendants; and offers of executive clemency had been made. How high up in the White House did complicity extend? Despite some testimony involving Ehrlichman and Haldeman, the two former chief aides denied that they had done anything illegal or wrong.

Still more murky was the question of the President's role in the affair. Was it conceivable that he had known nothing of White House involvement before March, 1973, as he claimed? Exactly what had John Dean said to him, and what had he said to Dean, in their numerous meetings and telephone conversations? Precisely what warning had L. Patrick Gray, acting director of the FBI, given to Nixon in a July, 1972, telephone conversation? Dean and Gray testified as to their recollections; spokesmen for Nixon denied their stories. How could the truth be ascertained? The Senate committee was surprised to learn that the Secret Service had on

Nixon's orders been making regular tape recordings of everything said in the presidential offices and on the presidential telephones. By listening to these tapes the committee might be able to determine who was telling the truth. But the President claimed that the Executive had a right to confidentiality in conferring with his advisers and refused to release the tapes, either to the Senate committee or to Special Prosecutor Cox. On the other hand, he allowed Haldeman, by this time a private citizen, to use some of the tapes in preparing his testimony before the committee. Arguing that Nixon could not have it both ways—using a friendly summary of the tapes to defend himself while refusing to allow investigators to hear them, the Special Prosecutor and the Ervin Committee both appealed to the Federal courts for orders directing the President to turn over this vital evidence. The constitutional issues involved in these cases were of extraordinary gravity, involving the powers and privileges of the presidency itself.

Yet the question of the President's complicity tended to overshadow ramifications of the Watergate affair that were even more serious. It had been proved that the break-in at Democratic National Committee Headquarters was only one part of a wide range of covert, often illegal, activities being carried on by administration officials. They had employed secret agents to spy upon political opponents and disrupt the primary campaigns of Democratic candidates for the presidency; they had compiled lists of political "enemies" for possible harassment in income tax matters; they had installed electronic devices to listen in on the conversations of their own employees and associates; they had hired men to break into a psychiatrist's office to search his files for damaging information to use against a defendant accused of releasing classified documents about the Vietnam war to the newspapers; they had even sought help from the CIA and the FBI in carrying out some of these activities. Former Attorney General Mitchell called these "the White House horrors"; others described them merely as "dirty tricks" about which the voters must at all costs be kept in ignorance during the 1972 election. The Watergate affair thus proved to be more serious than any previous scandal in American history because it involved a corruption of the political process itself. After collecting huge sums of cash from wealthy contributors the Nixon lieutenants had used these secret funds in efforts to disrupt the opposition and insure the Nixon majority.

Public opinion polls—so favorable to Nixon throughout the crucial election year—revealed a precipitous drop of confidence in the President during the summer of 1973. This turnabout resulted mostly from the Watergate affair and the administration's erratic wage-price policy, but new revelations about his Cambodian policy and his personal finances also hurt Nixon. A Congressional committee discovered that the American air force had been carrying on bombing raids against Communist targets in supposedly neutral Cambodia for more than a year before the controversial invasion of that country in 1970—all the time concealing the fact by false reports to Congress and the public. Nixon's penchant for secrecy got him into still further trouble as the White House released piecemeal and conflicting reports about how the President had purchased his Key Biscayne and San Clemente estates through ingenious deals involving his rich business friends and how he had spent millions of the taxpayers' dollars on improvements, supposedly necessary for his security.

On August 15 Nixon defended himself in a TV speech and a supplementary statement to the press. Once again he denied any complicity in the Watergate incident or in the cover-up; once again he claimed that he had always ordered a thorough investigation by the proper agencies; once again he appealed to the nation to leave the matter to the courts and turn its attention to "more important" concerns. But he still refused to release the disputed tapes. Accordingly, his speech reassured only the Nixon faithfuls and did nothing to answer the questions of the doubters.

A further blow to the administration was delivered on October 10 when Vice President Agnew, against whom charges had been made of bribery, conspiracy, and extortion, going back to the period even before his governorship of Maryland, suddenly resigned. At the same time he pleaded nolo contendere to a charge of federal income tax evasion and was fined $10,000 and placed on three years' probation. Under the 25th Amendment President Nixon nominated Gerald R. Ford as Agnew's successor.

In the summer of 1973 the nation was obviously in a mood of serious discontent. People evidenced a growing distrust, not only of politicians but of business and professional people as well. What would follow so many disclosures of wrongdoing? Would a chastened President impose stricter standards on himself and his subordinates? Would Congress modernize its procedures and regain some of its lost authority? Would it pass more stringent laws on campaign financing and election practices? If the humiliations of these months could result in more honest and effective government, the nation might then resume its quest for the three goals that had persisted through twentieth-century American history—peaceful cooperation between the United States and the rest of the world, achievement of the full equality implicit in American democracy, and the liberation of the people from the handicaps of poverty and ignorance.

SUGGESTIONS FOR FURTHER READING

Chapter 1. The Good Old Days

GENERAL. For an overall view of American life during these years, see Harold U. Faulkner, *The Quest for Social Justice, 1898–1914* (N.Y.: Macmillan, 1931). Brief but stimulating is the treatment in Thomas Cochran and William Miller, *The Age of Enterprise: A Social History of Industrial America* (N.Y.: Macmillan, 1942). A brilliant analysis of the impact of new ideas is Henry F. May, *The End of American Innocence* (N.Y.: Knopf, 1959).

IMMIGRATION. The most scholarly general treatment is Carl Wittke, *We Who Built America: The Saga of the Immigrant* (Englewood Cliffs, N.J.: Prentice-Hall, 1940). Oscar Handlin, *The Uprooted* (Boston: Little, Brown, 1951), is a sensitive analysis of the immigrant experience. John Higham, *Strangers in the Land: Patterns of American Nativism, 1860–1925* (New Brunswick: Rutgers U.P., 1955), examines hostility to the immigrant.

BLACKS. The best general accounts are John H. Franklin, *From Slavery to Freedom: A History of American Negroes* (3d ed.; N.Y.: Knopf, 1969), and August Meier and Elliott M. Rudwick, *From Plantation to Ghetto* (N.Y.: Norton, 1969). C. Vann Woodward, *The Strange Career of Jim Crow* (2d ed.: N.Y.: Oxford U.P., 1966), is a succinct history of segregation. Conditions in the northern cities are described in Gilbert Osofsky, *Harlem: The Making of a Ghetto* (N.Y.: Harper, 1966), and Alan Spear, *Black Chicago: The Making of a Negro Ghetto, 1890–1920* (Chicago: U. of Chicago, 1967). Charles F. Kellogg, *NAACP: A History of the National Association for the Advancement of Colored People* (vol. 1; Baltimore: Johns Hopkins, 1967), and Guichard Parris and Lester Brooks, *Blacks in the City: A History of the National Urban League* (Boston: Little, Brown, 1971), provide accounts of two major organizations. August Meier. *Negro Thought in America, 1880–1915* (Ann Arbor: U. of Michigan, 1963) is excellent. On the two most important black leaders of the period see Booker T. Washington, *Up from Slavery* (Garden City: Doubleday, 1909); Samuel R. Spencer, *Booker T. Washington and the Negro's Place in American Life* (Boston: Little, Brown, 1955); W. E. Burghardt Du Bois, *Dusk of Dawn* (N.Y.: Harcourt, 1940); *The Autobiography of W. E. B. Du Bois* (N.Y.: International, 1968); Francis L. Broderick, *W. E. B. Du Bois: Negro Leader in a Time of Crisis* (Stanford: Stanford U.P., 1959); Elliott Rudwick, *W. E. B. Du Bois: Propagandist of the Negro Protest* (Philadelphia: U. of Pa., 1968).

ECONOMIC TRENDS. Excellent accounts are Harold U. Faulkner, *The Decline of Laissez Faire, 1897–1917* (N.Y.: Rinehart, 1951), and Fred A. Shannon, *The Farmer's Last Frontier* (N.Y.: Rinehart, 1945). Historically important discussions of the trust problem are John Moody, *The Truth About Trusts* (N.Y.: Moody, 1904), and William Z. Ripley, ed., *Trusts, Pools, and Corporations* (Boston: Ginn: 1916). See also Ralph W. and Muriel E. Hidy, *Pioneering in Big Business, 1882–1911: A History of the Standard Oil Company (New Jersey)* (N.Y.: Harper, 1955). The role of the bankers is explored in George W. Edwards, *The Evolution of Finance Capi-*

talism (N.Y.: Longmans, 1938), and in more popular form in Frederick L. Allen, *The Lords of Creation* (N.Y.: Harper, 1935). Excellent biographies of key business-men are Joseph F. Wall, *Andrew Carnegie* (N.Y.: Oxford U.P., 1970); Allen Nevins, *Study in Power: John D. Rockefeller, Industrialist and Philanthropist* (2 vols.; N.Y.: Scribners, 1953); Frederick L. Allen, *The Great Pierpont Morgan* (N.Y.: Harper, 1949).

LABOR. Good standard works are Selig Perlman and Philip Taft, *History of Labor in the United States, 1896–1932* (N.Y.: Macmillan, 1935), and Philip Taft, *The A.F. of L. in the Time of Gompers* (N.Y.: Harper, 1957). On radical unionism, see Paul F. Brissenden, *The I.W.W.: A Study of American Syndicalism* (N.Y.: Columbia U.P., 1919), and Melvyn Dubofsky, *We Shall Be All: A History of the Industrial Workers of the World* (Chicago: Quadrangle, 1969). On individual leaders see Samuel Gompers, *Seventy Years of Life and Labor: An Autobiography* (2 vols.; N.Y.: Dutton, 1925); Bernard Mandel, *Samuel Gompers: A Biography* (Yellow Springs, Ohio: Antioch, 1963); *The Autobiography of William D. Haywood* (N.Y.: International, 1929).

RELIGION. A good survey is William W. Sweet, *The Story of Religion in America* (N.Y.: Harper, 1939). Brief but thoughtful surveys are Winthrop S. Hudson, *American Protestantism* (Chicago: U. of Chicago, 1961), and John T. Ellis, *American Catholicism* (Chicago: U. of Chicago, 1956). Herbert W. Schneider, *Religion in 20th Century America* (Cambridge: Harvard U.P., 1952), provides thoughtful inter-pretation. On revivalism see William G. McLoughlin, Jr., *Billy Sunday Was His Real Name* (Chicago: U. of Chicago, 1955). Excellent studies are Charles H. Hopkins, *The Rise of the Social Gospel in American Protestantism, 1865–1914* (New Haven: Yale U.P., 1940); Henry F. May, *Protestant Churches and Industrial America* (N.Y.: Harper, 1949); Frank H. Foster, *The Modern Movement in American Theology* (N.Y.: Revell, 1939); Robert D. Cross, *The Emergence of Liberal Catholicism in America* (Cambridge: Harvard U.P., 1958).

SCIENCE AND EDUCATION. Bernard Jaffe, *Men of Science in America* (N.Y.: Simon & Schuster, 1944), is a useful survey. Richard H. Shryock, *The Development of Modern Medicine* (N.Y.: Knopf, 1947), is outstanding. On education, the best analysis is Lawrence A. Cremin, *The Transformation of the School* (N.Y.: Knopf, 1961). Merle Curti, *The Social Ideas of American Educators* (N.Y.: Scribners, 1935) is interesting. On higher education, see Frederick Rudolph, *The American College and University: A History* (N.Y.: Random, 1962), and Laurence R. Veysey, *The Emergence of the American University* (Chicago: U. of Chicago, 1965).

LITERATURE AND ART. On literature, the following are excellent studies: Willard Thorp, *American Writing in the Twentieth Century* (Cambridge: Harvard U.P., 1960); Alfred Kazin, *On Native Grounds: An Interpretation of Modern American Prose Literature* (N.Y.: Reynal, 1942); Heinrich Staumann, *American Literature in the Twentieth Century* (3d ed.; N.Y.: Harper, 1965); Frederick J. Hoffman, *The Modern Novel in America* (Chicago: Regnery, 1951). On art, see Oliver W. Larkin, *Art and Life in America* (N.Y.: Rinehart, 1949); John Burchard and Albert Bush-Brown, *The Architecture of America: A Social and Cultural History* (Boston: Little, Brown, 1961); Henry Geldzahler, *American Painting in the Twentieth Century* (N.Y.: Metropolitan Museum, 1965). On music, see Gilbert Chase, *American Music: From the Pilgrims to the Present* (N.Y.: McGraw-Hill, 1955); David Ewen, *Music Comes to America* (N.Y.: Crowell, 1942); Rudi Blesh, *Shining Trumpets: A History of Jazz* (N.Y.: Knopf, 1946).

Chapter 2. Roosevelt and Reform

GENERAL. George E. Mowry, *The Era of Theodore Roosevelt* (N.Y.: Harper, 1958), is the best overall account. Richard Hofstadter, *The Age of Reform: From Bryan to F.D.R.* (N.Y.: Knopf, 1959), and Eric Goldman, *Rendezvous with Destiny:*

A History of Modern American Reform (N.Y.: Knopf, 1956), are important interpretations. The role of business in the progressive movement is explored in Robert
H. Wiebe, *Businessmen and Reform* (Cambridge: Harvard U.P., 1962), and Gabriel
Kolko. *The Triumph of Conservatism: A Reinterpretation of American History,
1900–1916* (Chicago: Quadrangle, 1963).

SOCIALISM. The American movement is extensively examined in the following:
Ira Kipnis, *The American Socialist Movement, 1897–1912* (N.Y.: Columbia U.P.,
1952); Howard H. Quint, *The Forging of American Socialism* (Columbia: U. of
S.C., 1953); David A. Shannon, *The Socialist Party of America: A History* (N.Y.:
Macmillan, 1955); Donald D. Egbert and Stow Persons, eds., *Socialism in American
Life* (2 vols.; Princeton: Princeton U.P., 1952).

THEODORE ROOSEVELT. Theodore Roosevelt, *An Autobiography* (N.Y.: Scribners,
1924), is an interesting self-appraisal, but must be used with caution. The best biographies are Henry F. Pringle, *Theodore Roosevelt, a Biography* (N.Y.: Harcourt,
1931), and William H. Harbaugh, *Power and Responsibility: The Life and Times
of Theodore Roosevelt* (N.Y.: Farrar, 1961). Brief but shrewd is John M. Blum,
The Republican Roosevelt (Cambridge: Harvard U.P., 1954).

OTHER KEY FIGURES. On Brandeis, see Alpheus T. Mason, *Brandeis: A Free Man's
Life* (N.Y.: Viking, 1946), and Melvin I. Urofsky, *A Mind of One Piece: Brandeis
and American Reform* (N.Y.: Scribners, 1971). On Bryan: Paolo E. Coletta, *William
Jennings Bryan, Political Evangelist, 1860–1908* (Lincoln: U. of Nebraska, 1964),
and Paul M. Glad, *The Trumpet Soundeth: William Jennings Bryan and His
Democracy, 1896–1912* (Lincoln: U. of Nebraska, 1960). On Debs: Ray Ginger, *The
Bending Cross: A Biography of Eugene Victor Debs* (New Brunswick, N.J.: Rutgers
U.P., 1949). On Hanna: Herbert Croly, *Marcus Alonzo Hanna: His Life and Work*
(N.Y.: Macmillan, 1912). On LaFollette: Robert M. LaFollette, *Autobiography*
(Madison, Wis.: LaFolle, 1913); Belle and Fola LaFollette, *Robert M. LaFollette,
June 14, 1855–June 18, 1925* (2 vols.; N.Y.: Macmillan, 1953). On Norris: Richard
Lowitt, *George W. Norris: The Making of a Progressive* (Syracuse: Syracuse U.P.,
1963). On Root: Philip C. Jessup, *Elihu Root* (2 vols.; N.Y.: Dodd, 1938), and
Richard W. Leopold, *Elihu Root and the Conservative Tradition* (Boston: Little,
Brown, 1954). On Steffens: *The Autobiography of Lincoln Steffens* (N.Y.: Harcourt,
1963). On Root: Philip C. Jessup, *Elihu Root* (2 vols.; N.Y.: Dodd, 1938), and
on White: *The Autobiography of William Allen White* (N.Y.: Macmillan, 1946).

PROGRESSIVISM IN THE STATES. Excellent studies are George E. Mowry, *The Cali-
fornia Progressives* (Berkeley: U. of California, 1951); Ransom E. Noble, Jr., *New
Jersey Progressivism Before Wilson* (Princeton: Princeton U.P., 1946); Robert S.
Maxwell, *LaFollette and the Rise of the Progressives in Wisconsin* (Madison: State
Hist. Soc. of Wisconsin, 1956); Russell B. Nye, *Midwestern Progressive Politics:
A Historical Study of Its Origins and Development, 1870–1950* (East Lansing:
Michigan S.C., 1951).

KEY ISSUES. On regulation of business, see H. R. Seager and C. A. Gulick, *Trust
and Corporation Problems* (N.Y.: Harper, 1929), and William Z. Ripley, *Railroads:
Rates and Regulation* (N.Y.: Longsman, 1913). On conservation, see Samuel P.
Hayes, *Conservation and the Gospel of Efficiency* (Cambridge: Harvard U.P., 1959).

Chapter 3. The Battle of the Progressives

GENERAL. Most of the titles recommended for Chapter 2 are still useful for the
Taft period. These should be supplemented with two other outstanding studies:
Kenneth W. Hechler, *Insurgency: Personalities and Policies of the Taft Era* (N.Y.:
Columbia U.P., 1940), and George E. Mowry, *Theodore Roosevelt and the Progres-
sive Movement* (Madison: U. of Wisconsin, 1946). The best biography of Taft is
Henry F. Pringle, *The Life and Times of William Howard Taft* (2 vols.; N.Y.:
Farrar, 1939).

CONTEMPORARY WORKS. One of the best ways of understanding the ideals of the progressives is through the reading of such works as the following: Louis D. Brandeis, *Other People's Money* (Washington, D.C.: National Home Library, 1933); Louis D. Brandeis, *The Curse of Bigness* (N.Y.: Viking, 1934); Herbert Croly, *The Promise of American Life* (N.Y.: Macmillan, 1909); Charles McCarthy, *The Wisconsin Idea* (N.Y.: Macmillan, 1912); Walter E. Weyl, *The New Democracy* (N.Y.: Macmillan, 1912); J. W. Davidson, ed., *A Crossroads of Freedom: The 1912 Campaign Speeches of Woodrow Wilson* (New Haven: Yale U.P., 1956).

KEY ISSUES. Alpheus T. Mason, *Bureaucracy Convicts Itself: The Ballinger-Pinchot Controversy of 1910* (N.Y.: Viking, 1941); James Penick, Jr., *Progressive Politics and Conservation: The Ballinger-Pinchot Affair* (Chicago: U. of Chicago, 1968); L. Ethan Ellis, *Reciprocity, 1911: A Study in Canadian-American Relations* (New Haven: Yale U.P., 1939); examine important episodes.

Chapter 4. The American Empire

GENERAL. Foster Rhea Dulles, *America's Rise to World Power* (N.Y.: Harper, 1955); Jules David, *America and the World of Our Time* (rev. ed.; N.Y.: Random, 1962); and Robert E. Osgood, *Ideals and Self-Interest in America's Foreign Relations* (Chicago: U. of Chicago, 1953); deal with United States foreign relations in the twentieth century. George F. Kennan, *American Diplomacy, 1900–1950* (Chicago: U. of Chicago, 1953), and William A. Williams, *Tragedy of American Diplomacy* (N.Y.: Dell, 1962), are severe critiques. Howard K. Beale, *Theodore Roosevelt and the Rise of America to World Power* (Baltimore: Johns Hopkins, 1956), and Walter and Marie V. Scholes, *The Foreign Policies of the Taft Administration* (N.Y.: Columbia U.P., 1970), are both excellent. Tyler Dennett, *John Hay: From Poetry to Politics* (N.Y.: Dodd, 1933), is a very good biography.

IMPERIALISM. Julius W. Pratt, *Expansionists of 1898* (Baltimore: Johns Hopkins, 1936), and the same author's *America's Colonial Experiment* (Englewood Cliffs, N.J.: Prentice-Hall, 1950), are good. For a very different interpretation, see Walter La Feber, *The New Empire: An Interpretation of American Expansion, 1860–1898* (Ithaca: Cornell U.P., 1968). An entertaining account of the role of newspapers in bringing on the Spanish-American War is Walter Millis, *The Martial Spirit* (Cambridge, Mass.: Riverside, 1931). W. D. Puleston, *Mahan: The Life and Work of Captain Alfred Mahan* (New Haven: Yale U.P., 1939), traces the career of an influential figure. See also Harold and Margaret Sprout, *The Rise of American Naval Power, 1776–1919* (Princeton: Princeton U.P., 1939). Interesting recent studies are Rubin F. Weston, *Racism in U.S. Imperialism: The Influence of Racial Assumptions on American Foreign Policy, 1893–1946* (Columbia: U. of S.C., 1972), and E. Berkeley Tompkins, *Anti-Imperialism in the United States: The Great Debate, 1893–1946* (Philadelphia: U. of Pa., 1970).

CUBA AND THE DEPENDENCIES. A good overall view is contained in William H. Haas, ed., *The American Empire: A Study of the Outlying Territories of the United States* (Chicago: U. of Chicago, 1940). Critical discussion of relations with particular areas are Daniel F. Healy, *The United States in Cuba: 1898–1902* (Madison: U. of Wisconsin, 1963); Moorfield Story and Marcial Liachauco, *The Conquest of the Philippines by the United States, 1898–1925* (N.Y.: Putnam, 1926); Leon Wolff, *Little Brown Brother: How the United States Purchased and Pacified the Philippines at the Century's Turn* (Garden City: Doubleday, 1961); Edward J. Berbusse, *The United States in Puerto Rico, 1898–1900* (Chapel Hill U. of N.C., 1966).

THE FAR EAST. The best study of the period is A. Whitney Griswold, *The Far Eastern Policy of the United States* (N.Y.: Harcourt, 1938). Outstanding studies of special phases are Raymond A. Eathus, *Theodore Roosevelt and Japan* (Seattle:

U. of Washington, 1967); Tyler Dennett, *Roosevelt and the Russo-Japanese War* (Garden City: Doubleday, 1925); Thomas A. Bailey, *Theodore Roosevelt and the Japanese-American Crises* (Stanford: Stanford U.P., 1934); Charles Vevier, *The United States and China, 1906–1913* (New Brunswick: Rutgers U.P., 1955).

Chapter 5. Search for Security and Peace

GENERAL. The general works recommended for Chapter 4 are still useful. Excellent biographies of leading diplomatists are Jessup, *Elihu Root,* cited above; and Allan Nevins, *Henry White: Thirty Years of American Diplomacy* (N.Y.: Harper, 1930).

RELATIONS WITH LATIN AMERICA. The best interpretative study is Samuel F. Bemis, *The Latin American Policy of the United States, an Interpretive Study* (N.Y.: Harcourt, 1943). On the fundamental policy underlying American action, the indispensable authority is Dexter Perkins, *The Monroe Doctrine, 1867–1907* (Baltimore: Johns Hopkins, 1927); more general is the same author's *Hands Off: A History of the Monroe Doctrine* (Boston: Little, Brown, 1941). The following are able studies: Howard C. Hill, *Roosevelt and the Caribbean* (Chicago: U. of Chicago, 1927); Wilfrid H. Calcott, *The Caribbean Policy of the United States, 1890–1920* (Baltimore: Johns Hopkins, 1942); Dexter Perkins, *The United States and the Caribbean* (Cambridge: Harvard U.P., 1947). An outstanding study of canal diplomacy is Dwight C. Miner, *The Fight for the Panama Route* (N.Y.: Columbia U.P., 1940). An historically important indictment of American policy is Sumner Welles, *Naboth's Vineyard: The Dominican Republic, 1844–1924* (2 vols.; N.Y.: Payson, 1928).

ANGLO-AMERICAN RELATIONS. Lionel M. Gelber, *The Rise of Anglo-American Friendship: A Study in World Politics, 1896–1906* (N.Y.: Oxford U.P., 1938), is narrowly diplomatic. Of more general interest are Forest Davis, *The Atlantic System: The Story of Anglo-American Control of the Seas* (N.Y.: Reynal, 1941), and Charles S. Campbell, Jr., *Anglo-American Understanding, 1898–1903* (Baltimore: Johns Hopkins, 1957).

Chapter 6. The New Freedom

GENERAL. The best studies of the period are Frederic Paxson, *American Democracy and the World War* (3 vols.; Boston: Houghton Mifflin, 1936–1948), and Arthur S. Link, *Woodrow Wilson and the Progressive Era* (N.Y.: Harper, 1954). Wilson's own speeches and letters are indispensable sources for his ideals and political methods. For these, consult Ray S. Baker and William E. Dodd, eds., *The Public Papers of Woodrow Wilson* (6 vols.; N.Y.: Harper, 1925–1926); and Ray S. Baker, *Woodrow Wilson, Life and Letters* (8 vols.; Garden City: Doubleday, 1927–1938). The best and most detailed biography is Arthur S. Link, *Wilson* (4 vols.; Princeton: Princeton U.P., 1947–1964). Other good ones are Arthur Walworth, *Woodrow Wilson* (2 vols.; N.Y.: Longmans, 1958); Herbert C. F. Bell, *Woodrow Wilson and the People* (Garden City: Doubleday, 1945); John A. Garraty, *Woodrow Wilson: A Great Life in Brief* (N.Y.: Knopf, 1956); John M. Blum, *Woodrow Wilson and the Politics of Morality* (Boston: Little, Brown, 1956). For an unusual psychological study, see Alexander L. and Juliette L. George, *Woodrow Wilson and Colonel House: A Personality Study* (N.Y.: Day, 1956).

MEMOIRS. Wilson's secretary provides an intimate portrait in Joseph Tumulty, *Woodrow Wilson as I Knew Him* (Garden City: Doubleday, 1925). His son-in-law and Secretary of the Treasury deals with the period in William G. McAdoo, *Crowded Years* (Boston: Houghton Mifflin, 1931). Important memoranda on Cabinet discussions are provided by David Houston, *Eight Years with Wilson's Cabinet* (Garden City: Doubleday, 1926); and E. David Cronon, ed., *The Cabinet Diaries of Josephus Daniels, 1913–1921* (Lincoln: U. of Nebraska, 1963). Josephus Daniels, *The Wilson Era: Years of Peace* (Chapel Hill: U. of N.C., 1944), provides an engaging discussion of personalities and politics.

REFORM LEGISLATION. Two key figures in the creation of the Federal Reserve System discuss its origins in Carter Glass, *An Adventure in Constructive Finance* (Garden City: Doubleday, 1915), and H. P. Willis, *The Federal Reserve: A Study of the Banking System of the United States* (Garden City: Doubleday, 1915). The functioning of the system is elucidated in Edwin W. Kemmerer, *The ABC of the Federal Reserve System* (Princeton: Princeton U.P., 1938). Thomas C. Blaisdell, Jr., *The Federal Trade Commission: An Experiment in the Control of Business* (N.Y.: Columbia U.P., 1932), is a valuable monograph.

FOREIGN AFFAIRS. Wilson's basic attitudes and principles are discussed in Harley Notter, *The Origins of the Foreign Policy of Woodrow Wilson* (Baltimore: Johns Hopkins, 1937); Arthur S. Link, *Wilson the Diplomatist* (Baltimore: Johns Hopkins, 1957); Edward H. Buehrig, *Woodrow Wilson and the Balance of Power* (Bloomington: Indiana U.P., 1955). Merle Curti, *Bryan and World Peace* (Northampton, Mass.: Smith College, 1931), is a sympathetic study. For American policy in key areas, see Howard F. Kline, *The United States and Mexico* (Cambridge: Harvard U.P., 1953); Robert F. Quirk, *An Affair of Honor: Woodrow Wilson and the Occupation of Veracruz* (Lexington: U. of Kentucky, 1962); Charles C. Tansill, *The Purchase of the Danish West Indies* (Baltimore: Johns Hopkins, 1932); Ludwell L. Montague, *Haiti and the United States, 1900–1935* (Durham: Duke U.P., 1940).

Chapter 7. The Road to War

GENERAL. Ernest R. May, *The World War and American Isolation, 1914–1917* (Cambridge: Harvard U.P., 1959), is the best balanced study. For the Wilsonian point of view, see Baker, *Wilson, Life and Letters,* cited above; Charles Seymour, *American Diplomacy During the World War* (Baltimore: Johns Hopkins, 1935); and the same author's *American Neutrality, 1914–1917* (New Haven: Yale U.P., 1935). The pioneer revisionist work is C. Hartley Grattan, *Why We Fought* (N.Y.: Vanguard, 1929). A highly readable account, but with overemphasis on the role of newspapers and propaganda, is Walter Millis, *Road to War: America, 1914–1917* (Boston: Houghton Mifflin, 1935). Critical of Wilson's policies is Alice M. Morrissey, *The American Defense of Neutral Rights, 1914–1917* (Cambridge: Harvard U.P., 1939). Most complete of all these revisionist studies is Charles C. Tansill, *America Goes to War* (Boston: Little, Brown, 1938). For intelligent summaries, see Newton D. Baker, *Why We Went to War* (N.Y.: Harper, 1936), and Dexter Perkins, *America and Two Wars* (Boston: Little, Brown, 1944).

PROPAGANDA. An important study is Horace C. Peterson, *Propaganda for War: The Campaign Against American Neutrality, 1914–1917* (Norman: U. of Oklahoma, 1937). Interesting, but to be used with caution because of its author's record as a German propagandist in two wars, is George S. Viereck, *Spreading Germs of Hate* N.Y.: Liveright, 1930). See also Arthur Willert, *The Road to Safety: A Study in Anglo-American Relations* (N.Y.: British Book Centre, 1953), and Armin Rappaport, *The British Press and Wilsonian Neutrality* (Palo Alto: Stanford U.P., 1950).

MEMOIRS. The influence upon policy of key United States officials may be traced in Charles Seymour, ed., *The Intimate Papers of Colonel House* (4 vols.; Boston: Houghton Mifflin, 1926–1928); Burton J. Hendrick, ed., *The Life and Letters of Walter Hines Page* (3 vols.; Boston: Houghton Mifflin, 1924–1925); James W. Gerard, *My Four Years in Germany* (N.Y.: Doran, 1920); Robert Lansing, *War Memoirs* (N.Y.: Bobbs, 1935). The activities of the British Embassy may be followed in Stephen Gwynn, ed., *The Letters and Friendships of Sir Cecil Spring-Rice* (2 vols.; Boston: Little, Brown, 1929); while the problems of the German ambassador are discussed in Count J. H. von Bernstorff, *My Three Years in America* (N.Y.: Scribners, 1920) and *Memoirs of Count Bernstorff* (N.Y.: Random, 1936).

Chapter 8. The War for Democracy

GENERAL. Preston W. Slosson, *The Great Crusade and After, 1914–1928* (N.Y.: Macmillan, 1931), and Paxson, *American Democracy and the World War,* cited above (vol. 2), are of particular value for this period. For the policies of Wilson's Secretaries of War and Navy, see Frederick Palmer, *Newton D. Baker: America at War* (2 vols.; N.Y.: Dodd, 1931); C. H. Cramer, *Newton D. Baker: A Biography* (Cleveland: World, 1961); and Josephus Daniels, *The Wilson Era: Years of War and After, 1917–1923* (Chapel Hill: U. of N. C., 1946). For wartime politics, see Seward Livermore, *Politics Is Adjourned: Woodrow Wilson and the War Congress, 1916–1918* (Middletown, Conn.: Wesleyan U.P., 1966).

ECONOMIC MOBILIZATION. The report of the War Industries Board is included in Bernard M. Baruch, *American Industry in the War* (Englewood Cliffs, N.J.: Prentice-Hall, 1941). See also the same author's *Baruch: The Public Years* (N.Y.: Holt, 1960), and Margaret L. Coit, *Mr. Baruch: The Man, the Myth, the Eighty Years* (Boston: Houghton Mifflin, 1957). Two wartime railroad administrators tell their stories in McAdoo, *Crowded Years,* cited above: and Walker D. Hines, *War History of the American Railroads* (New Haven: Yale U.P., 1928). Charles Gilbert, *American Financing of World War I* (Westport, Conn.: Greenwood, 1970), is the work of an economist.

MOBILIZATION OF THOUGHT. George Creel's own account is in his *How We Advertised America* (N.Y.: Harper, 1920). More objective are Harold D. Lasswell, *Propaganda Techniques in the World War* (N.Y.: Whittlesey, 1927), and James R. Mock and Cedric Larson, *Words That Won the War: The Story of the Committee on Public Information* (Princeton: Princeton U.P., 1940). For the antiwar movement, see H. C. Peterson and G. C. Fite, *Opponents of War, 1917–1918* (Madison: U. of Wisconsin, 1957), and Donald Johnson, *The Challenge to American Freedom: World War I and the Rise of the American Civil Liberties Union* (Lexington: U. of Kentucky, 1963).

THE WAR FRONTS. Most authoritative account of the AEF is John F. Pershing, *My Experiences in the World War* (2 vols.; N.Y.: Stokes, 1931). Also good is James G. Harbord, *The American Army in France, 1917–1919* (Boston: Little, Brown, 1936). For the war at sea, Thomas C. Frothingham, *The Naval History of the World War,* (3 vols.; Cambridge: Harvard U.P., 1925–1926), is recommended. On intervention in Russia, see William S. Graves, *America's Siberian Adventure, 1918–1920* (N.Y.: Smith, 1941), and Betty M. Unterberger, *America's Siberian Expedition, 1918–1920* (Durham: Duke U.P., 1956).

Chapter 9. Peace and Disillusionment

GENERAL. An excellent study is Harry R. Rudin, *Armistice 1918* (New Haven: Yale U.P., 1944). Basic documents for tracing the peace negotiations are in H. W. V. Temperley, *A History of the Peace Conference of Paris* (6 vols.; London: Hodder and Stoughton, 1920–1924), and Ray S. Baker, *Woodrow Wilson and the World Settlement* (3 vols.; Garden City: Doubleday, 1922). An interpretive study favorable to Wilson is Paul Birdsall, *Versailles Twenty Years After* (N.Y.: Reynal, 1941). Many contrary judgments are in Thomas A. Bailey, *Woodrow Wilson and the Lost Peace* (N.Y.: Macmillan, 1944).

MEMOIRS AND LETTERS. Highly critical of Wilson is Robert Lansing, *The Peace Negotiations: A Personal Narrative* (Boston: Houghton Mifflin, 1921). Less controversial accounts are given by the other members of the American delegation: Seymour, *Intimate Papers of Colonel House,* cited above; Nevins, *Henry White,* cited above; Frederick Palmer, *Bliss, Peacemaker: The Life and Letters of General Tasker Howard Bliss* (N.Y.: Dodd, 1934). Other informative works by Americans attached to the peace commission are David H. Miller, *The Drafting of the Covenant* (2 vols.; N.Y.: Putnam, 1938); Bernard M. Baruch, *The Making of the Reparations and Economic Sections of the Treaty* (N.Y.: Harper, 1920); James T. Shotwell, *At the Paris Peace Conference* (N.Y.: Macmillan, 1937). One of the liveliest portraits of the conference is the memoir of an English diplomatist, Harold Nicolson, *Peacemaking, 1919* (N.Y.: Harcourt, 1939).

THE TREATY FIGHT. The most extensive account, highly sympathetic to Wilson, is Denna Frank Fleming, *The United States and the League of Nations, 1918–1920* (N.Y.: Putnam, 1932). More critical is Thomas A. Bailey, *Woodrow Wilson and the Great Betrayal* (N.Y.: Macmillan, 1945). The conduct of the Senate is analyzed in W. Stull Holt, *Treaties Defeated by the Senate* (Baltimore: Johns Hopkins, 1933), and Kenneth Colgrove, *The American Senate and World Peace* (N.Y.: Vanguard, 1934). Wilson's most dangerous antagonist defends his course of action in Henry Cabot Lodge, *The Senate and the League of Nations* (N.Y.: Scribners, 1925). John A. Garraty, *Henry Cabot Lodge: A Biography* (N.Y.: Knopf, 1953), is excellent. On the tragic failure of Wilson and the pro-League Republicans to make a workable alliance, consult Ruhl J. Bartlett, *The League to Enforce Peace* (Chapel Hill: U. of N. C., 1944).

POSTWAR PROBLEMS. Paxson, *American Democracy and the World War,* cited above, vol. 3), and James R. Mock and Evangeline Thurber, *Report on Demobilization* (Norman: U. of Oklahoma, 1944), are excellent studies. The excesses associated with the Red scare are discussed in Zechariah Chaffee, Jr., *Free Speech in the United States* (Cambridge: Harvard U.P., 1941); Robert K. Murray, *Red Scare* (Minneapolis: U. of Minnesota, 1955); William Preston, Jr., *Aliens and Dissenters: Federal Suppression of Radicals, 1903–1933* (Cambridge: Harvard U.P., 1963); Stanley Coben, *A. Mitchell Palmer: Politician* (N.Y.: Columbia U.P., 1963). Theodore Draper, *The Roots of American Communism* (N.Y.: Viking, 1957), is an outstanding work. On the most critical industrial dispute of the period, see David Brody, *Labor in Crisis: The Steel Strike of 1919* (Philadelphia: Lippincott, 1965). Aileen S. Kraditor, *The Ideas of the Woman Suffrage Movement, 1890–1920* (N.Y.: Columbia U.P., 1966), is excellent.

Chapter 10. The Republican Restoration

GENERAL. The following provide excellent accounts: William E. Leuchtenburg, *The Perils of Prosperity, 1914–1932* (Chicago: U. of Chicago, 1958); John D. Hicks, *The Republican Ascendancy, 1921–1933* (N.Y.: Harper, 1960); Harold U. Faulkner, *From Versailles to the New Deal* (New Haven: Yale U.P., 1950). Highly critical is Karl Schriftgiesser, *This Was Normalcy: An Account of Party Politics During Twelve Republican Years* (Boston: Little, Brown, 1948). Samuel Hopkins Adams, *Incredible Era: The Life and Times of Warren Gamaliel Harding* (Boston: Houghton Mifflin, 1939), is entertaining and shrewd. Andrew Sinclair, *The Available Man: The Life Behind the Mask of Warren G. Harding* (N.Y.: Macmillan 1965), and Robert K. Murray, *The Harding Era: Warren G. Harding and His Administration* (Minneapolis: U. of Minnesota, 1969) are based on new sources. Calvin Coolidge, *Autobiography* (N.Y.: Cosmopolitan, 1929), is of very limited usefulness, but the following are excellent: William Allen White, *A Puritan in Babylon* (N.Y.: Macmillan, 1938); Claude M. Fuess, *Calvin Coolidge, the Man from Vermont* (Boston: Little, Brown, 1940); Donald R. McCoy, *Calvin Coolidge: The Quiet President* (N.Y.: Macmillan, 1967).

THE PROGRESSIVE OPPOSITION. On the most significant liberal of the twenties, see George W. Norris, *Fighting Liberal* (N.Y.: Macmillan, 1945), and Richard Lowitt, *George W. Norris: The Persistence of a Progressive* (Urbana: U. of Illinois, 1971).

For the 1924 third party movement, see Kenneth C. McKay, *The Progressive Movement of 1924* (N.Y.: Columbia U.P., 1947).

THE FARM PROBLEM. The best introduction to the farm problem is Wilson Gee, *The Social Economics of Agriculture* (N.Y.: Macmillan, 1942). See also James H. Sheidler, *Farm Crisis, 1919–1923* (Berkeley: U. of California, 1957); Theodore Saloutos and John D. Hicks, *Agrarian Discontent in the Middle West, 1900–1939* (Madison: U. of Wisconsin, 1951); Gilbert C. Fite, *George N. Peek and the Fight for Farm Parity* (Norman: U. of Oklahoma, 1954).

OTHER ISSUES. On the election of 1920, see William T. Hutchinson, *Lowden of Illinois: The Life of Frank O. Lowden* (2 vols.; Chicago: U. of Chicago, 1957); James M. Cox, *Journey Through My Years* (N.Y.: Simon & Schuster, 1946); W. M. Bagley, *The Road to Normalcy: The Presidential Campaign and Election of 1920* (Baltimore: Johns Hopkins, 1962). On the immigration issue, see Wittke, *We Who Built America*, and Higham, *Strangers in the Land*, both cited for Chapter 1. On the bonus, see Marcus Duffield, *King Legion* (N.Y.: Cape, 1931). M. E. Savage, *The Story of Teapot Dome* (N.Y.: New Republic, 1924), and Burt Noggle, *Teapot Dome and Politics in the 1920's* (Baton Rouge: Louisiana S.U., 1962), describe the oil scandal. For various aspects of the power controversy, see Stephen Rauschenbush, *The Power Fight* (N.Y.: New Republic, 1932); Ernest Gruening, *The Public Pays: A Study of Power Propaganda* (N.Y.: Vanguard, 1931); Judson King, *The Conservation Fight from Theodore Roosevelt to the Tennessee Valley Authority* (Washington: Public Affairs, 1959); Preston J. Hubbard, *Origins of the TVA: The Muscle Shoals Controversy* (Nashville: Vanderbilt U.P., 1961). Sidney Ratner, *American Taxation: Its History as a Social Force in Democracy* (N.Y.: Norton, 1942), is authoritative on tax policy.

Chapter 11. Foreign Affairs, 1921–1929

GENERAL. The diplomatic histories by Dulles, David, and Osgood, cited for Chapter 4, are very useful. These may be supplemented by Selig Adler, *The Uncertain Giant: American Foreign Policy Between the Wars* (N.Y.: Macmillan, 1965), and Frank H. Simonds, *American Foreign Policy in the Post-War Years* (Baltimore: Johns Hopkins, 1935). Betty Glad, *Charles Evans Hughes and the Illusions of Innocence* (Urbana: U. of Illinois, 1967), discusses the most important figure of the period.

INTERNATIONAL COOPERATION. Denna F. Fleming, *The United States and World Organization, 1920–1935* (N.Y.: Columbia U.P., 1938), and Russell M. Cooper, *American Consultation in World Affairs* (N.Y.: Macmillan, 1934), are competent discussions. Denna F. Fleming, *The United States and the World Court* (Garden City: Doubleday, 1945), emphasizes the irresponsibility of the Senate. A more creditable record is that discussed in Benjamin H. Williams, *The United States and Disarmament* (N.Y.: McGraw-Hill, 1931), and Merze Tate, *The United States and Armaments* (Cambridge: Harvard U.P., 1948). Also important for the disarmament issue are Thomas H. Buckley, *The United States and the Washington Conference, 1921–1922* (Knoxville: U. of Tennessee, 1970), and Harold and Margaret Sprout, *Toward a New Order of Sea Power: American Naval Policy and the World Scene, 1918–1922* (Princeton: Princeton U.P., 1940). On the Paris Pact, the most valuable studies are James T. Shotwell, *War as an Instrument of National Policy and Its Renunciation in the Pact of Paris* (N.Y.: Harcourt, 1929), and Robert H. Ferrell, *Peace in Their Time: The Origins of the Kellogg-Briand Pact* (New Haven: Yale U.P., 1952). Two outstanding economists discuss the debts issue in Harold G. Moulton and Leo Pasvolsky, *War Debts and World Prosperity* (N.Y.: Century, 1932).

SPECIAL AREAS. The background of Soviet-American relations is discussed in George F. Kennan, *Soviet-American Relations, 1917–1920* (Vol. 1; Princeton:

Princeton U.P., 1956). For the nonrecognition policy, consult Robert P. Browder, *The Origins of Soviet-American Diplomacy* (Princeton: Princeton U.P., 1953); Frederick L. Schuman, *American Policy toward Russia since 1917* (N.Y.: International, 1928); Foster Rhea Dulles, *The Road to Teheran: The Story of Russia and America, 1781–1943* (Princeton: Princeton U.P., 1944). The leader of the Philippine independence movement tells his story in Manuel Luis Quezon, *The Good Fight* (N.Y.: Appleton, 1946). Graham H. Stuart, *Latin America and the United States* (N.Y.: Appleton-Century, 1938), and Herbert Feis, *The Diplomacy of the Dollar: First Era, 1919–1932* (Baltimore: Johns Hopkins, 1950), are useful on relations with Latin America. See also Isaac J. Cox, *Nicaragua and the United States* (Boston: World Peace Foundation, 1927), and Henry L. Stimson, *American Policy in Nicaragua* (N.Y.: Scribners, 1927). On the easing of tensions between Mexico and the United States, see the excellent biography, Harold Nicolson, *Dwight Morrow* (N.Y.: Harcourt, 1935). For the Japanese-American crisis of 1924, see Rodman W. Paul, *The Abrogation of the Gentlemen's Agreement* (Cambridge: Harvard U.P., 1936).

Chapter 12. Reactionaries and Rebels
GENERAL. Mark Sullivan, *Our Times: The United States, 1900–1925* (Vol. 6; N.Y.: Scribners, 1926–1935), and Slosson, *The Great Crusade and After,* cited for Chapter 8, have interesting material. A treasury of stimulating data and comment is provided by President's Research Committee, *Recent Social Trends in the United States* (2 vols.; N.Y.: McGraw-Hill, 1933). Frederick L. Allen, *Only Yesterday* (N.Y.: Harper, 1931), is highly entertaining. A harsher judgment of the period is Henry M. Robinson, *Fantastic Interim: A Hindsight History of American Manners, Morals and Mistakes between Versailles and Pearl Harbor* (N.Y.: Harcourt, 1943). Robert S. and Harold M. Lynd, *Middletown: A Study in Contemporary American Culture* (N.Y.: Harcourt, 1929), is a well-known sociological study of Muncie, Indiana, during the twenties. An interesting comparison is with Angie Debo, *Prairie City: The Story of an American Community* (N.Y.: Knopf, 1944). André Siegfried, *America Comes of Age, a French Analysis* (N.Y.: Harcourt, 1927), is the work of an able foreign observer. Severely critical judgments are contained in Harold E. Stearns, ed., *Civilization in the United States: An Inquiry by Thirty Americans* (N.Y.: Harcourt, 1922).
PROTEST MOVEMENTS. For the labor unions, see Perlman and Taft, *History of Labor in the United States, 1896–1932,* and Taft, *The A. F. of L. in the Time of Gompers,* both cited for Chapter 1. Philip Taft, *The AFL from the Death of Gompers to the Merger* (N.Y.: Harper, 1959), and Irving Bernstein, *The Lean Years: A History of the American Worker, 1920–1933* (Boston: Houghton Mifflin, 1960), are excellent. On the problems of the Socialist party, see Bernard K. Johnpoll, *Pacifist's Progress: Norman Thomas and the Decline of American Socialism* (Chicago: Quadrangle, 1970). Important on civil liberties are Chafee, *Free Speech in the United States,* cited for Chapter 9, and Arthur Garfield Hayes, *Let Freedom Ring* (N.Y.: Boni, 1928). See also Felix Frankfurter, *The Case of Sacco and Vanzetti* (Boston: Little, Brown, 1927), and G. Louis Joughlin and Edmund F. Morgan, *The Legacy of Sacco and Vanzetti* (N.Y.: Harcourt, 1949).
PROHIBITION AND THE KLAN. Herbert Asbury, *The Great Illusion: An Informal History of Prohibition* (Garden City: Doubleday, 1950), is an interesting popular account. See also Herman Feldman, *Prohibition: Its Economic and Industrial Aspects* (N.Y.: Appleton, 1927), and Charles Merz, *The Dry Decade* (Garden City: Doubleday, 1931). David M. Chalmers, *Hooded Americanism: The First Century of the Ku Klux Klan, 1865–1965* (Garden City: Doubleday, 1965), is good.
RELIGION AND MORALS. Useful studies are Paul A. Carter, *The Decline and*

Revival of the Social Gospel (Ithaca: Cornell U.P., 1956); Stewart G. Cole, *The History of Fundamentalism* (N.Y.: Smith, 1931); Ray Ginger, *Six Days or Forever? Tennessee v. John Thomas Scopes* (Boston: Beacon, 1931); Nelson M. Blake, *The Road to Reno: A History of Divorce in the United States* (N.Y.: Macmillan, 1962); and David M. Kennedy, *Birth Control in America: The Career of Margaret Sanger* (New Haven: Yale U.P., 1970).

LITERATURE AND ART. For the major literary trends, see Frederick J. Hoffman, *Twenties: American Writing in the Postwar Decade* (N.Y.: Viking, 1965), and Joseph Beach, *American Fiction, 1920–1940* (N.Y.: Macmillan, 1941). On individual writers, the following are outstanding studies: Carlos Baker, *Ernest Hemingway: A Life Story* (N.Y.: Scribners, 1969); Cleanth Brooks, *William Faulkner: The Yoknapatawpha Country* (New Haven: Yale U.P., 1963); Mark Schorer, *Sinclair Lewis, an American Life* (N.Y.: McGraw-Hill, 1961); Andrew Turnbull, *Scott Fitzgerald* (N.Y.: Scribners, 1962). In addition to the histories of art cited for Chapter 1 the following are recommended: Wayne Andrews, *Architecture, Ambition and Americans* (N.Y.: Harper, 1955); Vergil Barker, *American Painting* (N.Y.: Macmillan, 1950); John A. Kouwenhoven, *Made in America: The Arts in Modern Civilization* (Garden City: Doubleday, 1948).

Chapter 13. Prosperity

GENERAL. George Soule, *Prosperity Decade: From War to Depression, 1917–1929* (N.Y.: Rinehart, 1947), is a valuable account. A contemporary study of importance is *Recent Economic Changes in the United States* (2 vols,; N.Y.: McGraw-Hill, 1929). A useful summary of this is Edward E. Hunt, *An Audit of America* (N.Y.: McGraw-Hill, 1930). Lewis Corey, *The Decline of American Capitalism* (N.Y.: Covici, 1934), is a Marxian interpretation. Important monographs by economists are Simon Kuznets, *National Income and Capital Formation, 1919–1935: A Preliminary Report* (N.Y.: National Bureau of Economic Research, 1937), and Spurgeon Bell, *Productivity, Wages and National Income* (Washington, D.C.: Brookings Inst., 1940). On the intellectual climate, see James W. Prothro, *The Dollar Decade: Business Ideas in the 1920's* (Baton Rouge: Louisiana S.U., 1954).

AUTOMOBILE INDUSTRY. Good general accounts are John B. Rae, *The Automobile* (Chicago: U. of Chicago, 1966), and David L. Cohn, *Combustion on Wheels: An Informal History of the Automobile Age* (Boston: Houghton Mifflin, 1944). Allan Nevins and F. E. Hill, *Ford: Expansion and Challenge, 1915–1933* (N.Y.: Scribners, 1957), is a sympathetic study. Brief but good is Reynold M. Wik, *Henry Ford and Grassroots America* (Ann Arbor: U. of Michigan, 1972).

AVIATION. Fred C. Kelley, *The Wright Brothers* (N.Y.: Harcourt, 1943), is a well-written acount of the origins of aviation, while a critical and informative study of the whole industry is Elsbeth F. Freudenthal, *The Aviation Business: From Kitty Hawk to Wall Street* (N.Y.: Vanguard, 1940). Kenneth S. Davis, *The Hero: Charles A. Lindbergh and the American Dream* (Garden City: Doubleday, 1959), is excellent.

OTHER INDUSTRIES. On the movies, see Margaret F. Thorp, *America at the Movies* (New Haven: Yale U.P., 1939); Lewis Jacobs, *The Rise of the American Film: A Critical History* (N.Y.: Harcourt, 1939). On radio: Erik Barnouw, *A Tower in Babel: A History of Broadcasting in the United States* (N.Y.: Oxford U.P., 1966). The following are important studies: Paul M. Zeis, *American Shipping Policy* (Princeton: Princeton U.P., 1938); Twientieth Century Fund, *The Power Industry and the Public Interest* (N.Y.: Twentieth Century Fund, 1944); Corporation Survey, *Big Business: Its Growth and Its Place* (N.Y.: Twentieth Century Fund, 1937); Thurmond W. Arnold, *The Folklore of Capitalism* (New Haven: Yale U.P., 1937); Robert Sobel, *The Great Bull Market* (N.Y.: Norton, 1969).

Chapter 14. Hoover and the Great Depression

GENERAL. Harris G. Warren, *Herbert Hoover and the Great Depression* (N.Y.: Oxford U.P., 1959), and Albert U. Romasco, *The Poverty of Abundance: Hoover, the Nation, the Depression* (N.Y.: Oxford U.P., 1966), are fair and thoughtful. Hoover's record is sturdily defended in William S. Myers and Walter Newton, *The Hoover Administration: A Documented Narrative* (N.Y.: Scribners, 1936). Hoover's own writing reveals both his assets and limitations as statesman; see: Herbert C. Hoover, *Memoirs* (3 vols.; N.Y.: Macmillan, 1952); William S. Myers, ed. *The State Papers and Other Public Writings of Herbert Hoover* (2 vols.; N.Y.: Scribners, 1934); Ray Lyman Wilbur and Arthur M. Hyde, eds., *The Hoover Policies* (N.Y.: Scribners, 1937). Useful but not definitive biographies are Eugene Lyons, *Our Unknown Ex-President: A Portrait of Herbert Hoover* (Garden City: Doubleday, 1948), and Harold Wolfe, *Herbert Hoover, Public Servant and Leader of the Opposition* (N.Y.: Exposition, 1956). For the election of 1928, see Edmund A. Moore, *A Catholic Runs for President: The Campaign of 1928* (N.Y.: Ronald, 1956).

DEPRESSION. Broadus Mitchell, *Depression Decade: From New Era Through New Deal, 1929–1941* (N.Y.: Rinehart, 1947), and John K. Galbraith, *The Great Crash 1929* (Boston: Houghton Mifflin, 1961), are excellent studies. There are vivid descriptions in Caroline Bird, *The Invisible Scar: The Great Depression and What It Did to American Life, from Then Until Now* (N.Y.: McKay, 1966); Gilbert Seldes, *The Years of the Locust (American 1929–1932)* (Boston: Little, Brown, 1933); Frederick L. Allen, *Since Yesterday* (N.Y.: Harper, 1940). A historically important interpretation is that of the Harvard economist Alvin Hansen, *Fiscal Policy and Business Cycles* (N.Y.: Norton, 1941). Josephine C. Brown, *Public Relief, 1929–1939* (N.Y.: Holt, 1940), discusses problems of government policy. Roger Daniels, *The Bonus March: An Episode of the Great Depression* (Westport, Conn.: Greenwood, 1971), is excellent. For a highly critical discussion of Republican policies, see Arthur M. Schlesinger, Jr., *The Crisis of the Old Order* (Boston: Houghton Mifflin, 1957). Jordan X. Schwartz, *The Interregnum of Despair: Hoover, Congress, and the Depression* (Urbana: U. of Illinois, 1970), discusses conflicts over policy.

Chapter 15. Hoover's Quest for World Stability

GENERAL. William S. Myers, *The Foreign Policies of Herbert Hoover* (N.Y.: Scribners, 1940), is laudatory. More balanced accounts are to be found in the diplomatic histories of Dulles, David, and Osgood, cited for Chapter 3. On Hoover's Secretary of State, see Henry L. Stimson and McGeorge Bundy, *On Active Service in Peace and War* (N.Y.: Harper, 1948); Richard N. Current, *Secretary Stimson: A Study in Statecraft* (New Brunswick: Rutgers U.P., 1954); Elting E. Morison, *Turmoil and Tradition: A Study of the Life and Times of Henry L. Stimson* (Boston: Houghton Mifflin, 1960); Robert H. Ferrell, *American Diplomacy in the Great Depression: Hoover-Stimson Foreign Policy, 1929–1933* (New Haven: Yale U.P., 1957).

SPECIAL PHASES. On the London Naval Conference, there is much valuable information in Charles G. Dawes, *Journal as Ambassador to Great Britain* (N.Y.: Macmillan, 1939). An important reorientation of American policy may be traced in Bemis, *Latin American Policy of the United States*, cited for Chapter 5, and Alexander De Conde, *Herbert Hoover's Latin-American Policy* (Stanford: Stanford U.P., 1951). For the Far Eastern crisis, see Armin Rappaport, *Henry L. Stimson and Japan, 1931–33* (Chicago: U. of Chicago, 1963); Robert Langer, *Seizure of Territory: The Stimson Doctrine and Related Principles in Legal Theory and Diplomatic Practice* (Princeton: Princeton U.P., 1947); Reginald Bassett, *Democracy and Foreign Policy, The Sino-Japanese Dispute, 1931–33* (N.L.: Longmans, 1952); Henry

L. Stimson, *The Far Eastern Crisis: Recollections and Observations* (N.Y.: Council on Foreign Relations, 1936).

Chapter 16. New Deal Triumphant

GENERAL. Indispensable not only for documentary material but for Roosevelt's subsequent comments on events is Samuel I. Rosenman, ed., *The Public Papers and Addresses of Franklin D. Roosevelt* (13 vols.; N.Y.: Random, Macmillan, Harper, 1938–1950). The most detailed account is Arthur M. Schlesinger, Jr., *The Age of Roosevelt* (3 vols.; Boston: Houghton Mifflin, 1957–1960). Basil Rauch, *The History of the New Deal* (N.Y.: Creative Age, 1944), is a clear, well-organized account. William E. Leuchtenburg, *Franklin D. Roosevelt and the New Deal, 1932–1940* (N.Y.: Harper, 1963), is the best brief interpretation. Other concise studies are Dexter Perkins, *The New Age of Franklin Roosevelt, 1932–1945* (Chicago: U. of Chicago, 1957), and Denis W. Brogan, *The Era of Franklin D. Roosevelt* (New Haven: Yale U.P., 1950). The most complete and competent biography of Roosevelt is Frank B. Freidel, *Franklin D. Roosevelt* (Boston: Little, Brown, 1952–), of which three volumes have now been published. Also excellent for the early years is Kenneth S. Davis, *FDR: The Beckoning of Destiny 1882–1928* (N.Y.: Putnam, 1972). Among numerous shorter studies, the following are recommended: Alden Hatch, *Franklin D. Roosevelt, an Informal Biography* (N.Y.: Holt, 1947); James M. Burns, *Roosevelt, the Lion and the Fox* (N.Y.: Harcourt, 1956); James M. Burns, *Roosevelt, the Soldier of Freedom* (N.Y.: Harcourt, 1970). Rexford G. Tugwell, *The Democratic Roosevelt: A Biography of Franklin D. Roosevelt* (Garden City: Doubleday, 1957). Edgar E. Robinson, *The Roosevelt Leadership, 1933–1945* (Philadelphia: Lippincott, 1955), is a severe indictment. Joseph P. Lash, *Eleanor and Franklin* (N.Y.: Norton, 1971), is a fascinating account of the influence of FDR's wife. Also excellent is Otto L. Graham, Jr., *An Encore for Reform: The Old Progressives and the New Deal* (N.Y.: Oxford U.P., 1967).

MEMOIRS. Particularly useful are the following: Frances Perkins, *The Roosevelt I Knew* (N.Y.: Viking, 1946); Robert E. Sherwood, *Roosevelt and Hopkins: An Intimate History* (N.Y.:Harper, 1948); Samuel I. Rosenman, *Working with Roosevelt* (N.Y.: Harper, 1952); *The Secret Diary of Harold I. Ickes* (3 vols.; N.Y.: Simon & Schuster, 1953–1954); Raymond Moley, *After Seven Years* (N.Y.: Harper, 1939). James A. Farley, *Behind the Ballots: The Personal History of a Politician* (N.Y.: Harcourt, 1938), is useful for the 1932 and 1936 campaigns. Its sequel, *Jim Farley's Story: The Roosevelt Years* (N.Y.: Whittlesey, 1948), is a record of disillusionment.

RELIEF AND SECURITY. The best discussion of the activities of the various New Deal agencies is Merle Fainsod and Lincoln Gordon, *Government and the American Economy* (N.Y.: Norton, 1941). On special phases, see Donald S. Howard, *The PWA and Federal Relief Policy* (N.Y.: Russell Sage, 1938); Harold L. Ickes, *Back to Work: The Story of PWA* (N.Y.: Macmillan, 1935); Searle F. Charles, *Minister of Relief: Harry Hopkins and the Depression* (Syracuse: Syracuse U.P., 1963); John A. Salmond, *The Civilian Conservation Corps, 1933–1942* (Durham: Duke U.P., 1967); Arthur M. Altmeyer, *The Formative Years of Social Security* (Madison: U. of Wisconsin, 1936); Roy Lubove, *The Struggle for Social Security, 1900–1935* (Cambridge: Harvard U.P., 1968).

NRA AND THE TRUST PROBLEM. Indispensable for understanding the point of view of NRA's most important administrator is Hugh S. Johnson, *The Blue Eagle from Egg to Earth* (Garden City: Doubleday, 1935). Johnson's successor adds his comment in Donald R. Richberg, *The Rainbow* (Garden City: Doubleday, 1936). Excellent studies are Sidney Fine, *The Automobile under the Blue Eagle* (Ann Arbor: U. of Michigan, 1963), and Ellis W. Hawley, *The New Deal and the Problem of Monopoly* (Princeton: Princeton U.P., 1966).

TVA AND THE UTILITIES ISSUE. The broad objectives and administrative philosophy of the TVA are lucidly set forth by its principal director, David E. Lilienthal, *TVA: Democracy on the March* (N.Y.: Harper, 1944). The following are important studies: Wilmon H. Droze, *High Dams and Slack Waters: TVA Rebuilds a River* (Baton Rouge: Louisiana S.U., 1965), Thomas K. McCraw, *TVA and the Power Fight* (Philadelphia: Lippincott, 1971); C. Herman Pritchett, *The Tennessee Valley Authority: A Study in Public Administration* (Chapel Hill: U. of N.C., 1943).

FISCAL AND MONETARY POLICY. Marriner S. Eccles, *Beckoning Frontiers: Public and Personal Recollections* (N.Y.: Knopf, 1951), is an excellent memoir dealing in part with the activities of the Federal Reserve Board. See also Fine, *American Taxation,* cited for Chapter 10; G. Griffith Johnson, *The Treasury and Monetary Policy, 1933–1938* (Cambridge: Harvard U.P., 1939); Gerard Cohn and Fritz Lehmann, *Economic Consequences of Recent American Tax Policy* (N.Y.: New School for Social Research, 1938).

AGRICULTURE. The philosophy of the New Deal Secretary of Agriculture is in Henry A. Wallace, *New Frontiers* (N.Y.: Reynal, 1934). Severely critical on many phases is Edwin G. Nourse, *Government in Relation to Agriculture* (Washington, D.C.: Brookings Inst., 1940). For intellectual influences, see Richard S. Kirkendall, *Social Scientists and Farm Politics in the Age of Roosevelt* (Columbia: U. of Missouri, 1966). For political aspects, see Wesley McCune, *The Farm Bloc* (Garden City: Doubleday, 1934), and Christina M. Campell, *The Farm Bureau and the New Deal* (Urbana: U. of Illinois, 1962). On the agricultural poor, see David E. Conrad, *The Forgotten Farmers: The Story of Sharecroppers and the New Deal* (Urbana: U. of Illinois, 1965).

Chapter 17. New Deal on the Defensive

GENERAL. See titles listed for Chapter 16. See also James T. Patterson, *Congressional Conservatism and the New Deal* (Lexington: U. of Kentucky, 1967). On the election of 1936, see Donald R. McCoy, *Landon of Kansas* (Lincoln: U. of Nebraska, 1966).

SUPREME COURT CRISIS. For essential background, Alfred H. Kelly and Winfield A. Harbison, *The American Constitution: Its Origins and Growth* (N.Y.: Norton, 1955), is good. On the two most influential justices, see Max Lerner, *The Mind of Faith of Justice Holmes* (Boston: Little, Brown, 1945), and Mason, *Brandeis,* cited for Chapter 2. A leading authority on the Supreme Court criticizes its conduct in Edward S. Corwin, *The Twilight of the Supreme Court* (New Haven: Yale U.P., 1934) and *Court Over Constitution* (Princeton: Princeton U.P., 1938). The best account of the court controversy from the New Deal point of view is Robert H. Jackson, *The Struggle for Judicial Supremacy* (N.Y.: Knopf, 1941). Detailed and well-informed, although unsympathetic to Roosevelt, is Joseph Alsop and Turner Catledge, *The 168 Days* (Garden City: Doubleday, 1938). The role of Chief Justice Hughes may be studied in Merlo J. Pusey, *Charles Evans Hughes* (2 vols.; N.Y.: Macmillan, 1951), and Samuel Hendel, *Charles Evans Hughes and the Supreme Court* (N.Y.: King's Crown, 1951). The sequel of the controversy is dealt with in Edward S. Corwin, *Constitutional Revolution, Ltd.* (Claremont, Calif.: Pomona College, 1941), and C. Herman Pritchett, *The Roosevelt Court* (N.Y.: Macmillan, 1948).

OTHER ISSUES. The neurotic fringe in American politics is studied in David H. Bennett, *Demagogues in the Depression: American Radicals and the Union Party, 1932–1936* (New Brunswick; Rutgers U.P., 1969); Alfred M. and Elizabeth B. Lee, eds., *The Fine Art of Propaganda: A Study of Father Coughlin's Speeches* (N.Y.: Harcourt's, 1939); Hartnett T. Kane, *Louisiana Hayride: The American Rehearsal for Dictatorship* (N.Y.: Morrow, 1941); T. Harry Williams, *Huey Long* (N.Y.: Knopf, 1969).

Chapter 18. Depression America

GENERAL. The best survey of social trends during the thirties is Dixon Wecter, *The Age of the Great Depression, 1929–1941* (N.Y.: Macmillan, 1948). See also Mitchell, *Depression Decade*, cited for Chapter 14. "Recent Social Trends," *American Journal of Sociology,* 47 (May, 1942), 803–980, does for this decade what the more extensive work of the same name did for the twenties. Frederick L. Allen, *Since Yesterday* (N.Y.: Harper, 1940), is a lively account. Harold F. Stearns, ed., *America Now: An Inquiry into Civilization in the United States by Thirty-six Americans* (N.Y.: Literary Guild, 1938), gives a more optimistic picture than the similar survey under Stearns's editorship in 1922 (cited for Chapter 12). Robert and Helen Lynd, *Middletown in Transition* (N.Y.: Harcourt, 1937), provides an important sequel to the Lynds' earlier study.

LABOR. The best study is Irving Bernstein, *Turbulent Years: A History of the American Worker 1933–1941* (Boston: Houghton Mifflin, 1970). Also recommended: Saul Alinsky, *John L. Lewis* (N.Y.: Putnam, 1949); Nels Anderson, *Men on the Move* (Chicago: U. of Chicago, 1940); Jerold S. Auerbach, *Labor and Liberty: The LaFollette Committee and the New Deal* (Indianapolis: Bobbs, 1966); Milton Derber and Edwin Young, eds., *Labor and the New Deal* (Madison: U. of Madison, 1957); Sidney Fine, *Sit-Down: The General Motors Strike of 1936–1937* (Ann Arbor: U. of Michigan, 1970); Walter Galenson, *The CIO Challenge to the AFL: A History of the American Labor Movement, 1935–1941* (Cambridge: Harvard U.P., 1960); Eli Ginzberg, *The Unemployed* (N.Y.: Harper, 1943); James O. Morris, *Conflict Within the AFL: A Study of Craft versus Industrial Unionism, 1901–1938* (Ithaca: Cornell U.P., 1958).

COMMUNISM. The best analysis is Irving Howe and Lewis Coser, *The American Communist Party* (Boston: Beacon, 1957). James Oneal and G. A. Werner, *American Communism: A Critical Analysis of Its Origins, Development and Programs* (N.Y.: Dutton, 1947), tells the story from the viewpoint of an anti-Stalinist radical. Theodore Draper, *American Communism and Soviet Russia, the Formative Period* (N.Y.: Viking, 1960), is objective and scholarly. Memoirs by one-time party members are Granville Hicks, *Where We Came Out* (N.Y.: Viking, 1954), and Whittaker Chambers, *Witness* (N.Y.: Random, 1952). Earl Latham, *The Communist Controversy in Washington: From the New Deal to McCarthy* (Cambridge, Harvard U.P., 1966), and Daniel Aaron, *Writers on the Left* (N.Y.: Harcourt, 1961), are excellent studies.

SPECIAL PHASES. On the revolution in economic thought, see Seymour E. Harris, ed., *The New Economics: Keynes' Influence on Theory and Public Policy* (N.Y.: Knopf, 1947); and Robert Lekachman, *The Age of Keynes* (N.Y.: Random, 1966). On literature, see Leo Gurko, *The Angry Decade* (N.Y.: Dodd, 1947); Walter B. Rideout, *The Radical Novel in the United States, 1900–1954* (Cambridge: Harvard U.P., 1956); Maxwell Geismar, *Writers in Crisis: The American Novel, 1925–1940* (Boston: Houghton Mifflin, 1942). On the arts, see works cited for Chapters 1 and 12.

Chapter 19. Gathering Clouds

GENERAL. For competent accounts, see works by Dulles, David, and Osgood, cited for Chapter 4. Allan Nevins, *The New Deal and World Affairs* (New Haven: Yale U.P., 1950), is an objective account. The official defense of American policy is State Department, *Peace and War: United States Foreign Policy, 1931–1941* (Washington, D.C.: GPO, 1943). Edgar B. Nixon, ed., *Franklin D. Roosevelt and Foreign Affairs* (3 vols.; Cambridge: Harvard U.P., 1969), is a valuable collection of documents. On the Secretary of State, see *The Memoirs of Cordell Hull* (2 vols.; N.Y.: Macmillan, 1948), and Julius W. Pratt, *Cordell Hull, 1933–44* (2 vols.; N.Y.: Cooper Square, 1964). Critical analyses of Roosevelt's foreign policy are Charles A. Beard, *American*

Policy in the Making, 1932–1940 (New Haven: Yale U.P., 1946), and Lloyd C. Gardner, *Economic Aspects of New Deal Diplomacy* (Madison: U. of Wisconsin, 1964). For a more sympathetic view, consult William L. Langer and S. Everett Gleason, *The Challenge to Isolation, 1937–1940* (N.Y.: Harper, 1952).

ISOLATIONISM. Robert A. Divine, *The Illusion of Neutrality* (Chicago: U. of Chicago, 1962); Manfred Jonas, *Isolationism in America, 1935–1941* (Ithaca: Cornell U.P., 1966); Charles Chatfield, *For Peace and Justice: Pacifism in America* (Knoxville: U. of Tennessee, 1971); and Adler, *Uncertain Giant,* cited for Chapter 11; are excellent studies. See also Wayne S. Cole, *Senator Gerald P. Nye and American Foreign Relations* (Minneapolis: U. of Minnesota, 1962). Contemporary academic support for isolationism was provided by Charles A. Beard, *The Open Door at Home* (N.Y.: Macmillan, 1934), and Edwin Borchard and William P. Lage, *Neutrality for the United States* (New Haven: Yale U.P., 1937).

RELATIONS WITH EUROPE. The following are recommended: Joseph E. Davis, *Mission to Moscow* (N.Y.: Simon & Schuster, 1941); William E. Dodd, Jr., and Martha Dodd, *Ambassador Dodd's Diary, 1933–1938* (N.Y.: Harcourt, 1941); Arnold A. Offner, *United States Foreign Policy and Germany, 1933–1938* (Cambridge: Harvard U.P., 1969); F. Jay Taylor, *The United States and the Spanish Civil War* (N.Y.: Bookman Associates, 1956); Brice Harris, Jr., *The United States and the Italo-Ethiopian Crisis* (Stanford: Stanford U.P., 1964).

LATIN AMERICA AND THE FAR EAST. On Latin America, see Gordon Connell-Smith, *The Inter-American System* (N.Y.: Oxford U.P., 1966); Edward O. Guerant, *Roosevelt's Good Neighbor Policy* (Albuquerque: U. of N.M., 1950). On the Far East: Joseph C. Grew, *Ten Years in Japan* (N.Y.: Simon & Schuster, 1944), and Dorothy Borg, *The United States and the Far Eastern Crisis of 1933–1938* (Cambridge: Harvard U.P., 1964). On general trade policy, see Raymond L. Buell, *The Hull Trade Program* (N.Y.: Foreign Policy Assn., 1938); Herbert Feis, *The Changing Pattern of International Economic Affairs* (N.Y.: Harper, 1940).

Chapter 20. The Prelude to Pearl Harbor

GENERAL. The titles recommended for Chapter 19 may be supplemented with *The United States in World Affairs, 1939, 1940, 1941* (N.Y.: Council on Foreign Relations 1940–1942). The most scholarly study is William L. Langer and S. Everett Gleason, *The Undeclared War, 1940–1941* (N.Y.: Harper, 1953). Roosevelt's policies are defended in Basil Rauch, *Roosevelt, From Munich to Pearl Harbor* (N.Y.: Creative Age, 1950), and Herbert Feis, *The Road to Pearl Harbor* (Princeton: Princeton U.P., 1950). Roosevelt's policies are severely criticized in Charles A. Beard, *President Roosevelt and the Coming of the War* (New Haven: Yale U.P., 1948), and Charles C. Tansill, *Backdoor to War: The Roosevelt Foreign Policy, 1933–1941* (Chicago: Regnery, 1952). Donald F. Drummond, *The Passing of American Neutrality* (Ann Arbor: U. of Michigan, 1955), is a balanced account. Sumner Welles, *The Time for Decision* (N.Y.: Harper, 1944), is an able discussion of American policy.

POLICY DEBATE. Much valuable information is contained in the account of the lend-lease administrator Edward R. Stettinius, Jr., *Lend Lease, Weapon for Victory* (N.Y.: Macmillan, 1944). The controversy between the interventionists and the isolationists may be traced in Charles A. Beard, *A Foreign Policy for America* (N.Y.: Knopf, 1940); Allen W. Dulles and H. F. Armstrong, *Can America Stay Neutral?* (N.Y.: Harper, 1939); Raymond L. Buell, *Isolated America* (N.Y.: Knopf, 1940); Walter Johnson, *The Battle Against Isolation* (Chicago: U. of Chicago, 1944); Wayne S. Cole, *America First: Battle Against Intervention, 1940–1941* (Madison: U. of Wisconsin, 1953).

THE FAR EAST. Essential background is provided in C. A. Buss, *War and Diplomacy in Eastern Asia* (N.Y.: Macmillan, 1941); W. C. Johnstone, *The United States and Japan's New Order* (N.Y.: Oxford U.P., 1941); Harold S. Quigley, *Far Eastern War,*

1937–1941 (Boston: World Peace Foundation, 1942). Grew, *Ten Years in Japan,* cited for Chapter 19, may be supplemented with Joseph C. Grew, *Turbulent Era: A Diplomatic Record of Forty Years* (2 vols.; Boston: Houghton Mifflin, 1952).

PEARL HARBOR. In addition to the discussion provided in the works listed above, consult Walter Millis, *This Is Pearl! The United States and Japan–1941* (N.Y.: Morrow, 1947), and Walter Lord, *Day of Infamy* (N.Y.: Holt, 1957). Roosevelt's policy is indicted in George E. Morgenstern, *Pearl Harbor, the Story of the Secret War* (N.Y.: Devin-Adair, 1947), and Robert A. Theobold, *Final Secret of Pearl Harbor: The Washington Contribution to the Japanese Attack* (N.Y.: Devin-Adair, 1954).

Chapter 21. The Global War

·GENERAL. The various services employed professional historians to collect materials and prepared a comprehensive account of the conflict. The Historical Division of the Department of the Army has published an extensive series of special studies under the title *The United States Army in World War II.* Forrest C. Pogue, *The Supreme Command* (Washington, D.C.: Office of the Chief of Military History, 1954), is an especially valuable work. Also useful is Wesley F. Craven and James L. Cate, eds., *The Army Air Forces in World War II* (7 vols.; Chicago: U. of Chicago, 1948–1958). Samuel E. Morison, *History of United States Naval Operations in World War II* (15 vols.; Boston: Little, Brown, 1947–1962), is the work of a leading historian. This account is condensed in Samuel E. Morison, *The Two-Ocean War: A Short History of the United States Navy in the Second World War* (Boston: Little, Brown, 1963). A. Russell Buchanan, *The United States and World War II* (2 vols.; N.Y.: Harper, 1964), is a good overall history. Briefer accounts are Francis T. Miller, *History of World War II* (Philadelphia: Winston, 1946), and Fletcher Pratt, *War for the World* (New Haven: Yale U.P., 1950). Hanson W. Baldwin, *Great Mistakes of the War* (N.Y.: Harper, 1950), and Chester Wilmot, *The Struggle for Europe* (N.Y.: Harper, 1952), criticize Allied strategy. On American campaigns in the Far East, see Barbara Tuchman, *Stilwell and the American Experience in China, 1911–47* (N.Y.: Macmillan, 1971).

REPORTS AND MEMOIRS. The clearest as well as the most authoritative brief account of the American effort is *General Marshall's Report: The Winning of the War in Europe and the Pacific* (N.Y.: Simon & Schuster, 1945). On the European campaign, an essential source is Dwight D. Eisenhower, *Report by the Supreme Commander to the Combined Chiefs of Staff on Operations in Europe of the Allied Expeditionary Force 6 June 1944 to 8 May 1945* (Washington, D.C.: GPO, 1946). On naval operations, see Ernest J. King, *U.S. Navy at War, 1941–1945: Official Reports to the Secretary of the Navy* (Washington, D.C.: U.S. Navy Dept., 1946). The wartime Secretary of War contributed an important memoir in Stimson and Bundy, *On Active Service in Peace and War,* cited for Chapter 15. Several of the major commanders have written accounts of their experiences: Dwight D. Eisenhower, *Crusade in Europe* (Garden City: Doubleday, 1948); Omar N. Bradley, *A. Soldier's Story* (N.Y.: Holt, 1951); Theodore H. White, ed., *The Stilwell Papers* (N.Y.: Sloan, 1948); Henry H. Arnold, *Global Mission* (N.Y.: Harper, 1949). A fascinating document, part memoir and part history in the grand manner, is Winston Churchill, *The Second World War* (6 vols.; Boston: Houghton Mifflin, 1948–1953).

WARTIME DIPLOMACY. The following are important studies: Stephen E. Ambrose, *Eisenhower and Berlin, 1945: The Decision to Halt at the Elbe* (N.Y.: Norton, 1967); Robert A. Divine, *Roosevelt and World War II* (Baltimore: Johns Hopkins, 1969); Herbert Feis, *Churchill, Roosevelt, Stalin* (Princeton: Princeton U.P., 1957); Gabriel Kolko, *The Politics of War: The World and United States Foreign Policy* (N.Y.: Vintage, 1970); William Langer, *Our Vichy Gamble* (N.Y.: Knopf, 1947); Gaddis Smith, *American Diplomacy During the Second World War, 1941–1945*

(N.Y.: Wiley, 1965); John L. Snell, *Illusion and Necessity: The Diplomacy of the Global War, 1939-1945* (Boston: Houghton Mifflin, 1963).

Chapter 22. The Home Front

GENERAL. Jack Goodman, ed., *While You Were Gone: A Report on Wartime Life in the United States* (N.Y.: Harcourt, 1946), is uneven in quality but has good chapters. Mercedes Rosebery, *This Day's Madness: A Story of the American People Against the Background of the War Effort* (N.Y.: Macmillan, 1944), is chaotic and impressionistic in treatment but captures something of the spirit of the times. Valuable contemporary accounts are provided in Selden Menefee, *Assignment: U.S.A.* (N.Y.: Reynal, 1943), and John Dos Passos, *State of the Nation* (Boston: Houghton Mifflin, 1944).

ECONOMIC POLICY. Allan Nevins and Louis Hacker, eds., *The United States and Its Place in World Affairs, 1918-1943* (Boston: Heath, 1943), has good chapters on the wartime economy. The most important authority for industrial mobilization is the memoir of WPB chief, Donald Nelson, *Arsenal of Democracy: The Story of American Production* (N.Y.: Harcourt, 1946). See also Seymour E. Harris, *Economics of America at War* (N.Y.: Norton, 1943), and the same author's *Price and Related Controls in the United States* (N.Y.: McGraw-Hill, 1945).

JAPANESE-AMERICANS. On the war's most serious infringements of civil liberties, see Roger Daniels, *Concentration Camps USA: Japanese-Americans and World War II* (N.Y.: Holt, 1971); Carey McWilliams, *Prejudice: Japanese-Americans, Symbol of Intolerance* (Boston: Little, Brown, 1944); Dillon S. Meyer, *Uprooted Americans: The Japanese Americans and the War Relocation Authority During World War II* (Tucson: U. of Arizona, 1971).

Chapter 23. The Mirage of Peace

GENERAL. Truman's handling of foreign problems has been warmly praised and sharply criticized. For favorable views, see John L. Gaddis, *The United States and the Origins of the Cold War* (N.Y.: Columbia U.P., 1972); John W. Spanier, *American Foreign Policy Since World War II* (N.Y.: Praeger, 1960); Robert W. Tucker, *The Radical Left and American Foreign Policy* (Baltimore: Johns Hopkins, 1971). For various critical views, see Gar Alperovitz, *Atomic Diplomacy* (N.Y.: Simon & Schuster, 1965); Barton J. Bernstein, ed., *Politics and Policies of the Truman Administration* (Chicago: Quadrangle, 1970); Denna F. Fleming, *The Cold War and Its Origins, 1917-1960* (2 vols.; Garden City: Doubleday, 1961); Lloyd C. Gardner, *Architects of Illusion: Men and Ideas in American Foreign Policy, 1941-1949* (Chicago: Quadrangle, 1970); Joyce and Gabriel Kolko, *The Limits of Power: The World and United States Foreign Policy, 1945-1954* (N.Y.: Harper, 1972); Walter LaFeber, *America, Russia, and the Cold War* (N.Y.: Wiley, 1967).

YALTA CONFERENCE. For a criticism of Roosevelt's concessions to the Russians, see William H. Chamberlin, *America's Second Crusade* (Chicago: Regnery, 1950), and Baldwin, *Great Mistakes of the War*, cited for Chapter 21. Roosevelt's conduct is defended in Diane S. Clemens, *Yalta* (N.Y.: Oxford U.P., 1970); Feis, *Churchill, Roosevelt, Stalin*, cited for Chapter 21; John L. Snell, ed., *The Meaning of Yalta: Big Three Diplomacy and the Balance of Power* (Baton Rouge: Louisiana S.U., 1956); Edward R. Stettinius, *Roosevelt and the Russians: The Yalta Conference* (Garden City: Doubleday, 1949).

INTERNATIONAL ORGANIZATION. Robert A. Divine, *Second Chance: The Triumph of Internationalism During World War II* (N.Y.: Atheneum, 1967), gives essential background. The genesis of the United Nations Organization is well traced in Vera M. Dean, *The Four Cornerstones of Peace* (N.Y.: Whittlesey, 1946), and Ruth B. Russell, *A History of United Nations Charter: The role of the United States, 1940-1945* (Washington, D.C.: Brookings Inst., 1958).

OCCUPATION PROBLEMS. On Germany, see Julian Bach, Jr., *America's Germany: An Account of the Occupation* (N.Y.: Random, 1946), and Saul K. Padover, *Experiment in Germany: The Story of an American Intelligence Officer* (N.Y.: Duell, 1946). Robert H. Jackson, *The Nürnberg Case* (N.Y.: Knopf, 1947), is the account of the chief American prosecutor. On Japan, see Thomas A. Bisson, *Prospects for Democracy in Japan* (N.Y.: Macmillan, 1949); Edwin O. Reischauer, *The United States and Japan* (Cambridge: Harvard U.P., 1950); Frederick S. Dunn, *Peacemaking and the Settlement with Japan* (Princeton: Princeton U.P., 1963). American policy in the Philippines is criticized by Hernando Abaya, *Betrayal in the Philippines* (N.Y.: Wyn, 1946).

CONTAINMENT POLICY. The difficulties involved in dealing with the Russians are related in W. Bedell Smith, *My Three Years in Moscow* (Philadelphia: Lippincott, 1950). Drew Middleton, *The Struggle for Germany* (Indianapolis: Bobbs, 1949), is the work of a well-informed journalist. Joseph M. Jones, *The Fifteen Weeks February 21 June 5, 1947* (N.Y.: Viking, 1955), deals with the Truman Doctrine and the Marshall Plan. Concise and informative is Halford L. Hoskins, *The Atlantic Pact* (Washington: Public Affairs, 1949).

CHINA AND KOREA. Essential to an understanding are Herbert Feis, *The China Tangle: The American Effort in China from Pearl Harbor to the Marshall Mission* (Princeton: Princeton U.P., 1953); John K. Fairbank, *The United States and China* (Cambridge: Harvard U.P., 1948); Tang Tsou, *America's Failure in China, 1941–1950* (Chicago: U. of Chicago, 1963). On Korea, consult Leland M. Goodrich, *Korea: A Study of U.S. Policy in the United Nations* (N.Y.: Council on Foreign Relations, 1956); Glenn D. Paige, *The Korean Decision, June 24–30, 1950* (N.Y.: Free Press, 1968); Mark W. Clark, *From the Danube to the Yalu* (N.Y.: Harper, 1954). On MacArthur's controversial role in Korea, see Trumbull Higgins, *Korea and the Fall of MacArthur* (N.Y.: Oxford U.P., 1960); John W. Spanier, *The Truman-MacArthur Controversy and the Korean War* (Cambridge: Belknap, 1959); Courtney Whitney, *MacArthur: His Rendezvous with Destiny* (N.Y.: Knopf, 1956).

MEMOIRS AND BIOGRAPHIES. Principal participants justify their action in the following: Harry S. Truman, *Memoirs* (2 vols.; Garden City: Doubleday, 1955–1956); James F. Byrnes, *Speaking Frankly* (N.Y.: Harper, 1947); Dean Acheson, *Present at the Creation: My Years in the State Department* (N.Y.: Norton, 1969); George Kennan, *Memoirs, 1925–1950* (Boston: Little, Brown, 1967); Walter Millis, ed., *The Forrestal Diaries* (N.Y.: Viking, 1951); Arthur H. Vandenberg, Jr., ed., *The Private Papers of Senator Vandenberg,* (Boston: Houghton Mifflin, 1952). See also Robert H. Ferrell, *George C. Marshall* (N.Y.: Cooper Square, 1966).

Chapter 24. Tribulations of Truman

GENERAL. Eric F. Goldman, *The Crucial Decade: America, 1945–1955* (N.Y.: Knopf, 1956), is a well-written account. Truman, *Memoirs,* cited for Chapter 23, states the President's case forcefully. William Hillman, *Mr. President* (N.Y.: Farrar, 1952), and Jonathan Daniels, *The Man from Independence* (Philadelphia: Lippincott, 1950), contain interesting material.

THE LOYALTY ISSUE. Robert Griffith, *The Politics of Fear: Joseph R. McCarthy and the Senate* (Lexington: U. of Kentucky, 1970), is excellent. Richard M. Freeland, *The Truman Doctrine and the Origins of McCarthyism* (N.Y.: Knopf, 1972), blames the administration for contributing to popular hysteria. A prominent ex-Communist makes his accusations in Louis F. Budenz, *Men Without Faces: The Communist Conspiracy in the U.S.A.* (N.Y.: Harper, 1950). Alistair Cooke, *A Generation on Trial: U.S.A. v. Alger Hiss* (N.Y.: Knopf, 1950). The two protagonists tell their stories in Alger Hiss, *In the Court of Public Opinion* (N.Y.: Knopf, 1957), and Chambers, *Witness,* cited for Chapter 18. Owen Lattimore, *Ordeal by Slander* (Boston: Little, Brown, 1950), is a vigorous defense of the author and counteroffensive against Senator McCarthy. David A. Shannon, *The Decline of American Communism: A History of the Communist Party in the United States since 1945* (N.Y.: Harcourt, 1959), is a thoughtful narrative.

OTHER ISSUES. To understand the issues involved in the civil rights controversy, the essential document is *To Secure These Rights: The Report of the President's Committee on Civil Rights* (Washington, D.C.: GPO, 1947). On economic policy, see Edward S. Flash, Jr., *Economic Advice and Presidential Leadership: The Council of Economic Advisers* (N.Y.: Columbia U.P., 1965); and George A. Steiner, *Government's Role in Economic Life* (N.Y.: McGraw-Hill, 1953). On labor policy, see R. Alton Lee, *Truman and Taft-Hartley: A Question of Mandate* (Lexington: U. of Kentucky, 1966), and Harry A. Millis and E. C. Brown, *From the Wagner Act to Taft-Hartley* (Chicago: U. of Chicago, 1950). For agriculture, consult Allen J. Matusow, *Farm Policies and Politics in the Truman Administration* (Cambridge: Harvard U.P., 1967). Excellent on Senator Robert Taft, as leader of the Republican opposition, is James T. Patterson, *Mr. Republican* (Boston: Houghton Mifflin, 1972). On the election of 1948, see Curtis D. MacDougall, *Gideon's Army* (3 vols.; N.Y.: Marzani, 1965), and Karl M. Schmidt, *Henry Wallace, Quixotic Crusader* (Syracuse: Syracuse U.P., 1960).

Chapter 25. Changing America

GENERAL. Max Lerner, *America as a Civilization: Life and Thought in the United States Today* (N.Y.: Simon & Schuster, 1957), is a brilliant and comprehensive work.

ECONOMIC TRENDS. Harold G. Vatter, *The U.S. Economy in the 1950's: An Economic History* (N.Y.: Norton, 1963), is an excellent analysis. A popular explanation of the new capitalism is Frederick L. Allen, *The Big Change: America Transforms Itself, 1900–1950* (N.Y.: Harper, 1952). See also John Brooks, *The Great Leap: The Past Twenty-five Years in America* (N.Y.: Harper, 1966), and A. D. H. Kaplan, *Big Enterprise in a Competitives System* (Washington, D.C.: Brookings Inst., 1964). More thoughtful interpretations are Adolph A. Berle, Jr., *The 20th Century Capitalist Revolution* (N.Y.: Harcourt, 1954); John K. Galbraith, *The New Industrial State* (N.Y.: Signet, 1968); Bernard D. Nossiter, *The Mythmakers: An Essay on Power and Wealth* (Boston: Houghton Mifflin, 1964). Vance Packard, *The Hidden Persuaders* (N.Y.: McKay, 1957), criticizes advertising methods.

SCIENCE AND THOUGHT. James P. Baxter, 3d, *Scientists Against Time* (Boston: Little, Brown, 1946), is a fine account of the American scientific effort in World War II. On nuclear research, see George Gamow, *Atomic Energy in Cosmic and Human Life* (Garden City: Doubleday, 1948); Daniel Lang, *Early Tales of the Atomic Age* (Garden City: Doubleday, 1948); Robert Jungk, *Brighter Than a Thousand Suns* (N.Y.: Harcourt, 1958). For criticism of educational practices, see Arthur E. Bestor, *Educational Wastelands: The Retreat from Learning in Our Public Schools* (Urbana: U. of Illinois, 1953). General discussions of the problems of higher education are R. Freeman Butts, *The College Charts Its Course* (N.Y.: McGraw-Hill, 1939), and Robert L. Kelly, *The American Colleges and the Social Order* (N.Y.: Macmillan, 1940). On literature and art, see John W. Aldridge, *In Search of Heresy: American Literature in an Age of Conformity* (N.Y.: McGraw-Hill, 1956), and Andrew C. Ritchie, *Abstract Painting and Sculpture in America* (N.Y.: Museum of Modern Art, 1951).

Chapter 26. Eisenhower Republicanism

GENERAL. The presidential viewpoint is well presented in Dwight D. Eisenhower, *The White House Years* (2 vols.; Garden City: Doubleday, 1963–1965). Robert L. Branyan and Lawrence H. Larson, *The Eisenhower Administration: A Documentary History* (2 vols.; N.Y.: Random, 1971), is an extensive record. A thoughtful appraisal is provided in Herbert S. Parmet, *Eisenhower and the American Crusades* (N.Y.:

Macmillan, 1972). For accounts written while Eisenhower was still President, see Robert J. Donovan, *Eisenhower: The Inside Story* (N.Y.: Harper, 1956); Merlo J. Pusey, *Eisenhower the President* (N.Y.: Macmillan, 1956); Marquis Childs, *Eisenhower: Captive Hero* (N.Y.: Harcourt, 1958); Richard H. Rovere, *Affairs of State: The Eisenhower Years* (N.Y.: Farrar, 1956). For a persuasive statement of the New Republicanism, see Arthur Larsen, *A Republican Looks at His Party* (N.Y.: Harper, 1956). For the Democratic opposition, see Stuart G. Brown, *Conscience in Politics: Adlai Stevenson in the 1950's* (Syracuse: Syracuse U.P., 1961).

MEMOIRS. Three key figures in the Eisenhower administration have told their stories in Sherman Adams, *First Hand Report: Story of the Eisenhower Administration* (N.Y.: Harper, 1961); Ezra T. Benson, *Crossfire: The Eight Years with Eisenhower* (Garden City: Doubleday, 1962); Richard M. Nixon, *Six Crises* (Garden City: Doubleday, 1962). Emmet J. Hughes, *The Ordeal of Power: A Political Memoir of the Eisenhower Years* (N.Y.: Atheneum, 1963), records the disillusionment of an Eisenhower speechwriter.

SPECIFIC ISSUES. On the utilities issue, see Aaron B. Wildavsky, *Dixon-Yates: A Study in Power Politics* (New Haven: Yale U.P., 1962). For the McCarthy controversy, see Michael Straight, *Trial by Television* (Boston: Beacon, 1954); Michael P. Rogin, *The Intellectuals and McCarthy: The Radical Spector* (Cambridge: MIT., 1967); James Rorty and Moske Decter, *McCarthy and the Communists* (Boston: Beacon, 1954); William F. Buckley and L. Bent Bozell, *McCarthy and His Enemies* (Chicago: Regnery, 1954).

Chapter 27. The United States in a Troubled World
GENERAL. Most of the general works cited for Chapter 26 have material on diplomatic problems. Indispensable are the annual publications of the Council on Foreign Relations, *The United States in World Affairs, 1953–1960* and *Documents on American Foreign Relations.* Spanier, *American Foreign Policy since World War II,* and Fleming, *The Cold War and Its Origins,* both cited for Chapter 23, present conflicting points of view. On Eisenhower's Secretary of State, see Richard Gool-Adams, *John Foster Dulles: A Reappraisal* (N.Y.: Appleton, 1962). For a criticism, see Dean Acheson, *Power and Diplomacy* (Cambridge: Harvard U.P., 1958). William G. Carleton, *The Revolution in American Policy* (rev. ed.; N.Y.: Random, 1957), and Walt W. Rostow, *The United States in the World Arena* (N.Y.: Harper, 1960), provide intelligent analysis.

SPECIFIC AREAS AND PROBLEMS. Useful books are Herman Finer, *Dulles Over Suez: The Theory and Practice of His Diplomacy* (Chicago: Quadrangle, 1964); Jack M. Schick, *The Berlin Crisis 1958–1962* (Philadelphia: U. of Pa., 1971); Harold Vinacke, *Far Eastern Politics in the Postwar Period* (N.Y.: Appleton, 1956); Henry A. Kissinger, *Nuclear Weapons and Foreign Policy* (N.Y.: Harper, 1957). On the Korean armistice, see Charles T. Joy, *How Communists Negotiate* (N.Y.: Macmillan, 1955). On the Cuban problem, see Herbert L. Matthews, *The Cuban Story* (N.Y.: Braziller, 1961), and Theodore Draper, *Castro's Revolution* (N.Y.: Praeger, 1962).

Chapter 28. A New Age of Reform
GENERAL. Arthur M. Schlesinger, Jr., *A Thousand Days: John F. Kennedy in the White House* (Boston: Houghton Mifflin, 1965), and Theodore Sorensen, *Kennedy* (N.Y.: Harper, 1965), are excellent works, written by Kennedy's White House assistants. A shorter affectionate portrait is Pierre Salinger, *With Kennedy* (Garden City: Doubleday, 1966). For the viewpoint of contemporary journalists, see William Manchester, *Portrait of a President: John F. Kennedy in Profile* (Boston: Little, Brown, 1962); Helen Fuller, *Year of Trial: Kennedy's Crucial Decisions* (N.Y.: Harcourt, 1962); Hugh Sidey, *John F. Kennedy, President* (New ed.; N.Y.: Atheneum, 1964). Lyndon B. Johnson, *The Vantage Point: Perspectives of the Presidency,*

1963–1969 (N.Y.: Holt, 1971), is a sturdy defense of his policies. A historian who served in the White House makes a critical appraisal in Eric Goldman, *The Tragedy of Lyndon Johnson* (N.Y.: Knopf, 1969). Another memoir by a historian is Henry Graff, *The Tuesday Cabinet: Deliberation and Decision on Peace and War under Lyndon Johnson* (Englewood Cliffs, N.J.: Prentice-Hall, 1970). The following are appraisals by good journalists: Rowland Evans and Robert Novak, *Lyndon Johnson, the Exercise of Power: A Political Biography* (N.Y.: New American Library, 1966); Hugh Sidey, *A Very Personal Presidency: Lyndon Johnson in the White House* (N.Y.: Atheneum, 1968); Tom Wicker, *JFK and LBJ: The Influence of Personality upon Politics* (N.Y.: Morrow, 1968).

KENNEDY'S ASSASSINATION. For the report of the Commission headed by Chief Justice Earl Warren, see *Report of the President's Commission on the Assassination of President Kennedy* (Washington, D.C.: GPO, 1964). There are vivid descriptions of the event in Jim Bishop, *The Day Kennedy Was Shot* (N.Y.: Funk, 1968); William Manchester, *The Death of a President, November 20–November 25, 1963* (N.Y.: Harper, 1967).

DOMESTIC POLITICS. Brilliant accounts of the elections are Theodore H. White, *The Making of the President 1960* (N.Y.: Atheneum, 1961), and the same author's *The Making of the President 1964* (N.Y.: Atheneum, 1965). On the problem of poverty, see Michael Harrington, *The Other America* (N.Y.: Macmillan, 1962). On economic policy, see Jim F. Heath, *John F. Kennedy and the Business Community* (Chicago: U. of Chicago, 1969).

FOREIGN AFFAIRS. Roger Hillsman, *To Move a Nation: The Politics of Foreign Policy in the Administration of John F. Kennedy* (Garden City: Doubleday, 1967), is written by a man who held an important post. Harold K. Jacobson and Eric Stein, *Diplomats, Scientists, and Politicians: The United States and the Nuclear Test Ban Negotiations* (Ann Arbor: U. of Michigan, 1967), is useful. On Cuba, see Graham T. Allison, *Essence of Decision: Explaining the Cuban Missible Crisis* (Boston: Little, Brown, 1971); Louise Fitzsimons, *The Kennedy Doctrine* (N.Y.: Random, 1972); Robert F. Kennedy, *Thirteen Days: A Memoir of the Cuban Missile Crisis* (N.Y.: Norton, 1969). John B. Martin, *Overtaken by Events: The Dominican Crisis from the Fall of Trujillo to the Civil War* (Garden City: Doubleday, 1966), is the memoir of the American diplomat on the scene.

Chapter 29. Struggle of the Blacks

GENERAL. There are good accounts in Franklin, *From Slavery to Freedom,* and Meier and Rudwick, *From Plantation to Ghetto,* both cited for Chapter 1. See also Lerone Bennett, Jr., *Confrontation: Black and White* (N.Y.: Penguin, 1965); Louis E. Lomax, *The Negro Revolt* (N.Y.: New American Library, 1963); Benjamin Muse, *The American Negro Revolution* (Bloomington: Indiana U.P., 1968); Jack Newfield, *A Prophetic Minority* (N.Y.: New American Library, 1966); Charles E. Silberman, *Crisis in Black and White* (N.Y.: Random, 1964).

BACKGROUND. The most complete and objective study is the work of a Swedish sociologist, Gunnar Myrdal, *An American Dilemma: The Negro Problem and Modern Democracy* (2 vols.; N.Y.: Harper, 1944). See also Kenneth Clark, *Dark Ghetto* (N.Y.: Harper, 1965); Harold Cruse, *The Crisis of the Negro Intellectual* (N.Y.: Morrow, 1967); E. Franklin Frazier, *Black Bourgeoisie: The Rise of a New Middle Class in the United States* (N.Y.: Free Press, 1957); S. P. Fullinwider, *The Mind and Mood of Black America: Twentieth Century Thought* (Homewood, Ill.: Dorsey, 1969); Robert C. Weaver, *Negro Labor: A National Problem* (N.Y.: Harcourt, 1946).

CIVIL RIGHTS MOVEMENT. Martin Luther King, Jr., *Stride Toward Freedom* (N.Y.: Harper, 1958), and the same author's *Why We Can't Wait* (N.Y.: New American Library, 1964), are eloquent statements. See also William C. Berman, *The Politics of Civil Rights in the Truman Administration* (Columbus: Ohio S.U., 1970); Jerome H. Holland, *Black Opportunity* (N.Y.: Weybright, 1969); Howard Zinn, *SNCC: The New Abolitionists* (Boston: Beacon, 1964); Lerone Bennett, Jr., *What Manner of Man: A Memorial Biography of Martin Luther King, Jr.* (N.Y.: Pocket, 1968).

BLACK NATIONALISM. Alex Haley, ed., *The Autobiography of Malcolm X* (N.Y.: Grove, 1966), is a fascinating document. See also Stokely Carmichael and Charles V. Hamilton, *Black Power: The Politics of Liberation in America* (N.Y.: Random, 1968); Eldridge Cleaver, *Soul on Ice* (N.Y.: McGraw-Hill, 1968); C. Eric Lincoln, *The Black Muslims in America* (Boston: Beacon, 1961); E. U. Essien-Udom, *Black Nationalism: The Search for an Identity* (Chicago: U. of Chicago, 1962); Nathan Wright, Jr., *Black Power and Urban Unrest* (N.Y.: Hawthorn, 1967); *Report of the National Commission on Civil Disorders* (N.Y.: Bantam, 1968).

Chapter 30. The Vietnam Tragedy

GENERAL. Frances Fitzgerald, *Fire in the Lake: The Vietnamese and the Americans in Vietnam* (Boston: Atlantic-Little, Brown, 1972), is a brilliant narrative and analysis. See also George M. Kahin and John E. Lewis, *The United States in Vietnam* (N.Y.: Dial, 1967), and David Halberstam, *The Best and the Brightest* (N.Y.: Random, 1972).

THE VIETNAM BATTLEFRONTS. Among the many books resulting from the war, the following are particularly recommended: Bernard Fall, *Viet-Nam Witness, 1953–1966* (N.Y.: Praeger, 1966); David Halberstam, *The Making of a Quagmire* (N.Y.: Random, 1965); Robert Shaplen, *Time Out of Hand; Revolution and Reaction in Southeast Asia* (N.Y.: Harper, 1969); Robert Thompson, *No Exit from Vietnam* (N.Y.: McKay, 1969).

UNITED STATES POLICY. For major revelations, see *The Pentagon Papers: As Published by the New York Times* (N.Y.: Bantam, 1971). Other important studies are Anthony Austin, *The President's War: The Story of the Tonkin Gulf Resolution and How the Nation Was Trapped in Vietnam* (Philadelphia: Lippincott, 1971); Townsend Hoopes, *The Limits of Intervention: As Inside Account of How the Johnson Policy of Escalation in Vietnam Was Reversed* (N.Y.: McKay, 1969); Raphael Litauer and Norman Uphoff, eds., *The Air War in Indochina* (Boston: Beacon, 1972).

Chapter 31. The Computer Age and Its Critics

GENERAL. William L. O'Neill, *Coming Apart: An Informal History of America in the 1960s* (Chicago: Quadrangle, 1972), is excellent on the social ferment of the decade. For other aspects, see Ronald Berman, *America in the Sixties: An Intellectual History* (N.Y.: Free Press, 1968), and Emma S. Woytinsky, *Profile of the U. S. Economy: A Survey of Growth and Change* (N.Y.: Praeger, 1967).

THE COMPUTER AND AUTOMATION. The following are useful: Committee on Economic Policy, CIO, *The Challenge of Automation* (Washington, D.C.: Public Affairs, 1955); Donald M. Michael, *Cybernation: The Silent Conquest* (Santa Barbara, Calif.: Center for the Study of Democratic Institutions, 1962); John Pfeiffer, *The Thinking Machine* (Philadelphia: Lippincott, 1962); Gerald Rabow, *The Era of the System: How the Systems Approach Can Help Solve Society's Problems* (N.Y.: Philosophical Library, 1969); Alice K. Smith, *A Peril and a Hope: The Scientists Movement in America* (Chicago: U. of Chicago, 1965); Norman Wiener, *The Human Use of Human Beings: Cybernetics and Society* (Garden City: Doubleday, 1954).

EXPLORING THE MOON. For various points of view, see Philip Bono and Kenneth Gatland, *Frontiers of Space* (N.Y.: Macmillan, 1969); Cornelius T. Leondes, ed., *Lunar Missions and Explorations* (N.Y.: Wiley, 1964); Norman Mailer, *Of a Fire on the Moon* (Boston: Little, Brown, 1970); Hugo Young, Bryan Silcock, and Peter Dunn, *Journey to Tranquility* (Garden City: Doubleday, 1970).

UNIVERSITY PROBLEMS. Christopher Jencks and David Riesman, *The Academic Revolution* (N.Y.: Doubleday, 1968), and James Ridgeway, *The Closed Corporation: American Universities in Crisis* (N.Y.: Random, 1968), are important discussions. For troubles at Berkeley, see Seymour M. Lipset and Sheldon S. Wolin, eds., *The Berkeley Student Revolt: Facts and Interpretations* (Garden City: Doubleday, 1965); and Michael V. Miller and Susan Gilmore, eds., *Revolution at Berkeley: The Crisis in American Education* (N.Y.: Dial, 1965). For events at Columbia, see Jerry L. Avorn, *Up Against the Ivy Wall: A History of the Columbia Crisis* (N.Y.: Atheneum, 1969), and *Crisis at Columbia: Report of the Fact-Finding Commission Appointed to Investigate the Disturbances at Columbia University in April and May, 1968* (N.Y.: Vintage, 1968).

THE NEW LEFT. The following studies are recommended: David T. Bazelon, *Power in America: The Politics of the New Class* (N.Y.: New American Library, 1967); Kenneth Keniston, *Young Radicals: Notes on Committed Youth* (N.Y.: Harcourt, 1968); Christopher Lash, *The Agony of the American Left* (N.Y.: Knopf, 1969); Seymour Lipset, ed., *Student Politics* (N.Y.: Basic, 1967); Theodore Roszak, *The Making of a Counter Culture* (Garden City: Anchor, 1969).

OTHER SOCIAL MOVEMENTS. For the background of the women's liberation movement, see Betty Friedan, *The Feminine Mystique* (N.Y.: Norton, 1963). On changes in the Catholic Church, see Desmond Fisher, *The Church in Transition* (Notre Dame, Ind.: Fides, 1967).

Chapter 32. The Nixon Majority

GENERAL. Earl Mazo, *Richard Nixon: A Political and Personal Portrait* (N.Y.: Harper, 1959), is an admiring account of Nixon's early life. See also Nixon, *Six Crises,* cited for Chapter 26. Garry Wills, *Nixon Agonistes: This Crisis of the Self-Made Man* (Boston: Houghton Mifflin, 1970), is a penetrating character study. Rowland Evans and Robert D. Novak, *Nixon in the White House: The Frustrations of Power* (N.Y.: Random, 1971), is the work of well-informed journalists.

THE ELECTION OF 1968. The best account is Theodore H. White, *The Making of the President 1968* (N.Y.: Atheneum, 1969). Also informative are Joe McGinniss, *The Selling of the President, 1968* (N.Y.: Trident, 1969); Jules Witcover, *The Resurrection of Richard Nixon* (N.Y.: Putnam, 1970). David Halberstam, *The Unfinished Odyssey of Robert Kennedy* (N.Y.: Random, 1969), deals with Kennedy's campaigning and death during the presidential primaries.

THE COURT ISSUE AND CIVIL RIGHTS. On the Warren Court, see Richard C. Cortner, *The Apportionment Cases* (Knoxville: U. of Tennessee, 1970); Clifford Lytle, *The Warren Court and Its Critics* (Tucson: U. of Arizona, 1968); Paul L. Murphy, *The Constitution in Crisis Times, 1918–1969* (N.Y.: Harper, 1972). Reg Murphy and Hal Gulliver, *The Southern Strategy* (N.Y.: Scribners, 1971), deals with the political motivations at work. Leon Panetta and Peter Gall, *Bring Us Together: The Nixon Team and the Civil Rights Retreat* (Philadelphia: Lippincott, 1971), is the memoir of a disillusioned HEW official.

OTHER ISSUES. On welfare reform, see Christopher Green, *Negative Taxes and the Poverty Program* (Washington, D.C.: Brookings Inst., 1967); George H. Hildebrand, *Poverty, Income Maintenance, and the Negative Income Tax* (Ithaca: New York State School of Industrial and Labor Relations, 1967). On economic policy, see Roger L. Miller, *The New Economics of Richard Nixon: Freezes, Floats, and Fiscal Policy* (N.Y.: Harper, 1972). On foreign policy, see David Landau, *Kissinger: The Uses of Power* (Boston: Houghton Mifflin, 1972). James Keough, *President Nixon and the Press* (N.Y.: Funk, 1972), deals with one of the friction points of the administration.

INDEX